SLANG AMERICAN STYLE

More than 10,000 Ways to Talk the Talk

Richard A. Spears

McGraw-Hill

New York Chicago San Francisco Lisbon London Madrid Mexico City Milan New Delhi San Juan Seoul Singapore Sydney Toronto

The McGraw-Hill Companies

Library of Congress Cataloging-in-Publication Data

Spears, Richard A.
[NTC's dictionary of American slang and colloquial expressions]
Slang American style : more than 10,000 ways to talk the talk / Richard A. Spears.
p. cm.
Previously published: NTC's dictionary of American slang and colloquial expressions. 2nd ed. 1995.
Includes index.
ISBN 0-8442-0907-4 (pbk.)
1. English language—United States—Slang—Dictionaries. 2. Figures of speech—Dictionaries. 3. Americanisms—Dictionaries. I. Title. II. Series.
PE2846.S643 1996
427'.973—dc20 96-26180
CIP

8 9 10 11 12 13 14 15 16 17 18 19 DSH/DSH 0 9 8

ISBN 0-8442-0907-4

This book is printed on acid-free paper.

CONTENTS

ABOUT THIS DICTIONARY

This dictionary is a collection of slang and colloquial expressions in frequent use in the United States in the twentieth century. It contains expressions that are familiar to many Americans and other expressions that are used primarily within small groups of people. The entries represent the language of the underworld, the nursery, the college campus, California beaches, urban back streets, and Wall Street. We hear from prisoners, surfers, junkies, Valley Girls, blacks, weight lifters, surfers, and just plain folks. Fad words, metaphors, wordplay, and various figures of speech make up the body of the dictionary.

The second edition of the dictionary contains approximately 2,000 new senses. These comprise the expressions that have become popular in the last five years—including many new expressions used in everyday talk on the streets and the college campus. Notable among the collegiate expressions are numerous new ways to speak about vomiting. At the same time, the output of new drug slang has slowed or has become more private in its use. The Phrase-Finder Index has been completely revised to make finding the location of phrasal entries in the dictionary easier.

There is no standard test that will decide what is slang or colloquial and what is not. Expressions that are identified as slang are often some type of entertaining wordplay, and they are almost always an alternative way of saying something. Colloquial expressions are usually spoken and are often thought of as being direct, earthy, or quaint. Slang and colloquial expressions come in different forms: single words, compound words, simple phrases, idioms, and complete sentences. Slang is rarely the first choice of careful writers or speakers or anyone attempting to use language for formal, persuasive, or business purposes. Nonetheless, expressions that can be called slang or colloquial make up a major part of American communication in movies, television, radio, newspapers, magazines, and informal conversation.

Localized fad words usually have a short life, but other kinds of slang expressions may spread and last for a long time. The farther they spread, the longer they will last. If they last long enough, they may become so well known that they become standard English unavoidably. Most such expressions simply join an enormous pool of similar expressions, and they are used until displaced by newer terms. At some point the old ones are put on hold until they are forgotten by everyone or revived by a new generation. Many expressions that hang around for decades will pop up again and again in novels and movies or in sporadic use in the speech of the older generation.

For more than two hundred years, the jargon of criminals has been a major source of everyday slang words. Alcohol, drugs, and crime have been firmly fixed in the public consciousness since the time of prohibition in the United States. The entertainment value of crime and law enforcement has brought a constant stream of criminal slang into novels, movies, radio, and television over the last half century. This dictionary contains many of the expressions from these areas that have made public appearances over the years. Even more remain hidden behind closed doors. Matters of social taboo have also provided many slang expressions. Although strictly speaking taboo words are not slang, the major taboo words have been included in this dictionary. Young people are responsible for a high proportion of the fad expressions and collegiate wordplay found here. Clever or insulting nicknames for types of people are the major linguistic product of this subgroup.

Whereas many of the entries are humorous or clever, others simply represent the everyday turns of phrase common to informal speech in the United States. Where possible, the examples are given in natural slangy language, even if it is ungrammatical in formal writing. The examples are to be taken as representative of slang usage, not of standard, formal English usage.

The grammar and syntax of each expression are best determined from the examples that accompany each entry. The notion of "part of speech" is relevant to the function of individual words. The words within the clauses and phrases that are entries in the dictionary can be given part-of-speech labels, but it is the grammar and syntax of the entire phrase that is important. Each expression in the dictionary is assigned a "function code" that serves to indicate the functional potential of the entry expression. These codes represent function independently from form. That is to say, expressions that function the same get the same label. For instance, nouns, noun compounds, noun phrases, and noun clauses are all marked *n.* for "nominal." The codes are described and illustrated in the section Guide to the Use of the Dictionary.

Unlike standard English, few slang or colloquial expressions are standardized in spelling or punctuation. Standard dictionaries differ considerably as to whether a standard English compound is printed as one word, two words, or a hyphenated word. The spelling of slang entries is even more variable. This dictionary usually represents slang expressions in the form in which they were found in print, except for rhyming compounds, e.g., "fat-cat" or "funny-money," which are always hyphenated.

The entries come from many sources. Many have been collected and submitted by college students and other individuals. Much of the latest material has come directly from television and a lesser amount from contemporary radio. Standard reference works have been used to verify the meanings and spellings of older material. A surprising amount of old material has been verified in reruns of old movies. Many attestations have come from contemporary journalism, especially human interest and Sunday supplement material. Few of the examples are verbatim quotes of the original. Some are concocted, and many more have been edited to exemplify an expression's meaning more concisely than the original quote. The examples exist to illustrate meaning, not to prove the earliest date of print or broadcast dissemination.

Guide to the Use of the Dictionary

1. Entries are alphabetized according to an absolute alphabetical order that ignores all punctuation. The hyphen is treated the same as a space. Entries beginning with numerals precede the alphabetic entries.

2. The first step in finding an expression is to try looking it up in the dictionary. Entries that consist of two or more words are entered in their normal order, such as **chill someone's action.** Phrases are never inverted or reordered like **action, chill someone's** or **track, off the.**

3. If you do not find the expression you want, or if you cannot decide on the exact form of the expression, look up any major word in the expression in the Phrase-Finder Index, which begins on page 461. There you will find all the multiword expressions

that contain the word you have looked up. Pick out the expression you want and look it up in the dictionary.

4. Entry expressions appear in **boldface type**. When words or expressions that are not entries in this dictionary are cited, they appear in *italics*. Function codes [see item 9 below] and examples appear in *italics*.

5. A main entry may have one or more alternative forms. The alternatives are printed in **boldface type** and are preceded by "AND." Alternative forms are separated by a semicolon. For example:

> **spondulicks** AND **spondulix; spondulics** [spɑn'dulɪks] *n.* money. □ *How much spondulicks will this set me back?* □ *I don't have enough spondulix to swing the deal.*

6. Definitions are in roman type. Alternative or closely related definitions are separated by semicolons. For example:

> **take a hike** AND **take a walk** *tr.* to leave; to beat it. □ *Okay, I've had it with you. Take a hike! Beat it!* □ *I had enough of the boss and the whole place, so I cleaned out my desk and took a walk.*

7. Some definitions contain restrictive comments in parentheses that help to make the definition clearer. These comments limit the context in which the expression can be used. For example:

> **blindside** *tr.* (for someone or something) to surprise someone, as if sneaking up on the blind side of a one-eyed person (or animal). □ *The new tax law blindsided about half the population.* □ *The mugger came up and blindsided her with a blow to the head before she knew what had happened.*

8. A definition may be followed by comments in parentheses. These comments give additional information about the expression,

including any cautions, comments on origins, or indications of cross-referencing. Each numbered sense can have its own comments. For example:

> **dickens** **1.** *n.* the devil. (Always with *the.*) □ *She was going to kick the dickens out of me.* □ *I felt as bad as the dickens, but what could I do?* **2.** *n.* a devilish or impish child. (Also a term of address.) □ *Come here, you little dickens.* □ *You are such a cute little dickens!*

9. Every expression is followed by a function code that indicates the grammatical or syntactic function of the expression. These codes are in *italics*. The function codes provide a way of determining the grammatical or syntactic function of a particular expression as it occurs in its examples. Expressions functioning as nominals (nouns, noun phrases, etc.) are marked *n.* Expressions serving to modify, restrict, or qualify (adjectives, adjective phrases, adverbs, adverb phrases, etc.) are marked *mod.* Expressions that are transitive verbs or transitive verb phrases (a transitive verb, its auxiliaries, object(s), and modifier(s) are marked *tr.* Expressions that are intransitive verbs or intransitive verb phrases (an intransitive verb, its auxiliaries, and modifiers) are marked *in.* Other abbreviations are explained in the section titled **Terms and Symbols**. For example:

> **ace** **1.** *mod.* (of persons) best; top-rated. □ *She is an ace reporter with the newspaper.* □ *Frank is an ace swimmer.* **2.** *n.* one dollar. □ *Give me an ace. I have to get some telephone change.* □ *It only costs an ace. Buy two.* □ **3.** *tr.* to pass a test easily, with an A grade. (Compare to *ace out.*) □ *Man, I really aced that test.* □ *I knew I wouldn't ace it, but I never thought I'd flunk it!* **4.** *n.* a nickname for a foolish and ineffectual person. (Sarcastic. Usually a term of address.) □ *Hey, ace, hand me that monkey wrench—if you know what one is.* □ *Look, ace, you can't expect to fix an engine without*

getting dirty. **5.** *tr.* to surpass someone or something; to beat someone or something; to *ace someone out.* □ *The Japanese firm aced the Americans by getting the device onto the shelves first.* □ *Fred aced Tom in the contest for the best beard.*

10. Some expressions that are modifiers (marked *mod.*) can occur before or after the things they modify. Other modifiers can occur both before and after the things they modify. The distribution of modifiers is illustrated in the examples. For example:

sad *mod.* poor; undesirable. □ *This is a sad excuse for a car!* □ *That was a sad pitch there at the end of the last inning.* □ *This steak is really sad.*

11. Many expressions have more than one major sense or meaning. These meanings are numbered with boldface numerals. For example:

sting 1. *tr.* to cheat or swindle someone; to overcharge someone. □ *That street merchant stung me, but good.* □ *They are likely to sting you in any of those hockshops.* **2.** *n.* a well-planned scheme to entrap criminals. □ *The sting came off without a hitch.* □ *It was a well-planned sting and shouldn't have failed.* **3.** *tr.* to entrap and arrest someone. □ *The feebies stung the whole gang at once.* □ *"We've been stung!" they hollered.*

12. Sometimes a numbered sense will have an alternative form that does not apply to the other senses. In such cases the AND and the alternative forms follow the numeral. For example:

birdbrain 1. *n.* a stupid-acting person. □ *You silly birdbrain. Stop it!* □ *I'm such a birdbrain. I forgot my driver's licence, officer.* **2.** AND **birdbrained** *mod.* stupid. □ *I've never* *heard such a birdbrain idea in my life.* □ *Look, you birdbrained idiot, you are dead wrong!*

13. Entries that contain unfamiliar words and entries whose spelling is misleading have an indication of pronunciation in International Phonetic Alphabet symbols. See the symbols and their values in the Pronunciation Guide.

Pronunciation may be for the entire expression . . .

triple whammy [ˈtrɪpl̩ ˈʍæmi]

. . . or only part of it:

beer and skittles [. . . ˈskɪdl̩z]

Alternative pronunciations are separated by OR:

anti [ˈænti OR ˈæntaɪ]

Pronunciation coordinated with alternative entry forms are separated by AND:

legal-beagle AND **legal-eagle** [ˈligl̩-ˈbigl̩ AND ˈligl̩ˈigl̩]

14. In some entries comments direct the user to other entries for additional information through the use of the terms "compare to," "see," or "see also." The expressions mentioned are in *slanted sans serif* type. For example:

B-ball *n.* basketball; a basketball. (See also *hoops.* Compare to *V-ball.*) □ *Let's go play some B-ball.* □ *Toss me the B-ball, huh?*

15. When additional forms of an expression are to be found at another entry, a comment beginning with "More at . . ." is found at the end of the entry. For example:

bamboozle [bæmˈbuzl̩] *tr.* to deceive someone; to confuse someone. □ *Don't try to bamboozle me! I know* *what I want!* □ *The crooks bamboozled the old man out of his life savings.* (More at *bamboozled.*)

16. In some instances an expression that is an entry in the dictionary is used to define another word. Such expressions are in *slanted sans serif* type. For example:

> **bear trap** *n.* a hidden speed trap that was set by a *bear.* (Citizens band radio.) □ *That whole town is a glorified bear trap.* □ *I got caught in a bear trap.*

17. If an entry has a grammatical structure that requires a nominal to serve as a subject or object, the nominal is represented by **someone** for human nominals or **something** for nonhuman nominals. When both human and nonhuman nominals are possible, **someone or something** is used. For example:

> **saddled with someone or something** *mod.* burdened with someone or something. □ *I've been saddled with the children all day. Let's go out tonight.* □ *I don't want to be saddled with your work.*

18. Sometimes the numbered senses refer to only people or things, but not both. In such cases the numeral is followed by "[with *someone*]" or "[with *something*]." For example:

> **lay someone or something out 1.** *tr.* [with *someone*] to scold someone severely. □ *Don't lay me out! I didn't do it!* 🅃 *She really laid out the guy but good. What did he do, rob a bank?* (More at *laid out.*) **2.** *tr.* [with *someone*] to knock someone down with a punch. □ *I can't wait to get into that ring and lay the guy out.* 🅃 *The boxer laid out his opponent with a blow to the head.* **3.** *tr.* [with *something*] to spend some amount of money. □ *I can't lay that kind of money out every day!* 🅃 *She laid out*

about $24,000 for that beemer. **4.** *tr.* [with *something*] to explain a plan of action or a sequence of events. □ *Let me lay it out for you.* Ⓣ *Lay out the plan very carefully, and don't skip anything.* □ **5.** *tr.* [with *someone*] to prepare someone for burial. (Not slang.) □ *The undertaker did not lay Aunt Fanny out to my satisfaction.* Ⓣ *The women of the town helped the young widow lay out her husband.* (More at *laid out.*)

19. In an entry phrase, parentheses can be used to collapse two or three semantically related phrases into one. The phrase **waffle (around)** stands for **waffle** and **waffle around**. The phrase **(baby) boomer** stands for **boomer** and **baby boomer**. The phrase **come clean (with someone) (about something)** stands for **come clean, come clean with someone, come clean about something,** and **come clean with someone about something.**

TERMS AND SYMBOLS

□ marks the beginning of an example.

T marks the beginning of an example in which two elements of the phrase, usually a particle and an object, are transposed.

acronym an abbreviation consisting of a set of initials pronounced as a single word, as with *UNESCO*, the United Nations Educational, Scientific, and Cultural Organization.

advertising used in advertisements or marketing jargon.

Amerindian related to American Indian languages or cultures.

AND indicates an alternative element, either an alternative entry form or an alternative pronunciation. See items 5 and 12 in the **Guide to the Use of the Dictionary**.

baby talk used by infants or children or, more typically, by adults when talking to infants or children.

black typically used by or originated by African Americans.

blend made up of sounds from two other words, such as *smoke* + *fog* = *smog*.

California originating among the young people of California.

catch phrase an expression that is meant to catch attention because of its cleverness or aptness.

collegiate typically heard on college campuses.

combining form a sense of a word used only in combination with another word, as with **bug** in *camera bug*.

deliberate spoonerism a deliberate interchanging of initial consonants in a pair of words, such as "queer old dean" for "dear old queen."

drugs having to do with illegal drugs and the sale and use of drugs.

euphemistic relatively refined and having no negative connotations.

exclam. exclamation.

eye-dialect a type of respelling of a word so that it appears to have been spoken with a regional accent, as with "sez" for "says."

folksy in the manner of country people; rustic and quaint.

function code an indication of the grammatical or syntactic potential of a particular sense of an expression. See item 9 in the Guide to the Use of the Dictionary and *exclam., in., interj., interrog., mod., n., phr., prep., pro., sent.,* and *tr.* in this section.

in. intransitive. Expressions that are intransitive verbs or intransitive verb phrases (an intransitive verb, its auxiliaries, and modifiers) are marked *in*.

interj. interjection.

interrog. interrogative.

initialism an abbreviation consisting of the initial letters of the words being shortened. The letters are pronounced one by one, as with "IBM."

jargon the specialized terminology of an occupation; shoptalk.

journalistic as used in popular journalism—newspapers and magazines.

juvenile as might be said by a child.

mod. modifier. Expressions serving to modify, restrict, or qualify (adjectives, adjective phrases, adverbs, adverb phrases, etc.) are marked *mod.*

n. nominal. Expressions functioning as nominals (nouns, noun phrases, etc.) are marked *n.*

onomatopoetic having to do with a word with a sound suggesting the meaning of the word, as with *vroom,* the sound of an engine.

phr. phrase.

Pig Latin a form of wordplay where the second part of a word is placed before the initial sound, which then ends in "ay," as with "unkjay" for "junk."

play on referring to wordplay that is based on a particular expression. For instance, "eagle-freak" is a play on "eco freak."

police from the speech of law enforcement officers.

prep. preposition.

pro. pronoun.

prohibition indicates an expression that came into use during the prohibition of alcohol in the United States during the 1920's and early 1930's.

securities market(s) having to do with the stock markets, the bond markets, or the sale of other financial instruments.

see Go to the entry indicated.

see also Find additional information at the entry indicated.

sent. sentence.

standard English widely known English, not usually considered slang or colloquial.

streets originating in the streets of urban America.

taboo indicates an expression that is regarded as out of place in public use.

term of address an expression that can be used to address someone directly.

tr. transitive. Expressions that are transitive verbs or transitive verb phrases (a transitive verb and its auxiliaries, object(s), and modifier(s)) are marked *tr.*

underworld from criminal speech or law enforcement.

verbal weapon an expression that is typically used to insult or malign someone.

Western speech typical of Western movies or other stereotypes of the Old West.

PRONUNCIATION GUIDE

Some expressions in the dictionary are followed by a phonetic transcription in International Phonetic Alphabet (IPA) symbols. These expressions include words whose pronunciation is not predictable from their spellings, difficult or unfamiliar words, and words where the stress placement is contrastive or unique. The style of pronunciation reflected here is informal and tends to fit the register in which the expression would normally be used. A [d] is used for the alveolar flap typical in American pronunciations such as [wadɚ] 'water' and [ə'naɪəledəd] 'annihilated.' The transcriptions distinguish between [a] and [ɔ] and between [w] and [ʍ] even though not all Americans do so. In strict IPA fashion, [j] rather than the [y] substitute is used for the initial sound in "yellow." The most prominent syllable in a multisyllabic word is *preceded* by a ['].

The use of AND or OR in a phonetic transcription echoes the use of AND or OR in the preceding entry phrase. The use of "..." in a transcription indicates that easy-to-pronounce words have been omitted. Parentheses used in a transcription either correspond to parentheses in the preceding entry phrase or indicate optional elements in the transcription. For instance, in ['artsi 'kræf(t)si] 'artsy-craftsy,' the "t" may or may not be pronounced.

The following chart shows the American English values for each of the IPA symbols used in the phonetic transcriptions. To use the chart, first find the large phonetic symbol whose value you want to determine. The three English words to the right of the symbol contain examples of the sound for which the phonetic symbol stands. The letters in boldface type indicate where the sound in question is found in the English word.

[ɑ]	stop top	[ɚ]	bird turtle	[n]	new funny	[tʃ]	cheese pitcher
[æ]	sat track	[f]	feel if	[n̩]	button kitten	[θ]	thin faith
[ɑʊ]	cow now	[g]	get frog	[ŋ]	bring thing	[u]	food blue
[ɑɪ]	bite my	[h]	hat who	[o]	coat wrote	[ʊ]	put look
[b]	beet bubble	[i]	feet leak	[ɔɪ]	spoil boy	[v]	save van
[d]	dead body	[ɪ]	bit hiss	[ɔ]	caught yawn	[w]	well wind
[ð]	that those	[j]	yellow you	[p]	tip pat	[ʍ]	wheel while
[dʒ]	jail judge	[k]	can keep	[r]	rat berry	[z]	fuzzy zoo
[e]	date sail	[l]	lawn yellow	[s]	sun fast	[ʒ]	pleasure treasure
[ɛ]	get set	[l̩]	bottle puddle	[ʃ]	fish sure	[ˈ]	ˈwater hoˈtel
[ə]	but nut	[m]	family slam	[t]	top pot		

SLANG AMERICAN STYLE

A

10-4 See *ten-four.*

20/20 hindsight See *twenty-twenty hindsight.*

411 ['for'wən'wən] *n.* information; the details about something or someone. (In the U.S., the telephone number of directory assistance or "information" is 411.) ☐ *What's the 411 on the new guy in the front office?* ☐ *I heard some interesting 411 on the guy down the street.*

773H *n.* "hell." (This is the printed word *hell* rotated 180 degrees. Jocular.) ☐ *What the 773H is going on around here?* ☐ *This place is one 773H of a mess!*

86 *tr.* to dispose of someone or something; to *nix* someone or something. ☐ *Please take this out and 86 it.* ☐ *He wants $400? 86 that! We can't afford it.*

A-1 AND **A number 1** ['e 'wən AND 'e 'nəmbɚ 'wən] *mod.* of the highest rating. ☐ *This steak is really A-1!* ☐ *I would like to get an A number 1 secretary for a change.*

A number 1 See the previous entry.

A-OK ['e'o'ke] *mod.* in the best of condition. ☐ *I really feel A-OK.* ☐ *Show me the most A-OK canary you have.*

abbreviated piece of nothing *n.* an insignificant person or thing. ☐ *Tell that abbreviated piece of nothing to get his tail over here, but fast.* ☐ *Why don't you drive your abbreviated piece of nothing over to the service station and have a muffler put on?*

able to cut something *phr.* able to manage or execute something. (Often negative.) ☐ *He's not able to cut his responsibilities like we thought.* ☐ *We thought he could cut it.* ☐ *Do you think you're able to cut it?*

abs [æbz] *n.* the abdominal muscles. (Bodybuilding.) ☐ *Look at the abs on that guy. Like a crossword puzzle.* ☐ *I do situps to harden my abs.*

abso-bloody-lutely ['æbsoblədi'lutli] *mod.* absolutely; emphatically. ☐ *Do I like pizza? Abso-bloody-lutely!* ☐ *We are abso-bloody-lutely sick to death of your wishy-washy attitude.*

absotively (posilutely) ['æbsə'tɪvli 'pɑzə'lutli] *mod.* absolutely; decidedly. ☐ *I will be there at ten, absotively posilutely.* ☐ *I am absotively exhausted!*

A.C.-D.C. AND **A.C./D.C.** *mod.* bisexual. (Initialism.) ☐ *I didn't realize at first that we were in an A.C.-D.C. bar!* ☐ *Clare said Tom is A.C./D.C., but I don't believe it.*

accidentally-on-purpose *mod.* deliberate, but meant to look like an accident. ☐ *Then I accidentally-on-purpose spilled water on him.* ☐ *I knew it was done accidentally-on-purpose. That kind of thing doesn't just happen.*

ace 1. *mod.* (of persons) best; top-rated. ☐ *She is an ace reporter with the newspaper.* ☐ *Frank is an ace swimmer.* **2.** *n.* one dollar. ☐ *Give me an ace. I have to get some telephone change.* ☐ *It only costs an ace. Buy two.* **3.** *tr.* to pass a test easily, with an A grade. (Compare to *ace out.*) ☐ *Man, I really aced that test.* ☐ *I knew I wouldn't ace it, but I never thought I'd flunk it!* **4.** *n.* a nickname for a foolish and ineffectual person. (Sarcastic. Usually a term of address.) ☐ *Hey, ace, hand me that* *monkey wrench—if you know what one is.* □ *Look, ace, you can't expect to fix an engine without getting dirty.* **5.** *tr.* to surpass someone or something; to beat someone or something; to *ace someone out.* □ *The Japanese firm aced the Americans by getting the device onto the shelves first.* □ *Fred aced Tom in the contest for the best beard.*

ace in the hole *n.* something important held in reserve. □ *The twenty-dollar bill I keep in my shoe is my ace in the hole.* □ *Mary's beautiful singing voice was her ace in the hole in case everything else failed.*

ace in (to something) *in.* to happen onto something good; to manage to get into something. □ *I hope I can ace into the afternoon physics class.* □ *I don't know how I aced in. I guess I was just lucky.*

ace out *in.* to be fortunate or lucky. □ *I really aced out on that test in English.* □ *Freddy aced out at the dentist's office with only one cavity.*

ace someone out *tr.* to maneuver someone out; to win out over someone. (See also *ace.*) □ *I plan to ace you out in the first lap.* □ *Martha aced out Rebecca to win the first place trophy.* (More at *aced.*)

aced [est] **1.** *mod.* outmaneuvered; outscored. □ *Rebecca really got aced in the track meet.* □ *"You are aced, sucker!" shouted Rebecca as she passed Martha in the 100-yard sprint.* **2.** *mod.* alcohol intoxicated. □ *How can anybody be so aced on three beers?* □ *I've never seen anybody that aced in my life.*

acid *n.* lysergic acid diethylamide (*L.S.D.*). (Drugs.) □ *Acid and pot! That's all you think about.* □ *Freddy got hold of some bad acid and freaked out.*

acid test *n.* a very thorough test. (From a test for determining true gold using acid.) □ *We put your invention through the acid test, and—I am extremely sorry to tell you—it failed miserably.* □ *I'll take this home to my kids and let them give it the acid test. If it survives them, it's a winner.*

action **1.** *n.* excitement; activity in general; whatever is happening. □ *This place is dull. I want some action.* □ *How do I find out where the action is in this town?* **2.** *n.* a share of something; a share of the winnings or of the booty. (See also *piece of the action.*) □ *I did my share of the work, and I want my share of the action.* □ *Just what did you do to earn any of the action?* **3.** *n.* sex; copulation. □ *Paul is over at Martha's house looking for some action.* □ *All those guys play around with girls just trying for a little action.* **4.** *n.* illegal activity; commerce in drugs; acts of crime. (Underworld.) □ *You want a fast buck, you get in on that action over on Fourth Street.* □ *Things have been a little slow here, but there's some action on the East Coast.*

activated *mod.* tipsy; alcohol intoxicated. □ *All four of them went out and got a little activated.* □ *Will this stuff get me seriously activated?*

addict ['ædıkt] *n.* someone showing a marked preference for something or someone. (A combining form not related to drug addiction.) □ *Sam is a real opera addict. He just loves the stuff.* □ *My uncle is a mystery addict.*

adios muchachos [ɑdi'os mu'tʃɑtʃos] *phr.* "the end"; "good-bye everyone." (Spanish.) □ *If you step out in front of a car like that again, it's adios muchachos.* □ *I've got a gun aimed at your navel. If you move so much as one muscle, you can just say adios muchachos.*

adobe dollar [ə'dobi 'dɑlɚ] *n.* a Mexican peso. □ *How many of these adobe dollars does it take to buy a can of pop here?* □ *One greenback will get you about 2400 adobe dollars these days.*

aggie ['ægi] **1.** *mod.* agricultural. □ *She spent a year at some aggie college, but didn't like it.* □ *Her aggie interests faded fast.* **2.** *n.* a student of an agricultural (college) training program. (Specifically, Texas A. and M.) □ *More and more aggies are going back for their M.B.A.s.* □ *What kind of a job can an aggie get these days?* **3.** *n.* an agricultural futures contract. (Securities markets. Usually plural.) ☐ *The March aggies are looking good right now.* ☐ *Let's take a look at the aggies and see how the bellies are doing.* **4.** *n.* an agate marble or a glass imitation of one. ☐ *I found the old aggies I played with when I was a kid.* ☐ *Somebody stolè my prize aggie!*

agree to disagree *phr.* to agree to discuss something, but retain one's opinions. ☐ *We have accomplished nothing except that we agree to disagree.* ☐ *The two political parties agreed to disagree in 1971, and that was the last agreeable thing either one of them did.*

AH *n.* a really wretched person, male or female; an abbreviation of *ass-hole.* (Initialism. Both written and pronounced.) ☐ *Stop being such an AH.* ☐ *Bill is a total AH, and he is getting on everyone's nerves.*

ahead of the game *mod.* being early; having an advantage in a competitive situation; having done more than necessary. (Especially with *get* or *keep.*) ☐ *Without a car telephone, I find it hard to get ahead of the game.* ☐ *If being ahead of the game is important to you and to your business, lease a mobile telephone from us.*

aim for the sky AND **reach for the sky; shoot for the sky** *in.* to aspire to something; to set one's goals high. (See a different sense at *reach for the sky.*) ☐ *Shoot for the sky, son. Don't settle for second best.* ☐ *Set your sights high. Aim for the sky!*

air-bags *n.* the lungs. ☐ *Fill those air-bags with good Colorado air!* ☐ *I've had a cold or something in my air-bags for about three days now.*

air ball *n.* a basketball throw that misses everything, especially the basket. ☐ *Old Fred has become a master with the air ball. The net will never get worn out.* ☐ *Another air ball for Fred Wilson. That's his fourth tonight.*

air guitar *n.* an imaginary guitar, played along with real music. ☐ *Dave stood near the window while his roommate played air guitar in front of the mirror.* ☐ *Jed, who sees himself as some sort of rock star, plays air guitar when he's happy or sad.*

air hose *n.* invisible socks; no socks. ☐ *All these kids run around campus in air hose. You'd think they'd get blisters.* ☐ *How do you like my new air hose? One size fits all.*

air one's belly *tr.* to empty one's stomach; to vomit. ☐ *What was in that hamburger? I think I've got to air my belly.* ☐ *That must have been some party. I heard you airing your belly for most of the night, after you got home.*

air one's pores *tr.* to undress oneself; to become naked. ☐ *I'm fixing to air my pores and take a shower.* ☐ *Me and Wilbur, that's my brother, both fell in the creek and had to air our pores a while so our pants could dry out.*

airbrain See the following entry.

airhead AND **airbrain** *n.* a stupid person. (Someone with air where there should be brains.) ☐ *What is that loony airhead doing there on the roof?* ☐ *Some airbrain put mustard in the ketchup squeezer.*

airheaded *mod.* stupid; giddy. ☐ *You are the most airheaded twit I have ever met!* ☐ *That was an airheaded idea if I ever heard one.*

airy-fairy ['ɛri'fɛri] *mod.* insubstantial; of wishful thinking. ☐ *Haven't you outgrown that kind of airy-fairy thinking yet?* ☐ *Her ideas are too airy-fairy.* ☐ *I don't care to hear any more of your airy-fairy ideas.*

ak AND **ok** [ɑk] *n.* October. (Securities markets: options and futures trading.) ☐ *The ak futures are looking worse by the hour.* ☐ *When the oks expire on Friday, we'll start looking at the dec index.*

alchy AND **alkie; alky** ['ælki] **1.** *n.* alcohol; an alcoholic beverage. ☐ *He showed up with a week's supply of alkie.* ☐ *The crooks stole most of the alchy from the bar at the club.* **2.** *n.* a drunkard. ☐ *You see alchy after alchy all up and down Maxwell Street.* ☐ *Some alkie came in and asked for a quarter.*

alkie See the previous entry.

alkied (up) ['ælkid . . .] *mod.* alcohol intoxicated. □ *That old bum looks completely alkied up.* □ *She spends a lot of time alkied.*

alky See *alchy.*

all-nighter 1. *n.* something that lasts all night, like a party or study session. □ *After an all-nighter studying, I couldn't keep my eyes open for the test.* □ *Sam invited us to an all-nighter, but we're getting a little old for that kind of thing.* **2.** *n.* a place of business that is open all night. □ *We stopped at an all-nighter for a cup of coffee.* □ *I worked in an all-nighter for a month. I just couldn't keep those hours though.* **3.** *n.* a person who often stays up all night. □ *Fred is an all-nighter. He's not worth much in the mornings though.* □ *I'm no all-nighter. I need my beauty sleep, for sure.*

all right 1. *interj.* "yes"; "okay." □ *All right. I'll do it.* □ *All right. I'm coming.* **2.** *mod.* for sure; for certain. □ *He's the one who said it, all right.* □ *I was there, all right.* **3.** *mod.* okay. (This is hyphenated before a nominal. Slang when used before a nominal.) □ *Wally is an all-right guy.* □ *I'm all right.* □ *We had an all-right time at your party.* **4.** *exclam.* "That's good!"; "Keep it up!" (A general expression of approval, often cried out from the audience during a performance or at applause time. Usually **All right!** The *right* is drawn out and falling in pitch.) □ *After the last drumbeat, the entire audience exploded into a roaring "All right!"* □ *"All right!" cried the crowd when they heard the announcement about the pay increase.*

(all) shook up *mod.* excited; disturbed; upset. □ *She stole my heart, and I'm all shook up.* □ *They were pretty shook up after the accident.*

all that jazz *n.* all that stuff; all that nonsense. □ *I need some glue, paper, string, and all that jazz, to make a kite.* □ *She told me I was selfish, hateful, rude, ugly, and all that jazz.*

all (that) meat and no potatoes *phr.* said of a tremendously fat person. (A rude catch phrase.) □ *Look at that guy—all meat and no potatoes.* □ *All that meat and no potatoes. She should go on a diet.*

all the way *mod.* with everything on it, as with a hamburger. (See also *go all the way.*) □ *I'd like one double cheeseburger—all the way.* □ *Make mine all the way, too.*

all the way live *mod.* very exciting; excellent. (California.) □ *Man, this place is all the way live.* □ *Oh, Tiffany is just, like, all the way live!*

alley apple 1. *n.* a piece of horse manure. (See also *road apple.*) □ *The route of the parade was littered with alley apples after about twenty minutes.* □ *Harry is collecting alley apples for his garden.* **2.** *n.* a brick or stone found in the rubble of the streets. □ *"Drop it!" the cop called to the kid with an alley apple in his hand.* □ *Kelly kicked an alley apple so that it struck a garbage can with a metallic crash.*

almighty dollar *n.* the dollar viewed as a symbol of power or greed. □ *You don't care about anything but the almighty dollar.* □ *The world's economy seems to depend on an adequate supply of the almighty dollar.*

alphabet soup *n.* initialisms and acronyms in general. □ *The names of these government offices are just alphabet soup.* □ *Just look at the telephone book! You can't find anything because it's filled with alphabet soup.*

ambulance chaser 1. AND **chaser** *n.* a lawyer or entrepreneur who hurries to the scene of an accident to try to get the business of any injured persons. □ *The insurance companies are cracking down on ambulance chasers.* □ *Two minutes after the spectacular wreck, seven chasers with police radios showed up and began harassing the victims.* **2.** *n.* a derogatory term for any lawyer. (Also a rude term of address.) □ *That ambulance chaser is trying to charge me for reaching his office when I called a wrong number!* □ *Look here, you* *ambulance chaser, I can't afford your rates.*

amigo [ə'migo] *n.* a friend. (Spanish. Also a term of address.) □ *Me and my amigo want to rent a couple of horses.* □ *Hey, amigo, let's go somewhere for a drink.*

ammo ['æmo] **1.** *n.* ammunition. □ *There they were, trapped in a foxhole with no ammo, enemy all over the place. What do you think happened?* □ *I don't know. They sent out for ammo, maybe?* **2.** *n.* information or evidence that can be used to support an argument or a charge. □ *I want to get some ammo on the mayor. I think he's a crook.* □ *Try to keep my traffic tickets a secret. The opposition will use them as ammo in the next election.*

ammunition 1. *n.* toilet tissue. □ *Could somebody help me? We're out of ammunition in here!* □ *The ammunition in Europe is better these days than it used to be.* **2.** *n.* liquor. (See also *shot.*) □ *The cowboy walked in, downed a shot, and called for more ammunition.* □ *He's had about all the ammunition he can hold.*

amps *n.* amphetamines. (Drugs.) □ *I never do any drugs except maybe a few amps now and then, and the odd downer, and maybe a little grass on weekends, but nothing really hard.* □ *Paul is on a roller coaster of amps and damps.*

anchor-clanker *n.* a sailor. (Army.) □ *The bar was suddenly filled with anchor-clankers, and the army guys began looking for a way out.* □ *How can you anchor-clankers stand being cooped up on those cans?*

ancient history *n.* someone or something completely forgotten, especially past romances. (See also *history.*) □ *Bob? I never think about Bob anymore. He's ancient history.* □ *That business about joining the army is ancient history.*

and change *phr.* plus a few cents; plus a few hundredths. (Used in citing a price or other decimal figure to indicate an additional fraction of a full unit.) □ *This one only costs ten bucks and change.* □ *The New York Stock Exchange was up seven points and change for the third broken record this week.*

And how! *exclam.* "I agree!" □ *I am really excited you are here. And how!* □ BILL: *I am pleased you are here.* BOB: *Me, too! And how!*

angel 1. *n.* a secret financier. □ *Who was the angel for your new play?* □ *I was hoping for an angel to see this project through, but all the fat-cats seem to have disappeared.* **2.** *n.* a sweetheart. (Also a term of address.) □ *See my angel standing over there? Isn't he gorgeous?* □ *Okay, angel, let's get in the car.*

angel dust AND **angel hair; dust of angels** *n.* the common name for phencyclidine (P.C.P.). (Originally drugs.) □ *Angel dust is getting to be quite a problem in this town.* □ *I thought that angel hair and stuff like that was a problem of the sixties.*

angel hair See the previous entry.

angle 1. *n.* selfish motive; ulterior motive. □ *Okay, Ted, I know you better than to think that you are doing this out of the kindness of your heart. What's your angle?* □ *I don't have any angle. I have reformed.* **2.** *n.* slant; bias; focus. □ *Let's try to get a good angle on this news story so the wire service will buy it from us.* □ *I think that by studying the Maya I will be able to develop a new angle on why they disappeared.*

animal *n.* a male who acts like a beast in terms of manners, cleanliness, or sexual aggressiveness. (Also a term of address.) □ *You are an animal!* □ *Stop picking your nose, animal.*

ankle 1. *n.* an attractive woman or *girl.* (Typically with *some.*) □ *Now, there's some ankle I've never seen around here before.* □ *Do you get ankle like that around here all the time?* **2.** *in.* to walk away from one's employment; to leave. (Compare to *walk.*) □ *One more day like this, and I'm gonna ankle.* □ *I didn't fire her. I told her she could ankle if she wanted.*

annihilated *mod.* very drunk; intoxicated with a drug. □ *The boys came in annihilated and their father had plenty to say to them.* □ *Pete and Gary went out and got annihilated.*

another peep (out of you) *n.* another complaint, word, or sound from someone. (Usually in the negative.) □ *I don't want to hear another peep out of you!* □ *I've heard enough! Not another peep!*

ante ['ænti] **1.** *n.* an amount of money that must be contributed before playing certain card games such as poker. □ *What's the ante to join this game?* □ *That's a pretty high ante. Forget it!* **2.** *n.* the charge or cost. □ *What's the ante for a used 1985 four-door?* □ *The ante is marked on the sticker.*

anti ['ænti OR 'æntɑɪ] **1.** *n.* someone who is against someone or something. □ *She's an anti. Don't even ask her.* □ *All the antis are going to vote for it this time.* **2.** *mod.* against someone or something. (Sometimes with the force of a preposition.) □ *I'm not anti the proposal, I just have some questions.* □ *Four are in favor, and two are anti.*

antifreeze *n.* liquor; any legal or illegal alcohol. □ *With enough antifreeze, I can stand the cold.* □ *Here's some antifreeze to stop your teeth from chattering.*

antifreezed *mod.* alcohol intoxicated. □ *Man, I feel totally antifreezed.* □ *He appears to be frozen even though he's antifreezed.*

antsy ['æntsi] *mod.* nervous; restless. (See also *have ants in one's pants.*) □ *You look a little antsy. What's wrong?* □ *Who is that antsy guy?* □ *She gets antsy before a test.*

Anytime. *interj.* "You are welcome."; "Happy to oblige." (Sometimes said in response to "Thank you.") □ MARY: *Thanks for the ride.* PAUL: *Anytime. Think nothing of it.* □ TOM: *You've been a real friend, Sally. I can't thank you enough.* SALLY: *Anytime.*

ape *n.* a hoodlum or strong-arm man, especially if big and strong. (Underworld.) □ *Tell your ape to let me go!* □ *You take your apes and get out of here!*

ape hangers *n.* long steering handles on a bicycle or motorcycle. □ *Who is that guy riding the bike with ape hangers?* □ *Aren't ape hangers sort of dangerous?*

aped [ept] *mod.* alcohol intoxicated. □ *I've never seen my brother so totally aped before.* □ *He comes home aped about once a month.*

app *n.* an application; a computer software application. □ *Ted bought a new app for word-processing and he says it's a killer.* □ *Ted's killer app can run circles around your old WordSun program.*

apple **1.** *n.* a baseball. □ *Jim slammed the apple over the plate, but the ump called it a ball.* □ *Just when I raised my arm to throw to second, the damn apple slipped out of my hand and rolled down my arm. Now, explain that!* **2.** *n.* an Amerindian who behaves more like a European than an Amerindian. (Like the apple, the person is red on the outside and white on the inside. Patterned on *oreo.* See also *banana.* Potentially offensive. Use only with discretion.) □ *Stop acting like an apple all the time!* □ *Sam is your typical apple. Can't decide who he really is.*

apple-polisher *n.* a flatterer. □ *Doesn't that wimpy apple-polisher know how stupid he looks?* □ *Everybody at the office seems to be an apple-polisher but me.*

applesauce *n.* nonsense. □ *Don't give me that applesauce. I know better.* □ *That's just applesauce!*

arb [ɑrb] *n.* an arbitrageur; a market speculator. (Securities markets.) □ *The arbs are at it again, buying up companies like hot cakes.* □ *I wanted to be an arb, but it takes about forty million to get in the door.*

Are we away? *interrog.* "Shall we go?"; "Let's go." (Really a command to "depart" expressed as a question.) □ *Well, it's late. Are we away?* □ *The car's warmed up. Are we away?*

ark [ɑrk] *n.* an old car. □ *Why don't you*

get rid of that old ark and get something that's easier to park? □ *This ark is the most comfortable car I've ever had. I'll drive it till it falls apart.*

arm *n.* a police officer. (Underworld. See also *long arm of the law.*) □ *What'll you do if the arms come in while you're sawing the bars of your cell?* □ *So this arm says to me, "Going to a fire?"*

arm-twister *n.* someone who uses strong persuasion. □ *I hate to seem like an arm-twister, but I really need your help on this project.* □ *My aunt works as an arm-twister collecting overdue bills for the telephone company.*

arm-twisting *n.* powerful persuasion. □ *The boss is very good at arm-twisting.* □ *If nice talk won't work, try a little arm-twisting.*

armpit *n.* any undesirable place. (A nickname for an undesirable town or city.) □ *Who wants to spend a weekend in an armpit?* □ *The town should be called the armpit of the nation.*

army brat *n.* a child born to a parent in the army. (Such a child will live in many different places.) □ *I was an army brat and went to seven different schools before I got out of high school.* □ *We army brats tend to stick together.*

(a)round the bend 1. *mod.* crazy; beyond sanity. □ *I think I'm going around the bend.* □ *She sounds like she's round the bend already.* **2.** *mod.* alcohol or drug intoxicated. □ *One more of those, and you'll be around the bend.* □ *From the look in her eye, I'd say she is completely round the bend now.*

artillery 1. *n.* guns; grenades. (Underworld.) □ *Where does Max stash the artillery?* □ *All the artillery is locked in the trunk of the getaway car.* **2.** *n.* flatware; cutlery. □ *Who put out the artillery? I didn't get a fork.* □ *Go get your own artillery. This ain't the Ritz.*

[artist] *n.* a combining form meaning "specialist." See also *booze artist, bullshit artist, burn artist, castor oil artist, con artist, flimflam artist, hype artist, make-out artist, off artist, rip-off artist, takeoff artist.*

artsy-craftsy ['ɑrtsi 'kræf(t)si] *mod.* dabbling in arts and crafts; artistic. □ *Wally is sort of artsy-craftsy.* □ *Gary's an artsy-crafty kind of guy with lots of talent.* □ *The artsy-craftsy crowd held a show in the library parking lot last Sunday.*

artsy (fartsy) ['ɑrtsi ('fɑrtsi)] *mod.* obviously or overly artistic. (Use caution with *fart.*) □ *The decorations were sort of artsy fartsy, but the overall effect was quite nice.* □ *Things are a little artsy fartsy in the south dorm, but most of the residents are really nice.*

asleep at the switch *mod.* inattentive to duty. (Not literal.) □ *Donald was asleep at the switch when the call came in.* □ *He sat there reading—asleep at the switch as usual.*

asphalt jungle *n.* the paved landscape of the city; the city viewed as a savage place. □ *I don't look forward to spending the rest of my days in an asphalt jungle.* □ *I want to go back to Kansas. I hate the asphalt jungle.*

asshole (Potentially offensive. Use only with discretion.) **1.** *n.* the anus. □ *He threatened to kick me in the asshole, or something like that, if I didn't leave at once.* □ *He had to tell the doctor about the pain in his asshole because he simply didn't know any other word for it.* **2.** *n.* an obnoxious person. (Crude and provocative. Also a rude term of address.) □ *Shut up and get out, you asshole!* □ *Some days it seems like only the assholes got up, and everyone else stayed in bed.*

astronomical *mod.* extremely expensive; of any very high figure. □ *The prices here are astronomical!* □ *The market indexes have all reached astronomical heights for the second time.*

at a snail's gallop See the following entry.

at a snail's pace AND **at a snail's gallop** *mod.* very slowly. □ *Things are moving along at a snail's pace here, but we'll* *finish on time—have no fear.* □ *Poor old Wally is creeping at a snail's gallop because his car has a flat tire.*

at loose ends *mod.* nervous and anxious; bored with nothing to do. □ *Tom usually works puzzles whenever he's at loose ends.* □ *I'm at loose ends on weekends.*

attic *n.* the head, thought of as the location of one's intellect. □ *She's just got nothing in the attic. That's what's wrong with her.* □ *Ken has an attic full of fear and resentment he needs to clean out before he will feel comfortable again.*

attitude-adjuster *n.* a police officer's nightstick; any club. □ *The officer said he would bring order to the gathering with his attitude-adjuster.* □ *Andy had a black attitude-adjuster hanging from his belt, and I wasn't going to argue with him.*

Aunt Flo [. . . 'flo] *n.* a woman's menstrual period. (Used especially in expressions. See also *visit from Flo.* Refers to the menstrual flow.) □ *I am sorry to announce that Aunt Flo has come for a visit.* □ *It's Aunt Flo again. She is such a pest.*

avs [ævz] *n.* chance; the law of averages. (Streets. Always with *the.*) □ *The avs say that I ought to be dead by now.* □ *It looks like the avs finally caught up with him.*

(Aw) shucks! *exclam.* a mild oath. (Folksy.) □ *Shucks, ma'am. It wasn't anything at all.* □ *Aw shucks, I ain't never been this close to a woman before.*

away 1. *mod.* out (in baseball). □ *Jim put the last one away, and that is three outs retiring the side.* □ *There's one away and two men left on base.* **2.** *mod.* in prison. (Underworld.) □ *My cousin is away for a year.* □ *The judge wanted to put him away for two years, but decided on one instead.*

awesome 1. *exclam.* "Great!"; "Excellent!" (Usually **Awesome!** Standard English, but used often in slang.) □ *You own that gorgeous hog? Awesome!* □ *Awesome! I'm impressed.* **2.** *mod.* impressive. □ *Let me have a look at this awesome new box of yours.* □ *That thing is really awesome.*

AWOL [e 'dəblju 'o 'ɛl OR 'ewɑl] *mod.* "absent without leave"; escaped from prison or from the military. (Acronym or initialism.) □ *The kid the cops picked up was AWOL. He's had it.* □ *If I don't get back to the base, they're going to think I'm A.W.O.L.*

Aztec two-step *n.* diarrhea, specifically that contracted in Mexico or South America by tourists; *Montezuma's revenge.* □ *I was there for only two days before I was struck down with the Aztec two-step.* □ *I spent a week in Cancun and never even heard of anybody with Aztec two-step.*

B

B. and B. *mod.* "breast and buttock," having to do with entertainment featuring female nudity. ☐ *There were some picketers in front of the store protesting the sale of B. and B. mags over the counter.* ☐ *Many movies contain a little B. and B. just to get an R-rating.*

B-ball *n.* basketball; a basketball. (See also *hoops.* Compare to *V-ball.*) ☐ *Let's go play some B-ball.* ☐ *Toss me the B-ball, huh?*

BA *n.* "bare ass"; the naked buttocks. (See also *hang a BA (at someone).*) ☐ *Cover up your BA and see who's at the door.* ☐ *The guy was running around with his BA showing.*

babe **1.** AND **babes** *n.* a term of endearment for a woman or a man. (Also a term of address. See also *baby.*) ☐ *Look, babe, get in there and tackle that guy! We're losing!* ☐ *Say, babes, bring me a beer, would you?* **2.** *n.* a good-looking woman. ☐ *Who is that babe standing on the corner over there?* ☐ *That babe happens to be my sister.*

babes See the previous entry.

baboon *n.* a jerk; a stupid person. (Also a rude term of address.) ☐ *Stop acting like a baboon! Grow up!* ☐ *Tell that ugly baboon to get out of here.* ☐ *Hey, baboon, get off my lawn!*

baby **1.** *n.* a lover; one's sweetheart. (Also a term of address.) ☐ *Come over here and kiss me, baby.* ☐ *Look, baby, I think we can work this out.* **2.** *n.* a term of address for a friend or pal of either sex. ☐ *Come on, baby, push this thing—hard!* ☐ *Hey, baby! Getting any action?* **3.** *n.* a thing; a gadget; a machine, such as a car. (Similar to *sucker.*) ☐ *This baby is a real bear.* ☐ *Hand me that baby with the sharp point, will you?* ☐ *What kind of tranny does that baby have?* **4.** *n.* a project thought of as an offspring. (Always with a possessor.) ☐ *Whose baby is the Johnson account?* ☐ *You give the report. This project is your baby.*

baby bear *n.* a beginning highway patrol officer; a *rookie* cop. (Citizens band radio. See also *Smokey (the Bear).*) ☐ *Some baby bear tried to arrest me for speeding, but I conned him out of it.* ☐ *He may be just a baby bear, but he can still bite hard.*

Baby Bell *n.* one of the new, regional telephone companies that were formerly a part of American Telephone and Telegraph Company. (Compare to *Ma Bell.*) ☐ *The Baby Bells are doing better than the parent company.* ☐ *"If the Baby Bells get into long distance service, say good-bye to Ma Bell," the hotshot money manager muttered in his third martini.*

(baby) boomer *n.* someone born during the baby boom—from the last years of World War II until the early 1960's. ☐ *When the baby boomers get around to saving up for retirement, you're going to see a lot of investment scams.* ☐ *At about age forty-five the boomers will start putting money away.*

baby-kisser *n.* a politician. ☐ *Once those baby-kissers get in office, they spend, spend, spend.* ☐ *There were lots of promises at the town square today when four local baby-kissers tried to rally interest in the upcoming election.*

babycakes AND **honeycakes** *n.* a term of endearment; sweetie; dear. (Also a term of address.) ☐ *My babycakes gave me a flimsy nightie for my birthday.* ☐ *Look, honeycakes, I found some lipstick on your collar.*

bach (it) See *ba(t)ch (it).*

back *n.* one's support or second in a fight. (From *back-up.*) ☐ *Fred served as Tom's back in the scuffle.* ☐ *I need a back I can depend on.*

back-door trot(s) *n.* a case of diarrhea. (From the time when people had to go out the backdoor to the outhouse.) ☐ *I can't go out tonight. I got a case of the back-door trots.* ☐ *She gets the back-door trot when she drinks wine.*

back-ender See *rear-ender.*

back number *n.* an old-fashioned person. (Like an out-of-print issue of a magazine.) ☐ *Some old back number wearing gaiters wants to have a word with you.* ☐ *Oh, Dad! You're getting to be such a back number!*

back to square one *phr.* back to the beginning. (Often with *go.*) ☐ *Well, it looks like it's back to square one.* ☐ *We've got to get this done without going back to square one.*

back to the salt mines *phr.* back to the workplace. ☐ *Well, it's Monday morning. Back to the salt mines.* ☐ *Break's over! Back to the salt mines, everybody.*

back up *in.* to refuse to go through with something; to back out (of something). ☐ *Fred backed up at the last minute, leaving me with twenty pounds of hot dogs.* ☐ *Don't back up now, man. It's too late.*

backbone *n.* courage; integrity. ☐ *If you had any backbone, you would be able to deal with this.* ☐ *She lacks backbone, that's all.*

backed up *mod.* drug intoxicated. ☐ *Oh my God, I am really backed up!* ☐ *Old Benny's really backed up.*

backer *n.* a supporter; a financier of a play, political campaign, etc. ☐ *I had a lot of generous backers for the play.* ☐ *I was hoping for a backer, but the project was too chancy.*

backfire *in.* to release intestinal gas anally, perhaps audibly. (Use caution with the topic.) ☐ *Whew! Somebody backfired!* ☐ *It was noisy when Dave backfired, and hardly anyone heard what happened.*

backfire (on someone) *in.* [for a scheme meant to cause harm to someone or something] to harm the person who runs the scheme. ☐ *I hope this plan doesn't backfire on me.* ☐ *Her attempt to frame Bill for the crime backfired.*

backhander *n.* a backhand slap in the face. ☐ *Then she gave me a powerful backhander without even looking to see who I was.* ☐ *Yes, officer, a perfectly strange woman came up and clobbered me with a backhander that loosened a tooth.*

backlash *n.* the negative response to something. ☐ *Was there any backlash aimed at your suggestion?* ☐ *We weren't prepared for the backlash we got.*

backroom *mod.* secret; concealed. ☐ *I am going to watch for backroom deals.* ☐ *All the candidates were selected in backroom meetings.*

backroom boys See *boys in the backroom.*

backseat driver *n.* an annoying passenger who tells the driver how to drive; someone who tells others how to do things. ☐ *I don't need any backseat driver on this project.* ☐ *Stop being a backseat driver!*

backside *n.* the buttocks; one's rear. ☐ *She fell right on her backside.* ☐ *There is some mustard or something on your backside.*

backslapper *n.* someone who is overly friendly and outgoing. ☐ *At election time, city hall is filled with backslappers and baby-kissers.* ☐ *In the used car dealership, this backslapper comes up to me and tells me he's got something that will last me a lifetime.*

bacon *n.* the police; a police officer. (Compare to *pig.*) ☐ *Keep an eye out* *for the bacon.* □ *That bacon is hassling me!*

bad 1. *mod.* powerful; intense. (Black.) □ *Man, that is really bad music!* □ *This grass is bad!* **2.** *mod.* suitable; excellent; good. (Black.) □ *I got some new silks that are really bad.* □ *That is a bad man dancing there.* □ *Look at those really bad shoes on that guy.*

bad egg *n.* a repellent person. □ *You're not such a bad egg after all.* □ *She's a real bad egg.*

bad hair day *n.* a bad day in general. (Also used literally when one's inability to do anything with one's hair seems to color the events of the day.) □ *I'm sorry I am so glum. This has been a real bad hair day.* □ *It's just one bad hair day after another.*

bad-mouth 1. *tr.* to speak ill of someone or something. (See also *dirty mouth, poor-mouth.*) □ *I wish you would stop bad-mouthing my car.* □ *Harry bad-mouths everything he doesn't understand.* **2.** *n.* someone who speaks ill of someone or something. □ *Harry is such a bad-mouth!* □ *The world is filled with bad-mouths. We need more caring people.*

bad news 1. *n.* the bill for something. □ *Here comes the bad news.* □ *Okay, let's see what the bad news is.* **2.** *mod.* unpleasant; unfortunate. □ *That poor guy is really bad news.* □ *It's bad news Freddy on the phone again.*

bad paper *n.* bad checks; a bad check. □ *She got six months for passing bad paper.* □ *There is more bad paper passed in this town in one month than in all of Sweden for a whole year!*

bad rap 1. *n.* a false criminal charge. (Underworld. The same as *bum rap.*) □ *Freddy got stuck with a bad rap.* □ *All those guys get nothing but bad raps. Nobody's ever guilty.* **2.** *n.* unjustified criticism. □ *This car has gotten a bad rap, and I don't know why.* □ *Butter has been getting sort of a bad rap lately.*

bad trip 1. *n.* a bad experience with a drug. (Drugs.) □ *My first trip was a bad trip, and I never took another.* □ *The guide is supposed to talk you down from a bad trip.* **2.** *n.* any bad experience or person. □ *This class is a bad trip.* □ *Harry can be such a bad trip.*

badass ['bæd'æs] **1.** *mod.* tough; bad; belligerent. □ *Tom is one badass cop!* □ *Stop acting like such a badass punk!* **2.** *n.* a tough guy; a belligerent and arrogant person, usually a male. □ *Don't be such a badass all the time.* □ *Tom is the classic badass. A real bum.*

baddie See the following entry.

baddy AND **baddie** ['bædi] *n.* a bad thing or person. □ *Using butter is supposed to be a real baddy.* □ *Marty has become such a baddie that no one speaks to her anymore.*

bafflegab ['bæfl̩gæb] *n.* confusing jargon. □ *Don't throw that bafflegab at me. Use English.* □ *Watch out for the bafflegab they use to try to sell that stuff.*

bag 1. *tr.* to capture and arrest someone. (Underworld.) □ *They bagged the robber with the loot still on him.* □ *We'll be able to bag the alleged killer when we have more evidence.* (More at *bagged.*) **2.** *n.* an ugly woman. (Derogatory.) □ *Tell the old bag to mind her own business.* □ *She has turned into an absolute bag.* **3.** *n.* one's preference; something suited to one's preference. □ *My bag is things with whipped cream.* □ *That kind of stuff is just not my bag.* **4.** *tr.* to obtain something. □ *I'll try to bag a couple of tickets for you.* □ *See if you can bag one of the red ones.* **5.** *n.* a container of drugs. (Drugs. Not necessarily a real bag.) □ *Two bags of H. for two dimes?* □ *The man flipped a couple of bags out from a little stack he had held under his wrist by a rubber band.* **6.** *in.* to die. □ *The guy was coughing so hard that I thought he was going to bag right there.* □ *The old man bagged on the way to the hospital.*

Bag it! 1. *exclam.* "Drop dead!" (California. See also *Bag your face!, Bag that!*) □ *You are not rad, and you are not awesome, so, like, bag it!* □ *Bag it yourself!* **2.** *exclam.* "Shut up!" □ *Bag* *it! I'm reading.* ☐ *Oh, bag it! I've heard enough.*

bag of bones *n.* an extremely skinny person or animal. ☐ *I'm just turning into a bag of bones.* ☐ *Get that old bag of bones off the racetrack!*

bag of wind See *windbag.*

bag on someone *in.* to criticize someone. ☐ *Stop bagging on me! I'm tired of all your complaining.* ☐ *If you are going to bag on everyone all the time, I don't want to hear about it.*

bag some rays See *catch some rays.*

Bag that! *tr.* "Forget that!" ☐ *Bag that! The number I gave you was wrong.* ☐ *There are four—no, bag that!—six of the red ones and three blue ones.*

Bag your face! *exclam.* "Go away!" (See also *Bag it!*) ☐ *You outrage me. Bag your face!* ☐ *You are in the way. Bag your face!*

bagged 1. AND **in the bag** *mod.* alcohol intoxicated. ☐ *How can anybody be so bagged on four beers?* ☐ *She just sat there and got bagged.* **2.** *mod.* arrested. ☐ *"You are bagged," said the officer, clapping a hand on the suspect's shoulder.* ☐ *"I'm not bagged yet, copper," said the crook.*

bagman ['bægmæn] **1.** *n.* a tramp. ☐ *Two old bagmen wandered slowly down the lane.* ☐ *The bagman asked politely for some work that he would be paid for in food.* **2.** *n.* a drug dealer. (Drugs.) ☐ *Sam was a bagman for a well-known dealer for a while.* ☐ *We don't just want the bagman. We want to arrest Mr. Big.* **3.** *n.* any racketeer. ☐ *Some bagman from the mob was pulled out of the river yesterday.* ☐ *So you think you and your bagmen can just walk in here and take over!*

Bahama-mama [bə'hamə'mamə] *n.* an obese black woman. ☐ *Clare has turned into a real Bahama-mama. She's gonna have to lay off eating so much.* ☐ *That Bahama-mama who was just in here ordered four chocolate shakes.*

bail (out) *in.* to resign or leave; to get free of someone or something. ☐ *I can't take any more. I'm going to bail out.* ☐ *Albert bailed just before he got fired.*

baked 1. *mod.* sunburned. ☐ *I was out in the sun until I got totally baked.* ☐ *If you would use some lotion, you wouldn't get so baked.* **2.** *mod.* alcohol or drug intoxicated. ☐ *All four of them went out and got baked.* ☐ *I've never seen anybody so baked.*

baldie See the following entry.

baldy AND **baldie** ['bɔldi] *n.* a bald-headed man. ☐ *I'm getting to be an old baldie.* ☐ *I turned into a baldy in my twenties.*

ball 1. *n.* a wild time at a party; a good time. ☐ *We really had a ball. See ya!* ☐ *Your birthday party was a ball!* **2.** *in.* to enjoy oneself. (Ambiguous with the next sense.) ☐ *The whole crowd was balling and having a fine time.* ☐ *We balled the whole evening.* **3.** *tr.* & *in.* to copulate (with someone). (Potentially offensive. Use only with discretion.) ☐ *Isn't there anything more to you than balling?* ☐ *I hear she balled him but good.* **4.** *n.* a testicle. (Usually plural. Potentially offensive. Use only with discretion.) ☐ *He got hit right in the balls.* ☐ *The teacher preferred 'testicles' to 'balls,' if they had to be mentioned at all.*

ball and chain *n.* a wife. (Mostly jocular.) ☐ *I've got to get home to my ball and chain.* ☐ *My ball and chain is mad at me.*

ball-breaker AND **ball-buster** (Potentially offensive. Use only with discretion.) **1.** *n.* a difficult task demanding hard work or effort. (Originally for males, now for either sex.) ☐ *This job is a real ball-breaker.* ☐ *The task I got assigned was a ball-buster, for sure.* **2.** *n.* a hard or cruel boss. (Originally for males, now for either sex.) ☐ *The boss is a real ball-breaker, and I don't know how long I can go on with this job.* ☐ *They have special management schools to train ball-breakers.* **3.** *n.* someone who is threatening or abusive. (Originally for males, now for either sex.) ☐ *She is a ball-buster. Just forget about her.* ☐

Claire can be such a ball-buster. What's her problem?

ball-buster See the previous entry.

ball-busting (Potentially offensive. Use only with discretion.) **1.** *mod.* difficult or challenging. □ *I am tired of this ball-busting job and I want out.* □ *I was given a ball-busting assignment, and it has kept me very busy.* **2.** *mod.* obnoxious and threatening. (Originally for males, now for either sex.) □ *Tell that ball-busting bitch to mind her own business.* □ *Wally is a ball-busting guy who is probably just very insecure.*

ball is in someone's court *phr.* to be someone else's move, play, or turn. (Always with *the*.) □ *The ball's in your court now. You do something.* □ *I can't do anything as long as the ball is in John's court.*

ball of fire AND **fireball** *n.* an energetic and ambitious person; a go-getter. □ *That guy is a real ball of fire when it comes to sales.* □ *I don't want to hire some young fireball. I need wisdom and thoughtfulness.*

ball park estimate AND **ball park figure** *n.* a rough estimate. □ *I can only give you a ball park estimate at this time.* □ *All I need is a ball park figure. Exactness comes later.*

ball park figure See the previous entry.

balled up *mod.* confused; mixed up. (This is hyphenated before a nominal.) □ *That dame is so balled up she doesn't know anything.* □ *This is really a balled-up mess you've made.*

baller *n.* an athlete. (One who plays with footballs, basketballs, baseballs, etc.) □ *You will make a lot of money as a professional baller.* □ *Most of the high-paid ballers are out of a job by the age of forty.*

ballhead *n.* an athlete. (Perhaps a stupid one.) □ *My dorm is full of ballheads.* □ *If you want to be a ballhead, you have to have talent and stamina.*

ballyhoo ['bælihu] **1.** *n.* publicity. □ *I have never heard so much ballyhoo for such a lousy movie.* □ *After the ballyhoo died down, we realized that nothing at all had really changed.* **2.** *tr.* to promote or publicize someone or something. □ *They ballyhooed this movie on television for a month before it came out.* □ *We promise to ballyhoo John at election time.*

balmed *mod.* alcohol intoxicated. (See also *bombed (out), embalmed.*) □ *Tom was totally balmed and went to bed.* □ *Fred and Wilma went out and got totally balmed.*

balmy 1. *mod.* crazy; giddy. □ *You are totally balmy if you think I will put up with that stuff.* □ *What a balmy idea!* **2.** *mod.* alcohol intoxicated. □ *She's not just drunk, she's a little balmy.* □ *How can anybody be so balmy on four beers?*

baloney AND **bologna** [bə'loni] *n.* nonsense. (Also as an exclamation.) □ *Don't give me all that baloney!* □ *That's just a lot of bologna. Don't believe it for a minute.* □ *Baloney! You're nuts!*

bamboozle [bæm'buzl̩] *tr.* to deceive someone; to confuse someone. □ *Don't try to bamboozle me! I know what I want!* □ *The crooks bamboozled the old man out of his life savings.* (More at *bamboozled*.)

bamboozled [bæm'buzl̩d] **1.** *mod.* confused. □ *This stuff sure has me bamboozled.* □ *I don't know who's more bamboozled, you or me.* **2.** *mod.* alcohol intoxicated. (Collegiate.) □ *She's not just drunk, she's totally bamboozled.* □ *She just sat there and got bamboozled as the dickens.*

banana *n.* an American of East Asian descent who acts "too much" like a Caucasian. (The person is yellow on the outside and white on the inside. Patterned on *oreo*. See also *apple*. Use discretion with racial and ethnic terms.) □ *Stop acting like such a banana!* □ *Dave is the classic banana. Can't quite figure out who he really is.*

banana-head *n.* a stupid person. □ *Kelly can be such a banana-head!* □ *Ask that banana-head why she is wearing a coat like that in July.*

banana oil *n.* nonsense. □ *That is the silliest banana oil I have ever heard!* □ *I refuse to listen to any more of your childish banana oil.*

banana republic **1.** *n.* a stereotypic small Central American country having continual political turmoil. (Formerly of interest to the U.S. only because it supplied bananas.) □ *This is no banana republic! Things like this aren't supposed to happen here!* □ *If you want to change governments like underwear, maybe you should emigrate to some banana republic.* **2.** *mod.* in turmoil, like a stereotypic small Central American country. □ *Who would think that you would have banana republic politics in your own backyard?* □ *We've had enough of your banana republic tactics!*

bananas (Often with *go*, see also *go bananas*.) **1.** *mod.* crazy. □ *You are driving me bananas!* □ *You were bananas before I ever showed up on the scene.* **2.** *mod.* enthusiastic. □ *The audience was bananas over the new star.* □ *The kids were bananas when they saw their presents.*

bang **1.** *n.* a bit of excitement; a thrill; some amusement. □ *We got a bang out of your letter.* □ *What a bang the party was!* **2.** *n.* the degree of potency of the alcohol in liquor. □ *This stuff has quite a bang!* □ *The bang is gone from this wine.* **3.** *n.* an injection of a drug; any dose of a drug. (Drugs.) □ *I need a bang pretty fast.* □ *If Max doesn't have a bang by noon, he gets desperate.* **4.** *tr. & in.* to inject a drug. (Drugs.) □ *They were in the backroom banging away.* □ *She banged herself and went on with her work.* **5.** *n.* a drug *rush*. (Drugs.) □ *One snort and the bang will knock you over.* □ *There was one sudden bang and then nothing.*

(bang) dead to rights *mod.* in the act; (guilty) without question. □ *We caught her dead to rights with the loot still on her.* □ *There he was, bang dead to rights with the gun still smoking.*

bang for the buck *n.* value for the money spent; excitement for the money spent; the cost-to-benefit ratio. □ *I didn't get anywhere near the bang for the buck I expected.* □ *How much bang for the buck did you really think you would get from a twelve-year-old car—at any price?*

bang in the arm *n.* an injection of narcotics. (Drugs. See also *bang*. Compare to *shot in the arm*.) □ *The guy looked like he needed a bang in the arm right then!* □ *One good bang in the arm leads to another, they always say.*

bang-up *mod.* really excellent. □ *We had a bang-up time at your bash.* □ *I like to throw a bang-up party once or twice a year.* □ *Another bang-up day at the factory!*

banger **1.** *n.* the front bumper of a vehicle. □ *Other than a dent or two in the banger, this buggy's okay.* □ *How much for a used banger like this old heap?* **2.** *n.* a hypodermic syringe. (Drugs.) □ *Jed dropped his banger and really panicked when it broke.* □ *His banger and other stuff were upstairs under a loose board.*

banjaxed ['bændʒækst] **1.** *mod.* demolished; ruined. □ *My car is totally banjaxed. What a mess!* □ *Everything I worked for is now banjaxed.* **2.** *mod.* alcohol intoxicated. □ *She just sat there and got banjaxed.* □ *All four of them went out and got banjaxed.*

bank *n.* money; ready cash. □ *I can't go out with you. No bank.* □ *I'm a little low on bank at the moment.*

banker's hours *n.* short work hours: 10:00 A.M. to 2:00 P.M. □ *When did you start keeping banker's hours?* □ *There aren't many bankers who keep banker's hours these days.*

bankroll **1.** *n.* a roll or wad of currency; one's cash assets. □ *My bankroll is getting a little low.* □ *Don't show that bankroll around here!* **2.** *tr.* to finance something. □ *We were hoping to find somebody who would bankroll the project.* □ *Wilson Sanderson, famous for bankrolling struggling acting companies, could not be reached for comment.*

barb *n.* a barbiturate; a barbiturate capsule. (Drugs.) □ *Old Joey is hooked on barbs.* □ *You got a barb I can bum?*

Barbie doll *n.* a pretty, giddy *girl* or woman. ☐ *She's just a Barbie doll.* ☐ *Ask that little Barbie doll if she wants a drink.*

bare-assed *mod.* naked. (Potentially offensive. Use only with discretion.) ☐ *Man, that little store has the biggest display of bare-assed girlie magazines I have ever seen.* ☐ *And she stood there at the window, drunk and bare-assed for all the world to see.*

barf [bɑrf] **1.** *in.* to empty one's stomach; to vomit. ☐ *I think I'm going to barf!* ☐ *Don't barf here.* **2.** *n.* vomit. ☐ *Is that barf on your shoe?* ☐ *Whatever it is, it looks like barf.* **3.** *in.* [for a computer] to fail to function. ☐ *The whole system barfed about noon, and all the data was lost.* ☐ *My little computer barfs about once a day. Something is wrong.* **4.** AND **barfola** [bɑrf'olə] *interj.* "dammit"; "Good grief!" (Often **Barfola!**) ☐ *Oh they're late. Barfola!* ☐ *Barfola! You're out of your mind!*

barf bag *n.* a bag available on an airplane for persons who are nauseated. ☐ *I hope I never even have to see anyone use a barf bag.* ☐ *What do they do with used barf bags?*

Barf City *n.* someone or something disgusting or undesirable. (*Barf* = vomit.) ☐ *The guy is gross! Just plain Barf City!* ☐ *The movie was really bad; Barf City, I'd say.*

Barf out! *exclam.* "This is awful!" (California.) ☐ *Look at that scrungy wimp! Barf out!* ☐ *Barf out! Get a life!*

barf-out *n.* an unpleasant person or thing. ☐ *What a barf-out! I want my money back.* ☐ *That guy is a real barf-out.*

barf someone out *tr.* to disgust someone. (California.) ☐ *This whole scene like, so, like, barfs me out.* 🅃 *The movie barfed out everybody in the theatre.*

barfly **1.** *n.* a person who frequents bars. ☐ *Who will trust the word of an old barfly like Wally?* ☐ *There were only a few of the regular barflies hanging over their drinks when I walked into Mike's place.* **2.** *n.* a drunkard. ☐ *You're nothing but an old barfly!* ☐ *Some barfly staggered out of the tavern straight into the side of a car.*

barfola See *barf.*

(bargaining) chip *n.* something to be used in negotiations. ☐ *I want to use this incident as a bargaining chip in future negotiations.* ☐ *I need a few chips to use when we get down to drawing up the contract.*

bari AND **bary** ['bæri] *n.* a baritone saxophone, the saxophone with a pitch range approximating that of the human baritone voice. (Musicians.) ☐ *Wally played the bari when he was in college.* ☐ *A fine bary will cost thousands of dollars.*

barking spider AND **trumpet spider** *n.* the imaginary source of the sound of an audible release of intestinal gas. ☐ *Hey, Chuck! Did I hear a barking spider over there?* ☐ *Heidi, do you know anything about the trumpet spider I keep hearing?*

barnburner *n.* an attention-getting event or development. ☐ *The current barnburner in Washington is the Wilson investigation.* ☐ *This is a real barnburner! Everyone will want to see it.*

Barney *n.* a *nerd;* a *wimp.* (From the Flintstones character or the children's dinosaur character.) ☐ *Sam's an old Barney—a real loser.* ☐ *If you weren't such a Barney, you'd stick up for your own rights.*

barnstorm **1.** *tr. & in.* [for an entertainer] to perform in small towns for short engagements. ☐ *My great-uncle used to barnstorm Kansas and Oklahoma with his medicine show.* ☐ *He barnstormed for three years before his death.* **2.** *in.* to perform stunts in a biplane in small towns. (Presumably swooping around barns.) ☐ *When we used to barnstorm, everybody thought we were kooks.* ☐ *The old biplane we used to barnstorm with is the safest plane ever built.*

barnyard *mod.* smutty; obscene. (Refers to the dung found in barnyards. See also *barnyard language.*) ☐ *Those* *barnyard movies belong in the barnyard.* □ *You are thinking barnyard thoughts again. I see it in your eyes.*

barnyard language *n.* dirty language. □ *We don't allow any barnyard language in the house!* □ *I don't care to hear so much barnyard language.*

barracuda *n.* a predatory person, especially a predatory woman. □ *She's a barracuda. Better watch out!* □ *I wouldn't get involved with those barracudas if I were you.*

barrel **1.** *tr. & in.* to drink liquor to excess. □ *Those guys are barreling like beer was going out of style.* □ *Stop barreling beer and let's go home.* **2.** *n.* a drunkard. □ *The barrel was full up and through for the evening.* □ *A tired and weepy barrel staggered in and fell into a booth in the corner.* **3.** *in.* to go fast; to speed while driving. □ *He was barreling along at about ninety.* □ *She barreled out of here like a bat out of hell.*

barrel ass *in.* to move or drive carelessly and rapidly. (Potentially offensive. Use only with discretion.) □ *He was barrel assing along at nearly ninety.* □ *I'm gonna barrel ass outa here in just one minute.*

barrel fever **1.** *n.* drunkenness. □ *She seems to get barrel fever about once a week.* □ *I think she has figured out what caused her barrel fever.* **2.** *n.* a hangover. □ *Man, have I ever got barrel fever.* □ *That business last night gave me a touch of barrel fever.* **3.** *n.* the delirium tremens. □ *The old man is down with barrel fever again.* □ *The barrel fever hit him in the middle of the night.*

barrel of fun *n.* a tremendous amount of fun. □ *Tracy is just a barrel of fun on dates.* □ *We had a barrel of fun at your party.*

barreled (up) *mod.* alcohol intoxicated. □ *Those guys are really barreled up!* □ *She spends a lot of time barreled.*

bary See *bari.*

base **1.** *mod.* rude; gross. (California.) □ *You are so, like, base!* □ *What a base creep!* □ *Oh, how base!* **2.** See *free base.*

base binge [... bɪndʒ] *n.* a binge on *free base,* a form of cocaine. (Drugs.) □ *Clare is off on another base binge.* □ *Base binges are very expensive.*

baseballing See *free-basing.*

basehead See the following entry.

baseman AND **basehead** *n.* someone who is using *free base,* a form of cocaine; someone who is "on *base.*" (Drugs.) □ *They say that all those rich guys are basemen.* □ *The baseheads in the dorm finally got caught.* □ *The stuff is so powerful that one whiff and you're a basehead.* □ *Basemen shouldn't drive.*

bash [bæʃ] **1.** *n.* a wild party; a night on the town. □ *What a bash! I'm exhausted!* □ *There's a big bash over at Wally's place.* **2.** *in.* to *party;* to celebrate. □ *Let's go out and bash, how 'bout it?* □ *No more bashing for me till I recover from last night.*

bashed [bæʃt] **1.** *mod.* crushed; struck. □ *His poor car was bashed beyond recognition.* □ *Give me that bashed one, and I'll straighten it out.* **2.** *mod.* alcohol intoxicated. □ *All four of them went out and got bashed.* □ *I've never seen anybody so bashed.*

bashing *n.* criticizing; defaming. (A combining form that follows the name of the person or thing being criticized.) □ *I am sick of your college-bashing!* □ *I hope you'll excuse the broker-bashing, but some of these guys don't play fair.* □ *On T.V. they had a long session of candidate-bashing, and then they read the sports news.*

basing See *free-basing.*

basket *n.* the stomach. (See also *breadbasket.*) □ *I got a pain in the basket.* □ *You've got a lot of something in your basket. It's huge.*

basket case *n.* a person who is a nervous wreck. (Formerly referred to a person who is totally physically disabled.) □ *After that meeting, I was practically a basket case.* □ *The waiting was so intense that I was a real basket case.*

Basra belly ['bɑsrə 'bɛli] *n.* diarrhea; a case of diarrhea. □ *The Basra belly hit* *me while I was on the bus.* ☐ *How do you tell Basra belly from Montezuma's revenge?*

basted ['bestəd] **1.** *mod.* beaten; harmed. ☐ *The team got basted three games in a row.* ☐ *We were really basted in the market crash.* **2.** *mod.* alcohol intoxicated. ☐ *I got totally basted.* ☐ *I got so basted I vowed never to touch another drop.*

bat [bæt] **1.** *n.* a drinking bout. ☐ *She was on a bat that lasted over a week.* ☐ *What's the longest bat you've ever heard of?* **2.** *n.* a drunkard; a person on a drinking spree. ☐ *Somebody give that bat a hand before he falls down.* ☐ *A tired old bat—still waving a bottle—met me on the stairs.*

ba(t)ch (it) [bætʃ . . .] *tr. & in.* to live alone like a bachelor. ☐ *I tried to bach it for a while, but I got too lonely.* ☐ *I didn't want to batch, but I had to.*

bathtub scum *n.* a totally despised person. (See also *pond scum; shower scum.* Also a term of address.) ☐ *Look out, bathtub scum, outa my way!* ☐ *John is bathtub scum at its worst.*

bats [bæts] **1.** AND **batty** ['bædi] *mod.* crazy. ☐ *You're bats!* ☐ *You are driving me batty!* **2.** AND **batty** *mod.* alcohol intoxicated; confused and drunk. ☐ *The guy was bats—stewed to his ears.* ☐ *She was sort of batty from the wine.* **3.** *n.* the delirium tremens. (Always with *the.*) ☐ *My buddy is shaking because of a slight case of the bats.* ☐ *The bats getting you down again, Jed?*

batted 1. *mod.* alcohol intoxicated. ☐ *She spends a lot of time batted.* ☐ *Will this stuff get me batted?* **2.** AND **batted out** *mod.* arrested. (Underworld.) ☐ *I got batted out on my first day as a booster.* ☐ *This gal got batted twice last year on the same rap.*

batted out See the previous entry.

battered *mod.* alcohol intoxicated. ☐ *Man, was I battered. I will never drink another drop.* ☐ *Those guys really got battered at the party.*

battle-ax ['bædl̩ 'æks] *n.* a belligerent (old) woman. (Derogatory.) ☐ *Tell the old battle-ax she can go straight to blazes.* ☐ *I can handle any battle-ax. Send her on in.*

battle of the bulge *n.* the attempt to keep one's waistline normal. (Named for a World War II battle.) ☐ *She appears to have lost the battle of the bulge.* ☐ *I've been fighting the battle of the bulge ever since I had the baby.*

battleships See *gunboats.*

batty See *bats.*

bay window *n.* a belly; an abdomen. ☐ *You are going to have to do something about that bay window.* ☐ *Your bay window is getting out of hand.*

bazillion [bə'zɪljən] *n.* an indefinite, enormous number. ☐ *Ernie gave me a bazillion good reasons why he shouldn't do it.* ☐ *Next year's bazillion-dollar budget should make things even worse.*

bazoo ['bɑ'zu OR bə'zu] **1.** *n.* a jeer; a raspberry. ☐ *They gave Ted the old bazoo when he fumbled the ball.* ☐ *A chorus of bazoos and hoots rebuked the coach when he threw the chair on the court.* **2.** *n.* the mouth. ☐ *You would have to open your big bazoo and tell everything.* ☐ *Don't talk with a full bazoo.* **3.** *n.* the stomach or belly. ☐ *Look at the bazoo on that guy!* ☐ *You can tell that his bazoo came from too much beer.* **4.** *n.* the anus. (Use caution with the topic.) ☐ *You wanna get kicked in the bazoo?* ☐ *Max threatened to install something in Bruno's bazoo.* **5.** *n.* the buttocks. (Use caution with the topic.) ☐ *She fell down right on her bazoo.* ☐ *Put your bazoo on this chair and let's have a little talk.*

bazoom(s) *n.* the breasts. (Potentially offensive. Use only with discretion. Jocular or euphemistic.) ☐ *This doll has real bazooms.* ☐ *She has quite a—ah—bazoom.*

B.B. brain *n.* a stupid person; a person with a brain the size of shot. (Also a rude term of address.) ☐ *What B.B. brain left the door open?* ☐ *Look here, B.B. brain, straighten up and fly right!*

BCNU ['bi'si'ən'ju] *phr.* "Be seeing you." (An initialism. Appears in informal written contexts.) □ *Bye for now. BCNU.* □ *Todd always closes his notes with "BCNU."*

be a drag (on someone) *phr.* to be a burden (to someone). □ *I wish you wouldn't be such a drag on your friends.* □ *I don't want to be a drag on the department.*

be casper *n.* to be leaving; to be disappearing. (In the manner of Casper, the friendly ghost—a cartoon character.) □ *We'll be casper in just a minute.* □ *I'm casper. See you later.*

be down (with someone) *n.* be friends with someone; to be okay or on good terms with someone. (*Down* = okay.) □ *It's okay. I'm down with Chuck.* □ *Chuck and I are down.*

be dust *n.* to be in trouble; to be worthless as dust; to be dead and turned to dust. □ *You keep acting like that and you'll be dust.* □ *Bruno said that Max was going to be dust if Mr. Big ever heard about what happened.*

be-in ['bi ɪn] *n.* a gathering of hippies. □ *A meeting of happy people, yes; a be-in this is not.* □ *This is just like a sixties be-in. Lots of phony love.*

be in someone's face *mod.* irritating someone. (See also *get in someone's face; Get out of my face!; in your face.*) □ *You are in my face too much, and I don't like it.* □ *I wish that the coach wasn't always in my face about something.*

Be my guest. *sent.* "Please go in front of me."; "Please make yourself comfortable in my home." □ *John stood aside at the open door and said to Walter, "Be my guest."* □ *Help yourself to whatever you need. Be my guest.*

beach bum *n.* a young man who frequents beaches. □ *A bronzed beach bum helped me find my lotion.* □ *Some of those beach bums are getting to look sort of old.*

beach bunny *n.* a young woman who frequents beaches. □ *This little beach bunny bounced up and offered to put lotion on me.* □ *They say that most of those beach bunnies have some degree of sun blindness.*

beak **1.** *n.* a nose. □ *What a beak on that guy!* □ *I want some glasses that sit in just the right place on my wonderful beak.* **2.** *v.* to gossip; to chatter. □ *We stood around and beaked for a while.* □ *Stop beaking and get to work.*

beam See *(I-)beam.*

Beam me up, Scotty! *sent.* "Get me out of here!"; "Take me away from this mess!" (From the television program *Star Trek.*) □ *This place is really crazy! Beam me up, Scotty!* □ *I've heard enough! Beam me up, Scotty!*

beam up *in.* to die. (From the television program *Star Trek.*) □ *Pete Dead? I didn't think he was old enough to beam up.* □ *I was so exhausted after climbing four flights that I was afraid I would beam up.*

beamer *n.* a user of IBM computers; one who is knowledgeable about IBM computers. (See also *beemer.*) □ *I'm no beamer! I'm a Mac fan.* □ *Fred is a confirmed beamer, especially now that computers are cheaper.*

beaming See *on the beam.*

bean **1.** *n.* the head. □ *I got a bump right here on my bean.* □ *Put your brim on your bean and cruise.* **2.** *tr.* to hit someone on the head. (See also *bean ball.*) □ *The lady beaned me with her umbrella.* □ *A board fell off the scaffold and beaned the worker.* **3.** See *beans.*

bean ball *n.* a pitched baseball that strikes the batter on the head, usually by accident. (Baseball.) □ *He got hit by a bean ball and went after the pitcher with a bat.* □ *The guy is a master at throwing a bean ball and living to tell about it.*

bean-counter *n.* a statistician; an accountant. □ *When the bean-counters get finished with the numbers, you won't recognize them.* □ *The bean-counters predict a recession sometime in the next decade.*

bean head 1. *n.* an oaf. (Also as one word.) ☐ *You are such a bean head!* ☐ *Why I keep running around with a bean head like you is beyond me.* 2. *n.* a drug user who uses pills habitually. (Drugs.) ☐ *You beanheads are just as much junkies as the jerks who shoot.* ☐ *There's no harm in being a bean head.*

bean time *n.* dinnertime. ☐ *Hey, you guys! It's bean time!* ☐ *I'm hungry. When's bean time around here?*

Bean Town *n.* Boston, Massachusetts. (From *Boston baked beans.*) ☐ *I plan to hit Bean Town about noon.* ☐ *I got a lot of buddies in Bean Town.*

beaned up *mod. high* on amphetamines. (Drugs.) ☐ *Ernie is beaned up again.* ☐ *Two students were beaned up and were sent home.*

beanery *n.* a cheap eating establishment. (Where baked beans are served.) ☐ *I stopped in for a cup of brew at a little all-night beanery on Thirty-fourth. Barlowe was waiting.* ☐ *I'm tired of eating in beaneries.*

beanpole *n.* a skinny person. ☐ *I'm getting to be such a beanpole.* ☐ *I used to be a beanpole. Look at me now—both of me!*

beans 1. *n.* nothing. ☐ *You act like you don't know beans about it.* ☐ *I have nothing I can give you. Nothing, zotz, beans!* 2. *n.* nonsense. (Refers to beans that produce *gas,* which is *hot air* or nonsense.) ☐ *Come on, talk straight. No more beans!* ☐ *Stop feeding me beans.* 3. *n.* soybean futures contracts. (Securities markets. Usually with *the.*) ☐ *The beans are headed south.* ☐ *Buy the jan beans and sell puts on the bellies.*

bear 1. *n.* a difficult task. ☐ *This problem is a real bear.* ☐ *This is a bear of a job. I'll be glad when it's over.* 2. *n.* an ugly woman. (Derogatory.) ☐ *Tell the old bear to hold her tongue.* ☐ *How can a bear like that be allowed to run around loose?* 3. *n.* a highway patrol officer. (See also *Smokey (the Bear).*) ☐ *There's a bear hiding under that bridge.* ☐ *A bear is overhead, watching your speed from a helicopter.*

bear cage *n.* a police station. (Citizens band radio.) ☐ *Have you ever been in a country bear cage?* ☐ *I sat for two hours in that stinking bear cage.*

bear in the air *n.* a police officer in an airplane or a helicopter. (Citizens band radio.) ☐ *They've got a bear in the air on duty in northern Indiana.* ☐ *There's a bear in the air and another regular one keeping watch over your speed.*

bear trap *n.* a hidden speed trap, one set by a *bear.* (Citizens band radio.) ☐ *That whole town is a glorified bear trap.* ☐ *I got caught in a bear trap.*

beast 1. *n.* an ugly person. ☐ *Who is that beast with the big hat?* ☐ *That beast should give the monkey back its face before it bumps into something.* 2. *n.* a crude, violent, or sexually aggressive male; an *animal.* ☐ *That beast scares the hell out of me.* ☐ *Oh, Martin, you're such a beast!* 3. *n.* liquor. ☐ *I feel a little overcome by the beast.* ☐ *Pour me some more of that beast.*

beasty *mod.* (of a person) undesirable; *yucky.* (California.) ☐ *You are like, so like, beasty!* ☐ *I can't stand that gross beasty jerk!*

beat 1. *mod.* exhausted; worn-out. ☐ *I'm just beat!* ☐ *The whole family was beat after the game.* 2. *mod.* down and out; ruined. ☐ *This thing is beat. I don't want it.* ☐ *Who wants a beat hat?* 3. *n.* the area that a worker, a police officer, reporter, etc., is assigned to cover. ☐ *That's not on my beat. You'll have to talk to someone else.* ☐ *Your store is on my beat, and I want to make sure everything is okay.* 4. *n.* (in music) the rhythm, especially the bass. ☐ *Man, that is just the kind of beat I like.* ☐ *The notes are nice, but it has no beat!* 5. *mod.* having to do with the Bohemian youths of the 1950's. ☐ *My brother looked sort of beat, but I was neat as a pin.* ☐ *Actually, I don't think I ever saw anybody who I would call beat.* ☐ *The beat guys are all gone now.* 6. *mod.* broke. ☐ *Man, I'm beat. I got no copper, no bread.* ☐ *All we need is another beat mouth to feed.* 7. *tr.* to get free from a specific criminal charge or *rap.* ☐ *I* *tried, but I couldn't beat the rap.* ☐ *I beat it twice, but there is no third time.* **8.** *mod.* having to do with counterfeit or bogus drugs. (Drugs.) ☐ *This stuff is beat. Ditch it!* ☐ *Whose ever it is, it's beat.* **9.** *mod.* having to do with marijuana after the smokable substance is exhausted; *cashed.* ☐ *This stuff is beat. Who wants it?* ☐ *Who sold you this beat dope?* **10.** *mod.* lousy; unfortunate. (Collegiate.) ☐ *This has been a beat day.* ☐ *What a beat deal you got!*

beat box *n.* the person who provides the (verbal) rhythmic beat in a rap song. ☐ *What makes him sound so good is his beat box.* ☐ *Let me be the beat box this time.*

Beat it! *exclam.* "Get out!"; "Go away!" ☐ *You bother me. Beat it!* ☐ *Beat it! I've had it with you.*

beat one's brains out (to do something) *tr.* to work hard at a task. ☐ *I'm tired of beating my brains out to do what you want.* 🅃 *He beat out his brains to get here on time!*

beat one's gums *tr.* to waste time talking a great deal without results. ☐ *I'm tired of beating my gums about this stuff.* ☐ *You're just beating your gums. No one is listening.*

beat someone or something out 1. *tr.* [with *someone*] to outdistance someone; to perform better than someone. ☐ *We have to beat the other company out, and then we'll have the contract.* 🅃 *I beat out Walter in the footrace.* **2.** *tr.* [with *something*] to type something or play something on the piano. ☐ *It'll just take me a few minutes to beat this out.* 🅃 *He beat out a cheery song on the old ivories.*

beat someone's brains out 1. *tr.* to beat someone severely. ☐ *She threatened to beat my brains out.* ☐ *Those thugs nearly beat his brains out.* **2.** *tr.* to drive oneself hard (to accomplish something). ☐ *I beat my brains out all day to clean this house, and you come in and track up the carpet!* ☐ *Don't beat your brains out. Just give it a good try.*

beat the drum for someone or something *tr.* to promote or support someone or something. ☐ *I spent a lot of time beating the drum for our plans for the future.* ☐ *The senator is only beating the drum for his special interests.*

beat up *mod.* visibly worn; shabby. (This is hyphenated before a nominal.) ☐ *Get your beat-up car painted or something!* ☐ *My coat is too beat up to wear to the opera.*

beater 1. *n.* a junky old car. ☐ *I like my old beater even if it has no bumpers.* ☐ *I want an old beater that doesn't cost more than 800 bucks.* **2.** See *beatnik.*

beatnik AND **beater** ['bitnɪk AND 'bitɚ] *n.* a member of the Bohemian subculture that flourished in the 1950's. (The *nik* is from Russian via Yiddish.) ☐ *Those beatniks back in the fifties were something to behold.* ☐ *This beater comes up to me and mumbles something I can't hear.*

beats me *phr.* (the answer is) not known to me. (The emphasis is on *me.*) ☐ *I don't know the answer. Beats me!* ☐ *Beats me how those things stay in the air.*

beauhunk *n.* a good-looking male. (Based on *bohunk.* A play on *beau* = boyfriend, and *hunk.*) ☐ *Who is that gorgeous beauhunk over there?* ☐ *Jennifer went out with a real beauhunk who turned out to be a dipwad.*

beaut [bjut] *n.* someone or something excellent, not necessarily beautiful. ☐ *Man, this fishing rod's a beaut!* ☐ *This is a beaut of a day!*

beautiful *mod.* very satisfying; excellent. ☐ *This wine is really beautiful!* ☐ *Man, this place is beautiful. You got your own sink and toilet right in the room and good strong bars to keep the riffraff out.*

beauty sleep *n.* sleep; the sleep one requires. (Usually mentioned by nonbeautiful men as a joke.) ☐ *I gotta get home and get my beauty sleep.* ☐ *You really need some beauty sleep. Why don't you try a week of it and see if that works?*

bed of roses *n.* a luxurious situation; an easy life. ☐ *Who said life would be a* *bed of roses?* □ *If I had a million bucks, I would be in a bed of roses.*

bedrock 1. *n.* fundamentals; solid facts. □ *Let's get down to bedrock and quit wasting time.* □ *This is bedrock—the truth.* **2.** *mod.* fundamental. □ *You've been avoiding the bedrock issues all your life.* □ *Let's hear some more about these bedrock ideas.*

bedroom eyes *n.* seductive eyes. □ *Beware of bedroom eyes. They mean trouble.* □ *She batted those bedroom eyes at me, and I knew I was a goner.*

bedtime story See *fairy tale.*

beecher *n.* a man who chews Beechnut (brand) tobacco. (Usually derogatory.) □ *Some old beecher wandered in and looked like he was going to leave a remembrance on the floor.* □ *The lobby of the county courthouse was populated by beechers and old hound dogs.*

beef 1. *n.* a complaint; a quarrel. □ *I gotta beef against you.* □ *Okay, what's the beef?* **2.** *n.* a criminal charge or complaint. □ *Well, officer, what's the beef?* □ *The beef is that you appear to have left the bank Monday with about seventy-five grand that isn't yours. That's the beef!* **3.** *n.* a large and muscular male. □ *Let's get one of those beefs in here to help.* □ *The two beefs pushed and pushed, but couldn't budge the crate.* **4.** *in.* to complain. □ *Stop your beefing!* □ *What's he beefing about now?* **5.** *in.* to break wind; to release intestinal gas audibly. (Use caution with the topic.) □ *Who beefed?* □ *Wally warned everybody that he was going to beef.* **6.** *n.* an act of breaking wind. (Use caution with the topic.) □ *All right! Who's beef was that?* □ *Jimmy made another beef!* **7.** *in.* to crack up and get injured as in a skateboard accident. □ *Chuck beefed and wrecked his elbow.* □ *Be careful or you'll beef!*

beef-head *n.* an oaf; a *meathead.* □ *Look you beef-head, lay off!* □ *This beef-head here thinks he knows how to do my job.*

beef something up *tr.* to add strength or substance to something. □ *Let's beef this up with a little more on the drums.* 🅃 *They beefed up the offer with another thousand dollars.*

beefcake 1. *n.* a display of the male physique. (Compare to *cheesecake.*) □ *There was some beefcake at the party just to liven things up.* □ *There was one calendar showing beefcake rather than the usual cheesecake.* **2.** *n.* a muscularly handsome male. □ *She's been going out with a real beefcake.* □ *I prefer skinny guys to a beefcake.*

beemer ['bimɚ] *n.* a B.M.W. automobile. (See also *beamer.*) □ *I had to sell my beemer when the stock market crashed.* □ *Tiffany's beemer was leased, but no one was supposed to know.*

been had AND **was had 1.** *phr.* been copulated with; been made pregnant. □ *I've been had, and I'm going to have the baby.* □ *When she said she was had, I didn't know it was on her honeymoon.* **2.** *phr.* been mistreated, cheated, or dealt with badly. (See also *taken.*) □ *Look at this shirt! I was had!* □ *I've been had by that lousy gyp joint.*

beeper *n.* a portable telephone signal. □ *I have somebody call me during a meeting so my beeper will go off and get me out of it.* □ *My beeper went off, and I had to leave the meeting.*

beer 1. *in.* to drink beer. □ *Fred and Tom sat in there watching the game and beering and belching like two old whales.* □ *Let's just sit here and beer for a while.* **2.** *tr.* to get oneself drunk on beer. □ *I beered myself, but good.* □ *Let's go beer a few.*

beer and skittles [...'skɪdl̩z] *n.* something very easy to do; an easy time of it. □ *Did you think life was all beer and skittles?* □ *All you want is beer and skittles. Don't you know you have to work hard for what you want?*

beer belly AND **beer gut** *n.* a large belly. □ *You're going to end up with a real beer belly hanging over your belt if you don't let up on that stuff.* □ *Look at the beer belly on that guy.*

beer blast AND **beer bust** *n.* a beer-drinking party; a beer binge. □ *Kelly's* *having a beer blast at his place, starting tonight.* □ *There is a beer bust somewhere around here almost every night.*

beer bust See the previous entry.

beer goggles [...'gaglz] *n.* a condition of the eyes of someone wherein all persons of the opposite sex look very attractive. (Usually said about the eyes of males.) □ *Three beers and it's beer goggles for Walter.* □ *See how Wally is looking at that bowser. He's got his beer goggles on!*

beer gut See *beer belly.*

beerbong ['birbɔŋ] **1.** *n.* a can of beer prepared for drinking in one gulp. (An opening is made in the bottom of a can of beer. The can, with the opening placed in the mouth, is turned upright, and the tab opener is pulled, releasing all the beer directly into the mouth.) □ *Do you know how to make a beerbong?* □ *A beerbong is a great way to liven up a party.* **2.** *in.* to drink beer as described in sense 1. □ *Those guys who were beerbonging all barfed after it was over.* □ *I tried beerbonging once, just once.*

beeswax ['bizwæks] *n.* business; concern. (See also *mind your own beeswax, none of someone's beeswax.*) □ *Is this any of your beeswax?* □ *Tend to your own beeswax.*

beetle *n.* a Volkswagen automobile. □ *We wanted to buy a beetle, but decided on a domestic model.* □ *I remember when people used to put big windup keys on their beetles to make them look like windup toys.*

beetlebrain ['bidlbren] *n.* a stupid person. □ *Some beetlebrain left a can of paint in the hall, and guess who knocked it over?* □ *Why are you such a beetlebrain when it comes to math?*

beeveedees See *B.V.D.s.*

beezer ['bizɚ] *n.* the nose. □ *I've got a zit on my beezer.* □ *I was afraid he would bop me on the beezer.*

begathon *n.* a televised appeal for contributions, especially as conducted by U.S. public television stations. □ *It seems like this station is one long begathon all year long.* □ *They made two million in the begathon last month.*

behind *n.* the posterior; the buttocks. □ *I've got a boil on the behind that's driving me crazy.* □ *She needs some jeans that will flatter her behind.*

behind bars *mod.* in jail; in prison. □ *You belong behind bars, you creep!* □ *I've got something here that will keep you behind bars for years.*

behind the eight ball **1.** *mod.* in trouble; in a weak or losing position. □ *I'm behind the eight ball again.* □ *John spends a lot of time behind the eight ball.* **2.** *mod.* broke. □ *Sorry, I'm really behind the eight ball this month. I can't make a contribution.* □ *I was behind the eight ball again and couldn't make my car payment.*

beige [beʒ] *mod.* boring; insipid. (California. See also *vanilla.*) □ *The party is beige. Let's cruise.* □ *Let's blow this beige joint!* □ *This day is way beige! Bag it!*

belch [bɛltʃ] **1.** *in.* to bring up stomach gas. (See also *berp.*) □ *They swallow beer by the can and see who can belch the loudest.* □ *I belched, and everybody stared.* **2.** *n.* a burp; an upwards release of stomach gas. □ *That was the loudest belch I've ever heard.* □ *What I really need is a good belch.* **3.** *n.* beer, especially bad beer. □ *Where did you get this belch?* □ *Pass the belch. Anything's good on a hot day.*

belcher ['bɛltʃɚ] **1.** *n.* a beer drinker. □ *Look at the belly on that belcher!* □ *Harry is a confirmed belcher.* **2.** *n.* a hard drinker; a drunkard. □ *A couple of belchers wandered in about midnight. Other than that, the night is dead.* □ *I'm a belcher, and I know it.*

Believe you me! *exclam.* "You should believe me!" □ *Believe you me, that was some cake!* □ *This is a fine picnic. Believe you me!*

bellies *n.* pork bellies; pork belly futures. (Securities markets. Often with *the.*)

☐ *What are the dec bellies doing?* ☐ *Buy the bellies and sell the beans.*

bells and whistles *n.* extra, fancy gadgets. ☐ *I like machines with all the bells and whistles.* ☐ *All those bells and whistles add to the cost.*

belly button *n.* the navel. ☐ *Is your belly button an insy or an outsy?* ☐ *Do dogs have belly buttons?*

belly flop **1.** *n.* a failed dive where there is a loud noise when the flat of the stomach hits the water. ☐ *Wow, I never knew that a belly flop hurts!* ☐ *A belly flop gets zero points in a dive meet.* **2.** *in.* to dive into the water so that the flat of the stomach hits the water, usually making a loud noise. ☐ *Sam belly flopped again.* ☐ *I get so embarrassed when I belly flop!*

belly laff See the following entry.

belly laugh AND **belly laff** *n.* a loud, deep, uninhibited laugh. ☐ *I don't want to hear giggles when I tell a joke. I want long belly laughs.* ☐ *I let out a loud belly laff at the preacher's joke. A no-no, for sure.*

belly up **1.** *mod.* alcohol intoxicated. ☐ *Sylvia was boiled—belly up—glassy-eyed.* ☐ *After four beers, I was belly up, for sure.* **2.** *mod.* dead. ☐ *That's the end. This company is belly up.* ☐ *After the fire the firm went belly up.* **3.** See *belly up (to something).*

belly up (to something) *in.* to move up to something, often a bar. ☐ *The man swaggered in and bellied up to the counter and demanded my immediate attention.* ☐ *As he bellied up, he said, "Do you know who I am?"*

bellyache ['beliek] **1.** *n.* a stomachache. ☐ *Oh, mama, do I have a bellyache!* ☐ *That stuff will give you one fine bellyache.* **2.** *in.* to complain. ☐ *You are always bellyaching!* ☐ *Don't bellyache to me about it!*

bellyful *n.* more than enough; more than one needs. ☐ *I've had a bellyful of your excuses.* ☐ *You've given us all a bellyful. Now, good night.*

belt **1.** *n.* a blow with the fist or hand. ☐ *Quiet or I'll give you a belt in the chops.* ☐ *I got a belt in the gut for my trouble.* **2.** *tr.* to strike someone. ☐ *Quiet or I'll belt you one!* ☐ *Don't belt me!* **3.** *n.* a kick or a thrill. ☐ *We all got quite a belt from your jokes.* ☐ *Kelly gets a belt from roller coasters.* **4.** *n.* the *rush* or *jolt* from an injection of a drug. (Drugs.) ☐ *This stuff has one hell of a belt.* ☐ *The belt nearly knocked her over.* **5.** *n.* an injection of a drug. (Drugs.) ☐ *I could use a belt of smack to hold off the pain.* ☐ *Gimme a belt in the leg, will you? My arms are finished.* **6.** *n.* a swallow of liquor. ☐ *He took a belt and rolled it around in his mouth before draining it down into his rumbling belly.* ☐ *Three more quick belts and he was ready to sit down and talk.* **7.** *tr.* to drink (something). (See also *belt the grape.*) ☐ *He belted his drink and asked for another.* ☐ *Don't belt it! Savor it! Go slowly.*

belt the grape *tr.* to drink wine or liquor heavily and become intoxicated. ☐ *He has a tendency to belt the grape—twenty-four hours a day.* ☐ *She's been belting the grape more than she wants.*

belted *mod.* alcohol or drug intoxicated. ☐ *How many belts does it take to get belted?* ☐ *We were belted out of our minds.*

bench **1.** *tr.* to take someone out of a ball game. ☐ *The coach benched Jim, who injured his arm.* ☐ *If you don't stop fouling, I'll bench you!* **2.** *tr.* to retire someone; to withdraw someone from something. ☐ *I worked as a bridge painter for twenty-five years until they benched me.* ☐ *The manager benched the entire sales staff for cheating on their expense reports.*

bench jockey *n.* a player who sits on the bench and calls out advice. ☐ *The coach told all the bench jockeys to shut up.* ☐ *Do what you are told, or be a bench jockey for the rest of the season!*

bench warmer *n.* a ballplayer who spends most of the game on the bench waiting to play; a second-rate player. ☐ *You'll never be anything but a bench warmer.*

☐ *I do what I'm told so I can play every game. I don't want to be a bench warmer.*

bend one's elbow AND **bend the elbow; lift one's elbow** *tr.* to take a drink of an alcoholic beverage; to drink alcohol to excess. ☐ *He's down at the tavern, bending his elbow.* ☐ *Paul gets lots of exercise. He bends his elbow thirty times a day.*

bend the elbow See the previous entry.

bend the law *tr.* to cheat a little bit without breaking the law. (Jocular.) ☐ *I didn't break the law. I just bent the law a little.* ☐ *Nobody ever got arrested for bending the law.*

bender **1.** *n.* a drinking binge. (See also *twister.*) ☐ *Her benders usually last about ten days.* ☐ *Paul is off on a bender again.* **2.** *n.* a heavy drinker; a drunkard. ☐ *This bender comes up to me and nearly kills me with his breath, asking for a match.* ☐ *In the dim light I could make out a few of the regular benders, but Harold wasn't there.*

benies *n.* benefits. (See also *benny.*) ☐ *The salary is good, but the benies are almost nonexistent.* ☐ *Are retirement contributions one of your benies?*

bennie See the following entry.

benny AND **bennie** *n.* a Benzedrine™ capsule or tablet. ☐ *You got a benny or two you could spare a poor man?* ☐ *A couple of bennies will chase away the blues.*

bent **1.** *mod.* alcohol or drug intoxicated. ☐ *I've never seen two guys so bent.* ☐ *I can get bent on a glass of wine.* **2.** *mod.* dishonest; crooked. ☐ *I'm afraid that Paul is a little bent. He cheats on his taxes.* ☐ *A lot of those officeholders get bent in office—if they weren't before.* **3.** *mod.* angry. ☐ *He was so bent there was steam coming out of his ears.* ☐ *Come on, don't get bent. I was only kidding.*

bent out of shape **1.** *mod.* angry; insulted. ☐ *Man, there is no reason to get so bent out of shape. I didn't mean any harm.* ☐ *I got bent out of shape because of the way I was treated.* **2.** *n.* alcohol or drug intoxicated. ☐ *I was so bent out of shape I thought I'd never recover.* ☐ *I've been polluted, but never as bent out of shape as this.*

benz [bɛnz] **1.** *n.* Benzedrine™. (Drugs.) ☐ *Benz will pep you up, but you give it all back later.* ☐ *Stay off the benz. Coffee is enough to perk anybody up.* **2.** AND **Benz** *n.* a Mercedes Benz automobile. ☐ *I traded in my Benz for a beemer.* ☐ *My uncle had a Benz that he took back to Germany every two years for service.*

berp AND **burp** [bɚp] **1.** *in.* to bring up stomach gas. (See also *belch.*) ☐ *She burped quietly behind her hanky, so no one would notice.* ☐ *Try not to burp at the table.* **2.** *n.* an upward release of stomach gas. ☐ *The burp did not go unnoticed.* ☐ *What can you do when you berp in church?*

berps AND **burps** [bɚps] *n.* liquor; beer. (See also *belch.*) ☐ *Did you bring the berps for the party?* ☐ *Hey, this is pretty good berps.*

berpwater *n.* beer; ale; champagne. ☐ *I don't care for all that berpwater.* ☐ *Berpwater is for sissies.*

berries **1.** *n.* the best; the finest. (Always with *the*. A noun with the force of an adjective.) ☐ *Those people are really the berries.* ☐ *Man, this stuff is the berries!* **2.** *n.* wine. (Originally black. Compare to *grape(s).*) ☐ *Lemme stop at the liquor store for some berries.* ☐ *No berries for me. Where's the belch?*

bet one's bottom dollar *tr.* to be very certain of something; to bet in complete certainty of winning. (Need not refer to an actual bet.) ☐ *I bet my bottom dollar you never ever went to Alaska!* ☐ *He bet his bottom dollar on that horse, and it died at the gate.*

bet someone dollars to doughnuts *tr.* to bet something of value against something worth considerably less. ☐ *I bet you dollars to doughnuts that she is on time.* ☐ *He bet me dollars to doughnuts that it would snow today.*

better half *n.* one's wife, and occasionally, one's husband. ☐ *My better half* *disapproved of the movie.* □ *I gotta go home to my better half.*

Better luck next time. *sent.* "I wish you luck when you try again." □ *So you goofed up. Better luck next time.* □ *You blew it, you stupid twit. Better luck next time.*

between a rock and a hard place *mod.* in a very difficult position; facing a hard decision. □ *You got him caught between a rock and a hard place, for sure.* □ *I'm between a rock and a hard place. I don't know what to do.*

between you, me, and the bedpost See the following entry.

between you, me, and the lamppost AND **between you, me, and the bedpost** *phr.* "just between you and me." □ *Between you, me, and the lamppost, things are going to get worse before they get better.* □ *They're worse than you think now, just between you, me, and the bedpost.*

bewottled *mod.* alcohol intoxicated. □ *Sam was so bewottled that he could hardly walk.* □ *Garth and Wayne were severely bewottled.*

B.F. *n.* "best friend." (Initialism. Collegiate.) □ *You would have thought you and she were B.F.s to hear her talk.* □ *Sharon is my B.F.*

BG *interj.* "big grin." (An initialism used on computer bulletin boards to show that the writer is joking or happy. Not pronounced. Often enclosed, <BG>.) □ *I haven't seen you on the board. I thought you had run away from home.* <BG> □ *Your last message was filled with misspelled words, but I think I could understand what you meant.* <BG>

bhang [bæŋ OR bɑŋ] **1.** *n.* the marijuana plant. (Drugs. From Hindi.) □ *Martha grows bhang in a pot in her room.* □ *She farms bhang for her own use.* **2.** *n.* a marijuana cigarette; the smoking of a marijuana cigarette. □ *Max had to stop for a bhang.* □ *The kids found an old bhang in Fred's car.*

bhang ganjah [bæŋ 'gændʒə OR bɑŋ 'gɑndʒə] *n.* marijuana; marijuana resin. (Drugs.) □ *It's the bhang ganjah that gives the stuff its kick.* □ *Can you get bhang ganjah by itself?*

bhong See *bong.*

bicarb ['bɑɪkɑrb] *n.* bicarbonate of soda, used for an upset stomach. □ *I sure could use a little bicarb after that chili she served.* □ *I can't stand that sweet-tasting stuff. I want bicarb.*

biff [bɪf] **1.** *tr.* to hit someone. □ *Tom biffed Fred on the snoot.* □ *Fred got biffed, and that really made him mad.* **2.** *n.* a blow. □ *The biff on the nose gave Fred a nosebleed.* □ *Tom got a biff in the gut for his trouble.*

biffy ['bɪfi] *n.* a toilet. □ *Where's the biffy?* □ *The house we toured has a pink biffy. Can you believe it?*

Big Apple *n.* New York City. (Always with *the.*) □ *The Big Apple is filled with young kids trying to get into show biz.* □ *Max and his gang went to the Big Apple to lie low for a while.*

big blue *n.* the stock of International Business Machines or the company itself. (Securities markets. See also *(I-)beam.*) □ *I have 400 shares of big blue that I would like to sell.* □ *Big blue led the market lower again today.*

big board *n.* the New York Stock Exchange. (Securities markets.) □ *On the big board, stocks were down again today, bringing the loss this week on the Dow to nearly 175 points.* □ *Is that stock on the big board or where?*

big brother **1.** *n.* a personification of the totalitarian state. (From George Orwell's *1984.*) □ *Big brother has changed the tax laws again.* □ *Now big brother has fixed it so you can't even baby-sit without paying taxes.* **2.** *n.* someone who personifies the totalitarian state: the police, parents, teachers. □ *Old big brother grounded me for a week.* □ *Big brother says the paper is due tomorrow, or else.*

big bucks *n.* a lot of money. (See also *megabucks.*) □ *To me, $400 is big bucks.* □ *She gets paid big bucks to worry about stuff like that.*

big-C. **1.** *n.* cancer. (Usually with *the.*) ☐ *She was struck with the big-C.* ☐ *The big-C. will finish off quite a few of us.* **2.** *n.* cocaine. (Drugs.) ☐ *When she started taking big-C., she was only eight.* ☐ *They use kids to deliver big-C. because they know they're not going to get put in prison.*

big cheese *n.* the boss; the key figure; the leader. ☐ *Here's a note from the big cheese telling me to come in for a chat.* ☐ *The big cheese is giving everyone a bonus at the end of the year.*

big-D. *n.* Dallas, Texas. ☐ *Kelly is from big-D.* ☐ *What is big-D. famous for?*

big deal **1.** *n.* something really important. ☐ *Don't make such a big deal out of it!* ☐ *This isn't a big deal as I see it.* **2.** *exclam.* "So what!"; "What does it matter?" (Usually **Big deal!**) ☐ *So he snores! Big deal! Snore back!* ☐ *She says to me, "Your socks don't match." And I says back, "Big deal!"*

big drink *n.* the Atlantic Ocean; an ocean. ☐ *We flew over the big drink in an hour or two.* ☐ *When you're over the big drink you really get to feel how tiny we humans are.*

big drink of water **1.** *n.* a very tall person. (Folksy.) ☐ *Tim is sure a big drink of water.* ☐ *Kelly grew into a big drink of water.* **2.** *n.* a boring person or thing. (A pun on "hard to take.") ☐ *She is a big drink of water, but she could be worse.* ☐ *The lecture was a big drink of water.*

big enchilada [...ɛntʃə'lɑdə] *n.* the boss; the leader. (See also *big cheese.*) ☐ *I wanna see the big enchilada!* ☐ *The big enchilada has sent word that it's safe to return.*

big fish *n.* the boss; the leader. (Underworld.) ☐ *We took in the little guys, but the big fish got away.* ☐ *The big fish ordered the killing.*

big gun *n.* an important and powerful person, such as an officer of a company. (Often with *bring in* as in the example.) ☐ *It went up to the big guns, who said no immediately.* ☐ *I knew they would bring in the big guns at the last minute.*

big-H. *n.* heroin. (Drugs.) ☐ *She's on big-H. now. Soon she'll be hooked for good.* ☐ *The big-H. in this town is so watered down, you can joy pop for years and never get hooked.*

big house *n.* a state or federal penitentiary. (Always with *the.*) ☐ *It's either go straight now or spend the rest of your life in the big house.* ☐ *Two years in the big house is like two years in a custom-made hell.*

big iron *n.* a large, mainframe computer. (Computers. See also *iron.*) ☐ *We'll have to run this job on the big iron over at the university.* ☐ *What kind of big iron do they have over there?*

big John *n.* the police; a police officer. ☐ *Big John is going to have to deal with you.* ☐ *Big John took her in and hit her with a vice rap.*

big juice *n.* a big-time crook. (See also *juice.*) ☐ *Marty's big juice now that he's got himself a gang.* ☐ *So, you're the big juice around here.*

big league **1.** *n.* a situation where competition is keen and a high level of performance is expected. (Usually plural. Referred originally to major league sports.) ☐ *In the big leagues you've got to know what you're worth.* ☐ *You're in the big leagues now—no more penny-ante stuff.* **2.** AND **big-league** *mod.* professional; *big time.* (From baseball.) ☐ *He works for one of the big-league accounting firms.* ☐ *When I'm a big-league star, I'll send you free tickets.*

Big Mac attack *n.* a sudden and desperate need for a Big Mac sandwich, a product of the McDonald's restaurant chain. (*Big Mac* is a protected trade name of McDonald's.) ☐ *I feel a Big Mac attack coming on!* ☐ *I just can't fight off a Big Mac attack.*

big man on campus *n.* an important male college student. (See more examples at *B.M.O.C.*) ☐ *Hank acts like* *such a big man on campus.* □ *Let some big man on campus do the dirty work for a change.*

big mouth 1. *n.* a person who talks too much or too loudly; someone who tells secrets. (Also a term of address.) □ *Okay, big mouth! Shut up!* □ *Tell that big mouth to shut up.* **2.** *tr.* to spread secrets around. □ *Why do you always have to big mouth everything around?* □ *Don't you big mouth this, but I'm going to have a baby.*

big name 1. *n.* a famous and important person. □ *Lots of big names were there lending their support to the cause.* □ *One of the big names invited for the event canceled out at the last minute.* **2.** AND **big-name** *mod.* famous; important. □ *Some big-name star I've never heard of was there pretending to serve dinner.* □ *The big-name ballplayers make millions.*

big noise 1. *n.* an important person. □ *If you're such a big noise, why don't you get this line moving?* □ *She's the big noise in Washington right now.* **2.** *n.* the important current news; the current scandal. □ *What's the big noise around town now?* □ *There's a big noise up on Capitol Hill. Something about budget cuts.*

big-O. *n.* opium. □ *The big-O. is making a comeback, I hear.* □ *Most of the users of big-O. died out thirty years ago.*

big of someone 1. *mod.* magnanimous of someone. □ *That is really big of you, Fred.* □ *It was big of Tom to come back and apologize.* **2.** *mod.* nice of someone. (Often sarcastic.) □ *A whole pound. Wow, that is really big of you!* □ *Three daisies he gave me! "Oh, that's big of you!" I said, batting my eyes.*

big shot (Also spelled as one word.) **1.** *n.* a very important person. □ *So, you really think you're a big shot.* □ *I'm no big shot, but I do have a little power around here.* **2.** *mod.* mighty; overbearing; overly-important. □ *If you think that a big shot title impresses me, you're wrong.* □ *Your bigshot ideas are getting us nowhere.*

big spender *n.* someone who spends much money. (Often sarcastic.) □ *The big spender left me a whole quarter tip!* □ *It's the big spenders who get themselves into money trouble.*

big stink *n.* a major issue; a scandal; a big argument. □ *There was a big stink made about my absence.* □ *Don't make such a big stink about it.*

big talk 1. *n.* boasting; exaggerated claims. □ *No more big talk. I want action!* □ *I heard nothing but big talk since you got here.* **2.** *tr.* to boss other people around. □ *Don't big talk me. I know who you are.* □ *She came in and big talked everybody, and we just naturally thought she was the owner.*

big-ticket *mod.* having to do with something expensive. □ *Will the government cut back on the big-ticket programs?* □ *In a survey taken last month, heads of families said they were unwilling to put big-ticket items at the bottom of their shopping lists.*

big time 1. *n.* the high level of success. □ *I've finally reached the big time!* □ *When the pressure in the big time got to be too much, the guy simply retired.* **2.** AND **big-time** *mod.* outstanding; extravagant. □ *This is one of your real big-time stars.* □ *I can't stand any more of this big-time living.* **3.** AND **big-time** *mod.* felonious. (Underworld.) □ *Max is into big-time stuff now.* □ *The gang pulled a real big-time job and got away with it.*

big-time operator AND **B.T.O. 1.** *n.* someone who does business in a big way. (The abbreviation is an initialism.) □ *If you're such a B.T.O., why are we standing here in the rain?* □ *He's no big-time operator!* **2.** *n.* a man who chases women. □ *This big-time operator comes up and asks me to go home with him.* □ *That twit thinks he's a big-time operator. A stud he's not.*

big-time spender *n.* someone who spends a lot of money. □ *Martin is the original big-time spender.* □ *A big-time spender doesn't look at the prices on the menu.*

big top 1. *n.* a circus tent; the circus, in general. □ *The best acts take place under the big top.* □ *And now, one of the greatest acts under the big top.* 2. *mod.* having to do with the circus. □ *Big top life doesn't appeal to me at all.* □ *One big top experience is enough to last me a lifetime.*

big wheel *n.* a very important person. □ *Some big wheel wrote the order. Don't blame me.* □ *Kelly was a big wheel with the gas company for a while.*

big with someone *mod.* preferred by someone. □ *Soup is big with everybody in cold weather.* □ *This kind of ice cream is really big with my family.*

big Z's *n.* sleep. □ *I need me some of them big Z's.* □ *The big Z's must have set in before I could finish the movie.*

biggie 1. *n.* something or someone important. □ *This one's a biggie. Treat him well.* □ *As problems go, this one's a biggie.* 2. *n.* copulation. (Usually with *the*.) □ *But I don't think I'm ready for the biggie.* □ *He wanted to do the biggie!*

biggity ['bɪgədi] *mod.* haughty; aloof. □ *Kelly is too biggity for my taste.* □ *Who is that biggity guy with the mustache?*

bighead *n.* a headache and other ill effects from drinking. □ *I got a case of the bighead. Too much soda in my drinks, I guess.* □ *You look like you have the bighead this morning.*

bigheaded 1. *mod.* conceited. □ *Now don't get bigheaded, but you are a top drummer in my book.* □ *Look at him swagger. He is so bigheaded.* □ *What a bigheaded jerk!* 2. *mod.* having a hangover. □ *Tiffany is a little bigheaded this morning.* □ *I feel sort of bigheaded.*

bigwig *n.* an important person; a self-important person. □ *The bigwig in charge of that sort of thing will be in tomorrow.* □ *Some bigwig in a pinstripe suit waltzed through and asked me to leave.*

bike *n.* a motorcycle; a bicycle. □ *How much did that bike set you back?* □ *You have to wear a helmet with a bike that size, don't you?*

biker *n.* a motorcycle rider. □ *Four bikers roared by and woke up the baby.* □ *That biker is wearing about a dozen earrings.*

bill and coo *in.* to kiss and cuddle. (In the manner of love birds.) □ *Keep an eye on those kids. They aren't going to be satisfied with billing and cooing forever, you know.* □ *If they bill and coo enough now, maybe they will remember how when they're older.*

billie AND **bill(y)** ['bɪli] *n.* paper money; a bill. (California.) □ *Do you have any billies on you?* □ *Nope, no billies on me.*

bill(y) See the previous entry.

bimbo ['bɪmbo] 1. *n.* a clown-like person. □ *What a silly bimbo!* □ *If that bimbo doesn't keep quiet, I'll bop him.* 2. *n.* a giddy woman; a sexually loose woman. □ *So she's a bimbo. She still has rights. Have a heart!* □ *Now the bimbo is a star in the movies.*

bind *n.* a problem; a *wrinkle.* □ *I've got a little bind here I didn't anticipate.* □ *Unfortunately, a new bind has slowed down the project.*

bindle 1. *n.* a packet or bundle; a hobo's pack. □ *The guy had a bindle tied to a stick, just like an old-time tramp.* □ *Throw your bindle over yonder, and plunk your butt on that empty crate.* 2. *n.* a packet of drugs. (Drugs.) □ *She had a bindle of H. in her purse.* □ *That bindle was more important than money.*

binge [bɪndʒ] 1. *n.* a drinking or drugging spree. □ *Larry is the type who likes a good binge every now and then.* □ *A coke binge can cost a lot of cabbage.* 2. *n.* any spree of self-indulgence: emotional, gluttonous, etc. □ *About Thanksgiving time I start a month-long eating binge.* □ *The crying binge started when Marty got off the train.* 3. *in.* to drink heavily. □ *He has been binging since June.* □ *She binges about once a month and is stone cold sober the rest of the time.*

binged ['bɪndʒd] *mod.* alcohol intoxicated. □ *She sat there, binged out of her mind.* □ *I'm gonna go out and get myself binged, but good.*

Bingo! ['bɪŋgo] *exclam.* "Yes!"; "That's right!" (From the game "Bingo.") □ *Bingo! I've got the answer!* □ *And we put this little jobber here, another one here, and bingo! We're done.*

bird **1.** *n.* a woman; a *girl.* □ *I like the bird you were with last night.* □ *What a bird! I want one.* **2.** *n.* a derisive noise made with the lips; a *raspberry.* □ *The third time he fumbled, he was greeted by two thousand mouths making the bird.* □ *You guys making the bird aren't perfect either.* **3.** *n.* an odd person. □ *Some old bird came up to me and tried to sell me a cookbook.* □ *This bird is too much for me. I'm leaving.* **4.** *n.* a rude gesture made with the middle finger. (Usually with *the.* See comments at *finger wave.*) □ *The kid gave me the bird, so I bopped him.* □ *A lot of little kids give people the bird all the time because they see it on television.* **5.** *n.* an airplane. □ *I like this bird. She's a dream to fly.* □ *The bird crashed on takeoff.*

bird-dog **1.** *tr.* to take away another man's girlfriend. □ *Why'd you have to go and bird-dog me, your best buddy?* □ *I didn't bird-dog you. I'm just more loveable, that's all.* **2.** *tr.* to supervise someone; to tail someone. □ *I wish you would stop bird-dogging me!* □ *Barlowe knew somebody was bird-dogging him, but he was too smart to show it.*

bird watcher *n.* a *girl* watcher; someone, usually a man, who enjoys watching women go by. □ *Harry is a dedicated bird watcher.* □ *You bird watchers should just mind your own business.*

birdbrain **1.** *n.* a stupid-acting person. □ *You silly birdbrain. Stop it!* □ *I'm such a birdbrain. I forgot my driver's license, officer.* **2.** AND **birdbrained** *mod.* stupid. □ *I've never heard such a birdbrain idea in my life.* □ *Look, you birdbrained idiot, you are dead wrong!*

birdbrained See the previous entry.

birdie See *birdy.*

birdseed **1.** *n.* a small amount of money. (Compare to *chicken feed.*) □ *That's just birdseed compared to what I spend.* □ *Forty billion is birdseed to a government with a 600 billion dollar budget.* **2.** *n.* nonsense. (Based on *B.S.*) □ *Cut the birdseed. I'm not stupid, you know.* □ *I've heard enough birdseed here to last for a lifetime.*

birdturd **1.** *n.* an obnoxious person. (Potentially offensive. Use only with discretion. Derogatory. Also a term of address.) □ *You silly birdturd. Wake up!* □ *Clare can be such a birdturd when she wants.* **2.** *mod.* stupid; obnoxious. (Potentially offensive. Use only with discretion. Derogatory.) □ *Of all the stupid, underhanded, birdturd tricks—this takes the cake!* □ *Get your ugly birdturd car out of my driveway!*

birdy AND **birdie** *mod.* crazy; strange. □ *She acts a little birdy from time to time.* □ *Would you kindly take your birdie friends and go?*

biscuit ['bɪskət] *n.* the head. □ *She got a nasty little bump on the biscuit.* □ *He wears a tin can on his biscuit in case he tumbles.*

bit **1.** *n.* a jail sentence. (Underworld.) □ *I did a two-year bit in Sing Sing.* □ *He got only a four-year bit. He was afraid of getting worse.* **2.** *n.* a small theatrical part. (From *bit part.*) □ *I worked in bits for a year and then started selling used cars.* □ *It was just a bit, but I needed the money.* **3.** *n.* any part of an act; any business or presentation. □ *I didn't like that bit concerning penalties.* □ *Now, in this next bit, you are to move stage center.*

bit-bucket *n.* the imaginary place where lost computer data goes. (Computers.) □ *I guess my data went into the bit-bucket.* □ *I bet the bit-bucket is filled with some of the best stuff in the world.*

bit much *mod.* more than enough; more than good taste allows. (Always with *a.*) □ *That was a bit much, Paul. After all there is such a thing as good taste.* □ *Your birthday card was a bit much, but thank you just the same.*

bit of the action See *piece (of the action).*

bitch (Potentially offensive. Use only with discretion.) **1.** *n.* a derogatory term for a woman. (A verbal weapon. Derogatory.) □ *The stupid bitch doesn't know from nothing.* □ *You bitch! Stop it!* **2.** *n.* the queen at cards and at chess. (Mostly jocular.) □ *You dealt me the bitch.* □ *And I take your bitch.* **3.** *in.* to complain. □ *You are always bitching!* □ *If I couldn't bitch, I would blow my top.* **4.** *n.* a difficult thing or person. □ *Life's a bitch.* □ *This algebra problem is a real bitch.* **5.** *tr.* to ruin something. (See also *bitch something up*.) □ *You really bitched this coil of wire.* □ *Here's a clean one. Don't bitch it.* **6.** *n.* one's girlfriend. (Crude and mostly jocular.) □ *She's my bitch, and I love her.* □ *Me and my bitch really like this kind of stuff.*

bitch box *n.* a loudspeaker, especially one that announces orders in the armed services. (From World War II and still heard.) □ *The bitch box was blaring out messages and I couldn't sleep.* □ *I hate to hear the Sarge's voice over the bitch box.*

bitch of a someone or something *n.* a really difficult person or thing. (Potentially offensive. Use only with discretion.) □ *What a bitch of a day!* □ *He is really a bitch of a boss.*

bitch session *n.* an informal gathering where people gripe and air their grievances. (Potentially offensive. Use only with discretion.) □ *The bitch session went on for forty minutes.* □ *I learned never to open my mouth in those office bitch sessions.*

bitch someone off *tr.* to make someone angry. (Potentially offensive. Use only with discretion.) □ *You really bitch me off, do you know that?* Ⓣ *That foul temper of yours could bitch off anybody.*

bitch something up *tr.* to ruin something; to mess something up. (Potentially offensive. Use only with discretion.) □ *You really bitched my day up!* Ⓣ *How can one person bitch up something this easy?*

bitchen See the following entry.

bitchin' AND **bitchen** ['bɪtʃn̩] (Potentially offensive. Use only with discretion.) **1.** *mod.* excellent; great; classy. □ *This is a totally bitchin' pair of jeans!* □ *This is a way bitchen rally, my man!* **2.** *exclam.* "Terrific!" (Usually **Bitchin'!**) □ *Bitchin'! Let's do it again!* □ *Four of them? Bitchen!*

bitchy ['bɪtʃi] *mod.* spiteful; moody; rude; complaining. (Potentially offensive. Use only with discretion.) □ *Don't be so bitchy!* □ *Who needs a house full of bitchy kids?*

bite 1. *in.* to accept a deception; to fall for something; to respond to a come-on. □ *I knew somebody would bite.* □ *We put up a sign advertising free pop, but nobody bit.* **2.** *in.* [for someone or something] to be bad or threatening. □ *Watch out for Gloria. She bites!* □ *My dad bites, but don't worry, he's in a good mood.* **3.** *in.* to be irritating. (More severe than to *suck*, as in *It sucks*.) □ *This movie is really dumb. It bites.* □ *This party bites. Sko.* **4.** *tr.* to copy something without permission; to steal something. □ *Sue bit a copy of my term paper, and I almost got in trouble.* □ *Somebody bit my jacket!*

bite on something *in.* to copy something that someone else has done; to dress the same way someone else does. □ *Nobody will bite on Sally. She has terrible taste.* □ *Jennifer is always biting on Anne, who is a careful dresser.*

bite the big one *tr.* to die. □ *I was so tired that I thought I was going to bite the big one.* □ *I hope I am old and gray when I bite the big one.*

bite the bullet *tr.* to accept something difficult and try to live with it. □ *You are just going to have to bite the bullet and make the best of it.* □ *Jim bit the bullet and accepted what he knew had to be.*

bite the dust 1. *tr.* to die. □ *A shot rang out, and another cowboy bit the dust.* □ *I'm too young to bite the dust.* **2.** *tr.* to break; to fail; to give out. □ *My car finally bit the dust.* □ *This pen has bitten the dust.*

Bite the ice! *exclam.* "Go to hell!" □ *If that's what you think, you can just bite the ice!* □ *Get a life! Bite the ice!*

Bite your tongue! *exclam.* "Be sorry you said that!"; "Take back what you said!" □ *Me a thief? Oh, bite your tongue!* □ *Why do you say that this will fail? Bite your tongue!*

biter *n.* a thief. (See also *bite.*) □ *Some biter made off with my algebra book.* □ *Who's the biter who took my jacket?*

biters *n.* the teeth. □ *My biters need a little work.* □ *I gotta get my biters to the dentist while there are still a few left.*

biz [bɪz] **1.** *n.* a business; business. □ *What biz you in?* □ *I'm in the plumbing biz.* **2.** *n.* apparatus for injecting drugs. (Drugs.) □ *The biz is right there in the towel on top of the stack.* □ *Use your own biz. I got that disease, I think.*

blab [blæb] **1.** *n.* talk; chatter; meaningless talk. □ *I never pay any attention to blab like that.* □ *Cut the blab and get to work.* **2.** *tr.* to tell a secret; to reveal something private in public. □ *I'll tell you if you promise not to blab it.* □ *Tiffany blabbed the whole thing.*

blabbermouth 1. *n.* someone who talks too much and tells secrets. □ *You are such a blabbermouth!* □ *See if you can keep your brother—who is a blabbermouth—to keep this still.* **2.** *tr.* to tell secrets in public. □ *Don't blabbermouth this to everybody.* □ *Somebody blabbermouthed the story all over town.*

black *mod.* without cream or milk. (Said of coffee.) □ *I'd like mine black, please.* □ *Black coffee, good and hot, please.*

black and blue *mod.* bruised, physically or emotionally. □ *I'm still black and blue from my divorce.* □ *What is that black and blue area on your leg?*

black and white *n.* the police; a black and white police patrol car; any police car. □ *A black and white pulled up to the curb.* □ *Call the black and whites. We got trouble here.*

black eye *n.* a moral blemish; an injury to the prestige of someone or something. □ *The library has gotten a black eye from this incident.* □ *That kind of behavior can give us all a black eye.*

blackball *tr.* to vote against someone in a secret ballot. □ *Someone blackballed the prospective member.* □ *I chose to blackball her, and I'm not sorry.*

blacklist 1. *n.* a list of the names of banned people; a list of people undesirable to some group. □ *Am I on your blacklist?* □ *I hear they keep a blacklist on all the people they disagree with.* **2.** *tr.* to put someone's name on a list of undesirables. □ *They blacklisted me for not belonging to the right organizations.* □ *Nobody else I know was blacklisted.*

blade 1. *n.* a knife. □ *Bring your blade over here and cut this loose.* □ *What are you carrying a blade for?* **2.** *n.* a young man, witty and worldly. □ *One of those blades kept winking at me.* □ *A couple of blades from the international jet set ordered vintage wine for everyone.* **3.** *n.* a homosexual man. (From "gay blade.") □ *This blade comes up and says, like, "Gotta match?"* □ *Some blade came over and offered to buy me a drink.*

blah [blɑ] **1.** *mod.* bland; dull. □ *What a blah performance!* □ *After a blah day like this I need something really exciting like a hot bath.* **2.** *mod.* depressed; worn out. □ *When I get into a blah mood like this, I just want to cry.* □ *I'm really blah. Would you mind awfully if I just went home?* **3.** *mod.* alcohol intoxicated; very drunk. □ *I got myself blah in about twenty minutes.* □ *We are going to get totally blah tonight.*

blah-blah [ˈblɑˈblɑ] *phr.* a phrase echoic of gibberish or incessant chattering. (It can be repeated many times.) □ *Why all this blah-blah-blah?* □ *She's going blah-blah on the phone all the time.*

blahs [blɑz] *n.* a state of mental depression. (Always with *the.*) □ *I've had the blahs about as long as I can stand.* □ *You look like you've got the blahs.*

blanco *n.* a white person; a Caucasian. (From Spanish. Potentially derogatory.) □ *Adios, blanco.* □ *The blancos arrived in droves.*

blanket drill *n.* a night's sleep; sleep. (Military.) □ *Fred is still on blanket* *drill. He's in for it.* ☐ *Blanket drill is the only thing I like in the army.*

blankety-blank AND **blankity-blank** ['blæŋkədi'blæŋk] *mod.* damned. (From the past practice of printing blank spaces in place of banned words. See also *blasted.*) ☐ *I'm tired of your blankety-blank bad humor.* ☐ *Get this blankity-blank cat out of here!*

blankity-blank See the previous entry.

blast 1. *n.* an exciting party. ☐ *Fred knows how to put on a real blast!* ☐ *What a blast we had!* **2.** *n.* a thrill; a *kick.* ☐ *That gag gave me a blast.* ☐ *The roller coaster was a blast.* **3.** *tr.* to shoot someone with a gun. ☐ *The speeding car drove by, and somebody tried to blast him with a machine gun.* ☐ *The cops blasted the crook till there was nothing left.* **4.** *tr.* to attack or criticize someone or something verbally. ☐ *She really blasted the plan in front of the board.* ☐ *He blasted his brother until we all left in embarrassment.* **5.** *n.* a verbal attack. ☐ *The senator leveled a blast at the administration.* ☐ *The administration delivered an enormous blast at the senate hearing.* **6.** *n.* the kick or *rush* from taking or injecting a drug. (Drugs.) ☐ *That stuff really gives me a blast.* ☐ *With a blast like that, somebody's gonna get hooked fast.*

blasted 1. *mod.* alcohol or drug intoxicated. ☐ *I got myself blasted. I'm really sorry.* ☐ *I got so blasted I swore never to blow another joint.* **2.** *mod.* damned. ☐ *I asked her to get her blasted stockings off the shower curtain.* ☐ *Shut your blasted mouth!*

blaster See *(ghetto) blaster.*

blazes See *(blue) blazes.*

bleed *tr.* to drain someone of money through extortion or continuous demands for payment. ☐ *You can't bleed me anymore. I'm tapped.* ☐ *I'm going to bleed you till I get what I deserve.*

bleed for someone *in.* to sympathize with someone. ☐ *I really bleed for you, but there's nothing I can do.* ☐ *We bleed for you, we really do.*

bleed someone dry See the following entry.

bleed someone white AND **bleed someone dry** *tr.* to take all of someone's money; to extort money from someone. (See also *bleed.*) ☐ *The creeps tried to bleed me white.* ☐ *Max got some picture of Fred and Paul together and tried to bleed both of them dry.*

blimp *n.* a nickname for an obese person. (Cruel.) ☐ *Look at that blimp who just came in.* ☐ *This enormous blimp managed to get on the plane, but couldn't get into a seat.*

blimp out *in.* to overeat. ☐ *I love to buy a bag of chips and just blimp out.* ☐ *I only blimp out on weekends.*

blimped *mod.* alcohol intoxicated; swollen with drinking. ☐ *I am still a little blimped from our party last night.* ☐ *I'm bigheaded and still blimped this morning.*

blind drunk *mod.* heavily alcohol intoxicated. ☐ *You came in blind drunk last night. What's going on?* ☐ *They drank till they were blind drunk.*

(blind) munchies *n.* a craving for food or snacks. (Originally drugs.) ☐ *There is nothing like potato chips when you've got the munchies.* ☐ *By midnight I had the blind munchies.*

blind(ed) *mod.* alcohol or drug intoxicated. ☐ *I guess she was blinded. She couldn't stand up.* ☐ *They were both blind as they come.*

blindside *tr.* [for someone or something] to surprise someone, as if sneaking up on the blind side of a one-eyed person (or animal). ☐ *The new tax law blindsided about half the population.* ☐ *The mugger came up and blindsided her with a blow to the head before she knew what had happened.*

blinkers *n.* the eyes. ☐ *As I opened my blinkers, guess who I saw?* ☐ *Look at those classy blinkers!*

blinky AND **winky** ['blɪŋki AND 'wɪŋki] *n.* a device for smoking *free base,* a form of cocaine. (Drugs.) ☐ *He broke his blinky and is desperate for a new one.* ☐

Hold the winky here and wait till I tell you.

blip [blɪp] **1.** *n.* an intermittently appearing light on a radar screen. ☐ *A blip caught the controller's eye for an instant.* ☐ *Did you see that blip, Freddy?* **2.** *n.* anything quick and insignificant; a onetime thing of little importance. ☐ *It was nothing, just a blip. The press blew it out of proportion.* ☐ *It wasn't really a fight. It was just a blip.*

bliss ninny ['blɪs 'nɪni] *n.* a giddy and disoriented person; a *blissed out* person. ☐ *You silly bliss ninny. Who watches over you, anyway?* ☐ *Tiffany is such a bliss ninny—all heart though.*

bliss out *in.* to become euphoric. ☐ *I blissed out just because it is spring and I am with you.* ☐ *I always bliss out from talk like that, but I still love Wally.* (More at *blissed (out)*.)

blissed (out) AND **blissed-out** [blɪst . . .] **1.** *mod.* in a state of emotional bliss. ☐ *After the second movement, I was totally blissed out.* ☐ *What a blissed-out dame!* ☐ *I know a gal who can get blissed from a sunset.* **2.** *mod.* alcohol or drug intoxicated. ☐ *She is more than blissed. She is stoned.* ☐ *My friend is a little blissed out. Can she sit here?*

blisterfoot *n.* someone who walks a lot: a police patrol officer, a soldier, etc. ☐ *This blisterfoot puts his hand on my shoulder and says, "What's the rush, chum?"* ☐ *So this blisterfoot just falls down right there on the parade ground.*

blithering idiot ['blɪðəɪŋ . . .] *n.* a crazy person; a totally disoriented person. ☐ *How can you be such a blithering idiot?* ☐ *You blithering idiot! You've buttered the tablecloth!*

blitz [blɪts] **1.** *n.* a devastating attack. ☐ *After that blitz from the boss, you must feel sort of shaken.* ☐ *That's my second blitz this week. I feel like London.* **2.** *tr.* to attack and defeat someone or something. ☐ *Two of your friends came by and blitzed my refrigerator.* ☐ *The team from downstate blitzed our local team for the third year in a row.*

blitzed (out) [blɪtst . . .] *mod.* alcohol or drug intoxicated. ☐ *To say she is blitzed out is putting it mildly!* ☐ *I want to go out and get totally blitzed. I'll show her who's in charge!*

blivit ['blɪvət] *n.* someone or something annoying and unnecessary. ☐ *The dame's a blivit. She adds up to one too many.* ☐ *Don't be a blivit. Just calm down.*

blixed [blɪkst] *mod.* mildly drug intoxicated. (Drugs.) ☐ *He was a little blixed when I last saw him.* ☐ *He has been blixed for hours.*

blob [blɑb] **1.** *n.* a fool; an oaf. ☐ *Don't be a blob. Get up and get going.* ☐ *This blob just sits there and lets me do all the work.* **2.** *n.* a useless dishrag of a person; a wimp. ☐ *You blob! Show some spunk!* ☐ *I'm amazed that blob can tie his own shoes.* **3.** *n.* a very fat person. ☐ *What a blob!* ☐ *You'd think being a blob like that would get old after a while.*

block **1.** *n.* the head. (See also *knock someone's block off*.) ☐ *That block of yours is pretty dense.* ☐ *Try to get this stuff through your block before the test.* **2.** *n.* the auction block. ☐ *The painting went on the block and sold for nearly fifty-three million dollars.* ☐ *The house had just gone on the block, and the first bid was already opened.* **3.** *n.* a stupid person. (Possibly a back formation on *blockhead*.) ☐ *You silly block! Get out of the way.* ☐ *Wally acts like such a block!*

blockbuster **1.** *n.* something enormous, especially a movie or book that attracts a large audience. ☐ *That blockbuster should make about twenty million.* ☐ *I need two blockbusters like that to pay for the last flop.* **2.** *mod.* exciting and successful. ☐ *The new blockbuster movie made about a zillion bucks in a month.* ☐ *With a blockbuster novel like that in print, you should make quite a bundle.*

blocked *mod.* alcohol or drug intoxicated. ☐ *Man, he is really blocked.* ☐ *How can anybody get so blocked on four beers?*

blockhead *n.* a stupid person. (See also *block.*) □ *Without a blockhead like you to remind me of the perils of stupidity, I might be less efficient than I am.* □ *Why did he call me a blockhead? I didn't do anything.*

blood 1. *n.* catsup. □ *Somebody pass the blood.* □ *How 'bout some blood for my burger?* **2.** See *blood (brother).* **3.** *n.* a black buddy or fellow gang member. (Also a term of address.) □ *Hey, blood! Where you been?* □ *The bloods aren't going to like this.*

blood and guts 1. *n.* strife; acrimony. □ *There is a lot of blood and guts around here, but we get our work done.* □ *Cut out the blood and guts and grow up.* **2.** *mod.* acrimonious. (This is hyphenated before a nominal.) □ *There are too many blood-and-guts arguments around here.* □ *Old blood-and-guts Wally is here making threats again.*

blood bath *n.* a battle; a great decimation. □ *What a blood bath! The whole town collapsed after the bank failed.* □ *There was a blood bath at the office when the manager fired twenty people.*

blood (brother) *n.* a fellow black male. □ *One of the bloods came up to say hello.* □ *This blood brother keeps asking me for money.*

blooey ['blui] **1.** *mod.* gone; destroyed. □ *Everything is finished, blooey!* □ *All my plans are blooey!* **2.** *mod.* alcohol intoxicated. □ *Bruno is totally blooey. He can't even open his eyes.* □ *Man, I'm blooey. I'm stoned to the bones.*

blooper ['blupɚ] **1.** *n.* an embarrassing broadcasting error that must be bleeped or blooped out of the program. □ *I made a blooper, and they cut it out of the program.* □ *There is a record you can buy that lets you hear the famous bloopers of the past.* **2.** *n.* an error. □ *Another day, another blooper.* □ *That was a real blooper. Did you get fired?*

blot someone out *tr.* to kill someone. (Underworld.) □ *Sorry, chum, we got orders to blot you out.* [T] *They blotted out the witness before the trial.*

blotter 1. *n.* a drunkard. (See also *sponge.*) □ *The guy's a blotter. He'll drink anything and lots of it.* □ *They say that Mr. Franklin is a blotter and needs treatment.* **2.** *n.* the drug *L.S.D.,* sold on bits of blotting paper. (Drugs.) □ *Most of the acid in this town is blotter.* □ *Blotter can bring one to five dollars a pop.* **3.** *n.* a police station log of arrests; a police blotter. □ *We went downtown to have a look at the blotter. There was no Matthew Wilson on it anywhere.* □ *The blotter is full of the names of petty criminals and drunks.*

blotto ['blado] **1.** *n.* strong liquor. □ *Let's go get a little of that blotto.* □ *Let's get some blotto and get blocked.* **2.** *mod.* alcohol intoxicated; dead drunk. □ *Let's get some smash and get blotto.* □ *She just lay there—blotto.*

blow 1. *tr. & in.* to leave (someplace) in a hurry. (See also *blow town, blow the joint.*) □ *It's late. I gotta blow.* □ *They blew this place before you got here.* **2.** *tr.* to ruin something; to ruin an opportunity. □ *You really blew it!* □ *It was my last chance, and I blew it.* **3.** *n.* a setback; an attack. □ *It was a real blow to our prestige.* □ *Acme Systems Industries suffered a blow to its plans to acquire A.B.C. Steel Widgets.* **4.** *tr.* to waste money; to spend money. □ *Mary blew forty bucks on a second-hand radio.* □ *We blew it all at a fancy restaurant.* **5.** *in.* to become very angry; to lose one's temper. (See also *blow a fuse.*) □ *Finally I had had enough, and I blew.* □ *The brass blew, and we heard the noise all the way down here.* **6.** *in.* to play a musical instrument, not necessarily a wind instrument. □ *Man, listen to her blow.* □ *She blows, and everybody listens.* **7.** AND **blow-out** *n.* a drinking party. □ *What a blow over at Joe's. I'll never get sober.* □ *Man, come to my blow-out. It's the best place to go.* **8.** *tr.* to *snort* any powdered drug; to take snuff. (Drugs.) □ *Those guys spend all their time blowing coke.* □ *Are you blowing something good?* **9.** *in.* to smoke marijuana. (Drugs.) □ *He sits there blowing by the hour. How can he afford it?* □ *They say that blowing that much *will affect your brain.* **10.** *n.* cocaine. (Drugs.) ☐ *You can get some good blow over at that crack house.* ☐ *What's blow cost around here?*

blow a fuse AND **blow one's fuse; blow a gasket; blow one's cork; blow one's lid; blow one's top; blow one's stack** *tr.* to explode with anger; to lose one's temper. ☐ *Come on, don't blow a fuse.* ☐ *Go ahead, blow a gasket! What good will that do?*

blow a gasket See the previous entry.

blow a hype *tr.* to overreact; to *spaz out.* ☐ *I was afraid she would blow a hype about the broken window.* ☐ *Come on, don't blow a hype. It's only a car.*

blow beets *tr.* to empty one's stomach; to vomit. ☐ *What was in that stew? I feel like I gotta blow beets.* ☐ *She wasted a few minutes blowing beets, just to make things worse.*

blow chow See the following entry.

blow chunks AND **blow chow; blow grits; blow lunch** *tr.* to vomit. ☐ *She drank too much and left the room to blow chunks.* ☐ *Who's been blowing lunch in the john?* ☐ *The smell was so bad I thought I was going to blow chow.* ☐ *Where's Kim? She was blowing grits in the john the last time I saw her.*

blow cold *in.* [for a person] to display disinterest. ☐ *Lately, he's sort of blown cold when I'm around.* ☐ *The committee blew cold as my plan unfolded.*

blow grits See *blow chunks.*

blow in *in.* to arrive. ☐ *I just blew in last night. Where can I find a room?* ☐ *When I blew in, nobody was here.*

Blow it out your ear! *exclam.* "Go away!"; "I don't believe it!" ☐ *Oh, blow it out your ear, you cornball!* ☐ *You are not way rad, you're just way out, twit! Blow it out your ear!*

blow jive [...dʒaɪv] *tr.* to smoke marijuana. (See also *jive.*) ☐ *Man, let's go out and blow some jive!* ☐ *You would rather blow jive than eat, I think.*

blow lunch See *blow chunks.*

blow off 1. *in.* to goof off; to waste time; to procrastinate. ☐ *You blow off too much.* ☐ *All your best time is gone—blown off.* **2.** *n.* a time-waster; a *goof-off.* (Usually **blow-off.**) ☐ *Fred is such a blow-off!* ☐ *Get busy. I don't pay blow-offs around here.* **3.** *n.* something that can be done easily or without much effort. (Usually **blow-off.**) ☐ *Oh, that is just a blow-off. Nothing to it.* ☐ *The test was a blow-off.* **4.** *n.* the final insult; an event that causes a dispute. (Usually **blow-off.**) ☐ *The blow-off was a call from some dame named Monica who asked for Snookums.* ☐ *When the blow-off happened, nobody was expecting anything.* **5.** *n.* a dispute; an argument. (Usually **blow-off.** See also *blow up.*) ☐ *After a blow-off like that, we need a breather.* ☐ *There was a big blow-off at the plant today.*

blow off (some) steam AND **let off (some) steam** *tr.* to release emotional tension by talking or getting angry. ☐ *Don't worry. She's just blowing off steam.* ☐ *Let off some steam. Get it out of your system.*

Blow on it! *exclam.* "Cool it!"; "Take it easy!" ☐ *It's all right, Tom. Blow on it!* ☐ *Hey, man. Relax. Blow on it!*

blow (one's) cookies *tr.* to empty one's stomach; to vomit. ☐ *I think I'm going to blow my cookies.* ☐ *Okay, if any you guys gotta blow your cookies or something, do it here, not inside!*

blow one's cool *tr.* to become angry. ☐ *Now, now, don't blow your cool.* ☐ *I almost blew my cool when the dog wet my pants leg.*

blow one's cork See *blow a fuse.*

blow one's doughnuts AND **lose one's doughnuts** [...'donəts] *tr.* to empty one's stomach; to vomit. ☐ *The stuff was so vile, I thought I would blow my doughnuts.* ☐ *Who lost their doughnuts in the hall?*

blow one's fuse See *blow a fuse.*

blow one's groceries *tr.* to empty one's stomach; to vomit. ☐ *I gotta blow my groceries. Look out!* ☐ *She blew her groceries all over the front seat.*

blow one's lid See *blow a fuse.*

blow one's lines *tr.* to forget one's lines in a play; to speak one's lines incorrectly in a play. □ *There I was in my first major role, and I blow my lines!* □ *If you blow your lines, just try to cover it up.*

blow (one's) lunch AND **lose one's lunch** *tr.* to empty one's stomach; to vomit. □ *I almost lost my lunch, I ran so hard.* □ *I wanted to blow my lunch, that's how rotten I felt.*

blow one's own horn AND **toot one's own horn** *tr.* to brag. □ *Gary sure likes to toot his own horn.* □ *"I hate to blow my own horn," said Bill, lying through his teeth.*

blow one's stack See *blow a fuse.*

blow one's top See *blow a fuse.*

blow-out See *blow.*

blow smoke 1. *tr.* to state something in a way that conceals the truth. (See also *smoke and mirrors.*) □ *She is a master at blowing smoke. She belongs in government.* □ *When they began to figure him out, he began to blow smoke.* **2.** *tr.* to smoke marijuana. (Drugs.) □ *Max sits around blowing smoke when he's not selling.* □ *The whole sales force blows smoke during office hours.*

blow someone away 1. *tr.* to kill someone; to shoot someone. (Underworld.) □ *The boss said we was to blow you away if you gives us any trouble.* 🅃 *We blow away guys like you every day.* **2.** *tr.* to overwhelm someone; to amaze someone. □ *The music about blew me away.* □ *The whole idea just blew her away.*

blow someone or something off 1. *tr.* to neglect or ignore someone or something. □ *Get it done now. Don't blow it off!* □ *Don't blow me off. Listen! I want it done now!* **2.** *tr.* [with *someone*] to cheat someone; to deceive someone. □ *Don't try to blow me off! I know what's what.* 🅃 *They blew off a young couple and conned a hundred bucks out of them.*

blow someone out of the water *tr.* to utterly destroy someone. (As a ship is blown up by a torpedo.) □ *This is too much. I'm gonna blow that guy out of the water.* □ *How does it feel to be blown out of the water like that?*

blow someone to something *tr.* to treat someone to something, such as a meal, a movie, a drink, etc. □ *Let me blow you to a meal.* □ *I think I'll blow myself to a fancy dessert.*

blow someone's cover *tr.* to reveal someone's true identity; to ruin someone's scheme for concealment. □ *The dog recognized me and blew my cover.* □ *I didn't mean to blow your cover.*

blow someone's doors off *tr.* to defeat someone; to surpass someone. (As if someone were going by another vehicle on the highway at such a high speed that the doors would be blown off in passing.) □ *We're gonna really blow your doors off in the next game.* □ *They blew our doors off in sales last year.*

blow someone's mind 1. *tr.* to impress someone; to overwhelm someone. □ *This whole business just blows my mind.* □ *Your credentials really blow my mind!* **2.** *tr.* [for a drug] to intoxicate someone. □ *This stuff will blow your mind.* □ *That blue acid blew my mind.*

blow something wide open AND **bust something wide open** *tr.* to expose corrupt practices or a scheme; to put an end to corruption. □ *The press is trying to blow the town wide open, and the feebies are trying to hush them up so they can move about in secret.* □ *I'm going to bust this racket wide open.*

blow the joint *tr.* to get out of a place, probably in a hurry. (Underworld. See also *joint.*) □ *Come on, let's blow the joint before there's trouble.* □ *They blew the joint about an hour ago.*

blow the lid off something *tr.* to expose a scandal or corrupt practice; to expose political dishonesty. □ *I'm going to blow the lid off another phony candidate.* □ *The reporter blew the lid off the latest city hall scandal.*

blow town *tr.* to get out of town, probably in a hurry. (Underworld.) □ *He* *blew town yesterday.* ☐ *I gotta pack and blow town. The cops are on to me.*

blow up 1. *in.* to burst into anger. ☐ *I just knew you'd blow up.* ☐ *So she blew up. Why should that affect you so much?* **2.** *n.* an angry outburst; a fight. (Usually **blowup.**) ☐ *After the third blowup, she left him.* ☐ *One blowup after another. Yuck!* **3.** *n.* an enlarged version of a photograph, map, chart, etc. (Usually **blowup.**) ☐ *Here's a blow up of the scene of the crime.* ☐ *Kelly sent a blowup of their wedding picture to all her relatives.* **4.** *n.* the ruination of something; the collapse of something. (Usually **blowup.**) ☐ *The blowup in the financial world has ruined my chances for early retirement.* ☐ *After the blowup, they called one another to compare notes.*

blow Z's [. . . ziz] *tr.* to sleep. ☐ *I got to blow Z's for a while; then we'll talk.* ☐ *Him? Oh, he's in the back blowing Z's.*

blowed (away) *mod.* alcohol or drug intoxicated. (See also *blown away.*) ☐ *I was so blowed away I couldn't see straight.* ☐ *I'm afraid I am way blowed.*

blower 1. *n.* a cocaine user. (Drugs.) ☐ *I can spot a blower any day.* ☐ *Max is a blower, among other things.* **2.** *n.* cocaine. (Drugs.) ☐ *What's the best quality blower around here?* ☐ *George says he can't live without blower.* **3.** *n.* a cigarette. ☐ *You got a blower I can bum?* ☐ *That's the third blower in ten minutes!* **4.** *n.* a handkerchief. ☐ *He pulled a crusty blower from his back pocket.* ☐ *And what does he do when he doesn't have a blower?*

blowhard ['blo'hɑrd] *n.* a braggart; a big talker. ☐ *You're just a big blowhard.* ☐ *When and if this blowhard finishes, let's go.*

blown See the following entry.

blown away 1. *mod.* dead; killed. (Underworld.) ☐ *Four of the mob were blown away when the cops got there.* ☐ *That guy was blown away weeks ago.* **2.** AND **blown** *mod.* alcohol or drug intoxicated. ☐ *I drank till I was blown, and then I drank some more.* ☐ *Whatever that pill was, Cecilia is totally blown away.* **3.** *mod.* overwhelmed; greatly impressed. (Often with *with* or *by.*) ☐ *We were just blown away by your good words.* ☐ *Like it? I was blown away.*

blown (out) *mod.* alcohol or drug intoxicated. ☐ *Fred is totally blown out and will have a huge hangover tomorrow.* ☐ *Fred stood at the door and told us he was blown—something that was totally obvious anyway.*

blown (up) *mod.* alcohol intoxicated. (See also *blown away.*) ☐ *I guess I'm a little too blown up to drive.* ☐ *You are blown as blazes, you twit!*

blubber gut(s) ['bləbɚ 'gət(s)] *n.* a fat person. (Also a rude term of address.) ☐ *Hey, blubber guts! Get a girdle.* ☐ *Why doesn't that blubber gut do something about all that weight?*

blue 1. *mod.* depressed; melancholy. ☐ *That music always makes me blue.* ☐ *I'm feeling sort of blue.* ☐ *I'm in a blue mood.* **2.** *mod.* obscene; vulgar; dirty. ☐ *Those blue jokes don't go over very well around here.* ☐ *Enough of your blue interests. Get out and take all these magazines with you.* ☐ *That one was really blue.* **3.** *n.* the sky; the heavens. ☐ *I just look up at the blue and hope for the best.* ☐ *The idea came to me right out of the blue.* **4.** *mod.* alcohol intoxicated. ☐ *What have you been drinking? You're getting a little blue.* ☐ *You might say I'm blue. Others might note that I am stoned.* **5.** *n.* an amphetamine tablet or capsule, especially a blue one. (Drugs.) ☐ *How are blues different from reds and yellows?* ☐ *I'm sort of wired. You got any blues?* **6.** *n.* a police officer; the police. ☐ *The blues will be here in a minute.* ☐ *One blue isn't enough to handle the job.* **7.** *n.* a 10-mg tablet of Valium™. (Drugs.) ☐ *A blue is enough to put most people into a stupor. Why do you want two?* ☐ *In treatment they kept giving me blues to calm me down. Now I can't live without them.*

blue and white *n.* a police car; the police. (Patterned on *black and white* and used in cities where the police cars are painted blue and white.) ☐ *A blue and white suddenly appeared, and I knew we* *were finished.* □ *I can usually spot a blue and white before anyone else.*

blue around the gills AND **green around the gills** **1.** *mod.* ill; nauseated. □ *You are looking a little blue around the gills.* □ *How about a little air? I feel a little green around the gills.* **2.** *mod.* alcohol intoxicated. □ *In the middle of the drink, I knew I was getting blue around the gills.* □ *Marty—now thoroughly green around the gills—slid neatly under the table, and everyone pretended not to notice.*

(blue) blazes *n.* hell. □ *You can go straight to blue blazes as far as I care.* □ *It's as hot as blazes here.*

blue boys AND **blue coats** *n.* the police. (See also *men in blue.*) □ *Four blue boys held me while a fifth slipped the cuffs on me. I ain't no pushover.* □ *The blue coats climbed out of the black and white and just stood there.*

blue chip **1.** *n.* stock shares of a large company that has a high value. (Securities markets.) □ *The blue chips took another nose dive in today's trading.* □ *I buy nothing but blue chips.* **2.** *mod.* having to do with the stock of large, valuable companies. (Securities markets.) □ *The blue chip rally ran for a third day.* □ *It was another blue chip led sell off.*

blue coats See *blue boys.*

blue devils **1.** *n.* melancholia; depression. □ *Hank is down with the blue devils again.* □ *How do you get rid of the blue devils?* **2.** *n.* the delirium tremens. □ *You wouldn't think that a society dame like that would have the blue devils, would you?* □ *The shakes, or the blue devils, are a sure sign of a serious drinking problem.* **3.** *n.* capsules of Amytal™, a barbiturate. □ *How much for a little box of blue devils?* □ *Got no red devils. Will blue devils do it to you?*

blue-eyed *mod.* innocent. □ *Look, you little blue-eyed sweetie, I know your game!* □ *He's sure his blue-eyed wonder couldn't have hit my child.* □ *Don't try to look so blue-eyed.*

blue flu ['blu 'flu] *n.* an imaginary disease afflicting police officers who call in sick during a work stoppage or slowdown. (Journalistic. Done where strikes are illegal.) □ *Another epidemic of the blue flu struck the city's police officers early today.* □ *It seems that the city's criminals and lawbreakers are immune to the blue flu. Their work goes on totally unaffected.*

blue funk ['blu 'fəŋk] *n.* a state of depression. □ *I'm glad I'm out of my blue funk.* □ *You've got to get out of your blue funk and get back to work.*

blue in the face *mod.* pale from exhaustion or exertion. □ *I laughed until I was blue in the face.* □ *She worked hard enough to be blue in the face.*

blue suit *n.* a police officer. (Usually plural.) □ *The blue suits showed up about twenty minutes after I called them!* □ *Watch out for the blue suits if you are going to drive this fast!*

bluehair ['bluher] *n.* an old lady, especially one whose hair is tinted blue. □ *The cruise was nice but sort of dull because of all the bluehairs aboard.* □ *The bluehairs all crowded up to the door, each one trying to be first.*

BM *n.* a disgusting and annoying person. (Potentially offensive. Use with caution. Initialism and euphemism. From *bowel movement.* A way of calling a person a *shit.* Derogatory.) □ *The guy's a real BM. A total pain.* □ *The new guy has to be the world's worst BM.*

B.M.O.C. *n.* "big man on campus," an important or self-important male college student. (Initialism. Collegiate. See also *B.W.O.C.*) □ *Who's the B.M.O.C. who keeps trying to get elected class president?* □ *When this B.M.O.C. asked me to leave, I ignored him.*

B.O. **1.** *n.* (bad) "body odor." (Initialism.) □ *Man, do you have B.O.!* □ *Now here is a product that will end your worries about B.O.* **2.** *n.* "box office," where tickets to some event are sold. □ *The show was a big hit at the B.O.* □ *If you want your money back, you'll have to go to the B.O.* **3.** AND **BO** *n.* "HBO,"

Home Box Office, the cable television channel. (Initialism and dysphemism.) ☐ *Is there a good movie on BO tonight?* ☐ *There is boxing on BO but no movie.*

B.O. juice *n.* a deodorant; an underarm deodorant. (Collegiate. See also *B.O.*) ☐ *Who took my B.O. juice? I've got to go to class.* ☐ *Help this man find his B.O. juice, fast! He really needs it.*

boat **1.** *n.* a big shoe. (See also *gunboats.*) ☐ *Whose boat is that under the coffee table?* ☐ *Those boats are special made, in fact.* **2.** *n.* a big car; a full-size car. ☐ *I don't want to drive a big boat like that.* ☐ *How do you stop that boat? Throw out an anchor?*

bod [bad] **1.** *n.* a body, especially a nice body. (Compare to *odd-bod.*) ☐ *You got a nice bod, Tom.* ☐ *If you got a good bod and enough money, why are you depressed?* **2.** *n.* a person. ☐ *How many bods are coming over tonight?* ☐ *Who's the bod with the tight slacks?*

bodacious [bo'deʃəs] *mod.* assertive; audacious. ☐ *That is a bodacious plan, for sure.* ☐ *Yes, sir! That is really bodacious.*

body count **1.** *n.* the total of dead bodies after a battle. ☐ *The body count at Hill 49 was three.* ☐ *The body count seems to go down during the rainy season.* **2.** *n.* the total number of casualties after some kind of shake-up.. ☐ *The pink slips are coming out every day. The body count on Monday was twenty-three.* ☐ *Most everybody is flunking quan. The body count after the last test was in the twenties.* **3.** *n.* a count of people present. ☐ *The body count was about forty-five at the meeting.* ☐ *The body count seems to go down each month.*

body shake *n.* a shakedown of the body; a skin-search. (Underworld. See also *shakedown.*) ☐ *You can't give me a body shake. I want my lawyer!* ☐ *They give everybody who passes through these doors a body shake.*

boff [baf] **1.** *tr.* to punch someone. ☐ *I was afraid she was going to boff me.* ☐ *Ted boffed Harry playfully.* **2.** *in.* to empty one's stomach; to vomit. (See also *barf.*) ☐ *She boffed and boffed, until she was exhausted.* ☐ *I think I'm gonna boff!*

boffo ['bafo] **1.** *n.* a box-office hit; a successful play, musical, movie, etc. ☐ *The last one was a tremendous boffo, but we only broke even.* ☐ *I need a boffo just once in my life.* **2.** *mod.* successful; tremendous. ☐ *We had a boffo time at your rally.* ☐ *Another boffo success for Wally!* ☐ *That was really boffo!*

bogard See the following entry.

bogart AND **bogard** ['bogart AND 'bogard] **1.** *in.* to monopolize a communal marijuana cigarette; to hold a communal marijuana cigarette so long—Bogart style—that one drools on it. (From *Humphrey Bogart,* the screen actor.) ☐ *Come on, man. Don't bogart on us!* ☐ *Stop bogarding and take a hit!* **2.** *in.* to stall. ☐ *Stop bogarting. Let's get this done!* ☐ *The lawyer for the other side is bogarding, and it will take weeks to get it settled.* **3.** *in.* to act in a tough manner like Humphrey Bogart. ☐ *Look at him bogarting! Who needs tough guys?* ☐ *There's nothing funnier than a wimp trying to bogard around.*

bogue [bog] *mod.* *bogus;* fake. ☐ *Keep your bogue gold watch. I don't want it!* ☐ *She is so, like, bogue!*

bogus ['bogəs] **1.** *mod.* phony; false; undesirable. ☐ *I can't eat any more of this bogus food.* ☐ *This class is really bogus.* **2.** *mod.* great; excellent. ☐ *Man, this place is really bogus!* ☐ *Sam and Charlie had a really bogus time at the jig.*

boheme [bo'him] *n.* a (feminine) personal style consisting of no makeup, large baggy clothing, long skirts, and comfortable shoes. (Collegiate.) ☐ *She looks so good in boheme!* ☐ *Boheme is not you.*

bohunk *n.* an oaf; a simpleton. (From *Bohemian* and the source of *hunky,* probably *Hungarian.* Derogatory or teasing.) ☐ *Some bohunk put the wrong label on this box.* ☐ *Come here, you silly bohunk.*

boiled **1.** *mod.* angry. ☐ *I am so boiled at you!* ☐ *Now, don't get boiled. It was* *only a joke.* **2.** *mod.* alcohol intoxicated. ☐ *How can you get so boiled on wine?* ☐ *The two were boiled and not much use to us.*

boiling (mad) *mod.* very mad. ☐ *Mad, I not mad. I'm just boiling.* ☐ *She is really boiling mad.*

bokoo AND **boku** ['bo'ku] *mod.* many. (A play on French *beaucoup.*) ☐ *I've got bokoo things to do today.* ☐ *There are already boku people invited.*

boku See the previous entry.

bold *mod.* great; outstanding. ☐ *Bold move, Charles. You outfoxed them.* ☐ *The movie we saw last night was really bold.*

bologna See *baloney.*

bolt *in.* to leave; to go away. (Not necessarily fast.) ☐ *Time to go, man. Let's bolt.* ☐ *Time to bolt. Got to get home.*

bolus ['boləs] *n.* a physician. (From the Latin name for a pill.) ☐ *The bolus kept trying to get me to lose weight.* ☐ *There is a new bolus in town.*

bomb **1.** *n.* a bad performance or an inherently bad show. ☐ *They tried as hard as they could, but the thing was a bomb from act one on.* ☐ *The latest bomb on Broadway, like all bombs, will only go off once. This one finished to a chorus of boos before the final curtain.* **2.** *in.* to fail. ☐ *My first try bombed, but things got better.* ☐ *It bombed the minute the first curtain went up.* **3.** See *bomb(shell).*

bomb (out) *in.* [for a computer or computer program] to fail. ☐ *You expect a program to bomb a time or two.* ☐ *The whole thing bombed out at just the wrong time.*

bombed (out) *mod.* alcohol or drug intoxicated. (Possibly from *embalmed.*) ☐ *They were bombed and looked nearly dead.* ☐ *How can I drive when I'm bombed out?*

bomb(shell) *n.* a stunning piece of news that is "dropped" without warning. ☐ *I am still recovering from your bomb of last evening.* ☐ *After you left us with the bombshell about your marriage to the Christmas tree farmer in Montana, we began to realize that it's your life and you should do what you want.*

bone [bon] *n.* a trombone. (Musicians. See also *bones.*) ☐ *Herman is just a wonder on the bone.* ☐ *She plays the bone like nobody's business.*

bone factory **1.** *n.* a hospital. ☐ *Lemme outa this bone factory!* ☐ *After about two months in the bone factory, I was back on the job.* **2.** *n.* a cemetery. ☐ *We must have passed by forty bone factories going across Missouri.* ☐ *I know I'll end up in the bone factory just like everyone else.*

bone idle *mod.* very lazy; completely idle or unproductive. ☐ *Your problem is that you are bone idle.* ☐ *Take your bone idle brother and move out!*

bone orchard *n.* a cemetery. ☐ *That is a very pleasant bone orchard.* ☐ *Does it really matter how comfortable a bone orchard looks?*

bone out *in.* to leave. ☐ *It's time we boned out and got home.* ☐ *Ted and Bill boned out after midnight.*

bonehead **1.** *n.* a stupid or stubborn person. ☐ *You are such a bonehead when it comes to buying cars.* ☐ *Don't be a bonehead. Cooperate!* **2.** AND **boneheaded** *mod.* stupid; stubborn. ☐ *Of all the boneheaded things to do!* ☐ *Why am I married to the world's greatest all-time bonehead klutz?* ☐ *Don't be so boneheaded.*

boneheaded See the previous entry.

boner ['bonɚ] *n.* a silly error; a gaffe. (See also *pull a boner.* There are other taboo meanings.) ☐ *Well, that was a bad boner.* ☐ *What a boner! You must be embarrassed.*

bones **1.** *n.* dice. (See also *bone.*) ☐ *Toss me the bones and get out your checkbooks.* ☐ *Throw them bones and hope for the best.* **2.** *n.* a nickname for a ship's physician. (From *sawbones.* Also the nickname of the doctor on the starship *Enterprise* of *Star Trek* fame.) ☐ *This fat bones actually wanted me to lose* *weight.* □ *This is quite a cut. You'll have to go over to the bones in Adamsville.* **3.** *n.* a nickname for a skinny person. (Also a term of address.) □ *Well, bones, how about a nice big meal?* □ *Ask bones there what he wants to drink.* **4.** *n.* dollars; money; cash. □ *You got any bones on you I can borrow?* □ *The tickets only cost a few bones, but the play was lousy and I want my money back.*

boneyard 1. *n.* a cemetery. □ *I'd like to be planted in a boneyard like that.* □ *I'll take a boneyard with a view of the lake.* **2.** *n.* a junkyard. □ *I got a used right-hand door from a boneyard.* □ *This old car's ready for the boneyard.*

bong AND **bhong** [bɔŋ] **1.** *n.* a marijuana smoking device that cools the smoke by passing it through water. (Drugs.) □ *This bong is really getting sort of nasty.* □ *Fill up your bong and let's get going.* **2.** *tr. & in.* to smoke marijuana or other drugs with a *bong* or other device. (Drugs.) □ *You can't just bong for the rest of your life!* □ *Wanna go bong a bowl?* **3.** *n.* a puff or *hit* of marijuana taken through a *bong.* (Drugs.) □ *I'll take two bongs, and then I gotta go.* □ *I only got one bong!* **4.** *tr. & in.* to drink keg beer through a hose. (California. See also *beerbong.*) □ *Everybody bonged till the keg was empty.* □ *There were no cups, so people had to bong their beer.*

bonged (out) [bɔŋd . . .] *mod.* exhausted from too much marijuana. (Drugs.) □ *I was bonged all through the holidays.* □ *She was still bonged out after the first week of classes.*

bonk [bɔŋk] **1.** *tr.* to strike one's head. □ *He bonked his head on the shelf.* □ *I bonked my bean.* **2.** *tr.* to strike someone on the head. □ *I bonked John on the head.* □ *He wouldn't move, so I bonked him.*

bonkers ['bɔŋkɚz] **1.** AND **crackers** *mod.* insane; crazy. □ *Get this bonkers brother of yours out of here!* □ *I think I am going crackers.* **2.** *mod.* slightly intoxicated. □ *I'm just a little bonkers, nothing really serious.* □ *She's too bonkers to drive.*

Bonus! ['bonəs] *exclam.* "That's great!"; "That's good enough to earn a bonus!" □ *Bonus! That's the best news I've heard in a long time!* □ *The teacher's sick? Bonus!*

bonzo ['banzo] *mod.* crazy. □ *You are completely bonzo!* □ *I want out of this bonzo place!*

boo-bird ['bu'bɚd] *n.* a person who boos frequently at games or other public events. □ *It was a big day for the boo-birds at Wrigley Field.* □ *The catcher turned and stared right at the loud-mouthed boo-bird. Everybody knew what he was thinking.*

boo-boo ['bubu] *n.* an error. (See also *make a boo-boo.*) □ *It's only a small boo-boo. Don't stress yourself.* □ *Another boo-boo like that, and you are through.*

boob [bub] **1.** *n.* a stupid person; a rural oaf. □ *You boob! What have you done?* □ *Why did I marry a boob like you?* **2.** AND **booby** ['bubi] *n.* a breast. (Usually plural. Potentially offensive. Use only with discretion.) □ *My boobs aren't what I might have wished for.* □ *With boobs like that, she can go anywhere she likes.*

boob-tube ['bub'tub] *n.* a television set. (Something for a *boob* to watch.) □ *You spend too much time in front of the boob-tube.* □ *What's on the boob-tube tonight?*

booby See *boob.*

booby hatch ['bubi . . .] *n.* a mental hospital. □ *I was afraid they would send me to the booby hatch.* □ *Don't you mean send you back to the booby hatch?*

booby trap 1. *n.* a concealed trap. (Both literal and figurative.) □ *This clause in the contract is a real booby trap. Let's rewrite it.* □ *Some kind of booby trap in the warehouse kept the robber from getting away.* **2.** *tr.* to install a concealed trap in a place. (Usually **booby-trap.**) □ *The agents booby-trapped the cellar.* □ *They booby-trapped the elevator so it turned into a cell if you didn't know the code to open the door.*

boodie See *boody.*

boodle ['budl] *n.* loot; the proceeds from a crime. (Underworld.) ☐ *All of the boodle was recovered in a suitcase.* ☐ *They divvied up the boodle and got out of town.*

boody AND **boodie; bootie; booty** ['budi] **1.** *n.* the buttocks. (Potentially offensive. Use only with discretion.) ☐ *Look at the nice little boody on that guy.* ☐ *Get your boodie out on that dance floor and shake it.* **2.** *n.* someone or something disliked. (From sense 1.) ☐ *Why don't you clean up all this boody? This place is a mess.* ☐ *Who are those boodies blocking the doorway?*

booger See the following entry.

boogie ['bugi OR 'bugi] **1.** *n.* a kind of rock dance. ☐ *I didn't like the boogie until I learned how to do it right.* ☐ *The boogie will tire you out, but good!* **2.** *in.* to dance rock-style. ☐ *I don't like to boogie.* ☐ *I'm too old to boogie.* **3.** *n.* a party where the *boogie* is danced. ☐ *There's a boogie over at Steve's tonight.* ☐ *One more boogie and I'm through for the year.* **4.** *in.* to get down to work; to get down to business. ☐ *All right, it's time to boogie. Cool it!* ☐ *The whistle blew. Time to boogie.* **5.** AND **booger** ['bugɚ] *n.* a piece of nasal mucus. (Crude. Use only with discretion.) ☐ *That's no way to take care of a booger!* ☐ *Is that a boogie on your lip, or what?* **6.** *in.* to leave. ☐ *Come on, man. Let's boogie.* ☐ *Time to boogie. It's late.* **7.** *n.* a tumor. (Medical slang. See also *guber.*) ☐ *Looks like a little boogie down in the lung.* ☐ *I've got to take out three boogies before lunch and look at x-rays all afternoon.*

boogie-board ['bugibord OR 'bugibord] **1.** *n.* a surfboard. (California.) ☐ *Get your boogie-board out there in that tube.* ☐ *She cracked her boogie-board apart on that big one.* **2.** *n.* a skateboard. (Teens.) ☐ *He fell off his boogie-board and broke his tailbone.* ☐ *Can you imagine a boogie-board costing 600 dollars?*

boogie down (to somewhere) *in.* to hurry (to somewhere); to go (somewhere). ☐ *So, why don't you boogie down to the store and load up with bud and berries for the weekend?* ☐ *I'm gonna boogie down and see what's going on.*

boogieman ['bugimæn OR 'bugimæn] *n.* an imaginary man who is said to frighten people; a false threat of any kind. ☐ *Don't turn me into a boogieman. Spank the child yourself.* ☐ *The press has made the secretary into some sort of boogieman.*

book 1. *in.* to leave. ☐ *Time's up. Gotta book.* ☐ *Let's book. I'm late.* **2.** *tr.* to charge someone with a crime. ☐ *The cop booked him for vagrancy.* ☐ *She looked sort of scroungy, and they wanted to book her for something, but didn't know what.* **3.** *in.* to study. (See also *book it.*) ☐ *I gotta book. Bye.* ☐ *I hate to book all night.*

book it *tr.* to study hard; to spend a period of time studying. (Collegiate.) ☐ *I am so tired of booking it every night of my life.* ☐ *I've got to spend the rest of the night booking it.*

bookie *n.* a bookmaker for betting. ☐ *Max was a bookie till he got into drugs.* ☐ *My bookie wants his money on the spot.*

boom *in.* to listen to music, as with a *boom box.* ☐ *You don't do anything but hang around and boom all day!* ☐ *If you're going to boom all the time, why don't you get some headphones?*

boom box *n.* a portable stereo radio. (See also *box, thunderbox.*) ☐ *Turn down that damn boom box, or I'll kick it in.* ☐ *Hey, man! You even gonna take your boom box to church, or what?*

boom sticks *n.* drumsticks. (Musicians.) ☐ *He always carries his boom sticks in his back pocket, and he beats on walls, radiators, desks—you name it.* ☐ *I need new boom sticks. They keep breaking.*

boomer 1. *n.* a laborer who moves from one economic boom to another. ☐ *Fred's great uncle was a boomer in the days of the Oklahoma oil rush.* ☐ *Most of the old boomers settled down and raised families.* **2.** See *(baby) boomer.*

boondocks AND **boonies** ['bundaks AND 'buniz] *n.* an isolated area; an area of wild terrain; suburbs distant from a city. (From the word for mountain in the Tagalog language. Since World War II.) □ *The weather out in the boonies looks cold and dry.* □ *I don't want to be stuck out in the boondocks!*

boondoggle ['bundɔgl̩] *n.* a waste of time and money; a project for spending public money. □ *Another Washington boondoggle came to light today as investigators revealed plans for a dam in a California canyon that doesn't have any water.* □ *This is another boondoggle—just the thing every single baby-kisser pledged to stop.*

boonies See *boondocks.*

boosiasm(s) *n.* a woman's breasts. (A blend of *bosom* and *enthusiasm*. Occurs both as a count and a noncount noun. Old but recurrent. Potentially offensive. Use only with discretion.) □ *Did you see the boosiasms on that dame?* □ *What a remarkable boosiasm!*

boost **1.** *tr. & in.* to steal or shoplift something. (Underworld.) □ *He specializes in boosting meat for resale.* □ *He boosts for a living.* **2.** *tr.* to praise or *hype* someone or something; to support someone or something. □ *She is always boosting some cause.* □ *If she would boost me as well, I wouldn't object to the time she spends hyping other people.*

booster **1.** *n.* a shoplifter. □ *The cops hauled in two boosters by noon.* □ *Gary was a part-time booster till he got into dope.* **2.** *n.* a supporter (of someone or some cause). □ *We don't have enough boosters to have any effect.* □ *I'm a booster of lots of good causes.*

boot **1.** *n.* a thrill; a charge. □ *I get a real boot out of my grandchildren.* □ *Their little games give me a real boot.* **2.** *tr.* to dismiss or eject someone. □ *I booted him myself.* □ *Bruno, boot that guy at once!* **3.** *n.* a dismissal or ejection. □ *I got the boot even though I had worked there for a decade.* □ *Seven people got the boot.* **4.** *tr. & in.* to start the operating system of a computer. □ *I booted the thing, but it just sat there.* □ *When I booted, all I got was a feep.* **5.** *in.* to empty one's stomach; to vomit. □ *The kid booted and booted and will probably never smoke another cigar.* □ *I think I'm gonna boot. Gangway!*

boot someone out *tr.* to throw someone out; to kick someone out. □ *Are you going to boot me out?* 🅃 *I don't boot out anybody. Bruno does that. Bruno, come here.*

bootie See *boody.*

booty See *boody.*

booze [buz] **1.** *n.* beverage alcohol. (Slang since the 1500's.) □ *I don't care for booze. It makes me sneeze.* □ *Where's the booze?* **2.** AND **booze up** *in.* to drink alcohol to excess; to go on a bash. □ *Let's go out and booze up!* □ *Stop boozing for a minute and listen up, guys.*

booze artist *n.* a drunken person; a drunkard. □ *Pete was a booze artist for a decade before he realized what he was doing.* □ *A wobbly booze artist sat musing on the stool in the corner.*

booze it (up) *tr.* to drink excessively; to drink to intoxication. □ *You come home every night and booze it up. How can you keep on this way?* □ *Let's go out and booze it, okay?*

booze up See *booze.*

boozed *mod.* alcohol intoxicated. □ *Wow, is he ever boozed!* □ *I think I am a little boozed.*

boozy-woozy ['buzi'wuzi] *mod.* alcohol intoxicated. □ *The boozy-woozy man clung to the railing and sang at the top of his voice.* □ *I think I am just an itty-bitty boozy-woozy.*

bop [bap] **1.** *tr.* to strike someone or something. □ *I bopped the car on the hood and made a dent.* □ *You wanna get bopped in the beezer?* **2.** *n.* a style of jazz popular in the 1940's. □ *We heard some bop in an old movie.* □ *Bop is not popular, but it is by no means dead.* **3.** *n.* a drug in pill form; a dose of a drug. (See also *hit.*) □ *Give me a bop of that* *stuff, will ya?* □ *You gonna drop both of them bops?*

bore the pants off (of) someone *tr.* to bore someone exceedingly. □ *You bore the pants off me!* □ *The lecture bored the pants off of everybody.*

bosh [bɑʃ] *n.* nonsense; idle talk. (Also an exclamation, **Bosh!**) □ *That is enough of your bosh!* □ *Oh, bosh! You don't know what you're talking about.*

bosom buddy *n.* a very close male or female friend. □ *We are bosom buddies, but we can still get into a big fight every now and then.* □ *Oh, yes, Sharon is my bosom buddy.*

bosom chums AND **bosom friends** *n.* lice. □ *The old guy sat there scratching at his bosom chums.* □ *"Nobody seems to like my bosom friends," he muttered.*

bosom friends See the previous entry.

boss *mod.* excellent; powerful; superior. □ *That is a boss tune.* □ *This rally is really boss.*

boss lady *n.* the woman in charge. □ *You'll have to ask the boss lady.* □ *The boss lady asked again for volunteers.*

boss man *n.* the man in charge. □ *The boss man's coming. Watch out!* □ *I guess the boss man is about ready to retire.*

both sheets in the wind *mod.* alcohol intoxicated. (See also *three sheets in the wind.*) □ *She's both sheets in the wind at the moment.* □ *She's not just both sheets in the wind—they're all in the wind.*

bottle 1. *n.* a drunkard. □ *The bar was empty save an old bottle propped against the side of a booth.* □ *That old girl is just a bottle. There's more booze in her than outside.* **2.** *n.* liquor. (Always with *the* in this sense.) □ *Her only true love is the bottle.* □ *The bottle plays a big role in his life.* **3.** *in.* to drink liquor to excess. □ *I wish there was a way I could get through the day without bottling.* □ *Let's go out and bottle into oblivion.*

bottle baby *n.* an alcoholic. □ *The bottle babies sat there, waiting to be thrown out at closing time.* □ *There is help for bottle babies.*

bottleache [ˈbɑdlek] *n.* a hangover; the delirium tremens. □ *A lot of these guys really suffer from the bottleache, but what can they do?* □ *I got a touch of the bottleache this morning.*

bottom 1. *n.* the buttocks. □ *Ted fell on his bottom and just sat there.* □ *My bottom is sore from sitting too long.* **2.** *n.* the second half of a baseball inning. □ *It's the bottom of the second, Wilbur's up.* □ *Wilbur hit a double-bagger in the bottom of the second.* **3.** *tr.* to drink something to the bottom. □ *He bottomed the beer and ordered another one.* □ *Come on. Bottom that beer, and let's get out of here.*

bottom dollar *n.* one's last dollar. (See also *bet one's bottom dollar.*) □ *I lost my bottom dollar on that deal.* □ *I'm down to my bottom dollar. How about a little loan?*

bottom fishing *n.* seeking something at its lowest price; seeking something at a low cost and willing to accept inferior quality. □ *I don't think bottom fishing for stocks is always wise. There is always a good reason why the price is low.* □ *Bottom fishing probably won't get you anything of value.*

bottom line 1. *n.* the grand total; the final figure on a balance sheet. (Securities markets. Always with *the.*) □ *The company's bottom line is in bad shape.* □ *If the bottom line is positive, everything is okay.* **2.** *n.* the result; the *nitty-gritty;* the score. □ *The bottom line is that you really don't care.* □ *Well, when you get down to the bottom line, it's only money that matters.*

bottom of the barrel AND **bottom of the heap** *n.* the location of persons or things of the very lowest quality. (Usually with *from.* See also *scrape the bottom of the barrel.*) □ *That last secretary you sent me was really from the bottom of the barrel.* □ *I don't need any candidates from the bottom of the heap.*

bottom of the heap See the previous entry.

bottom out *in.* to reach the lowest or worst point of something. ☐ *All my problems seem to be bottoming out. They can't get much worse.* ☐ *Interest rates bottomed out last February.*

bottomless pit 1. *n.* a very hungry person. ☐ *The guy is a bottomless pit. There isn't enough food in town to fill him up.* ☐ *I've got two boys, and they're both bottomless pits.* **2.** *n.* an endless source of something, usually something troublesome. ☐ *This house is a bottomless pit. Keeping it up is endless.* ☐ *Our problems come from a bottomless pit. There is just no end to them.*

Bottoms up. *sent.* "Let us drink up!" (A drinking toast.) ☐ *Well, bottoms up.* ☐ *They all raised their glasses, and the host said, "Bottoms up."*

bounce 1. *in.* [for a check] to be returned from the bank because of insufficient funds. (See also *rubber (check).*) ☐ *The check bounced, and I had to pay a penalty fee.* ☐ *If your check bounces, you'll have to bring us cash.* **2.** *tr.* [for a bank] to refuse to honor a check. ☐ *They bounced another of my checks today.* ☐ *The bank won't bounce any more checks because I closed the account.* **3.** *tr.* to throw someone out. ☐ *Bruno bounced me, and I ran to my car and beat it.* ☐ *The owner came out and bounced us.* **4.** *n.* pep; energy. ☐ *All these kids have a lot of bounce.* ☐ *I never have any bounce when I wake up early.*

bounce for something See *spring for something.*

bounce something off (of) someone *tr.* to try out an idea on someone; to get someone's opinion of an idea. ☐ *Let me bounce this off of you.* ☐ *I bounced the idea off Gary, but he wasn't at all impressed.*

bouncer *n.* a strong man hired to eject unruly people from a bar or similar place. (People supposedly bounce when thrown out.) ☐ *I saw the bouncer looking at me, and I got out of there fast.* ☐ *He was the biggest bouncer I've ever seen.*

bow to the porcelain altar *in.* to empty one's stomach; to vomit. (The *porcelain altar* is the toilet bowl.) ☐ *He spent the whole night bowing to the porcelain altar.* ☐ *I have the feeling that I will be bowing to the porcelain altar before morning.*

bow-wow ['bɑuwɑu] **1.** *n.* a dog. (Juvenile.) ☐ *The bow-wow frightened me.* ☐ *We're going to get you a bow-wow!* **2.** *n.* an ugly woman; a *dog.* (Derogatory.) ☐ *What a bow-wow!* ☐ *I would have chosen a better nose if I had been given a chance, but—all in all—I'm not such a bow-wow.*

bowl *n.* a pipe or other device for smoking cannabis. (Drugs.) ☐ *Where is my bowl? I got some real Q. gold.* ☐ *There's somebody's bowl out in the hall. Go get it before the neighbors call the fuzz.*

bowser ['bɑuzɚ] *n.* a person with a dog face or ugly face. (Typically applied to females.) ☐ *What a bowser! She belongs in a stable!* ☐ *Fred went out with a real bowser, but said he had a good time anyway.*

box 1. *n.* a coffin. ☐ *I want the cheapest box they sell.* ☐ *Put him in a box and put the box in a hole. Then the matter is closed.* **2.** See *(squeeze-)box.* **3.** *n.* a phonograph player. ☐ *My box is old, but still good.* ☐ *Yours is old! My box still has tubes!* **4.** *n.* a portable stereo radio; a *(ghetto) box.* (See also *(ghetto) blaster.*) ☐ *Where did you get that box?* ☐ *Does that damn box have to be so loud?* **5.** *n.* a piano. ☐ *Man, he plays a mean box.* ☐ *She sure can pound the devil out of that box!* **6.** *in.* to die. ☐ *I laughed so hard I thought I would box.* ☐ *The old man looks like he's going to box at any minute.*

box someone in *tr.* to put someone into a bind; to reduce the number of someone's alternatives. ☐ *I don't want to box you in, but you are running out of options.* 🅃 *I want to box in the whole staff, so they'll have to do it my way.* (More at *boxed in.*)

boxed *mod.* dead; died. ☐ *My old dog is boxed. A car hit her.* ☐ *He's boxed. There's nothing that can be done.*

boxed in *mod.* in a bind; having few alternatives. ☐ *I really feel boxed in around here.* ☐ *I got him boxed in. He'll have to do it our way.*

boxed on the table *mod.* died on the (operating) table. (Medical. See also *boxed.*) ☐ *The surgeon did the best job possible, but the patient boxed on the table.* ☐ *Another patient boxed on the table. That's three today.*

boxed (up) **1.** *mod.* alcohol or drug intoxicated. ☐ *I am way boxed, and I feel sick.* ☐ *She got boxed up on gin.* **2.** *mod.* in jail. ☐ *I did it, and I was boxed for a long time for it. Now lay off!* ☐ *Pat was boxed up for two days till we got bond money.*

boys in blue See *men in blue.*

boys in the backroom AND **backroom boys** *n.* any private male group making decisions, usually politicians. ☐ *The boys in the backroom picked the last presidential candidate.* ☐ *The backroom boys have decided too many things in the past. Their day is over.*

bozo ['bozo] *n.* a clown; a *jerk;* a fool. (Also a term of address.) ☐ *Look, you bozo, I've had enough of your jabber.* ☐ *Those bozos are at it again. Spend, spend, spend.*

bra-burner *n.* a nickname for a woman who supported the women's liberation movements of the 1960's and 1970's. (Derogatory.) ☐ *Didn't the bra-burners give way to whale-savers in the seventies?* ☐ *Mike wants to know if the bra-burners took them off first.*

brack-brain ['brækbren] *n.* a fool. ☐ *The brack-brains in Washington have done it again!* ☐ *One brack-brain around here is enough. Do you want me to leave?*

brain **1.** *n.* a good student; a very intelligent person. (See also *brains.*) ☐ *I'm no brain, but I get good grades.* ☐ *Who was the brain who figured this out?* **2.** *tr.* to hit someone (in the head). ☐ *I ought to brain you for that!* ☐ *She almost brained me with her umbrella.*

brain-burned AND **brain-fried** *mod.* brain-damaged from drugs. (Drugs. See also *burnout.*) ☐ *The kid is a little brain-burned, but still has a chance at an independent life.* ☐ *Man, you're gonna get brain-burned from this stuff.*

brain-dead *mod.* stupid. ☐ *I don't know why he's so dull. He's seems brain-dead half the time.* ☐ *I think that half my students are brain-dead.*

brain-drain *n.* the movement of intellectuals from one country to another where the pay and job opportunities are better. ☐ *It looks like the brain-drain of the fifties is reversing with more and more academics leaving the U.S. to join British universities.* ☐ *Where there is a good education system, there will always be a brain-drain.*

brain-fried See *brain-burned.*

brain-teaser See the following entry.

brain-twister AND **brain-teaser** *n.* a puzzle. ☐ *This Maltese falcon case is a real brain-twister.* ☐ *Can you help me with this brain-teaser?*

brainchild **1.** *n.* someone's good idea viewed as an offspring of the brain. ☐ *Is this your brainchild? It won't work.* ☐ *Listen to this. It's my best brainchild.* **2.** *n.* a person who has good ideas. ☐ *The boss's new brainchild seems to have gone dry.* ☐ *You can't just go out and hire a brainchild. They've got to want to work for you.*

brains *n.* the person(s) in charge of thinking something through. ☐ *Who's the brains around this joint?* ☐ *Bruno is not what I would call the brains of the gang.*

brainstorm **1.** *n.* a good idea; an idea that enters one's head suddenly. ☐ *I had a sudden brainstorm and got out of bed to write it down.* ☐ *This brainstorm hit me while I was in the shower.* **2.** *in.* to try to think up good ideas, especially as a group. ☐ *Let's brainstorm on this for a little while.* ☐ *They are in the meeting room now, brainstorming.*

(brand) spanking new *mod.* completely new. ☐ *My car is spanking new.* ☐ *Look at that brand spanking new car!*

brass *n.* high-ranking military or civilian officers. (See also *top brass.*) ☐ *We'll see what the brass has to say first.* ☐ *The brass said no to your promotion.*

brass hat *n.* a member of the *brass.* ☐ *When are the brass hats going to start paying attention to the important things?* ☐ *A brass hat came up to me and asked me where I was going.*

brass tacks *n.* essential business. (Usually in "get down to brass tacks.") ☐ *Now that we are talking brass tacks, how much do you really want for this watch?* ☐ *Since we haven't gotten down to brass tacks, would it be unethical for me to buy you lunch?*

brassed (off) *mod.* angry; disgusted. ☐ *You look so brassed off at the world. Smile!* ☐ *I'm not brassed in the least, really.*

BRB *interj.* "Be right back."(Used in electronic mail and computer bulletin board messages. Not pronounced aloud. Often enclosed, <BRB>.) ☐ *I have to get off the computer for a minute.* <BRB> ☐ *I have to get off the computer to use the phone. BRB*

bread *n.* money. ☐ *I need to get some bread to live on.* ☐ *You got any bread you can spare?*

bread and butter *n.* one's livelihood. ☐ *It's bread and butter to me. I have to do it.* ☐ *I can't give it up. It's my bread and butter.*

breadbasket AND **dinner basket** *n.* the belly; the stomach. ☐ *I hit him, pow, right in the breadbasket.* ☐ *With a dinner basket like that, he must have a devil of a time buying clothes.*

break 1. *n.* a chance; an opportunity. ☐ *Come on, give me a break!* ☐ *I got my first break in show biz when I was only twelve.* 2. *n.* an escape from prison; a prison breakout. ☐ *I hear there's a break planned for tonight.* ☐ *Two cons got shot in the break.* 3. *in.* [for a news story] to unfold rapidly. (Journalism.) ☐ *As the story continues to break, we will bring you the latest.* ☐ *Something is breaking on the Wilson murder. Get over to the D.A.'s office, quick.* 4. *n.* a solo played when the rest of the band stops. ☐ *This is your break, Andy. Let's hear it, man.* ☐ *It wasn't much of a break, but I gave it everything.*

Break a leg! *exclam.* "Good luck!" (A special theatrical way of wishing a performer good luck. Saying "good luck" is a jinx.) ☐ *"Break a leg!" shouted the stage manager to the heroine.* ☐ *Let's all go and do our best. Break a leg!*

Break it up! *exclam.* "Stop it!" (An order to two or more people to stop doing something, such as fighting.) ☐ *All right you two, break it up!* ☐ *She told the boys to break it up or get sent to the principal's office.*

break one's balls to do something See *bust (one's) ass (to do something).*

break out *in.* to leave. ☐ *It's late, man. Time to break out.* ☐ *We broke out a little after midnight.*

break someone's balls *tr.* to wreck or ruin someone; to overwork someone; to overwhelm someone. (Usually used with males, but not necessarily. See also *ball.* Potentially offensive. Use only with discretion.) ☐ *The boss acts like he's trying to break everybody's balls all the time.* ☐ *No need to break my balls. I'll do it!*

break the ice 1. *tr.* to be the first one to do something. ☐ *No one wants to break the ice. I guess I will be first.* ☐ *Well, I guess we should break the ice and start dancing.* 2. *tr.* to attempt to become friends with someone. ☐ *He tried to break the ice, but she was a little cold.* ☐ *A nice smile does a lot to break the ice.*

breaker 1. *n.* a break dancer. (Break dancing is a rhythmic and energetic impromptu performance usually done by untrained urban youths.) ☐ *He is one of the best breakers in the city.* ☐ *I'm too fat to be a breaker.* 2. *n.* someone attempting to use a citizens band radio channel. ☐ *There's a breaker trying to use this channel. Let's drop down to eleven.* ☐ *You got it, breaker.*

breakfast of champions *n.* a first alcoholic drink of the day, taken in the morning, instead of breakfast. (Collegiate.) ☐ *Well, here it goes—the breakfast of champions.* ☐ *He calls it the breakfast of champions. I call it a bad sign of something out of hand.*

breather *n.* a rest period; a lull. ☐ *I really need a breather.* ☐ *As soon as we've had a breather, it's back to work.*

breeder *n.* a nonhomosexual. (In a homosexual context.) ☐ *Don't invite Wally. He's a breeder.* ☐ *Why not? The breeders invited us to their party.*

breeze *n.* an easy task. ☐ *Nothing to it. It was a breeze.* ☐ *I went through it like a breeze.*

brew 1. *n.* coffee; occasionally, tea. ☐ *I could use a nice cup of brew.* ☐ *This is my kind of brew, hot, black, and aromatic.* **2.** *n.* beer; a can, bottle, or glass of beer. ☐ *Hey, give me a cold brew, will ya?* ☐ *This is my favorite brew, and it's at just the right temperature.*

brew-ha ['bruhɑ] *n. brew;* a beer. ☐ *One brew-ha over here, innkeeper!* ☐ *How 'bout some brew-ha, Mike?*

brew-out *n.* a beer blast; a beer *blowout.* ☐ *Were you at Tom's brew-out? I was too bombed to see who was there.* ☐ *Was that Tom's brew-out I was at?*

brewed *mod.* alcohol intoxicated. ☐ *Fred is brewed every evening by 9:00. I think he has a problem.* ☐ *He tries to get brewed as soon as he can after work.*

brews brothers *n.* (male) beer-drinking college students. (A play on *The Blues Brothers,* a popular movie released in 1980.) ☐ *The brews brothers were making a lot of noise last night. Don't those guys do anything but drink?* ☐ *You guys look like the devil and you smell like the brews brothers.*

brewski AND **brewsky** ['bruski] *n.* beer; a beer. ☐ *Hey, how 'bout a brewski?* ☐ *I'll take a nice cold brewsky.*

brewsky See the previous entry.

brewster ['brustɚ] **1.** *n* a beer drinker; a beer drunkard. ☐ *Fred has become a committed brewster. He pounds one beer after another.* ☐ *A dedicated brewster can put away a six-pack in half an hour.* **2.** *n.* beer; a can of beer. ☐ *I need another brewster over here, and another one for my buddy.* ☐ *Toss me a cold brewster, will you?*

brick 1. *n.* a failed shot in basketball. ☐ *Chalk up another brick for Michael.* ☐ *It looked close, but it was a brick.* **2.** *n.* any failure. ☐ *Charlie is responsible for another brick in the accounting department.* ☐ *This whole thing is a mess. Whose brick is this anyway?* **3.** *in.* to fail. ☐ *The whole project bricked because we sat on the contract too long.* ☐ *The company almost bricked because of delays in signing contracts.*

brickhouse *n.* a large-breasted woman. (A confused or euphemistic reference to *built like a brick shithouse.* Potentially offensive. Use only with discretion.) ☐ *Clara's a real brickhouse. I don't see how she stands up.* ☐ *Look at the boosiasms on that brickhouse!*

brig [brɪg] *n.* jail. (From the term for a naval prison or a shipboard jail.) ☐ *Throw this jerk in the brig.* ☐ *The brig in that one-horse town is a mess.*

bright and breezy *mod.* cheery and alert. ☐ *You look all bright and breezy. What happened?* ☐ *Bright and breezy people on a day like this make me sick.*

bright-eyed and bushy-tailed *mod.* alert and ready to do something; as alert and as active as a squirrel. ☐ *You look all bright-eyed and bushy-tailed this morning.* ☐ *The child—bright-eyed and bushy-tailed—woke everyone up at dawn.* ☐ *Tell that bright-eyed and bushy-tailed brat to shut up!*

brim *n.* a hat. ☐ *Man, that is one fine brim you got.* ☐ *New silks call for a new brim.*

bring-down 1. *n.* something that depresses someone. ☐ *The news was a terrible bring-down.* ☐ *Just to see your face was a bring-down.* **2.** *n.* something that brings someone back to reality. ☐ *The bill for the week's stay was a real* *bring-down.* □ *I have had one bring-down after another today.*

bring home the bacon *tr.* to earn a livelihood; to earn money to buy food. □ *When I have to bring home the bacon, I hope I have an interesting job.* □ *I have to bring home the bacon for six kids.*

bring someone down 1. *tr.* to terminate one's own or someone else's drug experience. (Drugs.) □ *It took a lot to bring her down.* 🅃 *We brought down the two of them carefully.* **2.** *tr.* to depress someone. □ *The news really brought me down.* 🅃 *The failure of the business brought down the staff.*

bring someone on *tr.* to arouse sexually; to turn someone on. □ *She was trying to bring her date on, but he saw her game.* □ *This kind of music brings me on.*

bring something up 1. *tr.* to mention something. (Standard English.) □ *Why did you have to bring that up?* 🅃 *Then they brought up the question of money.* **2.** *tr.* to vomit something up; to cough something up. 🅃 *See if you can get him to bring up the penny.* 🅃 *I did, and he brought up a nickel instead!*

broad *n.* a woman. (Originally derogatory. Now usually derogatory.) □ *This pushy broad comes up to me and asks if I have any manners!* □ *So—come on, what'd you tell the broad?*

Bronx cheer ['braŋks 'tʃir] *n.* a rude noise made with the lips; a *raspberry.* □ *The little air compressor in the corner of the parking lot made a noise like a Bronx cheer.* □ *He got only a Bronx cheer for his efforts.*

brother See *(soul) brother.*

brown-bag 1. *n.* a bag lunch. □ *Bring a brown-bag, and we'll talk and eat at the same time.* □ *I lost my brown-bag, but I'll come to talk anyway.* **2.** *in.* to carry a bag lunch. □ *He's back to brown-bagging while he saves up for his vacation.* □ *I like to brown-bag. I don't eat so much when I do.* **3.** *mod.* having to do with an event during which people eat their own bag lunches. □ *These brown-bag affairs seem so tacky.* □ *The brown-bag meeting wasn't very useful.* □ *It's brown-bag. Come if you can.*

brown bottle flu *n.* a hangover or sickness from drinking. (Probably from beer, which is often sold in brown bottles.) □ *The jerks in the back row of my history class show up every Monday morning with the brown bottle flu.* □ *Wayne had a case of the brown bottle flu and didn't make the meeting.*

brown-nose 1. AND **brown-noser** *n.* a sycophant; one who flatters for self-serving motives. □ *You are just a plain old brown-nose.* □ *That brown-noser actually gave the boss a bottle of wine for her birthday.* **2.** *tr. & in.* to curry favor with someone; to be a sycophant. □ *Don't you brown-nose me!* □ *Don keeps brown-nosing, and the professor pretends not to notice.*

brown-noser See the previous entry.

brown out 1. *in.* [for the electricity] to fade and dim down. (Something less than a black out.) □ *The power kept browning out.* □ *The lights started to brown out, and I thought maybe I didn't pay the bill for the juice.* **2.** *n.* a period of dimming or fading of the electricity. □ *There was another brown out today.* □ *They keep building all these expensive power stations, and then we still have brown outs.*

brown someone off *tr.* to make someone angry. □ *That whole business with the cab really browned me off.* 🅃 *I'm afraid I'm going to brown off everyone, but here goes anyway.* (More at *browned (off).*)

browned (off) *mod.* angry. □ *I am really browned off at you!* □ *The boss is browned—to say the least.*

brownie points *n.* imaginary credit for doing something well. (Originally "demerits" in railroading.) □ *How many brownie points do I get for not frowning when you take my picture?* □ *No brownie points for you, twit!*

bruised [bruzd] *mod.* alcohol intoxicated. □ *I am bruised. My head hurts, and my gut feels yucky.* □ *How can anybody get so bruised on so little booze?*

bruiser ['bruzɚ] *n.* a big rough male. ☐ *That big bruiser must weigh a ton.* ☐ *They call that 320-pound bruiser "The Fridge."*

brush *n.* an encounter; a *close shave.* ☐ *My brush with the bear was so close I could smell its breath—which was vile, I might add.* ☐ *It seemed like a brush with death.*

brushoff ['brəʃɔf] *n.* a dismissal; an act of ignoring someone. (See also *give someone the brushoff.*) ☐ *No brushoff for her. I told her to beat it.* ☐ *I got the brushoff, but I can take it.*

brutal *mod.* excellent; powerful. ☐ *Man, what a brutal tune!* ☐ *That last wave was brutal to the max.*

B.S. *n.* nonsense; *bullshit.* (Initialism.) ☐ *I've heard enough of your B.S.* ☐ *Less B.S. and more facts, please.*

B.T.O. See *big-time operator.*

BTW *interj.* "By the way." (Used in electronic mail and computer bulletin board messages. Not pronounced aloud.) ☐ *BTW, have you heard about the new communications software upgrade?* ☐ *I am, BTW, very interested in what you said about the high cost of software.*

bubble water AND **bubbles** *n.* champagne. ☐ *More bubble water, or do you want something stronger?* ☐ *I want about a gallon of bubbles, thanks.*

bubblehead 1. *n.* a fool; a giddy person. ☐ *You silly bubblehead. Watch where you are going!* ☐ *If you can't say anything without coming off like a bubblehead, keep your mouth shut.* **2.** *n.* a heavy drinker of champagne. ☐ *It takes a pretty good bankroll to be a real high-class bubblehead.* ☐ *Part-time bubbleheads go into operation at weddings and other celebrations.*

bubbles See *bubble water.*

bubbly *n.* champagne. (Often with *the.*) ☐ *I'd like a big glass of bubbly, if you don't mind.* ☐ *The bubbly will brighten up any party.*

buck 1. *n.* a dollar. ☐ *Gimme a buck for a bottle of wine, will you mister?* ☐ *Here's a buck; get me some cigarettes.* **2.** *tr.* to resist something. ☐ *Don't buck it. Do what you are told.* ☐ *He enjoys bucking the system.* **3.** *n.* a buckskin (leather) shoe. (Usually plural.) ☐ *Look at my new bucks!* ☐ *You don't see many red bucks. Are you sure you got the right thing?*

buck for something *tr.* to work ambitiously for something, such as a promotion. ☐ *I'm just bucking for recognition, and of course, a 20 percent raise.* ☐ *You can tell she's bucking for promotion.*

buck naked *mod.* entirely naked. (Folksy. From the color of buckskin leather.) ☐ *He stood there buck naked, scratching his belly.* ☐ *They all slipped off their trousers and went swimming buck naked.* ☐ *Who's that buck naked dancer?*

buck up *in.* to cheer up; to perk up. ☐ *Come on, now, buck up. Things can't be all that bad.* ☐ *She began to buck up when I showed her the results of the tests.*

buckage *n.* money. (See also *buck.*) ☐ *I am a little low on buckage at the moment.* ☐ *Can you spare a little buckage until payday?*

bucket 1. *n.* the goal (hoop and net) in basketball. (Sports.) ☐ *Freddy arced one at the bucket and missed.* ☐ *When he holds his arm up, his hand is as high as the top of the bucket.* **2.** *n.* a hoop or basket in basketball. (Sports.) ☐ *Four buckets in two minutes. Is that a record, or what?* ☐ *The last bucket put Adamsville ahead by two points.* **3.** *n.* the buttocks. (See also *can.*) ☐ *Sam's getting a real fat bucket, isn't he?* ☐ *Haul your bucket over here and have a seat.*

bucko ['bəko] *n.* friend; pal. (Also a term of address. Can also be used with a sneer to convey contempt.) ☐ *Hey, bucko, come here a minute.* ☐ *Ask your bucko there if he wants to join us.*

buckpasser *n.* someone who cannot accept the responsibility for something. (See also *pass the buck.*) ☐ *You are the most irresponsible buckpasser I have ever had to deal with!* ☐ *When something* *really goes wrong, everybody suddenly becomes a buckpasser.*

bud [bəd] *n.* a Budweiser™ beer; any beer. (See also *budhead.*) ☐ *How 'bout one of them buds in a green bottle?* ☐ *I got four kinds of bud here. Which do you want?*

buddy-buddy ['bədi'bədi] *mod.* friendly; too friendly. ☐ *Why is that guy so buddy-buddy with me?* ☐ *Don't try to get too buddy-buddy with these people. They don't like strangers.* ☐ *What a buddy-buddy phony!*

buddy up to someone *in.* to become very friendly toward someone. ☐ *Why are you buddying up to me? I don't even know you.* ☐ *Try to buddy up to him and pretend you are interested in what he is doing.*

buddy up (with someone) *in.* to share living space with someone; to share something with someone. ☐ *Let's buddy up, okay?* ☐ *There weren't enough to go around, so we had to buddy up.*

budget crunch See the following entry.

budget squeeze AND **budget crunch** *n.* a situation where there is not enough money in the budget. ☐ *Facing another budget squeeze, the legislators were forced to put off their pay increase.* ☐ *The budget crunch hasn't begun to affect us yet.*

budhead ['bədhɛd] *n.* a beer drinker. (See also *bud.*) ☐ *You're a budhead, and you're getting worse.* ☐ *Here comes Charlie, my favorite budhead. How about a brew, Charlie?*

buffaloed ['bəfəlod] *mod.* confused; stumped. ☐ *These tax forms really have me buffaloed.* ☐ *He was so buffaloed by the problem that he didn't get any work done.*

buff(ed) [bəft] *mod.* strong; muscular. ☐ *Bill is buffed and short-tempered. Stay away from him.* ☐ *He has such buff legs! Does he have a job or does he just work out?*

bug 1. *n.* a flaw in a computer program. ☐ *As soon as I get the bugs out, I can run my program.* ☐ *There is a little bug still, but it hardly causes any problems.* **2.** *n.* someone who is enthusiastic about something. (A combining form.) ☐ *Mary is a camera bug.* ☐ *Al has turned into a real compact disc bug.* **3.** *n.* an obsession or urge. ☐ *I've got this bug about making money.* ☐ *I have a bug that causes me to eat tons of pasta.* **4.** *n.* a spy device for listening to someone's conversation. ☐ *I found a little bug taped under my chair.* ☐ *The agency bulls put bugs everywhere.* **5.** *tr.* to conceal a microphone somewhere. ☐ *Who bugged my office?* ☐ *We will have to bug the bookie joint to get the goods on those guys.* **6.** *tr.* to annoy someone. ☐ *Stop bugging me, you twit!* ☐ *This kind of thing really bugs me.*

Bug off! *exclam.* "Get out!"; "Go away!" ☐ *Bug off! Get out of here!* ☐ *Bug off and leave me alone!*

bug out 1. *in.* to pack up and retreat. (Military, Korean War.) ☐ *Orders are to bug out by oh-nine-hundred.* ☐ *Okay, everybody, move it! We're bugging out.* **2.** *in.* to get out of somewhere fast. ☐ *I gotta find a way to bug out of here without getting caught.* ☐ *Okay, it's clear. Let's bug out.*

buggy ['bəgi] *n.* an automobile. ☐ *Other than a dent in the front bumper, this buggy is in A-1 condition.* ☐ *It's time to buy a new buggy.*

buick *in.* to vomit. (Onomatopoetic. Based on the automobile name.) ☐ *Dave buicked on the lawn and then stumbled into the house.* ☐ *Oh, lordy! I feel like I'm going to buick.*

built like a brick outhouse AND **built like a brick shithouse** *mod.* well-built —either strong or attractive. (The second entry is potentially offensive. Use only with discretion.) ☐ *That guy's built like a brick shithouse.* ☐ *This garage is built like a brick outhouse. It'll last for years.*

built like a brick shithouse See the previous entry.

bull 1. *n.* nonsense; *bullshit.* ☐ *That's just a lot of bull.* ☐ *Don't give me that* *bull! I won't buy it.* **2.** *tr. & in.* to lie to or deceive someone. □ *Stop bulling me!* □ *Is she bulling again?* **3.** *n.* a police officer; a private detective or guard. □ *Here come the bulls. Get out.* □ *And this bull comes up and says, "Where's the fire?"*

bull-pucky ['bulpəki] **1.** *n.* bull dung. □ *Why didn't you watch where you were going? Didn't you expect to find bull-pucky in a barnyard?* □ *How can you tell it's bull-pucky?* **2.** *n.* nonsense; *bull-shit.* □ *Don't give me that bull-pucky!* □ *That's all just bull-pucky. Don't believe a word of it.*

bull session *n.* a session of casual conversation. □ *The gals were sitting around enjoying a bull session.* □ *The bull session ran on late into the night.*

bulldoze *tr.* to apply pressure or force to get someone to do something. □ *You think you can bulldoze people into doing what you want!* □ *Don't bulldoze me! I push back.*

bullet-stopper *n.* a U.S. Marine. (From the Persian Gulf War.) □ *The bullet-stoppers shipped out before we even got to the desert.* □ *About a dozen bullet-stoppers came into the bar and the army guys tried to start a fight.*

bullheaded *mod.* stubborn. □ *Don't be so bullheaded.* □ *You are the most bull-headed man I've ever known.*

bullshit (Potentially offensive. Use only with discretion.) **1.** *n.* nonsense; lies; deception. □ *Don't give me all that bullshit!* □ *That's just bullshit.* **2.** *tr.* to deceive someone; to lie to someone. □ *Stop bullshitting me!* □ *You wouldn't bullshit us, would you?*

bullshit artist AND **bullshitter** *n.* someone who excels at boasting or lying. (Potentially offensive. Use only with discretion.) □ *Jim is such a bullshit artist!* □ *He can't talk straight—nothing but a bullshitter.*

bullshitter See the previous entry.

bullyrag ['buliræg] *tr. & in.* to harass someone. □ *Don't bullyrag me just because you're upset.* □ *Pete is bully-ragging again.*

bum **1.** *n.* a vagrant; a good-for-nothing. □ *You had better get your finances in order unless you want to become a bum.* □ *There is a bunch of bums on the corner, just doing nothing.* **2.** *mod.* bad; faulty. □ *This is a bum fuse. No wonder it won't run.* □ *The screw has a bum head and won't turn.* **3.** See *bum something (off someone).*

bum around *in.* to wander around; to *kick around.* □ *I thought I'd bum around for a few years before I settled down.* □ *Those two kids bummed around Europe for two months.*

bum check *n.* a bad check; a forged check. (See also *paper.*) □ *I never wrote a bum check in my life.* □ *We took in four bum checks today.*

bum out **1.** *in.* to have a bad experience with drugs. (Drugs.) □ *I bummed out on angel dust.* □ *She bummed out once too often and gave up the stuff altogether.* **2.** *in.* to have any bad experience. □ *We bummed out at the concert. I dropped my music, and Larry broke a string.* □ *The test was horrible. I bummed out, for sure.*

bum rap **1.** *n.* a false criminal charge. (Underworld. The same as *bad rap.*) □ *This is a bum rap, and you know it.* □ *If a crook didn't scream that he got a bum rap, I might think he was really innocent.* **2.** AND **bum-rap** *tr.* to talk ill about someone; to accuse someone of something falsely. □ *You're always bum-rapping your car!* □ *Don't bum rap me! I'll sue!*

bum someone out *tr.* to discourage someone. □ *That darn blow-out bummed me out.* Ⓣ *The failure of his tires bummed out the race driver.* (More at *bummed (out).*)

bum something (off someone) *tr.* to beg or borrow something (from someone). □ *Can I bum a cigarette off you?* □ *Can I bum a quarter for a phone call?*

bum steer ['bəm 'stir] *n.* a false lead; false information. □ *You sure gave me a bum steer when you told me who he* *was.* □ *We spent all day checking out what turned out to be a bum steer.*

bum trip See *bummer.*

bummed (out) *mod.* discouraged; depressed. □ *I feel so bummed. I think I need a nice hot bath.* □ *When you're feeling bummed out, think how many problems I have.*

bummer 1. AND **bum trip** *n.* a bad drug experience. (Drugs.) □ *She almost didn't get back from a bum trip.* □ *This bummer comes from mixing pills.* **2.** *n.* a disagreeable thing or person. □ *My coach is a real bummer.* □ *The game was a bummer you wouldn't believe.*

bumming *mod.* down; depressed; suffering from something disagreeable. (Collegiate.) □ *I'm really bumming. I think I need somebody to talk to.* □ *Everybody's bumming. It must be the weather.*

bump *tr.* to remove someone from an airplane flight, usually involuntarily, because of overbooking. □ *They bumped me, but gave me something to make up for it.* □ *Is this airline in the habit of bumping old ladies?*

bump someone off *tr.* to kill someone. (Originally underworld.) □ *What am I supposed to do, bump her off?* 🅃 *The mob bumped off the witness before the trial.*

Bump that! *tr.* "Forget that!" □ *Bump that! I was wrong.* □ *I gave you the wrong number. Bump that!*

bum's rush *n.* the ejection of a person from a place. □ *I got the bum's rush at that bar. Do I look that bad?* □ *Give this dame the bum's rush. She can't pay for nothin'.*

bunch of fives *n.* the fist. □ *How would you like a bunch of fives right in the kisser?* □ *He ended up with a bunch of fives in the gut.*

bunco ['bəŋko] **1.** *n.* a scheme to swindle people. (From *banca,* the name of a card game in Spanish.) □ *He's been fiddling with bunco on the West Coast.* □ *All the stuff relating to bunco comes across this desk.* **2.** *tr.* to swindle someone. □ *They buncoed an old lady and left her penniless.* □ *Fred tried to bunco a chick in Frisco, but felt sorry for her at the last minute.*

buncombe See *bunkum.*

bundle *n.* a large amount of money. (See also *lose a bundle, make a bundle, package.*) □ *He still has a bundle from the sale of his house.* □ *You must think I have a real bundle.*

bundle from heaven See the following entry.

bundle of joy AND **bundle from heaven** *n.* a baby. □ *We are expecting a bundle of joy next September.* □ *When your little bundle from heaven arrives, things will be a little hectic for a while.*

bundle of nerves *n.* a very nervous person. □ *I'm just a bundle of nerves. I wish this were over.* □ *Paul's been a bundle of nerves ever since his wreck.*

bunkie ['bəŋki] *n.* a roommate. □ *My bunkie is from Iowa.* □ *I wish I had a bunkie. Things get lonely in a single room.*

bunkum AND **buncombe** ['bəŋkəm] *n.* nonsense. □ *That's just plain bunkum.* □ *Another candidate for governor means just that much more buncombe.*

buns *n.* the buttocks, especially shapely buttocks, particularly male buttocks. (This word was a euphemism for *buttocks* in the 1980's, but the rude *butt* has become the word of choice in general speech.) □ *What cute little buns!* □ *His face looks like a mule kicked him, but have you seen his buns!*

burb [bɚb] *n.* a suburb. (Usually plural.) □ *I've lived in the burbs all my life.* □ *Our burb is too far from the city for much pollution.*

burbed out [bɚbd . . .] *mod.* looking very middle-class and suburban; decked out like a suburban citizen. □ *She's all burbed out with new clothes and a fancy car.* □ *He looks sort of burbed out for a city guy.*

burg [bə·g] *n.* a small town. (Disdainful.) □ *I can't stand another day in this burg.* □ *This burg is getting on my nerves.*

burger *n.* a hamburger sandwich; a hamburger patty. □ *You ready for another burger?* □ *He's cooking burgers out on the grill right now.*

burn **1.** *n.* a cigarette. □ *Gimme a burn, huh?* □ *Fred just stood there with a burn on his lower lip and his hands in his pockets.* **2.** *tr.* to smoke a cigarette. □ *I need to burn a fag. Just a minute.* □ *This nicotine fiend needs to burn one for a fix!* **3.** *tr.* to smoke cannabis. (Drugs.) □ *Jim spent Saturday out in the field burning grass.* □ *The two of them sat there burning reefers for hours on end.* **4.** *tr.* to execute someone in the electric chair. (Underworld.) □ *I'll see that they burn you for this!* □ *The D.A. tried to burn me, but I got off with six months.* **5.** *in.* to die by electrocution in the electric chair. (Underworld.) □ *I ain't afraid I'll burn, copper!* □ *I'll see that you burn for this.* **6.** *tr.* to cheat or rob someone. □ *Tom tried to burn me by selling me a bum watch, but I'm too clever.* □ *He will burn you if you're not careful.* **7.** *tr.* to shoot someone. (Underworld.) □ *He burned the guy with a pistol, but it didn't stop him.* □ *Hold it! I've burned one guy tonight, and I ain't afraid of puttin' a hole through you.* **8.** *n.* a deception; an instance of being cheated. □ *Man, that was a burn. That guy was really mad.* □ *We pulled off the burn without a hitch. It was a gas.* **9.** *n.* the charge or *rush* after the injection of a drug into a vein. (Drugs.) □ *Man, wait'll you taste the burn from this stuff.* □ *I don't want a big burn; just drag it out for about an hour.* **10.** *tr.* to cook food. □ *Why don't you burn some chow for me?* □ *Burn your own stuff, you lazy good-for-nothing man!*

burn artist *n.* someone who cheats or harms someone else; an informer. (Underworld.) □ *Never trust a known burn artist.* □ *The fuzz rounded up all the burn artists in the district and pumped them for info.*

burn rubber *tr.* to run a car engine so fast that one spins the tires so that rubber is left on the street. (Compare to *lay (some) rubber.*) □ *Man, this hog can really burn rubber.* □ *When George was at the age when the greatest thrill was burning rubber, he began to shave once a week.*

burn someone down *tr.* to humiliate someone. □ *Man, don't you ever burn me down like that again!* 🆃 *You just want to burn down everybody to make yourself seem better.*

burn someone up *tr.* to make someone very angry. □ *That kind of thing just burns me up.* □ *This whole business burns all of us up.*

burn with a low blue flame **1.** *in.* to be heavily alcohol intoxicated. □ *Yeah, he's burning with a low blue flame.* □ *He's not just drunk, he's burning with a low blue flame.* **2.** *in.* to be quietly and intensely angry. □ *She just sat there with her steak in her lap, burning with a low blue flame.* □ *She was quiet, but everyone knew she would soon burn with a low blue flame.*

burned **1.** *mod.* cheated; betrayed. □ *Man, did I get burned in that place!* □ *We sure got burned on that deal.* **2.** *mod.* disappointed; humiliated; put down. □ *Whenever we rap, you're never happy till I'm burned.* □ *Ha! You're burned!* **3.** AND **burned up** *mod.* very angry. □ *I've never been so burned up at anyone.* □ *Boy, was I burned!*

burned out AND **burnt out** **1.** *mod.* tired; bored. □ *I'm burned out after all that partying.* □ *I don't want to work with burnt out people. I need energy.* **2.** *mod.* having to do with the ruined veins of an addict. (Drugs.) □ *These old ropes are just burned out. I don't know what to do.* □ *My veins are burnt out so I shoot in the jug.* **3.** *mod.* ruined by marijuana smoking. (Drugs. See also *burnout.*) □ *The poor kid was burned out at the age of twelve.* □ *What's left for these burned out kids?* **4.** *mod.* no longer affected by a particular drug. (Drugs.) □ *It's no good. I'm just burned out. The stuff doesn't affect me at all.* □ *She was burned out on Q.*

burned up See *burned.*

burnout ['bə-naut] **1.** *n.* a person who is ruined by drugs. ☐ *The kid's a burnout. What can you do?* ☐ *Two burnouts sat on the school steps and stared at their feet.* **2.** *n.* someone no longer effective on the job. ☐ *As a teacher, Fred is a burnout.* ☐ *We try to find some other employment for the burnouts.*

burnt offering *n.* burned food; a badly cooked meal. ☐ *Everything I try to cook turns out to be a burnt offering.* ☐ *All I have to look forward to after work is a burnt offering.*

burnt-out See *burned out.*

burp See *berp.*

burps See *berps.*

bury the hatchet **1.** *tr.* to make peace. (From an alleged Amerindian practice.) ☐ *I'm sorry. Let's stop arguing and bury the hatchet.* ☐ *Tom and I buried the hatchet and we are good friends now.* **2.** *tr.* to leave surgical instruments in the patient. (Medical.) ☐ *Did Dr. Smith bury the hatchet again?* ☐ *The idea that a doctor would bury the hatchet is a very old joke.*

bush bitch AND **bush pig** *n.* an ugly or unpleasant female. (Derogatory.) ☐ *Tom's been dating some bush pig from Adamsville.* ☐ *Who is that bush bitch I saw Tom with last night?*

bush patrol **1.** *n.* a session of necking and petting. (Here *patrol* has the military meaning of assignment.) ☐ *Tom is out on bush patrol tonight. I don't know who with.* ☐ *Martha and Paul spent the evening on bush patrol.* **2.** *n.* an imaginary search through campus shrubbery to flush out the necking couples. ☐ *The dean of women put on her housecoat and went out on bush patrol.* ☐ *Bush patrol starts at midnight, so be in by then.*

bush pig See *bush bitch.*

bushed [buʃt] *mod.* exhausted. ☐ *I am just bushed.* ☐ *Another hard day! I am more bushed than ever.*

business end (of something) *n.* the dangerous end of something; the part of something that does something as opposed to the part one holds on to. ☐ *Harry burned himself on the business end of a soldering iron.* ☐ *The robber pointed the business end of the gun right at Kelly.*

bust **1.** *n.* a failure. ☐ *The whole project was a bust from the beginning.* ☐ *My whole life is a bust.* **2.** *tr.* to reduce someone's rank. (Originally military, now also in civilian use as with the police.) ☐ *I'm going to bust you to private!* ☐ *The brass busted her on the spot.* **3.** *n.* a riotous drinking party. ☐ *There was a big bust in the park until two in the morning.* ☐ *There was no beer at the bust. Only wine.* **4.** *n.* a raid by the police. ☐ *The cops staged a bust on Max's place.* ☐ *I knew it was a bust the minute they broke in the door.* **5.** *tr.* [for the police] to raid a place. ☐ *The bacon busted Bill's bar and put Bill in the slammer.* ☐ *We're gonna bust every bookie joint in town.* **6.** *tr.* to arrest someone. ☐ *The feds finally busted Max on a tax rap.* ☐ *A smokey busted Fred for not having a taillight.* **7.** *n.* an arrest. ☐ *The bust was carried off without much stress.* ☐ *What a bust! The man was hollering and the kids were scoffing like mad.* **8.** *tr.* to inform on someone, leading to an arrest. ☐ *I guess I busted Max, but they threatened me.* ☐ *Tom busted Sam because there's bad blood between them.* **9.** *n.* the police. ☐ *The bust is gonna find you no matter where you hole up.* ☐ *Here comes the bust. Beat it!* **10.** See *busted.*

bust a gut (to do something) *tr.* to make a great effort (to do something). (Potentially offensive. Use only with discretion.) ☐ *I busted a gut trying to get just the thing you wanted!* ☐ *Don't bust a gut, but try to get here on time.*

bust a move *tr.* to leave (a place). ☐ *Let's go. Time to bust a move.* ☐ *Let's bust a move. Lots to do tomorrow.*

bust ass out of some place *in.* to get out of some place in a hurry. ☐ *I had to bust ass out of the house and run all the way to school.* ☐ *Wayne bust ass out of the classroom and headed for home.*

bust (one's) ass (to do something) AND **break one's balls to do something; bust**

one's butt to do something; bust one's nuts to do something *tr.* to work very hard to do something. (The expressions with *balls* and *nuts* are said typically, but not necessarily, of a male. Potentially offensive. Use only with discretion.) □ *I've been busting my nuts to get this thing done on time, and now they don't want it!* □ *You are expected to bust your nuts every minute you are at work.*

bust one's butt to do something See the previous entry.

bust one's nuts to do something See *bust (one's) ass (to do something).*

bust (some) suds **1.** *tr.* to drink some beer. □ *Let's go out and bust some suds.* □ *I'm tired of busting suds. Let's play cards.* **2.** *tr.* to wash dishes. □ *I don't want to spend the rest of my life busting suds.* □ *You get into that kitchen and bust some suds to pay for your meal!*

bust someone one *tr.* to punch someone; to give someone a punch, probably in the face. □ *You better shut up, or I'll bust you one!* □ *You want me to bust you one? I will if you do that again.*

bust something up *tr.* to ruin something; to break something up. □ *She tried to bust my marriage up!* 🆃 *I hate to bust up the party, but we gotta go.*

bust something wide open See *blow something wide open.*

busted **1.** AND **bust** *mod.* arrested. □ *Max is bust again. The third time this month.* □ *I got busted for speeding.* **2.** *mod.* alcohol intoxicated. □ *I went to a beer bust and got busted.* □ *Jim is busted again—really boiled.*

but *mod.* totally; very. (Note position in the sentence.) □ *Tell him to get his tail over here but fast.* □ *This thing has to be done but good.*

but-boy *n.* someone, usually a male, who raises objections frequently. (The opposite of a *yes-man.*) □ *I wish you wouldn't be such a but-boy, Higgins. Can't you ever agree with anyone?* □ *Hank is such a but-boy. He doesn't know when to just let something go by.*

butch [butʃ] **1.** *n.* a physician. (Derogatory. From *butcher.*) □ *The butch at the infirmary was no help at all.* □ *What does it take to be a butch besides an office and a degree?* **2.** *mod.* virile and masculine. (In a homosexual context.) □ *That's a real butch haircut, Claude.* □ *Really, Clare. How butch!*

butcher *n.* a surgeon; a physician. (Usually derogatory, possibly jocular.) □ *I won't go back to that butcher for anything at all.* □ *He's been a butcher for seven years and pays 80 percent of his income for insurance.*

butt [bət] **1.** *n.* the buttocks. (Potentially offensive, although heard almost everywhere. Colloquial.) □ *She fell right on her butt.* □ *The doctor gave her a shot in the butt.* **2.** *n.* a cigarette butt. □ *Whose butts are those in the car ashtray?* □ *Don't leave your butts in the houseplants!* **3.** *n.* a cigarette of any kind. □ *You got a butt I can bum?* □ *What kind of butt is that, anyway?* **4.** *n.* someone or something that is disliked. (Potentially offensive. Use only with discretion. See also *boody.*) □ *The guy's a real butt. A real squid.* □ *I wish you didn't act like such a butt all the time.*

butt naked ['bət 'nekəd] *mod.* totally nude. (Collegiate. Potentially offensive. Use only with discretion.) □ *She just stood there butt naked, looking at us.* □ *My roommate sleeps butt naked.*

Butt out! *exclam.* "Get out of my affairs!"; "Mind your own business!" □ *Go away! Butt out!* □ *Butt out! I'm busy.*

butt-ugly *mod.* very ugly. (Potentially offensive. Use only with discretion.) □ *That is the most butt-ugly car I've ever seen.* □ *She is one butt-ugly woman.*

butterfingers *n.* someone who cannot hold on to things. (Also a term of address.) □ *I'm such a butterfingers. I dropped my papers.* □ *Hang on to this tight, butterfingers!*

buttinski See the following entry.

buttinsky AND **buttinski** [bəˈtɪnski] *n.* someone who interrupts; someone who gets involved in other people's business. □ *Frank is such a buttinsky.* □ *I hate to be a buttinski, but what are you talking about?*

buttlegging ['bətlɛgɪŋ] *n.* the transportation of untaxed or undertaxed cigarettes across a state line. (Patterned on *bootlegging.*) □ *There's another news story about buttlegging in northern Indiana tonight.* □ *Most of the guys at the plant do buttlegging on the way home from work.*

buttload AND **shitload** *mod.* a lot; a large amount. (Potentially offensive. Use only with discretion.) □ *I know we can sell a buttload of these recordings—if we can only get a shipment of them in time.* □ *I want to get a really good job and earn a shitload of money.*

button **1.** *n.* the termination of a recitation; the punch line of a joke; a *zinger.* (The equivalent of a button punched to signal a response.) □ *When I got to the button, I realized that I had told the whole joke wrong.* □ *When I came to the button, I knew I was really going to insult the guy.* **2.** *n.* a police officer's badge or shield. □ *The guy flashed his button, so I let him in.* □ *Just because you got a button, it doesn't mean you can push innocent citizens around!*

buttonhole *tr.* to accost someone; to make someone listen to one. (As if grabbing someone by the coat lapel to keep them from getting away.) □ *The guy buttonholed me on my way out, and started asking me a lot of questions.* □ *See if you can buttonhole a cop and get some directions.*

buy **1.** *n.* a purchase. □ *Man, this is a great buy.* □ *What a buy, two for the price of one.* **2.** *tr.* to believe something. □ *Nobody'll buy that story.* □ *It sounds good to me, but will your wife buy it?*

buy it *tr.* to die. (See also *buy the farm, buy the big one.*) □ *For a minute, I thought I was going to buy it.* □ *He lay there coughing for a few minutes, and then he bought it.*

buy someone's wolf ticket *tr.* to challenge someone's boast or taunt. (Black. See also *sell a wolf ticket.*) □ *He wants me to buy his wolf ticket bad.* □ *He's such a fighter. He'll buy anybody's wolf ticket.*

buy the big one *tr.* to die. □ *I don't plan to buy the big one for at least another thirty years.* □ *She conked out for good—you know, bought the big one.*

buy the farm *tr.* to die; to get killed. □ *He bought the farm on San Juan Hill.* □ *I'm too young to buy the farm.*

buy time *tr.* to use a tactic to postpone something. □ *You are just doing this to buy time.* □ *Maybe I can buy some time by asking for a continuance.*

buy trouble *tr.* to encourage trouble; to bring on trouble. □ *I don't want to buy trouble. I have enough already.* □ *Saying something like that is just buying trouble.*

buzhie ['buʒi] **1.** *n.* a middle-class person. (From *bourgeoisie.*) □ *My mother was a buzhie, but my father was a Bohemian type.* □ *I live in a neighborhood of buzhies.* **2.** *mod.* middle-class. □ *I can't stand this buzhie neighborhood.* □ *I live in a buzhie house and drive a buzhie car.* □ *She is so buzhie!*

buzz **1.** *n.* a call on the telephone. (Usually with *give.* See also *jingle.*) □ *I'll give you a buzz tomorrow.* □ *I got a buzz from him yesterday.* **2.** *tr.* to call someone on the telephone. □ *Buzz me about noon.* □ *I'll buzz Mary and see if she can go.* **3.** *tr.* to signal someone with a buzzer. □ *I'll buzz my secretary.* □ *Did you buzz, Gloria?* **4.** *n.* a thrill. □ *I got a real buzz out of that.* □ *The dancers gave the old man a buzz.* **5.** *n.* a chuckle. □ *She gets a buzz out of reading the comics.* □ *Here's a little joke that'll give you a buzz.* **6.** *n.* the initial effects of drinking alcohol or taking certain drugs. □ *Sam got a little buzz from the wine, but he still needed something stronger.* □ *She took a hit and leaned back, waiting for the buzz.*

buzz along **1.** *in.* to depart. □ *Well, I must buzz along.* □ *It's time to buzz along to work now.* **2.** *in.* to drive or move along rapidly. □ *We were buzzing* *along at about seventy when we heard a siren.* □ *"You were buzzing along at eighty-two miles per hour," said the cop.*

buzzard *n.* an old man; a mean old man. (Especially with *old.*) □ *Who's the buzzard in the wingtip shoes?* □ *Some old buzzard is at the door asking for Mary Wilson.*

buzzard meat *n.* someone or something that is dead or outdated. □ *If you don't watch out, you're going to become buzzard meat!* □ *That old car is buzzard meat. It will hardly run.*

buzzing *mod.* drunk. □ *Sally was buzzing after only a few drinks.* □ *She was really buzzing and Molly had to take her home.*

buzzword *n.* a specialist word; a technical word; a jargon word. (Compare to *fuzzword.*) □ *Your constant use of buzzwords makes your work sound quite trivial.* □ *What's the latest buzzword?*

B.V.D.s AND **beeveedees** *n.* underwear; men's underwear. (The first entry is an initialism. From *Bradley, Voorhies, and Day*, the manufacturers. Always plural.) □ *He stood there in his B.V.D.s, freezing.* □ *If you don't wear a belt, your B.V.D.s will show.*

B.W.O.C. *n.* "big woman on campus," an important or self-important female college student. (Initialism. Collegiate. See also *B.M.O.C.*) □ *Some B.W.O.C. came in and asked us to leave.* □ *It's always the same B.W.O.C.s you see in the paper.*

B.Y.O.(B.) *mod.* "bring your own (booze or bottle)."(Initialism.) □ *A note on the invitation says that the party is B.Y.O.B.* □ *I hate B.Y.O.B. parties. There's never enough to drink.*

C

C. *n.* the sum of one-hundred dollars, as in *C-note.* (Underworld. The "C" is the Roman numeral 100.) ☐ *Four C.s for an old junker like that? You're crazy!* ☐ *This suit cost me two C.s.*

C-head **1.** *n.* a cocaine user. (Drugs.) ☐ *I don't want any C-head operating on me!* ☐ *How much money does a C-head need to get through the day?* **2.** *n.* an *L.S.D.* user who takes *L.S.D.* on sugar cubes. (Drugs.) ☐ *Frank was a C-head in the sixties.* ☐ *Why don't you C-heads grow up?*

C-note AND **C-spot** *n.* a one-hundred-dollar bill. (The "C" is the Roman numeral for "100." See also *century note.*) ☐ *How much ammo will a C-note buy these days?* ☐ *That guy wanted a C-spot to fix my muffler.*

C-spot See the previous entry.

cabbage *n.* money. (Originally underworld. See also *green, spinach.*) ☐ *How much cabbage you want for this heater?* ☐ *I don't make enough cabbage to go on a trip like that!*

cabbagehead *n.* a fool; a stupid person. ☐ *What cabbagehead put this thing on upside down?* ☐ *I'm such a cabbagehead. I mailed my paycheck back to the office by mistake.*

cabbie AND **cabby** *n.* a taxi driver. (Also a term of address.) ☐ *Ask the cabbie if he can change a twenty.* ☐ *Say, cabby, do you know the way to St. Joseph's Hospital?*

cabby See the previous entry.

caboose [kə'bus] *n.* the buttocks. (From the name of the car at the end of a railroad train.) ☐ *You just plunk your caboose over there on the settee and listen up to what I have to tell you.* ☐ *My caboose is bigger than I want it, but life is too short to fret about stuff like that.*

caca AND **kaka** ['kɑkɑ] **1.** *n.* dung; feces. (Juvenile. From Spanish. Use caution with the topic.) ☐ *There's fresh caca in the front yard.* ☐ *Don't worry. It's dog kaka.* **2.** *in.* to defecate. (Juvenile. Use caution with the topic.) ☐ *Jimmy kakad in his diaper!* ☐ *It's time you learned to caca in the potty.*

cack [kæk] **1.** *n.* dung; feces. (Use caution with the topic. See also *caca.*) ☐ *Wipe that cack off your shoes before you come in here!* ☐ *The sidewalks are just covered with cack!* **2.** *in.* to defecate. (Use caution with the topic.) ☐ *The dog cacked right there on Fifth Avenue.* ☐ *"Dogs can't cack here," hollered the police officer.* **3.** AND **kack; kak** *in.* to empty one's stomach; to vomit. ☐ *I cacked all night with the flu.* ☐ *I've never heard anybody cack so loud in my life!* **4.** AND **kack; kak** *tr.* to kill someone. ☐ *Max threatened to cack Veronica if she didn't straighten up.* ☐ *The witness got kacked before she could testify.*

cactus (buttons) *n.* peyote cactus containing mescaline. (Drugs.) ☐ *Gert came back from vacation with a bag of cactus buttons.* ☐ *"Who ate all my cactus?" screamed Gert.*

cactus juice *n.* tequila. (A Mexican liquor.) ☐ *Ernie brought back a big jug of cactus juice from Mexico.* ☐ *This cactus juice will make your hair stand on end.*

caddy ['kædi] *n.* a Cadillac automobile. ☐ *What I really want is a caddy. Keep* *your yuppie beemer.* □ *Who's the chick in the caddy?*

Cadillac ['kædlæk] **1.** *n.* the name of something powerful or superior. (From the name of the automobile.) □ *This product is the Cadillac of plastic kitchenware.* □ *Acme is the Cadillac of monochrome closed-circuit retail surveillance equipment.* **2.** *n.* a powerful drug, especially cocaine. (Drugs.) □ *Just a pinch of Cadillac in my junk seems to keep me a little more lively.* □ *Nothing but Cadillac for Max!*

cagey ['kedʒi] *mod.* sneaky; shrewd. □ *Bruno is pretty cagey. You have to keep an eye on him.* □ *He's too cagey for me. I don't trust him at all.*

cake *n.* money. (From *bread, dough.*) □ *I can't scrape together enough cake to do the job.* □ *I don't have cake in my pocket, in the bank, or under my mattress. What am I going to do?*

cakewalk *n.* something very easy. (Compare to *sleepwalk.*) □ *Nothing to it. It's a cakewalk.* □ *The game was a cakewalk from beginning to end.*

calaboose ['kæləbus] *n.* jail. (From a Spanish word.) □ *One night in the calaboose is enough.* □ *Are we going to tell what happened, or are we going to spend the night in the calaboose?*

calendar *n.* a month. □ *Okay, man. I'll see you in one calendar.* □ *One more calendar, then you get your jack.*

call 1. *n.* a decision; a prediction. □ *That was a good call, Mike.* □ *The market behaved just as you said it would. Good call.* **2.** *tr.* to challenge someone. □ *I called him, but he ignored me.* □ *Are you the guy who called me? Who do you think you are?* **3.** *n.* the early effects of a drug; the beginning of a *rush;* a *rush.* (Drugs.) □ *You may not get the call on this stuff for twenty minutes or more.* □ *A guy like this is only happy when he senses the call.*

call (all) the shots *tr.* to decide on the course of action; to be in charge. □ *Why do you have to call all the shots?* □ *Do what you're told. I'll call the shots.*

call earl See *call hughie.*

call girl *n.* a prostitute; a prostitute who is always on call. □ *The snatcher hauled her in because she looked like a call girl.* □ *Most of the really sharp call girls look like M.B.A.s and drive beemers.*

call house *n.* a brothel. □ *The cops busted a call house on Fourth Street last week.* □ *The madame of the call house certainly looked like a lady to me.*

call hughie AND **call earl** [...'hyui AND ...'ɚl] *tr.* to vomit. (Onomatopoetic from the sound of wretching.) □ *Fred spent an hour in the john calling hughie.* □ *Yuck! I have to go call earl.*

Call my service. *sent.* "Please call me through my answering service." (Not a friendly or encouraging invitation.) □ *Good to talk to ya, babe. Call my service. Love ya!* □ *I can't talk now. Call my service.*

call of nature See *nature's call.*

call ralph See *cry ruth.*

call ruth See *cry ruth.*

call someone out *tr.* to challenge someone to a fight. □ *Max wanted to call him out, but thought better of it.* □ *Did you call me out? What are you going to do about it?*

cam (red) See the following entry.

Cambodian red AND **cam (red)** *n.* a reddish brown marijuana grown in Cambodia. (Drugs.) □ *Where did you get cam red?* □ *Cam is hard to find in the last few years.*

camp 1. *n.* something cute and out-of-fashion; something of such an anachronistic style as to be intriguing. □ *Camp is dull and was never interesting.* □ *My brother thinks camp is just a joke.* □ *Nobody really knows what style camp really is, and very few even care.* **2.** AND **campy** *mod.* overdone; out-of-fashion and intriguing. □ *Most camp entertainment is pretentious and overdrawn.* □ *Who needs camp movies?* **3.** *mod.* having to do with homosexual persons and matters. □ *What a camp way of* *walking!* ☐ *She is so camp, I could scream!*

camp it up 1. *tr.* to overact. ☐ *Can you make it a little more lively without camping it up?* ☐ *She's so dull that she could camp it up and still look half asleep.* **2.** *tr.* to overdo effeminacy; [for a homosexual male] to act too effeminate in public. ☐ *Can't you even walk across the room without camping it up?* ☐ *John just loves to burst into the most sedate hotel in town and camp it up in the lobby.*

campi ['kæmpaɪ] *n.* campuses. (The Latin plural of *campus* = field.) ☐ *I'll see you about the campi. Ciao!* ☐ *When will you return to the campi after vacation?*

campus ['kæmpəs] *tr.* to restrict someone to the grounds of a college campus. (Collegiate.) ☐ *The dean threatened to campus the entire fraternity for a month.* ☐ *"We will campus you for a year, if necessary," shouted the dean, who really didn't understand young people.* (More at *campused.*)

campus queen *n.* a good-looking and popular female college student. ☐ *I always thought I wanted to be a campus queen, but all that has changed.* ☐ *I wonder what some of those campus queens look like when they get up in the morning.*

campused ['kæmpəst] *mod.* restricted to the campus. (Collegiate.) ☐ *I can't go to town. I'm campused.* ☐ *She's campused and can only go to the library.*

campy See *camp.*

can 1. *n.* the head. ☐ *What do you have in your can, anyway? Lard?* ☐ *Jerry landed one on Frank's can. Frank crumpled.* **2.** *n.* toilet. ☐ *Hell, I ain't tired! Where's the can?* ☐ *I gotta use the can before we leave.* **3.** *n.* the buttocks. (Use caution with the topic. See also *bucket.*) ☐ *The guy slipped on the ice and fell on his can.* ☐ *Look at the can on that guy!* **4.** *n.* jail. (Usually with *the.*) ☐ *I had to spend the night in the can, but it wasn't too bad.* ☐ *You've seen one can, you've seen 'em all.* **5.** *tr.* to dismiss someone from employment. ☐ *The jerk canned everybody who played a part in the gag.* ☐ *I'll can anybody who tries a stunt like that again.* **6.** *n.* a car. ☐ *That's a good-looking can he's driving.* ☐ *Please don't park your old can in front of my house.* **7.** See *cans.* **8.** *n.* a breast. (Use caution with the topic. Usually plural.) ☐ *Man, look at the cans on that dame!* ☐ *Those cans can't be real!* **9.** *n.* a measurement of marijuana. (Drugs.) ☐ *How much do you want for a can?* ☐ *A can is too much except for a party.*

Can it! *exclam.* "Shut up!" ☐ *I've heard enough. Can it!* ☐ *That's enough out of you! Can it!*

can of worms *n.* an intertwined set of problems; an array of difficulties. (Often with *open.*) ☐ *This whole business is a real can of worms.* ☐ *When you brought that up, you opened a whole new can of worms.*

can-shaker *n.* a fund-raiser. (As if a person were holding a can for the solicitation of coins from passersby.) ☐ *John was the mayor's can-shaker in the last election.* ☐ *Fred was a professional can-shaker for a museum. Maybe he has some ideas as to how we can raise some money.*

canary [kə'nɛri] **1.** *n.* a female singer. ☐ *The band had a cute canary who could really sing.* ☐ *The drummer and the canary just don't seem to be able to get along.* **2.** *n.* a capsule of Nembutal™, a barbiturate. (Drugs. The capsule is yellow.) ☐ *You got any canaries? I need a downer.* ☐ *There are a couple of blues, which ought to do the same as canaries.*

cancel someone's Christmas *tr.* to kill someone; to destroy someone. (Underworld. The dead person will miss Christmas.) ☐ *If he keeps bugging me, I'm gonna cancel his Christmas.* ☐ *Bruno threatened to cancel Max's Christmas if Max didn't pay up.*

cancer stick *n.* a tobacco cigarette. (From the notion that cigarette smoking is a major cause of lung cancer. Old but recurrent.) ☐ *Kelly pulled out his ninth cancer stick and lit it up.* ☐ *A lot of people are addicted to cancer sticks.*

candied ['kændid] *mod.* addicted to cocaine. (Drugs. See also *nose (candy)*.) ☐ *Unfortunately, Paul is candied, and he lost his job so he can't buy toot.* ☐ *He is one of those people who gets candied at first snort.*

candy *n.* drugs in general. (Drugs. See also *nose (candy)*.) ☐ *I gotta go get some candy from the candy man.* ☐ *This candy is powerful stuff.*

candy-ass (Potentially offensive. Use only with discretion.) **1.** *n.* a coward. ☐ *You are such a candy-ass! Stand up for your rights.* ☐ *Ralph seems tough, but he's just a candy-ass.* **2.** *mod.* cowardly. ☐ *The candy-ass approach just isn't going to work.* ☐ *Stop the candy-ass stuff. Handle this issue directly.*

candy man *n.* a drug dealer. (Drugs.) ☐ *Lefty said he had to go meet with the candy man.* ☐ *Max is sort of a candy man.*

candy store *n.* a liquor store. ☐ *Let's stop at this candy store and get some bubbles.* ☐ *Somebody robbed the candy store on the corner.*

cane *n.* cocaine. (Drugs.) ☐ *What the hell did you pay for this cane?* ☐ *Even the kids can afford to buy cane now. The social problems of the twenty-first century are starting right here.*

canned 1. *mod.* alcohol intoxicated. ☐ *I'll drive. I'm too canned to walk.* ☐ *Man, am I canned!* **2.** *mod.* having to do with prerecorded laughter or applause that is added to the sound track of a television program. ☐ *Canned laughter really sounds phony.* ☐ *The dialogue was funny enough that they didn't need to have the laughter canned.*

cannon *n.* a gun; a revolver. (Underworld.) ☐ *Rocko pulled out his cannon and aimed it at Barlowe's throat.* ☐ *The cops found Rocko's cannon where Barlowe had kicked it during the struggle.*

cannot see (any) further than the end of one's nose See *see no further than the end of one's nose.*

cans *n.* earphones. ☐ *The guy with the cans on his head is the radio operator.* ☐ *I bought a new set of cans for my stereo.*

can't hit the (broad) side of a barn *phr.* "cannot aim something accurately." ☐ *You're way off. You couldn't hit the broad side of a barn.* ☐ *Carry the paper to the wastebasket. You can't hit the side of a barn.*

can't win (th)em all *phr.* (one should) expect to lose every now and then. ☐ *It doesn't really matter. You can't win them all.* ☐ *Well, I can't win 'em all.*

cap 1. *tr.* to exceed something; to surpass something. ☐ *I know I can't cap that. That's just super!* ☐ *Who could ever cap a joke like that?* **2.** *n.* a capsule of a drug. ☐ *Do you want it in caps or elixir?* ☐ *She spilled the caps on the floor and had to find every single one of them.* **3.** *tr.* to make a capsule. ☐ *I must have capped 300 placebos today.* ☐ *Max capped some H. for a pal.*

caper ['kepɚ] **1.** *n.* any stunt or event; a trick or a *scam*. ☐ *That little caper the kids did with the statue from the town square was a dandy.* ☐ *Another caper like that and I call your parents.* **2.** *n.* a criminal job: theft, kidnapping, blackmail, etc. (Underworld.) ☐ *Who did you work with on that bank caper?* ☐ *The black and whites pulled up right in the middle of the caper.*

capish [kə'piʃ] *in.* to understand. (Usually as a question. From an Italian dialect.) ☐ *The matter is settled. No more talk. Capish?* ☐ *Now, if you don't capish, let's get it clear right now.*

capital *n.* cash; money. ☐ *I'm a little short of capital right now.* ☐ *Do you think I could borrow a little capital until payday?*

capper ['kæpɚ] *n.* the climax or *clincher* of something. ☐ *The capper of the evening was when the hostess got lathered before midnight and couldn't celebrate the New Year.* ☐ *When the butler tripped and served Mr. Wilson the entire dessert, in his lap, that was the capper to an exciting evening.*

captain of industry *n.* a corporation officer; a capitalist. ☐ *The captains of industry manage to hang on to their money no matter what.* ☐ *It's fun to see* *those captains of industry drive up in their benzes.*

carb [karb] *n.* an engine carburetor. □ *This can needs a new carb.* □ *I learned how to clean and adjust a carb by the time I was in high school.*

carbos ['karboz] *n.* carbohydrates. (Bodybuilding.) □ *You need more protein and less carbos.* □ *Too many carbos will make you fat.*

carburetor *n.* a device for smoking cannabis that mixes the smoke with air. (Drugs.) □ *I have a carburetor with the rest of my stash.* □ *Max showed Walter how to use a carburetor.*

carcass ['karkəs] *n.* one's body; a large or heavy body. □ *He hauled his carcass out of the car and lumbered into the bank.* □ *Put your carcass on a chair, and let's chew the fat.*

card 1. *n.* a funny person. □ *Tracy is such a card. She cracks me up.* □ *Gee, Fred. You're a card. Somebody's gonna have to deal with you.* **2.** *tr.* to check people's ID cards for age or other eligibility. □ *They card everybody at the football games, even the parents.* □ *The bartender was carding people so we left quietly.* (More at *carded.*)

carded AND **proofed** *mod.* [for an ID card to be] examined to determine whether one has reached the legal drinking age. □ *Dave got carded at the party even though he is thirty and looks it.* □ *All the students were proofed at the door.*

carrier *n.* a narcotics seller or transporter. (Drugs. See also *courier.*) □ *The carrier has the most dangerous job of all.* □ *You'll never see an old carrier.*

carrot top *n.* a person with red hair. (Also a term of address.) □ *Sam is a carrot top with the most beautiful hair I've ever seen.* □ *Hey, carrot top, where are you going?*

carry 1. *in.* to carry drugs on one's person. (Drugs.) □ *If you get busted while you're carrying, you are in big trouble with the man.* □ *You gotta learn when you can carry and when you can't.* **2.** *n.* drugs carried on the person as an emergency supply in case of arrest. (Underworld.) □ *I lost my carry somewhere.* □ *The cops found my carry, and I spent three days in the clink climbing the walls.*

carry the stick *tr.* to live as a hobo, on the streets. (Streets. From the stick that supports the hobo's bundle.) □ *I even carried the stick for a while in the sixties.* □ *I was afraid I'd be carrying the stick if I got laid off.*

carry weight *tr.* to have influence. □ *I don't carry much weight around here, but Walter does.* □ *Tom carries weight with the mayor. Ask him.*

carrying a (heavy) load *mod.* alcohol intoxicated. □ *Marty is carrying a heavy load.* □ *Your father's carrying a load again. What are we going to do?*

cartwheel *n.* a round, white cross-scored amphetamine tablet. (Drugs.) □ *He took cartwheels in the morning and fender-benders at night.* □ *Cartwheels were the favorite diet pill of the 1960's.*

carved in stone *mod.* permanent or not subject to change. (Often in the negative.) □ *Now, this isn't carved in stone yet, but this looks like the way it's going to be.* □ *Is this policy carved in stone?*

cas [kæz] *mod.* okay; fine. (From *casual.* See also *cazh.*) □ *That's cas, man. Good to hear it.* □ *I agree. Cas. Totally cool.*

case of the shorts See *shorts.*

case the joint 1. *tr.* to look over someplace to figure out how to break in, what to steal, etc. (Underworld. See also *joint.*) □ *First of all you gotta case the joint to see where things are.* □ *You could see he was casing the joint the way he looked around.* **2.** *tr.* to look a place over. □ *The dog came in and cased the joint, sniffing out friends and foes.* □ *The old lady entered slowly, casing the joint for the face of someone of her era, and finally took a seat.*

cash cow *n.* a dependable source of money; a good investment. □ *I put most of my money in a dependable cash cow that pays off once a month.* □ *Mr.*

Wilson turned out to be the cash cow we needed to start our repertoire company.

cash flow *n.* cash; ready money. ☐ *When I get a little cash flow at the end of the week, I'll treat you to a hamburger.* ☐ *There wasn't enough cash flow to pay the rent.*

cash in one's checks See the following entry.

cash in one's chips AND **cash in one's checks** *tr.* to die; to finish the game (of life). ☐ *He opened his eyes, said goodbye, and cashed in his chips.* ☐ *I'm too young to cash in my checks.*

Cash is king. *sent.* "It is best to keep one's investment money in cash." (Said when the prices in the securities market are too high. It is better to build up cash and wait for a break in the market.) ☐ *Things look a little pricy now. I'd say that cash is king for the moment.* ☐ *I'm holding a little cash for a little bottom fishing, but I wouldn't say that cash is king.*

Cash is trash. *sent.* "It is unwise to keep one's investment money in cash." (Said when there are good opportunities in securities and it is foolish to stay on the sidelines in cash.) ☐ *If you've got money sitting around in a money market fund while the market is steaming ahead, you are losing dollars. Right now cash is trash.* ☐ *Cash is trash. Get into the market or you stand to lose a bundle.*

cashed 1. *mod.* having to do with marijuana whose active ingredients have been exhausted. (Drugs.) ☐ *This stuff is cashed. Trash it.* ☐ *Max sold the wrong guy some cashed grass.* **2.** *mod.* exhausted. ☐ *I'm just cashed—really pooped.* ☐ *After the game, the team was cashed and couldn't even celebrate.*

Casper Milquetoast ['kæspɚ 'mɪlktost] *n.* a very timid man. (From the name of a character in a cartoon.) ☐ *I'm a little sensitive—not a Casper Milquetoast, but I have feelings.* ☐ *He's no Casper Milquetoast. He's quite a tennis player in fact.*

cast-iron stomach *n.* a very strong stomach that can withstand bad food or anything nauseating. ☐ *If I didn't have a cast-iron stomach, I couldn't eat this stuff.* ☐ *Fred—known for his cast-iron stomach—ate all of his pepper soup.*

casting-couch *n.* a legendary couch found in the offices of casting directors for use in seducing young people by offering them roles. ☐ *They say she got the job on the casting-couch.* ☐ *They say the director got his job on the casting-couch, too.*

castor oil artist *n.* a medical doctor. ☐ *This two-bit castor oil artist tried to get me to lose weight.* ☐ *Check with your personal castor oil artist to see if you should be taking this medication.*

cat 1. *n.* a fellow; a *guy;* a *dude.* ☐ *Now, this cat wants to borrow some money from me. What should I do?* ☐ *Ask the cat what he's got for security.* **2.** *in.* to empty one's stomach; to vomit. ☐ *I think I'm gonna cat.* ☐ *Looks like somebody catted in the bushes.* **3.** *n.* a gossipy woman. (See also *catty.*) ☐ *She is such a cat!* ☐ *Mary can be such a cat, you know.*

cat-soup ['kætsup] *n.* catsup; ketchup. ☐ *Do you want some cat-soup on your burger?* ☐ *No, I never use cat-soup.*

catch 1. *n.* a drawback. ☐ *Okay, that sounds good, but what's the catch?* ☐ *There's no catch. It's all on the up and up.* **2.** *tr.* to view something; to attend something. ☐ *We'll take the chicks to catch a film after we eat.* ☐ *Did you catch "Gone with the Wind" on T.V.?*

catch-22 *n.* a directive that is impossible to obey without violating some other, equally important, directive. ☐ *There was nothing I could do. It was a classic catch-22.* ☐ *I had my choice between catch-22s. What do you call that kind of a dilemma?*

catch hell (for something) *tr.* to get severely reprimanded for (doing) something. ☐ *I knew I'd catch hell for it.* ☐ *Somebody is going to catch hell for this!*

catch some rays AND **bag some rays** *tr.* to get some sunshine; to tan in the sun. ☐ *We wanted to catch some rays, but* *the sun never came out the whole time we were there.* ☐ *I went to Hawaii to bag some rays.*

catch some Z's AND **cop some Z's; cut some Z's** *tr.* to get some sleep. ☐ *I gotta catch some Z's before I drop.* ☐ *Why don't you stop a little bit and try to cop some Z's?*

catch something *tr.* to see or listen to something. (More specific than the colloquial sense, to *manage to hear something.*) ☐ *I will try to catch that new movie this weekend.* ☐ *Did you catch that radio program about cancer last night?*

catch up *in.* to break the drug habit; to withdraw from drugs. (Drugs.) ☐ *Bruno never tried to catch up. He's just too far gone.* ☐ *I just know I can catch up, if I can just get through the first week.*

Catch you later. *sent.* "I will talk to you again when I next see you." ☐ *Can't talk now. Catch you later.* ☐ *Sorry, gotta rush. Catch you later.*

cats and dogs *n.* slow selling or undesirable merchandise. ☐ *During the Christmas season, the merchants try to get rid of all their cats and dogs.* ☐ *When people are buying up even the cats and dogs, you know business is good.*

cat's meow [...mi'ɑʊ] *n.* something really fine. ☐ *This stuff is really the cat's meow.* ☐ *Hearing all the old big band music again is the cat's meow.*

cattle-rustler *n.* a thief who steals meat from supermarkets for resale. (Underworld.) ☐ *Marty is a cattle-rustler, and she's got some stuff for sale.* ☐ *She's a cattle-rustler to support her habit.*

catty *mod.* spiteful; snotty. ☐ *You know how catty Mary is—almost as catty as Gloria—well, she told me something about you that really shocked me.* ☐ *How can anybody be so catty?*

cave man *n.* a strong, virile man. ☐ *He's sort of a cave man, big and hairy.* ☐ *I don't care for cave men.*

cazh [kæʒ] *mod.* casual. (From *casual.* See also **cas.**) ☐ *I tend to dress cazh in warm weather no matter what the occasion.* ☐ *Tom showed up dressed cazh and all the other guys were in tuxes.*

cee [si] *n.* cocaine. (Drugs. See also *C.*) ☐ *Where can I get a little bit of cee?* ☐ *Ask Max for some cee, but ask him nice.*

celeb [sə'lɛb] *n.* a celebrity. ☐ *They hired a few celebs to shill for their new computer.* ☐ *There were celebs all over the place, but nobody I recognized.*

cement city *n.* a cemetery. ☐ *I'm too young to end up in cement city.* ☐ *There's a cement city outside town, and our house is just a half mile east of it.*

cent *n.* one dollar. (Underworld.) ☐ *One cent for one joint? Not bad.* ☐ *A cent for this thing?*

century note *n.* a one-hundred-dollar bill. (Underworld. The "C" is the Roman numeral for "100." See also *C-note.*) ☐ *I got a couple of century notes for driving these guys home from the bank.* ☐ *Here's a century note for your trouble, young man.*

certain party *n.* "someone whom I do not wish to name; you can guess whom." (Always with *a.*) ☐ *I spoke to a certain party about the matter you mentioned.* ☐ *If a certain party finds out about you-know-what, what on earth will you do?*

cets AND **sets** [sɛts] *n.* tablets of Darvocet™, a painkiller. (Drugs.) ☐ *You got any cets I can bum off you?* ☐ *I don't know anything about sets or any of that stuff.*

chain(-smoke) *in.* to smoke cigarette after cigarette. ☐ *I never wanted to chain-smoke, but I got addicted.* ☐ *I used to chain, and my husband threatened to leave me if I didn't give it up. I quit when he left.*

chain-smoker *n.* someone who smokes cigarette after cigarette. ☐ *She was a chain-smoker for thirty years, and then suddenly, boom. She's gone.* ☐ *There are fewer chain-smokers now than there were just a few years ago.*

chain(saw) *tr.* to destroy something; to cut something up severely. ☐ *The senatorial committee tried to chainsaw the* *nominee, but the full senate voted for confirmation.* ☐ *We didn't think they'd come in and chain all our plans.*

chair *n.* the electric chair, as used in the execution of the death penalty. (Underworld. Always with *the*.) ☐ *You'll fry in the chair for this, Lefty!* ☐ *I don't wanna go to the chair!*

cham AND **chammy; sham; shammy** [ʃæm AND 'ʃæmi] *n.* champagne. ☐ *Would you like a little more shammy?* ☐ *This is a stunning cham you picked for us, Tiffany. Is it famous?*

chammy See the previous entry.

champ [tʃæmp] **1.** *n.* a champion. (Also a term of address.) ☐ *Mark is a real champ—always there to help.* ☐ *Hey, champ, welcome home!* **2.** *n.* a dependable member of the underworld. (Underworld. See also *thoroughbred*.) ☐ *Bruno would never sing. He's a champ.* ☐ *Lefty is a champ. He stood by me the whole time.*

champers AND **shampers** ['ʃampə·z] *n.* champagne. ☐ *I could live on shampers.* ☐ *My dad sent us a bottle of French champers.*

change *n.* money. (See also *and change*.) ☐ *It takes a lot of change to buy a car like that.* ☐ *I don't have the change to get one of those videotape machines.*

change the channel *tr.* to switch to some other topic of conversation. ☐ *Just a minute. I think you changed the channel. Let's go back to the part about you owing me money.* ☐ *Let's change the channel here before there is a fight.*

changes *n.* an alteration in one's mental state. (See also *go through the changes*.) ☐ *The changes have sort of got me down.* ☐ *I'm forty and I'm finished with the changes, and if there's anything I don't want it's to be young again.*

channel hopping AND **channel surfing; channel zapping** *n.* to use a remote control to move quickly from one television channel to another, pausing only a short time on each channel. ☐ *I wish you would stop channel hopping!* ☐ *Channel zapping is a way to keep up with a number of television shows at the same time.*

channel surfer *n.* a person who practices *channel hopping*. ☐ *My husband is a confirmed channel surfer. I can't understand why he does it.* ☐ *Channel surfers try to keep up with many programs at one time.*

channel surfing See *channel hopping*.

channel zapping See *channel hopping*.

chap *tr.* to anger or annoy someone. ☐ *That whole business really chapped me.* ☐ *I didn't mean to chap you.* (More at *chapped*.)

chapped *mod.* angry; annoyed. ☐ *I was chapped. There was no way to get around it.* ☐ *Don't get so chapped. Nothing can be done now.*

chapter and verse *mod.* in the finest detail. (From the "chapter and verse" organization of the Bible.) ☐ *He could recite the law concerning state-funded libraries, chapter and verse.* ☐ *She knew her rights, chapter and verse.*

charge **1.** *n.* a dose or portion of a drug. (Drugs.) ☐ *I need a charge to tide me over.* ☐ *Just a little charge till I can get to my candy man.* **2.** *n.* a drug's *rush*. (Drugs.) ☐ *This stuff has no charge at all.* ☐ *What kind of charge do you expect out of half-cashed weed?* **3.** *n.* a thrill. ☐ *Seeing my kid up there on that stage was a real charge.* ☐ *I got a tremendous charge out of your last letter.*

charged (up) **1.** *mod.* slightly overdosed with drugs. (Drugs.) ☐ *He was talking fast and nodding his head back and forth. I think he was charged.* ☐ *The kid is usually charged up by class time.* **2.** *mod.* drug intoxicated. (Drugs.) ☐ *The way she sat there nodding, you knew she was completely charged up.* ☐ *Paul was one charged up guy after the session.* **3.** *mod.* excited. ☐ *The audience was charged up and ready for the star to come out.* ☐ *The charged up quarterback made some wonderful plays.*

Charles **1.** *n.* cocaine. (Drugs.) ☐ *I want to meet Charles somewhere.* ☐ *Is there* *a house where I can buy some Charles somewhere close?* **2.** *n.* a Caucasian. (Black. Not necessarily derogatory.) □ *And what is Charles gonna say about what you did to his car?* □ *That brother's so backward, he's still afraid to go to Charles' front door.*

Charley *n.* the Viet Cong in Vietnam. (Military. From "Victor Charley," which is from "V.C.") □ *How come Charley never gets bit to death by those snakes?* □ *What if we meet up with Charley down there?*

Charlie Irvine *n.* a police officer. (Black. See also *Irv.*) □ *Charlie Irvine was around asking after you.* □ *Look smart, dude, here comes Charlie Irvine.*

charmer *n.* a seducer; a *make-out artist.* □ *You always have to act like some half-ass charmer scamming like it really mattered! Grow up!* □ *Willard is such a charmer! Too bad he's married.*

chart *n.* a musical score. (Musicians. See also *map.*) □ *Come on, man! Look at the chart! You're making clinkers like hot cakes.* □ *Lemme borrow your chart for a while, okay?*

charts *n.* the trade magazine rankings of current pop music. □ *The big one is back on the charts this week. Give it a listen.* □ *Number five on the charts again this week—it's "My Blue Heaven" with the Andrews Sisters.*

chas AND **chez** [tʃæz AND tʃɛz] *n.* matches. (Collegiate. A clipping of "matches.") □ *Where are my chas?* □ *You got a couple of chez?*

chase the dragon *tr.* to inhale opium fumes through a straw. (Drugs.) □ *Harry thinks that chasing the dragon sounds like real fun.* □ *Chasing the dragon may sound good, but it smells awful.*

chaser **1.** *n.* an alcoholic drink taken after a nonalcoholic one; beer, water, or some similar liquid drunk after a *shot* of hard liquor. (See also *wash.*) □ *I could use a little chaser with this soda.* □ *I'd like a double scotch and a beer chaser.* **2.** See *ambulance chaser.*

cheap shot *n.* a remark that takes advantage of someone else's vulnerability. □ *It's easy to get a laugh with a cheap shot at cats.* □ *People who wouldn't dare utter anything negative about blacks, Poles, or women just love to take a cheap shot at yuppies.*

cheapie *n.* a cheaply made article. (See also *el cheapo.*) □ *I don't want a cheapie. I can afford better.* □ *It broke. I guess it was a cheapie.*

cheapskate ['tʃipsket] *n.* a miserly person; a very cheap person. (Compare to *piker.*) □ *A 5 percent tip! What a cheapskate!* □ *I don't think of myself as a cheapskate, but I do try to watch my cash flow.*

cheaters *n.* sunglasses. (Formerly all spectacles. See also *shades, sunshades.*) □ *Get your cheaters on. The sun's really bright.* □ *Somebody sat on my cheaters!*

check **1.** *n.* a dose of a drug in a capsule or folded in a paper. (Drugs.) □ *Max handed me a check, and I slipped him some long green.* □ *How much you want for a check?* **2.** *interj.* okay; yes; "yes, it is on the list." □ BILL: *Four quarts of oil.* TOM: *Check.* □ FRED: *Are you ready?* PAUL: *Check.*

check out the plumbing AND **visit the plumbing** *tr.* to go to the bathroom. □ *I think I'd better check out the plumbing before we go.* □ *I want you kids to visit the plumbing as soon as we get there.*

check something out *tr.* to examine something; to think about something. □ *It's something we all have to be concerned with. Check it out.* Ⓣ *Check out this Billy Biggles album.*

check that *tr.* cancel that; ignore that (last remark). □ *Check that. I was wrong.* □ *At four, no, check that, at three o'clock this afternoon, a bomb exploded at the riverside.*

cheese **1.** *n.* vomit. □ *There's cheese on the sidewalk. Look out!* □ *In there, there's cheese on the bathroom floor. So gross!* **2.** *in.* to empty one's stomach; to vomit. □ *Somebody cheesed on the* *sidewalk.* □ *She popped into the bushes and cheesed soundlessly.*

cheese-eater *n.* an informer; a *rat fink.* (Rats eat cheese.) □ *Some cheese-eater called the clerk and warned her we were coming.* □ *Tracy, the cheese-eater, called the police.*

Cheese it (the cops)! *exclam.* "Run away, the cops are coming!" □ *Look out! Cheese it, the cops!* □ *If you see the fuzz coming, you're supposed to yell, "Cheese it, the cops!" But I don't know why. Then they know we're doing something wrong.*

cheesecake **1.** *n.* a display of the female form, probably wearing little clothing, often in photographs. (Compare to *beefcake.*) □ *Women don't like to see all that cheesecake on the walls when they bring their cars in here to be fixed.* □ *Now they're even putting the magazines with cheesecake under the counter.* **2.** *n.* a good-looking woman; good-looking women. □ *Who's the cheesecake in that low-cut job?* □ *Bring on the cheesecake!*

cheesed off *mod.* angry; disgusted. □ *Clare was really cheesed off at the butler.* □ *The butler was cheesed off at the cook.*

cheesehead *n.* a stupid-acting person. □ *Is this cheesehead bothering you?* □ *Why do all the cheeseheads in town ride in my cab in the same day?*

cheesy *mod.* cheap; *tacky.* □ *I wouldn't live in a cheesy place like this if I could afford better.* □ *That was a cheesy trick to pull on somebody.*

cherry *n.* an inexperienced person; a novice. □ *He's just a cherry. He don't know from nothing.* □ *She's a cherry when it comes to computers.*

chew *in.* to eat. □ *She's in the kitchen, chewing.* □ *Man, I'm hungry. It's time to chew!*

chew face *tr.* to kiss. (More jocular than crude.) □ *A couple of kids were in a doorway chewin' face.* □ *Hey Tracy! Wanna go chew face?*

chew someone out *tr.* to scold someone. □ *I knew my dad was going to chew me out.* 🅃 *The dean chewed out the whole fraternity.*

chew something over **1.** *tr.* to talk something over. □ *Why don't we do lunch sometime and chew this over?* □ *We can chew it over at lunch.* **2.** *tr.* to think something over. □ *I'll have to chew it over for a while. I'm not sure now.* □ *Don't chew it over too long. The offer is only good till Friday.*

chew the cheese *tr.* to vomit. □ *Fred's out in the bushes, chewing the cheese.* □ *The cat's chewing the cheese on the living room carpet again.*

chew the fat AND **chew the rag** *tr.* to chat or gossip. □ *Put your carcass over on the chair, and let's chew the fat for a while.* □ *We were just chewing the rag. Nothing important.*

chew the rag See the previous entry.

chewed *mod.* abused. □ *After that argument at the office yesterday, I really felt chewed.* □ *After an interview like that, I am too chewed to even cry.*

chez See *chas.*

chi-chi [ˈʃiʃi] *mod.* elegant. □ *Oh, you look so chi-chi in that lace blouse.* □ *Her living room is so chi-chi that you are afraid to go in.*

chick *n.* a *girl* or woman. □ *Who's the chick driving the ragtop?* □ *We're gonna take some chicks to dinner and then catch a flick.*

chicken *n.* a coward. □ *Come on, let's go. Don't be a chicken.* □ *He's no fun. He's a chicken.*

chicken feed *n.* a small amount of money. (See also *peanuts.*) □ *Sure I can afford it. It's just chicken feed.* □ *It may be chicken feed to you, but that's a month's rent to me.*

chicken-hearted *mod.* cowardly. □ *Yes, I'm a chicken-hearted softie. I hope you don't want to make something of it.* □ *He's chicken-hearted, but I still love him.*

chicken out (of something) *in.* to manage to get out of something, usually because of fear or cowardice. □ *Come on! Don't chicken out now!* □ *Freddy chickened out of the plan at the last minute.*

chicken powder *n.* powdered amphetamine. (Drugs.) □ *Those kids seem to be satisfied with chicken powder.* □ *Nobody is satisfied with chicken powder for very long.*

chief [tʃif] *n.* the person in charge. (Also a term of address.) □ *Okay, chief, where to?* □ *You got a couple of clams to pay the toll with, chief?*

chief cook and bottle washer See *head cook and bottle washer.*

chill 1. AND **chilly** *n.* a cold can of beer. □ *Hey, toss me a chill, would ya, buddy?* □ *You ready for another chill?* **2.** *tr.* to kill someone. (Underworld.) □ *Rocko had orders to chill Barlowe or not to show his face again.* □ *I'll chill you with one blast from my cannon, you creep.* **3.** *tr.* to frighten someone. (Standard English.) □ *The specter chilled everyone who saw it.* □ *The prospect of having to go in there alone chilled Wally, but good.* **4.** *tr.* to reject someone. □ *The whole gang chilled him, and this really made him come home.* □ *She chilled me once too often. I won't take that from a dame.* **5.** See *chill (out).* **6.** *tr. & in.* to relax; to cause someone to relax. (See also *chill (out).*) □ *Go out there and chill those people. They are getting wild!* □ *They are chilling now. For a while they were real rowdy.*

chill (out) *in.* to calm down; to be *cool;* to get *cool;* to relax. □ *All right now, people, chill . . . chill.* □ *Before we can debate this matter, you're all gonna have to chill out.*

chill someone's action *tr.* to squelch someone; to prevent someone from accomplishing something. □ *Freddie is trying to chill my action, and I'm a little steamed about that.* □ *Just wait! I'll chill his action—just you wait.*

chillin' *mod.* great; excellent. □ *I had one chillin' time last night.* □ *Everybody there was chillin'.*

chillum ['tʃɪləm] *n.* a pipe or device used for the smoking of marijuana. (Drugs.) □ *He keeps a chillum in his stash.* □ *Ernie carries a chillum with him. He's trying to sell it.*

chilly See *chill.*

chin music *n.* talk; idle chatter. □ *That's enough chin music back there.* □ *Okay, chum, make with the chin music. Let's have the whole story.*

China *n.* the teeth. (See also *ivories.*) □ *I spent a dumn fortune trying to get this China fixed up.* □ *If you would brush your China every day, you'd be okay.*

China white 1. AND **Chinese white** *n.* pure or nearly pure heroin. (Drugs.) □ *Beware of that China white.* □ *You never see Chinese white anymore. There's too many other kinds of junk for anybody to bother with it.* **2.** *n.* fentanyl, a synthetic narcotic analgesic. (Drugs.) □ *That Chinese white can paralyze your lungs.* □ *All the hopheads I know of stay away from China white.*

Chinese red *n.* heroin. (Drugs.) □ *Chinese red is really high quality.* □ *No, Chinese red is cheap.*

Chinese white See *China white.*

chintzy ['tʃɪntsi] **1.** *mod.* cheap; shoddy. □ *Nobody's gonna buy this chintzy stuff. Throw it out.* □ *What a chintzy car! The door fell off!* **2.** *mod.* stingy; miserly. □ *The chintzy guy left me no tip!* □ *Don't be chintzy. Give the man a dollar for a cup of coffee.*

chip See *(bargaining) chip.*

chipper 1. *mod.* jolly, fresh, and alert. (Standard English.) □ *Well, you look chipper this morning.* □ *This chipper young man will show you around.* **2.** *mod.* alcohol intoxicated. □ *Larry here is chipper already!* □ *A glass of wine will make her chipper almost immediately.* **3.** AND **chippie; chippy (user)** *n.* an occasional user of an addictive drug. (Drugs.) □ *The chippy users rarely end up in the hospital.* □ *Who can stay a chippie very long?*

chippie See the previous entry and the following entry.

chippy AND **chippie 1.** *n.* a part-time prostitute. □ *Yeah, so I'm a chippie. So what's that make you?* □ *Some little chippie stopped us to ask for a match.*

How amateurish. **2.** *in.* to play around sexually. ☐ *She won't even chippie.* ☐ *So me and my boyfriend was chippying a little in the hall. Why was ya watching?*

chippy around *in.* to be sexually promiscuous. ☐ *She has been known to chippy around, but not with just anyone and never for money.* ☐ *She figures it's her right to chippy around.*

chippy-chaser *n.* a man who chases sexually loose women. ☐ *He tried to be such a charmer—you know, a chippy-chaser, but he is so inept.* ☐ *Max used to be a chippy-chaser, but the scag has him sort of debilitated these days.*

chippy (user) See *chipper.*

chips **1.** *n.* money. (See also *(bargaining) chip.*) ☐ *I managed to put away a few chips when I worked for Acme Systems.* ☐ *She saved some chips over the years and bought herself a little place on the beach.* **2.** *n.* a carpenter. (Also a term of address.) ☐ *Tell our chips to come up here and put in a new floorboard.* ☐ *Tell me, chips, how fast can you build a coffin?*

chisel [ˈtʃɪzl̩] *tr. & in.* to extort (money). ☐ *Lefty tried to chisel forty bucks outa me.* ☐ *He's always chiseling. That's his hustle.*

chiseler *n.* a small-time crook; a cheater. (Originally underworld. Also a rude term of address.) ☐ *You dirty, two-bit chiseler! Give me my money back!* ☐ *Why did you trust a known chiseler like him?*

chit [tʃɪt] **1.** *n.* a bill or tabulation of charges that one signs rather than paying. ☐ *I don't have any cash. Can I sign a chit for it?* ☐ *Fred came in to pay for his chits about once a week.* **2.** *n.* a check. ☐ *She wrote out a chit for the balance due.* ☐ *I have your chit for the full amount.*

chitchat [ˈtʃɪttʃæt] **1.** *n.* talk; idle talk. ☐ *That's enough chitchat. Please get to work.* ☐ *Please stop the chitchat there in the back row.* **2.** *n.* a short, friendly conversation. ☐ *I'd like to have a little chitchat with you when you have time.* ☐ *We had a chitchat about the problem, and I think things will work out.*

Chi(town) [ˈʃaɪtaʊn OR ˈtʃaɪtaʊn] *n.* Chicago, Illinois. ☐ *I can't wait to get back to old Chitown.* ☐ *I was born in Chi.*

chiv See *shiv.*

chiz [tʃɪz] *in.* to relax. (Collegiate.) ☐ *I gotta get back to my room and chiz a while.* ☐ *Chiz, guys, things are getting a little rough.*

chock-full *mod.* totally full. ☐ *The new musical is just chock-full of laughs.* ☐ *The trunk is chock-full. There's no more room.*

chocoholic *n.* a person who craves chocolate. (Patterned on *alcoholic.*) ☐ *Cake, ice cream, pie—make it chocolate. I'm a chocoholic and I'm glad.* ☐ *I have a real treat for you chocolate lovers—triple chocolate cheesecake.*

choice *mod.* nice; *cool.* ☐ *We had a choice time at Tom's party.* ☐ *This new tunage is real choice.*

choke *in.* [for a computer] to fail to take in information being fed to it. (Computers.) ☐ *If you don't have your modem and your software set the same way as the host, your machine will choke.* ☐ *I did what you told me, but it choked anyway.*

choked *mod.* having to do with overly diluted drugs. ☐ *This stuff is choked. Don't score with that guy again.* ☐ *Why is this stuff so stepped on—you know, choked?*

choker *n.* a cigarette; a cigarette butt. ☐ *Put that damn choker out in my house!* ☐ *I can smell a choker the minute somebody lights it.*

chop *n.* a rude remark; a cutting remark. ☐ *Jerry made some chop about the way I dress.* ☐ *That was a rotten chop! Take it back!*

chop-shop *n.* a place where stolen cars are cut or broken up into car parts for resale. ☐ *The state is cracking down on these chop-shops.* ☐ *Once a stolen car gets to a chop-shop, there's no hope of identifying it.*

chopper *n.* a helicopter. □ *The chopper that monitors the traffic goes over my house every morning at 6:00.* □ *I never want to ride in a chopper. Those things scare me.*

choppers *n.* the teeth. □ *I may be on my last legs, but my choppers are still my own.* □ *That horse has a nice set of choppers.*

chow 1. *n.* food. □ *I need some chow before I go out and shovel snow.* □ *What time is chow served around here?* **2.** *tr. & in.* to eat (something). (See also *chow down.*) □ *I've been chowing canned tuna and stale bagels to save money.* □ *When do we chow?* **3.** See *ciao.*

chow down *in.* to eat; to take a meal. □ *Over there is where we chow down.* □ *It's past my time to chow down.*

chow hound *n.* someone who loves to eat; a heavy eater. □ *Harry is a real chow hound, and he's got love handles to prove it.* □ *Okay, listen up all you chow hounds. There's extra beans tonight!*

chow something down *tr.* to eat something, probably quickly or without good manners. □ *We can chow this pizza down in about two minutes!* □ *I found a box of cookies and chowed it down before anybody knew what I was doing.*

chowderhead *n.* a stupid person. □ *Look, chowderhead, do what I told you.* □ *Don't be such a chowderhead.*

Christmas tree *n.* a drunkard. (From being *lit* like a Christmas tree.) □ *Some old Christmas tree staggered by, muttering to herself.* □ *A well-dressed Christmas tree sat in the corner—lit up, of course.*

chrome-dome *n.* a shiny, bald head; a man with a bald head. (Also a rude term of address.) □ *The guy with the chrome-dome suddenly grasped his chest and made a face.* □ *Hey, chrome-dome, you're blinding me!*

chubbo ['tʃəbo] *n.* a fat person. (From *chubby.*) □ *Mary is a happy little chubbo. She'll probably outgrow all her baby fat.* □ *Look at those chubbos gobbling all those French fries.*

chuck 1. AND **chuck up** *in.* to empty one's stomach; to vomit. (See also *upchuck.*) □ *Look! Somebody chucked.* □ *I think I gotta chuck!* **2.** *tr.* to throw something away. □ *Chuck this thing. It's no good.* □ *The wrinkle-rod was so twisted we had to chuck it.* **3.** *in.* to eat voraciously. □ *Don't just chuck, man, enjoy your food.* □ *The two guys sat guzzling and chucking till they were full.* **4.** *n.* food. □ *Man, this chuck is okay.* □ *Who cooked this chuck, man? It's garbage!*

chuck a dummy *tr.* to empty one's stomach; to vomit. □ *He left the room—to chuck a dummy, I guess.* □ *Somebody chucked a dummy on the patio.*

chuck it in *tr.* to quit; to give up. (See also *throw in the towel.*) □ *I was so depressed, I almost chucked it in.* □ *If I didn't have to keep the job to live, I'd have chucked it in long ago.*

chuck up See *chuck.*

chucked *mod.* alcohol intoxicated. □ *I'm too chucked to drive.* □ *How did you get so chucked?*

chuckers AND **chucks** *n.* a great hunger; an enormous appetite. (Usually with *the.*) □ *Oh, man, I really got the chucks. What time is chow?* □ *The chuckers got my stomach asking if my throat is cut.*

chucks See the previous entry.

chug(-a-lug) ['tʃəgələg] *tr. & in.* to drink down a whole beer (or other drink) without stopping. □ *The two guys tried to see who could chug-a-lug the most beer.* □ *Wally chugged two cans in a row.* □ *All four of them sat there chugging.*

chum *n.* a pal; a good friend. □ *This is my chum, Wally.* □ *We've been chums for years. Went to college together.*

chummy ['tʃəmi] *mod.* friendly. □ *I'm glad to see that you are a little more chummy this morning.* □ *Don't get too chummy with me. I'm a real son of a bitch.*

chump [tʃəmp] *n.* a stupid person; a gullible person. □ *You are such a chump.* □ *See if that chump will loan you some money.*

chump change *n.* a small amount of money; the kind of salary or amount of money a *chump* would work for. □ *I refuse to work for chump change! I want a real job.* □ *It may be chump change, but it's better than nothing.*

chumphead *n.* a stupid person. □ *John is not my favorite chumphead, but he's close.* □ *What a chumphead. You painted over the windows.*

chunk 1. *in.* to empty one's stomach; to vomit. (Collegiate.) □ *I think I gotta chunk.* □ *The cat chunked all over the carpet.* **2.** *in.* to do badly; to blunder. □ *Sorry. I really chunked on that last deal.* □ *She is so afraid of chunking that she will hardly do anything.*

chunky *mod.* stout; fat. □ *Harry—the chow hound—is getting a little chunky.* □ *It's not all fat! He's always been a chunky brute.*

church key *n.* a beer can opener. □ *Where is the church key when I need it?* □ *I have a church key in my glove compartment.*

churn *tr.* [for a stockbroker] to cause a heavy turnover in the portfolio of an investor. (The broker collects commissions on each transaction.) □ *I reported my broker for churning my account.* □ *They churn accounts to earn the commissions.*

ciao AND **chow** [tʃaʊ] "Good-bye"; "Hello." (Italian.) □ *See ya. Ciao.* □ *Chow, baby. Call my service.*

cid AND **sid** [sɪd] *n.* the hallucinogenic drug *L.S.D.* (Drugs. From *acid. Sid* can be capitalized.) □ *Where can I go to drop a little cid?* □ *Bruno can tell you where Sid is these days.* □ *You know where I can rap with Sid?*

cig [sɪg] *n.* a cigarette; a cigar. □ *Barlowe fumbled for a cig and thought better of it.* □ *Toss me my pack of cigs, will ya?*

cigarette with no name AND **no brand cigarette; no name cigarette** *n.* a marijuana cigarette. (Drugs.) □ *You got one of them cigarettes with no name?* □ *He spends his whole life burning those no name cigarettes.*

ciggie See the following entry.

ciggy AND **ciggie** ['sɪgi] *n.* a cigarette. □ *How 'bout a ciggy before we take off?* □ *Where is my pack of ciggies?*

cinch [sɪntʃ] **1.** *n.* something very easy. □ *No sweat! It was a cinch!* □ *What a cinch. Anybody can do it.* **2.** *tr.* to have something settled and secured. □ *He cinched it with a simple signature and date.* □ *It only took a handshake to cinch the deal.*

cinched [sɪntʃt] *mod.* settled; secured; *sealed (up).* (As one tightens the saddle girth on a horse.) □ *I've got it cinched! No sweat!* □ *This is a cinched deal—a done deal. No one can stop it from going through.*

circular file *n.* a wastebasket. (See also *file 13.*) □ *That letter went straight into the circular file.* □ *Most of the junk mail sits here until I can put it into the circular file.*

civil serpent *n.* a civil servant. □ *You have no idea the kinds of things civil serpents have to put up with.* □ *I'm a civil serpent with the state.*

civvies ['sɪviz] *n.* civilian clothes rather than a uniform. (Originally military.) □ *I feel sort of funny in civvies.* □ *I re-upped because I couldn't stand the thought of civvies and stuff like that.*

clam 1. *n.* a dollar. (Underworld.) □ *Forty clams for a sweater that doesn't even have arms!* □ *You got a couple of clams I can bum for a little bottle?* **2.** *n.* a tight-lipped person. □ *Suddenly, she became a clam and wouldn't talk anymore.* □ *Rocko's a clam. He won't say a word.*

clam up *in.* to get quiet. (See also *dummy up.*) □ *The minute they got him inside the cop-shop, he clammed up.* □ *You'll clam up if you know what's good for you.*

clanked *mod.* exhausted; pooped. □ *At the end of the race, the chick was totally clanked.* □ *I'm really clanked, man. Gotta take a rest.*

clanks *n.* the delirium tremens. ☐ *He's suffering with the clanks again.* ☐ *Who's the old buzzard shaking with the clanks?*

clap *n.* gonorrhea. (Use caution with the topic.) ☐ *Max has had the clap a dozen times.* ☐ *A case of the clap can change your life for a while.*

claptrap *n.* nonsense; something worthless. ☐ *This is enough claptrap. I'm leaving.* ☐ *I know claptrap when I see it, and your play was claptrap.*

class 1. *n.* high style; elegance. ☐ *The dame's got class, but no brains.* ☐ *Class isn't worth much in this neighborhood.* **2.** *mod.* first-rate; high-class. ☐ *I've always regarded the firm as a class outfit.* ☐ *This was a class suburb just a few years ago.*

class act *n.* a high-quality act; a high-quality way of doing things. ☐ *I like the way you move on the field, Jerry. It's a real class act.* ☐ *The prof puts on a real class act, but he grades very hard.*

classis-chassis AND **classy-chassy** ['klæsi'tʃæsi AND 'klæsi'ʃæsi] *n.* an attractive female figure. ☐ *Who's the classis-chassis in the mink?* ☐ *Now there is a classy-chassy if I ever saw one.*

classy *mod.* elegant; dandy. ☐ *Pretty classy place you got here.* ☐ *How much does a classy car like this cost?*

classy-chassy See *classis-chassis.*

clay *n.* good-quality hashish. (Drugs.) ☐ *I like the feel of this clay. I'll take it.* ☐ *Ask Bruno where you can dig up some clay.*

clay pigeon *n.* a gullible person; a *pigeon.* (Underworld.) ☐ *We need a clay pigeon to divert attention from the snatch.* ☐ *Who's gonna be the clay pigeon for the bank caper?*

clean 1. *mod.* not using drugs; not involved with drugs. ☐ *There's a success story. Kelly is one clean guy if I ever saw one.* ☐ *I've been clean for more than a month now.* **2.** *mod.* sober; not intoxicated with drugs at the moment. (Almost the same as sense 1.) ☐ *He's clean right now, but he'll get the call in an hour or two.* ☐ *Just being clean for a day is an accomplishment.* **3.** *mod.* not breaking any law. (Police and underworld.) ☐ *I'm clean, officer. You can't charge me with anything.* ☐ *This guy is clean. Let him go.* **4.** *mod.* not carrying a weapon. (Police and underworld.) ☐ *I frisked him. He's clean.* ☐ *Bugsy's gang was clean except for Bugsy himself who had a small pistol.* **5.** *mod.* well-dressed. ☐ *Now there's a clean dude!* ☐ *New threads, huh? Clean, baby, clean!*

clean-cut *mod.* having to do with a person who is neat and tidy. ☐ *He's a very clean-cut guy, and polite too.* ☐ *He's sort of clean-cut looking, but with bushy hair.*

clean one's act up *tr.* to reform one's conduct; to improve one's performance. ☐ *We were told to clean our act up or move out.* Ⓣ *I cleaned up my act, but not in time. I got kicked out.*

clean someone out 1. *tr.* to get all of someone's money. ☐ *The bill for supper cleaned me out, and we couldn't go to the flick.* Ⓣ *The robbers cleaned out everybody on the train.* (More at *cleaned out.*) **2.** *tr.* to empty someone's bowels. ☐ *That medicine I took really cleaned me out.* ☐ *A couple of those little burgers will clean me out.* (More at *cleaned out.*)

clean sweep *n.* a broad movement clearing or affecting everything in the pathway. (Usually figurative.) ☐ *The boss and everybody in the front office got canned in a clean sweep from upstairs.* ☐ *Everybody got a raise. It was a clean sweep.*

clean up (on something) *in.* to make a lot of money on something. ☐ *The promoters cleaned up on the product.* ☐ *If we advertise, we can clean up.*

cleaned out 1. *mod.* broke; with no money. ☐ *I'm cleaned out. Not a cent left.* ☐ *Tom's cleaned out. He's broke. He'll have to go home.* **2.** *mod.* with one's digestive tract emptied. ☐ *That medicine really left me cleaned out.* ☐ *I feel better now that I'm cleaned out.*

clear 1. *mod.* alcohol intoxicated. ☐ *Man, is she ever clear!* ☐ *He was clear,* *you know, polluted.* **2.** *mod.* (of liquor) undiluted; neat. □ *No soda. Clear, please.* □ *I like mine clear with just one ice cube.* **3.** *tr.* to earn a specific net amount of money. □ *She cleared a cool forty thousand on that Wilson deal.* □ *We just want to clear a decent profit. Nothing greedy.*

clear as mud *mod.* not clear at all. (Often with *as.*) □ *All of this is clear as mud to me.* □ *I did all the reading, but it's still as clear as mud.*

clear as vodka **1.** *mod.* very clear. □ *The weather is as clear as vodka.* □ *The river wasn't exactly as clear as vodka because it had just rained.* **2.** *mod.* very understandable. □ *Everything he said is as clear as vodka.* □ *I understand what John said, but everything you say is clear as vodka.*

clear out *in.* to leave; to depart. □ *Time for you people to clear out. It's past midnight.* □ *The boss gave me till next week to clear out. I'm fired—canned.*

clear sailing *mod.* easy going. □ *It'll be clear sailing from now on.* □ *When this is finished, it'll be clear sailing.*

click (with someone) *in.* to catch on with someone; to intrigue someone; to become popular with someone. □ *The pink hair and multiple earrings never really seemed to click with many kids.* □ *Sam and Mary are getting along fine. I knew they'd click.*

cliff-dweller *n.* someone who lives in a tall apartment building. □ *I could never survive as a cliff-dweller in a big city.* □ *The majority of cliff-dwellers wouldn't choose to live in any other way.*

climb **1.** *n.* a marijuana cigarette. (Drugs. The means to a *high.*) □ *I need a climb to set me straight.* □ *Here, have a swallow of this climb.* **2.** *tr.* to scold someone. □ *The boss climbed Harry for being late.* □ *Don't climb me! The train broke down!*

climb the wall(s) *tr.* to do something desperate when one is anxious, bored, or excited. □ *He was home for only three days; then he began to climb the wall.* □ *I was climbing the walls to get back to work.*

clinch [klɪntʃ] *tr.* to settle something; to make something final. □ *I was able to clinch the deal, and I got a raise for it.* □ *I want to clinch this contract before the weekend.*

clincher [ˈklɪntʃɚ] *n.* the final element; the straw that broke the camel's back. (See also *capper.*) □ *The clincher was when the clerk turned up the volume.* □ *Eating garlic by the bushel was the clincher. I had to get a new roommate.*

clink *n.* jail. □ *We'll throw you in the clink if you don't talk.* □ *One night in the clink was enough.*

clinker **1.** *n.* a mistake; (in music) a misplayed note. □ *That was a bad clinker in the middle of the soft passage.* □ *Look at the score, man! That series of clinkers just isn't there.* **2.** *n.* a worthless person or thing. (From the term for a cinder.) □ *This guy is such a clinker. Who needs him?* □ *Ralph has turned out to be a real clinker. We'll have to pink slip him.*

clip **1.** *tr.* to cheat someone. (See also *clip joint.*) □ *That guy in there clipped me for a fiver.* □ *I didn't clip you or anybody else!* (More at *clipped.*) **2.** *tr.* to kill someone. □ *Rocko had orders to clip both Max and Bruno.* □ *Max and Bruno had set out to clip Rocko first.* **3.** *n.* a holder for a marijuana cigarette butt. (Drugs. See also *roach clip.*) □ *She's got a clip if you need it.* □ *My clip's at home in my stash.* **4.** *n.* a music video; a short film. □ *This next clip is something you'll all recognize.* □ *Stay tuned for more great clips.* **5.** *n.* a fast rate of speed. □ *By traveling at a good clip, we managed to get there before the wedding started.* □ *You were moving at a pretty good clip when you ran into the truck.*

clip a butt *tr.* to pinch out a cigarette for later smoking. (Also with *the.*) □ *Like an old soldier, Wally took a puff and then clipped the butt for later.* □ *You learn to clip a butt so you won't waste what you can't finish.*

clip joint *n.* a business establishment that cheats customers. ☐ *That place is a clip joint. Stay away.* ☐ *The clip joint on Fourth Street was busted last night.*

clip someone's wings *tr.* to restrain someone; to reduce or put an end to a teenager's privileges. ☐ *One more stunt like that, and I'm going to clip your wings for a couple of weeks.* ☐ *Her father clipped her wings for getting into trouble with the cops.*

clipped 1. *mod.* cheated. ☐ *When Marty counted his change, he found he'd been clipped.* ☐ *You weren't clipped by me. I just made a mistake.* **2.** *mod.* arrested. ☐ *Max got clipped as he got out of his car.* ☐ *He was clipped and no one read him his rights, so off he went.*

clobber *tr.* to strike someone; to beat someone; to outscore someone. ☐ *I ought to clobber you, but good.* ☐ *She clobbered him over the head with her bouquet.*

clobbered *mod.* alcohol intoxicated. ☐ *He's the kind of guy who goes home and gets clobbered after work.* ☐ *The whole fraternity celebrated by getting themselves clobbered.*

clock *tr.* to earn, score, or total up someone or something. (As if the person or thing gained were being metered or clocked.) ☐ *Sam clocked a date with Sally, and is he ever proud!* ☐ *Amy clocked nearly $12 an hour in overtime last weekend.*

clock in *in.* to record one's arrival at a set time. ☐ *He clocked in three minutes late.* ☐ *When they clock in, give them this envelope.*

clock watcher *n.* someone—a worker or a student—who is always looking at the clock. ☐ *There are four clock watchers in our office.* ☐ *People who don't like their jobs can turn into clock watchers.*

clodhopper 1. *n.* a big shoe. ☐ *Wipe the mud off those clodhoppers before you come in here.* ☐ *Look at the clodhoppers she's wearing!* **2.** *n.* a stupid person; a rural oaf. ☐ *Some clodhopper came into town and fell in with the wrong crowd.* ☐ *You don't know it, but that clodhopper is worth about two million bucks.*

Close, but no cigar. [klos . . .] *phr.* "Close, but not close enough to win a prize!" ☐ *You almost did it. Close, but no cigar.* ☐ *Close, but no cigar! Give it another try.*

close call See the following entry.

close shave AND **close call** *n.* a narrow escape. ☐ *Wow, that was a close shave.* ☐ *The car passed this close to us—a real close call.*

closet *mod.* secret; concealed. ☐ *Marty is a closet chocolate fiend.* ☐ *I'm a closet hard rock fan.*

clotheshorse ['klozhors] *n.* someone who is obsessed with clothing and looking good in it. ☐ *Her brother is the real clotheshorse.* ☐ *Mary is such a clotheshorse! Look at her now.*

clout *n.* influence; power. (See also *wallop.*) ☐ *You have clout with the mayor. You try it.* ☐ *I don't have any clout at all.*

clouted *mod.* arrested. ☐ *Some old wino got clouted for spitting on the sidewalk.* ☐ *They do things like that to get clouted so they can have a warm place to stay overnight.*

clown *n.* a fool. ☐ *Some clown threw our paper in a puddle this morning.* ☐ *Tell that clown in the front row to can it.*

clown around *in.* to act silly; to mess around. ☐ *Please stop clowning around and get to sleep.* ☐ *We were just clowning around. We didn't mean to break anything.*

cluck AND **kluck** [klək] *n.* a stupid person; a person as stupid as a chicken. ☐ *Why did they send me a dumb cluck to do this work?* ☐ *Some kluck came in and asked for a left-handed monkey wrench.*

cluckhead *n.* a stupid oaf. ☐ *What cluckhead put sugar in the salt shaker?* ☐ *I'm getting to be such a cluckhead!*

clucky *mod.* stupid; oafish. ☐ *What a clucky dame!* ☐ *The plan you submitted to this office was rejected by the policy committee. They noted that it was the cluckiest idea they had ever seen.*

clue someone in *tr.* to set someone straight (about something); to inform someone of the facts. □ *What's going on? Clue me in.* 🅃 *I think I'd better clue in Sam about the rally.*

clueless *mod.* unaware. □ *She is so dense. Totally clueless.* □ *I have never seen anyone so totally clueless. What a dunce.*

cluelessness *n.* total stupidity. (See also *totally clueless.*) □ *I just shake my head in wonder at the cluelessness of my fellow humans.* □ *This place is just infested with juvenile cluelessness!*

clunk 1. *tr.* to strike someone or something. □ *A small truck clunked me from behind.* □ *The branch clunked the roof as it fell.* **2.** *n.* a hit; the sound of a hit. □ *I heard a clunk on the roof. Must be reindeer.* □ *The clunk on the roof was a falling branch.*

clunker 1. *n.* an old car. □ *He drives an old clunker and doesn't have any insurance.* □ *I gotta get rid of this clunker pretty soon.* **2.** *n.* someone or something worthless; a *clinker.* □ *We have to get the clunkers off the payroll.* □ *Fred? There's another clunker we don't need.*

clunkhead *n.* an oaf; a stupid dolt. □ *What clunkhead put sugar in the salt shaker?* □ *My brother can be such a clunkhead.*

clunky *mod.* ponderous and inefficient. □ *The whole plan is too clunky. Try to prune it down.* □ *I got rid of all the clunky stuff. Now it's lean and mean.*

clutch (up) *in.* to become very tense and anxious; to freeze with anxiety. □ *I have been known to clutch up before a race.* □ *Cool it, babe! Don't clutch!*

clutched *mod.* nervous. □ *I get so clutched before a test.* □ *George is clutched most of the time. He's in bad shape.*

Clyde [klaɪd] *n.* an oaf; a *square,* usually a male. (Compare to *Zelda.* Also a term of address.) □ *Well, Clyde, I think you're way off base.* □ *A dull Clyde, that's my old Bill, but I still love him.*

coaster *n.* someone who lives near the ocean. (California.) □ *Tiffany is a coaster now, but she was born, like, somewhere else.* □ *The coasters just don't want to be beige, that's all.*

cock *n.* the penis. (Taboo. Potentially offensive. Use only with discretion. Mainly in the South, this refers instead to the female genitals.) □ *He made some joke about a cock, but nobody laughed.* □ *The streaker covered his cock and ran across the field.*

cockamamie ['kɑkəmemi] *mod.* ridiculous; inconceivable. □ *What a cockamamie idea!* □ *That is the most cockamamie thing I ever heard of.*

cockeyed ['kɑkaɪd] *mod.* crazy. □ *Who came up with this cockeyed idea, anyway?* □ *If you didn't act so cockeyed all the time, you'd have more friends.*

coed ['koɛd] *n.* a female college student. (From *coeducational.*) □ *Some of these coeds are pretty strong-minded.* □ *My daughter is a coed at Midwest University.*

coffee and *n.* coffee and a doughnut or a pastry. □ *I'll have coffee and.* □ *We stopped at a little shop for coffee and.*

coffin-dodger ['kɔfn̩ dɑdʒɚ] *n.* a heavy smoker. □ *I just hate these damn coffin-dodgers who light up a cigarette in a restaurant!* □ *Coffin-dodgers, chain-smokers—who cares? Let 'em commit suicide—in the privacy of their own homes, of course.*

coffin nail 1. AND **coffin tack** *n.* a cigarette. □ *No more coffin nails for me.* □ *Every coffin tack you smoke takes a little off the end of your life.* **2.** *n.* a drink of liquor. □ *How about another coffin nail?* □ *Coffin nail sounds bad. Drink sounds good.*

coffin tack See the previous entry.

coffin varnish *n.* inferior liquor. □ *You want some more of this coffin varnish?* □ *Do you see what that coffin varnish you serve here has done to some of those guys?*

coin *n.* money. (See also *hard coin, do some fine coin.*) □ *I'm sort of short of coin right now. Can it wait?* □ *He made a lot of coin on the last picture.*

coke party *n.* a gathering where cocaine is consumed. (Drugs.) □ *There's a coke party in the warehouse after closing tonight.* □ *Tom's hosting a coke party for his yuppie friends.*

cokeaholic [kokə'hɑlɪk] *n.* a cocaine addict. (Drugs.) □ *It's hard to get a cokeaholic to get treatment.* □ *When I realized I was a cokeaholic, I decided to stop, but I couldn't.*

cokehead *n.* a heavy cocaine user; a cocaine addict. (Drugs.) □ *We get a few depressed cokeheads in the emergency room who have tried suicide.* □ *As a banker, I see two or three cokeheads file for bankruptcy each year.*

cokespoon AND **(flake) spoon** *n.* a small spoon used to carry powdered cocaine to a nostril. (Drugs.) □ *Wally wears a cokespoon around his neck.* □ *The principal wrote a letter to Mrs. Simpson telling her that Jimmy had brought a flake spoon to school.*

cold 1. *mod.* (stopping something) suddenly and totally. □ *I stopped cold—afraid to move further.* □ *That remark stopped her cold.* **2.** *mod.* dead. □ *This parrot is cold—pifted!* □ *When I'm cold and buried, I hope people will think of me fondly.* **3.** *mod.* not good. □ *That new CD is real cold. The sound is bad and the performance is too.* □ *The lecture was cold and dull.* **4.** *mod.* excellent. (Very *cool*.) □ *That last pitch was cold, man.* □ *Hey, G! That's a cold ride.*

cold blood AND **cold coffee** *n.* beer. □ *How would you like a little cold blood to start things off?* □ *A nice big cold coffee would do me fine.*

cold call *tr.* to call a sales prospect from a list of persons one has never met. □ *The broker cold called a number of people each evening for two months.* □ *Things have to be pretty bad when the senior brokers at a major house have to cold call people to get business.*

cold coffee See *cold blood*.

cold feet *n.* a wave of timidity or fearfulness. □ *Suddenly I had cold feet and couldn't sing a note.* □ *You sort of expect a candy-ass like that to have cold feet.*

cold fish *n.* a dull and unresponsive person. □ *I hate to shake hands with a cold fish like that. He didn't even smile.* □ *I hate going out with a cold fish.*

cold pop *n.* beer. □ *How about another can of that cold pop?* □ *A few cans of cold pop and John began to wobble a little.*

cold shoulder 1. *n.* a cool reception; the brushoff. □ *I didn't expect to be greeted by such a cold shoulder.* □ *I got the cold shoulder at the office today.* **2.** *tr.* to ignore someone; to give someone a cool reception. □ *The hostess cold shouldered me, so I spilled my appetizers in the swimming pool.* □ *Tiffany cold shouldered the guy who was putting the moves on Roberta.*

cold sober *mod.* sober; completely sober. (See also *sold cober*.) □ *Of course, I'm cold sober!* □ *He had a fine head on and wanted more than anything to be cold sober and alert.*

cold turkey *mod.* (stopping something) suddenly, without tapering off. (Said especially of stopping an addictive drug intake. Originally drugs.) □ *Martha stopped cold turkey and survived.* □ *I stopped smoking cigarettes cold turkey and had to be hospitalized.* □ *I gave up rich desserts cold turkey and lived to tell about it.*

coldcock *tr.* to knock someone out. □ *The guy who called Max out wanted to coldcock him for shorting him, but got coldcocked himself.* □ *The clerk coldcocked the would-be robber with a champagne bottle.*

coli ['kɑli] *n.* marijuana. (Drugs. From *broccoli*.) □ *There's a little bag of coli in the fridge.* □ *Who got into my stash and took the coli?*

collar 1. *tr.* to arrest someone. □ *The cops collared her as she was leaving the hotel.* □ *The nark tried to collar Max, but Max moved away too fast.* (More at *collared*.) **2.** *n.* an arrest. □ *It was a* *tough collar, with all the screaming and yelling.* □ *I made the collar in broad daylight.*

collared *mod.* arrested. □ *Willard Babbit? Oh, yes. He's collared. Got him last night.* □ *Got collared during a routine traffic stop.*

Colombian (gold) AND **Columbian (gold)** *n.* a potent marijuana from Colombia. (*Columbian* is a misspelling.) □ *Colombian gold seems to be a favorite around here.* □ *Columbian is cheap and abundant in almost every city.*

color of someone's money *n.* the amount of money someone has in hand. □ *Well, I can tell if we can make a deal if I could see the color of your money.* □ *Lemme see the color of your money. Then we'll talk.*

Columbian (gold) See *Colombian (gold).*

combo ['kɑmbo] **1.** *n.* a small group of musicians; a small band. (From *combination.*) □ *Andy started his own combo and made money from day one.* □ *You can make a good living with a combo.* **2.** *n.* a combination of people or things. □ *Those two make an interesting combo.* □ *The dish was a combo of fish, garlic, and cream.* **3.** *n.* a bisexual person. □ *Nobody would have thought that Fred's a combo.* □ *He's not a combo, he's just confused.*

comboozelated [kəm'buzəledəd] *mod.* alcohol intoxicated. (Collegiate.) □ *I believe I am just a little comboozelated.* □ *How did you get so comboozelated?*

come clean (with someone) (about something) *in.* to admit (something) to someone. □ *I wish you'd come clean with me about this problem.* □ *You're gonna have to come clean eventually.*

come down **1.** *in.* to happen. □ *Hey, man! What's coming down?* □ *When something like this comes down, I have to stop and think things over.* **2.** *n.* a letdown; a disappointment. (Usually **comedown.**) □ *The loss of the race was a real comedown for Willard.* □ *It's hard to face a comedown like that.* **3.** *in.* to begin to recover from the effects of alcohol or drug intoxication. □ *She came down slow, which was good.* □ *It was hard to get her to come down.*

come down hard *in.* to come out of a drug use session badly. (Drugs.) □ *Mike came down hard, and it took them a long time to calm him down.* □ *Some kids who come down hard will need treatment, but none of them get it unless they look like they are bad off.*

come-hither look [kəm'hɪðɚ lʊk] *n.* an alluring or seductive look or glance, usually done by a woman. □ *She blinked her bedroom eyes and gave him a come-hither look.* □ *She had mastered the come-hither look, but was not ready for the next part.*

Come off it! **1.** *exclam.* "Stop acting arrogantly!" □ *Oh, you're just one of us. Come off it!* □ *Come off it, Tiff. You're not the Queen of England.* **2.** *exclam.* "Give up your incorrect point of view!" □ *Come off it! You're wrong, and you know it.* □ *You are arguing from a foolish position. You're dead wrong. Come off it!*

come on ['kəmɔn] **1.** *n.* a lure; bait. (Usually **come-on.**) □ *Forty people responded to the come-on published in the Sunday paper.* □ *It's just a come on. Nobody is giving away a decent color TV just for listening to a sales pitch.* **2.** *n.* an invitation; a sexual invitation. (Usually **come-on.**) □ *She stared at him with her bedroom eyes, giving him that age-old come-on.* □ *Who could resist a come-on like that?* **3.** *in.* to begin to perform well. □ *In the second scene, the entire cast came on, and the audience loved it.* □ *The singer came on immediately. We knew we had a star.* **4.** *in.* to begin to become friendly. □ *After a few minutes, they began to come on to each other.* □ *When the nervousness of meeting a blind date passed, Sam and Mary began to come on, and we could see it would be a success.* **5.** *in.* to feel the effects of a drug; for a drug to take effect. (Drugs.) □ *After what seemed a long time, I began to come on to the stuff.* □ *When I came on, I decided I didn't like it, but then it was too late.* **6.** [kəm'ɑn] *exclam.*

"You are wrong!" (Usually **Come on!**) ☐ *Come on! This is a good set of clubs!* ☐ *Come on! Wasteful spending occurs at all levels of all governments! Nobody is innocent!*

come on like gangbusters See the following entry.

come on strong AND **come on like gangbusters** *in.* to seem aggressive; to impress people initially as very aggressive and assertive. (See explanation at *like gangbusters.*) ☐ *She has a tendency to come on strong, but she's really a softie.* ☐ *The new president comes on strong at first.*

come on to someone *in.* to make advances to a person. ☐ *He came on to her, but she beat it outa there fast.* ☐ *She didn't even know he was coming on to her, till they got to his place.*

come out ahead *in.* to end up with a profit; to end up with some benefit. ☐ *I never seem to come out ahead at the end of the month.* ☐ *We'll come out ahead in the end. Just you wait.*

come out in the wash *in.* to be dealt with in the normal chain of events. (As if someone were counselling someone who had caused a clothing stain.) ☐ *All of these things will come out in the wash.* ☐ *Whatever it is, it'll come out in the wash. Don't worry.*

come out on top *in.* to end up to the better; to win. ☐ *Tim always has to come out on top—a classic poor loser.* ☐ *She made all the wrong moves and still came out on top.*

come up for air *in.* to pause for a break. ☐ *The kissers—being only human—had to come up for air eventually.* ☐ *They were taking in money so fast at the box office that there wasn't a minute to come up for air.*

comeback ['kəmbæk] **1.** *n.* a retort; back talk. ☐ *Hank is pretty fast with the comeback.* ☐ *One more snotty comeback like that and you're finished.* **2.** *n.* a return to a former state. ☐ *The aging singer tried to sober up and make a comeback.* ☐ *Her comeback was not a financial success, but it improved her spirits.*

comer ['kəmɚ] *n.* someone with a bright future. ☐ *Fred is a real comer. You'll be hearing a lot about him.* ☐ *A comer like that can command a high salary.*

comeuppance [kəm'əpənts] *n.* a well-deserved rebuke. ☐ *He finally got the comeuppance that he's needed for so long.* ☐ *I gave her a comeuppance she'll never forget.*

comfort station **1.** *n.* a restroom; toilet facilities available to the public. ☐ *Do you have a comfort station in this store?* ☐ *We need to stop and find a comfort station in the next town.* **2.** *n.* an establishment that sells liquor. ☐ *Let's get some belch at a comfort station along here somewhere.* ☐ *There's cops all around that comfort station. Somebody must have robbed it.*

comfy ['kəm(p)fi] *mod.* comfortable. ☐ *This is a very comfy chair.* ☐ *I find myself in a not too comfy position with regard to your further employment here.*

coming out of one's ears *mod.* in great abundance. ☐ *Mr. Wilson has money coming out of his ears.* ☐ *Borrow some paper from Chuck. He's got it coming out of his ears.*

comma-counter *n.* a pedantic person. ☐ *Comma-counters can be such a pain.* ☐ *When you need a proofreader, you need a comma-counter.*

commie ['kami] *n.* a communist. ☐ *What are the commies up to now?* ☐ *The commies are selling gold today, and the price went down a lot.*

commode-hugging drunk *mod.* heavily alcohol intoxicated; drunk and vomiting. ☐ *Bruno got commode-hugging drunk in the space of two hours.* ☐ *I could tell by the sounds coming from the bathroom that Ernie had come home commode-hugging drunk again.*

company bull *n.* a detective or guard who works for a private firm. ☐ *Pete is a company bull for Acme Systems. He works nights.* ☐ *The company bull asked what we were doing there.*

company man *n.* a man who always sides with his employers. ☐ *Ken's a company* *man—he'll always take management's side.* ☐ *You can depend on a company man to do as he is told.*

con 1. *n.* a convict. ☐ *One of the cons keeps a snake in his cell for a pet.* ☐ *Is that guy in the gray pajamas one of the escaped cons?* 2. *n.* a confidence scheme. ☐ *They pulled a real con on the old lady.* ☐ *This is an okay con you got going.* 3. *tr.* to swindle or deceive someone. ☐ *Don't try to con me. I know the score.* ☐ *Bruno conned him out of his money.*

con artist See *con man.*

con job *n.* an act of deception. ☐ *What a con job he tried to pull on us!* ☐ *This is not an annual report! It's a con job!*

con man AND **con artist** *n.* someone who makes a living by swindling people. ☐ *Gary is a con artist, but at least he's not on the dole.* ☐ *He looks like a con man, but he's just a sweetie.*

conehead 1. *n.* a fool; an oaf. ☐ *Some conehead put sugar in the salt shaker.* ☐ *You can be pretty much of a conehead yourself sometimes, you know.* 2. *n.* an intellectual; a *pointy-head.* ☐ *The coneheads have decided that we are all making too much money.* ☐ *They build fences around universities to keep the coneheads in.*

conk AND **konk** *n.* the head. ☐ *Put your brim on your conk, and let's cruise.* ☐ *Where'd you get that nasty bump on your konk?*

conk-buster [ˈkɔŋkbəstɚ] *n.* inferior liquor. ☐ *Another shot of that conk-buster and I will just pass out.* ☐ *Jed kept a jar of conk-buster under his bed against night sweats.*

conk out 1. *in.* [for someone] to collapse. ☐ *I was so tired I just went home and conked out.* ☐ *I was afraid I would conk out while I was driving.* 2. *in.* [for something] to break down; to quit running. ☐ *My car conked out finally.* ☐ *I hope my computer doesn't conk out.*

connect (with someone or something) 1. *in.* [with *someone*] to meet someone; to talk to someone on the telephone. ☐ *Let's try to connect on this matter tomorrow.* ☐ *We connected over a drink and discussed the matter fully.* 2. *in.* [with *something*] [for a batter] to hit a ball. ☐ *Wally connected for a double.* ☐ *He swung, but didn't connect with the ball.*

connection *n.* a seller of drugs; someone who is a source for drugs. (Originally drugs.) ☐ *Max's connection got rousted.* ☐ *This connection you keep taking about—is he dependable?*

conniption (fit) [kəˈnɪpʃən . . .] *n.* a burst of anger; a *spaz.* ☐ *He had a conniption fit over the question of my marriage to Wally.* ☐ *Come on, don't have a conniption!*

constitutional *n.* the first drink or dose of drugs of the day. (See also *breakfast of champions.*) ☐ *He downed a constitutional and made ready to set out for the office.* ☐ *He never fails to drop a constitutional in the morning.*

coo-coo AND **cuckoo** 1. *mod.* unconscious. ☐ *I socked him on the snoot and knocked him coo-coo.* ☐ *Rocko was cuckoo for a minute; then he was up and swinging.* 2. *mod.* insane. ☐ *The chick is just cuckoo, that's all.* ☐ *How did I ever get involved in this cuckoo scheme, anyway?*

cooked *mod.* alcohol or drug intoxicated. ☐ *Pete is cooked, fried, boiled, baked—drunk.* ☐ *Gary is calling a cab. He's too cooked to drive.*

cooked up *mod.* contrived. (This is hyphenated before a nominal.) ☐ *The whole thing seems so cooked up.* ☐ *What a cooked-up story! Of course, you don't believe it.*

cookie pusher 1. *n.* a bootlicker; someone who flatters other people for self-serving motives. ☐ *When you've got a whole office full of cookie pushers, there's always someone to take you to lunch.* ☐ *Another cookie pusher came in today to tell me what a great teacher I am.* 2. *n.* a lazy do-nothing. ☐ *Is Martin a couch potato or a cookie pusher? That is the question!* ☐ *I'm just looking for a cookie pusher to fire today.*

cooking with gas *in.* doing exactly right. (Always with *-ing*.) □ *That's great! Now you're cooking with gas!* □ *I knew she was finally cooking with gas when she answered all the questions correctly.*

cool 1. *mod.* unabashed; unruffled; relaxed. (See also *keep one's cool, lose one's cool*.) □ *This chick is so cool—no matter what happens.* □ *She is totally cool and easygoing.* **2.** *mod.* good; excellent. □ *This is a really cool setup!* □ *Then this, like, cool muscleman comes over and asks Tiffany if she'd like to dance.* **3.** *mod.* (of music) mellow; smooth. □ *This stuff is so cool, I'm just floating.* □ *Doesn't he blow a cool trumpet?* **4.** *mod.* no less than (some amount of money). □ *He earns a cool million every year.* □ *She cleared a cool forty thousand on the Wilson deal.* **5.** *in.* to die; to become cold after death. (Medical euphemism.) □ *The patient cooled during surgery.* □ *We were afraid that he would cool.*

Cool bananas! See the following entry.

Cool beans! AND **Cool bananas!** *exclam.* "Wow!" □ *Cool beans, man. That's great!* □ *You got a car? Cool bananas!*

cool, calm, and collected *mod. cool;* unabashed. □ *Albert is almost always cool, calm, and collected.* □ *Before a race I am anything but cool, calm, and collected.*

cool cat *n.* someone who is *cool,* usually a male. □ *Monty is a cool cat. I really like him.* □ *There is a shortage of cool cats on this turf.*

cool down *in.* to calm down. □ *Now, just cool down. Chill, chill. Everything's gonna be real cool.* □ *When things cool down around here, life will be much more liveable.*

Cool it! *exclam.* "Calm down!" □ *Take it easy! Cool it!* □ *Come on, cool it, man!*

cool off *in.* to calm down. □ *Now, it's all right. Cool off!* □ *I knew things would cool off eventually.*

cool out *in.* to calm down; to relax. □ *Now, just cool out, man. This will pass.* □ *Everybody cooled out after the emergency, and everything was fine.* (More at *cooled out.*)

cool someone out *tr.* to calm someone; to appease someone. □ *Cool yourselves out, you people. We gotta be sensible.* 🅃 *The manager appeared and tried to cool out everybody, but that was a waste of time.*

cooled out *mod.* calm; unabashed. □ *Ted is a really cooled out kind of guy.* □ *When she's cooled out, she's great.*

cooler *n.* jail. (Usually with *the*.) □ *Do you want to talk, or do you want to spend a little time in the cooler?* □ *Let me outa this cooler!*

cooties ['kudiz] *n.* real or imagined lice. □ *Randy pulled back from me like I had cooties or something. What's wrong with me?* □ *You have cooties, crotch-pheasants, and bad breath. What do you expect?*

cop 1. *tr.* to take or steal something. (Originally underworld.) □ *Somebody copped the statue from the town square.* □ *Who copped the salt from this table?* **2.** *n.* a theft. (Underworld.) □ *They pulled the cop in broad daylight.* □ *It was a lousy cop. No skill. No finesse.* **3.** *n.* a poliee officer. □ *The cop wasn't in any mood to put up with any monkey business.* □ *You call the cops. I've got enough trouble.* **4.** *tr.* to arrest someone. □ *The officer copped him and read him his rights.* □ *They copped Bruno with the evidence right on him.* (More at *copped.*) **5.** *n.* an arrest. □ *It was a smooth cop. No muss, no fuss.* □ *The cop went off without a hitch except for a few little insults.*

cop a drag *tr.* to smoke a cigarette. (See also *drag*.) □ *She kept going off to the john to cop a drag.* □ *Smokers who have to leave the office to cop a drag must cost this nation billions each year.*

cop a fix *tr.* to obtain a dose of drugs. □ *She was gonna, like, die if she didn't cop a fix pretty soon.* □ *She carries her apps so she can cop a fix whenever.*

cop a head *tr.* to become alcohol or drug intoxicated. □ *He was mad and depressed and went home having decided* *to cop a head.* ☐ *The two old codgers sat there copping a head, or trying to anyway.*

cop a plea *tr.* to plead guilty to a lesser charge. ☐ *Rocko copped a plea and got off with a week in the slammer.* ☐ *I wanted to cop a plea, but didn't have the chance.*

cop a squat *tr.* to sit down. ☐ *Hey, man! Come in and cop a squat.* ☐ *Cop a squat and crack a tube.*

cop a tube *tr.* to catch a perfect tubular wave. (Surfers.) ☐ *He was a real pro at copping a tube, and always just the right one.* ☐ *Mark—as drunk as all get out—said he was gonna go out and cop a tube.*

cop an attitude *tr.* to take a negative or opposite attitude about something. (See also *tude*.) ☐ *Look, chum, don't cop an attitude with me!* ☐ *I think you're copping an attitude. Not advised, man. Not advised.*

cop out 1. *in.* to plead guilty (to a lesser charge). (Underworld. See also *cop a plea*.) ☐ *Frank copped out and got off with a night in the cooler.* ☐ *I decided not to cop out and got a mouthpiece instead.* **2.** *in.* to give up and quit; to *chicken out (of something)*. ☐ *Why do you want to cop out just when things are going great?* ☐ *I couldn't cop out on you guys if I wanted to.* **3.** *n.* a poor excuse to get out of something. (Usually **cop-out** or **copout**.) ☐ *This is a silly copout.* ☐ *That's not a good reason. That's just a cop-out.*

cop-shop *n.* a police station. ☐ *They hauled off everybody to the cop-shop.* ☐ *The pigs down at the cop-shop tried to act like they didn't know who Max was.*

cop some Z's See *catch some Z's*.

copasetic [kopəˈsɛdɪk] *mod.* agreeable; satisfactory. (Originally black. Probably from French.) ☐ *Everything is copasetic. Couldn't be better.* ☐ *This is one fine copasetic day.*

copped *mod.* arrested. ☐ *Jed got himself copped—a speeder.* ☐ *I was copped for doing absolutely nothing at all.*

copper 1. *n.* a police officer. (Originally underworld. Because the *copper* "cops" or "takes." See also *cop*.) ☐ *See that copper over there? He busted me once.* ☐ *The coppers will catch up with you some day.* **2.** *n.* money. (From *copper penny*. See also *rivets*.) ☐ *How much copper you got on you?* ☐ *That car takes too much copper to run.*

copy *n.* a piece, as in an item produced. ☐ *We sell the toy at $14 a copy.* ☐ *These cars cost over $20,000 a copy.*

copycat *n.* someone who mimics or copies the actions of others. ☐ *Don't be such a copycat. Find a style that suits you.* ☐ *Jim is a real copycat. He can say anything you say, just the way you say it.*

corked (up) AND **corky** *mod.* alcohol intoxicated. ☐ *You seem to be a little corked.* ☐ *You'd be corked up, too, if you'd drunk as much as I have.*

corker *n.* someone or something good, funny, or entertaining. ☐ *That was a real corker. I thought I'd die laughing.* ☐ *Tracy is quite a corker. I bet she's fun at parties.*

corkscrewed (up) *mod.* courageous because of alcohol; with one's courage screwed by alcohol. ☐ *After getting himself corkscrewed up, he went into the boss's office for a word.* ☐ *He used a bit of vodka to get corkscrewed enough to demand a raise.*

corky See *corked (up)*.

cornball 1. *n.* a stupid or corny person. ☐ *He's a cornball, but he's fun.* ☐ *Who invited this cornball to my party?* **2.** *mod.* stupid or corny. ☐ *What a cornball idea!* ☐ *Ken is such a cornball hick!*

corned *mod.* alcohol intoxicated. ☐ *The old timer is corned on moonshine.* ☐ *Let's go out and get corned.*

cornfed *mod.* rural; backwards; unsophisticated. ☐ *I enjoy her honest, cornfed humor.* ☐ *Jed is a homey, cornfed kind of guy. Don't know anybody who bears him any ill will.*

corny 1. *mod.* having to do with simple-minded, overdrawn humor. ☐ *This corny dialog has to be revised before I'll act in this play.* ☐ *Don't be corny. This is* *serious.* **2.** *mod.* having to do with over-done sentiment. ☐ *The love scenes were your corny hands-off-the-naughty-parts events, but nobody laughed.* ☐ *Harry always laughs at corny mush in a movie.*

corpse 1. *n.* an empty liquor or beer bottle. (See also *dead soldier.*) ☐ *Sam tossed another corpse out the window.* ☐ *Throw your corpses in the trash can, you jerk!* **2.** *n.* a cigarette butt. ☐ *The wino picked up the corpse and put it in a little box of them he carried with him.* ☐ *He is saving corpses to build a real smoke.*

corral dust *n.* nonsense, lies, and exaggeration. (A euphemism for *bullshit.*) ☐ *The way Judy handles the corral dust, she must be running for political office.* ☐ *That stuff is all corral dust. Don't believe a word of it.*

cosmic *mod.* excellent; powerful. ☐ *This pizza is absolutely cosmic!* ☐ *Who wants to see a really cosmic movie?*

cotton-pickin' See the following entry.

cotton-picking AND **cotton-pickin'** *mod.* worthless; damned. (Folksy.) ☐ *What's the cotton-pickin' idea?* ☐ *Who is this cotton-picking bigwig pushing us around?*

couch-doctor AND **couch-turkey** *n.* a psychiatrist; a psychoanalyst. ☐ *Some couch-doctor told her to go out and find a lover.* ☐ *I finally walked out on my couch-turkey. Now I'm getting it all together.*

couch potato *n.* a lazy, do-nothing television watcher. (See also *sofa spud.*) ☐ *If there was a prize for the best couch potato, my husband would win it.* ☐ *You are turning into a perfect couch potato.*

couch-turkey See *couch-doctor.*

cough something up *tr.* to produce something (which someone has requested), usually money. ☐ *Come on, buster, cough it up, now!* ☐ *You owe me seven stereo amplifiers. Now, cough them up!* 🅃 *Cough up what you owe me!*

country drunk *mod.* alcohol intoxicated; drunk and disorganized. (Folksy.) ☐ *Them good old boys know how to get country drunk.* ☐ *The cowboy, really country drunk this time, got to town somehow and started a fight.*

county-mounty *n.* a highway patrol officer. (Citizens band radio.) ☐ *There's a county-mounty waiting under that bridge ahead of you.* ☐ *The county-mounty wrote me seven tickets in that one roust.*

courier *n.* a small-time drug seller; a drug runner; a carrier of contraband. (Drugs.) ☐ *The cops can catch the couriers whenever they want. It's the big guys they're after.* ☐ *The couriers are expendable.*

cover-up *n.* an act of concealing something. ☐ *The cover-up drew more attention than whatever it was that was covered up.* ☐ *The candidate accused her opponent of a cover-up.*

cow *n.* a fat or ugly woman. (Cruel.) ☐ *That cow can hardly get through the door.* ☐ *Wouldn't you think a cow like that would go on a diet?*

cow chips *n.* dried cow dung. ☐ *There's a whole field of cow chips out there! Why do you want to buy a bag of the stuff at a nursery?* ☐ *Break up these cow chips and work them into the soil around the base of the bushes.*

cow-doots [...'duts] *n.* cow dung; masses of cow dung. ☐ *Don was walking through the pasture gathering cow-doots to use as fertilizer.* ☐ *Don't step in the cow-doots.*

cow flop AND **cow plop** *n.* a mass of cow dung. ☐ *Mrs. Wilson is out in the pasture gathering cow flops for her garden.* ☐ *Cow plops are not all the same, you know.*

cow juice See *moo juice.*

cow plop See *cow flop.*

cowboy *n.* a reckless and independent man; a reckless driver. (Also a term of address.) ☐ *Come on, cowboy, finish your coffee and get moving.* ☐ *Some cowboy in a new caddy cut in front of me.*

coyote-ugly ['kaɪot 'əgli OR 'kaɪoti 'əgli] *mod.* extremely ugly. (Crude, cruel, and potentially offensive. Said of people. See also *double-bagger, triple-bagger.* Supposedly, if one woke up and found one's arm around a *coyote-ugly* person, one would chew off one's arm—in the manner of a coyote escaping from a steel-jaw trap—rather than pull it back away from this person.) □ *Is that your pet monkey, or is your date just coyote-ugly?* □ *Isn't that the most coyote-ugly creep you've ever seen?*

cozy up (to someone) *in.* to become overly friendly with someone in hope of gaining special favors. □ *Tracy cozied up to the prof, hoping for a good grade at least.* □ *She failed to read the syllabus, which advised students not to cozy up to the professor or call him at home.*

crab *n.* a louse. (Usually plural.) □ *He's scratching like he's got crabs.* □ *The old wino and his crabs wandered into the flop house for a little peace and quiet.*

crack 1. *n.* a joke; a smart-aleck remark. □ *Another crack like that and your nose will be a little flatter than it is.* □ *Who made that crack?* **2.** *n.* a try (that may or may not succeed). □ *Have another crack at it.* □ *One more crack and I'll have it.* **3.** *n.* a unit of something (for a particular price); a use (of something). □ *You would think twice, too, if you remembered that it's seven dollars a crack.* □ *At two dollars a crack, this is the best game on the midway.* **4.** *n.* crystalline, smokable cocaine. (Drugs.) □ *This crack seems to have become the drug of choice for punks of all ages.* □ *Crack became popular when it became easy and cheap to process. It's been around for years in medicinal form.* **5.** *in.* to break down and talk under pressure. (Underworld.) □ *They kept at her till she finally cracked and talked.* □ *We knew you'd finally crack.* **6.** *mod.* (of a person) excellent; top-flight. □ *The dealer's crack salesman was no help at all.* □ *With our crack staff, we can have everything worked out in no time.* **7.** *tr.* to break into something. (Underworld.) □ *We almost cracked the safe before the alarm went off.* □ *His specialty is cracking car trunks and stealing tires.*

crack a book *tr.* to open a book to study. (Usually in the negative.) □ *I never cracked a book and still passed the course.* □ *Sally didn't crack a book all semester.*

crack a tube *tr.* to open a can of beer. (See also *tube.*) □ *Why don't you drop over this evening, and we'll crack a few tubes?* □ *Would you crack a tube for me? My hands are too cold.*

crack house *n.* a house or dwelling where *crack* is sold and used. (Drugs.) □ *The police are continuing their efforts to close down crack houses in the area.* □ *In one dilapidated neighborhood, there is a crack house on every block.*

crack open a bottle *tr.* to open a bottle of liquor. (Also with *the.*) □ *Let's crack open a bottle and celebrate.* 🅃 *He cracked the bottle open and poured a little for everyone to try.*

crack some suds *tr.* to drink some beer. □ *Let's go out tonight and crack some suds.* □ *The guys wanted to watch the game and crack some suds.*

crack someone up *tr.* to make someone laugh. □ *She giggled, and that cracked us all up.* 🅃 *The lecturer would talk along sort of boring like, and then all of a sudden he would crack up everybody with a joke.*

crack up [kræk'əp] **1.** *in.* to have a wreck. □ *The plane cracked up and killed two of the passengers.* □ *Whose car cracked up on the expressway?* **2.** *in.* to break out in laughter. □ *The whole audience cracked up.* □ *I knew I would crack up during the love scene.* **3.** *in.* to have a nervous breakdown. □ *The poor guy cracked up. It was too much for him.* □ *You would crack up, too, if you had been through all he went through.* **4.** ['krækəp] *n.* an accident; a wreck. (Usually **crack-up**.) □ *There was a terrible crack-up on the expressway.* □ *There were four cars in the crack-up.*

crackbrain *n.* a fool; a stupid oaf. □ *Did you hear about the crackbrain who found part of the sky floating in the lake?* □

Sometimes you are quite a crackbrain yourself.

crackbrained *mod.* stupid; ridiculous. □ *I've heard enough of your crackbrained schemes.* □ *One more crackbrained idea and you're fired.*

cracked *mod.* crazy. □ *You're cracked if you think I'll agree to that.* □ *You gotta be cracked if you think I'm going back in there.*

cracked up to be *mod.* supposed to be. □ *This pizza isn't what it's cracked up to be.* □ *I wanted to find out whether this stuff was what it is cracked up to be.*

crackerjack ['krækəʳdʒæk] *mod.* excellent; industrious. □ *Fred is a crackerjack stockbroker, but his personal life is a mess.* □ *Clare is a crackerjack teacher, but she is looking for something that pays a real salary.*

crackers See *bonkers.*

crackhead *n.* a user of *crack.* (Drugs.) □ *They brought an eight-year-old crackhead in for treatment.* □ *Crackheads are a very serious problem in the nation's work force.*

crackpot **1.** *n.* a fake; a person with strange or crazy plans. □ *Some crackpot called to tell us that the sky is falling in.* □ *I'm no crackpot! I saw some of the sky floating in the lake. If it had fallen on land, someone might have been killed.* **2.** *mod.* having to do with crazy things, mainly ideas. □ *We need a crackpot idea around here just so we'll have something to compare your ideas to.* □ *Why not start a crackpot idea contest?*

cram *in.* to study hard at the last minute for a test. □ *She spent the night cramming for the test.* □ *If you would study all the time, you wouldn't need to cram.*

crank **1.** *n.* a *crackpot;* a bothersome person with a bogus message. □ *A crank called with a bomb threat.* □ *A crank came in and offered to punch me in the nose for a quarter.* **2.** *mod.* bogus. □ *We had four crank calls threatening to blow up the Eiffel tower.* □ *A crank letter promised us a million dollars if we would play "My Blue Heaven" for two hours each morning.* **3.** *n.* a crabby person. (Collegiate.) □ *Why are you such a crank? Is something wrong in your life?* □ *The prof is such a crank; he jokes only about once a semester.*

crank bugs *n.* a drug-induced hallucination that insects are crawling under one's skin. (Drugs.) □ *I have crank bugs, and I'm cartooning, too.* □ *There's no such thing as crank bugs, so stop scratching them.*

crank something out *tr.* to produce something; to make a lot of something. □ *She can crank mystery novels out like fury. They're all good, too.* 🅃 *That man does nothing but crank out trouble.*

crank something up **1.** *tr.* to start something up. □ *I'll go out and crank the car up so it can warm up.* 🅃 *Crank up the copying machine. We've got a big job to do.* **2.** *tr.* to increase the volume of an electronic device. □ *He cranked it up a little more and CRACK, there went both speakers!* 🅃 *Kelly cranked up his stereo until we were nearly deafened.*

cranking *mod.* exciting; excellent. □ *This record is really cranking!* □ *We had a massively cranking time at your set.*

cranky *mod.* irritable; fretful. □ *Don't be cranky. We're almost there.* □ *Max is cranky today. The fuzz is on his tail.*

crap [kræp] **1.** *n.* junk; worthless matter. □ *Why don't you just throw this crap away?* □ *Get your crap off my bed!* **2.** *n.* dung. (Potentially offensive. Use only with discretion. Colloquial.) □ *There's dog crap on the lawn.* □ *Don't step in that crap.* **3.** *n.* nonsense; lies. □ *I've had enough of your crap. Now talk straight, or out you go.* □ *Cut the crap!* **4.** *in.* to defecate. (Crude. Potentially offensive. Use only with discretion.) □ *Your dog crapped on my lawn!* □ *I have to crap; then I'll be right with you.*

crap out *in.* to evade something; to chicken out (of something). □ *Now, don't crap out on me at the last minute.*

☐ *Fred crapped out, so there are only three of us.*

craphouse *n.* a privy. (Potentially offensive. Use only with discretion. Colloquial.) ☐ *Wally's out in the craphouse reading, I guess.* ☐ *Where's the craphouse that used to be out there?*

crapper 1. *n.* a toilet, privy, or restroom. (Potentially offensive. Use only with discretion. See also *crap.* Colloquial.) ☐ *Where's the crapper around here?* ☐ *Old Jed never passes up a chance to use an indoor crapper.* **2.** *n.* a braggart. (Crude.) ☐ *The guy is a crapper and can't be trusted at all.* ☐ *Don't listen to the crapper.*

crapper dick *n.* a police officer or detective who patrols public toilets. ☐ *When he flubbed up the Wilson case, they made him a crapper dick in the central business district.* ☐ *What's a crapper dick get paid?*

crappy *mod.* bad; lousy; junky. ☐ *This is sure one crappy day!* ☐ *Shut your crappy mouth!*

crapshoot *n.* a gamble; a matter of chance. (Like a crap (dice) game.) ☐ *Basically, life is a crapshoot.* ☐ *The stock market isn't concerned with value anymore. It's just a crapshoot.*

crash 1. *tr. & in.* to attend a party or other event uninvited. ☐ *Some clown tried to crash the rally, but my dad called the cops.* ☐ *The boys who tried to crash also broke a window.* (More at *crasher.*) **2.** *in.* to spend the night. (See also *crash pad.*) ☐ *I crashed at a friend's place in the city.* ☐ *You have a place I can crash?* **3.** *n.* a place to sleep. ☐ *I think I know of a crash for tonight.* ☐ *Molly's on the phone, looking for a crash.* **4.** *in.* [for a computer] to stop working. ☐ *This thing crashes every time I hit a certain key.* ☐ *My machine hasn't crashed since I got it.* **5.** *n.* a total failure of a computer. ☐ *Most of my data was lost in the crash.* ☐ *Crashes are to teach you to back up your data.* **6.** *in.* [for any electronic device] to fail. ☐ *My stereo crashed, so I've been watching T.V.* ☐ *My T.V. crashed, and I had to go out to watch at somebody else's house.* **7.** *in.* [for a securities market] to lose a significant portion of its value in a short time. ☐ *The market crashed and scared the stuffing out of everybody.* ☐ *When the bond market crashed, the press didn't even realize it.* **8.** *n.* a collapse of a securities market. ☐ *After the crash, a lot of people swore off the market for good.* ☐ *A crash like that was too much for a lot of people.* **9.** *in.* to pass out from drinking alcohol to excess. ☐ *About midnight I crashed, and I woke up here.* ☐ *Let's get Wilbur home before he crashes for good.*

crash and burn *in.* [for a young man] to fail brilliantly with a romance. (Collegiate. See also *go down in flames.*) ☐ *I knew I would crash and burn with her.* ☐ *It stands to reason that if Ken hadn't shot me down, I wouldn't have crashed and burned.*

crash pad *n.* a place to stay the night on short notice. ☐ *I've got a crash pad in the city for emergencies like this.* ☐ *I gotta find a crash pad for tonight.*

crashed 1. *mod.* alcohol intoxicated. ☐ *Fred is crashed. Leave him alone.* ☐ *There were two crashed freshmen asleep on the lawn.* **2.** *mod.* raided by the police. (See also *bust.*) ☐ *Our pad got crashed, and a lot of kids were arrested.* ☐ *After the place was crashed, it was a mess.*

crasher *n.* a person who attends a party uninvited. (See also *crash.*) ☐ *The crashers ruined the party, and my dad called the cops.* ☐ *The crashers were no more rude than the guests.*

crate *n.* a dilapidated vehicle. ☐ *Where'd you get that old crate?* ☐ *This crate gets me to work and back. That's good enough.*

crater 1. *n.* an acne scar. ☐ *Ted has a nasty crater on his cheek.* ☐ *Walter was always sort of embarrassed about his craters.* **2.** *in.* to collapse and go down as with a falling stock price. ☐ *The stock cratered and probably won't recover for a year or two.* ☐ *When my portfolio cratered, I thought it was the end of the* *world. Then most of the prices came back up in a month.*

crater-face AND **pizza-face; pizza-puss** *n.* someone with an acne-scarred face. (Cruel. Collegiate. Also a term of address.) □ *Who's the crater-face putting the moves on Sally?* □ *Pizza-puss over there is talking sort of loud.*

crawling with someone or something *mod.* covered with someone or something; alive with someone or something. □ *The place was crawling with police and F.B.I. agents.* □ *The room was just crawling with ants.*

crazy 1. *n.* a crazy person. □ *The guy's a crazy, and he keeps coming in here asking for money.* □ *I think the crazies are taking over the world.* **2.** *mod.* cool. □ *This stuff is really crazy, man. I love it!* □ *What a crazy dress. It makes you look like a million.*

crazy bone *n.* the elbow. □ *Ouch! I hit my crazy bone!* □ *Ken hit his crazy bone as he went into church, and was yelling "Oh! Oh! Oh!" as if the Spirit had got into him or something.*

cream *tr.* to beat someone; to outscore someone. □ *The other team creamed us, but we had better team spirit.* □ *We'll cream 'em next week.*

cream puff 1. *n.* a weakling; a *wimp.* □ *Don't be a cream puff all your life! Join a health club!* □ *We're having a cream puff special this week for you clowns who can't climb stairs without panting.* **2.** *n.* a used car that is in very good condition. □ *This one is a real cream puff. Only driven to church by a little old lady.* □ *This cream puff is loaded, air and everything.*

creamed 1. *mod.* beaten; outscored. □ *We were really creamed in that last game, and the coach is steamed.* □ *Midwest U. got creamed again today by the Podunk Badgers.* **2.** *mod.* alcohol intoxicated. □ *Man, Tony is totally creamed!* □ *I got myself creamed last night, didn't I?*

creased *mod.* exhausted. □ *What a day. I am totally creased.* □ *Here is one creased football player. Let him hit the rack.*

creep *n.* a weird person; an eerie person. □ *Charlie is such a creep when he's stoned.* □ *I thought Charlie was a creep no matter what.*

creep dive See the following entry.

creep joint AND **creep dive** *n.* an unpleasant place populated by creeps. □ *You shouldn't go into a creep joint like that alone.* □ *Why would anyone want to work in a creep dive like that?*

creeping-crud 1. *n.* any unidentified disease. □ *There is some kind of creeping-crud between my toes.* □ *I got the creeping-crud growing in my armpit.* **2.** *n.* a repellent person. □ *Wally has become such a creeping-crud since he inherited all that money.* □ *Don't be a creeping-crud. Just go back to being a plain crud.* **3.** *n.* any nasty, slimy substance. □ *You got creeping-crud all over my pants leg.* □ *That's not creeping-crud! That's my pecan pie!*

creeps *n.* the jitters; a case of nerves. (Always with *the*.) □ *These movies always give me the creeps.* □ *The creeps always make me have to go to the john.*

creepy *mod.* eerie; frightening. □ *I have this creepy feeling that someone is just this very moment reading something that I wrote.* □ *This is the creepiest old house I have ever been in.*

crib 1. *n.* a location where thieves gather to plot; a dwelling for thieves, prostitutes, etc. (Underworld.) □ *The police busted a crib over on Fourth Street.* □ *They use a basement over there for a crib.* **2.** *n.* a dwelling. (Underworld.) □ *Where's your crib, man?* □ *My good threads are all back at my crib.*

crib course *n.* an easy course in college. □ *Tom signed up for three crib courses and gym. What a twit!* □ *Andy thought he was getting into a crib course, but it turned out to be really hard.*

cricket *mod.* acceptable. (Compare to *kosher.* See negative examples at *not cricket.*) □ *Is it really cricket to play under two different names?* □ *Who cares if it's cricket!*

crisco ['krɪsko] *n.* a fat person. (Cruel. Also a rude term of address. The brand name of a baking shortening.) □ *Some crisco came in and ordered ten large fries.* □ *Hey, crisco! Go on a diet!*

crisp *mod.* drug intoxicated. □ *The crisp guy waving the bra is the one we are after.* □ *Man, is he crisp!*

crispy-critter *n.* a person under the effects of marijuana. (From the brand name of a breakfast cereal.) □ *He's fried all right. A real crispy-critter.* □ *A crispy-critter came in and tried to sell me his watch.*

croak **1.** *in.* to die; to expire; to succumb. □ *I was afraid I'd croak.* □ *The parrot croaked before I got it home.* **2.** *tr.* to kill someone. □ *The car croaked the cat just like that.* □ *Somebody croaked my parrot.*

crock **1.** *n.* nonsense. (See also *crock of shit.*) □ *What a crock! You don't know what you are talking about!* □ *This whole business is a crock. Hell, life's a crock!* **2.** *n.* a drunkard. □ *Give the old crock some money, anything to get him outa here before he barfs or something.* □ *The crock wants booze, not money.*

crock of shit (Potentially offensive. Use only with discretion.) **1.** *n.* something really awful; a great mass of nonsense. □ *That whole place is just a crock of shit. Nobody knows what's what.* □ *You went on vacation and left this office with a real crock of shit.* **2.** *n.* a worthless person. □ *Who is that crock of shit who brought in the dead cat?* □ *Some crock of shit put my coat on the floor!*

crocked [krakt] *mod.* alcohol intoxicated. □ *What do you get out of getting crocked very night?* □ *Oh, my God! You're crocked again!*

crockery *n.* the teeth. (See also *China.*) □ *I gotta go to the dentist for some work on my crockery.* □ *Is that your own crockery?*

cromagnon [kro'mægnən] *n.* an ugly male. (Collegiate.) □ *Who is that cromagnon you were with last night?* □ *That was no cromagnon. That was your blind date for next weekend.*

cross-eyed (drunk) *mod.* alcohol intoxicated. □ *What's the point of getting cross-eyed drunk?* □ *He sat on the bar stool, cross-eyed and crying.*

cross someone (up) AND **cross up someone** *tr.* to go against someone; to thwart someone. □ *Don't cross me up if you know what's good for you.* □ *I told you not to cross me again!*

cross up someone See *cross someone (up).*

crotch-pheasant ['kratʃfɛzn̩t] *n.* a louse. (Usually in the plural.) □ *He appears to be afflicted with what you might call crotch-pheasants.* □ *There is a special medicine that will get rid of crotch-pheasants.*

crotch-rot *n.* a skin irritation or disease characterized by itching in the genital area, usually said of males. (See also *grunge.*) □ *What will get rid of crotch-rot?* □ *Here's some medicine for crotch-rot.*

crowd **1.** *tr.* to pressure or threaten someone. □ *Don't crowd me!* □ *Max began to crowd Bruno, which was the wrong thing to do.* **2.** *tr.* to gang up on someone. □ *Some guys were crowding Todd, so we chased them off.* □ *They moved in from all sides, carrying clubs, and began to crowd us.*

crown *tr.* to hit someone on the head. □ *The clerk crowned the robber with a champagne bottle.* □ *The bride, at the end of her patience, crowned the stuttering cleric with her bouquet, shouted "I do," and began kissing the groom.*

crud [krəd] **1.** *n.* nastiness; junk; worthless matter. □ *This is just crud. Get rid of it.* □ *Get all that old crud out of the attic so we can have room for newer stuff.* **2.** *n.* a repellent person. □ *Don't be such a crud!* □ *That crud kept trying to paw me!*

cruddie See the following entry.

cruddy AND **crudy; cruddie** ['krədi] *mod.* nasty; awful. □ *What is this cruddy stuff on my plate?* □ *It's just chocolate mousse, and it's not cruddie.*

crudy See the previous entry.

cruise **1.** *in.* to travel at top speed. □ *This old caddy can really cruise.* □ *We cruised all the way to Philly.* **2.** *in.* to drive around looking for friends or social activity. □ *We went out cruising, but didn't see anybody.* □ *Let's go cruise for a while.* **3.** *tr.* to pursue a member of the opposite sex. □ *Tom was cruising Tiffany, but she got rid of him.* □ *Are you cruising me, Tom? You know you just barf me, like, out!* **4.** *in.* to move on; to leave. □ *Listen, I gotta cruise.* □ *Time to cruise. Monty Python's on in ten minutes.* **5.** *in.* to move through life at a comfortable pace. □ *I just want to get a good job and cruise for a while.* □ *I'm cruising just the way I want now.* **6.** *tr.* to pass a course easily. □ *I'm gonna cruise that math course.* □ *Tom really cruised English this semester.*

cruiser *n.* a car; a fast car. □ *This old hog is a real cruiser.* □ *I don't want a yuppie cruiser, just an old family wagon.*

cruisin' for a bruisin' See the following entry.

cruising for a bruising AND **cruisin' for a bruisin'** ['kruzn̩ for ə 'bruzn̩] *in.* asking for trouble. □ *You are cruising for a bruising, you know that?* □ *Who's cruisin' for a bruisin'?*

crum something up *tr.* to mess something up; to make something crummy. □ *Who crummed the bird feeder up?* 🅃 *Now don't crum up this deal.*

crumb [krəm] *n.* a repellent person. □ *The old man was a crumb and tried to cheat us.* □ *Micky is a crumb, and he treats me like dirt.*

crumbum ['krəmbəm] **1.** *n.* a repellent person; a bum. □ *A skid row crumbum asked us for a buck.* □ *I gave the crumbum a buck and hoped he would leave.* **2.** *mod.* inferior; lousy. □ *I sent the crumbum food back to the kitchen. There was a bug in it.* □ *I want out of this crumbum place.*

crumby See the following entry.

crummy AND **crumby** ['krəmi] *mod.* lousy; bad; inferior. □ *You know, this stuff is pretty crummy.* □ *It's worse than crumby.*

crumped (out) **1.** *mod.* alcohol intoxicated. □ *She was too crumped out to drive herself home.* □ *Are you crumped out again?* **2.** *mod.* dead. □ *Our old dog crumped out at age fourteen.* □ *Uncle Dave is crumped and now there's nobody left to drive that 1952 Cadillac.* □ *I am so tired. I feel half-crumped.*

crunch *n.* a crisis; a time of pressure or tightness, especially of a budget. □ *We seem to be in a crunch of one kind or another all the time.* □ *The budget crunch meant that we couldn't take trips to Europe anymore.*

crunchers *n.* the feet. □ *My crunchers are sore from all this walking.* □ *New shoes can be hard on your crunchers.*

crunchie *n.* a soldier; a marching infantry soldier. (Military. See also *crunchers.*) □ *A couple of crunchies were complaining about the Army.* □ *Crunchies have a pretty hard life.*

crust *n.* nerve; gall. □ *She's got a lot of crust—coming in here like that.* □ *It takes crust to sell this stuff to somebody. You really gotta push.*

crusty *mod.* feisty; gruff. □ *Jed is a crusty old man.* □ *Unlike most crusty, avuncular old men, Jed hasn't a single redeeming quality.*

crutch *n.* a device to hold a marijuana cigarette butt. □ *Here's a crutch so you can finish your smoke.* □ *I lost my crutch.*

cry hughie ['krɑɪ 'hjui] *in.* to empty one's stomach; to vomit. □ *He is in the john crying hughie.* □ *I think I gotta go cry hughie.*

cry in one's beer *in.* to feel sorry for oneself. □ *She calls up, crying in her beer, and talks on and on about her problems.* □ *Don't cry in your beer. Get yourself straightened out.*

cry ralph See the following entry.

cry ruth AND **call ruth; call ralph; cry ralph** [...'ruθ AND...'rɑlf] *tr.* to empty one's stomach; to vomit. (See also *ruth*. Also with capital *r*.) ☐ *Someone is in the bushes crying ruth.* ☐ *I think I have to cry ruth! Stop the car!*

crying drunk *mod.* alcohol intoxicated and weeping. ☐ *She was crying drunk and feeling sorry for herself.* ☐ *I really hate it when they come in here crying drunk.*

crying towel *n.* someone or something used to comfort someone. ☐ *I guess I really need a crying towel today.* ☐ *I'm the kind of person who has to carry a crying towel at all times.*

crying weed *n.* marijuana. (Compare to *up pot.*) ☐ *I must have got hold of some crying weed. This stuff leaves me cold.* ☐ *On a rainy day, crying weed seems just right.*

crystal **1.** *n.* crystallized cocaine. (Drugs. See also *crack.*) ☐ *I wonder how much crystal is used in this country each day.* ☐ *Crystal—an older name for crack—was a favorite many years ago.* **2.** *n.* liquid Methedrine™ in glass ampoules. (Drugs.) ☐ *I hear that Wally's shooting crystal. Is that true?* ☐ *Max has lots of crystal right now.*

cube [kjub] **1.** *n.* a very *square* person. ☐ *This nerd was the most unbelievable cube you have ever seen.* ☐ *Not just an L7, a real cube.* **2.** *n.* a die, one of a pair of dice. (Usually in the plural.) ☐ *Toss me the cubes.* ☐ *She shook the cubes, saying "Baby needs shoes!"* **3.** *n.* a sugar cube impregnated with *L.S.D.* (Drugs. Often in the plural.) ☐ *First they took it on cubes. Then on little bits of paper.* ☐ *The cubes were usually bluish.*

cuckoo See *coo-coo*.

cuddle bunny *n.* a female lover. ☐ *All you want is a cuddle bunny with big tits! Grow up, Maxwell Wilson!* ☐ *Who is that cuddle bunny driving the caddy?*

cuff *tr.* to put a charge on one's bill. ☐ *Would you cuff this for me, please?* ☐ *Sorry, I can't cuff anymore for you.*

cuff quote *n.* an off-the-cuff quote of a financial instrument price. (Securities markets.) ☐ *This is just a cuff quote, but I would say it's about ninety-four.* ☐ *I can give you a cuff quote of ninety-two, but don't hold me to it.*

cuffs *n.* handcuffs. ☐ *I felt the cuffs tighten and snap shut on my wrists.* ☐ *The cuffs carried the cold of the night to my bare skin. Of course, I was innocent, but that's not the way it works in real life.*

cull *n.* a socially unacceptable person. ☐ *Who's the cull driving the Edsel?* ☐ *This place is filled with culls. Let's split.*

culture-vulture **1.** *n.* an avid supporter of the arts. ☐ *A gaggle of culture-vultures gawked its way into the gallery.* ☐ *Many culture-vultures seem to be long on enthusiasm and short on taste.* **2.** *n.* someone who exploits the arts for monetary gain. ☐ *Mr. Babbit, a well-known culture-vulture in art circles, never could pass up a chance to grab up all the works of an up-and-coming young artist.* ☐ *Some culture-vultures are throwing a wine and cheese party on behalf of some of the young dolts they have grubstaked.*

cum See the following entry.

cume AND **cum** [kjum] *n.* a cumulative average, such as a grade-point average. ☐ *My cume is not high enough to get into law school.* ☐ *My cum is a straight A.*

cup of tea *n.* something preferred or desired. (Often negative.) ☐ *This drug scene stuff is just not my cup of tea.* ☐ *Driving children around all afternoon is not my cup of tea.*

cupcake *n.* an attractive woman. (Also a term of address.) ☐ *Hey, cupcake, what ya doing?* ☐ *Who is that cupcake driving the beemer?*

curl up and die *in.* to retreat and die. (Often figurative.) ☐ *I was so embarrassed, I thought I would just curl up and die.* ☐ *The old cat, finishing up the last of its nine lives, just curled up and died.*

curse *n.* the menses. (Always with *the*.) ☐ *The curse struck this morning.* ☐ *Oh, the woes of the curse!*

curtains *n.* death. (Underworld.) ☐ *It's curtains for you if you don't come across.* ☐ *Okay, Barlowe, this time it's curtains.*

cushy ['kuʃi] *mod.* soft; easy. (From *cushion.*) ☐ *He's got sort of a cushy job.* ☐ *That's a cushy kind of life to lead.*

cut 1. *mod.* alcohol intoxicated. ☐ *She's too cut to drive.* ☐ *He got cut on beer, which is unusual for him.* **2.** *tr.* to dilute something. ☐ *She always cuts her eggnog with cola. Yuck!* ☐ *You can cut the saltiness with a little sugar.* **3.** *n.* a share of the loot or the profits. (Originally underworld.) ☐ *I want my cut now.* ☐ *You'll get your cut when everybody else does.* **4.** *n.* a single song or section of music on a record. ☐ *This next cut is one everybody likes.* ☐ *Let's listen to another cut of the same album.* **5.** *tr.* to eliminate something; to stop (doing something). ☐ *Okay, chum, cut the clowning.* ☐ *Cut that noise! Not another peep out of you.*

cut a check *tr.* to write a check. ☐ *We'll cut the check tonight and send it out in tomorrow's mail.* ☐ *Please cut a check for Mr. Babbit. Here's the amount.*

cut a deal *tr.* to arrange a deal; to seal a bargain. ☐ *Maybe we can cut a deal. Let's talk.* ☐ *The two lawyers cut a deal that left me with the furniture, although she got the house.*

cut and run *in.* to stop what one is doing and flee. ☐ *The cops were coming, so we cut and run.* ☐ *At the first warning, we cut and run.*

cut corners *tr.* to do something more easily; to take shortcuts; to save money by finding cheaper ways to do something. ☐ *They're always finding ways to cut corners.* ☐ *I won't cut corners just to save money. I put quality first.*

Cut it out! *exclam.* "Stop it!" ☐ *That's enough! Cut it out!* ☐ *Get your hands off me! Cut it out!*

cut loose *in.* to let go; to become independent. ☐ *It was hard to cut loose from home.* ☐ *I guess it's time I cut loose.*

cut no ice (with someone) *tr.* to have no influence on someone; to fail to convince someone. ☐ *I don't care who you are. It cuts no ice with me.* ☐ *So you're the mayor's daughter. It still cuts no ice.*

cut one's losses *tr.* to do something to stop a loss of something. ☐ *I knew I had to do something to cut my losses, but it was almost too late.* ☐ *Sell some of the high-priced stuff to cut your losses.*

cut one's own throat *tr.* to do something that harms oneself. ☐ *If I do that, I'd be cutting my own throat.* ☐ *He's just cutting his own throat, and he knows it.*

cut one's wolf loose *tr.* to go on a drinking bout; to get drunk. ☐ *I'm gonna go out and cut my wolf loose tonight.* ☐ *You're going to cut your wolf loose too often and really get into trouble.*

cut out *in.* to leave; to run away. ☐ *It's late. I think I'll cut out.* ☐ *Don't cut out now. The night is young.*

cut-rate *mod.* cheap; low-priced. ☐ *I don't want any cut-rate stuff.* ☐ *Where are your cut-rate sweaters?*

cut some Z's See *catch some Z's.*

cut someone a break *tr.* to give someone a break. ☐ *Come on, cut me a break! I'm a good guy!* ☐ *I was only a few minutes late! Cut me a break! Don't dock my pay!*

cut someone in (on something) *tr.* to permit someone to share something. ☐ *You promised you would cut me in on this caper.* ☐ *We can't cut you in. There's not enough.*

cut the cheese AND **cut the mustard** *tr.* to release intestinal gas. (Crude. Use caution with the topic.) ☐ *Who cut the cheese?* ☐ *People who cut the mustard in the car have to get out and walk.*

Cut the comedy! *exclam.* "Get serious!"; "Stop acting silly!" ☐ *That's enough, you guys. Cut the comedy!* ☐ *Cut the comedy and get to work!*

Cut the crap! *exclam.* "Stop the nonsense!" ☐ *I've heard enough. Cut the crap!* ☐ *Cut the crap. Talk straight or get out.*

cut the dust *tr.* to take a drink of liquor. ☐ *I think I'll stop in here and cut the dust.* ☐ *I want to cut the dust. Can I have a snort?*

cut the mustard **1.** *tr.* to be able to do something requiring youth or vigor. (Usually in the expression **too old to cut the mustard.**) ☐ *Do you really think he can cut the mustard?* ☐ *She's not too old to cut the mustard.* **2.** See *cut the cheese.*

cut to the chase *in.* to focus on what is important; to abandon the preliminaries and deal with the major points. ☐ *All right, let's stop the idle chatter and cut to the chase.* ☐ *After a few introductory comments, we cut to the chase and began negotiating.*

cut (up) *mod.* having well-defined abdominal muscles. ☐ *Greg is really cut up. He works out every day.* ☐ *Andy works hard to try to get a gut that's cut.*

cut up (about someone or something) *mod.* emotionally upset about someone or something. ☐ *She was all cut up about her divorce.* ☐ *You could see how cut up she was.*

cutie *n.* a cute thing or person. (Also a term of address.) ☐ *Your baby is a real cutie.* ☐ *Come here, cutie, let me fix your collar.*

cutie pie *n.* a cute person, typically a woman or a baby. (Also a term of address.) ☐ *She is such a cutie pie.* ☐ *What's your name, cutie pie?*

cuz [kəz] *n.* cousin. (Old colloquial.) ☐ *I've got to go to Denver to visit my cuz.* ☐ *My cuz came to visit for the weekend.*

D

dad *n.* one's father; any father; any old man. (Also a term of address. Capitalized when referring to one's own father.) ☐ *Hey, Dad, can I use the car tonight?* ☐ *Well, dad, how's it going?*

daddy (of them all) See *(grand)daddy (of them all).*

daffy ['dæfi] *mod.* silly; crazy. ☐ *Kelly was acting daffy because she was so happy.* ☐ *Oh, don't be daffy!*

dagwood (sandwich) ['dægwud . . .] *n.* a tall sandwich with many layers of food. (From the comic strip character *Dagwood* by Chick Young.) ☐ *I really like to make an old-fashioned dagwood sandwich every now and then.* ☐ *How many calories are there in a dagwood, on the average?*

daily dozen *n.* a short set of daily exercises. ☐ *I need to do my daily dozen before breakfast.* ☐ *A daily dozen would be good for you.*

daily grind *n.* the tedious pattern of daily work. (See also *rat race.*) ☐ *Well, it's Monday. Time to start another week of the daily grind.* ☐ *The daily grind really gets me down.*

daisy *n.* an excellent thing. (Compare to *doosie.*) ☐ *This little car is a real daisy.* ☐ *I want a daisy of a haircut. Something unusual with bangs or something.*

damage *n.* the cost; the amount of the bill (for something). (Compare to *bad news.*) ☐ *Okay, waiter. What's the damage?* ☐ *As soon as I pay the damage, we can go.*

dank [dæŋk] **1.** *mod.* very good. ☐ *We stopped for a while in this real dank little bistro on the main boulevard.* ☐ *This wine is so dank!* **2.** *mod.* very bad. ☐ *Class was so dank today. I thought I would die of terminal boredom.* ☐ *This is a real dank day. I hope it's over soon.*

dap [dæp] *mod.* well-dressed. (From *dapper.*) ☐ *Who is that dap looking dude?* ☐ *Man, you look dap!*

darb [dɑrb] *n.* an excellent person or thing. ☐ *Carl is a real darb. I'm glad to know him.* ☐ *What a swell darb of a car!*

dark horse **1.** *n.* an unknown entrant into a contest; a surprise candidate for political office. ☐ *The party is hoping that a dark horse will appear before the election.* ☐ *You'd be surprised at how eagerly people will vote for a dark horse.* **2.** *mod.* previously unknown. ☐ *Who would vote for a dark horse candidate?* ☐ *A dark horse player can win if all the others are creeps.*

Dash it all! *exclam.* "Oh, phooey!"; "To hell with it all!" ☐ *Oh, dash it all! I'm late.* ☐ *I broke it! Dash it all!*

day one *n.* the first day. ☐ *You haven't done anything right since day one! You're fired!* ☐ *She was unhappy with her new car even on day one.*

day person *n.* a person who prefers to be active during the daytime. (Compare to *night person.*) ☐ *I am strictly a day person. Have to be in bed early.* ☐ *The Count insisted that he was not a day person, and he had to remain on his home ground until nightfall.*

day the eagle flies See *when the eagle flies.*

day-tripper *n.* a tourist who makes one-day trips. ☐ *At about 4:00* P.M. *the day-trippers start thinning out.* ☐ *Being a* *day-tripper is hard on your feet sometimes.*

dead 1. *mod.* quiet and uneventful; boring. ☐ *The day was totally dead.* ☐ *What a dead day!* ☐ *Things were sure dead around this town this summer.* 2. *mod.* very tired. ☐ *I am just dead from all that jogging.* ☐ *I went home from the office, dead as usual.* 3. *mod.* dull; lifeless; flat. ☐ *This meal is sort of dead because I am out of onions.* ☐ *The pop went dead because someone left it open.* ☐ *Who wants dead pop?* 4. *mod.* no longer effective; no longer of any consequence. ☐ *You're dead, Fred. You can't help us anymore.* ☐ *That guy is dead—out of power.* 5. *mod.* (of an issue) no longer germane; no longer of any importance. ☐ *Forget it! It's a dead issue.* ☐ *The project is dead. Don't waste any more time on it.*

dead and gone 1. *mod.* (of a person) long dead. ☐ *Old Gert's been dead and gone for quite a spell.* ☐ *When I'm dead and gone, I hope folks remember me at my best.* 2. *mod.* (of a thing) gone long ago. ☐ *That kind of thinking is dead and gone.* ☐ *The horse and buggy days are dead and gone.*

dead broke *mod.* completely broke; without any money. ☐ *I'm dead broke—not a nickel to my name.* ☐ *I've been dead broke for a month now.*

dead-catty *mod.* with only a slight bounce. (See the explanation at *dead-cat bounce.* Securities markets.) ☐ *We expected the stock to go up a lot today, but the increase was no better than dead-catty.* ☐ *It was just a dead-catty day in spite of the good economic news.*

dead cinch *n.* an absolute certainty; an easy thing to do. ☐ *It's a dead cinch. I foresee no problems.* ☐ *The job was no dead cinch, but we did it on time.*

dead drunk *mod.* alcohol intoxicated; totally inebriated. ☐ *They were both dead drunk. They could only lie there and snore.* ☐ *Marty is dead drunk again.*

dead duck *n.* a person or thing doomed to failure or disaster. ☐ *This whole plan was a dead duck from the beginning.* ☐ *Wally is a dead duck because he flunked astronomy.*

dead easy *mod.* very easy. ☐ *This whole job is dead easy.* ☐ *It was so dead easy, Frank did it with one hand.*

dead-end kid *n.* a youth with no future, usually a male. ☐ *Kelly wasn't your typical dead-end kid.* ☐ *Max was a dead-end kid from the day he was born.*

dead from the neck up 1. *mod.* stupid. (With a "dead" head.) ☐ *Beavis seems dead from the neck up.* ☐ *She acts like she is dead from the neck up.* 2. *mod.* no longer open to new ideas. ☐ *My uncle is dead from the neck up. A real fossil.* ☐ *Everyone on the board of directors is dead from the neck up.*

dead horse *n.* a *dead issue,* especially one that is referred to continually. (Often with *beat, whip.*) ☐ *Forget it! Don't waste time whipping a dead horse.* ☐ *The whole business is a dead horse. Forget it.*

dead in the water *mod.* stalled; immobile. (Originally nautical.) ☐ *This whole company is dead in the water.* ☐ *The project is dead in the water for the time being.*

dead issue *n.* an issue that doesn't matter anymore. ☐ *It's a dead issue. Forget it.* ☐ *The question of my late arrival is a dead issue.*

dead letter 1. *n.* a letter that cannot move through the post office because the addressee does not exist or because the address is wrong or illegible. (Standard English.) ☐ *Every now and then they open the dead letters to see if they can figure out who they were meant for.* ☐ *Sometimes dead letters have return addresses in them.* 2. *n.* an issue that does not matter anymore. ☐ *This contract is a dead letter. Forget it!* ☐ *The mayor's plan for our raises is a dead letter.*

dead man See *dead soldier.*

dead marine See *dead soldier.*

dead on *mod.* exactly right; on target. ☐ *That's a good observation, Tiffany. You are dead on.* ☐ *Your criticism is dead on!*

dead one See *dead soldier.*

(dead) ringer (for someone) *n.* someone who is an exact duplicate of someone else. ☐ *You are sure a dead ringer for my brother.* ☐ *Isn't he a ringer for Chuck?*

dead soldier AND **dead man; dead marine; dead one** **1.** *n.* an empty liquor or beer bottle. ☐ *Toss your dead soldiers in the garbage, please.* ☐ *A dead marine fell off the table and woke up all the drunks.* **2.** *n.* a cigarette butt. (Less common than sense 1.) ☐ *The bum found a dead soldier on the ground and picked it up.* ☐ *He collected dead soldiers to use in building a whole smoke.*

dead to rights See *(bang) dead to rights.*

dead to the world **1.** *mod.* sound asleep. ☐ *After all that exercise, he's dead to the world.* ☐ *He's dead to the world, and I can't rouse him.* **2.** *mod.* alcohol intoxicated. ☐ *Six beers and he was dead to the world.* ☐ *By midnight almost everybody was dead to the world.*

deadbeat *n.* someone who doesn't pay debts or bills. ☐ *Some deadbeat with the same name as mine is ruining my credit rating.* ☐ *Pay up! Don't be a deadbeat.*

deadcat bounce *n.* a small, knee-jerk rally in one of the financial markets. (A dead cat—or any other animal—will bounce only slightly after being dropped. Refers to a stock index or security price that bounces up only slightly after a precipitous fall. Securities market.) ☐ *The whole market gave only a deadcat bounce after the string of losses this last week.* ☐ *I was expecting more than a deadcat bounce because of the good news.*

deadhead **1.** *n.* a stupid person. ☐ *Who's the deadhead in the plaid pants?* ☐ *Wow, are you a deadhead!* **2.** *tr. & in.* [for someone] to return an empty truck, train, airplane, etc., to where it came from. ☐ *I deadheaded back to Los Angeles.* ☐ *Who is supposed to deadhead this truck to Miami?* **3.** *n.* a follower of the rock group "The Grateful Dead." ☐ *What do these deadheads see in that group?* ☐ *My son is a deadhead and travels all over listening to these guys.*

deadly (dull) *mod.* very dull. ☐ *The lecture was deadly dull, and I went to sleep.* ☐ *What a deadly dull prof.* ☐ *Her story was really deadly. I am sorry I was awake for part of it.*

deadneck *n.* a stupid person. ☐ *What deadneck put sugar in the salt shaker?* ☐ *Who's the deadneck who painted the fence purple?*

deadpan **1.** *n.* an expressionless face. (See also *pan.*) ☐ *This guy has a super deadpan.* ☐ *Remember the deadpan she used to put on?* **2.** *n.* a person with an expressionless face. ☐ *The guy's a perfect deadpan.* ☐ *When you come on stage, look like a deadpan.* **3.** *mod.* dull and lifeless. (Usually said of a face, expression, etc.) ☐ *What a deadpan expression!* ☐ *Her face is totally deadpan.* ☐ *He has such a deadpan approach to everything.*

deadwood *n.* nonproductive or nonfunctional persons. ☐ *We'll have to cut costs by getting rid of the deadwood.* ☐ *Is there any way to make the deadwood productive again?*

deal stock *n.* a stock that is a takeover candidate. (Securities markets.) ☐ *I try to spot the deal stocks early and buy them before others do.* ☐ *You can lose a lot of money on deal stocks, too.*

Dear John letter *n.* a letter a woman writes to her boyfriend in the military service telling him that she does not love him anymore. ☐ *Wally got a Dear John letter today.* ☐ *Sally sends a Dear John letter about once a month.*

death on someone or something **1.** *n.* causing the death or destruction of someone or something. ☐ *This kind of road is just death on tires.* ☐ *This candy is death on my teeth.* **2.** *n.* [with *something*] moving very fast or skillfully on something, such as wheels. ☐ *He is way fast—just death on wheels.* ☐ *Pete is death on skis. You ought to see him go.*

deathly *mod.* excellent. ☐ *Did you see Kelly's deathly new convertible?* ☐ *That's a deathly idea!*

decent *mod.* good; very good. ☐ *This is some pretty decent jazz.* ☐ *Your threads are decent, all right.*

deck **1.** *tr.* to knock someone to the ground. ☐ *Fred decked Bob with one blow.* ☐ *I was so mad I almost decked him.* **2.** *n.* a pack of cigarettes. ☐ *Can you toss me a deck of fags, please?* ☐ *Why don't you stop in there and buy a deck?*

deduck ['didək] **1.** *n.* a tax deduction. (From *deduct.*) ☐ *Interest is no longer a deduck.* ☐ *I need a few more deducks this year.* **2.** AND **duck** *n.* a deduction from one's paycheck. ☐ *More of my pay goes to deducks than I get myself.* ☐ *What's this duck for?*

deejay See *disk jockey.*

deep *mod.* intense; profound. ☐ *She gave this really deep speech to us about how we should stay off drugs.* ☐ *All these comments are too deep for me.*

deep pockets **1.** *n.* a good source of money. ☐ *We need to find some deep pockets to finance this venture.* ☐ *Deep pockets are hard to find since the stock market crashed.* **2.** *n.* a rich person. ☐ *The lawyer went after the doctor who was the deep pockets of the organization.* ☐ *I want to find the deep pockets who arranged all this.*

deep six **1.** *tr.* to jettison something, including a corpse, from a ship at sea. ☐ *The captain had them deep six the garbage.* ☐ *They deep sixed the body of the first mate, who had died of the shakes.* **2.** *n.* burial at sea. (Always with *the.*) ☐ *They gave her the deep six with full honors.* ☐ *I think I'd want the deep six, but I'll probably kick off on dry land.* **3.** *tr.* to kill or dispose of someone. (Underworld.) ☐ *Mr. Big ordered Bruno to deep six Max.* ☐ *The thugs tried to deep six the witness, but failed.* **4.** *tr.* to throw something away. ☐ *Take this old thing out and deep six it.* ☐ *I've got to deep six this old T.V. set.* **5.** *n.* a grave. (Always with *the*. Graves are usually six feet deep.) ☐ *When you know the deep six is at the end of the line no matter who you are, it makes you take life less seriously.* ☐ *The deep six can't be made attractive to many people.*

def [dɛf] **1.** *mod.* better; *cool.* (Originally Black. From *definitive.*) ☐ *Man, that yogurt is def!* ☐ *What a def set of threads!* **2.** *mod.* definitely. ☐ *I will be there. Def.* ☐ *This is def the best there is.*

defrosted *mod.* "even" with someone who has insulted, embarrassed, or angered one. (See also *chill, ice.*) ☐ *He yelled at her till he was defrosted, and then things settled down.* ☐ *Bob was finally defrosted when he insulted Heidi.*

Delhi belly ['dɛli bɛli] *n.* diarrhea, as suffered by tourists in India. ☐ *I've got a touch of the Delhi belly and will have to miss the Taj Mahal.* ☐ *I've got something you can take for Delhi belly.*

delish [də'lɪʃ] *mod.* delicious. ☐ *Oh, this cake is just delish.* ☐ *What a delish meal.*

delts [dɛlts] *n.* the deltoid muscles. (Bodybuilding.) ☐ *Look at the delts on that dame!* ☐ *How do you get delts like that?*

dem See the following entry.

demo ['dɛmo] **1.** AND **dem** [dɛm] *n.* a member of the Democratic Party. ☐ *A couple of dems are running for the caucus, but no other party is represented.* ☐ *Which demos are they?* **2.** *n.* a demonstration (of something). ☐ *Can I have a demo of this model?* ☐ *Hey, Chuck, give this man a demo.* **3.** *n.* an automobile or other machine or device that has been used by a dealer for demonstration purposes. ☐ *I can give you a demo for half price.* ☐ *Do you have any demos?* **4.** *tr.* to demonstrate something (to someone). ☐ *Let me demo this for you so you can see how it works.* ☐ *Will someone please demo this computer?* **5.** *tr.* to demonstrate (something) to someone. ☐ *I've got to go demo these people on this software.* ☐ *Can you demo me before you go?*

des [dis] *n.* December. (Securities markets. Futures and options trading.) ☐ *The bean futures for des fell out of bed yesterday.* ☐ *Are these figures des or March?*

desert cherry *n.* a new soldier in a desert war; a soldier new to the desert in wartime. (From the Persian Gulf War. See also *cherry*.) □ *About 5,000 desert cherries arrived last week. Something is going to happen soon.* □ *The desert cherries are complaining about the scorpions again.*

desk jockey *n.* someone who works at a desk in an office. (Patterned on *disc jockey*.) □ *I couldn't stand being a cooped-up desk jockey.* □ *The desk jockeys at our place don't get paid very well.*

destroyed *mod.* drug intoxicated. □ *Wow, what happened to Tracy? She looks destroyed.* □ *The kid who took angel dust is destroyed most of the time.*

deuce [dus] **1.** *n.* the devil. (Always with *the*.) □ *I'll knock the deuce out of you if you come around here again.* □ *Get the deuce out of here!* **2.** *n.* the two in playing cards. □ *If I could only get a deuce.* □ *Ah, here's the deuce I need.* **3.** *n.* two dollars. □ *Can you loan me a deuce till payday?* □ *Sure, here's a deuce. Don't spend it all in one place.* **4.** *n.* a two-year prison sentence. (Underworld.) □ *Lefty served a deuce up the river.* □ *The D.A. made sure that Bruno got more than a deuce.* **5.** *n.* a table for two. □ *Give the next couple the deuce over in the corner.* □ *You can't put three people at a deuce!*

devil of a time *n.* a very difficult time. (Always with *a*.) □ *I had a devil of a time with my taxes.* □ *This cold has been giving me a devil of a time.*

devil's own time *n.* a very difficult time; a hellish time. (Always with *the*.) □ *I had the devil's own time with these tax forms.* □ *My gout is giving me the devil's own time.*

dew See *(mountain) dew.*

dialog *tr.* to attempt to deceive someone; to attempt to seduce someone. □ *Just let me dialog her for a while; then you'll see some action.* □ *Ron was dialoging this dame when her brother came in.*

diamond in the rough *n.* a person who is wonderful despite a rough exterior; a person with great potential. □ *Sam looks a little tacky, but he's a diamond in the rough.* □ *He's a diamond in the rough—a little hard to take at times, but okay mostly.*

diarrhea of the jawbone See the following entry.

diarrhea of the mouth AND **diarrhea of the jawbone** *n.* an imaginary disease involving constant talking. □ *Wow, does he ever have diarrhea of the mouth!* □ *You're getting diarrhea of the jawbone again.*

dibs on something *phr.* a claim on something. □ *I've got dibs on the yellow one!* □ *Dibs on the front seat!*

dicey ['dɑɪsi] *mod.* touchy; chancy; *touch and go.* □ *Things are just a little dicey right now.* □ *I'm working on a dicey deal with the city right now.*

dick 1. *n.* a detective; a police officer. (Underworld. From *detective*.) □ *Some dicks were around looking for you.* □ *Barlowe is a private dick who has to keep one step ahead of the cops.* **2.** *n.* the penis. (Widely heard, but potentially offensive. Use only with discretion.) □ *She told some dirty joke about a dick, but everybody just sat there and looked straight ahead.* □ *He covered his dick and stooped down, then reached up to pull down the shade.* **3.** *n.* a stupid person, usually a male. (Potentially offensive. Use only with discretion.) □ *You stupid dick!* □ *What stupid dick put this thing here in the way?* **4.** *n.* nothing. (Potentially offensive. Use only with discretion.) □ *The whole idea isn't worth dick.* □ *I was supposed to get a lot of money out of this deal, but all I got was dick!*

dickens 1. *n.* the devil. (Always with *the*.) □ *She was going to kick the dickens out of me.* □ *I felt as bad as the dickens, but what could I do?* **2.** *n.* a devilish or impish child. (Also a term of address.) □ *Come here, you little dickens.* □ *You are such a cute little dickens!*

dicty ['dɪkti] *mod.* snobbish. (Black.) □ *Those people can be so dicty!* □ *That* *dicty lady told me I could come to the back to get a tip if I wanted.*

diddle 1. *tr.* to cheat someone; to deceive someone. ☐ *The clerk diddled me so I reported her.* ☐ *That's a good place to get diddled. You gotta watch them in there.* **2.** *tr. & in.* to copulate (with someone). (Use caution with the topic. Old slang.) ☐ *I didn't think they'd diddle right there in the film.* ☐ *I'm tired of hearing who has diddled whom in Hollywood.*

diddle with something *in.* to play with something; to toy with something. ☐ *Here, don't diddle with that watch.* ☐ *Stop diddling with your nose, Jimmy!*

diddly-squat AND **(doodly-)squat** ['dɪdliskwɑt AND 'dudliskwɑt] *n.* nothing. (Folksy. Originally black or southern.) ☐ *This contract isn't worth diddly-squat.* ☐ *I get paid almost doodly-squat for a full day's work.*

DIDO *phr.* "dreck in, dreck out"; garbage in, garbage out. (Computers. Acronym. See also *dreck.* If you get *dreck* out of a computer, it's because you put *dreck* in. See also *GIGO.*) ☐ *Look at this stuff that the printer put out. What is it? Oh, well. D.I.D.O.* ☐ *As a programmer, I specialize in DIDO.*

die *in.* to die (figuratively) from laughter or some other emotionally intense response. ☐ *The whole audience died laughing.* ☐ *He laughed till he died.*

die on someone 1. *in.* [for a patient] to die under the care of someone. ☐ *Get that medicine over here fast, or this guy's gonna die on me.* ☐ *Come on, mister, don't die on me!* **2.** *in.* [for something] to quit running for someone. ☐ *My car died on me, and I couldn't get it started.* ☐ *My stereo died on me, and I had to listen to the radio.*

diesel ['dizl̩] *mod.* really good. ☐ *Fred had a really diesel idea, but no money to carry it out.* ☐ *I am set for a diesel evening and I intend to enjoy it.*

diff [dɪf] *n.* difference. ☐ *Aw, come on! What's the diff?* ☐ *The diff is about twenty dollars worth of repairs, that's what.*

different strokes for different folks *phr.* "different things please different people." (Catch phrase.) ☐ *Do whatever you like. Different strokes for different folks.* ☐ *Different strokes for different folks. That's what I always say.*

differential *n.* the buttocks; the *rear (end).* ☐ *I got a little ache in the differential.* ☐ *You're walking like there's something wrong with your differential.*

dig 1. *tr. & in.* to understand something. ☐ *I just don't dig what you are saying.* ☐ *Sorry. I just don't dig.* **2.** *tr.* to appreciate something; to like something. ☐ *He really digs classical music.* ☐ *Do you dig chocolate?*

Dig up! *exclam.* "Listen up!"; "Pay attention!" ☐ *Dig up, man! This is important.* ☐ *Shut up and dig up!*

digits *n.* numbers; phone number. ☐ *Tell me your digits and I'll call you and let you know the time.* ☐ *If I can find her digits, I'll call her.*

digs *n.* a dwelling; a dwelling and its furnishings. ☐ *You got some pretty swell digs, here.* ☐ *Nice digs. You like it here?*

dike [daɪk] *n.* a lesbian; a homosexual woman, especially one with masculine traits. (Derogatory. Potentially offensive. Use only with discretion. Resented by lesbians.) ☐ *Why does she work so hard to look like a dike?* ☐ *Who's the dike in the cowboy boots?*

dildo ['dɪldo] *n.* a stupid person, usually a male. (Potentially offensive. Use only with discretion. The term refers to an artificial penis.) ☐ *Hank can be such a dildo sometimes.* ☐ *You silly dildo!*

dilly *n.* something excellent. ☐ *This little car is a real dilly.* ☐ *What a dilly of an apartment!*

dilly-dally *in.* to waste time. ☐ *Stop dilly-dallying around.* ☐ *I like to dilly-dally over a cup of coffee.*

dim bulb *n.* a dull person; a stupid person. ☐ *George seems to be a dim bulb, but he's a straight-A student.* ☐ *I feel like such a dim bulb when I do things like that.*

dime-dropper *n.* an informer. (Underworld. Because an informer at one time could drop a dime in a public telephone and call the police or drop a dime on the sidewalk as a signal for the police to move in and make an arrest. See also *drop a dime*.) □ *I think that Tracy is the dime-dropper who caused the roust.* □ *The fuzz protects its dime-droppers with everything they've got.*

dime store *n.* an establishment that is chaotic because of its small scale. □ *I can't stand this dime store anymore. This is no way to run a law firm.* □ *Things move so fast around here that we have become a dime store rather than an accounting office.*

dimwit ['dɪmwɪt] *n.* an oaf; a dullard. (Also a rude term of address.) □ *Oh, Dave, you can be such a dimwit!* □ *Come on, now, you're not really a dimwit.*

dinero [dɪ'nɛro] *n.* money. (Spanish.) □ *I don't have as much dinero as I need, but other than that, I'm doing okay.* □ *You got some dinero I can borrow?*

ding **1.** *tr.* to shoot, dent, or knock something. □ *The rock dinged my left fender.* □ *The bullet dinged Rocko's right arm.* **2.** *tr.* to negate; to cast out; to blemish. □ *Please stop dinging my little brother. He's a good kid.* □ *The reviewer dinged the book, but it sold well anyway.*

ding-a-ling ['dɪŋəlɪŋ] *n.* a stupid person; a giddy person who hears bells. □ *This ding-a-ling comes up and asks me for a dollar for the orphans. I tell her I got all the orphans I can use at any price.* □ *Who's the ding-a-ling who painted the windows stuck?*

dingbat **1.** *n.* a name for a gadget. □ *Isn't there supposed to be a little red dingbat that goes in this hole?* □ *Is this the dingbat you mean?* **2.** *n.* a stupid person. □ *Who is the dingbat with Bob?* □ *That's no dingbat; that's his sister.* **3.** *n.* any undesirable person. (Also a rude term of address.) □ *Look, dingbat, stop laughing!* □ *I'm tired of reading about that dingbat in the paper every day.*

dinged out *mod.* alcohol intoxicated. □ *Gary is dinged out and can't drive.* □ *He got dinged out on a couple of quarts of foam.*

dinghead *n.* a stupid person. □ *Shut up, you stupid dinghead.* □ *Frank was a real dinghead when he cheated on the exam.*

dingleberry *n.* a weird person. (From a term for unclean matter clinging to anal hairs. Many users of this term do not know its source. Potentially offensive. Use only with discretion.) □ *Stop acting like such a dingleberry!* □ *Frank is such a dingleberry!*

dingus ['dɪŋgəs] *n.* a thing or gadget. □ *I have a little dingus that helps me clean venetian blinds.* □ *Toss me one of those dinguses that holds the wire in the groove, will ya?*

dingy ['dɪŋi] *mod.* loony; giddy. □ *That friend of yours sure does act dingy sometimes.* □ *Tell the dingy drip to forget it.* □ *I'm not dingy, I'm just in love.*

DINK AND **dink** [dɪŋk] *n.* "double income, no kids"; a (young) married couple with two incomes and no children. (Acronym.) □ *The whole neighborhood is populated by dinks. Not a single child on the block.* □ *Most dinks are young. Older couples whose children are grown up are just called old.*

dink someone off *tr.* to make someone angry. □ *Whatever you do, don't dink her off!* 🅃 *Why did you have to start out your speech by dinking off the entire audience?*

dinky ['dɪŋki] *mod.* small; undersized. □ *Isn't this a little dinky for a $14 steak?* □ *I'll take the dinky one. I'm on a diet.*

dinner basket See *breadbasket.*

dip **1.** *n.* a drunkard. (From *dipsomaniac*.) □ *Buy the dip a drink. That'll shut him up for a while.* □ *A dip hung around outside the tavern, mooching coin for drinks.* **2.** *n.* a pickpocket. (Underworld.) □ *Watch out for dips at the racetrack.* □ *The dip tried a snatch, but the dupe turned around at the wrong time.* **3.** *n.* a pinch or helping of snuff. □ *He* *took a dip just before he picked up the bat.* □ *After the hit, he got another dip.* **4.** *n.* a wad of chewing tobacco. □ *You could see he had a big dip in his cheek.* □ *I won't tell you what he did with the dip when he was finished with it.* **5.** See *dip(shit).*

dip(head) See *dip(shit).*

dippy *mod.* crazy; loony. □ *Who is that dippy chick with the lamp shade on her head?* □ *Tom is dippy, but fun.*

dip(shit) AND **dip(head); dipstick** *n.* an oaf; a *jerk.* (The first entry is potentially offensive. Use only with discretion.) □ *Why are you acting like such a diphead?* □ *Is there a convention of dipsticks or something here today?*

dipso ['dɪpso] *n.* a drunkard; an alcoholic. (From *dipsomaniac.* See also *dip.*) □ *Oh, I didn't realize she was a dipso.* □ *She's sort of a closet dipso.*

dipstick See *dip(shit).*

dipsy ['dɪpsi] *mod.* tipsy; alcohol intoxicated. (See also *dip.*) □ *I think that Jed is permanently dipsy.* □ *The cop pulled the dipsy dame over and arrested her.* □ *He was too dipsy to drive.*

dipwad ['dɪpwɑd] *n.* a *jerk;* a *nerd.* (Euphemistic for *dip(shit).*) □ *Fred is such a dipwad. Why doesn't he wise up?* □ *If you weren't a big dipwad, you would give me a hand with this.*

dirt 1. *n.* low, worthless people. □ *He is just dirt.* □ *I am not dirt. I'm just temporarily financially embarrassed.* **2.** *n.* scandal; incriminating secrets; *dirty linen.* □ *What's the dirt on Tracy?* □ *I don't want to know about anybody's dirt!*

dirt cheap *mod.* very cheap. □ *I picked this thing up dirt cheap.* □ *Get one of these while they're dirt cheap.*

dirty 1. *mod.* obscene. □ *You have a dirty mind.* □ *The movie was too dirty for me.* □ *How would you know what's dirty and what's not?* **2.** *mod.* low and sneaky. □ *What a dirty trick!* □ *That was really dirty!* □ *What a dirty thing to do!* **3.** *mod.* illegal; on the wrong side of the law. (Compare to *clean.*) □ *The cops knew that Max was dirty and they searched his car until they found something they could use against him.* □ *You just look at Bruno and you know he is dirty. The question is, what's he done now?*

dirty crack *n.* a rude remark. □ *Who made that dirty crack?* □ *Another dirty crack like that and I'll leave.*

dirty deal *n.* an unfair deal. □ *That was a dirty deal. I feel cheated.* □ *I got a dirty deal at that shop, and I won't go back.*

dirty dog *n.* a low and sneaky person. □ *What a low, dirty dog.* □ *That dirty dog tried to get fresh with me!*

(dirty) dozens *n.* a game of trading insulting remarks about relatives. (Originally Black. Always with *the.*) □ *Man, what's with you? Always the dirty dozens. You just gotta start something all the time.* □ *Freddy is out giving the dozens to Marty.*

dirty joke 1. *n.* an obscene joke. □ *Fred told a dirty joke that shocked almost everyone.* □ *No dirty jokes around here. We get enough of that on television.* **2.** *n.* a very ugly or very stupid person. □ *Look at that face. That's a dirty joke.* □ *Beavis is sort of a dirty joke that nobody can laugh at.*

dirty laundry See the following entry.

dirty linen AND **dirty laundry** *n.* scandal; unpleasant private matters. □ *I wish you wouldn't put our dirty linen out for everyone to see.* □ *I've heard enough about her dirty laundry.*

dirty look *n.* a frown meant to show displeasure with something that has been said or done. □ *I gave him a dirty look, and he took his arm off my shoulder.* □ *What is that dirty look meant to mean?*

dirty-minded *mod.* having a tendency to see the lewd or obscene aspects of anything; having a tendency to place an obscene interpretation on the words and actions of others. □ *Bruno is sort of dirty-minded, but he wouldn't do anything really vile.* □ *He's a vile, dirty-minded jerk.* □ *Most of those guys are dirty-minded.*

dirty mouth 1. *n.* a person who talks dirty. (See also *bad-mouth.*) ☐ *You are getting to be quite a dirty mouth, Gary.* ☐ *Some dirty mouth yelled out the most obscene things during the meeting.* 2. *tr.* to speak ill of someone or something. (See also *bad-mouth.*) ☐ *Please stop dirty mouthing my friends.* ☐ *You have dirty mouthed cats just about enough.*

dirty old man *n.* a lecherous old man. (Usually jocular.) ☐ *Jimmy, you are getting to be a dirty old man!* ☐ *What a terrible joke. You are a dirty old man!*

dirty pool *n.* activities conducted using unfair or sneaky tactics. ☐ *They're playing dirty pool now. This calls for a new plan.* ☐ *When they start playing dirty pool, it's time to get mean.*

dirty word *n.* a curse word; an informal word concerned with sex or excrement. ☐ *No dirty words are allowed on this computer bulletin board.* ☐ *Some kid got the microphone and yelled a dirty word into it.*

dirty work 1. *n.* menial work; hard work. ☐ *Why do I always get stuck with the dirty work?* ☐ *We should share the dirty work evenly.* 2. *n.* sneaky activities. ☐ *I hear that Sam is up to his old dirty work again.* ☐ *He is a master at dirty work.*

disc jockey See *disk jockey.*

discipline *n.* drugs. ☐ *Max has been on a little too much of that discipline lately.* ☐ *She smokes this stuff she calls discipline. Smells like pot to me.*

discombobulate [dıskəm'bɑbjəlet] *tr.* to confuse or perplex someone. ☐ *That kind of discussion discombobulates me something awful.* ☐ *Don't let the heat of the argument discombobulate you.*

discombobulated AND **discomboobulated** [dıskəm'bɑbjəledəd AND dıskəm'bubjəledəd] 1. *mod.* confused. ☐ *I get completely discombobulated when I think of figures that big.* ☐ *I'm so discomboobulated these days!* ☐ *She is one discombobulated gal.* 2. *mod.* alcohol intoxicated. ☐ *From the way she is walking, I'd say she is discombobulated.* ☐ *You'd be discomboobulated, too, if you'd drunk as much as she has.*

discomboobulated See the previous entry.

dish 1. *n.* a good-looking woman. ☐ *Wow, isn't she a dish?* ☐ *Now there's a good-looking dish.* 2. *tr.* to criticize someone or something; to spread gossip about someone or something. (Compare to *dis.* Probably short for *dish the dirt.*) ☐ *The critics all dished the opening of the play mercilessly.* ☐ *I wish you would stop dishing me all the time.*

dish something out 1. *tr.* to serve up food to people. (Standard English.) ☐ *I'll dish it out, and you take it to the table.* 🅃 *Careful how you dish out the mashed potatoes. There may not be enough.* 2. *tr.* to distribute information, news, etc. ☐ *The press secretaries were dishing reports out as fast as they could write them.* 🅃 *The company dishes out propaganda on a regular basis.* 3. *tr.* to give out trouble, scoldings, criticism, etc. ☐ *The boss was dishing criticism out this morning, and I really got it.* 🅃 *The teacher dished out a scolding to each one who was involved in the prank.*

dish the dirt *tr.* to spread gossip; to gossip. ☐ *Let's sit down, have a drink, and dish the dirt.* ☐ *David goes down to the tavern to dish the dirt.*

dishrag See *(limp) dishrag.*

disk jockey AND **deejay; disc jockey; D.J.** *n.* a radio announcer who introduces music from phonograph records. (The abbreviations are initialisms. Compare to *desk jockey.* See also *veejay.*) ☐ *The disk jockey couldn't pronounce the name of the singing group.* ☐ *I was a D.J. for a while, but I didn't like it.*

dis(s) (on someone) ['dıs . . .] *tr.* to belittle someone; to show disrespect for someone. (From either a nonstandard transitive verb *disrespect* or from *dismiss [as insignificant]*.) ☐ *Gary is such a complainer. All he does is diss on people.* ☐ *Please stop dissing my little sister. She didn't do any of those things.* ☐ *Don't dis my ride! It's only temporary.*

ditch 1. *tr.* to dispose of someone or something; to abandon someone or something. □ *The crooks ditched the car and continued on foot.* □ *The flyboy ditched the plane in the lake and waded ashore.* 2. *tr. & in.* to skip or evade someone or something. □ *Pete ditched class today.* □ *If you ditch too often, they'll throw you out of the organization.*

dither ['dɪðɚ] *n.* a state of confusion. (See also *in a dither.*) □ *A dither like that is hard to break out of. Maybe a good night's sleep would help.* □ *I'm too far gone with this dither to sleep.*

ditsy See *ditzy.*

ditz AND **ditzo** [dɪts(o)] *n.* a giddy, absent-minded person. □ *You silly ditz!* □ *I'm getting to be such a ditz!* □ *Who is the ditzo on the phone? Another wrong number?*

ditzo See the previous entry.

ditzy AND **ditsy** ['dɪtsi] mod. giddy; unaware; flighty. □ *You are such a ditzy geek!* □ *Betty has been acting a little ditsy lately. What's wrong?*

dive *n.* a low drinking establishment; a cheap saloon. □ *I don't think I want to spend the whole evening in this dive.* □ *Hey, this dive ain't bad.*

divot ['dɪvət] *n.* a toupee; a partial toupee. (See also *rug.*) □ *I think that Sam is wearing a little divot.* □ *His divot slipped, but no one laughed.*

divvy ['dɪvi] *n.* a share of something. (See also *divvy something up.*) □ *How much is my divvy?* □ *Give me my divvy so I can go home.*

divvy something up *tr.* to divide something up. □ *We had to divvy my aunt's things up after her death.* 🅃 *They divvied up the fish and drove back to the city.*

dizzy *mod.* stupid; scatterbrained. □ *The prof is a little dizzy, but entertaining.* □ *Who is that dizzy dame?*

D.J. See *disk jockey.*

do 1. *n.* a party; a social event. □ *We had a smashing time at your little do.* □ *I'm having a do for a friend this weekend. Would you like to come?* 2. *tr. & in.* to use a drug or drugs in general. (See also *do a line, do drugs.*) □ *Is Tracy doing dust again?* □ *Tracy never stopped doing. She just switched from dust to splash.* 3. AND **doo** *n.* a hairdo. □ *Nice do. Is it new?* □ *I can't go out in this rain and get my doo wet!* 4. See *(must) do.* 5. *in.* to serve (a purpose) well. (Usually with *will* or *won't.*) □ *This will do quite nicely.* □ *Oh, yes, this will do.* □ *That won't do at all!* 6. See *doo-doo.*

do a dump on someone or something AND **dump all over someone or something; dump on someone or something** *tr.* to criticize someone or something; to destroy someone or something. □ *There is no need to do a dump on me. I didn't wreck your car.* □ *The boss—mad as a wet hen—dumped all over me.* □ *That rotten jerk really did a dump on my car. Look at that fender!*

do a fade *tr.* to leave; to sneak away. □ *Max did a fade when he saw the pigmobile.* □ *It's time for me to do a fade.*

do a job on someone or something 1. *tr.* to ruin someone or something; to give someone or something a thorough working over. □ *The cops did a job on Rocko, but he still wouldn't talk.* □ *There's no need to do a job on me, man, I'll tell you everything I know—which is zip.* □ *That punch sure did a job on my nose.* 2. See *do a number on someone.*

do a line *tr.* to *snort* a dose of a powdered drug, usually cocaine. (Drugs.) □ *Max slipped into a doorway to do a line.* □ *Ernie has to do a line about every four hours—night and day.*

do a number on someone AND **do a job on someone** *tr.* to harm or deceive someone. □ *The IRS really did a number on me.* □ *My local friendly plumber did a job on me cleaning out my drain.*

do a slow burn *tr.* to be quietly angry. (See also *slow burn.*) □ *I did a slow burn while I was getting my money back.* □ *I was doing a slow burn, but I didn't let it show.*

do a snow job on someone *tr.* to deceive or confuse someone. □ *Don't try to do* *a snow job on me. I know all the tricks.* ☐ *She thought she did a snow job on the teacher, but it backfired.*

(do-)do See *doo-doo.*

do dope See the following entry.

do drugs AND **do dope** *tr.* to take drugs; to use drugs habitually. (Drugs and now general.) ☐ *Rocko doesn't do drugs, and he doesn't drink.* ☐ *Max started doing dope when he was very young.*

do-gooder ['dugudɚ] *n.* a person who is always trying to help others. (Often derogatory.) ☐ *The do-gooders are demanding a bigger cut of the pie.* ☐ *I don't consider myself a do-gooder, but I try to help people.*

Do I have to draw (you) a picture? See the following entry.

Do I have to paint (you) a picture? AND **Do I have to draw (you) a picture?** *interrog.* "Do you understand yet?"; "How simple do I have to make it for you?" ☐ *This is supposed to be easy. Do I have to paint a picture?* ☐ *Do I have to draw you a picture, or can you visualize this?*

do one's (own) thing *tr.* to do what one wants; to do what pleases oneself no matter what others think. ☐ *She's going to start doing her own thing for a change.* ☐ *I've always done my thing, and I don't see a great amount of benefit from it.*

do oneself proud *tr.* to have done a very fine job. ☐ *That's super! You've done yourself proud!* ☐ *I feel like I've done myself proud.*

do or die *mod.* having to try as hard as one can. ☐ *He has the obsessive do or die attitude.* ☐ *I was determined to get there—do or die.*

do-re-me See the following entry.

do-re-mi AND **do-re-me** ['do're'mi] *n.* money. (From *dough.*) ☐ *It takes too much do-re-mi to live in this part of town.* ☐ *Do you have a little do-re-me you could loan me?*

do some bongs *tr.* to smoke some marijuana, usually with a water pipe. (Drugs. See also *bong.*) ☐ *All the kids think that doing bongs is the greatest thing on earth.* ☐ *Hey, dude, wanna do some bongs?*

do some fine coin *tr.* to make a large sum of money. ☐ *When I get my big break, I'm going to do some fine coin.* ☐ *Max did some fine coin on that last house painting job.*

do someone dirt *tr.* to do ill to someone; to harm someone's reputation. ☐ *You really did me dirt.* ☐ *It seemed that the lawyer was determined to do me dirt right there in the courtroom.*

Do tell. *sent.* "Is that so?" (A disinterested way of holding up one end of a conversation.) ☐ *So, you're a dentist. Do tell.* ☐ *Do tell. I've never heard that before. Nice talking to you.*

do the drink thing *tr.* to drink alcohol heavily. ☐ *He's been doing the drink thing quite a lot lately.* ☐ *He started doing the drink thing when he got out of prison.*

do the drug thing *tr.* to be involved with drugs; to take drugs. ☐ *Man, you gotta stop doing the drug thing.* ☐ *All she thinks about is doing the drug thing.*

do the trick *tr.* to do exactly what is needed. ☐ *This about does the trick.* ☐ *Does this little dudenwhacker do the trick?*

do time *tr.* to serve a sentence in prison; to serve a specific amount of time in prison. (Underworld. See also *hard time.*) ☐ *Lefty had done time on a number of occasions.* ☐ *You'd better talk and talk fast if you don't want to do time.*

(Do) you eat with that mouth? AND **(Do) you kiss your momma with that mouth?** *interrog.* "Do you actually eat with the mouth you use to talk that filth?"; "Do you actually use that filthy mouth to kiss your mother?" (A catch phrase said to someone who talks dirty all the time.) ☐ *That's a lot of foul talk. Do you eat with that mouth?* ☐ *You talk dirt a lot. You eat with that mouth?*

(Do you) get my drift? *interrog.* "Do you understand me?" ☐ *Get my drift?*

Should I explain it again? □ *Do you get my drift, or shall I run through it again?*

(Do) you kiss your momma with that mouth? See *(Do) you eat with that mouth?*

DOA 1. *mod.* "dead on arrival." (Hospitals. Initialism.) □ *The kid was DOA, and there was nothing anybody could do.* □ *Do you want to end up D.O.A.?* **2.** *n.* a person who is dead on arrival at a hospital. □ *They brought in two D.O.A.s Saturday night.* □ *Drugs increase the number of D.O.A.s considerably.* **3.** *n.* phencyclidine (P.C.P.). (Because it is deadly.) □ *Stay away from D.O.A. There's a good reason why it's called that.* □ *The kids use D.O.A. no matter what.*

doc(s)-in-a-box *n.* a walk-in emergency health care center, as found in shopping centers. (See also *McDoctor(s)*.) □ *I was cut and went immediately to the docs-in-a-box in the mall.* □ *The doc-in-the-box finally closed because of lack of customers.*

doctor's orders *n.* something that one is strongly advised to do. (Refers here to any advice given by anyone but a doctor.) □ *I have to spend a month in Arizona. Doctor's orders.* □ *I'm doing this on doctor's orders, but I don't like it.*

dode [dod] *n.* a *nerd;* a simpleton. □ *Wally is such a dode.* □ *My roommate is a loser. I was afraid I'd end up with a dode.*

dodge [dadʒ] *n.* a swindle; a *scam;* a deception. □ *What sort of dodge did you get flimflammed with?* □ *Gary has a new dodge to make money, but he hasn't made any yet.*

dog 1. *n.* a foot. (Usually plural.) □ *My dogs are killing me.* □ *I gotta get home and soak my dogs.* **2.** *n.* an ugly *girl.* □ *I'm no dog, but I could wish for some changes.* □ *So she's not a movie star; she's not a dog either!* **3.** *n.* something undesirable or worthless; merchandise that no one wants to buy. □ *Put the dogs out on the sale table so people will see them.* □ *They even bought all the dogs this year. Sales were great.* **4.** *n.* dog dung. (See also *dog-doo*.) □ *There's some dog on the lawn.* □ *Don't step in the dog.* **5.** *tr.* to follow someone. □ *The cop dogged Lefty for a week.* □ *Stop dogging me, you twit!* **6.** *tr.* to stay with one and haunt one. □ *Will this memory dog me all the days of my life?* □ *The thought of all that cake and ice cream dogged me all during my diet.* **7.** *tr.* to eat something; to eat something as a dog eats. □ *He dogged his hamburger and ran out the door to catch the bus.* □ *Here, dog a couple of crackers and cheese. That should keep you from starving.*

dog and pony show *n.* a demonstration; a speech, skit, or other presentation that is presented often. □ *Wally was there with his dog and pony show about water safety.* □ *I've seen that dog and pony show so many times, it's like I know all the words.*

dog-dew See *dog-doo*.

dog-do See the following entry.

dog-doo AND **dog-dew; dog-do** ['dɔgdu] *n.* dog dung. □ *Don't step in the dog-doo.* □ *When the snow melts, the sidewalks are covered with dog-doo.*

dog-eat-dog *mod.* cruel; highly competitive. □ *This is a dog-eat-dog world.* □ *It's dog-eat-dog out there.*

dog meat *n.* a dead person. (Typically in a threat.) □ *Make one move, and you're dog meat.* □ *They pulled another hunk of gangland dog meat out of the river.*

dogface *n.* infantry soldier. (World War II. Also a term of address.) □ *Get those dogfaces over here on the double.* □ *Did I see a salute, dogface?*

doggo ['dɔgo] *mod.* hidden away; quiet and waiting. (See also *lie doggo*.) □ *This error was there, doggo, for nearly thirty years.* □ *Here is another one of your doggo deadbeats on this list.*

doggone(d) ['dɔ'gɔn(d)] *mod.* darn(ed); damn(ed). □ *I sort of wish my hooter wasn't so doggone big.* □ *Who made this doggoned mess?*

doggy bag ['dɔgibæg] *n.* a bag—supplied by a restaurant—in which uneaten food can be carried home. □ *Do you have a* *doggy bag for my mousse?* □ *We do not have doggy bags, but we do supply foil.*

dog's mother *n.* a *bitch;* a *bitchy* person. (Euphemism.) □ *If Sally insists on being a dog's mother on this matter, I'll tell her what I think of her.* □ *Stop being a dog's mother and chill out!*

dojigger AND **doojigger** ['dudʒɪgɚ] *n.* a name for a gadget. □ *A doojigger like this is worth about a quarter, but you'll pay 100 times that for it.* □ *What's this little dojigger called?*

doll 1. *n.* a pretty girl or woman. □ *Who's the doll I saw you with last night?* □ *That doll was my sister, jerk.* **2.** *n.* a pill. (Drugs. Usually plural.) □ *She took stuff, yeah, but only dolls.* □ *Taking dolls is different from shooting up.*

dome-doctor *n.* a psychologist or psychiatrist. □ *They sent me to a dome-doctor, but it didn't help.* □ *The dome-doctor lets me talk while he keeps score.*

done by mirrors AND **done with mirrors** *mod.* illusory; purposefully deceptive. □ *The whole budgetary process is done with mirrors.* □ *The self-review was done by mirrors and didn't come off too bad.*

done deal *n.* a completed deal; something that is settled. □ *It's too late. It's a done deal.* □ *The sale of the property is a done deal. There is nothing that can be done now.*

done for *mod.* lost; dead; doomed. □ *I'm sorry, this whole scheme is done for.* □ *I knew I was done for.*

done over *mod.* beat; outscored. □ *The other team was done over, and they knew it.* □ *Bruno felt that Max would get the idea if he was done over a little.*

done to a turn 1. *mod.* well-cooked; nicely cooked. □ *The entire meal was done to a turn.* □ *The turkey was done to a turn.* **2.** *mod.* beaten. □ *When Wilbur's opponent was done to a turn, Wilbur was declared the winner.* □ *Max was done to a turn, and Bruno walked away.*

done with mirrors See *done by mirrors.*

donkey's breakfast *n.* something made of straw: a straw hat, a straw mattress, etc. □ *I don't really want to sleep on a donkey's breakfast, but it's better than the floor.* □ *The tourist was wearing a red dress and had a donkey's breakfast on her head.*

donkey's years *n.* a long time. □ *I haven't seen you in donkey's years.* □ *It's been donkey's years since we talked.*

donnybrook *n.* a big argument; a brawl. □ *There was a big donnybrook at the concert, and the police were called.* □ *Who started this donnybrook?*

Don't ask. *sent.* "The answer is so depressing, you don't even want to hear it." □ *How am I? Don't ask.* □ *This has been a horrible day. How horrible, you say? Don't ask.*

Don't ask me. *sent.* "I don't know either." (With the emphasis on *me.*) □ *I don't know. Don't ask me.* □ *Don't ask me. I wasn't there.*

Don't call us, we'll call you. *sent.* a formulaic expression given to job applicants who have just interviewed or auditioned for a job. □ *Thank you, Eddie Evans. Don't call us, we'll call you.* □ *Stupendous, Gloria, just stupendous. What glamour and radiance! Don't call us, we'll call you.*

Don't have a cow! *exclam.* "Calm down!"; "Don't get so excited!" (Made famous in the television show, *The Simpsons.*) □ *Chill out, man! Don't have a cow!* □ *Aw, don't have a cow, dad!*

Don't I know it! *exclam.* "That is really true!" □ *It's bad all right. Don't I know it!* □ *Late? Don't I know it. I'm yawning like hot cakes.*

Don't make me laugh! *exclam.* "That is a stupid suggestion!" □ *You a judge? Don't make me laugh!* □ *Don't make me laugh. Tom could never do that.*

Don't sweat it! *exclam.* "Don't worry about it!" □ *No problem. Don't sweat it!* □ *Don't sweat it! We'll take care of it.*

(Don't) you wish! *exclam.* "I'm sure you wish it were true." □ *You think you'll win? Don't you wish!* □ *There's no school tomorrow? You wish!*

doo See *do.*

doo-doo ['dudu] **1.** AND **(do-)do** ['dudu] *n.* dung, especially animal dung. (See also *dog-doo.*) ☐ *Don't step in the doo-doo.* ☐ *There's a lot of pigeon doo-doo in the attic.* **2.** *in.* to defecate. (Juvenile.) ☐ *Jimmy was reminded that he had to remember to doo-doo in the potty.* ☐ *He has to doo-doo before he goes to bed, too.*

doobage See *dubage.*

doobie AND **dooby; duby** ['dubi] *n.* a marijuana cigarette; a fat marijuana cigarette. (Drugs.) ☐ *Max sells doobies like they were candy.* ☐ *Want a doobie?*

dooby See the previous entry.

doodad ['dudæd] *n.* a name for a gadget. ☐ *What are these little doodads?* ☐ *I don't know what they're called. If they had names, they wouldn't be doodads, now would they?*

(doodly-)squat See *diddly-squat.*

doofer AND **dufer** ['dufɚ] *n.* a (found or borrowed) cigarette saved for smoking at another time. (It will "do for" later.) ☐ *Sam always has a doofer stuck behind his ear.* ☐ *He takes two fags, one to smoke and a dufer.*

doofus ['dufəs] *n.* a *jerk;* a *nerd.* ☐ *Hank, you are acting like a doofus. Stop standing on your head.* ☐ *My roommate is a doofus and I'm tired of putting up with her.*

doohickey See the following entry.

doojigger AND **doohickey; doohickie** ['dudʒɪgɚ AND 'duhɪki] *n.* a name for a gadget. ☐ *Toss me that little red doohickey, will you?* ☐ *Jim has one of those doohickies that will tighten the bit in the drill.*

dook [duk] *mod.* really bad. (Probably related to *duky.*) ☐ *No more of your dook ideas!* ☐ *This day was really dook!*

doormat *n.* a weak-willed person who is abused by others. ☐ *I always feel like a doormat.* ☐ *Why do people treat me like a doormat?*

doosie AND **doozie; doozy** ['duzi] *n.* something extraordinary, good or bad. ☐ *The trade show was a real doozy this year.* ☐ *Old Gert was a real doozy.*

doowacky ['duwʌæki] **1.** *n.* a thing; a nameless gadget. ☐ *Where is the doowacky I laid here?* ☐ *Is this your doowacky? I was going to throw it away.* **2.** *n.* money. ☐ *You got some doowacky I can borrow?* ☐ *I'm out of doowacky myself.*

doozie See *doosie.*

doozy See *doosie.*

dope 1. *n.* a stupid person. ☐ *I'm not such a dope.* ☐ *That dope has done it again!* **2.** *n.* drugs in general; marijuana. ☐ *Lay off the dope, will ya?* ☐ *How much dope do you do in a week anyway?* **3.** *n.* news; *scuttlebutt.* ☐ *What's the dope on the new mayor?* ☐ *I got some dope on the tavern fire if you want to hear it.* **4.** *mod.* best; most excellent. ☐ *My roommate is really dope. Great guy!* ☐ *We had a great time there. It was dope and dudical.*

dope something out *tr.* to figure out something from the *dope* (information) available. ☐ *I think I can dope this thing out from the evidence available.* 🅃 *We can dope out the truth from her testimony if we have to.*

dope up 1. *in.* to inject drugs; to take a dose of a narcotic. (Drugs.) ☐ *I'm hurting, man, I gotta dope up, now!* ☐ *She slipped into the back room to dope up.* **2.** *in.* to purchase a supply of drugs. (Drugs.) ☐ *Where's my old friend Max? I gotta dope up.* ☐ *Max is doping up, himself. He doesn't grow it himself, you know.*

dopey 1. *mod.* stupid. ☐ *What a dopey guy!* ☐ *That was a dopey thing to do.* **2.** *mod.* sleepy. ☐ *I feel sort of dopey.* ☐ *The soft music made him dopey.* **3.** *mod.* drug intoxicated. ☐ *He looks sort of dopey.* ☐ *The chick is too dopey to drive. See that she gets home, Ralphy, huh?*

dorf [dorf] *n.* a stupid person; a weird person. ☐ *You are a prize-winning dorf.* ☐ *Is there a convention of dorfs here today or something?*

dork [dork] **1.** *n.* the penis. (Potentially offensive. Use only with discretion.) ☐ *Paul told a joke about a dork, but everybody just sat there and looked straight ahead.* ☐ *He covered his dork and squatted down; then he reached up and pulled down the shade.* **2.** *n.* a *jerk;* a strange person. (See also *megadork.*) ☐ *Ye gods, Sally! You are a dork!* ☐ *Here comes the king of dorks again.*

dork off *in.* to waste time; to *goof off.* ☐ *Stop dorking off and get busy.* ☐ *The whole class was dorking off and the teacher got furious.*

dorkmeier AND **dorkmunder** ['dorkmaɪr AND 'dorkməndɚ] *n.* a total *jerk;* a simpleton. ☐ *Ellen, stop acting like such a dorkmeier!* ☐ *Fred is my idea of the perfect dorkmunder.*

dorkmunder See the previous entry.

dorkus maximus ['dorkəs 'mæksɪməs] *n.* a simpleton or fool; a great fool. ☐ *Tim is now the dorkus maximus of our dorm since he broke the dorm's television set.* ☐ *Sally is a dorkus maximus and spaced out to boot.*

dorky ['dorki] *mod.* strange; weird; undesirable; stupid. ☐ *That is a real dorky idea. Just forget it.* ☐ *It's just too dorky.* ☐ *Let me out of this dorky place!* ☐ *I wouldn't be caught dead wearing that dorky hat.*

dorm *n.* dormitory. ☐ *Which dorm do you live in?* ☐ *Fred lives in a co-ed dorm.*

do's and don'ts *n.* the rules; the things that should be done and those that should not be done. ☐ *I must admit that a lot of the do's and don'ts don't make much sense to me either.* ☐ *Better learn the do's and don'ts immediately.*

double *n.* a drink consisting two servings of liquor. ☐ *Make mine a double, bartender.* ☐ *Sam usually has two doubles on the way home.*

double-bagger 1. *n.* a hit good for two bases in baseball. ☐ *Wilbur hit a nice double-bagger in the top of the fourth.* ☐ *The hit was good for a double-bagger.* **2.** *n.* a very ugly person. (Cruel. With a face so ugly that it takes two paper bags to conceal it. See also *Bag your face!; triple-bagger, coyote-ugly.*) ☐ *Fred is what I would call a double-bagger. What a mug!* ☐ *I am no double-bagger!*

double-barreled slingshot *n.* a brassiere. ☐ *Why does she wear a red double-barreled slingshot?* ☐ *Who dropped a double-barreled slingshot on the floor?*

double buffalo See *double nickels.*

double cross 1. *tr.* to betray someone. (Originally a more complicated switching of sides in a conspiracy wherein the *double-crosser* sides with the victim of the conspiracy—against the original conspirator.) ☐ *Don't even think about double crossing me!* ☐ *Max double crossed Mr. Big a few years back.* **2.** *n.* a betrayal. (See comments with sense 1.) ☐ *He always remembered that double cross.* ☐ *It's one double cross Max is sorry about.*

double-crosser *n.* a person who betrays someone. (Often with *dirty.* See comments at *double cross.*) ☐ *You dirty, lowdown double-crosser, you!* ☐ *Max is the classic double-crosser.*

double-decker 1. *n.* a two-level bus. ☐ *I like to ride in double-deckers.* ☐ *Some double-deckers don't have tops.* **2.** *n.* a sandwich of two layers. ☐ *He put away a giant double-decker and a glass of milk.* ☐ *How can anybody eat a double-decker that is so thick?*

double-deuces *n.* the number 22. ☐ *The National Weather Service says it's going down to the double-deuces tonight.* ☐ *He's double-deuces today, that's right twenty-two years old!*

double-dipper *n.* a person who collects two salaries; a federal employee who collects a federal pension and Social Security. ☐ *The voters of the state were shocked to learn that there were no laws against double-dippers.* ☐ *The double-dippers say they weren't doing anything wrong.*

double-dome 1. *n.* an intellectual. ☐ *It's not that what the double-domes say is wrong, it's that they are so sure that they are right that scares me.* ☐ *I'd rather* *be just folks than a double-dome.* **2.** *mod.* intellectual. ☐ *No more of your double-dome ideas.* ☐ *Most kids need to be exposed to double-dome profs at college for a while.*

double-gaited *mod.* weird; eccentric. ☐ *Carl is a little double-gaited at times. Tries too hard for a laugh.* ☐ *Wow, is he ever double-gaited!* ☐ *She is one of the most successful double-gaited comedians I've ever seen.*

double nickels AND **double buffalo** *n.* the number 55; the 55-mile-per-hour speed limit. (Originally citizens band radio. The buffalo is on one side of the nickel and accounts for the 5.) ☐ *You'd better travel right on those double nickels in through here. The bears are hungry.* ☐ *The double buffalo is enforced on this road.*

double saw(buck) *n.* a twenty-dollar bill. (See also *sawbuck.*) ☐ *This whole thing only cost a double sawbuck.* ☐ *Can you loan me a double sawbuck till payday?*

double take *n.* a surprised second look at something. ☐ *I did a double take and blushed.* ☐ *Fred did a double take, then recognized Tracy.*

double-trouble *n.* a very troublesome thing or person. ☐ *Oh, oh. Here comes double-trouble.* ☐ *That car you got is double-trouble.*

double up (with laughter) *in.* to laugh so hard that one bends over. ☐ *We all just doubled up with laughter.* ☐ *I doubled up when I heard the punch line.*

double whammy ['dəbḷ 'ʍæmi] *n.* a double portion of something, especially something troublesome. (From *Li'l Abner,* a comic strip by Al Capp.) ☐ *We got a real double whammy of trouble down at the office.* ☐ *This morning was bad, but this afternoon the boss gave us a double whammy.*

douche bag *n.* a repellent person; a disliked person. (Crude.) ☐ *Oh, shut up, you old douche bag!* ☐ *Don't be a douche bag!*

dough [do] *n.* money. (See also *bread.*) ☐ *I got a lot of dough for that ring I found.* ☐ *I need some dough to buy groceries.*

dough head *n.* a *nerd;* a simpleton. ☐ *Tom, don't be such a dough head. Read the instructions and do it right.* ☐ *Fred, you are a real dough head! Why did you do that?*

dove [dəv] *n.* someone who supports a peace-seeking U.S. defense policy. (Compare to *hawk.*) ☐ *The doves want to sell the tanks and distribute the money to the poor.* ☐ *The hawks want to ignore the poor and the doves and buy tanks with the money.*

down 1. *mod.* depressed; melancholy. (See also *down with something.*) ☐ *I feel sort of down today.* ☐ *We're all a little down.* **2.** *mod.* (of a machine) inoperative. (Originally said of a computer.) ☐ *The system is down. Come back later.* ☐ *How long has it been down?* **3.** *tr.* to eat or drink something down quickly. ☐ *He downed a can of soda and burped like a thunderclap.* ☐ *She downed her sandwich in record time.* **4.** *tr.* to throw someone down, as in wrestling; to knock someone down as in a fight. ☐ *Wilbur downed his opponent and won the match.* ☐ *Paul downed the guy with one blow.* **5.** *mod.* behind in a score. ☐ *We're three points down with two minutes to play.* ☐ *They're twenty points down, and it looks like the Adamsville team has won.* **6.** *mod.* finished; completed; behind one. ☐ *Well, I've got the test down. Now what?* ☐ *One down and three to go.* **7.** *mod.* learned; memorized. (From sense 6.) ☐ *I got all the dates down pat.* ☐ *I've got the dates down, but not the names.* **8.** *mod.* okay; satisfactory; *cool;* in agreement. (See also *be down (with someone).* The grammar error in the second example is part of the typical context.) ☐ *We had a fight, but we're down now.* ☐ *Me and him is down and always will be.* ☐ *This guy is really down.* **9.** *mod.* prepared; knowledgeable. (From sense 7 and 8.) ☐ *Are you down for the test tomorrow?* ☐ *Everything's down for the party.* **10.** *mod.* alcohol intoxicated. ☐ *Five beers and he was down.* ☐ *They were all down by midnight.* **11.** See *downer.*

down for the count *mod.* inactive for the duration (of something). (From boxing.) ☐ *I've got a terrible cold, and I think I'm down for the count.* ☐ *Fred is down for the count. He's in jail.*

down the drain *mod.* gone; wasted. ☐ *Well, there's 400 bucks down the drain.* ☐ *A lot of money went down the drain in that Wilson deal.*

Down the hatch! *exclam.* "Let's drink it!" (A drinking toast. See also *hatch.*) ☐ *Down the hatch! Have another?* ☐ *Bottoms up! Down the hatch!*

down time *n.* the time when a computer is not operating. (Compare to *up time.*) ☐ *I can't afford a lot of down time in the system I buy.* ☐ *We had too much down time with the other machine.*

down to the wire *mod.* until the very last minute. ☐ *It came down to the wire before I turned the proposal in.* ☐ *We went right down to the wire on that one.*

down trip *n.* any bad experience. (Compare to *downer.*) ☐ *Today was a classic down trip.* ☐ *My vacation was a down trip.*

down under *n.* the area of Australia; Australia. ☐ *I've always wanted to visit down under.* ☐ *We spent Christmas down under.*

down with something **1.** *mod.* comfortable with something; comfortable. (Usually with *get.*) ☐ *Let's get down with some good music.* ☐ *Pete wanted to get down with some grapes.* **2.** *mod.* ill with something; sick in bed with something. ☐ *I was down with the flu for two weeks.* ☐ *Fred and his wife were down with colds for weeks at a time.*

downbeat *mod.* *cool;* easygoing. (Compare to *upbeat.*) ☐ *He is sort of a downbeat character—no stress.* ☐ *I wish I was downbeat like he is.* ☐ *I had sort of a downbeat day. Not your typical Monday.*

downer AND **down; downie** **1.** *n.* a barbiturate or a tranquilizer. (Drugs.) ☐ *She favors downers.* ☐ *Too much booze with those downers, and you're dead.* **2.** *n.* a bad drug experience; a *down trip.* (Drugs.) ☐ *That stuff you gave me was a real downer.* ☐ *Dust is a downer for most people.* **3.** *n.* a depressing event; a bad situation; a *down trip.* ☐ *These cloudy days are always downers.* ☐ *My birthday party was a downer.*

downie See the previous entry.

doxy ['dɑksi] *n.* a gangster's woman. (Underworld. Old.) ☐ *Lefty's doxy dropped off this package. It's ticking.* ☐ *Does Max have a doxy?*

dozens See *(dirty) dozens.*

D.Q. *n.* "Dairy Queen," a trade name for a franchise fast-food store specializing in frozen desserts. (Initialism. Teens and collegiate.) ☐ *Let's go to D.Q., okay?* ☐ *The D.Q. is closed for the winter.*

draft board *n.* a tavern; a saloon. (Alludes to draft beer.) ☐ *Larry is down at the draft board, slamming some beers.* ☐ *Let's stop in the local draft board and toss a couple.*

drafty *n.* a draft beer; beer. ☐ *How about a cold drafty?* ☐ *Another drafty, Tom?*

drag **1.** *n.* something dull and boring. ☐ *This day's a drag.* ☐ *What a drag. Let's go someplace interesting.* **2.** *n.* an annoying person; a burdensome person. (Compare to *schlep.*) ☐ *Gert could sure be a drag when she wanted.* ☐ *Clare was a drag whether she wanted to be or not.* **3.** *n.* a (female) date. ☐ *You got a drag for the dance yet?* ☐ *My drag finked out on me.* **4.** *n.* a puff of a cigarette. ☐ *He took a big drag and scratched at his tattoo.* ☐ *One more drag and he coughed for a while and stubbed out the fag.* **5.** *tr.* to pull or puff on a cigarette. ☐ *She dragged a couple and sat in the funk for a while.* ☐ *When she dragged a fag, you could see her relax and get straight.* **6.** *tr.* to race a car against someone; to race someone in a car. ☐ *I'm planning to drag you at the fairgrounds next Saturday. Better be there.* ☐ *I don't drag anybody anymore. I lost my license.*

dragged *mod.* anxious or frightened after smoking marijuana. (Drugs. Compare to *wired.*) ☐ *The kid was dragged. You* *could tell he didn't have much experience with the real world.* □ *Some of these burnouts really look dragged.*

dragged out *mod.* exhausted; worn out. □ *I feel so dragged out. I think I need some iron.* □ *After the game, the whole team was dragged out.*

draggin'-wagon *n.* a fast car; a car customized for racing. □ *My draggin'-wagon is in the shop.* □ *Your draggin'-wagon can't be driven in town, can it?*

drain 1. *n.* someone or something that exhausts one. □ *Harry is such a drain on me.* □ *What a drain these meetings are.* **2.** *tr.* to wear someone out. □ *Arguing like that drains me something awful.* □ *Your constant bickering is meant to drain me till I submit. Is that it?*

drain the bilge *in.* to empty one's stomach; to vomit. □ *Fred left quickly to drain the bilge.* □ *Who drained the bilge in the bushes?*

Drat! [dræt] *exclam.* "Damn!" □ *Drat! I'm late!* □ *Oh, drat! Another broken nail!*

dreamboat *n.* just the kind of lover one has always dreamed of. (Also a term of address.) □ *Oh, Pete is my dreamboat.* □ *A face man makes a great dreamboat, as long as you never get to know him.*

dreck [drɛk] *n.* dirt; garbage; feces. (From German via Yiddish.) □ *What is all this dreck in the corner?* □ *I've had enough of this dreck around here. Clean it up, or I'm leaving.*

dressed to kill *mod.* dressed in fancy or stylish clothes to impress someone. □ *She is always dressed to kill.* □ *I'm never dressed to kill. I just try to be neat.*

dressed to the nines AND **dressed to the teeth** *mod.* dressed very stylishly with nothing overlooked. □ *She showed up for the picnic dressed to the nines.* □ *Clare is usually dressed to the teeth in order to impress people.*

dressed to the teeth See the previous entry.

Drink up! *exclam.* "Finish your drink!"; "Finish that drink, and we'll have another!" □ *Okay, drink up! It's closing time.* □ *Drink up, and let's get going.*

drinkies ['drɪŋkiz] *n.* drinks; liquor. □ *Okay, kids, it's drinkies all around.* □ *What time is drinkies around here?*

drinkypoo ['drɪŋkipu] *n.* a little drink of liquor. □ *Wouldn't you like just one more drinkypoo of Madeira?* □ *Just a little drinkypoo, my dear.*

drip *n.* an oaf; a *nerd.* □ *Oh, yuck. He's such a drip.* □ *Bob is a drip, I guess, but he's harmless.*

drippy *mod.* weak; ineffective; undesirable. □ *Bob can be so drippy without even trying.* □ *You are proposing some pretty drippy ideas.*

drive someone around the bend *tr.* to drive someone crazy. (See also *(a)round the bend.*) □ *This tax stuff is about to drive me around the bend.* □ *Gert tried to drive us all around the bend.*

drive someone bonkers AND **drive someone nuts** *tr.* to drive someone crazy. (See also *bonkers, nuts.*) □ *This cold is driving me bonkers.* □ *These tax forms are driving me nuts.*

drive someone nuts See the previous entry.

drive someone up the wall *tr.* to frustrate someone; to drive someone to distraction. □ *These days of waiting drive me up the wall.* □ *Staying in the house drove us all up the wall.*

drive the big bus AND **drive the porcelain bus; ride the porcelain bus** *tr.* to vomit into the toilet. □ *Harry's in the john driving the big bus.* □ *Who do I hear driving the porcelain bus in the john?*

drive the porcelain bus See the previous entry.

droid [drɔɪd] *n.* a robot-like person; a *nerd.* (From *android.*) □ *Beavis is as close to a droid as we'll ever see.* □ *The droids are taking over this campus.*

droob AND **drube** [drub] *n.* a dullard; an oaf. □ *Who's the droob standing by the punch bowl?* □ *That drube is my brother!*

drool (all) over someone or something *tr.* to show enormous desire for someone or something. ☐ *He was just drooling all over that new car.* ☐ *Sam was drooling over Martha like a love-sick calf.*

droopy-drawers *n.* someone—usually a child—whose pants are falling down. (Also a term of address.) ☐ *Hey, droopy-drawers, pull up your pants.* ☐ *Jimmy is a regular droopy-drawers. Maybe he needs suspenders.*

drop 1. *tr.* to kill someone or something. ☐ *He dropped the deer with one shot.* ☐ *Lefty tried to drop the leader of the gang.* **2.** *in.* to get arrested. (Underworld.) ☐ *I'm not going to drop for you.* ☐ *Bruno dropped, but Mr. Big got him off.* **3.** *tr.* to knock someone down. ☐ *Jim dropped Willard with a punch to the shoulder.* ☐ *The swinging board hit him and dropped him.* **4.** *n.* a small drink of liquor; a small serving of liquor. ☐ *I'll take just another drop of that dew, if you don't mind.* ☐ *Can I give you another drop?* **5.** *n.* a place at which drugs, alcohol, or other contraband is left to be claimed by the recipient. ☐ *The police discovered the drop and waited for the runner.* ☐ *They switched drops constantly just in case of discovery.* **6.** *tr.* to take a drug, specifically *acid.* (Drugs.) ☐ *Ted dropped some stuff and went on a trip.* ☐ *Now he doesn't drop even once a month.*

drop a bomb(shell) See *drop a brick.*

drop a bop *tr.* to take a drug in pill form. (See also *bop.*) ☐ *Tyrone dropped a bop and went on his way.* ☐ *Wanna come over and drop a bop or two?*

drop a brick AND **drop a bomb(shell)** *tr.* to reveal startling information. ☐ *Tracy came in and dropped a brick that scared us all.* ☐ *You really dropped a bombshell!*

drop a bundle (on someone or something) 1. *tr.* [with *someone*] to spend a lot of money pleasing or entertaining someone. ☐ *I dropped a bundle on the candidate, and it didn't help me at all.* ☐ *Over the years, I've dropped a bundle on clients at that restaurant.* **2.** *tr.* [with *something*] to pay a lot of money for something. ☐ *Pete dropped a bundle on this car.* ☐ *I always buy el cheapo. I've never dropped a bundle on anything.*

drop a dime *tr.* to inform the police of criminal activity. (Underworld. See explanation at *dime-dropper.*) ☐ *We were pretty sure that Tracy is the one who dropped the dime.* ☐ *No, almost anybody will drop a dime these days.*

Drop dead! *exclam.* "No!"; "Beat it!"; "Go away and don't bother me!" ☐ *I don't care. Just drop dead!* ☐ *Drop dead! Beat it!*

drop-dead 1. *mod.* stunning enough to make one drop dead. (Not literal.) ☐ *I had my living room done in a bright drop-dead red that makes your blood run cold!* ☐ *She stood up and made this drop-dead announcement about getting married, and I thought I would just scream.* **2.** *mod.* rude, as if telling someone to drop dead. ☐ *I couldn't stand the boss's drop-dead attitude, so I quit.* ☐ *She looked at me with that kind of drop-dead look that really made me mad.*

drop-dead list *n.* an imaginary list of annoying people whom one could live happily without. ☐ *You are right at the top of my drop-dead list.* ☐ *I put Max on my drop-dead list.*

Drop it! *exclam.* "Forget it!"; "Never mind!" ☐ *Never mind! Just drop it!* ☐ *Drop it! I should never have brought it up.*

drop one's cookies *tr.* to empty one's stomach; to vomit. (See also *toss one's cookies.*) ☐ *The runner went off to the side and dropped her cookies.* ☐ *If you feel like you're going to drop your cookies, don't do it on the carpet.*

drop one's teeth *tr.* to react with great surprise. ☐ *I almost dropped my teeth when she told me her news.* ☐ *They dropped their teeth when I told them I was married.*

drop out 1. *in.* to withdraw from a conventional lifestyle. ☐ *Sometimes I just want to drop out and raise pigs or something.* ☐ *Ted dropped out and bought a farm.* **2.** *in.* to drop out of school or some organization. ☐ *I dropped out before I got promoted.* ☐ *Don't drop out of school. You'll regret it.* **3.** AND **dropout** *n.* someone who has dropped out of school. ☐ *Dropouts find it very hard to get a job.* ☐ *Some dropouts make great successes of themselves, but not very many.*

drop someone *tr.* to knock someone down; to punch and knock down a person. ☐ *Fred dropped Bruno with one punch to the jaw.* ☐ *Max lost his cool and dropped Bruno.*

drop someone or something like a hot potato *tr.* to disassociate oneself with someone or something instantly. ☐ *When we learned of the conviction, we dropped him like a hot potato.* ☐ *I dropped the idea like a hot potato.*

drop the ball *tr.* to fail at something; to allow something to fail. ☐ *I didn't want to be the one who dropped the ball, but I knew that someone would flub up.* ☐ *Sam dropped the ball, and we lost the contract.*

dropped *mod.* arrested. ☐ *Max was dropped only once last year.* ☐ *He got himself dropped on a speeding ticket.*

drube See *droob.*

drug 1. *in.* to use drugs. (Drugs.) ☐ *There is no way that she will stop drugging by herself.* ☐ *Why does she drug so heavily?* **2.** AND **drug out** *mod.* down; depressed. ☐ *Man, am I drug!* ☐ *We are all drug out after that meeting.*

drug lord *n.* a drug dealer high up in the distribution chain. ☐ *The drug lords like Mr. Big seem never to get arrested.* ☐ *Max had always admired the sheer power of the domestic drug lord.*

drug out See *drug.*

druggie AND **druggy** *n.* a drug addict or user. ☐ *That druggy loves to hang out here.* ☐ *There are too many druggies in this neighborhood.*

druggy See the previous entry.

drughead *n.* a heavy drug user; an addict. (Drugs.) ☐ *They find a drughead in the river about once a month.* ☐ *The drugheads are taking over this neighborhood.*

drugola [drəg'olə] *n.* a bribe paid by drug dealers to the police for protection. (Patterned on *payola.*) ☐ *Max pays a little drugola, but mostly the cops never come into this area anyway.* ☐ *A lot of drugola is simply paid in drugs.*

drugstore cowboy *n.* a male who hangs around drugstores and other public places trying to impress women. ☐ *You don't see the old drugstore cowboys around this part of town anymore.* ☐ *The drugstore cowboys of years ago are all hidden away shooting up something.*

drunk back *mod.* alcohol intoxicated; very drunk. ☐ *The whole bunch was drunk back by midnight.* ☐ *Larry was drunk back and couldn't drive us home.*

drunk tank *n.* a jail cell where drunks are kept. (Compare to *junk tank.*) ☐ *A couple of hours in the drunk tank really made me think about alcohol.* ☐ *They hose down the drunk tank every hour on Friday and Saturday nights.*

dry 1. *mod.* sober; no longer alcohol intoxicated. ☐ *Tracy's dry, I hear.* ☐ *How long will Ernie stay dry?* **2.** *n.* a prohibitionist; an abstainer from alcohol. ☐ *The drys are in an increasing majority.* ☐ *Do you know even one dry?* **3.** *mod.* having to do with a region where alcoholic beverages cannot be purchased. (Compare to *wet.*) ☐ *Is Kansas still dry?* ☐ *I hate to get stuck in a dry town.* ☐ *Some small towns are dry, but not many.*

dry-as-dust *mod.* dull; lifeless. ☐ *I can't take another one of his dry-as-dust lectures.* ☐ *All her ideas are dry-as-dust.* ☐ *Some dry-as-dust old crock talked endlessly about old bones.*

Dry up! *exclam.* "Shut up!"; "Go away and don't bother me!" ☐ *Aw, dry up! I've heard enough.* ☐ *Dry up and beat it!*

dub [dəb] **1.** *tr. & in.* to duplicate something; to copy something. ☐ *Dub this and keep a copy yourself.* ☐ *He's busy dubbing right now.* **2.** *n.* a duplicate; a copy. ☐ *The dub was so poor we* *couldn't understand the dialog.* ☐ *This is an almost perfect dub of the original.*

dubage AND **doobage** ['dubɪdʒ] *n.* drugs; marijuana. (See also *doobie.*) ☐ *I detect the smell of dubage in the hallway!* ☐ *Bill kept his doobage in an old shoe in his closet.*

duby See *doobie.*

duc-ducs See the following entry.

ducats AND **duc-ducs** ['dəkəts AND 'dəkdəks] *n.* money. (See also *gold.*) ☐ *Who's got enough ducats to pay for the tickets?* ☐ *I've got duc-ducs galore!*

duck 1. *n.* a male urinal bedpan. (Hospitals.) ☐ *Somebody in room 212 needs a duck.* ☐ *Take this duck down there quick.* **2.** *tr.* to avoid someone or something. ☐ *Clare is ducking her responsibility.* ☐ *You can't duck this investigation. They're on to you.* **3.** See *deduck.*

duck butt AND **dusty butt** *n.* a short person, especially someone with large buttocks. (Also a rude term of address. Potentially offensive.) ☐ *The duck butt who just came in reminds me of somebody I once knew.* ☐ *Hey, dusty butt, where you been keeping yourself?*

duck-squeezer *n.* someone with strong concerns about the environment and conservation, especially rescuing oil-covered ducks. (See also *eagle freak.*) ☐ *Some duck-squeezers were complaining about what the new dam might do.* ☐ *The duck-squeezers were picketing the dam site.*

ducks *n.* tickets. ☐ *You got the ducks for Friday?* ☐ *There were no ducks left.*

ducky *mod.* okay; good. (Often used sarcastically.) ☐ *Now, isn't that just ducky?* ☐ *That's a ducky idea!*

dud [dəd] **1.** *n.* a failure; something that fails to perform as intended. ☐ *The whole idea turned out to be a dud.* ☐ *The play was a dud from start to finish.* **2.** See *duds.*

dude [dud] **1.** *n.* a male friend; a guy. (Also a term of address.) ☐ *Who's the dude with the cowboy boots?* ☐ *Hey, dude, what's happ?* **2.** *mod.* excellent. (See also *dudical.*) ☐ *The game was severely dude! We won!* ☐ *This whole day has been dude and fat.*

dude up *in.* to dress up. ☐ *Let's get all duded up and go out.* ☐ *I got to dude up a little before we go.*

dudette ['dudɛt] *n.* a young woman; the feminine of *dude.* ☐ *Susan is one fine-looking dudette.* ☐ *The place was filled with good-looking dudettes, just waiting for the right guy to come along.*

dudical ['dudɪkl̩] *mod.* really good. (Derived from *dude.*) ☐ *It is truly dudical to see you here, Dave.* ☐ *What a dudical crib!*

duds [dədz] *n.* clothes. (Folksy. Always plural.) ☐ *Are those new duds?* ☐ *I need some new duds, too.*

dufer See *doofer.*

duff [dəf] *n.* the buttocks. ☐ *Get off your duff and get busy.* ☐ *Don't you get tired of sitting around on your duff?*

duffer ['dəfɚ] **1.** *n.* a foolish oaf; a bumbler. ☐ *Some old duffer is weeding our garden for us. He's lost, I think.* ☐ *Pete's just a duffer—he's not really serious at it.* **2.** *n.* an unskilled golfer. ☐ *Those duffers up ahead are holding up the game.* ☐ *Don't call me a duffer!*

duke 1. *in.* to empty one's stomach; to vomit. (Collegiate. Rhymes with *puke.*) ☐ *He left to duke. I saw how green he was.* ☐ *She's in the john, duking like a goat.* **2.** See *dukes.*

duke someone out *tr.* to knock someone out. (See also *dukes.*) ☐ *Wilbur tried to duke the guy out first.* 🅃 *Bob duked out the mugger with a jab to the cheek.*

dukes 1. *n.* the fists. ☐ *Okay, brother, put your dukes up.* ☐ *The guy's got dukes like hams.* **2.** *n.* the knees. ☐ *He went down on his dukes and prayed for all sorts of good stuff.* ☐ *He cracked one of his dukes on the railing.*

duky ['duki] *n.* feces. (Originally black and primarily juvenile.) ☐ *The doggie made duky in the backyard.* ☐ *Mommy, there's duky in Jimmy's diaper.*

dull as dishwater *mod.* very dull. ☐ *She's cute, but dull as dishwater.* ☐ *Life can be as dull as dishwater.*

dull roar *n.* a relatively quiet degree of noisiness. ☐ *Hey, simmer down to a dull roar!* ☐ *Try to keep it at a dull roar if you can.*

dullsville ['dəlzvɪl] **1.** *n.* a dull place. ☐ *This place is just dullsville!* ☐ *Home is dullsville to a teenager.* **2.** *n.* something dull. ☐ *The lecture was downtown dullsville for sure.* ☐ *When each movie I see turns into dullsville, I want to give up seeing them.*

dum-dum See *dumb-dumb.*

dumb-ass AND **stupid-ass** *mod.* stupid. (Potentially offensive. Use only with discretion.) ☐ *That was a dumb-ass thing to do!* ☐ *You can be such a stupid-ass jerk!*

dumb bunny *n.* a stupid person; an oaf. ☐ *Who's the dumb bunny in the double-knits?* ☐ *Don't be a dumb bunny. Pay attention to what's going on.*

dumb cluck *n.* a stupid oaf; a person as stupid as a chicken. ☐ *Sally is not a dumb cluck, but she is sort of slow.* ☐ *What a dumb cluck!*

dumb-dodo ['dəm'dodo] *n.* a very stupid person. ☐ *What a dumb-dodo you are!* ☐ *I'm no dumb-dodo!*

dumb Dora *n.* a stupid woman; a giddy woman. ☐ *I'm no dumb Dora. I'm just learning.* ☐ *Who's the dumb Dora with the blonde hair and long fingernails?*

dumb-dumb AND **dum-dum** *n.* a stupid oaf; a dullard. ☐ *You can be such a dumb-dumb without even trying.* ☐ *Marvin is no dum-dum. He just looks that way.*

dumb ox *n.* a large and stupid person, usually a man. ☐ *What does that dumb ox want?* ☐ *Do you think I'm going to argue with that big dumb ox?*

dumbbell *n.* a stupid oaf. (Also a rude term of address.) ☐ *Look, dumbbell, pay attention!* ☐ *I'm afraid I come on like a dumbbell sometimes.*

dumbhead *n.* a stupid person. ☐ *Bob is no dumbhead, but he sure is strange.* ☐ *I'm no dumbhead. Just a little slow.*

dumbo ['dəmbo] **1.** *n.* a stupid oaf. (Also a rude term of address.) ☐ *Say, dumbo, could you move out of the way?* ☐ *Who's the dumbo in the plaid pants?* **2.** *n.* someone with large ears. (Also a rude term of address. The name of a cartoon character elephant whose ears were large enough to fly with.) ☐ *Wow, look at that dumbo with size twenty ears!* ☐ *I better get new glasses, or I'm going to be a dumbo when my head starts growing.*

dumbski ['dəmski] **1.** *n.* a stupid person. ☐ *He's not the dumbski he seems to be.* ☐ *They used to think Gert was a dumbski.* **2.** *mod.* stupid; dumb. ☐ *What a dumbski jerk!* ☐ *It is not a dumbski idea!*

dummy 1. *n.* an empty liquor or beer bottle. ☐ *Toss your dummies over here, and I'll put them in the bin.* ☐ *That was a sixty dummy party. I counted.* **2.** *n.* a cigarette butt. ☐ *The tramp collected dummies until he had enough for a smoke.* ☐ *The guy tossed a dummy out the window of his car.* **3.** *n.* a stupid person. ☐ *Don't be such a dummy.* ☐ *I'm no dummy!*

dummy up *in.* to refuse to talk. (Underworld. See also *clam up.*) ☐ *Tracy dummied up when they got her into the station.* ☐ *Rocko dummied up right away. He's a real thoroughbred.*

dump 1. *tr. & in.* to empty one's stomach; to vomit. ☐ *He ran straight to the john and dumped his dinner.* ☐ *She turned green, and I knew she was going to dump.* **2.** *in.* to defecate. (Crude. Potentially offensive. Use only with discretion. See also *dump one's load.*) ☐ *He dumped and then came back.* ☐ *He said he had to dump.* **3.** *n.* an act of defecation. (Potentially offensive. Use only with discretion.) ☐ *He said he needed a dump.* ☐ *He had a dump and then came back.* **4.** *n.* a low or cheap establishment; a *joint.* ☐ *I want out of this dump.* ☐ *My mama didn't raise me to spend the rest of my days in a run-down dump like this.*

dump all over someone or something See *do a dump on someone or something.*

dump on someone or something 1. *in.* to snow on someone or something. □ *Well, it dumped on us again last night.* □ *The cold front dumped on the northeast again today.* 2. See *do a dump on someone or something.*

dump one's load 1. *in.* to empty one's stomach; to vomit. □ *He's in the john dumping his load.* □ *Why can't he learn to dump his load silently?* 2. *in.* to defecate. (Crude. Potentially offensive. Use only with discretion. Also with *a.*) □ *He had to go dump a load.* □ *He dumped his load and settled back down to work.*

dumped on 1. *mod.* maligned; abused. □ *I really feel dumped on.* □ *The jerk who designed this stupid congested stairway hasn't been dumped on enough.* 2. *mod.* snowed on. □ *The entire Midwest was dumped on with about ten inches of snow.* □ *Our town really got dumped on last night.*

dupe 1. *n.* a potential victim of a confidence trick; a *patsy.* □ *The crooks found a good dupe and started their scheme.* □ *I don't want to be a dupe for anybody.* 2. *tr.* to trick someone; to swindle someone. □ *You tried to dupe me!* □ *I did not try to dupe you. It was an honest mistake.* 3. *n.* a duplicate; a copy. □ *Make a dupe of this before you send it off.* □ *I've got a dupe in the files.* 4. *tr.* to duplicate something; to copy something. □ *Dupe this and send the original back.* □ *Just a minute, I have to dupe a contract for the boss.*

dust 1. *in.* to leave; to depart. □ *Well, it's late. I gotta dust.* □ *They dusted out of there at about midnight.* 2. *tr.* to defeat someone; to win out over someone. □ *We dusted the other team, eighty-seven to fifty-four.* □ *In the second game, they dusted us.* 3. *tr.* to kill someone. (Underworld.) □ *The gang set out to dust the witnesses, but only got one of them.* □ *Max knew that Bruno was out to dust him.* 4. *n.* fine tobacco for rolling cigarettes. (Prisons.) □ *How about a little dust for this candy bar?* □ *I don't want dust. I need chocolate.* 5. *n.* a powdered drug: heroin, phencyclidine (P.C.P.), cocaine; fine cannabis. (Drugs.) □ *It's the dust that can really do you damage.* □ *Wally got hold of some kind of dust and took it to the police.* 6. *tr.* to add a powdered drug to the end of a (tobacco or cannabis) cigarette. (Drugs.) □ *Pete dusted one, then lit it up.* □ *Max never dusts them before he sells them.*

dust of angels See *angel dust.*

dust someone off *tr.* to give someone a good pounding or beating. □ *Bruno threatened to dust Max off.* 🅃 *Bob dusted off Larry; then he started for Tom.*

dust someone's pants *tr.* to spank someone, usually a child. □ *My dad will dust my pants if he hears about this.* □ *I'm too old for somebody to dust my pants.*

dust-up *n.* a fight. □ *Max got in a dust-up with Bruno.* □ *There was a dust-up at the party that ruined the evening for everyone.*

duster *n.* the buttocks. (See also *rusty-dusty.*) □ *She fell down right on her duster.* □ *My duster is sore from all that riding.*

dusty butt See *duck butt.*

Dutch act AND **Dutch cure** *n.* suicide. (Always with *the.*) □ *Well, Ken took the Dutch cure last week. So sad.* □ *She had tried the Dutch act many times in the past.*

Dutch courage 1. *n.* liquor; false courage from drinking liquor. □ *A couple of shots of Dutch courage, and he was ready to face anything.* □ *How about a little Dutch courage to help you through the first act?* 2. *n.* drugs. □ *Max deals in Dutch courage, as he calls it.* □ *Too much Dutch courage and you're in permanent trouble.*

Dutch cure See *Dutch act.*

Dutch treat *n.* an outing for two or more where the cost is split among the participants, either evenly or in proportion to what is consumed. (See also *go Dutch.*) □ *I propose a Dutch treat to celebrate the day.* □ *We had a Dutch* *treat, which gave us a chance to get to know one another better.*

Dutch uncle *n.* someone who gives avuncular advice; a man who gives advice with the directness of one of one's own relatives. ☐ *If I can be a Dutch uncle for a minute, I could give you some good advice.* ☐ *Dutch uncles can be as big of a pain as parents.*

dweeb [dwib] **1.** *n.* an earnest student. (Collegiate.) ☐ *Don't call Bob a dweeb! Even if he is one.* ☐ *The dweebs get all the A's, so why work?* **2.** *n.* a strange or eccentric person; a *nerd.* ☐ *This place is filled with dweebs of all sizes.* ☐ *Here comes a dweeb. Ask him for some money.*

dynamic duo [daɪˈnæmɪk ˈduo] *n.* a very special pair of people or things. (From the *Batman* television program. Used mostly for humor.) ☐ *The dynamic duo, Beavis and Fred, showed up late and without the beer.* ☐ *Next time tell the dynamic duo to come earlier.*

dynamite [ˈdaɪnəmaɪt] **1.** *n.* anything potentially powerful: a drug, news, a person. ☐ *This chick is really dynamite!* ☐ *The story about the scandal was dynamite and kept selling papers for a month.* **2.** *mod.* excellent; powerful. ☐ *I want some more of your dynamite enchiladas, please.* ☐ *These tacos are dynamite, too.*

E

86 *tr.* to dispose of someone or something; to *nix* someone or something. ☐ *Please take this out and 86 it.* ☐ *He wants $400? 86 that! We can't afford it.*

eager-beaver *n.* a person who is very eager to do something. ☐ *Rocko is an eager-beaver when it comes to collecting money for Mr. Big.* ☐ *The eager-beavers were trying to buy tickets yesterday!*

eagle-eye **1.** *n.* a busybody; a person who watches or monitors other people's actions: a floorwalker, a detective, a hall-monitor. ☐ *Some old eagle-eye across the street saw me standing in the cold and called my wife who came down and let me in.* ☐ *The store detective is an eagle-eye and caught the kleptomaniac.* **2.** *n.* an eye or eyes with very keen vision. ☐ *Keep your eagle-eye trained on the entrance.* ☐ *My eagle-eye tells me there's trouble over there.*

eagle freak *n.* someone with strong concerns about the environment and conservation, especially the preservation of the eagle. (A play on *eco freak.*) ☐ *The eagle freaks oppose building the dam.* ☐ *They call me an eagle freak, which doesn't bother me at all.*

ear candy *n.* soft and pleasant popular music; music that is sweet to the ear. ☐ *I find that kind of ear candy more annoying than heavy metal.* ☐ *People joke about it, but ear candy is restful.*

ear-duster *n.* a gossipy person. ☐ *Sally is sort of an ear-duster, but she's all heart.* ☐ *I can be an ear-duster, I know, but have you heard about Sally and her you-know-what?*

earful ['irful] **1.** *n.* a tremendous amount of gossip. ☐ *I got a big earful about Sally.* ☐ *I can give you an earful about the mayor.* **2.** *n.* a scolding. ☐ *Her mother gave her an earful when she finally got home.* ☐ *Tom got an earful for his part in the prank.*

earl [ɚl] *n.* to vomit. (Onomatopoetic.) ☐ *I think I gotta go earl!* ☐ *Who's earling in the john?*

early bird **1.** *n.* a person who gets up early. ☐ *I never miss sunrise. I'm an early bird.* ☐ *The early birds saw the corpse on the street and called the cops.* **2.** *n.* a person who arrives early. ☐ *The early birds get the best seats.* ☐ *There were some early birds who arrived before the tea things were laid.* **3.** *mod.* having to do with early arrival. ☐ *Early bird arrivals will be given a free cup of coffee.* ☐ *The early bird special this week is a free six-pack of pop for the first 100 visitors.*

earp AND **urp** [ɚp] **1.** *in.* to empty one's stomach; to vomit. (Onomatopoetic.) ☐ *Somebody earped here!* ☐ *I wish people could urp silently.* **2.** *n.* vomit. ☐ *There's earp on your shoe.* ☐ *Throw something over the urp in the flower bed.*

Earp slop, bring the mop. *phr.* "Someone has vomited." (Juvenile catch phrase.) ☐ *See what's in the hall? Earp slop, bring the mop.* ☐ *Earp slop, bring the mop. Somebody was sick.*

earth to ____ *phr.* "Hello ____, are you listening?" (A means of getting the attention of someone who is ignoring you or who is daydreaming. As if one were on the earth, trying to contact someone in a spaceship. The implication is that the person being addressed is *spacy.*) ☐ *Earth to Mom! Earth to Mom! What's* *for dinner?* ☐ *Earth to Fred! Are you asleep? Say something, Fred!*

easy *mod.* easy to please; flexible. ☐ *Don't worry about me. I'm easy.* ☐ *Fred's easy. He'll eat anything.*

Easy does it. **1.** *phr.* "Calm down."; "Relax." ☐ *Chill, man, easy does it.* ☐ *Easy does it! Relax and go slow!* **2.** *phr.* "Be gentle."; "Handle with care." ☐ *Easy does it. Go slow, and you won't dent anything.* ☐ *Easy does it. Two people can handle this heavy old thing if they go slow.*

easy mark *n.* a likely victim. ☐ *Martin looks like an easy mark, but he's really quite savvy.* ☐ *Mary is an easy mark because she is so unsuspecting.*

easy money *n.* money earned or gained with little or no difficulty. ☐ *You know where I can get some easy money?* ☐ *All you guys want easy money. Don't you want to work for it?*

easy street *n.* a place or position in life where living is easy. (See also *fat city, on easy street.*) ☐ *Easy street is no place for an active guy like Sam.* ☐ *Easy street is exactly what I want out of life.*

eat **1.** *tr.* [for something] to bother or worry someone. ☐ *What's eating you, Bill?* ☐ *Nothing's eating me. I'm just the nervous type.* **2.** *tr.* to absorb the cost or expense of something. ☐ *It was our mistake, and we'll have to eat it.* ☐ *We'll eat the costs on this one. It's the least we can do.*

eat crow *tr.* to display total humility, especially when shown to be wrong. ☐ *Well, it looks like I was wrong, and I'm going to have to eat crow.* ☐ *I'll be eating crow if I'm not shown to be right.*

eat face *tr.* to kiss deeply. (Compare to *suck face.*) ☐ *There were some kids eating face over in the corner.* ☐ *Tim and Karen were in the back seat eating face.*

eat nails *tr.* to look and act really tough or angry. ☐ *Bruno looked mad enough to eat nails.* ☐ *They were all eating nails by the time the IRS got the mess straightened out.*

eat one's hat *tr.* to do something extraordinary. ☐ *If she wins, I'll eat my hat.* ☐ *I'll eat my hat if our advertisement actually brings us a president.*

eat one's heart out **1.** *tr.* to suffer from sorrow or grief. ☐ *She has been eating her heart out over that jerk ever since he ran away with Tracy.* ☐ *Don't eat your heart out. You really didn't like him that much, did you?* **2.** *tr.* to suffer from envy or jealousy. (Usually a command.) ☐ *Yeah, this one's all mine. Eat your heart out!* ☐ *Eat your heart out! I won it fair and square.*

eat something up **1.** *tr.* to consume something rapidly, such as food or money. ☐ *Running this household eats my income up.* 🅃 *The car really eats up gas.* **2.** *tr.* to believe something. ☐ *Those people really eat that stuff up about tax reduction.* 🅃 *They'll eat up almost anything you tell them.* **3.** *tr.* to appreciate something. ☐ *The audience really ate it up.* 🅃 *The stuff about the federal budget went over well. They really ate up the whole story.*

eat up *in.* to eat in enjoyment. (Usually a command.) ☐ *Come on, now. Sit down and eat up!* ☐ *Eat up! There's plenty more where this came from.*

eco freak AND **eco nut** ['iko frik AND 'iko nət] *n.* someone with strong concerns about the environment and conservation. (Mildly derogatory. From *ecology.*) ☐ *They call me an eco freak, which is okay by me.* ☐ *It's we eco nuts who think about the future of our planet.*

eco nut See the previous entry.

Ecstasy ['ɛkstəsi] *n.* a hallucinogen similar to *L.S.D.* (Drugs.) ☐ *Chemicals with names like "Ecstasy" are being put on the streets every day.* ☐ *Ecstasy is just one of a dozen drugs with similar formulas.*

edge *n.* drunkenness; the early stage of intoxication from alcohol or drugs. (See also *have an edge on.*) ☐ *She was beginning to show a little edge, but she obviously still could drive.* ☐ *The edge was starting, so Kelly slowed down her drinking.*

edged *mod.* alcohol or drug intoxicated. ☐ *They set out to be edged by midnight.* ☐ *We were edged and full of rich food. We needed only to sleep.*

edgy *mod.* nervous; anxious and uncertain. ☐ *I feel sort of edgy about the race.* ☐ *I'm just an edgy guy.* ☐ *Don't let yourself get so edgy.*

egg-beater 1. *n.* an outboard boat motor. ☐ *My egg-beater has been acting up, so I didn't go out on the lake today.* ☐ *By the time you get about twenty egg-beaters on the lake at once, it's really pretty noisy.* 2. *n.* a helicopter. (See also *rotorhead*.) ☐ *The egg-beater landed on the hospital roof.* ☐ *I would think that egg-beaters all over the place would disturb the patients.*

egg-sucker *n.* a flatterer; a sycophant. ☐ *The guy is a chronic egg-sucker. Ignore him.* ☐ *Who's the egg-sucker who brought the teacher candy?*

egghead *n.* an intellectual person. ☐ *The eggheads aren't exactly taking over the world.* ☐ *My uncle was an egghead, but nobody in our family thought he knew very much.*

ego trip *n.* a public expression of one's feelings of importance or superiority. ☐ *The guy is on another ego trip. Pay no attention.* ☐ *Sorry, I guess I'm on another ego trip.*

ego tripper *n.* a person who habitually goes on an *ego trip.* ☐ *Not another ego tripper running for public office!* ☐ *You have to be an ego tripper to be a palm-presser.*

eighteen wheeler *n.* a large trailer truck. (There are a total of eighteen wheels on the cab and trailer.) ☐ *An eighteen wheeler almost ran me off the road.* ☐ *The eighteen wheelers rule the road at night.*

[eighty-six] See *86.*

el cheapo [ɛl 'tʃipo] 1. *n.* the cheap one; the cheapest one. (Mock Spanish.) ☐ *I don't want one of those el cheapos.* ☐ *I can only afford el cheapo.* 2. *mod.* cheap. ☐ *The el cheapo brand won't last.* ☐ *This is el cheapo. I don't want it.* ☐ *Is this the el cheapo model?*

(el) primo [(ɛl) 'primo] *mod.* having to do with something that is top quality. (From Spanish for "the first.") ☐ *This stuff is primo.* ☐ *I want some more of that el primo C.*

elbow-bending *n.* drinking liquor; drinking liquor to excess. ☐ *She spends quite a bit of time at elbow-bending.* ☐ *That's a lot of elbow-bending for one sitting.*

elbow-grease *n.* effort. ☐ *Put out a little elbow-grease.* ☐ *All this job needs is a little more elbow-grease.*

electrified *mod.* alcohol intoxicated. ☐ *Her eyes were staring straight ahead, and I knew she was electrified.* ☐ *By midnight we were all electrified.*

elevated *mod.* alcohol intoxicated; tipsy. ☐ *Jerry was too elevated to drive home.* ☐ *Sam was elevated from the drinking he did.*

elevator music *n.* dull, uninteresting music of the type that can be heard in elevators or shops. (As compared to exciting jazz or rock.) ☐ *I don't want to have to hear elevator music all day.* ☐ *Elevator music is better than listening to someone chewing food.*

eliminated 1. *mod.* killed. ☐ *Mr. Big wanted Max eliminated.* ☐ *When Max is eliminated, there will be no competition.* 2. *mod.* alcohol intoxicated. ☐ *By midnight, Wally was eliminated.* ☐ *How can anybody get eliminated on four beers?*

em [ɛm] *n.* AND **emm** an empty liquor bottle. ☐ *Put your ems in the garbage, not on the floor.* ☐ *Whose emms are all these?*

embalmed *mod.* alcohol intoxicated. ☐ *By morning they were all embalmed.* ☐ *Bob was too embalmed to stand up.*

embalming fluid *n.* strong liquor; raw whiskey. ☐ *Jed seemed to favor some cheap embalming fluid as his poison.* ☐ *Bartender, pour out this embalming fluid and get me your best.*

emm See *em.*

[emoticon] See the discussion at *Smiley.*

empties *n.* empty bottles. □ *Throw your empties in the trash.* □ *Whose empties are these, and how many are there?*

empty-nesters *n.* parents whose children have grown and moved out. □ *There are a few adjustments that empty-nesters have to make.* □ *I don't mind being an empty-nester. There's more room.*

end *n.* the final insult; too much; the last straw. □ *This is just the end. I'm leaving.* □ *When she poured her drink down my back, that was the end.*

end of the ball game *n.* the end of everything. □ *Well, the car broke down. I guess that's the end of the ball game.* □ *It looked like the end of the ball game as we sped too fast around the curve.*

ends 1. *n.* money. (Streets.) □ *You got enough ends to get you through the week?* □ *We don't have enough ends to pay the gas bill.* **2.** *n.* shoes. □ *You even got holes in your ends.* □ *Could you use some new ends?*

enforcer *n.* a bully; a thug or bodyguard. □ *Bruno is the perfect enforcer. Meaner than all get out.* □ *Rocko is too tenderhearted to be a good enforcer.*

enhanced *mod.* *high* on marijuana. (Drugs.) □ *Max is sort of enhanced, as usual.* □ *Fred is enhanced by dinnertime each day.*

equalizer *n.* a gun; a pistol. (Underworld.) □ *Rocko carried an equalizer, but wouldn't dream of using it.* □ *An equalizer can be dangerous in Max's business.*

erase *tr.* to kill someone. □ *Bruno had orders to erase Max.* □ *Mr. Big decided who was gonna erase who.*

erb See *herb.*

Ervine See *Irv.*

eternal checkout *n.* death. (Usually with *the.*) □ *When the time comes for the eternal checkout, I hope I am ready to go.* □ *Hank knew the eternal checkout was just around the corner, and he suddenly got religion.*

eternity-box *n.* a coffin. □ *When I'm in my eternity-box, then you can have my stereo.* □ *I have my eternity-box all picked out.*

euchre ['jukɚ] *tr.* to cheat or deceive someone. □ *Those guys'll try to euchre you, so watch out.* □ *I think the clerk euchred me.*

even-Steven 1. *mod.* evenly divided. □ *He made the two piles of diamonds even-Steven and then let me chose which one I wanted.* □ *The cake is not exactly cut even-Steven.* **2.** *mod.* even; balanced. □ *Now we're even-Steven.* □ *Now that we've given each other black eyes, are we even-Steven?*

evened out *mod.* back to normal; restored to sanity. □ *When things are evened out after the holidays, we can settle down.* □ *Finally, at about age thirty, you could say that Sam was evened out.*

everything from soup to nuts *n.* everything imaginable. □ *It looks like she brought everything from soup to nuts.* □ *I have everything from soup to nuts in my briefcase.*

evidence *n.* liquor. (Usually with *the.* Incorporated into a suggestion that the evidence be destroyed by drinking it.) □ *There is only one thing to do with evidence like this, and that's drink it.* □ *They knocked back all the evidence very quickly.*

evil *mod.* excellent. (See also *wicked.*) □ *This wine is really evil!* □ *Man, what evil fronts!*

ex [ɛks] *n.* a former spouse or lover. □ *My ex is in town, but we don't talk much anymore.* □ *Her ex remarried.*

Excellent! *exclam.* "Fine!" (Like *awesome,* this expression is a standard word used frequently in slang contexts.) □ *A new stereo? Excellent!* □ *Excellent! Way rad!*

Excuse my French. See *Pardon my French.*

exec [ɛg'zɛk] *n.* an executive. □ *The execs are well-treated around here.* □ *They are even firing the execs now.*

eye-opener 1. *n.* a real surprise. □ *Her confession was a real eye-opener.* □ *This day has been an eye-opener for me.* **2.** *n.* a wake-up drink of liquor; a strong drink any time. □ *He knocked back a quick eye-opener and finished dressing.* □ *One eye-opener led to another.*

eye-popper 1. *n.* something astonishing. □ *The description of the theft was a real eye-popper.* □ *What an eye-popper of a story!* **2.** *n.* a very good-looking woman or *girl.* □ *Isn't that foxy lady an eye-popper?* □ *I may not be an eye-popper, but my virtue is exemplary.*

eyeball *tr.* to look hard at someone or something. □ *I eyeballed the contract and saw the figures.* □ *The two eyeballed each other and walked on.*

eyeball to eyeball *mod.* face to face. □ *They approached each other eyeball to eyeball and frowned.* □ *Let's talk more when we are eyeball to eyeball.*

eyeful *n.* the sight of something that one was not meant to see. □ *I got an eyeful of that contract. Yikes! What a giveaway!* □ *She really gave us an eyeful. Shame.*

eyewash 1. *n.* nonsense; deception. □ *Aw, that's just a lot of eyewash!* □ *It's not eyewash! It's true!* **2.** *n.* liquor. □ *How about some of that nice eyewash?* □ *You've been putting away a lot of that eyewash, haven't you?*

F

411 ['for'wən'wən] *n.* information; the details about something or someone. (In the U.S., the telephone number of directory assistance or "information" is 411.) □ *What's the 411 on the new guy in the front office?* □ *I heard some interesting 411 on the guy down the street.*

fab [fæb] *mod.* fabulous. □ *Man, what a fab stereo!* □ *Your pad is not what I'd call fab. Just okay.*

face card *n.* an important person; a self-important person. (As with the royal characters in playing cards.) □ *Who's the face card getting out of the benz?* □ *Mr. Big is the face card in the local mob.*

(face) fungus ['fes fəŋgəs] *n.* whiskers; a beard. □ *If John would shave off that face fungus, he'd look a lot better.* □ *What do you need all that fungus for anyway?*

face man *n.* a good-looking young man with no personality. (Collegiate.) □ *Harry is just a face man and as dull as dishwater.* □ *Norm is the perfect face man—all looks and no brains.*

face-off ['fesɔf] *n.* a confrontation. (From hockey.) □ *For a minute it looked like we were headed toward a nasty face-off.* □ *The face-off continued for a few moments till both of them realized that there was no point in fighting.*

face the music *tr.* to receive the rebuke that is due one. □ *You had better go in and face the music now.* □ *You have to face the music eventually.*

faced **1.** *mod.* alcohol intoxicated. (From *shit-faced.*) □ *Lord, is he faced!* □ *Who is that guy on the corner who looks so faced?* **2.** *mod.* rejected by a member of the opposite sex. (Collegiate.) □ *I've been faced again, and I hate it!* □ *Sally was faced by Todd, and she won't speak to him or anybody else.*

facilities *n.* toilet facilities. □ *Where are the facilities around here?* □ *Can I use your facilities?*

fack [fæk] *in.* to state the facts; to tell (someone) the truth. (Black.) □ *That dude is not facking with me.* □ *Now is the time to start facking. Where were you?*

facts of life **1.** *n.* an explanation of human reproduction, especially as presented to a child. □ *No one ever explained the facts of life to me. I read books about it.* □ *She is so naive. She doesn't even know the facts of life.* **2.** *n.* the truth about life's difficulties. □ *You had better face up to the facts of life and get a job.* □ *They taught me everything in college except the facts of life.*

fade **1.** *in.* to leave. □ *I think that the time has come for me to fade. See ya.* □ *Hey, man, let's fade.* **2.** *in.* to lose power; to lose influence. □ *Ralph is fading, and someone else will have to take over.* □ *The positive effect of the weekend faded fast.*

fadoodle [fə'dudl̩] *n.* something ridiculous; nonsense. □ *Oh, stop your silly fadoodle!* □ *That's nothing but fadoodle!*

fag [fæg] **1.** *n.* a cigarette. □ *Hey, pal, gimme a fag.* □ *Go buy your own fags!* **2.** AND **faggot** *n.* a homosexual. (Potentially offensive. Use only with discretion. Usually derogatory. Resented by homosexuals.) □ *Who's the fag with the fancy hat?* □ *Don't act like a faggot,*

Gary. **3.** *n.* a repellent male. ☐ *You creepy fag. Stop it!* ☐ *Bruno is such a fag!*

fag-busting *n.* doing violence to homosexuals. (Potentially offensive. Use only with discretion.) ☐ *Those bums get some kind of pleasure out of fag-busting.* ☐ *What's this strange need you have for fag-busting? What's your problem?*

fagged out *mod.* exhausted. ☐ *I'm really fagged out after all that running.* ☐ *John, you sure look fagged out.*

faggot See *fag.*

fail *n.* a failing grade; a grade of F. (Compare to *pass.*) ☐ *Sorry, this paper's a fail if I ever saw one.* ☐ *I pulled a fail in stat.*

fair-haired boy *n.* a promising young man; a young man who receives favoritism. ☐ *Ted is the boss's fair-haired boy now, but he'll be just like the rest of us in a month.* ☐ *He'd have been fired if he wasn't the fair-haired boy.*

fair shake *n.* a fair chance. (From shaking dice.) ☐ *I want to give you both a fair shake.* ☐ *All I want from you is a fair shake.*

fair-weather *mod.* temporary; insincere. (From *fair-weather sailor.*) ☐ *I need something more than a fair-weather friend to help me through all this.* ☐ *Well, I see you are just a fair-weather golfer like me.*

fairy *n.* a homosexual. (Potentially offensive. Use only with discretion. Derogatory. Resented by homosexuals.) ☐ *I hear that you-know-who is a fairy.* ☐ *Who goes around calling people fairies?*

fairy tale AND **bedtime story** *n.* a simplistic and condescending explanation for something; a lie. ☐ *I don't want to hear a fairy tale, just the facts, ma'am.* ☐ *What you're telling me sounds like a bedtime story. Come back when you can be more straightforward.*

fake book *n.* a book with basic melody and chord changes for hundreds of popular songs. ☐ *Somebody lifted my fake book.* ☐ *I thought fake books were illegal.*

fake it *tr.* to pretend (to do something). ☐ *If you don't know the right notes, just fake it.* ☐ *I can't fake it anymore. I've got to be honest with you.*

fake off *in.* to waste time; to *goof off.* ☐ *Hey, you guys, quit faking off!* ☐ *All you clowns do is fake off. Now, get busy!*

fake someone out *tr.* to deceive someone, as with a football pass. ☐ *They faked me out, and then I stumbled over my own feet. The coach was fuming.* 🅃 *We faked out the teacher who thought we had gone out in the hall.*

fakus ['fekəs] *n.* a gadget; something with no name or a forgotten name. ☐ *This little fakus goes right in here.* ☐ *Hand me that long fakus with the hole in one end.*

falderal AND **folderol** ['fɑldəɑl] *n.* wasted effort; nonsense. ☐ *I had about enough of your falderal.* ☐ *Stop the folderol and get to work.*

fall 1. *in.* to be arrested; to be charged with a crime. (Underworld. See also *fall guy.*) ☐ *I heard that Bruno fell. Is that right?* ☐ *Bruno would never fall easily. Must be a frame.* **2.** *n.* one's arrest; being arrested and charged. (Underworld.) ☐ *Who took the fall for the bank job?* ☐ *Rocko will never accept a fall willingly.*

fall guy *n.* a victim; a *dupe.* (Originally underworld.) ☐ *Rocko wasn't going to be the fall guy for this caper.* ☐ *I didn't want to be the fall guy, so I sat out the last job.*

fall off the wagon *in.* to resume drinking after having stopped. ☐ *Poor Jed fell off the wagon again.* ☐ *It looks to me like he wanted nothing more than to fall off the wagon.*

fall out *in.* to depart. (Probably from the military command meaning "disperse.") ☐ *It's late, G. I have to fall out.* ☐ *Let's fall out. I have to get up early in the morning.*

fall out of bed *in.* to fall far down, as with the drop in some measurement. ☐

The temperature really fell out of bed last night! It was twenty-three below! ☐ *The stock market fell out of bed last year at this time.*

falling-down drunk **1.** *mod.* alcohol intoxicated; very drunk. ☐ *Poor Fred is falling-down drunk and has no way to get home.* ☐ *She's not just tipsy; she's falling-down drunk.* **2.** *n.* a drunken person who falls down. ☐ *Poor old Jed is turning into a falling-down drunk.* ☐ *One more falling-down drunk in this neighborhood will not be anything new.*

falling-out *n.* a disagreement. ☐ *Tom and Bill had a little falling-out.* ☐ *They patched up their little falling-out.*

fallout *n.* the results of something; the *flack* from something. ☐ *The fallout from this afternoon's meeting was not as serious as some expected.* ☐ *It's not the crisis itself, but the fallout from the crisis that concerns us all.*

fan *tr.* to ignore someone or something; to cut a class; to *blow someone or something off.* ☐ *You have to meet with your teacher? Oh, fan that. It doesn't matter.* ☐ *Mary fanned her history class and missed an important test.*

fan the breeze *tr.* to chat or gossip. ☐ *We're just fanning the breeze, so you didn't interrupt anything.* ☐ *Stop fanning the breeze and get to work.*

fancy footwork AND **fast footwork** *n.* artful maneuvering; fast and clever thinking. ☐ *Ken did a lot of fancy footwork to get out of that one.* ☐ *Fast footwork is the key to success in politics.*

Fancy meeting you here. *sent.* "Just imagine meeting you here!"; "I am surprised to meet you here!" ☐ *Well, hello, Tom. Fancy meeting you here!* ☐ *Fancy meeting you here, Bill. How have you been?*

fancy-schmancy ['fæntsi'ʃmæntsi] *mod.* fancy; very fancy. ☐ *This one is just too fancy-schmancy for Heidi.* ☐ *She likes everything fancy-schmancy.* ☐ *I don't care for these fancy-schmancy get-togethers.*

Fancy that! *exclam.* "Imagine that!" ☐ *So, you're a bus driver now. Well, fancy that!* ☐ *Fancy that! There's a piece of pie left in the fridge.*

fanigle See *finagle.*

fanny *n.* the buttocks. (Euphemistic in the U.S. The term has taboo implications in the U.K.) ☐ *He fell down right on his fanny.* ☐ *There's dust or something on your fanny.*

fanny-bumper *n.* an event that draws so many people that they bump into one another. ☐ *The fire on Thirty-fourth Street turned into a real fanny-bumper.* ☐ *There was a typically dull fanny-bumper in the village last night.*

fanny-dipper *n.* a swimmer, as opposed to a surfer. (California.) ☐ *The fanny-dippers are not supposed to go out that far.* ☐ *It's too windy for fanny-dippers, let alone surfers.*

Fantabulous! *exclam.* "Great!" (A blend of *fantastic* and *fabulous.*) ☐ *You're here at last. Fantabulous!* ☐ *Fantabulous! It's finished.*

far gone **1.** *mod.* in an extreme state. ☐ *Wow, that chick is far gone. Listen to her rave.* ☐ *He was too far gone to make any sense.* **2.** *mod.* alcohol intoxicated. ☐ *Larry's far gone and looking sick.* ☐ *Wow, is she ever far gone!*

far out **1.** *mod. cool;* great; extraordinary. ☐ *This jazz is really far out!* ☐ *You want to hear some far out heavy metal?* **2.** *mod.* very hard to understand; arcane; highly theoretical. ☐ *This stuff is too far out for me.* ☐ *I can't follow your far out line of reasoning.* **3.** *mod.* alcohol or drug intoxicated. ☐ *How'd you get so far out?* ☐ *Three beers and Wally was really far out.*

fart [fɑrt] (Potentially offensive in all senses. Use only with discretion. Less offensive in the U.K., and it is now used more openly in the U.S.) **1.** *n.* a release of intestinal gas, perhaps with a noise. ☐ *Did I hear a fart?* ☐ *Who is responsible for that fart?* **2.** *in.* to release intestinal gas, perhaps with a noise. ☐ *Who farted?* ☐ *Somebody farted.* **3.** *n.*

an obnoxious or a stupid person. (Also a provocative term of address.) □ *Who's the old fart with the enormous mustache?* □ *Who called me an old fart?*

fart sack *n.* a sleeping bag; a bed. (Potentially offensive. Use only with discretion.) □ *Well, it's time I was getting into the old fart sack.* □ *Get out of that fart sack and get up and get going!*

farts *n.* "fine arts." (Use discretion with *fart.*) □ *Ted is studying over in the farts department.* □ *Fred took a course in farts and hated it.*

fast buck See *quick buck.*

fast footwork See *fancy footwork.*

fast one *n.* a clever and devious trick. (See also *pull a fast one.*) □ *That was a fast one. I didn't know you were so devious.* □ *This was the last fast one like that you'll ever pull on me.*

fat 1. *mod.* great; excellent. □ *The fireworks in the park were really fat this year!* □ *Mary thought the rally was fat, but left early anyway.* **2.** *mod.* well supplied with something; having an overabundance of something. □ *When it comes to printer paper, this place is fat.* □ *We're fat with paper, but there's not a ribbon in sight.* **3.** *mod.* sexy. □ *She is one fat sister!* □ *You are truly fat, Wendy.*

fat-cat 1. *n.* someone with great wealth and the accompanying success. □ *I like to watch the fat-cats go by in their beemers.* □ *I'm no fat-cat. I'm usually financially embarrassed in fact.* **2.** *mod.* having to do with wealth or a wealthy person. □ *You'll never see me driving any of those fat-cat cars.* □ *I just have a bank account. No fat-cat investments.*

fat chance *n.* a very poor chance. (Sarcastic.) □ *Fat chance I'll ever get a new car.* □ *Me, get an A? Fat chance.*

fat city 1. *n.* a state of wealth and comfort; easy street. □ *She's living in fat city ever since she inherited her fortune.* □ *I could settle down in fat city without any trouble.* **2.** *n.* fatness (expressed as a place). □ *I've had it with fat city. I'm going on a diet.* □ *Sally is well on her way to fat city.*

fathead *n.* a stupid person; someone who has fat where brains ought to be. □ *You can be such a fathead!* □ *Paul, you are being a perfect fathead.*

fatheaded *mod.* stupid. □ *Now that is really a fatheaded idea.* □ *It's not fatheaded!* □ *Let's not come up with a fatheaded plan. This one has to make sense.*

fatso ['fætso] *n.* a fat person. (Cruel. Also a rude term of address.) □ *Hey, fatso! Go on a diet!* □ *Some fatso tried to get on the plane and couldn't even get through the door!*

fatty *n.* a derogatory nickname for a fat person. (Cruel. Also a rude term of address.) □ *Okay, fatty, you get the biggest piece of cake because you deserve it.* □ *That fatty over there is going to eat up all the snacks.*

fattygews ['fætigjuz] *n.* fatigues. (Originally military.) □ *I'll slip into some fattygews and be right with you.* □ *Whose fattygews are piled here in the corner?*

feather brain *n.* a stupid person. (Also a rude term of address.) □ *Gary is such a feather brain.* □ *Hey, feather brain. Wake up and get busy!*

fed 1. AND **the feds** *n.* a federal agent concerned with narcotics, tax collection, customs, etc. □ *Some fed was prowling around asking questions about you.* □ *The feds are onto Rocko and his gang.* **2.** *n.* the Federal Reserve Board. (Usually **Fed.** Always with *the.*) □ *The Fed is not likely to raise interest rates very soon again.* □ *There is no way to predict what the Fed is going to do.*

federal diploma *n.* a U.S. bank note. □ *I could use a few extra of those federal diplomas.* □ *How many federal diplomas you got with you?*

federal jug *n.* a federal prison. (Underworld. See also *jug.*) □ *Rocko was set to spend the next twenty years in the federal jug.* □ *Lefty is fresh and sweet—just out of the federal jug.*

feeb [fib] *n.* an oaf; a stupid person. (From *feebleminded.*) □ *Don't be a feeb. Wake up!* □ *You are such a feeb!*

feebee See the following entry.

feeby AND **feebee** ['fibi] *n.* the F.B.I., the Federal Bureau of Investigation. ☐ *The locals were going to call in the feebies, but the D.A. said to wait.* ☐ *The feeby is in on this already.*

feed one's face *tr.* to put food in one's mouth; to eat (something). ☐ *You're always feeding your face. You're going to get fat.* ☐ *Stop feeding your face and listen to me.*

feel a draft *tr.* to sense that one is being rejected; to sense that someone is cool toward one, possibly for racial reasons. ☐ *Oh, man, I feel a draft in here. Let's leave.* ☐ *What a reception! I sure feel a draft.*

feel groovy **1.** *in.* to feel really good and mellow. ☐ *It's a beautiful day, and I really feel groovy.* ☐ *Everybody is feeling groovy and smiling and all.* **2.** *in.* to be alcohol or drug intoxicated. ☐ *Looks like Kelly is feeling groovy on gin again.* ☐ *Bruno feels groovy because of what he is smoking.*

feeling no pain **1.** *mod.* numbed by alcohol and feeling nothing; alcohol intoxicated. ☐ *She fell off the wagon and is feeling no pain.* ☐ *He drank the whole thing, and he's feeling no pain.* **2.** *mod.* feeling nothing; dead. ☐ *Now, poor Jed is feeling no pain.* ☐ *Your aunt is feeling no pain now. She slipped away before dawn.*

feep [fip] **1.** *n.* the beep made by a computer. ☐ *This thing only makes a feep when I try to run my program.* ☐ *What does the feep mean?* **2.** *in.* [for a computer] to make a little beep. ☐ *It feeps when it's angry, I think.* ☐ *Naw! It just feeps to get your attention.*

fella ['fɛlə] *n.* a fellow; a *guy.* (Also a term of address.) ☐ *Who's the fella with the dark glasses?* ☐ *Hey, fella. Got a match?*

fence hanger *n.* someone who cannot decide which side to be on. ☐ *We need to find a way to persuade the fence hangers to come over to our side.* ☐ *The senator stated he would be a fence hanger until the very minute of the vote.*

fenced *mod.* angry. (California.) ☐ *Boy, was that old man fenced!* ☐ *Too many people around here are fenced all the time.*

fender-bender ['fɛndɚbɛndɚ] **1.** *n.* a minor accident. (Compare to *rear-ender.*) ☐ *There are a couple of fender-benders on the expressway this morning, so be careful.* ☐ *A minor fender-bender blocked traffic for a while.* **2.** *n.* a reckless driver (who causes minor accidents). ☐ *I can't get insurance on my seventeen-year-old, who is a hopeless fender-bender.* ☐ *Don't give up on young fender-benders.*

fer shur [fɚ 'ʃɚ] *phr.* "*for sure*"; "absolutely." (Eye-dialect. Used in writing only for effect. See also *for sure.*) ☐ *This is way rad, fer shur.* ☐ *I'll be there. Fer shur!*

feshnushkied [fɛ'ʃnuʃkid] *mod.* alcohol intoxicated. ☐ *Wow, is that guy ever feshnushkied!* ☐ *Gert is too feshnushkied to drive home.*

fetch up *in.* to empty one's stomach; to vomit. ☐ *I really felt like I was going to fetch up.* ☐ *Somebody fetched up in here and didn't clean it up.*

fib [fɪb] **1.** *n.* a small lie. ☐ *It was just a little fib. I'm sorry.* ☐ *Is this another one of your fibs?* **2.** *in.* to tell a small lie. ☐ *Stop fibbing and tell me the truth.* ☐ *Did you fib to the teacher?*

fibber ['fɪbɚ] *n.* a liar. ☐ *Harry can be a fibber sometimes. You got to watch him.* ☐ *Jimmy is turning into a little fibber.*

FIFO. *phr.* "first in, first out," the first items placed in the stack are the first items to be retrieved. (Computers. Acronym. See also *GIGO, LIFO.*) ☐ *Of course the wrong thing came out. That register is FIFO.* ☐ *Oh, I thought this thing was FIFO, and I put the stuff in the wrong order.*

fifth wheel *n.* an extra and unneeded person. ☐ *I feel like such a fifth wheel around here.* ☐ *Hank is just a fifth wheel. Send him home.*

file See *(pro)file.*

file thirteen *n.* the wastebasket. (See also *circular file.*) ☐ *Please throw this in* *file thirteen. I don't need it anymore.* □ *I'm afraid that the papers you want went into file thirteen two days ago.*

fill-mill *n.* a tavern. □ *She stopped off at the fill-mill again this evening.* □ *She spends a lot of time at that fill-mill.*

fill or kill AND **F.O.K.** *phr.* a broker's notation advising the stock exchange to fill a stock order or kill it. (The abbreviation is an initialism. Securities markets.) □ *Get rid of this order. It was fill or kill, and it should have been killed yesterday.* □ *Where? I don't see that it's marked F.O.K.*

filling station *n.* a liquor store. (From an old name for an automobile service station.) □ *Please stop at the filling station and get some suds on your way home.* □ *The filling station on the corner does a big business on Fridays.*

filthy lucre [...'lukɚ] *n.* money. □ *I sure could use a little of that filthy lucre.* □ *I don't want to touch any of your filthy lucre.*

filthy rich 1. *mod.* very wealthy. □ *I wouldn't mind being filthy rich.* □ *There are too many filthy rich people now.* □ *Ken is filthy rich because of the money his uncle left him.* **2.** *n.* people who are very wealthy. □ *The filthy rich can afford that kind of thing, but I can't.* □ *I sort of feel sorry for the filthy rich.*

fin AND **finn** [fɪn] *n.* a five-dollar bill. (Germanic via Yiddish.) □ *Who says I owe you a fin?* □ *I gave the old guy a finn, and he nearly passed out.*

finagle AND **fanigle** [fɪ'negl̩ AND fə'nɪgl̩] **1.** *in.* to plot and plan; to conspire; to arrange (something). □ *He's pretty good at finagling.* □ *She'd rather fanigle than ask outright.* **2.** *tr.* to acquire something through conniving. □ *She spent a lot of time trying to finagle a ride to work.* □ *Can I fanigle a buck from you?*

financially embarrassed *mod.* broke. □ *I'm a bit financially embarrassed at the moment.* □ *Gary found himself financially embarrassed when the time came to pay the bill.*

fine and dandy *mod.* nice; good; well. (Often sarcastic.) □ *Well, that's just fine and dandy. Couldn't be better.* □ *I feel fine and dandy, and I'm going to have a good time here.*

finger 1. *tr.* to point someone out; to identify someone (as having done something, been somewhere, etc.). □ *Pete fingered Marty as being the one who arrived first.* □ *Nobody would dare finger Rocko as the one who did it.* **2.** *n.* someone who identifies criminals for the police; a police informer. (Underworld.) □ *Tracy has become a finger for the cops.* □ *Yup, she turned finger after her last vacation.* **3.** *n.* an amount of liquor poured into a glass equal to the width of a finger. □ *Tracy said she only drank one finger, but the glass was five inches in diameter!* □ *No fingers for you, chum. You've had enough.*

finger wave *n.* the act of giving someone the finger; displaying the middle finger upright as a sign of derision. (The gesture is taboo. See also *give someone the finger.*) □ *Two little kids gave the cop the finger wave.* □ *The salute turned into a finger wave when the Major turned away.*

fink [fɪŋk] **1.** *n.* an informer; a *stool (pigeon).* (From *Pinkerton.* See also *rat fink.*) □ *Tracy has turned into a fink.* □ *Mr. Big doesn't think much of finks.* **2.** See *fink (on someone).* **3.** *n.* any strange or undesirable person. □ *You are being such a fink. Stop it!* □ *Martin is a strange kind of fink.*

fink (on someone) *in.* to inform on someone. □ *You won't fink on me, will ya?* □ *Rocko never finks on his friends.*

fink out (on someone or something) *in.* to decide not to cooperate with someone or something (after all). □ *Come on, don't fink out on us now.* □ *Bob finked out on the plan.*

finn See *fin.*

fire a line *tr.* to snort a *line* of cocaine. (Drugs.) □ *Max left to fire a line.* □ *Rocko has never fired a line in his life.*

fire away *in.* to start asking questions; to start talking. ☐ *Okay, I'm ready. Fire away.* ☐ *The cops fired away at him for an hour.*

fire someone or something up **1.** *tr.* [with *someone*] to motivate someone; to make someone enthusiastic. ☐ *See if you can fire John up and get him to paint the house.* Ⓣ *I have to fire up the electorate if I want them to vote for me.* (More at *fired up.*) **2.** *tr.* [with *something*] to start something such as an engine; to light something. ☐ *Fire this thing up, and let's get going.* Ⓣ *Andy fired up the snow blower and started to clear a path.*

fire up *in.* to light a marijuana cigarette. ☐ *Max fires up at every chance.* ☐ *Rocko says he never fired up in his life.*

fireball See *ball of fire.*

fired up *mod.* excited; enthusiastic. ☐ *How can you be so fired up at this time of the morning?* ☐ *It's impossible to get Martin fired up at all.*

firewater *n.* whiskey. (From cowboy and Indian talk.) ☐ *This firewater leaves a lot to be desired.* ☐ *This isn't gin; it's firewater!*

fireworks **1.** *n.* excitement. ☐ *When the fireworks are over, come in and we'll talk.* ☐ *What're all the fireworks about around here?* **2.** *n.* trouble; a display of temper. ☐ *After Bruno's fireworks, we calmed down a little.* ☐ *Cut out the fireworks, Sally. Calm down and get back to work.*

firstest with the mostest *mod.* the earliest and in the largest numbers; the earliest with more of what's needed. (Always with *the.*) ☐ *Pete got the prize for being the firstest with the mostest.* ☐ *I always like to be there early—the firstest with the mostest.*

fish *n.* a stupid and inept person. (Derogatory.) ☐ *The guy's a fish. He can't do anything right.* ☐ *Don't be such a fish, Martin. Anyone can work a can opener.*

fish-fight *n.* a fight between females. ☐ *There's a fish-fight over by the biology building.* ☐ *Those fish-fights can get brutal.*

fish-kiss **1.** *tr. & in.* to kiss (someone) with puckered up lips. (Collegiate.) ☐ *He can fish-kiss like an expert, which is like being an expert at nothing.* ☐ *He fish-kissed me, then ran back to his car.* **2.** *n.* a kiss made with puckered up lips. (Collegiate.) ☐ *One more fish-kiss tonight, and I am going to scream.* ☐ *The actor planted a big fish-kiss right on her lips and frightened her.*

Fish or cut bait. *sent.* "Do something or get out of the way." ☐ *Fish or cut bait, Chuck. There's work to be done here.* ☐ *Decide whether you're going to watch or help. Fish or cut bait.*

fish story AND **fish tale** *n.* a great big lie. (Like the fisherman who exaggerates the size of the fish that got away.) ☐ *That's just a fish story. Tell me another!* ☐ *He's a master at the fish tale. Maybe he should be a politician.*

fish tale See the previous entry.

fishing expedition *n.* an exploratory search for facts. (This involves asking questions with no preconceived notion of what the answers might reveal.) ☐ *The lawyer was on a fishing expedition. There was no real wrong committed to justify a lawsuit.* ☐ *Your honor, counsel is just on a clumsy fishing expedition. I move for dismissal.*

fishtail *in.* [for the rear of a car] to whip back and forth like a fish moving its tail. ☐ *The caddy fishtailed on the curb and almost spun around.* ☐ *It's easy to fishtail in wet weather.*

fishy *mod.* dubious; questionable; likely to be improper or illegal. (See also *smell fishy.*) ☐ *Something here is fishy.* ☐ *That was a pretty fishy story you told us.*

five-finger discount *n.* the acquisition of something by shoplifting. ☐ *Bruno used his five-finger discount to get the kind of ring Tracy wanted.* ☐ *I got this thingy with my five-finger discount.*

five it See *take the fifth.*

fiver ['fɑɪvɚ] *n.* a five-dollar bill. (See also *tenner.*) ☐ *This thing only cost me a fiver.* ☐ *Give him a fiver, and let's get outa here.*

fix 1. AND **fix-up** *n.* a dose of a drug, especially for an addict who is in need of drugs. (Drugs. It fixes the suffering of withdrawal.) ☐ *It was clear that the prisoner needed a fix, but there was nothing the cops would do for him.* ☐ *Max arranged to get a fix-up into the con.* **2.** *in.* to buy a dose of drugs; to take drugs. (Drugs.) ☐ *Max had to fix before he could even talk to me.* ☐ *Tracy was in the other room fixing.* (More at *fixed.*) **3.** *tr.* to castrate or spay an animal, especially a pet. (Jocularly of people.) ☐ *Get somebody to fix your cat!* ☐ *Sally suggested that someone ought to fix Beavis—if he isn't already.* (More at *fixed.*) **4.** *n.* a bribe. ☐ *Rocko never took a fix in his life.* ☐ *The agent payed a fix to the cops.* (More at *fixed.*) **5.** *tr.* to influence the outcome of a contest or an election. ☐ *Who fixed this race?* ☐ *Bruno knows what it takes to fix an election—cash.* (More at *fixed.*) **6.** *n.* a scheme to influence the outcome of a contest or an election. ☐ *Something is wrong with this game. I smell a fix.* ☐ *Bruno planned a great fix, but the cops got wise.* **7.** *n.* a repair made to a computer program. (Computers.) ☐ *This little fix should make the whole program run faster.* ☐ *I wrote a fix to make the program more efficient.* **8.** *n.* a "cure" for a social ill. (See also *quick fix.*) ☐ *There is no easy fix for a problem like this.* ☐ *Some people think there is no fix at all.*

fix-up See the previous entry.

fixed 1. *mod.* doped; intoxicated. ☐ *Max is comfortable now that he's fixed.* ☐ *He was fixed and broke—in a real mess, I'd say.* **2.** *mod.* bribed. ☐ *Don't worry, the night watchman is fixed.* ☐ *The cop is fixed and won't give you guys any trouble.* **3.** *mod.* having the outcome pre-arranged. (Said of a contest, race, or election.) ☐ *The election was fixed, and we are going to protest.* ☐ *It was not fixed!* ☐ *The race was fixed, but we won anyway.* **4.** *mod.* neutered. ☐ *Now that the cat is fixed, she seems even meaner.* ☐ *I wouldn't buy anything but an already-fixed dog.*

fixed up *mod.* provided with a date. ☐ *Sam got fixed up with Martha.* ☐ *Okay, Sam is fixed up with a date for Saturday.*

fixer *n.* a lawyer. ☐ *I'll get my fixer on it first thing in the morning.* ☐ *Bruno's fixer didn't show up in court.*

fizzle ['fɪzl̩] **1.** *n.* a failure; something that sputters away. ☐ *The whole project was a fizzle.* ☐ *Her first play was no fizzle.* **2.** *in.* to fail; to peter out. ☐ *The whole plan fizzled, and we had to start over.* ☐ *The play began to fizzle in the second act.*

flabbergasted ['flæbɚgæstəd] **1.** *mod.* surprised; baffled. ☐ *We were flabbergasted by your proposal.* ☐ *They all sat there flabbergasted.* **2.** *mod.* alcohol intoxicated. ☐ *I thought you were cutting down, and here you are totally flabbergasted again.* ☐ *After about six beers, Harry became flabbergasted and slid under the table.*

flack See *flak.*

flack (out) *in.* to collapse in exhaustion; to go to sleep. ☐ *I just have to go home now and flack out.* ☐ *Betsy flacked out at nine every night.*

flackery ['flækɚi] *n.* an advertising agency. ☐ *Ted works for a flackery over on Maple Street.* ☐ *It seems like the whole political campaign was directed by some New York flackery.*

flag [flæg] **1.** *tr.* to fail a course. ☐ *Pat flagged English again.* ☐ *I'm afraid I flagged algebra.* **2.** *n.* the grade of F. ☐ *I'll get a flag on algebra for the semester.* ☐ *I got three flags and an A.* **3.** *tr.* to arrest someone. ☐ *The cop flagged Tracy for soliciting.* ☐ *They flagged Bob for speeding even though he was a judge.* (More at *flagged.*)

flagged [flægd] *mod.* arrested. ☐ *Max almost got himself flagged for speeding.* ☐ *Sally was flagged, and she called her fixer to come get her out.*

flak AND **flack** [flæk] **1.** *n.* complaints; criticism; negative feedback. ☐ *Why do*

I have to get all the flak for what you did? ☐ *We're getting a lot of flack for that news broadcast.* **2.** *n.* publicity; *hype.* ☐ *Who is going to believe this flack about being first-rate?* ☐ *It's all flak and no substance.* **3.** *n.* a public relations agent or officer. ☐ *The flak made an announcement and then disappeared.* ☐ *There were flacks all over the place telling lies and making false promises.*

flake [flek] **1.** *n.* a person who acts silly or giddy. ☐ *Sally is such a flake!* ☐ *Who's the flake in the plaid pants?* **2.** *n.* a medicinal form of crystallized cocaine. (Drugs. Similar to *crack.*) ☐ *Where can I get some flake around here?* ☐ *Max specializes in flake.* **3.** *tr.* [for the police] to place drugs or traces of drugs on a person during an arrest. (Underworld. The person is then charged with possession of drugs.) ☐ *That's not mine! You flaked me!* ☐ *The fuzz must have flaked Rocko. He never touches the stuff.* **4.** AND **flakes** *n.* phencyclidine (P.C.P.), an animal tranquilizer. ☐ *Even Max won't sell flake, and he's not what I would call a concerned citizen.* ☐ *Sometimes they smoke a cigarette with flakes on it.*

flake down *in.* to go to bed; to go to sleep. ☐ *Look at the time. I gotta go home and flake down.* ☐ *After I flake down for about three days, I'll tell you about my trip.*

flake (out) **1.** *in.* to pass out from exhaustion; to fall asleep. ☐ *I just flaked out. I had had it.* ☐ *After jogging, I usually flake for a while.* **2.** *in.* to fall asleep after drug use. (Drugs.) ☐ *An hour after she took the stuff, she just flaked.* ☐ *Pete popped a few pills and flaked out.*

(flake) spoon See *cokespoon.*

flaked See the following entry.

flaked out **1.** *mod.* alcohol intoxicated. ☐ *You are too flaked out to drive home. Give me your keys.* ☐ *Man, is she flaked out!* **2.** AND **flaked** *mod.* passed out because of drugs. (Drugs.) ☐ *Sally was flaked out on the sofa.* ☐ *Jerry took the stuff and ended up flaked.* **3.** *mod.* unconscious; exhausted; tired out. ☐ *Tom? He's upstairs flaked out from work.* ☐ *There are too many flaked out people working at dangerous machines.*

flakes See *flake.*

flako See the following entry.

flaky ['fleki] **1.** *mod.* unreliable. ☐ *She's too flaky to hold the job.* ☐ *He's a flaky dude.* ☐ *I'm getting so flaky. Must be old age.* **2.** *mod.* habituated to the use of cocaine. (Drugs.) ☐ *He looks a little flaky. Look at his eyes and nose.* ☐ *Max is flaky. He's a walking advertisement for what he sells.* **3.** AND **flako** ['fleko] *mod.* alcohol intoxicated. ☐ *Man, is she flako!* ☐ *Paul was flaky and couldn't drive.*

flamdoodle See *flapdoodle.*

flame *in.* to write an excited and angry note on a computer bulletin board. ☐ *Barb is flaming again. It doesn't take much to set her off.* ☐ *Stop flaming a minute and try to explain your position calmly.*

flame-war *n.* an angry and excited exchange of notes on a computer bulletin board. ☐ *A flame-war erupted on the board last night and a lot of people said some pretty rude things.* ☐ *The SYSOP tried to stop the flame-war, but it kept going anyway.*

flamer **1.** *n.* a blatantly obvious homosexual person. (Primarily and originally for males.) ☐ *Todd is such a flamer!* ☐ *He tries not to be a flamer, but what can he do?* **2.** *n.* a person who writes excited and angry notes on a computer bulletin board. ☐ *There are too many flamers on this board to make it interesting and entertaining.* ☐ *The flamers turn everything into a screaming battle.*

flap *n.* an argument; a minor scandal. ☐ *I'm sorry about that flap we had yesterday, but it was all your fault.* ☐ *Who started this flap anyway?*

flapdoodle AND **flamdoodle** ['flæpdudl̩ AND 'flæmdudl̩] *n.* nonsense. ☐ *I've heard enough of this flapdoodle.* ☐ *Cut out the flamdoodle and speak the truth.*

flapjaw ['flæpdʒɔ] **1.** *n.* a talkative person. ☐ *Who is the flapjaw who has Sally* *cornered?* □ *Martin is anything but a flapjaw. I bet he doesn't say a dozen words per hour.* **2.** *n.* chatter; gossip. □ *Too much flapjaw for me to concentrate in here.* □ *Could you all turn down the flapjaw a little?*

flash [flæʃ] **1.** *n.* something suddenly remembered; something suddenly thought of. □ *I had a flash and quickly wrote it down.* □ *After we talked a while, a flash hit me. Why don't we sell the house?* **2.** *n.* a very short period of time; an instant. (See also *in a flash*.) □ *I'll be there in a flash.* □ *It was just a flash between the time I said I'd be there and when I showed up.* **3.** *tr.* to display something briefly. □ *You'd better not flash a wad like that around here. You won't have it long.* □ *The cop flashed her badge and made the pinch.* **4.** *in.* to display one's private parts briefly. (Use caution with the topic.) □ *The guy flashed and moved on down the street.* □ *She flashed briefly, providing the show that people came to see, and left the stage.* **5.** *n.* a drink of liquor. □ *I'll have just a flash; then I've got to run.* □ *Here, have a flash, and let's chat a little longer.*

flash on something *in.* to remember something suddenly and vividly. □ *Then I flashed on a great idea.* □ *I was trying to flash on it, but I couldn't bring it to mind.*

flash the hash *tr.* to empty one's stomach; to vomit. □ *Dave left quickly to go out and flash the hash, I think.* □ *Who's in there flashing the hash?*

flashback *n.* a memory of the past; a portrayal of the past in a story. □ *Suddenly, Fred had a wonderful flashback to his childhood.* □ *The next scene in the film was a flashback to the time of Ivan the Terrible.*

flasher *n.* a man who exhibits his genitals. □ *The cops caught the flasher and took him away.* □ *Sarah said she thought she saw a flasher in the library.*

flat broke *mod.* having no money at all. □ *Sorry, I'm flat broke. Not a cent on me.* □ *You may be flat broke, but you will find a way to pay your electricity bill or you will live in the dark.*

flat on one's ass **1.** *mod.* completely exhausted. (Potentially offensive. Use only with discretion.) □ *I'm just flat on my ass. I need some rest.* □ *After the day of the marathon, Pete was flat on his ass for a week.* **2.** *mod.* broke; financially destroyed. (Potentially offensive. Use only with discretion. An elaboration of *flat broke*.) □ *Sorry, I can't help you. I'm broke—flat on my ass.* □ *The guy's flat on his ass. Can you help him out with a loan?*

flat out **1.** *mod.* totally. □ *She was flat out mad as hell.* □ *We were all flat out disgusted.* **2.** *mod.* at top speed. □ *They drove the thing flat out for an hour.* □ *If we run flat out, we can get there before dusk.*

flatfoot AND **flatty** ['flætfut AND 'flæti] *n.* a police officer, especially a foot patrol officer. □ *Think about how the flatfoot on the beat is affected by this cold.* □ *The flatty stopped at the door, tried the lock, and moved on.*

flathead *n.* a stupid person. □ *Carl, don't act like such a flathead.* □ *He may seem slow, but Carl is no flathead.*

flatheaded *mod.* stupid. □ *That is really a flatheaded idea, you know?* □ *Martin seems flatheaded, but he's quite brilliant.*

flatline *in.* to die. (From the flatness of the line on an EEG monitor.) □ *It appeared that the patient flatlined during the night.* □ *She just grabbed at her chest and flatlined.*

flatten *tr.* to knock someone down with a blow. □ *Max flattened the kid with a jab to the nose.* □ *Wilbur will flatten his opponent.*

flatty See *flatfoot*.

fleabag ['flibæg] *n.* a cheap hotel; a *flop house*. □ *I won't stay in this fleabag for one minute.* □ *Rocko never stays in fleabags. He's too proud. Bruno doesn't care.*

fleece *tr.* to cheat someone; to steal everything from someone. (Underworld.) □ *Bruno fleeced the kids for a* *lot of money.* □ *Rocko never tried to fleece anybody.*

flesh-presser AND **palm-presser** *n.* a politician. □ *It's that time of the year when the flesh-pressers really go to work.* □ *A palm-presser came to our door to ask us what we thought about his issues.*

flexed out of shape *mod.* very angry; *bent out of shape.* □ *The boss was completely flexed out of shape.* □ *I am truly flexed out of shape.*

flick [flɪk] *n.* a movie. □ *That was a pretty good flick, right?* □ *Let's go see that new Woody Allen flick.*

flimflam ['flɪmflæm] **1.** *n.* a confidence trick or deception. □ *The whole business sounds like a bit of flimflam to me.* □ *The crooks pulled a nasty flimflam on Betsy.* **2.** *n.* nonsense; deception. □ *Beware of the flimflam they will try to pull on you.* □ *I can spot flimflam a mile away.* **3.** *tr. & in.* to cheat or deceive (someone). □ *Don't try to flimflam me. I wasn't born yesterday, you know.* □ *She is flimflamming over at the Adamsville fair this week.*

flimflam artist *n.* someone who practices confidence tricks or deceptions on someone else. □ *I don't trust that flimflam artist at all.* □ *Pretty soon, you'll learn how to spot a flimflam artist.*

fling up *in.* to empty one's stomach; to vomit. □ *I was afraid I was going to fling up.* □ *Who flung up on the sidewalk?*

fling-wing *n.* a helicopter. □ *The fling-wing from the radio station is hovering over the traffic jam.* □ *There must be a dozen fling-wings up there making all that noise.*

flip *in.* to go crazy. □ *Wow, I've got so much to do, I may just flip.* □ *The guy flipped. He was the nervous type.*

flip-flop **1.** *n.* a reversal. □ *The President denied making a flip-flop. He said he simply forgot his earlier position.* □ *The manager did a flip-flop on the personnel policy.* **2.** *n.* the return trip of a long journey. (Citizens band radio. See also *flip side.*) □ *Nice talking to you, Silver Streak. Catch you on the flip-flop.* □ *Didn't we chat on the flip-flop last week?* **3.** *in.* to change direction or intensity. □ *He flip-flopped again, leaving us quite confused.* □ *Jed flip-flopped twice in the evening, leaving us where we started.* **4.** *in.* to waiver in one's decisions. □ *I'm sorry I'm flip-flopping on this matter. I just can't seem to decide.* □ *Well, you just flip-flop all you want. I know what I want.*

flip one's wig *tr.* to go crazy; to lose control. □ *Tom nearly flipped his wig.* □ *I flipped my wig when I got the news.*

flip (out) *in.* to lose control of oneself. □ *Wow, I almost flipped out when I heard about it.* □ *He got so mad that he flipped.*

flip side **1.** *n.* the "other" side of a phonograph record. □ *On the flip side, we have another version of "Love Me Tender" sung by Beverly Mills.* □ *Give a listen to the flip side sometime.* **2.** *n.* the "other" side of something, such as an argument. □ *I want to hear the flip side of this before I make a judgement.* □ *On the flip side, he is no bargain either.* **3.** *n.* the return trip of a long journey. (Citizens band radio.) □ *See ya. Catch you on the flip side, maybe.* □ *Didn't I talk to you on the flip side last week?*

flip someone off AND **flip someone out** *tr.* to *give someone the finger.* (Collegiate.) □ *Did you flip me off?* □ *Ernie flipped Tom out, and Tom flattened Ernie. Ah, life in the big city.*

flip someone out See the previous entry.

flip someone the bird *tr.* to *give someone the finger;* to display the *digitus impudicus* to someone. □ *Max flipped the cop the bird—and that was just the wrong thing to do.* □ *The little kid flipped the cop the bird and didn't even know what it meant.*

flipping *mod.* damnable. (Euphemistic for *fucking.*) □ *Get this flipping dog out of here!* □ *What's the flipping idea?*

flivver ['flɪvɚ] *n.* an old car. (Once a nickname for the Model-T Ford.) □ *Whose flivver is that parked out in the street?* □ *I got an old flivver to get to school and back.*

FLK ['ɛf 'ɛl 'ke] *n.* "funny looking kid." (Initialism. A strange looking child, especially one being treated for social or physical problems.) □ *The therapist had two FLKs in a row.* □ *When the mother came in with an FLK in tow, Jane knew her afternoon would be busy.*

flog [flɑg] *tr.* to promote something; to try to sell something aggressively. □ *Fred was flogging this car so hard, I figured he was trying to get rid of it.* □ *Don't flog it so hard. It makes people suspicious.*

flooey ['flui] *mod.* alcohol intoxicated. □ *You're flooey again. That's every night this week.* □ *Wow, is she flooey!*

floored **1.** *mod.* surprised. □ *I was really floored by what she had to say.* □ *You looked floored when I came in. Wasn't I invited?* **2.** *mod.* knocked to the floor by a blow. □ *Wilbur was floored by his opponent.* □ *The guy was floored and didn't move a muscle—ever again.* **3.** *mod.* alcohol intoxicated. □ *He's totally floored. Can't see a hole in a ladder.* □ *You'd be floored, too, if you'd drunk a dozen beers.*

floozie ['fluzi] *n.* a promiscuous woman. □ *Tracy was enraged when Rocko called her a floozie.* □ *"I didn't call you a floozie," said Rocko. "I said you were boozy."*

flop **1.** *n.* a failure. □ *What do you mean your life is a flop?* □ *The play was a flop. The entire audience left during the second act.* **2.** *n.* a place to sleep for the night; a bed in a *flop house.* (Streets.) □ *The old man was looking for a flop for the night.* □ *Do you know where I can find a flop?*

flop house *n.* a very cheap hotel offering only rows of beds. □ *This place is a flop house! I won't stay here for a moment.* □ *All some of those guys need in life is a flop in a flop house.*

flopper-stopper *n.* a brassiere. □ *Hey, Jimmy, does your sister wear a flopper-stopper yet?* □ *She's very shy. She won't even hang her flopper-stoppers out on the line to dry.*

flub something up *tr.* to do something incorrectly; to *mess up* a procedure. □ *Now don't flub this up.* 🅃 *I never flub up anything.*

flub the dub ['fləb ðə 'dəb] *tr.* to fail to do the right thing. □ *Martin is flubbing the dub with the fund-raising campaign.* □ *Please don't flub the dub this time.*

flub (up) **1.** AND **flub-up** *n.* an error; a blunder. □ *I tried not to make a flub, but I did.* □ *Who is responsible for this flub-up?* **2.** *in.* to *mess up;* to *foul up.* □ *You are flubbing up again, aren't you?* □ *I do my best to keep from flubbing.*

flub-up See the previous entry.

fluff [fləf] **1.** *n.* nonsense; irrelevant stuff; *hype.* □ *This is just a lot of fluff. Nothing substantial at all.* □ *Cut out the fluff and talk straight.* **2.** *tr. & in.* to make an error; to do something incorrectly. □ *Todd fluffs his lines in the same place every night.* □ *Don't fluff again, please.*

fluff-stuff ['fləfstəf] *n.* snow. □ *There is supposed to be an inch of fluff-stuff tonight.* □ *Fluff-stuff looks pretty, but it's no fun to shovel it.*

flunk [fləŋk] **1.** *tr. & in.* to earn a failing grade in a course. □ *I'm flunking in English lit.* □ *Wilbur is flunking everything.* **2.** *tr.* to assign someone a failing grade. □ *Good grief! She flunked me!* □ *I'm sorry, but I am going to have to flunk half the class.*

flunk out (of something) *in.* to leave school or a course because of failure. □ *Fred flunked out of school and never tried to go back.* □ *That's it. All F's. I've flunked out.*

flush *mod.* wealthy; with plenty of money. □ *Today I am flush. By tomorrow, I'll be broke.* □ *I'm not exactly flush, but I can pay the bills.*

flusher *n.* a toilet. (Folksy. Compared to an outhouse.) □ *I hear they put in a flusher over at the Babbits'.* □ *That's silly. They've always had a flusher.*

fly **1.** *mod.* knowledgeable; alert and in the know. □ *This dude is fly; there's no question about it.* □ *We don't need any more fly birds around here.* **2.** *mod.* nice-looking; stylish. □ *I like your fly shoes, Sam.* □ *This guy is really fly.*

fly-by-night *mod.* undependable; dishonest. □ *Bruno seems like such a fly-by-night character.* □ *He's not fly-by-night at all.* □ *Don't do business with fly-by-night people.*

fly kites *tr.* to distribute or pass bad checks. (Underworld. See also *kite*.) □ *Marty was picked up for flying kites in three different cities.* □ *She got caught flying kites in Philadelphia.*

fly light *in.* to skip a meal or eating. □ *Nothing for me, thanks. I'm flying light today.* □ *I fly light until about dinnertime.*

fly the coop *tr.* to escape from somewhere; to get away. □ *I was afraid he would fly the coop if I didn't tie him up.* □ *I flew the coop before my dad got home.*

fly trap *n.* the mouth. □ *Close your fly trap. You talk too much.* □ *Don't talk with your fly trap full.*

flyboy ['flaɪbɔɪ] *n.* a pilot. (Military.) □ *Rocko was a flyboy in Korea.* □ *Those flyboys have it easy.*

foam *n.* beer. □ *How about some more foam?* □ *All the guy thinks about is foam.*

F.O.B. *mod.* "Fresh off the boat"; as gullible and trusting as a new immigrant. (Initialism. A play on the initials of "Free on Board.") □ *That new guy is really F.O.B. What a wimp!* □ *Where did you get those F.O.B. shoes? Blue suede is back?*

foggiest (idea) *n.* (even) a hazy idea. (Usually in the negative. Always with *the*.) □ *I'm sorry I don't know. I haven't the foggiest.* □ *I don't have the foggiest idea of how to do this.*

F.O.K. See *fill or kill*.

fold **1.** *in.* to fail; to close. □ *The play folded in the second week.* □ *I was afraid my business would fold because of the recession.* **2.** *in.* to collapse from drinking. □ *Dave had just one more drink, and then he folded.* □ *She folded neatly and slid beneath the table.*

folded *mod.* alcohol intoxicated. □ *Pete is folded. That's the third time this week.* □ *Man, is he folded!*

folderol See *falderal*.

folding money AND **folding stuff** *n.* U.S. paper bank notes, as opposed to coins. □ *Sorry, I don't have any folding money with me. Can you pick up the bill?* □ *I sure could use some more of that folding stuff.*

folding stuff See the previous entry.

folks *n.* one's parents. (Always with the possessive.) □ *I'll have to ask my folks if I can go.* □ *Her folks are sort of mad at her.*

fomp [fɑmp] *in.* to play around sexually. (Collegiate.) □ *Who are those two over there fomping?* □ *Jerry wanted to fomp, and I wanted to get him out of my sight.*

foo-foo water ['fufuwɑdɚ] *n.* aftershave lotion; cologne. □ *Don't use so much of that foo-foo water.* □ *I got three bottles of foo-foo water for my birthday.*

foodaholic *n.* a glutton. □ *Kelly is a foodaholic and has a real eating problem.* □ *What a foodaholic! She ate a whole large pizza!*

fooey See *phooey*.

foot-in-mouth disease *n.* the tendency to say the wrong thing at the wrong time. □ *I suffer a lot from foot-in-mouth disease.* □ *Well, Ralph has foot-in-mouth disease again.*

foot it *tr.* to go somewhere by foot; to walk or run. (Compare to *ankle*, *shank it*.) □ *I have to foot it over to the drugstore for some medicine.* □ *I'm used to footing it wherever I go.*

foozle ['fuzl̩] **1.** *n.* an error; a messed up task. □ *Who made this foozle?* □ *What a stupid foozle!* **2.** *tr.* to mess something up; to bungle something. □ *I'm afraid I'll foozle the camera if I open it up.* □ *Who foozled the copying machine?* (More at *foozlified*.)

foozlified ['fuzlɪfɑɪd] **1.** *mod.* bungled. □ *This job is really foozlified. Who was in* *charge?* □ *I've never seen such a foozlified mess in my life!* **2.** *mod.* alcohol intoxicated. □ *Why do you always come home foozlified?* □ *Fred is foozlified and can't see his hand in front of him.*

for all I know *phr.* "as far as I know"; "I really don't know." □ *For all I know, they just did it for a lark.* □ *She came in late because she had an accident, for all I know.*

for (all) one's trouble *phr.* in spite of one's efforts; in very poor payment for one's efforts. □ *He got a punch in the jaw for all his trouble.* □ *For her trouble, she got only honorable mention.*

for chicken feed See *for peanuts.*

for free *mod.* free from monetary charge; gratis. □ *And I get all this for free?* □ *Is all this really mine for free?*

for keeps *mod.* forever. □ *Does that mean I'm going to have this scar for keeps?* □ *This is yours for keeps. Enjoy it.*

for kicks *mod.* for fun; for a thrill. □ *We just did it for kicks. We didn't mean to hurt anyone.* □ *Let's drive over to Wally's place, just for kicks.*

for peanuts AND **for chicken feed** *mod.* for practically no money at all. (See also *chicken feed.*) □ *I won't work for peanuts.* □ *You surely don't expect me to do this for chicken feed, do you?*

For Pete's sake! AND **For pity's sake!; For the love of Mike!** *exclam.* "Good grief!" □ *For Pete's sake! How've ya been?* □ *For pity's sake! Ask the man in out of the cold!*

For pity's sake! See the previous entry.

for real *mod.* genuine; not imaginary. □ *Ken is really strange. Is he for real?* □ *This whole day just isn't for real.*

for sure *phr.* "absolutely." (The same as *fer shur.*) □ *I'll be there, for sure.* □ *Am I happy? For sure!*

for the birds *mod.* undesirable. □ *This pizza is for the birds.* □ *I don't like this kind of life. It's for the birds.*

for the devil of it AND **for the heck of it; for the hell of it** *mod.* because it is slightly evil; for no good reason. (Use caution with *hell.*) □ *The kids broke the window just for the devil of it.* □ *We just drove over for the heck of it.*

for the heck of it See the previous entry.

for the hell of it See *for the devil of it.*

For the love of Mike! See *For Pete's sake!*

forbidden fruit *n.* something that is attractive because it is denied to one. (From the Garden of Eden in the Bible.) □ *A new car became Ralph's forbidden fruit.* □ *Liquor was forbidden fruit for Jed.*

Forget it! 1. *exclam.* "Never mind, it wasn't important!" □ *Forget it! It wasn't important.* □ *I had an objection, but just forget it!* **2.** *exclam.* "Never mind, it was no trouble at all!" □ *No trouble at all. Forget it!* □ *Forget it! It was my pleasure.*

Forget you! *exclam.* "Drop dead!"; "Beat it!" □ *Oh, yeah! Forget you!* □ *Forget you! Get a life!*

fork something over *tr.* to hand something over (to someone). □ *Okay, fork it over. It's mine!* 🅃 *Okay, fork over the dough and be quick about it!*

forty winks *n.* a nap; sleep. (Usually with a quantifier. Either *forty* or *some, a few, a bunch of,* etc.) □ *I could use forty winks before I have to get to work.* □ *I need forty winks before I get started again.*

fossil 1. *n.* an old-fashioned person. □ *Some old fossil called the police about the noise.* □ *Oh, Tad, you are such a fossil.* **2.** *n.* a parent. □ *My fossils would never agree to anything like that.* □ *Would your fossils permit that?*

foul mouth *n.* a person who uses obscene language habitually. □ *Terry, don't be such a foul mouth.* □ *Sally is turning into a real foul mouth.*

foul up 1. *in.* to blunder; to *mess up.* □ *Please don't foul up this time.* □ *The quarterback fouled up in the first quarter, and that lost us the game.* **2.** *n.* a blunder;

an error. (Usually **foul-up**.) □ *That was a fine foul-up! Is that your specialty?* □ *I can produce a serious foul up with both hands tied behind me.*

fouled up *mod.* messed up; ruined; tangled up. □ *This is sure a fouled up mess.* □ *You sure are fouled up, you know.*

four-bagger *n.* a home run in baseball. □ *Wilbur hit his third four-bagger of the season.* □ *Another four-bagger for Wilbur!*

four-bits *n.* fifty cents. (A bit is equal to twelve and one-half cents.) □ *You got four-bits I can borrow?* □ *Here's four-bits. Keep the change.*

four-eyes *n.* someone who wears glasses. (Also a rude term of address.) □ *Well, I've got to the age where I'm a four-eyes.* □ *Hey, four-eyes, betcha you can't see this!*

four-flusher *n.* a cheater. □ *Bruno is a lousy four-flusher, among other unpleasant things.* □ *You dirty four-flusher!*

[four-one-one] See *411.*

four sheets in the wind AND **four sheets (to the wind)** *mod.* alcohol intoxicated. (See comments at *three sheets in the wind.*) □ *She's not just tipsy. She's four sheets!* □ *After only three beers, Gary was four sheets to the wind.*

four sheets (to the wind) See the previous entry.

four wheels *n.* a car; transportation. (Compare to *wheels.*) □ *I need four wheels to get me around town.* □ *Without four wheels at my disposal, I feel trapped.*

fox *n.* an attractive *girl* or young woman. □ *Man, who was that fox I saw you with?* □ *That fox was my sister. Next question?*

fox trap *n.* an automobile customized and fixed up in a way that will attract women. □ *I put every cent I earned into my fox trap, but I still repelled women.* □ *To you it's a fox trap; to me it's a pimpmobile.*

foxy ['faksi] **1.** *mod.* sexy, especially having to do with a woman. □ *Man, isn't she foxy!* □ *What a foxy dame!* **2.** *mod.* smelly with perspiration odor. □ *Somebody in this taxi is a little foxy.* □ *Who's got the foxy pits?* □ *Subway cars can sure get foxy in the summer.* **3.** *mod.* alcohol or drug intoxicated. □ *Gary is a little foxy. Let him rest awhile.* □ *He's worse than foxy—he's stinking drunk.*

foxy lady *n.* a sexually attractive woman or *girl.* □ *You are really a foxy lady, Tracy.* □ *A couple of foxy ladies stopped us on the street.*

fracture *tr.* to cause someone to laugh very hard. □ *Now, this joke'll fracture you.* □ *I like to tell a few that fracture everybody.*

fractured **1.** *mod.* alcohol intoxicated. □ *This is the third night this week that Pete has rolled in fractured.* □ *He was so fractured he couldn't see.* **2.** *mod.* demolished by laughter. □ *The class was fractured, and the laughter didn't stop until the teacher managed to get up off the floor.* □ *The whole audience was fractured by the time my ten minutes were up.*

frag [fræg] *tr.* to assassinate an unpopular military officer in Vietnam. (Military.) □ *The guy was so certain that nobody was going to frag him that he got careless and Charlie got him.* □ *I saw some creeps frag a guy once.*

fragged [frægd] *mod.* destroyed; ruined. □ *Why does your room look so fragged?* □ *My clothes are fragged, and I need a haircut.*

fraidy cat ['fredi . . .] *n.* a coward; a person who is frightened of everything. (Used in children's taunts.) □ *Don't be a fraidy cat. Go ahead, jump!* □ *Carl is such a fraidy cat.*

frame **1.** *tr.* to cause an innocent person to be blamed for a crime; to contrive evidence so that someone appears to be guilty. (Originally underworld.) □ *Jimmy tried to frame his sister for painting the cat yellow.* □ *You won't frame me and get away with it!* **2.** AND **frame-up; frameup** *n.* a scheme where an innocent person is made to take the blame for something; incrimination caused by contrived evidence. (Underworld.) □ *Bruno would never fall easy. Must be a frame.* □ *The frame-up would have worked if it weren't for one little thing.*

frame-up See the previous entry.

frantic *mod.* great; *wild.* □ *We had a frantic time at Chez Freddy.* □ *That rally was really frantic.*

frat [fræt] **1.** *n.* a fraternity. (Collegiate.) □ *Are you going to join a frat?* □ *My brother is in a frat.* **2.** *mod.* having to do with fraternities and their members. (Collegiate.) □ *Is there a frat party tonight?* □ *Frat life is not for me.*

frat-rat ['frætræt] *n.* a member of a fraternity. (Collegiate.) □ *The frat-rats are having a rally tonight.* □ *Is Frank a frat-rat, or is he independent?*

freak daddy *n.* a good-looking male. □ *Tony is a real freak daddy, and I intend to get him to take me out.* □ *Jane wants to get her hands on the freak daddy in her history class.*

freak mommy *n.* a good-looking female. □ *Wendy, you are a freak mommy, and I want to get to know you better.* □ *Sally is such a freak mommy. My eyes just water!*

freak (out) **1.** *in.* to panic; to lose control. □ *I was so frightened, I thought I would freak.* □ *Come on, relax. Don't freak out.* **2.** *n.* a bad drug experience; a psychotic reaction to the drug *L.S.D.* (Drugs. Usually **freak-out** or **freakout.**) □ *The poor kid had a freak-out and never really recovered.* □ *Some of them get turned off to drugs by a really good freakout.* **3.** ['frikaut] *n.* a wild party of any type; any exciting happening. (Usually **freak-out** or **freakout.**) □ *There is a big freak-out at Freddy's joint tonight.* □ *What a frantic freakout!* **4.** ['frikaut] *n.* a *freaked (out)* person. (Usually **freak-out** or **freakout.**) □ *Some poor freak-out sat in the corner and rocked.* □ *Who's the freakout in the corner?*

freak someone out *tr.* to shock or disorient someone. □ *The whole business freaked me out.* [T] *I didn't mean to freak out everybody with the bad news.*

freaked (out) **1.** *mod.* shocked; disoriented. (Perhaps from drugs or alcohol.) □ *I was too freaked out to reply.* □ *Man, was I freaked.* **2.** *mod.* tired out; exhausted. □ *I'm too freaked out to go on without some rest.* □ *The chick is really freaked. Let her rest.*

freaker ['frikɚ] **1.** *n.* an incident that causes someone to *freak (out).* (Collegiate.) □ *Wasn't that weird? A real freaker.* □ *Did you see that near miss? What a freaker!* **2.** *n.* a freaked (out) person. (Collegiate.) □ *Some poor freaker sat in the corner and rocked.* □ *Who's the freaker in the corner?*

freaking *mod.* damned. (Euphemistic for *fucking.*) □ *Get your freaking socks off my bed.* □ *What is this freaking mess on my plate?*

freaky *mod.* strange; eccentric. □ *I get a freaky feeling whenever I hear that music.* □ *That's really freaky.* □ *What a freaky movie.*

free base AND **(free)base** ['fribes] **1.** *n.* a smokable, pure extract of cocaine. □ *Max is real big on free base.* □ *Bruno likes base, too.* **2.** *in.* to smoke a pure extract of cocaine. □ *Rocko has never freebased in his life.* □ *Rocko won't base, smoke, or anything.*

free base party *n.* a gathering where *free base* is used. (Drugs.) □ *Max has a free base party about once a week.* □ *The cops broke up a free base party in Beverly Hills.*

free-baser *n.* a user of *free base.* (Drugs.) □ *Of course Max is a free-baser! What doesn't he do?* □ *Some of these free-basers have heart attacks.*

free-basing AND **baseballing; basing** *n.* using *free base* as a recreational drug. (Drugs.) □ *Rocko refuses to try free-basing.* □ *He saw what basing did to his brother.*

free for all AND **free-for-all** *n.* a brawl; a general fight. □ *A free for all started on the beach over near the concession stand.* □ *The cops broke up the free-for-all.*

free lunch *n.* something free. (Often negative.) □ *There is no such thing as a* *free lunch.* □ *There's always somebody who'll do anything to get a free lunch.*

free ride *n.* an easy time; participation without contributing anything. □ *You've had a free ride long enough. You have to do your share of the work now.* □ *No more free rides around here. Get off your duff and get a job!*

free show *n.* a peek at a private part of someone's body, usually a woman. □ *Martin looked like the type who was always waiting for a free show that was never to be.* □ *A true gentleman takes no notice of a "free show."*

free trip *n.* an echo or a *flashback* of an *L.S.D.* experience. (Drugs.) □ *The kid got a free trip, and it scared her to death.* □ *If these free trips continue, we may have to run some tests.*

free-wheeling *mod.* lacking restraint; flamboyant and uncontrolled. □ *These high-spending, free-wheeling palm-pressers appear out of nowhere at election time.* □ *She's too free-wheeling.* □ *She's a free-wheeling executive type.*

(free)base See *free base.*

freebee See the following entry.

freebie AND **freebee; freeby** ['fribi] *n.* something given away free. □ *They gave me a freebie with my purchase.* □ *I expect a freebee when I spend a lot of money like that.*

freeby See the previous entry.

freeload *in.* to sponge off someone else; to eat and drink at someone else's expense; to live off someone else. □ *Don't come around here and expect to freeload.* □ *My brother-in-law has been freeloading at our house for months.*

freeloader *n.* someone who eats and drinks at someone else's expense; a parasitic person. □ *Ken is sort of a freeloader, but he's a lot of fun anyway.* □ *There are a lot of freeloaders here. We are going to have to ask to see tickets.*

freeze 1. *n.* the act of ignoring someone; the *cold shoulder.* □ *Everybody seems to be giving me the freeze.* □ *I got the freeze from Julie. What did I do wrong?* **2.** *tr.* to ignore someone; to give someone the *cold shoulder.* □ *Don't freeze me, gang! I use a mouth wash!* □ *They froze him because he didn't send thank-you notes for his birthday presents.* **3.** *in.* to hold perfectly still. (Also a command given by a police officer that implies there is a gun pointed at a suspect.) □ *I froze, and the bull didn't see me.* □ *The fuzz shouted, "Freeze, or you're dead meat!"*

freeze someone out 1. *tr.* to make it too cold for someone, usually by opening windows or through the use of air conditioning. (See also *play freeze-out.*) □ *Turn up the heat unless you're trying to freeze us out.* 🅃 *Are you trying to freeze out everybody? Close the door.* **2.** *tr.* to lock someone out socially. □ *We didn't want to freeze you out. You failed to pay your dues, however.* 🅃 *They froze out the newcomers.*

freezing cold *mod.* very cold. □ *It's freezing cold out there.* □ *I won't go out in freezing cold weather.* □ *Why does it have to be so freezing cold?*

French kiss 1. *n.* kissing using the tongue; open mouth kissing. □ *What's French about a French kiss?* □ *I didn't know whether I was going to get a French kiss or a fish-kiss.* **2.** *tr.* to kiss someone using the tongue. □ *Kids like to try to French kiss each other at an early age. It's part of growing up.* □ *He tried to French kiss me, but I stopped him.*

fresh 1. *mod.* cheeky; impudent. □ *Ken sure is fresh sometimes.* □ *Kids get some pretty fresh ideas.* **2.** *mod.* a little aggressive sexually; prone to caress too eagerly. □ *Hey, buster! Don't get fresh with me!* □ *He got fresh, so I slapped him.* **3.** *mod.* cool; okay. □ *Gee, that's not fresh. Too bad.* □ *That stuff's really fresh. It's a winner.* **4.** *mod.* good-looking. □ *Wendy is fresh and smart too.* □ *Tom is fresh and buff.*

fresh and sweet *mod.* just out of jail. (Streets.) □ *Tracy is fresh and sweet and back on the street.* □ *Hey, Lefty, you look all fresh and sweet.*

fresh as a daisy *mod.* someone who is always alert and ready to go. ☐ *How can you be fresh as a daisy so early in the morning?* ☐ *I always feel fresh as a daisy.*

fridge [frɪdʒ] *n.* a refrigerator. ☐ *Put this in the fridge so it won't spoil.* ☐ *What's in the fridge for dinner tonight?*

fried *mod.* alcohol or drug intoxicated. (See also *brain-burned, southern-fried.*) ☐ *How the hell did you get so fried?* ☐ *The chick got totally fried on three beers.*

frigging **1.** *mod.* damnable. (A euphemism for *fucking.*) ☐ *Who made this frigging mess?* ☐ *I smashed up my frigging car!* **2.** *mod.* damnably. ☐ *What a frigging stupid thing to do!* ☐ *That is a dumb frigging thing to do!*

Frisco ['frɪsko] *n.* San Francisco, California. ☐ *Have you ever been in Frisco?* ☐ *My cousin lives in Frisco.*

friz [frɪz] *n.* a frizbee. ☐ *If I could find my friz, we could go out and whirl a few.* ☐ *Whose friz is that in the tree?*

frog face *n.* a *nerd;* a *geek.* (Especially as a rude term of address.) ☐ *Look here, frog face, what makes you think you can talk to me that way?* ☐ *Wally is such a frog face. Does he take nerd classes or what?*

frog slicing *n.* biology class; a biology course. (A dysphemism.) ☐ *Dave dreaded going to frog slicing. The smell got to him.* ☐ *Mary found frog slicing to be interesting. She especially liked the study of conservation and ecology.*

from A to Z *mod.* of a complete and wide variety. ☐ *We have just about everything from A to Z.* ☐ *She ordered everything on the menu from A to Z.*

from hunger See *(strictly) from hunger.*

from (the) git-go *mod.* from the very start. (See also *git-go, jump (street).*) ☐ *This kind of thing has been a problem from the git-go.* ☐ *I warned you about this from git-go.*

front **1.** *in.* to pay out money in advance of receiving goods; to pay up front. (See also *front money.*) ☐ *I fronted about $550 for the new computer.* ☐ *How much do you want her to front for this?* **2.** *n.* a respectable appearance. ☐ *Jan can put up a good front, but most of us know the real Jan.* ☐ *The front she put up collapsed as she heard the bad news.* **3.** *in.* to pretend. ☐ *Wendy, you are not real. You're just fronting all the time.* ☐ *Stop fronting and be yourself.* **4.** *tr.* to challenge someone; to confront someone, perhaps in anger. ☐ *Don't front me unless you are ready for a fight.* ☐ *You better not front any of your teachers.*

front man *n.* a respectable and well-known man who represents a less respectable person or organization. ☐ *The former adviser now serves as a front man for a large foundation.* ☐ *The front man came out and made an announcement.*

front money *n.* money paid in advance; earnest money. ☐ *How much front money do you need?* ☐ *I put up a lot of front money and have nothing to show for it.*

front off about something *in.* to be brash and resentful about something. ☐ *Todd was fronting off about his assignment and got a detention for it.* ☐ *You will wish you hadn't fronted off about your supervisor.*

front runner *n.* the leader; the person or thing most likely to win. ☐ *The press found out some juicy secrets about the front runner and made them all public.* ☐ *Who is the front runner in the race for senator?*

fronts *n.* clothing; a sports jacket. ☐ *You got some good-looking fronts there.* ☐ *I need some new fronts.*

froody ['frudi] *mod.* grand; wonderful. ☐ *The curtains parted to the most froody, funky set I've ever seen.* ☐ *Man, is this froody!* ☐ *Oh, you have some froody ideas, all right. But can you carry them out?*

frosh [frɔʃ] **1.** *n.* a freshman. ☐ *Ken is just a frosh, but he looks older.* ☐ *Get some frosh to do it for you.* **2.** *mod.* having to do with freshmen. ☐ *The* *frosh dorm is full again this year.* □ *This is a frosh dance. You can't come in.*

frost *tr.* to make someone angry. □ *That really frosts me.* □ *The little car frosted me by zooming into my parking place.* (More at *frosted (over)*.)

frosted (over) *mod.* angry; annoyed. □ *The clerk was really frosted over when I asked for a better one.* □ *Why was he so frosted?*

frosty 1. AND **frosty one** *n.* a beer; a cold beer. □ *Hey, toss me a frosty, will ya?* □ *I need a frosty one after all that work.* **2.** *mod.* cool; really *cool* and *mellow.* □ *That music is really frosty.* □ *We had a frosty time, didn't we?*

frosty one See the previous entry.

froth *n.* a beer. □ *Would you like some froth?* □ *How about another pitcher of frost, innkeeper?*

fruit 1. *n.* a strange person. (Now overwhelmed by sense 2.) □ *Ted is such a fruit.* □ *Sam comes on like a fruit, but it's just his sense of humor.* **2.** *n.* a homosexual person. (Objected to by homosexual persons.) □ *Bob thinks that you-know-who is a fruit.* □ *Who's the fruit who just came in?*

fruit loop See the following entry.

fruitcake 1. AND **fruit loop** *n.* a foolish oaf. (Someone who is as *nutty as a fruitcake.*) □ *What a fruitcake! Doesn't even know where his head is at.* □ *Carl acts like such a loony fruit loop.* **2.** *n.* a homosexual person. (Objected to by homosexual persons.) □ *Ken said that you-know-who is a fruitcake.* □ *Who's the fruitcake who just came in?*

fry 1. *in.* to die in the electric chair. (Underworld.) □ *The D.A. is determined that you will fry.* □ *I don't want to fry!* **2.** *tr.* to execute someone in the electric chair. (Underworld.) □ *They're gonna fry you for this.* □ *Nobody's gonna fry Rocko!*

fuck [fək] *tr. & in.* to copulate (with someone or some creature). (Taboo. Potentially offensive. Use only with discretion. A highly offensive word to many people. There are many additional meanings and constructions with the word. Colloquial.) □ *Two dogs were fucking out on the lawn.* □ *He actually said in public that he had—you know—fucked her.*

fucking *mod.* "damnable." (Taboo. Potentially offensive. Use only with discretion. Colloquial.) □ *Get this fucking idiot outa here!* □ *What the fucking hell do you think you are doing?*

fud See the following entry.

fuddy-duddy AND **fud** ['fədidədi AND fəd] *n.* a stuffy person; an old-fashioned person, especially a male. □ *Pay no attention to him. He's just an old fud.* □ *There seems to be a convention of fuddy-duddies in the park today.*

fudge [fədʒ] **1.** *in.* to cheat; to deceive (someone). □ *Bill, you're fudging. Wait till the starting gun fires.* □ *No fair fudging!* **2.** *n.* nonsense; deception. □ *Cut out the fudge and talk straight.* □ *I've heard enough of your fudge. Let's get honest, okay?*

fudge factor *n.* a margin of error. □ *I never use a fudge factor. I measure correctly, and I cut the material exactly the way I measured it.* □ *I built in a fudge factor of three inches.*

fugly ['fəgli] *mod.* "fat and ugly." (Collegiate.) □ *Man, is that dog of yours ever fugly! What or who did it eat?* □ *This is a real fugly problem we're facing.*

full blast *mod.* as strongly as possible. □ *He honked the horn full blast for a long time.* □ *The whistle blew full blast and woke everyone up.*

full of beans *mod.* full of nonsense; *full of hot air.* □ *Oh, be quiet. You're just full of beans.* □ *Pay no attention to John. He's full of beans.*

full of bull See *full of hot air.*

full of hops *mod.* full of nonsense. (As if one were full of beer, which contains hops.) □ *Aw, you're just full of hops!* □ *The guy was full of hops. Nothing he said made any sense.*

full of hot air AND **full of bull; full of it** *mod.* full of nonsense. ☐ *You're full of hot air. I don't believe you.* ☐ *Aw, you're just full of it! Be quiet!*

full of it See the previous entry.

full of Old Nick See *full of the devil.*

full of prunes *mod.* full of nonsense. (See also *full of beans.*) ☐ *You're just silly. Completely full of prunes.* ☐ *Oh, you're full of prunes. Get a life!*

full of the devil AND **full of Old Nick** *mod.* always making mischief. ☐ *Little Chuckie is sure full of the devil.* ☐ *In this weather, the kids are always full of Old Nick.*

full sesh ['ful 'sɛʃ] *mod.* totally; completely. (California.) ☐ *He was really out of it full sesh.* ☐ *It was a great game. They went at it full sesh the whole time.*

full steam ahead *mod.* with determination. ☐ *We started moving full steam ahead on the project.* ☐ *Full steam ahead! Let's see how fast this will go!*

fun *mod.* pleasant; entertaining. ☐ *We had a real fun time.* ☐ *His party was fun.* ☐ *What a fun evening!*

fun and games *n.* nonsense; a waste of time. ☐ *I've had enough fun and games. Let's get on with the business.* ☐ *You spend too much time with fun and games!*

fungus See *(face) fungus.*

fungus-face *n.* a bearded man. (See also *(face) fungus.* Compare to *fuzz-face.*) ☐ *Who's the fungus-face in the striped blazer?* ☐ *Hey, fungus-face! Who is that behind all the fuzz?*

funk [fəŋk] **1.** *n.* a bad odor; a stench. ☐ *What is that ghastly funk in here?* ☐ *Open the windows and clear out this funk.* **2.** *n.* tobacco smoke. ☐ *The funk was so thick I couldn't see across the room.* ☐ *Most of those important decisions are made by party hacks in funk-filled back rooms.* **3.** *n.* a depressed state. ☐ *I've been in such a funk that I can't get my work done.* ☐ *As soon as I get out of my winter funk, I'll be more helpful.* **4.** *n.* cowardice; terror. ☐ *She suffers this terrible funk whenever she has to give a talk.* ☐ *The dog was in such a funk that it was crying.* **5.** *n.* a kind of blues rock; jazz based on gospel music. ☐ *Man, groove on that funk, would ya?* ☐ *Now this is the kind of funk I've been looking for.*

funked out *mod.* alcohol or drug intoxicated. ☐ *Do you think you can go through life funked out all the time?* ☐ *Are you funked out again?*

funking *mod.* "damnable." (Euphemistic for *fucking.* Use only with caution.) ☐ *Who put this funking milk crate in the hall?* ☐ *Get the funking hell out of here.*

funky **1.** *mod.* strange; *far out.* ☐ *I like your funky hat.* ☐ *Is he funky?* ☐ *He's such a funky guy.* **2.** *mod.* basic and simple; earthy. ☐ *Everything she does is so funky.* ☐ *I like to be around funky people.* **3.** *mod.* smelly; obnoxious. ☐ *Get your funky old socks outa here.* ☐ *This place is really funky. Open some windows.* **4.** *mod.* unkempt. ☐ *Your hair is sort of funky. Comb it.* ☐ *John's room is funky and disorganized.*

funky-drunk *mod.* alcohol intoxicated; stinking drunk. ☐ *The guy is funky-drunk, and I think he's going to be sick.* ☐ *Wow, is she ever funky-drunk!*

funky-fresh *mod.* very good. (See also *fresh.*) ☐ *This tunage is funky-fresh—to my ears anyway.* ☐ *Mary is funky-fresh when she works out, but a real slow runner when she's been lazy.*

funny business See *monkey business.*

funny-farm *n.* an insane asylum; a mental hospital. ☐ *I think they ought to send you to the funny-farm.* ☐ *He's too far gone for the funny-farm.*

funny-money *n.* any substitute money: counterfeit money, military script, etc. ☐ *I don't want any funny-money. Real U.S. greenbacks or forget the deal.* ☐ *Who'll change my funny-money back to bucks?*

fur *n.* the police. (See also *fuzz.*) ☐ *I think the fur is onto you, Rocko.* ☐ *The fur ain't never gonna get Rocko.*

furball See *hairball.*

furphy ['fɚfi] *n.* a groundless rumor. □ *I heard a furphy about you yesterday.* □ *Who started that furphy anyway?*

fuse box ['fjuz bɑks] *n.* the head; the brain. □ *I'm afraid she's missing a little something in the fuse box.* □ *Jed acts like his fuse box is completely blown.*

fussbudget ['fəsbədʒət] *n.* someone who fusses all the time, especially a baby. □ *Oh, Gary, don't be such a fussbudget.* □ *He is such a fussbudget. Get him a passy.*

futz See *phutz.*

fuzz [fəz] **1.** AND **fuzz man; fuzzy (tail)** *n.* the police; a jail keeper; a detective. □ *The fuzz is onto you.* □ *See if you can distract the fuzz man while I lift his keys.* **2.** AND **fuzzle** *in.* to get drunk. □ *They were just sitting there fuzzling away the day.* □ *Stop fuzzing and listen.*

fuzz-face *n.* a man with a beard. (Compare to *fungus-face.*) □ *Hey, fuzz-face, come here a minute.* □ *A couple of fuzz-faces came in and asked for mustache wax.*

fuzz man See *fuzz.*

fuzz station *n.* a police station. □ *He had to spend about an hour at the fuzz station, but nothing happened to him.* □ *Drop by the fuzz station and pick up a copy of the driving rules.*

fuzzed AND **fuzzled; fuzzy** *mod.* alcohol intoxicated. □ *You are too fuzzed all the time to hold the job. Pack!* □ *Why do you come home every night fuzzled?*

fuzzle See *fuzz.*

fuzzled See *fuzzed.*

fuzzword ['fəzwɚd] *n.* a confusing term usually meant to obscure meaning. (Compare to *buzzword.*) □ *The current crop of fuzzwords contains a few that have come back from the twenties.* □ *Don't sling those fuzzwords at me!*

fuzzy See *fuzzed.*

fuzzy (tail) See *fuzz.*

FWIW *interj.* "for what it's worth." (Used in electronic mail and computer bulletin board messages. Not pronounced aloud.) □ *FWIW, I understand exactly what you are saying.* □ *I think you are just too sensitive, FWIW.*

G

G 1. *n.* "guy." □ *What's up G?* □ *Tom's a real chilled out G.* **2.** *interj.* grin. (An initialism used on computer bulletin boards to show that the writer is grinning or happy. Usually enclosed, <G>. Not pronounced.) □ *I guess you are not interested in what I was saying to you.* <G> □ *When are you going to learn to spell?* <G> **3.** See *grand.*

G-man ['dʒimæn] *n.* a government investigative agent; an F.B.I. agent. □ *The G-men busted in and started shooting.* □ *When I was a kid, I wanted to be a G-man.*

gab [gæb] **1.** *in.* to chatter; to gossip. □ *Can you stop gabbing just for a minute?* □ *We like to gab. Leave us alone.* **2.** *n.* mindless chatter; gossip. □ *I like to listen in on other people's gab.* □ *Enough of this gab—on with the show!*

gab room *n.* a women's restroom where women are said to chatter. □ *She went to the gab room to powder her nose.* □ *There was a small commotion in the gab room.*

gabfest ['gæbfɛst] *n.* an event where much chattering or gossip takes place. □ *There's a gabfest going on in Clare's room.* □ *Say, your gabfest is a little loud.*

gabmeister *n.* a talk show host or hostess. □ *Todd Remington, a late night gabmeister, startled his audience by suddenly walking off stage.* □ *There are so many of these gabmeisters that I can hardly keep them straight.*

gaffer ['gæfɚ] *n.* an old man; a rustic old man. (From *grandfather.*) □ *Nobody out there but some old gaffer with a cane.* □ *The old gaffer smiled and moved on.*

gaffled ['gæfl̩d] *mod.* arrested. □ *Fred got himself gaffled for speeding.* □ *I can just picture Fred gaffled and acting all humble.*

gag [gæg] **1.** *in.* to retch or choke, especially with much noise. (Standard English.) □ *The food was so horrible I almost gagged on it.* □ *Don't eat so fast. You'll gag.* **2.** *n.* a joke; a trick. □ *She tells the best gags.* □ *What a great gag! Everybody will love it.*

gaga ['gɑgɑ] **1.** *mod.* crazy; eccentric. □ *Sometimes you are so gaga!* □ *Sally is just naturally gaga.* **2.** *mod.* dazzled. □ *The family was gaga about my success.* □ *Tom was totally gaga after he got promoted.*

galloping dandruff See *walking dandruff.*

galumph (around) [gə'lʊmpf . . .] *in.* to walk around; to *schlep* around. □ *I spent all day galumphing around, looking for a present for Ted.* □ *Stop galumphing long enough to eat some dinner.*

game *mod.* willing to do something. □ *Is anybody game for some pizza?* □ *I'm game, what about you?*

game plan *n.* a plan of action; a scheme. (From sports.) □ *The game plan for the election was beginning to shape up.* □ *Our game plan had to be scrapped.*

game time *n.* time to go do what has to be done; time to go to work. (From sports.) □ *Okay, gang, let's get going. It's game time.* □ *Will this report be ready by game time?*

gams [gæmz] *n.* a woman's legs, especially if attractive. □ *Is she the one with* *the gorgeous gams?* □ *Look at the gams on that chick!*

gander *n.* a look. □ *Let me take a gander at it and see if it's done right.* □ *We should all take a gander to see what one is like.*

gang-bang **1.** *n.* an act of group rape. □ *The fuzz was around investigating that gang-bang on the next block.* □ *There were reports of a gang-bang in the prison.* **2.** *tr. & in.* to rape in a group. □ *The pack of thugs set out to gang-bang some innocent victim.* □ *Why can't they stop gang-banging people?* **3.** *tr. & in.* to gang up on someone or something. □ *They looked like they were going to gang-bang me.* □ *They're always gang-banging. The punks!*

gangbanger *n.* a member of a street gang. □ *The gangbangers threatened the old lady too often, and finally she pulled out a can of mace and gave them a little lesson in good manners.* □ *Unless you want to grow up to be a gangbanger, you'd better go to school every day.*

gangbusters [ˈgæŋbəstɚz] *n.* a wild, busy, and successful event. (See also *like gangbusters.*) □ *Our party was truly gangbusters, for sure.* □ *The explosion and fire two streets over was really gangbusters for a while.*

GAPO [ˈgæpo] *n.* "giant armpit odor"; a bad underarm odor. □ *Who's got the GAPO?* □ *That cab driver really has the GAPO.*

garbage **1.** *n.* nonsense; gibberish. □ *He's just talking garbage.* □ *I've heard too much garbage here today.* **2.** *n.* jumbled computer code. □ *All I get is garbage on the screen.* □ *If you put garbage into the computer, you'll get garbage out.*

garbage freak AND **garbagehead** *n.* an addict who will take any drug. (Drugs.) □ *We don't know what she took. She was such a garbage freak.* □ *The garbageheads will take beans or anything else.*

garbage mouth *n.* someone who uses obscene language. □ *Quiet, garbage mouth! Watch your language.* □ *Who's the garbage mouth making all the noise?*

garbage something down *tr.* to gobble something up; to bolt something down. □ *Don't garbage your food down!* T *That guy will garbage down almost anything.*

garbagehead See *garbage freak.*

gargle **1.** *in.* to drink liquor. □ *They sat and gargled for an hour or two.* □ *Let's go out and gargle for a while.* **2.** *n.* liquor; a drink of liquor. □ *You want some more gargle?* □ *Pour me a little of that gargle, if you please.*

gargle factory *n.* a saloon; a tavern. □ *Gary spends a lot of time at the gargle factory.* □ *He should open his own gargle factory.*

gargler *n.* a drinker; a drunkard. □ *You are going to turn into a gargler if you don't let up on your drinking.* □ *Some old gargler froze to death last night.*

gas **1.** *n.* intestinal gas. □ *The baby has gas and will cry for a while longer.* □ *I'm not too well, but I think it's just gas.* **2.** *n.* nonsense. □ *All we got in class today was gas.* □ *Hey, that's about enough of your gas.* **3.** *in.* to talk nonsense; to brag. (See also *gasbag.*) □ *Pay no attention. She's just gassing.* □ *Stop gassing for a minute and listen.* **4.** *in.* to have a good time. □ *We gassed all evening.* □ *Let's go out and gas tonight, how about it?* **5.** *n.* a joke; a prank; a wild time. □ *The party was a gas.* □ *What a gas! I had a great time.* **6.** *n.* liquor, especially inferior liquor. □ *You want some more gas?* □ *Pour me a little more of that gas, will you?* **7.** AND **gas up** *in.* to drink excessively; to get drunk. □ *Let's go out and gas up!* □ *I come home every night and find that you've been gassing all day.*

gas-guzzler *n.* a large automobile that uses much gasoline. □ *I got rid of my gas-guzzler and got a smaller car.* □ *The old gas-guzzlers were certainly comfortable.*

gas-passer *n.* a jocular nickname for an anesthetist. (Hospitals.) □ *My gosh! The gas-passer charged almost as much* *as the surgeon.* ☐ *The gas-passer put a needle in my arm.*

gas up See *gas.*

gasbag *n.* a braggart. ☐ *What's the old gasbag going on about now?* ☐ *Harry is such a gasbag when he gets going about himself.*

gash bucket *n.* a refuse bucket; a bucket used as a urinal. (Underworld and military.) ☐ *Don't kick over the gash bucket over there!* ☐ *Why don't you go dump the gash bucket?*

gassed (up) *mod.* alcohol or drug intoxicated. ☐ *Fred is gassed up and very wobbly.* ☐ *He was too gassed up to drive home.*

gate *n.* sending (someone) away. (Always with *the.*) ☐ *I could see in his eyes that it was the gate for me.* ☐ *I got the gate, but I was going to leave anyway.*

gaucho ['gɑutʃo] *tr. & in.* to expose the buttocks (at someone), usually through a car window; to *moon.* ☐ *Victor gauchoed the cops as they went by.* ☐ *Victor would gaucho at the drop of a hat —so to speak.*

gay as pink ink *mod.* having to do with an obviously homosexual person, usually a male. ☐ *Who said Ron's as gay as pink ink?* ☐ *These two guys—as gay as pink ink—came in together.*

gazinkus AND **gazunkus** [gə'zɪŋkəs AND gə'zəŋkəs] *n.* a gadget. ☐ *Where is the gazinkus I use for opening paint cans?* ☐ *Is this the little gazunkus you were looking for?*

gazizzey AND **gazob** [gə'zɪzi AND gə'zɑb] *n.* a fool. ☐ *What gazizzey put the sugar in the salt shaker?* ☐ *Don't call me a gazob!*

gazob See the previous entry.

gazoo [gə'zu] *n.* the buttocks; the anus. ☐ *He fell down flat, smack on his gazoo.* ☐ *Look at the monstrous gazoo on that guy.*

gazoony [gə'zuni] *n.* a bully or strong-arm man. (Underworld.) ☐ *Bruno didn't like being called a gazoony, although that is what he is.* ☐ *A couple of gazoonies stood outside looking menacing.*

gazumph [gə'zʊmpf] **1.** *tr.* to raise the price of a house after it is sold. ☐ *They tried to gazumph the price at the closing.* ☐ *I just knew that the owner was going to gazumph the final figure.* **2.** *tr.* to subject someone to the raising of the price of a house after it is sold. ☐ *They tried to gazumph me!* ☐ *If they try to gazumph you, tell them to forget the deal.*

gazunkus See *gazinkus.*

G.B.'ed ['dʒi'bid] *mod.* "goofballed"; drug intoxicated. (Initialism. Drugs.) ☐ *Pete is G.B.'ed again.* ☐ *Gert got G.B.'ed fairly often before the accident.*

GBG *interj.* a "great big grin." (An initialism used on computer bulletin boards to show that the writer is grinning, joking, or happy. Not pronounced. Often enclosed, <GBG>.) ☐ *I think you are just talking nonsense.* <GBG> ☐ *You are such a kook!* <GBG>

gear 1. *mod.* excellent. ☐ *This jazz is really gear!.* ☐ *Man, what a gear pizza!* **2.** *n.* an asterisk (*). ☐ *Why is there a gear after this word?* ☐ *The gear stands for anything you want it to stand for.*

gee [dʒi] **1.** *n.* a portion of liquor, a gallon or a single drink. ☐ *You want another gee of this booze?* ☐ *How about a gee for me?* **2.** *exclam.* "Wow!" (An abbreviation of *Jesus!*, although not always recognized as such. Usually **Gee!**) ☐ *Gee! What a mess!* ☐ *Golly gee, do I have to?* **3.** *mod.* "gross"; disgusting. (The initial letter of *gross.*) ☐ *This is just too gee!* ☐ *Tiffany is acting way gee lately.*

geedunk [gi'dəŋk OR 'gidəŋk] *n.* ice cream. ☐ *Let's go out and get some geedunk for dessert.* ☐ *Pineapple on chocolate geedunk? Yuck!*

geedus See *geetis.*

geegaw AND **gewgaw; googaw** ['gigɔ AND 'gugɔ] *n.* a gadget; a bauble. ☐ *Now that's a cute little geegaw.* ☐ *What do you do with these gewgaws? Hang them on a tree?*

geek AND **geke** [gik] **1.** *n.* a disgusting and repellent person; a *creep.* □ *The convention was a seething morass of pushy sales geeks and glad-handers.* □ *Who's the geek who just came in?* **2.** *n.* an earnest student; a hardworking student. □ *Martin is a geek, but he will go places with his brains.* □ *It looks like the geeks are taking over this campus. How gross!*

geek-chic ['gik'ʃik] *n.* stylish or fashionable only for social outcasts. (See also *geek.*) □ *Tom is the guy who always wears the tacky geek-chic jacket.* □ *Why do you have to buy all this geek-chic stuff? Don't they give it away somewhere?*

geek out *in.* to study hard. (See also *geek.*) □ *Big test tomorrow. I've got to get home and geek out.* □ *Bill's a geekazoid. He geeks out all the time.*

geekazoid ['gikəzoɪd] *n.* a social outcast; a *nerd.* □ *Don't be such a geekazoid!* □ *If you weren't such a geekazoid, I'd be surprised at the dumb things you do!*

geekdom *n.* the realm of the hard-studying students or *geeks.* □ *This dorm is not exactly geekdom. Almost all the guys here are on academic probation.* □ *I spent all last semester in the hallowed halls of geekdom, studying my buns off.*

Geesh! [giʃ] *exclam.* "Good grief!" (Shows shock and disgust.) □ *What a mess! Geesh!* □ *Geesh! I love my work but hate my job!*

geetis AND **geedus; geetus** ['gidəs] *n.* money. □ *That kind of car takes a lot of geetis, doesn't it?* □ *I don't have the geetis to throw around on something like that.*

geetus See the previous entry.

geezer ['gizɚ] **1.** *n.* a strange old man; a *buzzard.* □ *Who's the old geezer with the straw hat on?* □ *He is a nice geezer, but a little talkative.* **2.** *n.* a drink of liquor. □ *Toss down a geezer of this stuff and see how you like it.* □ *Can I have another geezer of this firewater?*

geke See *geek.*

gel [dʒɛl] *in.* to relax and let one's hair down. □ *I've got to go home and gel for a while. Things are too stressful just now.* □ *If I don't get to gel a little every day, I tend to fall apart.*

gender-bender **1.** *n.* a device that changes electrical plugs or sockets to the opposite gender—male to female, female to male. □ *You need what's called a gender-bender to match those plugs.* □ *I tried a gender-bender, but it won't work.* **2.** *mod.* having to do with something that obscures male/female distinctions. □ *Those gender-bender hairstyles can be confusing.* □ *He always wears gender-bender clothes.*

generic [dʒə'nɛrɪk] *mod.* cheap; plain; undesirable. □ *I don't want any old generic car, I want something with power and good looks.* □ *This cereal is generic. It has no taste at all.* □ *This pizza is completely generic. I can't stand it.*

genuine article ['dʒɛnjəwən 'ɑrtɪkl̩ OR 'dʒɛn'ju'waɪn 'ɑrtɪkl̩] *n.* the real thing rather than a substitute. □ *Is this the genuine article or some cheap made-in-U.S.A. substitute?* □ *I'll take the genuine article, thanks.*

george **1.** *tr. & in.* to seduce and copulate (with someone, usually a woman). (Use caution with the topic.) □ *They say he georges her a lot.* □ *They were off somewhere georging.* **2.** *n.* a bowel movement. (Euphemistic. Use caution with the topic.) □ *I gotta go take a george. Back in a minute.* □ *I'm okay. Nothing a good george wouldn't cure.*

GERK AND **gerk** [gɚk] *n.* an elderly simpleton; an old *nerd.* (Acronym. From *geriatric* and *jerk.*) □ *Old man Johnson is a real GERK—ill-tempered and rude.* □ *A couple of gerks sat on the park bench, snoozing.*

German goiter See *Milwaukee goiter.*

Geronimo! [dʒə'rɑnəmo] *exclam.* "Here I go!" (Originally said by parachutists leaving a plane. From Spanish for *Jerome.*) □ *There's my cue. Geronimo!* □ *Here goes nothing. Geronimo!*

get a bang out of someone or something AND **get a kick out of someone or something** *tr.* to get a thrill from someone or something. □ *I always get a bang out of her jokes.* □ *She gets a kick out of her grandchildren.*

get a buzz out of someone or something *tr.* to get some humor from someone or something. (See also *give someone a buzz.*) □ *I thought you'd get a buzz out of that gag.* □ *I hope you get a buzz out of Ted. He's a funny guy.*

get a can on *tr.* to get drunk. (Compare to *tie one on.*) □ *Let's go out tonight and get a can on.* □ *The entire office staff got a can on to celebrate the contract.*

get a fix AND **get a gift** *tr.* to buy drugs; to take a dose of drugs. (Drugs.) □ *Gert had to get home and get a fix.* □ *What did Tracy mean when she said she had to get a gift fast?*

get a gift See *get a fix.*

get a kick out of someone or something See *get a bang out of someone or something.*

Get a life! *exclam.* "Change your life radically!" (Compare to *Get real!*) □ *You are such a twit! Get a life!* □ *Get a life, you clown!*

get a load of something or someone *tr.* to look at someone or something. □ *Wow, get a load of Fred!* □ *Get a load of the chrome on that set of wheels!*

get a load off one's feet AND **take a load off one's feet** *tr.* to sit down and relax. □ *Sit down and get a load off your feet.* □ *Take a load off your feet and have a drink.*

get a load off one's mind *tr.* to say what one is thinking; to speak one's mind; to talk something out. □ *I'm sorry, but I just had to get a load off my mind.* □ *I think you'll feel better after you get a load off your mind.*

get a toehold *tr.* to work one's way into some association or relationship. □ *As soon as I get a toehold in the company, I'll be more relaxed.* □ *Once he gets a toehold, you'll never get rid of him.*

Get a wiggle on! *exclam.* to hurry up. □ *Get a wiggle on! We don't have all day!* □ *Hey, you guys! Get a wiggle on! We gotta finish before nightfall.*

get an eyeball on someone or something *tr.* to manage to spot someone or something; to catch sight of someone or something. □ *When I finally got an eyeball on the speeding car, it was too far away for me to read the license plate.* □ *When Jane first got an eyeball on her blind date, she almost cringed in disappointment.*

Get away! ['gɛt ə'we] *exclam.* "Stop being a pest!"; "I don't believe you!" □ *Don't bother me! Get away!* □ *Get away! Nobody is that stupid!*

get behind someone or something 1. *in.* to support someone or something. □ *Let's all get behind the party in the next election.* □ *Everybody got behind Todd and cheered him on.* **2.** *in.* [with *something*] to enjoy something, such as a drug or music. (Originally drugs.) □ *I'm really getting behind heavy metal.* □ *Sam got behind some acid and got stuck there.*

get down 1. *in.* to lay one's money on the table. (Gambling.) □ *Okay, everybody get down.* □ *Get down, and let's get going!* **2.** *in.* to concentrate; to do something well. □ *I'm flunking two subjects, man. I gotta get down.* □ *Come on, Sam, pay attention. Get down and learn this stuff.* **3.** *in.* to copulate. □ *Hey, let's get down!* □ *All Steve wants to do is get down all the time.*

get down on someone *in.* to be critical of someone; to *get on someone's case.* □ *Don't get down on me. I didn't do it!* □ *I'm gonna get down on him for that.*

get down to some serious drinking *in.* to settle down to a long session of drinking. □ *Well, now we can get down to some serious drinking.* □ *When the kids go to bed, let's get down to some serious drinking.*

get down to the nitty-gritty *in.* to get down to the basic facts. (See also *nitty-gritty.*) □ *Stop messing around and get down to the nitty-gritty.* □ *If we could only get down to the nitty-gritty and stop wasting time.*

get face *tr.* to gain respect; to increase one's status. (The opposite of *lose face.*) □ *He's doing his best in life to get face.* □ *Let's do something to help her get face.*

get hot 1. *in.* to begin to get lucky, as in gambling. □ *I knew I was getting hot when I got all the right cards.* □ *If I could only get hot, I might win back everything I lost.* **2.** *in.* to become busy or hectic. □ *Things always get hot around here toward the end of the month.* □ *When things start getting hot, we have to hire more people.*

get in bad (with someone) *in.* to get into trouble with someone. □ *I tried not to get in bad with Wally.* □ *We got in bad with each other from the start.*

get in on the act *in.* to become involved in something with someone else. (The involvement is not necessarily welcome.) □ *Everybody wants to get in on the act.* □ *Why are you trying to get in on the act?*

get in someone's face *tr.* to provoke someone. □ *Ted's a real pain. He likes to get in your face. He'll argue about anything.* □ *I know you are angry, but don't get in my face. I had nothing to do with it.*

get in the groove *in.* to become attuned to something. □ *I was uncomfortable at first, but now I'm beginning to get in the groove.* □ *Fred began to get in the groove, and things went more smoothly.*

get into something *in.* to become deeply involved with something. □ *I got into computers when I was in junior high school.* □ *When did you get into foreign films?*

get it 1. *tr.* to understand a joke; to understand a point of information. □ *Sorry. I don't get it.* □ *Don't you get it?* **2.** *tr.* to get punished. □ *I just know I'm going to get it when I get home.* □ *You're going to get it all right!*

get it (all) together *tr.* to get oneself organized; to get mentally adjusted. □ *When I get it together, I'll try to go back to school.* □ *Try to get it all together and come back to work next week, okay?*

get it in the neck *tr.* to receive something bad, such as punishment or criticism. (See also *pain in the neck.*) □ *You are going to get it in the neck for that remark.* □ *Jimmy was afraid he'd get it in the neck for being late.*

get it off *tr.* to ejaculate; to achieve sexual release; to copulate. (Potentially offensive. Use only with discretion.) □ *Harry kept saying he had to get it off or die. What's wrong with Harry?* □ *The entire crew of the yacht came ashore to get it off.*

get it on 1. *tr.* to begin something. □ *Time to go back to work. Let's get it on!* □ *Get it on, you guys! Time to start your engines.* **2.** *tr.* to begin dancing. □ *Let's go out there and get it on!* □ *He wanted to get it on, but my feet hurt.* **3.** *tr.* [for people] to copulate. (Potentially offensive. Use only with discretion.) □ *Come on, baby, let's get it on.* □ *I don't want to get it on with you or any other creep.* **4.** *tr.* to undertake to enjoy oneself. □ *I can really get it on with that slow jazz.* □ *Let's go listen to some new age and get it on.*

get it out *tr.* to tell (someone) about a problem; to pour out one's grief. □ *Come on, get it out. You'll feel better.* □ *He would feel better if he could get it out.*

get it up *tr.* to get excited about something. (Other taboo meanings, also.) □ *I just couldn't get it up about going off to college.* □ *Paul just couldn't get it up about life in general.*

get lip *tr.* to get some kissing; to *neck.* (Teens.) □ *Jim's been out getting lip again. Look at the lipstick.* □ *These kids talk about getting lip. Ye gods, how crude!*

Get lost! *exclam.* "Go away!"; "Beat it!" □ *Get lost, you're bothering me!* □ *Quit following me. Get lost!*

get mad (at something) *in.* to muster great physical strength and determination in order to do something. □ *You're gonna have to get mad at it if you want to move it.* □ *Come on, you guys. Get mad.*

Get my drift? See *(Do you) get my drift?*

get naked *in.* to enjoy oneself thoroughly; to relax and enjoy oneself. □ *Let's all go out and get naked tonight.* □ *Man, I feel like getting naked tonight.*

get narkied [. . .'narkid] *in.* to inject drugs; to become addicted. (Drugs.) □ *Rocko only got narkied once in his life.* □ *Gert couldn't wait to get narkied.*

get nowhere fast *in.* to make very poor progress. □ *We are getting nowhere fast around here.* □ *I'm getting nowhere fast in this job. I quit.*

get off 1. *in.* to reach an understanding with someone. (Not slang.) □ *We just weren't getting off well at all.* □ *How well do you get off with Ralph?* **2.** See *get off (on something).*

get off (on something) 1. *in.* to get pleasure from something. □ *I don't get off on music anymore.* □ *I listen, but I just don't get off.* **2.** *in.* to take a drug and experience a *rush.* (Drugs.) □ *Max likes to get off, but he's got his business to run.* □ *Tracy likes getting off better than anything else.* **3.** *in.* to do well on something. □ *Wayne is getting off on history, much to everyone's surprise.* □ *Bill got off on fixing up his car, and I may let him do mine too.*

get off one's rear *in.* to get up and get busy. □ *It's time to get off your rear and get to work.* □ *Hey, Chuck, get off your rear! There's work to be done.*

get off someone's back AND **get off someone's case** *in.* to stop annoying someone. □ *I wish you'd get off my back.* □ *Get off my case! You aren't my mother.*

get off someone's case See the previous entry.

get off the dime *in.* [for something or someone] to start moving. (To get off the dime that one stopped on in "stop on a dime.") □ *I wish this organization could get off the dime.* □ *If this project gets off the dime, we'll be okay.*

get on someone's case *in.* to start harassing someone about a personal problem; to annoy someone. □ *I'll get on Tom's case about being late so much.* □ *I'm sorry, I won't get on your case anymore.*

get on the stick *in.* to get organized and get busy. □ *Get on the stick and get this job done!* □ *Come on, you guys. Let's get on the stick!*

get one right here *tr.* to affect one deeply in a specific way. (Usually accompanied with a hand gesture showing exactly where one is affected: the heart = lovingly, the stomach or bowels = sickeningly.) □ *That sort of thing gets me right here.* □ *Pete clasped his hand to his chest and said, "That sort of thing gets me right here."*

get one's act together AND **get one's shit together; get one's stuff together 1.** *tr.* to organize oneself; to get one's possessions organized. (Use caution with *shit.*) □ *Let me get my act together, and I'll be right with you.* □ *I'll get my stuff together and be right with you.* **2.** AND **get one's head together** *tr.* to calm down and get mentally organized. (Use caution with *shit.*) □ *As soon as I get my head together, I can be of more help.* □ *Get your act together and start living again.*

get one's bowels in an uproar *tr.* to become overly anxious or excited. □ *Cool it! Don't get your bowels in an uproar.* □ *Fred's always getting his bowels in an uproar about nothing.*

get one's head together See *get one's act together.*

get one's hooks into someone or something 1. *tr.* to get a hold of someone or something; to gain control of someone or something. □ *I want to get my hooks into the operation of this organization.* □ *If I could get my hooks into the control of the company, I would change things for the better.* **2.** *tr.* [with *someone*] [for a woman] to succeed in "capturing" a specific man. □ *She just can't wait to get her hooks into Chuck.* □ *When she* *got her hooks into him, she decided he wasn't so great after all.*

get one's kicks (from someone or something) *tr.* to get pleasure from someone or something. ☐ *Do you get your kicks from this sort of thing?* ☐ *I get my kicks from Billy Simpson. What a great entertainer!*

get one's lumps *tr.* to get the result or punishment one deserves. (Compare to *take one's lumps.*) ☐ *If she keeps acting that way, she'll get her lumps.* ☐ *We will see that Dave gets his lumps.*

get one's nose cold *tr.* to *snort* cocaine. (Drugs.) ☐ *Max is always ready to get his nose cold.* ☐ *Rocko has never gotten his nose cold in his life.*

get one's nose out of joint *tr.* to feel slighted by something someone has done; to take offense at something. (See also *put someone's nose out of joint.*) ☐ *You get your nose out of joint too easily about stuff like that.* ☐ *Now, don't get your nose out of joint. She didn't mean it.*

get one's rocks off (on something) *tr.* to enjoy something. (Other taboo meanings, also.) ☐ *I really get my rocks off on heavy metal.* ☐ *I've listened to the stuff, but I sure don't get my rocks off on it.*

get one's shit together See *get one's act together.*

get one's stuff together See *get one's act together.*

get one's teeth into something AND **sink one's teeth into something** *tr.* to undertake to do something. ☐ *I can't wait to sink my teeth into that Wallace job.* ☐ *Here, sink your teeth into this and see if you can't manage this project.*

get one's ticket punched *tr.* to die; to be killed. (Literally, to be cancelled.) ☐ *Poor Chuck got his ticket punched while he was waiting for a bus.* ☐ *Watch out there, or you'll get your ticket punched.*

get one's wings *tr.* to use heavy drugs for the first time; to succeed in becoming a drug addict. (Drugs.) ☐ *Gert got her wings after fiddling around with stuff for a long time.* ☐ *Max got his wings at about age twelve.*

get out of Dodge *in.* to leave a place. (Refers to Dodge City, Kansas, and a catch phrase from Western entertainment adventures about this town.) ☐ *Come on, G. Let's get out of Dodge.* ☐ *Things are looking bad here. It's time to get out of Dodge.*

Get out of my face! *exclam.* "Stop arguing with me!"; "Stand back! Don't confront me with your arguments and challenges!" (See also *get in someone's face.*) ☐ *Beat it! Get out of my face!* ☐ *Get outa my face if you know what's good for you.*

Get out of town! *exclam.* "Beat it!"; "Get out of here!" ☐ *Go away, you bother me! Get out of town!* ☐ *You'd better get out of town, my friend. You are a pest.*

get (out) while the gettin(g)'s good AND **get (out) while the goin's good** *phr.* to leave while it is still safe or possible to do so. ☐ *I could tell that it was time for me to get while the gettin's good.* ☐ *I told her she should get out while the goin's good.*

get (out) while the goin's good See the previous entry.

Get real! *exclam.* "Start acting realistically!" (Compare to *Get a life!*) ☐ *Hey, chum! You are way off base! Get real!* ☐ *Get real! Wake up to reality!*

get right See *get straight.*

get smart (with someone) *in.* to become fresh with someone; to talk back to someone. ☐ *Don't you get smart with me!* ☐ *If you get smart again, I'll bop you.*

get some shut-eye *tr.* to get some sleep. ☐ *I need to get home and get some shut-eye before I do anything else.* ☐ *We all could use some shut-eye.*

get someone going *tr.* to get someone excited; to get someone talking excitedly. ☐ *I guess I really got him going on the subject of politics.* ☐ *The whole business really makes me mad. Don't get me going.*

get someone's goat *tr.* to irritate someone. □ *Don't let Mary get your goat. She's just irritable today.* □ *Everybody seems to be getting my goat today.*

get someone's motor running **1.** *tr.* to get someone excited. □ *What'll I have to do to get your motor running about algebra?* □ *I've got some news that'll really get your motor running.* **2.** *tr.* to get someone sexually aroused. □ *She knows how to get his motor running.* □ *It's funny how that wild music gets her motor running.*

get something going (with someone) *tr.* to start a romance with someone. □ *Heidi wants to get something going with Pete.* □ *Mary and Sam got something going.*

get straight AND **get right** *in.* to take a dose of a drug to end drug craving. (Drugs.) □ *Gert needed a fix to get straight.* □ *I need to get right before anything else.*

get stupid *in.* to become intoxicated; to make oneself alcohol or drug intoxicated. □ *Garth had the habit of going out and getting stupid every Friday night.* □ *It's been one totally screwed up week. I think I'll just stay home tonight and get stupid.*

get the ax See *get the sack.*

get the drop on someone **1.** *tr.* to succeed in getting an advantage over someone. □ *I guess I got the drop on you because I was early.* □ *I got the drop on almost everybody by sending in my registration by mail.* **2.** *tr.* [for person A] to manage to get a gun aimed at person B before person B can aim back at person A. (The gun is then "dropped" by person B.) □ *Rocko got the drop on Max in a flash.* □ *Max was too stoned to get the drop on Rocko.*

get the goods on someone *tr.* to uncover incriminating evidence against someone. □ *The fuzz has the goods on Mr. Big.* □ *The IRS tried to get the goods on Rocko, but Rocko knows all the angles.*

Get the lead out! *exclam.* "Get moving!"; "Hurry up!" (Crude. It is assumed that one has bowels full of lead. Use with caution.) □ *Come on, you turkeys. Get the lead out!* □ *Shake the lead out! I want it done today, not next week.*

Get the message? AND **Get the picture?** *interrog.* "Do you understand?"; "Are you able to figure out what is meant?" □ *Things are tough around here, and we need everyone's cooperation. Get the picture?* □ *We don't need lazy people around here. Get the message?*

get the nod *tr.* to be chosen. (See also *give someone the nod.*) □ *Fred got the nod for class treasurer.* □ *I hope I get the nod for the job.*

Get the picture? See *Get the message?*

get the sack AND **get the ax** *tr.* to be dismissed from one's employment. □ *Poor Tom got the sack today. He's always late.* □ *I was afraid that Sally was going to get the ax.*

get the show on the road *tr.* to get (something) started. □ *Let's get started! Get the show on the road!* □ *Get the show on the road. We don't have all day.*

get there *in.* to get drunk. □ *Another hour of drinking and Pete knew he was going to get there.* □ *Those guys have all got there. Now what?*

get to someone **1.** *in.* [for someone or something] to annoy someone. □ *The whole business began to get to me after a while.* □ *Her remark got to me after a while.* **2.** *in.* [for someone or something] to please or entice someone. □ *Lovely flowers and things like that get to me.* □ *Sad music gets to me and makes me cry.*

get with it **1.** *in.* to modernize one's attitudes and behavior. □ *Get with it, Martin. Get real!* □ *You really have to get with it, Ernie.* **2.** *in.* to hurry up and get busy; to be more industrious with something. □ *Get with it; we've got a lot to do.* □ *Let's get with it. There's a lot of work to be done.*

get with someone *in.* to find out about someone; to get to know someone. □ *I'd really like to get with her, but she's so distant.* □ *I was just beginning to get with Heidi when she left.*

get with the program *in.* follow the rules; do what you are supposed to do. ☐ *Come on, Mark. Get with the program. Do what you are told.* ☐ *Jane just can't seem to get with the program. She has to do everything her way, right or wrong.*

getaway ['getəwe] **1.** *n.* an escape from the law. (Originally underworld.) ☐ *Lefty made a quick getaway.* ☐ *There was no time to make a getaway, so we had to talk to Mrs. Wilson.* **2.** *n.* a quick vacation. ☐ *We took a little getaway to the Bahamas.* ☐ *What you need is a weekend getaway.*

gewgaw See *geegaw.*

(ghetto) blaster AND **(ghetto) box** ['gɛdo blæstɚ AND 'gɛdo bɑks] *n.* a portable stereo radio. (Often carried on the shoulder, especially by blacks.) ☐ *Hey, turn down that ghetto blaster in here!* ☐ *You can't bring that box on this bus!*

(ghetto) box See the previous entry.

ghost turd *n.* a wad of lint, as found under a bed. (Use caution with *turd.*) ☐ *There's a lot of ghost turds under the bed.* ☐ *Sweep out those ghost turds and get rid of them.*

GIB *mod.* "good in bed"; good as a sexual partner. (Use caution with the topic. Initialism.) ☐ *Pete lets on that he's GIB.* ☐ *How does he know he's GIB?*

gibber-gabber ['dʒɪbɚdʒæbɚ] *n.* nonsense; gossip and chatter. ☐ *There sure is a lot of gibber-gabber coming from your room, Jimmy.* ☐ *What's all this gibber-gabber about?*

Giddy up! ['gɪdi . . .] *exclam.* "Move faster!" (Said to a horse to start it moving. Also said to people or things as a joke.) ☐ *Giddy up, Charlie! It's time to start moving.* ☐ *Let's get going, chum. Giddy up!*

giffed [gɪft] *mod.* alcohol intoxicated. (From *TGIF* "Thank God it's Friday." Said of people who celebrate the end of the workweek with liquor.) ☐ *He left the tavern pretty giffed.* ☐ *She was pretty giffed for just a few beers.*

gift of gab *n.* the ability to speak well in public; the ability to persuade people verbally; the ability to speak well extemporaneously. ☐ *Gary has the gift of gab, but it doesn't get him anywhere.* ☐ *I wish I had the gift of gab. I'm just so shy.*

gig 1. *n.* a onetime job; an engagement. (Musicians.) ☐ *I had a gig out on the west side, but I couldn't get there.* ☐ *The gig was canceled because of the snow.* **2.** *in.* to play or perform. (Musicians.) ☐ *I didn't gig at all last week. I'm getting hungry for a job.* ☐ *I'm happiest when I'm gigging.* **3.** *n.* any job of an assignment nature; a onetime job such as when a newspaper reporter is assigned to write a particular story. ☐ *I didn't want that election gig, but I got it anyway.* ☐ *Wally is tired of getting the crime gigs.* **4.** *n.* a bother; an annoyance; a job. ☐ *Man, this paperwork is such a gig.* ☐ *This day's a gig. I've had it.* **5.** *n.* a giggle; a bit of laughter. ☐ *Her little story gave us all a good gig.* ☐ *I had a nice little gig over what happened to Tom.*

giggle goo ['gɪgl̩ gu] *n.* liquor. ☐ *Can I pour you a little of that giggle goo?* ☐ *Haven't you had about enough of that giggle goo?*

GIGO *phr.* "garbage in, garbage out." (Computers. Acronym. If you get garbage out of a computer, it's because you put garbage in. See also *DIDO.*) ☐ *The program failed, and I know it's my fault. You know, GIGO.* ☐ *G.I.G.O. is my theme song. I get out just what I deserve.*

gimme ['gɪmi] *phr.* "give me." (Eye-dialect. Typical spoken English. Used in writing only for effect. Used in the examples of this dictionary.) ☐ *Do you wanna gimme the thingy and lemme go ahead with my work?* ☐ *Gimme another one.*

Gimme a break! See *Give me a break!*

gimp [gɪmp] **1.** *n.* a lame person. (Originally underworld. Otherwise derogatory.) ☐ *Lefty tried to mug an old gimp with a cane.* ☐ *The gimp came hobbling along, muttering something under his breath.* **2.** *in.* to limp about. ☐ *I've been gimping a little bit since my accident.* ☐ *I'll gimp over there as soon as I can. It'll take a while on these crutches.*

gimpy ['gɪmpi] **1.** *mod.* crippled; lame. ☐ *I got a gimpy leg. I'll catch up in a minute.* ☐ *He's sort of gimpy since the football season.* **2.** *n.* a police officer. (Also a rude term of address. A pun on *lame,* an inept person.) ☐ *Here comes gimpy, swinging his stick.* ☐ *Gimpy has been around asking about you.*

gin dive See the following entry.

gin mill AND **gin dive; gin palace** *n.* a saloon; a low liquor establishment. ☐ *Fred hit every gin mill on the way home.* ☐ *You'll find Bob in some gin dive on the west side of town.*

gin palace See the previous entry.

ginhead *n.* a drunkard. ☐ *Gert could have ended up a ginhead, but she went another route instead.* ☐ *A couple of ginheads sat in the corner booth silently.*

girl 1. *n.* a woman; a young woman. (Objectionable to some as demeaning to women.) ☐ *A bunch of us girls got together for coffee today.* ☐ *Would you girls care to come over to my house next week?* **2.** *n.* the queen of playing cards. (See also *bitch.*) ☐ *What I needed in that last hand was the girl.* ☐ *Come on, dealer, I need that girl!*

girlie magazine *n.* a magazine featuring pictures of nude women. ☐ *The girlie magazines were hidden under the counter.* ☐ *Some creepy character asked Sally if she would pose for a girlie magazine.*

girlie show *n.* a performance featuring nude women. ☐ *Bob and Pete went to the city and tried to get into a girlie show.* ☐ *This movie has turned out to be nothing but a girlie show.*

git-go ['gɪtgo] *n.* the very beginning. (See also *from (the) git-go.*) ☐ *Clear back at the git-go, I told you this wouldn't work.* ☐ *He's been gritching ever since git-go.*

Give it a rest! *exclam.* "Shut up!" (The "it" is a mouth. Compare to *Give me a rest!*) ☐ *I've heard enough. Give it a rest!* ☐ *Give it a rest! You talk too much.*

give it the gun *tr.* to gun an engine; to rev an engine up. ☐ *Give it the gun for a minute.* ☐ *I gave it the gun, and it backfired.*

Give it up! *exclam.* "Quit now!"; "Enough is enough!" ☐ *Oh, give it up! You can't do it right.* ☐ *Give it up! You can't pitch!*

Give me a break! AND **Gimme a break! 1.** *exclam.* "That is enough!"; "Stop it!" ☐ *Do you have to go on and on? Give me a break!* ☐ *Give me a break, you guys! That's enough!* **2.** *exclam.* "Don't be so harsh!"; "Give me a chance!" ☐ *I'm sorry! I'll do better! Give me a break!* ☐ *I was only late once! Give me a break!* **3.** *exclam.* "I don't believe you!"; "You don't expect anyone to believe that!" ☐ *You say a gorilla is loose in the city? Gimme a break!* ☐ *Tom said he was late again because the back stairs caved in. His boss said, "Gimme a break!"*

Give me a rest! *exclam.* "Lay off!"; "That is enough!" (Compare to *Give it a rest!*) ☐ *Haven't I told you everything you need to know? Give me a rest.* ☐ *Give me a rest! I've heard enough.*

Give me five! See the following entry.

Give me (some) skin! AND **Give me five!; Slip me five!** *exclam.* "Shake my hand!" (A request for some form of hand touching in greeting. See also *give someone five, high five.*) ☐ *Hey, man! Give me some skin!* ☐ *Give me five, my man!*

give (out) with something *in.* to give out information. ☐ *Come on, give out with the facts, man.* ☐ *Give with the info. We're in a hurry.*

give someone a buzz 1. *tr.* to give someone a telephone call. ☐ *Give me a buzz sometime.* ☐ *I'll give her buzz tonight and ask her.* **2.** *tr.* to give someone a chuckle or a bit of enjoyment. ☐ *It always gives me a buzz to watch Sally do her act.* ☐ *Your little joke gave me a buzz.*

give someone a (good) talking to *tr.* to scold someone; to lecture someone sternly. ☐ *I think I'll have to give Pete a good talking to.* ☐ *The teacher gave Jimmy a talking to.*

give someone a (good) working over *tr.* to scold or beat someone. □ *The boss gave me a good working over before firing me.* □ *Fred really gave her a working over about her performance on the project.*

give someone a melvin *tr.* to jerk up someone's pants or underwear, drawing the fabric up sharply between the buttocks. (It is assumed that some *geek* named Melvin goes about with his underwear in this uncomfortable position.) □ *If you even try to give me a melvin, I'll bust you one.* □ *Tom came up behind Fred, and with a deft motion, gave Fred a melvin that he would never forget.*

give someone a pain *tr.* to annoy or bother someone. □ *Please don't give me a pain. I've had a hard day.* □ *You give me a pain!*

give someone an earful 1. *tr.* to scold someone. □ *I'm going to give Ralph an earful for doing that.* □ *Sally gave Sam an earful for the way he treated Mary.* **2.** *tr.* to tell someone surprising secrets. □ *Sally gave Wally an earful about Pete and the things he said about Mary.* □ *Wally gave Sally an earful about Todd's tax problems.*

give someone five 1. *tr.* to give someone a helping hand. □ *Hey, give me five over here for a minute, will ya?* □ *I gotta give this guy five with the crate. Be right with you.* **2.** *tr.* to slap hands in greeting. (See also *high five, Give me five!*) □ *Jerry gave John five as they passed in the corridor.* □ *Don tried to give me five in class, but missed.*

give someone hell 1. *tr.* to bawl someone out; to scold someone severely. (Use caution with *hell.*) □ *The boss just gave me hell about it.* □ *I'm really going to give Tom hell when he gets home.* **2.** *tr.* to trouble someone. (Use caution with *hell.*) □ *My arthritis is giving me hell in this weather.* □ *This problem is giving us hell at the office.*

give someone the ax 1. *tr.* to dismiss someone from employment. □ *They had to give Paul the ax because he was so unproductive.* □ *I was afraid they would give me the ax.* **2.** *tr.* to divorce someone. □ *Mary gave Fred the ax after only six months.* □ *She gave him the ax because he wouldn't stop smoking like he promised.*

give someone the brushoff *tr.* to repel someone; to ignore someone. (See also *brushoff.*) □ *Sam was afraid that Mary was going to give him the brushoff.* □ *The manager gave her the brushoff when she asked for a raise.*

give someone the business 1. *tr.* to harass someone; to scold someone. □ *The guys have been giving me the business about my haircut.* □ *Sam was giving Tom the business about being late all the time.* **2.** *tr.* to kill someone. (Underworld.) □ *Lefty wanted to give Rocko the business for being so damn perfect.* □ *Mr. Big told Bruno to give Max the business.*

give someone the finger 1. *tr.* to display the middle finger upright as a sign of derision. (The gesture is taboo.) □ *Did one of you guys give Ted the finger?* □ *Somebody gave the cop the finger.* **2.** *tr.* to mistreat someone; to insult someone. □ *You've been giving me the finger ever since I started working here. What's wrong?* □ *I'm tired of everybody giving me the finger around here just because I'm new.*

give someone the gate *tr.* to get rid of someone. □ *The chick was a pest, so I gave her the gate.* □ *He threatened to give me the gate, so I left.*

give someone the go-by *tr.* to bypass someone; to ignore someone. (See also *go-by.*) □ *Gert gave us all the go-by when she was so sick.* □ *I didn't mean to give you the go-by. I'm preoccupied, that's all.*

give someone the nod 1. *tr.* to signal someone by nodding. (Not slang.) □ *I gave Pete the nod, and he started the procedure.* □ *Just give me the nod when you are ready.* **2.** *tr.* to choose someone. (See also *get the nod.*) □ *The committee gave Frank the nod for the job.* □ *They gave her the nod.*

give someone the raspberry *tr.* to make a rude noise with the lips at someone. (See also *Bronx cheer, raspberry.*) ☐ *The audience gave him the raspberry, which gave him some second thoughts about his choice of career.* ☐ *Even after his grandstand play, they gave him the raspberry.*

give someone the shaft *tr.* to cheat or deceive someone; to mistreat someone. (See also *shaft.*) ☐ *The boss really gave Wally the shaft.* ☐ *Somebody always gives me the shaft.*

give someone the slip *tr.* to escape from a pursuer. ☐ *We were on his tail until he gave us the slip.* ☐ *I can give her the slip in no time at all.*

giveaway *n.* something that reveals a fact that was meant to be concealed. (Often with *dead.*) ☐ *The way he was walking was a giveaway to the fact that he was the one who was injured.* ☐ *The look on her face was a dead giveaway.*

gizmo ['gɪzmo] *n.* a gadget. ☐ *What is this silly little gizmo on the bottom for?* ☐ *This gizmo turns it on.*

gizzy ['gɪzi] *n.* marijuana. (Drugs.) ☐ *The cops found a little gizzy in the guy's pocket.* ☐ *Where'd you get this gizzy?*

glad *mod.* alcohol intoxicated. ☐ *After a few beers she was a mite glad.* ☐ *In fact, she was too glad to stand up.*

glad-hand *tr.* to greet someone effusively. ☐ *The Senator was glad-handing everyone in sight.* ☐ *He glad-handed Ernie and got a real earful.*

glad-hander *n.* someone who displays effusive friendship. ☐ *What a morass of eager glad-handers and glitz!* ☐ *The glad-handers were out in full force at the Independence Day parade.*

glad rags *n.* fancy clothes; best clothing. (See also *rag.*) ☐ *You look pretty good in your glad rags.* ☐ *I'll get on my glad rags, and we'll go out tonight.*

glamour puss *n.* a person with a beautiful face. ☐ *I'm no glamour puss, but I'm no dog either.* ☐ *Now, Sally is what I would call a glamour puss.*

glass gun *n.* a hypodermic syringe. (Drugs.) ☐ *Gert broke her glass gun and had to improvise.* ☐ *A lot of those bangsters don't even use a glass gun.*

glass(y)-eyed *mod.* alcohol or drug intoxicated. ☐ *Mary is looking sort of glassy-eyed, and it's only midnight.* ☐ *Ernie is usually glass-eyed, but tonight it's much worse.*

glazed (drunk) AND **glazed (over)** *mod.* alcohol intoxicated. ☐ *She has had too much. She's glazed drunk.* ☐ *Fred looks a little glazed. I think he's done for.*

glazed (over) See the previous entry.

gleep [glip] *n.* a fool; an oaf. ☐ *What a gleep! Does he know what's what?* ☐ *Don't act like such a gleep!*

glick [glɪk] a strange person; a *nerd.* ☐ *Don't be a glick, Bill.* ☐ *Fred seems to be a classic glick, but he is really an all-right guy.*

glitch [glɪtʃ] *n.* a defect; a *bug.* ☐ *There is a glitch in the computer program somewhere.* ☐ *I'm afraid there's a glitch in our plans.*

glitz [glɪts] *n.* flashiness and glamour. ☐ *The place was a morass of eager sales geeks and phony glitz.* ☐ *The glitz was blinding, and the substance was invisible.*

glitzy ['glɪtsi] *mod.* fashionable; glamorous. ☐ *It was a real glitzy place to hold a meeting.* ☐ *Some glitzy blonde sang a couple of songs, and then the band played again.*

glom [glɑm] **1.** *tr.* to steal something. (Underworld.) ☐ *Lefty glommed a little car for the evening.* ☐ *He gloms just about everything he needs.* **2.** *tr.* to take a look at someone or something. (Underworld.) ☐ *Glom this layout for a minute.* ☐ *Come over here and glom the view of the bank from this window.*

glommed [glɑmd] *mod.* arrested. (Underworld.) ☐ *Max got glommed on a speeding charge. I didn't even know he could drive.* ☐ *Glommed again! That's the story of my life.*

gloomy Gus *n.* a sad or dismal person; a pessimist. ☐ *Don't be such a gloomy*

Gus, Wally. ☐ *Well, gloomy Gus just came in again.*

glop [glɑp] **1.** *n.* unappetizing food; *gunk;* anything undesirable. ☐ *Do we have the same old glop again tonight?* ☐ *No, this is different glop.* **2.** *tr.* to slop or plop something (onto something). ☐ *She glopped something horrible onto my plate.* ☐ *Don't glop any of that pink stuff anywhere near me.*

glorified *mod.* overblown; over-hyped; phony. ☐ *Why, this is just a glorified potato chip!* ☐ *She's just a glorified dance-hall girl.*

glow *n.* a mild state of drug or alcohol intoxication. ☐ *She had a nice glow, but was by no means stewed.* ☐ *What was supposed to be a nice glow turned out to be a terrifying hallucination.*

glow worm *n.* a drunkard; an alcoholic. (From *glow.*) ☐ *You are turning into a regular glow worm.* ☐ *Gary came out of the bar and tripped over a napping glow worm near the entrance to the alley.*

glue factory *n.* the place where old horses are sent so their bones can be made into glue; a similar, imaginary place for people. ☐ *I'm not as young as I used to be, but I'm not ready for the glue factory yet.* ☐ *If you can't keep up, we'll send you to the glue factory.*

glued 1. *mod.* arrested. (Underworld.) ☐ *Wally got glued for having over three hundred parking tickets.* ☐ *Max goes to great extremes to keep from getting glued.* **2.** *mod.* alcohol intoxicated. ☐ *Fred is glued and can't stand up.* ☐ *About three more beers and I'll be glued.*

gluer See the following entry.

gluey AND **gluer** *n.* a person, usually a teenager, who sniffs glue. (Drugs.) ☐ *Teddy is a gluey. That's why he's failing in school.* ☐ *The gluers stand a chance of having brain damage.*

glug [gləg] *n.* a gulp or shot of liquor. ☐ *Have another glug of this moonshine.* ☐ *I took one glug and spit it out.*

glutz [gləts] *n.* a slut; a woman of low morals. ☐ *I didn't say she is a glutz!* ☐ *Tracy knows some old dames she would call glutzes.*

(g)narly ['nɑrli] *mod.* excellent; great. (California.) ☐ *This pizza is too gnarly for words!* ☐ *Who is that narly guy in the white sweater?*

go 1. *n.* a try (at something). ☐ *Let me have a go at it this time.* ☐ *I'd like to have another go at it, if I can.* **2.** *in.* to urinate. ☐ *I gotta go!* ☐ *Jimmy's gonna go in his pants!* **3.** *tr.* to say or utter something. (Mostly teens. Used in writing only for effect.) ☐ *So I go, "Gross!"* ☐ *Then she goes, "Like . . . ," and just stops talking.*

go-ahead *n.* permission to proceed; the signal to go ahead. (Compare to *say-so.*) ☐ *We're ready to go as soon as we get the go-ahead.* ☐ *I gave him the go-ahead, and the tanks started moving in.*

go all the way *in.* to copulate; to carry necking all the way to copulation. (Euphemistic. Use caution with the topic.) ☐ *Did they go all the way?* ☐ *He keeps wanting me to go all the way.*

go ape (over someone or something) *in.* to become very excited over something. ☐ *I just go ape over chocolate.* ☐ *Sam went ape over Mary.*

go bananas *in.* to go mildly crazy. (See also *bananas.*) ☐ *Sorry, I just went bananas for a minute.* ☐ *I thought he was going to go bananas.*

go belly up See *turn belly up.*

go blooey AND **go flooey** [go 'blui AND go 'flui] *in.* to fall apart; to go out of order. ☐ *Suddenly, all my plans went blooey.* ☐ *I just hope everything doesn't go flooey at the last minute.*

go-by ['gobɑɪ] *n.* an instance of ignoring or passing by (someone). (See also *give someone the go-by.*) ☐ *I got the go-by from her every time I saw her.* ☐ *I find the go-by very insulting.*

Go chase your tail! See the following entry.

Go chase yourself! AND **Go chase your tail!; Go climb a tree!; Go fly a kite!; Go fry an egg!; Go jump in the lake!;**

Go soak your head!; Go soak yourself! *exclam.* "Beat it!"; "Go away!" □ *Oh, go chase yourself! Get out of my face!* □ *Go soak your head! You're a pain in the neck.*

Go climb a tree! See the previous entry.

go down 1. *in.* to happen. □ *Hey, man! What's going down?* □ *Something strange is going down around here.* **2.** *in.* to be accepted. (See also *swallow.*) □ *We'll just have to wait awhile to see how all this goes down.* □ *The proposal didn't go down very well with the manager.* **3.** *in.* to be arrested. (Underworld.) □ *Lefty didn't want to go down for a job he didn't do.* □ *Mr. Big said that somebody had to go down for it, and he didn't care who.*

go down in flames *in.* to fail spectacularly. (See also *shoot someone down in flames, crash and burn.*) □ *The whole team went down in flames.* □ *I'd hate for all your planning to go down in flames.*

go down the chute See *go down the tube(s).*

go down the line *in.* to *snort* a *line* of cocaine. (Drugs.) □ *Gert had to leave the office to go down the line.* □ *They found her in the john, going down the line.*

go down the tube(s) AND **go down the chute** *in.* to fail totally; to be ruined. □ *The whole project is likely to go down the tubes.* □ *All my plans just went down the chute.*

go downhill *in.* to decline. □ *This company is going downhill at a great rate.* □ *Things began to go downhill when the county cut the maintenance budget.*

go Dutch *in.* [for two people] to split the cost of something, such as a meal. (See also *Dutch treat.*) □ *How about dinner tonight? We'll go Dutch, okay?* □ *Yes, let's go Dutch.*

Go figure. *interj.* "Try to figure it out."; "Just try to explain that!" □ *She hung up on me again. Go figure.* □ *They heat the water to make the tea hot, then they put ice in it to make it cold, then they put lemon in it to make it sour, and then they put sugar in it to make it sweet. Go figure.*

go flooey See *go blooey.*

Go fly a kite! See *Go chase yourself!*

go for broke *in.* to choose to risk everything; to try to succeed against great odds. □ *I feel lucky today. I'll go for broke.* □ *We decided to go for broke, and that is exactly how we ended up.*

Go for it! *exclam.* "Do it!"; "Try it!" □ *Go for it! Give it a try!* □ *It looked like something I wanted to do, so I decided to go for it.*

Go fry an egg! See *Go chase yourself!*

go-getter *n.* an energetic person. □ *Wally is a real go-getter. He'll go places.* □ *Sally was really cut out to be a go-getter.*

go-go ['gogo] **1.** *mod.* having to do with fast-dancing young women on display in a nightclub. □ *I worked as a go-go girl for a while.* □ *Those go-go places have mostly changed their style.* **2.** *mod.* vigorous; energetic; frantically moving. □ *He's a real go-go guy, always up to something.* □ *I bought some silly go-go stock, and it collapsed immediately.*

go great guns *in.* to do very well; to go very fast. □ *Everything is going great guns around here. We're busy and making lots of money.* □ *The project is finally going great guns, just as we planned.*

go haywire 1. *in.* [for a person] to go berserk. □ *I thought for a minute that Pete was going to go haywire.* □ *Sorry, I guess I just went haywire for a minute.* **2.** *in.* [for something] to go out of order; to break down. □ *My stereo's gone haywire.* □ *I'm afraid my car's gone haywire. It won't start.*

go home in a box *in.* to be shipped home dead. □ *Hey, I'm too young to go home in a box.* □ *You had better be careful on this camping trip, or you'll go home in a box.*

go home to mama *in.* to give up something—such as a marriage—and return to one's mother's home. □ *I've had it. I'm going home to mama.* □ *Mary left him and went home to mama.*

go into orbit *in.* to become very excited. ☐ *Wow, I thought the manager was going to go into orbit, she was so mad.* ☐ *The entire staff went into orbit when they got the news.*

Go jump in the lake! See *Go chase yourself!*

go mental *in.* go crazy; to act stupid. ☐ *Don't go mental, Jane. Just calm down and think about it.* ☐ *Another day in that history class and I know I will go mental.*

go off half-cocked *in.* to proceed without knowing all the facts. ☐ *I waited because I didn't want to go off half-cocked.* ☐ *The boss went off half-cocked and exploded into a rage about the mess.*

go off the deep end *in.* to do or experience something in the extreme: to fall madly in love, to go crazy, to commit suicide, to fly into a rage, etc. ☐ *John is completely in love with Mary and wants to marry her. I was afraid he would go off the deep end, and he did.* ☐ *Sally was so depressed that we had to watch her day and night so she wouldn't go off the deep end.* ☐ *I saw what he had done, and I just went off the deep end. I was in a blind rage and didn't know what I was doing.*

Go on! *exclam.* "I don't believe you!"; "I deny it!" ☐ *Go on! You don't really know what you are talking about!* ☐ *Go on! You weren't even there.*

go on (and on) about someone or something *in.* to rave about someone or something endlessly. ☐ *He just went on and on about the trouble he was having with the post office.* ☐ *Why do you have to go on about your sister so?*

go over big *in.* to be appreciated as a success. ☐ *I'm sure this will go over big with the folks at home.* ☐ *Well, it didn't go over very big with the boss.*

go over like a lead balloon *in.* [for something meant to be good] to fail to be good. (Compare to *go over big.*) ☐ *The joke went over like a lead balloon.* ☐ *I'm afraid your plan went over like a lead balloon.*

go over the hill *in.* to escape from a prison or from the military service. (See also *over the hill, go over the wall.*) ☐ *Jim went over the hill, and they caught him.* ☐ *Jed and Tom planned to go over the hill last night. What happened?*

go over the wall *in.* to escape from a prison. ☐ *Lefty tried to go over the wall, but the warden got wind of it.* ☐ *Nobody goes over the wall in this joint.*

go overboard *in.* to do far more than is necessary. ☐ *He has a tendency to go overboard at these parties.* ☐ *Now don't go overboard for us. We're just folks.*

go-pills *n.* amphetamines. (Drugs.) ☐ *She took go-pills to start the day.* ☐ *After a while, these go-pills just demand to be taken.*

go places *in.* to become very successful. ☐ *I knew that Sally would go places.* ☐ *I really want to go places in life.*

go public **1.** *in.* to sell to the public shares of a privately owned company. (Securities markets.) ☐ *The company decided not to go public because the economy was so bad at the time.* ☐ *We'll go public at a later time.* **2.** *in.* to reveal something to the public. (Especially with *with,* as in the examples.) ☐ *It's too early to go public with the story.* ☐ *Just let me know when we can go public with this.*

go Rinso [...'rınso] *in.* to fail; to collapse in price. (A play on to go *down the drain. Rinso* is a laundry soap that goes down the drain after it is used. Used in the context of the securities markets or other financial setting.) ☐ *All my drug stocks went Rinso when the president attacked the drug industry.* ☐ *I knew my bank account would go Rinso after last month's bills came in.*

Go soak your head! See *Go chase yourself!*

Go soak yourself! See *Go chase yourself!*

go sour *in.* to turn bad or unpleasant. ☐ *It looks like all my plans are going sour.* ☐ *My whole life is going sour right now.*

go South AND **head South** **1.** *in.* to make an escape; to disappear. ☐ *Lefty went*

South the minute he got out of the pen. □ *The mugger headed South just after the crime.* **2.** *in.* to fall; to go down. (Securities markets.) □ *All the stock market indexes went South today.* □ *The market headed South today at the opening bell.* **3.** *in.* to quit; to drop out of sight. □ *Fred got discouraged and went South. I think he gave up football permanently.* □ *After pulling the bank job, Max went South for a few months.*

go straight 1. *in.* to stop breaking the law. □ *Lefty thought about going straight once, but pulled himself out of it.* □ *I think I'll give all this up and go straight—some day.* **2.** *in.* to get off drugs. (Drugs.) □ *Ernie wanted to go straight more than anything else in the world.* □ *I'll go straight one of these days.*

go the limit *in.* to do as much as possible; to get as much as possible. □ *Let's plan to do everything we can. Let's go the limit.* □ *We'll go the limit. To heck with the cost.*

go through someone like a dose of (the) salts *in.* to move through someone's digestive tract like a strong laxative. □ *That stuff they served last night went through me like a dose of salts.* □ *Careful of the coffee. It'll go through you like a dose of the salts.*

go through the changes 1. *in.* to experience life's changes. □ *A good day, a bad day—it's all part of going through the changes.* □ *Nothing new with me, just going through the changes.* **2.** *in.* to go through a reconstruction of one's life. □ *I went through the changes all last year. It was a real bad time.* □ *I've been going through the changes lately. It's tough to grow up at this age.*

Go to! *exclam.* "Go to hell!" □ *Oh, you're terrible. Just go to!* □ *Go to, you creep!*

Go to blazes! AND **Go to the devil!** *exclam.* "Go to hell!" □ *Go to blazes! Stop pestering me!* □ *I'm sick of your complaining. Go to the devil!*

Go to the devil! See the previous entry.

go to town *in.* to do something with gusto; to do something with great speed and energy. □ *The main office is really going to town on collecting overdue payments.* □ *Man, our team is really going to town.*

Go to your room! See *On your bike!*

go underground *in.* to go into hiding; to begin to operate in secret. □ *The entire operation went underground, and we heard no more about it.* □ *We'll go underground if we have to. Nothing will stop the movement.*

go up *in.* to start to feel the effects of a drug. (Drugs.) □ *Gert started to go up and suddenly fell asleep.* □ *The guy couldn't wait to get home and go up.*

go West *in.* to die. □ *Ever since Uncle Ben went West, things have been peaceful around here.* □ *When I go West, I want flowers, hired mourners, and an enormous performance of Mozart's "Requiem."*

go with it See the following entry.

go with the flow AND **go with it** *in.* to cope with adversity; to accept one's lot. □ *No, just relax and go with the flow.* □ *Go with it. Don't fight it.*

go zonkers *in.* to go slightly crazy. □ *What a day! I almost went zonkers.* □ *I went a little zonkers there for a minute.*

goat *n.* a fast and powerful car; a Pontiac GTO. □ *Hey, man, where'd you get that goat?* □ *His goat conked out on him.*

gob [gab] **1.** *n.* a blob or mass of something. □ *I'd like a big gob of mashed potatoes, please.* □ *Take that horrid gob of gum out of your mouth!* **2.** *n.* a large amount of something. (Often in the plural.) □ *I've just got gobs of it if you need some.* □ *I need gobs of money to get through school.*

gobbledygook ['gab|diguk] **1.** *n.* nonsense; officialese or government gibberish. □ *I can't understand all this gobbledygook.* □ *They must have a full time staff to dream up all this gobbledygook.* **2.** *n.* any mess, espcially of food. □ *Dinner was just gobbledygook again.* □ *Do we have the same old gobbledygook tonight?*

God's acre *n.* a cemetery. □ *When I end up in God's acre, I want everything to go on without me.* □ *They're planting somebody new in God's acre.*

gofer See *gopher.*

goggle-eyed AND **googly-eyed** ['gagḷaɪd AND 'guglɪaɪd] *mod.* alcohol intoxicated and staring. □ *Wally was goggle-eyed and couldn't stand up.* □ *He's too googly-eyed to drive home.*

going high *n.* a long-lasting type of drug *high.* (Drugs.) □ *Freddie had a going high and was in trouble.* □ *Gert was always after a real going high.*

going over **1.** *n.* an examination. □ *After a thorough going over, the doctor pronounced me alive.* □ *I gave your car a good going over, and I fixed a lot of little things.* **2.** *n.* a beating. □ *Bruno gave the guy a terrible going over.* □ *After a going over like that, the guy spent two weeks in the hospital.*

goings-on *n.* happenings; events. □ *There are sure some strange goings-on around here.* □ *Some big goings-on downtown tied up the traffic.*

gold *n.* money. (See also *ducats.*) □ *Do you have enough gold to pay the bill?* □ *There's no gold in my pockets.*

gold digger *n.* a woman who pays attention to a man solely because of his wealth. □ *Sam called Sally a gold digger, and she was devastated.* □ *"You little gold digger!" cried Sam.*

goldbrick **1.** *n.* a lazy person. □ *Pete is just a lazy goldbrick.* □ *Tell that goldbrick to get back to work.* **2.** *in.* to be lazy; to shirk one's duty. □ *Stop goldbricking and get back to work.* □ *Whoever is goldbricking when I come back gets a real talking to.*

goldbricker *n.* a loafer. (Also a term of address.) □ *Larry is such a goldbricker!* □ *Get moving, you goldbrickers.*

golden-ager *n.* an old person; a senior citizen. □ *The golden-agers sat on the benches and chatted.* □ *When I'm a golden-ager, I'm going to have a part-time job.*

golden handcuffs *n.* monetary inducements to stay on the job. (Usually for highly paid executives in large corporations. See also *golden parachute.*) □ *The company provided a variety of golden handcuffs to keep its execs happy through a takeover.* □ *The golden handcuffs included a half million in severance pay for one of the vice presidents.*

golden opportunity *n.* a very good opportunity. □ *This is my golden opportunity, and I can't pass it up.* □ *You get a golden opportunity like this very rarely.*

golden parachute *n.* a special kind of severance pay for persons who may be forced to leave a job. (Usually for highly paid executives in large corporations. If the company is taken over and the executives are fired, they are very well provided for. See also *golden handcuffs.*) □ *My golden parachute was so attractive that I wanted to get fired.* □ *If all the golden parachutes were used at the same time, it would bankrupt the company.*

goldie locks *n.* a policewoman. (Citizens band radio.) □ *Goldie locks pulled me over and gave me a citation.* □ *There was a goldie locks waiting under the bridge to spring on poor unsuspecting people like me.*

gomer ['gomɚ] **1.** *n.* a stupid oaf; a social reject. (From the television character Gomer Pyle.) □ *Who's that gomer in the overalls?* □ *That gomer is my Uncle Ben.* **2.** AND **goomer** ['gumɚ] *n.* a person unwelcome in a hospital. (Supposedly an acronym for "Get out of my emergency room.") □ *That goomer with the allergy is back in E.R.* □ *I don't want that goomer back in the emergency room.*

gone **1.** AND **gone under** *mod.* unconscious. □ *He's gone. Prop his feet up and call an ambulance.* □ *He's gone under. You can begin the procedure now.* **2.** AND **gone under** *mod.* alcohol or drug intoxicated. □ *Those chicks are gone—too much to drink.* □ *Ted is really gone under.* **3.** *mod.* cool; out of this world. □ *This ice cream is gone, man, gone!* □ *She is one real gone chick.*

gone goose *n.* someone or something finished or done for. (A play on *dead duck.*) □ *I'm afraid that your old car is a gone goose.* □ *This old thing is a gone goose.*

gone under See *gone.*

goner ['gɔnɚ] *n.* someone or something finished or nearly finished. □ *This one's a goner. Toss it.* □ *The horse was a goner, so it had to be destroyed.*

gonged [gɔŋd] *mod.* drug intoxicated. (Drugs. Originally on opium.) □ *Bruno found himself in the alley, gonged.* □ *Ernie was too gonged to stand up.*

gonna ['gɔnə OR 'gʊnə] *phr.* "going to." (Eye-dialect. Used in writing only for effect. Used in the examples of this dictionary.) □ *What time you gonna be home?* □ *I'm gonna get you, you little dickens!*

gonzo ['gɑnzo] **1.** *n.* a silly or foolish person. □ *Some gonzo is on the phone asking for the president of the universe.* □ *Tell the gonzo I'm out.* **2.** *mod.* crazy. □ *The guy is totally gonzo!* □ *Who drew this gonzo picture of me?*

goo [gu] *n.* some sticky substance; *gunk.* □ *What is this goo on my shoe?* □ *There is some sort of goo on my plate. Is that meant to be my dinner?*

goo-goo eyes ['gugu 'ɑɪz] *n.* flirtatious eyes. (Often with *make.*) □ *Mary was making goo-goo eyes at Sam.* □ *Who's the chick over there with the goo-goo eyes?*

goob [gub] **1.** *n.* a pimple. (Short for *guber.*) □ *The goobs are taking over my whole face.* □ *I have the world's greatest goob right on the end of my nose.* **2.** *n.* a nerd; a simpleton. (See also *guber.*) □ *Don't be a goob. Come to the party with me.* □ *Gary is such a goob. Why can't he do anything right?*

goober See *guber.*

goober-grabber ['gubɚgræbɚ] *n.* someone who picks peanuts. (Typically someone native to Georgia where peanuts are grown. From *guber.*) □ *My nephew moved from Chicago to Atlanta, where he became a goober-grabber in no time at all.* □ *One of the local goober-grabbers took us to a peanut boil.*

goober-grease ['gubɚgris] *n.* peanut butter. □ *Pass me some of that goober-grease, will ya?* □ *This goober-grease is stale.*

goobrain ['gubren] *n.* a fool; a stupid person. (Also a rude term of address.) □ *What silly goobrain put sugar in the salt shaker?* □ *Look, goobrain, think about a while. You'll catch on.*

good and something *mod.* thoroughly something. (Where *something* is an adjective.) □ *I am really good and mad at you for that.* □ *We are good and ready to do something about it.*

good buddy *n.* a friend; a partner. (Citizens band radio. Also a term of address.) □ *Well, good buddy, what's new with you?* □ *John's my good buddy.*

Good call! *exclam.* "That was a good decision!" □ *Good call, Walter! You picked the right company to deal with.* □ *I guess this was Jane's choice. Good call, Jane.*

Good deal! *n.* "That is good!" (Old, but still heard.) □ *Everyone is here on time! Good deal!* □ *Good deal! My tax refund just arrived!*

good-for-nothing 1. *mod.* worthless. (Usually having to do with a person.) □ *Let's get rid of this good-for-nothing car right now.* □ *Tell your good-for-nothing brother to find another place to live.* **2.** *n.* a worthless person. (Also a rude term of address.) □ *Tell the good-for-nothing to leave.* □ *Look, you good-for-nothing. Go out and get a job.*

Good golly, Miss Molly! *exclam.* "Good grief!"; "Wow!" □ *Good golly, Miss Molly! This place is a mess!* □ *Good golly, Miss Molly, that's awful!*

Good heavens! *exclam.* "My goodness!" (A mild exclamation of amazement, shock, etc.) □ *Good heavens! I didn't expect you to be here.* □ *Good heavens! There's a man at the window!*

good Joe *n.* a good fellow. ☐ *Fred's a little slow on the uptake, but he's a good Joe.* ☐ *Frank's a good Joe. He'll help us.*

(good) looker *n.* a good-looking person. ☐ *Fred is not exactly a good looker, but he is pleasant enough.* ☐ *Mary is really a looker. I sure would like to go out with her.*

good old boy AND **good ole boy** *n.* a good guy; a dependable companion. (Folksy.) ☐ *Old Tom is a good old boy. He'll help.* ☐ *One of these good ole boys will give you a hand.*

good ole boy See the previous entry.

good-time Charley *n.* a man who is always trying to have a good experience; an optimist. ☐ *Wally is such a good-time Charley. Who would believe the trouble he's had?* ☐ *Some good-time Charley is making a lot of noise.*

good-time it *tr.* to *party;* to spend money and have a good time. ☐ *You're always good-timing it. Don't you ever study?* ☐ *I just want to good-time it for the rest of my life.*

good-time man *n.* a man who sells drugs. (Drugs.) ☐ *Max is the main good-time man in this neighborhood.* ☐ *The fuzz wants to see all the good-time men behind bars.*

good trip **1.** *n.* a good session with *L.S.D.* or some other drug. (Drugs.) ☐ *Paul said he had a good trip, but he looks like the devil.* ☐ *One good trip deserves another. At least that's what my guru says.* **2.** *n.* any good time. ☐ *This meeting was a good trip.* ☐ *Compared to the last class, this one is a good trip.*

goody two-shoes *n.* someone who tries to behave better than anyone else. (Also a term of address.) ☐ *Well, goody two-shoes, so you decided to come sit with us.* ☐ *I'm no goody two-shoes. I just like to keep my nose clean.*

gooey AND **GUI** *n.* a "graphical user interface." (A type of computer control system that uses an orderly layout on the screen with icons and menus that are controlled by a computer mouse. *Gooey* is slang; *GUI* is a technical acronym. See also *WIMP.*) ☐ *Some of the older programs that lack a gooey require a lot less memory to run.* ☐ *Many new computer users find it much easier to use a gooey than to type in commands.*

goof [guf] **1.** *n.* a foolish oaf; a *goofy* person. ☐ *Sometimes I'm such a goof. I really messed up.* ☐ *Don't be a goof. Get with it.* **2.** *in.* to use heroin or some other addictive drugs without intending to become addicted; to play around (with heroin). (Drugs.) ☐ *Gert spent the first few years just goofing.* ☐ *She was goofing, and you know what that leads to.* **3.** *in.* to scratch, nod, and slobber after an injection of heroin. (Drugs.) ☐ *She just rocks and goofs for hours.* ☐ *She has been goofing for an hour.* **4.** AND **goof up** *in.* to make a blunder. ☐ *Whoops, I goofed!* ☐ *This time, you goofed.* **5.** *n.* a blunder; an error. ☐ *Who made this silly goof?* ☐ *This goof is yours, not mine.*

goof around See the following entry.

goof off **1.** AND **goof around** *in.* to waste time. ☐ *Quit goofing off.* ☐ *Get busy. Stop goofing around.* **2.** *n.* a time-waster; a *jerk.* (Usually **goof-off.**) ☐ *Pete is such a goof-off!* ☐ *I'm no goof-off, but I am no scholar either.*

goof on someone *in.* to play a prank on someone; to involve someone in a deception. ☐ *Hey, don't goof on me. I'm your buddy!* ☐ *The kid goofed on Chuck, and he thought it was a pretty good joke.*

goof-proof **1.** *mod.* foolproof; not subject to misuse. ☐ *I want a goof-proof scheme.* ☐ *This scheme is not goof-proof, but it's pretty sound.* ☐ *Now, this time I've made it goof-proof.* **2.** *tr.* to make something foolproof; to take action to see that something cannot be misused. ☐ *I'll try to goof-proof my scheme.* ☐ *See if this can be goof-proofed by Monday evening.*

goof something up AND **goof up on something** *tr.* to mess something up. ☐ *Now don't goof it up this time.* 🅃 *I hope I don't goof up the report again.* 🅃 *I hope I don't goof up on the report again.*

goof up See *goof.*

goof up on something See *goof something up.*

goofball AND **goofer** *n.* a stupid person; a fool. ☐ *You are such a silly goofball.* ☐ *Chuck acts like a goofer, but he's really with it.*

goofed (up) **1.** *mod.* messed up; out of order. ☐ *All my papers are goofed up.* ☐ *Everything on my desk is goofed. Who's been here?* **2.** *mod.* confused; distraught. ☐ *I'm sort of goofed up today. I think I'm coming down with something.* ☐ *I was up too late last night, and now I'm all goofed up.*

goofer See *goofball.*

goofus ['gufəs] **1.** *n.* a gadget. ☐ *Where is that little goofus I use to pry open these cans?* ☐ *Here's just the little goofus you're looking for.* **2.** AND **goopus** *n.* a foolish oaf. (Also a term of address.) ☐ *You're just acting like a goofus. Be serious!* ☐ *Hey, goopus! Come here!*

goofy ['gufi] **1.** *mod.* silly. ☐ *Stop acting so goofy! What will the neighbors say?* ☐ *You are really a goofy chick.* **2.** *mod.* alcohol intoxicated. ☐ *Wow, is she goofy!* ☐ *They went out and got themselves good and goofy.*

googaw See *geegaw.*

googly-eyed See *goggle-eyed.*

gook [guk OR gʊk] **1.** *n.* a slimy substance; a sediment or residue. ☐ *There was a lot of gook in my crankcase.* ☐ *Too much of that gook will ruin your engine.* **2.** *n.* a foolish oaf. ☐ *Wow, Chuck is turning into a real gook!* ☐ *Don't be such a gook, you twit!* **3.** *n.* a tramp. ☐ *Some old gook was asking for a handout.* ☐ *Give the gook some food and wish him well.* **4.** *n.* a prostitute. ☐ *Some old gook was standing around with too much leg on view.* ☐ *There are a lot of gooks around here in the center of town.* **5.** *n.* a derogatory nickname for various East Asians. (Crude.) ☐ *Nobody wanted to go to war against the gooks.* ☐ *Let the gooks fight it out amongst themselves.*

goombah ['gumbɑ] *n.* a buddy; a trusted friend. (Also a term of address. Ultimately from Italian.) ☐ *Hey, goombah! How goes it?* ☐ *He's my goombah. I can trust him.*

goomer See *gomer.*

goon [gun] **1.** *n.* a stupid person; a fool. ☐ *Oh, Wally, you're such a goon sometimes.* ☐ *Todd is a silly goon, but he's a lot of fun at parties.* **2.** *n.* a hooligan; a thug or bodyguard. (Underworld.) ☐ *Bruno is one of Mr. Big's goons.* ☐ *Call off your goons!*

goon-platoon *n.* a platoon of misfits; a platoon that is noted for its errors. (Military.) ☐ *Well, the goon-platoon's done it again!* ☐ *Which side is the goon-platoon on?*

goon squad **1.** *n.* an organized group of thugs; a gang of toughs. (Underworld.) ☐ *Bruno and his goon squad are lurking about.* ☐ *The goon squad Mr. Big sent around scared the devil out of Max.* **2.** *n.* the police. ☐ *Here comes the goon squad. Watch out!* ☐ *My old buddy on the goon squad tells me there'll be some action over on Maple Street tonight.*

gooned [gund] *mod.* drunk. ☐ *Wayne came home gooned, and his dad went loco and grounded him.* ☐ *His date was gooned by ten, and he had to take her home.*

gooner ['gunɚ] *n.* a term for an Asian. (Derogatory. Military.) ☐ *These gooners sure can cook.* ☐ *See if one of the gooners will show you how to do it.*

goop AND **goup** [gup] *n.* slop; *gunk;* bad food. ☐ *I refuse to eat this goop.* ☐ *You get used to this goup after a while.*

goophead ['guphɛd] *n.* an inflamed pimple. (Patterned on *blackhead.*) ☐ *Ye gods! I'm covered with goopheads.* ☐ *You ought to see the goophead on your nose.*

goopus See *goofus.*

goopy ['gupi] *mod.* gummy; syrupy. ☐ *I just love goopy desserts.* ☐ *This is not goopy enough.* ☐ *There is some goopy stuff coming out of the car's engine.*

goose **1.** *n.* a silly oaf; an oaf. □ *Oh, I'm such a silly goose!* □ *What a goose you are!* **2.** *tr.* to (attempt to) poke something, such as a finger, in someone's anus. □ *Freddy tried to goose me!* □ *Don't goose me!* **3.** *n.* an attempt to goose someone. (As in sense 2.) □ *Harry is a master of the rude goose.* □ *He tried to give me a goose.* **4.** *tr.* to rev up an engine; to press down hard on the accelerator of a car. □ *Why don't you goose the thing and see how fast it'll go?* □ *Don't goose it too much.* **5.** *n.* an act of suddenly pressing down the accelerator of a car. □ *Give it a good goose and see what happens.* □ *One more goose, but don't hold it down so long.*

goose egg **1.** *n.* a score of zero. □ *We got a goose egg in the second inning.* □ *It was double goose eggs for the final score.* **2.** *n.* a bump on the head. □ *You've got quite a goose egg there.* □ *I walked into a door and got a big goose egg on my forehead.* **3.** *n.* a failure; a zero. (Similar to sense 1.) □ *The outcome was a real goose egg. A total mess.* □ *The result of three weeks' planning is one big goose egg.*

goozlum ['guzləm] *n.* any gummy, sticky substance: syrup, gravy, soup, etc. □ *Do you want some of this wonderful goozlum on your ice cream?* □ *Just keep putting that goozlum on my spuds.*

gopher AND **gofer** ['gofɚ] **1.** *n.* someone who goes for things and brings them back. (From *go for.*) □ *You got a gopher who can go get some coffee?* □ *Send the gofer out for cigarettes.* **2.** *n.* a dupe; a pawn; an underling. □ *The guy's just a gopher. He has no say in anything.* □ *I'll send a gopher over to pick up the papers.*

gopher ball *n.* a baseball pitch that is hit as a home run. (When it is hit, the batter will "go for" home.) □ *Wilbur hit another long gopher ball straight across center field.* □ *The center fielder did a dive over the fence trying to get the gopher ball.*

gorilla biscuits AND **gorilla pills** *n.* amphetamines. (Drugs.) □ *Tracy is big on those gorilla pills.* □ *Stay away from gorilla biscuits.*

gorilla juice *n.* steroids. (Bodybuilding. Steroids build muscle tissue rapidly.) □ *Andy really wanted to get hold of some gorilla juice, but his parents said no.* □ *Do all those muscle-bound creatures take gorilla juice?*

gorilla pills See *gorilla biscuits.*

gork [gork] **1.** *n.* a fool; a dupe. □ *Martin acts like such a gork sometimes.* □ *The gorks are taking over the world!* **2.** AND **GORK** *phr.* an alleged hospital chart notation of the diagnosis "God only really knows." (Hospitals.) □ *I see old Mr. Kelly is in again with a hundred complaints. His chart says GORK.* □ *He's down with gork again.* **3.** *tr.* to give a patient sedation. (Hospitals.) □ *Dr. Wilson says to gork the patient in 226.* □ *He'll quiet down after we gork him.*

gorked (out) [gorkt . . .] *mod.* heavily sedated; knocked out. (Hospitals.) □ *Once the patient was gorked, he was more cooperative.* □ *The guy in 226 is totally gorked out now.*

gospel (truth) *n.* the honest truth. □ *You gotta believe me. It's the gospel truth!* □ *He speaks nothing but gospel. You can trust him.*

gotcha ['gɑtʃə] **1.** *phr.* "I got you!"; "I've caught you!" (Usually **Gotcha!**) □ *I gotcha, and you can't get away.* □ *Ha, ha! Gotcha! Come here, you little dickens.* **2.** *n.* an arrest. (Underworld.) □ *The cop reached out, grasped Bruno's shoulder, and made the gotcha.* □ *It was a fair gotcha. Bruno was nabbed, and he went along quietly.* **3.** *phr.* "I understand you." □ *Gotcha! Thanks for telling me.* □ *Seven pounds, four ounces? Gotcha! I'll tell everybody.*

gouch off [gɑutʃ . . .] *in.* to pass out under the influence of drugs. (Drugs.) □ *After taking the stuff, Gary gouched off.* □ *After the fix, Gert waited patiently to gouch off.*

goup See *goop.*

gourd [gord] *n.* the head. □ *I raised up and got a nasty blow on the gourd.* □ *My gourd aches something awful.*

goy [gɔɪ] **1.** *n.* a gentile. (From Hebrew. Not necessarily derogatory.) □ *But the goys can do anything they want on Sunday!* □ *Leave that kind of thing to the goys.* **2.** *mod.* gentile; non-Jewish. □ *I don't care for that goy stuff.* □ *Goy pickles are sort of blah.*

grabbers *n.* the hands. □ *Keep your grabbers to yourself.* □ *Wash your grubby little grabbers before coming to the table.*

grade-grubber 1. *n.* an earnest, hard-working student. (In the way a pig roots or grubs around for food.) □ *Martin is a grade-grubber and a real hard worker.* □ *If there are too many grade-grubbers in a class, it will really throw off the grading scale.* **2.** *n.* a student who flatters the teacher in hopes of a higher grade. □ *Toward the end of a semester, my office is filled with grade-grubbers.* □ *A few grade-grubbers help assure old professors that the world is not really changing at all.*

grade-grubbing 1. *n.* working hard at one's studies in hopes of a high grade. □ *If all you're here for is grade-grubbing, you're going to miss a lot.* □ *Get a hobby. All grade-grubbing in college is no good.* **2.** *n.* flattering a teacher in hopes of a higher grade. □ *Some teachers don't mind a lot of grade-grubbing.* □ *So you've come in to do some grade-grubbing.* **3.** *mod.* having to do with students who are only concerned with getting high grades. □ *Grade-grubbing college kids are driving me crazy.* □ *Two grade-grubbing seniors came in and begged me to change their grades.*

graduate ['grædʒuət] **1.** *n.* a person experienced in life, especially sexually experienced. □ *Tracy is a graduate. Nothing is new to her.* □ *You need someone who is a graduate for this kind of a job.* **2.** ['grædʒuet] *in.* to move from casual drug use to addiction. (Drugs.) □ *Gert graduated to smack after only a year of skin-popping.* □ *Pete graduated and went into treatment all in the same month.*

grand AND **G** *n.* one thousand dollars. □ *That car probably cost about twenty grand.* □ *Four Gs for that thing?*

Grand Central Station *n.* any busy and hectic place. (From Grand Central Station in New York City—a very busy place.) □ *This place is Grand Central Station on a Friday night.* □ *At just about closing time, this place becomes Grand Central Station.*

granddad *n.* old-fashioned; out-of-date. □ *Tom is just a silly granddad. He is dull and old-fashioned.* □ *Don't be such a granddad. Live a little.*

(grand)daddy (of them all) *n.* the biggest or oldest of all; the patriarch. □ *This old fish is the granddaddy of them all.* □ *This one is the daddy. Been here since the place was built.*

grandstand *in.* to make oneself conspicuous. □ *Stop grandstanding, Sally. Everyone can see you.* □ *Don't you just hate the way that Pat grandstands all the time?*

grandstand play *n.* something done exceedingly well to impress an audience or a group of spectators. □ *The grandstand play caught the attention of the crowd just as they were leaving.* □ *He tried one final grandstand play, but the auience continued to give him the raspberry.*

grape shot *mod.* alcohol intoxicated; drunk on wine. □ *After the reception, Hank found himself a little grape shot.* □ *Man, is that guy ever grape shot! How can he hold enough to get that way?*

grape(s) *n.* champagne; wine. (Compare to *berries*.) □ *These grapes are great!* □ *No more of the grapes for me. It tickles my nose.*

grapes of wrath *n.* wine. □ *Fred had taken a little too much of the grapes of wrath.* □ *How about another dose of the grapes of wrath?*

grapevine *n.* a mouth-to-mouth communications network. □ *I heard on the grapevine that Sam is moving to the east.* □ *The grapevine was right. He's already left.*

grass 1. *n.* marijuana. (Drugs and now widely known.) □ *These kids manage to find this grass somewhere.* □ *Almost *everybody knows that grass means marijuana.* **2.** *n.* lettuce; salad greens. (See also *rabbit food.*) ☐ *I could use a little more grass in my diet.* ☐ *Do you want some dressing on your grass?*

grass party *n.* a marijuana-smoking party. (Drugs.) ☐ *The goon squad raided Pete's grass party without any warning.* ☐ *Sally tried to have a grass party, but didn't have any grass.*

grasser See the following entry.

grasshead AND **grasser; grasshopper** *n.* a marijuana smoker. (Drugs.) ☐ *The grassheads are taking over this neighborhood.* ☐ *Imagine, a seven-year-old grasser!*

grasshopper See the previous entry.

grassroots 1. *n.* the common people, especially rural people. ☐ *We really haven't heard anything from the grassroots yet.* ☐ *The grassroots isn't organized on most issues.* **2.** *mod.* having to do with or originating with the common people. ☐ *A grassroots movement pushed Senator Del Monte toward the nomination.* ☐ *Politicians love to create grassroots movements.*

grave-dancer *n.* someone who profits over someone else's misfortune. (From *dance on someone's grave.*) ☐ *I don't want to seem like a grave-dancer, but his defeat places me in line for a promotion.* ☐ *The guy's a grave-dancer. Anything to get ahead.*

gravel-pounder *n.* an infantry soldier. (Military.) ☐ *Do you really want to join the Army and be a gravel-pounder?* ☐ *The life of a gravel-pounder is not for me.*

graveyard shift *n.* the night shift of work in a factory, usually starting at about midnight. (Compare to *swing shift.*) ☐ *I'd prefer not to work the graveyard shift.* ☐ *The pay is pretty good on the graveyard shift.*

gravy *n.* extra or easy money; easy profit. ☐ *Virtually every cent that came in was pure gravy—no expenses and no materials costs at all.* ☐ *After I pay expenses, the rest is pure gravy.*

gravy train *n.* a job that brings in a steady supply of easy money or *gravy.* ☐ *This kind of job is a real gravy train.* ☐ *The gravy train is just not for me.*

Graybar Hotel AND **Graystone College** *n.* a jail; a prison. ☐ *The two cops had to spend two years in Graybar Hotel with some of the inmates they had caught over the past few years.* ☐ *Max has graduated from Graystone College three times in the last ten years.*

grayhound *in.* [for a black] to date Caucasians. ☐ *Somebody said you were grayhounding. Is that so?* ☐ *I am not grayhounding.*

Graystone College See *Graybar Hotel.*

GR&D *interj.* "Grinning, running, and ducking." (Describes what one might be doing after having written a mischievous message on an electronic bulletin board. Used in electronic mail and computer bulletin board messages. Sometimes enclosed, <GR&D>. Not pronounced aloud.) ☐ *I'm GR&D, but I'm glad I said it.* ☐ *I guess that you got just the kind of answer that you deserve.* <GR&D>

grease *n.* protection money; bribery money. (See also *grease someone's palm.*) ☐ *Rocko was in charge of making sure that enough grease was spread around city hall.* ☐ *See that the commissioner of the park district gets a little grease to help us get the contract.*

grease monkey *n.* a mechanic. ☐ *I took my car to my favorite grease monkey who says I need a new something or other.* ☐ *How much money does a grease monkey make?*

grease someone's palm *tr.* to pay someone a bribe. ☐ *I had to grease the clerk's palm in order to get the job done.* ☐ *Are you trying to grease my palm?*

grease the skids *tr.* to help prepare for the success or failure of someone or something. (Compare to *put the skids under someone or something.*) ☐ *Ray set out to grease the skids for the right things to happen.* ☐ *We need someone to grease the skids for the Wilson contract.*

greased [grizd OR grist] *mod.* alcohol intoxicated. ☐ *He went out and got himself greased, even though he knew it would probably kill him.* ☐ *She is way too greased to drive.*

greased lightning 1. *n.* strong liquor. ☐ *This greased lightning of yours nearly blew my head off.* ☐ *No more greased lightning for me.* 2. *n.* something fast or powerful. ☐ *That little car is just greased lightning.* ☐ *That kid can run like greased lightning.*

greaser ['grizɚ OR 'grisɚ] *n.* a rough and aggressive male, usually with long greased down hair. ☐ *Who's the greaser who just swaggered in?* ☐ *Donna has been going out with a real greaser.*

greasy spoon *n.* an untidy and unappetizing diner or restaurant. ☐ *Let's eat at the greasy spoon over on Maple. The food is gross, but the people-watching is good.* ☐ *I wouldn't be caught dead in a greasy spoon like that.*

great divide *n.* a divorce. ☐ *How did Sam survive the great divide?* ☐ *The great divide cost over two grand.*

Great Scott! ['gret 'skɑt] *exclam.* "Good grief!" ☐ *Great Scott! What happened?* ☐ *I'm late again! Great Scott!*

great unwashed *n.* most of the common people; the hoi polloi. (Always with *the*.) ☐ *The great unwashed could probably tell us a lot about life in the big city.* ☐ *I usually find myself more in agreement with the great unwashed than with the elite.*

greefo AND **griefo** ['grifo] *n.* marijuana or a marijuana cigarette. (Drugs. Old. Mexican Spanish for *weed.* See also *reefer.*) ☐ *Max had a soggy greefo in his mouth.* ☐ *He tossed Fred a griefo and held out his hand for some bread.*

Greek to someone *n.* something incomprehensible to someone; something as mysterious as Greek writing. ☐ *I don't understand this. It's all Greek to me.* ☐ *She said it was Greek to her, and that it made no sense at all.*

green AND **green folding; green paper; green stuff** *n.* money; paper money. (See also *long green.*) ☐ *How much green you got on you?* ☐ *I have so much green stuff, I don't know what to do with it.*

green around the gills See *blue around the gills.*

green folding See *green.*

green light *n.* the signal to go ahead with something; the *okay.* (Compare to *go-ahead, high sign.*) ☐ *She gave the green light to the project.* ☐ *When we get the green light, we'll start.*

green paper See *green.*

green stuff See *green.*

green thumb *n.* a wonderful ability to garden and grow houseplants. ☐ *Heidi has a green thumb and can work wonders with plants.* ☐ *If I had a green thumb, I could grow my own bananas.*

greenback ['grinbæk] *n.* a dollar bill. ☐ *She came out of the bank and dropped this pack of greenbacks right there on the street.* ☐ *It's only ten greenbacks. Anybody can afford that.*

greenie ['grini] *n.* a Heineken (brand) beer. (It comes in a green bottle.) ☐ *Tom ordered a greenie and had it put on his tab.* ☐ *Can I have a couple of greenies over here, please?*

greenmail *n.* a money-making scheme wherein a very wealthy person buys a large number of shares of a company, threatens to take control of the company, and then offers to sell the stock to the company at an exorbitant price in lieu of a takeover. (Securities markets.) ☐ *Mr. Smith made about twenty million in greenmail last year.* ☐ *One state is trying to outlaw greenmail to protect its industrial base.*

greenwash *tr.* to *launder* money; to obliterate the illegal sources of money by moving it through a variety of financial institutions. (Underworld.) ☐ *It was shown in court that the mayor had been involved in greenwashing some of the bribe money.* ☐ *The treasurer hired someone to greenwash the cash.*

greldge [grɛldʒ] 1. *n.* something nasty or *yucky.* ☐ *What is this greldge on my* *shoe?* □ *That's not greldge, that's just plain mud.* **2.** *exclam.* "Nuts!"; "Darn!" (Usually **Greldge!**) □ *Oh, greldge! I'm late!* □ *This is the last straw! Greldge!*

griefo See *greefo.*

gripe one's soul *tr.* to annoy someone. □ *That kind of thing really gripes my soul!* □ *John, have I ever told you that you gripe my soul?*

grit *n.* courage; nerve. □ *It takes a lot of grit to do something like that.* □ *Well, Pete has lots of grit. He can do it.*

gritch [grɪtʃ] **1.** *in.* to complain. (A blend of *gripe* and *bitch.*) □ *Stop gritching all the time.* □ *Are you still gritching about that?* **2.** *n.* a complainer; a griper. □ *You are getting to be such a gritch.* □ *Don't be such a gritch!*

gritchy ['grɪtʃi] *mod.* complaining; irritable. □ *I don't feel as gritchy today as I did yesterday.* □ *You seem quite gritchy to me.*

groan box *n.* an accordion. (See also *(squeeze-)box.*) □ *Clare is pretty good at the groan box.* □ *I used to play the groan box when I was a kid.*

groaty See *grody.*

grod AND **groddess** [grɑd AND 'grɑdəs] *n.* an especially sloppy man or woman. (Patterned on *god* and *goddess.*) □ *Hello, grods and groddesses, what's new?* □ *She is the groddess of scraggly ends.*

groddess See the previous entry.

grody AND **groaty** ['grodi] *mod.* disgusting. (From *grotesque.* See also *grotty.*) □ *What a grody view of the street from this window.* □ *These shoes are getting sort of groaty. I guess I'll throw them out.*

grody to the max ['grodi tu ðə 'mæks] *mod.* totally disgusting. (California. From *grotesque.* See also *groaty, grody.*) □ *Oo, this is grody to the max!* □ *This pizza is, like, grody to the max!*

grog [grɑg] *n.* liquor. □ *Here, have some more of this grog.* □ *That's enough grog for me.*

groggery ['grɑgəri] *n.* a tavern; a place to buy liquor. □ *Sam stopped at the groggery for a snort.* □ *All the groggeries are closed on Sundays.*

groggified See the following entry.

groggy 1. *mod.* tired; in a stupor. □ *He was too groggy to care what happened to him.* □ *Who's that groggy guy?* □ *I'm still groggy by ten in the morning.* **2.** AND **groggified** ['grɔgifɑɪd] *mod.* alcohol intoxicated. □ *John was a little groggy—from the grog, of course.* □ *He was too groggified to drive.*

groghound *n.* a drunkard. □ *I'm afraid that Ernie is getting to be a groghound.* □ *I'm an old groghound from way back.*

grok [grɔk] *tr.* to appreciate someone or something; to relate to someone or something. □ *I can really grok what you're saying.* □ *I don't quite grok that. Run it by again, would you?*

gronk [grɔŋk] *n.* a nasty substance, such as dirt that collects between the toes. □ *I don't want to hear any more at all about your gronk.* □ *What is this gronk here?*

gronk (out) *in.* to *conk out;* to crash, as with a car or a computer. □ *My car gronked out on the way to work this morning.* □ *The program gronks every time I start to run it.*

groove *n.* something pleasant or *cool.* (See also *in the groove.*) □ *This day has been a real groove.* □ *Man, what a groove!*

groove on someone or something *in.* to show interest in someone or something; to relate to someone or something. □ *Fred was beginning to groove on new age music when he met Phil.* □ *Sam is really grooving on Mary.*

grooved [gruvd] *mod.* pleased. □ *I am so grooved. I'll just kick back and meditate.* □ *You sure look grooved. What's been happening in your life?*

grooving *mod.* enjoying; being *cool* and laid back. □ *Look at those guys grooving in front of the television set.* □ *They were just sitting there grooving.*

groovy 1. *mod. cool;* pleasant. □ *Man, this music is groovy.* □ *What a groovy day!* **2.** *mod.* drug intoxicated. (Drugs.)

☐ *Three beers and he was a little groovy.* ☐ *She's groovy, but she can still stand up.* **3.** *mod.* out-of-date; passé. (California.) ☐ *Your clothes are so groovy. It barfs me out.* ☐ *Oh, how groovy!*

gross [gros] *mod.* crude; vulgar; disgusting. (Slang only when overused.) ☐ *This food is gross!* ☐ *What a gross thing to even suggest.*

gross-out 1. *n.* something disgusting. ☐ *This whole day has been a total gross-out.* ☐ *That horror movie was a real gross-out.* **2.** *mod.* disgusting; *gross.* ☐ *What a gross-out day this has been!* ☐ *Well, it looks like another gross-out movie.*

gross someone out *tr.* to disgust someone. ☐ *Those horrible pictures just gross me out.* 🅃 *Jim's story totally grossed out Sally.*

grotty ['gradi] *mod.* highly undesirable. (Originally British. From *grotesque*. See also *grody*.) ☐ *Let's not see another grotty movie tonight.* ☐ *What is this grotty stuff they serve here?* ☐ *It's not grotty!*

ground-pounder *n.* an infantry soldier. (Military.) ☐ *If you join the Army, it means a lot of your life spent as a ground-pounder.* ☐ *You won't find me among the ground-pounders. I have flat feet.*

grounded *mod.* confined to one's home. (The standard punishment for a teenager. See also *campused*.) ☐ *Tracy is grounded for a week because she came in late.* ☐ *You are grounded, and I don't want to hear another word about it!*

group-grope *n.* a group of people engaged in sexual activities. ☐ *That party turned into a hopeless group-grope.* ☐ *The group-grope was busted up by you-know-who.*

groupie *n.* a young woman who follows a band seeking romance with the band members. ☐ *Would you believe that Sally was a groupie when she was 19?* ☐ *You mean all those young girls are groupies?*

grouse [graus] **1.** *in.* to complain. ☐ *Paul is always grousing about something.* ☐ *Stop grousing and look on the good side of things.* **2.** *n.* a woman; women considered sexually. ☐ *Who's the grouse I saw you with last night?* ☐ *Look at that grouse over there.* **3.** *in.* to *neck*; to pet and kiss. ☐ *They stopped grousing in order to come up for air.* ☐ *They were grousing in the back seat the whole trip.*

grovel ['gravl̩] *in.* to fondle or pet. ☐ *They spent the whole time in the back seat groveling.* ☐ *He always wants to go out and grovel.*

growler *n.* a toilet. ☐ *Where's the growler around here?* ☐ *We only have one growler in this house.*

grub [grəb] **1.** *n.* food. ☐ *Hey, this grub's pretty good.* ☐ *What time's grub?* **2.** *in.* to eat (a meal). ☐ *When do we grub?* ☐ *Let's grub and get going.* **3.** *n.* an earnest student. (Collegiate. See also *grade-grubber*.) ☐ *Martin is not exactly a grub. He gets good grades without trying.* ☐ *The test was so hard, even the grubs did poorly.* **4.** *n.* a sloppy person. (From *grub worm*.) ☐ *Don is such a grub all the time.* ☐ *Sorry I look like a grub. I've been doing some plumbing.* **5.** See *grubbies*.

grubbers See the following entry.

grubbies AND **grubbers; grubs** ['grəbiz AND 'grəbəz, grəbz] *n.* worn-out clothing; clothing one wears for the occasional dirty job. ☐ *I have to go home, put some grubbies on, and paint the house.* ☐ *There I was, running around in my grubs when the Senator stops by to say hello!*

grubby ['grəbi] *mod.* unclean; untidy; unshaven. ☐ *Pete looks sort of grubby today. What's wrong?* ☐ *Who's that grubby guy?* ☐ *I feel grubby, and I want a shower.*

gruesome-twosome ['grusəm'tusəm] *n.* two people or things. (Jocular. Neither the things or the people have to be "gruesome.") ☐ *Well, it's the gruesome-twosome. Come in and join the party.* ☐ *The gruesome-twosome will both start in tonight's game.*

grunch See the following entry.

grunge AND **grunch** [grəndʒ AND grəntʃ] **1.** *n.* any nasty substance; dirt; *gunk.* □ *There's some gritty grunge on the kitchen floor.* □ *What's that grunch on your tie?* **2.** *n.* an ugly or nasty person; a repellent person. □ *Heidi thinks that Max is a grunge.* □ *Some grunch came by and dropped off this strange package for you.*

grungy ['grəndʒi] *mod.* dirty and smelly; *yucky.* □ *Get your grungy feet off the table!* □ *My feet are not grungy!* □ *What is this grungy stuff on the closet floor?*

grungy See *gungy.*

grunt [grənt] **1.** *n.* an infantry soldier. (Military. From the gutteral sound made by a pig, and anyone doing very heavy labor.) □ *Hey, you grunts! Get in line!* □ *Get those grunts out on the field at sunrise!* **2.** *n.* a low-ranking or subservient person. (Someone who is likely to utter a grunt because of the discomforts of menial labor.) □ *Get one of the grunts over here to clean this up.* □ *Let's hire a grunt to do this kind of work.* **3.** *n.* a belch. □ *I heard your grunt!* □ *Does that grunt mean you like my cooking?* **4.** *n.* a hard-working student. □ *Martin isn't a grunt. Everything's easy for Martin.* □ *The grunts got B's on the test. It was that hard!* **5.** *n.* a wrestler. (Possibly in reference to a grunting pig.) □ *Two big grunts wearing outlandish costumes performed for the television cameras.* □ *One grunt threw the other grunt out of the ring.*

grunt work *n.* hard, menial labor; tedious work. □ *I'm tired of doing grunt work for minimum wages.* □ *Who is supposed to do the grunt work around here? Not me!*

gubbish *n.* nonsense; useless information. (Computers. A combination of *garbage* and *rubbish*.) □ *There's nothing but gubbish on my printout.* □ *I can't make any sense out of this gubbish.*

guber AND **goober** ['gubɚ] **1.** *n.* a facial pimple. (See also *goob.*) □ *Wow, look at that giant guber on my nose.* □ *How does anybody get rid of goobers?* **2.** *n.* a tumor. (Jocular medical slang. Possibly because it grows beneath the surface like the goober—the peanut. See also *boogie.*) □ *Dr. Jones took a huge goober out of a lady this morning.* □ *The patient with the abdominal goober is going into surgery now.*

guck [gək] *n.* a thick, sticky substance; *yuck.* □ *What is this guck on the bottom of my shoe?* □ *The doctor painted some nasty guck on my throat and told me not to swallow for a while.*

gucky ['gəki] *mod.* thick and sticky; *yucky.* □ *This is a gucky day. Look at the sky.* □ *Yes, it is gucky.* □ *There is a lot of gucky oil and grease on the garage floor.*

guff [gəf] **1.** *n.* nonsense; *bunkum.* □ *Wow, that vice president guy can sure dish out the guff!* □ *No more guff outa you, okay?* **2.** *n.* back talk; complaining. □ *I don't want to hear any more of your guff.* □ *That's enough of your guff!* **3.** *n.* a strange person; a *nerd.* (Possibly related to *goof.*) □ *Wally acts like a guff when we go out. I am going to break up with him.* □ *Some old guff driving an Edsel yelled at us when we crossed the street.*

gug [gəg] *n.* a repellent person. □ *Oo, he's such a gug!* □ *Rocko is not a gug!*

GUI See *gooey.*

gulf *n.* heroin from the Persian Gulf region. (Drugs.) □ *This gulf is flooding the country.* □ *Those pushers can call anything gulf. How does anybody know where it's from?*

gumb(e)y ['gəmbi] *n.* a tall, squared-off and slanting haircut that looks like the Gumbey character's head. □ *Wayne came to school sporting a gumby and got a lot of attention.* □ *Ted got sent to the principal's office because of his gumbey.*

gumbeyhead ['gəmbihɛd] *n.* someone who does stupid things like the character, Gumbey. □ *Fred is a total gumbeyhead. He does all the wrong things.* □ *Don't be a gumbeyhead. Don't drink and drive.*

gump [gəmp] *n.* a fool; an oaf. □ *Who's the gump in the yellow slacks?* □ *Don't act like such a gump!*

gumshoe ['gəm'ʃu] *n.* a policeman or a detective. (Underworld. Also a term of address. So-named for wearing silent, gum-rubber soles.) □ *Has that gumshoe been around asking questions again?* □ *Look, gumshoe, what do you want with me?*

gun 1. *n.* a hired gunman; a bodyguard, an assassin, or a member of a gang of criminals. (Underworld and Western.) □ *Bruno and his guns came by to remind Gary of what he owed Mr. Big.* □ *Tell your guns to lay off.* 2. *n.* a leader; the key member of a group. □ *Who's the gun around here?* □ *Bruno is the gun, and what he says goes.* 3. *tr.* to race an engine; to rev up an engine. □ *See how loud it is when I gun it?* □ *Gun the thing again and let me hear it.*

gun for someone *in.* to be looking for someone, not necessarily with a gun. □ *Bruno is gunning for Max.* □ *The French prof is gunning for you.*

gunboats AND **battleships** *n.* big feet; big shoes. □ *Hasn't he got the biggest gunboats you ever saw?* □ *Whose battleships are these under the coffee table?*

gung-ho ['gəŋ'ho] *mod.* zealous; enthusiastic. □ *We're really gung-ho about the possibilities of this product.* □ *Pete always seems so gung-ho about everything.* □ *He's a gung-ho guy.*

gunge [gəndʒ] *n.* a skin irritation in the groin. (See also *crotch-rot.* Said of males.) □ *I got the gunge. What'll I do?* □ *The sawbones'll give you something for the gunge.*

gungeon ['gəndʒən] *n.* a potent type of marijuana from Africa or Jamaica; a cigarette made of this marijuana. □ *Where can I get some of that gungeon?* □ *Is this gungeon really from Africa?*

gungy AND **grungy** ['gəndʒi AND 'grəndʒi] *mod.* messy; nasty; worn out. (See also *grunge.*) □ *Get your grungy feet off the sofa.* □ *The weather is so grungy today.*

gunk [gəŋk] 1. *n.* any nasty, messy stuff. □ *What is this gunk on the counter?* □ *Get this gunk up off the floor before it dries.* 2. *n.* glue sniffed as a drug. (Drugs.) □ *This kid is high on gunk.* □ *I thought that it was illegal to sell gunk.*

gunner *n.* an earnest student. (Collegiate.) □ *Martin is a gunner, all right.* □ *The gunners in my algebra class always get the A's.*

gunny ['gəni] *n.* a potent marijuana from Jamaica or Africa. (Drugs.) □ *Is this gunny really from Jamaica?* □ *This gunny is just junk, plain old junk.*

gunzel-butt ['gənzl̩bət] *n.* a strange-looking person, usually a male. (Underworld.) □ *Bruno told the gunzel-butt where to get off.* □ *Rocko is no gunzel-butt. He's a thinker.*

guru ['guru] 1. *n.* an experienced *L.S.D.* user who guides someone else on a *trip.* □ *Max volunteered to serve as a guru, but he never showed up.* □ *A guru can be a big help.* 2. *n.* a stockbroker or other financial adviser. (Securities markets.) □ *My guru says to sell all my bonds.* □ *My guru just went bankrupt.* 3. *n.* a psychiatrist; a psychotherapist. □ *I go to this guru who gets a lot of money just to listen.* □ *I've started using my mirror for a guru. It's cheaper.*

gussied up ['gəsid . . .] *mod.* dressed up in one's best clothing. (Folksy.) □ *She was all gussied up in her finest.* □ *I like to get gussied up and go out on the town.*

gusto ['gəsto] 1. *n.* beer. □ *Can you stop at the filling station and get some gusto?* □ *How about another tube of gusto?* 2. *in.* to drink beer. □ *Don't you ever do anything but gusto?* □ *Let's go out and gusto all night!*

gut [gət] 1. *n.* the belly; the intestines. □ *What a gut that guy has.* □ *Tom poked Bill right in the gut.* 2. *mod.* basic; fundamental. □ *This is a gut issue, and we have to deal with it now.* □ *We are not dealing with what I would call one of the gut matters of the day.* 3. *mod.* easy. (Said of a course in high school or college.) □ *That's a gut course. Nothing to it.* □ *I won't take anymore gut economics courses. Even those are hard.* 4. *n.* an easy course in school. □ *That course is a gut.* □ *If it's a gut, it's for me.*

gut reaction (to something) *n.* a basic and immediate response to something. □ *Well, my gut reaction is quite negative.*

☐ *Her gut reaction to the plan is basically a good one.*

gutbucket ['gətbəkɪt] **1.** *n.* a chamber pot, especially one used in a prison cell. (Compare to *gash bucket.*) ☐ *You got something around here I can use as a gutbucket?* ☐ *I don't want any gutbucket around here.* **2.** *n.* a toilet. ☐ *Where's the gutbucket around here?* ☐ *The kid tried to flush his stash down the gutbucket.* **3.** *n.* the stomach. ☐ *Hey, your gutbucket's getting sort of big, isn't it?* ☐ *Sam poked Pete right in the gutbucket.* **4.** *n.* a fat person, usually a man. ☐ *Harry is getting to be a real gutbucket.* ☐ *Look at the gutbucket waddling down the street.* **5.** *n.* a cheap saloon; a low tavern. ☐ *Old Jed is probably stuck in some gutbucket someplace, talking his head off.* ☐ *The pinstriper needed a drink so bad he stopped at one of those gutbuckets on Maple Street.* **6.** *n.* an earthy style of music. ☐ *I'd like to hear some good old-fashioned gutbucket.* ☐ *You don't hear much gutbucket in public places these days.*

gutless wonder *n.* a totally spineless person. ☐ *George, don't be such a gutless wonder! Stand up for your rights!* ☐ *Here comes that gutless wonder, Martin.*

guts [gəts] **1.** *n.* courage; bravado. ☐ *Man, she's got guts!* ☐ *It takes guts to do something like that.* **2.** *n.* the belly; the intestines. ☐ *Ted poked Frank right in the guts.* ☐ *I've got some kind of pain in the guts.* **3.** *n.* the inner workings of anything. ☐ *There's something wrong in the guts of this clock.* ☐ *My tape recorder needs all new guts.* **4.** *n.* the essence of something. ☐ *Let's discuss the real guts of this issue.* ☐ *The guts of your proposal are really easy to understand.*

gutsy ['gətsi] *mod.* courageous; feisty. ☐ *She sure is a gutsy young thing.* ☐ *She is not gutsy.* ☐ *Ernie's acting sort of gutsy today. What happened?*

guy *n.* a fellow; a man or boy. (Not necessarily male in the plural.) ☐ *Hey you guys, let's go!* ☐ *When you guys finish getting your makeup on, we can go back to the guys.*

guzzery See *guzzlery.*

guzzle ['gəzl̩] **1.** *tr. & in.* to drink alcohol in great quantities. ☐ *Stop guzzling for a while and pay attention.* ☐ *Don't guzzle all that beer, or you'll turn into a guzzle-guts.* **2.** *n.* a drinking spree. ☐ *Fred's out on another of his guzzles.* ☐ *It's one guzzle after another, day after day.*

guzzle-guts *n.* a drunkard; a heavy drinker. ☐ *Old guzzle-guts here would like another drink.* ☐ *Don't call me guzzle-guts. I hardly ever have a drop.*

guzzled ['gəzl̩d] **1.** *mod.* arrested. (Underworld.) ☐ *Rocko got himself guzzled on a speeding rap.* ☐ *Lefty is guzzled again. He's so clumsy.* **2.** *mod.* alcohol intoxicated. ☐ *Sam was plenty guzzled when he got home.* ☐ *Todd was too guzzled to drive home.*

guzzler *n.* a heavy drinker. ☐ *Harry is getting to be quite a guzzler.* ☐ *A couple of guzzlers at the bar were carrying on a low conversation when Barlowe came in.*

guzzlery AND **guzzery** ['gəzlɚi AND 'gəzɚi] *n.* a bar; a liquor store. ☐ *Sam hit every guzzlery on Maple Street on the way home.* ☐ *I wouldn't be caught dead in a guzzery like that!*

gweeb [gwib] *n.* a studious student. (Collegiate. A variant of *dweeb.*) ☐ *I'm in a physics class full of gweebs.* ☐ *Martin is a gweeb, all right, but he's a good guy.*

gweebo ['gwibo] *mod.* feeble; despicable; in the manner of a *gweeb.* ☐ *I'm not a gweebo. I'm just eccentric.* ☐ *Who is that gweebo in the striped blazer?*

gym shoe *n.* a disliked person. ☐ *Who is the gym shoe who comes to class in a sport coat?* ☐ *Fred is such a gym shoe. Will he ever get with it?*

gynie ['gaɪni] *n.* a gynecologist. ☐ *My gynie says I'm fine.* ☐ *She went to a new gynie last week.*

gyve [dʒaɪv] *n.* marijuana; a marijuana cigarette. (Drugs. See also *jive.*) ☐ *Why are you always smoking gyve?* ☐ *How about a hit of that gyve?*

gyvestick See *jivestick.*

H

H. *n.* heroin. (Drugs.) □ *Now he's shooting H.* □ *First it was M.; now it's H.*

H-E-double-toothpicks ['etʃ'ɪ . . .] *n.* "hell." (A jocular euphemism. It is not usually written and can be spelled a number of different ways.) □ *Oh, H-E-double-toothpicks! I did it wrong again!* □ *Here she comes again. H-E-double-toothpicks!*

habit *n.* an addiction to a drug. □ *She has to steal to support her habit.* □ *There are many treatment programs to help with drug habits.*

hack 1. *n.* a taxi. □ *Go out to the street and see if you can get a hack.* □ *I drove a hack for a few months; then I quit.* **2.** *n.* a cough. □ *That's a nasty hack you've got there.* □ *A hack like that can lead to pneumonia.* **3.** *n.* a professional writer who writes mediocre material to order. □ *This novel shows that even a hack can get something published these days.* □ *That hack can't even write her name!* **4.** *n.* a reporter. □ *She was a hack for the newspaper for a while.* □ *Newspaper hacks have to know a little of everything.* **5.** *tr. & in.* to write clumsy or inefficient computer programs. □ *I can hack a program for you, but it won't be what you want.* □ *Well, I can hack myself.* **6.** *tr.* to annoy someone. □ *This really hacks me.* □ *That kind of behavior hacks her a lot.* (More at *hacked (off).*) **7.** *n.* anyone who does poor or undesirable work. □ *Oh, he's just a hack. What can you expect?* □ *There's always plenty of work for a hack.*

hack around *in.* to waste time. □ *You guys are always hacking around. Get busy!* □ *I wanted to hack around for a year after college, but my finances disagreed.*

hack it *tr.* to stand up to something; to endure something. □ *It's hard, but I'm sure I can hack it.* □ *I'm afraid you can't hack it. It just isn't working out.*

hacked [hækt] *mod.* worn out; ready to quit. □ *What a day! I'm hacked.* □ *We were all hacked at the end of the climb.*

hacked (off) *mod.* angry; annoyed. □ *Wally was really hacked off about the accident.* □ *Oh, Wally is always hacked about something.*

hacker 1. *n.* a taxi driver. □ *That hacker nearly ran into the back of my car!* □ *You wonder how some of these hackers keep their licenses.* **2.** *n.* a sloppy or inefficient computer programmer. □ *This program was written by a real hacker. It's a mess, but it works.* □ *I may be a hacker, but I get the job done.* **3.** *n.* a generally unsuccessful person. □ *Poor Pete is just a hacker. He'll never go any place.* □ *Hackers keep trying, but they never succeed.*

had See *taken.*

hairball AND **furball** *n.* an obnoxious person. □ *I wish that the guys I date didn't always turn out to be hairballs.* □ *Stop being such a furball, Wally.*

Hairball! *exclam.* "How awful!" (An exclamation of disgust. From the name of the undigested mass of fur vomited by a cat.) □ *Hairball! I did it wrong again!* □ *Oh, I hate that dork! Hairball!*

hairy *mod.* hazardous; difficult. □ *That was a hairy experience!* □ *Wow, that's hairy!* □ *What a hairy ride!*

hairy-ass(ed) (Potentially offensive. Use only with discretion.) **1.** *mod.* wild; exciting. □ *We had a real hairy-ass time on the roller coaster.* □ *The last part of the climb was really hairy-assed.* **2.** *mod.* virile. □ *This big hairy-ass guy started to push us around.* □ *He's not what I would call hairy-assed.* □ *Stop acting like a hairy-assed jerk.*

half a bubble off plumb *phr.* giddy; crazy. □ *She is acting about half a bubble off plumb. What is wrong with her?* □ *Tom is just half a bubble off plumb, but he is all heart.*

half-baked 1. *mod.* badly thought out. □ *That was a half-baked scheme. Was that the best you could do?* □ *It would have been approved if it weren't so half-baked.* **2.** *mod.* alcohol intoxicated. □ *We're getting half-baked, come hell or high water.* □ *Fred got himself sort of half-baked every Saturday night.*

half-blind *mod.* alcohol intoxicated. □ *Fred got himself half-blind in no time at all.* □ *Get that half-blind jerk out of here!* □ *Four cans of beer and she was half-blind.*

half-canned *mod.* alcohol intoxicated; tipsy. □ *He's half-canned and will be no help at all.* □ *Old Don is half-canned and can't drive home.*

half-cocked 1. *mod.* unprepared. (See also *go off half-cocked.*) □ *So he's half-cocked. So what?* □ *You're half-cocked for everything you do.* **2.** *mod.* alcohol intoxicated. □ *He just sat there, half-cocked and singing.* □ *Old Jed got himself half-cocked at the reception.*

half-crocked *mod.* alcohol intoxicated. □ *Sam and John set out to get half-crocked.* □ *They came home half-crocked at midnight.*

half in the bag *mod.* alcohol intoxicated. □ *Jerry was half in the bag when we found him.* □ *They were all half in the bag by midnight.*

half-lit *mod.* alcohol intoxicated. □ *John was half-lit in no time at all.* □ *Harry was half-lit by noon.*

half-sprung *mod.* tipsy; alcohol intoxicated. □ *Ted was half-sprung and could hardly stand up.* □ *They were half-sprung by noon.*

half-stewed *mod.* tipsy; alcohol intoxicated. □ *Poor Fred was half-stewed and still had to give a speech.* □ *We were half-stewed and had a lot of drinking yet to do.*

half under 1. *mod.* semi-conscious. □ *I was half under and could hear what the doctor was saying.* □ *I was afraid they would start cutting while I was only half under.* **2.** *mod.* alcohol intoxicated; tipsy. □ *He was half under and could barely stand up.* □ *Only four beers and she was half under.*

half up the pole *mod.* alcohol intoxicated; tipsy. □ *She drank till she was half up the pole.* □ *Don was half up the pole when we picked him up to come here.*

halvsies ['hævziz] *mod.* with each (of two) paying half. (See also *go Dutch.*) □ *Let's do it halvsies.* □ *Let's make it halvsies, and I pay for the parking, too.*

ham 1. *n.* an actor; a bad actor. (See also *hams.*) □ *What a ham! A real showoff.* □ *The cast was an assemblage of hams.* **2.** *n.* an amateur radio operator. □ *My brother is a ham, and he helped a lot during the emergency.* □ *The hams helped by providing communication to the outside world.*

ham-handed *mod.* lacking dexterity; clumsy. □ *If I wasn't so ham-handed, I could probably fix the thing myself.* □ *He is the most ham-handed guy I've ever seen.*

hamburg *n.* a hamburger. (See also *burger.*) □ *I'd like a couple of hamburgs and a shake.* □ *This hamburg is as greasy as they come.*

hamburger *n.* a stupid and worthless person—meat. □ *The guy is just hamburger. You can't teach him anything.* □ *There is a lot of hamburger around here. Who hired them?*

hamburgers *n.* shares in the McDonald's corporation. (Securities markets. New

York Stock Exchange jargon.) □ *I want 400 shares of hamburgers.* □ *Hamburgers just dropped a point.*

hammer *n.* the accelerator of a vehicle. □ *She pressed down the hammer, and off they went.* □ *The hammer went straight to the floor.*

hammer a beer See *pound a beer.*

hammer some beers See *pound a beer.*

hammered *mod.* alcohol intoxicated. □ *Man, old Fred was really hammered.* □ *She got so hammered she couldn't see.*

hammerhead 1. *n.* a stupid person; a person whose head seems to be as solid as a hammer. □ *You can be such a hammerhead!* □ *What a hammerhead! Totally dense!* **2.** *n.* a drunkard or a drug user. □ *These hammerheads can't even hold a simple job for the most part.* □ *A couple of hammerheads stood in the alley, looking suspicious.*

hams *n.* legs; hips. □ *Her great hams extended over the sides of the chair.* □ *I got to do something to get the size of these hams down.*

hand-in-glove *mod.* suiting one another naturally. □ *These two go hand-in-glove.* □ *The two parts went together like hand-in-glove.*

hand it to someone *tr.* to acknowledge someone's excellence (at something). □ *Well, I have to hand it to you. That was great!* □ *He had to hand it to her for her excellent performance.*

hand over fist *mod.* repeatedly and energetically, especially as with taking in money in a great volume. □ *We were taking in fees hand over fist, and the people were lined up for blocks.* □ *The money came in hand over fist at the B.O.*

hand someone something *tr.* to tell someone something; to tell someone nonsense. □ *Don't hand me that stuff! That's silly!* □ *She handed me a line about being a famous author.*

handful *n.* a difficult thing or person. □ *Little Jimmy is a handful.* □ *His dad can be a handful, too.*

handle 1. *n.* a person's name or nickname. (Western jargon and then citizens band radio.) □ *Well, what's your handle so I'll know what to call you?* □ *My handle is Goober. You can call me Goob.* **2.** *n.* a way of dealing with something; a grasp of a problem. □ *As soon as I get a handle on this Wilson matter, I'll give you a buzz.* □ *I can't seem to get a handle on what's wrong.*

handles See *(love) handles.*

handout 1. *n.* a gift of money, food, or other goods to a needy person. (Often in the negative, as in the examples.) □ *I don't want a handout, just a loan.* □ *Give him a handout and send him on his way.* **2.** *n.* an informational sheet of paper "handed out" to people. □ *As you can see on your handout, 40 percent of those who started never finished.* □ *I didn't get a handout.*

hands down *mod.* easily; unquestionably. □ *She won the contest hands down.* □ *They declared her the winner hands down.*

hands-on 1. *mod.* having to do with an instructional session where the learners are able to handle the device they are being trained to operate. □ *Please plan to attend a hands-on seminar on computers next Thursday.* □ *After three weeks of hands-on training, I still couldn't add two and two.* **2.** *mod.* having to do with an executive or manager who participates directly in operations. □ *We expect that he will be the kind of hands-on president we have been looking for.* □ *John is a hands-on manager. I wish he would stay in his office.*

Hands up! AND **Stick 'em up!** *exclam.* "Raise your hands in the air; this is a robbery!" (Underworld and Western.) □ *Hands up! Don't anybody move a muscle. This is a heist.* □ *Stick 'em up! Give me all your valuables.*

hang *in.* to hang around; to spend time aimlessly. □ *Is that all you did all summer? Just hang?* □ *My mom yelled at me because I spent all day hanging with the guys.*

hang a BA (at someone) *tr.* to display one's buttocks to someone in derision. (A *BA* is a "bare ass.") ☐ *Victor was angry and hung a BA at the cop.* ☐ *He went to the window and hung a BA—just for the hell of it.*

hang a few on *tr.* to take a few drinks; to have a few beers. ☐ *They went out to hang a few on.* 🅃 *Let's hang on a few and then go on to the meeting.*

hang a huey ['hæŋ ə 'jui AND 'hæŋ ə 'hjui] *tr.* to turn left. (The first pronunciation of *Huey* with no *h* is probably the original version. See also *hang a louie.*) ☐ *Hang a huey at the next corner.* ☐ *Right here! Hang a huey!*

hang a left *tr.* to turn left. ☐ *He hung a left at the wrong corner.* ☐ *Hey, here! Hang a left here!*

hang a louie ['hæŋ ə 'lui] *tr.* to turn left. ☐ *You have to hang a louie at the stop sign.* ☐ *Go another block and hang a louie.*

hang a ralph ['hæŋ ə 'rælf] *tr.* to turn right. ☐ *He skied down the easy slope and hung a ralph near a fir tree.* ☐ *Don't hang a ralph until you get past the traffic light.*

hang a right *tr.* to turn right. ☐ *Hang a right about here.* ☐ *I told him to hang a right at the next corner, but he went on.*

hang (around) *in.* to loiter; to waste away time doing nothing. ☐ *Don't just hang around. Get busy with something.* ☐ *Move. Don't just hang. There's work to be done.*

hang five AND **hang ten** *tr.* to stand toward the front of a surfboard or diving board and hang the toes of one or both feet over the edge. (Teens and collegiate.) ☐ *The coach told her to hang ten and not to look down.* ☐ *Get out there and hang five. You can swim. Nothing can go wrong.*

hang in there *in.* to keep trying; to persevere. ☐ *Hang in there. Keep trying.* ☐ *I'll just hang in there. Maybe things will get better.*

Hang it all! *exclam.* "Damn it all!" ☐ *Oh, hang it all! I'm late.* ☐ *He's late again! Hang it all!*

hang it up *tr.* to quit something. ☐ *I finally had enough and decided to hang it up.* ☐ *Oh, hang it up! It's hopeless.*

hang loose AND **stay loose** *in.* to relax and stay *cool.* ☐ *Just hang loose, man. Everything'll be all right.* ☐ *Stay loose, chum. See ya later.*

hang one on *tr.* to get drunk. ☐ *Fred was hacked and went out to hang one on.* ☐ *Fred hangs one on about once a month.*

hang ten See *hang five.*

hang tough (on something) *in.* to stick to one's position (on something). ☐ *I decided I'd hang tough on it. I tend to give in too easy.* ☐ *Yes, just hang tough.*

hang up 1. *n.* a problem or concern; an obsession. (Usually **hang-up**.) ☐ *She's got some serious hang-ups about cats.* ☐ *I don't have any hang ups at all. Well, almost none.* **2.** *in.* to say no; to cancel out of something. ☐ *I hung up. That's not for me anyway.* ☐ *If you don't want to do it, just hang up. I'll understand.*

hang with someone *in.* to hang around with someone. ☐ *Dave spent the afternoon hanging with Don, and neither one got anything done.* ☐ *I'm going down to the corner and hang with the guys.*

hangout ['hæŋaut] *n.* a place to loaf or *hang (around).* ☐ *I dropped by one of his favorite hangouts, but he wasn't there.* ☐ *We went over to the hangout and sat around talking.*

hankie See the following entry.

hanky AND **hankie** ['hæŋki] *n.* a handkerchief, especially if lacy and feminine. ☐ *Do you have a hanky I can borrow?* ☐ *Here, use my hankie.*

hanky-panky ['hæŋki'pæŋki] **1.** *n.* funny business; deceitfulness. ☐ *There's some hanky-panky going on in the treasurer's office.* ☐ *I am going to get this hanky-panky straightened out.* **2.** *n.* sexual play; sexual misconduct. (See also *mifky-pifky.*) ☐ *Sam and Mary are up to a* *little hanky-panky, I've heard.* □ *There's some hanky-panky going on in the storeroom.*

happening 1. *mod.* fashionable; trendy; positive. (Collegiate.) □ *Oh, Tiffany, your skirt is really happening.* □ *Wow, that's happening!* **2.** *n.* an event. □ *The concert was a real happening.* □ *Well, class is never a happening, but it's never dull.*

happy 1. *mod.* alcohol intoxicated; tipsy. □ *She seems a little happy. Must have had a few already.* □ *She's not happy. She's stewed.* **2.** *mod.* obsessed with something. (A combining form showing a strong interest in the thing that is named before *happy.*) □ *All those guys are girl-happy at this age.* □ *Pete's car-happy right now. That's all he thinks about.*

happy camper *n.* a happy person. (Often in the negative.) □ *Fred flunked algebra and he is not a happy camper.* □ *I am not a happy camper. I am tired, hungry, and I need a shower.*

happy hour *n.* cocktail time. □ *Happy hour starts at dawn for Harry.* □ *The hotel had a nice happy hour at five.*

happy juice *n.* liquor, beer, and wine. □ *A little more happy juice, John?* □ *Too much happy juice can make you very unhappy.*

happy pills *n.* tranquilizers. □ *She asked the doctor for some happy pills.* □ *She is now hooked on happy pills.*

happy shop *n.* a liquor store. □ *I need something from the happy shop.* □ *Let's stop off at the happy shop.*

hard 1. *mod.* fermented, as with cider. (See also *hard liquor.*) □ *This juice got hard. What shall I do with it?* □ *Where's the hard stuff?* □ *If it's hard, give it to me and I'll drink it.* **2.** *mod.* having to do with an addictive drug. (Compare to *soft.*) □ *Gert's on hard stuff now.* □ *Hard drugs are easier to get than ever before.* **3.** *mod.* tough. (Akin to *hard-hearted; hard as nails.*) □ *Sally is really hard. She can stand anything.* □ *Only the hard guys get through basic training.*

hard case 1. *n.* a case of liquor. □ *Pete wanted a hard case delivered to his house.* □ *There's a lot of beer and a hard case in the van.* **2.** *n.* a person who is a real problem. □ *Jed has turned into a hard case. He's fighting us at every turn.* □ *The hard case we dealt with last week is back again.*

hard coin *n.* lots of money. (See also *coin.*) □ *A car like that takes hard coin.* □ *Old Freddie is earning some hard coin these days.*

hard-core 1. *mod.* sexually explicit; pornographic. □ *You can't sell that hard-core stuff in a store like this!* □ *You think that's hard-core?* **2.** *mod.* extreme; entrenched. □ *She spent some time teaching hard-core illiterates in a medium-sized town.* □ *There are too many hard-core cases of poverty there.* **3.** *mod.* very good; stunning; great. □ *This new album is one hard-core piece of tunage.* □ *I'd like a really hard-core pizza with at least five kinds of cheese.*

hard head *n.* a stubborn person. □ *You are a classic hard head. Lighten up!* □ *I'm not really a hard head. You bring out the worst in me.*

hard liquor *n.* potent liquor such as whiskey, gin, rum, etc. □ *Hard liquor makes me sick.* □ *Stay off of hard liquor until your stomach feels better.*

hard-nosed *mod.* stern and businesslike; unsympathetic. □ *She's pretty hard-nosed and tends to put people off.* □ *It takes a hard-nosed manager to run a place like this.*

hard sell *n.* a high-pressure attempt to sell something. □ *I didn't want to listen to any hard sell, so I bought it from a mail order place.* □ *I'm afraid I'm very susceptible to the hard sell.*

hard time 1. *n.* a difficult experience. □ *I had a hard time at the doctor's office.* □ *She's having a hard time with her child.* **2.** *n.* a prison sentence. (Underworld.) □ *Lefty did hard time for his part in the robbery.* □ *How much hard time does he have behind him?*

hard to swallow *mod.* difficult to believe. □ *Your story is pretty hard to swallow,* *but I am beginning to believe it.* ☐ *The news was hard to swallow.*

hard up 1. *mod.* alcohol intoxicated. ☐ *After a couple of six packs, Wally found himself a little hard up.* ☐ *The whole gang was hard up by midnight.* **2.** *mod.* in need of drugs or alcohol. ☐ *Gert was hard up and needed a fix.* ☐ *The old hobo was hard up for a drink.* **3.** *mod.* desperate for companionship. ☐ *Freddie said he was hard up and needed a date.* ☐ *Mary must be hard up to date a jerk like that.*

hardboiled *mod.* tough; heartless. ☐ *She is a hardboiled old gal.* ☐ *Do you have to act so hardboiled?*

hardhat ['hɑrdhæt] **1.** *n.* a protective helmet worn around construction sites. (Standard English.) ☐ *You'll need a hardhat to come into this area.* ☐ *John swiped a hardhat from the construction site.* **2.** *n.* construction worker. (Usually derogatory.) ☐ *The hardhats didn't care much for the actress's politics.* ☐ *Some hardhat was waving a flag and shouting something I couldn't understand.*

hardheaded *mod.* stubborn. ☐ *Gary is a real hardheaded guy.* ☐ *Anybody that hardheaded is going to have trouble with everybody.*

hardliner *n.* a person who takes a strict position (on something). ☐ *Tom is sort of a hardliner when it comes to spending public money.* ☐ *The mayor is a hardliner on the question of care for the elderly.*

hardware 1. *n.* whiskey; potent liquor. ☐ *This hardware is enough to knock your socks off.* ☐ *Pour me some of that hardware, will ya?* **2.** *n.* hard drugs or hard liquor. ☐ *No wine for me. Give me the hardware.* ☐ *This hardware is pretty powerful.* **3.** *n.* a weapon; a gun. (Underworld and Western.) ☐ *I think I see your hardware showing.* ☐ *Lefty keeps his hardware under his mattress.* **4.** *n.* computer parts, as opposed to computer programs. ☐ *What kind of hardware are you running this program on?* ☐ *The software is okay, so it must be the hardware that's off.*

harsh *mod.* bad. ☐ *She's a harsh lady and doesn't care how you feel.* ☐ *Man, this hamburger is harsh. What did you put in it?*

harsh toke 1. *n.* an irritating puff of a marijuana cigarette. (Drugs.) ☐ *Wow, that was a harsh toke. Yuck!* ☐ *Pat got a harsh toke and coughed a lot.* **2.** *n.* anything or anyone unpleasant. ☐ *Sally can sure be a harsh toke when she wants.* ☐ *This meeting has been a real harsh toke.*

has-been ['hæzbɪn] **1.** *n.* someone who used to be important; a person whose career has ended. ☐ *Marty is just a has-been. There's no future for him.* ☐ *An old has-been was hired to host the midnight show.* **2.** *mod.* former; burnt-out. ☐ *Some has-been singer croaked through "The Star-Spangled Banner."* ☐ *Now I'm a has-been football player, and nobody even knows my name.*

hash [hæʃ] *n.* hashish; cannabis in general. (Drugs.) ☐ *The amount of hash that moves into this city in a single day would astound you.* ☐ *Hash is still the favorite first drug other than alcohol.*

hash cannon *n.* a device used in the smoking of cannabis. (Drugs. See also *shotgun*.) ☐ *Gert kept a hash cannon in her stash.* ☐ *Don had a hash cannon in his office as a sample of a device for smoking pot.*

hash-head *n.* a smoker of cannabis. (Drugs.) ☐ *You can't stay a hash-head all your life.* ☐ *Kelly was almost a hopeless hash-head.*

hash-house 1. *n.* a cheap diner. ☐ *Tom worked for two days as a hash-slinger in a hash-house.* ☐ *You see a lot of interesting people go in and out of a hash-house like this one.* **2.** *n.* a place where hashish is sold and used. (Drugs.) ☐ *This hash-house is due for a raid. Let's hit it.* ☐ *The fuzz raided a hash-house over on Maple Street.*

hash pipe *n.* a small pipe for smoking cannabis. (Drugs.) ☐ *John kept a hash pipe on the shelf just for show.* ☐ *The cops found a hash pipe in her pocket.*

hash-slinger *n.* a cook, waiter, or waitress in a *hash-house.* ☐ *I worked as a hash-slinger in an all-night diner.* ☐ *The life of a hash-slinger is pretty tough.*

hassle ['hæsl̩] **1.** *n.* a dispute; a bother. ☐ *The whole thing was a real hassle.* ☐ *It's a hassle every time I come here.* **2.** *tr.* to harass someone; to bother someone; to give someone a hard time. ☐ *Listen, please don't hassle me. I've had a hard day.* ☐ *Please make this dame stop hassling me!*

hatch *n.* the mouth. (See also *Down the hatch!*) ☐ *Shut your hatch!* ☐ *Pop this in your hatch.*

haul **1.** *n.* the proceeds from a theft; loot. (Underworld.) ☐ *They divvied up the haul from the bank job.* ☐ *The cops thought they must have got a pretty good haul.* **2.** *n.* the proceeds from any activity: a performance, a fishing trip, a collection of goods or money for charity, etc. ☐ *They got a good haul from the benefit.* ☐ *They surveyed the haul of cans and packages and decided they had done a pretty fair job.*

have a ball *tr.* to have an exciting time. (See also *ball.*) ☐ *I plan to have a ball while I'm there.* ☐ *Come on, everybody! Let's have a ball!*

have a big mouth *tr.* to speak loudly; to tell secrets. (*Have got* can replace *have.*) ☐ *Boy, do you have a big mouth!* ☐ *He has a big mouth. Don't tell him anything you don't want everybody else to know.*

Have a blimp! *exclam.* "Have a good year!" (A play on *Goodyear Tire and Rubber Company,* which operates the Goodyear blimp.) ☐ *Good-bye. Have a blimp!* ☐ *Have a blimp! See you next summer.*

have a buzz on *tr.* to be tipsy or alcohol intoxicated. (*Have got* can replace *have.*) ☐ *Pete has a buzz on and is giggling a lot.* ☐ *Both of them had a buzz on by the end of the celebration.*

have a crack at something See *take a crack at something.*

have a glow on *tr.* to be alcohol intoxicated; to be tipsy. (*Have got* can replace *have.*) ☐ *Since you already have a glow on, I guess you won't want another drink.* ☐ *Jed had a glow on and was just becoming civil.*

Have a good one. AND **Have a nice one.** *sent.* "Have a good morning, afternoon, or evening," as appropriate. (A general formulaic expression used at any time of the day or night.) ☐ *Thank you. Have a good one.* ☐ *See you tomorrow, Todd. Have a nice one.*

have a (big) head *tr.* to have a hangover. (*Have got* can replace *have.*) ☐ *Oh, man, do I have a head!* ☐ *Tom has a head this morning and won't be coming into work.*

Have a heart! *exclam.* "Be compassionate!"; "Be kind!" ☐ *Have a heart! Give me another chance.* ☐ *Come on! Have a heart!*

have a leg up on someone *tr.* to have an advantage over someone; to be ahead of someone. (*Have got* can replace *have.*) ☐ *Pete has a leg up on Wilbur because of his physical strength.* ☐ *I don't have a leg up on anyone. I'm a loser.*

have a little visitor *tr.* to have received the menses. (*Have got* can replace *have.*) ☐ *Mary said she has a little visitor.* ☐ *She has a little visitor and will call you later.*

have a load on *tr.* to be alcohol intoxicated. (*Have got* can replace *have.*) ☐ *Fred has a load on and is finished for the evening.* ☐ *You have a load on every time I see you.*

have a loose screw See *have a screw loose.*

have a monkey on one's back *tr.* to have a drug addiction. (Drugs. *Have got* can replace *have.*) ☐ *Gert has a monkey on her back.* ☐ *Do you think she wants to have a monkey on her back?*

Have a nice day. *sent.* a formulaic way of saying good-bye. (See also *Have a good one.*) ☐ *Thank you for shopping at Wallace's. Have a nice day.* ☐ *See you tomorrow. Have a nice day.*

Have a nice one. See *Have a good one.*

have a run-in (with someone or something) *tr.* to have trouble with someone or something. ☐ *I had a run-in with Mrs. Wilson. She's a hard case.* ☐ *We've had a run-in before.*

have a screw loose AND **have a loose screw** *tr.* to be silly or eccentric. (*Have got* can replace *have.*) ☐ *He's sort of strange. I think he's got a loose screw.* ☐ *Yes, he has a screw loose somewhere.*

have a short fuse *tr.* to be easy to anger. (*Have got* can replace *have.*) ☐ *He's got a short fuse, so watch out.* ☐ *Tracy has a short fuse and is likely to lose her temper at any time.*

have a skinful *tr.* [for someone] to contain too much alcohol; to be alcohol intoxicated. (See also *skinful. Have got* can replace *have.*) ☐ *Pete had a skinful and just sat there quietly.* ☐ *What is wrong with her is that she has a skinful, that's what.*

have a spaz [. . . spæz] *tr.* to get angry or hysterical; to have a *conniption (fit).* (Teens and collegiate.) ☐ *If my dad hears about this, he'll have a spaz.* ☐ *The teacher had a spaz when I came in so late.*

have a tiger by the tail *tr.* to have become associated with something powerful and potentially dangerous. (*Have got* can replace *have.*) ☐ *You have a tiger by the tail. You bit off more than you could chew.* ☐ *You've had a tiger by the tail ever since you took office.*

have a whale of a time *tr.* to have an exciting time; to have a big time. (See also *whaling* at *wailing.*) ☐ *We had a whale of a time at your party.* ☐ *Yes, we really had a whale of a time.*

have a yellow streak down one's back *tr.* to be cowardly. (*Have got* can replace *have.*) ☐ *I think that Wally has a yellow streak down his back. That's what's wrong.* ☐ *If you have a yellow streak down your back, you don't take many risks.*

have all one's marbles *tr.* to have all one's mental faculties; to be mentally sound. (See also *lose (all) one's marbles. Have got* can replace *have.*) ☐ *I don't think he has all his marbles.* ☐ *Do you think Bob has all his marbles?*

have an ace up one's sleeve *tr.* to have something useful in reserve; to have a special trick available. (*Have got* can replace *have.*) ☐ *I still have an ace up my sleeve that you don't know about.* ☐ *I don't have an ace up my sleeve. If it doesn't work, it doesn't work.*

have an edge on *tr.* to be alcohol intoxicated. (See also *edge. Have got* can replace *have.*) ☐ *I've got an edge on and shouldn't drive home.* ☐ *Bob has an edge on even though he hardly drank anything.*

have an itch for something *tr.* to have a desire for something. (*Have got* can replace *have.*) ☐ *I have an itch for some ice cream.* ☐ *We had an itch for a good movie, so we went.*

have ants in one's pants *tr.* to be nervous and anxious. (See also *antsy. Have got* can replace *have.*) ☐ *He seems to have ants in his pants before each game.* ☐ *All kids've got ants in their pants all the time at that age.*

have bats in one's belfry [. . .'bɛlfri] *tr.* to be crazy. (See also *bats. Have got* can replace *have.*) ☐ *You must really have bats in your belfry if you think I'll put up with that kind of stuff.* ☐ *Pay no attention to her. She has bats in her belfry.*

have egg on one's face *tr.* to be embarrassed by something one has done. (As if one went out in public with a dirty face. *Have got* can replace *have.*) ☐ *I was completely wrong, and now I have egg on my face.* ☐ *She's really got egg on her face!*

have good vibes [. . . vaɪbz] *tr.* to have good feelings (about someone or something). (*Have got* can replace *have.*) ☐ *I've got good vibes about Heidi.* ☐ *I know everything will go all right. I have good vibes.*

have it all together *tr.* to be mentally and physically organized; to be of sound mind. (*Have got* can replace *have.*) ☐ *I* *don't have it all together today.* □ *Try me again later when I have it all together.*

have it made *tr.* to have succeeded; to be set for life. (*Have got* can replace *have.*) □ *I have a good job and a nice little family. I have it made.* □ *He's really got it made.*

have it made in the shade *tr.* to have succeeded; to be set for life. (*Have got* can replace *have.*) □ *Wow, is he lucky! He has it made in the shade.* □ *Who's got it made in the shade?*

have kittens 1. *tr.* to become enraged. □ *When I heard the news, I had kittens. I was hacked!* □ *I almost had kittens, I was so mad.* **2.** *tr.* to laugh very hard; to enjoy something enormously. □ *It was so funny, I had kittens laughing.* □ *She had kittens laughing about it.* **3.** *tr.* to be surprised. □ *I nearly had kittens when I heard.* □ *She had kittens when she heard about the wedding.*

have-nots *n.* the poor; those who have little or nothing. (Always with *the*. Compare to *haves.*) □ *The have-nots seem never to be able to get ahead.* □ *What's in it for the have-nots?*

have one foot in the grave *tr.* to be near death. (*Have got* can replace *have.*) □ *I feel like I've got one foot in the grave.* □ *Uncle Ben has one foot in the grave, but he's still cheery.*

have one's ass in a crack *tr.* to be stranded in a very difficult or uncomfortable state of affairs. (Potentially offensive. Use only with discretion. *Have got* can replace *have.*) □ *He's got his ass in a crack and needs all the help he can get.* □ *Now he's really got his ass in a crack and doesn't know what to do.*

have one's ass in a sling *tr.* to be dejected or hurt; to be pouting. (Potentially offensive. Use only with discretion. *Have got* can replace *have.*) □ *She's got her ass in a sling because she got stood up.* □ *Why do you have your ass in a sling?*

have one's brain on a leash *in.* to be drunk. □ *Wayne had his brain on a leash before he even got to the party.* □ *Some guy who had his brain on a leash ran his car off the road.*

have one's mind in the gutter *tr.* to think or suggest something obscene. (*Have got* can replace *have.*) □ *Tiffany has her mind in the gutter. That's why she laughs at all that dirty stuff.* □ *You always have your mind in the gutter.*

have rocks in one's head *tr.* to be silly or crazy. (*Have got* can replace *have.*) □ *You have rocks in your head!* □ *She's got rocks in her head if she thinks that.*

have someone dead to rights *tr.* to have caught someone red-handed; to have irrefutable evidence about someone's misdeed. (*Have got* can replace *have*. See also *(bang) dead to rights.*) □ *We've got you dead to rights on this one.* □ *The cops had him dead to rights.*

have something cinched *tr.* to have something settled; to have the results of some act assured. (See also *cinched. Have got* can replace *have.*) □ *Don't worry. I've got it cinched.* □ *You just think you've got it cinched.*

have something on the brain *tr.* to be obsessed with something. (*Have got* can replace *have.*) □ *You've just got girls on the brain, you silly twit.* □ *I have money on the brain, I guess.*

have the wrong number 1. *tr.* to be wrong. (*Have got* can replace *have.*) □ *Boy, do you have the wrong number! Get with it!* □ *You have missed the boat again. You have the wrong number!* **2.** *tr.* to be addressing the wrong person. (This use is in addition to the same expression used for a wrong telephone number. *Have got* can replace *have.*) □ *You have the wrong number. Walter is my brother. We look alike, though.* □ *No, I'm Sally. You have the wrong number.*

have what it takes *tr.* to have the skills, power, intelligence, etc., to do something. (*Have got* can replace *have.*) □ *I know I've got what it takes.* □ *I guess I don't have what it takes to be a composer.*

haves *n.* the wealthy; those who have money. (Always with *the*. Compare to *have-nots.*) □ *The haves seem to be able to take care of themselves.* □ *I live in the western suburbs with the haves.*

hawk 1. *n.* someone who supports a warlike U.S. defense policy. (Compare to *dove.*) □ *The hawks want to raise taxes and buy tanks.* □ *The doves want to sell the tanks, ignore the hawks, and give the money to the poor.* 2. *in.* to cough mightily; to cough something up. □ *The cold has had me hawking for a week.* □ *He's been hawking all night.* 3. *n.* the cold winter wind. (Originally black. Always with *the*. See also *Mr. Hawkins.*) □ *Man, just feel the hawk cut through you!* □ *It's the time of the year when the hawk rules!*

hay burner 1. *n.* a worthless racehorse; any old and worn-out horse. □ *Send that old hay burner to the glue factory.* □ *I went to a dude ranch, and they gave me an old hay burner to ride.* 2. AND **hay head** *n.* a marijuana smoker. (Drugs.) □ *Some hay burner was around trying to sell raffle tickets that looked handmade.* □ *Another hay head came in and applied for the job.*

hay head See the previous entry.

hayseed *n.* a farmer; a rustic character, usually a male. □ *I'm not just some hayseed fresh off the farm.* □ *It's hard for these hayseeds to adjust to city life.*

haywire ['hewɑɪr] 1. *mod.* out of order. (Folksy.) □ *This telephone has gone haywire.* □ *My stereo is haywire, so I've been listening to the radio.* 2. *mod.* disoriented. (Often from marijuana.) □ *Wally is sort of haywire from the grass.* □ *Max has been haywire for years.*

hazel ['hezl̩] *n.* heroin. (Drugs. A variety of *H.*) □ *Gert needs some hazel, but anything will help her.* □ *She wants to spend the evening with hazel.*

head 1. *n.* a headache. □ *Man, do I have a head. You got any aspirin?* □ *Music that loud gives me a head.* 2. *n.* a hangover. (Always with *a*.) □ *Boy, do I have a head this morning.* □ *How do you get rid of a head so you can go to work?* 3. *n.* a toilet; a restroom. (Originally nautical. Usually with *the*.) □ *Where's the head around here?* □ *Ralph is in the head. He'll be back in a minute.* 4. *n.* a member of the drug culture; a hippie or a person who drops out of mainstream society because of drug use. (From the 1960's and 1970's.) □ *You still see a few heads around, even today.* □ *Some of the heads became very, very straight.*

head cook and bottle washer AND **chief cook and bottle washer** *n.* someone who is in charge of something trivial. □ *I'm the head cook and bottle washer around here.* □ *I want to see the chief cook and bottle washer.*

head drug *n.* a drug that affects the mind rather than the body; a psychoactive drug. □ *It's these head drugs that get the kids into so much trouble.* □ *Head drugs are just as addictive as other drugs, but in a different way.*

head hunt *tr. & in.* to recruit someone (for a job). □ *He went to the conference to head hunt a new employee.* □ *All the managers were there to head hunt.*

head South See *go South*.

head trip 1. *n.* a session with a *head drug*. (Drugs.) □ *Bob had his first head trip last night.* □ *He says it will be his last head trip.* 2. *n.* an ego trip. □ *Wally is on another of his head trips.* □ *Come down from your head trip and see if you can get along with the rest of us.*

headache 1. *n.* an annoying person or thing. □ *Here comes that Ken Johnson. He's a real headache.* □ *Cars can be such a headache.* 2. *n.* liquor. □ *Pour me some more of that headache, will you?* □ *Give the man some more headache.*

headache department 1. *n.* a central source of unnecessary problems; a person who habitually causes problems. □ *Here's another memo from the headache department.* □ *Mrs. Wilson is my least favorite headache department.* 2. AND **headache house** *n.* a liquor store or department. □ *I stopped in at the headache department for some supplies.* □ *The headache house is having a special on gin.*

headache house See the previous entry.

headache man *n.* a male law enforcement agent. □ *The headache man was here to see you, Ernie.* □ *Who gave that hot tip to the headache man?*

headbone *n.* the skull. □ *I got a nasty bump on my headbone.* □ *Do you want I should conk your headbone, or will you be coming along politely?*

headfucker ['hɛdfəkɚ] *n.* a potent psychoactive drug; *L.S.D.* (Drugs. Potentially offensive. Use only with discretion.) □ *This stuff is a real headfucker. Stay away from it.* □ *John's first experience with a headfucker was not one he's likely to forget.*

headhunter *n.* someone who recruits executives for employment. (*Head* means "boss" here.) □ *The board of directors hired a headhunter to get a new manager.* □ *The headhunter brought in a few candidates, but nobody promising.*

Heads up! *exclam.* "Look out!" □ *Heads up! Watch out for the swinging bucket!* □ *Here's a rough spot on the trail. Heads up!*

heads will roll *phr.* someone will be punished. □ *When I find out who did this, heads will roll.* □ *Heads will roll when I get back to the office.*

Headstone City *n.* a cemetery. □ *Unless you want to move into a furnished flat in Headstone City, you had better fasten your seatbelt when you drive or ride in a car.* □ *Our house is just one block after the large Headstone City on the left.*

heap **1.** *n.* an old car. (See also *load.*) □ *I've got to get my heap fixed up.* □ *Is this old heap yours?* **2.** *n.* any dilapidated thing or person. □ *Marty is turning into a heap.* □ *We have to fix up this heap if we're really going to live in it.* **3.** AND **heaps** *n.* lots (of something). □ *I have a whole heap of papers for you.* □ *Mr. Wilson has heaps of money.*

heaps See the previous entry.

heart *tr.* to love someone or something. (Teens.) □ *Oh, I just, like, heart your letter.* □ *She's hearting him more every day.*

heart-to-heart (talk) *n.* a serious and intimate discussion. □ *We sat down and had a nice heart-to-heart for about an hour.* □ *A little heart-to-heart talk is just what you need.*

hearts and flowers *n.* sentimentality. □ *The movie was so full of hearts and flowers that I was bored.* □ *I didn't care for the hearts and flowers part.*

heat **1.** *n.* the police. (Underworld. Always with *the.*) □ *The heat is gonna catch up with you, Ernie.* □ *Who tipped the heat off about me?* **2.** *n.* pressure. □ *There's a lot of heat on Fred right now.* □ *The boss put some heat on Wally, and things are moving faster now.* **3.** *n.* a gun; armaments. (Underworld. Compare to *heater.*) □ *Lefty has his heat on him at all times.* □ *Rocko never carries heat.*

heater *n.* a pistol. (Underworld.) □ *Lefty carried his heater with him that day.* □ *Put your heaters away, boys. This is a job for reason.*

heave [hiv] *in.* to empty one's stomach; to vomit. □ *He heaved and heaved and sounded like he was dying.* □ *I think I have to go heave.*

heaven dust *n.* cocaine. (Drugs.) □ *A little heaven dust and Pat was as good as new.* □ *She left her desk to take on a little heaven dust.*

heavy **1.** *n.* a villain. (Especially in movies, etc.) □ *He is well-known for playing heavies in the movies.* □ *Do I always have to be the heavy?* **2.** *mod.* important; profound; serious. □ *This is a very heavy matter.* □ *This matter is too heavy.* □ *I have some heavy things to talk over with you, Sam.* **3.** *mod.* really fine. □ *Man, this is some heavy chocolate cake!* □ *This stuff is really heavy!* □ *This is a real heavy thing you're doing for me.*

heavy artillery *n.* powerful or persuasive persons or things. □ *Finally, the mayor brought out the heavy artillery and quieted things down.* □ *The heavy artillery seemed to know how to handle matters.*

heavy bread AND **heavy money** *n.* a great deal of money. ☐ *Man, that car cost some heavy bread.* ☐ *It takes heavy money to run a household like this.*

heavy date *n.* an important date with someone; a date with someone important. ☐ *Mary has a heavy date with Sam tonight.* ☐ *Pete and Sally were out on a heavy date together.*

heavy-handed *mod.* tactless; forceful; unfair. ☐ *Paul is a little heavy-handed at times, but mostly he's reasonable.* ☐ *That was a pretty heavy-handed thing to do.*

heavy hash *n.* potent cannabis. (Drugs.) ☐ *Man, you came up with some real heavy hash.* ☐ *This is heavy hash, and it will cost you.*

heavy into someone or something *mod.* much concerned with someone or something; obsessed with someone or something. ☐ *Freddie was heavy into auto racing and always went to the races.* ☐ *Sam is heavy into Mary.*

heavy joint *n.* a marijuana cigarette tipped with phencyclidine (P.C.P.). (Drugs.) ☐ *He said something about smoking a heavy joint just before he passed out.* ☐ *Bob found something on the sidewalk he called a heavy joint.*

heavy metal **1.** *n.* a type of rock music characterized by enormous volume and a throbbing beat. ☐ *I just don't care for that heavy metal.* ☐ *Heavy metal is just too loud.* **2.** *mod.* having to do with *heavy metal* music or musicians. ☐ *Heavy metal stuff is a little harsh for my old ears.* ☐ *Those heavy metal guys must have made a fortune.*

heavy money See *heavy bread.*

heavy necking *n.* hugging and kissing, plus intimate caresses. ☐ *Mary and Sam are past heavy necking.* ☐ *The teacher caught them at some heavy necking in the closet.*

heavy scene *n.* a serious state of affairs; an emotionally charged situation. ☐ *Man, that meeting was really a heavy scene.* ☐ *Another heavy scene like that and I quit.*

heavy soul *n.* heroin. (Black.) ☐ *Tyrone is hung up on some heavy soul.* ☐ *That heavy soul will be on your back forever.*

heavyweight **1.** *n.* an important person; a successful person; a leader. ☐ *Mr. Wilson is a heavyweight in local government.* ☐ *They'll bring out the heavyweights next time. Just wait and see.* **2.** *mod.* important; successful. ☐ *Vince is one of the heavyweight operators in this business.* ☐ *He's good, but he's no heavyweight.*

heebie-jeebies AND **heeby-jeebies** ['hibi-'dʒibiz] *n.* an extreme case of anxiety or fear. ☐ *I have the heebie-jeebies whenever I go to the dentist.* ☐ *These movies give me the heebie-jeebies.*

heeby-jeebies See the previous entry.

heel *n.* a low and despicable man. ☐ *You are the most impossible heel!* ☐ *The guy is a heel, and he seems to work at it, too.*

heeled **1.** *mod.* alcohol intoxicated. ☐ *Sally was too heeled to drive home.* ☐ *Man, were those guys heeled!* **2.** *mod.* carrying drugs. (Drugs.) ☐ *Max is heeled and ready to deal.* ☐ *Gert was heeled when they arrested her.*

heesh [hiʃ] *n.* hashish; cannabis. (Drugs.) ☐ *Ernie started out on heesh and moved on from there.* ☐ *Who's dealing heesh around here?*

Heinz 57 (variety) [hɑɪnz . . .] *n.* a mongrel breed of dog. (From the trade name of a condiment company.) ☐ *We have one pedigreed dog and one Heinz 57 variety.* ☐ *My Heinz 57 is the greatest dog of all.*

heist [hɑɪst] **1.** *n.* a theft; a robbery; a *lift.* (Underworld.) ☐ *Lefty just had to pull one last heist.* ☐ *The heist went off without a hitch.* **2.** *tr.* to steal something; to rob a person or place; to *lift* something. (Underworld.) ☐ *The thugs heisted her and took her purse and watch.* ☐ *Lefty heisted a car and then drove around in it all evening.*

heister ['hɑɪstɚ] *n.* a drunkard. ☐ *Two old heisters were lifting drink after drink and tossing them down.* ☐ *Wally is getting to be quite a heister.*

helium head ['hiliəm 'hɛd] *n.* a fool; an airhead. ☐ *Well, what's that helium head done now?* ☐ *You can be such a helium head without even trying.*

hell 1. *n.* trouble. (Use caution with *hell.*) ☐ *I went through all sorts of hell to get this done on time.* ☐ *This day was real hell.* **2.** *exclam.* "Damn!" (Usually **Hell!** Use caution with *hell.*) ☐ *Oh, hell. I'm late.* ☐ *Hell, I'm too early.*

hell of a mess *n.* a terrible mess. (See also *mell of a hess.* Use caution with *hell.*) ☐ *This is really a hell of a mess you've gotten us into.* ☐ *I never dreamed I'd come back to such a hell of a mess.*

hell of a note *n.* a surprising or amazing piece of news. (Use caution with *hell.*) ☐ *Well, that's a hell of a note!* ☐ *You forgot it. That's a hell of a note.*

hell of a someone or something AND **helluva someone or something 1.** *n.* a very bad person or thing. (Use caution with *hell.*) ☐ *That's a hell of a way to treat someone.* ☐ *He's a hell of a driver! Watch out!* **2.** *n.* a very good person or thing. (Use caution with *hell.*) ☐ *He is one hell of a guy. We really like him.* ☐ *We had a helluva good time.*

hell-on-wheels *n.* a very impressive person or thing; an extreme type of person or thing. (Use caution with *hell.*) ☐ *Fred is really hell-on-wheels when it comes to getting those little jobs done on time.* ☐ *This little machine is hell-on-wheels for general woodworking purposes.*

hell raiser See *heller.*

hellacious [hɛl'eʃəs] **1.** *mod.* wild; excellent. (Use caution with *hell.*) ☐ *What a hellacious good time we had!* ☐ *Sally throws one hellacious party.* **2.** *mod.* terrible. ☐ *The food was just hellacious. Yuck!* ☐ *The heat was hellacious, and the mosquitoes wouldn't leave us alone.*

hellbender ['hɛlbɛndɚ] **1.** *n.* a drinking bout. (Use caution with *hell.*) ☐ *Jed is off on another of his hellbenders.* ☐ *One of his hellbenders can last for a week.* **2.** *n.* a heavy drinker; a drunkard. (The *bender* refers to bending the elbow with a drink in hand. Use caution with *hell.*) ☐ *Wally is a hellbender from way back.* ☐ *Jed is a world-class hellbender.*

heller AND **hell raiser** *n.* a rowdy person; a hell-raising person. (Use caution with *hell.*) ☐ *Ernie was a real heller when he was younger.* ☐ *A bunch of hell raisers kept me up late last night.*

hellhole *n.* a hot and crowded place; any unpleasant place. (Use caution with *hell.*) ☐ *I want out of this hellhole.* ☐ *The theater was an over-crowded hellhole. Lucky there was no fire.*

hellpig *n.* a fat and ugly girl or woman. (Derogatory.) ☐ *Who was that hellpig you were out with last night?* ☐ *Comb your hair. You look like some hellpig!*

Hell's bells (and buckets of blood)! *exclam.* "Dammit!" (Use caution with *hell.*) ☐ *Oh, hell's bells and buckets of blood! I forgot my keys.* ☐ *Hell's bells! I'm late.*

helluva someone or something See *hell of a someone or something.*

hemp 1. *n.* a smelly cigar. ☐ *Get that vile hemp out of here!* ☐ *Can you imagine somebody bringing an old hemp like that in here?* **2.** *n.* cannabis. (Drugs.) ☐ *The guy sort of smells like hemp.* ☐ *I smell hemp in here.*

hen fruit *n.* hen's eggs. ☐ *I always have hen fruit for breakfast.* ☐ *There's nothing like hen fruit and bacon.*

hen party *n.* a gossipy party attended by women. ☐ *I have a hen party every few weeks. We love to get together.* ☐ *I wouldn't be caught dead at one of those hen parties.*

hep [hɛp] *mod.* aware; informed. ☐ *The chick is simply not hep.* ☐ *Fred is one of the most hep guys you're going to run into.*

hepped (up) *n. mod.* alcohol intoxicated. ☐ *Wally is a little too hepped up to drive home.* ☐ *Harry's too hepped to stand up.*

herb AND **erb** *n.* marijuana. (Drugs.) ☐ *Bruno is very fond of herb.* ☐ *Carl has found a way to synthesize the erb.*

Herb and Al *n.* marijuana and alcohol. □ *I'm afraid that Tom's best friends are Herb and Al.* □ *Wally asked us over to meet Herb and Al.*

Here's looking at you. *sent.* "I salute you." (A polite drinking toast.) □ *Well, here's looking at you.* □ *Here's looking at you. Bottoms up!*

Here's mud in your eye. *sent.* "I salute you." (A jocular drinking toast.) □ *Here's mud in your eye. Bottoms up!* □ *Well, here's mud in your eye. Care for another?*

hero (of the underworld) *n.* heroin. □ *Don says he knows the hero of the underworld well.* □ *Bruno stays away from hero.*

herped up *mod.* infected with the *herpes simplex* virus. □ *Why do all the boys treat me like I was herped up or something?* □ *They say all those frat guys are herped up.*

herpie ['hɚpi] *n.* a person infected with the *herpes simplex* virus. □ *Oo, somebody said he's a herpie!* □ *Stay away from that chick. She's a herpie.*

hey *interj.* hello. (A standard greeting in much of the South, and now, among the young.) □ *Hey, Walter. How are you?* □ *Hey, Chuck! Living large.*

Hey, bum! *interj.* hello. □ *Hey, bum! What's poppin'?* □ *Hey, bum! So good to see your smiling face.*

hi-res See *high-res.*

hickey AND **hicky** ['hɪki] **1.** *n.* a love bite; a mark on the skin caused by biting or sucking. (See also *monkey bite.*) □ *He's mad at her because she gave him a hicky.* □ *She wore a high collar to cover up a hickey.* **2.** *n.* a pimple, especially if infected. □ *There is a hickey on my nose!* □ *Wouldn't you know I'd get a hickey like this right when I have to have my picture taken!*

hicky See the previous entry.

hiddy AND **hidi** ['hɪdi] **1.** *mod.* hideous. □ *That skirt is just hiddi! Get a life!* □ *What hidi wheels! That car's owner has more money than sense.* **2.** *mod.* hideously drunk; very drunk. □ *Fred was totally hidi. He fell asleep under the table.* □ *Susan was not just drunk, she was hiddy—you know bombed.*

hide *n.* the skin. □ *I need to get some rays on my hide.* □ *Your hide looks pretty pale, all right.*

hides *n.* drums. (See also *skins.*) □ *Andy can really bang those hides.* □ *They say his hides are worth about 4,000 clams.*

hidi See *hiddy.*

high **1.** *mod.* alcohol or drug intoxicated. □ *Wally is a little high for so early in the evening.* □ *They went out for the evening to get high, and for no other reason.* **2.** *n.* a state of euphoria caused by drugs or alcohol. □ *His life is nothing but one high after another.* □ *Her only goal is a high.*

high and dry *mod.* abandoned; unsupported. (Like a ship beached or stranded ashore.) □ *He went off and left me high and dry.* □ *Here I sit high and dry —no food, no money, no nothing.*

high five **1.** *n.* a greeting where the palm of the hand is raised and slapped against another person's palm similarly raised. (Compare to *low five.*) □ *They exchanged a high five and went on with the show.* □ *How about a high five, man?* **2.** *tr. & in.* to greet someone as described in sense 1. □ *They high fived and went off together.* □ *Ted high fived Sam, and they stopped to talk.*

high mucky-muck [...'məkimək] *n.* an important person; the person in charge. □ *When the high mucky-mucks meet, they will decide what to do about the problem.* □ *Ted's father is a high mucky-muck at the gas company.*

high on something *mod.* excited or enthusiastic about something. □ *Tom is really high on the idea of going to Yellowstone this summer.* □ *I'm not high on going, but I will.*

high-res AND **hi-res** ['haɪ'rɛz] *mod.* good; satisfying. (From *high-resolution,* referring to the picture quality of a computer monitor. Compare to *low-res.*)

☐ *This is a real high-res day for me.* ☐ *I sure feel hi-res today.*

high roller *n.* a big gambler who risks much money; anyone who takes risks. (Refers to rolling dice.) ☐ *Rocko is a high roller and isn't afraid to lose some money.* ☐ *He's a high roller from way back.*

high sign *n.* a hand signal meaning "okay." (The tip of the index or middle finger touches the tip of the thumb, and the hand is raised into the air.) ☐ *Tom got the high sign and began to open the door.* ☐ *Give me the high sign when you want me to start.*

high ups AND **higher ups** *n.* the people in charge. ☐ *I have to speak to the high ups about the refund.* ☐ *One of the higher ups is coming down to talk to you.*

high, wide, and handsome *mod.* happy; carefree. ☐ *Wally is high, wide, and handsome after his great triumph.* ☐ *He sure looks high, wide, and handsome. I'm glad he's happy.*

highbrow 1. *n.* an intellectual person; a person with refined tastes. (Compare to *lowbrow.* See also *longhair.*) ☐ *Sam used to be a highbrow, but he gave up his fancy ways.* ☐ *The highbrows usually congregate in there.* **2.** *mod.* having to do with an intellectual or a person with refined tastes. ☐ *I just don't care for highbrow music.* ☐ *Pete is sort of highbrow, but he's an okay guy.*

higher ups See *high ups.*

highjinks AND **hijinks** ['hɑɪdʒɪŋks] *n.* tricks; capers. ☐ *Enough of your hijinks! Get busy.* ☐ *I like to hear about the kids and their latest hijinks.*

highway robbery *n.* a charge that is unbelievably high, but nonetheless unavoidable. (As if one had been accosted and robbed on the open road.) ☐ *But this is highway robbery. I demand to see the manager.* ☐ *Four thousand dollars! That's highway robbery!*

hijinks See *highjinks.*

hike 1. *n.* a monetary increase. ☐ *I need a pay hike.* ☐ *Another hike in the electric rates takes place this spring.* **2.** *tr.* to increase an amount of money. ☐ *I wanted them to hike my salary, but they refused.* ☐ *The utilities all hike their rates at least once a year.*

Hill *n.* the U.S. Congress; the U.S. capitol building located on Capitol Hill in Washington, D.C. (Always with *the.*) ☐ *I really can't tell what's happening up on the Hill.* ☐ *The Hill moves at its own speed.*

hincty ['hɪŋkti] *mod.* snobbish; fussy; aloof. (Black.) ☐ *Some of those people are so hincty.* ☐ *That hincty lady told me to turn my radio down.*

hip 1. *mod.* informed; aware. (See also *hep.*) ☐ *The guy is just not hip. He's a nerd.* ☐ *Get hip, Tom!* **2.** *tr.* to tell someone; to inform someone. ☐ *Hey, man, hip me to what's going on!* ☐ *What's happening? Take a minute and hip me!*

hip-shooter *n.* someone who talks without thinking; someone who speaks very frankly. (See also *shoot from the hip.*) ☐ *He's just a loudmouth hip-shooter. Pay no attention.* ☐ *The press secretary was a hyper and a hip-shooter. She won't last long.*

hipe See *hype.*

hippie See the following entry.

hippy AND **hippie** ['hɪpi] *n.* a long-haired, drug-using youth of the 1960's and 1970's. ☐ *That guy looks like a hippy left over from the sixties.* ☐ *Who's that has-been hippie who just came in?*

hipster ['hɪpstɚ] *n.* a youth of the 1950's, characterized by an interest in jazz and cool things. ☐ *Can you imagine your father as a hipster?* ☐ *Were the hipsters the ones with the big shoulder pads?*

hired gun *n.* a paid assassin. (Underworld.) ☐ *Bruno is Mr. Big's hired gun.* ☐ *The cops are holding a well-known hired gun until they can prepare charges.*

history *n.* someone or something in the past. (See also *ancient history, I'm history.*) ☐ *Dave? Oh, he's just history. I never go out with him anymore.* ☐ *Susan is just history. We're through.* ☐

Don't make a move! If this gun goes off, you're history.

hit 1. *n.* a success; something that meets with approval. (Often with *with*.) ☐ *The play was a hit.* ☐ *The fudge with nuts in it was a great hit at the sale.* 2. *n.* a successful result; something that is exactly as intended. ☐ *It was a hit—a real winner.* ☐ *Your idea was right on target—a hit for sure.* 3. *n.* a drink of liquor; a dose of a drug. (See also *bop*.) ☐ *He had a hit of sauce and went out to finish his work.* ☐ *She popped a hit by the water cooler.* 4. *tr.* to reach something; to achieve something. ☐ *The car hit ninety in no time at all.* ☐ *I hit sixty next month, and I'm going to retire.* 5. *tr.* to kill someone; to assassinate someone. (Underworld.) ☐ *Bruno was told to hit Max.* ☐ *The thug set out to hit the mayor, but got nabbed first.* 6. *tr.* to attack or rob someone or something. (Underworld.) ☐ *Lefty and his gang hit the bank for the second time.* ☐ *Can you believe that they tried to hit a block party on Fourth Street?* 7. *n.* a robbery; an assassination. (Underworld.) ☐ *There was a hit at the bank on Maple Street last night.* ☐ *Somebody died in the hit last night, but they don't know who yet.*

hit list *n.* a list of people to whom something is going to happen. ☐ *Ralph is on my hit list for contributing money for the orphans.* ☐ *She's on our hit list for volunteers.*

hit man 1. *n.* a hired killer. (Underworld.) ☐ *Bruno was the perfect hit man. Hardly any brains or conscience.* ☐ *To look at Rocko, you'd never believe he was a hit man.* 2. *n.* a man hired by a helpless addict to inject drugs. (Drugs. See also *pinch hitter*.) ☐ *Gert needed a hit man when she was sick.* ☐ *Max refuses to be a hit man. He says that's not what he does best.*

hit me 1. AND **hit me again** *tr.* (in gambling) "Deal me a card." ☐ *Hit me again, dealer!* ☐ *Okay, hit me.* 2. *tr.* "Give me the high five." ☐ *Hit me! Where you been? Hit me again!* ☐ *Long time, no see. Hit me, man.* 3. AND **hit me again** *tr.* "Serve me (another) drink." ☐ *Hit me again, bartender.* ☐ *It's empty. Hit me.*

hit me again See the previous entry.

hit on someone *in.* to flirt with someone; to make a pass at someone. ☐ *The women were all hitting on George, but he didn't complain.* ☐ *I just knew he was going to hit on me—but he didn't.*

hit on something *in.* to discover something. ☐ *She hit on a new scheme for removing the impurities from drinking water.* ☐ *I hit on it when I wasn't able to sleep one night.*

hit pay dirt AND **strike pay dirt** 1. *tr.* to discover something of value. ☐ *At last, we hit pay dirt.* ☐ *When we opened the last trunk, we knew we had hit pay dirt.* 2. *tr.* to get to the basic facts of something. ☐ *Now we're beginning to hit pay dirt.* ☐ *When we figured out the code, we really struck pay dirt.*

hit (someone) below the belt *tr.* to deal with someone unfairly. (Boxing.) ☐ *Don't hit below the belt!* ☐ *You were hitting Tom below the belt when you said that.*

hit someone (up) for something *tr.* to ask someone for something. ☐ *I hit Fred up for some help with the committee.* ☐ *He hit me up for a loan, but I said no.*

hit someone with something *tr.* to present someone with an idea, plan, or proposal. ☐ *Pete hit me with a great idea just before we left.* ☐ *Fred hit his boss with a plan to save a bundle in the front office.*

hit the books AND **pound the books** *tr.* to study hard. ☐ *I spent the weekend pounding the books.* ☐ *I gotta go home and hit the books.*

hit the booze See the following entry.

hit the bottle AND **hit the booze** *tr.* to go on a drinking bout; to get drunk. ☐ *Jed's hitting the bottle again.* ☐ *He's been hitting the booze for a week now.*

hit the bricks AND **hit the pavement** 1. *tr.* to start walking; to go into the streets. ☐ *I have a long way to go. I'd better hit the bricks.* ☐ *Go on! Hit the pavement!*

EAN/UPC/Title

Batch 011

8/29/2008
9:31:09

2 A

Quantity
5

780844209074

Title
SLANG AMER STYLE

Title#
01605296

Pub – Item#

Category
QP

Author
PEARS R

O Number
00138963

Unit ID

* U D35470731 *

ll ID
CELL027A

Get going! **2.** *tr.* to go out on strike. ☐ *The workers hit the pavement on Friday and haven't been back on the job since.* ☐ *Agree to our demands, or we hit the bricks.*

hit the bull's eye See *hit the spot.*

hit the ceiling AND **hit the roof** *tr.* to get very angry. ☐ *She really hit the ceiling when she found out what happened.* ☐ *My dad'll hit the roof when he finds out about this.*

hit the deck 1. *tr.* to get out of bed. ☐ *Come on, hit the deck! It's morning.* ☐ *Hit the deck! Time to rise and shine!* **2.** *tr.* to fall down; to drop down. ☐ *Hit the deck. Don't let them see you.* ☐ *I hit the deck the minute I heard the shots.*

hit the fan *tr.* to become publicly known; to become a scandal. (From the phrase "when the shit hit the fan.") ☐ *I wasn't even in the country when it hit the fan.* ☐ *It hit the fan, and within ten minutes the press had spread it all over the world.*

hit the hay AND **hit the sack** *tr.* to go to bed. ☐ *I have to go home and hit the hay pretty soon.* ☐ *Let's hit the sack. We have to get an early start in the morning.*

hit the jackpot 1. *tr.* to win a large amount of money. ☐ *I hit the jackpot in the big contest.* ☐ *Sally hit the jackpot in the lottery.* **2.** *tr.* to be exactly right; to find exactly what was sought. ☐ *I hit the jackpot when I found this little cafe on Fourth Street.* ☐ *I wanted a small house with a fireplace, and I really hit the jackpot with this one.*

hit the panic button AND **press the panic button; push the panic button** *tr.* to panic. ☐ *She hit the panic button and just went to pieces.* ☐ *Don't press the panic button. Relax and keep your eyes open.*

hit the pavement See *hit the bricks.*

hit the road *tr.* to leave; to begin to travel on a road. (See also *smack the road.*) ☐ *We plan to hit the road about dawn.* ☐ *Let's hit the road. We have a long way to go.*

hit the roof See *hit the ceiling.*

hit the sack See *hit the hay.*

hit the skids *tr.* to decline; to decrease in value or status. ☐ *Jed hit the skids when he started drinking.* ☐ *The firm hit the skids when the dollar collapsed.*

hit the spot 1. AND **hit the bull's eye** *tr.* to be exactly right. (See also *ring the bell.*) ☐ *You really hit the spot with that prediction.* ☐ *Pete's prediction hit the bull's eye.* **2.** *tr.* to be refreshing. ☐ *This cold water really hits the spot.* ☐ *I want something hot—some coffee would really hit the bull's eye.*

hit the trail *tr.* to leave. (As if one were riding a horse.) ☐ *I have to hit the trail before sunset.* ☐ *Let's hit the trail. It's late.*

hit under the wing *mod.* alcohol intoxicated. (See also *shot.*) ☐ *Jed got hit under the wing.* ☐ *Sally was a little hit under the wing, but she wasn't bad off at all.*

hitched *mod.* married. (Folksy.) ☐ *Sam and Mary decided to get hitched.* ☐ *They went out of state to get hitched.*

Hiya! ['haɪjə] *exclam.* "Hi!" (From *Hi, you!*) ☐ *Hiya! Good to see ya!* ☐ *Hiya! Where you been keeping yourself?*

ho-hum ['ho'həm] *mod.* dull; causing yawns. ☐ *Clare played another ho-hum concert at the music hall last night.* ☐ *It was a ho-hum lecture.*

ho-jo('s) ['hodʒo(z)] *n.* a Howard Johnson's restaurant or hotel. (Collegiate. Often with *the.*) ☐ *Let's hit ho-jo's for some grub.* ☐ *We're going to meet the others at the ho-jo.*

hock 1. *tr.* to pawn something. ☐ *I tried to hock my watch to get some money.* ☐ *I've got nothing left to hock.* **2.** *n.* the state of having been pawned. (Usually with *in.*) ☐ *My watch is already in hock.* ☐ *Get it out of hock or go buy a new one.* **3.** *n.* a foot. ☐ *My hocks are sore from all that walking.* ☐ *Have you ever seen such humongous hocks?*

hock a luggie ['hak ɑ 'lugi] *tr.* to cough up and spit out phlegm. ☐ *Wayne hocked a luggie right outside the classroom door and the teacher sent him to the* *principal's office.* □ *Tom suppressed the urge to hock a luggie over the bridge railing.*

hockey AND **hocky** ['hɑki] *mod.* dung. (See also *horse hockey.*) □ *Watch out for that hocky there in the gutter.* □ *Don't step in the fresh hockey.*

hockshop *n.* a pawnshop. □ *We took the watch to a hockshop, but couldn't get enough money for it.* □ *The cops checked all the hockshops in town for the murder weapon.*

hocky See *hockey.*

hocus *tr.* to falsify something; to adulterate something. □ *Who hocused the check?* □ *Somebody has hocused the booze.*

hodad AND **hodaddy** ['hodæd AND 'hodædi] *n.* an obnoxious person; a repellent person. (California.) □ *Ted is a total hodad.* □ *Who's the hodaddy in the plaid pants?*

hodaddy See the previous entry.

hog 1. AND **hog cadillac** *n.* a large car; a *souped up* car. (See also *road hog.*) □ *How do you like my new hog?* □ *That hog cadillac needs new shocks.* **2.** *n.* a police officer; a *pig.* □ *The hogs are on to you.* □ *Who called the hogs?* **3.** *n.* an addict who requires very large doses to sustain the habit. (Drugs.) □ *Gert isn't a hog. She tries to keep her habit small.* □ *Ernie is turning into a hog. He just can't get enough.* **4.** *n.* phencyclidine (P.C.P.), an animal tranquilizer. (Drugs.) □ *We're glad to learn that the demand for hog is tapering off.* □ *Max won't sell hog to kids these days.*

hog cadillac See the previous entry.

hog-wild *mod.* wild; boisterous. □ *All the kids were completely hog-wild by the time I got there.* □ *Things got sort of hog-wild while you were away.*

hogwash 1. *n.* bad food or drink. □ *This stuff is hogwash. Take it away.* □ *How about some more of this high-quality hogwash?* **2.** *n.* nonsense. □ *Now that's just hogwash, and you know it.* □ *Hogwash! That's about enough of your lies!*

hoist one *tr.* to have a drink. □ *Let's go out and hoist one sometime.* □ *Hey, Sam. Let's you and me hoist one.*

hokey ['hoki] *mod.* contrived; phony. □ *What a hokey way to deal with a perfectly honest request.* □ *That idea is too hokey.* □ *That's a pretty hokey idea, but it may work.*

hokum ['hokəm] *n.* nonsense. □ *All that is just hokum.* □ *No more hokum. I want the truth.*

hold *tr. & in.* to possess drugs. (Drugs.) □ *Gert was holding coke when she was arrested.* □ *Max is holding and wants to deal.*

hold all the aces *tr.* to be in control of everything. □ *The boss holds all the aces on this deal.* □ *I'll come out okay. I hold all the aces.*

Hold everything! *exclam.* "Stop everything!" □ *Hold everything! I forgot my wallet.* □ *Hold everything! My door isn't closed.*

Hold it! *exclam.* "Stop right there!" □ *Hold it! Stop!* □ *That's enough! Hold it!*

Hold it, Buster! *exclam.* "Stop that, mister!" (Sometimes said by women in repulsing an arduous male.) □ *Hold it, Buster! Who do you think you are?* □ *Hold it, Buster! Who do you think I am?*

hold one's high *tr.* to behave reasonably well under the influence of drugs. □ *Gert is having a harder and harder time holding her high.* □ *Ernie can't hold his high. What a creep!*

hold one's horses *tr.* to wait up; to relax and slow down; to be patient. (Usually a command.) □ *Hold your horses! Don't get in a hurry.* □ *Now, just hold your horses and let me explain.*

hold one's liquor *tr.* to be able to drink alcohol in quantity without ill effects. □ *Old Jed can sure hold his liquor—and a lot of it, too.* □ *I asked him to leave because he can't hold his liquor.*

Hold some, fold some. *sent.* to hold some of your stocks and sell some. (Securities markets.) □ *My best advice right now is to hold some, fold some. There is no real* *trend to the market.* □ *The stock market was so lackluster that I decided to hold some, fold some.*

hold the fort *tr.* to remain behind and take care of things. □ *Hold the fort. I'll be there in a while.* □ *I left John there to hold the fort.*

hold water *tr.* [for an idea, plan, etc.] to survive evaluation or scrutiny. □ *Nothing you've said so far holds water.* □ *Her story doesn't hold water.*

hole *n.* a despised person; an *asshole.* (Use caution with the topic. Also a term of address.) □ *Sam is such a hole. He needs human being lessons.* □ *You stupid hole! Watch what you're doing!*

hole in the wall *n.* a tiny shop, not much wider than its doorway. □ *I went into this little hole in the wall where they had the nicest little gifts.* □ *His office is just a hole in the wall.*

hole up *in.* to hide (somewhere). □ *Lefty wanted to hole up somewhere till things cooled down.* □ *I just want to hole up until the whole matter is settled.*

holiday cheer *n.* liquor, especially liquor drunk at Christmas and New Year's. □ *I think he had a little too much holiday cheer.* □ *Would you care for a little holiday cheer?*

holier-than-thou *mod.* superior in piety; condescending. □ *She has such a holier-than-thou attitude.* □ *Tracy can act so holier-than-thou sometimes.*

Hollywood **1.** *mod.* having phony glitter. □ *Who is this Hollywood dame who just came in?* □ *This whole thing is just too Hollywood.* **2.** *n.* a gaudily dressed person in sunglasses. (Also a term of address.) □ *Hey, Hollywood! What's cooking?* □ *Ask Hollywood over there to take off his shades and make himself known.*

holmes [homz] *n.* one's pal or friend. (A variant of *homes.* See also *Sherlock.* Usually a term of address.) □ *Hey, holmes, how ya living?* □ *What do you think about that, holmes?*

Holy cow! *exclam.* "Wow!" □ *Holy cow! A red one!* □ *Give me a chance! Holy cow, don't rush me!*

holy Joe **1.** *n.* a chaplain; a cleric; a clergyman. □ *I went to see the holy Joe, and he was a lot of help.* □ *Old holy Joe wants to see all of us at services.* **2.** *n.* a very pious person. □ *Martin looks stuffy, but he's no holy Joe.* □ *Don't let that holy Joe hear about what you've done.*

Holy mackerel! ['holi 'mækrəl] *exclam.* "Wow!" □ *Holy mackerel! What a day!* □ *Holy mackerel! What's this?*

Holy moley! ['holi 'moli] *exclam.* "Wow!" □ *Holy moley! A whole quarter!* □ *Look, here's another one! Holy moley!*

holy stink *n.* anything repellent. □ *You really created a holy stink with that silly remark.* □ *What is this holy stink about broken windows?*

holy terror *n.* a devilish person; a badly behaving child. □ *Jimmy has become a holy terror lately.* □ *Why is the boss such a holy terror today?*

hombre ['ɑmbre] *n.* a man. (From Spanish.) □ *Who's that hombre who just came in?* □ *Now, he's a strange sort of hombre.*

home-brew *n.* homemade liquor or beer. □ *Is this your own home-brew, Wally?* □ *My uncle makes his own home-brew.*

homeboy AND **homegirl** *n.* a buddy; a pal. (Originally between blacks. Also a term of address. *Homeboy* is for males and *homegirl* is for females.) □ *Come on, homeboy. Help out a friend.* □ *She's my homegirl, and I'd do anything for her.*

homegirl See the previous entry.

homegrown **1.** *mod.* local; folksy; amateur. □ *Everyone enjoyed Sally's homegrown humor.* □ *The homegrown talent at the fair was just as entertaining as anything could have been.* **2.** *n.* marijuana grown domestically or locally. (Drugs.) □ *She'd rather use homegrown than have to deal with Max.* □ *This homegrown is from the pots in her room.*

homer [ˈhomɚ] **1.** *n.* a home run in baseball. ☐ *Wilbur hit one homer after another.* ☐ *Another homer for our team!* **2.** *tr. & in.* to hit a home run. ☐ *Wilbur homered another one and brought in two runs with him.* ☐ *Sam has never homered in six years of playing,*

homes AND **homey; homie** *n.* a buddy; a pal. (Originally between blacks. Also a term of address. See also *holmes.*) ☐ *Hey, homes! How's it going?* ☐ *Me and my homie want to go with you.*

homeslice *n.* a *homeboy;* a *homegirl.* ☐ *Ask my homeslice over there if he wants to go with you.* ☐ *Well, homeslice, what now?*

homespun *n.* homemade liquor or beer. ☐ *Jed offered a little of his homespun round the table.* ☐ *How about a swig of homespun?*

homey See *homes.*

homie See *homes.*

homo [ˈhomo] **1.** *mod.* homosexual. (Often derogatory. Resented by homosexual persons.) ☐ *Is this one of those homo bars?* ☐ *Where'd you get those homo shoes?* **2.** *n.* a homosexual person. (Often derogatory. Resented by homosexual persons.) ☐ *Somebody said she is a homo.* ☐ *So what if he's a homo? He can still vote, can't he?*

honcho [ˈhɑntʃo] **1.** *n.* the head man; the boss. (Useable for either sex.) ☐ *The marketing honcho couldn't say when the product would be on the shelves.* ☐ *The top honcho at the water department was no help at all.* **2.** *tr.* to manage or boss something. ☐ *Who's supposed to honcho this affair?* ☐ *I'll honcho it until Larry gets here.*

honest injun [ˈɑnəst ˈɪndʒən] *interj.* "It is true." ☐ *You actually did that? Honest injun?* ☐ *Sure I did, honest injun.*

honey [ˈhəni] *n.* beer. ☐ *Let's stop at the happy shop and get some honey.* ☐ *You want another can of honey?*

honey cart See *honey wagon.*

honey of a something *n.* a very special something; an excellent example of something. ☐ *This is a honey of a car. Wanna drive it?* ☐ *Now here's a honey of a little stereo receiver.*

honey wagon **1.** AND **honey cart** *n.* any vehicle used for or designed for carrying excrement: a farm manure wagon; a tank truck used to pump out septic tanks; a tank truck used to pump out airplane toilets; a portable latrine truck used in movie making. ☐ *I drove a honey wagon in Hollywood for a year. How's that for glamour?* ☐ *The honey cart was stalled with a flat tire in front of the plane.* **2.** *n.* a beer truck. ☐ *What time does the honey wagon bring in new supplies?* ☐ *I drove a honey cart in the city for a while.*

honeybunch *n.* a sweetheart. (Also a term of address.) ☐ *Look, honeybunch, let's hurry up. We're late.* ☐ *I can't wait to get back and see my honeybunch.*

honeycakes See *babycakes.*

honeymoon (period) AND **honeymoon stage** *n.* an early stage in any activity, before problems set in. ☐ *Of course, this is still the honeymoon stage, but everything seems to be going all right.* ☐ *The honeymoon is over, Carl. You have to produce now.*

honeymoon stage See the previous entry.

Hong Kong dog [ˈhɔŋ ˈkɔŋ ˈdɔg] *n.* diarrhea; a case of diarrhea. ☐ *Andy has a touch of the Hong Kong dog and needs some medicine.* ☐ *I got rid of the Hong Kong dog by meditating.*

honk **1.** *n.* a drinking spree; a *toot.* ☐ *Jed's last honk lasted nearly a week.* ☐ *The guys went off on the honk to end all honks.* **2.** *n.* a white male; a *honky.* (Black. Not necessarily derogatory.) ☐ *Who's the honk who keeps driving by?* ☐ *There are mainly honks where I work.* **3.** *in.* to vomit. (Onomatopoetic.) ☐ *I can hear someone in the john honking like mad.* ☐ *Who honked on the driveway?*

honked AND **honkers** *mod.* alcohol intoxicated. ☐ *Wally was too honked to stand up.* ☐ *Man, is that guy honkers!*

honker **1.** *n.* a goose. (Juvenile.) ☐ *A whole flock of honkers settled on our* *pond.* □ *Can we have honker for Thanksgiving dinner?* **2.** *n.* a strange or eccentric person. □ *Clare is a real honker these days. Is she all right?* □ *Martin is a classic honker.*

honkers See *honked.*

honkey See *honky.*

honkie See the following entry.

honky AND **honkey; honkie; hunky** ['hɔŋki] **1.** *n.* a Caucasian. (Black. Not necessarily derogatory. Probably a pronunciation variant of *hunky.*) □ *The honkies are taking over this neighborhood.* □ *Some honky was around asking for you.* **2.** *mod.* in the manner of a Caucasian; white-like. □ *Where'd you get that honky car?* □ *That's honky music. I want to hear soul.*

honyock ['hɑnjɑk] *n.* someone, usually a male, who acts like a peasant; a crude or unsophisticated person; a rustic oaf. (Old. Also a rude or playful term of address.) □ *Steve seems like such a honyock until you get to know him.* □ *Come here, you silly honyock.*

hoo-ha ['huhɑ] **1.** *n.* a commotion. □ *What is all this hoo-ha about?* □ *A deer created quite a hoo-ha by running frantically through the department store.* **2.** *n.* nonsense. □ *What is all this hoo-ha about your leaving the company?* □ *Stop talking hoo-ha and tell the truth.*

hooch AND **hootch** [hutʃ] *n.* hard liquor; any alcoholic beverage. □ *Let's go guzzle some hooch.* □ *More hootch for you?*

hooch head See the following entry.

hooch hound AND **hooch head** *n.* a drunkard. □ *Jed is a classic hooch hound. He lives for the stuff.* □ *The party turned into a drinking session for hooch heads.*

hooched (up) *mod.* alcohol intoxicated. □ *Sally is too hooched to drive.* □ *She got herself hooched up and couldn't give her talk.*

hoocher AND **hootcher** *n.* a drunkard. □ *Ernie isn't a hoocher, you can say that for him.* □ *A hootcher staggered in and staggered right out again.*

hood *n.* a hoodlum. □ *A couple of hoods hassled us on the street.* □ *That hood should be behind bars.*

hooey ['hui] *n.* nonsense. □ *The whole newspaper is nothing but hooey today.* □ *What's all this hooey about getting a new car?*

hoof it 1. *tr.* to run away. □ *I saw them coming and hoofed it home.* □ *Lefty hoofed it when he saw the uniform.* **2.** *in.* to walk instead of ride. □ *My car's broken down, so I had to hoof it to work today.* □ *Let's hoof it over to the library.*

hoofer *n.* a (professional) dancer. □ *Clare was a hoofer when she was younger and lighter.* □ *She was a hoofer on Broadway.*

hoofing *n.* walking; running. □ *My car's in the shop, so I'm hoofing for a few days.* □ *Two or three of the kids were hoofing around the mall, so I joined them.*

hook 1. *tr.* to cheat someone. □ *Watch the clerk in that store. He might try to hook you.* □ *They hooked me on the car deal.* **2.** *tr.* to steal something. □ *Lefty hooked a couple of candy bars just for the hell of it.* □ *What did they hook last night?* **3.** *tr.* to addict someone (to something). (Not necessarily drugs.) □ *The constant use of bicarb hooked him to the stuff.* □ *The pot hooked him.* **4.** *n.* the grade of C. □ *I didn't study at all and I still got a hook!* □ *I got three hooks and a D this semester.* **5.** *tr.* to earn or "pull" the grade of C on something in school. □ *History? I hooked it without any trouble.* □ *If I can just hook algebra, I'll stay off probation.*

hook, line, and sinker *mod.* totally. □ *She fell for it hook, line, and sinker.* □ *They believed every word hook, line, and sinker.*

hook shop *n.* a brothel. (See also *hooker.*) □ *Guess who I saw coming out of a hook shop?* □ *There is a secret hook shop over on Maple Street.*

hook something down *tr.* to swallow something down. □ *He hooked a drink* *down and turned to face his brother.* T *Hook down one of these cookies and see what you think about them.*

hooked (on someone or something) 1. *mod.* [with *something*] addicted (to a drug). □ *Gert is hooked on horse.* □ *Everybody knows she is hooked.* **2.** *mod.* preferring someone or something; enamored of someone or something. □ *I'm really hooked on chocolate anything.* □ *Sam is hooked on Mary for good.* **3.** *mod.* [with *something*] cheated. □ *I was really hooked on this travel deal.* □ *You were hooked all right.*

hooker *n.* a prostitute. □ *There were some hookers standing right on that corner.* □ *Clare dresses like a hooker.*

hooks *n.* the hands. (See also *meathooks.*) □ *Get your hooks off my newspaper!* □ *Don't stand there with your hooks in your pocket. Get busy!*

hoopla ['hupla OR 'huplə] *n.* an outcry; a fuss or a *to-do.* □ *What's all this hoopla about?* □ *There is too much hoopla in these elections.*

hoops *n.* the game of basketball. □ *You wanna go play some hoops?* □ *Welcome to another evening of college hoops, brought to you by the Nova Motor Company.*

hoosegow ['husgau] *n.* a jail. □ *Learning to read can shorten one's time in the hoosegow.* □ *The judge threw the punk in the hoosegow for a few days.*

hoot 1. *in.* to laugh loudly. □ *The audience screamed and hooted with their appreciation.* □ *They howled and hooted. I know they just loved it.* **2.** *n.* a joke; something laughable. □ *The whole business was a terrific hoot.* □ *The skit was a hoot, and everyone enjoyed it.* **3.** *in.* to boo at someone's performance. □ *The audience hooted until the performer fled the stage in disgrace.* □ *They hooted for a few minutes after she left the stage.*

hootch See *hooch.*

hootcher See *hoocher.*

hoo(t)chfest *n.* a drinking bout; a drinking party. □ *We stopped by Sally's to join in the hoochfest for a while.* □ *Let's throw a big hootchfest next month.*

hooted *mod.* alcohol intoxicated. □ *Jed got himself good and hooted.* □ *Ted is too hooted to drive.*

hooter 1. *n.* a nose; a big nose. □ *I sort of wish my hooter wasn't so doggone big.* □ *He blew his hooter and went back to his reading.* **2.** *n.* a drink of liquor. □ *He tossed back a big hooter of booze and stood there a minute.* □ *Have another hooter?* **3.** *n.* cocaine. (Drugs.) □ *Max is known for his high-quality hooter.* □ *Where can I get some hooter around here?*

hop 1. *n.* beer. □ *Pretty good hops, Tom.* □ *How about some hop with your hamburger?* **2.** *n.* a dancing party for young people. □ *The kids are out at some school-sponsored hop.* □ *The hop was a lot of fun.* **3.** *tr.* to get aboard a plane or train. □ *I'll hop a plane and be there in a couple of hours.* □ *Hop a train or anything, but get here as soon as you can.*

Hop to it! *exclam.* "Get moving!"; "Hurry up!" □ *Hop to it! I don't pay you to stand around.* □ *I need it now! Hop to it!*

hopfest *n.* a beer-drinking party. □ *We went to a big hopfest over at Wally's, but it broke up early.* □ *That was some hopfest! No potato chips!*

hophead 1. *n.* an alcoholic or a drunkard. □ *I'm afraid that Wally is becoming a hophead.* □ *Ernie is a well-established and incurable hophead.* **2.** *n.* a drug user; someone under the effects of drugs. (Drugs.) □ *The hopheads are taking over this part of town.* □ *What happens to these hopheads when they grow up?*

hopped up 1. *mod.* stimulated by drugs. (Drugs.) □ *The two of them were hopped up most of the time.* □ *Two hopped up kids were hunkered down in the alley.* **2.** *mod.* (having to do with a car that is) customized and speeded up. □ *As soon as I get this hog hopped up, you'll see some real speed.* □ *Sam drives a hopped up old Ford.* **3.** *mod.* excited. □ *Paul is certainly hopped up* *about something.* □ *Why are you so hopped up?*

hopping mad *mod.* very angry; angry and jumping up and down. □ *I was hopping mad about the broken window.* □ *The boss was hopping mad at the secretary.*

horizontal *mod.* alcohol intoxicated. □ *The boss was horizontal at the Christmas party.* □ *Stewed? No, he's totally horizontal!*

horn 1. *n.* the nose. □ *He scratched his horn with his pencil and opened his mouth to speak.* □ *He had the most humongous horn I have ever seen on man or beast.* **2.** *n.* the telephone. □ *Get Mrs. Wilson on the horn, please.* □ *She's on the horn now. What'll I tell her?* **3.** *tr.* to sniff or *snort* a narcotic. (Drugs.) □ *Ernie horned a line and paused for a minute.* □ *He'd rather horn it than shoot it.*

horner 1. *n.* a heavy drinker; a drunkard. □ *Wally is a real horner. He has an enormous capacity.* □ *Jed is the king of horners around here.* **2.** *n.* a cocaine user. (Drugs.) □ *Sure, Max is a horner. He sells the stuff to support his own habit.* □ *I think the new employee is a horner.*

horny *mod.* sexually aroused. (Use caution with the topic.) □ *Tom said he was horny.* □ *Who is that horny jerk?* □ *All the guys in that fraternity are horny.*

horrors 1. *n.* the delirium tremens. □ *The old wino had the horrors all the time.* □ *He has a bad case of the horrors.* **2.** *n.* frightening hallucinations from drugs. (Drugs.) □ *Once he had gone through the horrors, he swore off for good.* □ *Pete had the horrors and had to be hospitalized.*

horse 1. *n.* heroin. (Drugs.) □ *Now, horse is all that Gert will touch.* □ *Horse is still very popular in the big cities.* **2.** *n.* horse dung. □ *I use horse on my vegetables.* □ *I got a job shoveling horse out of the stables.*

horse around *in.* to work inefficiently; to *goof around.* □ *Stop horsing around and get busy.* □ *You guys are always horsing around.*

horse doctor *n.* a doctor. (Derogatory. Originally referred to a veterinarian.) □ *That horse doctor says there's nothing wrong with me.* □ *My horse doctor says everything is wrong with me.*

horse hockey 1. *n.* horse dung. □ *I try to get horse hockey for my garden.* □ *You don't see horse hockey in the streets anymore.* **2.** *n.* nonsense. □ *I've heard enough of your horse hockey.* □ *The guy specializes in producing horse hockey for the gossip columns.*

horse laugh *n.* a mocking and sarcastic laugh. □ *He came out with a horse laugh that caused some eyebrows to raise.* □ *The horse laugh from the back of the room did not go unnoticed.*

horse opera *n.* a Western movie. (See also *oater.*) □ *They're showing a series of old horse operas at the theater tonight.* □ *Haven't I seen this horse opera before? About a hundred times maybe?*

horsed AND **on the horse** *mod.* under the effects of heroin; addicted to heroin. (Drugs.) □ *Gert was totally horsed.* □ *How long have you been on the horse?*

Horsefeathers! *exclam.* "Phooey!"; "Nonsense!" □ *Oh, horsefeathers! You're nuts!* □ *Horsefeathers! I did no such thing!*

horseradish *n.* heroin. (See also *horse.*) □ *Max can get you some horseradish.* □ *Gert is hooked on horseradish.*

horses *n.* horse power, as in an engine. □ *How many horses does this thing have?* □ *Isn't 400 horses a lot for just one car?*

horse's ass *n.* a fool. (Crude. Potentially offensive. Use only with discretion.) □ *My ex-husband was a real horse's ass.* □ *Stop being such a horse's ass and listen to some sense.*

hose someone down *tr.* to kill someone. (Underworld. From the image of spraying someone with bullets.) □ *Mr. Big told Bruno to hose Max down.* 🅃 *The thugs tried to hose down the witness.*

hoser ['hozɚ] **1.** *n.* a good guy or buddy. ☐ *You're a real hoser, Ted.* ☐ *Old Fred is a good hoser. He'll help.* **2.** *n.* a cheater or deceiver. ☐ *Stop acting like a hoser and tell me the truth!* ☐ *You dirty lying hoser!*

hoska See *(ma)hoska.*

hot 1. AND **hot under the collar** *mod.* angry. ☐ *Don't get so hot under the collar. Chill, man.* ☐ *What a hot dude!* ☐ *Gee, that guy is really hot. What did I do?* **2.** *mod.* wanted by the police. (Underworld.) ☐ *Lefty is hot because of his part in the bank job.* ☐ *Bruno was hot and wanted somebody to hide him.* **3.** *mod.* stolen. ☐ *This watch is hot. Keep it.* ☐ *Rocko won't touch a hot watch or anything else hot.* **4.** *mod.* carrying contraband and subject to arrest if caught. ☐ *Max was hot and on the run.* ☐ *Lefty was hot and needed a place to stay.* **5.** *mod.* having a run of good luck in gambling. ☐ *I'm hot tonight! Here I go again.* ☐ *I was hot when I started. I'm broke now.* **6.** *mod.* of great renown; doing quite well for the time being. ☐ *The opera tenor was hot, and even the lowbrows would pay to hear him.* ☐ *The dancer was hot and was offered movie roles and all sorts of things.* **7.** *mod.* alcohol intoxicated. ☐ *You could see that Wally was pretty hot from all the whisky.* ☐ *He was too hot to stand up.* **8.** *mod.* selling well. ☐ *These things are really hot this season.* ☐ *Now, here's a hot item.* **9.** *mod.* sexy; sexually aroused. ☐ *Man, is that chick hot!* ☐ *She's not my idea of hot.* ☐ *Wow, who was that hot hunk you were with?*

hot air *n.* boasting; lying; nonsense. ☐ *I've heard enough of your hot air.* ☐ *That's just a lot of hot air. Ignore it.*

hot check *n.* a bad check. ☐ *The crook got picked up after passing a hot check.* ☐ *The clerk got in trouble for taking a hot check.*

Hot diggety (dog)! ['hɑt 'dɪgədi ('dɔg)] *exclam.* "Wow!" ☐ *Hot diggety dog! I won!* ☐ *I made it on time. Hot diggety!*

Hot dog! *exclam.* "Wow!" ☐ *Hot dog! It's my turn.* ☐ *Look at that! Hot dog! It's coming this way!*

hotdog *in.* to show off. ☐ *The coach said, "Stop hotdogging and play ball, you guys."* ☐ *It's just like Wayne to hotdog when he should be paying attention to the game.*

hot head *n.* a person with a bad or quick temper. ☐ *Max is a hot head. Watch out.* ☐ *Don't be such a hot head, Chuck.*

hot item 1. *n.* an item that sells well. ☐ *This little thing is a hot item this season.* ☐ *Now here's a hot item that everybody is looking for.* **2.** *n.* a romantically serious couple. ☐ *Sam and Mary are quite a hot item lately.* ☐ *A hot item like Bill and Clare isn't likely to show up for the party.*

hot number 1. *n.* an exciting piece of music. ☐ *Now here's a hot number by the Wanderers.* ☐ *Another hot number after this message.* **2.** *n.* an attractive or sexy *girl* or woman. ☐ *She's quite a hot number.* ☐ *Who's that hot number I saw you with last night?*

hot paper *n.* bad checks; a bad check. (Underworld. See also *hot check.*) ☐ *Tracy got caught passing hot paper.* ☐ *That teller can spot hot paper a mile away.*

hot potato *n.* a difficult problem. ☐ *I sure don't want to have to deal with that hot potato.* ☐ *This one is a hot potato. Ignore it for a while.*

(hot) rod *n.* a car that has been customized for power and speed by the owner. ☐ *My rod'll outrun yours any day.* ☐ *Is that a hot rod or a junk heap?*

hot seat 1. *n.* the electric chair. (Underworld.) ☐ *Lefty, you're headed for the hot seat.* ☐ *The hot seat is just waiting for you, Lefty.* **2.** *n.* the position of being scrutinized. ☐ *I was in the hot seat for about an hour, but they didn't learn anything from me.* ☐ *This new information puts Tom in the hot seat, doesn't it?*

(hot) skinny *n.* inside information. ☐ *What's the skinny on the tower clock?* ☐ *I've got the hot skinny on Mary and her boyfriend.*

hot stuff *n.* a person who acts superior (to others). (Also a term of address.) ☐ *What makes you think you're such* *hot stuff?* □ *Hey, hot stuff, come down here and say that.*

hot tip *n.* a special bit of information that ought to be reliable. □ *Ted got a hot tip on a horse.* □ *I phoned in a hot tip about a news story to the papers.*

hot under the collar See *hot.*

hot wire *tr.* to start a car without a key. □ *Lefty hot wired the car and used it for an hour or two.* □ *Isn't it illegal to hot wire a car?*

Hot ziggety! ['hɑt 'zɪgədi] *exclam.* "Wow!" □ *Hot ziggety! I made it!* □ *The plane's on time! Hot ziggety!*

hotbed of something *n.* a nest of something; a gathering place of something. □ *This office is a hotbed of lazy people.* □ *My class is a hotbed of nerds.*

hotkey *n.* one or more keys on a computer keyboard that will bring forth a special computer applications program. (Computers.) □ *The hotkeys for my thesaurus are "control" and "F2."* □ *Press the hotkey to bring up a calendar.*

hotshot 1. *n.* an important and energetic person. (Often used sarcastically. Also a term of address.) □ *If you're such a hotshot, why not straighten out the whole thing?* □ *Look, hotshot, get busy, will you?* **2.** AND **hot-shot** *mod.* brilliant; great. □ *Wally is becoming a real hot-shot tenor with the local opera company.* □ *So, you're the hot-shot guy who's going to straighten this place out?*

hotsy-totsy ['hɑtsi'tɑtsi] *mod.* fine; great. □ *Well, isn't that just hotsy-totsy.* □ *I don't feel so hotsy-totsy.*

house moss *n.* little blobs of lint. (See also *ghost turd.*) □ *There is some house moss under the sofa.* □ *Sweep up this house moss, please.*

house of many doors *n.* a prison. □ *Max faced a sentence of a few years in the house of many doors.* □ *Bruno just got out of the house with many doors and is looking for somebody to pull a job with.*

How does that grab you? *interrog.* "What do you think of that?" □ *Looks good, okay? How does that grab you?* □ *How does that grab you? Enough salt?*

How goes it? *interrog.* "How are you?"; "How are things going?" □ *Nice to see you. How goes it?* □ *How goes it? Everything okay?*

how the other half lives *n.* how poorer people live; how richer people live. □ *Now I am beginning to understand how the other half lives.* □ *Most people don't care how the other half lives.*

How ya living? *interrog.* "How are you doing?" (The response is *Living large.*) □ *How ya living, man?* □ *Yo! How ya living?*

howdy *interj.* "hello." (Folksy.) □ *Howdy, friend.* □ *Well, howdy. Long time, no see.*

howl 1. *n.* something funny. (See also *scream.*) □ *What a howl the surprise party turned out to be when the guest of honor didn't show up.* □ *The gag was a real howl.* **2.** *in.* to laugh very hard. □ *Everybody howled at my mistake.* □ *John howled when the joke was told.*

howler *n.* a serious and funny mistake. □ *Who is responsible for this howler on the Wilson account?* □ *That howler cost us plenty.*

howling (drunk) *mod.* alcohol intoxicated; loudly drunk. □ *Wally got howling drunk and ran in the streets with his coat off.* □ *He was just howling!*

H.T.H. *n.* "hometown honey," a sweetheart from home or still at home. (Initialism. Collegiate.) □ *Wally is my H.T.H., but I think I've outgrown him.* □ *I heard that Mary is Sam's H.T.H.*

hubbas *n.* crystallized cocaine; *crack.* (Drugs.) □ *A ten-year-old died yesterday from hubbas.* □ *They arrested an eight-year-old for selling hubbas.*

hubby ['həbi] *n.* a husband. □ *My hubby will be late tonight.* □ *Where is your hubby tonight?*

huffer ['həfɚ] *n.* a person (teenager) who inhales glue vapors or some other solvent for a *high.* (Drugs.) □ *The age of the huffers has come to an end. Now* *they start out on crack.* □ *His school work suffered because he was a huffer.*

huffy *mod.* angry; haughty. □ *Now, don't get huffy. I said I was sorry, didn't I?* □ *Who's the huffy old lady?* □ *She was so huffy about it.*

hug the porcelain god(dess) AND **hug the throne** *tr.* to vomit; to vomit while holding on to the toilet seat. □ *The girls drank a lot of beer and two of them spent the night hugging the porcelain god.* □ *I don't want to get drunk and have to hug the porcelain goddess all night.*

hug the throne See the previous entry.

hughie ['hjui] *in.* to empty one's stomach; to vomit. (See also *cry hughie.*) □ *I gotta go hughie.* □ *Oo, who hughied?*

humdinger AND **hummer** ['həm'dɪŋɚ AND 'həmɚ] *n.* someone or something excellent. □ *Now, this one is a real humdinger.* □ *Yup, he's a hummer all right.*

hummer See the previous entry.

humongous [hju'mɑŋgəs] *mod.* huge. □ *She lives in a humongous house on the hill.* □ *Wally has a humongous nose.* □ *That nose is not humongous.*

hump (along) *in.* to move along in a hurry. □ *I guess I'd better hump along over there.* □ *Come on, move it! Hump to the main office and be fast about it!*

hump it (to somewhere) *tr.* to move rapidly (to somewhere). □ *I have to hump it over to Kate's place right now.* □ *You'll have to hump it to get there in time.*

hung 1. *mod.* hungover. □ *John is really hung this morning.* □ *I'm miserable when I'm hung.* **2.** *mod.* annoyed. □ *Fred is hung and looking for somebody to take it out on.* □ *How can you get so hung about practically nothing?*

hungover *mod.* having a hangover from too much alcohol. □ *John is really hungover today.* □ *I can't eat when I'm hungover.*

hungries *n.* hunger. (Always with *the*. See also *munchies.*) □ *Jimmy's crying because he's got the hungries.* □ *I get the hungries about this time every day.*

hungry 1. *mod.* eager to make money. □ *He doesn't sell enough because he's not hungry enough.* □ *When he gets hungry for wealth, he'll get busy.* **2.** *mod.* ambitious. □ *He gets ahead because he's hungry.* □ *We like to hire the hungry ones.*

hunk *n.* a strong and sexually attractive male. □ *Larry is a real hunk.* □ *Who was that hot hunk I saw you with?*

hunky See *honky.*

hunky-dory ['həŋki'dori] *mod.* fine; okay. □ *As a matter of fact, everything is just hunky-dory.* □ *That is a hunky-dory idea all right.*

hurl *in.* to empty one's stomach; to vomit. (Like the *throw* in *throw up.*) □ *I think I gotta go hurl.* □ *Who's in the john hurling so loud?*

hurry up and wait *phr.* to be alternately rushed and delayed in a hectic situation. (Often with the force of a modifier.) □ *I hate to hurry up and wait.* □ *It's always hurry up and wait around here.*

hurt 1. *mod.* very ugly; damaged and ugly. (Black. Similar to *hurting.*) □ *Man, are you hurt!* □ *That poor girl is really bad hurt.* **2.** *mod.* drug intoxicated. (Black.) □ *Gert was really hurt and nodding and drooling.* □ *One hit of that horse trank and he was really hurt.*

hurt for someone or something *in.* to long after someone or something; to need someone or something. □ *Sam really hurts for Mary.* □ *I sure am hurting for a nice big steak.*

hurting 1. *mod.* very ugly; in pain from ugliness. (Similar to *hurt.*) □ *That dog of yours is something to behold. It's really hurting.* □ *Man, is she hurting!* **2.** *mod.* seriously in need of something, such as a dose of drugs. (Drugs.) □ *Gert is hurting. She needs something soon.* □ *When Ernie is hurting, he takes barbs.*

hush-hush ['həʃ'həʃ] **1.** *mod.* secret; undercover. □ *The matter is so hush-hush I can't talk about it over the phone.* □ *What is all this hush-hush stuff?* **2.** *mod.* secretly. □ *They did it so hush-hush that no one knew for a long time.* □

What are all these hush-hush plans you have made?

hush money *n.* money paid to buy someone's silence. ☐ *They paid enough hush money to silence an army.* ☐ *There was some hush money paid to someone in city hall.*

hush someone or something up 1. *tr.* [with *someone*] to kill someone. ☐ *Nobody knew how to get to Mr. Big to hush him up.* 🅃 *Mr. Big told Bruno to hush up Max.* **2.** *tr.* [with *something*] to keep something a secret; to try to stop a rumor from spreading. ☐ *We just couldn't hush it up.* 🅃 *We wanted to hush up the story, but there was no way to do it.*

husky ['həski] *n.* a strong man; a thug. ☐ *Tell your husky to lay off, Bruno.* ☐ *A couple of huskies helped me get my car unstuck.*

hustle ['həsl̩] **1.** *in.* to move rapidly; to hurry. ☐ *Come on, hustle, you guys.* ☐ *It's late. I've got to hustle.* **2.** *n.* hurried movement; confusion. ☐ *All the hustle and confusion made it hard to concentrate.* ☐ *I can't work when there is all this hustle around me.* **3.** *n.* a scheme to make money; a special technique for making money. (Underworld. This includes drug dealing, prostitution, and other vice activities.) ☐ *Each of these punks has a hustle—a specialty in crime.* ☐ *We all know what Max's hustle is.* **4.** *in.* to use one's special technique for making money. ☐ *He's out there on the streets hustling all the time.* ☐ *I gotta go hustle. I need some bread.* **5.** *tr.* to use a scheme on a person to try to make money; to *con* someone. ☐ *Don't try to hustle me, sister. I know which end is up.* ☐ *Sam is always trying to hustle people.* **6.** *tr.* to attempt to seduce someone. ☐ *Max is hustling Tracy.* ☐ *I think that Tracy's hustling Max.*

hustler ['həslɚ] **1.** *n.* a gambler in a pool hall. ☐ *Wasn't he the guy who played the hustler in that famous movie?* ☐ *He made a lot of money as a hustler.* **2.** *n.* a swindler; a con artist. ☐ *The chick is a real hustler. I wouldn't trust her at all.* ☐ *The hustler conned me out of a month's pay.* **3.** *n.* a prostitute. ☐ *Gert almost became a hustler to pay for a habit.* ☐ *A lot of hustlers are hooked on horse.* **4.** *n.* a *stud;* a man who is notoriously good with women. ☐ *That guy's a hustler. Watch out.* ☐ *He thinks he's a hustler. The chicks think he's a wimp.*

hut *n.* a house. ☐ *I've got to go to my hut and pick up some bills.* ☐ *Where's your hut? I'll come and visit you.*

hype [hɑɪp] **1.** *n.* publicity; sales propaganda; promotion, especially if blatant and aggressive. ☐ *There was so much hype before the picture was released that the picture itself was a letdown.* ☐ *There is hype for the election all over the place.* **2.** *tr.* to publicize or promote someone or something aggressively; to overpraise someone or something. ☐ *Don't hype the thing to death.* ☐ *Let's hype it until everyone in the country has heard about it.* **3.** AND **hipe** *n.* a hypodermic syringe and needle. (Drugs.) ☐ *She forgot to clean the hype.* ☐ *He got an infection from a dirty hipe.* **4.** *n.* an injection of drugs. (Drugs.) ☐ *Ernie needed a hype real bad.* ☐ *Max told him who could help him with a hype.* **5.** *n.* a drug addict who injects drugs. (Drugs.) ☐ *Gert's been a hype for about a year.* ☐ *The hypes have a rough time in prison.* **6.** *mod.* really good; excellent. ☐ *Now this is a truly hype pizza!* ☐ *This rally is really hype!*

hype artist *n.* someone who produces aggressive promotional material for a living. ☐ *She is a hype artist for a public relations firm.* ☐ *How much does a hype artist get paid for all that junk?*

hype something up *tr.* to overpraise something; to propagandize something. ☐ *They hyped it up too much.* 🅃 *Why do they hype up an election?*

hyped (up) 1. *mod.* excited; stimulated. ☐ *They were all hyped up before the game.* ☐ *She said she had to get hyped before the tennis match.* **2.** *mod.* contrived; heavily promoted; falsely advertised. ☐ *I just won't pay good money to see these hyped up movies.* ☐ *If it has to be hyped so much, it probably isn't very good.* **3.** *mod.* drug intoxicated. (Drugs.) ☐ *Gert is happiest when she's* *hyped.* □ *Here comes another hyped up musician.*

hyper ['haɪpɚ] **1.** *mod.* excited; overreacting. □ *I'm a little hyper because of the doctor's report.* □ *Here's another hyper patient.* □ *Now, now, don't get hyper.* **2.** *n.* a person who praises or promotes someone or something. □ *She's a hyper, and she doesn't always tell things the way they are.* □ *As a hyper, she is a whiz.* **3.** *n.* a person who is always overly excited or hyperactive. □ *Pat is such a hyper. Just can't seem to relax.* □ *My dad is a hyper.* **4.** *n.* a drug user who injects drugs with a hypodermic syringe. (Drugs.) □ *How long have you been a hyper, Gert?* □ *Max has been a hyper since he was twenty-four.*

I

I am so sure! *exclam.* "I am right!" (California.) □ *You are way rad! I am so sure!* □ *This is too much. I am so sure!*

(I-)beam ['aɪbim AND bim] *n.* "IBM," International Business Machines stock shares. (Securities markets. See also *big blue.*) □ *I-beam fell out of bed and took the market with it.* □ *How much beam do you own?*

I could(n't) care less. *sent.* "I don't care!" (The affirmative version does not make sense, but is widely used, nonetheless.) □ *So you're late. I couldn't care less.* □ *I could care less if you fell off a cliff.*

I don't believe this! *exclam.* "What is happening right now is unbelievable!" □ *Gross! I don't believe this!* □ *I don't believe this! It can't be happening.*

I don't know. *sent.* "I disagree." □ *I don't know. I like it. What's wrong with it?* □ *I don't know. It looks good to me.*

I don't mean maybe! *exclam.* "I am not kidding!" □ *You get over here right now, and I don't mean maybe!* □ *I will spank you if you ever do that again, and I don't mean maybe.*

I hear what you are saying. 1. AND **I hear you.** *sent.* "I know just what you are trying to say." □ *Yes, yes. I hear what you are saying, and I'm with you.* □ *Yeah! I hear you!* **2.** *sent.* "I understand your position, but I am under no obligation to agree." □ *I hear you. So do what you want.* □ *I hear you, but it doesn't matter.*

I hear you. See the previous entry.

I kid you not. *sent.* "I am not kidding." (Attributed to the entertainer Jack Paar.) □ *She is a great singer. I kid you not.* □ *I kid you not. This is the best.*

(I) love it! *exclam.* "That is wonderful!" (A catch phrase.) □ *It's wonderful, Ted. I love it!* □ *Love it! More, more!* □ *You're so clever! Love it! Love it!*

I smell you. *sent.* "I understand you." □ *I smell you. No need to go on and on.* □ *That's enough. I smell you. Don't go on and on.*

IAC See the following entry.

IAE AND **IAC** *interj.* "in any event"; "in any case." (Initialisms. Used in electronic mail and computer bulletin board messages. Not pronounced aloud.) □ *IAE I will give you the answer tomorrow.* □ *I will be there IAC.*

ice 1. *n.* diamonds; jewels. (Underworld.) □ *That old dame has tons of ice in her hotel room.* □ *Look at the ice on her!* **2.** *n.* cocaine; crystalline cocaine. (Drugs.) □ *Max deals mostly in ice, but can get you almost anything.* □ *This ice isn't good enough.* **3.** *tr.* to kill someone; to kill an informer. (Underworld. See also *chill.*) □ *Mr. Big ordered Bruno to ice you-know-who.* □ *Somebody set out to ice Tracy—the dirty squealer.* **4.** *tr.* to ignore someone. (Underworld. See also *chill.*) □ *Max iced Bruno for obvious reasons.* □ *The members of the gang iced Bruno, and that really made him worry.* **5.** *tr.* to embarrass someone; to make someone look foolish. □ *Don't ice me in front of my friends.* □ *Why does she feel like she has to ice everybody?* **6.** *n.* money given as a bribe, especially to the police. (Underworld.) □ *Did you give Ervine the ice?* □ *A lot of those cops take ice.* **7.** *mod.* excellent; very cool. □ *Her answer was ice, and she really put down that guy.* □ *Man this stuff is ice!*

ice queen *n.* a cold and haughty woman. □ *Tracy is not exactly an ice queen, but comes close.* □ *It's Kim who's the ice queen.*

iceberg *n.* a cold and unemotional person. □ *Sally can be such an iceberg!* □ *What an insensitive iceberg!*

iceberg slim 1. *n.* a *pimp.* □ *When iceberg slim came by in his pimpmobile, Jed made a rude sign at him.* □ *No iceberg slim is gonna push me around!* **2.** *n.* a person who exploits others; a cold, heartless person. □ *The guy's a regular iceberg slim.* □ *Rocko is a perfect example of an iceberg slim. He's heartless.*

iced *mod.* settled once and for all; done easily. □ *I've got it iced. Nothing to it.* □ *The whole business is iced. Don't fret.*

iceman *n.* a killer. (Underworld. See also *ice.*) □ *It's hard to believe that Rocko is a professional iceman.* □ *The mob employs a number of icemen.*

icicles ['ɑɪs sɪklz] *n.* pure cocaine in a crystallized form. (Drugs.) □ *Are icicles the same as crack?* □ *Icicles are probably more pure than crack.*

icing on the cake *n.* an extra enhancement. □ *Oh, wow! A tank full of gas in my new car. That's icing on the cake!* □ *Your coming home for a few days was the icing on the cake.*

ick [ɪk] **1.** *n.* any nasty substance. □ *What is this ick on my shoe?* □ *That's not ick; it's good clean mud.* **2.** *exclam.* "Nasty!" (Usually **Ick!**) □ *Oh, ick! What now?* □ *Ick! I'm late!* **3.** *n.* a disliked person. □ *Tell that ick to leave. He's polluting the place.* □ *Oh, Todd, don't be an ick.*

icky ['ɪki] *mod.* distasteful; nasty. □ *What is this icky old stuff?* □ *This is icky.* □ *This was an icky day.*

icky-poo ['ɪkipu] **1.** *mod.* disgusting. □ *I don't like all this icky-poo talk.* □ *What is that icky-poo stuff in the soup bowl?* **2.** *exclam.* "Nasty!" (Usually **Icky-poo!**) □ *Icky-poo! What a mess!* □ *Oh, icky-poo! I missed my bus!*

ID 1. *n.* some kind of identification card. (Initialism.) □ *Can you show me an I.D.?* □ *I don't have any ID on me.* **2.** *tr.* to determine the identity of someone; to check someone for a valid identification card. □ *They IDed us at the door.* □ *I hate being I.D.ed.* □ *The cops IDed the driver in less than thirty minutes.*

idiot box *n.* a television set. □ *You spend too much time watching the idiot box.* □ *What's on the idiot box tonight?*

idiot card *n.* a large card that shows people on television what to say. □ *The floor director held up an idiot card so I could read out the telephone number.* □ *I couldn't read the number off the idiot card.*

idiot juice AND **idiotic** ['ɪdiət dʒus AND ɪdi'ɑdɪk] *n.* a mixture of ground nutmeg and water. (Prisons.) □ *Somehow a bunch of these guys got hold of some idiot juice.* □ *He drank about a gallon of idiotic to get the kick of one beer.*

idiot light *n.* a light (instead of a meter) on a car's dashboard that indicates the state of various things concerning the operation of the car. □ *I don't want idiot lights. I want meters!* □ *The idiot light went on, and I knew I was in some sort of trouble.*

idiot oil *n.* alcohol. □ *She drinks too much of that idiot oil.* □ *Idiot oil can wreck you as much as smack does.*

idiot pills *n.* barbiturates. (Drugs.) □ *Lay off those idiot pills, why don't you?* □ *She takes idiot pills every night.*

idiotic See *idiot juice.*

if I've told you once, I've told you a thousand times *phr.* "I know I have told you many, many times." □ *If I've told you once, I've told you a thousand times, don't lean back in that chair.* □ *If I've told you once, I've told you a thousand times, wipe your feet!*

if one knows what's good for one *phr.* "one had better do what is expected of one." □ *You'd better be on time if you know what's good for you.* □ *If you know what's good for you, you'll call and apologize.*

if one's a day *phr.* a phrase attached to an expression of someone's age. □ *She's fifty if she's a day!* □ *I'm sure he's forty-five if he's a day.*

if push comes to shove See *when push comes to shove.*

If you can't stand the heat, keep out of the kitchen. *sent.* "If you cannot accept the problems of involvement, do not get involved." □ *Yes, it's difficult to be a candidate. If you can't stand the heat, keep out of the kitchen.* □ *Relax. If you can't stand the heat, keep out of the kitchen.*

if you'll pardon the expression *phr.* "excuse the expression I am about to say." □ *This thing is—if you'll pardon the expression—loused up.* □ *I'm really jacked, if you'll pardon the expression.*

iffy ['ɪfi] *mod.* marginally uncertain. □ *Things are still sort of iffy, but we'll know for sure in a few days.* □ *It's sort of an iffy matter, but things will get straightened out.*

ill *mod. lame;* dull; bad. □ *This is an ill pizza and I won't eat it.* □ *That broad is ill and has a face that would stop a clock.*

I'll bite. *sent.* "You want me to ask what or why, so, what or why?" □ *Okay, I'll bite. What's the answer?* □ *I'll bite. Why did the chicken cross the road?*

illin' ['ɪlən] **1.** *mod.* being ill; being sick. □ *She was illin' big time and could not come to class.* □ *I was illin' so I called in sick.* **2.** *mod.* ill-behaved. □ *You are most illin' and you are bugging me, Kim. Stop it!* □ *She is the most illin' homeslice I know.* **3.** *in.* behaving badly. □ *Stop illin' and pay attention.* □ *You are always illin'!* **4.** *mod.* upset. □ *What are you illin' about? Everything is ice.* □ *Tom was illin' and angry about the broken window.*

illuminated *mod.* alcohol intoxicated. (A play on *lit.*) □ *Paul is a bit illuminated.* □ *He's too illuminated to drive home.*

I'm history. *sent.* "Good-bye, I am leaving." (See also *history.*) □ *I'm history. See you tomorrow.* □ *Later. I'm history.*

I'm listening. *sent.* "Keep talking."; "Make your explanation now." □ *You did it wrong. I'm listening.* □ *I'm sure there's an explanation. Well, I'm listening.*

I'm not kidding. *sent.* "I am telling the truth." □ *Get over here now! I'm not kidding.* □ *I'm not kidding. It was this big!*

I'm out of here. AND **I'm outa here.** *sent.* "I am leaving this minute." □ *In three minutes I'm outa here.* □ *I'm out of here. Bye.*

I'm outa here. See the previous entry.

I'm shaking (in fear). *sent.* "You don't really frighten me at all." (A mocking response to a threat.) □ *Oh, what you said! I'm shaking. Not!* □ *Your threats really scare me. I'm shaking in fear.*

I'm there! *sent.* "I will accept your invitation and I will be there." □ *Sounds like it will be a great rally. I'm there!* □ *If you and Tom are going to get together and watch the game, I'm there!*

IM(H)O *interj.* "in my (humble) opinion." (Initialism. Used in electronic mail and computer bulletin board messages. Not pronounced aloud. Compare with *IYHO.*) □ *IMHO, you are dead wrong.* □ *She is the person to choose, IMO.*

impaired *mod.* alcohol intoxicated. (Borrowed from the euphemistic *impaired physician.*) □ *Don is a bit impaired because he drinks like a fish.* □ *He was so impaired he couldn't see his hand in front of his face.* □ *The impaired driver was arrested.*

in 1. *mod.* current; fashionable. □ *This kind of thing is in now.* □ *What's in around here in the way of clothing?* **2.** *mod.* private. □ *Is this in information?* □ *If it's in or something, I'm sure they won't spread it around.* **3.** *n.* someone in a special position; someone who is serving in an elective office. □ *Well, now that I am an in, there's going to be* *some changes.* □ *When Ralph is one of the ins, he'll throw the crooks out.* **4.** *n.* a ticket or means of getting in (someplace). □ *I lost my in. Can I still see the show?* □ *Lemme see your in or give me a buck.*

in a bad way See *in bad shape.*

in a big way *mod.* very much; urgently. □ *I'm really interested in her in a big way.* □ *He plays to win—in a big way.*

in a blue funk *mod.* sad; depressed. □ *I've been in a blue funk all week.* □ *Don't be in a blue funk. Things'll get better.*

in a cold sweat *mod.* in a state of fear. □ *He stood there in a cold sweat, waiting for something to happen.* □ *I was in a cold sweat while they counted the ballots.*

in a dither *mod.* confused; undecided. □ *Mary is sort of in a dither lately.* □ *Don't get yourself in a dither.*

in a familiar way *mod.* pregnant. (Euphemistic for *in a family way.*) □ *Tracy is in a familiar way, have you heard?* □ *In a familiar way again?*

in a family way AND **in the family way** *mod.* pregnant. □ *I hear that Tracy is in a family way.* □ *Is she in the family way again?*

in a flash *mod.* right away; immediately. (See also *flash.*) □ *Get over here in a flash, or else.* □ *I'll be there in a flash.*

in a heap *mod.* alcohol intoxicated. □ *Poor Jed's in a heap again.* □ *The guys were all in a heap after the blast.*

in a jam *mod.* in a difficult situation. □ *I think I'm sort of in a jam.* □ *Sam is in a jam.*

in a jiff(y) *mod.* right away; immediately. (See also *jiffy.*) □ *I'll be there in a jiffy.* □ *The clerk'll be with you in a jiff.*

in a snit *mod.* in a fit of anger or irritation. □ *Don't get in a snit. It was an accident.* □ *Mary is in a snit because they didn't ask her to come to the shindig.*

in a tizzy *mod.* in a state of mental disorder. □ *Fred is all in a tizzy.* □ *The whole office is in a tizzy today.*

in a twit *mod.* upset; frantic. □ *She's all in a twit because she lost her keys.* □ *Pete was in a twit and was quite rude to us.*

in a twitter *mod.* in a giddy state; silly. □ *Don't get yourself in a twitter.* □ *We were all in a twitter over the upcoming event.*

in action **1.** *mod.* healthy and getting around. □ *After I got well, I was in action again immediately.* □ *When will she be in action again?* **2.** *mod.* selling or using drugs. (Drugs.) □ *Max is in action about twenty hours a day.* □ *In this neighborhood, somebody is in action twenty-four hours a day.*

in bad shape AND **in a bad way** **1.** *mod.* injured or debilitated in any manner. □ *Fred had a little accident, and he's in bad shape.* □ *Tom needs exercise. He's in bad shape.* **2.** *mod.* pregnant. □ *Tracy's in bad shape again, I hear.* □ *Yup, she's in bad shape all right—about three months in bad shape.* **3.** *mod.* alcohol intoxicated. □ *Two glasses of that stuff and I'm in really bad shape.* □ *Fred is in bad shape. I think he's going to toss his cookies.*

in business *mod.* operating; equipped to operate. □ *We're in business now, and things are running smoothly.* □ *Now it works. Now we're in business.*

in cold blood *mod.* without feeling; with cruel intent. □ *Rocko kills in cold blood and never gives it a thought.* □ *The prof flunked me in cold blood.*

in cold storage *mod.* dead; in a state of death. □ *Rocko gets paid for putting his subjects in cold storage.* □ *Poor old Jed is in cold storage.*

in deep **1.** *mod.* deeply involved (with someone or something). □ *Mary and Sam are in deep.* □ *Max is in deep with the mob.* **2.** *mod.* deeply in debt. (Often with *with* or *to.*) □ *Bruno is in deep with his bookie.* □ *I'm in deep to the department store.*

in deep doo-doo *mod.* in real trouble. (*Doo-doo* = dung.) □ *See what you've done. Now you are in deep doo-doo.* □ *I broke the window. Now I'm in deep doo-doo.*

in drag *mod.* wearing the clothing of the opposite sex. (Usually refers to women's clothing.) □ *Two actors in drag did a skit about life on the farm.* □ *Gary looks better in drag than he does in a suit.*

in dribs and drabs *mod.* in small portions; bit by bit. □ *I'll have to pay you what I owe you in dribs and drabs.* □ *The whole story is being revealed in dribs and drabs.*

in Dutch *mod.* in trouble. □ *I think I'm in Dutch with my folks.* □ *I didn't want to get in Dutch with you.*

in fine feather 1. *mod.* well dressed; of an excellent appearance. □ *Well, you are certainly in fine feather today.* □ *I like to be in fine feather when I have to give a speech.* **2.** *mod.* in good form; in good spirits. □ *Mary is really in fine feather tonight.* □ *I feel in fine feather and ready to go!*

in nothing flat *mod.* immediately. □ *I'll be there in nothing flat.* □ *She changed the tire in nothing flat.*

in one's blood *mod.* inborn; part of one's genetic makeup. □ *It's in my blood. I can't help it.* □ *Running is in his blood. He loves it.*

in one's something mode *phr.* behaving in a specified mode. (The *something* can be replaced by *work, sleep, hungry, angry,* etc.) □ *I'm not very alert because I'm still in my sleep mode.* □ *Todd is always in his play mode when he should be working.*

in orbit 1. *mod.* ecstatic; euphoric. □ *She was just in orbit when she got the letter.* □ *Pete was in orbit over the promotion.* **2.** *mod.* alcohol or drug intoxicated. □ *Gary is in orbit and can't see a hole in a ladder.* □ *After having a six-pack all to herself, Julie was in orbit.*

in play 1. *mod.* being played; inbounds. (Said of a ball in a game.) □ *The ball's in play, so you made the wrong move.* □ *No, it wasn't in play, you twit!* **2.** *mod.* having to do with a company (or its stock) that is a candidate for acquisition by another company. (Securities markets.) □ *The company was in play, but nobody was buying it.* □ *These deal stocks—which are in play right now—offer excellent buying opportunities.*

in rare form 1. *mod.* well-tuned for a good performance; at one's best. □ *He is in rare form today.* □ *We are not exactly in rare form on Monday mornings.* **2.** *mod.* alcohol intoxicated. □ *Gert is in rare form, but she'll have time to sleep it off.* □ *When Harry was finally in rare form, he slid beneath the table.*

in spades *mod.* in the best way possible; extravagantly. □ *He flunked the test in spades.* □ *They won the championship in spades.*

in tall cotton *mod.* successful; *on easy street.* □ *I won some money at the track, and I'm really in tall cotton.* □ *We were in tall cotton until the IRS caught up with us.*

in the bag 1. *mod.* *cinched;* achieved. □ *It's in the bag—as good as done.* □ *The election is in the bag unless the voters find out about my past.* **2.** *mod.* alcohol intoxicated. (See also *bagged.*) □ *Kelly looks like he is in the bag.* □ *John is in the bag and mean as hell.*

in the black *mod.* financially solvent; profitable; not in debt. □ *Now that the company is in the black, there's a good chance it will become a deal stock.* □ *We're in the black now and making a profit.*

in the buff *mod.* naked. □ *You-know-who sleeps in the buff.* □ *You can save hundreds of dollars in a lifetime by not buying pajamas and sleeping in the buff instead.*

in the catbird seat *mod.* in a dominant or controlling position. □ *Sally's in the catbird seat—telling everybody where to go.* □ *I hold all the aces. I'm in the catbird seat.*

in the chips *mod.* wealthy; with lots of money. □ *I'm in the chips this month. Let's go squander it.* □ *If I was in the chips, I'd buy a jag.*

in the driver's seat *mod.* in control. □ *She's just not comfortable unless she's in* *the driver's seat.* □ *I'm in the driver's seat now, and I get to decide who gets raises.*

in the family way See *in a family way.*

in the grip of the grape *mod.* drunk on wine; drunk. □ *Wayne was in the grip of the grape and couldn't talk straight.* □ *Sue was in the grip of the grape after only three glasses of wine.*

in the groove *mod. cool; groovy;* pleasant and delightful. □ *Man, is that combo in the groove tonight!* □ *Get in the groove! Relax.*

in the gun *mod.* alcohol intoxicated. (See also *shot.*) □ *Ted is in the gun again.* □ *When Fred is in the gun, he's mean.*

in the hole *mod.* in debt; running a deficit. □ *Looks like we are in the hole again this month.* □ *We always end the month in the hole.*

in the (home) stretch *mod.* in the last stage of the process. (From horse-racing.) □ *We're in the home stretch with this project and can't change it now.* □ *We're in the stretch. Only three more days till we graduate.*

in the hopper *mod.* in process; in line to be processed. (A hopper is an "in-basket" for incoming work.) □ *It's in the hopper. I'll get to it.* □ *Your job is in the hopper, and your turn is next.*

in the know *mod.* knowledgeable (about something); having inside knowledge (about something). □ *Ask Harry. He's usually in the know.* □ *Sure I'm in the know. But I'm not telling.*

in the ozone *mod.* alcohol or drug intoxicated. □ *Four beers and Tom is in the ozone.* □ *We were in the ozone, but we still made a lot of sense.*

in the pink 1. *mod.* feeling quite well; feeling on top of the world. □ *I'm in the pink today. Feeling great.* □ *When she's in the pink again, she'll give you a ring.* **2.** *mod.* alcohol intoxicated. □ *Pete is in the pink and singing at the top of his lungs.* □ *When he's in the pink, he's a handful.*

in the pipeline *mod.* backed up somewhere in a process; in process; in a queue. □ *There's a lot of goods still in the pipeline. That means no more orders for a while.* □ *Your papers are in the pipeline somewhere. You'll just have to wait.*

in the soup *mod.* in trouble. □ *Now you're in the soup.* □ *I'm in the soup with the boss.*

in the suds *mod.* alcohol intoxicated. □ *Fred is in the suds and can't see.* □ *When Bob is in the suds, he's mean.*

in the tube 1. *mod.* in the tube of a large wave. (Surfing.) □ *Pete is in the tube and looks great.* □ *On a day like today, I want to be out there in the tube.* **2.** *mod.* at risk. □ *He's in the tube now, but things should straighten out soon.* □ *If you find yourself in the tube in this matter, just give me a ring.*

in there *mod.* sincere; likeable. □ *Martha is really in there. Everybody likes her.* □ *I like a guy who's in there—who thinks about other people.*

in thing to do *n.* the fashionable or orthodox thing to do. (Always with *the.* See also *in.*) □ *Cutting your hair short on the sides is the in thing to do.* □ *Smoking is no longer the in thing to do.*

in-your-face *mod.* confrontational. □ *I'm really tired of this in-your-face attitude of yours.* □ *Fred is just an in-your-face kind of guy. He means no harm.*

incense *n.* marijuana. (Drugs.) □ *I think I smell some incense somewhere in this building.* □ *Hank likes to burn a little incense every now and then.*

incentive *n.* cocaine. (Drugs. See also *initiative.*) □ *Maybe a little of that incentive would make me work harder.* □ *That's pretty expensive incentive.*

incy-wincy ['intsi'wintsi] *mod.* tiny. (Compare to *itty-bitty, itsy-bitsy.*) □ *Just give me an incy-wincy bit. I'm on a diet.* □ *Well, maybe an incy-wincy bit more wouldn't hurt.*

initiative *n.* cocaine. (Drugs. See also *incentive.*) □ *Maybe I need some more of that initiative to get me going.* □ *That kind of initiative is pretty expensive.*

ink 1. *n.* cheap red wine. ☐ *The old wino prefers ink to anything else.* ☐ *All I have is some ink. Is that okay?* 2. *n.* publicity; print media coverage of someone or something. ☐ *The movie star's divorce got a lot of ink for a few days.* ☐ *The new president managed to get some ink everyday, but it wasn't always good.*

ink slinger *n.* a professional writer; a newspaper reporter. ☐ *The ink slingers have been at the candidates again.* ☐ *The problem is that there are too many ink slingers around.*

ins and outs *n.* the fine points (of something); the details; the intricacies. ☐ *I'm learning the ins and outs of this business.* ☐ *My father taught me the ins and outs of hog calling.*

inside dope *n.* the inside story; special or privileged information. (Compare to *(hot) skinny.*) ☐ *Can you give me the inside dope on Marty?* ☐ *What's the inside dope on the candidate's drug addiction?*

inside job *n.* a crime perpetrated against an establishment by someone associated with the victimized establishment. (Underworld.) ☐ *The cops figured that it was an inside job.* ☐ *It was an inside job all right. The butler did it.*

inside out *mod.* drunk. ☐ *Wayne spends every weekend inside out.* ☐ *Beavis looked forward to the day he could go out and get inside out.*

insy ['ɪnzi] *n.* a navel that recedes and does not protrude. (Compare to *outsy.*) ☐ *Is yours an insy or an outsy?* ☐ *It's an outsy. So what?*

intense *mod.* serious; heavy. ☐ *That man is so intense!* ☐ *This is an intense matter.* ☐ *Oh, wow! Now that's what I call intense!*

IOW *interj.* "in other words." (Initialism. Used in electronic mail and computer bulletin board messages. Not pronounced aloud.) ☐ *IOW, you are angry at me.* ☐ *I have heard enough on this point. IOW, shut up.*

iron 1. *n.* a gun; a revolver. (Underworld.) ☐ *Rocko never carries iron unless he's going to use it.* ☐ *What kind of iron do you carry?* 2. *n.* computer hardware. (See also *big iron.*) ☐ *What kind of iron are you people running over there?* ☐ *This is good old compatible iron.*

Irv AND **Ervine; Irvine** *n.* a police officer. (Black. See also *Charlie Irvine.*) ☐ *Irv is after you, did you know?* ☐ *Tell Ervine to go catch a speeder or something.*

Irvine See the previous entry.

It cuts two ways. *sent.* "There are two sides, you know."; "There are two people involved." ☐ *You have to help, too. It cuts two ways.* ☐ *It cuts two ways, you know. It can't always all be my fault.*

It will be your ass! *sent.* "It will cost you your ass!"; "You will pay dearly!" (Potentially offensive. Use only with discretion.) ☐ *If you do that again, it will be your ass!* ☐ *It will be your ass if it isn't done right this time.*

It's been a slice! *sent.* "It's been good." ☐ *Good-bye and thank you. It's been a slice!* ☐ *It's been a slice. I hope to see you again some day.*

It's your funeral! *exclam.* "If you do it, you will suffer all the consequences!" ☐ *Go if you want. It's your funeral!* ☐ *Go ahead, swim to Cuba. It's your funeral!*

itsy-bitsy See the following entry.

itty-bitty AND **itsy-bitsy** ['ɪdi'bɪdi AND 'ɪtsi'bɪtsi] *mod.* tiny. ☐ *What an itty-bitty car!* ☐ *Give me an itsy-bitsy piece. I'm on a diet.*

I've been there. *sent.* "I know from experience what you are talking about." ☐ *I know what you mean. I've been there.* ☐ *I've been there. You don't need to spell it out for me.*

I've got to fly. AND **I('ve) gotta fly.** *sent.* "I have to leave right now." ☐ *Time's up. I've got to fly.* ☐ *I've gotta fly. See you later.*

I've got to split. *sent.* "I have to leave now." ☐ *See you later. I've got to split.* ☐ *I've got to split. Call my service.*

I('ve) gotta fly. See *I've got to fly.*

ivories [ˈɑɪvriz] **1.** *n.* the teeth. (See also *China.*) □ *I gotta go brush my ivories.* □ *Look at those nice white ivories!* **2.** *n.* piano keys. (From when piano keys were made from real elephant ivory.) □ *She can really bang those ivories.* □ *I'd say she has mastered the ivories.*

ivory tower *n.* an imaginary location where aloof academics are said to reside and work. □ *Why don't you come out of your ivory tower and see what the world is really like?* □ *Better yet, stay in your ivory tower.*

IYHO *interj.* "in your humble opinion." (Initialism. Used in electronic mail and computer bulletin board messages. Not pronounced aloud. Compare with *IM(H)O.*) □ *Things are in bad shape IYHO, but I think they are great.* □ *IYHO, everyone else is wrong!*

J

J. AND **jay** *n.* a marijuana cigarette; marijuana. (Drugs. From the initial letter of *joint.*) □ *Toss me a jay, huh?* □ *A jay is two clams.*

J. Edgar (Hoover) ['dʒe 'ɛdgɚ ('huvɚ)] *n.* the police; federal officers. (Underworld.) □ *Max got out of town when he heard that the J. Edgars were on his tail.* □ *Well, J. Edgar Hoover, looks like you got me!*

jab pop ['dʒæb'pɑp] *in.* to inject (drugs). (Drugs.) □ *Gert was jab popping when she died.* □ *Jab popping is a ticket to cement city.*

jabber ['dʒæbɚ] **1.** *n.* mindless chatter. □ *Stop all this jabber and get to work.* □ *I've heard enough of your jabber.* **2.** *in.* to chatter. □ *Come over and we'll jabber about things over coffee.* □ *What are those kids jabbering about?* **3.** *n.* a drug addict who injects drugs. (Drugs.) □ *The guy's a jabber. Look at those tracks.* □ *These scars show that the victim was a jabber.*

jack **1.** *n.* money. □ *I don't have the jack for a deal like that.* □ *How much jack will it take?* **2.** *n.* tobacco for rolling cigarettes. □ *You got some jack I can bum?* □ *I don't use jack at all.* **3.** *n.* nothing. (Probably from *jackshit.*) □ *This new television program isn't worth jack!* □ *Your last idea wasn't worth jack. Do I pay you to come up with stuff that bad?* **4.** *n.* a strange person; an annoying person. (Possibly from *jackass* or *jackshit.*) □ *Wally, stop acting like such a jack!* □ *Ted is a total jack. He doesn't know his head from a hole in the ground.*

jack around *in.* to waste time; to mess around. □ *Stop jacking around and get busy.* □ *The gang was jacking around and broke your window.*

jack someone around *tr.* to hassle someone; to harass someone. (Compare to *jerk someone around.*) □ *The IRS is jacking my brother around.* 🅃 *The boss was jacking around Gert, so she just walked out.*

jack someone or something up **1.** *tr.* [with *someone*] to motivate someone; to stimulate someone to do something. □ *I'll jack him up and try to get some action out of him.* 🅃 *What does it take to jack up that lazy guy?* **2.** *tr.* [with *something*] to raise the price of something. □ *They kept jacking the price up with various charges, so I walked.* 🅃 *How can they jack up the published price?*

jack-ups *n.* capsules of a barbiturate drug. (Drugs.) □ *Walter took a few jack-ups and went on to work.* □ *Gert took her jack-ups with whiskey. She's gonna get pifted.*

jackal *n.* a low and devious person. □ *You are nothing but a slimy jackal!* □ *What does that jackal want here?*

jacked See *jacked up.*

jacked (out) *mod.* angry; annoyed. □ *Boy was that old guy jacked out at you.* □ *Yup, he was jacked all right.*

jacked up **1.** AND **jacked** *mod.* excited. □ *Don was really jacked up about the election.* □ *The gang was jacked up and ready to party.* **2.** *mod.* arrested. (Underworld.) □ *What time did Bruno get himself jacked up?* □ *He was jacked up at midnight.* **3.** *mod.* upset; stressed. □ *I was really jacked up by the bad news.* □ *Don't get jacked up. It'll work out.* **4.**

mod. *high* on drugs. □ *He's jacked up, and he may have O.D.ed.* □ *The poor kid is jacked up most of the time now.*

jackshit *n.* nothing. (Potentially offensive. Use only with discretion. See also *jack*.) □ *This car isn't worth jackshit.* □ *Your comments aren't worth jackshit. Keep them to yourself.*

jag **1.** *n.* a Jaguar automobile. □ *What I really want is a jag.* □ *How much will a jag set me back?* **2.** *n.* a drinking bout; a prolonged state of alcohol or drug intoxication. □ *Is he off on another jag, or is this the same one?* □ *One more jag will kill her. Try to keep her away from the stuff.* **3.** *n.* a prolonged state of emotional excess. □ *I've been on a jag and can't get my work done.* □ *She's off on a jag again.* **4.** *n.* a drug *rush*. (Drugs.) □ *This stuff has no jag at all.* □ *How big a jag do you want?*

jagged *mod.* alcohol intoxicated. □ *Man, is that chick jagged!* □ *Let's go out and get jagged.*

jagster *n.* someone on a drinking spree; a heavy drinker. □ *Gary is a typical jagster. Drunk for a week and sober for three.* □ *There's not a lot that a doctor can do for a jagster like that.*

jake **1.** *n.* a toilet; a men's restroom. □ *Where's the jake?* □ *The jake is around the corner.* **2.** *n.* a stupid person, usually a male. □ *Some loony jake told me we are going the wrong way.* □ *Who's the jake in the plaid pants?* **3.** *mod.* okay; satisfactory. □ *All right? Then everything is jake.* □ *If you get here by nine, it'll be just jake.* **4.** *n.* illegal liquor. (Prohibition.) □ *You know where I can get some jake?* □ *Why, there's no jake around here. There's a law against it, you know.*

jam **1.** *n.* a problem; trouble. □ *I hear you're in a bad jam.* □ *Well, it's not a bad jam.* **2.** *in.* [for musicians] to play together, improvising. □ *They jammed until the neighbors complained.* □ *Come over and let's jam, okay?* **3.** *tr.* & *in.* to force a basketball into the basket; to *slam dunk* a basketball. □ *He tried to jam it, but blew it.* □ *Andy broke the rim by trying to jam.* **4.** *n.* an act of forcing a basketball into the basket; a *slam dunk*. □ *The jam didn't work, and Fred's team rebounded the ball.* □ *One more jam for Wilbur!* **5.** *in.* to depart. □ *It's time to jam. Let's go.* □ *I gotta jam, Tom. See ya.*

jambled [ˈdʒæmbl̩d] *mod.* alcohol intoxicated. □ *Jerry was too jambled to stand up.* □ *Let's go out and get good and jambled.*

jammed [ˈdʒæmd] **1.** *mod.* arrested. (Underworld.) □ *Bruno got jammed for speeding.* □ *When did he get jammed?* **2.** *mod.* alcohol intoxicated. □ *I'm a little jammed, but I think I can still drive.* □ *They were jammed by midnight.* **3.** See *jammed up*.

jammed up **1.** AND **jammed** *mod.* in trouble. □ *He got himself jammed up with the law.* □ *I'm sort of jammed and need some help.* **2.** *mod.* glutted; full of food or drink. □ *I'm jammed up. I can't eat another bite.* □ *After dinner, I am so jammed up that I need a nap.*

jamming *mod.* excellent. □ *This music is really jamming.* □ *What a jamming class session.*

jampacked AND **jam-packed** *mod.* full. □ *This day has been jampacked with surprises.* □ *The box was jam-packed with goodies.*

jan [dʒæn] *n.* January in the financial futures markets. (Securities markets.) □ *The bean futures for jan fell out of bed yesterday.* □ *Are these figures jan or March?*

jane **1.** *n.* marijuana. (Drugs.) □ *You got any jane?* □ *Max has jane coming out of his ears.* **2.** *n.* a women's restroom; the *ruth*. □ *Where's the jane around here?* □ *The jane is upstairs.*

Jane Doe [ˈdʒen ˈdo] *n.* a general term for a woman. (The mate of *John Doe*.) □ *A Jane Doe was pulled out of the river this morning.* □ *There was an accident involving a Jane Doe.*

Jane Q. Public [ˈdʒen ˈkju ˈpəblɪk] *n.* a general term for a female representative of the public. (The mate of *John*

Q. Public.) ☐ *And what does Jane Q. Public think about all this?* ☐ *Jane Q. Public doesn't care at all.*

jarhead *n.* a U.S. Marine. ☐ *The jarheads got there first and let them know what was what.* ☐ *Do you want to spend a few years as a gravel-pounder or a jarhead? You get free clothes with both jobs.*

java ['dʒɑvə] *n.* coffee. ☐ *How about a cup of java?* ☐ *Some black java would be real good.*

jaw 1. *n.* a chat. ☐ *Come over for a jaw this weekend.* ☐ *I could use a good jaw with my old friend.* **2.** *in.* to chat. ☐ *Stop jawing and get to work.* ☐ *Come over, and we can jaw for a while.* **3.** See *jaw(bone).*

jaw(bone) *tr.* to try to persuade someone verbally; to apply verbal pressure to someone. ☐ *They tried to jawbone me into doing it.* ☐ *Don't jaw me. I won't do it.*

jay See *J.*

jazz someone or something up *tr.* to make someone or something more exciting or sexy; to make someone or something appeal more to contemporary and youthful tastes. ☐ *Let's jazz this up a little bit.* Ⓣ *They jazzed up the old girl till she looked like a teenager.* Ⓣ *Don't jazz up the first number too much.*

jazzed (up) 1. *mod.* alert; having a positive state of mind. ☐ *I am jazzed up and ready to face life.* ☐ *Those guys were jazzed and ready for the game.* **2.** *mod.* alcohol or drug intoxicated. ☐ *Dave was a bit jazzed up, but not terribly.* ☐ *Gert was jazzed out of her mind.* **3.** *mod.* enhanced; with something added; having been made more enticing. ☐ *The third act was jazzed up with a little skin.* ☐ *It was jazzed enough to have the police chief around asking questions.* **4.** *mod.* forged or altered. (Underworld. See also *tinseled.*) ☐ *This check is jazzed. Deep six it!* ☐ *Better not try to cash a jazzed check at this bank.*

jazzy ['dʒæzi] *mod.* stimulating; appealing. ☐ *That's a jazzy sweater you got.* ☐ *He's a real jazzy guy.*

JCL See *Johnnie-come-lately.*

J.D. 1. *n.* "Jack Daniels" whiskey. (Initialism. *Jack Daniels* is a protected trade name for a brand of whiskey.) ☐ *He poured a little J.D. into a glass, set it aside, and drank all of what was in the bottle.* ☐ *Then he poured the glass of J.D. back into the bottle.* **2.** *n.* a "juvenile delinquent." (Initialism.) ☐ *Some J.D. broke my window.* ☐ *The J.D.s are taking over the neighborhood.*

Jeepers(-creepers)! ['dʒipɚz'kripɚz] *exclam.* "Wow!" ☐ *Jeepers-creepers! I'm sorry!* ☐ *Jeepers, she's wonderful!*

Jeez! See *Jesus!*

jeff [dʒɛf] **1.** *n.* a Caucasian. (All senses originally black. From *Jefferson Davis.* Potentially derogatory.) ☐ *The jeffs are coming around more often. What's up?* ☐ *Those jeffs like you, man.* **2.** *n.* a boring or *square* person. ☐ *That jeff bugs me.* ☐ *Don't be a jeff, man!* **3.** *tr.* to persuade or deceive someone. ☐ *The guy tried to jeff me!* ☐ *You're just jeffing us!* **4.** *in.* to gentrify; to take on the ways of whites. ☐ *Cool it man; stop your jeffing.* ☐ *I'm not jeffing.*

jel [dʒɛl] *n.* a stupid person. (Someone who has "Jello," a protected brand name of gelatin, where brains ought to be. ☐ *The guy's a jel. Forget him.* ☐ *Oh, Wallace, don't act like such a jel.*

jellies See *jelly shoes.*

jelly babies *n.* an amphetamine tablet or capsule. (Drugs.) ☐ *You got any jelly babies?* ☐ *Are there any jelly babies in this neighborhood?*

jelly sandals See the following entry.

jelly shoes AND **jellies; jelly sandals** *n.* colorful shoes made from soft, flexible plastic. (From *jelly bean.*) ☐ *It's too cold to wear jelly shoes.* ☐ *Jellies will crack in this weather.*

jerk *n.* a stupid or worthless person. (Now both males and females.) ☐ *What a loony jerk!* ☐ *You are such a classic jerk!*

jerk around *in.* to waste time. ☐ *Stop jerking around and get to work.* ☐ *All you do is jerk around. Get a move on!*

jerk someone around AND **jerk someone over** *tr.* to hassle someone; to waste someone's time. □ *Stop jerking me around and give me my money back.* Ⓣ *They sure like to jerk around people in that music shop.*

jerk someone over See the previous entry.

jerker 1. *n.* a drunkard; an alcoholic. □ *Some of the jerkers have the D.T.s.* □ *Ask the jerker to come in and have a drink.* **2.** *n.* a heavy user of cocaine. (Drugs.) □ *The new guy is a jerker. You can see it in his eyes.* □ *The jerkers who need immediate treatment are sent from E.R. up to detox.*

jerks *n.* the delirium tremens. □ *The old guy has the jerks.* □ *What can they do for the jerks—other than hospitalize the victims?*

jerkwater *mod.* backwoodsy; insignificant. (See also *one-horse town*.) □ *I'm from a little jerkwater town in the Midwest.* □ *He's sort of the jerkwater type.*

jerry-built *mod.* carelessly and awkwardly built. □ *This is an old, jerry-built house, but we love it.* □ *The lawyer's case was jerry-built, but the jury bought it anyway.*

Jesus! AND **Jeez!** [ˈdʒizəs AND ˈdʒiz] *exclam.* "Wow!" (Use caution with *Jesus* in profane senses.) □ *Jesus, what a jerk!* □ *Jesus! I'm late.*

Jesus boots *n.* sandals. (Use caution with *Jesus* in profane senses.) □ *Jesus boots are okay in the summer.* □ *Who is the kook in Jesus boots?*

jet *in.* to leave a place rapidly; to go somewhere fast. □ *I will jet to Tom's house and show him these pictures.* □ *Let's jet. It's late.*

jet-set(ters) *n.* young and wealthy people who fly by jet from resort to resort. □ *The jet-set doesn't come here anymore.* □ *Jet-setters have turned to other kinds of excitement.*

jibe [dʒaɪb] *in.* to agree; to be in harmony. (Compare to *track*.) □ *Your story just doesn't jibe with the facts.* □ *These things just don't jibe.*

jiffy [ˈdʒɪfi] *n.* a very short time. (See also *in a jiff(y)*.) □ *That was a pretty long jiffy I had to wait!* □ *Just a jiffy, I'll be there.*

jig [dʒɪg] *tr. & in.* to copulate (with someone). (Use caution with the topic.) □ *He's telling everybody that he didn't jig her.* □ *She's claiming they jigged twice.*

jig is up *phr.* the game is ended; the scheme has been found out. (Always with *the*.) □ *Okay, you kids. The jig's up!* □ *Who says the jig is up?*

jigger 1. *n.* a drink of whiskey. (The standard term for a small container used for measuring the right amount of liquor for a drink.) □ *How about another jigger of that shine?* □ *Okay, I'll have a jigger.* **2.** *n.* a cigarette. □ *You got a jigger I can bum?* □ *Here's a pack of jiggers. Help yourself.* **3.** *n.* a gadget. □ *Toss me one of those copper jiggers there in the box.* □ *This kind of jigger?*

jiggered 1. *mod.* damned. □ *Get that jiggered cat out of here!* □ *Well, I'll be jiggered!* **2.** *mod.* alcohol intoxicated. (See also *jigger*.) □ *Todd was more than just a little jiggered.* □ *Bill was too jiggered to stand up.*

jillion [ˈdʒɪljən] *n.* an enormous, indefinite number. □ *I've got a jillion things to tell you.* □ *This car cost me about a jillion bucks.*

jingle 1. *n.* a buzz or tingle from alcohol. □ *He had a little jingle, but he wasn't even tipsy.* □ *This stuff gives me a little jingle, but that's all.* **2.** *n.* a drinking bout. □ *Jack was out on a jingle all night.* □ *The guys planned a big jingle for Friday.* **3.** *n.* a call on the telephone. (See also *buzz*.) □ *Give me a jingle when you get into town.* □ *I got a jingle from Gert today.*

jingled *mod.* alcohol intoxicated. □ *She was a little jingled, but not worse than that.* □ *Let's go out and get good and jingled.*

jingler *mod.* a drunkard; an alcoholic. □ *The jinglers have taken over the streets.* □ *Where do all these jinglers sleep?*

jitters ['dʒɪdɚz] *n.* the nervous shakes. (Always with *the*.) □ *I get the jitters when I have to talk in public.* □ *Too much booze gives me the jitters.*

jive [dʒaɪv] **1.** *n.* drugs; marijuana. (Drugs. See also *gyve*.) □ *Stop using all that jive all the time.* □ *That jive is gonna be the end of you.* **2.** *n.* back talk. □ *Cut the jive, man!* □ *Don't you give me any of that jive!* **3.** *n.* lies; deception; nonsense. □ *No more of your jive. Talk straight or don't talk.* □ *I've listened to your jive for years. You'll never change.* **4.** *mod.* deceptive; insincere. □ *Don't give me all those jive excuses.* □ *I listened to her little jive speech and then fired her.*

jive-ass *mod.* foolish. (Potentially offensive. Use only with discretion.) □ *You can tell that jive-ass jerk to forget it.* □ *Don't pay any attention to that jive-ass jeff.*

jive talk *n.* slang; contemporary fad words. □ *I like to hear jive talk. It's like trying to work a puzzle.* □ *He stands by the window with a pad of paper and takes down the jive talk he hears.*

jive turkey *n.* a stupid person. □ *What jive turkey made this mess?* □ *Get that jive turkey out of here!*

jivestick AND **gyvestick** *n.* a marijuana cigarette. (Drugs.) □ *Max flipped a jivestick to Bruno and smiled.* □ *He had a gyvestick stuck behind his ear.*

job 1. *n.* a drunkard. □ *What does this old job want besides a drink?* □ *Give the job a drink and make somebody happy today.* **2.** *n.* a theft; a criminal act. (Police and underworld. See also *pull a job*.) □ *Max and Lefty planned a bank job over in Adamsville.* □ *Who did that job at the old mansion last week?*

jobber AND **jobby** ['dʒabɚ AND 'dʒabi] **1.** *n.* a gadget. □ *Where is the little jobber I use to tighten this?* □ *Do you mean this little jobber?* **2.** *n.* a bowel movement. (Juvenile.) □ *Don't forget to jobber, Jimmy.* □ *Mommy, I gotta jobby.*

jobby See the previous entry.

jober as a sudge ['dʒobɚ æz ə 'sədʒ] *mod.* sober. (A deliberate spoonerism on *sober as a judge*.) □ *Me? I'm as jober as a sudge.* □ *What I mean to shay is that I am shertainly as jober as a sudge!*

jock 1. *n.* an athlete. (See also *strap, jockstrap*. Now of either sex.) □ *The jocks are all at practice now.* □ *She's dating a jock who has to be home by ten.* **2.** *n.* an athletic supporter (garment). □ *Somebody dropped a jock in the hall.* □ *Whose jock is that out there on Tracy's clothesline?*

jock(e)y *n.* an addictive drug. (Drugs. Because such a drug rides one like a jockey rides a horse.) □ *That jockey rode her for years.* □ *She fought that jocky, and it finally won.*

jockstrap 1. AND **jockstrapper** *n.* an athlete. (From the name of the supporting garment worn by male athletes.) □ *The jockstrappers are all at practice now.* □ *Here comes one of the best jockstrappers on the team.* **2.** *in.* to work as a professional athlete. □ *I jockstrapped for a few years and then lost my interest in it.* □ *I made a lot of money jockstrapping.*

jockstrapper See the previous entry.

joe 1. *n.* coffee. □ *How about a cup of joe?* □ *Yeah, a cup of black joe would be great.* **2.** *n.* an ordinary man. □ *What does the everyday joe make of all this nonsense?* □ *Do you know even one everyday joe?*

Joe Blow AND **Joe Doakes** ['dʒo 'blo AND 'dʒo 'doks] *n.* a typical or average male American citizen. □ *What do you think Joe Blow really thinks about all this?* □ *According to surveys, Joe Doakes can hardly read.*

Joe Citizen ['dʒo 'sɪtəsn̩] *n.* a general term for a male representative of the public. (Compare to *John Q. Public*.) □ *Joe Citizen hasn't spoken yet.* □ *Joe Citizen is watching T.V.*

Joe College *n.* a typical or average male college student. □ *You sure look like Joe College from the good old days.* □ *Joe College never had a computer or a* *laser-powered record player in the good old days.*

Joe Doakes See *Joe Blow.*

Joe Schmo ['dʒo 'ʃmo] *n.* a jerk. ☐ *Joe Schmo doesn't really care.* ☐ *Let's say Joe Schmo wants a new car. What does he do?*

Joe Six-pack *n.* the average guy who sits around drinking beer by the six-pack. ☐ *Joe Six-pack likes that kind of television program.* ☐ *All Joe Six-pack wants is a good game on T.V.*

john **1.** *n.* a toilet; a bathroom. ☐ *Somebody's in the john.* ☐ *Is there another john around here?* **2.** *n.* a man. ☐ *Some john was around asking for you.* ☐ *This john came up and asked if I had seen the girl in a picture he had.* **3.** *n.* a prostitute's customer. ☐ *She led the john into an alley where Lefty robbed him.* ☐ *The john looked a little embarrassed.* **4.** *n.* a victim of a crime or deception; a *sucker.* ☐ *The john went straight to the cops and told the whole thing.* ☐ *Clobber the john a good one when he turns around.*

John Doe ['dʒɑn 'do] *n.* a general term for a man. (The mate of *Jane Doe.*) ☐ *John Doe was the name at the bottom of the check.* ☐ *Oh, you mean John Doe isn't his real name?*

John Hancock *n.* one's signature. (Refers to the signature of John Hancock, one of the signers of the Declaration of Independence.) ☐ *Put your John Hancock right here, if you don't mind.* ☐ *Mr. Wilson's John Hancock is worth about thirty million.*

John Q. Public ['dʒɑn 'kju 'pəblɪk] *n.* a general term for a male representative of the public. (The mate of *Jane Q. Public.*) ☐ *John Q. Public doesn't seem to like the new tax forms.* ☐ *John Q. Public tends not to like regimentation.*

Johnnie-come-lately AND **JCL** *n.* someone new to a situation or status. ☐ *This Johnnie-come-lately doesn't know what it was like in the old days.* ☐ *I'm just a Johnnie-come-lately, but I'm eager.*

Johnny-be-good *n.* a police officer. ☐ *Here comes Johnny-be-good, so be good.* ☐ *Johnny-be-good went through my pockets.*

John(ny) Law *n.* a law officer. ☐ *Johnny Law is supposed to be your friend.* ☐ *John Law showed up with a piece of paper that says you are in trouble.*

johnson **1.** *n.* a thing. (See also *jones.*) ☐ *What is this johnson about you snitching?* ☐ *He's got this smack johnson riding him.* **2.** *n.* a penis. (Again, a "thing." Use caution with the topic.) ☐ *Zip up, or your johnson'll get out.* ☐ *He covered his johnson and ran for the dressing room.*

joined at the hip *mod.* closely connected; as thick as thieves. (As Siamese twins are joined.) ☐ *Those two are joined at the hip. They are always together.* ☐ *Sam and Martha are joined at the hip.*

joint **1.** *n.* a tavern; a speakeasy. (Prohibition.) ☐ *Lefty has his own joint over on Fourth Street.* ☐ *I wanted to open a joint, but I don't have the cash.* **2.** *n.* a low-class establishment; a *dive.* ☐ *Let's get out of this crummy joint.* ☐ *This joint bores me.* **3.** *n.* a tobacco cigarette. ☐ *You got a filter joint on you?* ☐ *Why are beggars being choosers about their joints all of a sudden?* **4.** *n.* a marijuana cigarette. ☐ *He always has a joint with him.* ☐ *The joint wasn't enough to carry him very long.* **5.** *n.* a penis. (Use caution with the topic.) ☐ *He told some joke about a joint, but people just turned away.* ☐ *He covered his joint and ran for the dressing room.* **6.** *n.* a jail; a prison. (Underworld.) ☐ *Lefty just got out of the joint.* ☐ *He learned a lot in the joint that he was anxious to try out.*

joke *tr.* to tease someone; to make fun of someone. ☐ *Everybody was joking my roommate because of her accent.* ☐ *Don't joke me, man. I do the best I can.*

joker *n.* a man; a guy. ☐ *Who was that joker I saw you with last night?* ☐ *Some joker was at the door selling something.*

jollies *n.* a charge or thrill; a sexual thrill; *kick.* ☐ *He got his jollies from skin flicks.*

☐ *This gyvestick gives Ernie all the jollies he wants.*

jollop ['dʒɑləp] *n.* a drink of liquor ☐ *She poured a big jollop into each of the glasses and then drank them one by one.* ☐ *"Have another jollop," she said to herself.*

jolly *mod.* alcohol intoxicated; tipsy. ☐ *Everybody was jolly and singing by the time the food arrived.* ☐ *Kelly was a little too jolly, and her sister told her to slow down.*

jolly-well *mod.* certainly. ☐ *You jolly-well better be there on time.* ☐ *I jolly-well will.*

jolt 1. *n.* the degree of potency of the alcohol in liquor. ☐ *It doesn't have much of a jolt.* ☐ *Watch out. This stuff has quite a jolt.* **2.** *n.* a drink of strong liquor. ☐ *Can you give me a little jolt of shine?* ☐ *He knocked back a jolt and asked for another.* **3.** *n.* a portion or dose of a drug. (Drugs.) ☐ *How about a little jolt as a taste?* ☐ *A jolt costs.* **4.** *n.* the *rush* from an injection of drugs. (Drugs.) ☐ *This stuff doesn't have much jolt.* ☐ *What kind of jolt do you want?*

jones 1. *n.* a thing. (See also *johnson.*) ☐ *There's a big turf jones down on the corner.* ☐ *This get-rich-quick jones will land you in the joint, Lefty.* **2.** *n.* a penis. (Use caution with the topic.) ☐ *Zip up, man. You want your jones getting out?* ☐ *Cut out all this talk about joneses!* **3.** *n.* a drug habit; drug addiction. (Drugs. See also *skag jones.*) ☐ *That jones is really riding that guy.* ☐ *He's got a real bad jones with that dust.*

joog [dʒug] *tr.* to stab someone. (Prisons.) ☐ *Lefty jooged the screw.* ☐ *Man, who'd you joog?*

josh [dʒɑʃ] *tr. & in.* to tease someone; to kid someone. ☐ *Stop joshing. Be serious.* ☐ *You're just joshing me!*

joy dust See the following entry.

joy flakes AND **joy dust** *n.* powdered or crystallized cocaine. (Drugs. See also *crack.*) ☐ *Is joy flakes the same as crack?* ☐ *Joy dust is sort of crack without the press coverage.*

joy juice *n.* liquor; beer. ☐ *Joy juice makes Ted sad.* ☐ *Can I pour some more of this joy juice?*

joy ride 1. *n.* a drinking bout or party. ☐ *There's a little joy ride over at Tom's.* ☐ *Some joy ride! They ran out of booze.* **2.** *n.* a state of euphoria from drug use. (Drugs.) ☐ *This stuff is a real joy ride.* ☐ *Ernie's on a little joy ride right now and can't come to the phone.* **3.** *n.* a ride where the passenger does not return alive. (Underworld.) ☐ *Mr. Big wanted Bruno to take Max on a joy ride.* ☐ *You're going on a little joy ride with me. Now, get moving.*

joy water *n.* liquor; strong liquor. ☐ *How about some more joy water?* ☐ *No more joy water for me, thanks.*

joybox *n.* a piano. (See also *tinklebox.*) ☐ *Can you play this joybox at all?* ☐ *Your joybox needs some tuning.*

jug 1. *n.* jail. (Usually with *the.*) ☐ *Take it easy. I don't want to end up in the jug.* ☐ *A couple of days in the jug would do you fine.* **2.** *n.* a jug of liquor; a jar of *moonshine;* a can of beer. ☐ *Where's my jug? I need a swig.* ☐ *Pass her the jug, Sam.* **3.** AND **jug up** *in.* to drink heavily. ☐ *Let's jug up and have a good time.* ☐ *We jugged till about noon and then went to sleep.* (More at *jugger.*) **4.** *n.* a glass vial of liquid amphetamine intended for injection. (Drugs.) ☐ *His mother found a jug and took it to a drugstore to find out what it was.* ☐ *Any kid can get jugs just by asking around.* **5.** *n.* the jugular vein, used for the injection of narcotics. (Drugs.) ☐ *Now Ernie has to take it in the jug.* ☐ *He's even got scars on his jugs.*

jug up See the previous entry.

jug wine *n.* cheap wine that is sold in volume, usually in gallon jugs. ☐ *We're having a little do tomorrow—nothing special. A little jug wine and chips.* ☐ *Can you stop by the juice shop and nick some jug wine?*

jugged (up) *mod.* alcohol intoxicated. ☐ *I'm not jugged up. I'm not even tipsy.* ☐ *Fred was too jugged to drive home.*

jugger *n.* an alcoholic; a drunkard. □ *A couple of old juggers sat in the alley, trying to figure out how to get some more.* □ *He's a jugger, and he will never change.*

jughead 1. *n.* a stupid person. □ *You can be such a jughead!* □ *I guess I'm sort of a jughead lately.* **2.** *n.* a drunkard. □ *Buy the jughead a drink. That'll shut him up.* □ *You don't see jugheads at parties as much as you used to.*

juice 1. *n.* liquor; wine. □ *Let's go get some juice and get stewed.* □ *You got any juice in your room?* **2.** *in.* to drink heavily. □ *Both of them were really juicing.* □ *Stop juicing and listen to me.* **3.** *n.* electricity. □ *The juice has been off since dawn.* □ *Turn on the juice, and let's see if it runs.* **4.** *n.* energy; power; political influence. □ *The boss has the juice with the board to make the necessary changes.* □ *Dave left the president's staff because he just didn't have the juice anymore to be useful.* **5.** *n.* orange juice futures market. (Securities markets. Usually with *the*.) □ *The juice opened a little high today, but fell quickly under profit taking.* □ *It's time to sell the juice and buy bellies.*

juice freak *n.* someone who prefers alcohol to drugs. (Drugs.) □ *Freddy is a juice freak. He won't touch dolls.* □ *Juice freaks end up with addictions, too.*

juice house *n.* a liquor store. □ *Would you stop by the juice house for some foam?* □ *The juice house was held up last night.*

juice joint *n.* a liquor establishment; a speakeasy. (Prohibition.) □ *His grandfather ran a juice joint during prohibition.* □ *The cops raided the juice joints over and over.*

juice racket *n.* a racket where exorbitant interest is charged on loans. (Underworld.) □ *The cops got one of the leaders of the juice racket.* □ *The juice racket is no picnic, I guess.*

juice something back *tr.* to drink alcohol. □ *He's been juicing it back since noon.* Ⓣ *Juice back your drink, and let's go.*

juicehead AND **juicer** *n.* a heavy drinker; a drunkard. □ *Hank is turning into a regular juicehead.* □ *The tavern is always filled with juicers on Friday night.*

juicer See the previous entry.

juicy *mod.* alcohol intoxicated. □ *Mary is just a little bit juicy, I'm afraid.* □ *She's so juicy she can't stand up!*

jump bail *tr.* to fail to show up in court and forfeit bail. □ *Lefty jumped bail, and now he's a fugitive.* □ *Once you've jumped bail, everybody is after you.*

jump smooth *in.* to give up illegal activities; to become *straight*. (Underworld.) □ *Freddy jumped smooth just in time.* □ *After a night in the junk tank, I knew I had to jump smooth.*

jump-start 1. *n.* the act of starting a car by getting power—through jumper cables—from another car. □ *I got a jump-start from a friend.* □ *Who can give me a jump-start?* **2.** *tr.* to start a car by getting power from another car. □ *I jump-started her car for her.* □ *I can't jump-start your car. My battery is low.*

jump (street) *n.* the beginning; the start (of something). (Prisons and streets.) □ *I knew from jump that you were going to be trouble.* □ *Way back at jump street, I spotted you as a troublemaker.*

jump the gun *tr.* to start too soon; to start before the starting signal. □ *Don't jump the gun again. Wait till I tell you.* □ *The secretary jumped the gun and gave out the letters too soon.*

jump-start someone or something *tr.* to get someone or something going or functioning. □ *I need to jump-start Bill early in the morning to get him going in time to get on the road by a decent hour.* □ *I am looking for someone to jump-start my car.*

jumpy *mod.* nervous. □ *I'm a little jumpy today, and I don't know why.* □ *Now, don't be jumpy. Everything will be all right.*

jungle *n.* a vicious area of confusion; the real world. □ *The place is a jungle out there. You'll grow up fast out there.* □ *Once you're out in that jungle, you'll appreciate home more.*

jungle juice *n.* homemade liquor; any strong liquor. ☐ *This jungle juice will knock you for a loop.* ☐ *Jungle juice will do in a pinch.*

jungle mouth *n.* a case of very bad breath; breath like the rotting jungle floor. ☐ *My husband woke up with jungle mouth, and I could hardly stand to be around him.* ☐ *Wow, Wayne really has a bad case of jungle mouth.*

jungled *mod.* alcohol intoxicated; affected by *jungle juice.* ☐ *Pete is a little jungled.* ☐ *He was jungled before he came here.*

juniper juice *n.* gin. (From the juniper berry flavoring of gin.) ☐ *He just lived for his daily ounce of juniper juice.* ☐ *Tracy used to like juniper juice before she went on the dust.*

junk bond *n.* a low-rated corporate bond that pays higher interest because of greater risk. (Parallel to *junk food.*) ☐ *Don't put all your money into junk bonds.* ☐ *Junk bonds pay a lot of interest.*

junk fax *n.* an unwanted and irritating fax message. ☐ *We got nothing but a whole pile of junk faxes today.* ☐ *I wish they would outlaw junk faxes.*

junk food *n.* food that is typically high in fats and salt and low in nutritional value; food from a fast-food restaurant. ☐ *Stay away from junk food. It's bad for you.* ☐ *Junk food tastes good no matter how greasy it is.*

junk heap *n.* a dilapidated old car; a dilapidated house or other structure. ☐ *They lived in that junk heap for thirty years and never painted it.* ☐ *Why don't you fix up that junk heap?*

junk mail *n.* unwanted or annoying advertising mail. ☐ *All we got was junk mail today.* ☐ *I read everything that comes in the mail, even the junk mail.*

junk squad *n.* police who enforce the narcotics laws. (Underworld.) ☐ *The junk squad has more than it can handle trying to keep up with the hard stuff.* ☐ *We need a bigger junk squad in this part of town.*

junk tank *n.* a jail cell where addicts are kept. (Compare to *drunk tank.*) ☐ *That junk tank is a very dangerous place.* ☐ *Nobody sleeps in the junk tank.*

junkie AND **junky** ['dʒəŋki] **1.** *n.* a drug dealer. (Drugs.) ☐ *Max is a junkie.* ☐ *Junkies should be put into the jug.* **2.** *n.* a drug user; an addict. (Drugs.) ☐ *The junkies can be helped, you know.* ☐ *Junkies have to steal to support their habits.*

junky See the previous entry.

just off the boat *mod.* to be freshly immigrated and perhaps gullible and naive. (See also *F.O.B.*) ☐ *I'm not just off the boat. I know what's going on.* ☐ *He may act like he's just off the boat, but he's all right.*

just the ticket *n.* just the perfect thing. ☐ *This little jigger is just the ticket.* ☐ *A nice cup of tea will be just the ticket.*

just what the doctor ordered *n.* exactly what is needed. ☐ *This nice cool beer is just what the doctor ordered.* ☐ *A nice chat with friends is just what the doctor ordered.*

juvie ['dʒuvi] **1.** *n.* a police officer concerned with juveniles. (Underworld.) ☐ *I'm a juvie in the Shakespeare district.* ☐ *The juvies have to know juvenile law cold.* **2.** *n.* a youth; a teenager under age eighteen. (Underworld.) ☐ *I work with juvies a lot. I try to get them back on the track.* ☐ *They brought in a juvie and charged him with shoplifting.* **3.** *mod.* juvenile. ☐ *That was sort of a juvie thing to do.* ☐ *Don't be so juvie.* ☐ *She still has a lot of juvie attitudes.*

K

K. [ke] **1.** AND **kee; key; ki** [ki] *n.* a kilogram of cannabis. (Drugs.) ☐ *You want a whole K?* ☐ *Well, how much is a ki?* **2.** *n.* ketamine hydrochloride, a drug similar to *L.S.D.* (Drugs.) ☐ *You want to try this K stuff?* ☐ *What is this K anyway?* **3.** *n.* a thousand (of anything, such as dollars, bytes, etc.) ☐ *This car is worth at least twenty K.* ☐ *I have 640 K memory in my computer.*

kack See *cack.*

kafooster [kəˈfustɚ] *n.* nonsense. ☐ *We've heard enough of your kafooster.* ☐ *This kafooster about me being a cheater is too much.*

kak See *cack.*

kaka See *caca.*

kangaroo court **1.** *n.* a bogus or extralegal court. ☐ *Is this a newspaper office or a kangaroo court?* ☐ *You have turned this interview into a kangaroo court.* **2.** *n.* a legally convened court operating unjustly. ☐ *"Let me out of this kangaroo court," muttered Fred.* ☐ *The judge held Fred in contempt for calling the proceedings a kangaroo court.*

kayo See *K.O.*

kee See *K.*

keep cool *in.* to keep calm. ☐ *Now, keep cool. It's going to be all right.* ☐ *Just keep cool, man. Chill.*

Keep in touch. *sent.* "Good-bye." (Sometimes a sarcastic way of saying good-bye to someone one doesn't care about.) ☐ *Nice talking to you. Keep in touch.* ☐ *Sorry, we can't use you anymore. Keep in touch.*

Keep on trucking. *sent.* "Keep doing what you are doing."; "Keep taking care of business." ☐ *See ya, man. Keep on trucking.* ☐ *Keep on trucking. Things'll get better.*

keep one's cool *tr.* to remain calm and in control. (See also *keep cool.* Compare to *lose one's cool.*) ☐ *Relax, man! Just keep your cool.* ☐ *It's hard to keep your cool when you've been cheated.*

keep one's head right *tr.* to maintain control of oneself. ☐ *Chill, man, chill. You've got to keep your head right.* ☐ *I can keep my head right. I'm mellow.*

keep one's nose clean *tr.* to keep out of trouble, especially trouble with the law. ☐ *Okay, chum. Keep your nose clean.* ☐ *I can keep my nose clean. Don't worry.*

Keep out of this! *exclam.* "Mind your own business!" ☐ *This is not your affair. Keep out of this!* ☐ *Keep out of this! I'll settle it.*

Keep the faith (baby)! *exclam.* a statement of general encouragement or solidarity. ☐ *You said it! Keep the faith, baby!* ☐ *Keep the faith! See ya later.*

Keep your hands to yourself. **1.** *sent.* "Do not touch things that are not yours."; "Do not touch breakable things." (Said to a child.) ☐ *You can look, but don't touch. Keep your hands to yourself.* ☐ *Put that down and keep your hands to yourself.* **2.** *sent.* "Don't poke or hit other children." (Said to a child.) ☐ *Jimmy! Leave him alone and keep your hands to yourself.* ☐ *Keep your hands to yourself when you go to school.* **3.** *sent.* "No intimate caressing is allowed." (Said to an adult, usually a male.) ☐

Keep your hands to yourself, Buster. □ *Just keep your hands to yourself or take me home.*

Keep your pants on! See the following entry.

Keep your shirt on! AND **Keep your pants on!** *exclam.* "Just wait a minute!" □ *I'll be right with you. Keep your shirt on!* □ *Keep your pants on! You're next.*

keeper *n.* something that can be kept; something that qualifies. □ *This fish is a keeper. Throw the others out.* □ *The chipped one is not a keeper.*

keester AND **keyster; kiester** ['kistɚ] **1.** *n.* a chest; a suitcase. □ *The old lady was hauling the most enormous keester.* □ *The keester was full of cash.* **2.** *n.* the buttocks; the anus. □ *Get your keester over here!* □ *He fell flat on his keyster.*

keg party *n.* a party where liquor, especially beer, is served. □ *There is a free keg party at Freddy's.* □ *The keg party ended early owing to the arrival of uninvited nabs.*

kegger 1. *n.* a party where beer is served from a keg. (Teens and collegiate.) □ *Tiffany is having a kegger, and a few of her intimates are invited.* □ *Isn't there a kegger somewhere tonight?* **2.** AND **keggers** *n.* a keg of beer. (Collegiate.) □ *We need another kegger. It's only nine o'clock.* □ *We came here because somebody said there was keggers.*

keggers See the previous entry.

Kentucky fried *mod.* alcohol intoxicated. (An elaboration of *fried.* Based on the trade name "Kentucky Fried Chicken.") □ *Man, is that guy really Kentucky fried!* □ *I've never seen anybody so downright Kentucky fried on six beers.*

key See *K.*

key figure *n.* an important person in an event; a person central to an event. □ *Wally is a key figure in the investigation.* □ *Bruno is not exactly a key figure, but he can lead us to Mr. Big.*

key grip *n.* the head laborer on a movie set. (Filmmaking.) □ *The key grip has a complaint that could hold up production.* □ *What is the key grip's beef?*

keyed (up) 1. *mod.* nervous; anxious. □ *Sally was a little keyed up before the meet.* □ *When I get keyed, I meditate.* **2.** AND **keyed up to the roof** *mod.* alcohol or drug intoxicated. □ *He was a mite keyed, but still technically sober.* □ *She was so keyed up she could hardly stand up.*

keyed up to the roof See the previous entry.

keyster See *keester.*

ki See *K.*

kibosh ['kaɪbaʃ OR kə'baʃ] **1.** *tr.* to end something; to squelch something. □ *Please don't try to kibosh the scheme this time.* □ *Fred kiboshed our plan.* **2.** *n.* the end; the final blow; the thing that terminates something. (Usually with *the.* See also *put the kibosh on something.*) □ *The kibosh was a real corker.* □ *They thought the kibosh was overdone.*

kick 1. *n.* a charge or good feeling (from something); pleasure or enjoyment from something. (See also *get a kick out of someone or something.*) □ *That song really gives me a kick. I love it!* □ *What a kick that gives me!* **2.** *n.* the *jolt* from a drug or a drink of strong liquor. □ *This stuff really has a kick.* □ *The kick nearly knocked Harry over.* **3.** *tr.* to break a drug addiction voluntarily. (Drugs.) □ *I knew I had the guts in me somewhere to kick juice.* □ *It's hard to kick that stuff.* **4.** *n.* a complaint. □ *What's the kick, man?* □ *You got another kick, troublemaker?* **5.** *in.* to complain. □ *Why are you always kicking?* □ *Ernie kicks about everything.* **6.** See *kicks.*

kick around See *knock around.*

kick back 1. *in.* to relax (and enjoy something). □ *Now you just kick back and enjoy this.* □ *I like to kick back and listen to a few tunes.* **2.** *n.* money received in return for a favor. (Usually **kickback.**) □ *The kickback the cop got wasn't enough, as it turned out.* □ *You really don't believe that the cops take* *kickbacks!* **3.** *in.* [for an addict] to return to addiction after having been detoxified and withdrawn. (Drugs.) □ *Gert stopped and kicked back a number of times.* □ *They may kick back a dozen times before it takes.*

kick cold (turkey) *in.* to stop taking drugs without tapering off. (Drugs.) □ *Tracy tried to kick cold turkey, but it was just too much.* □ *Kicking cold may be the only way to do it.*

kick freak *n.* a nonaddicted drug user. (Drugs.) □ *Ernie used to be a kick freak, but all that has changed.* □ *Yeah, the kick freak became a junky.*

kick in the ass See *kick in the (seat of the) pants.*

kick in the butt See *kick in the (seat of the) pants.*

kick in the guts *n.* a severe blow to one's body or spirit. □ *The news was a kick in the guts, and I haven't recovered yet.* □ *I didn't need a kick in the guts like that.*

kick in the (seat of the) pants AND **kick in the ass; kick in the butt; kick in the teeth** *n.* a strong message of encouragement or demand. (Use *ass* and *butt* with discretion.) □ *All he needs is a kick in the seat of the pants to get him going.* □ *A kick in the butt will get her moving.*

kick in the teeth See the previous entry.

kick in the wrist *n.* a drink of liquor. □ *You want another kick in the wrist?* □ *I'll take another kick in the wrist.*

kick off *in.* to die. □ *We've been waiting for years for that cat to kick off.* □ *The old girl finally kicked off.*

kick party *n.* a party where some drug is used. (Drugs.) □ *The kick party broke up early with the help of Johnny-be-good.* □ *There was a kick party at one of the crack houses, and even little children went in.*

kick some ass (around) *tr.* to take over and start giving orders; to *raise hell.* (Potentially offensive. Use only with discretion.) □ *Do I have to come over there and kick some ass around?* □ *Bruno is just the one to kick some ass over there.*

kick the bucket *tr.* to die. □ *I'm too young to kick the bucket.* □ *The cat kicked the bucket last night.*

kick the habit *tr.* to voluntarily end any habit or custom, especially a drug habit. (See also *knock the habit.*) □ *She tried and tried to kick the habit.* □ *It's hard to kick the habit.*

kick up a storm *tr.* to create a disturbance; to put on an angry display. □ *My dad will just kick up a storm when he finds out.* □ *The demand made us all kick up a storm.*

kicken See *kickin'.*

kicker *n.* a clever but stinging remark; a sharp criticism; a *zinger.* □ *I waited for the kicker, and finally it came.* □ *The kicker really made me mad.*

kickin' AND **kicken** ['kɪkn̩] *mod.* wild; super; excellent. □ *Your rally was really kickin'.* □ *I don't know where you get your clothes, but that jacket's kickin'.*

kicks *n.* cleats or shoes; gym shoes. (Collegiate. See also *kick.*) □ *Don't you dare wear those kicks in here!* □ *Take your kicks off before coming in.*

kicky ['kɪki] *mod.* exciting and energetic. □ *Man, what a kicky idea!* □ *She is a real kicky gal.*

kid stuff *n.* marijuana, a drug for "beginners." (Drugs.) □ *That grass is kid stuff.* □ *He's still using kid stuff.*

kid-vid ['kɪdvɪd] *n.* children's television; television programming aimed at children. □ *Kid-vid isn't good for anything other than selling cereal.* □ *I don't know. Kid-vid is fun.*

kidney-buster **1.** *n.* a rough ride; a rough road. □ *This road is a kidney-buster. I wish they'd fix it.* □ *That kidney-buster damaged my car.* **2.** *n.* an uncomfortable or poorly built seat in a vehicle. □ *I have to get this kidney-buster replaced.* □ *This kidney-buster is going to ruin my back.*

kiester See *keester.*

kill 1. *tr.* to be very successful with an audience; to perform very well for an audience. ☐ *She really killed them with that last joke.* ☐ *She killed them, and they died with laughter.* **2.** *tr.* to eat all of something; to drink all (of a bottle) of something. ☐ *Kill this bottle so we can get another.* ☐ *We finally killed the last of the turkey.* **3.** *tr.* to douse a light. ☐ *Kill that light!* ☐ *Would you kill the light so they can't see we're home?* **4.** *tr.* to stop or terminate something; to quash a story; to stop a story from being printed in a newspaper. ☐ *Kill that story. It's got too many errors.* ☐ *This issue has gone to press. Too late to kill it.*

killed (off) *mod.* alcohol or drug intoxicated. (Drugs.) ☐ *The team went out drinking and came home killed off.* ☐ *Man, were those guys killed.*

killer 1. *n.* a marijuana cigarette. ☐ *How about a killer, Max?* ☐ *He's always smoking a killer.* **2.** *n.* a very funny joke. ☐ *That last one was a killer!* ☐ *She told a killer about a red-nosed juicer.* **3.** *n.* something extraordinary. ☐ *That jacket is a real killer!* ☐ *That car is a killer. I like it!* **4.** *mod.* extraordinary; great. ☐ *What a killer jacket you're wearing!* ☐ *This is a killer hamburger all right.*

killer-diller *n.* an excellent thing or person. ☐ *She is just a real killer-diller.* ☐ *This story is a real killer-diller.*

killer weed 1. *n.* very potent marijuana. (Drugs.) ☐ *Wow, this stuff is killer weed!* ☐ *This killer weed is oregano, I think.* **2.** *n.* phencyclidine (P.C.P.), an animal tranquilizer. (Drugs.) ☐ *Killer weed seems to be a favorite around here just now.* ☐ *Killer weed, K.J.—it's all exactly the same stuff.*

killing *n.* a great financial success. ☐ *Sally made a real killing in the stock market.* ☐ *Fred made a killing in real estate.*

killjoy *n.* a person who takes the fun out of things for other people; a *party-pooper.* ☐ *Don't be such a killjoy!* ☐ *Larry is such a killjoy when he gets nervous.*

kilobucks *n.* a tremendous sum of money. (See also *megabucks.*) ☐ *These boondoggles waste kilobucks!* ☐ *How many kilobucks does a set of wheels like that cost?*

King Grod [... grɑd] *n.* a very repellent male. (California.) ☐ *You are just King Grod! So gross!* ☐ *Ralph is almost King Grod!*

King Kong pills AND **King Kong specials** *n.* barbiturates. (Drugs. See also *gorilla biscuits.*) ☐ *Watch out for those King Kong pills.* ☐ *Don't mix these King Kong specials with booze.*

King Kong specials See the previous entry.

kingpin *n.* a major figure in organized crime. (Underworld.) ☐ *Mr. Big is not your typical kingpin. He likes to play the stock market, too.* ☐ *The drug kingpins are well protected.*

kink 1. *n.* a strange person; a *kinky* person. ☐ *The guy's a kink. Watch out for him.* ☐ *There are kinks all over this place.* **2.** *n.* a sexually deviant person. ☐ *He was a kink, and I broke up with him.* ☐ *The kinks congregate two streets over.*

kinky 1. *mod.* having to do with someone or something strange or weird. ☐ *The guy is so kinky that everyone avoids him.* ☐ *Who is that kinky dame in the net stockings?* **2.** *mod.* having to do with unconventional sexual acts or people who perform them. ☐ *She seems to have a morbid interest in kinky stuff.* ☐ *He showed her a picture of some kind of kinky sex thing.*

kip *in.* to sleep. ☐ *He's upstairs kipping. Can he call you back?* ☐ *He'll kip for about another hour.*

kipe *tr.* to steal something. ☐ *Where did you kipe this thing?* ☐ *The punk kiped a newspaper just for the heck of it.*

kiper ['kɑɪpɚ] *n.* a thief; someone who steals. ☐ *The punk is a two-bit kiper and needs to be taught a lesson.* ☐ *You dirty little kiper. Give it back!*

kiss-ass 1. *mod.* subservient. (Potentially offensive. Use *ass* with discretion.) ☐ *Don't be such a kiss-ass jerk. Tell off your boss.* ☐ *He is a little kiss-ass bastard who'll do anything to get ahead.* **2.**

in. to act subservient (to someone). (Potentially offensive. Use only with discretion.) □ *Stop kiss-assing around and stand up to your employer.* □ *That guy will kiss-ass his way to the top.*

kiss of death *n.* the direct cause of the end of someone or something. □ *The ordinance was the kiss of death for our budding jazz band.* □ *Your attitude was the kiss of death for your employment here.*

kiss off **1.** ['kɪs ɔf] *n.* the dismissal of someone or something. (Usually **kiss-off.**) □ *The kiss-off was when I lost the Wilson contract.* □ *Pete got the kiss off and is now looking for a new job.* **2.** ['kɪs ɔf] *n.* death. (Usually **kiss-off.**) □ *When the time comes for the kiss-off, I hope I'm asleep.* □ *The kiss-off came wrapped in lead, and it was instant.* **3.** ['kɪs 'ɔf] *in.* to die. □ *The cat is going to have to kiss off one of these days soon.* □ *The cat kissed off after eighteen years of joy and devotion.*

kiss someone or something off **1.** *tr.* [with *someone*] to kill someone. □ *Bruno had instructions to kiss Max off.* 🅃 *Max wanted to kiss off Bruno, too.* **2.** *tr.* [with *something*] to forget about something; to ignore something. □ *Just kiss it off. You've lost your chance.* 🅃 *Just kiss off any idea you might have had about running for office.*

kiss someone's ass *tr.* to fawn over someone; to flatter and curry favor with someone. (Potentially offensive. Use ass with discretion.) □ *What does he expect me to do? Kiss his ass?* □ *I won't kiss your ass for anything.*

kiss something good-bye *tr.* to face and accept the loss of something. □ *Well, you can kiss that 100 bucks good-bye.* □ *I kissed my chance for success good-bye.*

kiss the dust *tr.* to fall to the earth, because of death or because of being struck. (Western movies. See also *bite the dust.*) □ *I'll see that you kiss the dust before sunset, cowboy!* □ *You'll kiss the dust before I will, Sheriff.*

kiss the porcelain god *tr.* to empty one's stomach; to vomit. □ *He fled the room to kiss the porcelain god, I guess.* □ *Who's in there kissing the porcelain god?*

kiss up to someone *in.* to flatter someone; to make over someone. □ *I'm not going to kiss up to anybody to get what's rightfully mine.* □ *If I have to kiss up to her, I guess I will.*

kisser *n.* the face; the mouth. (See also *right in the kisser.*) □ *I poked him right in the kisser.* □ *There he stood with a bloody kisser.*

kissyface ['kɪsifes] **1.** *n.* kissing. □ *There was a lot of kissyface going on in the back seat.* □ *They're mostly involved with kissyface at this age.* **2.** *mod.* feeling the need to kiss and be kissed. □ *I feel all kissyface.* □ *They were both sort of kissyface, so they left.*

kit and caboodle ['kɪt n̩ kə'budl̩] *n.* everything; all parts and property. (Often with *whole.*) □ *I want you out of here—kit and caboodle—by noon.* □ *She moved in to stay, kit and caboodle.* □ *She plunked her whole kit and caboodle right in my way.*

kite **1.** *n.* a drug user who is always *high.* (Drugs.) □ *The guy's a kite. He won't make any sense no matter what you ask him.* □ *Gert is a kite, and she's getting worse.* **2.** *tr.* to write worthless checks; to raise the amount on a check. (Underworld. See also *fly kites.*) □ *Chuck made a fortune kiting checks.* □ *He kited a check for $50,000.* **3.** *n.* a worthless check. (Underworld.) □ *He finally wrote one kite too many, and they nabbed him.* □ *She passed kites from one end of town to the other, then dyed her hair, took off her glasses, and did it all over again.*

kited *mod.* alcohol intoxicated. (From *high as a kite.*) □ *Tracy was too kited to see her hand in front of her.* □ *Both guys were kited by midnight.*

kitsch [kɪtʃ] *n.* any form of entertainment—movies, books, plays—with enormous popular appeal. □ *This kitsch sells like mad in the big city.* □ *Most people prefer kitsch to art.*

kitschy ['kɪtʃi] *mod.* trivial in spite of enormous popular appeal. □ *A lot of* *people like kitschy art.* □ *This stuff is too kitschy for me.*

klepto ['klɛpto] *n.* a kleptomaniac; one who steals small things obsessively. □ *The cops thought Gert was a klepto until she showed them her receipts.* □ *The jury awarded Gert five grand for being falsely arrested as a klepto.*

klotz See *klutz.*

kluck See *cluck.*

kludge AND **kluge** [kləd3 OR klud3] **1.** *n.* a patch or a fix in a computer program or circuit. □ *This is a messy kludge, but it will do the job.* □ *Kluges which are invisible don't bother anybody.* **2.** *tr.* to patch or fix a computer program circuit. □ *I only have time to kludge this problem.* □ *The kid kluged a program for us in an hour.*

kludgy ['kləd3i OR 'klud3i] *mod.* having to do with an inefficient or sloppily written computer program. □ *This program is too kludgy to be acceptable.* □ *Who wrote this kludgy mess?* □ *I don't care if it's kludgy. Does it work?*

kluge See *kludge.*

klutz AND **klotz** [kləts AND klɑts] *n.* a stupid and clumsy person. □ *Don't be a klutz!* □ *Some klotz put mustard in the stew.*

klutzy ['klətsi] *mod.* foolish; stupid. □ *That was really a klutzy thing to do.* □ *You are so klutzy!* □ *Whose klutzy idea was this?*

knee-deep in something *mod.* having lots of something. (See also *up to one's knees.*) □ *We are knee-deep in orders and loving it.* □ *Right now, we are knee-deep in trouble.*

knee-high to a grasshopper *mod.* of very short stature. (Folksy.) □ *I knew you when you were knee-high to a grasshopper.* □ *I was knee-high to a grasshopper when I first heard that joke.*

knee-jerk *mod.* automatic; quick and without thought. □ *That was only a knee-jerk response. Pay no attention.* □ *My knee-jerk response is that you should not go.*

knock *tr.* to criticize someone or something. □ *Don't knock it if you haven't tried it.* □ *The papers are knocking my favorite candidate again.*

knock around 1. *in.* to waste time. □ *Stop knocking around and get to work!* □ *I need a couple of days a week just for knocking around.* **2.** AND **kick around.** *in.* to wander around; to *bum around.* □ *I think I'll knock around a few months before looking for another job.* □ *We're just knocking around and keeping out of trouble.*

knock back a drink *tr.* to drink a beer; to have a quick drink of liquor. □ *He knocked back three beers in a row.* □ *Let's knock back another one or two and leave.*

Knock it off! *exclam.* "Be Quiet!"; "Shut up!" □ *Hey, you guys! Knock it off!* □ *I'm trying to sleep! Knock it off!*

knock off (work) *tr. & in.* to quit work, for the day or for a break. □ *What time do you knock off work?* □ *I knock off about five-thirty.*

knock one back See the following entry.

knock one over AND **knock one back** *tr.* to take a drink of liquor. □ *He knocked one over right away and demanded another.* 🅃 *He knocked back one and belched grossly.*

knock some heads together *tr.* to scold some people; to get some people to do what they are supposed to be doing. □ *Do I have to come in there and knock some heads together, or will you kids settle down?* □ *I knocked some heads together and got the proposal out on time.*

knock someone dead *tr.* to put on a stunning performance or display for someone. □ *She knocked us dead with her stunning performance.* □ *Go out on that stage and knock them dead, Sally.*

knock someone or something off 1. *tr.* [with *something*] to manufacture or make something, especially in haste. (See also *knock someone or something out.*) □ *I'll see if I can knock another one off before lunch.* 🅃 *They knocked off four window frames in an hour.* **2.**

tr. [with *someone*] to kill someone. (Underworld. See also *bump someone off.*) □ *The mob knocked the witnesses off.* 🅃 *The cops would be happy if someone wanted to knock off Mr. Big.* **3.** *tr.* [with *something*] to lower the price of something; to knock off some dollars or cents from the price of something. □ *The store manager knocked 30 percent off the price of the coat.* □ *Can't you knock something off on this damaged item?*

knock someone or something out 1. *tr.* [with *someone*] to surprise someone. □ *Her stunning beauty knocked us all out.* 🅃 *The news knocked out the entire crowd.* **2.** AND **knock something off** *tr.* [with *something*] to write something quickly. □ *Would you please knock a speech out for the senator?* 🅃 *I'll knock out a letter explaining the whole thing.*

knock someone some skin *tr.* to shake hands with someone. □ *Hey, man, knock me some skin!* □ *Pete knocked Sam some skin, and they left the building together.*

knock someone up *tr.* to make a woman pregnant. (Crude.) □ *They say it was Bruno who knocked her up.* 🅃 *He did not knock up Tracy. I did.* (More at *knocked up.*)

knock someone's block off *tr.* to hit someone hard in the head. (See also *block.*) □ *Wilbur almost knocked Tom's block off by accident.* □ *He threatened to knock my block off if I didn't do as I was told.*

knock someone's socks off *tr.* to surprise or startle someone; to overwhelm someone. □ *Wow, that explosion nearly knocked my socks off.* □ *This news'll knock your socks off.*

knock something down 1. *tr.* to drink a portion of liquor. □ *Here, knock this down and let's go.* 🅃 *He knocked down a bottle of beer and called for another.* **2.** *tr.* to earn a certain amount of money. 🅃 *I'm lucky to knock down twenty thousand.* 🅃 *She must knock down about twenty thou a year.*

knock something into a cocked hat *tr.* to demolish a plan, a story, etc. □ *I knocked his plans into a cocked hat.* □ *You've knocked everything into a cocked hat.*

knock something together AND **throw something together** *tr.* to assemble something—such as a meal—at the last moment. □ *I'll see if I can throw something together.* 🅃 *I knocked together a vegetable dish at the last minute.*

knock the habit *tr.* to stop using drugs; to break a drug addiction. (Drugs. See also *kick the habit.*) □ *I just can't knock the habit.* □ *He tried to knock the habit by drinking lots of booze.*

knockdown drag-out fight *n.* a prolonged and hard fight. □ *Trying to get my proposal accepted was a knockdown drag-out fight.* □ *I don't want to get involved in a knockdown drag-out fight over this business.*

knocked in *mod.* arrested. (Underworld.) □ *Would you believe that Rocko has never been knocked in?* □ *When Lefty was knocked in, they found his heater on him.*

knocked out 1. *mod.* exhausted. □ *We were all knocked out at the end of the day.* □ *I'm knocked out after just a little bit of work.* **2.** *mod.* overwhelmed. □ *We were just knocked out when we heard your news.* □ *Were we surprised? We were knocked out—elated!* **3.** *mod.* alcohol or drug intoxicated. □ *They were all knocked out by midnight.* □ *Gary was knocked out when we dropped by, so we tried to sober him up.*

knocked up 1. *mod.* battered; beaten. □ *Sally was a little knocked up by the accident.* □ *This book is a little knocked up, so I'll lower the price.* **2.** *mod.* alcohol intoxicated. □ *Bill was knocked up and didn't want to drive.* □ *Wow, was that guy knocked up!* **3.** *mod.* pregnant. □ *Tracy got knocked up again.* □ *Isn't she knocked up most of the time?*

knockers 1. *n.* the breasts. (Potentially offensive. Use only with discretion.) □

Nice knockers, huh? □ *All you think about is knockers.* **2.** *n.* the testicles. (Potentially offensive. Use only with discretion.) □ *Pow, right in the knockers. Ye gods, it hurt!* □ *He turned sideways to protect his knockers.*

knockout 1. *n.* something that is quite stunning. □ *Your new car is a knockout.* □ *Isn't her dress a knockout?* **2.** *n.* a good-looking man or woman. □ *Your date is a real knockout.* □ *Who is that knockout I saw you with last weekend?* **3.** *mod.* very exciting. □ *It was a real knockout evening.* □ *What a knockout idea!*

knothead *n.* a stupid person. □ *Don't be such a knothead!* □ *You're no knothead. You're just great!*

know all the angles *tr.* to know all the tricks and artifices of dealing with someone or something. □ *Ask my mouthpiece about taxes. He knows all the angles.* □ *Rocko knows all the angles, That's how he keeps out of the slammer.*

know from something *in.* to know about something. (See also *not know from nothing.*) □ *Do you know from timers, I mean how timers work?* □ *I don't know from babies! Don't ask me about feeding them!*

know-how ['nohau] *n.* the knowledge of how to do something. □ *I don't have the know-how to do this job.* □ *You'll get the know-how on the job.*

know-it-all *n.* someone who gives the impression of knowing everything. □ *Pete is such a know-it-all!* □ *That know-it-all isn't of much use to our committee.*

know shit from Shinola AND **tell shit from Shinola** [. . . ʃaɪ'nolə] *tr.* to know what's what; to be intelligent and aware. (Always in the negative. Shinola is a brand of shoe polish. A person who doesn't *know shit from Shinola* is very stupid. See also *No Shinola!*) □ *Poor Tom doesn't know shit from Shinola.* □ *Fred can't tell shit from Shinola, and he's been made my boss.*

know the score *tr.* to know the way things work in the hard, cruel world. □ *Don't try to con me. I know the score.* □ *She knows the score. She wasn't born yesterday.*

know what's what *tr.* to be aware of what is going on in the world. □ *Heidi knows what's what. She can help.* □ *We don't know what's what around here yet.*

know where it's at *tr.* to know the way things really are. □ *I know where it's at. I don't need to be told.* □ *We know where it's at, and we want to change it.*

know where one is coming from *tr.* to understand someone's motivation; to understand and relate to someone's position. □ *I know where you're coming from. I've been there.* □ *We all know where he's coming from. That's why we are so worried.*

know which end is up *tr.* to be alert and knowledgeable. □ *Don't try to hustle me, sister. I know which end is up.* □ *Poor Jed doesn't even know which end is up.*

knowledge-box *n.* the head. □ *Now, I want to get this into your knowledge-box once and for all.* □ *My knowledge-box is just spinning with all this information.*

knuckle down (to something) *in.* to get busy doing something. □ *Please knuckle down to your studies.* □ *You have to knuckle down if you want to get ahead.*

knuckle-dragger *n.* a strong, ape-like man. □ *Bruno is Mr. Big's favorite knuckle-dragger.* □ *Call off your knuckle-draggers. I'll pay you whatever you want.*

knuckle sandwich *n.* a blow struck in the teeth or mouth. □ *How would you like a knuckle sandwich?* □ *He threatened to give me a knuckle sandwich.*

knuckle under (to someone or something) *in.* to give in to or accept someone or something. □ *She always refused to knuckle under to anyone.* □ *You have to knuckle under to the system sometimes.*

knucklehead *n.* a stupid person. □ *Oh, I feel like such a knucklehead!* □ *Don't worry, you're not a knucklehead.*

K.O. AND **kayo** ['ke'o] **1.** *n.* a knockout. (The abbreviation is an initialism. Boxing.) □ *It was a quick K.O., and Wilbur was the new champ.* □ *It was a classic kayo. It was quick and effective.* **2.** *tr.* to knock someone out. (Boxing.) □ *Wilbur planned to K.O. Wallace in the third round.* □ *Wilbur usually kayos his opponent.* (More at *K.O.ed*.)

K.O.ed ['ke'od] **1.** *mod.* "knocked out." (Initialism. Originally from boxing.) □ *Wilbur was K.O.ed and got a cut over his eye.* □ *He stayed K.O.ed for about two minutes.* **2.** *mod.* alcohol or drug intoxicated. (Initialism.) □ *Both guys were K.O.ed and spent the night.* □ *How could anybody get so K.O.ed on a six-pack?*

Kojak ['kodʒæk] *n.* a police officer. (From the television character of the same name.) □ *Ask Kojak in for a cup of coffee.* □ *Here comes Kojak. Beat it!*

kong [kɔŋ] *n.* strong whiskey; illicit whiskey. (From the movie ape King Kong.) □ *How about a big swallow of that kong?* □ *Here, have some kong.*

konk See *conk*.

kook [kuk] *n.* a strange person. □ *She seems like a kook, but she is just grand, really.* □ *Todd's a kook, but I love him.*

kookish ['kukɪʃ] *mod.* strange; eccentric. □ *There's a lot of kookish things going on around here.* □ *He is just too kookish.* □ *Who is the kookish one over there with the purple shades?*

koshe See the following entry.

kosher ['koʃɚ OR 'koʒɚ] **1.** AND **koshe** *mod.* acceptable; orthodox; *cricket.* (From Hebrew *kasher,* "proper," via Yiddish.) □ *Is it kosher to do this?* □ *It's a kosher thing, okay.* □ *Her party was koshe. Everyone loved it.* □ *Of course, it's kosher. Everybody does it.* **2.** *tr.* to make something acceptable. □ *Do you want me to kosher it with the boss for you?* □ *Look, if you can kosher this stuff with my parents, I agree.* **3.** *mod.* having to do with undiluted alcohol. □ *I'll take mine kosher with a little ice.* □ *Do you want this kosher or with soda?*

kvetch AND **quetch** [kvɛtʃ AND kʍɛtʃ] **1.** *in.* to complain. (From German *quetschen,* "to squeeze," via Yiddish.) □ *Quit your kvetching!* □ *He quetches from dawn to dusk.* **2.** *n.* a complainer. □ *What a kvetch you are!* □ *We don't need another kvetch around here.*

L

L7 ['ɛl 'sɛvn̩] **1.** *n.* a *square;* a dull person. ☐ *That guy is an L7.* ☐ *Who is that L7 in the wingtip shoes?* **2.** *mod.* dull; *square.* ☐ *This guy was real, like, you know, L7.* ☐ *Who is the most L7 person you know?*

label mate *n.* someone who records on the same label (as the speaker). (Record industry.) ☐ *Frank Duke is my label mate, and we like to get together and gossip about the record industry.* ☐ *I feel like a real success because my label mates are so good.*

labonza [lə'bɑnzə] **1.** *n.* the buttocks. ☐ *Good grief, what a gross labonza!* ☐ *She fell flat on her labonza.* **2.** *n.* the pit of the stomach. ☐ *That kind of beautiful singing really gets you right in the labonza.* ☐ *She experienced the kind of gut-wrenching anger that starts in your labonza and cuts through right to the tip of your noggin.* **3.** *n.* the belly. ☐ *I feel the effects of last night's celebration in my wallet and in my labonza.* ☐ *Look at the labonza on that creep! He's gonna deliver triplets.*

lace **1.** *tr.* to add alcohol to coffee or tea; to add alcohol to any food or drink. ☐ *Who laced the punch?* ☐ *I think I'll lace my coffee with a little whisky.* **2.** *tr.* to add a bit of one drug to another; to add drugs to any food or drink. (Drugs.) ☐ *Somebody laced the ice cubes with acid.* ☐ *This fag is laced with opium.* **3.** *n.* money. (Underworld.) ☐ *You got any lace in those pockets?* ☐ *My lace won't reach that far. I can't afford it.*

lacy *mod.* feminine; effeminate. ☐ *He's sort of lacy, but when he settles down to work, the sparks fly.* ☐ *This place is too lacy.* ☐ *The hotel lobby is a little lacy, but it's clean.*

ladies' room *n.* the women's restroom. ☐ *Is there a ladies' room somewhere close?* ☐ *Sally has gone to the ladies' room.*

lady bear *n.* a female officer of the law. (See also *Smokey (the Bear), mama bear.*) ☐ *This lady bear asks me if I'm going to a fire.* ☐ *These two lady bears walked in and took a booth by the door.*

lady-killer *n.* a man who is very successful with women. ☐ *Bruno is anything but a lady killer.* ☐ *We saw an old-time lady-killer with a close-cut black mustache and everything.*

Lady Snow *n.* cocaine. (Drugs.) ☐ *I spent the afternoon with Lady Snow.* ☐ *Lady Snow is about the only friend I have left.*

ladyfinger *n.* a marijuana cigarette. (Drugs.) ☐ *Bruno knows how to roll a ladyfinger.* ☐ *Hell, any old joint is a ladyfinger. Don't be so particular.*

lah-di-dah ['lɑ'di'dɑ] **1.** *mod.* casual; relaxed and uncaring. ☐ *He is so lah-di-dah with financial matters.* ☐ *She's not all that calm about her possessions, but she is very lah-di-dah with men.* **2.** *interj.* a jeer; a mocking response. ☐ *So you have a new car! Well, lah-di-dah.* ☐ *Lah-di-dah! Excuse me!*

laid **1.** AND **layed** *mod.* drug intoxicated. (See also *laid out.*) ☐ *Man, did I get myself laid.* ☐ *Are you too layed to drive home?* **2.** *mod.* copulated with. (Crude. Potentially offensive. Use only with discretion.) ☐ *Well, you look laid, all right.*

☐ *If you come home laid, don't say I didn't warn you.*

laid back 1. *mod.* calm and relaxed. ☐ *Bruno is not what I would call laid back.* ☐ *You are really one laid back guy!* **2.** *mod.* alcohol or drug intoxicated. ☐ *He's a little laid back and can't come to the phone.* ☐ *How can those guys work when they are laid back by noon?*

laid out 1. *mod.* alcohol or drug intoxicated. ☐ *Man, you got yourself laid out!* ☐ *I'm too laid out to go to work today.* **2.** *mod.* well-dressed. ☐ *Look at those silks! Man are you laid out!* ☐ *She is all laid out in her Sunday best.* **3.** *mod.* dead; having to do with a corpse arranged for a wake. (Not slang.) ☐ *When the remains were laid out, the children were allowed to come in.* ☐ *When I'm laid out and ready to be planted, make sure this little book is in my hand.* **4.** *mod.* knocked down (by a punch). ☐ *He was down, laid out, and the cowboy just stood there panting.* ☐ *There he was, laid out on the sidewalk, and no one made a move to help him.*

laid to the bone *mod.* alcohol intoxicated. ☐ *He got himself laid to the bone.* ☐ *We were all laid to the bone by midnight.*

laine See the following entry.

lame AND **laine; lane 1.** *mod.* inept; inadequate; undesirable. ☐ *That guy's so lame, it's pitiful.* ☐ *This mark is about as laine as they come.* **2.** *n.* a square person. (Streets. Underworld.) ☐ *Let's see if that lame over there has anything we want in his pockets.* ☐ *He won't drink anything at all. He is such a lame!* **3.** *n.* an inept person. ☐ *The guy turned out to be a lame, and we had to fire him.* ☐ *Maybe the lane can work in the front office answering phones or something.*

lame duck 1. *n.* someone who is in the last period of a term in an elective office. ☐ *You can't expect much from a lame duck.* ☐ *As a lame duck, there's not a lot I can do.* **2.** *mod.* having to do with someone in the last period of a term in an elective office. ☐ *You don't expect much from a lame duck president.* ☐ *Lame duck Congresses tend to do things they wouldn't dare do otherwise.*

lamebrain AND **lame-brain 1.** *n.* a fool. ☐ *Please don't call me a lamebrain. I do my best.* ☐ *What a lame-brain! She put scallops in scalloped potatoes!* **2.** AND **lamebrained** *mod.* foolish. ☐ *No more of your lamebrain ideas!* ☐ *My last scheme looked lamebrained at first, but it worked, didn't it?*

lamebrained See the previous entry.

lamp *tr.* to look at someone or something. (The *lamps* are the eyes.) ☐ *I lamped the paper and then threw it away.* ☐ *Here, lamp this tire for a minute.*

lamps *n.* the eyes. (Crude.) ☐ *His lamps are closed. He's asleep or dead.* ☐ *Look at them blue lamps that dame's got.*

land a blow 1. *tr.* to strike someone. ☐ *He kept moving, and I found it almost impossible to land a blow.* ☐ *The boxer landed a blow to the face of his opponent.* **2.** *tr.* to make a point. ☐ *I think I really landed a blow with that remark about extortion.* ☐ *The point about justice landed a blow.*

land a job *tr.* to find a job and be hired. ☐ *As soon as I land a job and start to bring in some money, I'm going to get a stereo.* ☐ *I managed to land a job.*

land office business *n.* a large amount of business done in a short period of time. ☐ *We always do a land office business at this time of year.* ☐ *We keep going. Never do land office business—just enough to make out.*

landowner ['lændonɚ] *n.* a corpse; a dead person. (See also *buy the farm.*) ☐ *Now old Mr. Carlson was a landowner for real.* ☐ *"How would you like to become a landowner?" snarled the mugger.*

lane See *lame.*

lap of luxury *n.* a luxurious situation. ☐ *I rather enjoy living in the lap of luxury.* ☐ *You call this pigpen the lap of luxury?*

lapper *n.* a drunkard. ☐ *The street was empty except for an old lapper staggering* *home.* □ *The party was ruined by the antics of a few lappers.*

lard *n.* the police. (Streets. Derogatory. See also *bacon, pig, pork.*) □ *Here comes the lard!* □ *If the lard catches you violating your parole, you're through.*

lard ass *n.* a fat person. (Crude. Derogatory. Also a rude term of address. Potentially offensive. Use only with discretion. Compare to *crisco.*) □ *Who's the lard ass with the sixty-inch waist?* □ *Hey, lard ass, get moving!*

lardhead 1. *n.* a stupid person. □ *What a lardhead! Where are your brains?* □ *I'm not a lardhead. I dwell in a different dimension.* **2.** *mod.* foolish. □ *Now here's something from the lardhead department.* □ *No more of those lardhead ideas!*

last roundup *n.* death. (Western.) □ *To everyone's surprise, he clutched the wound and faced the last roundup with a smile.* □ *When I know I'm headed for the last roundup, I'll write a will.*

last straw *n.* the final act or insult; the act that finally calls for a response. □ *This is the last straw. I'm calling the police.* □ *Someone's leaving the egg shells in the sink was the last straw.*

latch onto something 1. *tr.* to obtain something. □ *I have to latch onto a hundred bucks by Friday night.* □ *I latched onto a good book about repairing plumbing.* **2.** *tr.* to begin to understand something. □ *When Fred finally latched onto the principles of algebra, he began to get better grades.* □ *Sue doesn't quite latch onto the proper stance in golf.*

Later. *interj.* "Good-bye." □ *It's time to cruise. Later.* □ *Later. Gotta go.*

lathered ['læðɚd] *mod.* alcohol intoxicated. □ *The two brothers sat there and got lathered.* □ *She is too lathered to drive.*

latrine lips [lə'trin 'lɪps] *n.* a person who uses dirty language. □ *Hey, latrine lips! Cool it!* □ *When old latrine lips finishes shocking everyone, I have something to say.*

latrine rumor [lə'trin 'rumɚ] *n.* any rumor, especially one that is alleged to spread at the latrine [general toilet facilities]. (Military.) □ *Somebody started spreading a latrine rumor about the Colonel's wife.* □ *That's just a latrine rumor. The Colonel isn't married.*

latrine wireless [lə'trin 'wɑɪɚləs] *n.* the free exchange of information and gossip at the general toilet facilities. (See also *latrine rumor.*) □ *It came over the latrine wireless this morning. We're all shipping out.* □ *The latrine wireless was virtually silent while you were in sick bay.*

latrino(gram) [lə'trino(græmʒ)] *n.* a *latrine rumor.* □ *There was a latrino yesterday about the Colonel and his golf game.* □ *There's another latrinogram that says we're moving out.*

lats [læts] *n.* the *latissimus dorsi;* the muscles of the back. (Bodybuilding.) □ *Your lats are coming along fine. Now let's start working on your delts.* □ *Nice lats on that guy.*

laugh at the carpet *in.* to vomit; to vomit on a carpet. □ *Tom bent over and laughed at the carpet, much to the embarrassment of the entire group.* □ *Wayne laughed at the carpet, and people moved away—not knowing what he was going to do next.*

laughing academy *n.* a mental hospital; an insane asylum. □ *About four years in the laughing academy would get you straightened out.* □ *I'm not ready for the laughing academy. A little while longer around here and I will be, though.*

laughing soup AND **laughing water** *n.* liquor; champagne. □ *Laughing soup flowed like fury at the reception.* □ *How about some more laughing water?*

laughing water See the previous entry.

launch (one's lunch) *tr. & in.* to empty one's stomach; to vomit. □ *When I saw that mess, I almost launched my lunch.* □ *Watch out! She's going to launch!*

launder *tr.* to conceal the source and nature of stolen or illicitly gotten money by moving it in and out of different financial institutions. (Underworld.

See also *greenwash.*) ☐ *The woman's sole function was to launder the money from drug deals.* ☐ *When you finish laundering the last job, we want you to do another.*

laundry list *n.* any long list of things. (Compare to *shopping list.*) ☐ *He came to the interview with a laundry list of things.* ☐ *Now I have a laundry list of items we have to discuss.*

law *n.* the police. (Always with *the.*) ☐ *She is in a little trouble with the law.* ☐ *Mrs. Wilson finally called the law in on her old man.*

lawn *n.* poor quality marijuana. (Drugs.) ☐ *This isn't good grass; it's lawn.* ☐ *Put this lawn in your pipe and smoke it.*

lay 1. *tr.* to copulate (with someone). (Crude. Use caution with the topic.) ☐ *She laid him on the spot.* ☐ *He said he was going to lay her. I thought he was just talking tough.* **2.** *n.* a sexual act. (Crude. Use caution with the topic.) ☐ *I could use a good lay about now.* ☐ *All the shipwrecked sailor could think about was a lay.* **3.** *n.* a person considered as a potential sex partner. (Crude. Use caution with the topic.) ☐ *He actually said that she was a good lay.* ☐ *If anybody said I was a good lay, I'd sue—probably.*

lay a guilt trip on someone See the following entry.

lay a (heavy) trip on someone 1. *tr.* to criticize someone. ☐ *There's no need to lay a trip on me. I agree with you.* ☐ *When he finally does get there, I'm going to lay a heavy trip on him like he'll never forget.* **2.** *tr.* to confuse or astonish someone. ☐ *After he laid a heavy trip on me about how the company is almost broke, I cleaned out my desk and left.* ☐ *After Mary laid a trip on John about her other self, he sat down and stared at his feet.* **3.** AND **lay a guilt trip on someone** *tr.* to attempt to make someone feel very guilty. ☐ *Why do you have to lay a guilt trip on me? Why don't you go to a shrink?* ☐ *Of course, she just had to lay a trip on him about being bossy, self-centered, and aloof.*

lay an egg 1. *tr.* [for someone] to do something bad or poorly. ☐ *I guess I really laid an egg, huh?* ☐ *The cast laid an egg in both performances.* **2.** *tr.* [for something] to fail. ☐ *The community theater laid an egg last night with the opening performance of* Death of a Salesman. ☐ *The film was fun to make, but it laid an egg at the box office.* **3.** *tr.* to laugh very hard; to cackle long and loudly. (As if one were a chicken.) ☐ *Half the audience laid an egg when I told this one.* ☐ *I didn't know whether to cry or lay an egg.*

lay down *in.* to give up. ☐ *Do you expect me to just lay down?* ☐ *You really think I should just lay down and let them walk all over me?*

lay it on the line *tr.* to speak very frankly and directly. ☐ *I'm going to have to lay it on the line with you, I guess.* ☐ *Go ahead; lay it on the line. I want to know exactly what you think.*

lay off (someone or something) *in.* to stop bothering or harming someone or something; to stop being concerned about someone or something. ☐ *Lay off the booze for a while, why don't ya?* ☐ *Lay off me! I didn't do anything!*

lay one on See *tie one on.*

lay (some) rubber *tr.* to spin one's car tires when accelerating, leaving black marks on the street. (Compare to *burn rubber.*) ☐ *At that age all they want to do is get in the car and lay some rubber.* ☐ *You wanna know how well I can lay some rubber in this thing?*

lay some sweet lines on someone AND **put some sweet lines on someone** *tr.* to speak kindly to someone; to *soft soap* someone. ☐ *I just laid some sweet lines on her, and she let me use her car.* ☐ *If you put some sweet lines on him, maybe he won't ground you.*

lay someone or something out 1. *tr.* [with *someone*] to scold someone severely. ☐ *Don't lay me out! I didn't do it!* 🅃 *She really laid out the guy but good. What did he do, rob a bank?* (More at *laid out.*) **2.** *tr.* [with *someone*] to knock someone down with a punch. □ *I can't wait to get into that ring and lay the guy out.* Ⓣ *The boxer laid out his opponent with a blow to the head.* **3.** *tr.* [with *something*] to spend some amount of money. □ *I can't lay that kind of money out every day!* Ⓣ *She laid out about $24,000 for that beemer.* **4.** *tr.* [with *something*] to explain a plan of action or a sequence of events. □ *Let me lay it out for you.* Ⓣ *Lay out the plan very carefully, and don't skip anything.* **5.** *tr.* [with *someone*] to prepare someone for burial. (Not slang.) □ *The undertaker did not lay Aunt Fanny out to my satisfaction.* Ⓣ *The women of the town helped the young widow lay out her husband.* (More at *laid out.*)

lay someone out in lavender *tr.* to scold or rebuke someone severely. □ *She really laid him out in lavender for that.* □ *No need to lay me out in lavender. I wasn't there.*

lay something on someone **1.** *tr.* to present a plan or an idea to someone. □ *Here is this century's greatest idea. Let me lay it on you.* □ *I'm going to lay a great idea on you.* **2.** *tr.* to attempt to make someone feel guilty about something. □ *Don't lay that stuff on me. Face your own problem.* □ *Every week she calls up to lay a guilt trip on me about something or other.*

layed See *laid.*

layout **1.** *n.* a place; a place to live. (Compare to *setup.*) □ *How much does a layout like this set you back a month?* □ *This is a nice layout you got here.* **2.** *n.* a floor plan. □ *Let's see if the layout is what we want.* □ *The layout looks awkward and wasteful of space.* **3.** *n.* a scheme. (Underworld.) □ *Now here's the layout. Lefty goes in this side, and Ratface comes in the other way.* □ *The layout's no good. The cops are wise to your style, boss.*

lazybones *n.* a lazy person. □ *I'm just a lazybones, but I don't eat much.* □ *That lazybones is out there sleeping in the shade.*

LBO *n.* "leveraged buy-out." (Initialism. Securities markets.) □ *The money used for the LBO came from the issuance of junk bonds.* □ *Mr. Boone specializes in L.B.O.s. He's made a fortune at it.*

lead poisoning *n.* death caused by being shot with a lead bullet. (Underworld.) □ *He pifted because of a case of lead poisoning.* □ *The fourth mobster to die of lead poisoning this month was buried today in a private service.*

leadfoot *n.* a speeder in an automobile. □ *There is a leadfoot driving behind me and wanting to pass.* □ *Tom was a real leadfoot until he got a few speeding tickets.*

leaf *n.* cocaine. (Sometimes with *the*. Cocaine is extracted from the leaves of the *coca* plant.) □ *Sure I like plants. I am especially fond of the leaf.* □ *The entire shipment of leaf was seized by the feds.*

lean and mean *mod.* capable and ready for hard, efficient work. □ *Ron got himself lean and mean and is ready to play in Saturday's game.* □ *The management is lean and mean and looks to turn a profit next year.*

leapers *n.* amphetamines. (Drugs.) □ *You can tell Bruno's on leapers. He's wired as hell.* □ *He needs some barbs to balance the leapers, or maybe he just ought to go cold turkey and go straight.*

leave someone cold *tr.* to leave someone unaffected. □ *He said it was dull, and it left him cold.* □ *The music's good, but the story left the producer cold.*

leeky store ['liki stor] *n.* a liquor store. (Black. From *liquor.* See also *take a leak.*) □ *Get me some grapes at the leeky store.* □ *The leeky store is closed till 10:00 A.M.*

leerics ['lirɪks] *n.* sexually suggestive song lyrics. □ *For those of you out there who go in for leerics, listen carefully to this tune.* □ *A group of parents has banded together in the eastern suburbs to fight the naughty leerics of some of the current hot rock tunes.*

left-handed monkey wrench *n.* a nonexistent tool. (New workers are sometimes sent to fetch nonexistent tools. See also *sky hook.*) □ *Hand me the left-handed monkey wrench, huh?* □ *Do you think you can dig up a left-handed monkey wrench?*

leg work *n.* the physical work accompanying a task. □ *I don't mind making the phone calls if you do the leg work.* □ *I have a gopher to do the leg work for me.*

legal-beagle AND **legal-eagle** ['ligl'bigl AND 'ligl'igl] *n.* a lawyer. □ *I've got a legal-beagle who can get me out of this scrape.* □ *She keeps a whole bunch of legal-eagles to handle that sort of thing.*

legal-eagle See the previous entry.

legit [lə'dʒɪt] *mod.* honest; legal. □ *If she's not legit, I won't work with her.* □ *Is this deal legit?*

lemme ['lɛmi] *phr.* "let me." (Eye-dialect. Typical spoken English. Used in writing only for effect. Used in the examples of this dictionary.) □ *Do you wanna gimme the thingy and lemme go ahead with my work?* □ *If you won't give me one of my own, make him lemme use his.*

Let her rip! AND **Let it roll!** ['lɛdɚ 'rɪp AND 'lɛdɪt 'rol] *exclam.* "Let it go!"; "Let it start!" □ *Time to start. Let her rip!* □ *There's the signal! Let it roll!*

let it all hang out *tr.* to be yourself, assuming that you generally are not. □ *Come on. Relax! Let it all hang out.* □ *I let it all hang out, but I still feel rotten.*

Let it roll! See *Let her rip!*

let off (some) steam See *blow off (some) steam.*

let something ride *tr.* to let something remain as is; to ignore something (for a while). □ *Don't bother with it now. Let it ride for a day or two.* □ *Let it ride. It's not that important.*

Let's bump this place! *tr.* "Let's get out of this place!"; "Let's leave!" □ *Time to go. Let's bump this place!* □ *Let's bump this place! It's dead here.*

Let's do lunch (sometime). *sent.* "Let us have lunch together sometime." □ *Great seeing you, Martin, absolutely great. Let's do lunch.* □ *Let's do lunch sometime so we can catch up.*

Let's dump. *interj.* "Let's go." □ *It's late. Let's dump.* □ *Let's dump. I've still got a lot to do at home tonight.*

Let's have it! *exclam.* "Please tell (us) the news!" □ *What's happened? Let's have it!* □ *Don't beat around the bush. Let's have it!*

let's say *phr.* introduces an estimate or a speculation. □ *I need about—let's say—twenty pounds.* □ *Let's say I go over and talk to him. What do you think?*

lettuce *n.* money. □ *Put your lettuce on the table; then we'll talk.* □ *How much lettuce do you have left?*

level best *n.* one's very best effort. □ *I will do my level best to find your husband.* □ *Don't go to a whole lot of trouble. Your level best is good enough.*

level with someone *in.* to speak truly and honestly with someone. □ *Okay, I'm gonna level with you. This thing is a steal at this price!* □ *I want you to level with me. Did you do it?*

libber ['lɪbɚ] *n.* a woman who advocates woman's liberation movements; a feminist. (Usually derogatory.) □ *She sure sounds like a libber.* □ *This libber on the radio says men are unnecessary.*

liberate *tr.* to steal something. (Originally military.) □ *We liberated a few reams of paper and a box of pens.* □ *The privates liberated a jeep and went into town.*

library *n.* a bathroom; an outhouse. □ *John is in the library at the moment.* □ *He keeps stuff like that to read in the library.*

lick and a promise *n.* a very casual treatment. (Always with *a.*) □ *A lick and a promise isn't enough. Take some time and do it right.* □ *She gave it a lick and a promise and said she was done.*

lick something into shape AND **whip something into shape** *tr.* to put something into good condition, possibly with considerable effort. □ *I've got about two days more to lick this place into shape so I can sell it.* □ *I want to whip this house into shape for Saturday night.*

lickety-split [lɪkɪdi'splɪt] *mod.* very fast. □ *They ran across the field lickety-split.* □ *We were there lickety-split in my new car.*

licorice stick ['lɪkrɪʃ stɪk] *n.* a clarinet. (Jazz musicians.) □ *Man, can he play the licorice stick.* □ *Frank makes the old licorice stick talk.*

lid 1. *n.* an eyelid. □ *Her lids began to close, and the professor raised his voice to a roar.* □ *Pop your lids open! It's morning!* **2.** *n.* one half to one ounce of marijuana. (Drugs. An amount that will fill a Prince Albert tobacco can lid. Often plural.) □ *How much a lid?* □ *It looks like a matchbox to me. Why do they call it a lid?*

lid poppers See the following entry.

lid proppers AND **lid poppers** *n.* amphetamine tablets or capsules. (Drugs. Refers to the eyelids.) □ *Kelly has to have a couple of lid proppers each morning.* □ *Are lid poppers habit-forming?*

lie doggo ['lɑɪ 'dɔgo] *in.* to remain unrecognized (for a long time). (See also *doggo*.) □ *This problem has lain doggo since 1967.* □ *If you don't find the typos now, they will lie doggo until the next edition.*

lifer ['lɑɪfɚ] *n.* someone who is attached to an institution for life, such as a lifetime soldier or a prisoner serving a life sentence. (Prisons and military.) □ *Me a lifer? Not in this army!* □ *The lifers begin to accept their fate after a few years.* □ *Most of the lifers are kept in this cell block.*

LIFO *phr.* "last in, first out." (Computers. Acronym. Refers to the order of data put in and returned from the processor.) □ *I can't remember whether the stack is LIFO or FIFO.* □ *This one is LIFO.*

lift 1. *n.* the potency of alcohol in liquor. □ *This stuff doesn't have much lift!* □ *Now, this imported stuff has enough lift to raise the dead.* **2.** *n.* a brief spiritual or ego-lifting occurrence. □ *Your kind words have given me quite a lift.* □ *I could use a lift today. I am glummer than usual.* **3.** AND **lift-up** *n.* drug euphoria; a *rush*. (Drugs.) □ *This stuff'll give you quite a lift.* □ *The lift-up from the shot jarred her bones.* **4.** *tr.* to steal something. □ *She had lifted this ring. We found it on her when we arrested her.* □ *Some of these really young kids will lift something just because they like it.* **5.** *tr.* to take something away. □ *It was his third offense, so they lifted his license.* □ *They lifted the rule about not having two different jobs.* **6.** *n.* a tall heel on shoes that makes someone seem taller. (Usually plural.) □ *I feel better in my lifts.* □ *Some people wear lifts just to make them a little more confident.* **7.** *n.* a surgical face-lift. □ *He had a lift on his vacation, but his face still looked two sizes too big.* □ *We've got three lifts and a nose job in O.R. this morning.* **8.** *n.* a device—worn under the hair at the temples—that provides some of the effects of a surgical face-lift. □ *Do you think she's wearing a lift?* □ *Lift, hell, she's got a damn pair of cranes under that hairdo.* **9.** *n.* a ride; transportation. □ *Can you give me a lift?* □ *Would you like a lift over to your apartment?*

lift one's elbow See *bend one's elbow*.

lift-up See *lift*.

light 1. *mod.* alcohol intoxicated. □ *I began to feel a little light along about the fourth beer.* □ *I feel a little light. You'd better drive.* **2.** *n.* an eye. (Crude. Usually plural.) □ *You want I should poke your lights out?* □ *Open your lights and watch for the turn off sign.* **3.** *n.* a police car. □ *A couple of lights turned the corner just as the robbers were pulling away.* □ *We could see the lights coming down the expressway behind us, so we pulled over to the right and let them pass.*

light bulb *n.* a pregnant woman. (Jocular. Refers to the shape of a pregnant woman.) □ *Who's the light bulb on the sofa?* □ *I can't possibly fit that light bulb out there. She'll have to wait a few months before buying expensive clothing.*

light into someone See *sail into someone.*

light stuff 1. *n.* low-proof liquor. ☐ *The light stuff is okay for parties, but not for serious drinking.* ☐ *Poor Sam is trying to cut down by drinking the light stuff. He drinks twice as much, though.* **2.** *n.* marijuana and nonaddictive drugs. ☐ *Sure, it's innocent. Sure, they're just kids. Do you know what kids do when they get through with the light stuff? They do coke, they shoot H., and they do the big one somewhere in an alley!* ☐ *The cops just found some light stuff in his pockets. They let him go.*

lighten up (on someone or something) *in.* to reduce the pressure (on someone or something); to calm down (about someone or something). ☐ *Cool it, man. Lighten up! We all gotta get along here.* ☐ *Lighten up on the guy. He only stepped on your toe.*

lights out 1. *n.* bedtime. ☐ *It's lights out, kids. Radios off, too!* ☐ *I was finished with it by lights out.* **2.** *n.* death; time to die. (Underworld.) ☐ *It's lights out for you, chum.* ☐ *When it's lights out, I want it to be fast.*

lightweight 1. *mod.* inconsequential. ☐ *This is a fairly lightweight matter.* ☐ *We need an executive here, not just a lightweight flunky.* **2.** *n.* an inconsequential person; someone who accomplishes very little. ☐ *Don't worry about her. She's just a lightweight.* ☐ *Those lightweights don't know how to run things right.*

like 1. *interj.* an emphatic or meaningless word that, when said frequently, marks the speaker as speaking in a very casual or slangy mode. (Use caution with *like.* Compare to *like, you know.* Used in writing only for effect.) ☐ *This is, like, so silly!* ☐ *She is like, so, like, way rad!* **2.** *interj.* a particle meaning roughly "saying." (Always with some form of *be*. Use caution with *like.* Never used in formal writing.) ☐ *Tiffany was like, "Wow!"* ☐ *And I'm like, "Well, you should have put your hat on!"*

like a bat out of hell *mod.* very fast or sudden. (Use caution with *hell.*) ☐ *The cat took off like a bat out of hell.* ☐ *The car pulled away from the curb like a bat out of hell.*

like a million (dollars) *mod.* very good or well. (Usually with *feel.*) ☐ *This old buggy runs like a million dollars.* ☐ *Man, I feel like a million.*

like a ton of bricks *mod.* like something very ponderous and heavy. ☐ *The whole thing hit me like a ton of bricks.* ☐ *Hitting the back end of that truck was like hitting a ton of bricks.*

like crazy AND **like mad** *mod.* furiously; very much, fast, many, or actively. ☐ *They're buying tickets like crazy.* ☐ *Look at those people on the bank. They're catching fish like mad!*

like death warmed over *mod.* horrible; deathlike. ☐ *Oh, my God! You look like death warmed over!* ☐ *A tall, black-garbed gentleman lay there, looking like death warmed over.*

like gangbusters *mod.* with great excitement and fury. (From the phrase "Come on like gangbusters," a radio show that "came on" with lots of noise and excitement.) ☐ *She works like gangbusters and gets the job done.* ☐ *They are selling tickets like gangbusters.*

Like hell! *exclam.* "That is not true!"; "I do not believe you!" (Use caution with *hell.*) ☐ *You're going to a Dead concert! Like hell!* ☐ *Like hell, you are!*

Like it or lump it! *exclam.* "Give up!"; "Shut up!"; "Accept it or go away!" (Compare to *Lump it!*) ☐ *If you don't want to do it my way, like it or lump it!* ☐ *Too bad! Like it or lump it!*

like mad See *like crazy.*

like nobody's business *mod.* very well; very much. ☐ *She can sing like nobody's business. What a set of pipes!* ☐ *My mom can cook chocolate chip cookies like nobody's business.*

like stink *mod.* rapidly. (As fast as a smell spreads.) ☐ *Those kids moved through the whole test like stink. Real eager-beavers.* ☐ *As long as she can run like stink, swim like stink, and smell like a flower, she gets my support.*

like there was no tomorrow *mod.* as if there would never be another opportunity. □ *She was drinking booze like there was no tomorrow.* □ *He lived like there was no tomorrow.*

like, you know *interj.* a combining of the expressions *like* and *you know*. (Never used in formal writing.) □ *She is, well, like, you know, P.G.* □ *This is, well, like, you know, too much!*

lily-livered *mod.* cowardly. □ *Don't be so lily-livered. Give it a try.* □ *That lily-livered guy is up hiding under his bed till this blows over.*

limbo See *lumbo.*

(limp) dishrag *n.* a totally helpless person; a cowardly and spineless person. □ *He's sweet, but he's a dishrag.* □ *A limp dishrag is no help at all in a crisis.*

line 1. *n.* a story or argument; a story intended to seduce someone. (See also *lines.*) □ *I've heard that line before.* □ *Don't feed me that line. Do you think I was born yesterday?* **2.** *n.* a dose of finely cut cocaine arranged in a line, ready for insufflation or *snorting.* *(Drugs.)* □ *Let's you and me go do some lines, okay?* □ *See these lines here? Watch what happens to them.*

line one's own pocket(s) *tr.* to make money for oneself in a greedy or dishonest fashion. □ *They are interested in lining their pockets first and serving the people second.* □ *You can't blame them for wanting to line their own pockets.*

lines *n.* words; conversation. (See also *line.*) □ *I like your lines, but I don't have the time.* □ *We tossed some lines back and forth for a while and then split.*

lineup *n.* a row of suspects arranged at a police station so that a witness can identify one of them. (Underworld.) □ *I had to stand in the lineup with this bunch of yahoos.* □ *When they round up all the likely suspects and put them in the lineup, they always stick in a desk sergeant to spy on the rest.*

lingo *n.* language; special vocabulary. □ *When you catch on to the lingo, everything becomes clear.* □ *If you don't like the lingo, don't listen.*

lion's share *n.* the largest portion. □ *I earn a lot, but the lion's share goes for taxes.* □ *The lion's share of the surplus cheese goes to school cafeterias.*

lip 1. *tr. & in.* to kiss someone intimately. □ *The two of them were in the corner, lipping intently.* □ *Hey, honeycakes, I really want to lip you.* **2.** *n.* a lawyer. (Underworld. See also *mouth.*) □ *So I brought in my lip, and he got me off the rap.* □ *How much do you pay your lip?* **3.** *n.* back talk; impudent talk. □ *Don't give me any more of your lip!* □ *I've had enough of her lip.*

lip gloss *n.* lies; deception; exaggeration; *B.S.* (From the name of a lipstick-like cosmetic.) □ *Everything he says is just lip gloss. He is a liar at heart.* □ *She doesn't mean it. Her words are just lip gloss.*

L.I.Q. *n.* a liquor store. (Initialism or acronym.) □ *Let's stop at the L.I.Q. and get some berries.* □ *I got a headache already. I don't need anything from any L.I.Q. to make it worse.*

liquefied *mod.* alcohol intoxicated. □ *Ten beers and I am absolutely liquefied!* □ *She is too liquefied to walk, let alone drive.*

liquid cork *n.* a medicine that stops diarrhea. □ *This nasty tasting stuff is a good liquid cork for what you have.* □ *This liquid cork isn't so bad if you get it good and cold before you take it.*

liquid laugh *n.* vomit. □ *If you drink much more, you're gonna come out with a liquid laugh.* □ *There's some liquid laugh on your shoe.*

liquidate *tr.* to kill someone. (Underworld.) □ *The boss wants me to liquidate Mr. Bruno.* □ *They used a machine gun to liquidate a few troublesome characters.*

listen up *in.* to listen carefully. (Usually a command.) □ *Now, listen up! This is important.* □ *Listen up, you guys!*

lit 1. *n.* literature, as a school subject. □ *I'm flunking English lit again.* □ *I hate* *lit. Give me numbers any day.* **2.** AND **lit up** *mod.* drunk. ☐ *She was always lit by bedtime.* ☐ *Todd was lit up like a Christmas tree at our office party.*

lit up See the previous entry.

little black book *n.* a book containing the names and addresses of acquaintances who are potential dates, usually put together by men. ☐ *I've got a nice collection in my little black book.* ☐ *Am I in your little black book, or can you already tell that I wouldn't go out with you?*

little boy blue *n.* a (male) police officer. ☐ *I hear that little boy blue is looking for you.* ☐ *Little boy blue is coming this way, and he's mad.*

little boys' room *n.* the boys' restroom; the men's restroom. ☐ *Can you tell me where the little boys' room is?* ☐ *Ted's in the little boys' room. He'll be right back.*

little girls' room *n.* the girls' restroom; the women's restroom. ☐ *Can you please tell me where the little girls' room is?* ☐ *Is there an attendant in the little girls' room?*

(little) pinkie AND **(little) pinky** *n.* the littlest finger on either hand. ☐ *Ouch! I smashed my pinky.* ☐ *My little pinkie nearly froze because there's a hole in my glove.*

live *mod. cool;* great. ☐ *Everything's live! No problem!* ☐ *It's live and ice. No problem, man.*

(live) wire *n.* an energetic and vivacious person. ☐ *Tracy is a real live wire.* ☐ *With a wire like Tracy in charge, things will get done, that's for sure.*

liveware ['laɪvwɛr] *n.* the human component of computer use. (Patterned on *software* and *hardware.*) ☐ *The hardware is okay. It's the liveware that's bad.* ☐ *If I don't get some sleep, you're going to see a liveware crash.*

Living large. *phr.* "Doing okay." (The response to *How ya living?*) ☐ *I'm living large. How you doing?* ☐ *Living large. So, how's it with you?*

lo-res See *low-res.*

load 1. *n.* as much liquor as one can hold. ☐ *Harry had quite a load of booze.* ☐ *Mary is carrying a load.* (More at *loaded.*) **2.** *n.* a drink of liquor. ☐ *Can I have a load from your bottle?* ☐ *Help yourself to a load.* **3.** *n.* a dose of drugs; an injection of drugs. (Drugs.) ☐ *She shoots a load every day or two.* ☐ *He scored enough for a load only yesterday.* (More at *loaded.*) **4.** *n.* a drug supply; a *stash.* (Drugs.) ☐ *My load is up in the closet.* ☐ *If his load dwindles, he gets more easily.* **5.** *n.* a large purchase of heroin. (Drugs.) ☐ *I've scored a load that'll last me a few days.* ☐ *That load must be worth about $50,000.* **6.** *n.* an automobile. (See also *heap.*) ☐ *Whose junky old load is that parked in front of the house?* ☐ *I'm saving money so I can replace this load with a new car.*

loaded 1. *mod.* alcohol or drug intoxicated. ☐ *If you're loaded, don't drive.* ☐ *I'm not loaded. I'm just a little tipsy.* **2.** *mod.* spiked with liquor; containing much alcohol. ☐ *There's a little rum in the eggnog, but it's certainly not what I would call loaded.* ☐ *Wow, this punch is loaded!* **3.** *mod.* having all available accessories. (Said of a car.) ☐ *Did you want to see a car that's loaded, or is this to be a budget car?* ☐ *Now, this little gem is loaded with everything.* **4.** *mod.* wealthy; loaded with money. ☐ *Mr. Wilson is loaded, but he is also generous with his money.* ☐ *My Uncle Fred is loaded, but he's going to take it all with him.*

loaded for bear 1. *mod.* alcohol intoxicated. ☐ *He is loaded for bear and anything else.* ☐ *He's been drinking mule since dawn, and he's loaded for bear.* **2.** *mod.* ready for the hardest problems. ☐ *Bring on the hard cases. I'm loaded for bear.* ☐ *I'm loaded for bear, and that's good because this is going to be a rough day.* **3.** *mod.* very angry. ☐ *By the time he finished talking, I was loaded for bear.* ☐ *I had been loaded for bear* *when I came into the room, and I left as meek as a lamb.*

loaded question *n.* a question to which an honest answer will reveal things the speaker might otherwise wish to conceal. ☐ *Now, that's a loaded question, and I don't think I have to answer it.* ☐ *I didn't mean it to be a loaded question.*

loaded remark *n.* a remark containing important implications. ☐ *Your loaded remark did not go over well with the host.* ☐ *In spite of your numerous loaded remarks, I do hope you will return sometime when it is convenient.*

loaded to the barrel See the following entry.

loaded to the gills AND **loaded to the barrel** *mod.* alcohol intoxicated. ☐ *He's loaded to the gills. Couldn't see a hole in a ladder.* ☐ *Man, he's loaded to the barrel and fighting mad.*

loadie See the following entry.

loady AND **loadie** ['lodi] *n.* a drinker or drug user. (Teens and collegiate. One who gets *loaded* frequently.) ☐ *I hear that Wally is a loady. Is that true?* ☐ *These loadies are all very difficult to deal with.*

local yokel ['lok| 'jok|] *n.* a local resident of a rural place. (Mildly derogatory.) ☐ *One of the local yokels helped me change the tire.* ☐ *The local yokels all listen to the same radio station.*

loco ['loko] *mod.* crazy. (From Spanish.) ☐ *Who is that loco kid jumping up and down in the front seat?* ☐ *This zit is gonna drive me loco.*

LOL *interj.* "laughing out loud." (Indicates that one is laughing in response to a previous remark. Used in electronic mail and computer bulletin board messages. Not pronounced aloud.) ☐ *I'm LOL about the last remark you made.* ☐ *LOL at your last message.*

lollapalooza [lɑləpə'luzə] **1.** *n.* something very big; something wondrous. ☐ *Look at that bump on your head. That's a lollapalooza!* ☐ *Her singing voice is a real dandy—a lollapalooza.* **2.** *n.* a big lie. ☐ *She just told a lollapalooza.* ☐ *What a lollapalooza! You expect me to believe that?*

lommix See *lummox.*

lone wolf *n.* a man who stays to himself. ☐ *Fred is sort of a lone wolf until he has a few drinks.* ☐ *It's the lone wolves you read about in the paper when they pull a drowning person from the river.*

long arm of the law *n.* the police; the law. (See also *arm.*) ☐ *The long arm of the law is going to tap you on the shoulder some day, Lefty.* ☐ *The long arm of the law finally caught up with Gert.*

long bread AND **long green** *n.* money. ☐ *Man, that must have cost you some long bread!* ☐ *Look at the long green you get for doing the job!*

long dozen *n.* thirteen; a baker's dozen. ☐ *Don't you sell a long dozen anymore?* ☐ *They used to give you a long dozen in that bakery.*

long green See *long bread.*

long knife **1.** *n.* an assassin. (Underworld.) ☐ *The boss sent one of his long knives to kill the guy.* ☐ *Some long knife showed up, but Marty took him out before he made his move.* **2.** *n.* a destroyer; a hatchet man. ☐ *The secretary was acting as a long knife for the President.* ☐ *One of his long knives came over to pressure us into cooperating.*

long shot *n.* a wild guess; an attempt at something that has little chance of succeeding. ☐ *Well, it was a long shot, but I had to try it.* ☐ *You shouldn't expect a long shot to pay off.*

long story short *phr.* "to make a long story short." ☐ *Okay, long story short: everything that goes up comes down, okay?* ☐ *Then the guy comes over, and —long story short—"You got a match?"*

long-tall-Sally *n.* a tall girl or woman. ☐ *Isn't she a gorgeous long-tall-Sally?* ☐ *She's quite a long-tall-Sally.*

Long time no see. *phr.* "I haven't seen you in a long time." □ *Hey, John! Long time no see!* □ *Long time no see! How ya been?*

longhair **1.** *n.* a *highbrow* with long hair; especially a musician. □ *There were a few longhairs at the bar, but none of the regulars.* □ *I am sort of a longhair, but I still watch T.V.* **2.** *mod.* highbrow; [of music] classical. □ *I don't care for longhair music.* □ *It's too longhair.* □ *Longhair stuff like symphonies and art galleries bores me to tears.* **3.** *n.* a *hippie;* a long-haired youth of the 1960's. (Usually derogatory.) □ *Tell that longhair to get out of here.* □ *There are fewer longhairs around here than there were in the sixties.*

look after number one *in.* to take care of oneself first. (See also *number one.*) □ *You gotta look after number one, right?* □ *It's a good idea to look after number one. Who else will?*

Look alive! *exclam.* "Move faster!"; "Look and act alert!" □ *There's work to be done! Look alive!* □ *Look alive! It's a long, hard day ahead!*

look-see *n.* a look; a visual examination. □ *Let's go and have a look-see at this monster of yours.* □ *Take a look-see at this one and see if you like it.*

Look who's talking! *exclam.* "You are just as guilty!"; "You are just as much at fault!" □ *Me a tax cheat? Look who's talking!* □ *Look who's talking. You were there before I was.*

looker See *(good) looker.*

loonie See the following entry.

loony AND **loonie** ['luni] **1.** *n.* a crazy person. (From *lunatic.*) □ *I'm beginning to feel like a loonie the longer I stay around here.* □ *Don't be a loony. Use common sense.* **2.** *mod.* crazy. □ *That is a loony idea. Forget it.* □ *I'm not really as loony as I seem.* **3.** *mod.* alcohol intoxicated. □ *She's acting a little loonie. Let's get her home before she's sick.* □ *A couple of drinks and she's as loonie as hot cakes.*

loony bin *n.* an insane asylum; a mental hospital. □ *I feel like I'm about ready for the loony bin.* □ *Today's loony bins are far different from those of just a few decades ago.*

loop-legged *mod.* alcohol intoxicated. □ *He's too loop-legged to drive.* □ *She has this strange tendency to get a little loop-legged when she has four or five drinks.*

looped AND **loopy** *mod.* alcohol intoxicated. □ *Sam is too looped to drive.* □ *She got loopy very quickly and had to be helped to a chair.*

loopy See the previous entry.

loose *mod.* very drunk. □ *Mary was a little loose and had to be driven home.* □ *Don is too loose to stand up.*

loose cannon *n.* a loudmouth; a braggart. □ *As it turned out, he's not just a loose cannon. He makes sense.* □ *Some loose cannon in the State Department has been feeding the press all sorts of crap as a diversion.*

loot **1.** *n.* stolen goods; stolen money. □ *The loot was stashed in the trunk of the getaway car.* □ *Where's the loot? I want my piece.* **2.** *n.* money in general. □ *I left home without any loot.* □ *It takes too much loot to eat at that restaurant.*

Lord love a duck! *exclam.* "Wow!" □ *Lord love a duck! It's Mary!* □ *Lord love a duck, I'm tired!*

lorg [lorg] *n.* a stupid person. □ *Why is Frank such a lorg? Can't he get with it?* □ *Tell that lorg to find his own chair.*

lose a bundle *tr.* to lose a lot of money. (See also *bundle.* Compare to *make a bundle.*) □ *Don lost a bundle on that land purchase.* □ *I know I would lose a bundle if I got on a riverboat and gambled.*

lose (all) one's marbles *tr.* to become crazy. (See also *have all one's marbles.*) □ *Have you lost all your marbles?* □ *She acts like she lost her marbles.*

lose it **1.** *tr.* to empty one's stomach; to vomit. (Collegiate.) □ *Oh, God! I think I'm going to lose it!* □ *Go lose it in the bushes.* **2.** *tr.* to get angry; to lose one's temper. □ *It was too much for him. Ted* *lost it.* □ *I sat there calmly, biting my lip to keep from losing it.*

lose one's cool *tr.* to lose control; to lose one's temper. (Compare to *keep one's cool.*) □ *Now, don't lose your cool. Relax.* □ *I'm trying not to lose my cool, but it's hard.*

lose one's doughnuts See *blow one's doughnuts.*

lose one's grip AND **lose one's hold** *tr.* to lose one's control over something. □ *When I begin to lose my grip, I will just quit.* □ *I'm losing my hold. It must be time to chuck it.*

lose one's hold See the previous entry.

lose one's lunch See *blow (one's) lunch.*

lose one's shirt *tr.* to go broke; to lose everything of value, even one's shirt. □ *I lost my shirt on that bank deal.* □ *Try not to lose your shirt in the market again.*

loser ['luzɚ] *n.* an inept person; an undesirable or annoying person; a social failure. □ *Dave is a real loser.* □ *Only losers wear clothes like that.* □ *Those guys are all losers. They'll never amount to anything.*

losing streak *n.* a period of bad luck, especially in gambling. □ *After a prolonged losing streak, Diamond Jane retired and opened some sort of manicure parlor outside Las Vegas.* □ *I've been on a three-year losing streak in my business. I'm just about done.*

lost-and-found badge *n.* a military identification tag; a military dog tag. (From the Persian Gulf War.) □ *Ted's lost-and-found badge was stolen while he was on leave.* □ *My father still keeps his lost-and-found badge from the Korean War.*

lost cause *n.* a hopeless or worthless thing or person. □ *The whole play began to wash out during the second act. It was a lost cause by the third.* □ *Max is just a lost cause. Just forget about him.*

lost in the sauce *mod.* alcohol intoxicated and bewildered. □ *Bill spends many days lost in the sauce.* □ *Sally got lost in the sauce at the party and made quite a spectacle of herself.*

Lots of luck! 1. *exclam.* "Good luck!" □ *I'm glad you're giving it a try. Lots of luck!* □ *Lots of luck in your new job!* **2.** *exclam.* "You don't have a chance!"; "Good luck, you'll need it!" (Sarcastic.) □ *Think you stand a chance? Lots of luck!* □ *You a senator? Lots of luck!*

loudmouth *n.* a person who talks too much or too loudly. □ *I try not to be a loudmouth, but I sometimes get carried away.* □ *There are a number of loudmouths in here who are competing with one another.*

louse [laus] *n.* a thoroughly repellent person, usually a male. □ *You can be such a louse!* □ *Max turned out to be a louse, and his wife of two weeks left him.*

louse something up *tr.* to botch something up. □ *Please don't louse the typewriter ribbon up this time.* 🅃 *Jack loused up my effort to win approval for my plan.*

lousy ['lauzi] *mod.* rotten; poor; bad. □ *This is a lousy day.* □ *This mushy stuff is lousy. Do I have to eat it?*

lousy with someone or something *mod.* having lots of someone or something. (Like an infestation of lice.) □ *Old Mr. Wilson is lousy with money.* □ *Tiffany is lousy with jewels and furs, but she's got bad teeth.*

love bombs *n.* affirmations of affection. □ *These two were dropping love bombs on each other, even though they hate each other's guts.* □ *What a phony bunch of kooks. They were throwing love bombs all over the place!*

(love) handles *n.* rolls of fat around the waist that can be held on to during lovemaking. □ *Ted worked out daily, trying to get rid of his love handles.* □ *Not only did he grow a belly, but he's got handles on his handles.*

love-in 1. *n.* an event during the 1960's where one or more couples made love in a public place. □ *My uncle was at one of those love-ins, and he said if anything was going on, it was going on under blankets.* □ *I think the only people who went* *to love-ins were reporters.* **2.** *n.* an event in the 1960's where everyone became euphoric—with the help of marijuana—about love and respect for their fellow humans. ☐ *The meeting was no love-in, but we got along.* ☐ *Everyone at the annual company love-in was throwing love bombs around at each other.*

Love it! See *(I) love it!*

Love you! *exclam.* "You are great!" (Almost meaningless patter.) ☐ *See ya around, Martin. Let's do lunch! Love ya! Bye-bye.* ☐ *Nice talking to you, babe. Love you!*

low-blow *n.* an unfair blow. (See also *hit (someone) below the belt.*) ☐ *No fair! That was a low-blow.* ☐ *Coming in like that unannounced was a pretty low-blow.*

low five *n.* the slapping of hands at waist level as a greeting. (Compare to *high five.*) ☐ *They turned to each other, throwing a quick low five as they passed.* ☐ *The two eight-year-olds tried to give each other a low five, but they both hurt their hands.*

low-key *mod.* not obvious. ☐ *Let's try to keep this low-key so as not to upset the family.* ☐ *It was a very low-key meeting, but we got a lot done.*

low-life **1.** *n.* a low person; a repellent person. ☐ *This low-life smells like bacon.* ☐ *Hey, low-life, keep out of my way.* **2.** *mod.* mean; belligerent. ☐ *Don't be so low-life, man!* ☐ *We don't need any low-life characters around here.*

low rent **1.** *n.* a low person; someone without grace or spirit. (Also a rude term of address.) ☐ *Look, low rent, where is what you owe me?* ☐ *This low rent here thinks he can push Bruno around, huh?* **2.** *mod.* cheap; unfashionable. ☐ *This place is strictly low rent.* ☐ *Why don't you go live with some of your low rent friends?*

low-res AND **lo-res** ['lo'rɛz] *mod.* poor; unpleasant. (From *low resolution* in a computer terminal. Compare to *high-res.*) ☐ *I feel sort of low-res today.* ☐ *The party is lo-res. Let's cruise.*

lowbrow ['lobrɑu] **1.** *n.* a nonintellectual person; an anti-intellectual person. ☐ *Some lowbrow came in and made a stink about not being able to find any Gene Autry records.* ☐ *Not that Gene Autry is lowbrow. The guy who came in was.* **2.** *mod.* nonintellectual; anti-intellectual. ☐ *I like my lowbrow music and my lowbrow friends!* ☐ *What's lowbrow about soft rock?*

lowdown **1.** *mod.* rotten; bad. ☐ *What a dirty, lowdown thing to do.* ☐ *You are a lowdown rat!* **2.** *n.* the facts on something; the *scuttlebutt* about something. ☐ *What's the lowdown on that funny statue in the park?* ☐ *Give me the lowdown on the project we just started.*

L.S.D. *n.* lysergic acid diethylamide, a hallucinogenic drug. (Initialism. Drugs. A mainstay of the 1960's and 1970's drug culture.) ☐ *Is there much L.S.D. still around?* ☐ *L.S.D. isn't the problem it used to be, but it's far from gone.*

L.T. *in.* "living together." (Initialism and euphemism.) ☐ *Guess who're LT?* ☐ *They have been L.T. for some time.*

lube *n.* butter. ☐ *Pass the lube, will ya, huh?* ☐ *We're outa lube.*

lubricated *mod.* alcohol intoxicated. ☐ *They are sufficiently lubricated for the night.* ☐ *He's not fit to talk to until he's lubricated a bit.*

lubrication *n.* liquor. ☐ *A little lubrication would help this party a lot.* ☐ *Wally has had a little too much lubrication.*

luck of the draw *n.* the results of chance; the lack of any choice. ☐ *Why do I always end up with the luck of the draw?* ☐ *The team was assembled by chance. It was just the luck of the draw that we could work so well together.*

luck out *in.* to be fortunate; to strike it lucky. ☐ *I really lucked out when I ordered the duck. It's excellent.* ☐ *I didn't luck out at all. I rarely make the right choice.*

lucky dog *n.* a lucky person, perhaps undeserving. (Also a term of address.) ☐ *You lucky dog!* ☐ *Max was a lucky dog because he won the football pool.*

lude [lud] *n.* a capsule of Quaalude™, a tranquilizer. (Drugs.) □ *A couple of ludes put Max in a better mood.* □ *I don't know what he gave me. Mary said it was a lude or something.*

lug [ləg] *n.* a stupid male. □ *Is this lug bothering you, lady?* □ *Some lug on a tractor was holding up traffic.*

lughead *n.* a stupid person. (Also a term of address.) □ *What a lughead! How can you be so dumb?* □ *Hey, lughead! Watch where you are going.*

lumbo AND **limbo** ['ləmbo AND 'lɪmbo] *n.* Colombian marijuana. (Drugs. See also *lum(s)*.) □ *He showed up with a bag of lumbo.* □ *Hey, Max! You are just in time with the limbo, man.*

lummox AND **lommix; lummux** ['ləmɑks AND 'ləməks] *n.* a heavy, awkward, stupid person. □ *He looks like a big lummox, but he can really dance.* □ *Bruno is what you would call a lummux —but not to his face, of course.*

lummux See the previous entry.

lump *n.* a stupid clod of a man. □ *I am not a lump! I am just sedate and pensive.* □ *Who is that lump leaning over the bar?*

Lump it! *exclam.* "Forget it!"; "Go away!" (See also *Like it or lump it!*) □ *Well, you can just lump it!* □ *Lump it! Drop dead!*

lumpus ['ləmpəs] *n.* a stupid oaf. □ *You are a silly lumpus!* □ *Is this lumpus giving you any trouble, ma'am?*

lum(s) [ləm(z)] *n.* cannabis from Colombia. (The "lum" is based on the misspelling "Columbia.") □ *Bruno preferred lums, but he would take what he could get.* □ *If it weren't for lum, our trade deficit wouldn't be so bad.*

lunger ['ləŋɚ] *n.* a large and nasty mass of phlegm coughed up from the lungs and spat out. (See also *nose-lunger.*) □ *Wayne loved to pretend that he was going to plant a lunger on somebody's shoe.* □ *Sharon walked around a lunger on the sidewalk, but Beavis stepped right in it.*

lush 1. *n.* liquor. □ *Who's bringing the lush to the party?* □ *Lead me to the lush.* **2.** AND **lush up** *in.* to drink alcohol to excess. □ *Come over sometime, and we'll lush.* □ *We sat lushing up for an hour waiting for the plane.* **3.** *n.* a drunkard. □ *I was afraid of it for some time, but now I know. Tracy is a lush.* □ *There were four confirmed lushes at the party, but they all passed out and didn't bother us much.*

lush up See the previous entry.

M

M. and M.s *n.* capsules of Seconal™, a barbiturate. (From the brand name of a type of brightly colored candy pellets.) □ *Is there somewhere around here I can get some M. and M.s?* □ *No M. and M.s for me. I'm on blues.*

Ma Bell *n.* AT&T, the American Telephone and Telegraph Company;. any telephone company. (Compare to *Baby Bell.*) □ *I forgot to pay Ma Bell this month.* □ *Ma Bell is still one of the largest firms in the nation.*

mac out *in.* to overeat, especially the type of food served at McDonald's fast-food restaurants. (From the Big Mac™ sandwich. Compare to *Big Mac attack.* See also *blimp out, pig out, pork out, scarf out.*) □ *I've been in Europe for a month, and I just want to get home and mac out.* □ *I mac out every weekend. It's like going to church.*

mace someone's face [mes . . .] *tr.* to do something drastic to someone, such as spraying mace in the face. (Chemical Mace™ is a brand of tear gas sold in pressurized cans for personal protection.) □ *Do you want me to mace your face? Then shut up!* □ *I look at him, and suddenly I just want to mace his face or something.*

macho ['matʃo] **1.** *mod.* masculine; virile. (From Spanish. Used as a derogation by feminists.) □ *Does the world really need one more macho man?* □ *He's hardly macho.* □ *You know—that bright-eyed macho type.* **2.** *n.* a masculine or virile male. □ *He's such a macho. He even chews tobacco.* □ *Watch out for that macho over there. He's cruising for a bruising.*

Mac(k) [mæk] *n.* a generic name for a man. (Also a term of address.) □ *Look, Mac, you want to make some big money?* □ *Hey, Mack! Come here a minute.*

mad money *n.* money to be spent in a frivolous fashion. □ *This is my mad money, and I'll do with it as I please.* □ *I got $100 in mad money for my birthday.*

madam *n.* the female keeper of a brothel. □ *The madam was caught in a sting operation.* □ *The cops led the madam away, followed by a parade of you-know-whats.*

Madison Avenue ['mædəsən 'ævənu] **1.** *n.* in the style or image of the major U.S. center for advertising agencies. (The agencies are located on Madison Avenue in New York City.) □ *It's too much like Madison Avenue. We want a calm, sincere mood.* □ *This is plain old Madison Avenue. I want something more subtle.* **2.** *mod.* in the manner of intense promotion; propagandalike. □ *More and more people simply do not respond to Madison Avenue hype.* □ *Can Madison Avenue techniques sell a political candidate?*

mag *n.* magazine. □ *I gotta stop and get a computer mag.* □ *I've seen your face in the mags, haven't I?*

maggot **1.** *n.* a cigarette. (Probably a play on *faggot.*) □ *Can I bum a maggot off of you?* □ *Get your own maggots.* **2.** *n.* a low and wretched person; a vile person. □ *You maggot! Take your hands off me!* □ *Only a maggot would do something like that.*

maggot(t)y *mod.* alcohol intoxicated; very drunk. (A play on *rotten.*) □ *Rotten, hell. They were absolutely maggotty!*

☐ *How can anybody reach the state of being maggoty on three beers?*

magic bullet See *silver bullet.*

magic mushrooms AND **sacred mushrooms** *n.* mushrooms' of the genus *Psilocybe,* which cause visions or hallucinations when eaten. (Drugs.) ☐ *Magic mushrooms are okay because they are natural, or something like that.* ☐ *This is the so-called "sacred mushroom," named for its use in Amerindian ritual.*

magpie *n.* a person who chatters; a person who annoys others by chattering. ☐ *Sally is such a magpie!* ☐ *Why do those horrendous magpies all go to the same movies I go to?*

(ma)hoska [mə'hɑskə] **1.** *n.* narcotics; any contraband. (Underworld.) ☐ *The tall pinstriper asked where he could get some mahoska.* ☐ *The hoska must be for a friend. He's a blower if I ever saw one.* **2.** *n.* energy; strength; *moxie.* ☐ *The guy's got mahoska and guts!* ☐ *She's quick and has lots of mahoska.*

main drag *n.* the main street. ☐ *I have a shop over on the main drag.* ☐ *The main drag is solid with traffic on Saturday nights.*

main squeeze **1.** *n.* one's boss; the person in charge. ☐ *The main squeeze has a lot of responsibility.* ☐ *The main squeeze is out of town for a week.* **2.** *n.* one's steady girlfriend or boyfriend. ☐ *My main squeeze is coming over to talk tonight.* ☐ *She plans to marry her main squeeze.*

main stash *n.* the home of a drug user described in terms of where one's major store of drugs is kept. (Drugs. See also *stash.*) ☐ *His apps are in his main stash.* ☐ *My main stash is on Maple, but I'm usually not there.*

major *mod.* excellent; serious; severe. (Collegiate.) ☐ *This rally is, like, major!* ☐ *Wally is one of the most major beach guys!*

make **1.** *tr.* to identify someone. (Underworld.) ☐ *We tried to make him down at the station but came up with nothing.* ☐ *Given another second or two I could have made the guy—but he covered his face.* **2.** *n.* an identification. (Underworld.) ☐ *We ran a make on her. She's got two priors.* ☐ *The make didn't come through until after she was released.* **3.** *tr.* to arrive at a place; to cover a distance. ☐ *Can we make Boston by sunset?* ☐ *We made forty miles in thirty minutes.* **4.** *tr.* to achieve a specific speed. ☐ *See if this thing can make ninety.* ☐ *This buggy will make twice the speed of the old one.*

make a boo-boo *tr.* to make an error. (See also *boo-boo.*) ☐ *Everybody makes a boo-boo every now and then.* ☐ *Whoops! I made a boo-boo.*

make a bundle AND **make a pile** *tr.* to make a lot of money. (See also *bundle.*) ☐ *I made a bundle off that last deal.* ☐ *I want to buy a few stocks and make a pile in a few years.*

make a federal case out of something *tr.* to exaggerate the importance of an error; to overdo something. ☐ *Do you have to make a federal case out of everything?* ☐ *I only spilled my milk. Why make a federal case out of it?*

make a killing *tr.* to make an enormous profit; to become an enormous success. ☐ *The company made a killing from the sale of its subsidiary.* ☐ *I wanted to make a killing as a banker, but it didn't work out.*

Make a lap! *exclam.* to sit down. ☐ *Hey, make a lap and get out of the way!* ☐ *Pull up a chair and make a lap!*

make a pig of oneself *tr.* to overeat; to take more of something than anyone else gets; to be selfish. ☐ *Please don't make a pig of yourself.* ☐ *I have a tendency to make a pig of myself at affairs like this.*

make a pile See *make a bundle.*

make a score *tr.* to do a criminal act: to buy or sell drugs, to rob someone, to perform a *scam.* (Underworld.) ☐ *We made a score with that bank job in Adamsville, didn't we?* ☐ *They made quite a score off that junky.*

make a stink (about someone or something) See *raise a stink (about someone or something).*

make book on something *tr.* to make or accept bets on something. ☐ *Well, she might. But I wouldn't make book on it.* ☐ *Don't make book on my success in this game.*

make for somewhere *in.* to set out for somewhere; to run or travel to somewhere. ☐ *Max made for Philadelphia when he heard the pigs in the Big Apple were after him.* ☐ *Barlowe made for the stairs, but two shots rang out, and he knew it was all over for Mary.*

make hamburger out of someone or something AND **make mincemeat out of someone or something** *tr.* to beat someone or something to a pulp; to destroy someone or something. ☐ *The puppy made mincemeat out of my paper.* ☐ *They threatened to make hamburger out of me.*

make it **1.** *tr.* to achieve one's goals. (See also *make (it) big.*) ☐ *I can see by looking around this room that you have really made it.* ☐ *I hope I make it someday. But if not, I tried.* **2.** *tr.* to copulate (with someone). ☐ *There was no doubt in his mind that those bedroom eyes were telling him their owner wanted to make it.* ☐ *She wanted to make it, but he convinced her they should wait.*

make (it) big *tr. & in.* to become successful, especially financially. ☐ *I always knew that someday I would make it big.* ☐ *My brother made big, but it has just led to tax problems.*

make it hot for someone *tr.* to make things difficult for someone; to put someone under pressure. (Note the variation in the examples.) ☐ *The cops were making it hot for him, so he blew town.* ☐ *The boss is making it a little hot for me, so I had better get to work on time.*

Make it snappy! *exclam.* "Hurry up!"; "Make it fast!" ☐ *We're late, Tracy. Make it snappy!* ☐ *Make it snappy, Fred. The cops are headed up the walk now.*

make like a tree and leave *phr.* to leave; to depart. (A pun on the *leaf* of a tree.) ☐ *I have to leave now. It's time to make like a tree and leave.* ☐ *Hey, Jane. Don't you have an appointment somewhere? Why don't you make like a tree and leave?*

make like someone or something *in.* to act like someone or something. ☐ *Why don't you make like a bunny and run away? Beat it!* ☐ *Would you please make like a butler and hold the door open for me?*

make mincemeat out of someone or something See *make hamburger out of someone or something.*

Make my day! *exclam.* "Go ahead, do what you are going to do, and I will be very happy to do what I have to do!" (A catch phrase said typically by a movie police officer who has a gun pointed at a criminal. The police officer wants the criminal to do something that will justify pulling the trigger, which the police officer will do with pleasure. Used in real life in any context, and especially in sarcasm.) ☐ *Move a muscle! Go for your gun! Go ahead, make my day!* ☐ *Make my day. Just try it.*

Make no mistake (about it)! *sent.* an expression signifying the sincerity of the speaker's previous statements. ☐ *Make no mistake! This is the real thing.* ☐ *This is a very serious matter. Make no mistake about it.*

make one's bed *tr.* to be the cause of one's own misery. ☐ *Well, I guess I made my own bed. Now I have to lie in it.* ☐ *"We all make our own beds," said the minister.*

make oneself scarce *tr.* to leave; to be in a place less frequently. ☐ *Here come the boys in blue. I'd better make myself scarce.* ☐ *I suggest that you make yourself scarce before she returns.*

make out **1.** *in.* to neck and pet. ☐ *I still like to make out, but it's hard with dentures.* ☐ *He started making out when he was twelve.* **2.** *in.* to succeed. ☐ *How did you make out?* ☐ *I hope I make out okay tomorrow.*

make-out artist *n.* a seducer; a lecher, usually a male. (See also *lady-killer.*) ☐ *The guy thinks he's a make-out artist,* *but the women all think he's a nerd.* ☐ *He might have been a make-out artist in his youth, but I doubt it.*

make someone *tr.* to identify someone. ☐ *The cop stared at Max and tried to make him, but failed to identify him and let him go.* ☐ *The cops took Bruno downtown where the police chief made him for the third time in a month.*

make the scene **1.** *tr.* to attend an event. (See also *scene.*) ☐ *We plan to make the scene, but you know how things are.* ☐ *I hope everybody can make the scene.* **2.** *tr.* to understand a situation; to appreciate the situation. (Underworld. See also *make.*) ☐ *I can't quite make the scene, but it looks like Bruno punched the guy over here. Then he moved to the window over here, and that's when the old dame across the street saw him.* ☐ *I can make the scene. It's just like you said, except Bruno came in and found the guy laid out on the floor.*

make tracks *tr.* to move out of a place fast. ☐ *I gotta make tracks home now.* ☐ *Let's make tracks. We gotta hit Adamsville before noon.*

make waves *tr.* to cause difficulty. (Often in the negative.) ☐ *Just relax. Don't make waves.* ☐ *If you make waves too much around here, you won't last long.*

make with the something *in.* to make something visible; to use something. ☐ *Come on, make with the cash.* ☐ *I want to know. Come on, make with the answers!*

malark(e)y [mə'lɑrki] *n.* nonsense; flattery. ☐ *Don't give me that malarkey.* ☐ *What ridiculous malarkey!*

male chauvinist pig See *MCP.*

mallet *n.* a police officer. ☐ *Sam was struck by a mallet this noon.* ☐ *Some mallet is going around asking questions about you.*

mama bear *n.* a policewoman. (See also *lady bear.*) ☐ *As we came under the bridge, we saw a mama bear sitting in a pigmobile.* ☐ *A mama bear pulled the trucker over.*

man **1.** *n.* one's friend; a buddy, not necessarily male. (Also a term of address.) ☐ *Look, man, take it easy!* ☐ *Hey, man. That one's mine!* **2.** *exclam.* "Wow!" (Usually **Man!**) ☐ *Man, what a bundle!* ☐ *Man, what an ugly mug.* **3.** AND **the man** *n.* a drug seller or pusher. (Drugs.) ☐ *The man won't give you credit, you numskull!* ☐ *When your man doesn't show, there's always a good reason.* **4.** AND **the man** *n.* the police; the establishment. ☐ *You better check with the man before you get seen with me.* ☐ *We are about to rap a little with my man.*

man on the street **1.** *n.* the common man; just anyone selected at random. ☐ *But what does the man on the street think about all this?* ☐ *The man on the street really doesn't care about most of what you think is important.* **2.** *mod.* common; everyday. (This is hyphenated before a nominal.) ☐ *These man-on-the-street interviews all seem sort of phony.* ☐ *The man-on-the-street opinion spots are fun to make, but we can't show half of them.*

man-size(d) *mod.* large-size, especially in reference to the size of servings of food. ☐ *This is a man-sized steak! That's what I want.* ☐ *For a man-size meal, open a can of Wallace's Chili tonight!*

mañana [mə'njɑnə] *mod.* tomorrow. (Spanish.) ☐ *It's always mañana with you. Isn't there any 'today' or 'now' in your vocabulary?* ☐ *He's a mañana kind of guy. You know—real laid back.*

manicure **1.** *tr.* to trim and clean marijuana for smoking. (Drugs.) ☐ *Bruno never would manicure the stuff. Some people would buy it anyway.* ☐ *Max wants to manicure his own dope.* **2.** *n.* good-quality, cleaned marijuana. ☐ *Ah, this manicure should bring some good coin.* ☐ *You got any high Q. manicure?*

map **1.** *n.* one's face. ☐ *There was fear and hatred all over his map.* ☐ *With a map like that, she could really go somewhere.* **2.** *n.* sheet music. (Jazz musicians. See also *chart.*) ☐ *Check my map and see where you come in.* ☐ *I left the map at home. Can I look at yours?*

Marble City See *marble orchard.*

marble dome *n.* a stupid person. (Someone who has marble where brains should be.) ☐ *The guy's a marble dome. He has no knowledge of what's going on around him.* ☐ *Is this marble dome giving you any trouble?*

marble orchard AND **Marble City** *n.* a cemetery. ☐ *I already bought a little plot in a marble orchard.* ☐ *When I take a trip to Marble City, I want truckloads of flowers.*

marine officer See the following entry.

marine (recruit) AND **marine officer** *n.* an empty beer or liquor bottle. (See also *dead soldier, dead marine.*) ☐ *Every now and then the gentle muttering of the customers was accented by the breaking of a marine as it hit the floor.* ☐ *The guy in a uniform tossed the marine officer in the barrel and giggled.*

mark *n.* a *dupe;* a victim selected for a theft or a swindle. (Underworld.) ☐ *I bumped the mark on the shoulder, and he put his hand on his wallet just like always.* ☐ *We picked the marks out of the crowd in front of the two-dollar window.*

mark time *tr.* to wait; to do nothing but wait. ☐ *I'll just mark time till things get better.* ☐ *Do you expect me to just stand here and mark time?*

marker *n.* a personal promissory note; an IOU. ☐ *Max signed a marker for $3,000 and handed it to Bruno.* ☐ *Bruno said that he held Max's marker for three grand.*

marksman *n.* a serious college student who works hard to get good marks (grades). ☐ *Sally is a marksman. She's always studying.* ☐ *Bill kept saying that Todd was a geek and a marksman, until Todd flunked algebra.*

Mary J. See the following entry.

Mary Jane AND **Mary J.; Maryjane** *n.* marijuana. (Drugs. See also *jane.*) ☐ *I can't live another day without Mary Jane!* ☐ *I could sure rap with Mary Jane about now.*

mash *in.* to neck and pet. (Collegiate.) ☐ *Who are those two mashing in the corner?* ☐ *I can't spend every evening mashing with you!*

mashed *mod.* alcohol intoxicated. ☐ *Both guys were totally mashed. I called my brother, who came and rescued me.* ☐ *Bruno was mashed, but he wouldn't let anyone else drive.*

massive *mod.* excellent. (California.) ☐ *The bash at Tiffany's was, like, massive!* ☐ *That was a totally massive party, Tiff.*

massively *mod.* excellently; totally. ☐ *Max showed up for the meeting massively stoned and singing at the top of his lungs.* ☐ *Robert presented us with a massively gross belch that actually made the window rattle a little.*

maven AND **mavin** ['mevn̩] *n.* an expert; a self-proclaimed expert. (From Hebrew *mevin* via Yiddish.) ☐ *A maven in the stock market you are not.* ☐ *Harriet—a well-known clothing mavin in Rochester —keeps giving pointers on fabrics, but I don't listen.*

mavin See the previous entry.

maw [mɔ] *tr. & in.* to kiss and pet; to smooch. (Probably from *maul.*) ☐ *Come on, don't maw me. You've been watching too many movies—or two few.* ☐ *Let's go out somewhere and maw.*

max *n.* the maximum. (See also *to the max.*) ☐ *Is this the max I can have?* ☐ *I want the max. I'm hungry.*

max out *in.* to reach one's maximum in something, such as weight in weight lifting or credit on a credit card. ☐ *Andy finally maxed out at 300 pounds.* ☐ *Randy just knew when he had maxed out. Something in his body told him to stop.*

maxed out 1. *mod.* exhausted; tired. ☐ *I am just maxed out. I haven't been getting enough sleep.* ☐ *I had to stop work because I was too maxed out.* **2.** *mod.* alcohol intoxicated. ☐ *Sam was maxed out and seemed happy enough to sit under the table and whimper.* ☐ *I hadn't seen Barlowe so maxed out in years. He was nearly paralyzed.*

maxin' *in.* relaxing. □ *I spent Saturday just maxin' around the house and doing some tunage.* □ *I spent all day maxin' and drinking beer.*

mayo ['meo] *n.* mayonnaise. □ *You want mayo or mustard?* □ *I'll take both mayo and mustard, thank you.*

mazulla See the following entry.

mazuma AND **mazulla** [mə'zumə AND mə'zulə] *n.* money. (From Hebrew *mezu* via Yiddish.) □ *How much mazuma do you want for this?* □ *She's got more mazuma than she knows what to do with.*

McCoy See *(real) McCoy.*

McDoc(s) See the following entry.

McDoctor(s) AND **McDoc(s)** *n.* a jocular term for a walk-in, emergency medical clinic as found in shopping malls. (Compare to *doc(s)-in-a-box.*) □ *They took the kid to McDoctors, or whatever it is, over in the mall.* □ *McDocs is not cheap, but it's handy.*

McD's AND **McDuck's** *n.* McDonald's, the franchised fast-food restaurant. (Teens and collegiate. The *duck* is a play on the Walt Disney character "Donald Duck.") □ *Can you take McD's tonight, or do you want some slow food?* □ *I can always handle McDuck's.*

McDuck's See the previous entry.

McFly ['mɪk'flɑɪ] **1.** *n.* a stupid person; a simpleton. (Also a term of address.) □ *Oh, Donna, you are such a McFly!* □ *Hey, McFly. What do you think you are doing?* **2.** *mod.* stupid; simple-minded. □ *That was a McFly thing to do.* □ *Wayne is so McFly!*

MCP AND **male chauvinist pig** *n.* a male who acts superior to and aggressively toward women. (From the woman's liberation movements of the 1970's.) □ *The guy is just a male chauvinist pig, and he'll never change.* □ *Don't you just hate walking through a room filled with MCPs and just knowing what they are thinking about you?*

meadow muffin *n.* a mass of cow dung. □ *Jill stepped in a meadow muffin while she was bird-watching.* □ *Andy's mom gathered dried meadow muffins to put in her flower garden.*

mean 1. *mod.* having to do with someone or something that is very good; *cool.* □ *This music is mean, man, mean. What a great sound!* □ *This is the meanest wine I ever drank.* **2.** *mod.* having to do with an excellent example of the art of doing something well habitually. (Always with *a* as in the examples.) □ *John plays the piano quite well. Fred says that John plays a mean piano.* □ *You may say that your mother bakes delicious pies, but all my friends say she bakes a mean pie.* □ *Tom says that his father plays a mean game of golf.*

mean business *tr.* to be very, very serious. □ *Stop laughing! I mean business.* □ *I could tell from the look on her face that she meant business.*

meanie See the following entry.

meany AND **meanie** *n.* a mean or grouchy person. □ *Come on! Don't be such a meany.* □ *I don't want to be a meany, but if you don't turn down that radio, I don't know what I'll do.*

meat wagon *n.* an ambulance. □ *The meat wagon showed up just as they were pulling what was left of Marty out of what was left of her car.* □ *When the meat wagon stops at all the traffic lights on the way to the hospital, you know somebody's pifted.*

meathead *n.* a stupid oaf. □ *Don't call him a meathead. He does his best.* □ *Is this meathead bothering you, miss?*

meatheaded *mod.* stupid; simple-minded. □ *Of all the meatheaded ideas. This one takes the cake!* □ *How meatheaded!* □ *When someone conducts a meatheaded operation like this, we tend to lose faith in the whole system.*

meathooks *n.* the hands. (See also *hooks.*) □ *Get your meathooks off my car!* □ *If your meathooks so much as brush by my jacket again, you are finished!*

medico ['mɛdɪko] *n.* a doctor. (From Spanish.) □ *The medico says I should lose some weight.* □ *It's hard to take it* *seriously when a fat medico tells you to shed a few pounds.*

meet *n.* a meeting or an appointment. (Mostly underworld.) □ *If this meet works out, we could score a cool million.* □ *What time is the meet?*

meeting of the minds *n.* a consensus; an agreement. □ *At last we've reached a meeting of the minds.* □ *This meeting of the minds is nothing more than a truce.*

mega ['mɛgə] *mod.* large; serious. □ *Some mega beast boogied down to the front of the auditorium and started screaming.* □ *You see I have this, like, mega problem, ya know.*

megabitch *n.* a truly obnoxious *bitch.* □ *Bob, you are such a megabitch!* □ *Anne called herself a megabitch and said she didn't care what people thought of her.*

megabucks ['mɛgəbəks] *n.* a lot of money; *big bucks.* (See also *kilobucks.*) □ *A stereo that size must cost megabucks.* □ *Mr. Wilson has megabucks in pharmaceutical stocks.*

megadork ['mɛgədork] *n.* a very stupid person. (See also *dork.*) □ *What a wimpy megadork!* □ *Tiffany, you are, like, such a megadork!*

megillah [mə'gɪlə] *n.* a long and complicated story. (From Hebrew *megillah* via Yiddish.) □ *He struggled through this megillah and nobody believed him.* □ *Here you come in here with this megillah about a flat tire and how your brother-in-law stole your jack and how your arthritis is kicking up—what do you think I am, some sort of shoulder to cry on?*

mell of a hess *n. hell of a mess.* (A deliberate spoonerism.) □ *What a mell of a hess you've gotten us into this time.* □ *Have you ever seen such a mell of a hess?*

mellow 1. *mod.* relaxed; untroubled; *laid back.* □ *Being mellow is my only goal in life.* □ *She is the mellowest fox I know.* **2.** *mod.* slightly alcohol or drug intoxicated. □ *I got mellow and stopped drinking right there.* □ *I'm only mellow, but you drive anyway.*

mellow out 1. *in.* to calm down; to get less angry. □ *When you mellow out, maybe we can talk.* □ *Come on, man, mellow out!* **2.** *in.* to become generally more relaxed; to grow less contentious. □ *Gary was nearly forty before he started to mellow out a little and take life less seriously.* □ *After his illness, he mellowed out and seemed more glad to be alive.*

meltdown *n.* a total collapse of anything. (From the term used to describe the self-destruction of a nuclear reactor.) □ *There seems to have been a meltdown in the computer center, and all our records were lost.* □ *The meltdown in the securities markets was caused by a combination of things.*

melvin ['mɛlvən] **1.** *n.* a studious or unattractive male. (Teens and collegiate.) □ *Gary is such a melvin!* □ *Do you think I would go out with that melvin?* **2.** *n.* a situation where one's underpants ride up high between the buttocks. (Named for a person so stupid and unaware that he is comfortable with this arrangement. See also *give someone a melvin.*) □ *Look at that twit with the melvin.* □ *How could anybody go around all day with a melvin like that?*

men in blue AND **boys in blue** *n.* the police; policemen. (See also *blue boys.*) □ *The men in blue are looking for you.* □ *You can depend on the boys in blue to clean things up in this town.*

men's room *n.* a men's restroom. □ *Where's the men's room, please?* □ *I gotta use the men's room.*

mensch [mɛntʃ] *n.* a mature and responsible person. (From German via Yiddish.) □ *Now there goes a real mensch!* □ *I am honored to invite such a mensch into my home.*

mental 1. *mod.* mentally retarded. (Use caution with the topic. Derogatory.) □ *The girl's mental. Leave her alone.* □ *Everybody in this ward is mental.* **2.** *n.* a mentally retarded person. (Use caution with the topic. Derogatory.) □ *He's a mental. He'll need some help.* □ *Who doesn't need help? Mentals are normal on that point.* **3.** *n.* a stupid person. □ *You're such a mental lately.* □ *Don't be a mental.*

mental giant *n.* a genius. □ *I'm no mental giant, but I do know trouble when I see it.* □ *Don was a mental giant but didn't ever take advantage of it.*

mental midget *n.* a stupid person. □ *I hate to seem like a mental midget, but what's so great about that?* □ *This mental midget here thinks he can solve it for us.*

mep(s) *n.* meperdine, Demerol™, a painkiller. (Drugs and hospitals.) □ *The nurse was sneaking a little meps now and then.* □ *For some people, mep is highly addictive.*

merchandise *n.* any contraband. (Underworld.) □ *The merchandise is still at the boss's place.* □ *How much of the merchandise can you deliver by midnight?*

merger-mania *n.* an apparent need for companies to merge with one another. (Securities markets and journalism.) □ *Merger-mania is in the news again tonight with Ford's offer to take over GMC.* □ *The market meltdown put an end to merger-mania.*

mesc [mɛsk] *n.* mescaline, a hallucinatory substance. (Drugs.) □ *Tiffany is totally hooked on mesc. I don't know where she gets it.* □ *Jerry refuses to take mesc or any other dope.*

mesh *n.* a crosshatch or octothorpe, "#". (See also *pigpen.*) □ *Put a mesh on each end of your formula.* □ *What does the mesh stand for in this equation?*

meshuga AND **meshugah** [məˈʃʊgə] *mod.* crazy. (From Hebrew *meshuggah* via Yiddish.) □ *What a meshuga day!* □ *This guy is meshugah!*

meshugah See the previous entry.

mess 1. *n.* a hopeless, stupid person. □ *Harry has turned into a mess.* □ *The guy's a mess!* **2.** *n,* dung. (Usually with *a.*) □ *There is a dog mess on the lawn again this morning.* □ *There's a mess in Jimmy's diapers, Mom.*

mess about (with someone or something) See the following entry.

mess around (with someone or something) AND **mess about (with someone or something); monkey around (with someone or something) 1.** *in.* [with *someone*] to play with someone sexually. □ *Those two have been messing around.* □ *Pete was messing around with Maria, and now she's storked.* **2.** *in.* [with *someone*] to waste someone's time. □ *Don't mess around with me. Just answer the question, if you please.* □ *I don't have the time for this. Stop messing around.* **3.** *in.* [with *someone*] to waste time with someone else. □ *I was messing around with John.* □ *John and I were monkeying around.* **4.** *in.* [with *something*] to play with or fiddle with something. □ *Don't mess around with the ashtray.* □ *You'll break it if you don't stop messing about with it.*

mess someone or something up 1. *tr.* to put someone or something into disorder. □ *You messed me up a little bit, but I know you didn't mean to bump into me.* Ⓣ *Who messed up this place?* (More at *messed up.*) **2.** *tr.* [with *someone*] to beat someone up. (Underworld.) □ *The boss says me and the boys is supposed to mess you up a little.* Ⓣ *Is that your job—going around messing up people?*

mess someone's face up *tr.* to beat someone around the face. (Underworld.) □ *I had to mess his face up a little, boss, but he's been real cooperative since then.* Ⓣ *You want me to mess up your face, or do you want to come along quietly?*

mess up *in.* to make an error; to do something wrong; to *flub (up).* □ *I hope I don't mess up on the quiz.* □ *You really messed up!*

mess with someone or something AND **monkey with someone or something** *in.* to bother or interfere with someone or something. □ *Come on, don't monkey with it.* □ *Don't mess with me unless you want trouble.*

messed up 1. *mod.* confused. □ *I'm sort of messed up since my divorce.* □ *Most kids are sort of messed up at this age.* **2.** *mod.* alcohol or drug intoxicated. □ *Somehow I must have got messed up. What caused it, do you think?* □ *Everybody at the party was too messed up to drive home.*

meth **1.** *n.* denatured alcohol; methyl alcohol. (Streets and underworld.) ☐ *Oh, yeah, we drank meth. We drank anything we could get.* ☐ *Meth used to be pink. Now they put something in it to make you vomit.* **2.** *n.* methamphetamine. (Drugs.) ☐ *Usually meth is injected, having almost an immediate effect.* ☐ *Meth comes in little glass tubes.* **3.** *n.* methadone. (Drugs.) ☐ *Sometimes meth means methadone, a drug used in drug treatment.* ☐ *Jerry gets meth from a clinic in the city.*

meth monster *n.* a habitual user of methamphetamine. ☐ *Sometimes a meth monster will do okay in school.* ☐ *These teenage meth monsters can be a real menace when they need juice.*

metros ['metroz] *n.* the police; the metropolitan police. (Not used in all metropolitan areas.) ☐ *The metros took ten minutes to get to the scene of the crime, and the entire city is enraged.* ☐ *The metros showed up and managed traffic for the fire company.*

Mexican breakfast *n.* a cigarette and a cup of coffee or a glass of water. ☐ *After a Mexican breakfast, I went to Barlowe's hotel hoping to catch him before he went out.* ☐ *When some punk kid crosses the border into Mexico for a night of fun and games, all he can get to help him sober up and get out of the country the next day is a Mexican breakfast.*

mickey AND **micky** **1.** *n.* a hip flask for liquor. ☐ *He took a little swig out of a mickey he carries in his pocket.* ☐ *His micky made a clunk as he sat down.* **2.** See *Mickey (Finn).* **3.** *n.* a small bottle of wine. ☐ *See if you can get a mickey of something for a buck.* ☐ *The old guy just wants to get a micky to help with his wineache.* **4.** *n.* a tranquilizer. (Drugs.) ☐ *Whatever that mickey was you gave me, it helped.* ☐ *Maybe a little mickey would help me relax.*

Mickey D's *n.* McDonald's fast-food restaurant. (Teens and collegiate.) ☐ *Let's hit Mickey D's for chow this noon.* ☐ *We're going to Mickey D's for dinner, too.*

Mickey finished *mod.* alcohol intoxicated; totally drunk. (A play on *Mickey (Finn).*) ☐ *I guess the old guy is about Mickey finished. He's plootered!* ☐ *What gets into guys that makes them want to get Mickey finished before they stop?*

Mickey (Finn) **1.** *n.* a drink containing chloral hydrate; a drink containing a fast-acting laxative. ☐ *He slipped her a Mickey Finn, but she switched glasses.* ☐ *Once you've had a Mickey, you'll never forget it.* **2.** *n.* chloral hydrate as put in drinks to knock people out. ☐ *There was a Mickey Finn in this drink, wasn't there?* ☐ *Now where would I get a Mickey?*

mickey mouse **1.** *n.* nonsense; something trivial. (From the world-famous mouse character by the same name, owned by The Walt Disney Company.) ☐ *This is just a lot of mickey mouse.* ☐ *This mickey mouse is wasting my time.* **2.** *mod.* trivial; time wasting; lousy. ☐ *I want out of this mickey mouse place.* ☐ *No more mickey mouse questions if I agree to stay?* **3.** *n.* a police officer. (Streets.) ☐ *Mickey mouse is hanging around asking about you.* ☐ *Tell mickey mouse he knows where to find me.* **4.** *n.* a bit of blotter impregnated with *L.S.D.* with a picture of The Walt Disney Company's Mickey Mouse on it. (Drugs.) ☐ *How much is the mickey mouse?* ☐ *The mickey mouse is more than you want to pay.*

mickey mouse ears *n.* the two lights found on top of a police car. ☐ *There were no mickey mouse ears, but the jerk inside looked like your average ossifer.* ☐ *I could see the outline of the mickey mouse ears on the blue and white behind me.*

mickey mouse habit *n.* a trivial drug habit. (Drugs.) ☐ *Nothing to it. Just a little mickey mouse habit. I can stop any time I want.* ☐ *I don't care if it is a mickey mouse habit. It's a habit, and it's illegal.*

micky See *mickey.*

middle of nowhere *n.* an isolated place. ☐ *I don't want to stay out here in the middle of nowhere.* ☐ *I was stranded in the middle of nowhere for an hour with a flat tire.*

middlebrow *mod.* middle-class; average or mediocre. (Between *highbrow* and *lowbrow.*) ☐ *She has average middlebrow tastes and drives a mid-sized Chevrolet.* ☐ *He's just too middlebrow.* ☐ *There are some who look down on middlebrow interests as trivial.*

midi ['mɪdi] **1.** *n.* a mid-length woman's garment. ☐ *Shall I wear my midi, or is it too hot?* ☐ *The midi is okay.* **2.** *mod.* having to do with a mid-length woman's garment. ☐ *This midi style is out, and the mini is back in.* ☐ *The midi length was just transitional. Who decides on these things anyway?*

mifky-pifky (in the bushes) *n.* illicit sex; *hanky-panky.* ☐ *Jeff got caught again. Mifky-pifky in the bushes seems to be his style.* ☐ *Mifky-pifky is the way of the world in Hollywood.*

milk **1.** *tr.* to attempt to persuade an audience to laugh or applaud. ☐ *Mitzy tried to milk the audience for applause.* ☐ *She went on milking the crowd for adulation long after they had demonstrated their appreciation.* **2.** *tr.* to attempt to get recognition from an audience. ☐ *His performance was marred by an amateurish attempt to milk applause.* ☐ *If you're good, they'll let you know it. If not, don't milk cheers, applause, or laughter.*

milled *mod.* alcohol intoxicated. (See also *cut.*) ☐ *She was cut up with all that booze—milled, I guess.* ☐ *She was too milled to drive and couldn't walk either.*

milquetoast ['mɪlktost] *n.* a shy coward; an effeminate male. (See also *Casper Milquetoast.*) ☐ *This little milquetoast goes up to the biker, looks at him sort of sad like, and then karate chops him into a quivering pulp.* ☐ *Some guy who looked like a milquetoast came in and asked for a set of brass knuckles.*

Milwaukee goiter AND **German goiter** [mɪl'wɔki 'gɔɪdɚ AND 'dʒɚmən 'gɔɪdɚ] *n.* a beer belly. (Refers to Milwaukee, Wisconsin, a major beer-brewing city, and to Germany.) ☐ *By the time he was twenty-six, he was balding and had a Milwaukee goiter that would tip him over if he turned too fast.* ☐ *He was proud of his German goiter.*

mind-bender AND **mind-blower** *n.* a hallucinogenic drug, typically *L.S.D.* (Drugs.) ☐ *You wanna try some mind-blower?* ☐ *That mind-bender takes a long time to wear off.*

mind-blower See the previous entry.

mind your own beeswax [. . . 'bizwæks] *tr.* to "mind one's own business." (Juvenile.) ☐ *You just mind your own beeswax!* ☐ *Lay off! Mind your own beeswax!*

mingy ['mɪndʒi] *mod.* "mean" and "stingy." ☐ *Why can't you borrow it? I'm just mingy, that's all.* ☐ *What a mingy jerk!* ☐ *Aw, don't be so mingy!*

mini ['mɪni] **1.** *mod.* small; miniature. ☐ *I have a mini problem you can maybe help me with.* ☐ *This is just a mini office. I'll get a bigger one later.* **2.** *n.* a miniskirt. ☐ *I look pretty good in a mini.* ☐ *I'll try a mini this time. I was too plump the last time they were in style.*

mink *n.* a woman. (Black.) ☐ *I see your mink has some new silks, man.* ☐ *Take this home to your mink. She'll like it.*

Minnehaha [mɪni'hɑhɑ] *n.* champagne. (From Longfellow's *Song of Hiawatha.* "Minnehaha" means laughing waters.) ☐ *Have a glass of Minnehaha.* ☐ *Minnehaha tickles my nose.*

mint **1.** *n.* a lot of money. ☐ *He makes a mint. He can afford a little generosity.* ☐ *That kind of car costs a mint!* **2.** *mod.* good-looking; superior. (As *in mint condition.*) ☐ *Look at that guy. He's really mint, right?* ☐ *These tunes are mint, all right!*

mish-mash AND **mish-mosh** ['mɪʃmæʃ AND 'mɪʃmɑʃ] *n.* a mixture; a disorderly conglomeration. ☐ *What a mish-mash of colors and designs!* ☐ *There's no theme or focus. It's just a mish-mash.*

mish-mosh See the previous entry.

miss the boat *tr.* to have made an error; to be wrong. ☐ *If you think you can do that, you have just missed the boat.* ☐ *The guy's missed the boat. He's a lunkhead.*

mitt *n.* a hand. □ *Get your mitts off my glass.* □ *The kid's got mitts on him like a gorilla.*

mix it up (with someone) *tr.* to fight with someone; to quarrel with someone. □ *Max and Bruno mixed it up for a while, and then things calmed down.* □ *Max came out of the shop and began to mix it up with Bruno.*

mixed (up) **1.** *mod.* confused; mentally troubled. (This is hyphenated before a nominal.) □ *I was a little mixed up after the accident.* □ *This kid's just a little mixed. She'll straighten out.* □ *She's a crazy mixed-up kid.* **2.** *mod.* alcohol intoxicated. □ *I'm just a little mixed-up, nothing serious. No reason you should be swaying around like that.* □ *Jerry's too mixed to drive home.*

mob [mab] *n.* the crime syndicate. (Underworld and journalistic.) □ *The mob has held this city in abject terror for years.* □ *One of the biggest fish in the mob was pulled from the river yesterday.*

moby ['mobi] **1.** *mod.* enormous; unwieldy. (Like Herman Melville's great white whale, *Moby Dick.*) □ *This is a very moby old car.* □ *Why does he let himself get so moby?* **2.** *n.* a "megabyte," a measurement of computer memory size. (A megabyte is whale-sized compared to a kilobyte.) □ *My fixed disks give me a capacity of over seventy-five mobies.* □ *My new computer has one moby of random access memory.*

mod [mad] *mod.* contemporary and fashionable in clothing and ideas. □ *Your clothes are mod, but you're just a plain, old-fashioned prude.* □ *Your mod friends might appreciate this article in the paper.*

mod poser ['mad 'pozə-] *n.* someone who looks mod in dress only. (Collegiate.) □ *Tiffany is such a mod poser. At home it's jeans and a T-shirt.* □ *The more extreme the style gets, the more mod posers there are.*

moist around the edges *mod.* alcohol intoxicated. □ *Charlie is more than moist around the edges. He is soused.* □ *Didn't that guy seem a little moist around the edges?*

mojo ['modʒo] **1.** *n.* heroin; morphine; cannabis. (Drugs. See also *on the mojo.*) □ *This mojo is no good.* □ *Why don't you try to kick the mojo?* **2.** *n.* a narcotics addict. (Drugs.) □ *These mojos will rob you blind if you don't keep an eye on them.* □ *Bruno's no mojo, and if he was nobody'd mention it.*

moldy fig *n.* an old-fashioned person; a square. □ *Don't be a moldy fig! Lighten up!* □ *Some moldy fig objected to our music.*

mom *n.* a mother. (Also a term of address. Capitalized when used as the name of one's own mother.) □ *My mom is the greatest!* □ *Mom, can I have a bigger allowance?*

mondo ['mando] *mod.* totally; very much. (California.) □ *You are, like, mondo gross!* □ *This place is like, so, like, mondo beige.*

money from home **1.** *n.* easily gotten money. (Underworld.) □ *There is nothing to a simple con job like this. It's money from home.* □ *This job is like taking candy from a kid. It's money from home.* **2.** *n.* something as welcome as long-awaited money from home. □ *This cool drink is money from home right now.* □ *Having you visit like this is like getting money from home, Tracy.*

money grubber *n.* a stingy person. □ *Why is he such a money grubber? Is he going to take it with him?* □ *The boss is such a money grubber. He still has his first paper clip.*

money talks *phr.* "money can buy cooperation"; "having money makes one influential." □ *I know that money talks, but I don't have the scratch to say anything with.* □ *Like they say, money talks, but don't try making it talk to a cop.*

moneybags *n.* a nickname for a wealthy person. □ *When old moneybags does finally buy the farm, who gets the loot?* □ *When you get to be a big moneybags, don't forget those you left behind.*

moniker AND **monniker** ['mɑnəkɚ] *n.* a nickname. □ *What's your moniker, chum?* □ *With a monniker like that, you must get in a lot of fights.*

monkey **1.** *n.* a playful child. (Also a term of address.) □ *Come here, you little monkey!* □ *Hey, monkey, where are you going?* **2.** *n.* a drug addiction. (Drugs. See also *have a monkey on one's back.*) □ *That monkey of mine is getting hungry again.* □ *Why don't you try to get rid of that monkey?*

monkey around (with someone or something) See *mess around (with someone or something).*

monkey bite *n.* a kiss that leaves a blotch or mark. (See also *hickey.*) □ *Who gave you that monkey bite?* □ *Do you have some makeup that'll cover this monkey bite?*

monkey business AND **funny business** *n.* silliness; dishonest tricks. □ *That's enough monkey business. Now, settle down.* □ *Stop the funny business. This is serious!*

monkey swill *n.* inferior liquor; strong liquor. □ *This monkey swill will probably make me blind.* □ *Where did you get this monkey swill? This would kill a monkey anyway.*

monkey talk *n.* distorted speech, as uttered while drug intoxicated. (Drugs.) □ *Max slapped the poor junky to get him to stop the monkey talk.* □ *Their pupils are pinpoint-sized, and they talk monkey talk. That's how you can tell they're on H.*

monkey wagon *n.* drug addiction. (Drugs.) □ *I've been riding this monkey wagon long enough.* □ *Some of these treatment centers won't get you off the monkey wagon unless you have insurance.*

monkey wards *n.* "Montgomery Wards," a department store chain. □ *I get that kind of stuff at monkey wards.* □ *They closed the monkey wards near us.*

monkey with someone or something See *mess with someone or something.*

monkeyshines *n.* tricks; small acts of mischief. □ *You and your silly monkeyshines!* □ *These kids are a lot of fun despite their monkeyshines.*

monniker See *moniker.*

monolithic [mɑnəˈlɪθɪk] *mod.* heavily drug intoxicated. (Drugs. A play on *stoned.*) □ *She's not just stoned, she's monolithic!* □ *I was monolithic—dead drunk.*

monster **1.** *n.* any powerful drug affecting the central nervous system. (Drugs.) □ *This P.C.P. is a monster. Why don't the cops put a stop to it?* □ *That monster just about did me in.* **2.** *mod.* having to do with a powerful or addictive drug. (Drugs.) □ *Where the devil did you get that monster dust?* □ *That is monster C., and it will make you its slave.*

monster weed *n.* cannabis; powerful marijuana. (Drugs.) □ *Where on earth does she get that monster weed she's been blowing?* □ *This is what they call monster weed. Stay away from it. It may have angel dust on it.*

Montezuma's revenge [mɑntəˈzuməz rɪˈvɛndʒ] *n.* diarrhea; tourist diarrhea. (Refers to tourists in Mexico.) □ *I had a little touch of Montezuma's revenge the second day, but other than that we had a wonderful time.* □ *Most people blame Montezuma's revenge on the water.*

monthlies *n.* the period of menstruation. □ *It's her monthlies. You know how she feels then.* □ *The monthlies have struck again!*

moo juice AND **cow juice** *n.* milk. □ *How about another glass of moo juice?* □ *While you're at the store, get some more cow juice.*

mooch [mutʃ] **1.** *tr. & in.* to beg for money, liquor, or drugs in public places. □ *No mooching around here! Move along!* □ *Jed mooched drinks all evening.* **2.** *n.* a beggar. □ *The guy is a mooch. Get him out of here.* □ *I don't want to be a mooch, but could I borrow your lawn mower?* **3.** *n.* narcotics. (Drugs. Compare to *hooch.*) □ *Mooch is what Minnie the Moocher is famous for.* □ *He's gonna have to work hard to get off the mooch.*

moocher **1.** *n.* a beggar. □ *What do you usually give a moocher?* □ *I try to give every moocher a little change.* **2.** *n.* a drug addict. (Drugs.) □ *The guy's a moocher and can't be trusted.* □ *These moochers will do anything to get a few bucks for a load.*

moolah ['mulɑ] *n.* money. (Originally underworld.) □ *That is a whole lot of moolah!* □ *There was no moolah in that safe!*

moon **1.** *n.* the buttocks. □ *He rubbed a plump moon where he had been kicked, but said no more.* □ *She fell square on her moon and slowly broke into a smile.* **2.** *tr. & in.* to show (someone) one's nude posterior through a window (usually of an automobile). (Compare to *gaucho.*) □ *When the plane flew over Cuba, this guy named Victor actually mooned a Russian M.I.G. that flew by.* □ *The kids were mooning, and they got arrested for indecent exposure.* (More at *mooner.*)

mooner **1.** *n.* a drunkard. (From *moonshine.*) □ *This old mooner from up in the hills wandered into town last Friday and died in the town square.* □ *There must be dozens of mooners who beg in town in the day and drink in the woods at night.* **2.** *n.* an idler who stares at the moon. □ *If he ever outgrows being a mooner, he may be all right.* □ *I feel like a mooner tonight. There is nothing better to do.*

moonlight **1.** *n.* illicit liquor; *moonshine.* □ *Where's that bottle of moonlight you used to keep under the counter?* □ *How about a sip of moonlight?* **2.** *in.* to traffic in illicit liquor. (Best done under the cover of darkness.) □ *He moonlighted during prohibition.* □ *Jed was moonlighting around the clock.* **3.** *in.* to work at a second job. □ *Larry had to moonlight to earn enough to feed his family.* □ *A lot of people have to moonlight to make ends meet.*

moonlight requisition *n.* a nighttime theft. (Military. See also *liberate.*) □ *It took a moonlight requisition to get the medicine we needed.* □ *They got the spare part on a moonlight requisition.*

moonlit *mod.* alcohol intoxicated, with *moonshine.* □ *He's on the jug again. See, he's all moonlit.* □ *He's too moonlit to drive.*

moonrock *n.* a form of *crack* that contains heroin. □ *Max was caught with a supply of moonrock on him.* □ *He was trying to start the little kids out on moonrock.*

moonshine **1.** *n.* nonsense; humbug. □ *That's just moonshine! I don't believe a word.* □ *He's a master at moonshine.* **2.** *n.* homemade whisky; any cheap or inferior liquor. □ *This moonshine isn't the best you've made.* □ *Moonshine is supposed to be strong, not good.* **3.** *in.* to distill or traffic in illicit liquor. □ *Yeah, I moonshine a little. So what?* □ *You would be amazed at how much people moonshine back in the hills.* (More at *moonshiner.*)

moonshiner *n.* a maker of *moonshine.* □ *Moonshiners in the Georgia hills are using sophisticated electronic warning systems to keep one step ahead of the feds.* □ *I have an uncle who was a moonshiner for a while.*

moose *n.* a Japanese girlfriend; any girlfriend. (Crude. Military.) □ *She's my moose, and you'd better remember it!* □ *She's one fine moose, if you ask me.*

mop [mɑp] **1.** *n.* a drinking bout. □ *She is off somewhere on another mop.* □ *This mop lasted about a day and a half.* **2.** *n.* a heavy drinker; a drunkard. □ *The guy's a mop. There is nothing you can do till he decides he's had enough.* □ *The mops hang out here looking for handouts.* **3.** *n.* hair; a hairdo. □ *How do you like my new mop?* □ *Why don't you comb that mop?*

mop the floor up with someone AND **wipe the floor up with someone** *tr.* to beat someone to a pulp. (Also with other verbs: *clean, dust,* etc.) □ *One more crack like that, and I'll have Bruno wipe the floor up with you.* Ⓣ *Bruno's job is dusting up the floor with people who don't wipe off their feet before coming in.*

mope [mop] **1.** *n.* a tired and ineffectual person. □ *I can't afford to pay mopes* *around here. Get to work or get out!* ☐ *I feel like such a mope today.* **2.** AND **mope around** *in.* to move around slowly and sadly. ☐ *I feel like moping and nothing else.* ☐ *He just mopes around all day and won't eat anything.*

mope around See the previous entry.

mopped AND **moppy** *mod.* alcohol intoxicated. ☐ *Jack was a little moppy to be driving.* ☐ *He's not mopped; he's sloshed.*

mopping-up operation *n.* a clean-up operation; the final stages in a project where the loose ends are taken care of. ☐ *It's all over except a small mopping-up operation.* ☐ *The mopping-up operation should cost just under twenty million.*

moppy See *mopped.*

more than one bargained for *n.* (getting) more than one expected. ☐ *This is certainly more than I bargained for!* ☐ *Trouble and more trouble. I'm getting more than I bargained for when I took the job.*

morning after (the night before) *n.* a hangover. (Always with *the.*) ☐ *Do worries about the morning after keep you from having a good time at parties?* ☐ *She's suffering from the morning after the night before.*

mossback ['mɔsbæk] *n.* an old *square;* a *stick in the mud.* ☐ *Walter, you are such an old mossback.* ☐ *I enjoy appearing to be a mossback. People expect so little from you.*

most *n.* something that is the best. (Always with *the.*) ☐ *This noodle stuff is the most, Mom!* ☐ *Sally is the most! Can she dance!*

mother 1. *n.* marijuana. (Drugs. See also *mother nature('s).* ☐ *She grows her own mother in a pot in her room.* ☐ *This mother is way rad!* **2.** *n.* a drug dealer; one's own drug dealer upon whom one depends. (Drugs.) ☐ *Bruno is my mother.* ☐ *If you can't trust your mother, who can you trust?*

mother nature('s) *n.* marijuana. (Drugs.) ☐ *No chemicals for me. I find that mother nature is everything I need.* ☐ *See if you can get some of mother nature's.*

motion-lotion *n.* gasoline; motor fuel. (Citizens band radio.) ☐ *Let's stop up ahead for some motion-lotion.* ☐ *I'm about out of motion-lotion.*

motor *in.* to depart. ☐ *Well, let's motor, you guys. It's getting late.* ☐ *I've got to motor. It's a long walk home.*

motor-mouth See *ratchet-mouth.*

Motown ['motaun] *n.* "motor town," Detroit, Michigan. ☐ *Have you ever been to Motown?* ☐ *We went to Motown to buy a car once.*

(mountain) dew 1. *n.* Scotch whiskey. ☐ *Mountain dew is best when it's from the old country.* ☐ *The real mountain dew is smoky-tasting and amber.* **2.** *n.* illicit liquor; any liquor. ☐ *Mountain dew is what I want. As long as it's not store bought.* ☐ *My pappy made his own mountain dew.*

mouth 1. *n.* a hangover. (Always with *a.*) ☐ *I've got quite a mouth this morning. I guess I overdid it.* ☐ *What a mouth! It tastes like a bird slept in it!* **2.** See *mouth(piece).*

mouth-breather *n.* a stupid-acting person. ☐ *I always end up with a mouth-breather on a blind date.* ☐ *Who's the mouth-breather with Fred?*

mouth full of South *n.* a southern accent. ☐ *You sure do have a mouth full of South.* ☐ *I just love to hear a man with a mouth full of South.*

mouth off 1. *in.* to give (someone) back talk. ☐ *If you mouth off, I will ground you for three weeks.* ☐ *Don't mouth off at me, buster!* **2.** *in.* to speak out of turn. ☐ *Don't just mouth off. Wait your turn.* ☐ *Hold up your hand. I won't deal with people who mouth off.*

mouthful 1. *n.* a true statement. ☐ *You said a mouthful, and I agree.* ☐ *That is a mouthful, and I know it took courage to say it.* **2.** *n.* a tirade. ☐ *Paul really gave me a mouthful. I didn't know I hurt his feelings.* ☐ *She sure had a mouthful to say to you!*

mouth(piece) *n.* a lawyer specializing in criminal cases. (Underworld.) □ *The guy hired a mouthpiece and beat the rap.* □ *I won't answer anything without my mouth right here by me.*

mouthwash *n.* liquor; a drink of liquor. □ *I could use a shot of that mouthwash.* □ *You could use a little mouthwash after that long trip, I bet.*

move on someone *in.* to attempt to pick up someone; to attempt to seduce someone. (Collegiate.) □ *Don't try to move on my date, old chum.* □ *Harry is trying to move on Tiffany. They deserve each another.*

movers and shakers *n.* people who get things done; organizers and managers. □ *The movers and shakers in this firm haven't exactly been working overtime.* □ *Who are the movers and shakers around here?*

movies *n.* a case of diarrhea. □ *A case of the movies kept me going all night.* □ *I can't go too far from the little boys' room. I got the movies.*

moxie ['mɑksi] *n.* energy; spunk; spirit. □ *Now here's a gal with real moxie.* □ *Come on. Show some moxie!*

Mr. Big *n.* an important man; the boss man. □ *So you're Mr. Big. I thought you'd be taller.* □ *The office suite of Acme's Mr. Big was cold and ostentatious, as was its occupant.*

Mr. Hawkins *n.* the winter wind. (Originally Black. See also *hawk.*) □ *We have an appointment with Mr. Hawkins in January.* □ *Put something on your head, or Mr. Hawkins will cut you down.*

Mr. Nice Guy *n.* a friendly, forgiving fellow. □ *You'll find that I am Mr. Nice Guy as long as you play fair with me.* □ *Oh, my boss is Mr. Nice Guy. He'll let me off, I'm sure.*

Mr. Right *n.* the one man who is right for a woman. □ *Some day Mr. Right will come along and sweep you off your feet.* □ *I'm tired of waiting for Mr. Right. Where is Mr. Maybe?*

Mr. Whiskers AND **Uncle Whiskers; whiskers (man)** *n.* a federal agent. (Underworld. From the whiskers of Uncle Sam.) □ *Mr. Whiskers is trying to get me to pay tax on those few bucks.* □ *Mr. Whiskers is on our tail. Let's blow town.*

Mrs. Murphy *n.* a bathroom. □ *Whose turn is it at Mrs. Murphy's?* □ *When will Mrs. Murphy be free?*

M.T. *n.* an empty bottle. (Initialism.) □ *Put your M.T.s in the garbage.* □ *Here's another M.T. for your collection.*

mu *n.* marijuana. (Drugs.) □ *This mu is stale.* □ *Are mu and bu the same thing?*

mucho ['mutʃo] *mod.* very. (Spanish.) □ *This is a mucho happy young man.* □ *We are mucho disgusted with your performance.*

muck something up *tr.* to mess something up; to ruin something. □ *Try not to muck it up this time.* 🅃 *You seem to have mucked up this one, too.*

mudbud *n.* homegrown marijuana. (Drugs.) □ *Mudbud, hell! It's garbage.* □ *If you sell your mudbud, you're a pusher!*

muddled (up) *mod.* alcohol intoxicated. □ *I've had a little too much muddler, I think. Anyway, I'm muddled.* □ *Larry is too muddled up to drive.*

muddler *n.* liquor. □ *I've had a little too much muddler, I think. Anyway, I'm muddled.* □ *Let's stop here for some muddler.*

mug 1. *n.* the face. (Crude.) □ *Wipe that smile off your mug!* □ *What a gorgeous mug!* **2.** *n.* a thug; a *goon.* (Underworld.) □ *Call off your mugs. I'll come peacefully.* □ *Bruno is just another one of the mugs from the mob.* **3.** *tr.* to attack and rob someone. □ *Somebody jumped out of an alley and tried to mug me.* □ *Some punk mugged Mrs. Lopez last night.*

mug shot *n.* a photograph of one's face taken for police records. (Underworld.) □ *I'm going to have to ask you to come down to the station and go through some mug shots.* □ *How can a professional photographer take a portrait that looks like a mug shot?*

mugger *n.* someone, usually a male, who attacks and robs people. □ *I clobbered the mugger with a tire iron I carry just for such occasions.* □ *The muggers have the downtown almost to themselves after dark.*

muggy ['məgi] *mod.* alcohol intoxicated. □ *George is just a little muggy. It doesn't take much anymore.* □ *I'm too muggy to drive.*

mule *n.* someone who delivers or smuggles drugs for a drug dealer. (Drugs.) □ *The jerks use a twelve-year-old kid for a mule!* □ *A car drove by, and suddenly the mule was riddled with machine gun bullets.*

munch out *in.* to eat ravenously. (Drugs. See also *pig out.*) □ *I had to munch out after the party. I can't imagine why.* □ *I can munch out for no reason at all.*

munchies 1. See *(blind) munchies.* **2.** *n.* snacks, such as potato chips; any casual food. □ *What kind of munchies are we going to have?* □ *The munchies at the party were great!*

munchkin ['məntʃkən] *n.* a small or insignificant person. □ *You're not going to let that munchkin push you around, are you?* □ *Who is the munchkin holding the clipboard?*

mung 1. AND **MUNG** [məŋ] *n.* something that is "mashed until no good"; anything nasty or gloppy. (An acronym, but possibly a coinage before it became an acronym.) □ *Get this mung off my plate.* □ *This mung is cruel and unusual punishment. I demand to see the warden.* **2.** *tr.* to ruin something. □ *You munged my car!* □ *Look at it! You munged it!*

mung something up *tr.* to mess something up. □ *Don't mung it up this time.* [T] *The team munged up the play, and the coach blasted them but good.*

mungy ['məŋi] **1.** *mod.* gloppy; messy. □ *Get that mungy stuff off my plate!* □ *The spaghetti was cold and mungy by the time it was served.* **2.** *mod.* having to do with an oily feeling of the face of a person who has taken *L.S.D.* (Drugs.) □ *I feel so mungy after I take the stuff. Yuck!* □ *I can do without the mungy feeling and the flashbacks.*

murder AND **slaughter** *tr.* to overwhelm; to beat someone in a sports contest. □ *The other team murdered us.* □ *We went out on the field prepared to slaughter them.*

murphy ['mɚfi] **1.** *n.* a potato. □ *I spent half my tour of duty peeling murphies.* □ *Look, this murphy looks like my mother-in-law.* **2.** *n.* a breast. (Crude. Usually plural. Use caution with the topic.) □ *Look at the murphies on that dame!* □ *She stood about six feet tall and was turned in the light so her murphies stood out in silhouette.*

musclehead *n.* a stupid man; a man who has muscle where there should be brains. (Also a rude term of address.) □ *Look, musclehead, do exactly what I tell you!* □ *An overstuffed musclehead waddled over and offered to bend me in half if I didn't beat it.*

muscleman 1. *n.* a strong bully; a *goon.* (Underworld.) □ *Bruno is a muscleman for the kingpin of a local drug ring.* □ *Tell your muscleman to lay off.* **2.** *n.* a man who builds muscles through bodybuilding exercises. □ *That muscleman doesn't have a single ounce of fat on him.* □ *Being a muscleman requires most of your time.*

mush 1. *n.* nonsense. □ *What mush! Come on, talk straight!* □ *That's just mush. Don't believe it.* **2.** *n.* romance; lovemaking; kissing. □ *I can't stand movies with lots of mush in them.* □ *When an actor looks at an actress like that, you just know that there's gonna be some mush.* **3.** *n.* one's face. (Crude.) □ *Put some paint on your mush, and let's get going.* □ *With a mush like that, you ought to be in pictures. Maybe another King Kong remake.*

mushhead *n.* a stupid person. □ *Oh, good grief, I'm such a mushhead!* □ *Who is the mushhead in the cowboy boots?*

mushmouth *n.* a person who does not or cannot speak clearly. □ *Don't be a mushmouth. Talk plainly.* □ *How can a* *mushmouth like that get a job reading news on network television?*

musical beds *n.* acts of sexual promiscuity; sleeping with many people. (From the name of the game "musical chairs.") ☐ *Mary has been playing musical beds for about a year.* ☐ *She thinks that playing musical beds is the way to get ahead.*

must See the following entry.

(must) do AND **must** *n.* something that someone ought to do. (Always with *a*.) ☐ *Seeing the Eiffel tower is a must do in Paris.* ☐ *This is a do when you're in town.*

mutant *n.* a total *jerk;* a social outcast. (Also a term of address.) ☐ *Sam, you act like such a mutant!* ☐ *Hey, mutant! Get out of the way!*

My foot! *exclam.* "I do not believe it!"; "Like hell!" (An exclamation of contradiction.) ☐ *You're the best in town, my foot!* ☐ *She's going to marry you? My foot!*

my man *n.* my brother or buddy. (Originally black.) ☐ *This is my man Sam who's gonna show you how to boogie.* ☐ *Come on, my man, we have to be taking care of business.*

mystery meat *n.* any unidentified meat. (Collegiate.) ☐ *What is the mystery meat tonight?* ☐ *There are no hints as to what this mystery meat is—except its strange pinkish color.*

mystic biscuit *n.* a chunk of peyote cactus. (Drugs.) ☐ *Wally thought he got a piece of mystic biscuit, but it was just a moldy raisin.* ☐ *Max was selling mystic biscuit to the college kids.*

N

nab [næb] **1.** *tr.* to arrest someone. □ *They nabbed Tom with a stolen watch on him.* □ *I knew they would nab him sooner or later.* (More at *nabbed.*) **2.** AND **nabber** *n.* a police officer; a cop. □ *The nabs got him, and he had the evidence on his person.* □ *There's a nabber at the door who wants to talk to you.*

nabbed *mod.* caught by the police; arrested. □ *He got nabbed last night with a stolen watch on him.* □ *She's down at the police station. She's nabbed.*

nabber See *nab.*

nabe [neb] **1.** *n.* a neighborhood; one's own neighborhood. □ *I can't wait to get back to my own nabe.* □ *Hey, man, welcome back to the old nabe!* **2.** *n.* a neighborhood theater. □ *Do I have to go downtown to see that movie, or is it playing at the nabes yet?* □ *Why drive all the way out there when you can see it at the nabe for half the cost?*

nada ['nɑdɑ] *n.* nothing; none. (Spanish.) □ *I asked him, but he didn't say nada.* □ *The score was nada to nada.*

nag 1. *tr.* to pester someone constantly. □ *Stop nagging me!* □ *I'll nag him until he remembers on his own.* **2.** *n.* a worn-out horse. □ *I bet a week's pay on that nag. Look what happened!* □ *The cowboy came riding into town on an old gray nag.*

nail 1. *tr.* to arrest someone. □ *The cops nailed him right in his own doorway.* □ *"I'm gonna nail you," said the officer.* (More at *nailed.*) **2.** See *coffin nail.* **3.** *tr.* to identify someone. □ *They nailed him from his picture.* □ *The officer nailed Freddy, thanks to the description the victim provided.*

nail-em-and-jail-em AND **nailer** *n.* the police in general; a police officer. □ *The nailers caught Freddy last night.* □ *Old nail-em-and-jail-em is going to be knocking at your door any day now.*

nail someone to a cross AND **nail someone('s hide) to the wall** *tr.* to punish or scold someone severely. (Literally, to crucify someone or to nail someone's skin to the wall like that of a captured animal.) □ *That guy was really mad. He really nailed you to a cross.* □ *She must hate your guts. She sure nailed your hide to the wall.*

nail someone('s hide) to the wall See the previous entry.

nailed 1. *mod.* correctly identified. □ *The thugs sure got nailed fast.* □ *The killer was nailed with the help of the F.B.I.* **2.** *mod.* arrested. (See also *nail.*) □ *Okay, chum. You are nailed: Let's go.* □ *Why am I nailed? I didn't do anything.*

nailer See *nail-em-and-jail-em.*

naked *mod.* undiluted; having to do with neat liquor, especially gin. (See also *raw.*) □ *No ice, please. I want mine naked.* □ *Give me a naked whisky, if you don't mind.*

naked truth *n.* the complete, unembellished truth. □ *Sorry to put it to you like this, but it's the naked truth.* □ *I can take it. Just tell me the naked truth.*

Nam *n.* Vietnam. □ *How long were you in Nam?* □ *Things were pretty bad in Nam.*

namby-pamby ['næmbi'pæmbi] *mod.* overly nice; effeminate and weak, when said of a male. □ *Fred is too namby-pamby when it comes to making up his mind.* □ *A real namby-pamby guy.* □ *What a namby-pamby guy!*

name of the game *n.* the way things are; the way things can be expected to be. (Always with *the*.) □ *The name of the game is money, money, money.* □ *I can't help it. That's the name of the game.*

Name your poison. *sent.* "State what you want to drink." (Refers to alcoholic drinks only.) □ *Okay, friend, name your poison.* □ *Step up to the bar and name your poison.*

narc See *nark*.

narc(o) [nɑrk AND 'nɑrko] **1.** *n.* a narcotic. (See also *nark*.) □ *She's been taking narcs.* □ *How long has he been on narcs?* **2.** *mod.* having to do with narcotics. □ *Does he have a narc problem?* □ *She is a narco officer.* **3.** *n.* a federal narcotics agent; any narcotics enforcement officer. □ *The narcs caught him.* □ *There is a narco at our school.*

nark AND **narc** [nɑrk] **1.** *n.* a police informer. □ *Fred is a nark. He squealed.* □ *I'm going to get that narc for squealing.* **2.** *in.* to inform (on someone) to the police; to *squeal*. (Often with *on*.) □ *Don't nark on me!* □ *All right. Who narked?* **3.** *tr.* to annoy someone. □ *Stop narking me!* □ *Why are you always narcing someone?* (More at *narked*.) **4.** *n.* any unpleasant person. □ *Tell that narc to get lost.* □ *Stop being such a narc. Beat it!*

narked [nɑrkt] *mod.* annoyed. (Usually with *at* or *with*.) □ *He's really narked at us.* □ *She is narked with you and your car.*

narky ['nɑrki] *n.* a narcotic drug. □ *They caught him with a lot of narky in his pockets.* □ *The mugger wanted money to buy some narky.*

narly See *(g)narly*.

narrow squeak *n.* a success almost not achieved; a lucky or marginal success; a problem almost not surmounted. □ *That was a narrow squeak. I don't know how I survived.* □ *Another narrow squeak like that and I'll give up.*

natch [nætʃ] *interj.* "yes"; "naturally." □ *I guess it's okay. She said natch.* □ *Natch, you can borrow my car.*

natural *n.* someone with obvious natural talent. □ *That guy is a natural!* □ *Can she ever dance! What a natural!*

natural-born *mod.* born with talent or skill. □ *She is really a natural-born dancer.* □ *Mary is a natural-born artist.*

nature stop *n.* a stop to use the toilet, especially during road travel. (Euphemistic.) □ *I think I need a nature stop when it's convenient.* □ *I left my comb back at the last nature stop.*

nature's call AND **call of nature** *n.* the feeling of a need to go to the toilet. □ *I think I feel nature's call coming on.* □ *A call of nature forced us to stop along the way.*

nause someone out *tr.* to nauseate someone. □ *That horrible smell really nauses me out.* □ *Things like that nause me out, too.*

naw *interj.* "no." □ *Naw, I didn't do that.* □ *Naw, I won't go.*

nay *mod.* ugly; unfavorable. (From *nasty*.) □ *She is really nay.* □ *What a nay thing to say.*

NBD *interj.* "no big deal." (Initialism.) □ *Don't worry. NBD.* □ *So you're a little late. NBD.*

NBT *n.* "no big thing." (Initialism.) □ *Hey, man! Don't make a fuss! It's NBT.* □ *Listen up, Fred. This is NBT, but listen anyway.*

neanderthal [ni'ændəθɑl] *n.* a large and ugly male. □ *Tell that neanderthal to get out of here.* □ *Tom, don't act like such a neanderthal.*

near-beer *n.* beer with less than 1/2 percent alcohol content. (Originally from the Prohibition era.) □ *I read in the paper that near-beer is making a comeback.* □ *You can drink a lot of near-beer without getting drunk.*

neat 1. *mod.* great; *cool;* fine. □ *What a neat idea!* □ *That was not a very neat thing to do.* 2. *exclam.* "Wow!" (Usually **Neat!**) □ *Neat! I'm glad you came.* □ *Five of them! Neat!*

neato (canito) ['nito (kə'nito)] *exclam.* really fine. □ *Look at this! Neato canito!* □ *What a great present. Neato!*

neb(bish) ['nɛb(ɪʃ)] *n.* a dull person; a *jerk.* (From Yiddish.) □ *Tracy is such a nebbish. Why doesn't she just give up?* □ *You are such a neb!*

Nebraska sign *n.* a flat EEG indicating the death of the patient being monitored. (See also *flatline.* Medical.) □ *The lady in 203 is giving the Nebraska sign. I think she's boxed.* □ *I saw the Nebraska sign on my monitor, and knew it must not be hooked up right.*

necessary *n.* money; an income. (Always with *the.*) □ *I can always use more of the necessary.* □ *I gotta have more of the necessary, man.*

neck *in.* to cuddle and kiss. (Always in reference to lovers or boy-girl relationships.) □ *There are some teenagers in the back room, necking.* □ *Let's go somewhere quiet and neck.*

neck and neck *mod.* almost even. (See also *nip and tuck.*) □ *The horses were neck and neck at the finish line.* □ *They ran neck and neck for the entire race.*

needle *tr.* to annoy someone. □ *Tom is always needling Frank.* □ *Stop needling me!*

needle candy *n.* narcotics that are taken by injection. (Drugs. Compare to *nose (candy).*) □ *Max likes needle candy best of all.* □ *Some people prefer needle candy to food.*

negative *n.* any drawback or bad thing about someone or something. □ *There are too many negatives associated with your plan.* □ *I know another negative you didn't mention.*

nerd AND **nurd** [nɚd] *n.* a dull and bookish person, usually a male. □ *Fred can be such a nerd!* □ *That whole gang of boys is just a bunch of nurds.*

nerd magnet *n.* a girl or woman who attracts dull males. □ *Oh, Kim, sometimes I feel like such a nerd magnet.* □ *Sally is weary of dating total drips. She is a classic nerd magnet.*

nerd mobile *n.* a full-sized, uninteresting car; a family car. □ *My father always buys some kind of stupid nerd mobile.* □ *There is nothing but nerd mobiles on our block.*

nerd pack *n.* a plastic sheath for holding pens in a pocket, protecting the cloth from ink. (This is the classic symbol of a bookish *nerd.*) □ *A lot of engineers have nerd packs.* □ *A real nerd wears a nerd pack in the pocket of a dirty shirt.*

Nerts! [nɚts] *exclam.* "Nuts!" (Partly euphemistic.) □ *Oh, nerts! I forgot my wallet.* □ *Nerts! I dropped my keys.*

nerts See *nurts.*

nervous Nellie *n.* any nervous person, male or female. □ *Sue is such a nervous Nellie. She should calm down.* □ *Relax! Don't be such a nervous Nellie.*

nervy 1. *mod.* nervous. □ *Mary is so nervy. Anything will set her off.* □ *Now, don't get nervy.* 2. *mod.* daring; courageous. □ *What a nervy guy!* □ *Don't get nervy with me!*

nest egg *n.* money saved for some important purpose, such as retirement. □ *I lost most of my nest egg in the market crash.* □ *It takes years to build up a nest egg.*

net result *n.* the final result after all the assets and liabilities have balanced out. □ *The net result was that I was fired.* □ *I don't care about the little things. What is the net result?*

never mind *phr.* "Forget it."; "It doesn't matter anymore." □ *Never mind. I forget what I was going to say.* □ *Oh, never mind. Nobody really cares anyway.*

New York's finest *n.* a New York City police officer. □ *One of New York's finest gave me a parking ticket.* □ *Three of New York's finest were standing there at my door with my lost dog.*

newshound *n.* a newspaper reporter who pursues a story with the same diligence used by a bloodhound. ☐ *If the newshounds get hold of this story, we'll never have any peace.* ☐ *Tell that newshound that I'll sue her if she prints that!*

newt *n.* a stupid person; a dull and uninteresting person. ☐ *Look, you silly newt, you are wrong!* ☐ *Don't act like such a newt.*

nibble **1.** *n.* a cautious or preliminary response to something. (See also *nybble*.) ☐ *My advertisement got three nibbles this morning.* ☐ *We will see if anyone else gives it a nibble.* **2.** *in.* to reply cautiously or tentatively to something. ☐ *Someone nibbled at your want ad.* ☐ *I hope someone who wants to buy my car nibbles at the description I posted on the bulletin board.*

nice meeting you *phr.* "it is nice to have met you." (Said when leaving someone whose acquaintance you have just made.) ☐ *I must go now, Fred. Nice meeting you.* ☐ *Well, nice meeting you. I must get home now.*

nice talking to you *phr.* "it's been pleasant, good-bye." (A leave taking formula, sometimes with an air of dismissal.) ☐ *Do tell. Well, nice talking to you.* ☐ *Nice talking to you. Call my service.*

nick **1.** *tr.* to arrest someone. ☐ *The cops nicked Paul outside his house.* ☐ *They are going to nick Joe, too.* (More at *nicked*.) **2.** *tr.* to steal something. ☐ *The thugs nicked a couple of apples from the fruit stand.* ☐ *Don't ever nick anything! Do you hear me?* **3.** *tr.* to get or take something. ☐ *Would you please nick me a slice of bread?* ☐ *Tom nicked a copy of the test for Sam, who also needed one.*

nicked *mod.* arrested. ☐ *Paul was nicked last night.* ☐ *"Now I'm nicked," he said.*

nickel and dime someone (to death) *tr.* to make numerous small monetary charges that add up to a substantial sum. ☐ *Those waiters nickel and dimed me to death.* ☐ *Just give me the whole bill at one time. Don't nickel and dime me for days on end.*

nifty *mod.* neat; smart. ☐ *That is a pretty nifty car you have there.* ☐ *Yes, it is nifty.*

night person *n.* a person who prefers to be active in the nighttime. (The plural is with *people*. Compare to *day person*.) ☐ *I can't function in the morning. I'm strictly a night person.* ☐ *Night people prefer to sleep in the daytime.*

nimrod ['nɪmrɑd] *n.* a simpleton; a *nerd*. ☐ *Susan is a total nimrod. She does such dumb things!* ☐ *What stupid nimrod left the lid off the cottage cheese?*

nine-to-five *mod.* typical in terms of working hours; structured and scheduled, starting and ending at set times. (From the expression *from nine to five*, normal working hours.) ☐ *I work nine-to-five.* ☐ *I really wanted a nine-to-five job until I finally got one.* ☐ *I can't stand the nine-to-five rat race.*

nineteenth hole *n.* a place to buy an alcoholic beverage after a golf game. (Likely to be filled with golfers who have played eighteen holes of golf.) ☐ *All off us gathered at the nineteenth hole to celebrate a great match.* ☐ *I hit a hole-in-one on the first hole and went straight to the nineteenth hole to celebrate.*

nip **1.** *n.* a small, quick drink of liquor. ☐ *Here, have a nip of this stuff.* ☐ *One nip is enough. That is powerful!* **2.** *in.* to take small drinks of liquor periodically. (See also *nipped*.) ☐ *Paul has been nipping since noon.* ☐ *After nipping all day, Fred was pretty well stewed by dinnertime.* **3.** *tr.* to steal something. ☐ *The thief nipped my purse.* ☐ *The punk kid nipped two candy bars from the drugstore.*

nip and tuck *mod.* so close as to be almost the same; *neck and neck*. ☐ *They ran nip and tuck all the way to the finish line, but Tom won the race.* ☐ *It was too close to call—nip and tuck all the way.*

nipped *mod.* alcohol intoxicated. (See also *nip*.) ☐ *All four of them went out and got nipped.* ☐ *How can anybody be so nipped on four beers?*

nippers *n.* handcuffs; leg fetters. ☐ *The cops put the nippers on the crooks.* ☐ *No, not the nippers. They hurt my arms.*

nit-picker *n.* a person who is hypercritical. ☐ *Mary is such a nit-picker.* ☐ *Nit-pickers drive me crazy.*

nit-picking *n.* too much minor criticism; overly particular criticism; nagging. ☐ *I am tired of all your nit-picking.* ☐ *Enough nit-picking! What are the major problems?*

nitery ['naɪtəi] *n.* a nightclub. ☐ *We'll hit a few niteries and then come back to my place.* ☐ *There is a cheap nitery over on Twelfth Street where Chuck has a job.*

nitty-gritty ['nɪdi 'grɪdi] *n.* the essence; the essential points. (Usually in *get down to the nitty-gritty.*) ☐ *What's the nitty-gritty about the broken window?* ☐ *Once we are down to the nitty-gritty, we can begin to sort things out.*

nitwit *n.* someone who behaves stupidly. (Also a term of address.) ☐ *You are such a nitwit!* ☐ *Please stop acting like a nitwit all the time.*

nix [nɪks] (all senses from German *nichts.*) **1.** *interj.* "no." ☐ *The man said nix, and he means nix.* ☐ *Nix, I won't do it.* **2.** *exclam.* "No!"; "Stop it!"; "I disagree!" (Usually **Nix!**) ☐ *Nix! I won't do it.* ☐ *"Nix," said Paul. "I can't permit that."* **3.** *n.* nothing. ☐ *What did I get for all my trouble? Nix!* ☐ *I got nix for a tip. And after I was so helpful!* **4.** *tr.* to put a stop to something; to say no to something; to ban something; to turn something down. ☐ *The boss nixed my plan.* ☐ *I wanted to say a certain word in my speech, but the management nixed it.*

no-account 1. *mod.* worthless; no-good. ☐ *Her uncle is a no-account gambler.* ☐ *She is a no-account part-time dealer at the casino.* **2.** *n.* a worthless person. (Also a rude term of address.) ☐ *Ask that no-account to come over here and explain himself.* ☐ *Look, you no-account! Take your problems and go away!*

no bargain *n.* not an especially good person or thing. ☐ *Fred is okay, but he's no bargain.* ☐ *This car gets me to work and back, but it's no bargain.*

no big deal AND **no biggie** *n.* (something) not difficult or troublesome. (See also *NBT.*) ☐ *Don't worry. It's no big deal.* ☐ *No problem. It's no biggie.*

no biggie See the previous entry.

no-brainer *n.* an easy question that takes no thinking to answer; a simple problem that requires no intellect to solve; a dilemma that requires no pondering to resolve. ☐ *Of course, the question is a no-brainer. The answer has to be yes.* ☐ *His proposal of marriage was a no-brainer. She turned him down flat on the spot.*

no brand cigarette See *cigarette with no name.*

no-brow *n.* a stupid person. (Patterned on *lowbrow.*) ☐ *Sam is a complete no-brow. No culture, no sense of style, and no money.* ☐ *Max is a total drip. No-brow and a phony.*

no can do *phr.* "It can't be done."; "I can't do it." ☐ *Sorry. No can do.* ☐ *Lend you $200? No can do.*

no dice *interj.* "no"; not possible. ☐ *When I asked about a loan, he said, "No dice."* ☐ *No. It can't be done, no dice.*

no earthly reason *n.* no conceivable reason. ☐ *There is no earthly reason for your behavior.* ☐ *I can think of no earthly reason why the repairs should cost so much.*

no end of something *n.* an endless supply of something. ☐ *Have some candy. I have no end of chocolate drops.* ☐ *I've had no end of trouble ever since I bought this car.*

No fair! *exclam.* "That's not fair!" ☐ *No fair! I saw it first!* ☐ *That's no fair! We paid full price to see this movie.*

no go ['no 'go] *mod.* negative; inopportune. (This is hyphenated before a nominal.) ☐ *We're in a no-go situation.* ☐ *Is it go or no go?*

no-good 1. *n.* a worthless person. ☐ *Tell that no-good to leave.* ☐ *The no-good is* *back again.* **2.** *mod.* worthless; bad. ☐ *Get that no-good jerk out of here!* ☐ *I have never heard of such a no-good car dealership before.*

no-goodnik [no'gudnɪk] *n.* someone who is no good. (The *nik* is from Russian via Yiddish.) ☐ *That no-goodnik is pestering me again.* ☐ *Tell the no-goodnik to leave quietly, or I will call the police.*

no great shakes *n.* someone or something not very good. (There is no affirmative version of this.) ☐ *Your idea is no great shakes, but we'll try it anyway.* ☐ *Ted is no great shakes when it comes to brains.*

no holds barred *mod.* without restriction. (There is no affirmative version of this.) ☐ *I want you to get that contract. Do anything—no holds barred.* ☐ *Try anything that will work, no holds barred.*

No kidding! *exclam.* "I am not kidding."; "You are not kidding (are you)?" ☐ *No kidding! I never thought she would do that.* ☐ *No kidding, he's really going to join the Air Force.*

No lie! *exclam.* "Honest!"; "No kidding!" ☐ *I really did it! No lie!* ☐ *I was there on time. No lie! Ask my sister.*

no name cigarette See *cigarette with no name.*

no-no ['nono] *n.* something that is not (to be) done. (Essentially juvenile.) ☐ *You can't smoke in here. That's a no-no.* ☐ *She seems to delight in doing all the no-nos.*

No nukes! ['no 'nuks OR 'no 'njuks] *exclam.* a cry against nuclear energy, weapons, submarines, etc. ☐ *The marchers kept chanting, "No nukes! No nukes!"* ☐ *No nukes! Make my electricity the old-fashioned way.*

no sale *interj.* "no." ☐ *I wanted to go to Florida for the holidays, but my father said, "No sale."* ☐ *No sale. You can't do it.*

No Shinola! [. . . ʃaɪ'nolə] *exclam.* "You are kidding!"; "No shit!" (A play on the expression indicating that a stupid person doesn't know shit from Shinola. Shinola is a brand of shoe polish. Use with caution.) ☐ *So taxes are too high? No Shinola!* ☐ *He's late again? No Shinola!*

no show AND **no-show** *n.* someone who doesn't show up for something, such as an airline flight. ☐ *The flight was cancelled because there were too many no-shows.* ☐ *I have never been a no show, but my brother does it all the time.*

no soap *interj.* "no." ☐ *I can't do it. No soap.* ☐ *No soap, I don't lend anyone money.*

no stress *interj.* "no problem"; "no bother." ☐ *Don't worry, man, no stress.* ☐ *Relax. No stress. It doesn't bother me at all.*

no sweat *interj.* "no problem"; "Don't worry; it is no problem." ☐ *It's no big deal. No sweat.* ☐ *No sweat, don't fret about it.*

No way! *exclam.* "No!" (Compare with *Way!*) ☐ *Me join the Army? No way!* ☐ *She can't do that. No way!*

no-win situation *n.* a situation in which there is no hope of success. ☐ *I find myself in a no-win situation again.* ☐ *The team—in a no-win situation—punted.*

nobody *n.* an insignificant person. (Always with *a*. Compare to *somebody.*) ☐ *Don't pay any attention to him. He's just a nobody.* ☐ *That silly girl is a nobody and a pest.*

nodded out *mod.* in heroin euphoria; under the influence of heroin. (Drugs.) ☐ *Max nodded out after his fix.* ☐ *He is upstairs nodded out.*

noid *n.* a "paranoid" person. ☐ *Some of those noids write hilarious letters to the editor.* ☐ *Who's the noid screaming about Big Brother?*

noise 1. *n.* empty talk; nonsense. ☐ *I've had enough of your noise. Shut up!* ☐ *That's nothing but noise. I want the truth.* **2.** *n.* heroin. (Drugs.) ☐ *Man, I need some noise now! I hurt!* ☐ *Max is hooked on noise.*

non compos ['nɑn 'kɑmpos] **1.** *mod.* out of one's mind; *non compos mentis.* □ *She is strictly non compos!* □ *Don't pay any attention to her. She's non compos.* **2.** AND **non compos poopoo** *mod.* alcohol intoxicated. □ *That gal isn't just drunk. She's non compos poopoo.* □ *Two glasses and he was non compos.*

non compos poopoo See the previous entry.

none of someone's beeswax [...'bizwæks] *n.* none of someone's business. □ *It's none of your beeswax. I'm not telling.* □ *You'll never know. The answer is none of your beeswax.*

noodge See *nudge.*

noodle *n.* (one's) head. □ *That's using your noodle.* □ *Put your hat on your noodle, and let's go.*

nope *interj.* "no." □ *I won't do it! Nope. I won't!* □ *She asked him to do it, but he said, "Nope."*

nose-burner AND **nose-warmer** *n.* a marijuana cigarette stub; a *roach.* (Drugs.) □ *Hey, man! Can I have a hit of that little nose-burner?* □ *The cops found a nose-warmer under the chair.*

nose (candy) *n.* powdered drugs that are inhaled, primarily cocaine, sometimes heroin. (Drugs. See also *needle candy.*) □ *Max has some nose candy for sale.* □ *Hey, man! Where can I get some nose?*

nose habit *n.* an addiction to sniffed drugs, usually heroin or cocaine. (Drugs.) □ *Max is suffering with his nose habit.* □ *One sniff of that white powder and she'll get a nose habit, for sure.*

nose hit *n.* marijuana smoke taken through the nose from the burning end of the cigarette. (Drugs.) □ *Max likes to take nose hits.* □ *Come on, Max. Give me a nose hit!*

nose job *n.* a plastic surgery operation to change the appearance of one's nose. □ *How much does a nose job cost?* □ *I don't want a nose job. What I got is good enough.*

nose-lunger ['nozləŋɚ] *n.* a mass of nasal mucus. (See also *lunger.*) □ *Wayne blew a nose-lunger onto the wall and giggled.* □ *Beavis thought the funniest thing in the world was having a nose-lunger dangling from his chin.*

nose-warmer 1. *n.* a short tobacco pipe. □ *Fred smokes a nose-warmer, especially in the winter.* □ *His nose-warmer almost set his mustache on fire once.* **2.** See *nose-burner.*

nosedive *n.* a great drop; a great decline. (As with a bird or an airplane diving—nose first—toward the ground. See also *take a nosedive.*) □ *This year our profits have taken a nosedive.* □ *Confidence in the government took a sudden nosedive.*

nosh [nɑʃ] **1.** *n.* a snack. (From German via Yiddish.) □ *How about a little nosh?* □ *I don't want a nosh. I need a whole meal.* **2.** *in.* to snack. □ *You nosh too much.* □ *Every time I see you, you're noshing.*

nosh on something ['nɑʃ...] *in.* to make a snack of something. □ *After Thanksgiving, we noshed on turkey for three days.* □ *Who's been noshing on the chocolate cake?*

nosher ['nɑʃɚ] *n.* someone who is always eating snacks. (See also *nosh.*) □ *I don't know of a single nosher who's not fat.* □ *Fred's a nosher. He's always eating.*

nosy parker ['nozi 'pɑrkɚ] *n.* a nosy person. (Also a term of address.) □ *Mary can be such a nosy parker.* □ *Look, you nosy parker, mind your own business.*

Not! *interj.* "Not really so!" (A tag phrase added to the end of a statement, changing it from affirmative to negative. There is usually a pause before *Not!*, which is said on a level pitch somewhat higher than the sentence that comes before.) □ *Of course I'm going to pay $100 a ticket to see a rock concert. Not!* □ *I am deeply in love with Kim. Not!*

not a chance *interj.* "no." □ *Me lend you money? Not a chance!* □ *I won't go, not a chance. Don't ask.*

not all there *mod.* crazy; stupid acting. □ *Tom's not all there. Really dense.* □ *You can't depend on Paul for much help. He's really not all there.*

not cricket *mod.* unfair; illegitimate; unorthodox. (See affirmative examples at *cricket.*) □ *You can't do that! It's not cricket!* □ *What do you mean it's not cricket? You do it.*

not give a hoot *tr.* not to care at all. (Folksy.) □ *Go ahead. Do it if you want. I don't give a hoot.* □ *She doesn't give a hoot if you go into town without her.*

not grow on trees *in.* not to be abundant; not to be expendable. (Usually said about money.) □ *I can't afford that. Money doesn't grow on trees, you know.* □ *Don't waste the glue. That stuff doesn't grow on trees, you know.*

not just whistling Dixie [...'dıksi] *tr.* "not talking nonsense." (Folksy. Refers to a song titled "Dixie.") □ *Man, you are right! You're not just whistling Dixie.* □ *When you say she is wrong, you're not just whistling Dixie.*

not know beans (about something) *tr.* to know nothing about something. □ *Don't pay any attention to her. She doesn't know beans.* □ *I don't know beans about fixing cars.*

not know from nothing *in.* to be stupid, innocent, and naive. (Usually with *don't,* as in the examples. Always in the negative.) □ *Tom don't know from nothing. He is really dense.* □ *Don't pay any attention to her. She don't know from nothing.*

Not to worry. *phr.* "Don't worry." □ *You lost your ticket? Not to worry. I'll give you mine.* □ *Not to worry. Everything will be all right.*

not too shabby **1.** *mod.* (with emphasis on *shabby*) "nice"; "well done." □ *Is that your car? Not too shabby!* □ *That play was not too shabby.* **2.** *mod.* (with emphasis on *too*) very shabby; very poor indeed. (Sarcastic.) □ *Did you see that basket she missed? Not too shabby!* □ *What a way to treat someone. Not too shabby!*

not worth a damn *mod.* worthless. □ *This pen is not worth a damn.* □ *When it comes to keeping score, she's not worth a damn.*

not worth a plugged nickel *mod.* worth little or nothing. □ *This new battery is not worth a plugged nickel.* □ *Mary isn't worth a plugged nickel at baseball.*

not worth beans *mod.* worthless. □ *This paint is not worth beans. I'll have to buy another can.* □ *Sue, you're not worth beans as a painter.*

notch *tr.* to count up something; to add up or score something. □ *Well, it looks like we notched another victory.* □ *The crooks notched one more theft before they were caught.*

Nothing doing! *exclam.* "No!" □ *Me, go to the opera? Nothing doing!* □ *Nothing doing! I refuse to do it.*

Nothing to it! *exclam.* "It is very easy!" □ *Look, anybody can do it! Nothing to it!* □ *Changing a light bulb is easy. Nothing to it!*

nothing to sneeze at *n.* no small amount of money; something not inconsequential. □ *It's not a lot of money, but it's nothing to sneeze at.* □ *She worked hard and did not accomplish much, but it's nothing to sneeze at.*

nothing to write home about *n.* something small or inconsequential. □ *I got a little bit of a raise this year, but it was nothing to write home about.* □ *The party was nothing to write home about.*

nothing upstairs *phr.* no brains; stupid. □ *Tom is sort of stupid acting. You know—nothing upstairs.* □ *I know what's wrong with you. Nothing upstairs.*

now generation *n.* the (once current) generation of young people who seemed to want only instant gratification. □ *All those people in the now generation want to start out with fancy cars and nice houses.* □ *What will happen to the now generation when times are hard?*

Now what? *interrog.* "What is wrong now?" □ *I ran into the room and stopped in front of Tom. "Now what?"*

asked Tom. ☐ *I see you standing there. Now what?*

Now you're talking! *exclam.* "What you are saying is making sense!" ☐ *Now you're talking! You've got a great idea!* ☐ *"Now you're talking!" said the coach when I told him I was going to win.*

nowhere *mod.* bad; no good; dull. ☐ *This place is really nowhere. Let's go.* ☐ *I want to get out of this nowhere party.*

nudge AND **noodge** [nʊdʒ] **1.** *n.* someone who nags. ☐ *Sally can be such a nudge!* ☐ *I really can't stand a noodge.* **2.** *in.* to nag. ☐ *Don't noodge all the time.* ☐ *Stop always noodging.* **3.** *tr.* to nag someone. ☐ *Stop nudging me about that.* ☐ *I'll noodge him a little to remind him.*

nudie ['nudi] *n.* a movie featuring nudes. (See also *skin flick.*) ☐ *There is a nudie playing over at the Roxie Theater.* ☐ *I didn't know this movie was a nudie!*

nudnik ['nʊdnɪk] *n.* a bore; a pest; a crank. (From Russian via Yiddish. Also a term of address.) ☐ *Tell that nudnik to stay away from here. He is such a pest.* ☐ *Heidi can be such a nudnik!*

nuke 1. *n.* a nuclear weapon. ☐ *Are there nukes aboard that ship?* ☐ *The military establishment is working on a number of new nukes.* **2.** *tr.* to destroy someone or something. (As with a nuclear weapon.) ☐ *Your cat ran through my garden and totally nuked my flowers!* ☐ *I'm going to nuke that cat the next time I see it.* **3.** *tr.* to microwave something. ☐ *I have to nuke my dinner and then I will be right over.* ☐ *Let's nuke a bag of popcorn before we watch the movie you rented.*

nuke oneself [n(j)uk . . .] *tr.* to tan oneself at a tanning salon. ☐ *I nuke myself once a week in the spring so I will be ready for the summer bikini season.* ☐ *Leonard nuked himself in the middle of winter, and everyone thought he had been to Florida.*

nuker ['n(j)ukɚ] *n.* a microwave oven. ☐ *I tried to do a turkey in the nuker once and made a real mess of it.* ☐ *Who left the soggy bacon in the nuker?*

numbed out *mod.* nearly paralyzed by phencyclidine (P.C.P.). (Drugs.) ☐ *The teenager was nearly numbed out when they brought her in.* ☐ *Max was totally numbed out on angel dust.*

number 1. *n.* a *girl;* a sexually attractive *girl.* ☐ *Who is that cute little number I saw you with?* ☐ *She is really some number.* **2.** *n.* a marijuana cigarette. (Drugs.) ☐ *Max lit up a number just as the boss came in.* ☐ *Can I have a hit off your number?* **3.** *n.* any person or thing. ☐ *This is an interesting little number. You attach it to your bicycle handlebars.* ☐ *Yes, Tom can be a strange number when he wants.* **4.** *n.* an act or performance; a performance specialty. ☐ *Ann did her number and left the stage.* ☐ *I'll talk to you after my number.*

number-cruncher 1. *n.* someone who works with figures; an accountant. ☐ *The number-crunchers are trying to get the annual report ready.* ☐ *I enjoy being a number-cruncher. Math doesn't scare me.* **2.** *n.* a large and powerful computer. (Computers.) ☐ *They traded in the old computer for a powerful number-cruncher.* ☐ *The small one is reserved for minor projects. The really big and important jobs are run on the number-cruncher.*

number crunching *n.* using a computer to solve enormously complicated or complex mathematical problems. ☐ *I don't do a lot of number crunching, so I don't need a terribly fast machine.* ☐ *I use the big mainframe computer for number crunching.*

number one 1. *mod.* top rate; best; closest. (See also *numero uno.*) ☐ *We heard the number one high school band in the whole state last night.* ☐ *This is my number one buddy, Tom.* **2.** *n.* oneself. ☐ *I don't know who will pay for the broken window, but old number one isn't!* ☐ *Everything always comes back to number one. I have to solve everybody's problems.*

numero uno ['numɚo 'uno] **1.** *n.* "number one"; the best. (Spanish. See also *number one.*) ☐ *This coffee is numero* *uno in my book.* ☐ *Mary is numero uno in our office. You'll have to ask her.* **2.** *n.* oneself; *number one.* ☐ *I always look out for numero uno.* ☐ *What's in it for numero uno?*

nummy ['nəmi] tasty; yummy. (Also juvenile or baby talk.) ☐ *This cake is just nummy.* ☐ *Here, Jimmy, don't you want a spoon of this nummy food?*

nurd See *nerd.*

nurts AND **nerts** [nə·ts] *n.* nonsense. ☐ *Don't talk that kind of nurts to me!* ☐ *Oh, that's just nerts. I don't believe a word of it.*

nut 1. *n.* an odd or strange person; a crazy person. ☐ *Who is that nut over there in the corner?* ☐ *Some nut is going to try to fly from the top of one building to another.* **2.** *n.* (one's) head. ☐ *A brick fell and hit him on the nut.* ☐ *The baseball came in fast. Clonk! Right on the nut!* **3.** *n.* an enthusiast (about something). ☐ *Paul is a nut about chocolate cake.* ☐ *Mary is a party nut.*

nut factory See *nuthouse.*

nut-foundry See *nuthouse.*

nut up *in.* to go crazy; to go *nuts.* ☐ *I've got to have a vacation soon, or I'm going to nut up.* ☐ *Poor Sue nutted up and had to take it easy for a few months.*

nutcake *n.* a stupid person. (See also *fruitcake.*) ☐ *Stop acting like such a nutcake all the time.* ☐ *My sister can be a real nutcake if she tries.*

nuthatch See the following entry.

nuthouse AND **nut factory; nut-foundry; nuthatch** *n.* an insane asylum. ☐ *The judge spent three years in the nuthouse.* ☐ *They're going to send you to the nut-foundry some day.*

nutpick *n.* a psychoanalyst. ☐ *Bill pays a nutpick about $100 an hour just to listen.* ☐ *What do you have to know to be a nutpick?*

nuts 1. *mod.* crazy. ☐ *You're nuts if you think I care.* ☐ *That whole idea is just nuts!* **2.** *exclam.* "No!"; "I don't believe you!"; "I don't care!" (Usually **Nuts!**) ☐ *Nuts! You don't know what you are talking about.* ☐ *Oh, nuts! I forgot my wallet.* **3.** *n.* the testicles. (Potentially offensive. Use only with discretion.) ☐ *Chuck got kneed in the nuts in a football game.* ☐ *She tried to kick him in the nuts, like she'd seen on television, but he turned too quickly.*

nuts and bolts 1. *n.* the mundane workings of something; the basics of something. ☐ *I want you to learn how to write well. You have to get down to the nuts and bolts of writing.* ☐ *She's got a lot of good, general ideas, but when it comes to the nuts and bolts of getting something done, she's no good.* **2.** *n.* the subject of psychology in college. ☐ *I took a class in nuts and bolts and didn't learn anything at all about what makes me tick.* ☐ *Tom is flunking nuts and bolts because he won't participate in the required "experiments."*

Nuts to you! *exclam.* "Go away!"; "Drop dead!" ☐ *Well, nuts to you! You are just plain rude!* ☐ *Nuts to you! I will NOT lend you money!*

nutter *n.* a nutty person. ☐ *Sally is such a nutter. She would forget her head if it wasn't screwed on.* ☐ *That guy is a real nutter. Thinks he can get a cab at this hour.*

nuttery *n.* an insane asylum; the place where nuts are kept. (See also *nut.*) ☐ *If you keep acting so odd, we'll have to put you in a nuttery.* ☐ *This place is a nuttery! I've never seen so many silly people.*

nutty *mod.* silly; giddy; stupid. ☐ *What a nutty idea!* ☐ *That's nutty!* ☐ *Mary is a real nutty girl, but she is my best friend.*

nutty as a fruitcake *mod.* very silly or stupid. ☐ *The whole idea is as nutty as a fruitcake.* ☐ *Tom is as nutty as a fruitcake. They will put him in a nuttery someday.*

nybble ['nɪbl̩] *n.* four bits of computer memory. (Literally, one half of a "bite," i.e., a byte.) ☐ *My program wouldn't work just because I had one silly little nybble wrong!* ☐ *You don't program a nybble! It's just half a bite.*

O

O-sign *n.* the rounded, open mouth of a dead person. (A semi-jocular usage. Hospitals. See also *Q-sign.*) □ *The guy in room 226 is giving the O-sign.* □ *That's the third O-sign we've gotten since noon.*

oak(s) [oks] *mod.* "O.K."; satisfactory; worthy. (Prisons.) □ *That guy's oaks.* □ *This stuff is oak.*

oasis [o'esəs] *n.* a place to buy liquor. □ *Let's go into this oasis here and pick up a few bottles.* □ *There is an oasis on almost every corner in this district.*

oater ['odɚ] *n.* a Western movie. (From the oats that the horses eat. See also *horse opera.*) □ *I don't want to see an oater. Isn't anything else showing?* □ *Let's go out and see a good old-fashioned oater.*

ob [ɑb] *mod.* obvious. □ *Of course I understand it. It's completely ob.* □ *It's pretty ob that you are just trying to start something.*

obliterated *mod.* drunk. □ *Fred was obliterated and couldn't walk to his car, let alone drive it.* □ *Three beers and Sally became obliterated.*

obno(c) ['ɑb'nɑk AND 'ɑbno] *mod.* obnoxious; disgusting. □ *I wish you weren't so obnoc all the time!* □ *Beavis is totally obno, and he loves being that way.*

occifer See *ossifer.*

O.D. **1.** *n.* an overdose of a drug. (Initialism. Drugs.) □ *Max took an O.D. and was sent to the hospital.* □ *If you take an O.D. and no one is around, you may end up dead.* **2.** *in.* to purposely or accidentally give oneself a fatal dose of drugs. (Drugs.) □ *Max O.D.ed on heroin.* □ *I knew he would O.D. someday.* **3.** *in.* to die from an overdose of drugs. (Drugs.) □ *Two kids at my school O.D.ed last weekend.* □ *I think Max may O.D. in a week or two.* **4.** *n.* a person who has taken an overdose of drugs. (Hospitals.) □ *This O.D. has just stopped breathing.* □ *How many O.D.s did you get in here last weekend?*

odd bird AND **strange bird** *n.* a strange or eccentric person. □ *Mr. Wilson certainly is an odd bird.* □ *What a strange bird you are.*

odd-bod ['ɑdbɑd] **1.** *n.* a strange person. □ *Who is that odd-bod over in the corner?* □ *Ralph can be sort of an odd-bod now and then.* **2.** *n.* a person with a strange body. □ *I am such an odd-bod that it's hard to find clothes that fit.* □ *I've never seen anyone so tall. What an odd-bod!* **3.** *n.* a peculiar body. □ *I have such an odd-bod that it's hard to find clothes.* □ *With an odd-bod like that, he'll never make good in the movies.*

oddball **1.** *n.* an eccentric person. □ *Tom is sure an oddball. He ordered a pineapple and strawberry milkshake.* □ *We oddballs love concoctions like that.* **2.** *mod.* strange; peculiar. □ *What an oddball combination of things!* □ *It's too oddball for me.* □ *Your oddball ideas have cost us too much money.*

odds-on *mod.* having to do with the thing or person favored to win. □ *My horse is an odds-on favorite to win.* □ *My plan is odds-on to be selected.*

Of all the nerve! *exclam.* "I am shocked by your domineering and high-handed behavior." □ *You want me to do your* *laundry? Of all the nerve!* ☐ *Of all the nerve! Asking me to do a thing like that.*

off 1. *mod.* alcohol or drug intoxicated. ☐ *She is truly off.* ☐ *Tom is so off he can't stand up.* **2.** *tr.* to dispose of someone or something; to kill someone. ☐ *The crooks offed the witness before the trial.* ☐ *Forget the whole idea! Just off it once and for all.* **3.** *in.* to die. ☐ *The guy just falls down and offs, right there on Main Street.* ☐ *I don't want to off before my time.* (More at *outed.*)

off artist See *(rip-)off artist.*

off base *mod.* off target; wrong; not relevant. ☐ *Your answer was completely off base. Try again.* ☐ *You are off base. I will have to deal with someone else.*

off-brand cigarette *n.* a marijuana cigarette. (Drugs.) ☐ *Max smokes nothing but those off-brand cigarettes.* ☐ *I smell an off-brand cigarette in here.*

off color *mod.* dirty or smutty; *raunchy.* ☐ *That joke was sort of off color.* ☐ *Tom told an off color joke that embarrassed everyone.*

off one's chump *mod.* crazy; *nuts.* ☐ *You silly clown. You're off your chump.* ☐ *Am I off my chump, or did that car suddenly disappear?*

off one's nut 1. *mod.* crazy; out of one's head. ☐ *Shut up! You're off your nut!* ☐ *Don't pay any attention to her. She's off her nut.* **2.** *mod.* alcohol intoxicated. ☐ *Those guys are really off their nuts!* ☐ *She just sat there and got more and more off her nut.*

off one's rocker *mod.* silly; giddy; crazy. (See also *rocker.*) ☐ *That silly dame is off her rocker.* ☐ *You're off your rocker if you think I believe that!*

off one's trolley *mod.* silly; eccentric. ☐ *Don't mind Uncle Charles. He's a bit off his trolley.* ☐ *That silly old man is just off his trolley.*

off the hook *mod.* no longer in jeopardy; no longer obligated. ☐ *I'll let you off the hook this time, but never again.* ☐ *We're off the hook. We don't need to worry anymore.*

off-the-shelf *mod.* readily available; purchasable without any special difficulties or delays. ☐ *This is just plain old off-the-shelf hand lotion. Isn't it great?* ☐ *Is it off-the-shelf?* ☐ *I don't use off-the-shelf software in my computer. I write my own.*

off the track *mod.* not on a productive course; following the wrong lead. ☐ *You are off the track just a little. Let me help you.* ☐ *I was off the track for a while, but now everything is O.K.*

off the wagon 1. *mod.* drinking liquor after a period of abstinence. ☐ *Poor John fell off the wagon again. Drunk as a skunk.* ☐ *He was off the wagon for a year the last time before he sobered up.* **2.** *mod.* back on drugs after a period of abstinence. ☐ *Max is off the wagon and shooting up again.* ☐ *He can't be off the wagon, because he has never stopped using, even for a day.*

off-the-wall *mod.* strange; improbable; nonsensical. ☐ *What an off-the-wall guy!* ☐ *Your ideas are generally off-the-wall, but this one makes sense.*

offbeat *mod.* strange; unconventional. ☐ *That is really an offbeat idea.* ☐ *Tom is sort of offbeat. Well, he's weird.*

offed See *outed.*

Oh, boy! *exclam.* "Wow!" ☐ *Oh, boy! What a mess!* ☐ *Oh, boy! That was a great play!*

Oh, yeah? ['o 'jæə] *exclam.* "Is that what you think?"; "Are you trying to start a fight?" ☐ *Oh, yeah? What makes you think so?* ☐ *Oh, yeah? You want to start something?* ☐ *Tom said, "Bill, you are a numskull." Bill whirled around, saying, "Oh, yeah?"*

OIC ['o'ɑɪ'si] *phr.* "Oh, I see." (Initialism.) ☐ *OIC. That's very interesting.* ☐ *OIC. So that's how it's done.*

oil it *tr.* to study all night. (Literally, "burn the midnight oil.") ☐ *I have a test tomorrow, and I really have to oil it tonight.* ☐ *If you studied all semester long, you would still have to oil it before final exams.*

oiled *mod.* alcohol or drug intoxicated. ☐ *Will this stuff make me really oiled?* ☐ *She's not just drunk; she's totally oiled.*

oilhead *n.* a drunkard; an alcoholic. ☐ *There is an old oilhead over there on the street corner.* ☐ *Paul gave the oilhead a quarter, knowing it would be spent on cheap wine.*

oink [oɪŋk] *n.* a police officer. (A play on *pig.*) ☐ *There is an oink following us on a motorcycle.* ☐ *Here come the oinks!*

oink out *in.* to overeat. ☐ *I oink out every weekend.* ☐ *This Thursday starts a four-day weekend, and I plan to oink out every day.*

oinker *n.* a very fat person. (Refers to the fatness of a pig.) ☐ *Sally is getting to be quite an oinker, don't you think?* ☐ *Who is that oinker who just came into the cafeteria? There won't be any food left for the rest of us.*

O.J. **1.** *n.* orange juice. (Initialism.) ☐ *I like to have a big glass of fresh O.J. every morning.* ☐ *The price of O.J. is going to go up again soon.* **2.** See *overjolt.*

O.K. AND **okay** **1.** *interj.* "accepted." (Initialism. This may be originally from a jocular "oll kerrect," but no one really knows its origin.) ☐ *O.K., I'll do it.* ☐ *You want me to lend you $100? Okay.* ☐ *So, he said, like, "okay," and, like, I go "okay." So we both go "Okay." Okay?* **2.** *mod.* acceptable. ☐ *Fred is an O.K. guy.* ☐ *This cake is okay, but not what I would call first rate.* **3.** *mod.* acceptably. ☐ *She ran okay—nothing spectacular.* ☐ *They usually do it okay.* **4.** *n.* (someone's) acceptance. ☐ *I won't give the final okay until I see the plans.* ☐ *We got her O.K. and went on with the job.* **5.** *tr.* to approve something. ☐ *She refused to okay our plans.* ☐ *Please OK this bill so I can pay it.*

ok See *ak.*

okey-dokey ['oki'doki] *interj.* "yes"; *O.K.* (Folksy.) ☐ *Okey-dokey, I'll be there at noon.* ☐ *Okey-dokey. You sure can.*

old flame *n.* a former sweetheart or lover. ☐ *Mary's old flame, Tom, will be at the party.* ☐ *It is best to forget an old flame.*

old fogey *n.* an old-fashioned person; an old man. ☐ *My uncle is an old fogey. He must be the most old-fashioned man in the world.* ☐ *Don't be such an old fogey.*

old girl *n.* an old lady; a lively old lady. ☐ *That old girl is still going.* ☐ *What makes an old girl like that so feisty?*

old hand (at something) *n.* someone experienced at doing something. ☐ *I'm an old hand at fixing cars.* ☐ *Do you need help with your painting? I'm an old hand.*

old hat *n.* an old-fashioned thing or person; an outmoded thing or person. ☐ *That's just old hat. This is the modern world!* ☐ *Her latest work is nothing but old hat. She's through.*

old heave-ho ['old 'hiv'ho] *n.* a dismissal; a physical removal of someone from a place. ☐ *I thought my job was secure, but today I got the old heave-ho.* ☐ *You had better act right, or my friend will give you the old heave-ho.*

old lady AND **old woman** **1.** *n.* (one's) mother. ☐ *I'll ask my old lady if I can go.* ☐ *What time does your old lady get home?* **2.** *n.* (one's) wife. ☐ *I wonder what my old lady is cooking for dinner tonight.* ☐ *My old lady doesn't like for me to go out without her.* **3.** *n.* (one's) girlfriend. ☐ *My old lady and I are getting married next week.* ☐ *I got my old lady a bracelet for her birthday.*

old man **1.** *n.* (one's) father. ☐ *I'll ask my old man if I can go.* ☐ *What time does your old man get home?* **2.** *n.* (one's) husband. ☐ *My old man is downstairs fixing the furnace.* ☐ *My old man is sick and can't come with me.* **3.** *n.* (one's) boyfriend. ☐ *Ask your old man to come to the party, too.* ☐ *I got my old man to take me to see that movie I told you about.* **4.** *n.* the boss; a high-ranking officer. (Always with *the.*) ☐ *The old man says do it, so you had better do it.* ☐ *Quiet! Here comes the old man.*

old one-two **1.** *n.* a series of two punches delivered quickly, one after another.

(Always with *the*.) □ *Tom gave Bill the old one-two, and the argument was ended right there.* □ *Watch out for Tom. He's a master of the old one-two.* **2.** *n.* any destructive assault on an idea, thing, or person. □ *By the time the committee had given the plan the old one-two, there was nothing left I could do.* □ *I gave his proposal the old one-two. Next time he will be better prepared.*

old soldier 1. *n.* a cigarette or cigar butt; a hunk of tobacco. □ *The tramp bent over to pick up an old soldier off the pavement.* □ *He's never had anything but an old soldier for a smoke.* **2.** *n.* an empty liquor bottle; an empty beer bottle or can. □ *Larry hid all his old soldiers under the bed.* □ *Bill hit Tom over the head with an old soldier.*

old-timer *n.* an old person; an old man. (Also a term of address.) □ *Hey, old-timer, how's it going?* □ *Ask that old-timer over there if it has always been this bad around here.*

old woman See *old lady*.

oldie but goodie *n.* something (or even someone) that is old but still likeable. □ *I love that piece of music. It's an oldie but goodie.* □ *Mary is an oldie but goodie. I'm glad she's still around.*

on a roll *mod.* in the midst of a series of successes. (See also *roll*.) □ *Don't stop me now. I'm on a roll.* □ *Things are going great for Larry. He's on a roll now.*

on a shoestring *mod.* on practically no money; on a very tight budget. (See also *shoestring*.) □ *I run my business on a shoestring. I never know from day to day whether I will survive.* □ *We live on a shoestring—hardly any money at all.*

on a tank See *on the tank*.

on a tight leash 1. *mod.* under very careful control. □ *My father keeps my brother on a tight leash.* □ *We can't do much around here. The boss has us all on a tight leash.* **2.** *mod.* addicted to some drug. □ *Max is on a tight leash. He has to have the stuff regularly.* □ *Gert is kept on a tight leash by her habit.*

on easy street *mod.* in a state of financial independence and comfort. (See also *easy street*.) □ *I want to live on easy street when I grow up.* □ *When I get this contract signed, I'll be on easy street.*

on fire 1. *mod.* very attractive or sexy. □ *She is really on fire!* □ *Look at those jet-set people! Each one of them is just on fire.* **2.** *mod.* doing very well; very enthusiastic. □ *Jill's new book is really on fire. Everyone is buying it.* □ *Fred is on fire in his new job. He'll get promoted in no time.*

on ice *mod.* in reserve. □ *That's a great idea, but we'll have to put it on ice until we can afford to put it into action.* □ *I have two boyfriends. One I see every weekend, and the other I keep on ice for a rainy day.*

on it *mod.* really good. □ *Man, Weasel is really on it! What a rad lad!* □ *Susan is on it, and getting lots of attention for her running style.*

on one's high horse *mod.* in a haughty manner or mood. □ *Larry is on his high horse again, bossing people around.* □ *The boss is on her high horse about the number of paper clips we use.*

on one's or its last legs *mod.* about to expire or become nonfunctional. □ *This car is on its last legs. We have to get a new one.* □ *Poor old Chuck is on his last legs.*

on one's own hook *mod.* all by oneself. □ *I don't need any help. I can do it on my own hook.* □ *She did it on her own hook without having to call on anyone.*

on someone's case AND **on someone's tail** *mod.* nagging someone; annoying someone with criticism or supervision. □ *You have been on my case long enough. Mind your own business!* □ *The boss has been on my tail about the large number of telephone calls I make.*

on someone's tail 1. *mod.* following someone closely. □ *There is a huge truck on my tail. What should I do?* □ *Keep on her tail and don't let her out of your sight.* **2.** See *on someone's case*.

on someone's watch *mod.* while someone is on duty. □ *I am not responsible* *since it didn't happen on my watch.* ☐ *I guess I have to bear the blame since it happened on my watch.*

on tap 1. *mod.* having to do with beer sold from a barrel or keg. ☐ *Do you have any imported beers on tap here?* ☐ *I like beer on tap. The canned stuff tastes funny to me.* 2. *mod.* immediately available. ☐ *I have just the kind of person you're talking about on tap.* ☐ *The cook has any kind of food you might want on tap.*

on-target *mod.* timely; exact; incisive. ☐ *Your criticism is exactly on-target.* ☐ *We are on-target for a December completion date.*

on the back burner *mod.* out of the way; aside and out of consideration. (See also *on the shelf.*) ☐ *We will have to put this on the back burner for a while.* ☐ *She kept her boyfriend on the back burner until she decided what to do about him.*

on the ball 1. *mod.* knowledgeable; competent; attentive. ☐ *This guy is really on the ball.* ☐ *If you were on the ball, this wouldn't have happened.* 2. *mod.* in one's head or brain; at one's disposal. (Especially with *have a lot.*) ☐ *He sure has a lot on the ball.* ☐ *When you've got it on the ball the way she does, things generally go right.*

on the bandwagon *mod.* with the majority; following the latest fad. (Often with *hop, get, climb,* or jump.) ☐ *Come on! Hop on the bandwagon! Everyone else is joining.* ☐ *Tom always has to climb on the bandwagon. He does no independent thinking.*

on the beam 1. *mod.* homing in on an aviation radio beam. (No longer a major navigational device.) ☐ *The plane was on the beam and landed safely in the fog.* ☐ *I couldn't get on the beam, and I flew right over the airfield.* 2. *mod.* on the right course or track. (From sense 1.) ☐ *That is exactly right. You are right on the beam.* ☐ *You're on the beam. You will finish this with no problems.* 3. AND **beaming** *mod.* under the effects of marijuana. (Drugs.) ☐ *Walter is on the beam again. How can he hold a job?* ☐ *The only time that Max is happy is when he is beaming.* 4. *mod.* smart; clever. ☐ *That was well done, Tom. You're on the beam.* ☐ *She is really on the beam. Glad she came along.*

on the bean See *on the button.*

on the bird *mod.* available on the T.V. satellite channels. ☐ *There is a whole lot of good stuff on the bird, but you need a receiving dish to get it.* ☐ *I get a huge book every month listing what programs are on the bird.*

on the bleeding edge *phr.* having the most advanced technology; knowing about the most advanced technology. (Jocular. More advanced than *on the cutting edge.*) ☐ *This gadget is brand new. It's really on the bleeding edge.* ☐ *Tom is on the bleeding edge when it comes to optical storage technology.*

on the blink 1. *mod.* out of order; ill. (Compare to *on the fritz.*) ☐ *I was a little on the blink yesterday and decided to stay at home.* ☐ *My refrigerator is on the blink again.* 2. *mod.* alcohol intoxicated; on a drinking spree. ☐ *They all went out and got on the blink.* ☐ *My brother is a little bit on the blink this morning.*

on the button AND **on the bean** *mod.* exactly the right time or place. ☐ *He was there on time, right on the button.* ☐ *I want to see you here at noon—on the bean.*

on the chopping block *mod.* in serious and threatening straits. ☐ *Our whole future is on the chopping block.* ☐ *Until this is resolved, our necks are on the chopping block.*

on the double *mod.* very fast; twice as fast. (Originally military. Refers to "double time" in marching.) ☐ *Get over here right now—on the double!* ☐ *She wants to see you in her office on the double.*

on the fly *mod.* while something or someone is operating or moving. ☐ *I'll try to capture the data on the fly.* ☐ *Please try* *to buy some aspirin somewhere on the fly today.*

on the fritz **1.** *mod.* not functioning properly. □ *This T.V. is on the fritz again.* □ *My watch is on the fritz.* **2.** *mod.* alcohol intoxicated. □ *Sue is a bit on the fritz.* □ *She drank till she was totally on the fritz.*

on the horse See *horsed.*

on the juice *mod.* drinking heavily; on a drinking bout. (See also *juice.*) □ *Fred spent the whole week on the juice.* □ *She won't be able to return your call. I'm afraid she's on the juice again.*

on the junk *mod.* on drugs; addicted to drugs. (See also *junk.*) □ *Max has been on the junk for all of his adult life.* □ *He's not really on the junk. He's only addicted to cigarettes.*

on the lam [. . . læm] *mod.* running from the police. (Underworld.) □ *Max has been on the lam for a week now.* □ *When the boss found out you was on the lam, he got real mad.*

on the level *mod.* honest; straightforward. □ *Come on now. Be on the level with me.* □ *Is the ad on the level?*

on the make *mod.* ambitious; attempting to be great. □ *That young lawyer is sure on the make.* □ *This university is on the make.*

on the mojo [. . .'modʒo] *mod.* addicted to morphine; using morphine. (Drugs. See also *mojo.*) □ *How long you been on the mojo?* □ *How can you hold a steady job if you're on the mojo?*

on the money *mod.* exactly as desired; at the right amount of money. □ *Your new idea is right on the money.* □ *The bid for the new hospital came in on the money.*

on the natch [. . . nætʃ] *mod.* free of drugs; natural and *straight.* □ *Max says he wants to get on the natch, but I don't believe it.* □ *I have been on the natch for almost a year.*

on the needle *mod.* addicted to injectable drugs. (Drugs.) □ *My sister's on the needle, and I want to help her.* □ *Once you're on the needle, you've had it.*

on the nose *mod.* exactly on time; exactly as planned. □ *I want you there at noon on the nose.* □ *All three of them were at the appointed place right on the nose.*

on the outs (with someone) *mod.* in a mild dispute with someone; sharing ill will with someone. □ *Tom and Bill are on the outs again.* □ *Tom has been on the outs with Bill before. They'll work it out.*

on the pill *mod.* taking birth control pills. □ *Is it true that Mary is on the pill?* □ *She was on the pill, but she isn't now.*

on the prowl *mod.* looking for someone for sexual purposes, in the manner of a prowling cat. □ *Tom looks like he is on the prowl again tonight.* □ *That whole gang of boys is on the prowl. Watch out.*

on the rag **1.** *mod.* menstruating. (Potentially offensive. Use with caution.) □ *Kim's on the rag and in a bad mood.* □ *Sue doesn't go swimming when she's on the rag.* **2.** *mod.* ill-tempered. □ *Bill is on the rag and making trouble for everyone.* □ *Wow, Wayne, you are on the rag. What's eating you?*

on the road *mod.* traveling from place to place, not necessarily on the highways. (See also *get the show on the road.*) □ *I was on the road with the circus for six months.* □ *I don't work in the main office anymore. Now I'm on the road.*

on the rocks **1.** *mod.* (of an alcoholic drink) with ice cubes. (See also *rocks.*) □ *I'd like mine on the rocks, please.* □ *Give me a scotch on the rocks, please.* **2.** *mod.* in a state of ruin or bankruptcy. (Like a ship that has gone aground on the rocks and cannot be moved.) □ *That bank is on the rocks. Don't put your money in it.* □ *My finances are on the rocks just now.*

on the run **1.** *mod.* while one is moving from place to place. □ *I will try to get some aspirin today on the run.* □ *I will think about it on the run.* **2.** *mod.* running from the police. □ *Max is on the run from the cops.* □ *The gang of crooks is on the run. Probably somewhere in Florida.*

on the safe side *mod.* taking the risk-free path. □ *Let's be on the safe side and call first.* □ *I think you should stay on the safe side and call the doctor about this fever.*

on the same wavelength *mod.* thinking in the same pattern. □ *We're not on the same wavelength. Let's try again.* □ *We kept talking until we were on the same wavelength.*

on the sauce *mod.* drinking regularly; alcohol intoxicated. □ *Poor old Ron is on the sauce again.* □ *He is on the sauce most of the time.*

on the shelf 1. *mod.* not active socially; left to oneself in social matters. □ *I've been on the shelf long enough. I'm going to make some friends.* □ *She likes being on the shelf.* **2.** *mod.* postponed. (See also *on the back burner.*) □ *We'll have to put this matter on the shelf for a while.* □ *I have a plan on the shelf just waiting for an opportunity like this.*

on the side 1. *mod.* extra, such as with a job or a side order of food. □ *I would like an order of eggs with toast on the side, please.* □ *She is a bank teller and works as a waitress on the side.* **2.** *mod.* extramarital; in addition to one's spouse. □ *He is married, but also has a woman on the side.* □ *She has boyfriends on the side, but her husband knows about them.*

on the skids *mod.* on the decline. (See also *put the skids under someone or something.*) □ *My newly started business is on the skids.* □ *Her health is really on the skids, but she stays cheery anyway.*

on the sly *mod.* secretly and deceptively. □ *She was stealing little bits of money on the sly.* □ *Martin was having an affair with the maid on the sly.*

on the squiff [. . . skwɪf] *mod.* on a drinking bout. (See also *squiff.*) □ *Bob is out on the squiff again.* □ *Max is always on the squiff, except when he's shooting dope.*

on the street 1. *mod.* using drugs; selling drugs; looking for drugs. (Drugs.) □ *Fred spent a year on the street before he was arrested.* □ *Max will be on the street all his life.* **2.** *mod.* engaged in prostitution. □ *Mary said, "What am I supposed to do—go on the street?"* □ *All three of them went on the street to earn enough money to live.* **3.** *mod.* widely known. □ *Sue put it on the street, and now everyone knows.* □ *It's on the street. There isn't anyone who hasn't heard it.* **4.** *mod.* on Wall Street or elsewhere in the New York City financial districts. (Similar to sense 3, except that it refers to a specific street. Usually with a capital *s*.) □ *I heard on the Street today that Apple is buying IBM.* □ *It's on the Street that the market is due to crash again.* **5.** *mod.* at discount prices; as available from discounters. (As if some item were being sold on the street by a peddler.) □ *It lists at $2200 and can be got for about $1650 on the street.* □ *On the street it goes for about $400.*

on the take *mod.* taking bribes. (Underworld.) □ *I heard that the mayor is on the take.* □ *Everyone in city hall is on the take.*

on the tank AND **on a tank** *mod.* on a drinking bout. □ *All the guys were on the tank last Saturday.* □ *Paul spent all weekend on a tank.*

on the up-and-up *mod.* legitimate; open and aboveboard. □ *Is this deal on the up-and-up? What's the catch?* □ *Everything I do is on the up-and-up. I am totally honest.*

on the wagon *mod.* not now drinking alcoholic liquor. □ *How long has John been on the wagon this time?* □ *He's on the wagon again.*

on the warpath *mod.* very angry. □ *The boss is on the warpath again. Watch out!* □ *I am on the warpath about setting goals and standards again.*

On your bike! AND **Go to your room!** *imperative.* "Get out of here!"; "Get on your motorcycle and get out!" □ *What a bad joke! No puns allowed here! On your bike!* □ *That was a ridiculous remark. Go to your room!*

once and for all *mod.* permanently. □ *I'm gonna take care of you once and for* *all!* □ *I would like to get this ridiculous problem settled once and for all.*

once in a blue moon *mod.* rarely. □ *I do this only once in a blue moon.* □ *Once in a blue moon I have a little wine with dinner.*

once-over *n.* a visual examination, especially of a person of the opposite sex. (Always with *the*.) □ *The way she was giving him the once-over, I knew she would say something to him.* □ *Tom, you are always giving the girls the once-over.*

once over lightly **1.** *mod.* quickly and superficially; carelessly; cursorily. (This is hyphenated before a nominal.) □ *He looked at it once over lightly and agreed to do it.* □ *It needs more than a once-over-lightly look.* **2.** *n.* a perfunctory examination; a quick glance. □ *Please give it more than the usual once over lightly.* □ *Once over lightly is not enough.*

one *mod.* having to do with something unique or special. (Similar to a definite article.) □ *Tracy is one fine cook.* □ *He was left with one powerful hangover.* □ *Hank? Now there is one ugly son of a gun for you.*

one and one *mod.* having to do with the use of both nostrils in snorting a drug, usually cocaine. (Drugs.) □ *Max always takes it one and one. It's the only way he can get enough.* □ *He does it one and one because it hits him faster that way.*

one and only *n.* one's lover or sweetheart. □ *I bought a gift for my one and only.* □ *She's my one and only, and I love her.*

one brick shy of a load *mod.* stupid; dense. □ *Joyce has done some stupid things. Sometimes I think she is one brick shy of a load.* □ *Ted is one brick shy of a load. He can't seem to do what he is told without messing up.*

one for the road *n.* a drink; a drink before a journey. □ *Let's have one for the road.* □ *Don't have one for the road if you are going to be the driver.*

one-horse town *n.* a very small town; a small and backward town. □ *I refuse to spend a whole week in that one-horse town!* □ *I grew up in a one-horse town, and I liked it very much.*

one jump ahead of someone or something *n.* in advance of someone or something; a step ahead of someone or something. □ *I try to be one jump ahead of the problems.* □ *You have to keep one jump ahead of the boss in order to succeed.*

one-man show **1.** *n.* a performance put on by one person. □ *It was a one-man show, but it was very entertaining.* □ *For a one-man show, it was very long.* **2.** *n.* an exhibition of the artistic works of one person. □ *She is having a one-man show at the Northside Gallery.* □ *I'm having a one-man show next weekend. Come and see what I have done.*

one-night stand **1.** *n.* a performance lasting only one night. □ *The band did a series of one-night stands down the East Coast.* □ *You can't make a living doing one-night stands.* **2.** *n.* a romance or sexual relationship that lasts only one night. □ *It was not a romance, just a one-night stand.* □ *It looked like something that would last longer than a one-night stand.*

one of the faithful *n.* a drunkard. □ *Here comes Mr. Franklin—one of the faithful—staggering down the street.* □ *I saw one of the faithful standing at the bar.*

one smart apple *n.* a smart or clever person. □ *That Sue is one smart apple.* □ *My brother is one smart apple.*

one too many *n.* one drink of liquor too many, implying drunkenness. □ *I think I've had one too many. It's time to stop drinking.* □ *Don't drive if you've had one too many.*

one-track mind *n.* a (person's) mind obsessed with only one thing. □ *When it comes to food, Tom has a one-track mind.* □ *Mary has a one-track mind. All she thinks about is Tom.*

one's bag *n.* one's preferences; one's talents. □ *Working crossword puzzles is* *my bag.* □ *Hey, Tom, what's your bag? What do you like to do?*

one's best shot *n.* one's best attempt (at something). □ *That was his best shot, but it wasn't good enough.* □ *I always try to give something my best shot.*

only way to go *n.* the best way to do something; the best choice to make. □ *Get a four-wheel drive car. It's the only way to go.* □ *That's it! A new house. It's the only way to go.*

onto a good thing *mod.* having found something that is to one's advantage, such as something easy, profitable, inexpensive, etc. □ *I think that Bill got onto a good thing when he opened his own store.* □ *I won't quit now. I'm onto a good thing, and I know it.*

onto someone or something *mod.* alerted to or aware of a deceitful plan or person. □ *The cops are onto your little game here.* □ *Max thought he was safe, but the fuzz was onto him from the beginning.*

oodles ['udlz] *n.* lots (of something). □ *My uncle has just oodles and oodles of money.* □ *I don't have oodles, but I have enough to keep me happy.* □ *When I have spaghetti, I just love oodles of noodles.*

oof [uf] **1.** *exclam.* the sound one makes when one is struck in the abdomen. (Usually **Oof!**) □ *So, then Bob hit him in the belly. Oof!* □ *"Oof!" cried Tom. He couldn't talk any more after that.* **2.** *n.* the potency of the alcohol in liquor; the effect of potent alcohol. □ *This stuff really has oof. How old is it?* □ *Beer doesn't have enough oof for her anymore.*

oomph [ʊmpf] **1.** *n.* energy; drive and vitality. □ *Come on, you guys. Let's get some oomph behind it. PUSH!* □ *You need more oomph if you want to work at heavy labor.* **2.** *n.* sex appeal. (Euphemistic.) □ *She had a lot of oomph, but didn't wish to become a movie star.* □ *No amount of oomph can make up for a total lack of talent.*

open (up) one's kimono *phr.* to reveal what one is planning. (From the computer industry, referring especially to the involvement of the Japanese in this field.) □ *Sam isn't one to open his kimono much when it comes to new products.* □ *Even if Tom appears to open up his kimono on this deal, don't put much stock in what he says.*

O.P.s ['o'piz] *n.* other people's cigarettes; begged or borrowed cigarettes. (Initialism.) □ *My favorite kind of cigarettes is O.P.s. They're the cheapest, too.* □ *Ted only smokes O.P.s.*

or what? *phr.* or what else can it be? (Part of a special formula that asks if something is a good example or specimen of something. The expected answer is yes. The question "Is this an X or what?" means "If this isn't a really great X, what is it then?") □ *Look at what I am wearing! Is that a great jacket or what?* □ *That's my son. Is he a superman or what?*

oreo *n.* an American of African descent who behaves more white than black. (Like the Oreo brand cookie, the person is black on the outside and white on the inside. Potentially offensive. Use only with discretion. Also a derogatory term of address.) □ *They called Sam an oreo because he wears a suit and works downtown.* □ *I'm not an oreo, I'm just doing my best with what God gave me.*

org [org] **1.** *n.* the *rush* caused by potent drugs. (Drugs. From *orgasm*.) □ *Max hated the vomiting when he first took it, but he loved the org.* □ *Does this stuff give you a real org?* **2.** *n.* an organization. □ *She's a member of the org and can't be expected to use independent judgement.* □ *Come on, join the org.*

organic *mod.* great. □ *This is one fine, organic rally! I'm glad I stopped by.* □ *Wow, this whole day was organic!*

ork-orks ['orkorks] *n.* the delirium tremens. □ *He has the ork-orks. He's a real drunk.* □ *Whenever he gets the ork-orks, he gets himself arrested and put in jail where he can sober up.*

ossifer AND **occifer** ['ɑsəfɚ] *n.* a police officer. (Also an ill-advised term of address.) □ *Look here, ossifer, I was just having a little fun.* □ *Ask the occifer* *there if he wants to step outside and discuss it.*

ossified ['ɑsəfɑɪd] *mod.* alcohol or drug intoxicated. (From *stoned (out).*) □ *How can anybody be so ossified on four beers?* □ *I've never seen anybody so ossified.*

Otis ['otɪs] **1.** *n.* a drunkard. (From the name of a television character who is the town drunk. Also a term of address.) □ *Look at Otis over there, propped up against the wall.* □ *Have another beer, Otis?* **2.** *mod.* drunk. □ *Gary was completely Otis and couldn't walk straight.* □ *Fred was Otis by midnight and began looking like he was going to barf.*

OTL ['o'ti'ɛl] *phr.* "*out to lunch*"; *spacy;* giddy. (An initialism.) □ *Wally is the most OTL guy I have ever seen.* □ *Sue is OTL. She seems witless all the time.*

OTOH *phr.* "on the other hand." (An initialism. A computer abbreviation, not pronounced.) □ *That's one good idea. OTOH, there must be many other satisfactory procedures.* □ *OTOH, everyone is a little forgetful now and then.*

out 1. *mod.* alcohol or drug intoxicated. (Probably from *far out.*) □ *All four of them were totally out.* □ *Those guys are really out!* **2.** *mod.* out of fashion. (The opposite of *in.*) □ *That kind of clothing is strictly out.* □ *You need to tell me which of my dresses is out this season.*

out-and-out *mod.* complete or total; blatant. □ *Fred was an out-and-out liar.* □ *Don't be such an out-and-out stinker!*

out cold 1. *mod.* unconscious. □ *Paul was out cold when we found him.* □ *Who knocked him out cold?* **2.** *mod.* alcohol intoxicated. □ *Four beers and he was out cold.* □ *He sat in his chair at the table, out cold.*

out in left field *mod.* wrong; *off base; loony.* □ *Don't pay any attention to her. She's out in left field as usual.* □ *That guy is out in left field—a real nut.*

out like a light 1. *mod.* unconscious or sleeping soundly. □ *I fell and hit my head. I was out like a light for two minutes, they tell me.* □ *I closed my eyes and was out like a light in no time at all.* **2.** *mod.* heavily alcohol intoxicated. □ *Those guys are really out like a light!* □ *All four of them drank till they were out like a light.*

out of it 1. *mod.* not in with the real world. □ *You never pay attention to what's going on. You're really out of it.* □ *Fred is out of it most of the time. He even looks dull.* **2.** *mod.* alcohol or drug intoxicated. □ *Two drinks and she was totally out of it.* □ *When they are out of it, they are quite dangerous.*

out of kilter 1. *mod.* not functioning properly; *on the fritz; out of w(h)ack.* □ *My car's engine is out of kilter and needs some repair work.* □ *My coffeepot is out of kilter, so I have to make coffee in a pan.* **2.** *mod.* out of square. □ *That picture is out of kilter. Please straighten it.* □ *That corner is not square, and the wall even looks out of kilter.*

out of left field *mod.* suddenly; from an unexpected source or direction. □ *Most of your ideas are out of left field.* □ *All of his paintings are right out of left field.*

out of line *mod.* not in accord with what is appropriate or expected, especially in price or behavior. □ *Your behavior is quite out of line. I shall report you.* □ *Your price is out of line with the other stores.*

out of luck *mod.* unfortunate; in a hopeless position. □ *If you think you are going to get any sympathy from me, you're just out of luck.* □ *I was out of luck. There were no eggs left in the store.*

out of one's skull *mod.* alcohol intoxicated. □ *Oh, man, I drank till I was out of my skull.* □ *Two beers and he was out of his skull.*

out of sight 1. *mod.* heavily alcohol or drug intoxicated; *high.* □ *They've been drinking since noon, and they're out of sight.* □ *Man, is she ever out of sight!* **2.** *mod.* very expensive; high in price. □ *Prices at that restaurant are out of sight.* □ *The cost of medical care is out of sight.*

out of sync [... sɪŋk] *mod.* uncoordinated; unsynchronized. ☐ *Our efforts are out of sync.* ☐ *My watch and your watch are out of sync.*

out of the picture *mod.* no longer relevant to a situation; departed; dead. ☐ *Now that Tom is out of the picture, we needn't concern ourselves about his objections.* ☐ *With her husband out of the picture, she can begin living.*

out of the way 1. *mod.* dead; killed. ☐ *The crooks put the witness out of the way before the trial.* ☐ *Now that her husband was out of the way, she began to get out and about more.* **2.** *mod.* alcohol intoxicated. ☐ *She spends a lot of time out of the way.* ☐ *After a few more drinks, Bill will be out of the way.*

out of the woods *mod.* freed from a previous state of uncertainty or danger; no longer critical. ☐ *As soon as her temperature is down, she'll be out of the woods.* ☐ *We're out of the woods now, and things aren't so chancy.*

out of this world 1. *mod.* wonderful and exciting. ☐ *This pie is out of this world.* ☐ *My boyfriend is just out of this world.* **2.** *mod.* drug intoxicated. ☐ *Man, is she ever out of this world! What did she drink?* ☐ *He drank until he was out of this world.*

out of w(h)ack *mod.* out of adjustment; inoperative. (Compare to *out of kilter.*) ☐ *My watch is out of whack.* ☐ *I think my left eye is out of wack a little. Maybe I need glasses.*

out the gazoo [... gəˈzu] *phr.* in great plenty; everywhere. (*Gazoo* = anus. Potentially offensive. Use only with discretion.) ☐ *We have old magazines out the gazoo here. Can't we throw some of them away?* ☐ *Go away. I have problems out the gazoo. I don't need any more of them from you!*

out the window *mod.* gone; wasted. ☐ *All that work gone out the window.* ☐ *My forty dollars—out the window. Why didn't I save my money?*

out to lunch *mod.* absentminded; giddy; stupid acting. (See also *OTL.*) ☐ *Old Ted is so out to lunch these days. Seems to be losing his mind.* ☐ *Don't pay any attention to my uncle. He's out to lunch.*

outa [ˈaʊdə] *phr.* "out of." (Eye-dialect. Used in writing only for effect. Used in the examples of this dictionary.) ☐ *Get outa here!* ☐ *In two minutes I'm outa here!*

outed AND **offed** *mod.* dead; killed. ☐ *The witness was outed before a subpoena could be issued.* ☐ *The guy was offed when we found him.*

outfit 1. *n.* a group of people; a company. ☐ *That outfit cheated me out of my money.* ☐ *I will never deal with that outfit again.* **2.** *n.* a set of clothing. ☐ *You look lovely in that outfit.* ☐ *Should I wear my gray wool outfit?* **3.** *n.* a set of things; the items needed for some task. ☐ *I got a fine chemistry outfit for my birthday.* ☐ *My tool kit has everything I need. It's the whole outfit.*

outsy [ˈaʊtsi] *n.* a navel that protrudes. (Compare to *insy.*) ☐ *Is yours an insy or an outsy?* ☐ *I have an outsy. Why on earth do you ask?*

over easy *mod.* turned carefully, said of cooking eggs. ☐ *I want mine cooked over easy.* ☐ *Over easy eggs are better than scrambled.*

over my dead body *phr.* "not if I can stop you"; "you won't be able to do something if I am alive to prevent you." ☐ *You'll drop out of school over my dead body!* ☐ *Get married and move to Arizona? Over my dead body!*

over one's head *mod.* confusing; too difficult to understand. ☐ *This stuff is too hard. It's over my head.* ☐ *Calculus is all over my head.*

over-the-counter 1. *mod.* having to do with stocks that are sold through dealers rather than through a stock exchange. ☐ *You can make or lose a lot of money on over-the-counter stocks.* ☐ *Is this stock over-the-counter or available on the exchange?* **2.** *mod.* having to do with medication sold without a prescription. ☐ *Over-the-counter drugs can be helpful in some diseases.* ☐

Is this medication over-the-counter or by prescription only?

over the hill 1. *mod.* escaped from prison or the military. (See also *AWOL.*) □ *Two privates went over the hill last night.* □ *They broke out of jail and went over the hill.* **2.** *mod.* too old (for something). □ *You're only fifty! You're not over the hill yet.* □ *Some people seem over the hill at thirty.*

over the hump 1. *mod.* drug intoxicated. □ *Max is over the hump now. He is stoned.* □ *This stuff makes you sick at first. Then suddenly you are over the hump and floating.* **2.** *mod.* over the hard part; past the midpoint. □ *Things should be easy from now on. We are over the hump.* □ *When you get over the hump, life is much better.*

over the long haul *mod.* long term; over a long period of time. □ *Over the long haul, this one will prove best.* □ *This will last over the long haul.*

overamped *mod.* high on amphetamines; overdosed with amphetamines. (Drugs.) □ *Max is overamped again.* □ *Two students were overamped and got sent to the counselor.*

overjolt AND **O.J. 1.** *n.* an overdose of drugs, especially of heroin. (The abbreviation is an initialism. Drugs.) □ *Ted is suffering from a serious O.J.* □ *That overjolt nearly killed her.* **2.** *in.* to take an overdose of drugs, especially of heroin. (Drugs.) □ *She overjolted once too often.* □ *If you O.J. again, you will probably die.*

overkill *n.* too much. □ *That is enough. Any more is just overkill.* □ *Your policy of overkill is wasteful and expensive.*

overserved *mod.* having to do with a drunken person in a bar; alcohol intoxicated. (Euphemistic.) □ *Four customers were overserved and had to leave.* □ *The overserved guy there in the corner is going to be sick.*

P

pack *tr.* to carry something, usually a gun. (Underworld. Any of the slang terms for gun may be used: *rod, iron, heat,* etc.) ☐ *I can tell that guy's packing heat from the bulge in his jacket.* ☐ *I never pack a rod on Sunday.*

pack of lies *n.* a whole collection or series of lies. ☐ *I've heard you talk about this before, and it's all a pack of lies.* ☐ *Her story is nothing but a pack of lies.*

package 1. *n.* a combination of a variety of related things; a unified set of things. (See also *package deal.*) ☐ *You can't buy just one part. It comes as a package.* ☐ *The first college I applied to offered me a good aid package, so I went.* **2.** *n.* a lot of money; a *bundle.* ☐ *She made quite a package on that bank deal.* ☐ *I came away from the dog track with a nice little package.* **3.** *n.* someone who is cute or sexually attractive. (Primarily refers to females as bundles of sexual charms. Similar in meaning to sense 1.) ☐ *How do you like that little package who just came in?* ☐ *She's quite a package, if you like the giggly type.* **4.** *tr.* to position or display someone or something, as in marketing, to good advantage. ☐ *The agent packaged the actress so that everyone thought she only did dramatic roles.* ☐ *If you package your plan correctly, the committee will accept it.*

package deal *n.* a variety of goods or services sold as a unit. ☐ *I got all these tools in a package deal for only $39.95.* ☐ *What about giving me all three shirts as a package deal?*

packaged *mod.* alcohol intoxicated. ☐ *Man, Max was really packaged last night!* ☐ *By midnight she was totally packaged.*

pad 1. *n.* a place to live; one's room or dwelling. ☐ *Why don't you come over to my pad for a while?* ☐ *This is a nice pad you've got here.* **2.** *tr.* to lengthen a piece of writing with unnecessary material. ☐ *This story would be better if you hadn't padded it with so much chitchat.* ☐ *I think I can pad the report enough to make it fill twenty pages.* (More at *padded.*)

pad out *in.* to go to bed or to sleep. (See also *pad.*) ☐ *Man, if I don't pad out by midnight, I'm a zombie.* ☐ *Why don't you people go home so I can pad out?*

padded *mod.* plump or fat. ☐ *He didn't hurt himself when he fell down. He's well padded there.* ☐ *Your clothes would fit better if you weren't so—ah—padded.*

paddy *n.* a police officer, especially an Irish police officer. (Usually derogatory. Also an ill-advised term of address.) ☐ *Tell that paddy to go catch a crook or something.* ☐ *Look here, paddy, I wasn't doing anything.*

paddy wagon *n.* a police van used to take suspected criminals to the police station. ☐ *It took two paddy wagons to carry away the people they arrested.* ☐ *The cop put the woman in handcuffs and then called the paddy wagon.*

padre ['padre] *n.* any male religious cleric: priest, monk, or chaplain. (From Spanish. Typically military. Also a term of address.) ☐ *I went to see the padre for some advice.* ☐ *Hey, padre, anything new on the religion front?*

pafisticated [pəˈfistəkédəd] *mod.* alcohol intoxicated. (A corruption of "sophisticated.") ☐ *Whenever I drink champagne, I get totally pafisticated.* ☐ *Look* *at her drive. She is a real pafisticated lady.*

paid *mod.* alcohol intoxicated. □ *I think I'll go out and get paid tonight.* □ *Tom went to the tavern and spent all his money on getting paid.*

pain *n.* a bother; an irritating thing or person. □ *That woman is such a pain.* □ *Those long meetings are a real pain.*

pain in the ass AND **pain in the butt; pain in the rear** *n.* a very annoying thing or person. (Crude. Potentially offensive. Use only with discretion. An elaboration of *pain.* Use caution with *ass. Butt* is less offensive. *Rear* is euphemistic.) □ *That guy is a real pain in the ass.* □ *Things like that give me a pain in the butt.* □ *You are nothing but a pain in the rear.*

pain in the butt See the previous entry.

pain in the neck *n.* a difficult or annoying thing or person. (Compare to *pain in the ass.*) □ *This tax form is a pain in the neck.* □ *My boss is a pain in the neck.*

pain in the rear See *pain in the ass.*

painkiller *n.* liquor. (See also *feeling no pain.*) □ *Pass that bottle of painkiller over here. My throat hurts.* □ *He should look happy. He's full of painkiller.*

paint remover *n.* strong or inferior whiskey or other spirits. □ *That paint remover you gave me nearly burned out my throat.* □ *What do you call that paint remover anyway? It sure is powerful.*

paint the town (red) *tr.* to go out and celebrate; to go on a drinking bout; to get drunk. □ *I feel great. Let's go out and paint the town.* □ *They were out painting the town red last night.*

pal [pæl] **1.** *n.* a close, male friend or buddy. □ *Be nice to him. He's my pal.* □ *Hey, be a pal. Give me a match.* **2.** *n.* a term of address for a stranger, usually a male. □ *Hey, pal. Got a match?* □ *Look, pal, I was in line in front of you!*

pal around (with someone) *in.* to be friends with someone; to move about socially with someone. □ *Tom and Heidi have palled around for years.* □ *Young people like to pal around with one another.*

palimony ['pæləmoni] *n.* alimony—living expenses—paid to a common-law wife or to a former girlfriend. □ *He left her, and she took him to court to try to get him to pay palimony.* □ *With a good lawyer, she got more palimony than she could ever have gotten as alimony if they had been married.*

pally (with someone) *mod.* friendly or overly friendly with someone. □ *I don't know why Sue acts so pally. I hardly know her.* □ *She doesn't seem pally with me.*

palm *tr.* to conceal something in the hand as in a theft or the performance of a magic trick; to receive and conceal a tip or a bribe. □ *The kid palmed the candy bar and walked right out of the store.* □ *The waiter palmed the twenty-dollar bill and led us to a table.*

palm-oil *n.* a bribe; a tip. □ *How much palm-oil does it take to get this deed recorded in reasonable time?* □ *The messenger seemed to move his legs faster after an application of palm-oil.*

palm-presser See *flesh-presser.*

palm someone or something off (on someone) 1. *tr.* to transfer some unwanted person or thing to another person. □ *Don't palm her off on me. I don't want her.* Ⓣ *My uncle palmed off his old clothes on me.* **2.** *tr.* [with *something*] to succeed in spending counterfeit money; to succeed in cashing a bad check. (Underworld.) □ *Max palmed four phony twenties off in less than an hour.* Ⓣ *Somebody palmed off a rubber check on me yesterday.*

palooka AND **paluka** [pə'lukə] *n.* a stupid person; an unskilled prizefighter; any mediocre person. (Also a term of address. From the name of the comic-strip prizefighter "Joe Palooka.") □ *Tell that stupid palooka to sit down and shut up.* □ *Get out of here, you paluka. You're just in the way.*

palsy-walsy ['pælzi'wælzi] **1.** *n.* a good friend, *pal,* or buddy. (Also a term of address.) □ *Look here, palsy-walsy, let's you and me get out of here.* □ *Meet my old palsy-walsy, John. We've known each other since we were kids.* **2.** *mod.* friendly; overly friendly. (Often with *with.*) □ *Why is Tom so palsy-walsy with everyone?* □ *That guy is a little too palsy-walsy.*

paluka See *palooka.*

pan *n.* the face. (See also *deadpan.*) □ *Look at that guy! I've never seen such an ugly pan in my life.* □ *I stared her right in the pan and told her to shut up.*

pan out *in.* [for something] to work out or turn out all right. □ *Don't worry. Everything will pan out okay.* □ *Nothing seems to pan out for me anymore.*

panic *n.* a very funny or exciting person or thing. □ *John's party was a real panic.* □ *Paul is a panic. He tells a joke a minute.*

pants rabbits *n.* lice. (See also *seam-squirrels.*) □ *Max is sure scratching a lot. Do you think he's got pants rabbits?* □ *I don't want to be around people who have pants rabbits and stuff like that.*

paper 1. *n.* a written document; written evidence supporting something. (Often with *some.*) □ *Don't tell me over the phone! I want paper!* □ *Come on, send me some paper. Let's make this official.* **2.** *n.* a forged check. (See also *paper-pusher, paper-hanger.*) □ *She was arrested for passing paper.* □ *The police actually lost the paper and ended up with no evidence.*

paper-hanger *n.* someone who tries to pass bad checks. (Underworld. See also *paper, paper-pusher.*) □ *The cops caught the paper-hanger red-handed.* □ *He's wanted as a paper-hanger in four states.*

paper over something *tr.* to try to conceal something unpleasant; to try to cover up a misdeed. □ *You can't paper this over. It has to be dealt with now!* Ⓣ *This is a severe social problem. Don't try to paper over it.*

paper-pusher 1. *n.* a bureaucrat; a clerk in the military services; any office worker. (See also *pencil-pusher.*) □ *If those paper-pushers can't get their work done on time, make them stay late.* □ *I don't want to talk to some paper-pusher, I want to talk to the boss.* **2.** *n.* someone who passes bad checks. (See also *paper, paper-hanger.*) □ *The bank teller spotted a well-known paper-pusher and called the cops.* □ *The old lady was charged as a paper-pusher and sent to jail.*

paperhanging *n.* writing and spending bad checks. (Underworld.) □ *She was accused of paperhanging and didn't even know what the cops were talking about, so they let her go.* □ *She is good at both paperhanging and acting.*

parboiled *mod.* alcohol intoxicated. (See also *boiled.*) □ *Sally stayed at the bar just long enough to get parboiled.* □ *She's not really stewed, just parboiled.*

pard *n.* partner. (From *pardner.* Also a term of address.) □ *Come on, pard, let's go find some action.* □ *This is my old pard, Clarence.*

Pardon my French. AND **Excuse my French.** *sent.* "Excuse my use of swear words or taboo words." (Does not refer to real French.) □ *Pardon my French, but this is a hell of a day.* □ *What she needs is a kick in the butt, if you'll excuse my French.*

(parental) units *n.* parents. (Teens. Also a term of address. See also *rent(al)s.*) □ *I don't think my parental units will let me stay out that late.* □ *Hey, units! I need to talk to you about something really important.*

park *in.* to *neck* or to make love, especially in a parked car. □ *Do kids still park, or do they just watch television?* □ *They still park, but they don't have a name for it anymore.*

park it (somewhere) *tr.* sit down somewhere; sit down and get out of the way. □ *Hey, park it! You're in the way.* □ *Max, park it over there in the corner. Stop pacing around. You make me nervous.*

parting shot *n.* the last word; a final comment before departing. □ *For a parting* *shot, she called me a miser.* ☐ *His parting shot concerned some comments about my ability to do simple math.*

party 1. *n.* a combining form used in expressions to refer to certain kinds of activity carried on in groups or in pairs. (For examples, see *coke party, free base party, grass party, hen party, keg party, kick party, pot party, stag-party, tailgate party, tea party.*) 2. *in.* to drink alcohol, smoke marijuana, or use other drugs. (May also include sexual activity.) ☐ *Come on, man! Let's party!* ☐ *If you didn't party so much, you'd get better grades.*

party animal *n.* someone who loves parties. ☐ *My boyfriend and I are real party animals. Let's party!* ☐ *If you weren't such a party animal, you'd have more time for studying.*

party bowl *n.* a marijuana pipe large enough to serve a number of smokers. (Drugs.) ☐ *When they arrested Max, he had two pipes and a party bowl with him.* ☐ *The cops thought the party bowl was a flower vase!*

party-hearty *in.* to have a great time; to celebrate. (Originally teenage. The past tense is variable.) ☐ *Let's get some stuff and party-hearty.* ☐ *The whole class decided to celebrate and party-hearty.*

Party on! *exclam.* "That's right!" ☐ *Party on, Beavis! You are totally right!* ☐ *Party on, Waldo! You said it!*

party-pooper *n.* the first person to leave a party; someone who ruins a party because of dullness or by leaving early. ☐ *Don't leave! Don't be a party-pooper!* ☐ *Don't invite Martha. She's such a party-pooper.*

pass 1. *n.* a passing grade or mark on a test. (Compare to *fail.*) ☐ *Did you get a pass or a fail?* ☐ *This is my third pass this semester.* 2. *in.* to decline something; to decline to participate in something. ☐ *No, thanks. I pass.* ☐ *I'll have to pass. I am not prepared.* 3. *n.* an act of declining something. ☐ *I'll have to take a pass.* ☐ *Can I have a pass on that one? There is nothing I can do.* 4. *n.* a sexual advance or invitation. (Usually with *make.*) ☐ *He made a pass at me, so I slapped him.* ☐ *When he made a pass at me, he got a pass right back.* 5. *tr.* to succeed in spending counterfeit money; to succeed in cashing a bad check. ☐ *Beavis passed one bad check after another.* ☐ *He was arrested for passing bad checks.*

pass for something *in.* to pay for something; to treat someone by paying for something. ☐ *Come on. Let's go out. I'll pass for dinner.* ☐ *I'll pass for drinks if you want.*

pass go *tr.* to complete a difficult or dangerous task successfully. (From "pass go and collect $200" in the game Monopoly™.) ☐ *Man, I tried to get there on time, but I just couldn't pass go.* ☐ *You had better pass go with this job, or you've had it.*

pass the buck *tr.* to shift the responsibility for something to someone else; to evade responsibility. (See also *buck-passer.*) ☐ *When things get a little tough, do what I do. Pass the buck.* ☐ *Don't pass the buck. Stand up and admit you were wrong.*

passion-pit *n.* a drive-in movie theatre; any place where young people go to *neck,* such as an area where teenagers *park.* (Dated but still heard.) ☐ *She wanted me to drive down to the passion-pit, but I said I had a headache.* ☐ *My mother used to tell me about her trips to the passion-pit.*

passy *n.* a baby's pacifier. (Baby talk.) ☐ *Does little Johnnie want his passy?* ☐ *Mommy, Mary threw her passy on the floor.*

paste 1. *tr.* to strike someone, especially in the face. (See also *paste someone one.*) ☐ *I hauled off and pasted him right in the face.* ☐ *He tried to paste me, but I ducked.* 2. *tr.* to defeat a person or a team, usually in a game of some type. (See also *pasting.*) ☐ *The Warriors pasted the Rockets, 70-49.* ☐ *They really pasted our team in last week's game.* (More at *pasted.*)

paste someone one *tr.* to land a blow on someone. (See also *paste.*) ☐ *I pasted* *him one right on the nose.* ☐ *Next time you do that, I'll paste you one!*

pasted 1. *mod.* alcohol or drug intoxicated. (From *paste.*). ☐ *Poor Tom is totally pasted.* ☐ *Max got pasted on beer.* **2.** *mod.* beaten; outscored. ☐ *Our team really got pasted.* ☐ *He sure looked pasted the last time I saw him.*

pasting *n.* a beating; a defeat in a game. (See also *paste.*) ☐ *Our team took quite a pasting last weekend.* ☐ *I gave him a pasting.*

patsy ['pætsi] *n.* a victim of a *scam.* (Underworld. See also *dupe.*) ☐ *That guy over there looks like a perfect patsy.* ☐ *We got nearly twenty-five hundred bucks off that patsy.*

patter of tiny feet *n.* the sound of young children; having children in the household. ☐ *I really liked having the patter of tiny feet in the house.* ☐ *Darling, I think we're going to be hearing the patter of tiny feet soon.*

paw 1. *n.* someone's hand. (Jocular.) ☐ *Get your paws off me!* ☐ *That dog bit my paw.* **2.** *tr.* to feel someone or handle someone sexually. ☐ *If you paw me again, I'll slap you!* ☐ *I can't stand men who paw you to pieces.* **3.** *tr.* to touch someone more than is necessary or desired, without any sexual intent. ☐ *I don't like for people to paw me while they're shaking hands. There is no reason to shake my shoulder, too.* ☐ *Tom doesn't realize that he paws people and that it annoys them.*

pay a call *tr.* to go to the toilet; to leave to go to the toilet. (See also *call of nature, nature's call.*) ☐ *Excuse me. I have to pay a call.* ☐ *Tom left to pay a call. He should be back soon.*

pay one's dues 1. *tr.* to serve one's time in a menial role. ☐ *I spent some time as a bus boy, so I've paid my dues in the serving business.* ☐ *You have to start out at the bottom. Pay your dues, and then you'll appreciate better what you have.* **2.** *tr.* AND **pay one's dues to society** to serve a prison or jail sentence. ☐ *I served ten years in prison. I've paid my dues to society. The matter is settled.* ☐ *I took my medicine and paid my dues. Stop trying to punish me more.*

pay one's dues to society See the previous entry.

payola [pe'olə] *n.* a bribe paid to a *disk jockey* by record producers to get extra attention for their records; any bribe or payoff. ☐ *The announcer was fired for taking payola.* ☐ *There was a big scandal of payola in the 1950's.*

PDQ *mod.* "pretty damn quick"; very fast; very soon. (Initialism.) ☐ *You get those papers over here P.D.Q.!* ☐ *They had better get this mess straightened out PDQ if they know what's good for them.*

peach *n.* someone or something excellent. (Usually a person.) ☐ *That guy's a real peach.* ☐ *This is a peach of a car!*

peachy (keen) *mod.* fine; excellent. ☐ *Your idea is really peachy!* ☐ *What a peachy keen idea!*

peanut head *n.* an oaf; a *nerd.* ☐ *You are so silly, Kim. You're a real peanut head!* ☐ *What peanut head left the door open? It's freezing in here!*

peanuts *n.* practically no money at all; *chicken feed.* ☐ *They want me to do everything, but they only pay peanuts.* ☐ *The cost is just peanuts compared to what you get for the money.*

peckish *mod.* hungry. ☐ *I'm just a little peckish right now. I need a bite to eat.* ☐ *Wow, you look peckish!*

pecks AND **pecs; pects** [pɛks AND pɛkts] *n.* the pectoral muscles. (From weightlifting and bodybuilding.) ☐ *Look at the pecks on that guy!* ☐ *With pects like that he needs a bra.*

pee'd *mod.* alcohol intoxicated. (Euphemistic for *pissed.*) ☐ *This old boy is really pee'd.* ☐ *His old lady gets pee'd after a few beers.*

pecs See *pecks.*

pects See *pecks.*

pee'd off *mod.* extremely angry. (Euphemistic for *pissed (off).*) ☐ *I certainly was pee'd off!* ☐ *I've never been so pee'd off in my life!*

peel *in.* to strip off one's clothing. ☐ *I had to peel for my physical examination.* ☐ *She stood up on the stage and peeled right down to nothing!*

peep *n.* a noise; an utterance. ☐ *Don't you make another peep!* ☐ *I don't want to hear another peep out of you.*

peepers *n.* the eyes. ☐ *Come on, use your peepers. Take a good look.* ☐ *My peepers are tired.*

peg-leg *n.* a rude nickname for someone with a wooden peg for a leg. (Now used primarily in reference to theatrical pirates.) ☐ *See that peg-leg over there? He lost his foot to a shark.* ☐ *Hey, peg-leg. Race you to the bar!*

peg someone *tr.* to gossip about someone. ☐ *Kim is always pegging Jill. What's her problem?* ☐ *Don't peg me all the time. I've never done anything to you!*

pen *n.* a penitentiary; prison. (Underworld.) ☐ *Max got sent to the pen for fifteen years.* ☐ *After a few years in the pen, he began to appreciate freedom.*

pencil-pusher *n.* a bureaucrat; a clerk; an office worker. (See also *paper-pusher*.) ☐ *Look here, you lousy pencil-pusher, I want to talk to your boss!* ☐ *City Hall is filled with a bunch of over-paid pencil-pushers.*

Pennsy *n.* Pennsylvania. ☐ *I went to a conference in Pennsy last year.* ☐ *My cousin lives in Pennsy.*

penny *n.* a police officer. (A play on *copper*. See the note at *cop*.) ☐ *The penny over on the corner told the boys to get moving.* ☐ *We better get going before the pennies get here.*

penny-ante *mod.* trivial; cheap. (See also *ante*.) ☐ *I'm sick of this penny-ante stuff. Let's get serious.* ☐ *Max moved from penny-ante crimes into drugs.*

penny-pincher *n.* someone who is very miserly; someone who objects to the expenditure of every penny. ☐ *If you weren't such a penny-pincher, you'd have some decent clothes.* ☐ *Let's elect some penny-pinchers to Congress.*

peonied *mod.* alcohol intoxicated. (Related to *pee'd* and *pissed*.) ☐ *Man, was she peonied! Really stoned.* ☐ *Let's go get peonied, just for the hell of it.*

people watching *n.* observing different kinds of people as a pastime. ☐ *Let's eat at the greasy spoon over on Maple. The food is gross, but the people watching is good.* ☐ *I enjoy people watching, especially at airports.*

pep pill *n.* a stimulant pill or capsule, such as an amphetamine. ☐ *The doctor prescribed some kind of pep pills, but I refused to take them.* ☐ *Got any pep pills or anything?*

pep talk *n.* an informal speech of encouragement. ☐ *The coach gave the team a good pep talk, but they lost anyway.* ☐ *The pep talk grew into a real gripe session.*

pepped (up) AND **peppy** *mod.* alcohol intoxicated. (A euphemism. Compare to *perked (up)*.) ☐ *That guy looks a little pepped up. Don't give him any more booze.* ☐ *I feel sort of pepped up. Time to stop drinking.*

pepper-upper *n.* an amphetamine tablet or capsule; a *pep pill*. ☐ *I need me a little pepper-upper. Can I have a prescription?* ☐ *You need more sleep, not a pepper-upper.*

peppy 1. *mod.* vigorous; energetic. (Compare to *perky*.) ☐ *She's such a peppy thing.* ☐ *I sure don't feel very peppy right now.* **2.** See *pepped (up)*.

Period! *exclam.* "... and that's final!" (A way of indicating that there will be no more discussion or negotiation.) ☐ *I don't want to hear any more about it! Period!* ☐ *My final offer is $30.00. Period!*

perk *n.* an extra financial benefit; a monetary inducement or reward. (From *perquisite*. See also *benies*.) ☐ *I don't get paid much, but the perks are good.* ☐ *I don't get paid much, and I don't get any perks!*

perked (up) *mod.* alcohol intoxicated. (Compare to *pepped (up)*.) ☐ *Three* *beers and he's perked.* ☐ *No more. She's done. She's perked up for good.*

perky *mod.* energetic; alert. (Compare to *peppy.*) ☐ *Most poodles are quite perky.* ☐ *A perky hostess keeps parties alive.*

perp [pɚp] *n.* a perpetrator; someone who does something, such as committing a crime. ☐ *The cops were almost sure that Max was the perp in this job.* ☐ *The perp left a good set of prints on the doorknob.*

perpetrate ['pɚpətret] *in.* to pose; to pretend. ☐ *Terry is always walking around perpetrating. He sure wants people to think he's somebody.* ☐ *Look at her clothes. Have you ever seen anyone perpetrate like that?*

persuader *n.* a gun or other weapon used to threaten someone. (Underworld.) ☐ *He pulls out this persuader, see, and aims it right at me, see.* ☐ *Maybe my little persuader will help you remember where the money is.*

pesky *mod.* annoying; bothersome. ☐ *I am going to kill that pesky fly!* ☐ *I've had a pesky headache all day.*

pet peeve *n.* a major or principal annoyance or complaint. ☐ *Dirty dishes in restaurants are my pet peeve.* ☐ *He has no pet peeve. He hates everything.*

Peter Jay *n.* a nickname for a police officer. ☐ *You walk straight, or Peter Jay is going to bust you.* ☐ *Here comes Peter Jay in his pigmobile.*

peter out *in.* to give out; to wear out. ☐ *I'm about to peter out. I need a rest.* ☐ *What'll we do when the money peters out?*

petrified *mod.* alcohol intoxicated. (Literally, turned into stone. Another way of saying *stoned.*) ☐ *She's not drunk; she's petrified.* ☐ *He drank moonshine till he was petrified.*

petting-party *n.* a session of kissing and caressing. ☐ *I just want to watch the movie. I didn't come here for some teenage petting-party!* ☐ *We went to the passion-pit for a petting-party.*

P.F.D. *n.* a "potential formal date"; someone who looks good enough to be a date to a formal affair. (Initialism. Collegiate.) ☐ *That gal is a real P.F.D.* ☐ *Mike is no P.F.D., but he is a great friend anyway.*

PG *mod.* "pregnant." (Initialism.) ☐ *Do you think Sally's P.G.?* ☐ *I think I'm PG. You know, pregnant.*

phased See *phazed.*

PHAT *phr.* "pretty hips and thighs." (Initialism.) ☐ *Now, that's what I like, PHAT.* ☐ *PHAT is what it's all about.*

phazed AND **phased** [fezd] *mod.* intoxicated with marijuana. ☐ *Man, I was phazed out of my mind!* ☐ *How much booze does it take you to get really phased?*

phedinkus [fɪ'dɪŋkəs] *n.* nonsense. ☐ *Stop your silly phedinkus!* ☐ *That's just phedinkus. No one will believe you.*

phfft [ffft] **1.** *mod.* finished; done for. (See also *piffed.*) ☐ *There is my cat, and zoom comes a car. My cat is phfft.* ☐ *Yup. Deader than a doornail. Phfft!* **2.** *mod.* alcohol intoxicated. ☐ *You won't wake him up for hours yet. He's phfft.* ☐ *Three beers and she's phfft, for sure.*

Philly *n.* Philadelphia, Pennsylvania. ☐ *We stopped off in Philly for a day.* ☐ *We left Philly for the Big Apple at noon.*

phony **1.** *mod.* bogus; fake. ☐ *This money looks phony to me.* ☐ *I can't stand phony vanilla flavoring.* **2.** *n.* someone or something bogus. ☐ *That guy is a real phony!* ☐ *Look here, you phony, get out of my office!* ☐ *This is a phony. Get me a real one.* **3.** *n.* a phone call where the caller hangs up the minute the telephone is answered. ☐ *No one was on the telephone. It was just a phony.* ☐ *We have had phony after phony all evening.*

phony as a three-dollar bill AND **queer as a three-dollar bill** *mod. phony;* bogus. ☐ *This guy's as phony as a three-dollar bill.* ☐ *The whole deal stinks. It's as queer as a three-dollar bill.*

phooey AND **fooey** **1.** *n.* nonsense. ☐ *Your story is just a lot of phooey.* ☐ *I've heard* *enough fooey. Let's get out of here.* **2.** *exclam.* an expression of disgust, disagreement, or resignation. (Usually **Phooey!** or **Fooey!** Used typically when something smells or tastes bad.) ☐ *Who died in here? Phooey!* ☐ *This is the worst food I ever ate. Fooey!*

phumfed ['fəm(p)ft] *mod.* drug intoxicated. ☐ *You can't get your work done when you are totally phumfed.* ☐ *She gets phumfed on pot every afternoon.*

phutz AND **futz** [fəts] *tr.* to rob, swindle, or cheat someone. ☐ *Don't futz me! Tell the truth!* ☐ *The muggers phutzed his wallet and watch.*

pick-me-up *n.* any food or drink that boosts energy, such as a drink of liquor, candy, soda pop. ☐ *I'm pooped. I really need a pick-me-up.* ☐ *I can't finish the day without a little pick-me-up at lunch.*

pick up on something *in.* to become alert to something; to take notice of something; to learn or catch on to something. ☐ *She's real sharp. She picks up on everything.* ☐ *The cop picked up on the word "persuader."*

pickled *mod.* alcohol intoxicated. (Very common.) ☐ *She's usually pickled by noon.* ☐ *It only takes a few drinks to get him pickled.*

picklepuss *n.* a person who has a puckered up mouth; a child who is about to cry. ☐ *Don't be such a picklepuss. Smile!* ☐ *She is such a picklepuss. Nothing seems to please her.*

pickler *n.* a drunkard; an alcoholic. (See also *pickled.*) ☐ *What a pickler. He could drink all night.* ☐ *The cops brought in about thirty picklers last night.*

pickup **1.** *n.* something eaten or drunk to boost energy; a *pick-me-up.* ☐ *Bartender, I need a little pickup.* ☐ *She stopped at a candy machine for a pickup.* **2.** *n.* a sudden increase in something, such as speed or tempo in music. ☐ *We need a bit of a pickup at measure forty-three.* ☐ *There will be a pickup in sales during the Christmas season.* **3.** *mod.* spontaneous; unplanned. (Especially with ball games where the members of the team are "picked up" from whoever is available. Compare to *scratch.*) ☐ *He stopped at the basketball court for a pickup game with the boys.* ☐ *A pickup game can be fun if the sides are evenly matched.* **4.** *n.* an arrest. (Underworld.) ☐ *Send Sergeant Townsend out to make the pickup.* ☐ *The cop made a pickup right across the street.* **5.** *n.* someone whose acquaintance is made solely for sexual purposes. ☐ *She's no date. She's just a pickup.* ☐ *She had the gall to show up at the dance with a pickup in street clothes.* **6.** *n.* the power of a car's engine as reflected in the car's ability to reach a high speed quickly. ☐ *This car has more pickup than I really need.* ☐ *Little cars hardly ever have enough pickup.*

picky **1.** *mod.* choosy. ☐ *Don't be so picky. They're all the same.* ☐ *Red, blue, green! What's the difference? You are too picky.* **2.** *mod.* overly critical. ☐ *Complain, complain! What a picky old lady.* ☐ *I have to do it exactly right. My boss is very picky.*

picnic *n.* a good time; an easy time. ☐ *What a great class! Every day was a real picnic.* ☐ *Nothing to it. A real picnic.* ☐ *It wasn't a terrible day, but it was no picnic.*

piddle **1.** *in.* to urinate. (Said of children and pets.) ☐ *Mommy! Jimmy's got to piddle!* ☐ *Please, Jimmy, don't piddle on the floor.* **2.** *n.* urine. ☐ *Where's the dog? There's piddle on the carpet.* ☐ *Don't step in the puppy's piddle.* **3.** See *piddle (around).*

piddle (around) *in.* to waste time; to work aimlessly or inefficiently. ☐ *Stop piddling around! Get to work!* ☐ *Can't you get serious and stop piddling?*

piddler *n.* someone who wastes time. ☐ *Bob is such a piddler. He can't seem to get organized and get down to work.* ☐ *That piddler will never get anywhere in life.*

piddling *mod.* inadequate; meager; tiny. (Compare to *piss poor.* See also *piddle.*) ☐ *What a piddling amount of money! I can't live on that.* ☐ *That is a piddling steak. I want a big one.*

pie-eyed 1. *mod.* wide-eyed with amazement. □ *He didn't cry out. He just stood there pie-eyed.* □ *Why are all those people pie-eyed? What happened?* 2. *mod.* alcohol intoxicated. □ *That guy is really pie-eyed. Send him home.* □ *We've got a pie-eyed bus driver. I want to get off!*

pie in the sky 1. *n.* a reward; a special "heavenly reward." □ *Don't hold out for pie in the sky. Get realistic.* □ *If he didn't hope for some heavenly pie in the sky, he would probably be a real crook.* 2. *mod.* having to do with a hope for a special reward. (This is hyphenated before a nominal.) □ *Get rid of your pie-in-the-sky ideas!* □ *What these pie-in-the-sky people really want is money.*

piece 1. *n.* a sexually attractive (young) woman. (Crude.) □ *She's a real piece!* □ *Who's that piece I saw you with last night?* 2. *n.* a gun, especially a revolver. (Underworld.) □ *Is that guy carrying a piece?* □ *Okay, this gun is aimed at your head. Drop your piece.* 3. *n.* a tiny ponytail worn by males. □ *Even the little boys—six and seven years old—want to wear a piece.* □ *Tony pointed out that lots of pirates wore pieces.*

piece of cake 1. *n.* something easy to do. □ *No problem. When you know what you're doing, it's a piece of cake.* □ *Glad to help. It was a piece of cake.* 2. *exclam.* "It's a piece of cake!"; "It's easy!" (Usually **Piece of cake!**) □ *No problem, piece of cake!* □ *Rescuing drowning cats is my specialty. Piece of cake!*

piece (of the action) AND **bit of the action; slice of the action** *n.* a share in the activity or the profits. (Especially gambling activity.) □ *If you get in on that real estate deal, I want a piece, too.* □ *Deal Tom in. He wants a piece of the action.* □ *Don't be selfish. Give me a slice of the action.*

piffed [pɪft] 1. AND **pifted** ['pɪftəd] *tr.* killed. (Past tense only. See also *phfft.*) □ *He piffed his goldfish by mistake.* □ *The speeding car pifted the cat yesterday.* 2. AND **pifted** ['pɪftəd] *mod.* dead. □ *What will I do with a pifted cat?* □ *He's as piffed as they come.* 3. *mod.* alcohol intoxicated. (See also *piffled.*) □ *That guy is really piffed.* □ *How can anybody get that piffed on four beers?*

piffle ['pɪfl̩] 1. *n.* nonsense. □ *What utter piffle!* □ *The entire report was piffle from beginning to end.* 2. *exclam.* a mild exclamation or expression of distress. (Usually **Piffle!**) □ *You a stockbroker? Piffle!* □ *She finished her story, and I looked her straight in the eye and said, "Piffle!"*

piffled ['pɪfl̩d] *mod.* alcohol intoxicated. □ *Three glasses of booze and she was totally piffled.* □ *He was so piffled he couldn't talk!*

piff(l)icated ['pɪf(l)əkedəd] *mod.* alcohol intoxicated. □ *How can anybody drink so much and not get totally pifflicated?* □ *Get that pifficated stuffed shirt out of here!*

pifted See *piffed.*

pig (All senses are usually derogatory.) 1. *n.* someone who eats too much; a glutton. □ *Stop being a pig! Save some for other people.* □ *I try to cut down on calories, but whenever I see red meat I make a pig of myself.* 2. *n.* an ugly and fat woman. □ *Clare is a pig. Why doesn't she lose a ton or two?* □ *Every girl in that sorority is a pig.* 3. *n.* a dirty or slovenly person. □ *Max is a pig. I don't think he bathes enough.* □ *Jimmy, change your clothes. Look at that mud, you little pig!* 4. *n.* an officer; a police officer or a military officer. (Used mostly for a police officer. Widely known since the 1960's.) □ *The pigs are coming to bust up the fight.* □ *The pigs who aren't in pig heaven are driving around in pigmobiles busting innocent people like me.* 5. *n.* a Caucasian. (Black.) □ *Why do those pigs think they can walk in here like that?* □ *Who do those pigs think they are, tourists?*

pig heaven *n.* a police station. (Chiefly black.) □ *The man came and took my brother to pig heaven.* □ *All the bacon eventually goes home to pig heaven.*

pig out *in.* to overeat; to overindulge in food or drink. (Compare to *blimp out, mac out, pork out, scarf out.*) □ *I always pig out on Fridays.* □ *I can't help* *myself when I see ice cream. I have to pig out.*

pigeon 1. *n.* a *dupe;* a *sucker;* someone singled out to be cheated. (See also *patsy.*) □ *There's our pigeon now. Don't let him see us sizing him up.* □ *Be alert for pickpockets. Don't be some crook's pigeon.* **2.** *n.* a cute girl or woman. □ *What a cute little pigeon.* □ *Who was the dreamy little pigeon I saw you with last night?* **3.** See *stool (pigeon).*

pigeon-eyed *mod.* alcohol intoxicated. □ *How can anyone get so pigeon-eyed on so little booze?* □ *Who is that pigeon-eyed guy over there who is having such a hard time standing up?*

pighead *n.* someone who is both stupid and stubborn. (See also *pigheaded.*) □ *Stop acting like such a pighead!* □ *She'll never change her mind. She's a real pighead.*

pigheaded *mod.* stupidly stubborn. (From the notion that pigs are immovable.) □ *You are unbelievably pigheaded!* □ *What a stupid pigheaded position to take.*

pigmobile *n.* a police car. (See also *pig.*) □ *Look out, here comes the pigmobile.* □ *Hey, man! Have you ever ridden in a pigmobile?*

pigpen *n.* a crosshatch or octothorpe, "#." (Computers. See also *mesh.*) □ *Put a pigpen just after the gear.* □ *There is nothing on my printout but a whole string of pigpens.*

piker ['paɪkɚ] **1.** *n.* a miser; a *cheapskate.* (Also a term of address.) □ *You cheap little piker! Beat it!* □ *A 5 percent tip? You piker!* **2.** *n.* a lazy person; a shirker. □ *All right, you pikers. Pick up your shovels and get back to work.* □ *Come on, you lazy piker. There's plenty left for you to do.*

pile *n.* a large amount of money. □ *She really made a pile in the stock market.* □ *That old lady has a pile of money stashed in the bank.*

pileup *n.* a wreck; a vehicular crash where more than one vehicle is heavily damaged. □ *There is a serious pileup on the expressway.* □ *My car was ruined in a pileup on the highway.*

pilfered ['pɪlfɚd] *mod.* alcohol intoxicated. □ *I've had too much. I'm beginning to feel pilfered.* □ *That old boy is really pilfered.*

pill 1. *n.* a birth control pill. (Always with *the.*) □ *Is Sally on the pill?* □ *The pill has really changed my life.* **2.** *n.* a tobacco cigarette; a marijuana cigarette. □ *Hey, toss me a pill, huh?* □ *I'll trade you a pill for a match.* **3.** *n.* a drug in capsule form. □ *Stop taking those pills!* □ *The doctor prescribed these pills.* **4.** *n.* a football. □ *Hank tossed the pill to Wally, who promptly dropped it.* □ *Fred kicked the pill through the goal and won the game.*

pill-dropper See *pill-popper.*

pill freak See *pillhead.*

pill-peddler See *pill-pusher.*

pill-popper AND **popper; pill-dropper** *n.* anyone who takes pills frequently or habitually. □ *Poor Sue is a pill-popper.* □ *I knew she was always ill, but I didn't know she was a pill-dropper.* □ *The pill-popper thought she wouldn't get hooked.*

pill-pusher AND **pill-roller; pill-peddler** *n.* a nickname for a physician. □ *That pill-peddler charges too much.* □ *I went to the infirmary, but the pill-pusher wasn't in.*

pill-roller See the previous entry.

pillhead AND **pill freak** *n.* a drug user who prefers drugs in pill or capsule form. (Drugs.) □ *You pill freaks should try some of this stuff.* □ *I don't smoke. I'm strictly a pillhead.*

pillowed *mod.* pregnant. (Refers to the swelling in a pregnant woman's abdomen.) □ *She does look a bit pillowed, doesn't she?* □ *I think I'm more than a bit pillowed.*

pimp *n.* a man who solicits business for a prostitute. (Use caution with *pimp* and the topic.) □ *The guy with the diamond rings looks like a pimp.* □ *The cops took in three hookers and their pimp.*

pimpish ['pɪmpɪʃ] *mod.* flamboyant in dress and manner, as with a *pimp.* (Use caution with *pimp* and the topic.) □ *Where did you get that pimpish hat, Ron?* □ *Take the feathers off it, and it won't look quite so pimpish.*

pimpmobile *n.* a gaudy automobile, as might be driven by a *pimp.* (Use caution with *pimp.*) □ *You call that pimpmobile a car? Why all the chrome?* □ *He drove up in a pimpmobile and shocked all the neighbors.*

pimpstick *n.* a typical cigarette made by mass production. (Use caution with *pimp.* From an earlier time when *pimps* were likely to smoke machine-made cigarettes rather than the rugged roll-your-own type.) □ *Hey, chum. Why do you smoke those pimpsticks? Can't you roll one yourself?* □ *Real cowboys never smoke pimpsticks, and they don't have tattoos, either.*

pin 1. *n.* someone's leg. (Usually plural.) □ *My pins are a little wobbly.* □ *Stand up on your pins and speak your mind.* **2.** *n.* an important criminal leader. (From *kingpin.*) □ *The pin sent me. He says you're to come with me.* □ *The mob's getting careless. The cops think they caught the pin this time.*

pin someone's ears back 1. *tr.* to scold someone severely. □ *She really pinned his ears back.* □ *The teacher pinned the kids' ears back for chewing gum.* **2.** *tr.* to beat someone, especially about the head. □ *Lefty says I'm supposed to pin your ears back.* □ *You do something like that again, and I'll pin your ears back.*

pinch 1. *n.* a small amount of a powdered substance, such as salt, snuff, a spice, etc. (Not slang.) □ *He put a pinch under his lips and walked up to home plate.* □ *Do you have any oregano? I need a pinch.* **2.** *tr.* to arrest someone. □ *The cops pinched her in front of her house.* □ *The police captain pinched her for passing bad checks.* **3.** *n.* the arresting of someone. □ *They made the pinch in front of her house.* □ *The pinch was for forgery.* **4.** *tr.* to steal something. (See also *cop.*) □ *The kid pinched a candy bar right off the counter.* □ *I pinched these paper clips from my office.*

pinch hitter 1. *n.* a substitute batter in the game of baseball. □ *Sam is a pinch hitter for Ralph, who broke his wrist.* □ *Time to send in a pinch hitter.* **2.** *n.* any substitute person. □ *In school today we had a pinch hitter. Our teacher was sick.* □ *I want my own doctor, not a pinch hitter!*

pinched *mod.* arrested. (See also *cop, pinch.*) □ *I got pinched for speeding.* □ *Sam got pinched for a parole violation.*

pink elephants AND **pink spiders 1.** *n.* the delirium tremens. □ *He's screaming with pink elephants again.* □ *He was shaking something awful from the pink spiders.* **2.** *n.* hallucinatory creatures seen during the delirium tremens. □ *He said pink elephants were trying to kill him. He's really drunk.* □ *If you ever find yourself surrounded with pink elephants, you've got the D.T.s.* (More at *seeing pink elephants.*)

pink slip 1. *n.* a piece of paper giving notice of dismissal from employment; any dismissal from employment. □ *I got a pink slip today. I guess I had it coming.* □ *I hope I don't get a pink slip. I need this job.* **2.** *tr.* to dismiss someone from employment. □ *They pink slipped the whole office force today.* □ *If your work doesn't improve, I will be forced to pink slip you.* (More at *pink-slipped.*) **3.** *n.* a learner's permit for driving an automobile. (In some U.S. states.) □ *You can't even drive in your own driveway without a pink slip.* □ *He wrecked the car one day after getting his pink slip.*

pink-slipped *mod.* fired; dismissed from employment. □ *I guess I've done it. I'm pink-slipped.* □ *Now I'm a member of the young and pink-slipped crowd.*

pink spiders See *pink elephants.*

pinked *mod.* alcohol intoxicated; tipsy. □ *She's sitting there looking a bit pinked.* □ *I want to get pinked. Fill it up, bartender.*

pinkie See *(little) pinkie.*

pinko **1.** *n.* a communist. (Popular during the 1950's.) ☐ *Get out of here, you pinko!* ☐ *He called me a pinko, so I left.* **2.** *mod.* having communist tendencies; in the manner of a communist. ☐ *Get that pinko jerk out of here!* ☐ *Take your old pinko laws and go to hell.*

pinky See *(little) pinkie.*

pinned *mod.* arrested. (Underworld.) ☐ *The boys in blue pinned him and took him away.* ☐ *He had a gun in his belt when they pinned him.*

pinstriper *n.* a businessman or businesswoman wearing a pinstriped suit. (Compare to *suit, vest.*) ☐ *Who's the pinstriper driving the beemer?* ☐ *Wall Street is nothing but wall-to-wall pinstripers.*

pint-sized *mod.* small; miniature. ☐ *I won't fit into one of those pint-sized cars.* ☐ *My car is not pint-sized.* ☐ *Tell that little pint-sized guy to beat it.*

pip *n.* a pimple; a zit. ☐ *Good grief, I've got ear-to-ear pips!* ☐ *Do you ever outgrow pips?*

PIP [pɪp] *n.* "postindustrial person." (Acronym. Refers to a person as a member of a group that has become useless because of technological change.) ☐ *The world really doesn't really need more PIPs, except as consumers, of course.* ☐ *Not so! The world needs plenty of PIPs to pay taxes.*

pipe *n.* an easy course in school. ☐ *Take this course. It's a pipe.* ☐ *I don't want a full load of pipes. I want to learn something.*

pipe down *in.* to become quiet; to cease making noise; to shut up. (Especially as a rude command.) ☐ *Pipe down! I'm trying to sleep.* ☐ *Come on! Pipe down and get back to work!*

pipped (up) *mod.* alcohol intoxicated. ☐ *I'm not drunk. Just a little pipped up.* ☐ *She's pipped and ready to get sick.*

pipsqueak *n.* a small or timid man or boy. (Also a term of address.) ☐ *Shut up, you little pipsqueak, or I'll hit you.* ☐ *I may be a pipsqueak, but I am a gentleman.*

piss (All senses are potentially offensive. Use only with discretion.) **1.** *in.* to urinate. ☐ *He went out and pissed in the woods.* ☐ *Don't piss on the floor.* **2.** *n.* urine. ☐ *There's piss on the rug. Where's that cat?* ☐ *Hey, stupid! There's piss on your pants leg.* **3.** *n.* an act of urination. (Especially with *take.*) ☐ *He went out to take a piss.* ☐ *Man, I gotta stop here for a piss.*

piss-ant [ˈpɪsænt] **1.** *n.* an insignificant person. (Also a rude term of address. Regarded as impolite. A misunderstanding of French *pis-ant*, a "step ant." Use caution with *piss*, nonetheless.) ☐ *Get out of here, you little piss-ant.* ☐ *Tell that little piss-ant to come and see me.* **2.** *mod.* insignificant; unimportant. (Compare to *piss poor.*) ☐ *I don't have time for her little piss-ant problems.* ☐ *Take your piss-ant papers out of here and leave me alone.*

piss-ant around *in.* to move about in a timid fashion; to behave overly cautiously. (Potentially offensive. Use only with discretion.) ☐ *Don't just piss-ant around here. State your business or get out.* ☐ *Stop piss-anting around and get busy.*

piss elegant *mod.* falsely elegant; pretentious. (Crude. Potentially offensive. Use only with discretion.) ☐ *Here comes Paul in his piss elegant car.* ☐ *Do we have to go to a party at that piss elegant apartment with its corny decor?*

piss factory *n.* a saloon or a tavern. (Crude. Potentially offensive. Use only with discretion.) ☐ *What time did you leave that old piss factory?* ☐ *In my hometown there's a piss factory on every corner.*

piss poor *mod.* very inadequate. (Crude. An elaboration of *poor.* Potentially offensive. Use only with discretion.) ☐ *This is a piss poor excuse for fried chicken.* ☐ *It is really piss poor.* ☐ *That was a piss poor performance for a professional musician.*

piss someone off *tr.* to make someone angry. (Crude. Potentially offensive, even though it is widely used. Use only with discretion.) ☐ *She really pissed me off!* ⓣ *That's enough to piss off anybody.* (More at *pissed (off)*.)

pissed 1. *mod.* alcohol intoxicated. (Potentially offensive. Use only with discretion.) ☐ *He was really pissed.* ☐ *He was so pissed he could hardly stand up.* **2.** See *pissed (off)*.

pissed (off) *mod.* angry. (Crude. Potentially offensive, even though it is heard widely. Use only with discretion. Compare to *piss someone off*.) ☐ *I was so pissed off I could have screamed.* ☐ *He's come back, and he's sure pissed.*

pistol *n.* a person who is bright, quick, or energetic. (Implying "hot as a pistol" or "quick as a pistol.") ☐ *She's a bright kid. A real pistol.* ☐ *Ask that pistol to step over here for a minute, would you?*

pit stop 1. *n.* a pause in a journey (usually by car) to urinate. (From the name of a service stop in automobile racing.) ☐ *I think we'll pull in at the next rest area. I need a pit stop.* ☐ *Poor Max needs a pit stop every thirty miles.* **2.** *n.* an underarm deodorant. (Because it *stops* arm*pit* odor.) ☐ *Man, do you need some pit stop!* ☐ *Can I borrow your pit stop? I need it bad.*

PITA *n.* "pain in the ass." (Initialism. A computer abbreviation, not pronounced.) ☐ *The SYSOP here is a real PITA. I wish he would leave us alone.* ☐ *Who is the PITA who keeps asking the same question over and over?*

pitch a bitch *tr.* to make a complaint. (Crude.) ☐ *You really love to pitch a bitch, don't you? What makes you happy?* ☐ *Complain, complain! You could pitch a bitch all day long.*

pitch in (and help) *in.* to volunteer to help; to join in completing a task. ☐ *Come on, you guys! Pitch in.* ☐ *If more people would pitch in and help, we could get this job done in no time at all.*

pitch (the) woo *tr.* to kiss and caress; to woo (someone). (Old but still heard.) ☐ *They were out by the barn pitching woo.* ☐ *Old Ted can hardly see any more, but he can still pitch the woo.*

pits 1. *n.* the armpits. (Usually crude.) ☐ *Man, you have a problem in your pits.* ☐ *Who's got the smelly pits in here?* **2.** *n.* anything really bad. (Always with *the*.) ☐ *Life is the pits.* ☐ *This whole day was the pits from beginning to end.* **3.** *n.* the depths of despair. (Always with *the*. Often with *in* as in the example.) ☐ *It's always the pits with him.* ☐ *She's depressed and in the pits.*

pix [pɪks] *n.* pictures; photographs. ☐ *I got my pix back from the drugstore.* ☐ *Hold still and let me get your pix taken. Then you can jump around.*

pixilated AND **pixolated 1.** *mod.* bewildered. ☐ *That little old lady is pixilated.* ☐ *She seems a bit young to be so pixolated.* **2.** *mod.* alcohol intoxicated; tipsy. ☐ *She seems a bit pixilated. She's probably been drinking.* ☐ *Martha, you mustn't drive. I think you are pixilated.*

pixolated See the previous entry.

pizza-face See *crater-face*.

pizza-puss See *crater-face*.

pizzazz [pəˈzæz] *n.* punch; glitter and excitement. ☐ *Listen to the way she put pizzazz into that song!* ☐ *This script lacks pizzazz.*

P.J.s *n.* pajamas. (Initialism. Usually juvenile.) ☐ *Get your P.J.s on and get into bed right now.* ☐ *I can't find my P.J.s. Where are they?*

plant 1. *tr.* to strike a blow (to a particular place on someone). ☐ *I planted one right on his nose.* ☐ *The boxer planted a good blow on his opponent's shoulder.* **2.** *n.* a spy who secretly participates in criminal activities in order to inform on the criminals. ☐ *The crooks discovered the plant and fed him bogus information.* ☐ *Don't tell everything you know. You don't know who's a plant and who isn't.*

plant something on someone 1. *tr.* to hide incriminating evidence on a person for later discovery and use in prosecution. (Drugs. Allegedly a police practice used to entrap drug offenders. See also *flake.*) ☐ *The cops planted snow on Max and then arrested him for carrying it.* ☐ *Don't touch me! You'll plant something on me!* **2.** *tr.* to conceal narcotics or other contraband on an unsuspecting person for the purpose of smuggling. (This person will bear the risk of discovery and arrest.) ☐ *The crooks planted the stuff on a passenger, but couldn't find him when the plane landed.* ☐ *Someone had planted coke on me, and the airport security officer found it.*

plastered *mod.* alcohol intoxicated. ☐ *She's really plastered.* ☐ *She's so plastered she can't see.*

plastered to the wall *mod.* heavily alcohol intoxicated. (An elaboration of *plastered.*) ☐ *He's not just drunk; he's plastered to the wall!* ☐ *How can anybody get plastered to the wall on just four beers?*

plastic 1. *mod.* phony; false. ☐ *She wears too much makeup and looks totally plastic.* ☐ *I'm tired of living in such a plastic society.* **2.** *n.* a plastic credit card. ☐ *Our economy depends on plastic.* ☐ *I don't carry any cash, just plastic.* **3.** *mod.* having to do with credit cards and their use. ☐ *This plastic economy is dangerous.* ☐ *There is too much plastic debt in most households.*

plastic punk *n.* falsely stylish. ☐ *Most music videos are just plastic punk.* ☐ *Isn't all punk really plastic punk?*

plate See the following entry.

platter 1. AND **plate** *n.* home base or home plate in baseball. (Usually with *the.*) ☐ *The batter stepped up to the platter.* ☐ *The ump dusted off the plate.* **2.** *n.* a phonograph record. (Old but still heard.) ☐ *Now, here's an interesting platter.* ☐ *They call it a platter because it looks like a serving platter.*

play 1. *n.* a strategy; a plan of action. ☐ *That was a bad play, Bill. We lost the account.* ☐ *Here's a play that worked for us last year at this time.* **2.** *n.* an attractive investment; a way to make some money in the securities markets. ☐ *I just heard about a good play in the options market.* ☐ *Not talking it over with your friends first was a bad play.* ☐ *Buying bonds at a discount is an interesting play.*

play around (with someone) 1. *in.* to waste time; to waste someone's time. ☐ *Stop playing around and get to work.* ☐ *Don't play around with me!* **2.** *in.* to flirt or have an affair with someone. ☐ *Those two have been playing around for months.* ☐ *She only wants to play around with me.* **3.** *in.* to tease, deceive, or try to trick someone. ☐ *You're playing around with me. Leave me alone.* ☐ *Don't pay any attention to them. They're just playing around.*

play ball (with someone) *tr.* to cooperate with someone. ☐ *Are you going to play ball, or do I have to report you to the boss?* ☐ *You will be better off if you will play ball with me.*

play fast and loose (with someone or something) *in.* to treat someone or something carelessly or unfairly. ☐ *The broker played fast and loose with our money. Now we are nearly broke.* ☐ *He was playing fast and loose with his girl, so she left him.*

play for keeps *in.* to take serious and permanent actions. (Refers to playing a game where the money won is not returned at the end of the game.) ☐ *Wake up and face the fact that she's playing for keeps. She wants to get married.* ☐ *I always play for keeps.*

play freeze-out *tr.* to open windows and doors, or turn down a thermostat, making someone cold. (See also *freeze someone out.*) ☐ *Wow, it's cold in here! Who's playing freeze-out?* ☐ *Is someone trying to play freeze-out?*

play hardball (with someone) *tr.* to act strong and aggressive about an issue with someone. ☐ *Things are getting a little tough. The president has decided to play hardball on this issue.* ☐ *If he wants to play hardball with us, we can play that way, too.*

play hell with someone or something AND **play the devil with someone or something** *tr.* to cause difficulty for someone or something. ☐ *You know* *that this cake is going to play hell with my diet.* □ *Your decision plays hell with all my friends.*

play hooky [...'huki] *tr.* to not go to school; to not keep an appointment. □ *I played hooky today and did not go to work.* □ *Tommy is probably playing hooky from school again.*

play in the big leagues *in.* to become involved in something of large or important proportions. □ *You had better shape up if you want to play in the big leagues.* □ *The conductor shouted at the oboist, "You're playing in the big leagues now. Tune up or ship out."*

play it cool 1. *tr.* to do something while not revealing insecurities or incompetence. (See also *cool.*) □ *Play it cool, man. Look like you belong there.* □ *If the boss walks in, just play it cool.* **2.** *tr.* to hold one's temper. □ *Come on now. Let it pass. Play it cool.* □ *Don't let them get you mad. Play it cool.*

play someone for a fool *tr.* to treat someone like a fool; to act as if someone were a fool. □ *I know what you're trying to do. Don't try to play me for a fool.* □ *We played her for a fool, and she never knew it.*

play the devil with someone or something See *play hell with someone or something.*

play the dozens AND **shoot the dozens** *tr.* to trade insulting remarks concerning relatives with another person. (Chiefly black. See also *(dirty) dozens.*) □ *They're out playing the dozens.* □ *Stop shooting the dozens and go do your homework.*

play tonsil hockey *tr.* to kiss deeply, using the tongue. □ *Kids sit around in cars, playing tonsil hockey all evening.* □ *Sally's mother caught her playing tonsil hockey with George and grounded her.*

play with a full deck *in.* to operate as if one were mentally sound. (Usually in the negative. One cannot play cards with a partial deck.) □ *That guy's not playing with a full deck.* □ *Look sharp, you dummies! Pretend you are playing with a full deck.*

play with fire *in.* to do something dangerous or risky. □ *When you talk to me like that, you're playing with fire.* □ *Going out at night in a neighborhood like that is playing with fire.*

pleasantly plastered *mod.* mildly alcohol intoxicated; mellow with drink. (And elaboration of *plastered.*) □ *He wasn't really stoned. Just pleasantly plastered.* □ *I get to the point that I am pleasantly plastered, and then I stop.*

[please] See *Puh-leez!*

plonk *n.* white wine; cheap wine; any liquor. (From French *blanc*. See also *blank.*) □ *That plonk is really hard on the gut.* □ *How about a bottle of plonk?*

plonked (up) *mod.* alcohol intoxicated. (See also *plonk, blank.*) □ *He sure is plonked up.* □ *She is totally plonked.*

plonko *n.* a drunkard. (See also *plonk.*) □ *Get that smelly plonko out of here!* □ *He's a plonko if I ever saw one.*

plootered ['pludɚd] *mod.* alcohol intoxicated. □ *We went out and got totally plootered.* □ *How can anyone get so plootered on a bottle of wine?*

plop 1. *n.* the sound of dropping something soft and bulky, such as a hunk of meat. □ *When the roast fell on the floor, it made a nasty plop.* □ *When I heard the plop, I looked up and saw our dinner on the floor.* **2.** *tr.* to put or place something (somewhere). □ *I don't mind cooking a turkey. You only have to plop it in the oven and forget about it.* □ *I plopped my books on the table and went straight to my room.* **3.** *tr.* to sit oneself down somewhere; to place one's buttocks somewhere. (The *it* in the examples is the buttocks.) □ *Come in, Fred. Just plop it anywhere you see a chair. This place is a mess.* □ *Just plop it down right there, and we'll have our little talk.*

plotzed ['plɑtst] *mod.* alcohol intoxicated; really drunk. □ *They all came home plotzed.* □ *Two bottles and she was plotzed.*

plowed (under) *mod.* alcohol or drug intoxicated. ☐ *She was plowed under for a week.* ☐ *They went out and got ploughed.*

pluck AND **plug** *n.* wine; cheap wine. (Originally black.) ☐ *Where can I get some plug?* ☐ *You spilled plug all over my car seat.*

plug **1.** *n.* a bite-sized, pressed mass of chewing tobacco. ☐ *He put a plug in his cheek and walked away.* ☐ *Hey, gimme a piece of that plug!* **2.** *n.* a drink of beer; a *slug* of beer. ☐ *Let me have a plug out of that bottle.* ☐ *I just want a plug, not the whole thing.* **3.** *n.* a free advertisement or a commercial boost from someone for a product. (See also *plugola.*) ☐ *I managed to get a plug on the Mike Michael show.* ☐ *How about a free plug during your introduction?* **4.** *tr.* to give an advertisement or commercial boost for something without having to pay for it. ☐ *I want to get on that T.V. program and plug my new book.* ☐ *I can't plug your product until I have a sample I can test.* **5.** See *pluck.*

plug-ugly *mod.* very ugly. (Compare to *pug-ugly.*) ☐ *Your dog is just plug-ugly.* ☐ *My plug-ugly dog happens to be pedigreed.*

plugged in *mod.* excited by drugs; having to do with the drug culture; *turned on.* (Drugs.) ☐ *Those guys are really plugged in.* ☐ *That punker is plugged in, for sure.*

plugola [pləg'olə] *n.* a bribe paid to get a free advertising *plug* (worth far more than the amount of the bribe). ☐ *How much plugola did you have to pay for that mention?* ☐ *The announcer was charged with accepting plugola.*

plum *n.* a prize or reward; something that can be considered the spoils of a political office. ☐ *That appointment was quite a plum.* ☐ *My plum for getting elected was a big new office.*

plumb loco ['pləm 'loko] *mod.* completely crazy. (Folksy. *Loco* is from a Spanish word meaning mad.) ☐ *You're plumb loco if you think I'll go along with that.* ☐ *All those people were running around like they were plumb loco.*

PMJI *interj.* "Pardon me for jumping in." (This indicates that someone is responding to a message directed to someone else. Used in electronic mail and computer bulletin board messages. Not pronounced aloud.) ☐ *PMJI, but I have some information that would help you with your problem.* ☐ *PMJI. As long as we are talking about vacations, does anyone know the price of admission to EPCOT Center in Orlando, Florida?*

Podunk ['podəŋk] **1.** *n.* an imaginary rural town where everything and everyone is backward, old-fashioned, and inferior. ☐ *I don't want a job in Podunk.* ☐ *This is the big city, not Podunk.* **2.** *mod.* rural and backward. (Usually **podunk.**) ☐ *I want out of this podunk town.* ☐ *This podunk place is driving me crazy.*

poindexter ['poɪndɛkstɚ] *n.* a bookish person; a well-mannered good student, usually male. ☐ *Charles is a poindexter, but he's a good guy.* ☐ *I'm no poindexter. In fact, my grades are pretty low.*

point man **1.** *n.* a ballplayer who habitually scores points. ☐ *Fred is supposed to be point man for our team, but tonight he is not doing so well.* ☐ *Paul is our favorite point man.* **2.** *n.* anyone whose job it is to score successes against the opposition. ☐ *The president expects the secretary of defense to be point man for this new legislation.* ☐ *I am a diplomat, not a point man. Ask someone else to play your little games.*

pointy-head *n.* a studious thinker; an intellectual. (Compare to *conehead.*) ☐ *The pointy-heads seem to be living in a world of their own.* ☐ *Why do pointy-heads spend so much time arguing about nothing?*

poison **1.** *mod.* wicked; evil. ☐ *Stay away from her. She's poison.* ☐ *What a poison personality.* **2.** *n.* an alcoholic drink. ☐ *Name your poison.* ☐ *How about a drink of that poison there?*

poison pill *n.* an element introduced into the restructuring of a corporation so that it becomes undesirable for another corporation to take over. ☐

Acme Corporation approved a poison pill to prevent a hostile takeover. □ *Mr. Boone would have bought the company if it weren't for the poison pill.*

poke 1. *n.* a puff of a marijuana cigarette or pipe. (Drugs. Compare to *toke*.) □ *Can I have a poke of that?* □ *Hey! One poke is enough!* 2. *tr.* [for a male] to copulate (with a female). (Crude. Use caution with the topic.) □ *They say he poked her.* □ *Your dog poked my dog, then ran away.*

poky 1. *n.* jail; a jail cell. □ *She spent a day in the poky.* □ *Have you ever been in the poky?* 2. *mod.* slow; lagging and inefficient. □ *Hurry up! Don't be so poky.* □ *What a poky old horse.*

pol [pɑl] *n.* a politician. □ *The pols are spending my taxes like mad again.* □ *How many pols does a democracy require anyway?*

polecat *n.* a mean and deceitful person, usually male. (Folksy. *Polecat* is another U.S. word for skunk. See also *skunk, stinker*.) □ *You dirty polecat!* □ *Tell that polecat I want to talk to him.*

polished (up) *mod.* alcohol intoxicated. (See also *waxed*.) □ *One glass of that stuff and I was polished up.* □ *How much of that do I have to drink to get good and polished?*

polluted *mod.* alcohol or drug intoxicated. □ *Those guys are really polluted.* □ *Madam, you are polluted!*

pond scum *n.* a mean and wretched person; a worthless male. (Collegiate. An elaboration of *scum*, less crude than *scumbag*. Also a rude term of address.) □ *Tell that pond scum to beat it.* □ *Get your hands off me, you pond scum!*

poo 1. AND **poo-poo** *n.* fecal material. (See also *poop*. Mostly juvenile. Use caution with the topic.) □ *Don't step in that dog poo!* □ *There's poo on your shoe, I think.* 2. *in.* to defecate. (Use caution with the topic.) □ *That old dog pooed on our lawn.* □ *Don't let your dog poo here!* 3. *n.* nonsense. (From sense 1. See also *poo(h)-poo(h)*.) □ *Don't give me that poo!* □ *I've heard enough of your poo.* 4. *n.* champagne. (From shampoo.) □ *How about another glass of poo?* □ *Oh, I just love poo!* 5. See *poo(h)-poo(h)*.

poo-poo See the previous entry and *poo(h)-poo(h)*.

pooch *n.* a dog. (Also a term of address to a friendly dog.) □ *Hello, pooch. My goodness, you're friendly.* □ *Please take your pooch out of my garden.*

poo(h)-poo(h) [ˈpuˈpu] *tr.* to belittle someone or something. □ *He tends to pooh-pooh things he doesn't understand.* □ *Don't always poo-poo me when I express my opinions!*

poohead *n.* an obnoxious person. □ *Wally, don't be such a poohead!* □ *What poohead left the window open?*

pool-hopping *n.* sneaking into private or public swimming pools at night or during the off-hours. □ *The kids went pool-hopping, and one of them nearly drowned.* □ *Pool-hopping is illegal.*

poop 1. *n.* information; the detailed knowledge of something. □ *What's the poop on the broken glass in the hall?* □ *Tell me all the poop.* 2. *n.* fecal matter. (Use caution with the topic. See also *poo*.) □ *Don't step in the poop.* □ *There's poop on the sidewalk.* 3. *in.* to defecate. □ *Your dog pooped on my lawn.* □ *I tried to chase the cat away while it was pooping.*

poop out *in.* to quit; to wear out and stop. □ *He pooped out after about an hour.* □ *I think I'm going to poop out pretty soon.* (More at *pooped (out)*.)

poop sheet *n.* a sheet containing information. □ *Where is the poop sheet on today's meeting?* □ *You can't tell one from the other without a poop sheet.*

pooped (out) 1. *mod.* exhausted; worn out. (Said of a person or an animal.) □ *I'm really pooped out.* □ *The horse looked sort of pooped in the final stretch.* 2. *mod.* alcohol intoxicated. □ *How much of that stuff does it take to get pooped?* □ *He's been drinking all night and is totally pooped out.*

pooper-scooper *n.* a device used to pick up and carry away dog feces from public places. ☐ *I never leave home without my pooper-scooper.* ☐ *Tracy actually got a ticket for walking her dog without a pooper-scooper in sight!*

poophead *n.* a person who acts very stupidly. (Also a term of address.) ☐ *Sometimes you act like such a poophead.* ☐ *Look here, poophead, you're making a fool of yourself.*

poopied *mod.* alcohol intoxicated. (A euphemism for *shit-faced.*) ☐ *She was so poopied that she giggled all the way home.* ☐ *They got real poopied last night.*

poor-mouth 1. *tr.* to speak ill of someone. (See also *bad-mouth.*) ☐ *Please don't poor-mouth my brother.* ☐ *There's no need to poor-mouth your clothing.* **2.** *in.* to speak repeatedly of how little money one has; to plead poverty. ☐ *She's got money, but she's always poor-mouthing anyway.* ☐ *Spend more time looking for a job and less time poor-mouthing.*

pop 1. *tr.* to hit or strike someone. ☐ *Please don't pop me again.* ☐ *She popped him lightly on the shoulder.* **2.** *mod.* popular. ☐ *This style is very pop.* ☐ *I don't care for pop stuff.* **3.** *n.* popular music. ☐ *I like most pop, but not if it's too loud.* ☐ *Pop is the only music I like.* **4.** *n.* a time; a try; a piece. (Always with *a.*) ☐ *Twenty dollars a pop is too much.* ☐ *I love records, but not at $15.98 a pop.* **5.** *tr.* to take or swallow a pill, tablet, or capsule. ☐ *Here, pop a couple of these.* ☐ *He pops uppers from dawn to dusk.*

pop-eyed *mod.* alcohol intoxicated, with bulging eyes. ☐ *What's he been drinking? He's pop-eyed as hell.* ☐ *She drank until she was totally pop-eyed.*

pop for something *in.* to pay for a treat (for someone). (See also *spring for something.*) ☐ *Let's have some ice cream. I'll pop for it.* ☐ *It's about time you popped for coffee.*

pop off 1. *in.* to make an unnecessary remark; to interrupt with a remark; to sound off. ☐ *Please don't pop off all the time.* ☐ *Bob keeps popping off when he should be listening.* **2.** *in.* to lose one's temper. (Compare to *pop one's cork.*) ☐ *Now, don't pop off. Keep cool.* ☐ *I don't know why she popped off at me. All I did was say hello.* **3.** *in.* to die. ☐ *My uncle popped off last week.* ☐ *I hope I'm asleep when I pop off.* **4.** *in.* to leave; to depart in haste. ☐ *Bye, I must pop off.* ☐ *Got to pop off. I'm late.*

pop one's cork *tr.* to release one's anger; to *blow one's top.* ☐ *I'm just about to pop my cork.* ☐ *She tried to hold it back, but suddenly she popped her cork.*

pop (some) tops *tr.* to drink beer. ☐ *Wanna go out tonight and pop some tops?* ☐ *We are going to pop tops and watch the B-ball game.*

pop the question *tr.* [for a man] to ask a woman to marry him. (Could also be used by a woman asking a man.) ☐ *She waited for years for him to pop the question.* ☐ *Finally she popped the question.*

pop wine *n.* a cheap, flavorful, sparkling wine drink. ☐ *Even if you don't like fine wines, you'll like pop wine.* ☐ *They were drinking pop wine like it was water.*

popped 1. *mod.* arrested. (Similar to *busted.*) ☐ *Tom got popped for speeding.* ☐ *He was popped for hardly anything at all.* **2.** *mod.* alcohol or drug intoxicated. ☐ *She looks glassy-eyed because she's popped.* ☐ *They went out last night and got good and popped.*

popper 1. AND **popsie** *n.* an ampoule of amyl nitrite, a drug that is inhaled when the ampoule is broken. (Drugs.) ☐ *You got a popper I can have?* ☐ *He had a popsie in his pocket that broke when he sat down.* **2.** See *pill-popper.* **3.** *n.* a handgun. (Underworld. From the sound of a gunshot.) ☐ *He carries a popper under his coat.* ☐ *It's illegal to carry a popper in this state.* **4.** *n.* a can of beer (in a pop-top can). ☐ *Hey, toss me a popper, Fred!* ☐ *You ready for another popper, Tom?*

popping *in.* happening. ☐ *Is anything popping around here?* ☐ *Things are always popping at the gym.*

poppycock *n.* nonsense. (From Dutch.) □ *I've heard enough of your poppycock.* □ *That's nothing but poppycock.*

pops *n.* one's father; any older man. (Also a term of address.) □ *Hey, pops! How you doing?* □ *Well, pops, what do you think?*

popsie See *popper.*

popskull *n.* fiery liquor; inferior whiskey; *moonshine.* □ *This popskull will burn a hole in you.* □ *Where is that jug of popskull?*

pork 1. *n.* the police in general; a *pig.* (Underworld.) □ *Keep an eye out for the pork.* □ *The pork hauled all of them to the station.* **2.** *tr. & in.* to copulate (with someone). (Potentially offensive. Use only with discretion.) □ *He's telling everybody that he porked her.* □ *They pork all the time, just like bunnies.*

pork out *in.* to overindulge in food and drink. (A play on *pig out.*) □ *Whenever I see french fries, I know I'm going to pork out.* □ *We porked out on pizza.*

porker *n.* a fat person. □ *Sally is not exactly a porker, but she is not skinny either.* □ *I was a porker until I started exercising.*

porky *mod.* fat; obese; pig-like. □ *You are beginning to look a little porky.* □ *See that porky man over there?*

posse ['pɑsi] *n.* the group of teenagers or children that one plays with or hangs out with. □ *Hank and his posse are in the backyard playing.* □ *A whole posse of kids just ran through my flower garden.*

pot 1. *n.* a toilet. (Usually with *the.*) □ *Jimmy's on the pot, Mommy.* □ *Where's the pot around here?* **2.** *n.* a drinking vessel. (Old but still heard.) □ *How about a pot of beer?* □ *Care for another pot?* **3.** *in.* to drink heavily; to use a *pot* (sense 2) to excess. □ *He's been potting since dusk.* □ *Let's sit here and pot for a while.* **4.** *n.* a vessel, hat, basket, etc., used to collect or receive contributions. □ *Please pass the pot.* □ *How much is left in the pot?* **5.** *n.* a sum of money collected; a pool of money. □ *Clare won the whole pot.* □ *How large is the pot this month?* **6.** *n.* cannabis; marijuana. (Originally drugs, now widely known.) □ *She had pot on her when she was arrested.* □ *The cops found pot growing next to city hall.*

pot boiler *n.* a book or other literary work of no value except for the money it earns. □ *I can write one pot boiler every six months or so.* □ *Can you produce anything but pot boilers?*

pot hound AND **pot sniffer** *n.* a dog trained to sniff out cannabis. (Drugs.) □ *The pot hound at the airport is always busy finding marijuana.* □ *How do they train pot sniffers to find cannabis?*

pot party *n.* a communal marijuana smoking session; a party where marijuana is smoked. (Drugs.) □ *I didn't know you were taking me to a pot party!* □ *There was a bust at Max's pot party.*

pot sniffer See *pot hound.*

potato *n.* the head. □ *I got a nasty bump on my potato.* □ *Put your hat on your potato, and let's get out of here.*

potato soup *n.* vodka. □ *Have a bit of this potato soup, why don't you?* □ *Those Russians make fine potato soup.*

potatohead *n.* a stupid person. (Compare to *potato.*) □ *Stop acting like a potatohead.* □ *Look, potatohead, go home!*

potbelly *n.* a big belly. □ *He got a potbelly from eating fried chicken.* □ *Everyone in her family has a potbelly.*

potshot *n.* a sharp criticism; a wild shot of criticism. (Usually with *take.*) □ *Please stop taking potshots at me!* □ *He took a potshot at my old car.*

potty 1. *n.* a small toilet. (Usually juvenile.) □ *Mommy, I've got to go to the potty.* □ *I need to use the potty.* **2.** *in.* to use the toilet. (Always juvenile.) □ *I've got to potty.* □ *Be sure to potty before we leave.* **3.** *mod.* crazy. □ *She is acting a little potty.* □ *Who is that potty old man?* □ *He got more potty as he grew older.*

potty mouth AND **toilet mouth** *n.* someone who uses obscene or profane language in most social settings. (Also a term of address.) ☐ *That potty mouth is offending people again.* ☐ *Hey, toilet mouth! Cool it!*

pound *tr.* to drink something quickly. (See also *pound a beer*.) ☐ *Dan said he could pound the cup of coffee in thirty seconds.* ☐ *You don't have to pound your milk. Take your time.*

pound a beer AND **pound some beers; hammer a beer; hammer some beers; slam a beer; slam some beers** *tr.* to drink a beer; to drink a beer fast. ☐ *On a hot day like this, I want to go home and pound a beer.* ☐ *Let's go down to the tavern and pound some beers.* ☐ *We went out and hammered some beers.*

pound one's ear *tr.* to sleep. ☐ *I've got to spend more time pounding my ear.* ☐ *She went home to pound her ear an hour or two before work.*

pound some beers See *pound a beer*.

pound someone's head in *tr.* to beat someone. ☐ *Talk nice to him, or he'll pound your head in.* ☐ *I was afraid that the cop was going to pound my head in.*

pound something out **1.** *tr.* to play something loudly on the piano, perhaps with difficulty. ☐ *Here, pound this one out. A little softer, please.* [T] *She was pounding out a nice little tune.* **2.** *tr.* to type something on a typewriter. ☐ *I have finished writing it. Can I borrow your typewriter so I can pound it out?* [T] *All the reporters were pounding out stories for the next edition of the paper.*

pound the books See *hit the books*.

pounder *n.* a police officer; a cop on the beat. ☐ *The pounder gave me a parking ticket.* ☐ *Most pounders get sore feet.*

pounds *n.* dollars; money. ☐ *How many pounds does this thing cost?* ☐ *I don't have any pounds on me.*

pour cold water on something *tr.* to put an end to something; to dampen something. ☐ *I hate to pour cold water on your plan, but it won't work.* ☐ *I wanted to go to the party, but my brother poured cold water on that by taking the car.*

pow-wow **1.** *n.* a meeting; a conference. (From an Amerindian word.) ☐ *There's a big pow-wow about money at the home office.* ☐ *Let's have a pow-wow on that issue.* **2.** *in.* to hold a meeting or a conference. ☐ *Let's pow-wow on that tomorrow.* ☐ *The senators were pow-wowing on how to get the law passed.*

powder monkey *n.* a specialist in the use of dynamite. (See also *grease monkey*.) ☐ *I won't stay around while the powder monkey is working.* ☐ *How long do powder monkeys usually live?*

powder one's face See the following entry.

powder one's nose AND **powder one's face** *tr.* to depart to the bathroom. (Usually said by women, or jocularly by men.) ☐ *Excuse me, I have to powder my nose.* ☐ *She just went out to powder her face.*

powder room **1.** *n.* a small bathroom without bathing facilities in a private home, usually located for the convenience of guests. ☐ *Can I use your powder room?* ☐ *Excuse me, where is the powder room?* **2.** *n.* the ladies' restroom in a public place, especially a restaurant; the place women go to powder their noses. (The emphasis is on comforts other than toilet facilities, such as mirrors, places to rest, and even a maid to help with emergency repairs of makeup or clothing.) ☐ *The ladies went to the powder room. They'll be back in a minute.* ☐ *She went to the powder room to clean the spill off her dress.*

powder up *in.* to drink heavily; to get drunk. ☐ *Let's go out and powder up.* ☐ *He's at the tavern powdering up.*

powdered (up) *mod.* alcohol intoxicated. ☐ *Those guys are powdered up.* ☐ *Most of the bums in the gutter are really powdered.*

power hitter *n.* a batter in the game of baseball who can hit the ball great distances. ☐ *Ted is a real power hitter. They'll try to walk him.* ☐ *I'm no power hitter, but I can run like mad.*

powerhouse *n.* a very big strong person, usually a male. □ *Ted is a real powerhouse. I'd hate to have him mad at me.* □ *Each member of the football team is a powerhouse.*

power tool *n.* a student who studies most of the time. (An elaboration of *tool.*) □ *Willard is a power tool if there ever was one. Studies most of the night.* □ *All the power tools always get the best grades.*

pratfall *n.* a fall on the buttocks; a stage fall on the buttocks. □ *I took a pratfall right on the sidewalk.* □ *If you want to be in musical comedy, you should learn to take a pratfall.*

prat(t) *n.* the buttocks. □ *Get out before I kick you in the pratt.* □ *Your father will spank your prat.*

pray to the enamel god See the following entry.

pray to the porcelain god AND **pray to the enamel god** *in.* to empty one's stomach; to vomit. (Refers to being on one's knees [praying] in front of a porcelain toilet bowl.) □ *Boy, was I sick. I was praying to the porcelain god for two hours.* □ *Wayne was in the john, praying to the enamel god.* □ *I think I'd better go home and pray to the porcelain god.*

prayerbones *n.* the knees. □ *Okay, down on your prayerbones.* □ *He pushed one of his prayerbones into my gut.*

preemie *n.* a premature baby. (Medical.) □ *There were two preemies born today.* □ *I was a preemie.*

preg *mod.* pregnant. □ *Doesn't Sally look a little preg?* □ *Nobody is ever just a little preg.*

prelims *n.* preliminary examinations. (Collegiate.) □ *I hope I pass my prelims.* □ *What do you have to do to get the degree after you pass your prelims?*

preppie AND **preppy** **1.** *mod.* in the manner of a student at a preparatory school. □ *I just love your preppy coat.* □ *Preppy clothes are almost out of style.* **2.** *n.* a young person who dresses and acts like a student at a preparatory school. □ *Those preppies are having fun now, but how will they support themselves?* □ *Do all preppies become yuppies?*

preppy See the previous entry.

preserved *mod.* alcohol intoxicated. (See also *pickled.*) □ *He's really preserved.* □ *He drank a quart of vodka and is totally preserved.*

press (the) flesh *tr.* to shake hands. (See also *flesh-presser.*) □ *Hey, chum! Glad to press flesh with you!* □ *He wanted to press the flesh, but I refused even to touch him.*

press the panic button See *hit the panic button.*

pretty *mod.* very. □ *Bob's a pretty nice guy.* □ *I'm pretty busy at the moment.*

pretty penny *n.* a sizeable amount of money. □ *I imagine that your jacket cost you a pretty penny.* □ *This watch cost me a pretty penny, and I intend to take care of it.*

prexy *n.* a president. □ *The prexy broke the tied vote.* □ *This year's prexy will retire in March.*

pric(e)y *mod.* expensive. □ *This stuff is too pricey.* □ *That's a pretty pricy car.* □ *Do you have anything less pricy?*

primed *mod.* alcohol or drug intoxicated. □ *The entire fraternity got primed.* □ *The whole college was primed by midnight.*

primo ['primo] **1.** *mod.* great; first-class. □ *This pizza is really primo.* □ *Sally is primo. You can't do better than Sally.* **2.** See *(el) primo.*

Prince Albert *n.* cannabis in general, especially marijuana sold or transported in a Prince Albert™ pipe tobacco can. (From the 1960's, but still heard.) □ *I've heard that Max smokes Prince Albert.* □ *Where can I get a can of Prince Albert?*

prior *n.* a prior arrest. (Underworld.) □ *This guy has about fifteen priors.* □ *Have you ever had a prior, young man?*

private eye *n.* a detective who is licensed to work privately rather than for a police department. □ *I worked for a* *while as a private eye.* □ *The cops don't like private eyes much.*

privy *n.* an outdoor toilet; any toilet. □ *Uncle Paul was out in the privy.* □ *Where's the privy around here?*

pro 1. *n.* a "professional" (at anything); someone as good as a professional. □ *I'm a pro at photography.* □ *When it comes to typing, he's a pro.* **2.** *mod.* professional. □ *I hope to play pro ball next year.* □ *This is not what I'd call a pro hammer.* **3.** *n.* a prostitute. □ *Do you think she's a pro or just overly friendly?* □ *This pro comes up to me and acts like she's met me before.*

prod 1. *n.* a reminder. □ *She gave me a little prod about the report that is due Monday.* □ *Call me up and give me a little prod so I won't forget.* **2.** *tr.* to remind someone (about something). □ *Call me up and prod me just before the due date.* □ *Stop prodding me about these minor matters.*

prof *n.* a professor. (Collegiate.) □ *The prof was dull and the room was hot, and I kept closing my eyes.* □ *Who's the prof for that course?*

(pro)file *in.* to walk about and show something off; to walk carefully in a way that gets attention. (As if showing one's profile.) □ *Look at Albert profiling along! What a nerd.* □ *All those guys are filing and styling like they were a bunch of peacocks.*

pronto *mod.* fast; immediately. (From Spanish. Common in Western movies.) □ *You get over here, pronto.* □ *I want to see you in my office, pronto.*

proofed See *carded.*

prostie See the following entry.

prosty AND **prostie** *n.* a prostitute. □ *The cops haul in about forty prosties a night from that one neighborhood alone.* □ *This one prosty was high on something and started screaming.*

pseudo ['sudo] *mod.* false; bogus. □ *This is a very pseudo position that you are taking.* □ *She is just too pseudo.* □ *What a pseudo hairdo!*

psych out *in.* to have a nervous or emotional trauma; to go mad for a brief time. (Compare to *freak (out).*) □ *Another day like this one and I'll psych out for sure.* □ *He looked at the bill and psyched out.*

psych someone out *tr.* to try to figure out what someone is likely to do. □ *Don't try to psych me out.* Ⓣ *The batter tried to psych out the pitcher, but it didn't work.*

psych someone up *tr.* to get someone excited or mentally prepared for something. □ *I psyched myself up to sing in front of all those people.* Ⓣ *The coach psyched up the team for the game.* (More at *psyched (up).*)

psyched (out) 1. *mod.* excited; overwhelmed; thrilled. □ *She's really psyched out.* □ *That's great. I'm really psyched!* □ *What a psyched out way to talk!* **2.** *mod.* alcohol or drug intoxicated. (Drugs.) □ *She's just lying there psyched out.* □ *Two beers and a red devil and he was psyched out.*

psyched (up) *mod.* completely mentally ready (for something). □ *I'm really psyched for this test.* □ *The team isn't psyched up enough to do a good job.*

psycho *n.* a psychopathic person; a crazy person. □ *Get that psycho out of here!* □ *Pat is turning into a real psycho.*

ptomaine-domain AND **ptomaine-palace** ['tomen . . .] *n.* any institutional dining facility; a mess hall; a cafeteria. □ *I can't stand the food at the ptomaine-domain.* □ *Time to go over to the ptomaine-palace and eat—if you can call it that.*

ptomaine-palace See the previous entry.

puddinghead *n.* someone, usually a male, who acts very stupid. □ *Please stop being such a puddinghead.* □ *That puddinghead sold my antique table for junk!*

puddle jumper *n.* a small airplane. □ *I'm not going to fly 200 miles in that puddle jumper!* □ *My uncle has his own puddle jumper.*

puff *in.* to get drunk. □ *Those guys go out and puff every Friday night.* □ *I've been puffing since dinnertime, and I'm done.*

puffer *n.* a cigar. ☐ *Who's smoking that foul puffer?* ☐ *Can you imagine anyone smoking a puffer like that in a restaurant?*

pug-ugly **1.** *mod.* having to do with a very ugly person. ☐ *He is so pug-ugly.* ☐ *What a pug-ugly cat you have there!* **2.** *n.* a very ugly person. (Also a rude term of address.) ☐ *Ask that pug-ugly to leave. He will frighten the children.* ☐ *Hey, pug-ugly, try plastic surgery!*

puggled **1.** *mod.* exhausted; bewildered. ☐ *I have had a long day, and I'm really puggled.* ☐ *Who is that puggled old man?* **2.** *mod.* alcohol intoxicated. ☐ *When he started pouring his drink down his collar, I knew he was puggled.* ☐ *The whole gang got puggled last night.*

Puh-leez! [pəə 'liiiz] *exclam.* "Please!"; "That is enough! You can't expect me to accept that!" (A long drawn-out way of saying *Please!* The tone of voice shows exasperation and disgust. The spelling is highly variable.) ☐ *I am the one who's at fault? Puuuleeeze!* ☐ *Puh-leez! Don't try to make me believe that!*

puke [pjuk] **1.** *in.* to empty one's stomach; to vomit. ☐ *I think I am going to puke.* ☐ *Max went home and puked for an hour.* **2.** *n.* vomit. ☐ *There's puke on the floor!* ☐ *Good grief, Tom. Is that puke on your shoe, or what?* **3.** *n.* a disgusting person. ☐ *I can't stand that puke!* ☐ *Make that puke get out of here, or I will scream!*

puke hole ['pjuk . . .] **1.** *n.* a tavern. ☐ *Let's go in this puke hole and get a cold one.* ☐ *Carl spends almost every evening at the local puke hole.* **2.** *n.* a toilet. ☐ *Max tried to flush the dope down the puke hole, but the cops caught him.* ☐ *Who didn't flush the puke hole?* **3.** *n.* a mouth. (Rude.) ☐ *Shut your puke hole and listen to what I am telling you!* ☐ *Do you want me to punch you in the puke hole?*

pukes *n.* the feeling of nausea; the feeling of impending vomiting. (Especially with *have, get*. Always with *the*.) ☐ *Oh my God, I've got the pukes.* ☐ *I hate having the pukes.*

pukey AND **pukoid** *mod.* disgusting; repellent. ☐ *Who is that pukey looking guy?* ☐ *Gosh, it's pukoid!* ☐ *What a pukey day!*

pukish *mod.* nauseated. (Folksy.) ☐ *Oh, I feel so pukish.* ☐ *That old pukish feeling came over me, and I just let go.*

pukoid See *pukey*.

pull **1.** *n.* a drink; a *swig;* a drink from a flask. ☐ *He took another pull and kept on talking.* ☐ *Can I have a pull?* **2.** *tr.* to take a drink or a mouthful of liquor from a bottle or other container. ☐ *He pulled a slug from the bottle.* ☐ *She pulled a mouthful and then spat it out.* **3.** *n.* a mouthful of smoke from a cigarette; a *drag* on a cigarette. ☐ *A couple of pulls and she crushed out the cigarette.* ☐ *After a big pull, she blew an enormous smoke ring.* **4.** *tr.* to smoke a cigarette. ☐ *He pulled a long filter job and then went back to work.* ☐ *He stopped for a minute and pulled one.* **5.** *in.* to *pull one's punches.* (Martial arts.) ☐ *See, he pulled just at the last minute.* ☐ *If you pull during a fight, you're through as a fighter.*

pull a boner *tr.* to make a silly error. (See comment at *boner.*) ☐ *That was dumb. You really pulled a boner.* ☐ *Tom is always pulling boners.*

pull a fast one *tr.* to outwit or outsmart someone by a clever and timely maneuver. ☐ *Don't try to pull a fast one on me.* ☐ *So you think you can pull a fast one?*

pull a job *tr.* to carry out a crime, especially a robbery. (Police and underworld. Note the variations in the examples.) ☐ *Max decided that it was not a good time to pull a bank job.* ☐ *Bruno and Max left town after they pulled the job.*

pull an attitude *tr.* to be haughty; to put on airs. ☐ *Don't pull an attitude with me, chum!* ☐ *Mary pulled an attitude and sat around pouting all evening.*

pull down an amount of money *tr.* to earn a stated amount of money. ("An amount of money" is expressed as a figure or other indication of an actual amount.) ☐ *She pulls down about $40,000 a year.* ☐ *They pull down pretty good salaries.*

pull jive *tr.* to drink liquor. (See also *jive.*) ☐ *Let's go pull jive for a while.* ☐ *Don't you ever do anything but pull jive?*

pull one's belt in (a notch) See *take one's belt in (a notch).*

pull one's punches **1.** *tr.* to pull back during a boxing punch just before the full force of a blow is felt; to land lighter blows than normal upon an opponent. (Boxing and related sports.) ☐ *The boxer started pulling his punches, and the ref ended the fight.* ☐ *He got fined for pulling his punches.* **2.** *tr.* to hold back in one's criticism; to attenuate the intensity of one's remarks. (Also with *any* in the negative.) ☐ *I won't pull my punches with you. This is lousy.* ☐ *He never pulls any punches. He always talks straight.*

pull out all the stops *tr.* to use everything available; to not hold back. (Refers to pulling out all of the stops on an organ so that it will sound as loud as possible.) ☐ *Then the mayor decided to pull out all the stops.* ☐ *Don't pull out all the stops in the first round. Wait till he's tired in the third and clobber him good.*

pull someone's leg *tr.* to kid someone; to tease someone. ☐ *They're just pulling your leg. Relax!* ☐ *Stop it! I don't believe you! You're pulling my leg.*

pull something off *tr.* to make something happen. ☐ *I didn't think he could pull it off.* 🅃 *It takes a lot of skill to pull off something like that.*

pull the plug (on someone or something) *tr.* to put an end to someone or something as a problem; to defuse a problem caused by someone or something. (As if one were disconnecting an electrical appliance.) ☐ *It's time to pull the plug on this problem.* ☐ *I've heard enough from Mr. Jones. It's time to pull the plug on him.*

pummelled *mod.* alcohol intoxicated. (Collegiate.) ☐ *Can you imagine getting pummelled on peppermint schnapps?* ☐ *They get pummelled every Friday night.*

pump **1.** *tr.* to press someone for an answer or information. ☐ *Pump him until he talks.* ☐ *Don't pump me! I will tell you nothing!* **2.** *n.* the heart. (See also *ticker.*) ☐ *He has the pump of a forty-year-old.* ☐ *My pump's getting sort of weak.* **3.** *n.* a pumped up muscle. (Bodybuilding.) ☐ *Look at the size of that pump.* ☐ *He's tired and can't quite make a pump.*

pump ship **1.** *tr.* to urinate. (Crude. From an expression meaning to pump the bilge water from a ship.) ☐ *He stopped and pumped ship right in the alley.* ☐ *I'll be with you after I pump ship.* **2.** *tr.* to empty one's stomach; to vomit. (Crude. Less well known than the previous sense.) ☐ *After I pumped ship, I felt better.* ☐ *Oh, man! I think I gotta pump ship!*

pump (some) iron *tr.* to lift weights. ☐ *Andy went down to the gym to pump some iron.* ☐ *Mary's hobbies are pumping iron and running.*

pump (someone) up *tr.* to excite someone; to make someone enthusiastic. ☐ *The coach gave a pep talk to pump the players up for the big game.* ☐ *Tom pumped us up at the sales meeting.*

pump something up *tr.* to flex and tense a muscle until it is expanded to its fullest size, as with thighs and forearms. (Bodybuilding.) ☐ *He really can pump up his pecs.* 🅃 *She pumped up her thighs and struck a pose.*

pumped **1.** *mod.* pregnant; impregnated. (Crude.) ☐ *She was so pumped, she was out to here.* ☐ *Look at her! She's pumped and looks due any minute.* **2.** See *pumped (up).*

pumped (up) *mod.* excited; physically and mentally ready. (Sports.) ☐ *The team is really pumped up for Friday's game.* ☐ *She really plays well when she's pumped!*

punch-drunk AND **punchy** *mod.* unstable; stupid acting; bewildered. (From a term describing a boxer suffering from brain damage.) □ *I feel sort of punch-drunk after a roller coaster ride.* □ *Who is that punchy jerk?* □ *I feel punchy when I drink too much coffee.*

punch someone out *tr.* to knock someone out. (See also *punch someone's lights out*.) □ *He threatened to punch me out.* 🅃 *The thug punched out the cop and ran down an alley.*

punch someone's lights out *tr.* to knock someone out; to close someone's eyes with a hard blow. □ *Shut up, or I'll punch your lights out.* □ *He threatened to punch my lights out.* 🅃 *You want me to punch out your lights?*

punchy See *punch-drunk*.

punk 1. AND **punk kid** *n.* an inexperienced boy or youth. (Derogatory. Also a term of address.) □ *Ask that punk to come over here.* □ *Look here, punk, I need some help.* **2.** *n.* a petty (male) hoodlum; a (male) juvenile delinquent. □ *We know how to deal with punks like you.* □ *The jails are packed with crooks who were just punks a few years ago.* **3.** *mod.* poor; dull and inferior. □ *The party turned punk, and we left.* □ *This is pretty punk food.* **4.** *mod.* having to do with *punkers* or their music. □ *I am tired of your red punk hair. Try it brown for a change.* □ *This music sounds too punk for me.*

punk kid See the previous entry.

punk out 1. *in.* to chicken out. □ *He was supposed to ask her out, but he punked out at the last minute.* □ *Come on! Stick with it! Don't punk out!* **2.** *in.* to become a *punker*. □ *If I punked out, my parents would probably clobber me.* □ *If my kids ever punked out and looked like that, I think I'd clobber them.*

punker *n.* a *punk* rocker; a young person who dresses in the style of *punk* rockers. □ *It's not safe to walk on the street with all those weird punkers out there.* □ *The punkers don't even have a sense of rhythm.*

punt [pənt] *in.* to do something different in a pinch; to improvise. (From the act of kicking the ball in order to gain ground in football.) □ *When all else fails, punt!* □ *Everyone expected me to lose my temper, so I punted. I cried instead of getting mad.*

puppy 1. *n.* a *wimp*; a softie. □ *That silly puppy is still waiting outside your door.* □ *Oh, Paul, you're such a puppy!* **2.** *n.* a thing; a piece or part of something. □ *Put this little puppy right here.* □ *Where is that puppy?*

puppy love *n.* mild infatuation; infatuation as in a crush. □ *Is it really love or just puppy love?* □ *Look at them together. It may be puppy love, but it looks wonderful.*

pure and simple *mod.* basically; simply; essentially. □ *Max is a crook, pure and simple.* □ *It's a pure and simple fact. The guy is a bum.*

purr (like a cat) *in.* [for an engine] to run well and smoothly. □ *My car really purred after I got it tuned up.* □ *New spark plugs and this old heap will really purr like a cat.*

push 1. *tr.* to approach a particular age (in years). □ *She looked like she was pushing forty-eight or fifty.* □ *He's only pushing thirty, but he looks much older.* **2.** *in.* to recruit new drug users and sell drugs to them; to deal in drugs. □ *He was pushing for two years before the cops got him.* □ *Man, look at that guy push. He hooks two new kids every day.* **3.** *tr.* to *hype* something or someone; to pressure something or someone. □ *She's always pushing her own interests.* □ *The clerk was pushing one brand so hard that I finally bought it.*

push money *n.* extra money paid to a salesperson to sell certain merchandise aggressively. (See also *spiff*.) □ *The manufacturer supplied a little push money that even the store manager didn't know about.* □ *I got about $300 last month in push money for selling some low-grade sweaters.*

push off AND **shove off** *in.* to leave. (As if one were pushing away from a dock.) □ *Well, it looks like it's time to push off.* □ *It's time to go. Let's shove off.*

push the panic button See *hit the panic button.*

pushed 1. *mod.* alcohol intoxicated. ☐ *Tom is a little pushed and can't walk very straight.* ☐ *How can you be so pushed on so little booze?* **2.** *mod.* addicted to a drug. (Drugs. See also *push.*) ☐ *He's pretty pushed, and he needs some stuff now!* ☐ *He used H. for years before he really got pushed.*

pusher *n.* a drug dealer who works hard to establish new addicts and customers. (Drugs. See also *push.*) ☐ *That pusher over on Eighth Street was just mobbed by a group of angry parents.* ☐ *They said that pushers should be locked up forever.*

pushing up daisies *mod.* dead and buried. (Folksy. Usually in the future tense.) ☐ *I'll be pushing up daisies before this problem is solved.* ☐ *If you talk to me like that again, you'll be pushing up daisies.*

pushy *mod.* very aggressive in dealing with other people. ☐ *Stop being so pushy! Who do you think you are?* ☐ *Who is that pushy dame?* ☐ *If she weren't so pushy, she would get more cooperation.*

puss [pus] *n.* the face. ☐ *I ought to poke you right in the puss!* ☐ *Look at the puss on that guy! What an ugly face!*

pussycat 1. *n.* a woman or young woman; one's girlfriend. (Also a term of address.) ☐ *Hi, pussycat. Don't I know you from somewhere?* ☐ *Who was that yummy pussycat I saw you with last Friday?* **2.** *n.* a timid male; a mild-mannered and passive male. ☐ *That guy is a wimp, a real pussycat.* ☐ *He seems mean, but underneath he's a pussycat.*

pussyfoot (around) *in.* to behave in a very cautious manner; to (metaphorically) tread softly; to hedge or equivocate. ☐ *Come on and say what you mean! Stop pussyfooting.* ☐ *You can depend on the mayor to pussyfoot around while the crisis is on.*

put a con on someone *tr.* to attempt to deceive someone; to attempt to swindle someone. (Underworld.) ☐ *Don't try to put a con on me, Buster! I've been around too long.* ☐ *I wouldn't try to put a con on you. I'm not that dumb.*

put a damper on something *tr.* to reduce the intensity of something, such as a problem. ☐ *The death of the chief put a damper on the ceremony.* ☐ *I hate to put a damper on your party, but you are too loud!*

put a smile on someone's face *tr.* to please someone; to make someone happy. ☐ *We are going to give Andy a pretty good raise, and I know that'll put a smile on his face.* ☐ *I was able to pay a few dollars down, and that put a smile on the clerk's face.*

Put a sock in it! See *Stuff a sock in it!*

put balls on something *tr.* to make something more masculine or powerful; to give something authority and strength. (Potentially offensive. Use only with discretion.) ☐ *Come on, sing louder. Put some balls on it.* ☐ *This story is too namby-pamby. Put some balls on it.*

put-down *n.* an insult; an intentionally cruel and deflating insult. ☐ *Another put-down like that and I'm going home.* ☐ *Don't cry. It was just a little friendly put-down.*

put on the dog AND **put on the ritz** *tr.* to make things extra special for a special event. ☐ *Frank's really putting on the dog for the big party Friday night.* ☐ *They really put on the ritz for us.*

put on the feedbag AND **put on the nosebag; tie on the nosebag** *tr.* to prepare to eat; to eat a meal. (Refers to a bag of feed tied under a horse's mouth.) ☐ *I'm starved. Must be time to put on the feedbag.* ☐ *Let's go tie on the nosebag. It's nearly noon.*

put on the nosebag See the previous entry.

put on the ritz See *put on the dog.*

put one's nose in (where it's not wanted) AND **stick one's nose in (where it's not wanted)** *tr.* to interfere in someone else's business. ☐ *Why do you always* *have to stick your nose in?* ☐ *Please don't put your nose in where it's not wanted!*

put oneself straight *tr.* to take a needed dose of drugs. (Drugs. See also *straight.*) ☐ *I gotta get some stuff and put myself straight.* ☐ *Here take this and put yourself straight.*

put some distance between someone and someone or something *tr.* to lengthen the distance or time between oneself and someone or something (including a place). ☐ *I gotta put some distance between me and that cop, fast.* ☐ *You need to put some distance between you and your brother's death.* ☐ *She needed enough money to put some distance between herself and her hometown.*

put some sweet lines on someone See *lay some sweet lines on someone.*

put someone on **1.** *tr.* to tease or deceive someone innocently and in fun. ☐ *Come on! You're just putting me on!* ☐ *He got real mad even though they were only putting him on.* **2.** *tr.* to introduce someone to cannabis use, usually smoking. (Drugs.) ☐ *Where did you get that stuff? Who put you on?* ☐ *My brother uses it, and he put me on.*

put someone or something away **1.** *tr.* [with *someone*] to put someone in prison for a long time. (Underworld.) ☐ *They put Max away for fifteen years.* 🅃 *The judge put away the whole gang.* **2.** *tr.* [with *someone*] to knock someone unconscious. ☐ *One tap on the head and I put him away.* ☐ *The cowboy slugged the rancher in the jaw and put him away for a while.* **3.** *tr.* [with *something*] to eat something. ☐ *Are you going to put this cake away?* 🅃 *Did you put away that whole pizza?*

put someone or something out of the way **1.** *tr.* to remove someone or something as a barrier. ☐ *I will put the whole problem out of the way.* ☐ *Yes, she is a problem, but you'll just have to put her out of the way and concentrate on this issue.* **2.** *tr.* [with *someone*] to kill someone. ☐ *The crooks tried to put the witness out of the way.* ☐ *Sorry, my friend, we no longer need you. Bruno is going to have to put you out of the way.*

put someone to bed with a shovel *tr.* to bury someone; to kill and bury someone. ☐ *Shut up! You want me to put you to bed with a shovel?* ☐ *The leader of the gang was getting sort of tired and old, so one of the younger thugs put him to bed with a shovel.* (More at *put to bed with a shovel.*)

put someone up *tr.* to provide someone with temporary shelter; to let someone stay the night. ☐ *Can you put me up for a few days?* 🅃 *I could put up a football team, there's so much room here.*

put someone's nose out of joint *tr.* to cause someone to feel slighted; to cause someone to take offense. (See also *get one's nose out of joint.*) ☐ *I'm sorry we didn't invite you. We didn't mean to put your nose out of joint.* ☐ *Now, now, that shouldn't put your nose out of joint. We're sorry.*

put something on the street *tr.* to make something known publicly; to tell everyone one's troubles. ☐ *Man, can't you keep a secret? Don't put everything on the street.* ☐ *She gets a little problem, and she puts it on the street right away!*

Put that in your pipe and smoke it! *exclam.* "Take that!"; "See how you like that!" ☐ *Everybody thinks you're a phony! Put that in your pipe and smoke it!* ☐ *You are the one who made the error, and we all know it. Put that in your pipe and smoke it!*

put the arm on someone **1.** *tr.* to demand something of someone, especially money. ☐ *I know Tom wants some money. He put the arm on me, but I said no.* ☐ *She put the arm on her roommate for a loan.* **2.** *tr.* to arrest someone. (Underworld.) ☐ *They put the arm on Max for pushing pills.* ☐ *They're gonna put the arm on the whole gang at once.*

put the bite on someone *tr.* to try to get money out of someone. ☐ *You're always putting the bite on me for a few bucks. Go away.* ☐ *Don't put the bite on me. I'm broker than you are.*

put the chill on someone AND **put the freeze on someone** *tr.* to ignore someone. ☐ *She was pretty snooty till we all put the chill on her.* ☐ *Let's put the freeze on Ted until he starts acting better.*

put the finger on someone *tr.* to identify someone (for someone else, such as the police). (Underworld.) ☐ *The old lady put the finger on the punk who mugged her.* ☐ *Tyrone put the finger on the killer, then got out of town fast.*

put the freeze on someone See *put the chill on someone.*

put the heat on someone See *put the screws on someone.*

put the kibosh on something *tr.* to squelch something. ☐ *The mayor put the kibosh on the whole deal.* ☐ *Tom was starting his presentation when Bob put the kibosh on the plan.*

put the moves on someone *tr.* to attempt to seduce someone. (With *any* in the negative.) ☐ *At least he didn't try to put any moves on me.* ☐ *If somebody doesn't try to put the moves on her, she thinks she's a failure.*

put the pedal to the metal *tr.* to press a car's accelerator to the floor; to floor it. ☐ *Let's go, man. Put the pedal to the metal.* ☐ *Put the pedal to the metal, and we're out of here.*

put the screws on someone AND **put the heat on someone; put the squeeze on someone** *tr.* to pressure someone; to threaten someone to achieve something. ☐ *He told everything about the plan when they put the screws on him.* ☐ *The cops put the squeeze on Harry, and he spilled the beans.*

put the skids under someone or something *tr.* to cause someone or something to fail. (See also *on the skids.*) ☐ *The mayor put the skids under my plan.* ☐ *Tom tried to talk, but the boss put the skids under him.*

put the squeeze on someone See *put the screws on someone.*

put to bed with a shovel 1. *mod.* dead and buried. (From *put someone to bed with a shovel.*) ☐ *You wanna be put to bed with a shovel? Just keep talking that way.* ☐ *Poor old Jake. He was put to bed with a shovel last March.* **2.** *mod.* alcohol intoxicated. (From sense 1.) ☐ *He wasn't just tipsy. He was put to bed with a shovel!* ☐ *Dead drunk? Yes, put to bed with a shovel.*

put to it *mod.* in trouble or difficulty; hard up (for something such as money). (As if one's back were put to the wall.) ☐ *Sorry, I can't lend you anything. I'm a bit put to it this month.* ☐ *What a day. I'm really put to it.*

put-up job *n.* a deception; a deceptive event. ☐ *That's really phony. A put-up job if I ever saw one.* ☐ *No put-up job is clever enough to fool me.*

Put up or shut up! *exclam.* "Speak now or remain silent for good!" ☐ *I'm tired of your whining. What's your problem? Put up or shut up!* ☐ *Now is your chance. Put up or shut up!*

Put your money where your mouth is! *exclam.* "Stop talking big and make a bet!" (From gambling. Can also be said to someone giving investment advice.) ☐ *You want me to bet on that horse? Did you? Why don't you put your money where your mouth is?* ☐ *If this is such a good stock, you buy it. Put your money where your mouth is!*

putrid *mod.* alcohol intoxicated. (See also *rotten.*) ☐ *That guy is stinking drunk. Putrid, in fact.* ☐ *They went out last night and got putrid.*

putt-putt *n.* a small motorized vehicle, especially a small car. ☐ *I hear him coming in his putt-putt now.* ☐ *That's not a motorcycle; it's just a little putt-putt.*

puttyhead *n.* a stupid person. (As if the person's head were soft as putty. Also a term of address.) ☐ *Look, you silly puttyhead, shut up!* ☐ *Stop acting like a puttyhead.*

putz [pəts] **1.** *n.* a penis. (Yiddish. Use caution with *putz* and topic.) ☐ *Tell him to cover his putz and run and grab a towel.* ☐ *He told some joke about a* *putz, but nobody laughed.* **2.** *n.* a stupid person, typically a male; a *schmuck.* (Yiddish. Also a rude term of address.) □ *And this stupid putz just stood there smiling.* □ *Tell that putz to leave his card with the secretary.*

putz around [pəts . . .] *in.* to fiddle around; to mess around. (See also *putz.*) □ *Stop putzing around and get to work.* □ *Those guys spend most of their time just putzing around.*

Q

Q. *n.* a quart bottle of liquor. (An abbreviation.) □ *While you're there, get me a Q. of whiskey.* □ *She can knock off a Q. a day.*

Q-sign *n.* the rounded, open mouth of a dead person with the tongue hanging out like the tail of a capital Q. (A semi-jocular usage. Hospitals. See also *O-sign.*) □ *The old lady in the corner room is giving the Q-sign.* □ *I can't handle another Q-sign today.*

quack *n.* a fraudulent physician; a derogatory term for a physician. □ *I won't go back to that quack ever again!* □ *Tell that quack to heal himself!*

quaff a brew ['kwɑf ə 'bru] *tr.* to drink a beer. (See also *brew.*) □ *I went down to the bar to quaff a brew.* □ *Let's go somewhere and quaff a brew.*

quail *n.* any girl or woman, especially considered sexually. (Crude.) □ *Look at that cute little quail over there.* □ *Who was the quail I saw you with last night?*

qual [kwɑl] *n.* qualitative analysis. (Scientific.) □ *We'll have to turn to qual for that answer.* □ *She worked in qual for a while and then went on to management.*

quality Joe *n.* an innocent or straight (male) person. (Underworld.) □ *Lefty is not what I would call your average quality Joe.* □ *These quality Joes just don't understand how it is on the street.*

quan See the following entry.

quant 1. AND **quan** *n.* quantitative analysis. (Scientific and collegiate.) □ *I didn't study enough for my quant test.* □ *I flunked quan twice.* **2.** *n.* a technician who works in securities market analysis. □ *He was a quant on Wall Street for two years.* □ *The quants have been warning us about the danger for a month.*

quarterback *tr.* to manage, lead, or direct someone or something. □ *Who is going to quarterback this organization after you go?* □ *I quarterbacked the whole company for more years than I care to remember.*

quartzed *mod.* alcohol intoxicated. (Related to *stoned (out).*) □ *She is really quartzed!* □ *How can anybody get so quartzed on a bottle of wine?*

Que pasa? [ke 'pɑsə] *interrog.* "Hello, what's going on?" (Spanish.) □ *Hey, man! Que pasa?* □ *What's happening? Que pasa?*

queen *n.* a homosexual male. □ *Tom is getting to be such a queen.* □ *What kind of a queen is Tom?*

queer 1. *mod.* counterfeit. □ *This bill is queer.* □ *I don't want any queer money.* **2.** *n.* illicit liquor, especially whiskey. (Prohibition era.) □ *Can you get me a bottle of queer?* □ *This isn't queer; it's left over from before prohibition.* **3.** *mod.* alcohol intoxicated. □ *After a glass or two, he got a little queer.* □ *She was so queer she could hardly stagger home.* **4.** *tr.* to spoil something. □ *Please don't queer the deal.* □ *I was afraid his dirty look would queer his chances.* **5.** *mod.* homosexual. (Derogatory. Potentially offensive. Use only with discretion. Resented by homosexuals.) □ *Who is that queer character?* □ *Isn't he queer?* □ *She doesn't like being called queer.* **6.** *n.* a homosexual male, occasionally a female. (Derogatory. Usually offensive. Use only with discretion. Resented by homosexuals.) □ *Tell that queer to get out of here.* □ *She came to the dance with a queer.*

queer as a three-dollar bill 1. *mod.* See *phony as a three-dollar bill.* **2.** *mod.* definitely or obviously homosexual. (Usually derogatory. Potentially offensive. Use only with discretion. Resented by homosexuals.) □ *That guy is as queer as a three-dollar bill.* □ *He's wearing makeup. He's queer as a three-dollar bill.*

queer-beer 1. *n.* bad beer; beer of low alcohol content. □ *I hate this queer-beer. Get out the good stuff.* □ *Please don't serve me any of your queer-beer.* **2.** *n.* any strange person. (Also a term of address.) □ *Look, queer-beer, stop that right now!* □ *What does that queer-beer think he's doing?* **3.** *mod.* having to do with homosexuals; homosexual. (Usually derogatory. Resented by homosexuals.) □ *I won't wear that queer-beer outfit!* □ *Don't call me a queer-beer fruitcake!* **4.** *n.* a homosexual male, possibly a female. (See sense 3.) □ *They say she's a queer-beer.* □ *That queer-beer is staring at you.*

queer fish *n.* a strange person; an aloof person. □ *She's a bit odd. Sort of a queer fish.* □ *He's a queer fish. Don't you agree?*

queer for something *mod.* in the mood for something; desiring something. □ *I'm queer for a beer right now.* □ *She's queer for him because of his money.*

queered *mod.* alcohol intoxicated. (In the sense "made bogus.") □ *I feel sort of queered.* □ *How can anybody get so queered on two beers?*

quencher ['kwɛntʃɚ] *n.* a drink of liquor or beer. □ *I could really use a quencher about now.* □ *How about a nice cold quencher?*

quetch See *kvetch.*

quick-and-dirty *mod.* rapidly and carelessly done. □ *I'm selling this car, so all I want is a quick-and-dirty repair job.* □ *They only do quick-and-dirty work at that shop.*

quick buck AND **fast buck** *n.* a quickly or easily earned profit. □ *I'm always on the lookout to make a fast buck.* □ *I need to make a quick buck without much effort.*

quick fix 1. *n.* a quick and probably none too permanent or satisfactory solution to a problem. □ *The quick fix isn't good enough in this case.* □ *He's a master of the quick fix.* **2.** *mod.* having to do with a temporary or unsatisfactory solution or repair. (Usually **quick-fix.**) □ *Frank is a master of the quick-fix solution.* □ *This is no time for quick-fix efforts.*

quick one AND **quickie** *n.* a quick drink of booze; a single beer consumed rapidly. □ *I could use a quick one about now.* □ *I only have time for a quickie.*

quicker than hell *mod.* very fast. □ *You get over here quicker than hell.* □ *Be careful in the stock market. You can lose all your money quicker than hell.*

quickie See *quick one.*

quimp [kwɪmp] *n.* a total *jerk;* a social outcast. (Also a term of address.) □ *I don't want to live in a dorm full of quimps.* □ *Who is the quimp who packed this thing wrong?*

quit while one is ahead *in.* to stop doing something while one is successful. □ *When will I learn to quit while I'm ahead?* □ *Get into the market. Make some money and get out. Quit while you're ahead.*

quitter *n.* someone who gives up easily. □ *Don't be a quitter. Get in there and finish the job.* □ *Dave has a reputation as a quitter.*

quote, unquote *phr.* a parenthetical expression said before a word or short phrase indicating that the word or phrase would be in quotation marks if used in writing. □ *So I said to her, quote, unquote, it's time we had a little talk.* □ *I think my quote, unquote reputation is ruined.*

R

R. & R. *n.* "rest and recuperation"; "rest and relaxation." (Originally military.) □ *I could use about three years of R. & R. after that battle.* □ *I'll need a lot of R. & R. to recover from that stuff they fed us.*

rabbit food *n.* lettuce; salad greens. □ *I think I need a little more rabbit food in my diet.* □ *Rabbit food tends to have a lot of vitamin C.*

rabbit punch *n.* a quick little punch. (Boxing and general slang.) □ *That couldn't have hurt you! It was just a little rabbit punch.* □ *She battered him with about forty rabbit punches on the arm. Boy, is he ever sore!*

rack **1.** *n.* a bed. □ *I need some more time in the rack.* □ *You don't get to see the rack very much in the army.* **2.** See *rack (out).*

rack duty See *rack time.*

rack (out) *in.* to go to sleep or to bed. (See also *rack.*) □ *What time do you rack out?* □ *I've got to rack out or drop from exhaustion.* □ *If I don't rack by midnight, I'm dead the next day.*

rack something up **1.** *tr.* to accumulate something; to collect or acquire something. □ *They all racked a lot of profits up.* 🅃 *We racked up twenty points in the game last Saturday.* **2.** *tr.* to wreck something. □ *Fred racked his new car up.* 🅃 *He racked up his arm in the football game.*

rack time AND **rack duty** *n.* time spent in bed. (Military.) □ *I need more rack time than I'm getting.* □ *I was on rack duty for my entire leave.*

rack up *in.* to become alcohol intoxicated. □ *Let's go down to the tavern and rack up.* □ *I think I'll rack up.* (More at *racked (up).*)

racked (up) *mod.* alcohol or drug intoxicated. (See also *rack up.*) □ *They drank till they were good and racked.* □ *Man, are you racked. What did you drink? A gallon?* □ *They all got racked up last weekend.*

racket **1.** *n.* noise. □ *Cut out that racket! Shut up!* □ *Who's making all that racket?* **2.** *n.* a deception; a *scam.* □ *He operated a racket that robbed old ladies of their savings.* □ *This is not a service station; it's a real racket!* **3.** *n.* any job. □ *I've been in this racket for twenty years and never made any money.* □ *I'm a stockbroker. What's your racket?*

rad [ræd] **1.** *n.* a radical person. (California.) □ *He's such a rad! For sure!* □ *My brother is a rad, but he's a good guy.* **2.** *mod.* great; wonderful; excellent; exciting. (California. From *radical.*) □ *Oh my God, that's, like, really rad!* □ *What a rad swimsuit!*

radical *mod.* great; excellent. (California.) □ *It's so, like, radical!* □ *My boyfriend, he's, like, so radical!*

radioland *n.* an imaginary place where radio listeners dwell. □ *Hello out there in radioland. This is Martin Jones speaking.* □ *All you folks in radioland who enjoy country music will like this next one.*

rag **1.** *n.* a newspaper. □ *I'm tired of reading this rag day after day. Can't we get a different paper?* □ *What a rag! It's only good for putting in the bottom of bird* *cages!* **2.** *n.* ugly or badly styled clothing; an ugly garment. ☐ *I can't wear that rag!* ☐ *I need some new clothes. I can't go around wearing rags like these.* ☐ *I wouldn't be seen in last season's rags.* **3.** *n.* any clothing, even the best. (Always plural.) ☐ *Man, I got some new rags that will knock your eyes out!* ☐ *You got soda pop all over my new rags!*

rag on someone AND **rake on someone** *in.* to bother someone; to irritate someone; to criticize and humiliate someone. ☐ *I wish you would stop ragging on me. I don't know why you are so annoyed at me.* ☐ *Stop raking on me!*

rag out *in.* to dress up. ☐ *I like to rag out and go to parties.* ☐ *I hate to rag out. I like comfortable clothes.*

rage 1. *n.* the current fad; an irresistible fad. (Always with *the;* often with *all the.* Old but recurrent.) ☐ *Get a haircut like mine! It's all the rage!* ☐ *One rage after another. Can't I find something that will stay the same for a while?* **2.** *in.* to *party;* to celebrate. (Collegiate.) ☐ *Man, are we going to rage tonight!* ☐ *Fred and Mary were raging over at the frat house last weekend.*

ragtop *n.* a convertible car. ☐ *The ragtop is making a comeback.* ☐ *I wanted a ragtop, but they cost nearly $3,000 more.*

ragweed *n.* inferior marijuana. (Drugs.) ☐ *This stuff is ragweed. You can have it!* ☐ *Max just sells ragweed except to his friends.*

rah-rah ['rɑ'rɑ] *mod.* having to do with college and college enthusiasm. ☐ *That gal is so rah-rah. What energy!* ☐ *It was sort of a rah-rah party.*

railroad tracks 1. *n.* dental braces. ☐ *I can't smile because of these railroad tracks.* ☐ *My railroad tracks cost nearly $1,200.* **2.** *n.* rows of needle scars on the veins of the arms. ☐ *Look at those railroad tracks on his arm. That means he shoots drugs.* ☐ *Max has railroad tracks on both arms.*

rails *n.* powdered cocaine arranged into lines. (Drugs.) ☐ *Max makes the rails too messy.* ☐ *Max put the rails on something smooth.*

rain on someone or something See the following entry.

rain on someone's parade AND **rain on someone or something** *in.* to spoil something for someone. ☐ *I hate to rain on your parade, but your plans are all wrong.* ☐ *She really rained on our parade.* ☐ *Did anyone rain on the meeting?*

rain pitchforks *tr.* to rain very hard and heavy. ☐ *It rained pitchforks all day long.* ☐ *Every time I go out to rake leaves, it rains pitchforks.*

rainbow *n.* a bowlegged person. (Also a rude term of address.) ☐ *Hey, rainbow! Are you a cowboy?* ☐ *Ask that rainbow if he has to have special trousers made.*

raise a stink (about someone or something) AND **make a stink (about someone or something)** *tr.* to make a big issue about someone or something. ☐ *You can depend on Fred to raise a stink.* ☐ *I hope you don't plan to make a stink about the problem.*

raise Cain [. . . ken] *tr.* to make a lot of trouble; to *raise hell.* ☐ *Fred was really raising Cain about the whole matter.* ☐ *Let's stop raising Cain.*

raise hell 1. *tr.* to make a lot of trouble; to go on a rampage. ☐ *Stop raising hell so much of the time!* ☐ *Quiet! Don't raise hell around here.* **2.** *tr.* to go on a drinking spree and get drunk. ☐ *Let's go out and really raise hell.* ☐ *The boys went out to raise hell.*

raise hell (with someone or something) See the following entry.

raise the devil (with someone or something) AND **raise hell (with someone or something) 1.** *tr.* [with *someone*] to confront someone and complain or scold. ☐ *I really raised the devil with my brother for being late.* ☐ *It won't do any good to raise hell with me.* **2.** *tr.* [with *something*] to cause trouble with something. ☐ *That idea raises hell with my plan.* ☐ *The onions raised the devil with my stomach.*

rake on someone See *rag on someone.*

rake something in *tr.* to take in a lot of something, usually money. □ *Our candidate will rake votes in by the thousand.* Ⓣ *They were raking in money by the bushel.*

rally ['ræli] **1.** *n.* get-together of some kind; a party, usually informal, possibly spontaneous. □ *There's a rally over at Tom's tonight.* □ *The rally was a flop. Everyone left early.* **2.** *in.* to hold a get-together of some kind; to *party.* (Collegiate.) □ *Let's rally tonight about midnight.* □ *They rallied until dawn.*

ralph AND **rolf** [rælf AND rɔlf] *in.* to empty one's stomach; to vomit. (Teens and collegiate. See also *cry ruth.*) □ *She went home and ralphed for an hour.* □ *I think I'm going to rolf.*

ralph something up *tr.* to vomit (something). (Teens and collegiate.) □ *The doctor gave him some stuff that made him ralph it up.* Ⓣ *He ralphed up his dinner.*

ram something down someone's throat *tr.* to force something upon someone. (Not literal.) □ *Don't try to ram that nonsense down my throat.* □ *They're always trying to ram something down our throats.*

rambo(ize) ['ræmbo(aɪz)] *tr.* to (figuratively) annihilate someone or something; to harm someone or something. (Collegiate. From the powerful film character Rambo.) □ *The students ramboed the cafeteria, and the cops were called.* □ *Please don't rambo the other team. Just win the game.*

rammy ['ræmi] *mod.* sexually excited or aroused. (Refers to the ram, a symbol of arousal.) □ *Fred was looking a little rammy, so I excused myself and left.* □ *Your rammy boyfriend is on the telephone.*

ramrod *tr.* to lead something; to act as the driving force behind something. □ *Who is going to ramrod this project?* □ *Don't ramrod us into something we don't really want.*

randy ['rændi] *mod.* sexually excited or aroused. □ *The town is full of randy sailors when the fleet's in.* □ *Wow, does he look randy!* □ *There is a randy looking guy at the door asking for you.*

rank *tr.* to give someone a hard time; to *hassle* someone. □ *Stop ranking me!* □ *The dean was ranking the boys for pulling the prank.* □ *When he finished with the boys, he started ranking their parents.*

rank and file *n.* the common members of something. □ *What will the rank and file think of the proposal?* □ *The rank and file will vote on it tomorrow.*

rank on someone *in.* to attack someone verbally; to gossip about someone. □ *Please stop ranking on my family!* □ *Tom keeps ranking on Jennifer, and she is really mad about it.*

rank someone (out) *tr.* to annoy or chastise someone. (Compare to *rank.*) □ *He really ranks me out. What a pest!* Ⓣ *I ranked out the whole gang, but good!*

rap 1. *in.* to talk or chat about something. □ *Something wrong? Let's rap about it.* □ *The kids sat down and rapped for an hour or so.* **2.** *n.* a conversation; a chat. □ *How about a rap?* □ *Let's have a rap sometime.* **3.** *n.* sweet talk; seductive talk; *line.* □ *I like your rap, but that's all I like about you.* □ *Don't lay that rap on me! You're not my type.* **4.** *n.* a criminal charge; the blame for something. (Underworld.) □ *I won't take the rap for something you did.* □ *The cops tried to make the rap stick, but they didn't have enough evidence.*

rap session *n.* an informal conversation session. □ *The kids settled down for a long rap session.* □ *The rap session was interrupted by a fire drill.*

(rap) sheet *n.* a criminal record listing all recorded criminal charges. (See also *rap.*) □ *This guy has a rap sheet a mile long.* □ *The sergeant asked if there was a sheet on the prisoner.*

rare bird *n.* an unusual person; a person with rare talents or abilities. □ *An interesting kind of rare bird is the man who can take long vacations and still make money.* □ *She is a rare bird who* *enjoys opera and can understand most of it, too.*

rare old time *n.* a fine and enjoyable time at a party or something similar. (Folksy.) □ *That was a rare old time at Tom's the other night.* □ *I haven't had a rare old time like that in years.*

raring to go *mod.* anxious and eager to go. □ *Come on, I'm raring to go!* □ *The whole family is raring to go on vacation.*

raspberry ['ræzbɛri] *n.* the *Bronx cheer.* □ *The entire audience gave the performer the raspberry.* □ *The performer gave them a raspberry right back.*

rasty ['ræsti] *mod.* having to do with a harsh-looking young woman. (Collegiate.) □ *Who is that rasty dame I saw you with?* □ *That dark lipstick makes you look a little rasty.*

rat 1. *n.* a wretched acting person. (Also a term of address.) □ *You dirty rat, you!* □ *Stop acting like a dirty rat!* **2.** See *rat (on someone).*

rat around *in.* to waste time loafing around; to *kick around.* (Collegiate.) □ *I didn't do anything but rat around all summer.* □ *If kids don't have jobs, they just rat around.*

rat fink *n.* an informer. (Also a term of address. See also *rat.*) □ *That guy is nothing but a rat fink. A dirty squealer!* □ *Fred told the teacher about the plot, and everybody called him a rat fink for the next two years.*

rat (on someone) *in.* to inform (on someone). □ *Bill said he was going to rat on that punk.* □ *If you rat on me, I'll get you!* □ *Who ratted?*

rat out *in.* to quit; to *fink out (on someone or something).* □ *It's too late to rat out.* □ *He tried to rat out at the last minute.*

rat race *n.* a dull and repetitive situation; a dull and unrewarding job. (Compare to *daily grind.*) □ *I am really tired of this rat race—day after day.* □ *She dropped out of the rat race and moved to Vermont, where she opened a barber shop.*

ratchet-mouth AND **motor-mouth** *n.* someone who talks incessantly. (Also a term of address.) □ *Tell that ratchet-mouth to shut up!* □ *Hey, motor-mouth, quiet!*

rathole 1. *n.* a run-down place; a *dump* or a *joint.* □ *I refuse to live in this rathole any longer.* □ *Why don't you clean up this rathole?* **2.** *n.* a bottomless pit. (Typically with *throw* and *down* as in the examples.) □ *Why do they keep throwing money down that rathole?* □ *That rathole will absorb as much money as they can supply.* □ *The transportation system is beyond help. Giving it more subsidies is just throwing money down a rathole.*

Rats! *exclam.* "Oh, damn!" □ *Rats! I broke a nail!* □ *Oh, rats! I'm late.*

rats *n.* the delirium tremens. (Always with *the.*) □ *The way he was shaking, I knew he had the rats.* □ *Most of those old guys down on Fourth Street have the rats.*

rattle-trap *n.* a rattly (old) car; any rattly vehicle. □ *I hear Ted's rattle-trap in the driveway.* □ *I bought a rattle-trap for $400.*

rattlebones *n.* a nickname for a very skinny person. (Also a term of address.) □ *Hey, rattlebones, come over here a minute.* □ *Ask rattlebones over there to have a seat.*

rattlebrain *n.* a stupid person. □ *Is that rattlebrain here again?* □ *Please try not to be such a rattlebrain! Pay attention to what you are doing.*

rattled 1. *mod.* confused; bewildered. □ *He tends to get a little rattled at minor things.* □ *Try not to get her rattled.* **2.** *mod.* tipsy; alcohol intoxicated. □ *After an hour of drinking, Bill was more than a little rattled.* □ *Being rattled from beer, I stopped drinking beer and began on the rum.*

rattling *mod.* excellent. (Collegiate. Compare to *rocking.*) □ *Her party was really rattling.* □ *What a rattling place to live!*

raunch someone out [rɔntʃ . . .] *tr.* to disgust someone. (From *raunchy.*) ☐ *These dirty socks absolutely raunch me out!* ☐ *Wayne and Beavis enjoy raunching people out.*

raunchie See the following entry.

raunchy AND **raunchie; ronchie** [ˈrɑntʃi] **1.** *mod.* crude; tasteless; bad. ☐ *He told a very raunchy story at the party.* ☐ *Don't be so ronchie.* **2.** *mod.* alcohol intoxicated. ☐ *Those guys were raunchy as hell.* ☐ *Let's go out and get good and ronchie.* **3.** *mod.* sick; ill. ☐ *I feel sort of ronchy.* ☐ *After I ate dinner, my stomach felt a little raunchie, so I went home.* **4.** *mod.* untidy; unclean; crude; tasteless. ☐ *Get your ronchie socks out of the living room.* ☐ *We decided to leave the raunchy movie about halfway through.*

rave *n.* a party; a wild celebration. ☐ *What a rave! A real fine party.* ☐ *Let's have a little rave next Friday.*

raw 1. *mod.* inexperienced; brand new. ☐ *The raw recruit did as well as could be expected.* ☐ *She'll get better. She's just a little raw.* **2.** *mod.* vulgar; crude; raucous; untamed. ☐ *I've had enough of your raw humor.* ☐ *That joke was a little raw.* **3.** *mod.* (of alcoholic spirits) undiluted; neat. ☐ *No ice, please. I prefer it raw.* ☐ *I'll drink it raw—just the way it is now.* **4.** *mod.* (of alcoholic spirits) unaged; fiery and strong. ☐ *My gosh, this stuff is raw! It'll burn a hole in me.* ☐ *Give me something to drink that isn't quite so raw.*

raw deal *n.* an unfair deal; unfair treatment. (Always with *a.*) ☐ *You really got a raw deal.* ☐ *My last job was a raw deal. I hope this is better.*

rays *n.* sunshine. (Collegiate.) ☐ *I'm going to go out and get some rays today.* ☐ *I've had too many rays. I'm cooked.*

razz [ræz] *tr.* to tease someone. ☐ *Please stop razzing me.* ☐ *I was just razzing you. I didn't mean any harm.*

razzamatazz See *razzmatazz.*

razzle-dazzle [ˈræzl̩ˈdæzl̩] *n.* flamboyant publicity; *hype.* ☐ *After all the razzle-dazzle dies down, we'll see what things are really like.* ☐ *Hollywood is filled with razzle-dazzle and excitement.*

razzmatazz AND **razzamatazz** [ˈræzməˈtæz AND ˈræzəməˈtæz] *n.* deceptive talk; *hype.* ☐ *Cut out the razzamatazz. How dumb do you think I am?* ☐ *Don't give me all that razzamatazz!*

reach for the sky 1. See *aim for the sky.* **2.** *in.* (a command) to put one's hands up, as in a robbery. ☐ *Okay, you guys, reach for the sky!* ☐ *The bank teller reached for the sky without having to be told.*

Read my lips! See *Watch my lips!*

reader *n.* a piece of paper with writing on it; a note; a prescription; an I.O.U. (Underworld.) ☐ *Max has my reader for $500.* ☐ *I got a reader for some morphine.*

real *mod.* very; really. ☐ *This is a real fine party.* ☐ *You did a real good thing.*

real bitch *n.* a very difficult or annoying thing or person. (Can refer to male or female.) ☐ *This math problem is a real bitch.* ☐ *Fred is a true problem. A real bitch.*

real gone *mod.* really *cool;* mellow and pleasant. ☐ *Man, this music is real gone.* ☐ *That's a real gone drummer.* ☐ *You are something—real gone.*

(real) McCoy 1. *n.* something authentic. (Always with *the.*) ☐ *This is the real McCoy. Nothing else like it.* ☐ *This is no copy. It's the McCoy.* **2.** *n.* pure drugs or alcohol. (Always with *the.*) ☐ *Is this stuff the McCoy?* ☐ *If it's not the real McCoy, I don't want it.*

ream someone out *tr.* to scold someone severely. ☐ *The teacher really reamed him out.* 🅃 *The coach reamed out the whole team.*

rear (end) *n.* the tail end; the buttocks. (Euphemistic.) ☐ *She fell right on her rear.* ☐ *The dog bit her in the rear end.*

rear-ender AND **back-ender** *n.* an automobile wreck where one car runs into the back of another. (Compare to *fender-bender.)* □ *It wasn't a bad accident, just a rear-ender.* □ *My neck was hurt in a back-ender.*

red hot 1. *mod.* important; in great demand. □ *This is a red hot item. Everybody wants one.* □ *The stock market is a red hot issue right now.* **2.** *n.* a hot dog; a frankfurter. □ *"Get your red hots right here!" shouted the vendor.* □ *In Chicago they eat red hots with catsup. Imagine!*

red-hot mama *n.* an exciting woman; a sexually exciting or excited woman. □ *Clare is really a red-hot mama!* □ *I'm no red-hot mama, just a country girl.*

red ink *n.* debt; indebtedness as shown in red ink on a financial statement. □ *There is too much red ink in my financial statement.* □ *Too much red ink and the company will collapse.*

red-letter day *n.* an important day that might well be marked in red on the calendar. □ *Today was a red-letter day in our history.* □ *It was a red-letter day for our club.*

red tape *n.* bureaucratic annoyances; bureaucratic forms and procedures. (Typically with *cut* as in the example.) □ *If you deal with the government, you will have to put up with lots of red tape.* □ *I have a friend who knows how to cut through red tape.*

redneck 1. *n.* a stereotypic southern bigot. (Derogatory. Also a term of address.) □ *Those rednecks can hardly read.* □ *Look, you stupid redneck, try to understand.* **2.** *mod.* in the manner of a southern bigot. □ *I don't follow that kind of redneck thinking.* □ *The candidate didn't want the redneck vote.*

reef See the following entry.

reefer ['rifɚ] **1.** *n.* a refrigerator. □ *Please put the milk in the reefer.* □ *A new reefer costs nearly $1000!* **2.** AND **reef** *n.* cannabis; a marijuana cigarette. (Drugs.) □ *He had a reefer in his hand when he was busted.* □ *Don't stall the reefer. Pass it on.*

ref [rɛf] **1.** *n.* a referee. (Also a term of address.) □ *Hey, ref! Get some glasses!* □ *The ref did a fine job.* **2.** *tr.* to referee something, such as a game. □ *Are you going to ref this one, or am I?* □ *I don't like to ref night games.*

regs *n.* regulations. □ *Follow the regs or pay the penalty.* □ *There is a list of regs posted on the back of your door.*

reinvent the wheel *tr.* to make unnecessary or redundant preparations. □ *You don't need to reinvent the wheel. Read up on what others have done.* □ *I don't have time to reinvent the wheel.*

rent(al)s *n.* one's parents. (Teens. See also *(parental) units.* Also a term of address.) □ *I'll have to ask my rents.* □ *Hey, rentals, let's go out for dinner.*

rep [rɛp] **1.** *n.* a representative, usually a sales representative. □ *Please ask your rep to stop by my office.* □ *Our rep will be in your area tomorrow.* **2.** *n.* someone's reputation. □ *I hope this doesn't ruin my rep.* □ *I've got my own rep to think about.* **3.** *n.* repertory theater. □ *He spent a year in rep on the East Coast.* □ *Rep is the best place to get experience, but not to make connections.*

repo ['ripo] **1.** *n.* a repossessed car. □ *It's a repo, and I got it cheap.* □ *I'd rather have a plain used car than a repo.* **2.** *tr.* to repossess a car. □ *Some guy came around and tried to repo my car.* □ *She's good at repoing family cars.*

repo man ['ripo 'mæn] *n.* a man who repossesses cars for a living. □ *What kind of guy is lower than a repo man?* □ *I'd rather beg than get a job as a repo man.*

ret [rɛt] *n.* a tobacco cigarette. (Collegiate.) □ *You got a ret I can bum?* □ *Give my buddy a ret, will you?*

retard ['ritɑrd] **1.** *n.* a rude nickname for a retarded person. (Derogatory and unkind.) □ *That retard is having a rough time.* □ *Don't call my brother a retard!* **2.** *n.* a stupid person. (Also a term of address.) □ *Don't be a retard! Get with it!* □ *Look, you retard, get busy.*

retread ['ritrɛd] *n.* a burned-out person; a made-over person. □ *Chuck is just a retread. He's through.* □ *I need somebody fresh and alive, not some tired retread.*

rev something up *tr.* to speed up an engine in short bursts. ☐ *Rev it up a few times and see if it stalls.* 🅃 *Tom sat at the traffic light revving up his engine.*

reverse gears *tr.* to wretch as a prelude to vomiting. ☐ *The cat is reversing gears. Throw her out the back door.* ☐ *Beavis is reversing gears and might be going to vomit. You never know with Beavis.*

revved up *mod.* excited, perhaps by drugs. ☐ *Max is revved up from too much dope.* ☐ *The kids were all revved up, ready to party.*

rhubarb ['rubɑrb] *n.* a brawl, especially in a baseball game. ☐ *There's a noisy rhubarb down on the field.* ☐ *Ted got punched around a little bit in that rhubarb last week.*

rib 1. *n.* a joke; an act of teasing. ☐ *I didn't mean any harm. It was just a little rib.* ☐ *That's a great rib, Sam!* **2.** *tr.* to tease someone. ☐ *Please don't rib me anymore tonight. I've had it.* ☐ *Let's go rib Jennifer.*

rib-tickler *n.* a joke; something very funny. ☐ *That was a real rib-tickler. I'll remember that joke.* ☐ *She told a rib-tickler, and everybody laughed.*

ride *n.* a car. ☐ *What time are you coming by in your ride?* ☐ *Do you care if I leave my ride parked in your driveway?*

ride shotgun *tr.* to accompany and guard someone or something. (A term from the days of stage coaches and their armed guards. See also *shotgun*.) ☐ *I have to take the beer over to the party. Why don't you come along and ride shotgun?* ☐ *Who's going to ride shotgun with Bill?*

ride the porcelain bus See *drive the big bus*.

rif [rɪf] **1.** *tr.* to dismiss an employee. (From the euphemism *reduction in force*.) ☐ *They're going to rif John tomorrow.* ☐ *Who'll they rif next?* **2.** *n.* a firing; a dismissal. ☐ *Who got the rif today?* ☐ *There's a rif in your future.*

riff [rɪf] **1.** *n.* a short, repeated line of music played by a particular performer. ☐ *Jim just sat there and forgot his riff.* ☐ *Listen to this riff, Tom.* **2.** *n.* a digression while speaking. (From sense 1.) ☐ *Excuse the little riff, but I had to mention it.* ☐ *If she didn't make so many riffs while she spoke, we could understand her better.*

riffed [rɪft] **1.** *mod.* alcohol or drug intoxicated. ☐ *That guy is really riffed!* ☐ *I can't keep getting riffed every night like this.* **2.** AND **rift** *mod.* fired; released from employment. (From *R.I.F.*, "reduction in force.") ☐ *Poor Walter got riffed Friday.* ☐ *Most of the sales force was riffed last week.*

rift See the previous entry.

rig 1. *tr.* to arrange or tamper with the results of something. ☐ *The crooks rigged the election.* ☐ *Somebody rigged the contest so no one got first prize.* **2.** *n.* a large truck; an *eighteen wheeler*. ☐ *Jim drives a really big rig.* ☐ *There were three rigs sitting in the parking lot when we got there.*

right as rain *mod.* completely correct. (Folksy. Often with *as*.) ☐ *Yes, indeed! You are right as rain!* ☐ *She was right as rain about the score.*

right guy *n.* a good guy; a straight guy. ☐ *Tom is a right guy. No trouble with him.* ☐ *I'm glad you're a right guy. I can trust you.*

right in the kisser *mod.* right in the mouth or face. (See also *kisser*.) ☐ *Max poked the cop right in the kisser.* ☐ *He caught one right in the kisser.*

(right) up one's alley *mod.* exactly one's kind of thing; exactly what one is best equipped to do. ☐ *That job is right up her alley.* ☐ *It's not exactly up my alley, but I'll try it.*

righteous ['rɑɪtʃəs] *mod.* good; of good quality. (Originally black.) ☐ *She is a righteous mama.* ☐ *Max told me about some righteous grass he's got.* ☐ *This stuff is really righteous!*

righteous collar *n.* a justifiable arrest. (As opposed to a *setup* or a *frame*.) ☐ *Bruno was taken in, and the gang agreed it was a righteous collar. Bruno was* *caught red-handed.* ☐ *"I can't complain," said Bruno. "It was a righteous collar."*

ring a bell *tr.* to stir something in someone's memory. ☐ *Yes, that rings a bell. I seem to remember it.* ☐ *Maybe the name Marsha will ring a bell!*

ring off the hook *in.* [for a telephone] to ring endlessly or constantly. ☐ *The phone was ringing off the hook when I came in.* ☐ *We've been busy today. The phone's been ringing off the hook.*

ring the bell *tr.* to be just what is needed; to *hit the spot.* ☐ *This cold water really rings the bell.* ☐ *A good hot bowl of soup would ring the bell about now.*

ringer (for someone) See *(dead) ringer (for someone).*

ringtailed snorter *n.* someone or something energetic and powerful. ☐ *Old Charlie is a real ringtailed snorter.* ☐ *Ask that ringtailed snorter to calm down and come over here for a minute.*

rinky-dink ['rɪŋki'dɪŋk] *mod.* cheap; inferior; broken down. ☐ *I sold my rinky-dink old car yesterday.* ☐ *What a rinky-dink job! I quit!*

riot ['rɑɪət] *n.* someone or something entertaining or funny. ☐ *Tom was a riot last night.* ☐ *Her joke was a real riot.*

rip 1. *n.* a drinking bout. (See also *tear.*) ☐ *All four of them went out on a rip.* ☐ *Fred had another rip last night. He's rotten now.* **2.** *n.* the loot from a *rip-off.* ☐ *I want my share of the rip, now!* ☐ *Give him some of the rip and tell him to beat it.* **3.** *n.* a theft; a *rip-off.* ☐ *The crooks pulled a rip on Fourth Street last night.* ☐ *That was the third rip there this week.* **4.** *n.* a tear in the flesh of the hand, as in an athletic event where the flesh comes in contact with solid material, such as in gymnastics and weightlifting. ☐ *I keep getting rips from the bar.* ☐ *Sally has a rip on her palm.*

rip-off 1. *n.* a theft; a deception; an exploitation. (See also *rip.*) ☐ *This sandwich is a rip-off!* ☐ *What a rip-off! I want my money back.* **2.** *mod.* having to do with theft and deception. ☐ *I consider myself to be rip-off champion of North America.* ☐ *All I hear is rip-off stories. Isn't anybody honest?*

(rip-)off artist *n.* a con artist. ☐ *Fred is such an off artist.* ☐ *Beware of the rip-off artist who runs that shop.*

rip on someone *in.* to give someone a hard time; to *hassle* someone. ☐ *Fred was ripping on me, and I heard about it.* ☐ *Stop ripping on my friend!*

rip snorter *n.* a remarkable person or thing; a hilarious joke. (Folksy.) ☐ *Old Fred is a real rip snorter.* ☐ *Her new car is a rip snorter, I tell you.* ☐ *Let me tell you a rip snorter about a farmer and his cow.* ☐ *Judy can tell some rip snorters.*

rip someone or something off 1. *tr.* [with *someone*] to assault, kill, beat, rob, rape, or cheat someone. (Note the *for* in the example.) ☐ *They ripped me off, but they didn't hurt me.* ☐ *Man, they ripped me off for three hundred dollars.* **2.** *tr.* [with *something*] to steal something. ☐ *They ripped them all off.* 🅃 *The crooks ripped off the hubcaps of my car.*

ripe 1. *mod.* alcohol intoxicated. ☐ *Yes, they were ripe all right. Stinking drunk.* ☐ *Bill was so ripe that they took him home.* **2.** *mod.* foul; smelly. ☐ *Whooey! This place is ripe. What died?* ☐ *Get your ripe old socks out of here!* ☐ *The fish seems quite ripe.* **3.** *mod.* crude; raunchy. ☐ *Your jokes are a bit ripe.* ☐ *That was a ripe one!* ☐ *Stop acting so ripe.*

ripped (off) See the following entry.

ripped (up) AND **ripped (off)** *mod.* alcohol or drug intoxicated; under the effects of marijuana. ☐ *Why do you have to get ripped up like that?* ☐ *Max was ripped out of his mind on uppers.*

Rise and shine! *exclam.* "Get up and get going!" ☐ *Get up! Rise and shine! It's late.* ☐ *Okay, you guys, rise and shine!*

ritzy ['rɪtsi] *mod.* elegant; flamboyant. ☐ *That is a real ritzy car.* ☐ *It's really ritzy!* ☐ *What a ritzy coat! Is it new?*

rivets ['rɪvəts] *n.* dollars; money. (From copper rivets.) ☐ *You got enough rivets on you for a snack?* ☐ *Who can come up with that many rivets?*

roach 1. *n.* a police officer. (Derogatory. From *cockroach.*) ☐ *Watch out! The roaches are coming.* ☐ *A roach caught him while he was at work.* 2. *n.* the butt end of a marijuana cigarette. (Drugs.) ☐ *The cops found a roach on the bathroom floor.* ☐ *Hey, give me that roach!* 3. *n.* an ugly girl or woman. (Derogatory. From *cockroach.*) ☐ *Who was that roach you were with last night?* ☐ *That dame is a real roach.*

roach clip AND **roach pick** *n.* a device to hold a *roach* and make it smokable. (Drugs.) ☐ *When the cops find a roach clip on you, you've had it.* ☐ *They found two roach picks and a pipe.*

roach-coach *n.* a mobile snack truck. (The term was revived in the Persian Gulf War.) ☐ *Let's go get a sandwich at the roach-coach.* ☐ *Here comes the roach-coach! Let go spend some coin.* ☐ *The roach-coach pulled up in front of the dorm every night about eleven.*

roach pick See *roach clip.*

roached *mod.* hungover; exhausted. ☐ *I'm roached. I feel lousy.* ☐ *What a day! I've never been so roached.*

road apple *n.* a lump of horse excrement. (Compare to *alley apple.*) ☐ *Don't step on the road apples.* ☐ *There must be horses around here. I see road apples.*

road hog *n.* someone who takes too much space on a road or highway; someone who seems to run other people off the road. ☐ *Get over! Road hog!* ☐ *A road hog nearly ran me off the road.*

road pizza *n.* a dead animal on the road. ☐ *Every morning the highway is littered with road pizza.* ☐ *A bunch of crows were feasting on road pizza when we drove by.*

roadie AND **roady** ['rodi] 1. AND **roadster** ['rodstɚ] *n.* a young person who helps rock groups set up for performances. ☐ *I want to be a roadie when I grow up.* ☐ *I was a roadster for a while, but I didn't like it.* 2. AND **roadster** *in.* to help rock groups set up. ☐ *Let's go downtown and roadie tonight. The Red Drips are in town.* ☐ *I hate to roady. It's, like, work!* 3. *mod.* eager to travel; eager to get on the road. ☐ *I get a little roady when the weather gets warm.* ☐ *We'd better get going. Your father looks a little roadie.*

roadster See the previous entry.

roadtrip *n.* a sudden trip in a car. (Sometimes yelled; **Roadtrip!** to indicate an impending jaunt in an automobile.) ☐ *Let's make a little roadtrip to get some beer.* ☐ *"Roadtrip!" hollered Ken. "We're gonna go out and get some dames!"*

roady See *roadie.*

roast 1. *tr.* to put on an entertaining program where the guest of honor is teased and insulted. ☐ *They roasted Dave when he retired.* ☐ *If they roast me at the dinner, I'll cry.* 2. *n.* an entertaining program where the guest of honor is insulted all in fun. ☐ *It was a wonderful roast. The guest of honor was pleased with the quality of the insults.* ☐ *It was a little too polite for a real roast.*

roasted *mod.* alcohol intoxicated. ☐ *He was stewed, roasted, and boiled.* ☐ *He's out getting roasted with the boys.*

rob someone blind 1. *tr.* to steal freely from someone. ☐ *Her maid was robbing her blind.* ☐ *I don't want them to rob me blind. Keep an eye on them.* 2. *tr.* to overcharge someone. ☐ *You are trying to rob me blind. I won't pay it!* ☐ *Those auto repair shops can rob you blind if you don't watch out.*

rock 1. AND **rock candy** *n.* *crack,* a crystallized form of cocaine. (Drugs. See also *rocks.*) ☐ *Some call it rock, and some call it crack.* ☐ *Rock is pretty expensive.* 2. *n.* a crystallized form of heroin used for smoking. (Drugs.) ☐ *Max is hooked on rock—the kind that you smoke.* ☐ *Powder is everywhere, but you can hardly find rock anymore.* 3. *n.* a diamond or other gemstone. ☐ *Look at the size of that rock in her ring.* ☐ *How many rocks are there decorating the edges of your watch?* 4. See *rocks.* 5. *n.* a baseball; a basketball. ☐ *Michael shot the rock to Scottie who turned and dropped it in the basket.* ☐ *Hank hit the* *rock with the bat and broke the bat in half.*

rock bottom 1. *n.* the lowest point or level. □ *The value of the goods is at rock bottom right now.* □ *Prices have reached rock bottom.* 2. *mod.* absolute lowest, especially in reference to price. □ *Prices are rock bottom this month.* □ *I am offering you the rock bottom price.* □ *You can't beat these rock bottom deals.*

rock candy See *rock.*

rock-jock *n.* a mountain or rock climber. □ *The serious rock-jocks practice in North Wales.* □ *The sides of every mountain are covered with rock-jocks.*

rocker 1. *n.* a rocking chair. (Not slang.) □ *I love to spend a sunny afternoon in my rocker.* □ *Children love rockers, but they can tip over in them.* 2. *n.* a rock and roll singer, song, or fan. (See also *off one's rocker.*) □ *Do all rockers have red hair?* □ *Let's listen to a good rocker.*

rockhead *n.* someone who seems to have rocks in the head; a hardheaded or stubborn person. □ *What a rockhead! That's a stupid thing to do.* □ *Why do you always have to be such a rockhead?*

rocking *mod.* excellent. (Collegiate.) □ *Man, what a rocking party!* □ *This set is really rocking.* □ *We had a rocking time!*

rocks 1. *n.* ice cubes. (See also *on the rocks, rock.*) □ *No rocks, please. I like my drink warm.* □ *Can I have a few rocks in my drink, please?* 2. *n.* Xerox Inc. (Securities markets, New York Stock Exchange.) □ *When she says, "Buy me a thousand rocks at the market," that means she wants one thousand shares of Xerox at whatever the market price is at the moment.* □ *Rocks is down a point and a half.* 3. *n.* money; a dollar. (Underworld.) □ *How many rocks do you want for that?* □ *Twenty rocks for that?*

rod 1. *n.* a gun; a revolver. (Underworld.) □ *I got a rod in my pocket. Don't move.* □ *I don't have any bullets for my rod.* 2. See *(hot) rod.*

ROF See *RO(T)F(L).*

roger ['rɑdʒɚ] *interj.* "okay"; "That is correct." □ *Roger, I'll do it.* □ *Roger. Will do.*

rolf See *ralph.*

roll 1. *n.* a bankroll; lots of money. □ *I earned a roll off that last deal.* □ *He's got a roll right there in his pocket.* 2. *tr.* to rob a drunkard. □ *The muggers found a drunk and rolled him.* □ *Those punks can't get much money by rolling drunks.* 3. *n.* a sustained period of luck or productivity. (See also *on a roll.*) □ *I'm doing great! What a roll!* □ *The fantastic roll that this performer is on is truly exciting.* 4. *in.* to leave, perhaps in a car. □ *I can't wait around any longer. Let's roll.* □ *We have to roll, now. It's late.*

roll in 1. *in.* to pull in; to drive up; to arrive. □ *The car rolled into the parking lot at a high speed.* □ *Four station wagons rolled in at the same time.* 2. See *turn in.*

roller *n.* a police car. □ *There are rollers in the next block, driving slow, looking for someone.* □ *The roller pulled up in front of the boys, and two officers got out.*

rolling buzz *n.* a long-lasting drug high. (Drugs.) □ *What I want is a nice rolling buzz.* □ *That stuff will give you a rolling buzz without putting you to sleep.*

ronchie See *raunchy.*

rook [rʊk] *tr.* to cheat someone. □ *She tried to rook me when I paid my bill.* □ *Don't go into that store. They'll rook you.*

rookie AND **rooky** ['rʊki] 1. *n.* a person new at something; a neophyte, especially a police officer or a ballplayer. □ *Tom is a rookie on the police force.* □ *The rookie tackled the old-time player and earned a lot of cheering and applause.* 2. *mod.* new; inexperienced. □ *Fred is a rookie first baseman for the home team.* □ *A rooky cop can make arrests just like the other cops.*

rooky See the previous entry.

room for rent *n.* a person who acts very stupid. (Also a term of address. This implies that one's head is so empty of brains that the space could be rented out.) □ *Hey, room for rent, wake up and* *pay attention.* □ *My brother is a room for rent if I ever saw one. What a dope!*

rooster ['rustɚ] *n.* the posterior; one's butt end. (Old. Because one "roosts" on it.) □ *Don't just sit there on your rooster. Get to work.* □ *I fell down smack on my rooster.*

root 1. *n.* a cigarette or a cigar. □ *That root you're smoking sure stinks.* □ *You got a root I can borrow?* **2.** *in.* to eat food like a pig. □ *Don't root. Slow down and enjoy your food.* □ *Max is downstairs rooting now. It won't take that slob long to eat.*

rooting-tooting *mod.* exciting; renown; famous; illustrious. (A vague adjective of praise.) □ *We really had a rooting-tooting time last weekend.* □ *She's a rooting-tooting dancer from Omaha.*

rope someone in 1. *tr.* to cause someone to get involved in some project. □ *She's always trying to rope me into her club.* 🅃 *Let's rope in someone to help with cleaning up.* **2.** See *take someone in.*

roscoe ['rɑsko] *n.* a pistol, especially a revolver. (Underworld.) □ *He's got a roscoe in his pocket.* □ *I'm going down there to talk to Max, and I'm taking my roscoe.*

rosy *mod.* good; satisfactory. □ *Things are looking rosy now that the economy is improving.* □ *Doesn't look like a very rosy future.* □ *When the stock market crashed, nothing looked rosy.*

rot *n.* nonsense. □ *Don't give me any more of your rot. Speak straight with me.* □ *That's just rot. Don't believe any of it!*

RO(T)F(L) *interj.* "rolling on the floor laughing." (Used in electronic mail and computer bulletin board messages. Not pronounced aloud.) □ *I was ROTFL when I read your note. That was too much.* □ *Your comment had me ROTF.*

rotgut 1. *n.* strong or inferior liquor, especially whisky. (Folksy.) □ *Where is that jug of rotgut you used to keep around here?* □ *The old man nearly went blind drinking all that rotgut.* **2.** *mod.* (of liquor) strong or fiery. □ *You've got to stop drinking that rotgut liquor and think of your health.* □ *I won't pay for this rotgut whisky. Give me something better.* **3.** *n.* weak or otherwise inferior beer. □ *I need a can of beer, and you give me this rotgut?* □ *She can afford something better, but she drinks nothing but cheap rotgut.*

rotorhead *n.* a helicopter pilot or member of a helicopter crew. (Military. Also a term of address.) □ *Radio those rotorheads and tell them to get back to the base, now!* □ *Hey, rotorhead, where's your egg beater?*

Rots of ruck! ['rɑtsə'rək] *exclam.* "Lots of luck!" (Mocking a Japanese pronunciation.) □ *Have a good trip, and rots of ruck!* □ *Good-bye, and rots of ruck!*

rotsee ['rɑtsi] *n.* "R.O.T.C.," the Reserve Officers Training Corps. □ *I joined rotsee to help pay my way through school.* □ *How long have you been in the rotsee program?*

rotten 1. *mod.* smelly; disgusting. (Not slang.) □ *What is that rotten smell?* □ *Something rotten is under that board.* **2.** *mod.* alcohol intoxicated. (From sense 1. See also *putrid.*) □ *It takes a case of beer to get Wilbur rotten.* □ *When he gets rotten, he's sort of dangerous.* **3.** *mod.* poor or bad. (From sense 1.) □ *We have nothing but one rotten problem after another.* □ *This is the most rotten mess I've ever been in.*

rotten apple *n.* a single bad person or thing. □ *There always is a rotten apple to spoil it for the rest of us.* □ *Tom sure has turned out to be the rotten apple.*

rotten egg *n.* a bad or despised person; a stinker. □ *That guy is a real rotten egg.* □ *She sure has turned out to be a rotten egg.*

rotten luck *n.* bad luck. □ *Of all the rotten luck!* □ *I've had nothing but rotten luck all day.*

rotten to the core *mod.* really bad. (See also *rotten apple.*) □ *That lousy punk is rotten to the core.* □ *The entire administration is rotten to the core.*

rough and ready *mod.* vigorous and eager. □ *After a good night's sleep, I feel rough and ready—I could take on a bear.* □ *My friend is the rough and ready type. I'd rather sit and think about things.*

rough and tumble *mod.* disorderly; aggressive. □ *That was a rough and tumble football game.* □ *George is too rough and tumble for me. He doesn't know how to act around civilized people.*

rough it *tr.* to live for a short period of time in a relatively primitive state. □ *We went camping and had to rough it for a week.* □ *With no electricity in our house, I roughed it by burning candles.*

rough someone up *tr.* to beat someone up; to maltreat someone. □ *Am I going to have to rough you up, or will you cooperate?* 🅃 *The crooks roughed up the old lady before taking her purse.*

rough stuff *n.* unnecessary roughness; physical violence or threats of violence. □ *Okay, let's cut out the rough stuff!* □ *There was too much rough stuff in Friday's game.*

rough time *n.* a hard time; a bad time. □ *I didn't mean to give you such a rough time. I'm sorry.* □ *What a rough time we had getting the car started!*

roughhouse AND **roughneck** **1.** *n.* a mean kid; a boisterous child, usually male. □ *Jimmy! Stop acting like such a roughhouse.* □ *Tell that young roughneck to straighten up and behave.* **2.** *in.* to be boisterous. □ *Stop roughnecking in my living room.* □ *The boys broke the lamp when they were roughnecking around in the family room.*

roughneck See the previous entry.

round the bend See *(a)round the bend.*

round tripper *n.* a home run in baseball. □ *Ted is responsible for four round trippers in Saturday's game.* □ *He hit a round tripper in the fourth inning.*

roundhouse punch *n.* a punch to the head made by swinging the arm in an arc rather than by a jabbing punch. □ *Jim knocked Ted down with a roundhouse punch.* □ *He let him have a roundhouse punch that would have cracked a two-by-four.*

roundup *n.* a collection or summary of news items, such as a weather roundup, news roundup, etc. □ *Tune in at eleven for a roundup of the day's news.* □ *Now for a weather roundup.*

roust [raʊst] **1.** *tr.* [for a police officer] to bother or interfere with someone; to arrest someone. (Underworld.) □ *The cops rousted the gang without warning.* □ *I was walking along doing nothing, and this cop rousts me.* (More at *rousted.*) **2.** *tr.* to raid someone's residence; to *bust* a person or place. (Underworld.) □ *They rousted Max's place last night.* □ *That bar was rousted last week.* **3.** *n.* a raid or a *bust.* □ *Okay, stand still. This is a roust!* □ *They pulled a big roust down on Fourth Street.*

rousted [ˈraʊstəd] *mod.* arrested. (Underworld.) □ *Max got rousted last night.* □ *The cops rousted the dealers, but that didn't even slow down the drug trade.*

royal pain *n.* someone or something irritating; a severe annoyance. □ *You are a royal pain!* □ *Her questions were a royal pain, but I had to answer them as part of my job.*

RSN *interj.* "real soon now." (Used in electronic mail and computer bulletin board messages. Not pronounced aloud.) □ *I will post the rest of my trip report RSN.* □ *I will be finished RSN. I'll let you know.*

rub someone out *tr.* to kill someone. (Underworld.) □ *The gunman was eager to rub somebody out.* 🅃 *The crooks tried to rub out the witness.*

rub someone's nose in something *tr.* to remind someone of something constantly; to make a big issue about someone's mistake. (From the practice of training a puppy by rubbing its nose in the messes it makes.) □ *So I made a mistake! I wish you'd stop rubbing my nose in it.* □ *Rubbing my nose in it is not going to correct the mistake.*

rubber **1.** *n.* automobile tires; the rubber of automobile tires. □ *This car has* *some fine rubber on it.* □ *The rubber on my car is practically ruined.* **2.** See *rubber (check).*

rubber (check) *n.* a check that bounces; a forged check. (See also *bounce.*) □ *The bank says I wrote a rubber check, but I'm sure there was enough money on deposit.* □ *One rubber check after another! Can't you add?*

rubber sock *n.* a timid person; a passive and compliant person. □ *What a rubber sock. She's afraid of her own shadow.* □ *Come on! Stand up for your rights. Don't be such a rubber sock!*

rubberneck 1. *n.* one who stares at something or someone; a tourist. □ *At noon the sidewalks are crowded with rubbernecks.* □ *See if that rubberneck over there has the correct time.* **2.** *in.* to stare (at something or someone). □ *What are all those people rubbernecking at?* □ *Traffic is stalled because of all the drivers who are rubbernecking.*

rubbish *n.* nonsense. (Also an exclamation.) □ *I'm tired of listening to your rubbish.* □ *Rubbish! That's the stupidest thing I've ever heard.*

ruckus ['rəkəs] *n.* a commotion; an uproar. □ *Quiet, please. Don't raise such a ruckus.* □ *The boss kicked up quite a ruckus when I came in late.*

rude 1. *mod.* undesirable; unpleasant. □ *The prof in my history class is a rude dude, for sure.* □ *What a rude idea!* **2.** *mod.* cool; pleasant. □ *Man, that's a rude bike!* □ *Sally is a rude-looking girl!*

rug *n.* a wig or toupee. (See also *divot.*) □ *Is that guy wearing a rug, or does his scalp really slide from side to side?* □ *I wear just a little rug to cover up a shiny spot.*

rug rat *n.* a child. (Also a term of address.) □ *You got any rug rats at your house?* □ *Hey, you cute little rug rat, come over here.*

rule *in.* to dominate; to be the best. (Slang only in certain contexts. Typical in graffiti.) □ *The rockets rule!* □ *Pizza rules around here.*

rumble 1. *in.* to fight. □ *The gangs are rumbling over on Fourth Street.* □ *We're going to rumble tomorrow night.* **2.** *n.* a fight; a street fight; a gang fight. □ *If there is a rumble, get out of there fast.* □ *My brother was hurt in a gang rumble.*

rumdum AND **rum-dum** ['rəm'dəm] **1.** *n.* a drunkard; a ruined alcoholic. □ *Get that smelly rumdum out of here.* □ *I don't want to end up like a dirty rumdumb.* **2.** *n.* a stupid person. □ *Hey, rumdum, wise up and do what you are told.* □ *Don't be such a rum-dum.* **3.** *mod.* alcohol intoxicated. □ *The old lady got rumdum on gin.* □ *Two glasses and she was rumdum and asleep.*

rummed (up) *mod.* alcohol intoxicated. □ *Sailors like to go into town and get rummed up.* □ *Those boys are really rummed.*

rummy ['rəmi] **1.** *n.* a drunkard; an alcoholic; an alcoholic hobo. □ *Ask that rummy to leave before he throws up.* □ *There is a rummy at the door asking for a handout.* **2.** *mod.* alcohol intoxicated. □ *She's rummy, and she's going to be sick.* □ *Who's the rummy old girl?* □ *How long does it take a heavy drinker like Bob to get rummy?* **3.** *mod.* habitually confused and inept. □ *I get more rummy as I grow older.* □ *That rummy old man is here again.*

rump 1. *n.* the hindquarters; the buttocks; the posterior. □ *He fell on his rump.* □ *A dog doesn't have much rump.* **2.** *tr.* to flog someone on the buttocks. □ *They rumped him and made him run around the frat house.* □ *I'm going to get rumped when my dad gets home.*

rumpus ['rəmpəs] *n.* a commotion. □ *Please don't make such a rumpus.* □ *There was quite a rumpus in Jim's room.*

rumpus room *n.* a family recreation room. (Old but still heard.) □ *Our rumpus room has a pool table.* □ *If you kids are going to play rough, you'll have to go down to the rumpus room.*

run 1. *n.* a session or period of time spent doing something; a period of time when something happens. □ *The market had a good run today.* □ *We all* *have enjoyed a good run of luck.* □ *Max takes amphetamines and was on a run all week.* □ *A run like that can kill.* **2.** *tr.* to transport contraband, alcohol, or drugs. □ *Max used to run booze during prohibition.* □ *The soldiers were caught running guns.* **3.** *n.* an act of transporting contraband. □ *Four soldiers were killed during a run.* □ *In their final run the cocaine smugglers made over four million dollars.*

run a make on someone *tr.* to perform an identity check on someone. (Underworld.) □ *The cops ran a make on Lefty and learned about his prison record.* □ *We tried to run a make on him and came up with nothing.*

run amok ['rən ə'mək] *in.* to go awry. (From a Malay word meaning to run wild in a violent frenzy.) □ *Our plan ran amok.* □ *The whole company ran amok after the market crashed.*

run down some lines 1. *in.* to converse (with someone). □ *I was running down some lines with Fred when the bell rang.* □ *Hey, man, let's run down some lines.* **2.** *in.* to try to seduce someone; to go through a talk leading to seduction. (See also *run one's rhymes.*) □ *Go run down some lines with someone else.* □ *I was just standing there running down some lines with Mary when those guys broke in.*

run it down *tr.* to tell the whole story; to tell the truth. □ *Come on! What happened? Run it down for me!* □ *I don't care what happened. Run it down. I can take it.*

run-of-the-mill *mod.* average; typical. (Referring to the typical quality of a product that comes out of a mill.) □ *He is just a run-of-the-mill guy.* □ *I don't want just run-of-the-mill ice cream.* □ *This stuff is just run-of-the-mill.*

run off *in.* to have diarrhea. □ *Jimmy has been running off since midnight.* □ *At least I'm not running off anymore.*

run off at the mouth *in.* to talk too much; to have diarrhea of the mouth. □ *I wish you would stop running off at the mouth.* □ *Tom runs off at the mouth too much. I wish he would temper his remarks.*

run on all cylinders 1. *in.* to run well and smoothly. □ *This department is running on all cylinders now.* □ *My plan is now running on all cylinders.* **2.** *in.* to operate sensibly and intelligently. □ *Pay attention to what you are doing. Start running on all cylinders.* □ *She doesn't run on all cylinders this early in the morning.*

run one's rhymes *tr.* to say what you have to say; to give one's speech or make one's plea. (Collegiate.) □ *Go run your rhymes with somebody else!* □ *I told him to run his rhymes elsewhere.*

run out of gas *in.* to lose momentum or interest. □ *His program is running out of gas.* □ *I hope I don't run out of gas before I finish what I set out to do.*

run scared *in.* to act panicked. □ *All the politicians are running scared.* □ *Don't panic. There is no reason to run scared.*

run someone in *tr.* to arrest someone; to take someone to the police station. □ *Don't argue with me, or I'll run you in.* [T] *The cops ran in everybody in sight.*

Run that by (me) again. AND **Run that by (me) one more time.** *sent.* "Please tell it to me again." □ *I can't believe my own ears. Can you run that by again, please?* □ *It's noisy in here. Please run that by me one more time.*

Run that by (me) one more time. See the previous entry.

run-up *n.* a movement upward in the value of one or more securities. (Securities markets.) □ *The market's had a good run-up in the last week.* □ *I'm afraid that if it has a run-up to 3,000, it will fall to zero.*

runaround *n.* a wild-goose chase. (Especially with *give,* as in the examples.) □ *The IRS gave us the runaround when we asked for a review.* □ *The customer will never get a runaround at my store!*

rundown *n.* a summary bringing someone up to date. □ *Can you give me a rundown on what's happened since* noon? □ *I need a rundown on the current situation in Alaska.*

runner **1.** *n.* a messenger. □ *Send a runner over to the other office for supplies.* □ *I work as a runner in the financial district.* **2.** *n.* a person who transports contraband. (Underworld.) □ *The cops caught the runner red-handed.* □ *The runners got away, but we have the goods.*

runs *n.* diarrhea. (Always with *the*.) □ *That stuff we ate gave me the runs.* □ *I can't believe those cute little hamburgers could give anybody the runs.*

runt *n.* a small person; someone whose growth has been stunted. (Also a rude term of address.) □ *He can't play basketball. He's just a runt.* □ *Hey, runt. Come here!*

rush **1.** *n.* a quick print of a day's shooting of a film. (Film-making. Usually plural.) □ *After today's shooting, we'll watch yesterday's rushes.* □ *Rush these rushes right over to Mr. Hitchcock's office.* **2.** *n.* a period of time when fraternities and sororities are permitted to pursue new members. (Collegiate.) □ *When does rush start this year?* □ *I've got to be at school in time for rush.* **3.** *tr.* [for a fraternity or sorority member] to try to persuade someone to join. □ *The frat tried to rush me, but I'm too busy.* □ *They can't rush anyone except during rush week.* **4.** *tr.* to court or date someone, usually a woman. (From sense 3.) □ *Tom's trying to rush Betty, but she's not interested.* □ *He spent some time trying to rush her, but had to give up.* **5.** *n.* a burst of energy or good feeling from a drug; the explosive euphoria of some kinds of drugs. (Drugs.) □ *Man, this stuff really gives me a rush.* □ *What kind of rush does this have?* **6.** *n.* any excitement; any burst of good feeling. (From sense 5.) □ *I got a real rush from helping out.* □ *The wonderful ending to the movie gave me a rush.*

rust belt *n.* the industrial north of the U.S. (Patterned on *sun belt*.) □ *The economy in the rust belt is slowing down.* □ *The salt they put on the roads in the winter made my car all rusty. I guess that's why they call this area the rust belt.*

rust bucket *n.* a naval destroyer; any ship. (Military.) □ *I'm anxious to get off this old rust bucket.* □ *Why don't I ever get assigned to a new ship? It's always some crummy rust bucket!*

rusty-dusty *n.* the posterior; the buttocks. (See also *duster*.) □ *I fell down right on my rusty-dusty.* □ *I almost kicked him in the rusty-dusty.*

ruth [ruθ] **1.** *n.* a women's restroom. (Compare to *john*.) □ *Where's the ruth?* □ *Point me toward the ruth!* **2.** *in.* to empty one's stomach; to vomit. (See also *cry ruth, rolf*.) □ *I gotta go ruth!* □ *I just can't stand to ruth.*

S

773H *n.* "hell." (This is the printed word *hell* rotated 180 degrees. Jocular.) ☐ *What the 773H is going on around here?* ☐ *This place is one 773H of a mess!*

sack **1.** *n.* a bed. ☐ *I was so tired I could hardly find my sack.* ☐ *Somebody put a spider in my sack.* **2.** *tr.* to dismiss someone from employment; to fire someone. ☐ *The boss sacked the whole office staff last week.* ☐ *If I do that again, they'll sack me.* **3.** *n.* a dismissal. (Always with *the*.) ☐ *The boss gave them all the sack.* ☐ *The sack is what I am afraid of.* **4.** *tr.* to tackle someone in football. ☐ *I tried to sack him, but he was too fast.* ☐ *Sack that guy or else!* **5.** *n.* the completion of a tackle in football. ☐ *Andy made the sack on the ten-yard line.* ☐ *Who failed to make the sack?*

sack out *in.* to go to bed or go to sleep. ☐ *It's time for me to sack out.* ☐ *Let's sack out early tonight.* (More at *sacked out*.)

sack rat *n.* someone who spends a lot of time in bed; someone who does not ever seem to get enough sleep. ☐ *Tom is such a sack rat. He can't seem to get enough sleep.* ☐ *Mary is such a sack rat that she misses classes.*

sack time **1.** *n.* a period of time spent in bed. ☐ *I need more sack time than most people.* ☐ *How much sack time do you get?* **2.** *n.* time to go to bed. ☐ *Okay, gang, it's sack time. Go home so I can get some sleep!* ☐ *When is sack time around here?*

sacked out *mod.* asleep. ☐ *Mary is sacked out in her room.* ☐ *Here it is ten o'clock, and you are still sacked out!*

sacred mushrooms See *magic mushrooms.*

sad *mod.* poor; undesirable. ☐ *This is a sad excuse for a car!* ☐ *That was a sad pitch there at the end of the last inning.* ☐ *This steak is really sad.*

sad sack *n.* a sad person; a listless or depressed person. ☐ *Tom always looks like such a sad sack.* ☐ *Who is that sad sack moping in the corner?*

saddled with someone or something *mod.* burdened with someone or something. ☐ *I've been saddled with the children all day. Let's go out tonight.* ☐ *I don't want to be saddled with your work.*

sail into someone AND **light into someone** *in.* to beat or scold someone. ☐ *Jimmy's mother really sailed into him for breaking the window.* ☐ *Jimmy lit into the cat for getting in the way.*

sail (right) through something *in.* to get through something easily. ☐ *I sailed right through my homework.* ☐ *We sailed through the examination with no difficulty.*

salt *n.* a sailor. (Especially with *old*.) ☐ *A couple of salts came ashore and asked if they could buy some beer.* ☐ *I've sailed a little, but you could hardly call me an old salt.*

salt and pepper **1.** *n.* a black and white police car. ☐ *There is a salt and pepper around the corner waiting for speeders.* ☐ *There is a salt and pepper behind you, and it's too late to slow down.* **2.** *mod.* interracial, including black and white. ☐ *It was sort of a salt and pepper meeting, with representatives from all neighborhoods.* ☐ *We achieved a salt and* *pepper agreement that made everyone happy.*

salt horse *n.* corned or salted beef. ☐ *We had salt horse on toast for dinner.* ☐ *We made spaghetti sauce with salt horse because that was the only meat we could find.*

Sam *n.* federal agents; federal narcotics agents. (Also a term of address. From *Uncle (Sam).*) ☐ *Sam is on the trail of the dope smugglers.* ☐ *Sam is working hard to put an end to all this drug trouble.*

Sam and Dave *n.* the police; police officers. (Black.) ☐ *Mike got hit by Sam and Dave last night.* ☐ *And there at the door were my old buddies Sam and Dave with a warrant.*

same difference *n.* the same; no difference at all. ☐ *Pink, fuchsia, what does it matter? Same difference.* ☐ *Whether you go or I go, it's the same difference.*

same here *phr.* "me too"; "I agree." ☐ MARY: *I think I'll have the broiled halibut.* JANE: *Same here.* ☐ BILL: *I feel sort of cold. What about you?* SUE: *Same here.*

same o(l)' same o(l)' ['semo(l) 'semo(l)] *n.* the same old thing. ☐ *I'm getting tired of the same ol' same ol'.* ☐ *Why not something different? Do you like the same o' same o'?*

same old story *n.* an often repeated story or situation. ☐ *It's the same old story. Boy meets girl, girl gets consumption, girl dies.* ☐ *One after one they came in. It's the same old story with each of them, "Not enough time to do my homework."*

sand *n.* sugar. ☐ *Please pass the sand.* ☐ *Do you use sand in your coffee?*

sandbag 1. *tr.* to force someone to do something. ☐ *I don't want to have to sandbag you. Please cooperate.* ☐ *Don't let them sandbag you into buying something you don't need.* **2.** *tr.* to deceive someone; to fool someone about one's capabilities. ☐ *Don't let them sandbag you into expecting too little.* ☐ *The guy sandbagged me, and I wasn't expecting him to shoot the ball.*

sap 1. *n.* a stupid person. ☐ *That poor sap thinks he can convince them.* ☐ *Who is that miserable looking sap in the corner?* **2.** *n.* a blackjack. (Underworld.) ☐ *The thug bopped him on the head with a sap.* ☐ *Max had a sap in his pocket when they arrested him for possession.*

Saturday night special *n.* a small, easily obtainable pistol. ☐ *There was another killing last night with a Saturday night special.* ☐ *That's the tenth shooting done with a Saturday night special this week.*

sauce *n.* liquor; any alcoholic beverage. (See also *on the sauce.*) ☐ *Those guys have had too much sauce again.* ☐ *Did you bring the sauce? Can't have a good party without lots of sauce.*

sauce parlor *n.* a tavern. ☐ *You spend too much time in the sauce parlor, Fred.* ☐ *I wouldn't be caught dead in that sauce parlor.*

sauced *mod.* alcohol intoxicated. ☐ *She went out and got herself sauced.* ☐ *Man, do you look sauced.*

savage *mod.* excellent. (Collegiate.) ☐ *This is really a savage piece of music.* ☐ *Man, Fred is a totally savage guy.* ☐ *Wow, is he savage!*

Save it! *exclam.* "Be quiet!" ☐ *Save it! Keep quiet until this is over.* ☐ *I don't care what you think you have to say. Save it!*

saved by the bell *mod.* saved by the timely intervention of someone or something. ☐ *I was going to have to do my part, but someone knocked on the door and I didn't have to do it. I was saved by the bell.* ☐ *I wish I had been saved by the bell.*

savvy ['sævi] **1.** *tr. & in.* to understand (someone or something). (Adapted from Spanish *sabe,* "he knows.") ☐ *Do you savvy?* ☐ *Can you savvy at all what I am trying to tell you?* ☐ *I just can't savvy stuff like that.* **2.** *n.* knowledge; know-how. ☐ *She really has savvy when it comes to clocks.* ☐ *I don't have the savvy necessary to do the job.* **3.** *mod.* knowledgeable. ☐ *What a savvy gal!* ☐

She is truly savvy! ☐ *He is one of the most savvy directors in New York.*

sawbones *n.* a doctor. (Folksy. Referring to someone who amputates limbs.) ☐ *Call the sawbones. This is an emergency.* ☐ *Is there a sawbones in this town?*

sawbuck *n.* a ten-dollar bill. (From the time when the "10" was indicated by the Roman numeral "X", which looks like the crosspiece that supports wood that is being sawed.) ☐ *It cost me a sawbuck to have my car pulled out of the mud.* ☐ *Can I borrow a sawbuck till payday?*

sawed *mod.* alcohol intoxicated. (Perhaps an elaboration of *cut.*) ☐ *I got sawed last weekend, and I still have a headache.* ☐ *She drank a lot, but never got sawed.*

sawed-off *mod.* short of stature. ☐ *Mike is sawed-off.* ☐ *Tom called Mike a sawed-off little runt.* ☐ *Well, Mike is a sawed-off runt, isn't he?*

Say cheese! *exclam.* "Please smile!" (A phrase said by a photographer who is trying to get someone to smile for a photograph.) ☐ *Come on, now. Say cheese!* ☐ *Say cheese for the camera, please.*

say-so *n.* a command; an authorization. ☐ *I can't do it just on your say-so.* ☐ *We can begin as soon as we get the boss's say-so.*

say uncle *tr.* to admit defeat; to give up. ☐ *He held me down until I said uncle.* ☐ *I never say uncle. I just keep right on going.*

Say what? *interrog.* "What did you say?" ☐ *Say what? I didn't hear that.* ☐ *The old man held his hand to his ear and said, "Say what?"*

Says me! AND **Sez me!** *exclam.* a formulaic answer to *Says who?* ☐ TOM: *Says who?* FRED: *Says me, that's who!* ☐ TOM: *You?* FRED: *You got it, buster. Says me!*

Says who? AND **Sez who?** *interrog.* a formulaic challenge indicating disagreement with someone who has said something. (See also *Says you!*) ☐ TOM: *Says who?* FRED: *Says me, that's who!* ☐ *She drew herself up to her full height, looked him straight in the eye, and said, "Says who?"*

Says you! *exclam.* "That's just what you say!"; "You don't know what you are talking about!" ☐ FRED: *You are fat and ugly.* TOM: *Says you!* ☐ MARY: *People who go around correcting other people were found to be very annoying in a recent survey.* BILL: *Says you!*

scabbed ['skæbd] *mod.* cheated in a drug deal; having been sold bogus or inferior drugs. ☐ *Max got scabbed by a dealer who got arrested the next day.* ☐ *This junk is junk. I've been scabbed.*

scads [skædz] *n.* lots (of something). ☐ *I have just scads and scads of paper.* ☐ *Aunt Mary has scads of money.*

scag See *skag.*

scag jones See *skag jones.*

scale *n.* the regular union rate of pay; union wages. ☐ *Even the big stars work for scale.* ☐ *We pay scale and not a penny more. I don't care who you think you are!*

scam [skæm] **1.** *n.* a swindle; a *hustle.* ☐ *I lost a fortune in that railroad scam.* ☐ *What a scam! I'm calling the cops.* **2.** *tr.* to swindle someone; to deceive someone. ☐ *They were scammed by a sweet-talking southern lady who took all their money.* ☐ *She scammed them for every cent they had.* **3.** *in.* to seek out and pick up young women, said of males. (Collegiate.) ☐ *Bob was out scamming last night and ran into Clare.* ☐ *Those guys are always scamming around.* **4.** *in.* to copulate. ☐ *All you ever want to do is scam.* ☐ *I think those people over there are scamming.* **5.** *in.* to fool around and waste time. ☐ *Quit scamming and get busy.* ☐ *You'd get better grades if you didn't scam so much.*

scammer ['skæmɚ] **1.** *n.* a swindler; a *hustler.* ☐ *Max is a scammer if I ever saw one.* ☐ *There are a couple of scammers on the street corner. Watch out.* **2.** *n.* a lecher; a fast worker with the opposite sex. □ *Bob thinks he's a great scammer, but he's just a wimp.* □ *Do scammers have a great future? What's for an encore?*

scammered *mod.* alcohol intoxicated. □ *She is scammered out of her mind.* □ *Two bottles of that stuff and she was scammered.*

scamp [skæmp] *n.* a small child. □ *Come here, you little scamp!* □ *There are three little scamps at the door saying, "Trick or treat!"*

scandal sheet *n.* a tabloid newspaper featuring lurid news. □ *I like to read a scandal sheet every now and then.* □ *I'm tired of this scandal sheet. Let's get a classy newspaper today.*

scank See *skank.*

scare someone or something up *tr.* to find someone or something. (As if one were flushing wild game.) □ *I have to scare a date up for Friday night.* 🆃 *See if you can scare up a clean tablecloth.*

scare the hell out of someone *tr.* to frighten someone badly. (Use caution with *hell.*) □ *These figures scare the hell out of me.* □ *The door blew shut and scared the hell out of me.*

scare the pants off someone *tr.* to frighten someone suddenly. □ *The piano lid fell and scared the pants off my parents.* □ *It takes a lot to scare the pants off a hardened criminal.*

scared shitless *mod.* very frightened. (Potentially offensive. Use caution with *shit.*) □ *He wasn't just frightened. He was scared shitless!* □ *He had to go to court and was scared shitless about it.*

scared stiff *mod.* frightened; unable to move from fear. □ *The poor little kid stood there—scared stiff.* □ *I was scared stiff for hours after the accident.*

scarf 1. *tr.* to eat something. □ *Andy scarfed the whole pie.* □ *Are you going to scarf the whole thing?* **2.** *in.* to eat. □ *I'll be with you as soon as I scarf.* □ *I gotta go scarf now.* **3.** *n.* food. □ *I want some good scarf. This stuff stinks.* □ *No more fried scarf for me.* **4.** *tr.* to steal or swipe something. □ *The kid scarfed a candy bar, and the store owner called the cops.* □ *The plumber's assistant had been scarfing copper for months before they figured out what was going on.* **5.** *tr.* to discard something. □ *Scarf that thing. It's no good.* □ *Bill scarfed his girl. She was seeing somebody else at the same time.*

scarf out *in.* to overeat. (See also *blimp out, pig out, mac out.*) □ *I scarf out every weekend.* □ *My brother scarfs out every day—around the clock!*

scarf something down *tr.* to eat something, perhaps in a hurry; to swallow something, perhaps in a hurry. □ *Are you going to scarf this whole thing down?* 🆃 *Here, scarf down this sandwich.*

scary *mod.* (of women) ugly. □ *Man, is she scary!* □ *Why do I always end up with a scary woman?*

scat [skæt] **1.** *n.* nonsense syllables sung to music. (Refers to a [primarily black] jazz practice in the jazz era.) □ *She used to do scat but moved on to blues.* □ *He could sing scat like nobody's business.* **2.** *exclam.* "Go away!" (Usually **Scat!** Often said to a cat to get it to go away.) □ *Get out! Scat! Beat it, cat!* □ *Scat, you wretched animal!* **3.** *in.* to leave. □ *It's midnight. I gotta scat.* □ *You guys scat now. I have to go to work.* **4.** *n.* heroin. (Drugs. From an old term for dung. See also *shit.*) □ *Max is trying to sell scat in the neighborhood again.* □ *That scat's gonna get that man killed.* **5.** *n.* inferior whiskey. □ *That rotten scat nearly choked me.* □ *You got anything better than that scat, bartender?*

scatterbrain *n.* a forgetful person; someone who is mentally disorganized. □ *I'm getting to be such a scatterbrain, I think.* □ *Aunt Martha is a real scatterbrain. She always forgets where her glasses are.*

scattered *mod.* drug intoxicated; confused by drug use. (Drugs. See also *scat.*) □ *Those poor kids are so scattered, they can't even get themselves to class.* □ *Fred must spend half his life scattered and sleeping.*

scene [sin] **1.** *n.* a place; a setting. (See also *make the scene.*) ☐ *This scene is no good. Let's split.* ☐ *I need a different scene. Life is too hectic here.* **2.** *n.* the drug-use environment; the drug scene. ☐ *The longer you spend in a scene like this, the harder it is to sober up and go straight.* ☐ *This coke scene is a bad one. It will shorten your life.* **3.** *n.* one's preference. (Compare to *bag.*) ☐ *This nine-to-five stuff just isn't my scene. I quit.* ☐ *Your scene doesn't seem to involve much in the way of hard work.*

schicker See *shicker.*

schickered See *shicker.*

schizo ['skızo OR 'skıtso] **1.** *mod.* schizophrenic. ☐ *That gal is sort of schizo, isn't she?* ☐ *I have never dealt with such a schizo type before.* **2.** *n.* a schizophrenic person. ☐ *That guy is an absolute schizo!* ☐ *Keep that schizo away from me.*

schiz(z) out [skız . . .] *in.* to freak out; to lose mental control. ☐ *What a day! I nearly schizzed out.* ☐ *I schizzed out during the test. Got an F.*

schlemazel AND **schlemozzle; shlimazl** [ʃlə'mazl̩] *n.* an awkward, bumbling person; a *loser.* (Yiddish.) ☐ *And this poor schlemazel tries to get me to help him paint his fence!* ☐ *That schlemozzle is afraid of his own shadow.*

schlemiel AND **schlemihl; shlemiel** [ʃlə'mil] *n.* a gullible person; a *loser.* (From Hebrew *Shelumiel* via Yiddish.) ☐ *See if you can get that schlemiel to buy the Brooklyn Bridge.* ☐ *The stupid schlemiel says he already bought it yesterday.*

schlemihl See the previous entry.

schlemozzle See *schlemazel.*

schlep AND **shlep** [ʃlɛp] **1.** *tr.* to drag or carry someone or something. (From German *schleppen* via Yiddish.) ☐ *Am I supposed to schlep this whole thing all the way back to the store?* ☐ *I am tired of shlepping kids from one thing to another.* **2.** *n.* a journey; a distance to travel or carry something. ☐ *It takes about twenty minutes to make the schlep from here to there.* ☐ *That's a ten-mile schlep, and I won't go by myself.* **3.** *n.* a stupid person; a bothersome person. (Literally, a *drag.*) ☐ *What a schlep! The guy's a real pain.* ☐ *Ask that shlep to wait in the hall until I am free. I'll sneak out the back way.*

schlepper AND **shlepper** ['ʃlɛpɚ] *n.* an annoying person who always wants a bargain or a favor. (See also *schlep.*) ☐ *Why am I surrounded by people who want something from me? Is this a schlepper colony or what?* ☐ *Tell the shleppers that they'll get their money after I close the sale on my wife and kids.*

schlock [ʃlak] **1.** *n.* inferior merchandise. (From German *schlacke,* "dregs" via Yiddish.) ☐ *That store has nothing but schlock.* ☐ *For this schlock I should pay good money?* **2.** AND **schlocky** ['ʃlaki] *mod.* cheap; junky; inferior. ☐ *Schlocky stuff like this I can get from a no overhead mail order.* ☐ *That place is nothing but a schlock shop.* ☐ *This thing is really schlock.*

schlocky See the previous entry.

schloomp AND **schlump; shlump** [ʃlump OR ʃlʊmp] *n.* a stupid and lazy person. (From German via Yiddish.) ☐ *Tell that schloomp to get busy or get out.* ☐ *Do you work hard? I don't hire any schlumps.*

schlub AND **zhlub** [ʃləb OR ʒləb] *n.* a dull, unpolished person, usually a male. (Yiddish.) ☐ *I spent the whole evening listening to that schlub from New Hampshire.* ☐ *Hank's no zhlub. He's just eccentric.*

schlump See *schloomp.*

schmaltz AND **shmaltz** [ʃmalts] *n.* extreme sentimentality; corny sweetness. (From a Yiddish word meaning fat or oil.) ☐ *I didn't like that movie. Too much schmaltz.* ☐ *You aren't playing this piece right. It needs a little schmaltz.*

schmaltzy AND **shmaltzy** ['ʃmaltsi] *mod.* overly sweet and sentimental. (See also *schmaltz.*) ☐ *This movie is too schmaltzy for me.* ☐ *What a schmaltzy movie!*

schmegegge AND **schmegeggy** [ʃmə'gegi] **1.** *n.* a stupid person. (Yiddish.) ☐ *Who* *is that schmegegge in the plaid pants?* □ *Ask the schmegegge standing over by the workbench if he's seen my sky hook.* **2.** *n.* nonsense. □ *I've heard enough of your schmegegge. Out!* □ *I don't hear anything but schmegeggy coming out of Washington.*

schmegeggy See the previous entry.

schmendrick AND **shmendrick** [ˈʃmɛn-drɪk] *n.* a stupid and ineffectual nobody. (Yiddish.) □ *Some schmendrick from downstairs asked if you could turn down your stereo.* □ *Tell the schmendrick to drop dead.*

schmo AND **shmo; shmoe; schmoe** [ʃmo] *n.* a foolish and naive person, usually a male. (Yiddish. See also *Joe Schmo.*) □ *What a schmo! He thinks I caused the problem.* □ *Tell the silly schmoe to beat it.*

schmoe See the previous entry.

schmoose See the following entry.

schmooze AND **shmooze; schmoose** [ʃmuz] **1.** *in.* to chat; to *chew the fat.* (From Hebrew *schmuos* via Yiddish.) □ *You were schmoozing when you should have been listening.* □ *We were schmoozing before quitting time, and then the boss walked by.* **2.** *n.* a session of chatting or conversing. □ *Come over, and let's have a schmooze before you go.* □ *A good schmoose is what you need.*

schmoozer *n.* someone who chats or converses well. □ *Clare can't sing a note, but what a schmoozer!* □ *Two old schmoozers sat muttering to one another all afternoon by the duck pond.*

schmuck [ʃmək] **1.** *n.* a *jerk;* a repellent male. (Also a rude term of address. Yiddish.) □ *Who is that stupid schmuck over there?* □ *Ask that schmuck how long he will be on the phone.* **2.** *n.* a penis. (Yiddish. Use caution with the topic.) □ *If I hear that joke about a camel's schmuck one more time, I'm going to scream.* □ *There are probably better names than schmuck for what you are talking about.*

schnockered AND **schnoggered; shnockered; snoggered** [ˈʃnakə˞d AND ˈʃnagə˞d] *mod.* alcohol or drug intoxicated. □ *How can anybody be so schnockered on four beers?* □ *I've never seen anybody so schnockered.*

schnoggered See the previous entry.

schnook AND **schnuck; shnook** [ʃnʊk] *n.* a naive person; a dope. (Yiddish.) □ *The guy's a schnook with a heart of gold.* □ *What's a good-looking dame like her doing with a shnook like him?*

schnorrer [ˈʃnorə˞] *n.* a beggar; a person who sponges off of friends and relatives. (Yiddish.) □ *Here comes that schnorrer from down the street. Look poor.* □ *Buy your own ciggies if you don't like mine. Shnorrers can't be choosers.*

schnozz AND **schnozzle; schnozzola; shnozz** [ʃnaz AND ʃnazl̩, ʃnaˈzolə, ʃnaz] *n.* the nose. (From German *Schnauze* via Yiddish.) □ *Look at the schnozz on that guy!* □ *With a schnozzola like that he should be in the circus.*

schnozzle See the previous entry.

schnozzola See *schnozz.*

schnuck See *schnook.*

schoolboy Scotch *n.* wine. □ *Give me a pint of that schoolboy Scotch.* □ *Man, she is stoned out of her mind on schoolboy Scotch!*

schtick AND **shtik** [ʃtɪk] *n.* a routine or act that is the trademark of an entertainer, especially in vaudeville. (Yiddish.) □ *His schtick was a trained dog and cat act.* □ *Their shtik is so old! Maybe nobody will remember whose it was.*

schtoonk AND **shtoonk** [ʃtʊŋk] *n.* a detestable person. (Yiddish.) □ *The schtoonk from downstairs was here to talk to you. I told him you died.* □ *Who needs a shtoonk like that?*

Schwing! [ʃʍɪŋ] *exclam.* "How exciting!"; "How stimulating!"; "Wow!" (Originally said on seeing an extremely good-looking or sexually attractive girl. The word is onomatopoetic for the imaginary whishing sound of instant arousal. Many users are not aware of the origins. Potentially offensive. Use only with discretion.) □ *Did you see her? Schwing!* □ *Nice car. Schwing!*

scoff [skɔf] **1.** *tr. & in.* to eat (something). (Compare to *scarf.*) □ *He's upstairs scoffing in his room.* □ *She scoffed three hamburgers and a large order of fries.* **2.** *n.* food. □ *This scoff is gross!* □ *I want some good old American scoff.*

scooch [skutʃ] **1.** *in.* to move (oneself), while seated, forward, backward, or sideways by sliding. □ *Scooch over here by me.* □ *Why don't you scooch over here?* **2.** *tr.* to push or move something. □ *Scooch your chair over where the light is better.* □ *Scooch the potted palm to the edge of the deck and push it overboard.*

scoop 1. *n.* a news story gathered by a reporter before any other reporter hears of it. □ *I got a great scoop! I was right there when it happened.* □ *That was no scoop at all. It was on live television. Didn't you see the cameras?* **2.** *tr.* to beat someone—such as another reporter—in the race to get a news story first. □ *They scooped the other paper on both stories.* □ *Larry scooped me twice last month.* **3.** *n.* a general roundup and arrest of criminals; a *bust.* (Underworld.) □ *Max got picked up in that big drug scoop last month.* □ *There are some people who get dragged in every time there is a scoop. It cannot just be a coincidence.* **4.** *n.* liquor; a glass of beer. □ *I could use a good cold scoop about now.* □ *A little scoop helps pass the time when you're waiting.* **5.** *n.* a folded matchbook cover used to *snort* cocaine or heroin. □ *I need a scoop. It's no good without one.* □ *I burned up the scoop by accident. Sorry.* **6.** *tr. & in.* to *snort* cocaine or heroin, using a folded matchbook cover. □ *Max is scooping for the fourth time today.* □ *He scooped two lines together.*

scoot *in.* to run or scurry quickly from one place to another. □ *I scooted from the bank to the cleaners and then on to the dentist's.* □ *The shoppers scooted from store to store spending money like it was going out of style.*

scooters ['skutɚz] *mod.* crazy; confused. □ *It's days like this that make me think I'm scooters.* □ *You are driving me totally scooters with your constant beefing.*

scoots *n.* diarrhea. (Always with *the.*) □ *Our vacation was ruined by a case of the scoots.* □ *I've got just the thing for the scoots. Stay at home.*

scope (on) someone *tr.* to evaluate a member of the opposite sex visually. □ *He scoped every girl who came in the door.* □ *He wouldn't like it if somebody scoped on him. Or would he?*

scope someone out *tr.* to look someone over; to check someone out. □ *Nobody was scoping Dave out, though.* 🆃 *Dave was scoping out all the girls.*

scorched 1. *mod.* alcohol or drug intoxicated. □ *Who wants to go out and get scorched?* □ *How can anybody get so scorched on four beers?* **2.** AND **singed** [sɪndʒd] *mod.* having to do with hair burned while smoking marijuana. (Collegiate.) □ *Guess who scorched herself last night?* □ *If you go to sleep, you'll be singed for sure.*

scorcher 1. *n.* a very hot day. □ *This is really a scorcher, isn't it?* □ *Wow! What a scorcher!* **2.** *n.* a caustic remark. □ *Bob made a real scorcher about Tom's shoes.* □ *He is a master at the rude scorcher.*

scorching 1. *mod.* really hot; about to win something big. □ *Let me roll again. I'm really scorching.* □ *Here comes a scorching runner!* □ *He says he's scorching. Get out of his way.* **2.** *mod.* caustic. □ *That remark was really scorching.* □ *What a scorching glare you got from her!*

score 1. *in.* to succeed. □ *I knew if I kept trying I could score.* □ *It takes hard work and luck to score.* **2.** *tr. & in.* to obtain something; to obtain drugs or sex. (Very close to sense 1.) □ *Max spent an hour trying to score some pot.* □ *Fred is always trying to score with women.* **3.** *n.* the result of a scoring: drugs, loot, winnings, etc. □ *Where's the score? How much did you get?* □ *The crooks* *dropped the score as they made their getaway.* **4.** *in.* [for a male] to copulate with a female. (Use caution with the topic.) □ *Fred can't think about anything but scoring with Martha.* □ *He will spend his vacation trying to score.* **5.** *n.* the client of a male or female prostitute. □ *She conked the score over the head and robbed him.* □ *Three scores was a full day's work for Tracy.* **6.** *n.* a summary; a conclusion; the sum total. (Compare to *bottom line.*) □ *The score is that you are in trouble with the Internal Revenue Service.* □ *Okay, waiter, what's the score?*

scrag [skræg] **1.** *n.* the neck. (Underworld.) □ *The cop grabbed him by the scrag and pushed him along to the squad car.* □ *It's gonna be your scrag in the noose when this thing's over.* **2.** *tr.* to kill someone or something. (Originally underworld to "strangle.") □ *The gang decided that somebody was going to have to scrag the witness.* □ *A truck almost scragged Max.*

scraggy ['skrægi] *mod.* bony. □ *That dame is too scraggy for me.* □ *Who is that scraggy dame?* □ *I lost weight till I was scraggy as a hungry bear.*

scram [skræm] *in.* to exit fast; to get out of a place in a hurry. □ *I gotta scram. I'm late.* □ *Go on, scram! Get out of here fast!*

scrambled eggs *n.* decorations on a military officer's uniform. □ *I know his rank is high because of the scrambled eggs, but I don't know how high.* □ *I'll be glad when I get some scrambled eggs on me.*

scrape the bottom of the barrel *tr.* to utilize the last or only things or people available, even if unsatisfactory. (See also *bottom of the barrel.*) □ *They were really scraping the bottom of the barrel when they picked you.* □ *You scraped the bottom of the barrel for this one. I want something better.*

scratch 1. *n.* money. □ *I just don't have the scratch.* □ *How much scratch does it take to buy a car like this one?* **2.** *tr.* to eliminate something from a list; to cancel something. □ *Scratch Fred. He can't make the party.* □ *We decided to scratch the idea of a new car. The old one will have to do.* **3.** *mod.* impromptu; temporary. (Compare to *pickup.*) □ *We started a scratch game of basketball, but most of the girls had to leave at dinnertime.* □ *This is just a scratch tape. After you use it for your computer program, someone else will write something over it.*

scratch sheet *n.* a daily horse-racing newsletter at the racetrack. □ *I picked up a scratch sheet from Lucky Louie and proceeded to lay down my life's saving on a horse named Felicity Anne.* □ *Even the cost of a scratch sheet is going up, and I'm trying to economize!*

scream 1. *n.* someone or something very funny. (Always with *a.*) □ *The joke Tom told was really a scream.* □ *Tom is always a scream at parties.* **2.** *n.* ice cream. (Collegiate.) □ *How about a nice big dish of scream?* □ *It's too cold for scream. Ask me in June.*

scream bloody murder *tr.* to scream very loudly; to complain or protest loudly. □ *She screams bloody murder every time I get near her.* □ *Those guys scream bloody murder long before they're hurt.*

screamer 1. *n.* a newspaper headline. □ *Did you see the screamer in the paper today? "The King Died."* □ *I never read screamers.* **2.** *n.* an exclamation point. (Printing.) □ *Put a screamer at the end of the line.* □ *Clean up this copy. There are too many screamers. Looks like junior high stuff.* **3.** *n.* anything challenging. □ *What a horrible assignment I got. A classic screamer.* □ *Bring on the screamers. I can handle anything.* **4.** *n.* someone or something very exciting or attention getting. □ *This guy is a real screamer! Wait'll you meet him.* □ *Her political campaign is a real screamer.*

screaming-meemie AND **screamie-meemie** *n.* a screaming child or adult. □ *Oh, don't be such a screaming-meemie!* □ *Jennifer has been a terrible screamie-meemie all day long!*

screaming-meemies AND **screaming-meamies** *n.* the *willies*—a mental breakdown. ☐ *They sent Max away with the screaming-meemies.* ☐ *I need some sleep. I'm about to come down with the screaming-meamies.*

screeching (drunk) *mod.* alcohol intoxicated; very drunk. ☐ *How can anybody be so screeching drunk on four beers?* ☐ *She's not just drunk; she's screeching.*

screw 1. *n.* a jailer. (Underworld.) ☐ *See if you can get the screw's attention.* ☐ *I'm sick, screw! Let me out!* **2.** *tr. & in.* to copulate (with someone). (Use caution with *screw* and the topic.) ☐ *He's telling everybody that he screwed her.* ☐ *They screw all the time, just like bunnies.* **3.** *tr.* to cheat someone. ☐ *That salesman tried to screw me, but I just walked out on him.* ☐ *They didn't screw me. I got good value for my money.* (More at *screwed*.)

screw around *in.* to waste time. ☐ *Stop screwing around and get busy.* ☐ *John's always screwing around and never does anything on time.*

screw around with someone or something *in.* to fiddle with or *mess around (with someone or something)*. ☐ *Andy screwed around with his clock until he broke it.* ☐ *Look, chum! Don't screw around with me!*

screw someone or something up *tr.* to interfere with someone or something; to mess up someone or something. ☐ *Try again and don't screw it up this time.* 🅃 *You really screwed up my brother by not being on time.*

screw someone out of something *tr.* to cheat someone of something. ☐ *You are trying to screw me out of what is rightfully mine!* ☐ *I'm not trying to screw anybody out of anything!*

screw someone over *tr.* to give someone a very bad time; to scold someone severely. ☐ *Those guys really screwed you over. What started it?* 🅃 *Let's get those kids in here and screw over every one of them. This stuff can't continue.*

screw up 1. *in.* to mess up. ☐ *I hope I don't screw up this time.* ☐ *The waiter screwed up again.* **2.** *n.* a mess; a blunder; utter confusion. (Usually **screw-up.**) ☐ *This is the chef's screw-up, not mine.* ☐ *One more screw up like that and you're fired.* (More at *screwed up*.)

screwball 1. *n.* an eccentric person; a clown or a dunce. (Also a rude term of address.) ☐ *Tom is such a screwball!* ☐ *Look, you screwball, get out!* **2.** *n.* (in baseball) a (pitched) ball that does not travel in a straight line. ☐ *Jim threw another screwball, but somehow the batter hit it.* ☐ *Larry always seemed to be able to hit a screwball, no matter what.*

screwed 1. AND **screwed tight** *mod.* alcohol intoxicated. ☐ *She spends a lot of time screwed.* ☐ *She's not just drunk; she's screwed tight.* **2.** *mod.* bested; defeated; cheated. ☐ *I really got screwed at the garage.* ☐ *If you don't want to get screwed by somebody, you have to do it yourself.*

screwed, blued, and tattooed ['skrud 'blud æn tæ'tud] **1.** *mod.* badly mistreated; badly screwed. ☐ *I got a bad deal. I got screwed, blued, and tattooed.* ☐ *When John bought his wreck of a car, he got screwed, blued, and tattooed.* **2.** *mod.* alcohol intoxicated. ☐ *Who wants to go out and get screwed, blued, and tattooed?* ☐ *All four of them went out and got screwed, blued, and tattooed.*

screwed tight See *screwed*.

screwed up *mod.* ruined; messed up. ☐ *This is a really screwed up schedule. Let's start over again.* ☐ *Your schedule is completely screwed up.*

screwy 1. *mod.* crazy. ☐ *I've never heard such a screwy idea.* ☐ *It's really screwy.* ☐ *That's the screwiest looking hat I've ever seen.* **2.** *mod.* alcohol intoxicated. ☐ *How can anybody be so screwy on five beers?* ☐ *I've never seen anybody so screwy.*

script(t) *n.* a note; any piece of paper with a written message. (Underworld.) ☐ *Hey, Mike, here's a script for you from the boss.* ☐ *Make him sign this script before you let him in on the deal.*

scrog [skrɔg] *tr. & in.* to have sex; to copulate (with someone). (Use caution with the topic.) □ *You know what! I think those people over in the corner are scrogging!* □ *The movie showed scene after scene of this woman scrogging some guy.*

scronched [skrɔntʃt] *mod.* alcohol intoxicated. □ *She just sat there and got scronched.* □ *He spends a lot of time totally scronched.*

scrooge [skrudʒ] *n.* a stingy person; a *penny-pincher.* (From the character in Dickens's *A Christmas Carol.*) □ *Ask scrooge over there if you can borrow a quarter to call the cops.* □ *Don't be such a scrooge! All I want is a buck!*

scrounge (around (for someone or something)) [skrɑundʒ . . .] *in.* to look around for someone or something; to seek someone or something in every likely place. □ *Try to scrounge around for somebody to go to the party with, why don't you?* □ *I don't think there is anybody who will go with me, but I'll scrounge around.* □ *Ask John to scrounge around for a wrench.*

scrounge someone or something up *tr.* to get someone or something somehow. □ *I scrounged a doctor up in the middle of the night.* 🆃 *See if you can scrounge up a new carburetor by noon.*

scrub *tr.* to cancel something. □ *We had to scrub the whole plan because of the weather.* □ *The manager scrubbed the party because people wouldn't cooperate.*

scrud *n.* a serious disease; a venereal disease. (Military.) □ *Oh, hell! I think I got the scrud!* □ *Poor dumb Charlie can't tell scrud from crotch rot.*

scruff(y) ['skrəf(i)] *mod.* sloppy; unkempt. □ *Her boyfriend is a little scruffy, but he's got billies!* □ *Why don't you clean up this scruff car? It's—like—grody!*

scrump [skrəmp] *tr. & in.* to copulate (with someone). (Use caution with the topic.) □ *You know what! I think those people over by the garage are scrumping!* □ *The movie showed a scene of some woman scrumping her lover.*

scrumptious ['skrəmpʃəs] *mod.* excellent; tasty. □ *That cake is just scrumptious, Mary. What's in it?* □ *Who makes the most scrumptious chocolate chip cookies in the world—besides me, that is?*

scrunch [skrəntʃ] *tr.* to crush or crunch. □ *I sat on my cookies and scrunched them.* □ *I hate crowds. I am afraid people will scrunch me.*

scrunge [skrəndʒ] *n.* nastiness; gunk. □ *What is this scrunge on my shoe?* □ *When you find some scrunge on your shoe or something, never try to find out what it is. Just wipe it off.*

scrungy ['skrəndʒi] **1.** *mod.* filthy. □ *This place is too scrungy for me. I'm outa here.* □ *What a scrungy guy. Put him somewhere to soak for a day or two.* **2.** *mod.* inferior; bad. □ *I don't need scrungy merchandise like this. I'm going elsewhere.* □ *You have a very scrungy outlook on life.* □ *Life is scrungy.*

SCSI AND **scuzzy** ['skəzi] *n.* "small computer system interface." (Computers. Acronym.) □ *Come over and see my new SCSI. It lets me run a hard disc.* □ *Why do they call it a scuzzy? Why not just say what it is?*

scum [skəm] *n.* a wretched person. (Also a rude and provocative term of address. See also *pond scum.*) □ *Who is that scum? Who does she think she is?* □ *Look, you scum, I'm gonna fix you once and for all!*

scumbag *n.* a mean and wretched person, usually a male. (Also a rude term of address.) □ *That scumbag is going to get caught someday.* □ *All those guys are scumbags. I don't want to have anything to do with any of them.*

scupper up *in.* to drink liquor, especially beer. □ *Tom goes home to scupper up every evening.* □ *Come on, you guys. Scupper up, and let's get outa here.*

scurvy ['skɚvi] *mod.* repulsive; *gross.* (Collegiate.) □ *Who is that scurvy guy who just came in?* □ *That class is scurvy. You'll wish you hadn't taken it.*

scut [skət] *n.* a despicable person. (Teens and collegiate.) □ *How can you be, like, such a scut?* □ *It's scuts like that who give all us really rad kids a bad name.*

scuttlebutt *n.* gossip. □ *What's the scuttlebutt on the steeple clock? Why did it stop?* □ *Don't pay any attention to the scuttlebutt around here.*

scuz(z) [skəz] **1.** *n.* filth. □ *What is this scuzz all over the floor?* □ *There is some scuzz on your shoe.* **2.** *n.* a nasty person; an undesirable person; a scraggly person. □ *And this scuzz comes up to me and asks me to dance, and I'm like, "What?"* □ *I told the scuz, like, I was feeling sick, so I couldn't dance with anybody.*

scuzz someone out *tr.* to nauseate someone. □ *He had this unreal face that almost scuzzed me out!* T *It's not nice to scuzz out people like that, especially when you hardly know them.*

scuzzbag *n.* a despicable person. (Also a rude term of address.) □ *Who is that scuzzbag who just came in?* □ *Look, scuzzbag, we don't want your kind around here.*

scuzzo *n.* a repellent person. □ *There's the scuzzo who thinks I like him.* □ *How do you get rid of a scuzzo like that?*

scuzzy ['skəzi] **1.** *mod.* repellent; unkempt. □ *His clothes are always so scuzzy. He probably keeps them in a pile in his room.* □ *Whose scuzzy car is that in the driveway?* **2.** See *SCSI.*

sea *n.* cocaine. (Drugs. A spelling-out of *C.*) □ *There is a bunch using sea over at Fred's place.* □ *I never used sea before. I hear there's nothing like it.*

sealed (up) *mod.* settled; secured; *cinched.* □ *The matter was sealed by Monday morning.* □ *The contract was sealed up just in time.*

sealed with a kiss AND **SWAK** *mod.* written and sent with love and care. (The initialism is sometimes written on love letters. Also an acronym.) □ *All her letters come SWAK.* □ *I know they are sealed with a kiss, because she says so.*

seam-squirrels *n.* lice. (See also *pants rabbits.*) □ *I got an itch. Must be seam-squirrels.* □ *Where would you get seam-squirrels?*

Search me. *sent.* "I don't know." (There is a heavy stress on both words.) □ TOM: *How do crickets make that chirping noise?* BILL: *Search me.* □ *You can search me. How should I know?*

seat *n.* the buttocks. □ *Bob fell down on his seat.* □ *I was so angry. I wanted to kick him in the seat as he left.*

sec [sɛk] **1.** *n.* a second. (See also *tick.*) □ *I'll be with you in a sec. Keep your pants on!* □ *Just a sec. I'm on the phone.* **2.** AND **secs** *n.* a Seconal™ barbiturate capsule. (Drugs.) □ *Max likes amies better than secs.* □ *I started taking sec in the hospital and just couldn't stop.*

second fiddle *n.* a person in a secondary role; the second best. (Frequently with *play.*) □ *I won't stay around here playing second fiddle for someone half my age and ability!* □ *There are worse things than being second fiddle.*

second sacker *n.* the second baseman in baseball. □ *The second sacker missed the throw, and the runner went on home.* □ *The shortstop and the second sacker crashed into one another trying to catch a ball.*

secs See *sec.*

see *tr.* to equal or raise someone's bet in poker. □ *I see your five and raise you ten.* □ *Well, can you see me or not?*

see a man about a dog *tr.* to leave a place for a mysterious reason, usually to go to the toilet. □ *I gotta see a man about a dog.* □ *Fred went to see a man about a dog. I hope he remembers to put the seat down.*

see eye to eye *in.* [for two or more people] to agree on something or view something the same way. □ *We never seem to see eye to eye.* □ *Gary and Walter see eye to eye on this question.*

see no further than the end of one's nose AND **cannot see (any) further than the**

end of one's nose in. to be narrow-minded; to lack understanding and perception. □ *She is so selfish she can see no further than the end of her nose.* □ *You don't care about anyone but yourself. You can't see any further than the end of your nose.*

see red *tr.* to be angry. □ *When she hung up the phone, I saw red. I've never been so angry in my life.* □ *As he continued to talk, she began to see red.*

see stars *tr.* to be (knocked) unconscious. □ *If you talk to me like that again, you'll be seeing stars.* □ *I saw stars for a few seconds, and then someone threw cold water in my face.*

See ya. See the following entry.

See you. AND **See ya.** *interj.* "Good-bye." □ *Good game, Tom. See ya.* □ *See you, old chum. Give me a ring.*

See you later. *interj.* "Good-bye." (Common colloquial. Also said to people one knows one will never see again.) □ *Nice talking to you. See you later.* □ *Have a great trip, Mary. See you later.*

See you later, alligator. *interj.* "Good-bye." (From the 1930's. Answered with "After while, crocodile.") □ TOM: *Bye.* BILL: *See you later, alligator.* □ BILL: *See you later, alligator.* TOM: *After while, crocodile.*

seegar ['sigɑr] *n.* a cigar. (Folksy. The stress is on the first syllable.) □ *This dude came into this hamburger joint with a big seegar in his mouth, and the manager called the cops.* □ *There's nothing like a fine seegar after a nice bowl of hot chili.*

seeing pink elephants AND **seeing pink spiders; seeing snakes** *tr.* alcohol intoxicated; recovering from a drinking bout; having the delirium tremens. □ *When I got to the point of seeing pink elephants, I knew that something had to be done.* □ *The old one who's shaking —he's probably seeing snakes.*

seeing pink spiders See the previous entry.

seeing snakes See *seeing pink elephants.*

seen better days *tr.* showing signs of wear or exhaustion. (Always a past participle.) □ *This coat has seen better days.* □ *The pitcher has seen better days. He's about through on this team, I think.*

seeyabye ['sijə'bɑɪ] *interj.* "bye." (California.) □ *Oh, that's, like, so, like, rad. Okay, seeyabye.* □ *Gotta go now. Seeyabye.*

self-propelled sandbag *n.* a U.S. Marine. (Persian Gulf War.) □ *Once those self-propelled sandbags hit the bars, you army guys had better just go home.* □ *Those guys are just self-propelled sandbags. They are fearless.*

sell a wolf ticket AND **sell wolf tickets** *tr.* to boast, bluff, or lie. (Originally black. Compare to *buy someone's wolf ticket.*) □ *Freddie is out selling wolf tickets again.* □ *Are you trying to sell me a wolf ticket?*

sell someone out *tr.* to betray someone. □ *How could you sell me out like that?* Ⓣ *She would sell out her mother.*

sell wolf tickets See *sell a wolf ticket.*

sellout **1.** *n.* the event of selling all of something. (Advertising.) □ *Come to our gigantic sellout of all name brand merchandise!* □ *This is the sellout of the century. Everything must go.* **2.** *n.* a betrayal. (See also *sell someone out.*) □ *Any one of you could have stood up for me. What a sellout!* □ *How can you pull such a sellout?*

send someone from pillar to post *tr.* to send someone from place to place; to give someone the runaround. □ *Red tape everywhere I went. They sent me from pillar to post until closing time.* □ *Nobody is in charge there. They send you from pillar to post, and you don't complain for fear they'll start you all over again.*

send someone or something up *tr.* to perform a parody of someone or something. □ *Last week, he sent the president up.* Ⓣ *In his act, he sends up famous people.* (More at *send-up.*)

send someone to glory **1.** *tr.* to kill someone. □ *One shot sent him to glory.* □

You want me to send you to glory or something? **2.** *tr.* to officiate at the burial services for someone. □ *The preacher sent him to glory amidst the sobs of six or seven former fans.* □ *The preacher probably gets fifty bucks for every stiff he sends to glory.*

send someone up the river *tr.* to send someone to prison. (Underworld. As done by a judge or indirectly by the police.) □ *They tried to send me up the river, but my lip got me off.* □ *I'm gonna send you up the river if it's the last thing I do.*

send-up *n.* a parody. □ *It was his delightful send-up of the current administration that catapulted Roger Rogers to national fame.* □ *I enjoy a good send-up, even if it is about me.*

sense (bud) See *sinse*.

sent **1.** *mod.* alcohol or drug intoxicated. □ *Two glasses and she's sent.* □ *He's not just sent; he's stoned.* **2.** *mod.* carried away by mellow music. □ *She's really sent. Look at her as she listens.* □ *All the musicians were sent. Maybe they were on something.*

serious *mod.* good; profound; excellent. (See also *heavy*.) □ *He plays some serious guitar.* □ *Man, these tunes are, like, serious.*

serious about someone *mod.* in love, or almost in love, with someone. □ *I'm afraid I'm getting serious about Bill.* □ *Bill, unfortunately, is pretty serious about Mary.*

serve someone right *tr.* to be just what someone deserves. □ *It would serve you right if you lost your money.* □ *He fell down. It serves him right.*

session **1.** *n.* a drinking bout. □ *Your father's off on another session again.* □ *He was just sobering up from a session with the bottle.* **2.** *n.* a marijuana-smoking session; time spent on a drug high. (Collegiate.) □ *What a fine session that was!* □ *Max was terribly hungry after the session.*

set **1.** *n.* a period of time that a band plays without a break; a thirty-minute jam session. □ *I'll talk to you after this set.* □ *We do two sets and then take a twenty-minute break.* **2.** *n.* a party. □ *Your set was a totally major bash!* □ *Let's throw a set tonight and invite some chicks.*

set of pipes *n.* a very loud voice; a singing voice. □ *She has a nice set of pipes.* □ *With a set of pipes like that, she's a winner.*

set of wheels *n.* a car. □ *I need a new set of wheels.* □ *Man, look at that set of wheels that chick has!*

set someone back *tr.* to cost someone. □ *That must have set you back a mint!* □ *This bracelet set me back plenty.*

set someone up (for something) *tr.* to set the scene for something to happen to someone. □ *His buddies set him up for the gag—which ended up injuring two of them severely.* □ *Who set me up for this anyway?*

sets See *cets*.

settle someone's hash *tr.* to calm someone down, perhaps by threats or by violence. □ *If he comes in here, I'll settle his hash.* □ *Now, that ought to settle your hash.*

setup **1.** *n.* a place to live. □ *She's got a little setup over on Maple.* □ *This is a pretty nice setup. What's the rent?* **2.** *n.* a scheme; a plot. (Underworld.) □ *Okay, what's the setup for the bank job?* □ *I got a good little setup for earning some money.* **3.** *n.* a person who is set up for some swindle; a *mark*. (Underworld.) □ *Is he the setup? He's a cop!* □ *The setup got wise at the last minute.* **4.** *n.* a glass with ice for an alcoholic beverage. (Usually plural.) □ *Can we have a couple of setups brought to our room, please?* □ *Who ordered the setups?*

[seven-seven-three-H] See *773H* [at the beginning of this section].

seven-year itch *n.* a real or imagined longing for other women in a man's seventh year of marriage. □ *Looks like Jack has the seven-year itch.* □ *The seven-year itch is just a rumor.*

sew something up *tr.* to finalize something; to conclude something. □ *Let's sew this up and get out of here.* Ⓣ *I'm about ready to sew up this matter.* (More at *sewed up.*)

sewed up 1. *mod.* completed. □ *I've just about got this contract sewed up.* □ *When we get it sewed up, we'll go out for a drink.* **2.** *mod.* alcohol intoxicated. □ *She's not just drunk; she's sewed up.* □ *Will this stuff get me sewed up?*

sewer hog *n.* a ditchdigger; a sewer worker. □ *A sewer hog doesn't get a lot of chances to pal around with the gentry, but the pay's plenty good.* □ *Fred worked as a sewer hog and made a fortune.*

sewermouth *n.* someone who uses vile language constantly. (Also a rude term of address.) □ *If you're going to be a sewermouth, I wish you would leave.* □ *Who's the sewermouth in the plaid jacket?*

sex goddess *n.* a sexy looking female movie or television star. □ *I wonder what these sex goddesses look like when they get up in the morning.* □ *Sex goddesses get up in the afternoon.*

sex kitten *n.* a woman with enormous sexual potential. □ *He thought he was getting a sex kitten, but she turned out to be just a plain cat.* □ *Clare does everything she can to look like a sex kitten.*

sex-machine *n.* a sexually promising person; a person obsessed with sex. □ *Heidi looks like such a sex-machine, but she is a real wallflower.* □ *John thinks of himself as a sex-machine, but no one else does.*

sex pot *n.* one who flaunts one's sexuality, usually a woman. □ *Tiffany is such a sex pot.* □ *About 20,000 young sex pots hit Hollywood every year hoping to be discovered.*

sexy 1. *mod.* having great sex appeal. □ *What a sexy chick!* □ *He's not what I would call sexy, but I suppose it's a matter of taste.* **2.** *mod.* neat; exciting. □ *That's a sexy set of wheels.* □ *You play really sexy music.* □ *Your idea is real sexy.*

Sez me! See *Says me!*

Sez who? See *Says who?*

S.F. *mod.* alcohol intoxicated. (Initialism. From *shit-faced.*) □ *Fred was really S.F. last night.* □ *How can that guy get so S.F.?*

sgo See *sko.*

shack up (with someone) 1. *in.* to have a *one-night stand* with someone; to copulate (with someone). □ *Those two just wanted to shack up for a while.* □ *He only wanted to shack up with me.* **2.** *in.* to move in with someone temporarily, presumably for sexual purposes. □ *They shacked up for over a year until her parents found out and stopped sending her money.* □ *They decided to shack up.*

shades *n.* dark glasses. (See also *sunshades.*) □ *Where are my shades? The sun is too bright.* □ *The guy stood there —wearing shades and carrying a violin case. Barlowe grimaced.*

shaft 1. *n.* a bad deal; unfair treatment. □ *He really gave me the shaft.* □ *It's the shaft whenever you go into that place.* **2.** *tr.* to do wrong to someone. □ *The jerk shafted me, but good.* □ *We are going to shaft this guy in a way that he will remember.* (More at *shafted.*)

shafted *mod.* beaten; bested; cheated. □ *I really got shafted in that deal.* □ *I've been shafted!*

shag-nasty *mod.* nasty. □ *What a shag-nasty jerk!* □ *I want out of this shag-nasty mess.*

shag (off) *in.* to depart. □ *I gotta shag. It's late.* □ *Go on! Shag off!* □ *I gotta shag. Somebody's calling my name.*

shagged *mod.* alcohol intoxicated. □ *She is mucho shagged!* □ *Nobody is not too shagged to drive—or something like that.*

shagged out *mod.* exhausted. □ *What a day! I'm shagged out!* □ *You guys look sort of shagged out.*

shake *n.* a milkshake. □ *I'd like a chocolate shake, please.* □ *A shake only costs sixty cents.*

shake a leg **1.** *tr.* to hurry; to move faster. (Often as a command.) ☐ *Let's shake a leg, you guys. We gotta be there in twenty minutes.* ☐ *She told me to shake a leg, so I hurried the best I could.* **2.** *tr.* to dance. ☐ *Let's shake a leg. The music's great.* ☐ *Hey, Tracy! You wanna shake a leg with me?*

Shake it (up)! *exclam.* "Hurry!"; "Move faster!" ☐ *Get going, chum! Shake it up!* ☐ *We're late. Shake it!*

shake someone down **1.** *tr.* to blackmail someone. (Underworld.) ☐ *Fred was trying to shake Tracy down, but she got the cops in on it.* 🅃 *The police chief was trying to shake down just about everybody in town.* **2.** *tr.* to put pressure on someone to lend one money. ☐ *We tried to shake them down for a few hundred, but no deal.* ☐ *If you're trying to shake me down, forget it. I got a case of the shorts.*

shake-up *n.* a reorganization. ☐ *After a shake-up like the one we've just been through, everybody's a little upset.* ☐ *Fred and Clare both survived the shake-up.*

shakedown *n.* an act of extortion. (Underworld.) ☐ *Mary was giving Bruno the shakedown, so he tried to put her out of the way.* ☐ *Those bums are masters at the shakedown.*

shakeout *n.* an event that eliminates the weak or unproductive elements from a system. ☐ *After a shakeout that lasted a month, we went into full production.* ☐ *There was a big shakeout at the plant, and a whole lot of people got pink-slipped.*

shakes *n.* the delirium tremens. ☐ *I got the shakes again. That's what I get for putting soda water in my whisky.* ☐ *In the last stages, they have the shakes all the time.*

sham See *cham*.

sham(m)us [ˈʃeməs] *n.* a police officer or a detective. (Probably from Yiddish.) ☐ *One thing that a shamus always knows is when another shamus is following him.* ☐ *This is it, shammus, say your prayers.*

shammy See *cham*.

shampers See *champers*.

shampoo *n.* champagne. (See also *cham, champers, poo.*) ☐ *I just love this bubbly shampoo!* ☐ *There is nothing like shampoo to liven up a party!*

shank **1.** *n.* a knife. ☐ *The mugger pulled a shank on the victim.* ☐ *The cops found the shank in the bushes.* **2.** *in.* to dance. ☐ *They were busy shankin' and didn't hear the gunshots.* ☐ *We were all shankin' to a great reggae band.*

shank it *tr.* to use one's legs to get somewhere; to walk. ☐ *My car needs fixing so I had to shank it to work today.* ☐ *I like to shank it every now and then.*

shank's mare *n.* foot travel. ☐ *You'll find that shank's mare is the quickest way to get across town.* ☐ *Is there a bus, or do I have to use shank's mare?*

shape up **1.** *in.* to improve; to reform. ☐ *I want to get things shaped up around here.* ☐ *I guess I'd better shape up if I want to stay in school.* **2.** *in.* to assume a final form or structure. ☐ *The game plan for the election was beginning to shape up.* ☐ *Her objectives began to shape up in her senior year.*

shape up or ship out *phr.* "improve or get out." ☐ *I'll tell you one more time. Shape up or ship out!* ☐ *They told me I had to shape up or ship out.*

shark **1.** *n.* a swindler; a confidence operator. (Underworld.) ☐ *The sharks were lined up ten deep to get at the blue-eyed new owner of the bowling alley.* ☐ *The guy's a shark, and he's after your hard-earned money!* **2.** *n.* a lawyer. (Derogatory.) ☐ *Some shark is trying to squeeze a few grand out of me.* ☐ *Hire another shark to go after him.*

shark repellent *n.* something that prevents corporate takeovers. (Securities markets.) ☐ *Acme Systems tried again to get its board to approve a shark repellent to keep the Widget cartel from* *acquiring it.* □ *The shark repellent wasn't enough.*

sharp 1. *mod.* clever; intelligent. □ *She's a real sharp chick! Got lots of savvy.* □ *She's sharp enough to see right through everything you say.* **2.** *mod.* good-looking; well-dressed. □ *You really look sharp today.* □ *That's a sharp set of wheels you got there.*

sharpie *n.* a clever operator; a clever person. □ *She's a real sharpie. She'll take you for everything you've got.* □ *A young sharpie in the first row got the answer right away.*

shave *tr.* to reduce or lessen something. □ *They shaved the waiting time to six months.* □ *The coach thought that the other team was shaving points, so he complained the next day.*

shaved *mod.* alcohol intoxicated. □ *I feel a tad shaved.* □ *So what if I'm a bit shaved? I shtill have all my shenses.*

shavetail *n.* a second lieutenant; a noncommissioned officer in the army; any inexperienced person. (Military. From a nickname for an untrained mule that is marked by a shaved tail.) □ *This shavetail here is trying to tell me my job.* □ *Who's the shavetail dancing with the Colonel's daughter?*

Shazzam! [ʃəˈzæm] *exclam.* "Wow!"; "Would you believe?" □ *And there was my ring—Shazzam!—right on the sidewalk!* □ *Shazzam! I passed the test!*

sheen [ʃin] *n.* a car. (From *machine.*) □ *You have one fine sheen there.* □ *I have to get my sheen's oil changed today.*

sheepskin *n.* a high school or college diploma. □ *When you get that sheepskin on the wall, you'll feel like it was all worth something.* □ *Where is your sheepskin from?*

Sheesh! [ʃiʃ] *exclam.* "Damn!"; "*Shit!*" (A euphemism for *Shit!*) □ *Sheesh! What a mess!* □ *Sheesh! I'm getting out of here!*

sheet See *(rap) sheet.*

shekels [ˈʃɛkl̩z] *n.* dollars; money. □ *You got a few shekels you can spare?* □ *These things cost plenty of shekels.*

shell an amount of money out See the following entry.

shell out (an amount of money) AND **shell an amount of money out** *tr. & in.* to spend a certain amount of money. □ *I'm not going to shell $400 out for that!* □ *Come on. You owe me. Shell out!*

shellack [ʃəˈlæk] *tr.* to beat someone; to outscore someone. □ *We're gonna shellack those bums Friday night.* □ *We'll be shellacking every team in the league this year.* (More at *shellacked, shellacking.*)

shellacked 1. *mod.* beaten; outscored. □ *They were shellacked, and they knew it.* □ *The team got shellacked in last week's game.* **2.** *mod.* alcohol intoxicated; overcome by booze. □ *Ernie was so shellacked he couldn't see.* □ *How did he get so shellacked? I didn't see him drink anything.*

shellacking *n.* a beating. □ *We gave them a shellacking they'll never forget.* □ *Our team took a real shellacking.*

Sherlock [ˈʃɚlɑk] *n.* one's pal or buddy. (A play on *homes, holmes,* and *Sherlock Holmes.*) □ *Come on, Sherlock, let's go!* □ *What's happening, Sherlock?*

shicker [ˈʃɪkɚ] **1.** AND **schicker; schickered** [ˈʃɪkɚd] *mod.* alcohol intoxicated. (From Hebrew *shiqor* via Yiddish.) □ *It took her about ten minutes to get schicker and three days to get sober.* □ *He's schickered, and he's not going anywhere tonight.* **2.** *n.* liquor; beer. □ *Fill it up with shicker again.* □ *How do you know when you've had enough shicker?* **3.** *in.* to tipple; to become alcohol intoxicated. □ *I'm gonna go out and shicker till I'm silly.* □ *Fred is shickering again this weekend.*

shield *n.* a police officer's badge. □ *The fuzz flashed his shield, and I knew the game was over.* □ *If you're a cop, where's your shield?*

shill [ʃɪl] **1.** *n.* someone planted in the crowd to urge others to buy something, participate in something, etc. □ *The guy's a shill! Don't fall for this setup!* □ *There were more shills than suckers on the midway that day.* **2.** *in.* to advertise for something; to give a sales pitch for something. □ *Four stars of an old television show were there shilling for a major computer firm.* □ *They pay them a mint to shill like that.*

shindig ['ʃɪndɪg] *n.* a party; a dance. (Folksy.) □ *What a fancy shindig! They even have glass glasses!* □ *What time do we have to be at that shindig Saturday night?*

shine someone *tr.* to insult someone; to deceive someone. □ *Stop shining me. I'm cool, man, ice.* □ *Bill is always shining Carla.*

shined *mod.* alcohol intoxicated, especially by *moonshine.* □ *Tipsy? He's shined from dawn to dusk.* □ *The old farmer seemed a bit shined.*

shiner *n.* a black eye. □ *Wow, look at Marty's shiner!* □ *I got this shiner by walking into a door.*

shit (All senses are potentially offensive. Use only with discretion.) **1.** *n.* dung. □ *Don't step in that shit there.* □ *There's dog shit in my yard!* **2.** *n.* something poor in quality; junk. □ *This stuff is shit. Show me something better.* □ *What do you keep all this shit around here for?* **3.** *n.* nonsense; *bullshit.* □ *Don't give me that shit! I know you're lying.* □ *I'm tired of your shit!* **4.** *n.* drugs in general; heroin; marijuana. (Drugs.) □ *Lay off the shit, Harry! You're gonna end up hooked.* □ *So Marty scores a bag of shit—I mean skag—you know, H.—and we get out the apps to shoot.* **5.** *tr.* to deceive someone; to lie to someone. □ *Stop shittin' me, you bastard!* □ *You wouldn't shit me, would you?* **6.** *n.* a despicable person. (Crude. Also a rude and provocative term of address.) □ *Tell that stupid shit to get out of here, or I'll bust him one.* □ *What a shit you are!* **7.** *exclam.* a general expression of disgust. (Usually *Shit!* Potentially offensive. Use only with discretion.) □ *Oh, shit! What a mess!* □ *Shit! That's terrible.*

shit-faced AND **shitty** *mod.* alcohol intoxicated. (Potentially offensive. Use only with discretion. See also *poopied, S.F.*) □ *I'm shit-faced, and I know it.* □ *Move over. You're too shitty to drive.*

Shit happens. *interj.* "Bad things just happen." (Potentially offensive. Use only with discretion.) □ *Tough luck, but shit happens.* □ *Shit happens. There's nothing that can be done about it.*

shitcan (Potentially offensive. Use only with discretion.) **1.** *n.* a trash can; a garbage can. □ *Just throw this in the shitcan. It's worthless.* □ *The shitcan is full. Go dump it.* **2.** *tr.* to throw something in the garbage can. □ *Shitcan this thing, will you?* □ *Who shitcanned my dirty socks?*

shithead *n.* a despicable person. (Crude. Also a rude and provocative term of address. Potentially offensive. Use only with discretion.) □ *You stupid shithead!* □ *The guy is somewhere between an asshole and a shithead.*

shitload See *buttload.*

shitsky ['ʃɪtski] **1.** *n.* dung. (Potentially offensive. Use only with discretion.) □ *There's some shitsky on your shoe.* □ *Some rude dog has left a little pile of grade-A shitsky on the sidewalk.* **2.** *n.* a despicable person. (Provocative. Potentially offensive. Use only with discretion.) □ *The stupid shitsky is back on skag again.* □ *With a shitsky like that on your side, who needs enemies?*

shitty See *shit-faced.*

shiv AND **chiv** [ʃɪv] **1.** *n.* a knife. (Underworld.) □ *Swiftly and silently his shiv found its way up under Rocko's ribs. All for a silly dame.* □ *I could tell from the way his cuff broke that there was a chiv strapped to his leg.* **2.** *tr.* to stab someone. (Underworld.) □ *He shivved Rocko, and Rocko deserved it.* □ *The boss told Bruno to get Rocko one way or the other—shiv him, burn him, clobber him—but get him.*

shlemiel See *schlemiel.*

shlep See *schlep.*

shlepper See *schlepper.*

shlimazl See *schlemazel.*

shlump See *schloomp.*

shmaltz See *schmaltz.*

shmaltzy See *schmaltzy.*

shmen [ʃmen] *n.* freshmen. ☐ *A couple of shmen wandered by—looking sort of lost.* ☐ *The shmen are having a party all to themselves this Friday.*

shmendrick See *schmendrick.*

shmo See *schmo.*

shmoe See *schmo.*

shmooze See *schmooze.*

shnazz See *snazz.*

shnazzy See *snazzy.*

shnockered See *schnockered.*

shnook See *schnook.*

shnozz See *schnozz.*

shocker *n.* something shocking. ☐ *Now, here's a shocker for you.* ☐ *Her news was quite a shocker.*

shocks *n.* shock absorbers in an automobile. ☐ *That hog Cadillac needs new shocks.* ☐ *How much is a set of shocks for a buggy like this?*

shoe polish *n.* liquor; whiskey; inferior whiskey. ☐ *Why don't you give that cruddy shoe polish to the cat?* ☐ *The old lush would be delighted to get some of your shoe polish.*

shoestring *mod.* low-cost; cheap. (See also *on a shoestring.*) ☐ *This is just a shoestring operation. There is no capital involved.* ☐ *We have nothing but a shoestring budget this year.*

shoo-in [ˈʃuɪn] *n.* an easy winner. ☐ *She's a shoo-in. Nobody can touch her.* ☐ *My horse was a shoo-in. It won by a mile.*

shook up See *(all) shook up.*

Shoot! *exclam.* "Darn!" (An exclamation or a very mild curse.) ☐ *Oh, shoot! I left my shades in the car.* ☐ *Shoot! I'm late!*

shoot 1. AND **shoot up** *tr. & in.* to inject a specific drug into the bloodstream. (Drugs.) ☐ *He actually had to leave the meeting to shoot.* ☐ *The two of them were shooting up skag.* **2.** *n.* an injection of heroin. (Drugs. Usually **shoot-up.**) ☐ *The way Ernie was yawning, I knew he needed a shoot-up.* ☐ *"Just one more shot. That's all. Then, never again!" moaned Ernie, rather unconvincingly.* **3.** *tr.* to spike a drink with liquor. ☐ *I'm gonna shoot the punch with rum.* ☐ *Harry shot his date's coke with vodka.* **4.** *in.* to tell (something). ☐ *We're ready. Go ahead. Shoot!* ☐ *Okay, shoot. I'm all ears.* **5.** See *Shoot!*

shoot 'em up 1. *n.* a Western, action movie. ☐ *I like a good shoot 'em up every now and then.* ☐ *Most films are more sophisticated nowadays than the old shoot 'em ups.* **2.** *mod.* having to do with a Western, action film. ☐ *He was a shoot 'em up star in the thirties.* ☐ *I like the good old shoot 'em up movies.*

shoot for the sky See *aim for the sky.*

shoot from the hip *in.* to speak quickly and without thinking. (See also *hip-shooter.*) ☐ *She has a tendency to shoot from the hip, but that's not really a problem.* ☐ *I shot from the hip when I spoke. I'm sorry.*

shoot one's breakfast See the following entry.

shoot one's cookies AND **shoot one's breakfast; shoot one's supper** *tr.* to empty one's stomach; to vomit. ☐ *I think I'm gonna shoot my cookies.* ☐ *I shot my supper, and I was glad to get rid of it.*

shoot one's mouth off *tr.* to brag; to tell secrets. ☐ *Stop shooting your mouth off. Nobody believes you anymore.* 🅃 *So you had to go and shoot off your mouth about the bankruptcy proceedings!*

shoot one's supper See *shoot one's cookies.*

shoot one's wad *tr.* to spend or use everything. ☐ *I shot my wad on junk food.* ☐ *I can't afford a cab. I shot my wad at the restaurant.*

shoot oneself in the foot *tr.* to cause oneself difficulty; to be the author of one's own doom. ☐ *I am a master at shooting* *myself in the foot.* □ *Again, he shot himself in the foot with his open and honest dealings with the press.*

shoot-out 1. *n.* a gunfight. □ *There was a big shoot-out at the end of the movie.* □ *In this shoot-out, there were no survivors—not even a horse!* 2. *n.* an argument. □ *When the shoot-out was over, the boss—confident she had won—went back into her office.* □ *A big public shoot-out like that sours morale a lot.*

shoot someone down in flames *tr.* to ruin someone; to bring about someone's downfall. (See also *go down in flames.*) □ *It was a bad idea, okay, but you didn't have to shoot me down in flames.* □ *I didn't mean to shoot you down in flames.*

shoot someone or something down *tr.* to ruin someone or something; to debunk someone or something. □ *Just as I was making the final point, she shot me down with a simple fact I should have remembered.* 🅃 *The boss shot down my plan immediately.* (More at *shot down.*)

shoot the breeze *tr.* to chat casually and without purpose. □ *We spent the entire afternoon just shooting the breeze.* □ *It was good to shoot the breeze with you, Mary.*

shoot the bull AND **shoot the crap; shoot the shit** *tr.* to chat and gossip. (The same as *throw the bull.* Use caution with *crap, shit.*) □ *Let's get together sometime and shoot the bull.* □ *You spend too much time shooting the crap.*

shoot the cat *tr.* to empty one's stomach; to vomit. □ *I must have shot the cat a dozen times during the night.* □ *Shooting the cat is no fun when you're weak and dizzy.*

shoot the crap See *shoot the bull.*

shoot the dozens See *play the dozens.*

shoot the shit See *shoot the bull.*

shoot the works 1. *tr.* to do everything; to use everything; to bet all one's money. □ *Okay, let's go out to dinner and shoot the works.* □ *Don't shoot the works! Save some for a cab.* 2. *tr.* to empty one's stomach; to vomit. □ *Suddenly she turned sort of green, and I knew she was going to shoot the works.* □ *After she shot the works, she looked fine—but I was sort of pale.*

shoot up See *shoot.*

shoot up (on something) 1. *in.* to inject (a drug). (Drugs. See also *shoot.*) □ *About that time we both began shooting up on skag.* □ *He couldn't wait to get home and shoot up.* 2. *n.* an injection of narcotics. (Drugs. Usually **shoot-up**.) □ *Barlowe watched the dame do a shoot-up on H. and settle down so they could talk.* □ *A quick shoot-up was all she needed.*

shooting iron *n.* a pistol. (Cowboy and folksy.) □ *Millard "Shorty" Wilson always carried his shooting iron with him, except for one fateful day back in '92—1892, that is.* □ *He pulled out his shooting iron and got down to cleaning it.*

shopping list *n.* a list of things, especially questions or things one wants. (Compare to *laundry list.*) □ *I have a shopping list of absolute musts.* □ *He showed up for the interview with a shopping list so long that it took two pages.*

short 1. *n.* a small drink of hard liquor or of beer. □ *One short, bartender.* □ *I'll have a short and a pack of cigarettes.* 2. *mod.* having to do with a single drink of undiluted liquor. □ *I'll take mine short, innkeeper.* □ *Who ordered a short one?* 3. *n.* a purchase of drugs that counts or weighs out less than the amount agreed upon. □ *You gave me a short. Fix it now, or this thing goes off accidentally in your ear.* □ *Max knew that Bruno ended up with a short, and Bruno wasn't stable enough to talk about things like that. Max blew.* 4. *tr.* to give someone less of something than was agreed upon. □ *You shorted me!* □ *They shorted us on the last order, so we switched suppliers.* 5. *n.* a car. (Streets.) □ *Man, that's some short you got!* □ *Max gets his money cracking shorts.* 6. *n.* the sale of borrowed shares of stock; a short sale. (Securities markets.) □ *I think that IBM is a good short in here. The high-tech companies are in for a pullback.* □ *There is a lot of covering of* *shorts this week. After that the market is in for a steady decline.* **7.** *tr.* to sell borrowed stock. (Securities markets.) ☐ *I wouldn't short IBM. It's a long-term hold.* ☐ *The way the deficit is running, I'd short the whole market.*

short end of the stick *n.* the burden, responsibility, blame, etc., for something. (Always with *the*.) ☐ *Here I am stuck with the short end of the stick again.* ☐ *I am the one who plans all this stuff, and when you jerks drop the ball, I'm left holding the short end of the stick.*

short fuse *n.* a quick temper. ☐ *Fred's got a short fuse. Watch out.* ☐ *I knew she'd blow. She's got a short fuse.*

short one *n.* a small or quickly drunk drink of liquor, including beer. (Compare to *tall one*.) ☐ *How about a short one, innkeeper?* ☐ *Give my friend here a short one.*

short-snort *n.* a quick drink of whisky from a bottle, flask, or jug. ☐ *He grabbed a short-snort and went back to his carving.* ☐ *Jed offered the visitor a short-snort from a jar of shine.*

shorts AND **case of the shorts** *n.* the lack of money. (Always with *the*.) ☐ *Here I am with a case of the shorts again.* ☐ *The shorts always come around at the end of the month.*

shot 1. *n.* a try at something. ☐ *Go ahead. Give it another shot.* ☐ *Have a shot at this problem.* **2.** *mod.* exhausted; ruined. ☐ *I really feel shot today.* ☐ *Here's your pen back. It's shot anyway.* ☐ *This thing is shot. Let's get a new one.* **3.** *n.* a rocket launching. ☐ *The shot was canceled because of the weather.* ☐ *This shot, like the last, was a total failure.* **4.** *n.* a small or quickly drunk drink of liquor, usually whiskey. ☐ *Here, have a shot of this stuff.* ☐ *He stopped at every bar on the strip for a quick shot.* **5.** *n.* an injection of drugs. ☐ *Just one shot of that stuff and you're hooked for life.* ☐ *A shot of skag put the poor guy straight for a while.* **6.** *mod.* alcohol intoxicated. ☐ *They are a little noisy, I guess, but after all they are shot, you know, plastered.* ☐ *I am half shot now. I'll quit before I'm shot.*

shot-away See *shot-up*.

shot down 1. *mod.* demolished; destroyed. ☐ *Her idea was shot down after all her work.* ☐ *I felt shot down, even though I was sure of what I was getting into.* **2.** *mod.* rejected by a young woman. ☐ *Tiffany is a cruel chick. I was shot down from day one.* ☐ *Fred's shot down, thanks to his best girl. He'll get over it.*

shot in the arm 1. *n.* a drink of liquor. ☐ *I could use a little shot in the arm.* ☐ *How about a little shot in the arm, bartender?* **2.** *n.* an injection of narcotics. (The same as *bang in the arm*.) ☐ *You might say that I really needed this shot in the arm.* ☐ *It's nothing. Just a little shot in the arm.* **3.** *n.* a boost or act of encouragement. ☐ *The pep talk was a real shot in the arm for all the guys.* ☐ *The good test grade was a shot in the arm for Gary.*

shot in the dark *n.* a very general attempt; a wild guess. ☐ *It was just a shot in the dark. I had no idea I was exactly correct.* ☐ *Come on, try it. Even a shot in the dark may win.*

shot in the neck 1. *n.* a drink of straight whiskey. ☐ *Wally took a little shot in the neck before heading out into the cold.* ☐ *A shot in the neck was just what was needed.* **2.** *mod.* alcohol intoxicated. ☐ *He's shot in the neck, but he's not bleeding.* ☐ *What's wrong with Harry is that he's shot in the neck every day by supper.*

shot to hell *mod.* ruined; decimated. (An elaboration of *shot*.) ☐ *This thing is shot to hell. Let's get a new one.* ☐ *My car is shot to hell.*

shot-up AND **shot-away** *mod.* alcohol or drug intoxicated. ☐ *Well, you see, he's shot up and can't come to the phone.* ☐ *How can anybody get so shot-away in so little time?*

shot up 1. *mod.* severely injured by gunshots. ☐ *Tom got himself shot up in a hunting accident.* ☐ *He was pretty badly shot up in the police action.* **2.** See *shot-up*.

shotgun 1. *mod.* broad; general. □ *It was a shotgun attempt to include everyone.* □ *A shotgun approach to a problem like this is useless. You must get specific.* 2. *exclam.* a phrase called out by someone who claims the privilege of riding in a car's passenger seat. (Usually **Shotgun!**) □ *"Shotgun!" cried Jimmy, heading for the car.* □ *Whoever yelled "shotgun" has to sit holding the cake all the way.*

shotgun wedding *n.* a forced wedding, presumably because the bride is pregnant. □ *It was a shotgun wedding, but they sure are in love.* □ *I thought shotgun weddings went out with feuds and things like that.*

shouldn't happen to a dog *phr.* describes something that is so bad that no creature deserves it. □ *Poor guy. That shouldn't happen to a dog.* □ *This cold I got shouldn't happen to a dog.*

shout *n.* an exclamation point. (See also *screamer, shriek.*) □ *Put a shout at the end of the line. Make this dull story more sexy.* □ *This gal uses shouts like they were salt and pepper.*

shove *tr.* to pass counterfeit money. (Underworld.) □ *She got sent up for three years for shoving funny-money.* □ *He got away with shoving the stuff for months before they got onto him.*

shove off See *push off.*

show and tell *n.* a session where objects are presented and described. (Essentially a kindergarten or grade school activity.) □ *It was a short lecture with lots of show and tell.* □ *I can't take another show and tell session.*

show biz *n.* show business. □ *Well, that's show biz for you.* □ *Anybody who can make a living in show biz has to be clever and talented.*

shower scum *n.* a despised person; despised people. (See also *bathtub scum, pond scum.*) □ *Who is the shower scum who put a cigarette butt in my houseplant?* □ *I wish the shower scum of the neighborhood wouldn't throw trash in my yard.*

shpleef See *spliff.*

shredded *mod.* alcohol intoxicated. (Collegiate.) □ *We are all too shredded to drive home. What shall we do?* □ *I believe that each of us is shredded enough to fly home. Let's vote on that.*

shriek *n.* an exclamation point. (Printers. Compare to *screamer, shout.*) □ *Where is there a shriek at the end?* □ *Take off that shriek. You use too many of those things.*

shrimp *n.* a small person. □ *Who's the little shrimp over by the door?* □ *I'm such a shrimp. I just have short genes.*

shrink *n.* a psychoanalyst or psychotherapist. □ *I dropped a bundle on a shrink, but it didn't help me.* □ *The shrink says I have to take these pills to help me get off the drug habit.*

shroom [ʃrum] *in.* to take or eat peyote cactus. (Drugs.) □ *They spent all afternoon shrooming.* □ *You shroom too much.*

shrooms [ʃrumz] *n.* the tips of the peyote cactus that contain mescaline. (Drugs. From *mushrooms*. Not really a mushroom.) □ *I got some shrooms. Ya wanna come over?* □ *Shrooms and me don't mix.*

shtik See *schtick.*

shtoonk See *schtoonk.*

shuck [ʃək] 1. *n.* an insincere person. □ *The guy's a shuck. Don't believe a thing he says!* □ *Who needs a shuck for a legislator?* 2. *tr. & in.* to kid someone; to tease someone. □ *Cool it! I'm just shucking.* □ *Stop shucking me!* 3. *tr.* to swindle someone; to deceive someone. □ *The con man shucked a number of people in the town before moving on.* □ *He was going to shuck the mayor, but people were beginning to talk, so he blew town.* 4. *n.* a hoax. □ *What a stupid shuck!* □ *How could you fall for that old shuck?* 5. AND **shuck down** *tr. & in.* to undress oneself; to remove one's clothing. □ *He shucked himself quickly and jumped into bed.* □ *He shucked down and showered and was at work in twenty minutes.*

shuck down See *shuck.*

Shucks! See *(Aw) shucks!*

shuffler *n.* a drunkard; a *tippler.* □ *The tavern was full of aged shufflers hoping for a handout.* □ *Some shuffler barfed in the shrubbery.*

shush (up) *in.* to be quiet. □ *Shush! I want to hear the weather.* □ *Shush up and listen to the lecture.*

shut-eye *n.* sleep. □ *It's about time to get some shut-eye.* □ *I could use about another hour of shut-eye.*

shut up *in.* to be quiet. □ *Shut up and listen!* □ *Shut up yourself.*

Shut your face! *exclam.* "Shut up!"; "Be quiet!" □ *Oh, shut your face. I've heard enough.* □ *Can't you shut your face, you motor-mouth?*

shutout **1.** *n.* a game where one team prevents the other from scoring any points at all. □ *He was still reveling from last week's shutout.* □ *It was another shutout at Klum Field House last night.* **2.** *mod.* having to do with a game where one team has no score. □ *Another shutout game gave the fans nothing to cheer about this afternoon.* □ *I was hoping for a shutout contest, and I got one.*

shutters *n.* the eyelids. □ *Her shutters dropped slowly, and she was asleep.* □ *She blinked those yummy shutters over those bedroom eyes, and my knees turned to mush.*

shwench [ʃwɛntʃ] *n.* a female freshman. (Collegiate.) □ *A couple of giggling shwenches showed up to cheer on the team.* □ *There's a shwench in my English class who knows more than the prof.*

shyster ['ʃaɪstɚ] *n.* an unethical or unscrupulous lawyer. (Also a rude term of address.) □ *Look, you cheap shyster, I paid you to help me, not ruin me!* □ *My ex-wife's shyster called again today to say she wants more money.*

Siberian express *n.* an enormous mass of very cold air moving from Siberia, across the North Pole, and down onto North America. □ *The country braced itself for a return Friday of the Siberian express with temperatures dropping to twenty below in many areas.* □ *The Siberian express seems to be aimed right at our state.*

sick to death (of someone or something) *mod.* totally disgusted with someone or something. □ *I am sick to death of your constant bickering.* □ *This whole bribery business just has me sick to death.*

sick (up) *in.* to empty one's stomach; to vomit. □ *I think I'm going to sick up. Isn't there supposed to be a barf bag in one of these seat pockets?* □ *He's got to sick, and there's no air sickness bag. Help!*

sicks *n.* nausea; vomiting. □ *Oh man, I got the sicks.* □ *He's at home with the sicks.*

sicky *n.* someone who seems mentally deranged. □ *The dame's a sicky. Watch out for yourself.* □ *Some sicky drew these obscene pictures on the wall.*

sid See *cid.*

side *n.* a side of a record. □ *Let's cruise over to Sam's pad and hear some sides.* □ *Now here's a side you may remember.*

sidewalk superintendent **1.** *n.* someone who—out of curiosity—watches excavations being dug and buildings being built. □ *All day, the lines of sidewalk superintendents oozed by.* □ *I don't want any advice from a sidewalk superintendent.* **2.** *n.* any critic. □ *If another sidewalk superintendent comes in here and tries to tell me how to manage this office, heads will roll.* □ *I hate to be a sidewalk superintendent, but this plan is all wrong.*

sidewalk surfing *n.* skateboarding. □ *Bill spent a lot of time sidewalk surfing until the town passed an ordinance against it.* □ *The little kids started the summer sidewalk surfing, but gave it up after a few weeks.*

sidewinder *n.* a sneaky and despicable man. (Western jargon. From the name of the sidewinder rattlesnake.) □ *You dirty, lowdown sidewinder! That's too much!* □ *What sidewinder spilled my drink?*

sidney *n.* the hallucinogenic drug *L.S.D.* (Drugs. Also capitalized. See also *cid.*) □ *Is Sidney working tonight?* □ *Sidney and I have a little business trip planned.*

sieg-heil someone ['sɪg'haɪl] *tr.* to show homage to someone; to salute and obey someone. □ *The guy expects all his underlings to sieg-heil him and worship the ground he walks on.* □ *I won't sieg-heil her. She'll have to earn my respect.*

signify **1.** *in.* to cause trouble for fun; to stir things up. (Black.) □ *Why's that dude signifying over there?* □ *What are all these cats signifying about anyway?* **2.** *in.* to try to look more important than one really is; to brag; to *strut one's stuff.* (Black.) □ *See that dude signify like somebody important?* □ *First you gotta learn to signify.*

silk *n.* a Caucasian. (Black.) □ *Some silk was over here, looking around sort of suspicious.* □ *He told his mama that if she doesn't treat him better, he's gonna bring some silk home for dinner and let her see what the neighbors think.*

silks *n.* clothing. □ *Look at the silks on that dude!* □ *I gotta get some new silks before spring.*

silky *mod.* smooth; unctuous. □ *Beware of anybody that silky.* □ *What a silky character. He could talk his way into the heart of some unsuspecting chick.*

silo drippings *n.* alcohol allegedly obtained at the base of a silo containing fermenting corn. □ *You actually drink this stuff? This is silo drippings.* □ *The old-timer called his moonshine "silo drippings."*

silver *n.* money. □ *What kind of silver is that going to take?* □ *I have some silver stashed at home if you need it.*

silver bullet AND **magic bullet** *n.* a specific, failsafe solution to a problem. (From the notion that a bullet made of silver is required to shoot a werewolf.) □ *I'm not suggesting that the committee has provided us with a silver bullet, only that their advice was timely and useful.* □ *Okay, I've got the silver bullet you need for this. Your vote on the pork storage units for my district would be greatly appreciated, of course.*

silver goose *n.* a proctoscope. (Medical. See also *goose.*) □ *The patient seems to have a real phobia about the silver goose.* □ *When the nurse brought in the silver goose, the patient nearly fainted.*

simmer (down) **1.** *in.* to reduce one's anger. □ *Now, now! Just simmer! Cool it!* □ *Simmer down, you guys.* **2.** *in.* to get quiet. □ *I waited till things began to simmer down, and then I started.* □ *Hey, simmer down to a dull roar!*

simoleon [sɪ'moliən] *n.* a dollar. (Underworld.) □ *How many simoleons is this going to cost me?* □ *For only one simoleon, you get a ticket to the greatest show on earth.*

Simon Legree ['saɪmən lə'gri] *n.* a very hard taskmaster; a hard boss. (From the name of the slave driver in *Uncle Tom's Cabin.*) □ *She's a regular Simon Legree.* □ *Ask Simon Legree if I will be able to stop work and go home for breakfast now.*

simp *n.* a simpleton. □ *You are such a simp!* □ *Why did some simp feel it necessary to do this?*

sin *n.* synthetic marijuana. (Drugs. From *synthetic.*) □ *Most of this stuff the kids put down good money for is not sin, but angel dust.* □ *Max was caught up in the quest for sin.*

sin-bin *n.* a van fitted with bedding as a place for necking and love-making. □ *Wally said he was saving his money to buy a sin-bin so he could have more fun on dates.* □ *Some rusty old sin-bin was parked in front of the house when I got there.*

sing *in.* to inform (on someone). (Underworld.) □ *Rocko knew the stoolie would sing. He had to do something to stop her.* □ *Bruno would never sing. He's a champ.*

singed See *scorched.*

single **1.** *n.* one dollar; a dollar bill. □ *I don't have enough singles in the register* *to get me through the morning.* ☐ *I got a couple of singles I can lend you.* **2.** *n.* an unmarried person. (Usually plural.) ☐ *I'm holding a little party for singles.* ☐ *Todd's a single—just recently.*

sink *tr.* to swallow some food or drink. ☐ *Here, sink a bite of this stuff.* ☐ *Larry stopped at a tavern to sink a short one.*

sink one's teeth into something See *get one's teeth into something.*

sinker *n.* a doughnut. ☐ *This sinker must be four days old.* ☐ *All our sinkers are brought in fresh on Monday.*

sinse AND **sense (bud)** [sɪnts AND 'sɛnts (bəd)] *n.* seedless marijuana. (Drugs. From Spanish *sinsemilla*, "seedless.") ☐ *Where's the sinse I was saving?* ☐ *Sense bud is all that Tiffany will touch.*

sip **1.** *n.* a puff of a marijuana cigarette. (Drugs.) ☐ *How about a sip of your joint?* ☐ *He took a big sip and held it so long he almost turned blue.* **2.** *tr. & in.* to take a puff of a marijuana cigarette. ☐ *He sipped a big one, stopped a minute, then spoke.* ☐ *The alley was populated by a bunch of teeny-boppers sipping away the afternoon.*

sipster *n.* a *tippler*, a drunkard. ☐ *The old lady is a sipster who says she drinks a little wine to help her arthritis.* ☐ *Most sipsters have a really fine excuse like that.*

sis [sɪs] *n.* sister. (Also a term of address and a common pet name for one's sister.) ☐ *Come on, sis. We're going to be late.* ☐ *Well, sis, good luck.*

sissified ['sɪsifaɪd] *mod.* effeminate; sissy-style. ☐ *Don't act so sissified.* ☐ *I'm not comfortable in a sissified place like that.*

sister **1.** *n.* a (female) friend. (Originally underworld. Sometimes a term of address.) ☐ *Hi, sister! How ya doing?* ☐ *Come here, sister. I gotta have a word with you.* **2.** *n.* a fellow sorority member. ☐ *One of my sisters let me borrow her car.* ☐ *The junior sisters are putting on a skit.* **3.** *n.* a fellow feminist. ☐ *We can do this thing, sisters, we can do it!* ☐ *The sisters will be discussing it at tonight's meeting.* **4.** See *(soul) sister.*

sitcom ['sɪtkɑm] *n.* a situation comedy as found on television. (Compare to *kid-vid.*) ☐ *These sitcoms are made for juvenile minds.* ☐ *Sitcoms can be fun.*

sitting duck *n.* someone who waits unsuspectingly for doom or destiny; an easy target for something bad. ☐ *Get out of the way! You're a sitting duck.* ☐ *The guy was a sitting duck for a mugging.*

sitting pretty *mod.* doing very nicely; in a very pleasant and secure position. ☐ *If I get the job, I'll be sitting pretty for a long time.* ☐ *She married a millionaire, and now she's sitting pretty.*

six-bits *n.* seventy-five cents. (A *bit* is equal to twelve and one-half U.S. cents.) ☐ *You got six-bits I can borrow?* ☐ *Just try one of these things. It's only six-bits.*

six feet under *mod.* dead and buried. ☐ *Fred died and is six feet under.* ☐ *They put him six feet under two days after he died.*

six-pack **1.** *in.* to while away a specified period of time drinking a six-pack of beer. (See also *Joe Six-pack.*) ☐ *He sat in front of the television and six-packed the entire afternoon.* ☐ *He's in the back —six-packing, as usual.* **2.** *n.* a well-muscled abdomen. ☐ *Tom's gut is a real six-pack. He must work out every day.* ☐ *What do you do with a six-pack like that? Walk around with your shirt open?*

sixer *n.* a six-pack beverage container. (Usually refers to beer.) ☐ *Tom showed up with three sixers and a bushel of pretzels, and we all watched the game together.* ☐ *Please stop by the store and pick up a sixer.*

sixty-four-dollar question *n.* the most important question; the question that everyone wants to know the answer to. (Always with *the.*) ☐ *When? Now, that is the sixty-four-dollar question.* ☐ *Now for the sixty-four-dollar question. What's the stock market going to do this year?*

sizzled *mod.* alcohol intoxicated. (Compare to *fried.*) ☐ *I'd like to go out tonight and get sizzled—maybe that would help me forget Tiffany.* ☐ *Harold got* *himself sizzled and couldn't drive to the dance.*

sizzler *n.* a very hot day. □ *Today will be another sizzler. A low pressure center over Alabama is pumping hot and humid air into the area.* □ *What a sizzler! I'm sweating like a horse.*

skag AND **scag** [skæg] **1.** *n.* a rotten thing or person. □ *Don't be such a skag. Who do you think you are?* □ *Gary has become more of a scag than I can stand.* **2.** *n.* a very ugly woman. (Collegiate.) □ *What a skag! I wouldn't be seen with her.* □ *She looks like a scag without makeup.* **3.** *n.* a tobacco cigarette; a tobacco cigarette butt. (Military.) □ *Can I bum a scag off you?* □ *Here, have a scag on me.* **4.** *in.* to smoke (a tobacco cigarette). □ *He stopped scagging for about a week.* □ *I'll scag till I die.* **5.** *n.* heroin, especially poor quality heroin; any powerful drug. (Drugs.) □ *Just lay off the skag—if you can.* □ *Scag has sent a lot of my friends to the bone orchard.* **6.** *n.* hard liquor. □ *No beer for me. Tonight it's scag.* □ *The two of them put away a quart of my finest skag.*

skag jones AND **scag jones** *n.* an addiction to heroin. (Drugs. Here *jones* is a "thing.") □ *It's the scag jones that's got her down.* □ *She has a serious skag jones.*

skagged out *mod.* drug intoxicated; very high. (Drugs. See also **skag**.) □ *Max was rocking back and forth on the top step—skagged out, as usual.* □ *He got to the point where being skagged out was more important than eating.*

skank AND **scank** [skæŋk] **1.** *n.* an ugly (young) woman. (Collegiate.) □ *What a skank she is! Give her a comb or something.* □ *Look at her! Is she a skank or what?* **2.** *in.* to appear ugly. □ *My face is skanking like mad. Must be the zits.* □ *Both sisters skank. Must be hereditary.*

skanky ['skæŋki] *mod.* ugly; repellent, usually said of a woman. (Collegiate.) □ *She is so skanky! That grody hairdo doesn't help either.* □ *What's wrong with being a little skanky? It's what you can do with your brain that counts.* □ *She's skanky, nonetheless.*

skat [skæt] *n.* beer. □ *How about some skat, chum?* □ *You got any pretzels to go with the skat?*

skate **1.** *n.* a drinking bout. □ *He's off on another three-day skate.* □ *Jerry hopes that this will be his last skate. He wants to dry out for good.* **2.** *n.* a drunkard; a person on a drinking spree. □ *Jerry's a skate and he knows it.* □ *A couple of skates celebrating the new year ran into my car.* **3.** *in.* to get drunk. □ *Jerry's skating again. It's his whole life.* □ *Let's go out and skate, okay?*

skating *mod.* drug intoxicated. □ *He's high all right—I'd say he's skating.* □ *He took some wicked silo and is totally skating.*

skedaddle [skə'dædl̩] *in.* to get out; to leave in a hurry. (Folksy.) □ *Go on, skedaddle! Out!* □ *Well, I'd better skedaddle on home.*

skeet *n.* a blob of nasal mucus. (Collegiate. See also *skeet shooting*.) □ *God, Fred, there's a gross skeet hanging outta your nose!* □ *That wasn't stew; that was skeets!*

skeet shooting *n.* the act of blowing one's nose by pinching one nostril and using no tissue or handkerchief. (See also *skeet*.) □ *There is nothing more disgusting than a bunch of college boys belching and skeet shooting.* □ *Bill's mother caught him skeet shooting and really gave him a lot of trouble.*

skeeter ['skidɚ] *n.* a mosquito. (Folksy.) □ *A skeeter bit me on the arm.* □ *There are a lot of skeeters out tonight.*

skeevy ['skivi] *mod.* sleazy and disgusting. □ *This is a skeevy joint. Let's get out.* □ *Your coat looks so skeevy. Is it old?*

skeezer ['skizɚ] *n.* a weird person; a geek. (Also a term of address.) □ *Dave is a nice guy, but sort of a skeezer.* □ *Hey, skeezer, get out of the way!*

skid-lid *n.* a motorcycle helmet. □ *The law has no business telling me I gotta* *wear a skid-lid.* □ *Don't you use a skid-lid?*

skid marks *n.* unclean, brownish marks on one's underpants. □ *Just looking at him, you know he's the type who has skid marks and enjoys popping zits.* □ *There is hardly anything a genteel person can say about skid marks that is acceptable in public.*

skid row *n.* the name for a place populated with ruined alcoholics and other down-and-out people. □ *I don't want to end up on skid row. How can I get rid of this monkey?* □ *Just because they're on skid row, it doesn't mean they're beyond help.*

skid row bum *n.* a down-and-out person; a low alcoholic beggar. □ *Do you want to end up a skid row bum?* □ *Even a skid row bum has some pride.*

skillion ['skɪljən] *n.* an imaginary enormous number. □ *I have a skillion reasons why I won't marry you.* □ *About a skillion people are running in the marathon.*

skin **1.** *n.* a dollar bill. □ *This ticket cost me a couple of skins—and it's not worth it.* □ *You got a skin for the toll booth?* **2.** AND **skinhead** *n.* someone with a shaved or bald head. (Some such persons may also engage in political violence.) □ *Who's the skin with the earrings?* □ *That skinhead looks stoned.* **3.** *tr.* to cheat or overcharge someone. □ *The guy who sold me this car really skinned me.* □ *We skinned him on that stock deal.*

skin a goat *tr.* to empty one's stomach; to vomit. □ *Ralph went out to skin a goat.* □ *Was my cooking so bad that everybody had to skin a goat?*

skin flick *n.* a movie featuring nudity. (See also *nudie.*) □ *We took in a skin flick when we were in the city.* □ *Max likes skin flicks better than real girls.*

skin game *n.* any swindle. (Underworld.) □ *Bruno was mixed up in a skin game for a while.* □ *The con running the skin game got out of town.*

Skin me! *exclam.* "Give me some skin!"; "Shake my hand!" (Originally black.) □ *Hey, man, skin me!* □ *Hey, old buddy. Don't walk on! Skin me!*

skin-search *n.* a search of the naked body by legal authorities. (See also *strip-search.*) □ *These clowns were actually doing skin-searches on traffic offenders!* □ *Aren't there laws against frivolous skin-searches?*

skinful *n.* an intoxicating quantity of liquor; enough liquor. (See also *have a skinful.*) □ *He's got a skinful and can't drive.* □ *She knows enough to stop drinking before she gets a skinful.*

skinhead See *skin.*

skinny See *(hot) skinny.*

skinny dip **1.** *in.* to swim in the nude. □ *We used to go skinny dipping when I was a kid.* □ *There was an old creek on the farm where we used to skinny dip.* **2.** *n.* a swim in the nude. □ *A nice skinny dip in a quiet glade takes you back to nature.* □ *Randy, who fears fish, didn't take a skinny dip with the others.*

skins *n.* drums. (Musicians. The same as *hides.*) □ *Andy can really make the skins talk.* □ *Buddy could beat those skins like nobody's business.*

Skip it! *exclam.* "Forget it!"; "Never mind!" □ *I won't bother you with my question again. Skip it!* □ *Oh, skip it! It doesn't matter.*

skip (out) *in.* to leave; to run away without doing something, such as paying a bill. □ *The guy skipped when I wasn't looking.* □ *Fred skipped out, leaving me with the bill.*

skirt *n.* a woman. □ *Some skirt comes up to me and asks where the police station is.* □ *Who's the skirt I saw you with last night?*

skivvies ['skɪviz] *n.* underpants; underwear. □ *He stood there chattering in his skivvies waiting for additional indignities.* □ *I don't have any clean skivvies!*

sko AND **sgo** ['sko AND 'sgo] *phr.* "Let's go." (Now considered current slang even though it has been informal colloquial for decades.) □ *Sko. We're going to be late.* □ *It's time to hit the road. Sgo.*

skrag [skræg] *tr.* to murder someone. (Underworld.) □ *These thugs tried to skrag me, I swear.* □ *Barlowe wanted to skrag him right then and there.*

skrungy [ˈskrəndʒi] *mod.* disgusting. □ *What is this skrungy stuff they are serving here?* □ *That movie was too skrungy for me.*

skull-buster AND **skull-popper** **1.** *n.* a difficult course in school or college. □ *The course was a skull-buster, and I had to drop it.* □ *All the courses in that department are skull-busters.* **2.** *n.* a police officer. □ *Two skull-busters came up and started asking questions.* □ *Watch out for the skull-buster over there.*

skull-popper See the previous entry.

skullduggery [ˈskəlˈdəgəi] *n.* deceitful doings; dirty work. □ *It took a lot of skullduggery to bring it off, but that was no problem for Janice.* □ *Without skullduggery, politics wouldn't be interesting.*

skulled *mod.* alcohol or drug intoxicated. □ *He's too skulled to drive.* □ *He had got himself skulled in less than twenty minutes.*

skunk **1.** *n.* a mean and hateful person. (Compare to *polecat, stinker.*) □ *What a skunk!* □ *Must you be such a skunk in front of my friends?* **2.** *tr.* to outwit someone. □ *I skunked them. They'll never find me.* □ *That fish skunked me. I thought I caught him for sure this time.*

skunk-drunk *mod.* alcohol intoxicated. □ *He was skunk-drunk and didn't want to be bothered.* □ *Some skunk-drunk character came in and started talking big.*

skunked **1.** *mod.* alcohol intoxicated. □ *Kelly got skunked on suds—very unusual for him.* □ *He was so skunked he couldn't find his house.* **2.** *mod.* outwitted; outscored; defeated. □ *The home team skunked the visitors for the third year in a row.* □ *I was skunked on this year's fishing trip. Not even a bite.*

skurf [skəf] *in.* to skateboard. (From the words *skate* and *surf.*) □ *He skurfed from city hall to the post office.* □ *My mom won't let me skurf anymore.*

sky *in.* to travel (to somewhere) in an airplane. □ *I decided to sky down to Orlando for the weekend.* □ *Let's sky to New York and then go on to London.*

sky hook *n.* an imaginary tool. □ *I can't get this thing outa here without a sky hook.* □ *Go get me a sky hook, would ya?*

sky-pilot *n.* a chaplain. □ *The sky-pilot says we can park in the church's lot, if we don't mess anything up or make too much noise.* □ *The sky-pilot's a good guy.*

sky rug *n.* a toupee; a man's wig. □ *I think he is wearing a sky rug.* □ *He looks better in his sky rug, but that's not necessarily good.*

sky's the limit *phr.* "there is no upper limit." (Always with *the.*) □ *I can afford it. The sky's the limit.* □ *You can do anything you set your mind to, Billy. The sky's the limit.*

slam **1.** *tr.* to criticize someone or something. □ *Please don't slam my car. It's the best I can do.* □ *The secretary was slamming the boss in one room, and the boss was slamming the secretary in another.* **2.** *n.* a criticism. □ *Harry took another slam at the sales record the sales force had produced for the meeting.* □ *I don't want to hear another nasty and hateful slam at my sister. Is that clear?* **3.** *tr.* to drink something quickly. □ *Max slammed a couple of beers and left.* □ *Don't slam your coffee. You'll burn yourself.*

slam a beer See *pound a beer.*

slam-bang *mod.* wild; exciting. □ *It was a slam-bang weekend, and I loved every minute of it.* □ *Wow, did we ever have a slam-bang time!*

slam dunk **1.** *tr.* & *in.* to force a basketball into the basket from above. (See also *jam.*) □ *Wilbur slam dunked another one, raising the score from 108 to 110.* □ *Wilbur slam dunked his way to fame and riches.* **2.** *n.* an act of making a basket as in sense 1. □ *Another slam* *dunk and Wilbur ties the score again!* □ *The rim will probably not withstand another slam dunk.*

slam some beers See *pound a beer.*

slammer 1. *n.* a jail. □ *I got out of the slammer on Monday and was back in by Wednesday.* □ *The slammer in this town is like a hotel.* **2.** *n.* a slam dunk. □ *He really has that slammer perfected!* □ *It's another slammer for Wilbur!*

slant *n.* a biased view; a unique perception. □ *You can probably give us yet another slant on this problem.* □ *You provided us with a fresh slant on this question.*

slap-dab *mod.* directly. (See also *smack (dab) in the middle.*) □ *We put it slap-dab on his head.* □ *I found this pop bottle slap-dab on top of the car! How'd it get there?*

slap-dash *mod.* fast and careless. □ *I wish you hadn't done it in such a slap-dash fashion.* □ *This is a very slap-dash way to do something.*

slap happy *mod.* silly; giddy. □ *I get slap happy when I have to stay up this late.* □ *She's a little slap happy, but a tremendous dear.*

slap in the face *n.* an insult; a rejection. □ *That remark was a real slap in the face.* □ *Her departure was a slap in the face to the manager who had refused to give her a raise.*

slap someone on the wrist See the following entry.

slap someone's wrist AND **slap someone on the wrist** *tr.* to administer a minor reprimand. □ *The judge only slapped her wrist.* □ *The courts only slap them on the wrist and send them back out on the streets.*

slash *n.* a drink of liquor. □ *Just one slash, and I have to be going.* □ *How about a slash? You ready yet?*

slaughter See *murder.*

slaughtered *mod.* drunk. □ *Ted and Bill came home slaughtered and caught hell for it.* □ *Garth went out and got himself slaughtered again last night.*

slave away (at something) *in.* to work very hard (doing something). □ *I'm tired of slaving away at this and getting nowhere.* □ *I'm slaving away for $7.00 an hour and have no prospects for the future.*

slave market *n.* a job market where many candidates for jobs come face to face with potential employers. □ *I gotta go to the annual slave market this year. We're hiring for a change.* □ *There was little hope at the annual slave market. There were six jobs and 432 applicants.*

slay *tr.* to overwhelm someone with one's performance or other excellence. □ *These jokes always slay the audience.* □ *Oh, you slay me with your silly remarks.*

sleaze AND **sleez** [sliz] **1.** *n.* a low and despicable person. □ *God, what a sleaze! How can anybody be so skanky?* □ *You'd expect to find a sleaze like that in a sleazoid joint like this.* **2.** *n.* any junk. □ *I won't sell sleez like that! I won't even have it in my store.* □ *Look at this sleaze —and look at the price! Outrageous!* **3.** *in.* to act low; to be sexually promiscuous. □ *She looks like the type who will sleaze and lie to get her own way.* □ *She earned quite a reputation sleazing around with just anybody.*

sleaze-bucket *n.* a repellent person, thing, or place. □ *Gad, what a sleaze-bucket! Let me out of here!* □ *Gee, Sue, your date's a real sleaze-bucket!*

sleazebag *n.* a repellent person or place. □ *I won't go into a sleazebag like that.* □ *Who is the sleazebag leaning against the wall?*

sleazeball *n.* a repellent person. □ *He's okay if you're into sleazeballs.* □ *Who is that sleazeball with the earring?*

sleazo AND **sleazoid** ['slizo AND 'slizɔɪd] *mod.* low; disreputable; sleazy. □ *Let's get out of this sleazo joint.* □ *This place is really sleazo.* □ *Who wants a sleazoid car with no back seat?*

sleazoid ['slizɔɪd] **1.** *n.* a sleazy person. □ *Who is this sleazoid?* □ *Who was that sleazoid I saw you with last night?* **2.** See *sleazo.*

sleep it off *tr.* to sleep while the effects of drugs or alcohol wear off. □ *I'm polluted, I guesh. Have to get home and shleep it off.* □ *She'll be okay when she sleeps it off.*

sleeper **1.** *n.* a sleeping pill. □ *I just took one little sleeper.* □ *She took a handful of sleepers with a glass of booze, and that was it.* **2.** *n.* someone or something that achieves fame after a period of invisibility. □ *The movie "Red Willow" was undoubtedly the sleeper of the year, winning six awards.* □ *My candidate had been a sleeper, but he finally began to pull ahead in the polls.*

sleepfest *n.* something, such as a dull lecture, that induces a long period of sleep. □ *The history lecture today was a real sleepfest.* □ *The play was a sleepfest. Half the audience left before it was over.*

sleepwalk *n.* a movement toward something without effort. (A movement that could be done "in one's sleep." See also *cakewalk, walk.*) □ *Getting the degree was a sleepwalk. Getting a job was hell.* □ *It was no sleepwalk, but it didn't make me slave away either.*

sleez See *sleaze.*

slew **1.** *in.* to drink to intoxication. □ *They must have been slewing for an hour before one got up and left.* □ *Let's go out and slew till we forget who we are.* **2.** AND **slews** *n.* a lot; lots. □ *I have a whole slew of old computer programs at home in a box somewhere.* □ *She's got slews of money.*

slewed AND **slewy; slued; sloughed (up)** [slud AND 'slui, slud . . .] *mod.* alcohol intoxicated. □ *Wallace is too slewed to drive.* □ *She knows how to stop drinking before she gets slewy.*

slews See *slew.*

slewy See *slewed.*

slice of the action See *piece (of the action).*

slick **1.** *mod.* clever; glib. □ *He is a slick operator.* □ *His talk is slick, but his action is zotz.* **2.** *mod.* excellent. □ *This is a real slick setup you got here.* □ *That is a slick idea.* □ *The idea is not so slick!* **3.** *n.* a high-quality magazine printed on slick [coated] paper. □ *The slicks are all carrying ads for products and services that couldn't even be mentioned a few years ago.* □ *Most of the price increase for the slicks has been because of postage increases.* **4.** *n.* a racing tire. (Auto racing.) □ *That set of wheels has slicks. I wonder why.* □ *I have some slicks at home in the garage.*

slick-chick *n.* an attractive and cute *girl.* □ *Tiffany is a slick-chick. I wonder if she'd go out with me.* □ *Who was that slick-chick I saw you with the other night?*

slickum ['slɪkəm] *n.* hair dressing, especially if thick and heavy. □ *What kind of slickum do you have on your hair—bear grease?* □ *His hair was plastered down with slickum, and he looked like something in an old movie.*

slightly rattled **1.** *mod.* upset; confused. □ *Tom was slightly rattled by the trouble at the door.* □ *I'm slightly rattled. I'll get over it.* (More at *rattled.*) **2.** *mod.* tipsy; alcohol intoxicated. □ *He's only slightly rattled. He'll recover by morning.* □ *She can be stone blind and still seem only slightly rattled.*

slim *n.* a tobacco cigarette. (The same as *straight,* as opposed to a marijuana cigarette, which may be thicker.) □ *I'll take a slim and a little mist, thanks.* □ *You got a slim I can borrow?*

slime **1.** *n.* a worthless person; a low and wretched person. □ *What a slime that guy is!* □ *Who is the slime over there with the greasy hair?* **2.** *n.* degrading matters; corrupt people or situations. □ *I don't want to be involved in slime like that.* □ *The press uncovered even more slime at city hall.*

slime bag AND **slime bucket; slimebag; slimeball** *n.* a despicable person, usually a male. (See also *slime.*) □ *Gee, a slime bag like that in the same room with me! Yuck!* □ *Who's the slime bucket in the 1962 Bonneville?*

slime bucket See the previous entry.

slimebag See *slime bag.*

slimeball See *slime bag.*

sling the cat *tr.* to empty one's stomach; to vomit. □ *Suddenly Ralph left the room to sling the cat, I guess.* □ *That stuff will make you sling the cat.*

Slip me five! See *Give me (some) skin!*

slip one's trolley *tr.* to become a little crazy; to lose one's composure. (See also *off one's trolley.*) □ *I was afraid I would slip my trolley.* □ *He slipped his trolley and went totally bonkers.*

slip someone a Mickey *tr.* to secretly put a *Mickey Finn* in someone's alcoholic drink. (This drug either makes the victim ill or causes immediate diarrhea.) □ *Somebody slipped Barlowe a Mickey and sent him into action.* □ *For a ten-spot, the bartender slipped Rocko a Mickey.*

slip someone five *tr.* to shake someone's hand. □ *Billy slipped me five, and we sat down to discuss old times.* □ *Come on, man, slip me five!*

slip (up) **1.** *in.* to make an error. □ *Don't slip up and pay this bill twice, please.* □ *I slipped and gave the guy a 35 percent tip.* **2.** AND **slip(-up)** *n.* an error. □ *That was a silly slip-up. I'm sorry.* □ *That slip cost us nearly $2,000.*

slipstick *n.* a slide rule. □ *Who carries a slipstick these days?* □ *Who even knows what a slipstick is these days?*

slob [slɑb] *n.* a rude, fat, and unpleasant person. □ *What a slob! Comb your hair, if you can get a comb through it!* □ *Why doesn't that slob go on a diet or something? Anything!*

slob up *in.* to eat. □ *What time do you people slob up around here?* □ *Fred stopped slobbing up long enough to change the channel on the T.V. set.*

slobber *n.* nonsense. (From the term for saliva running out of the mouth.) □ *I've heard enough of your slobber. Can it!* □ *Another hour of professorial slobber!*

slopped *mod.* alcohol intoxicated. □ *I've never seen a senior citizen so inelegantly slopped as was Walter.* □ *He was so slopped, he could walk without his cane.*

slop(s) *n.* bad beer; inferior liquor. □ *Why do we have to drink slops like this? Can't Tom afford to give his guests something decent?* □ *Tom's slop is better than water—dishwater anyway.*

slosh **1.** *n.* beer; liquor. □ *How about a glass of slosh?* □ *No slosh for me. Just plain water.* **2.** *tr. & in.* to drink liquor, including beer; to drink to excess. □ *Are you going to slosh gin all night?* □ *I slosh just because I like the taste.*

sloshed (to the ears) *mod.* alcohol intoxicated. □ *Man, is he sloshed to the ears!* □ *He is as sloshed as they come.*

sloughed (up) See *slewed.*

slow burn *n.* the act of becoming angry very slowly or being resentful for a long period of time. (See also *do a slow burn.*) □ *His lips were pressed together and he was angry, but just having a slow burn.* □ *She wasn't angry yet, but she was doing a slow burn.*

sludgeball [ˈslədʒbɑl] *n.* a despicable and repellent person. □ *Mike is such a sludgeball! Why do you keep seeing him?* □ *He's no sludgeball; he's eccentric.*

slued See *slewed.*

sluff (off) *in.* to waste time; to *goof off.* □ *Watch him. He will sluff off if you don't keep after him.* □ *He won't sluff. I know I can trust him.*

slug **1.** *n.* a drink of liquor; a shot of whiskey. □ *Have a slug of this stuff. It will—I'm sorry to say, ma'am—put hair on your chest.* □ *A couple more slugs and he was ready to face the huge bull-necked ruffian.* **2.** *n.* a bullet. □ *Barlowe sent a couple of slugs into Rocko's chest. Rocko crumpled soundlessly.* □ *The medico dug out the slugs like he had done it a thousand times—which he probably had.*

slug it out *tr.* to fight something out; to fight about something figuratively. □ *They finally went outside to slug it out.* □ *We'll just have to sit down in the conference room and slug it out.*

slugfest **1.** *n.* a fight; a festival of slugging. ☐ *They went out in the alley for a real slugfest.* ☐ *You wanna see a slugfest, just stick around.* **2.** *n.* a festival of arguing. ☐ *The slugfest went on until both sides were willing to compromise.* ☐ *The president emerged from the slugfest with control of the company still hers.*

slugged *mod.* alcohol intoxicated. ☐ *I'm slugged—skunked, you know, corned. And I think I am going to sick up.* ☐ *Ted realized that he was slugged out of his mind, but tried to get the bartender to serve him another drink.*

slumgullion ['sləm'gəljən] *n.* a meat stew; any food. ☐ *What is this slumgullion tonight? It looks like what we had last night, only thinner.* ☐ *This is the best slumgullion I've ever had—which puts it right up there with dishwater.*

slummy ['sləmi] *mod.* lousy. ☐ *What a slummy place!* ☐ *This place is not slummy!* ☐ *That was a slummy trick to pull on her.*

slush fund *n.* a fund of money that can be used for various unofficial and discretionary purposes. ☐ *How much is left in the slush fund?* ☐ *The slush fund is bankrupt.*

slush up *in.* to drink liquor; to get drunk. ☐ *They slushed up for a while and went out to look for some chicks.* ☐ *Don't you ever get tired of going out and slushing up with those guys?*

slushed (up) *mod.* alcohol intoxicated. ☐ *I hate to come home slushed and wake up everybody. I have to sing, you see.* ☐ *This chick is so slushed that she doesn't know her name.*

sly *mod.* excellent; *cool.* ☐ *Look at Jim's sly new ride.* ☐ *That is really a sly jacket you got there.*

smack (dab) in the middle *mod.* exactly in the middle. (See also *slap-dab.*) ☐ *I came in smack dab in the middle of the play.* ☐ *Not too big and not too small. Just smack in the middle.*

smack the road *tr.* to leave; to *hit the road.* ☐ *Time to smack the road! Sgo!* ☐ *Let's smack the road. I have to get up early.*

smacker **1.** *n.* the face. (Compare to *kisser.*) ☐ *What a gorgeous smacker on that chick.* ☐ *She ought to give that ugly smacker back to the horse before it runs into something.* **2.** *n.* a dollar. (Underworld.) ☐ *You got a couple of smackers for the toll booth?* ☐ *Don't waste your hard-earned smackers like that. Run on through.* **3.** *n.* a kiss. ☐ *He planted a smacker square on her lips. She kicked him in the shins for his trouble.* ☐ *Barlowe was greeted at the door by a lovely, cuddly chick in a nightie—eyes closed and lips parted for a better than average smacker. He really wished—just for a moment—that he hadn't rung the wrong doorbell.*

small beer *n.* nothing or next to nothing; an insignificant person. ☐ *The guy is just small beer. Pay him no mind.* ☐ *Small beer or not, he's my customer, and I will see that he is taken care of.*

small change *n.* an insignificant person. (Also a rude term of address.) ☐ *Look, small change, why don't you just move along?* ☐ *The guy you think is small change happens to own this building you seem to be guarding so well.*

small fortune *n.* a rather sizeable amount of money. ☐ *This set of wheels cost me a small fortune.* ☐ *I've got a small fortune tied up in test equipment.*

small fry *n.* anything or anyone small or unimportant. (*Fry* are juvenile fish.) ☐ *Forget the small fry. I'm going after Mr. Big.* ☐ *Don't worry about the small fry. You have to please the fat-cats.*

small potatoes *n.* something or someone insignificant. ☐ *This contract is small potatoes, but it keeps us in business till we get into the real money.* ☐ *Small potatoes are better than no potatoes at all.*

small-time *mod.* insignificant; petty. ☐ *I was in a lot of small-time stuff at home, but never a Broadway hit before.* ☐ *Broadway is not small-time.* ☐ *Max was involved in a lot of small-time crime when he was twelve.*

smarmy ['smɑrmi] *mod.* insincere and obsequious. ☐ *He's obnoxious but brazen rather than smarmy.* ☐ *He's a smarmy creep.* ☐ *The guy is so smarmy, I can't stand him.*

smart aleck ['smɑrt 'ælək] *n.* someone who is saucy and acts cocky. ☐ *A smart aleck like you ought to have no trouble at all getting his face mashed in.* ☐ *Don't be such a smart aleck.*

smart ass *n.* someone who makes wisecracks and acts cocky. (Potentially offensive. Use only with discretion.) ☐ *Some smart ass came in here and asked for a sky hook.* ☐ *Don't be such a smart ass!*

smart cookie *n.* a clever person. ☐ *She's really a smart cookie if you give her a chance.* ☐ *Fred is a smart cookie and really ought to go far.*

smart guy *n.* a man who acts cocky; a wise guy. ☐ *All right, smart guy, see if you like this one.* ☐ *Some smart guy put fresh paint on this bench.*

smart money *n.* money belonging to smart or clever people. ☐ *Most of the smart money is going into utility stocks right now.* ☐ *Watch and see what the smart money is doing.*

smart mouth *n.* someone who makes wisecracks; a cocky person who speaks out of turn. ☐ *Don't be a smart mouth with me!* ☐ *Mr. Atkins is going to get a reputation as a smart mouth.*

smarts *n.* intelligence. ☐ *She's got plenty of smarts but no spunk.* ☐ *I got the smarts to do the job. All I need is someone to trust me.*

smarty *n.* a cocky person. (Also a term of address.) ☐ *Well, if you're such a smarty, why aren't you rich?* ☐ *Okay, smarty, do it yourself.*

smarty-pants *n.* a cocky person; a *smart aleck.* ☐ *Look, smarty-pants, let's cut the clowning around.* ☐ *That smarty-pants is going to get herself into big trouble.*

smash *n.* wine. (Black. Because it is made from smashed grapes.) ☐ *I got a bottle of smash in my car.* ☐ *This is great smash for a buck twenty-five.*

smash hit *n.* a play, movie, musical, etc., which is a big success. ☐ *Her first book was a smash hit. The second was a disaster.* ☐ *A smash hit doesn't always make people rich.*

smashed *mod.* alcohol or drug intoxicated. ☐ *He was so smashed he couldn't stand up.* ☐ *Tracy can drink a lot without ever getting smashed.*

smashing *mod.* excellent; really tremendous. ☐ *We had a smashing time at your little do.* ☐ *This whole meal has been smashing.*

smear *tr.* to defeat someone; to outscore someone. ☐ *We smeared them 50-20.* ☐ *They said they would smear us, but we smeared them.*

smeared *mod.* alcohol or drug intoxicated. ☐ *I feel sort of smeared. Maybe I should have drunk less.* ☐ *Bob and Jim found themselves smeared at the end of the day.*

smell a rat *tr.* to suspect that something is wrong. ☐ *He smelled a rat the minute he came into the room.* ☐ *Keep everything normal. I don't want her to smell a rat. She has never had a surprise party before.*

smell blood *tr.* to be ready for a fight; to be ready to attack; to be ready to act. (Like sharks, which are sent into a frenzy by the smell of blood.) ☐ *Lefty was surrounded, and you could tell that the guys from the other gang smelled blood.* ☐ *The lawyer heard the crash and came running—smelling blood and bucks.*

smell fishy *in.* to seem suspicious. (See also *fishy.*) ☐ *Barlowe squinted a bit. Something smells fishy here, he thought.* ☐ *Something about the deal smelled fishy.*

smell it up AND **smell the stuff** *tr.* to sniff or *snort* powdered drugs, usually cocaine. (Drugs.) ☐ *One of those guys shoots it; the other smells it up.* ☐ *You don't breathe it in; you just smell the stuff.*

smell like a rose *in.* to seem innocent. □ *I came out of the whole mess smelling like a rose, even though I caused all the trouble.* □ *Tiffany pretended that she was the only one who should smell like a rose, but I knew different.*

smell the stuff See *smell it up.*

smell to (high) heaven 1. *in.* to smell very bad. □ *This kitchen smells to high heaven. What besides garlic are you cooking?* □ *Where has this dog been? It smells to heaven.* **2.** *in.* to give signals that cause suspicion. □ *This deal is messed up. It smells to high heaven.* □ *Something's wrong here. Somebody blabbed. This setup smells to high heaven.*

smeller *n.* (one's) nose. □ *I think my smeller's gone bad because of my cold.* □ *He's got a fine strawberry on the end of his smeller.*

smidgen ['smɪdʒn̩] *n.* a tiny bit. □ *I just want a smidgen of cake. I'm on a diet.* □ *Oh, come on, more than a smidgen. Just a little?*

smile AND **smiler; smiley** *n.* a drink of liquor; liquor. □ *Come over and join me for a smiley.* □ *Here, have a smiler on me.*

Smile when you say that. *sent.* "Give some sort of a signal that you are only joking when you say something potentially offensive." □ *That's pretty rude. You'd better smile when you say that.* □ *I told him he'd better smile when he says that, or he's going to get in trouble.*

smiler See *smile.*

Smiley *n.* a circular, smiling yellow face. (The face appears in many forms, stick-on labels, pin-on buttons, hand-drawn, etc. It is possible to re-create the smiling face on any keyboard through the use of the punctuation symbols, as with :) or :-). All computer Smileys and their variants appear sideways. A major variant is the *Unsmiley,* which is basically :(or :-(. The following faces are a sample of the variants that can be seen in computer bulletin board messages and informal typewritten or word processed notes. This type of symbol is called an *emoticon* because it is intended to show "emotion" in what is otherwise a rather cold medium of communication. The typical use is to show that the writer is just joking or writing in good, well-intentioned spirits. The following Smileys are separated by slashes, and an equal sign separates the actual Smiley from its explanation.) :-] = Squarejaw Smiley / :-o = Singing Smiley; Shocked Smiley; Surprised Smiley / :-(= Sad Smiley / :-) = Happy Smiley / : -=) = Smiley with a Big Mustache / :-)' = Drooling Smiley; Smoking Smiley / :-)8 = Smiley Wearing a Bow Tie / :-D = Big-mouth Smiley / :-# = Smiley with Sealed Lips / :-* = Pursed-lips Smiley; Shocked Smiley / :-s = Twisted-mouth Smiley (after hearing or saying something strange) / :-" = Smiley with Walrus Mustache / :-| = Smiley Making Dull Response; "Have-a-dull-day" Smiley / :-> = Wry-faced Smiley / :-0 = Loudmouth Smiley; Big-mouth Smiley / :-x = Sealed-lips Smiley / :-Q = Smoking Smiley; Drooling Smiley / :> = Midget Smiley / ;-) = Winking Smiley / (-) = Smiley Needing a Haircut / ":-) Smiley with its Hair Parted in the Middle / +:-) Smiley Priest / *-(= Smiley Cyclops, Poked in the Eye / *:o) Bozo Smiley / <:I = Dunce Smiley / @-) = Cyclops Smiley / @:I = Smiley Wearing a Turban / |-) = Gleeful Smiley / |-| = Sleeping Smiley; Bored Smiley / 0-) = Smiley Wearing a Scuba Mask / 8-) = Smiley in Glasses / 8:-) A Smiley with Glasses on its Forehead / B-) = Smiley Wearing Horn-rim Glasses / 0-) = Cyclops Smiley / [:-) = Smiley Happily Listening to a Walkman / [:|] = Robot Smiley; Squarejaw Smiley Listening to a Walkman.

smiley See *smile.*

smithereens ['smɪðɚinz] *n.* many tiny pieces or splinters. □ *The mirror was broken to smithereens.* □ *I broke my crystal bell to smithereens.*

smoke 1. *n.* a tobacco cigarette; a pipe; a cigar. □ *I think I'll have a smoke now.* □ *You got a smoke I can owe you?* **2.** *n.* the act of smoking anything smokable, including drugs. □ *I need a smoke—of* *anything.* □ *I'm going to stop here for a smoke.* **3.** *n.* methyl alcohol; bad liquor; any liquor. □ *The old guy was drinking smoke, and it blinded him.* □ *They call it smoke because when you mix it with water and shake it, it's cloudy.* **4.** *n.* exaggeration; deception. (See also *blow smoke, smoke and mirrors.*) □ *That's not a report. That's just smoke.* □ *If the smoke is too obvious, they'll just get suspicious.* **5.** *tr.* to annihilate someone; to shoot someone. (Underworld.) □ *Rocko tried time and time again to smoke Barlowe, always without success.* □ *You want me to smoke you on the spot, or are you gonna cooperate?* **6.** *tr.* to beat someone in a contest; to outrun, outdistance, or outplay someone. □ *Jill smoked Dave in the bicycle race.* □ *I will smoke you in the race!*

smoke and mirrors *n.* a strategy of deception and cover up. □ *Her entire report was nothing but smoke and mirrors. Who could believe any of it?* □ *There is no plan. It's all just smoke and mirrors.*

smoke eater *n.* a fire-fighter. □ *A couple of off-duty smoke eaters wandered around the store doing a little shopping.* □ *The smoke eaters took a long time getting there.*

smoke-filled room *n.* a room where a small group of people make important decisions. (Usually used in reference to political parties.) □ *The smoke-filled rooms are still producing the candidates for most offices, even as we approach the year two thousand.* □ *The deal was cut in a smoke-filled room.*

smoke-in *n.* a young people's public gathering of the 1960's where marijuana was smoked in open defiance of the law. □ *My uncle was at a smoke-in. He says the reporters were getting kids to pose for shots.* □ *They say you could get a high just by being near a smoke-in.*

smoke like a chimney *in.* to smoke a great deal of tobacco or other smokable substances. □ *My uncle smoked like a chimney when he was living.* □ *Somebody who smokes like a chimney in a restaurant ought to be thrown out.*

Smokey (the Bear) *n.* a highway patrol officer; a police officer. (Citizens band radio. See also *bear, lady bear.*) □ *A Smokey was hiding behind a billboard!* □ *Smokey the Bear is after you!*

smokin' ['smokən] *mod.* really *hot;* overpowering. □ *Those threads on that dude are really smokin'.* □ *If you wanna hear some smokin' vinyl, just stay tuned.*

smoking gun *n.* the indisputable sign of guilt. □ *Mr. South was left holding the smoking gun.* □ *The chief of staff decided that the Admiral should be found with the smoking gun.*

smooch [smutʃ] **1.** *in.* to kiss and *neck.* □ *Too much smooching in a movie ruins it for me.* □ *I like to smooch myself, but I don't enjoy watching somebody else.* **2.** *n.* a kiss. □ *I like a good smooch from my hubby.* □ *Hey, sweetie, how about a smooch?*

smooth operator AND **smoothie** *n.* a clever and quiet person, especially in reference to romantic involvement. □ *Clare is an old smoothie till she thinks she's got everything the way she wants. Then you see the real Clare.* □ *Hank is a smooth operator. The girls just love him.*

smoothie See the previous entry.

smurf [smɚf] **1.** *n.* someone who "cleans" ill-gotten money by buying cashier's checks at banks and shifting funds from place to place. (Underworld. From the name of a type of cartoon character. See also *greenwash, launder.*) □ *I think the guy at the first window is a smurf. He's in here twice a week with $9,500 in cash each time.* □ *Did you get a good look at this alleged smurf?* **2.** *tr. & in.* to shift illicit money from place to place to conceal its origin. (Underworld.) □ *I smurf for a living. It doesn't pay much, but you meet some very interesting people.* □ *I smurfed a fortune for a famous drug kingpin and got fourteen years up the river—with some very interesting people.*

smurfbrain ['smɚfbren] *n.* a simple-minded person. (A *smurf* is an innocent little cartoon character.) □ *You can* *be such a smurfbrain!* □ *You're not a smurfbrain, I suppose?*

smurfed [smɚft] *mod.* having to do with a bank that has been used to *launder* money. (See also *smurf.*) □ *The teller came slowly into the office. "I think we were smurfed," she said.* □ *See that this dough is smurfed by Friday.*

snafu [snæ'fu] *n.* an accident; a foul-up. (Acronym. From *situation normal, all fouled (fucked) up*. Also capitalized.) □ *Your being last is not just a snafu. It's a disaster.* □ *What a SNAFU! All the power went off when you turned on the coffeepot.*

snag 1. *n.* a difficulty. □ *There's a little snag in our plan.* □ *We ran into a little snag, I'm sorry to say.* 2. *n.* an ugly (young) woman. □ *She's not a snag! She's lovely.* □ *Who's the snag your brother is running around with?* 3. *tr.* to grab or steal something. □ *Somebody snagged the jacket I just bought.* □ *See if you can snag a couple of good seats while I get the popcorn.*

snail-mail *n.* post office mail; regular mail as opposed to electronic mail. (Refers to the slowness of regular mail in comparison to electronic mail or faxes.) □ *I'll send you the full text by snail-mail.* □ *There are lots of color pictures in the article, so I will send you the original by snail-mail.*

snake *in.* to scheme; to plot and plan. (Prisons.) □ *Lefty is always snaking.* □ *He spent a lot of time snaking about that job.*

snake eyes *n.* the two in dice, one spot on each die. □ *Well, it's snake eyes again. That's all for me.* □ *The baby needs shoes, and all I get is snake eyes.*

snake in the grass *n.* a sneaky and despised person. □ *How could I ever have trusted that snake in the grass?* □ *John is such a snake in the grass.*

snakebite medicine *n.* inferior whiskey; strong whiskey; homemade whiskey. □ *That old-time snakebite medicine is good for what ails you.* □ *Snakebite medicine is a tremendous protection against snakebites if you can get the snake to drink the stuff before it bites you.*

snap 1. *n.* a snapshot. □ *I got some good snaps of the fish you caught.* □ *Here's a snap of my brother.* 2. *in.* to go crazy. □ *Suddenly Rocko snapped and began beating her savagely.* □ *His mind snapped, and he's never been right since.* 3. *n.* an easy thing to do. (Always with *a*.) □ *Nothing to it. It's a snap.* □ *The whole thing was a snap.*

snap course *n.* an easy course (in school). □ *I took a snap course in algebra and flunked it.* □ *I need at least one snap course a semester to pass.*

Snap it up! *exclam.* "Hurry up!" □ *We're late. Snap it up!* □ *Come on, snap it up! I don't have all day.*

snap one's cookies *tr.* to vomit; to regurgitate. □ *I think I'm gonna snap my cookies.* □ *Some jerk snapped his cookies on the sidewalk.*

snap out of something *in.* to recover from something. □ *I'll snap out of it in a while.* □ *It was an emotional blow, but he'll snap out of it in a while.*

snap something up *tr.* to buy up something. □ *People were snapping these things up like hot cakes.* 🅃 *The customers snapped up all the humidifiers on the second day of the cold spell.* (More at *snapped (up).*)

snap to (attention) *in.* to come to attention; to look alert immediately. □ *When they realized what was happening, they began to snap to.* □ *Snap to attention when the sarge comes in!*

Snap to it! *exclam.* "Get busy!" □ *Come on, snap to it!* □ *Snap to it, we've got lots to do.*

snapped (up) 1. *mod.* alcohol intoxicated. □ *Let's go out and get ourselves good and snapped.* □ *Pete was snapped up by eight-thirty.* 2. *mod.* arrested. □ *He got snapped up on a vag charge.* □ *The bacon busted the joint and snapped everybody in sight.*

snapper *n.* a strange person. □ *Wally is sort of a snapper, but a nice guy.* □ *Who is the snapper with the gumbey haircut?*

snappers *n.* the teeth. (Folksy.) □ *I couldn't talk to you on the phone till I got my snappers in.* □ *You got a mouthful of fine-looking snappers.*

snappy **1.** *mod.* quick. □ *You can get there if you're snappy.* □ *Make it snappy. I'm in a hurry.* **2.** *mod.* sharp-looking. □ *That's a real snappy outfit you're wearing.* □ *Who's driving that snappy car over there?* □ *That car's not snappy!*

snatch **1.** *tr.* to kidnap someone. (Underworld.) □ *We're gonna snatch the kid when the baby-sitter comes out to see what happened.* □ *The mob snatched Mrs. Davis and held her for ransom.* **2.** *n.* a kidnaping. (Underworld.) □ *The Bradley snatch had the detectives up all night for weeks.* □ *The snatch went off without a hitch.* **3.** *tr.* to grab something; to steal something. □ *Snatch me the paper there on the table as you walk by, would you please?* □ *Somebody snatched my car.* **4.** *n.* a theft. (Underworld.) □ *The snatch went off without a hitch except that the safe was empty.* □ *Are you the guys who pulled off that First National snatch?*

snatched *mod.* arrested. □ *Everybody in the crack house got snatched in the bust.* □ *Bruno was snatched for the umpteenth time yesterday.*

snatcher *n.* a police officer; a detective. (Underworld.) □ *One of the local snatchers came around to see if the door was locked.* □ *A snatcher hauled her away to the station.*

snaved in [snevd . . .] *mod.* drug intoxicated. □ *The poor guy was as snaved in as they come. Really fried.* □ *By midnight they were so snaved in they couldn't walk.*

snazz AND **shnazz** [snæz AND ʃnæz] *n.* class; glitter and excitement. □ *The curtain opened on a dazzling display of snazz and bright lights.* □ *There was lots of snazz and glitz, but no real substance.*

snazz something up *tr.* to make something classy or exciting. □ *Come on, let's try to snazz this up.* 🅃 *What can I do to snazz up my face?*

snazzy AND **shnazzy** ['snæzi AND 'ʃnæzi] *mod.* elegant; classy. □ *This is a snazzy place all right.* □ *This place is sure snazzy.* □ *Whose shnazzy new car is this?*

sneak *n.* a sneak preview of a movie. □ *There was a good sneak at the Granada last night.* □ *The sneak was better than the flick they had advertised.*

sneaks *n.* sneakers. □ *Are those sneaks new?* □ *She wore red sneaks and a mini.*

sneaky *mod.* unfair and sly. □ *That was a sneaky thing to do!* □ *Jerry is sneaky. Don't trust him.*

snide remark *n.* a caustic, haughty, or insulting remark. □ *You're really quick with the snide remark. Ever say anything nice to anybody?* □ *I did not appreciate that snide remark.*

sniff *n.* a drink of liquor. (See also *snort.*) □ *I'd like just a sniff of that Scotch.* □ *Sure, have a sniff of whatever you want.*

snipe [snɑɪp] *n.* a cigarette or cigar butt. □ *Down on skid row, a snipe won't be on the sidewalk for ten seconds.* □ *He saves a bunch of snipes until he gets enough for a real smoke.*

snit [snɪt] *n.* a state of resentment. □ *Don't work yourself into such a snit.* □ *She threw quite a snit.*

snitch [snɪtʃ] **1.** *n.* an informer. □ *Who needs a snitch? If he can't keep his mouth shut, he can beat it.* □ *The snitch went and told the teacher.* **2.** *in.* to inform (on someone). (Often with *on.*) □ *The cops were waiting for us. Who snitched?* □ *Tracy snitched on Bruno, and he nearly snuffed her.* **3.** *tr.* to steal something. □ *Who snitched my cake?* □ *Why don't you snitch the salt from one of the other tables?* **4.** *n.* a theft. (Underworld.) □ *The snitch went off without a hitch.* □ *How much loot did we get in the snitch?*

snitcher ['snɪtʃɚ] *n.* an informer. (Originally underworld.) □ *There's nothing worse than a snitcher.* □ *Clare is a snitcher. Watch what you say around her.*

snitzy ['snɪtsi] *mod.* classy; ritzy. □ *This is a pretty snitzy place—tablecloths and everything.* □ *Tiffany is too snitzy for me.*

snoggered See *schnockered.*

snookered ['snʊkɚd] *mod.* cheated; deceived. ☐ *I was snookered skillfully and quickly. It was almost a pleasure.* ☐ *I got snookered at the service station.*

snookums ['snʊkəmz OR 'snukəmz] *n.* a nickname for a child or a lover. (Also a term of address.) ☐ *Now, now, snookums, it's all right.* ☐ *Does my little snookums want to play?*

snoop 1. *in.* to prowl around looking for something. ☐ *What are you snooping around here for?* ☐ *Somebody was around here snooping and asking questions.* **2.** *n.* someone who prowls around looking for something. ☐ *Don't be a snoop.* ☐ *Fred is just a snoop. He went through my desk!*

snoot [snut] *n.* the nose. ☐ *You wanna get bopped on the snoot?* ☐ *That's one fine zit you got on your snoot.*

snooted ['snudəd] *mod.* alcohol intoxicated. ☐ *He got himself thoroughly snooted.* ☐ *She's snooted and will never get home by herself.*

snooty *mod.* haughty; conceited. ☐ *Don't be so snooty!* ☐ *Tiffany can be snooty if she wants to, and she usually wants to.* ☐ *What a snooty waiter!*

snoozamorooed ['snuzəmə'rud] *mod.* alcohol intoxicated. ☐ *Man, was she smoozamorooed!* ☐ *He went and got himself snoozamorooed before the wedding.*

snooze [snuz] **1.** *in.* to sleep; to take a little nap. ☐ *You can't snooze every afternoon!* ☐ *I snoozed a little bit before the party.* **2.** *n.* a little nap. ☐ *I need a little snooze.* ☐ *Why not go up and take a little snooze?* **3.** *n.* something that is boring enough to put someone to sleep. ☐ *The play was a snooze. I left before it was over.* ☐ *It wasn't a lecture; it was a snooze.*

snork [snork] *in.* to smoke marijuana or hashish. (Drugs.) ☐ *Let's get down to some serious snorking.* ☐ *They snorked until they could snork no more.*

snort 1. *tr. & in.* to sniff (insufflate) a powdered drug, now usually cocaine. (Drugs.) ☐ *Here, snort this.* ☐ *You're snorting every time I see you.* **2.** *n.* a nasal dose of a drug, usually cocaine. ☐ *Here, take a snort.* ☐ *I don't want a snort. I'm clean, and I'm going to stay that way.*

snot (Potentially offensive. Use only with discretion.) **1.** *n.* nasal mucus. (Crude.) ☐ *Oh, God, there's snot on your cheek.* ☐ *He sneezed and got snot all over the newspaper.* **2.** *n.* a nasty person; an obnoxious person. ☐ *You needn't be such a snot about it.* ☐ *What a snot!*

snotnose(d) (kid) *n.* a young child; a relatively young person. (Derogatory. Potentially offensive. Use only with discretion.) ☐ *Some little snotnose swiped my wallet.* ☐ *A little snotnosed kid came in and asked for money.*

snotrag *n.* a handkerchief. (Crude. Potentially offensive. Use only with discretion.) ☐ *I guess I should use my snotrag.* ☐ *Don't you carry a snotrag?*

snotted *mod.* alcohol intoxicated. (Potentially offensive. Use only with discretion.) ☐ *He got himself totally snotted in two hours.* ☐ *He was too snotted to stand up.*

snottie See the following entry.

snotty AND **snottie** ['snɑdi] (Potentially offensive. Use only with discretion.) **1.** *mod.* nasty with nasal mucus. ☐ *Keep your snotty old handkerchief to yourself.* ☐ *Don't leave your snotty tissues all over the house!* **2.** *mod. bitchy;* rude. ☐ *What makes her so snotty?* ☐ *What a snotty waiter!* ☐ *Now, there's no reason to get snottie with me.*

snow 1. *n.* deceitful talk; deception. ☐ *No snow, okay? I want straight talk.* ☐ *All I heard for an hour was snow. Now, what's the truth?* **2.** *tr.* to attempt to deceive someone. ☐ *Don't try to snow me!* ☐ *You can try to snow me if you want, but I'm onto your tricks.* (More at *snowed.*) **3.** AND **snowball; snowflakes; snow stuff** *n.* a powdered or crystalline narcotic: morphine, heroin, or cocaine. (Now almost always the latter.) ☐ *Now, snow is almost old-fashioned.* ☐ *The price of snow has come down a lot as South America exports more of it.*

snow bunny 1. *n.* someone learning to ski. □ *This little slope is for snow bunnies.* □ *Most of the snow bunnies come here to socialize.* 2. *n.* a female skier. □ *Some cute little snow bunny came over and sat beside me.* □ *This place is swarming with snow bunnies who have never even seen a ski.*

snow job *n.* a systematic deception. □ *You can generally tell when a student is trying to do a snow job.* □ *This snow job you call an explanation just won't do.*

snow stuff See *snow.*

snowball 1. *in.* to grow at an increasing rate. (As a snowball rolling down a hill might increase in size.) □ *The problem began to snowball, and we had to close down for a while.* □ *Offers to help with money and prayers began to snowball, and we had to get volunteers to help answer the phones.* 2. See *snow.*

snowball's chance in hell *n.* a very poor chance. (Usually in the negative.) □ *She doesn't have a snowball's chance in hell of getting it done on time.* □ *I know I don't have a snowball's chance in hell, but I'll try anyway.*

snowed *mod.* deceived. □ *He was one snowed coach. He still doesn't know what really happened.* □ *We really had him snowed!*

snowflakes See *snow.*

snozzle-wobbles ['snazl'wablz] *n.* a hangover; the delirium tremens. □ *Freddy had the snozzle-wobbles this morning. He had no idea what caused it.* □ *They say that a big glass of milk is good for the snozzle-wobbles.*

snozzled ['snazld] *mod.* alcohol intoxicated. □ *How can anybody be so snozzled on four beers?* □ *Those guys are really snozzled!*

snuff 1. *tr.* to kill someone. (Underworld.) □ *The mob tried to snuff Max, but he moved too fast for them.* □ *Somebody snuffed my cat!* 2. *mod.* having to do with death or killing. □ *Those snuff acts ought to be outlawed.* □ *All this snuff stuff is for sickies.*

snuff film *n.* a film that vividly portrays death or killing. □ *Who would watch a snuff film anyway?* □ *Some of these snuff films have a loyal following of real sickies.*

snuff it *tr.* to die. □ *The cat leapt straight up in the air and snuffed it.* □ *I was so sick they thought I was going to snuff it.*

snuffy ['snəfi] *mod.* alcohol intoxicated. □ *She was a little snuffy, but nothing debilitating.* □ *Who's the snuffy little guy in the corner booth?*

so-and-so *n.* a euphemistic way of addressing someone with an insulting term of address. (This is usually euphemistic for "son of a bitch." However, it is also used for good friends, especially male to male, to show affection.) □ *This lousy so-and-so tried to take me for 400 bucks.* □ *Terry, you old so-and-so, how ya been?*

so bad one can taste it *mod.* very much, indeed. □ *I want that car so bad I can taste it.* □ *He had to get to Philadelphia so bad he could taste it.*

So gross! *exclam.* "How disgusting!" (California.) □ *He put chocolate syrup on his pie! So gross!* □ *He's barfing! So gross!*

So long. *interj.* "Good-bye." □ *So long, see ya later.* □ *It's been good talking to you. So long.*

So much for that. *sent.* "That is all for that." (Also in other variants as in the examples.) □ *It's gone, ruined, broken—so much for that.* □ *He's finished as a friend of mine. So much for him!* □ *So much for you! Good-bye!*

so-so 1. *mod.* average; mediocre. □ *It was just so-so. Nothing to write home about.* □ *I don't need to pay $7.50 to see a so-so movie.* 2. *mod.* tipsy; alcohol intoxicated. □ *They were so-so after a while—in front of the television with all that beer and stuff.* □ *He's so-so, but he can still stand up.*

So what? *interrog.* "What does it matter?"; "What is the point of what you are saying?" □ *So what if I'm too old?*

Did that stop Rudolph Drew from trying it? □ *I'm a crook. So what?*

soak **1.** *in.* to drink heavily; to get drunk. □ *The two old ladies put on their coats and went out to soak.* □ *They sat quietly soaking for an hour.* (More at *soaked.*) **2.** *n.* a drinking bout. □ *They sat there quietly enjoying their soak.* □ *Both guys declined to go out and stayed home and enjoyed a soak in front of the T.V.* **3.** *n.* a drunkard. □ *Some old soak lay moaning in the gutter.* □ *Hank is getting to be a real soak.* **4.** *tr.* to overcharge someone; to extort money from someone. □ *They soaked me for twenty dollars for the parts, but at least it runs now.* □ *The cleaners soaked me for the cleaning job.*

soak one's face *tr.* to drink heavily. □ *They're down at the tavern soaking their faces.* □ *Well, I guess I'll go soak my face for a while.*

soaked *mod.* alcohol intoxicated. □ *All the guys came home soaked.* □ *Frank was too soaked to drive home.*

soaker *n.* a drunkard; a *tippler.* □ *Uncle Charlie was a soaker, and the family never realized it.* □ *Give the old soaker a drink to shut him up.*

soap *n.* a soap opera. □ *She won't schedule anything when her soap is on.* □ *Soaps are very popular on college campuses these days.*

S.O.B. *n.* a "son of a bitch"; a despised person, usually a male. (Initialism only. Crude. Also a rude and provocative term of address.) □ *Tell that S.O.B. to mind his own business.* □ *Look here, you S.O.B., get out!*

sob sister *n.* a weak woman who is prone to crying. □ *Mary is a sob sister. She wears you out fast.* □ *I had another sob sister in the office today. Went through half a box of tissues.*

sob story *n.* a sad story that is likely to draw tears. □ *I've heard nothing but sob stories today. Isn't anybody happy?* □ *She had quite a sob story, and I listened to the whole thing.*

sober as a judge *mod.* as sober (free from alcohol) as it is possible to be. □ *Kelly—who was starched as could be—claimed to be sober as a judge.* □ *The judge was not always sober as a judge, but he could get through his court call.*

sober up *in.* to recover from alcohol or drug intoxication. □ *Barlowe had one hour to sober up and get to the station.* □ *It took him a while to sober up.*

sobersides *n.* a very serious person; a grumpy old man. □ *Old sobersides can't manage to laugh at anything.* □ *Some sobersides came over and asked us to watch our language.*

social disease *n.* a venereal disease. □ *Many people find things like—ah—social diseases difficult to discuss in public.* □ *Others talk about private matters like social diseases till you're sick to death of it.*

sock *tr.* to punch someone or something. □ *Wally was so mad, he tried to sock Paul.* □ *He socked the door with his fist and began to howl with pain.*

sock hop *n.* a dance party where everyone dances in stocking feet. (From the 1950's.) □ *My mother told us about a sock hop she went to. It doesn't sound like fun at all.* □ *Sock hops were popular in schools that had new and expensive floors in their gymnasiums.*

Sock it to me! *exclam.* "Come on, let me have it!" (Refers to bad news.) □ *Come on! I can take it. Sock it to me!* □ *Sock it to me, man. I'm ready.*

socked *mod.* alcohol intoxicated. □ *I don't know what was in that punch, but I was socked.* □ *She got socked out of her mind.*

socked in *mod.* fogged in. □ *The airport was completely socked in.* □ *We couldn't take off because we were socked in.*

sofa spud ['sofə 'spəd] *n.* someone who spends a great deal of time sitting and watching television. (A play on *couch potato.*) □ *Sofa spuds have been getting a lot of attention in the newspapers.* □ *These sofa spuds usually watch sports on television.*

soft 1. *mod.* alcohol intoxicated. □ *After a few hours at the party, it appeared that most people were getting soft.* □ *Hard liquor makes people soft.* **2.** *mod.* having to do with nonaddictive drugs. (Compare to *hard*.) □ *The soft stuff just leads to hard stuff.* □ *This acid is not exactly soft.* □ *Soft drugs just take longer to turn you into a zombie.* **3.** *mod.* stupid. □ *The guy's soft in the head. He just can't think straight.* □ *She seems a little soft, but she's really bright.*

soft berth *n.* an easy situation; employment at an easy job. □ *Fred ended up with a real soft berth.* □ *I hope I can arrange a soft berth for my brother, who just applied for a job here.*

soft core 1. *mod.* referring to a mild type of pornography. □ *There are more and more soft core movies on cable television.* □ *This stuff I saw was just soft core.* □ *Now even the soft core stuff is getting harder to find at newsstands.* **2.** *n.* mild pornography. □ *They keep some soft core under the counter.* □ *The movie was a bit of soft core, but people still walked out.*

soft-hearted *mod.* tender-hearted; sympathetic. □ *She is too soft-hearted to handle this job.* □ *He is a soft-hearted guy who can help our cause a lot.*

soft in the head *mod.* stupid; witless. □ *George is just soft in the head. He'll never get away with his little plan.* □ *You're soft in the head if you think I'll go along with that.*

soft money *n.* easy money; money obtained without much effort. □ *Don't become dependent on soft money.* □ *There's not even very much soft money around now.*

soft on someone or something 1. *mod.* [with *someone*] romantically attracted to someone. □ *Fred is soft on Martha, I've heard.* □ *He looked like he was getting a little soft on Sally.* **2.** *mod.* too easy on someone or something. □ *The judge was viewed as being too soft on pushers.* □ *The cops are soft on speeders in this town.*

soft pedal something *tr.* to play something down; to de-emphasize something. (Refers to the soft pedal on the piano.) □ *Try to soft pedal the problems we have with the cooling system.* □ *I won't soft pedal anything. Everyone must know the truth.*

soft sell *n.* a polite attempt to sell something; a very gentle sales pitch. □ *Some people won't bother listening to a soft sell. You gotta let them know you believe in what you are selling.* □ *I tried the soft sell, but that didn't work.*

soft soap 1. *n.* flattering talk; sweet talk. □ *I don't mind a little soft soap. It won't affect what I do, though.* □ *Don't waste my time with soft soap. I know you don't mean it.* **2.** *tr.* to attempt to convince someone (of something) by gentle persuasion. □ *We couldn't soft soap her into it.* □ *Don't try to soft soap her. She's an old battle-ax.*

soft touch 1. *n.* a gentle way of handling someone or something. □ *Bess has a soft touch and can bring both sides together.* □ *Kelly lacks the kind of soft touch needed for this kind of negotiation.* **2.** *n.* a gullible person; a likely victim of a scheme. □ *John is a soft touch for a few bucks.* □ *Here comes the perfect soft touch—a nerd with a gleam in his eye.*

softie AND **softy 1.** *n.* a gentle person; a very agreeable person. □ *He shouldn't give you much trouble. He's such a softie.* □ *The judge who tried the case was anything but a softie.* **2.** *n.* a weakling; a coward. □ *He's too much of a softie to fight back.* □ *Don't worry—he's a softie.*

software rot *n.* an imaginary disease that causes computer programs to go bad over a long period of time. (Computers.) □ *I guess software rot finally got to my program!* □ *What you have here is not a bug, but just plain old software rot.*

softy See *softie*.

soggy ['sagi] *mod.* alcohol intoxicated. □ *The two old ladies got a little soggy, but nothing uncouth.* □ *They weren't sopping wet, just soggy.*

sold cober ['sold 'kobɚ] *mod.* sober. (A spoonerism on *cold sober.* Similar to *jober as a sudge.*) ☐ *What do you mean drunk? Why, I'm sold cober.* ☐ *Ted is always as sold cober as the next guy.*

sold on someone or something *mod.* convinced of the value of someone or something. ☐ *I'm not yet sold on your idea.* ☐ *The crowd was sold on Gary. Nothing he had done or could do would cool their enthusiasm.*

soldier **1.** *n.* a liquor bottle; an empty liquor bottle. (Compare to *dead soldier.*) ☐ *Toss your soldier into the garbage, please.* ☐ *There was a broken soldier on the floor and a cap on the table.* **2.** *n.* a whole tobacco cigarette. ☐ *The old man almost fell over trying to pick up the soldier from the sidewalk.* ☐ *"Look, Jed. A soldier. My lucky day!" said the old soak to his buddy.*

solid **1.** *mod.* good; great; *cool.* ☐ *Man, this music is solid!* ☐ *Listen to that solid beat.* **2.** *mod.* consecutive; consecutively. ☐ *Larry ate for four solid days.* ☐ *Then he "had the flu" for three days solid.*

some pumpkins AND **some punkins** *n.* someone or something great or special. ☐ *That chick is some punkins!* ☐ *Isn't this little gadget really some pumpkins?*

some punkins See the previous entry.

somebody *n.* an important person. (Often with *a.* Compare to *nobody.*) ☐ *Aren't you a somebody?* ☐ *If she was somebody, you wouldn't have to ask.*

someone or something from hell *n.* someone or something very intense, annoying, or challenging. (As if the person or thing were a demon from hell.) ☐ *She is the nurse from hell and just loves to give shots.* ☐ *I just came back from a cruise from hell and have lots of horror stories to tell about the trip.* ☐ *I worked for three years at that job from hell, and I'm glad to be out of it.*

Something's got to give. *sent.* "Things cannot go on like this."; "The stalemate will be broken." ☐ *The pressure on me is getting to be too much. Something's got to give.* ☐ *They keep arguing about money. Something's got to give.*

son of a bitch (All senses are potentially offensive. Use only with discretion.) **1.** *n.* a despicable person, usually a male. (Crude and provocative. Also a very insulting term of address. Abbreviated *S.O.B.*) ☐ *Tell that son of a bitch to get out of here, but fast.* ☐ *Look, you son of a bitch. I'm going to paste you one.* **2.** *n.* old buddy. (Used between close male companions.) ☐ *Why, you old son of a bitch! How are you?* ☐ *Where you been keeping yourself, you son of a bitch?* **3.** *exclam.* "Dammit!" (Usually **Son of a bitch!**) ☐ *Son of a bitch! Look at that drip!* ☐ *Look at that place burn. Son of a bitch!* ☐ *Son of a bitch! I didn't even see that car pull out.*

son of a gun **1.** *n.* a despicable person, usually a male. (Euphemistic for *son of a bitch.*) ☐ *If that son of a gun thinks he can boss me around like that, he's got another think coming.* ☐ *Some son of a gun tried to sell me a used car with no engine.* **2.** *n.* old buddy. ☐ *You old son of a gun! How are you?* ☐ *I went to school with this son of a gun! He's my old buddy.* **3.** *exclam.* "I am totally surprised!"; "I am shocked!" (Usually **Son of a gun!**) ☐ *Son of a gun! He did it!* ☐ *The thing just blew up! Son of a gun!*

sop **1.** *n.* a drunkard; an alcoholic. ☐ *What does the old sop want, a handout?* ☐ *Give the old sop a buck and tell him to beat it.* **2.** *tr. & in.* to guzzle (liquor). ☐ *Let's go out and do some serious sopping.* ☐ *You've sopped booze long enough. Go home.*

soph [sɔf] *n.* a sophomore. ☐ *The sophs are holding a meeting to decide on a plan.* ☐ *He's just a soph, so he still might grow a little.*

sopping (wet) AND **soppy** *mod.* alcohol intoxicated. (Compare to wet.) ☐ *After about six beers, Ralph found himself a little soppy.* ☐ *He's soused—you know, sopping wet.*

soppy See the previous entry.

sore *mod.* angry. ☐ *Come on! Don't get sore! I was only kidding.* ☐ *She is one* *sore old lady. You should give her teeth back.*

sorehead **1.** *n.* a grumpy person. (Also a term of address.) ☐ *She's sort of a sorehead right now. Wait a day or two and then ask her.* ☐ *The boss is a sorehead, but she's all we have.* **2.** *n.* a poor loser. ☐ *Don't be a sorehead. You knew what you're getting into.* ☐ *Some sorehead at the track tried to punch a cashier.*

sorry about that AND **sorry 'bout that** *interj.* "sorry"; "whoops." (A gross understatement, said more as a self-deprecating joke than as an apology.) ☐ *You spill hot cocoa on my coat, and all you can say is "Sorry 'bout that"?* ☐ *When the passenger stepped on my toe, she said, "Sorry about that."*

sorry-ass *mod.* inadequate. (Potentially offensive. Use only with discretion.) ☐ *This is a sorry-ass mess you've gotten us into.* ☐ *What a sorry-ass day this has been.*

sorry 'bout that See *sorry about that.*

So's your old man! *exclam.* "The same to you!"; "*Drop dead!* " (A catch phrase indicating basic disagreement or hostility.) ☐ BILL: *You're acting like an idiot!* TOM: *So's your old man!* ☐ *I don't know what you said, but so's your old man!*

sosh [soʃ] *n.* a (young female) socialite. ☐ *A young sosh in a beemer kept trying to get around me.* ☐ *Tiffany looks like a sosh, but she's just a working girl.*

sossled See *sozzled.*

(soul) brother *n.* a black person's male, black friend. ☐ *Another brother took a fall last night.* ☐ *Terry's a soul brother, and I'll do anything for him.*

soul kiss **1.** *n.* a kiss where the kissers' tongues interact; a *French kiss.* ☐ *He tried to give me a soul kiss, but I pulled away.* ☐ *Yes, a soul kiss sounds silly—till you try it with somebody you really like.* **2.** *in.* [for two people] to kiss with interacting tongues. ☐ *They were soul kissing and making noises.* ☐ *The creep had bad breath and wanted to soul kiss!*

(soul) sister *n.* a black person's female, black friend. (See also *sister.*) ☐ *One of the soul sisters dropped by to talk.* ☐ *A sister called, but didn't leave her name.*

sound off (about something) **1.** *in.* to complain about something; to gripe about something. ☐ *You are always sounding off about something that gripes your soul.* ☐ *Just sound off if you've got a beef.* **2.** *in.* to speak out of turn about something. ☐ *Who asked you to sound off about this?* ☐ *Don't just sound off without raising your hand.* **3.** *in.* to announce something. ☐ *Why did you have to go and sound off about the surprise party?* ☐ *Keep it a secret. Don't sound off about it.*

sounds *n.* music; records. ☐ *I got some new sounds. Ya wanna come over and listen?* ☐ *Man, these sounds are massive!*

soup *n.* nitroglycerin, a liquid explosive. (Underworld.) ☐ *Lefty was a master with the soup till he blew off his hand.* ☐ *Take care of that soup and treat it like eggs.*

soup something up *tr.* to increase the power of something. ☐ *He souped his car up so it will do nearly 120.* 🆃 *If only I could soup up this computer to run just a little faster.* (More at **souped up**.)

soup-strainer *n.* a mustache. ☐ *Jerry had a big bushy soup-strainer that he was very proud of.* ☐ *It's not a soup-strainer—just a neat little black line.*

souped up *mod.* made more powerful. ☐ *That souped up car of John's sure makes a lot of noise.* ☐ *Why do all cars driven by males under the age of twenty have to be souped up?*

soupy ['supi] *mod.* alcohol intoxicated; drunk and vomiting. ☐ *Then he got sort of soupy and broke up the party.* ☐ *These young kids tend to get soupy rather than pass out.*

sourpuss ['sauɚpus] *n.* a grouchy or frowning person. (Compare to *picklepuss.*) ☐ *What a sourpuss! He makes King Kong look sweet.* ☐ *Don't be a sourpuss, babycakes.*

souse [saus] **1.** *in.* to drink excessively; to go on a drinking bout; to get drunk. (From a word meaning "to soak or pickle.") □ *They sat sousing quietly in the corner.* □ *Let us retire from the table and souse in the parlor.* (More at *soused.*) **2.** *n.* a drinking bout. □ *The souse lasted longer than anyone would have thought.* □ *That was one fine souse we had.* **3.** *n.* a drunkard. □ *The best thing you can do for a souse like John is to take away his car keys.* □ *It's hard to live with a souse.*

soused *mod.* alcohol intoxicated. (See also *souse.*) □ *We were really soused.* □ *All we need right now is a soused bus driver.*

southern-fried *mod.* alcohol intoxicated. (An elaboration of *fried,* referring to fried chicken.) □ *Ted and Bill went out and got themselves southern-fried.* □ *When Bob came home southern-fried, his wife nearly killed him.*

southpaw *n.* a left-handed person. □ *Micky's a southpaw and writes sort of funny.* □ *My sister is a southpaw, but I'm not.*

sozzle ['sazl̩] *in.* to drink to excess. □ *The guys are sozzling over at John's place.* □ *I wish you'd stop coming home every night and sozzling to oblivion.* (More at *sozzled, sozzler.*)

sozzled AND **sossled; sozzly** ['sazl̩d AND 'sazl̩d, 'sazli] *mod.* alcohol intoxicated. □ *Man, was she sozzled.* □ *She was so sozzly she didn't even know her name, or my name, or anybody's name.*

sozzler ['sazlɚ] *n.* a drunkard. □ *The sozzler leaned against the tavern window. I thought he would break it.* □ *A sozzler staggered by—reeking of gin.*

sozzly See *sozzled.*

space See *space out.*

space cadet 1. *n.* a person who is always silly or giddy. □ *Mom, you are such a space cadet.* □ *Here comes a space cadet who looks like he has more money than he needs.* **2.** *n.* a person who is always high on drugs. □ *Max has been a space cadet since he was twelve.* □ *The space cadets can usually be found sitting on a bench outside the principal's office.*

space out 1. *n.* a giddy person. (Usually **space-out.**) □ *Terry is becoming such a space-out!* □ *What a space out you are!* **2.** AND **space** *in.* to become giddy; to become disoriented. □ *She is spacing again. She doesn't even know where she is.* □ *I spaced out after the long climb.*

space someone out *tr.* to cause someone to become giddy. □ *The whole business just spaced me out.* T *The spectacle spaced out the entire audience.*

spaced (out) AND **spacy** *mod.* silly; giddy. □ *I have such spaced out parents!* □ *He's so spaced!* □ *I love my spacy old dad.*

spacy See the previous entry.

spam *n.* something disliked, typically, but not necessarily, food. (From the brand name of a canned meat product.) □ *I can't eat this spam. It could be spoiled.* □ *This book is spam! I refuse to read it.*

spanking new See *(brand) spanking new.*

spare tire 1. *n.* a thickness in the waist; a roll of fat around one's waist. □ *I've got to get rid of this spare tire.* □ *The spare tire started when I was twenty-six.* **2.** *n.* an unneeded person; an unproductive person. □ *Gary is a spare tire. Send him home.* □ *You spare tires over there! Get to work.*

sparkler *n.* a diamond; gemstones. □ *Look at the sparklers on that old dame.* □ *Janice has a new sparkler on her finger.*

spastic *mod.* overly responsive; out of control. □ *She can get so spastic when I come in late.* □ *Tell the spastic jerk to shut up.* □ *My dad's spastic when it comes to drugs.*

spaz [spæz] **1.** *n.* a fit or an attack; a strong reaction to a bad or funny situation. □ *My father had a spaz when he heard.* □ *Take it easy! Don't have a spaz.* **2.** *n.* a total jerk; someone who overreacts to something. (Not used for a congenitally spastic condition.) □

Some spaz is in the other room screaming about a stolen car. □ *Relax! You don't need to be a spaz.*

spaz around *in.* to waste time; to mess around. □ *You kids are always spazzing around. Why don't you get a job?* □ *We're just spazzing around. Leave us alone.*

spaz down *in.* to relax. □ *Spaz down, man! Chill out!* □ *We tried to get the crowd to spaz down, but they were very excited.*

spaz out **1.** *in.* to overreact to something; to become overly excited about something. □ *I knew you would spaz out! It's not that bad!* □ *Come on, don't spaz out!* **2.** *n.* an emotional display. (Usually **spaz-out.**) □ *There's no need for a spaz-out!* □ *She threw a hell of a spaz-out.*

speak of the devil *phr.* said when someone whose name has just been mentioned appears or is heard from. (A catch phrase.) □ *And speak of the devil, here's Ted now.* □ *Speak of the devil, that was Mary on the phone.*

speak someone's language *tr.* to say something that one agrees with or understands. □ *I gotcha. Now you're speaking my language.* □ *Mary speaks Fred's language. They get along fine.*

speakeasy *n.* a nightclub during prohibition. □ *My grandfather remembers speakeasies. They were pretty crude places.* □ *You weren't supposed to talk about speakeasies so their locations would remain a secret.*

specs [spɛks] *n.* eyeglasses; spectacles. □ *I broke my specs.* □ *I need specs to find where I left my specs.*

speed **1.** *n.* methamphetamine; amphetamine in general. (Drugs.) □ *Speed is a monstrous problem in some cities.* □ *Kids think that speed won't get them into trouble.* **2.** *in.* to use methamphetamine; to be high on methamphetamine or amphetamine. (Drugs.) □ *Kids who speed think it is a harmless blow-off.* □ *If they speed rather than study—speed is a problem.*

speed demon **1.** *n.* a fast runner; a fast driver. □ *Tom is a speed demon. He qualified for the Olympics.* □ *Watch out, here comes another speed demon!* **2.** *n.* a habitual user of methamphetamine. (Drugs.) □ *A couple of speed demons mugged the old lady.* □ *When they are high, most speed demons don't know what they are doing.*

speed freak AND **speedhead** *n.* a drug user who injects methamphetamine; an amphetamine user. (Drugs and general slang.) □ *Hank is a speed freak, but he's not on skag.* □ *Speed freaks, not heroin addicts, account for a high proportion of drug-related crime.*

speed merchant *n.* someone who does something fast: a runner, pitcher, swimmer, driver, etc. □ *Look at her go! What a speed merchant!* □ *What a pitch! That guy is a speed merchant for sure.*

speedball *n.* (in baseball) a fast (pitched) ball. □ *The pitcher threw a speedball, and I didn't even see it!* □ *Tom can hit almost any speedball that Mike can throw.*

speeder **1.** *n.* a speeding ticket. □ *The cop that gave Mary a speeder Wednesday gave her another one Friday.* □ *Actually, that's three speeders in one week counting the one she got Monday.* **2.** *n.* an amphetamine or methamphetamine tablet, capsule, or ampoule. (Drugs. See also *speed.*) □ *Somebody dropped some speeders on the floor of the car, and my father spazzed out.* □ *Fred took a speeder before the exam, but he went to sleep anyway.* **3.** AND **speedster** *n.* a user of amphetamines or methamphetamine; a person who is hyperactive from amphetamine use. (Drugs.) □ *That kid is really hyped up—must be a speeder.* □ *The speeders can seem crazy when they're on a run.*

speedhead See *speed freak.*

speedster See *speeder.*

spending money *n.* cash, as opposed to money in the bank. □ *I'm a little short of spending money at the present. Could I borrow ten dollars?* □ *I don't have any spending money either.*

spew *in.* to empty one's stomach; to vomit. □ *After dinner, I suddenly had the urge to spew.* □ *Fred is up in the john spewing like mad.*

spew one's guts (out) **1.** *tr.* to empty one's stomach; to vomit. □ *Fred is spewing his guts out because of that lousy fish you served.* □ *He's spewing his guts because he has the flu, cabbagehead.* **2.** *tr.* to tell everything that one knows; to confess everything. (Underworld.) □ *Lefty was sitting there in the cop-shop spewing his guts out about the bank job.* □ *If he really is spewing his guts, the mob will cancel his Christmas.*

spiff *n.* extra money paid to a salesperson to sell certain merchandise aggressively. (See also *push money.*) □ *The manufacturer supplied a little spiff that even the store manager didn't know about.* □ *I got about $300 last month in spiff for selling some low-grade shoes.*

spiffed out *mod.* nicely dressed up; decked out. □ *I like to get all spiffed out every now and then.* □ *Wow, you look spiffed out! Where are you going?*

spiffed up *mod.* dressed up, brushed up, and polished up nicely. □ *See if you can get yourself a little spiffed up before we get to the front door. We wouldn't want the Wilmington-Thorpes to think you only have one suit.* □ *The house doesn't have to be too spiffed up for the Franklins. They are used to clutter.*

spifflicated AND **spificated** ['spɪfləkedəd AND 'spɪfəkedəd] *mod.* alcohol intoxicated. □ *Mrs. Wilmington-Thorpe drank champagne until she was nearly spifflicated.* □ *Being spificated on champagne is not as bad as it sounds.*

spiffy ['spɪfi] *mod.* excellent. □ *This is a real spiffy place you've got here, Sam.* □ *Come have a look at my spiffy new car.* □ *Doesn't look so spiffy to me.*

spificated See *spifflicated.*

spike **1.** *n.* a hypodermic needle; a hypodermic syringe and needle; a medicine dropper and a needle. (Drugs.) □ *The addict caught some strange disease from a dirty spike.* □ *What'll I do? I broke my spike.* **2.** *tr.* to add ether or alcohol to beer, originally by injecting it through the cork with a hypodermic needle; to add alcohol to a nonalcoholic drink. (From prohibition times.) □ *He found a man who would spike his beer for a small fee.* □ *He spiked the beer with ether, which is a dangerous thing to do.* (More at *spiked.*) **3.** *tr.* to puncture an idea. □ *I explained the plan, but the boss spiked it immediately.* □ *I hate to see my ideas spiked like that.*

spiked **1.** *mod.* having to do with a drink with alcohol added; having to do with a punch with an alcoholic content. □ *Is the punch spiked? I want some without.* □ *We only have spiked punch.* □ *Max's breakfast orange juice is usually spiked.* **2.** *mod.* alcohol or drug intoxicated. □ *I knew that Mrs. Wilmington-Thorpe was spiked when she belched like a real country thunder-boomer.* □ *Her old man was just as spiked, and he made worse noises.* **3.** *mod.* having to do with hair that stands up straight. □ *His spiked hair wouldn't look so bad if it wasn't orange.* □ *Both orange and spiked is too much.* □ *Is spiked hair a fad or the way of the future?*

spill *in.* to confess. (Underworld.) □ *The cops tried to get her to spill, but she just sat there.* □ *The gang was afraid she would spill, but she's a tough old thing.*

spill one's guts *tr.* to tell all; to confess. (Compare to *spew one's guts (out).*) □ *I had to spill my guts about the broken window. I didn't want you to take the blame.* □ *Mary spilled her guts about the window. She confessed that she was trying to shield Bob.*

spill the beans AND **spill the works** *tr.* to give away a secret or a surprise. □ *There is a surprise party for Heidi on Wednesday. Please don't spill the beans.* □ *Paul spilled the beans about Heidi's party.*

spill the works See the previous entry.

spin doctor *n.* someone who provides an interpretation of news or an event in a way that makes the news or event work to the advantage of the entity employing the *spin doctor*. (Usually in political contexts in reference to manipulating the news.) ☐ *Things were going bad for the president, so he got himself a new spin doctor.* ☐ *A good spin doctor could have made the incident far less damaging.*

spin one's wheels *tr.* to waste time; to remain in a neutral position, neither advancing nor falling back. ☐ *I'm just spinning my wheels in this job. I need more training to get ahead.* ☐ *The whole project was just spinning its wheels until spring.*

spinach *n.* money. (Because it is green. See also *cabbage, lettuce*.) ☐ *How much spinach you got on you?* ☐ *Look at this! One hundred dollars in good old American spinach!*

spit and polish *n.* orderliness; ceremonial precision and orderliness. ☐ *I like spit and polish. It comes from being in the military.* ☐ *There is no such thing as too much spit and polish.*

Spit it out! *exclam.* "Say it!" ☐ *Come on, don't be shy! Spit it out!* ☐ *Say what you have to say and leave. Hurry up! Spit it out!*

spizzerinktum [spɪzə˞'rɪŋktəm] *n.* energy; vitality. ☐ *The kid's got spizzerinktum! I like that.* ☐ *Put more spizzerinktum into it!*

spleef See the following entry.

spliff AND **shpleef; spleef; splim** [splɪf AND ʃplif, splif, splɪm] *n.* marijuana; a marijuana cigarette; hashish. (Originally Jamaican.) ☐ *They consume an enormous amount of spliff and try to sell it to the tourists.* ☐ *It's really high-quality splim.*

splim See the previous entry.

split *in.* to leave. ☐ *Look at the clock. Time to split.* ☐ *Let's split. We're late.*

split a gut 1. *tr.* to laugh very hard. ☐ *He laughed until he nearly split a gut.* ☐ *The audience split a gut laughing.* **2.** *tr.* to work very hard. ☐ *I split a gut to get this place fixed up in a week.* ☐ *Don't split a gut for me. I love things that are falling apart.*

split up [splɪt 'əp] **1.** *in.* to separate. ☐ *The two split up and went their separate ways.* ☐ *They couldn't get along, so they split up.* **2.** ['splɪtəp] *n.* an act of separating or breaking up. (Usually **split-up**.) ☐ *Everyone was mentally prepared for the company's split-up.* ☐ *The split-up caused neither surprise nor grief.*

splitting headache *n.* a severe headache, as if one's head were splitting open. ☐ *I'm sorry, I can't. I have a splitting headache. Maybe Fred will play bridge with you.* ☐ *This splitting headache has been going on for hours.*

splurge *in.* to indulge oneself with much spending or eating. ☐ *I have to splurge every now and then. I deserve it.* ☐ *I splurge every weekend.*

spoil *tr.* to kill someone. ☐ *It was Bruno's job to make sure that nobody got close enough to Mr. Big to spoil him.* ☐ *Rocko was determined to spoil Barlowe.*

spoiled rotten *mod.* indulged in; greatly spoiled. ☐ *This kid is spoiled rotten!* ☐ *I was spoiled rotten when I was a child, so I'm used to this kind of wasteful luxury.*

spoiling for a fight *phr.* argumentative; asking for a fight. ☐ *They were just spoiling for a fight, and they went outside to settle the matter.* ☐ *She was grouchy, and you could tell she had been spoiling for a fight all day.*

spondulicks AND **spondulics; spondulix** [spɑn'dulɪks] *n.* money. ☐ *How much spondulicks will this set me back?* ☐ *I don't have enough spondulix to swing the deal.*

spondulics See the previous entry.

spondulix See *spondulicks*.

sponge AND **spunge 1.** *in.* to drink heavily. ☐ *She was sponging like there was no tomorrow.* ☐ *What can you do with a woman who sits and spunges all day long?* **2.** *n.* a drunkard; a *tippler*. (See also *blotter*.) ☐ *She was a spunge, and she wasn't going to do anything about it.* ☐ *Is there treatment for spunges like* *her?* **3.** *n.* a parasitic person. ☐ *Don't be a sponge. Get your own!* ☐ *Here comes that sponge, Wally. Hide your wallet, pencils, glasses, and any clothes in his size.*

spoof [spuf] **1.** *n.* a parody. ☐ *The first act was a spoof of a Congressional investigation.* ☐ *The second act was a spoof of the first act.* **2.** *tr.* to make a parody of someone or something. ☐ *The comedian spoofed the executive branch by sitting in a big chair and going to sleep.* ☐ *I like to spoof myself. It helps break the ice at parties.*

spook 1. *tr.* to frighten or startle someone or something. ☐ *Something I did spooked the teller, and she set off the silent alarm.* ☐ *Don't spook the cattle. They'll stampede.* (More at *spooked*.) **2.** *n.* a spy; a C.I.A. (U.S. Central Intelligence Agency) agent. ☐ *I just learned that my uncle had been a spook for years.* ☐ *Fred is training to be a spook, but don't tell anybody.*

spook factory *n.* the C.I.A. (U.S. Central Intelligence Agency) in Washington D.C., where spies are said to be trained. ☐ *Tom got a job in the spook factory.* ☐ *Does the spook factory pay very well?*

spooked *mod.* frightened or startled. ☐ *The guy looked sort of spooked. He was sweating and panting like someone had scared him to death.* ☐ *The horse was spooked and rolled its eyes and snorted a lot.*

spoon 1. *in.* to neck and pet. ☐ *They like to go out and spoon under the stars.* ☐ *Do you remember spooning with me years ago?* **2.** See *cokespoon*.

sport *n.* friend; chum. (A term of address.) ☐ *Well, sport, looks like we have a little problem here.* ☐ *Hey, sport, what's new?*

spot 1. *n.* a small drink of liquor. ☐ *I'll just have a spot, please.* ☐ *Just a spot for me, too.* **2.** *n.* a nightclub; a night spot. ☐ *It was a nice little spot, with a combo and a canary.* ☐ *We went to a spot with a jukebox for entertainment.* **3.** See *spot someone (something)*.

spot market *n.* the open market where deals are made on the spot. (Securities markets.) ☐ *Oil reached nearly twenty-five dollars a barrel on the spot market.* ☐ *Gold prices on the spot market finally reached $600 per ounce and then promptly collapsed.*

spot of lunch *n.* a small amount of lunch. ☐ *How about a spot of lunch?* ☐ *I had a spot of lunch at my desk, thanks.*

spot someone (something) 1. *tr.* to give an advantage to someone. ☐ *I'll spot you twenty points.* ☐ *No need to spot me. I'm the greatest!* **2.** *tr.* to lend someone something. ☐ *Can you spot me a few bucks?* ☐ *I can spot you a whole hundred!*

sprain one's ankle *tr.* to become pregnant. ☐ *She has, ah, sprained her ankle.* ☐ *From the looks of her, she must have sprained her ankle some months ago.*

spring chicken *n.* a young and naive person, especially a young woman. (Usually in the negative.) ☐ *Well, I may not be a spring chicken, but I got some spizzerinktum left.* ☐ *I am a spring chicken, but I lie about my age to get served in bars.*

spring for something AND **bounce for something** *in.* to treat (someone) by buying something. (See also *pop for something*.) ☐ *I'm bouncing for pizza. Any takers?* ☐ *Ralph sprang for drinks, and we all had a great time.*

spring someone *tr.* to get someone out of jail on bond or permanently. ☐ *My wife came down and sprung me; otherwise, I'd still be in the slammer.* ☐ *The guy's mouthpiece tried to spring him, but the D.A. nixed it.*

sprout *n.* a child. ☐ *Where are the sprouts?* ☐ *A little sprout came up and tried to sell me a ticket to a game.*

sprout wings 1. *tr.* to die and become an angel. ☐ *I'm not ready to sprout wings yet. I've got a few more years.* ☐ *You wanna sprout wings, you just keep talking like that.* **2.** *tr.* to be so good as to become an angel. ☐ *The kid is not about to sprout wings, but he probably won't get* *into jail again.* □ *He was so good and helpful, I thought he would sprout wings.*

spud [spəd] **1.** *n.* a potato. □ *I'd like a few more spuds.* □ *Mashed spuds are the best of all.* **2.** *n.* vodka. (Presumed to be made from potatoes.) □ *How about a glass of spud?* □ *She keeps a big jug of spud in the reefer and drinks it like water.* **3.** *n.* a vodka drunkard. □ *That silly spud thinks we can't smell what's on her breath.* □ *The old spud on the third floor fell down a flight or two and broke his hip.* **4.** *n.* a short person. (Also a term of address.) □ *He can jump pretty high for a spud.* □ *Hey, spud! I almost didn't see you!*

spunge See *sponge.*

spunk [spəŋk] *n.* courage. □ *Show some spunk. Get in there and stand up for your rights.* □ *I have the spunk, but I don't have the brains.*

spunky ['spəŋki] *mod.* gutsy; courageous. □ *I like a spunky girl—one who can really dance.* □ *The guy's a shrimp, but he's spunky.*

square 1. *mod.* old-fashioned; law-abiding; stodgy. □ *Man, you are really square.* □ *I come from a very square family.* **2.** *n.* a person who behaves properly. □ *You are a square if I ever saw one.* □ *Ask that square what her favorite kind of music is.* **3.** AND **square joint** *n.* a tobacco cigarette, compared to a marijuana cigarette. □ *You got a square on you?* □ *I'll take a reefer. I've heard that squares will give you cancer.* **4.** *tr.* to settle or to make something right. □ *Let's talk about squaring this matter.* □ *Will twenty bucks square the matter?* **5.** See *square (meal).*

square apple See the following entry.

square john AND **square apple** *n.* someone who obeys the rules; a *square.* □ *Fred is a square john. There's no point in worrying about him.* □ *All those square apples can take care of themselves.*

square john broad *n.* an honest, straightforward woman. (Underworld.) □ *Betty is okay. She's a real square john broad.* □ *We need a square john broad to give this place a look of respectability.*

square joint See *square.*

square (meal) *n.* a good and nutritious meal. (Always with quantifier when *square* is used without *meal.*) □ *I need three squares a day—at least.* □ *The old soak looks like he could use a square meal.*

square off *in.* to prepare to fight; to prepare to argue or compete. □ *They were squaring off, so I asked them if they'd like to step outside.* □ *Let's square off and debate this thing properly.*

square peg (in a round hole) *n.* someone who does not fit in. □ *I'm a square peg in a round hole. Maybe I am meant to be eccentric.* □ *Kelly seems to be a square peg. What'll we do with him?*

square shooter *n.* an honest person. (See also *straight shooter.*) □ *I trust Sam. He's a square shooter.* □ *He wouldn't do anything shabby. He's a square shooter.*

square with someone *in.* to become honest with someone. □ *I want you to square with me. Tell the truth this time.* □ *Okay, I'll square with you. Terry did it.*

squared away *mod.* straightened out. □ *I'm not really squared away on this stuff, but I'm beginning to see the light.* □ *We'll get everything squared away in a few days.*

squared up *mod.* no longer taking drugs. (Drugs.) □ *Walter is squared up now and spends a lot of time trying to help others.* □ *Max'll never get himself squared up.*

squat 1. *in.* to sit (down). □ *Come on in and squat for a while.* □ *Squat over here by the fire.* **2.** *n.* nothing. (See also *diddly-squat.*) □ *I worked all day on this, and she didn't pay me squat.* □ *I earn just a little more than squat, but I am very pleased with my life.*

squawk 1. *in.* to complain. □ *Come on, don't squawk all the time!* □ *Some people squawk because they don't have anything else to do.* **2.** *n.* a complaint. □ *Here's another squawk from the lady on the third floor.* □ *I have a list of squawks from the mayor's office.* **3.** *tr.* & *in.* to reveal or *blab* something. □ *Watch*

Tracy. She may decide to squawk. □ *She squawked the whole business to the fuzz.*

squawk box *n.* a public address system; a loudspeaker, especially if installed in a box or other housing. □ *A raspy voice came over the squawk box announcing the arrival of what we had been waiting for.* □ *The squawk box was strangely quiet through the night.*

squeaky clean *mod.* very clean. (Like a clean glass that squeaks when one rubs a finger on it.) □ *I got this floor squeaky clean. Don't spill anything on it.* □ *Somebody tracked mud on my squeaky clean floor!*

squeal *in.* to inform (someone about something). □ *Who squealed to the cops?* □ *Tracy squealed on us.*

squealer 1. *n.* an informer. (Underworld.) □ *Tracy is a terrible squealer.* □ *Some squealer let the cops know what was going to happen.* **2.** *n.* a pig; a piglet. □ *They sent their squealers to market at just the right time.* □ *I was horrified to learn that bacon comes from squealers.*

squeeze 1. *n.* liquor. (Black. See also *grape(s)*.) □ *Let's stop on the way and get some squeeze.* □ *Freddie, where is your squeeze?* **2.** *tr.* to put pressure on someone. □ *The mob began to squeeze Max for money.* □ *The tight schedule squeezed us all.* **3.** *n.* a tight situation; a situation where pressure is felt. □ *I'm in sort of a squeeze. Can you wait a month?* □ *When the squeeze is over, we'll be able to get squared away.* **4.** *n.* one's lover. (See also *main squeeze*.) □ *I'll see if my squeeze wants to go.* □ *Get your squeeze, and let's go sink a few.*

(squeeze-)box *n.* an accordion. (Compare to *groan box*.) □ *My brother plays the squeeze-box—not very well, but who can tell?* □ *The band consisted of drums, clarinet, and a box. A real winner.*

squeeze play *n.* a special play in baseball where there is a runner on third base and the batter bunts. (With an early start the runner may reach home plate.) □ *They pulled off that squeeze play like the professionals they are.* □ *The crowd roared as the squeeze play paid off.*

squib [skʌɪb] *n.* a notice; a small advertisement. □ *There was a squib in the paper about your project.* □ *I read a squib about that yesterday.*

squid [skʌɪd] *n.* an earnest student; a collegiate wimp. (Collegiate. Refers to sliminess.) □ *This whole campus is populated by squids and nerds.* □ *I'm no squid. I went out on a date last month.*

squiff [skʌɪf] *n.* a drunkard. (See also *on the squiff*.) □ *It's no fun living with a squiff.* □ *Is there anything that can be done for a confirmed squiff?*

squiff out *in.* to collapse from drink. □ *Hank squiffed out at midnight, right on the dot.* □ *She kept from squiffing out because she didn't trust her date.*

squiffed AND **squiffy** [skʌɪft AND 'skʌɪfi] *mod.* alcohol intoxicated. □ *She was a little squiffed, but still entertaining.* □ *The hostess was so squiffed she could hardly stand.*

squiffy See the previous entry.

squiggle ['skʌɪgl̩] *n.* a wiggly mark. □ *What does this squiggle mean?* □ *That squiggle is my signature.*

squirrel 1. *n.* a strange or eccentric person. □ *Martin can be such a squirrel.* □ *Freddie is a squirrel, but I love him.* **2.** *n.* a car engine's horsepower. □ *What kind of squirrels you got under the hood?* □ *I got 440 squirrels and a gaggle of carburetors.*

squirrel-food *n.* a *nut;* a loony person. □ *The driver of the car—squirrel-food, for sure—just sat there smiling.* □ *Some squirrel-food came over and asked for a sky hook.*

squirrel out of something *in.* to wiggle out of something; to manage to extricate oneself from a situation one does not wish to be in. □ *He will do anything he can to squirrel out of going to the dance.* □ *Don't try to squirrel out of it. Go through with it.*

squirrel something away *tr.* to hide something in reserve. □ *Here is some* *food. I squirreled it away in my suitcase.* Ⓣ *She had squirreled away quite a fortune.*

squirrely *mod.* loony. ☐ *Who wrote this squirrely play?* ☐ *Good old squirrely Tom! Isn't he a wonder?* ☐ *No, he's just squirrely.*

squirt 1. *n.* a small person; a young child, especially a young boy. (Also a term of address.) ☐ *Hey, squirt, come over here.* ☐ *He sure is a cute little squirt.* **2.** *n.* beer or champagne. ☐ *I like squirt and things. It tickles my nose.* ☐ *How about a nice bubbly glass of squirt?*

squirts *n.* a case of diarrhea. (Always with *the*.) ☐ *He's got the squirts and can't go out.* ☐ *What do you take for the squirts?*

squooshy ['skʌmʃi AND 'skʌmʃi] *mod.* soft; squishy. ☐ *I can't stand squooshy food!* ☐ *Mush is supposed to be squooshy.* ☐ *I like to walk barefooted in squooshy mud.*

stack the deck *tr.* to arrange things secretly for a desired outcome. (From card playing where a cheater may arrange the order of the cards that are to be dealt to the players.) ☐ *The president stacked the deck so I would be appointed head of the finance committee.* ☐ *It's not fair when somebody stacks the deck.*

stacked *mod.* having to do with a person with a sexually attractive body, usually a female. ☐ *Wow, is she ever stacked!* ☐ *I like to see stacked dames like that starting to do business in this place.*

stag 1. *mod.* having to do with someone going to a party without a date. (Originally said of a male.) ☐ *He decided to ignore her and go stag.* ☐ *A bunch of the guys got together and went stag to the dance.* **2.** *mod.* having to do with a gathering for men only. ☐ *The party is stag, so Tom and I are going together.* ☐ *Stag parties cease to be fun after a while.*

stag line *n.* a line of dateless men at a dance. ☐ *She looked over the stag line and saw nobody she knew.* ☐ *The guys in the stag line looked so forlorn. She suddenly wanted to do something to make them all happy.*

stag-party *n.* a party for men only. (Thought to be *raunchy*.) ☐ *Sally was hired to dance at a stag-party.* ☐ *They hired a stripper for the stag-party—you know, the kind that jumps out of a cake.*

staggers 1. *n.* liquor. ☐ *He couldn't seem to get enough staggers.* ☐ *She poured herself a huge glass of staggers and mumbled something about cough medicine.* **2.** *n.* drunkenness; the delirium tremens. (Always with *the*.) ☐ *He seems to have a little touch of the staggers.* ☐ *Larry's laid up with the staggers again.*

stake someone or something out 1. *tr.* to position a person so that someone or something can be observed or followed. ☐ *The cops staked the car out and made the arrest.* Ⓣ *Barlowe staked out the apartment building and watched patiently for an hour.* **2.** *tr.* to position a person to observe someone or something. ☐ *He staked his best operative out in front of the building.* Ⓣ *We staked out two men to keep watch.*

stake someone to something 1. *tr.* to lend or give someone money to buy something. ☐ *Can you stake me to a decent meal?* ☐ *Stake the man to a meal and a flop, and he'll tell us what we want to know.* **2.** *tr.* to treat someone to something. ☐ *Can I stake you to a drink to celebrate?* ☐ *Let me stake you to a big ice cream cone.*

stakeout 1. *n.* a person who is positioned to observe someone or something. (See also *stake someone or something out*.) ☐ *The stakeout stuck out like a sore thumb—standing there under the streetlight reading a paper.* ☐ *The stakeout was one of Barlowe's best operatives.* **2.** *n.* a (police) assignment where someone is positioned to observe someone or something. ☐ *The two top cops were out on a stakeout.* ☐ *The stakeout at the warehouse backfired. They only found cats.*

stale drunk *n.* a long-standing and frequently renewed drunken state. ☐ *The guy's on a stale drunk. He is a mess.*

□ *Are you on a stale drunk again, or is this the same one?*

stallion *n.* a tall, good-looking woman. □ *Dana is really a stallion!* □ *Who is the stallion with that dude?*

stamping ground *n.* one's favorite or customary location. □ *Adamsville is my old stamping ground. I was born there, you know.* □ *I like to go back and look at my old stamping ground every now and then.*

stand-in *n.* a substitute; a temporary replacement. □ *I was a stand-in for the lead soprano, who had the sniffles.* □ *The audience booed the stand-in. They had paid to hear a star.*

stand-out *n.* an extraordinary thing or person. □ *Bob is a real stand-out in our bowling league.* □ *This car is a real stand-out as a speed machine.*

stand pat (on something) *in.* to stick firmly to one's position or opinions. □ *I am going to stand pat on this issue.* □ *I thought you would stand pat in the absence of new information.*

stand someone up *tr.* to break a date by not showing up. □ *She stood him up, and he was really angry.* 🅃 *He stood up his date while he played basketball with the guys.*

stand tall *in.* to be brave and proud. □ *I can still stand tall. I'm innocent.* □ *Our athletes stand tall in the knowledge that they did their best.*

stand there with one's bare face hanging out *phr.* to stand someplace looking helpless and stupid. □ *Say something. Don't just stand there with your bare face hanging out.* □ *She just stood there with her bare face hanging out while they took away everything she owned.*

standee *n.* someone who must stand (at some event). □ *There were about forty standees in addition to the full house.* □ *Can I get in as a standee, or do I have to wait for the next showing?*

standoffish [stænd'ɔfɪʃ] *mod.* aloof. □ *Bob is sort of standoffish until he gets to know you.* □ *Don't be so standoffish! Join in the fun.* □ *I am a standoffish guy.*

stanza ['stænzə] *n.* an inning in baseball or some other division of a ball game. □ *He's doing better than he was in the last stanza.* □ *Jerry Clay is pitching again in this stanza.*

starched AND **starchy** *mod.* alcohol intoxicated. (Compare to *stiff.*) □ *Man, was he starched!* □ *No, he wasn't quite stiff, but he was starched.*

starchy See the previous entry.

stash 1. *n.* a mustache. □ *Jerry has this enormous stash that he keeps waxed and trimmed.* □ *I cut my stash off because it was too much trouble to remember not to cut it off.* **2.** *tr.* to hide something (somewhere). □ *Stash this under the chair until I can think of a place to put it.* □ *Fred stashed his coat in a heap in the corner.* **3.** *n.* a concealed supply of drugs, especially marijuana; drugs and equipment to use them stored in a secret place. (Drugs.) □ *Max's stash was never located by the fuzz.* □ *My stash is down to nothing.*

stat [stæt] *n.* a thermostat. (See also *stats.*) □ *Who turned down the stat?* □ *I'm afraid you need a new stat.*

static *n.* complaints. □ *I don't expect any static because of the noise. I warned the neighbors about the party.* □ *Is this guy giving you any static?*

stats [stæts] *n.* statistics. □ *They're working out the stats now.* □ *The stats are expected to show that the trade balance is growing steadily worse.*

stay loose See *hang loose.*

Stay tuned. 1. *sent.* "Stay tuned in to this radio or television station." (A formula uttered before a commercial.) □ *I'll be right back after these announcements. Stay tuned.* □ *Stay tuned. Back in a minute.* **2.** *sent.* "Continue to pay attention to this matter."; "Watch for further developments." (From sense 1.) □ *Things are developing rapidly in this area. Stay tuned.* □ *Stay tuned. Pending legislation could change all this.*

steady *n.* a boyfriend or girlfriend. □ *She showed up with Tom, her steady for* *the last few months.* □ *My steady is laid up with a cold. I'll come alone.*

steal *n.* a bargain. (Always with *a*.) □ *At this price, it's a steal.* □ *This car wasn't exactly a steal at this price, but it's still a good value.*

steam 1. *tr.* to anger someone. □ *She steamed him by being two hours late.* □ *The prof steamed the class with the long assignment.* **2.** *in.* to be angry. □ *She was absolutely steaming.* □ *They steamed for a while and then did as they were told.*

steam someone up 1. *tr.* to get someone excited. □ *Steam yourselves up and get in there and win this game!* Ⓣ *The coach can really steam up those guys.* **2.** *tr.* to get someone angry. □ *This whole mess steamed me up but good.* Ⓣ *The long critical statement simply steamed up the opposition.* (More at *steamed (up)*.)

steam someone's beam *tr.* to make someone angry. □ *Being stood up really steams my beam!* □ *Come on, don't steam your beam. Remember how hard times are now.*

steam up *in.* to drink heavily; to get drunk. □ *Fred and Mike were steaming up in the back room.* □ *Let's go down to the tavern and steam up, okay?* (More at *steamed (up)*.)

steamed (up) 1. *mod.* angry. □ *Now, now, don't get so steamed up!* □ *She is really massively steamed.* **2.** *mod.* alcohol intoxicated and fighting. □ *He was really steamed—and could hardly stand up.* □ *By midnight, Larry was too steamed to drive home, and he had to spend the night.*

steamroller *tr.* to force something to be approved; to force something to happen. □ *He plans to steamroller this bill through Congress, but it just won't work.* □ *When you can't steamroller something, try soft soap.*

steamy *mod.* lewd; sensuous; passionate. □ *They cut a couple of steamy scenes out of the movie because of complaints.* □ *Hank and Bess were having a steamy session on the couch.* □ *The session was really steamy.*

steenth [stintθ] *n.* "one sixteenth," used in quoting securities prices. (Securities markets. See also *teenie*.) □ *This issue was only up a few steenths for the whole week.* □ *Acme Systems was down a steenth at midday.*

steep *mod.* (of a price) high; expensive. □ *Isn't that price sort of steep?* □ *I don't have steep prices here.* □ *Their prices are pretty steep, but their goods are of high quality.*

stellar ['stɛlɚ] *mod.* excellent; grand. □ *It was a stellar performance, and the applause was thunderous.* □ *Ronald Simpson gave us a stellar characterization of Boris, but the chorus was a disappointment.* □ *The chorus was stellar!*

stems *n.* legs. □ *Look at the stems on that dame!* □ *My feet are sore, and my stems ache all the time.*

step off the curb *in.* to die. □ *Ralph almost stepped off the curb during his operation.* □ *I'm too young to step off the curb.*

step out on someone *in.* to betray one's lover by going out with someone else. □ *Hank has been stepping out on Bess, and she doesn't know it yet.* □ *She would never step out on him.*

step outside *in.* to leave the present area and go to another place, presumably to fight. □ *The two—who had been arguing—stepped outside to settle the matter.* □ *Do you want to step outside, smart ass?*

step right up *phr.* "come forward and do not be bashful." □ *There are still a few of these left. Step right up and get yours.* □ *Step right up and buy a ticket to the greatest show on earth!*

stepped on *mod.* having to do with diluted drugs. (Drugs.) □ *That smack you bought was really stepped on.* □ *This stuff is too stepped on. It's sugar, and it won't do.*

stern *n.* the posterior. □ *The little airplane crashed right into the stern of an* *enormous lady who didn't even notice.* □ *Haul your stern over here and sit down.*

stet [stɛt] *mod.* just as it was originally. (Proofreading.) □ *No, mark that one stet. It was right the way it was.* □ *This says stet, but it's wrong.* □ *This one should look just like the other one, so mark one stet and ignore the other.*

stew 1. *n.* a drinking bout. □ *One more stew like that and I'll need a vacation to recover.* □ *These frequent stews must stop. You will ruin your health.* 2. *n.* a drunkard. □ *Who is that stew in the corner?* □ *There are three stews sleeping in the alley.* 3. See *stewed (up).* 4. *n.* a stewardess or steward on an airplane. □ *The stew brought the coffee and rolls.* □ *My sister is a stew for a major airline.* 5. *in.* to fret. □ *It's bad, but don't stew about it.* □ *I spent most of last night stewing about my job.* 6. *n.* a fretful state. □ *Don't work yourself into a stew.* □ *Look at her face. That is the result of a dreadful stew. I wonder what's wrong.*

stew bum *n.* a drunkard; an alcoholic. □ *You're going to end up a stew bum if you don't lay off the moonshine.* □ *Those stew bums could use a bath.*

stewed to the ears See the following entry.

stewed to the gills AND **stewed to the ears** *mod.* alcohol intoxicated. □ *Why does a grown man have to get stewed to the gills every night of his life if there isn't something a little wrong with him?* □ *Here's old Charlie—stewed to the ears, as always.*

stewed (up) AND **stew** *mod.* alcohol intoxicated. (See also sense 1 for *stew.*) □ *Gary was too stewed to remember his name.* □ *The kid was stewed up and scared to death of what his parents were going to do to him.*

stick 1. *n.* a baseball bat. (Baseball.) □ *He started to run and tripped over the stick.* □ *He holds the stick up higher than most batters.* 2. *n.* a pool cue. □ *He drew the stick back slowly, sighted again, and gave the cue ball a sharp knock.* □ *The guy was so mad he broke the stick over his knee!* 3. *n.* a golf club. □ *These aren't my sticks, and you aren't my caddy. What's going on around here?* □ *I wanted a new set of sticks for Christmas, but I got a snowmobile instead.* 4. *n.* the lever that controls the horizontal and vertical surfaces of the tail of an aircraft. □ *The pilot pulled back on the stick, and the plane did nothing—being that he hadn't even started the engine or anything.* □ *You pull back on the stick, which lowers the tail and raises the nose, and up you go.* 5. *n.* a gearshift lever in a car. (See also *stick shift.*) □ *I keep reaching for the stick in a car with automatic.* □ *Put the stick in reverse and move back slowly.* 6. *n.* a drunkard. □ *Some stick threw up on my car.* □ *Get that stick out of here before he makes a mess.* 7. *n.* a person's legs. (Always plural.) □ *Get those sticks moving! Get over here now!* □ *He's got good sticks under him, but he won't use them.* 8. *n.* a rural or backwoods area. (Always with *the* and always plural.) □ *I hated living in the sticks.* □ *You hear a lot about how things are in the sticks. They're worse.*

stick around *in.* to remain nearby. □ *Stick around. Things are bound to get better.* □ *I think if you'll stick around, you'll get a seat sooner or later.*

Stick 'em up! See *Hands up!*

stick in the mud *n.* a dull and old-fashioned person. □ *Don't be such an old stick in the mud.* □ *Some stick in the mud objected to the kind of music we wanted to play in church.*

stick it to someone *tr.* to give someone a problem; to confront someone. □ *They stuck it to me about the stopped up drain.* □ *He was late, and the boss really stuck it to him.*

stick man *n.* a police patrol officer (who carries a stick). □ *The stick man is due here in about three minutes. Hurry.* □ *I was a stick man for a few years till my feet went bad.*

stick one's nose in (where it's not wanted) See *put one's nose in (where it's not wanted).*

stick out like a sore thumb *in.* to be very obvious. □ *That zit really sticks out like* *a sore thumb.* ☐ *Do you think I would stick out like a sore thumb at the party if I wear this coat?*

stick shift 1. *mod.* having to do with a nonautomatic transmission or a car that has one. ☐ *I prefer a stick shift car—I don't know why.* ☐ *The stick shift models are cheaper—that's why.* ☐ *This one's stick shift.* **2.** *n.* a nonautomatic transmission. ☐ *I can't drive a stick shift!* ☐ *My husband took the other car and stuck me with the stick shift.*

stick someone with something *tr.* to burden someone with something. ☐ *Please don't stick me with the stick shift again.* ☐ *He left town and stuck me with the bill.*

sticker shock *n.* the shock at seeing just how much a new automobile costs as determined by looking at the price tag or sticker. ☐ *I went to a car dealer today, and I am still suffering from sticker shock.* ☐ *If sticker shock is getting you down, think about getting a used car.*

sticktoitiveness [stɪkˈtuɪtɪvnəs] *n.* tenacity. ☐ *The kid has sticktoitiveness. I like that in a kid.* ☐ *If I had more sticktoitiveness, maybe I could get a job.*

stickum [ˈstɪkəm] **1.** *n.* glue. ☐ *Put some stickum on this paper and paste it up where it can be seen.* ☐ *There's no stickum left on this stamp.* **2.** *n.* any thick and sticky substance, especially hair dressing. (Compare to *slickum.*) ☐ *Use some stickum on your hair!* ☐ *He uses too much stickum on his hair.*

sticky 1. *mod.* gooey. (Standard English.) ☐ *This stuff sure is sticky.* ☐ *What is this sticky stuff on my shoe? Oh, no!* **2.** *mod.* chancy; awkward. ☐ *Things began to get a little sticky, and Barlowe began to move toward the door.* ☐ *When the going got sticky, Freddy disappeared.* **3.** *mod.* sentimental. ☐ *Things were getting a little sticky the more Harriet drank. She tried to kiss me, and I left.* ☐ *There's a sticky part in the movie, but other than that it's pretty good.* **4.** *mod.* having to do with hot and humid weather. ☐ *It's so sticky today!* ☐ *I can't take another sticky day like this.*

sticky fingers *n.* a tendency to steal. ☐ *Bruno has sticky fingers and likes wallets especially.* ☐ *Watch these young kids with sticky fingers who come in here "just looking."*

stiff 1. AND **stiffed** *mod.* alcohol intoxicated; dead drunk. ☐ *Kelly was too stiff to find his keys.* ☐ *She knows how to stop drinking before she gets stiff.* **2.** *n.* a drunkard. ☐ *Some stiff staggered by —belching clouds of some beery smell.* ☐ *The guy's a stiff, and you want to run him for mayor? Even in this town that's going too far.* **3.** *mod.* dead. (Originally underworld.) ☐ *He's stiff. There's nothing that can be done.* ☐ *Yeah, he's stiff. Don't hit him no more.* **4.** *n.* a corpse. (Underworld.) ☐ *They pulled another stiff out of the river last night. Looks like another mob killing.* ☐ *They took me into a room full of stiffs to identify Rocko's bod.* **5.** *n.* a fellow worker; a fellow tramp. (Originally hobos.) ☐ *He's just another working stiff like me.* ☐ *This stiff wants some help finding a flop for the night.* **6.** *tr.* to fail to tip someone who expects it. ☐ *Ya know, you can tell right away when a guy's gonna stiff you—ya just know.* ☐ *I guess I get stiffed two-three times a day.* **7.** *tr.* to cheat someone. ☐ *The clown selling hot dogs stiffed me for about forty cents.* ☐ *I really got stiffed on that deal. Look at this cheap junk.*

stiffed See the previous entry.

sting 1. *tr.* to cheat or swindle someone; to overcharge someone. ☐ *That street merchant stung me, but good.* ☐ *They are likely to sting you in any of those hockshops.* **2.** *n.* a well-planned scheme to entrap criminals. ☐ *The sting came off without a hitch.* ☐ *It was a well-planned sting and shouldn't have failed.* **3.** *tr.* to entrap and arrest someone. ☐ *The feebies stung the whole gang at once.* ☐ *"We've been stung!" they hollered.*

stinger *n.* the drawback; the catch; the hitch. ☐ *Now, here's the stinger.* ☐ *Sounds good, but what's the stinger?*

stink 1. *in.* to be repellent. ☐ *This whole setup stinks.* ☐ *Your act stinks. Try* *another agent.* **2.** *n.* a commotion. (See also *raise a stink (about someone or something).*) ☐ *The stink you made about money has done no good at all. You're fired.* ☐ *One more stink like that and out you go.*

stink on ice *in.* to be really rotten. (So rotten as to reek even when frozen.) ☐ *This show stinks on ice.* ☐ *The whole idea stank on ice.*

stinker **1.** *n.* an unpleasant or wicked person. ☐ *Jerry is a real stinker. Look what he did!* ☐ *What stinker messed up my desk?* **2.** *n.* a serious problem. ☐ *This whole business is a real stinker.* ☐ *What a stinker of a problem.*

stinking **1.** See *stinking (drunk).* **2.** *mod.* lousy; rotten. ☐ *What a stinking mess you've got yourself into.* ☐ *That was a mean stinking thing to do. Really stinking!*

stinking (drunk) *mod.* alcohol intoxicated. ☐ *He was really stinking.* ☐ *She came within an inch of getting stinking drunk.*

stinking rich *mod.* very rich. ☐ *I'd like to be stinking rich for the rest of my life.* ☐ *Tiffany is stinking rich, and she acts like it.*

stinking with something *mod.* with lots of something. ☐ *Mr. Wilson is just stinking with dough.* ☐ *Those guys are stinking with grass.*

stinkpot **1.** *n.* a baby with a dirty diaper. (Also a term of address.) ☐ *Jimmy's a stinkpot. Better change him.* ☐ *Come here, you little stinkpot. I'll fix you.* **2.** *n.* anything smelly. ☐ *What are you barbecuing in this old stinkpot?* ☐ *Why don't you drive this stinkpot into a service station and get it tuned?* **3.** *n.* a motorboat. (Because the engine smells bad, especially when compared to a sailboat.) ☐ *Those guys in their stinkpots sure make a lot of noise.* ☐ *Those stinkpots just have to be polluting the lake.*

stinky *mod.* bad. ☐ *That was a stinky thing to do.* ☐ *You have a very stinky attitude. Really stinky.*

stir *n.* prison. (Underworld.) ☐ *I can't stand being in stir!* ☐ *Stir is very dull—and dangerous.*

stir crazy *mod.* anxious and mentally disturbed from being confined, as in prison. (See also *stir.*) ☐ *I was going stir crazy in my little room, so I moved to a bigger place.* ☐ *I get sort of stir crazy in the winter.*

stitch **1.** *n.* a very funny person. (Always with *a.*) ☐ *Harry is a stitch. What a sense of humor!* ☐ *Clare is a stitch, too. Her jokes can slay you.* **2.** *n.* a sharp pain, usually in the side. ☐ *I got a stitch and had to drop out of the marathon.* ☐ *A stitch in the side can be very painful.*

stocking-stuffer *n.* a small gift that is suitable for putting inside a Christmas stocking. ☐ *This will make the perfect stocking-stuffer.* ☐ *I got some little stocking-stuffers for the kids.*

stogie ['stogi] *n.* a cigar. ☐ *Then this guy pulls out a big stogie and starts to smoke it right there in the restaurant.* ☐ *Some activist type tried to get the customers to walk out if the manager didn't make the jerk put out his stogie.*

stoked (on someone or something) *mod.* excited by someone or something. (Compare to *stokin'.*) ☐ *We were stoked on Mary. She is the greatest.* ☐ *Everyone is stoked on spring.* ☐ *Now, don't get too stoked, you are the one who has to run.*

stoked out *mod.* exhausted. ☐ *I ran all the way and got stoked out.* ☐ *Alex is totally stoked out.*

stokin' *mod.* excellent; wild. ☐ *That car is really stokin'.* ☐ *We had a stokin' time at Fred's house.*

stomach *tr.* to tolerate someone or something. (Usually negative.) ☐ *Bruno couldn't stomach the opera, and he left after the first ten minutes.* ☐ *I can't stomach movies like that.*

stomp (on) someone *tr. & in.* to beat someone; to misuse someone. ☐ *We are gonna stomp you guys next game.* ☐ *One team stomped on the other so hard* *and fast, the scoreboard couldn't keep up.*

stone *mod.* completely; totally. (See additional examples in the following entries.) □ *This lecture is stone dull.* □ *I am stone mad at you.*

stone blind *mod.* heavily alcohol intoxicated. □ *Jerry drank the sauce till he was stone blind.* □ *When he was stone blind, he drank some more.*

stone broke *mod.* completely broke. □ *I'm sorry, I'm stone broke. Can I send you a check?* □ *What could I do? She was stone broke.*

stone (cold) sober *mod.* absolutely sober. □ *I am stone cold sober, or I will be by morning anyway.* □ *I found the secret to being stone sober. Don't drink.*

stone dead *mod.* dead; unquestionably dead; long dead. □ *The cat was stone dead and stiff as a board by the time we got to him.* □ *Old Tom is stone dead and in the ground.*

stone fox *n.* an attractive woman; a very sexy woman. □ *She is a stone fox if I ever saw one.* □ *Who is that stone fox I saw you with last night?*

stone groove *n.* something really *cool;* a fine party or concert. □ *This affair is not what I would call a stone groove. Stone beige, maybe.* □ *Ted's do was a stone groove.*

stoned (out) *mod.* alcohol or drug intoxicated. □ *Fred is really stoned out.* □ *I have never seen anybody so stoned who could still talk.*

stoned out of one's gourd See the following entry.

stoned out of one's head AND **stoned out of one's gourd** *mod.* under the effects of marijuana. □ *Tiffany was stoned out of her head and started giggling.* □ *The guy was stoned out of his gourd and should never have been driving.*

stoned out of one's squash *mod.* alcohol or drug intoxicated. □ *Tracy will drink a little now and then, but she never gets stoned out of her squash.* □ *Well, she was stoned out of her squash last night!*

stoned silly *mod.* alcohol or drug intoxicated. □ *I hate to get stoned silly in public. At home—ah, that's a different matter.* □ *He got stoned silly at the rally, and for all I know is still there on the floor in the corner.*

stonewall **1.** *tr.* to obstruct something or someone. □ *And again, the mayor tried to stonewall the investigation.* □ *If you continue to stonewall, we'll call in the FBI.* **2.** *n.* an obstructionist act. □ *His answer to the committee was another stonewall that caught them all by surprise.* □ *The stonewall they were faced with was almost too much.*

stonkered ['stɔŋkɚd] **1.** *mod.* killed. □ *The car crashed into him and he was stonkered for sure.* □ *He was stonkered before the plane hit the ground.* **2.** *mod.* alcohol intoxicated. □ *My buddy here is stonkered and needs a ride, and can I have one, too?* □ *Wally was stonkered beyond any help.*

stooge [studʒ] **1.** *n.* someone's pawn; someone controlled or maneuvered by someone else. □ *I'm not going to be your stooge!* □ *The guy's a stooge for the mob's Mr. Big. Ignore him.* **2.** *in.* to work as someone's underling; to serve as someone's pawn. □ *I'm not gonna stooge for you, no sirree!* □ *You will do what I tell you, and if it's stooging you will do it, and you will smile and say thank you.*

stool (on someone) *in.* to inform (on someone). □ *Tracy would stool on anybody, even her own mother.* □ *Somebody stooled and ruined the whole layout.*

stool (pigeon) AND **stoolie** ['stul 'pɪdʒən AND 'stuli] *n.* an informer. (Originally underworld.) □ *Some stool spilled the works to the boys in blue.* □ *There's nothing I hate worse than a stoolie.*

stoolie See the previous entry.

stoop See *stupe.*

stop on a dime *in.* to stop immediately. □ *This thing will stop on a dime.* □ *Imagine a bus that could stop on a dime.*

Stop the music! *exclam.* "Stop!"; "Stop whatever is happening!" (From an old radio game show called "Stop the Music!") ☐ *Stop the music! I have an announcement.* ☐ *"Stop the music!" hollered the conductor, making a little joke.*

storked *mod.* pregnant. ☐ *She got herself good and storked. Now what?* ☐ *I hear that Tracy is storked again.*

story stock *n.* shares in a company that are bought because of an appealing story about the company. ☐ *I never buy a story stock. By the time I hear about it, it's already gone up as much as it ever will.* ☐ *Acme Widgets is another story stock that I advise all my clients to buy.*

Stow it! *exclam.* "Shut up!" ☐ *Okay, stow it! I've heard enough.* ☐ *Stow it! That is enough of your applesauce.*

stozzled ['stɑzl̩d] *mod.* alcohol intoxicated. ☐ *My buddy is too stozzled to drive home. Can you give him a lift?* ☐ *Marty can drink and drink and never get stozzled or even tipsy.*

straddle the fence *tr.* to support both sides of an issue. ☐ *The mayor is straddling the fence on this issue, hoping the public will forget it.* ☐ *The legislator wanted to straddle the fence until the last minute, and that alone cost her a lot of votes.*

straight 1. *mod.* honest; unembellished. ☐ *This is the straight truth.* ☐ *Have I ever been anything but straight with you?* **2.** *n.* a tobacco cigarette; a tobacco cigarette butt. (As opposed to a marijuana cigarette. See also *slim*.) ☐ *No, I want a straight. That spliff makes me sneeze.* ☐ *Can I bum a straight off you?* **3.** *mod.* having to do with undiluted liquor. ☐ *I'll take mine straight.* ☐ *Make one straight with a little ice.* **4.** *mod.* relieved and satisfied by a dose of drugs. (Drugs.) ☐ *It only takes a few bucks and a little time to get straight.* ☐ *She will be straight for a few hours, and then the same struggle all over again—all through the night.* **5.** *mod.* off drugs; no longer addicted to drugs. ☐ *I'm straight now, and I'm gonna stay that way.* ☐ *I'm a straight guy.* ☐ *See how long you can stay straight, how 'bout it?* **6.** *n.* a square person (who does not use drugs, etc.). ☐ *The guy's a straight. He's gonna turn us over to the cops!* ☐ *The straights are putting pressure on city hall to clean up this neighborhood.* **7.** *n.* a nonhomosexual; a heterosexual. (Often from the homosexual point of view.) ☐ *Walter invited a few straights to the affair, just to keep things calm.* ☐ *The straights really get upset if you camp it up too much.* **8.** *mod.* excellent. ☐ *This news is truly straight and I am happy to hear it.* ☐ *You are a straight G.*

straight arrow *n.* an honest person; a law-abiding citizen. (See also *straight shooter*.) ☐ *Wally is really a straight arrow at heart—as long as he's not around Max.* ☐ *Max is not a straight arrow. Slime is more like it.*

straight dope *n.* the true information. ☐ *He gave us the straight dope.* ☐ *I want the straight dope. I can take it.*

straight-faced *mod.* with a serious, unsmiling face. ☐ *Mary couldn't stay straight-faced very long. It was just too funny.* ☐ *He was a very straight-faced prof, but he has a tremendous sense of humor.*

straight from the horse's mouth *mod.* directly from the source. (As if a racehorse were giving racing tips.) ☐ *Of course it's true. I got it straight from the horse's mouth.* ☐ *This came straight from the horse's mouth. It's Zeerocks Copy in the sixth race.*

straight from the shoulder *mod.* very direct, without attenuation or embellishment. ☐ *Okay, I'll give it to you straight from the shoulder.* ☐ *Right straight from the shoulder: clean out your desk; you're through.*

straight low *n.* the absolute truth; the true *lowdown*. (Prisons.) ☐ *Can you give me the straight low on this mess?* ☐ *Nobody ain't gonna tell no warden the straight low; you can be sure of that.*

straight man *n.* someone who sets up jokes or gags so that someone else can say the punch line. ☐ *I need a straight man to pick up on all my jokes.* ☐ *I'm* *tired of being a straight man for a has-been comic.*

straight shooter *n.* an honest person. (Compare to *straight arrow.*) ☐ *I trust Mike; he's a straight shooter.* ☐ *We need a straight shooter in office who will work for the people rather than some political party.*

straight talk *n.* direct and honest talk. ☐ *It's about time for a little straight talk around here.* ☐ *If they want straight talk and can handle straight talk, give 'em straight talk.*

straight up **1.** *mod.* upright. ☐ *A fine guy —really straight up.* ☐ *She is one of the most straight up brokers in town.* **2.** *mod.* without ice; neat. ☐ *I'll have a bourbon, straight up, please.* ☐ *No, not straight up. Just a little ice.* **3.** *mod. sunny-side up;* having to do with eggs cooked with yellow yolks facing straight up. ☐ *Two eggs, straight up, and a cup of coffee.* ☐ *I like my eggs straight up, but the white part has to be cooked solid.*

straighten up and fly right *in.* to get serious and start behaving properly. ☐ *It's time for you to straighten up and fly right!* ☐ *Straighten up and fly right before you get into difficulty.*

strange bird See *odd bird.*

strap *n.* an athlete, not necessarily male. (From *jockstrap.*) ☐ *A whole gang of straps came in the bar and ordered milk.* ☐ *The guy's a strap all right, but he's not dumb.*

strap someone with someone or something *tr.* to burden someone with someone or something. (Often passive.) ☐ *Don't you try to strap me with your baby brother!* ☐ *She was strapped with too many bills to pay each month.*

straphanger *n.* a subway passenger. ☐ *I didn't think I could get used to being a straphanger.* ☐ *Straphangers learn to blot out their surroundings.*

strapped *mod.* broke; short of money. ☐ *I'm sorry I can't pay you right now. I'm strapped.* ☐ *They're really strapped for money at the present time.*

straw **1.** *n.* marijuana. (Drugs.) ☐ *He stood right on the corner, selling straw by the handful from a bucket at his feet—and nobody even called the cops.* ☐ *This straw is not the best quality I've seen.* **2.** *n.* papers for rolling marijuana cigarettes. (Drugs.) ☐ *I need some straw.* ☐ *I can't manage the straw with one hand. How do these cowboys do it?*

straw boss *n.* a foreman; anyone who is second in command. ☐ *The straw boss gave the order, and off we went.* ☐ *I don't mind being a straw boss as long as they pay me.*

strawberry *n.* a pimple from drinking excessively. (See also *toddy blossom.*) ☐ *His disability made itself manifest by the occasional strawberry.* ☐ *That's a fine strawberry on your snoot.*

streak **1.** *in.* to move rapidly from one place to another. ☐ *The train streaked into the station and came to a stop just inches from the end of the track.* ☐ *I've got to streak over to the library in a big hurry.* **2.** *in.* to run about in a public place naked. ☐ *This kid was streaking back and forth until the cops caught him.* ☐ *He streaked on a dare.* **3.** *tr.* to grace or ornament a public place or event with a naked run. ☐ *Charles streaked the baseball game, but nobody noticed him.* ☐ *I wanted to streak her party but decided against it.* **4.** *n.* a naked run in a public place. ☐ *There was a streak at the end of the game, but people were leaving then and didn't see it.* ☐ *That was no streak; that was the coach in his long underwear being chased by the owner of the team.* (More at *streaker.*) **5.** *n.* an exciting time; a wild party. ☐ *That rally was a streak!* ☐ *We had a streak at Tom's.*

streaker *n.* someone who runs naked in public places. ☐ *The streaker ran through a glass door and was severely injured.* ☐ *Streakers seemed to take over the whole country in 1973.*

street **1.** *n.* the real, free world, as opposed to prison. (Always with *the.*) ☐ *The street just isn't the same as stir.* ☐ *It's good to be back on the street.* **2.** *n.* Wall Street in New York City. (Always with *the*. Usually capitalized.) □ *The Street doesn't seem to believe the policymakers in Washington.* □ *If you want excitement and stress, the Street is the place to be.*

street-casting *n.* selecting amateurs to be performers or models. □ *I do a lot of street-casting. Almost everybody can act a little.* □ *Street-casting is fun, and it's cheap.*

street people *n.* people who live in the streets; homeless people. □ *There are a lot of cold street people at this time of the year.* □ *Some of the street people prefer that kind of life.*

street pusher *n.* a drug dealer who works at the retail level on the streets. □ *It's the street pushers who take the risk and end up doing a few months in the pen.* □ *Max was a street pusher until he got busted.*

street smart *mod.* wise in the ways of urban life; wise in the ways of tough neighborhoods. □ *Freddy was street smart at age eight.* □ *Bess wasn't street smart enough to survive by herself.*

street smarts *n.* the knowledge and ability to survive on the urban street. □ *If you don't have street smarts, you won't last long out there.* □ *You either pick up street smarts, or you don't.*

street time *n.* time not spent in prison. (Underworld.) □ *I had three months street time; then they nailed me again.* □ *I want out of this place. I need a little street time to renew some old acquaintances.*

streeter *n.* an urban "street person." □ *These streeters have to be bright and clever just to survive.* □ *A couple of streeters taught me how to get a meal for nothing.*

stress 1. *in.* to suffer annoyance; to experience stress. □ *I'm stressing again! Please don't annoy me!* □ *Clare finds that she is stressing more and more about little things.* **2.** *tr.* to annoy or bother someone. □ *Don't stress Wally! He's had a hard day.* □ *The whole affair about my beemer stressed me a whole lot.* (More at *stressed*.)

stressed *mod.* upset; annoyed. □ *Come on, man, don't get stressed! It's only a gag.* □ *I am really stressed. I need a vacation.*

stretch 1. *n.* a period of time. (Folksy.) □ *Let's talk here for a stretch and then go up and see if dinner's ready.* □ *I sat there for a stretch and then got up and kept going.* **2.** *n.* a prison term. □ *I was away for a stretch of about seven years.* □ *That's quite a stretch for tax evasion.* **3.** *in.* to hang (as with a death sentence). □ *You will stretch for this, Lefty!* □ *I'll live to see you stretch, you rat!* **4.** *tr.* to cut or dilute a drug. □ *Max was known for stretching the stuff a little too much.* □ *Let's stretch this stuff, sell it, and then blow town.* **5.** *n.* a nickname for a tall person, usually male. □ *Well, stretch, think you'll go out for basketball this season?* □ *Come on, stretch, let's get it in the basket!*

stretch one's legs *tr.* to stand up and perhaps walk about. □ *I need to get out of here and stretch my legs for a while.* □ *Most of us stood up to stretch our legs at intermission.*

(strictly) from hunger *mod.* very strange; acceptable only when nothing else is available. □ *This kind of entertainment is from hunger.* □ *The singer was strictly from hunger.*

strike *n.* a dose of drugs. (Drugs. Compare to *hit*.) □ *I need a strike. You got any stumbles?* □ *Just one strike, Max, come on, just one. I'll pay you tomorrow, Max, come on, just one little strike. Anything, Max. I really hurt, Max.*

strike it rich *tr.* to become rich suddenly. □ *I never thought I would strike it rich.* □ *Pete is the kind of guy who wants to strike it rich and live in the lap of luxury for the rest of his life.*

strike out 1. *in.* [for a baseball batter] to be declared out after three strikes. (Baseball.) □ *And so Drew Wilson strikes out for his second time in this game!* □ *He struck out in the second inning, and manager Willy "Herky"*

Simpson read him out then. **2.** *in.* to fail. □ *Well, we struck out again, but we'll keep trying.* □ *I hear you struck out on that Acme proposal. Better luck next time.*

strike pay dirt See *hit pay dirt.*

stringbean *n.* a thin person. (Also a term of address.) □ *Wow, is he a stringbean.* □ *Who's the stringbean standing by the punch bowl? Somebody ought to feed him.*

strip-search *tr.* to search someone's entire naked body. (Compare to *skin-search.*) □ *The cops strip-searched the good-looking chick who ran a red light.* □ *Now it takes a court order to strip-search someone.*

stripper *n.* a striptease artist. □ *Tracy worked for a while as a stripper.* □ *Strippers from all over assembled here for their fourth annual convention and immediately took off on a sight-seeing tour.*

stroke *tr. & in.* to flatter someone; to soothe and comfort someone. □ *She strokes everybody to keep them on her side during the bad times.* □ *She learned long ago that stroking puts people at ease.*

strong-arm 1. *tr.* to force someone (to do something). □ *Bruno tried to strong-arm Frank into cooperating.* □ *Don't strong-arm me, you creep!* **2.** *mod.* forceful; by physical force. □ *The strong-arm approach got him nowhere.* □ *Too much strong-arm stuff isn't good.*

strong-arm man *n.* a bully; a man who is employed to use physical power to force someone to do something. □ *Bruno is Mr. Big's strong-arm man.* □ *The mob employs hundreds of strong-arm men.*

strong-arm tactics *n.* tactics based on the use of force. □ *No more strong-arm tactics. You need to be more subtle.* □ *Strong-arm tactics are out. The boss says be gentle and don't break anybody.*

strung out 1. AND **strung (up)** *mod.* drug intoxicated and bewildered. (Drugs.) □ *Bruno is really strung out lately. What's he shooting now?* □ *Tim is sort of strung out and doesn't even remember what he took.* **2.** *mod.* badly addicted to heroin; dissipated by heroin. (Drugs.) □ *Harry's strung out for good, I guess.* □ *Clare is strung out and can't deny her problem any longer.* **3.** *mod.* depressed; nervous. □ *I get strung out before tests and other traumatic things.* □ *I'm a little strung out—because of the accident, I guess.* **4.** *mod.* in love and disoriented. □ *Mary is strung out, and all because of Sam.* □ *Sam is strung out over Mary.*

strung-out shape *n.* a tired and exhausted condition. □ *They were sort of in strung-out shape, tired and ready for the sack.* □ *I've never been in such strung-out shape, but I've never run a marathon before.*

strung (up) See *strung out.*

strut one's stuff *tr.* to walk proudly and show off one's best features or talents. □ *Get out there on that stage and strut your stuff!* □ *I'm going to strut my stuff and become a star.*

stuccoed [ˈstəkod] *mod.* alcohol intoxicated. (A play on *plastered.*) □ *The guy was too stuccoed to drive and couldn't stand up to walk.* □ *I can drink without getting stuccoed, mainly because I drink soda.*

stuck on someone or something *mod.* enamored with someone or something; obsessed with someone or something. □ *Tom is stuck on himself—as conceited as can be.* □ *I'm really stuck on this stuff. It's just yummy.*

stuck-up *mod.* conceited. □ *Tom is really stuck-up.* □ *What a stuck-up jerk.* □ *Don't be so stuck-up. Unbend a little.*

stuck with someone or something *mod.* burdened with someone or something; left with the burden of someone or something. □ *It's your problem, and you're stuck with it.* □ *Am I stuck with this kid forever?*

stud [stəd] **1.** *n.* a male horse used for breeding purposes. (Not slang.) □ *Last spring, we rented out all our studs and made some money.* □ *The mare kicked the stud and put us all out of business for a while.* **2.** *n.* a human male viewed as very successful with women. (Parallel to sense 1.) □ *Fred thinks he is a real stud.* □ *Man, look at that stud over there. Think he's going steady with anyone?*

stud-muffin *n.* a really good-looking guy; a stud. □ *Who's the stud-muffin with Sally?* □ *Did you see that stud-muffin come in?*

studhammer *n.* a male who is successful sexually with women. □ *Alex is a real studhammer.* □ *The guy thinks he is a studhammer, but he is just a jerk.*

study animal *n.* someone who studies hard. (A play on *party animal.*) □ *All the geeks in the dorm were study animals. Dull, dull, dull.* □ *At the end of the school year every party animal turns into a study animal.*

Stuff a sock in it! AND **Put a sock in it!** *exclam.* "Shut up!" □ *I've heard enough. Stuff a sock in it!* □ *Stuff a sock in it! You are a pain.*

stuffed shirt *n.* a dull and stuffy person, usually a male. □ *Mr. Wilson is a stuffed shirt, and people would tell him so if he didn't have so much money.* □ *I don't want to listen to that stuffed shirt anymore.*

stum [stəm] **1.** *n.* marijuana. (Drugs.) □ *Where can I get some stum?* □ *This stum is cashed. Trash it.* **2.** See *stumbles.*

stumble-bumbles See *stumbles.*

stumblebum *n.* a tramp or bum, especially drunk and stumbling. □ *The poor old stumblebum got to the other side of the street the best he could.* □ *You are headed toward being a stumblebum if you don't lay off the sauce.*

stumbles ['stəmblz] **1.** AND **stum; stumble-bumbles** [stəm, 'stəmbl'bəmblz] *n.* barbiturates; sedatives; tranquilizers; alcohol. (Drugs.) □ *Kelly was shocked to find a handful of stumble-bumbles in his brother's jeans.* □ *I need a strike. You got any stum?* **2.** *n.* the inability to stand up and walk straight. □ *I guess I have the stumbles today. Not enough sleep, I guess.* □ *Whoops! I have a case of the stumbles.*

stump 1. *tr.* to confuse or puzzle someone. □ *That one really stumped me.* □ *I like to stump people with hard questions.* **2.** *tr.* to visit or tour a place. □ *We stumped all of Europe this summer.* □ *The team stumped the countryside before even practicing for the game.* **3.** *n.* a visit or tour. □ *The old girl is off on another stump.* □ *It was a fine stump; we didn't miss anything.* **4.** See *stumps.*

stumper *n.* a shoe. (Black. Usually plural.) □ *Make those stumpers shine!* □ *You like my new stumpers?*

stumps *n.* a person's legs. □ *My stumps are sore from all that walking.* □ *You need good strong stumps to do that kind of climbing.*

stung *mod.* alcohol intoxicated. □ *I'm a little stung by the mule, but I can find my way home if you'll just remind me how to open this door.* □ *She can drink that stuff all evening and never get stung.*

stunned *mod.* alcohol intoxicated. □ *I was simply stunned with the stuff.* □ *Kelly was stunned and had to be carried home to recover.*

stunner *n.* a stunningly good-looking woman. □ *Did you see that stunner who just came in?* □ *I think that she is a stunner, and I go to all her movies—over and over.*

stupe AND **stoop** *n.* a stupid person. (Also a term of address.) □ *Look, stoop, just do what you are told.* □ *Don't be a stupe! Use your head!*

stupehead *n.* a stupid person; a blockhead. (Also a term of address. See also *stupe.*) □ *What a stupehead!* □ *This stupehead keeps trying to sell me something.*

stupid *mod.* drunk. (See also *get stupid.*) □ *These kids are so stupid they can't see straight. They're all going to be sick.* □ *Wayne was too stupid to walk, let alone drive.*

stupid-ass See *dumb-ass.*

stupid fresh *mod.* very, very good. (See also *fresh; funky fresh.*) □ *Her looks were stupid fresh. Bonus!* □ *This ice* *cream is stupid fresh and needs to be eaten in great volumes.*

style *in.* to show off; to strut around. (Black. See also *strut one's stuff.*) ☐ *Look at that brother style!* ☐ *Why don't you style over here and meet my man?*

stylin(g) *n.* looking good; showing off how good one looks. ☐ *Dave thinks that stylin' is his sole occupation.* ☐ *When you finish styling in front of the mirror, would you please dump the garbage?*

stymie ['staɪmi] *tr.* to obstruct someone or something. ☐ *He did everything he could to stymie the investigation.* ☐ *The nose guard stymied the play all by himself.*

suave [swɑv] *n.* personal polish and smoothness. ☐ *Man, does that guy ever have suave!* ☐ *You need some suave to carry off this sham.*

sub **1.** *n.* a substitute. ☐ *I was a sub in the school system for a while.* ☐ *The coach sent in a sub for Wilbur.* **2.** *in.* to serve as a temporary replacement. ☐ *I subbed for Mary in a couple of games.* ☐ *Then she subbed for me to even the score.* **3.** *n.* a submarine. ☐ *I was aboard a sub for twenty minutes—and that was at Disney World.* ☐ *You have to have a special kind of personality to live on a sub.* **4.** See *submarine.* **5.** *n.* a subscription, as to a magazine. ☐ *I got a sub to a computer magazine for my birthday.* ☐ *Would you like to buy a sub to the local newspaper?*

submarine **1.** AND **sub** *n.* a long sandwich containing many different foods. ☐ *He ordered a submarine, but he couldn't finish it.* ☐ *He took what was left of the sub home with him.* **2.** *n.* a large marijuana cigarette. ☐ *Look at the size of that sub!* ☐ *Max makes a sub when he's got low-power straw.*

suck **1.** AND **suction** *n.* liquor; wine; beer; strong drink. ☐ *How about a little glass of suck before we leave?* ☐ *This is powerful suction!* **2.** AND **suck something up** *tr.* to drink beer or liquor. ☐ *Yeah, I'll suck one up with ya.* 🅃 *Let's go out and suck up a few.* **3.** *in.* [for someone or something] to be bad or undesirable. ☐ *This movie sucks!* ☐ *I think that the whole business sucks.* **4.** AND **suction** *n.* influence. ☐ *He thinks he has suck, but he's just a pain in the neck.* ☐ *Who has some suction with the boss?*

suck face *tr.* to kiss. (Compare to *swap spits.*) ☐ *The kid said he was going out to suck face. It sounds awful.* ☐ *Sally said she didn't want to suck face.*

suck (some) brew AND **suck (some) suds** *tr.* to drink beer. ☐ *Wanna go suck some brew?* ☐ *I'm tired of sucking suds. Got any staggers?*

suck (some) suds See *suck (some) brew.*

suck someone's hind tit *tr.* to do someone's bidding no matter how unpleasant or impossible; to *kiss someone's ass.* (Potentially offensive. Use only with discretion.) ☐ *What am I supposed to do—suck his hind tit?* ☐ *She acts like everybody has to suck her hind tit to keep their jobs.*

suck something up See *suck.*

suck up to someone *in.* to attempt to gain influence with or favor from someone. ☐ *In school, Max was always sucking up to the teacher.* ☐ *Don't suck up to me. It won't do any good.*

suckabuck *mod.* greedy; exhibiting greed. ☐ *I refuse to do business with this suckabuck company anymore.* ☐ *She is such a suckabuck landlady that it makes me want to move.*

sucker **1.** *n.* a dupe; an easy mark. ☐ *See if you can sell that sucker the Brooklyn Bridge.* ☐ *The sucker says he doesn't need a bridge, thank you.* **2.** *tr.* to trick or victimize someone. ☐ *That crook suckered me. I should have known better.* ☐ *They suckered him into selling half interest in his land.* **3.** *n.* an annoying person. (Also a rude term of address.) ☐ *Look, sucker, get out of my way!* ☐ *I am really sick of that sucker hanging around here.* **4.** *n.* a gadget; a thing. ☐ *Now, you put this little sucker right into this slot.* ☐ *Where is that sucker that looks like a screw?*

sucker for someone or something *n.* someone who is prejudiced in favor of someone or something. ☐ *I'm a sucker for a pretty face.* ☐ *Ted is a sucker for any dessert with whipped cream on it.*

sucker list *n.* a list of potential dupes; a list of people who might be taken in by deception. ☐ *I'm sure on their sucker list. They are trying to get me to go to a lecture and receive a free clock or something.* ☐ *Here's the sucker list. Call them all and try to get them interested.*

sucky *mod.* poor; undesirable. ☐ *This is the suckiest movie I ever saw.* ☐ *This food is sucky. It really sucks!*

suction See *suck.*

sudden death *mod.* having to do with something short, quick, and decisive. ☐ *The game ended in a sudden death playoff.* ☐ *Okay, you've got just one more sudden death chance.*

suds **1.** *n.* beer. ☐ *How about some suds, Bill?* ☐ *I can't get enough suds.* **2.** *in.* to drink beer. ☐ *How 'bout going out and sudsing for a while?* ☐ *They were sudsing when they should have been studying.*

suds-swiller *n.* a beer-drinker. ☐ *Ted is a suds-swiller and Bill won't touch the stuff. What strange roommates.* ☐ *Wayne's goal in life is to be a professional suds-swiller.*

sue the pants off (of) someone *tr.* to sue someone for a lot of money. ☐ *If they do it, I'll sue the pants off of them.* ☐ *He sued the pants off his landlord.*

sugar daddy *n.* an older man who takes care of a younger person, especially a young athlete or a young woman. ☐ *Mr. Wilson is sort of a sugar daddy to the whole team.* ☐ *I thought sugar daddies were illegal.*

sugarcoated *mod.* palatable; inoffensive; easy to take. ☐ *Math is so sugarcoated these days. Even I could learn it.* ☐ *Stop giving them sugarcoated knowledge.*

suit *n.* a businessman or businesswoman; someone who is in charge. ☐ *This suit comes up and asks to go to the airport.* ☐ *A couple of suits checked into a working-class hotel and caused some eyebrows to raise.*

summer complaint *n.* diarrhea, especially that experienced in the summer. ☐ *I've got a touch of the summer complaint.* ☐ *Does summer heat cause the summer complaint?*

sun belt *n.* the southern U.S. states, where it is generally warm and sunny. (Compare to *rust belt.*) ☐ *I want to retire to the sun belt.* ☐ *The population of the sun belt is exploding.*

Sunday best *n.* one's best clothing, which one would wear to church. ☐ *We are in our Sunday best, ready to go.* ☐ *I got mud on my Sunday best.*

Sunday driver *n.* a slow and leisurely driver who appears to be sightseeing and enjoying the view, holding up traffic in the process. (Also a term of address.) ☐ *I'm a Sunday driver, and I'm sorry. I just can't bear to go faster.* ☐ *Move over, you Sunday driver!*

Sunday punch *n.* a very solid and destructive blow; one's best blow. ☐ *Barlowe sent a Sunday punch straight into Rocko's gut. Rocko's eyes bugged out; then he crumpled to the floor and wretched.* ☐ *Ralph aimed a Sunday punch at Frederick's nose, but missed and spun about, striking his elbow on the banister.*

sunny-side up *mod.* (of eggs) with yolks facing up and still yellow and hot, but not cooked through; *straight up.* ☐ *I'll have my eggs sunny-side up, with toast and coffee.* ☐ *People who like sunny-side up eggs wouldn't dream of eating a whole raw egg.*

sunshades *n.* sunglasses. (See also *shades.*) ☐ *Where are my sunshades? Did you borrow them again?* ☐ *I left my sunshades in the car.*

Sup? See *(T)sup?*

super **1.** *mod.* fine; excellent. ☐ *This report is just super!* ☐ *Who made the super pie?* **2.** *n.* superintendent. ☐ *The super comes by every now and then to check on things.* ☐ *Call the super and ask for some help.*

super-dooper See the following entry.

super-duper AND **super-dooper** *mod.* excellent. □ *That's just super-duper. Couldn't have asked for better.* □ *Where is this super-dooper car of yours?*

super-strap *n.* an earnest and hard-working student. (As compared to a *jock, strap, superjock.*) □ *He's a Melvin, a super-strap, and he doesn't do anything but study.* □ *I couldn't be a super-strap even if I had the brains. I just don't care that much.*

superfly *mod.* excellent; wonderful. □ *This dude is really superfly.* □ *I don't care about this superfly gent of yours. If he doesn't have a job, I don't want you seeing him anymore. Ya hear?*

supergrass *n.* high-quality marijuana. □ *Tiffany picked up some pot she called supergrass. It looks like alfalfa to me.* □ *The cannabis that is the richest in resin is sometimes called supergrass.*

superjock **1.** *n.* an excellent athlete. □ *Mike is a real superjock. He plays four sports.* □ *All those superjocks get special meals and tutors to help them pass their classes.* **2.** *n.* a very well-built man regardless of athletic ability. □ *My boyfriend is a superjock, and does he look good!* □ *No nerd has ever been a superjock.*

sure as hell *mod.* absolutely certain. □ *I'm sure as hell he's the one.* □ *You sure as hell better get yourself over here.*

sure thing *n.* something that is absolutely certain. □ *It's a sure thing! You can't lose!* □ *Well, it looks like the sure thing didn't turn out to be so sure, after all.*

surefire *mod.* certain; effective; fail-safe. □ *I've got a surefire method for fixing cracks in drywall.* □ *Good, yes; surefire, no.* □ *This stuff is a surefire cure.*

surf **1.** *mod.* wonderful; with it. (California.) □ *This party is, like, surf.* □ *This is not what I would call a surf day.* **2.** *in.* to use a remote control to check a large number of T.V. stations. (See also *channel hopping.*) □ *Don spends almost an hour surfing before he falls asleep in front of the T.V.* □ *Mary surfed until she fell asleep.*

suss someone out ['səs . . .] *tr.* to try to figure someone out. □ *I can't seem to suss Tom out. What a strange guy.* 🅃 *I don't have any luck sussing out people I don't know well.*

Suzy *n.* a U.S. one-dollar coin bearing a likeness of Susan B. Anthony. □ *I've got two Suzys I want to get rid of.* □ *Someday I'm going to buy a car or something with a barrel of Suzys.*

swacked [swækt] *mod.* alcohol intoxicated. □ *Tracy is too swacked to drive home. Can somebody give her a lift?* □ *He walked straight out of the office and went straight into the bar with the intention of getting swacked.*

SWAK See *sealed with a kiss.*

swallow **1.** *n.* a puff of cigarette smoke. □ *He took just one swallow and started coughing.* □ *Can I have a swallow of your fag?* **2.** *tr.* to believe or accept something. (Compare to *eat something up.*) □ *Did they actually swallow that?* □ *Nobody's gonna swallow that nonsense.*

swallow the dictionary *tr.* to acquire an enormous vocabulary. (Usually in the past tense.) □ *My uncle says I've swallowed the dictionary. That's because I know so many big words.* □ *Did you just go to college to swallow the dictionary?*

swamped **1.** *mod.* very, very busy. □ *I can't handle it now. I'm swamped.* □ *We're always swamped at this time of the year.* **2.** *mod.* alcohol intoxicated. □ *Look at him! He's swamped—stoned out of his mind.* □ *Those old boys used to go out and get swamped every Saturday night.*

swamper *n.* a truck driver's helper or assistant. □ *This guy and his swamper showed up to deliver the stuff, but neither one of them would touch it.* □ *He told the swamper to get some coffee for everybody.*

swank [swæŋk] *n.* class; visible quality. □ *He doesn't have swank. He's a cornball!* □ *This place has swank. I like it.*

swanky ['swæŋki] *mod.* classy; *ritzy.* □ *What a swanky joint!* □ *This place is too swanky. I like to eat where I can pronounce the names of the food.*

swap notes (on someone or something) *tr.* to share information on someone or something. □ *The two chicks sat around swapping notes on guys they knew.* □ *The mechanics were swapping notes on rude customers they had dealt with in the last month.*

swap spits *tr.* to kiss with someone. □ *A couple of kids were in the car swapping spits.* □ *Tiffany and Wilbur were off somewhere swapping spits, I guess.*

swear like a trooper *in.* to curse and swear with great facility. □ *Mrs. Wilson was known to swear like a trooper on occasion.* □ *The clerk started swearing like a trooper, and the customer started crying.*

swear on a stack of Bibles *in.* to make a very solemn pledge of one's honesty. (Folksy. Official oaths are sometimes taken with one hand on a Bible. This phrase implies that more Bibles make an even stronger oath.) □ *I swear on a stack of Bibles that I was in Atlanta on the night of January sixteenth.* □ *It's true! I swear on a stack of Bibles it's true!*

sweat 1. *tr. & in.* to fret (about something) while waiting for an outcome. □ *Come on, don't sweat it. It'll work out.* □ *This whole promotion business really has me sweating.* **2.** *n.* trouble; bother. (See also *no sweat.*) □ *I can handle it. It won't cause me any sweat.* □ *You really caused a lot of sweat around here.*

sweat blood *tr.* to work very hard at something; to endure distress in the process of accomplishing something. □ *And here I sweated blood to put you through college, and you treat me like a stranger.* □ *Everybody in the office had to sweat blood that week.*

sweat bullets *tr.* to suffer about something; to be anxious or nervous about something; to *sweat blood.* □ *They were sweating bullets, waiting for the results.* □ *The kid sat in the waiting room, sweating bullets while the surgeons worked on his brother.*

sweat-shop *n.* a workplace where employees work long hours for low pay in poor conditions. □ *This office is a sweat-shop! I only got a 2 percent raise.* □ *The bank manager is unfair! I've been a teller in this sweat-shop for thirteen years, and I've never had a new carpet in my office.*

sweat sock *n.* an athlete; a *jock.* (Usually plural.) □ *I live in a dorm with a bunch of sweat socks. They feed us well, anyway.* □ *Both Bill's roommates are sweat socks and smell like it too.*

sweat something out *tr.* to wait out something; to fret and worry until the end of something. □ *You'll just have to sweat it out. There's no way to hurry it up.* 🅃 *We'll sweat out the wait—like everybody else.*

sweet *mod.* good; profitable; excellent. □ *I got involved in a sweet deal having to do with a better job.* □ *Fred offered Bill a sweet contract, but Bill turned it down.*

sweet nothings *n.* loving comments; pleasant remarks between lovers. □ *They are out on the porch swing whispering sweet nothings in each other's ears.* □ *Thank heavens most married people never remember the sweet nothings they were once told.*

sweeten *tr.* to make a bargain or agreement better or more attractive. □ *Okay, I'll sweeten the deal. I'll throw in a lighted mirror on the visor.* □ *Sweeten the deal with air, and I'll buy the car.*

sweetener *n.* extra encouragement, usually in the form of money. □ *Money makes the best sweetener around.* □ *Let me add a little sweetener, and we'll see if he goes for it.*

sweetheart AND **sweetie(-pie)** *n.* (one's) dear child, husband, wife, lover, etc. (Often a term of address.) □ *Look, sweetheart, can't we afford a new car?* □ *Pick up your toys, sweetie. Aunt Matilda is coming over for a visit.*

sweetheart deal *n.* a deal made between friends so that both may profit well. (Such deals usually involve illegal or unethical practices.) □ *They found that the mayor was involved in a number of sweetheart deals.* □ *Most of the general contractors in town would be out of business if they didn't offer sweetheart deals to the politicians.*

sweetie(-pie) See *sweetheart.*

swell *mod.* fine; excellent. (Also sarcastic use.) □ *Where did you get that swell hat?* □ *Oh that's just swell! Yuck!*

swellelegant ['swɛl'ɛləgənt] *mod.* really fine. (From *swell* and *elegant.*) □ *Gee, this place is sure swellelegant!* □ *It is not swellelegant.* □ *Her car is just swellelegant.*

swellhead *n.* a conceited person. □ *Tom is getting to be such a swellhead.* □ *I wish that swellhead would spend more time elsewhere!*

swift 1. *mod.* smart and clever. □ *Excuse my brother. He's not too swift.* □ *Dave is doing well in school. He's swift, and he likes his classes.* **2.** *mod.* sexually fast or easy, usually said of a woman. □ *Tracy is swift they say, but I find her to be a perfect lady.* □ *Clare is not only swift, she has a reputation.*

swig 1. *n.* a deep drink of liquor; a swallow of liquor. □ *She took a swig of rum and leaped into the lagoon.* □ *One swig of that stuff was enough for me.* **2.** *tr.* to drink liquor deeply. □ *He nearly swigged the whole bottle before he needed to take a breath.* □ *She swigged a big gulp and just stood there—bottle in her hand—and became paralyzed.*

swigged AND **swiggled** [swɪgd AND 'swɪg|d] *mod.* alcohol intoxicated; tipsy. □ *Man, is she ever swigged!* □ *He is too swiggled to drive.*

swiggled See the previous entry.

swill 1. *n.* liquor. □ *This swill is awful. Please give me some beer.* □ *The swill they serve here is better than you can get elsewhere.* **2.** *n.* a drink of liquor. □ *How about a swill out of your glass?* □ *Here, you can have a little swill of mine.* **3.** *tr. & in.* to drink liquor. □ *Ted is in his room swilling like a madman.* □ *He swilled a whole case of beer yesterday. Isn't he joyful yet?* **4.** *n.* any nasty food or drink. □ *Let's go over to the ptomaine-domain and get our evening swill.* □ *Man does not live by swill alone. Let's go to McDuck's instead.*

swill-up *n.* a drinking bout. □ *There was a swill-up at the frat house last week.* □ *I never miss a swill-up.*

swimming in something *in.* having lots of something. □ *Right now we are swimming in merchandise. In a month it will be gone.* □ *The Wilmington-Thorpes are just swimming in money.*

swimmingly *mod.* quite nicely. □ *I'm having a fine time here. Everything is going along just swimmingly.* □ *The plans are moving ahead swimmingly.*

swindle sheet *n.* an expense account record sheet or book. □ *I turned in my swindle sheet yesterday, and no one challenged the $400 for new shoes.* □ *The government makes it hard to put just anything on your swindle sheet these days.*

swing 1. *in.* [for a person] to be up to date and modern. □ *Tom really swings. Look at those blue suede shoes!* □ *I used to swing, but then age and good taste overtook me.* **2.** *in.* [for a party or other event] to be fun or exciting. □ *This party really swings!* □ *I've never been to a gathering that swings like this one.* **3.** *in.* to be involved in sexual fads, group sex, or the swapping of sexual partners. □ *Carol says that Tom, Ted, and Heidi swing. How does she know?* □ *There is a lot less swinging going on since these strange diseases have spread.* **4.** *tr.* to bring something off; to execute a deal. □ *This is a very important deal. I hope I can swing it.* □ *They want to elect me president of the club. I hope they can swing it.*

swing both ways *in.* to be bisexual. □ *They say that Gary swings both ways, but I wouldn't know.* □ *Since he swings both ways, he may stand a better chance at finding a date.*

swing into high gear *in.* to begin operating at a fast pace; to increase the rate of activity. □ *During the winter season we swing into high gear around here.* □ *The* *chef swings into high gear around eight o'clock in preparation for the theater crowd.*

swing shift *n.* an evening work shift in a factory, usually from mid-afternoon to midnight. (Compare to *graveyard shift.*) ☐ *I don't mind the swing shift. I'm a night person anyway.* ☐ *My brother works the swing shift, so I never get to see him.*

swing with someone or something *in.* to appreciate someone or something. (See also *swing.*) ☐ *Man, I can really swing with that color. Glorious!* ☐ *I can really swing with John. He and I are real close.*

swinger 1. *n.* a person who participates in innovative sexual activities. (See also *swing.*) ☐ *Is Gary a swinger? I've heard talk about him.* ☐ *We watched a movie about a swinger, but everything interesting happened in dim blue light.* **2.** *n.* a youthful, socially active, and knowledgeable person. ☐ *Those kids are real swingers.* ☐ *Tom is a swinger. Look at those mod shoes.*

swinging *mod.* great. ☐ *We had a swinging time at John's rally.* ☐ *The concert was swinging—nothing like it, ever.*

swingman *n.* a drug seller; a drug connection. ☐ *Max couldn't deliver till he met with his swingman.* ☐ *Bruno wants to be a swingman with the mob.*

swipe 1. *tr.* to drink liquor rapidly and to excess; to bolt a drink of liquor. ☐ *Ted swiped a quick one and ran out the door.* ☐ *Fred sat at the bar and swiped two gins and ate an egg.* **2.** *n.* moonshine; inferior liquor. ☐ *This swipe is gross. I'd rather drink water.* ☐ *I can't stand the swipe they serve here.* **3.** *tr.* to steal something. ☐ *Max swiped a pack of cigarettes from the counter.* ☐ *Somebody swiped my wallet!* **4.** *n.* a blow or an act of striking someone or something. (See also *take a swipe at someone or something.*) ☐ *Bob got a nasty swipe across the face.* ☐ *The cat gave the mouse a swipe with its paw.*

swish [swɪʃ] **1.** *mod.* overly fancy; effeminate; displaying effeminacy. ☐ *The lobby of the theater was a little swish, but not offensive.* ☐ *Who is your swish little friend?* **2.** *n.* elaborate decoration; effeminacy. ☐ *There's a little too much swish here. Get rid of the gold drapes.* ☐ *What this place needs is more swish. Hang some baubles here and there.*

switch *n.* a switchblade knife. ☐ *They found a switch in his pocket when they searched him.* ☐ *Max was arrested for carrying a switch.*

switch-hitter *n.* a ballplayer who bats either right-handed or left-handed. (Baseball.) ☐ *Monty is a switch-hitter, but he's batting right-handed today.* ☐ *I'm not a switch-hitter. In fact, I can hardly hit the ball at all.*

switch off *in.* to become oblivious to everything. ☐ *I want to go home and switch off—just forget this whole day.* ☐ *I have to switch off when I go home.*

switch on 1. *in.* to come alive. ☐ *She saw her child and immediately switched on.* ☐ *I don't switch on until about noon.* **2.** *in.* to become modern and participate in current fads and events. ☐ *I am too old to switch on.* ☐ *Most kids I know switched on when they went to high school.* **3.** *in.* to get high on drugs; to begin taking *L.S.D.* or some other hallucinogens. (Drugs. See also *turn on.*) ☐ *One by one, each of my friends switched on.* ☐ *There was some old man who seemed to get pleasure from getting kids to switch on. Maybe he was a dealer.* (More at *switched on.*)

switched on 1. *mod.* alert and up-to-date; with it. ☐ *My brother is switched on and has lots of friends.* ☐ *I'm not switched on. In fact, I am pretty dull.* **2.** *mod.* excited. ☐ *I get switched on by that kind of music.* ☐ *I am never switched on by raucous music.*

switcheroo ['swɪtʃə'ru] *n.* a reversal; a switching around. ☐ *He pulled a switcheroo on us and showed up at the other door, so we missed getting his autograph.* ☐ *She is a master at the old switcheroo.*

swizzle ['swɪzl] **1.** *tr. & in.* to drink (liquor), probably to excess; to *tipple.* ☐

Have you been swizzling again? □ *Fred's uncle is always swizzling a little drink.* **2.** *n.* liquor; beer; a drink of an alcoholic beverage. □ *What a hot day. I could use some swizzle.* □ *What I need is a nice cold swizzle.*

swizzle-stick *n.* a drunkard. (From the name of a short stick used to stir an alcoholic drink.) □ *That guy is a swizzle-stick. Don't give him any more.* □ *You had better slow down, or you will turn into a swizzle-stick.*

swizzled ['swɪz|d] *mod.* alcohol intoxicated. □ *Fred went out and got himself swizzled.* □ *Man, he is really swizzled!*

swoozled AND **swozzled** ['swuz|d AND 'swaz|d] *mod.* alcohol intoxicated. □ *How can anybody be so swozzled on three beers?* □ *Those guys are really swoozled!*

swozzled See the previous entry.

syrupy *mod.* overly sentimental. □ *I can't stand syrupy movies.* □ *That music is too syrupy.* □ *All this syrupy talk is making me tired.*

SYSOP ['sɪsap] *n.* "system operator," the person who manages a computer system or bulletin board. □ *The SYSOP tried to bring order to the bulletin board discussion but failed.* □ *I sent a message to the SYSOP complaining about the number of personal messages on the board.*

T

10-4 See *ten-four.*

20/20 hindsight See *twenty-twenty hindsight.*

T. *n.* marijuana. (Drugs. From *tea.*) ☐ *Can't you stay off that T.?* ☐ *All she thinks about is smoking T. and where she's gonna get more of it.*

T. and A. 1. *n.* an operation to remove one's tonsils and adenoids. (Hospitals.) ☐ *She was scheduled for a T. and A. this morning at six sharp.* ☐ *The T. and A. went off without a hitch.* **2.** AND **tits and ass** *n.* a display of "tits and ass," breasts and buttocks. (See also *B. and B.* Use caution with the topic.) ☐ *The magazines featuring tits and ass flourish in their under-the-counter trade.* ☐ *These silly T. and A. movies have no plot to interfere with the leers.*

T-man *n.* a federal narcotics agent; a treasury agent. (The "T" is from *treasury.*) ☐ *The T-men were at the front while Bruno crept out the back.* ☐ *It's curtains for you, T-man!*

Ta-ta. ['tɑ'tɑ] *interj.* "Good-bye." ☐ *See ya later. Ta-ta.* ☐ *Ta-ta. Take care.*

tab 1. *n.* a bill (for something). (From *tabulation.* See also *chit.*) ☐ *What's the tab for this?* ☐ *Barlowe paid the tab and left quietly.* **2.** *n.* a tablet (of medicine). ☐ *Take a couple of aspirin tabs and call me in the morning.* ☐ *These tabs must have got wet. They're ruined.* **3.** *tr.* to identify someone. ☐ *I couldn't quite tab her, but when she started talking I knew right away who she was.* ☐ *I tabbed him right away.*

tabbed *mod.* well-dressed. (Black.) ☐ *That dude is tabbed.* ☐ *She's really tabbed in some nice threads.*

table-hop *in.* to move from table to table in a restaurant, nightclub, bar, etc. ☐ *We used to table-hop, but nobody knows us anymore.* ☐ *They would table-hop—to the great dismay of the waiters.*

tackhead *n.* an overdressed male. (One who looks *tacky.*) ☐ *Gary is sort of a tackhead when it comes to clothing.* ☐ *Don't be such a tackhead, Tom. Loosen up.*

tacky 1. *mod.* cheap; crude. ☐ *That was a tacky thing to do to her.* ☐ *That was so tacky!* ☐ *This is sort of a tacky gift for a wedding.* **2.** *mod.* alcohol intoxicated. ☐ *Tom was a little tacky, so he gave me his car keys.* ☐ *Bruno seems tacky, but that's just the way he is.*

taco stand ['tɑko . . .] *n.* a lousy place; a tacky place. ☐ *It's time to get out of this taco stand and go somewhere decent.* ☐ *Why doesn't somebody clean up this taco stand?*

tad *n.* a bit; a small bit. ☐ *I'll take just a tad. I'm on a diet.* ☐ *That's a little more than a tad, but it's all right.*

tag 1. *n.* a name. ☐ *I know the face, but I forgot the tag.* ☐ *Everybody knows that tag well.* **2.** *n.* euphoria from drug use; a drug *rush.* ☐ *This tag from this mojo is something to behold.* ☐ *This trash has no tag at all.* **3.** *n.* a car license plate or sticker. ☐ *The car had Kansas tags and was towing a trailer.* ☐ *Don't forget to get a new tag for this year.* **4.** *n.* a blow to the body in boxing. ☐ *Wilbur landed another tag to the right shoulder before the gong sounded.* ☐ *Another tag on the head and Wilbur will be down.* **5.** *tr.* to punch someone in boxing. ☐ *Sam tagged his opponent on the cheek.* ☐ *The guy tagged him back right in the gut.* **6.** *tr.* (in baseball) to touch a runner with the baseball. ☐ *Wilbur tagged the runner and fell flat on his face.* ☐ *The catcher tagged the runner, but it was too late.* **7.** *n.* the coda or ending section of a piece of music. ☐ *Now, I want everybody to slow down and watch me on the tag.* ☐ *Give everything you've got on the tag.* **8.** *tr.* to charge someone with a crime. ☐ *The cop tagged him with the bank caper immediately.* ☐ *The cop tagged me with a ticket before I knew what hit me.*

Tah-dah! [tə'dɑ] *exclam.* "Look at this!"; "Look at me!"; "Presenting . . ." ☐ *Tah-dah! How do you like my new haircut?* ☐ *And here is—tah-dah!—our ever-late and never-punished executive secretary.*

tail-end *n.* the back end of something or someone. ☐ *He was at the tail-end of the long line.* ☐ *Tracy fell down on her tail-end.*

tailgate **1.** *tr. & in.* to follow (someone) too closely in a car. ☐ *That guy tailgating me is drunk, I think.* ☐ *Ease off a little; you're tailgating.* **2.** *in.* to have a tailgate party. ☐ *We planned to tailgate before the game, but it was massively cold.* ☐ *The people who were tailgating next to us asked to borrow our salt.*

tailgate party *n.* a small party held on the folded down tailgate of a station wagon in a parking lot. (Something that is done before a ball game, concert, etc.) ☐ *They had a tailgate party before the Bears game.* ☐ *The tailgate party was a success, except for the cold.*

tailor-made *n.* a machine-made cigarette. (From an expression for something, such as an article of clothing, that is custom made.) ☐ *They used to call these things tailor-made, meaning professionally made, as opposed to homemade.* ☐ *The cowboy in the movie refused to smoke a tailor-made.*

tails *n.* a tuxedo with long tails. ☐ *Shall I wear my tails?* ☐ *Ralph had to rent tails for the evening.*

take **1.** *n.* a section of a film that is pronounced acceptable just after it is shot. ☐ *It's a take. Get it over to the lab.* ☐ *After seven straight takes the crew demanded a break.* **2.** *n.* the amount of money taken in at some event; the money received for the tickets that have been purchased. ☐ *What was the take for the concert?* ☐ *The take was much larger than we expected.* **3.** *tr.* to cheat or deceive someone. ☐ *That clerk tried to take me.* ☐ *When they think you're going to count your change, they won't try to take you.* **4.** *tr.* to defeat someone, as in a fight. ☐ *Max thought he could take the guy, but he wasn't sure.* ☐ *I know I can take you. Make my day!*

take a bath (on something) *tr.* to have large financial losses on an investment. ☐ *Fred took a bath on that gold mining stock.* ☐ *The broker warned me that I might take a bath if I bought this stuff.*

take a beating *tr.* to be beaten, bested, or defeated. ☐ *The candidate took a beating in the runoffs.* ☐ *The team took quite a beating.*

take a break *tr.* to stop working for a rest period. ☐ *Let's take a break here. Be back in five minutes.* ☐ *I've got to take a break before I drop.*

take a chill pill *tr.* to calm down; to relax. (See also *chill (out)*.) ☐ *Take a chill pill, man! You are too excited.* ☐ *The police officer told Jim to take a chill pill and answer the questions.*

take a crack at something AND **have a crack at something** *tr.* to take a try at something. ☐ *She had a crack at food preparation, but that wasn't for her.* ☐ *Let me take a crack at it.*

take a dig at someone AND **take a jab at someone** *tr.* to insult or needle someone. ☐ *Why did you take a jab at Sam?* ☐ *You're always taking digs at people who think they're your friends.*

take a dirt nap *tr.* to die and be buried. □ *I don't want to end up taking a dirt nap during this operation.* □ *Isn't Tom a little young to take a dirt nap?*

take a dive See the following entry.

take a fall AND **take a dive** **1.** *tr.* to fake being knocked out in a boxing match. □ *Wilbur wouldn't take a fall. He doesn't have it in him.* □ *The boxer took a dive in the second round and made everyone suspicious.* **2.** *tr.* to get arrested. (Underworld. See also *take the fall.*) □ *Bruno took a fall for the bank robbery.* □ *I didn't wanna take a dive, but the cop left me no choice.*

take a flyer (on something) *tr.* to take a chance on something. □ *Kim was very reckless when she took a flyer on that airline stock.* □ *Fred is too wise an investor to take a flyer on some story stock like that.*

take a gander (at someone or something) *tr.* to look at someone or something. (See also *gander.*) □ *Wow, take a gander at this chick!* □ *I wanted to take a gander at the new computer before they started using it.*

take a hike AND **take a walk** *tr.* to leave; to beat it. □ *Okay, I've had it with you. Take a hike! Beat it!* □ *I had enough of the boss and the whole place, so I cleaned out my desk and took a walk.*

take a jab at someone See *take a dig at someone.*

take a leak *tr.* to urinate. (Crude. Use caution with the topic. Usually in reference to a male.) □ *I gotta go take a leak. Back in a minute.* □ *He just went out to take a leak.*

take a load off one's feet See *get a load off one's feet.*

take a lot of nerve **1.** *tr.* to be very rude; to require a lot of rudeness (to behave so badly). □ *He walked out on her, and that took a lot of nerve!* □ *That took a lot of nerve! You took my parking place!* **2.** *tr.* to require courage. □ *He climbed the mountain with a bruised foot. That took a lot of nerve.* □ *It took a lot of nerve to go into business for himself.*

take a nosedive *tr.* to collapse; to fail. □ *The market took a nosedive again today.* □ *She slipped on the ice and took a nosedive.*

take a page from someone's book *tr.* to copy or emulate. □ *I took a page from Edison's book and began inventing useful little things.* □ *Mind if I take a page from your book and apply for a job here?*

take a pop at someone *tr.* to punch at someone. □ *Bruno took a pop at me, but I ducked.* □ *The drunk took a pop at the cop—which was the wrong thing to do.*

take a powder *tr.* to leave; to leave town. (Underworld.) □ *Why don't you take a powder? Go on! Beat it!* □ *Bruno took a powder and will lie low for a while.*

Take a running jump (in the lake)! *exclam.* "Go away!"; "Get away from me!" □ *You know what you can do? You can take a running jump. Beat it!* □ *You can just take a running jump in the lake, you creep!*

take a shot (at something) *tr.* to try (to do) something. □ *I don't think I can do it, but I'll take a shot at it.* □ *Go ahead. Take a shot.*

take a swipe at someone or something *tr.* to poke at someone or something. (See also *swipe.*) □ *Max took a swipe at Bruno.* □ *The cat took a swipe at the ball.*

take a walk See *take a hike.*

take a whack at someone or something **1.** *tr.* [with *something*] to have a try at something. □ *Let me take a whack at it.* □ *Why don't you practice a little while and take a whack at it tomorrow?* **2.** *tr.* to hit at someone or something. □ *Wilbur took a whack at Martin and missed.* □ *Jerry got an ax and took a whack at the tree, but didn't do much damage.*

Take care. *phr.* "Good-bye, be careful." □ *See you later. Take care.* □ *Take care. See you in Philly.*

take care of number one AND **take care of numero uno** *tr.* to take care of oneself. (See also *number one, numero uno.*)

□ *Arthur, like everybody else, is most concerned with taking care of number one.* □ *If you don't take care of numero uno, who will?*

take care of numero uno See the previous entry.

take care of someone *tr.* to kill someone. (Underworld.) □ *The boss told Bruno to take care of Max.* □ *I'm gonna take care of you once and for all.*

take five *tr.* to take a five-minute break. □ *Okay, gang, take five. Be back here in five minutes, or else.* □ *She told them to take five, but they turned the five into fifty.*

take it *tr.* to endure something, physically or mentally. (See also *take it on the chin.*) □ *I just can't take it anymore.* □ *If you can't take it, quit.*

Take it down a thou(sand)! *in.* "Cool down!"; "Calm down!"; "Quiet down!" □ *Okay. Take it down a thousand, and let's talk this out.* □ *You are wild! Take it down a thou and let's try again to talk this out.*

take it easy **1.** *phr.* "relax and take care." □ *See you later. Take it easy.* □ *They told me to take it easy for a few days.* **2.** *exclam.* "Let up!"; "Not so hard!"; "Be gentle!" (Usually **Take it easy!**) □ *Take it easy! That hurts!* □ *Take it easy; he's just a kid!*

take it on the chin AND **take it on the nose** **1.** *tr.* to stand up to something adverse, such as criticism. □ *They laid some rude chops on him, but he took it on the chin.* □ *I knew he could take it on the nose.* **2.** *tr.* to receive the full brunt of something. □ *Why do I have to take it on the chin for something I didn't do?* □ *If you did it, you have to learn to take it on the chin.*

take it on the lam *tr.* to get out of town; to run away. (Underworld.) □ *Both took it on the lam when things got hot.* □ *Bruno knew that the time had come to take it on the lam.*

take it on the nose See *take it on the chin.*

Take it or leave it. *sent.* "There are no other choices."; "It is this or nothing." □ *This is what you get for the money. Take it or leave it.* □ *I told her that there was a shortage of these things and she had to take it or leave it.*

take it out on someone or something *tr.* to punish or harm someone or something because one is angry or disturbed about something. □ *I'm sorry about your difficulty, but don't take it out on me.* □ *Don't take it out on the cat.*

take it slow *tr.* to go slowly and carefully. □ *Just relax and take it slow. You've got a good chance.* □ *You'll make it. Take it slow and keep your spirits up.*

take it through the nose *tr.* to snort cocaine. (Drugs. A play on *take it on the nose* at *take it on the chin.*) □ *Max liked taking it through the nose better than anything, except maybe a shot in the arm.* □ *He went into the john, and most of us knew he had to take it through the nose right then.*

take it to the street *tr.* to tell everyone about your problems. (See also *on the street.*) □ *If there's something bothering her, she's gonna take it to the street, first thing.* □ *Come on, don't take it to the street.*

take names *tr.* to make a list of wrongdoers. (Often figuratively, as with a schoolteacher, whose major weapon is to take names and send them to the principal.) □ *The boss is madder than hell, and he's taking names.* □ *Gary is coming by to talk about the little riot last night, and I think he's taking names.*

take off **1.** *in.* [for someone] to leave in a hurry. □ *She really took off outa there.* □ *I've got to take off—I'm late.* **2.** *in.* [for something] to start selling well. □ *The fluffy dog dolls began to take off, and we sold out the lot.* □ *Ticket sales really took off after the first performance.* (More at *take-off.*)

take-off **1.** *n.* an imitation of something; a copy of something. □ *This robot is capable of producing 200 circuit board take-offs per hour.* □ *My machine is a* *take-off of the real thing.* **2.** *n.* a parody of someone or something. (Usually with *on.*) □ *The comedian did a take-off on the wealthy senator.* □ *The take-off on the dean didn't go over well.* **3.** *n.* a robbery. (Underworld.) □ *That was some take-off Lefty pulled, huh?* □ *Yeah, Lefty sure knows take-offs.* (More at *take off.*)

take-off artist *n.* a thief. (Underworld.) □ *A take-off artist known as the Cat is cleaning out closets and jewelry boxes all over town.* □ *He's not a sales agent. He's a take-off artist, pure and simple.*

take on fuel *tr.* to drink alcohol to excess. □ *They stopped at the tavern to take on fuel.* 🅃 *They went inside to take fuel on and then came back out to watch the horses.*

take one's belt in (a notch) AND **pull one's belt in (a notch)** *tr.* to prepare for lean times. (See also *tighten one's belt.*) □ *It was clear that we would have to bite the bullet and take our belt in a notch.* □ *We were able to take our belt in a notch, unlike other people who were already strained to the maximum.*

take one's lumps *tr.* to accept the result or punishment one deserves. (Compare to *get one's lumps.*) □ *You've got to learn to take your lumps if you're going to be in politics.* □ *I hate taking my lumps. I'd rather pretend nothing had happened.*

take pictures *tr.* for a highway patrol officer to use radar. (Citizens band radio.) □ *There's a smokey under the bridge taking pictures.* □ *I didn't see the creep was taking pictures. I got nabbed.*

take some doing *tr.* to require added effort and planning. □ *It'll take some doing, but it'll get done.* □ *It's not impossible. It'll just take some doing.*

take some heat See *take the heat.*

take someone in 1. AND **rope someone in** *tr.* to cheat or deceive someone. □ *He might try to take you in. Keep an eye on him and count your change.* □ *The con artists tried to rope in the old lady, but she was too clever.* **2.** *tr.* to give shelter to someone. □ *We took her in and gave her some soup and a place to stay.* □ *Mrs. Wilson takes in almost every young person who needs her help.*

take someone or something apart 1. *tr.* to criticize or defame someone or something. □ *They really took me apart, but what the hell?* □ *The editorial took the whole board apart.* **2.** *tr.* to beat or damage someone or something. □ *The mugger really took the old lady apart.* □ *The wreck took both cars apart.*

take someone or something off 1. *tr.* [with *someone*] to kill someone. (Underworld.) □ *The mob took the witness off a week before the trial.* 🅃 *Barlowe didn't want to have to take off Lefty—like hell, he didn't.* **2.** *tr.* to rob someone or something. (Underworld.) □ *Weren't you in that bunch that took the bank off in Philly?* □ *No, we never took off no bank, did we, Lefty?*

take someone or something on *tr.* to accept the task of handling a difficult person or thing. □ *I'll take it on if nobody else will do it.* 🅃 *Nobody wanted to take on Mrs. Franklin, but it had to be done.*

take someone or something out 1. *tr.* [with *someone*] to block someone, as in a football game. □ *I was supposed to take the left end out, but I was trapped under the center.* 🅃 *Okay, Andy, you take out the center this time.* **2.** *tr.* [with *someone*] to kill someone. (Underworld.) □ *The boss told Rocko to take out Barlowe.* □ *Barlowe was sure he could keep Rocko from taking him out.* **3.** *tr.* [with *something*] to bomb or destroy something. □ *The enemy took out one of the tanks, but not the one carrying the medicine.* □ *The last flight took out two enemy bunkers and a radar installation.* **4.** *tr.* [with *someone*] to date someone. □ *I hope he'll take me out soon.* □ *She wanted to take him out for an evening.*

take someone to the cleaners 1. *tr.* to take all of someone's money. □ *The lawyers took the insurance company to the cleaners, but I still didn't get enough to pay for my losses.* □ *The con artists took the old man to the cleaners.* **2.** *tr.* to defeat or best someone. □ *We took the other team to the cleaners.* □ *Look at *the height they've got! They'll take us to the cleaners!*

take something public 1. *tr.* to make something known to the public. ☐ *You gotta take it public—put it on the street—even when it's none of your business.* ☐ *Don't take it public. You'll just get talked about.* **2.** *tr.* to sell shares in a company to the general public. (Securities markets.) ☐ *The board decided not to take the company public.* ☐ *We're going to take it public whenever the market looks good.*

take the cure *tr.* to enter into any treatment program or treatment center. (Especially those dealing with drugs and alcohol.) ☐ *I wanted to take the cure, but I just couldn't bring myself to do it.* ☐ *It's hard to get them to realize that they are the ones who have to decide to take the cure.*

take the fall *tr.* to get arrested for a particular crime. (Especially when others are going unpunished for the same crime. See also *take a fall.*) ☐ *Bruno and Tony pulled the job off together, but Tony took the fall.* ☐ *You did it, and I won't take the fall!*

take the fifth 1. AND **five it** *tr.* to refuse to testify to a U.S. legislative committee under the protection of the Fifth Amendment to the U.S. Constitution. ☐ *His lawyer told him to take the fifth.* ☐ *The lawyer just sat there and said, "Five it." after every question.* **2.** *tr.* to decline to answer any questions. ☐ *I'll take the fifth on that one. Ask Fred.* ☐ *Don't ask me. I take the fifth.*

take the gas pipe See *take the pipe.*

take the heat AND **take some heat** *tr.* to receive criticism (for something). ☐ *The cops have been taking some heat about the Quincy killing.* ☐ *If you can't take the heat, stay out of the kitchen.*

take the heat off someone *tr.* to relieve the pressure on someone; to free someone from suspicion, responsibility, a deadline, etc. ☐ *The confession by Rocko took the heat off the cop-shop for a while.* ☐ *They took the heat off us by moving the deadline.*

take the (long) count *tr.* to die. ☐ *The poor cat took the long count at last.* ☐ *I'm too young to take the count.*

take the pipe 1. AND **take the gas pipe** *tr.* to commit suicide. (Originally by inhaling gas.) ☐ *The kid was dropping everything in sight and finally took the pipe.* ☐ *Some poor old guy took the gas pipe and nearly blew the place up.* **2.** *tr.* to fail to perform under pressure; to cave in. (From sense 1.) ☐ *He tends to take the pipe when the going gets rough.* ☐ *Don't take the pipe, man. Stick in there!*

take the pledge *tr.* to promise to abstain from beverage alcohol. ☐ *I'm not ready to take the pledge yet, but I will cut down.* ☐ *My aunt tried to get me to take the pledge.*

take the plunge *tr.* to marry someone. ☐ *I'm not ready to take the plunge yet.* ☐ *Sam and Mary took the plunge.*

take the rap (for something) *tr.* to take the blame for something. (Originally underworld. See also *rap.*) ☐ *I didn't want to take the rap for the job, but, after all, I was guilty.* ☐ *I threw the rock, but John took the rap.*

take the spear (in one's chest) *tr.* to accept full blame for something; to accept the full brunt of the punishment for something. ☐ *The Admiral got the short straw and had to take the spear in his chest.* ☐ *I sure didn't want to take the spear.*

take the starch out of someone *tr.* to reduce someone's self-assurance; to reduce someone's conceit. ☐ *I took the starch out of Kelly by telling him where he was headed if he didn't change his ways.* ☐ *That remark really took the starch out of him.*

take the wind out of someone's sails *tr.* to put a barrier in someone's path; to reduce the effectiveness of someone. ☐ *When the cops showed Max the evidence, it took the wind out of his sails.* ☐ *It really took the wind out of his sails when he didn't get promoted.*

take things easy 1. *tr.* to live well and comfortably. ☐ *I'll be glad when I can* *make enough money to take things easy.* □ *I make enough to take things easy.* **2.** *tr.* to relax temporarily and recuperate. □ *The doctor says I'm supposed to take things easy for a while.* □ *I want you to take it easy until the stitches heal.*

taken AND **had; took 1.** *mod.* cheated; deceived. □ *I counted my change, and I knew I was taken.* □ *You were really took, all right.* **2.** *mod.* drug intoxicated; unconscious from drugs. □ *The guy in the corner booth was taken and crying in his beer.* □ *His eyes were bloodshot, his hands were shaking—he was had.* **3.** *mod.* dead. □ *I'm sorry, your cat is taken —pifted.* □ *Your cat's took, lady, tough luck.* **4.** *mod.* already claimed as someone's mate or lover. □ *Sorry, Bill, I'm already taken. Sam and I are engaged.* □ *Forget it. She's taken.*

taker *n.* one who accepts an offer; a buyer. □ *Are there any takers for this fine, almost new caddy?* □ *Here's a taker. You'll not be sorry.*

takes two to tango *phr.* "requires two people to do certain things." □ *No, he didn't do it all by himself. Takes two to tango, you know.* □ *There's no such thing as a one-sided argument. It takes two to tango.*

taking care of business *tr.* doing what one is meant to do; coping with life as it is. (Black. See also *TCB.*) □ *If the dude is taking care of business, what else do you want out of him?* □ *Walter is taking care of business. Back in a minute.*

tale of woe *n.* a sad story; a list of personal problems; an excuse for failing to do something. □ *I listened to her tale of woe without saying anything.* □ *This tale of woe that we have all been getting from Kelly is just too much.*

talk a blue streak *tr.* to talk fast or a lot. □ *This crazy bird suddenly began talking a blue streak.* □ *Some parrots never talk. Others talk a blue streak whenever it's light.*

talk big *in.* to brag; to make grandiose statements. □ *She talks big, but can't produce anything.* □ *He has some deep need to talk big. He can't do anything.*

talk like a nut *in.* to say stupid things. □ *You're talking like a nut! You don't know what you are saying.* □ *Don't talk like a nut! We can't afford a trip to Florida!*

talk on the big white phone *in.* to vomit into a toilet. □ *One more beer and I'm gonna have to go talk on the big white phone.* □ *She was talking on the big white phone all night.*

talk someone ragged *tr.* to talk to someone too much; to bore someone. □ *That was not an interview. She talked me ragged.* □ *He always talks me ragged, but I always listen.*

talk someone's ear off *tr.* to talk to someone endlessly; to bore someone with too much talk. □ *My aunt always talks my ear off when she comes to visit.* □ *Stay away from Mr. Jones. He will talk your ear off if he gets a chance.*

talk one's head off *tr.* to talk endlessly; to argue persuasively or vigorously. □ *I talked my head off trying to convince them.* □ *Don't waste time talking your head off to them.*

talk through one's hat *in.* to say baseless things; to speak carelessly and tell lies. □ *Pay no attention to my friend here. He's just talking through his hat.* □ *You don't know what you are talking about. You're just talking through your hat.*

talk to earl [. . . ɚl] *in.* to vomit. (Onomatopoetic.) □ *I think I hear Pete in the john talking to earl.* □ *Oh, my gosh! I think I have to go talk to earl!*

talk to hear one's own voice *in.* to talk far more than is necessary; to talk much, in an egotistical manner. □ *Oh, he's just talking to hear his own voice.* □ *Am I just talking to hear my own voice, or are you listening to me?*

talk to Herb and Al *in.* to use marijuana and drink alcohol. (See also *herb. Al* is alcohol.) □ *I've been out talking to Herb and Al—that's where I've been.* □ *Let's go talk to Herb and Al while we're waiting.*

talk turkey *tr.* to talk serious business; to talk frankly. □ *We've got to sit down and talk turkey—get this thing wrapped up.* □

It's time to talk turkey and quit messing around.

talk until one is blue in the face *in.* to talk until one is exhausted. □ *You can talk till you're blue in the face, but it won't do any good.* □ *She talked until she was blue in the face, but could not change their minds.*

talking head *n.* a television news reader or announcer whose head and neck appear on the screen. □ *I've had it with talking heads. I can read the paper and learn as much in twenty minutes.* □ *Some of those talking heads make millions a year.*

tall 1. *mod. high* on drugs; intoxicated with marijuana. (Drugs.) □ *When Jerry gets a little tall, he gets overwhelmed with a sense of guilt.* □ *She seems a little tall. What's she on?* **2.** *mod.* high-quality. □ *This is one tall pizza, man.* □ *You're bringing in some tall ideas, man.*

tall in the saddle *mod.* proud. (Often with *sit*.) □ *I'll still be tall in the saddle when you are experiencing the results of your folly.* □ *Despite her difficulties, she still sat tall in the saddle.*

tall one *n.* a large drink; a long drink. (Compare to *short one*.) □ *She ordered a tall one and sat back to cool off.* □ *Give me a tall one, John.*

tall order *n.* a request that is difficult to fulfill. □ *That's a tall order. Do you think anyone can do it?* □ *Well, it's a tall order, but I'll do it.*

tall timbers *n.* some remote well-forested place; the *boondocks*. □ *Oh, Chuck lives out in the tall timbers somewhere. He only has a post office box number.* □ *You're not going to move me out into the tall timbers somewhere!*

tangle with someone or something *in.* to quarrel or fight with someone or something. □ *I didn't want to tangle with her, so I did what she wanted.* □ *It's like tangling with a grizzly.*

tank 1. AND **tank up** *in.* to drink too much beer; to drink to excess. □ *The two brothers were tanking up and didn't hear me come in.* □ *Let's go out this Friday and tank a while.* **2.** *n.* a drunkard. (Usually **tank-up**.) □ *You're turning into a real tank, Harry.* □ *Who's the tank-up carrying the thermos of whiskey?* **3.** *n.* a jail cell for holding drunks. □ *Maybe a night in the tank would give you a chance to think about being a full-time drunk.* □ *One night in the tank was enough to make John take the pledge.* **4.** *tr. & in.* to lose a game deliberately. □ *Wilbur would never tank.* □ *The manager got wind of a plan to tank Friday's game.* **5.** *in.* for something to fail. □ *The entire stock market tanked on Friday.* □ *My investments did not tank when the market collapsed.*

tank up See the previous entry.

tanked 1. AND **tanked up** *mod.* alcohol intoxicated. □ *She was too tanked to drive.* □ *That old codger is really tanked.* **2.** *mod.* defeated; outscored. □ *The team was tanked again—20-17.* □ *I just knew we'd get tanked today.*

tanked up See the previous entry.

tanker *n.* a drinker; a drunkard. □ *When I came into the bar, a few tankers were in the back.* □ *Who's the tanker carrying the thermos of gin?*

tanky *mod.* alcohol intoxicated. □ *The guy was just a little tanky.* □ *He found a way to slow down and keep from getting tanky at parties.*

tanned *mod.* alcohol intoxicated. (Preserved like a tanned hide of an animal.) □ *She was completely tanned.* □ *Tom is too tanned to drive. Get him out of that car.*

tap dance like mad *in.* to be busy continuously; to have to move fast to distract someone. □ *When things get tough, the whole Congress tap dances like mad.* □ *Any public official knows how to tap dance like mad without getting out of breath or sweating.*

tap out 1. *in.* to lose one's money in gambling or in the securities markets. □ *I'm gonna tap out in about three more rolls—just watch.* □ *I really tapped out on that gold-mining stock.* (More at *tapped*.) **2.** *in.* to die; to expire. □ *My* *dog tapped out after being hit by a car.* ☐ *Mary was so tired that she thought she was going to tap out.*

tap someone (for something) *tr.* to select someone for some purpose or position. ☐ *The committee tapped John to run for Congress.* ☐ *I had thought they were going to tap Sally.*

taped [tept] *mod.* finalized; *sealed (up)*; cinched. (As if one were taping a package.) ☐ *I'll have this deal taped by Thursday. Then we can take it easy.* ☐ *Until this thing is taped, we can't do anything.*

tapped [tæpt] **1.** AND **tapped out** *mod.* broke. ☐ *The consumer is just about tapped. Don't expect much buying in that sector.* ☐ *I'm tapped out. Nothing left for you or anybody else this month.* **2.** AND **tapped out** *mod.* exhausted. ☐ *I need a nap. I'm tapped out.* ☐ *I've had it. I'm tapped.* **3.** AND **tapped out** *mod.* ruined. ☐ *We are tapped. That really did it to us.* ☐ *The project is completely tapped out.* **4.** *mod.* arrested. (As if one were tapped on the shoulder by a police officer.) ☐ *I knew I was gonna get tapped eventually, but I just couldn't stop stealing.* ☐ *The whole gang was tapped in a police raid.*

tapped out See the previous entry.

taste *n.* a share; a *piece (of the action).* ☐ *I want a taste, too.* ☐ *Whatever the deal is, I want a taste.*

taste blood *tr.* to experience something exciting, and perhaps dangerous, for the first time. ☐ *She had tasted blood once, and she knew that the life of a racecar driver was for her.* ☐ *Once you taste blood, you're hooked.*

tawny ['tɔni] *mod.* excellent. ☐ *Who is throwing this tawny party anyway?* ☐ *This pizza is, like, tawny!*

TCB *phr.* "taking care of business"; doing things that have to be done. (Black. Initialism.) ☐ *He's TCB; that's where he is.* ☐ *If I am just TCB and keeping my nose clean, I know I'm gonna be all right.*

tea 1. *n.* liquor; alcoholic drink. ☐ *Would you care for more tea?* ☐ *Give the lady some more tea.* **2.** *n.* urine. (Use caution with the topic.) ☐ *There is some tea on the floor.* ☐ *Is that tea on your pants leg?* **3.** *n.* marijuana. (Drugs.) ☐ *Max has tea and canaries on him now. No dust.* ☐ *Can't you lay off that tea a while?*

tea party 1. *n.* a wild drinking party. (Like the Mad Hatter's party in Lewis Carroll's *Alice in Wonderland.*) ☐ *There was a loud tea party going on in the corner booth when Barlowe came in.* ☐ *I'm having a little tea party Friday. Wanna come?* **2.** *n.* something easy; a pleasant and unstressful event. ☐ *It was not a tea party, but it wasn't bad either.* ☐ *The test was a real tea party. No sweat.*

tear [tɛr] *n.* a wild drinking bout. (See also *rip.*) ☐ *Sally is off on a tear again.* ☐ *What a tear it was at Paul's on Saturday night!*

tear into someone or something 1. *in.* [with *someone*] to scold someone severely; to attack someone. ☐ *I was late, and the super tore into me like a mad dog.* ☐ *I don't know why she tore into me. I was at work when the window was broken.* **2.** *in.* [with *something*] to begin eating food with gusto. ☐ *The family tore into the mountain of food like they hadn't eaten since breakfast—which was true, in fact.* ☐ *Jimmy tore into the turkey leg and cleaned it off in no time.* **3.** *in.* [with *something*] to rush into a place. ☐ *I tore into the office and answered the phone.* ☐ *They tore into town and held up the bank.*

tear-jerker ['tɪrdʒɚkɚ] *n.* a very sad story or film. ☐ *The film was a real tear-jerker.* ☐ *I don't care to read a steady diet of tear-jerkers.*

tear loose (from someone or something) [tɛr . . .] *in.* to manage to break away from someone or something. ☐ *The quarterback tore loose and took twenty yards for a first down.* ☐ *Barlowe tore loose from Rocko and made for the door.*

tear off *in.* to break away; to run away. ☐ *I hate to tear off, but I'm late.* ☐ *Don't tear off without having some of my pie.*

tear someone or something apart *tr.* to criticize someone or something severely. ☐ *I was late, and the boss tore me* *apart.* □ *I thought my paper was good, but the prof tore it apart.*

tear someone or something up 1. *tr.* to rip someone or something to pieces. □ *The two drunks tore the bar up the best they could.* Ⓣ *The dog tore up the robber, and the robber sued.* 2. *tr.* [with *someone*] to cause someone much grief. □ *I know this news will tear him up.* Ⓣ *The situation really tore up his father.* (More at *tore (up)*.)

teaser ['tizɚ] 1. *n.* a (found) cigarette butt. □ *The hobo picked up the teaser from the street and put it in a little bag.* □ *He saves up teasers to make a big smoke out of them.* 2. *n.* a brief sample of something, such as a performance. □ *The teaser didn't look very promising, but the reviews were great.* □ *The teasers they showed before the film were the best part of the evening.*

tech-nerd ['tɛknɚd] *n.* a technically oriented, dull person, typically a male computer enthusiast. □ *My brother, who is a tech-nerd, spends more than ten hours a day on his computer.* □ *I had to consult a tech-nerd to get my VCR operating.*

techie ['tɛki] 1. *n.* a student in a technical or engineering college. □ *Does one guy like Martin prove that all techies are nerds?* □ *Of course, one groovy guy proves that techies aren't nerds, right?* 2. *n.* a person with technical skills or knowledge. □ *We'll have to take this problem to a techie.* □ *The techies say it should work, theoretically, that is.* 3. *mod.* having to do with technical people or things. □ *I don't like this techie jargon.* □ *This is the techie lounge. See how messy it is?*

technicolor yawn *n.* vomit. (See also *throw a technicolor yawn*.) □ *This garbage will bring on a few technicolor yawns if we serve it.* □ *Who did the technicolor yawn in the bushes?*

tee someone off *tr.* to make someone angry. □ *That really teed me off!* Ⓣ *Well, you sure managed to tee off everybody!* (More at *teed off*.)

tee-tee ['titi] 1. *in.* to urinate. (Juvenile. Use caution with the topic.) □ *Jimmy, please go tee-tee before we leave.* □ *Jimmy, you are supposed to flush it when you tee-tee.* 2. *n.* urine. (Juvenile. Use caution with the topic.) □ *There's tee-tee on the floor.* □ *Why is tee-tee yellow?*

teed off *mod.* angry. □ *I'm not teed off! I'm enraged.* □ *I was so teed off I could have spit!*

teed (up) *mod.* alcohol or drug intoxicated. □ *She was totally teed up by midnight.* □ *Tom was too teed to drive.*

teenie AND **teeny** *n.* a sixteenth. (Securities markets. From six*teen*th. One sixteenth of a point in a stock price. See also *steenth*.) □ *It's going at three and two teenies at the moment.* □ *My forty thousand shares have dropped to three teenies each, and I think I am going to go down to the beach and jump.*

teenie-weenie See *teeny-weeny*.

teensy-weensy See *teeny-weeny*.

teeny See *teenie*.

teeny-weeny AND **teenie-weenie; teensy-weensy** ['tini'wini AND 'tintsi'wintsi] *mod.* tiny. □ *It was just a teeny-weeny sin.* □ *This one is too teeny-weeny.* □ *Could you move just a teenie-weenie bit to the left?*

teenybopper ['tinibɑpɚ] *n.* a young teenager, usually a girl. □ *The teenyboppers moved around the mall in droves, not buying and not causing any trouble, just being available for anyone who wanted to see them.* □ *Somebody called Mary a, like, teenybopper, and she went, like, "So gross!"*

teepee See *TP*.

telegraph one's punches 1. *tr.* to signal, unintentionally, what blows one is about to strike. (Boxing.) □ *Wilbur used to telegraph his punches until his coach beat it out of him.* □ *Don't telegraph your punches, kid! You'll be flat on your back in twenty seconds.* 2. *tr.* to signal, unintentionally, one's intentions. □ *When you go in there to negotiate, don't telegraph your punches. Don't* *let them see that we're broke.* □ *The mediator telegraphed his punches, and we were prepared with a strong counter argument.*

Tell it like it is. *sent.* "Speak frankly."; "Tell the truth no matter how much it hurts." □ *Come on man, tell it like it is!* □ *Well, I've got to tell it like it is.*

Tell me another (one)! *exclam.* "Tell me another fairy tale!"; "That was a lie. Tell me another just as good!" □ *You a stockbroker? Tell me another one!* □ *There's no improvement in this problem! Tell me another!*

tell shit from Shinola See *know shit from Shinola.*

tell someone what to do with something *tr.* to tell someone to do something rude with something. (With the unspoken notion that one should stick it up one's ass.) □ *I'll tell you what you can do with it.* □ *If that's the way he wants to be, you can just tell him what to do with it.*

tell someone where to get off *tr.* to tell someone when enough is enough; to tell someone off. □ *I was fed up with her bossiness. I finally told her where to get off.* □ *He told me where to get off, so I walked out on him.*

tell the (whole) world *tr.* to spread around private business. □ *Well, you don't have to tell the whole world.* □ *Go ahead, tell the world!*

telly ['tɛli] *n.* a television set. (Originally British.) □ *What's on the telly tonight?* □ *I mean, what's showing on the telly tonight?*

ten *n.* the highest rank on a scale of one to ten. (Always with *a*.) □ *She's definitely a ten.* □ *On a scale of one to ten, this pizza's a ten.*

ten-four AND **10-4** *interj.* "okay." (Citizens band radio.) □ *Ten-four, old buddy. I will do that.* □ *Please, where the answer to the question is yes or no, don't write 10-4 for yes.*

ten percenter *n.* an agent who collects 10 percent. □ *I've been supporting that ten percenter for years, and he was robbing me blind.* □ *The life of a ten percenter is not easy.*

ten-spot *n.* a ten-dollar bill. □ *I slipped him a ten-spot, and suddenly there was a table available.* □ *It will cost you a ten-spot to get the book, in paperback, that is.*

tenner *n.* a ten-dollar bill. (See also *fiver.*) □ *For a tenner, the bum led Barlowe to the place where the crate still lay in the alley.* □ *Barlowe slipped him a tenner and faded into the fog.*

tennies *n.* tennis shoes; sneakers. □ *Let me get my tennies on, and I'll be right with you.* □ *What is that stuff on your tennies?*

terps See *turps.*

terrific *mod.* excellent. □ *Glad to hear it. That's just terrific.* □ *What a terrific idea!*

TGIF 1. *interj.* "Thank God it's Friday." (Initialism.) □ *It was a rough week. T.G.I.F.* □ *Everybody was muttering TGIF by Friday afternoon.* **2.** *n.* a party held on Friday in honor of the end of the workweek. □ *Everyone is invited to the TGIF tonight.* □ *Terry has a T.G.I.F. in his room every evening.*

thank you very much *phr.* a (sometimes sarcastic) tag added to a statement for emphasis. (Often used when there is really nothing to thank anyone for.) □ *I will manage somehow to find my own way out, thank you very much.* □ *We are probably the only people in town who might be able to help you, thank you very much.* □ *You've been quite annoying, thank you very much!*

thanks a bunch *phr.* "thanks." □ *Thanks a bunch for your help.* □ *He said "thanks a bunch" and walked out.*

that 1. *mod.* a stylistic replacement for *the.* (Especially in citizens band radio jargon and much daily colloquial speech. It is the pervasive overuse of this form that makes it notable as colloquial.) □ *Can you tell me where that next rest stop is?* □ *Put that can of stuff on that shelf and sweep that floor.* **2.** *mod.* a stylistic modifier of personal and place names and some other nouns that do not normally take modifiers. (Citizens band radio.) □ *How do I get to that Kansas City?* □ *That Mr. Silverflash is making good time.*

That-a-boy! *exclam.* "That is the way to do it." (Said to a boy or man.) □ *Come on, Chuck. That-a-boy!* □ *That-a-boy, Chuck. You can do it!*

That tears it! [. . . terz . . .] *exclam.* "That is too much!" □ *Well, that tears it! I'm leaving!* □ *I thought yesterday's error was bad enough, but that tears it!*

that way 1. *mod.* in love. □ *Sam and Martha are that way. They look so happy.* □ *Well, Martha's that way, but Sam's just out for a good time.* 2. *mod.* alcohol intoxicated. □ *Daddy's that way again.* □ *I'm sorry, but Fred's that way again and can't drive to work.* 3. *mod.* homosexual. □ *Ken said that you-know-who was acting sort of that way. What a gossip!* □ *Somebody said that Ken talks that way because he is that way.*

That'll be the day! *exclam.* "That will never happen!" □ *You win a medal? That'll be the day!* □ *When he gets his own car—that'll be the day!*

That'll teach someone. *sent.* "That is what someone deserves." □ *That'll teach you to pull out in front of me.* □ *I hit him on the head. That'll teach him.*

That's a new one on me. *sent.* "That is truly amazing."; "I did not know that." □ *A machine that copies in four colors. That's a new one on me.* □ *A talking camera? That's a new one on me.*

That's about the size of it. *sent.* "That is the way things are."; "That's all there is to tell." □ *Well, that's about the size of it. See you tomorrow.* □ *That's about the size of it. You've understood it perfectly.*

That's all she wrote. AND **That's what she wrote.** *sent.* "That is all of it." □ *Here's the last one we have to fix. There, that's all she wrote.* □ *That's what she wrote. There ain't no more.*

That's all someone needs. *sent.* "That is too much."; "That is the last straw." □ *Now the sewer's backing up. That's all I need.* □ *A new mouth to feed. That's all we need!*

That's my boy. *sent.* "That is my son of whom I am proud."; "I'm proud of this young man." □ *After the game, Tom's dad said, "That's my boy!"* □ *That's my boy! Always a winner!*

That's show business (for you). *sent.* "That is the way that life really is." (Also with *biz* and *show biz.*) □ *And now the car won't start. That's show business for you.* □ *Too bad about the bad investment. That's show biz.*

That's that! *exclam.* "That is final!"; "That is the end of it!" □ *I said no, and that's that!* □ *I won't go, and that's that!*

That's the stuff! *exclam.* "That is good work!" □ *Good shot, Wally! That's the stuff!* □ *That's the stuff! Way to go!*

That's the ticket! *exclam.* "That is exactly what is needed!" □ *Good! That's the ticket! Now you're cooking with gas.* □ *That's the ticket! Perfect!*

That's the way the ball bounces. *sent.* "That is life."; "That is the random way things happen." □ *It's tough, I know, but that's the way the ball bounces.* □ *That's the way the ball bounces. It could be worse.*

That's the way the cookie crumbles. *sent.* "That is life."; "That is typical of the unequal share of things you are likely to get in life." □ *I lost my job. Oh, well. That's the way the cookie crumbles.* □ *Oh, gee! Too bad. That's the way the cookie crumbles.*

That's the way the mop flops. *sent.* "This is the way things happen."; "This is typical of the random patterns of events." (Contrived.) □ *Sorry to hear about that, but that's the way the mop flops.* □ *That's tough, but that's the way the mop flops.*

(That's the) way to go! *exclam.* "Nicely done!" □ *Way to go, Charlie!* □ *That's the way to go! You did it!*

That's what I say. *sent.* "I agree with you." □ *Of course, Mary. That's what I* *say.* □ *That's what I say. The way to cut spending is just to do it.*

That's what she wrote. See *That's all she wrote.*

thawed *mod.* alcohol intoxicated. □ *Tad is sort of soppy, you might say, thawed.* □ *Do you think he's too thawed to drive us home?*

The baby needs shoes. *sent.* "Give me luck." (Said in games of chance, such as dice or bingo.) □ *He shook the bones, saying, "The baby needs shoes."* □ *All the players in the crap game must be poor, because they kept saying that the baby needs shoes.*

the feds See *fed.*

the man See *man.*

the way it plays *phr.* the way it is; the way things are. □ *The world is a rough place, and that's the way it plays.* □ *It's tough, but it's the way it plays.*

then and there *mod.* right then. □ *He dropped the box right then and there and walked out on us.* □ *Right then and there, he pulled up his shirt and showed everyone the jagged scar.*

There will be hell to pay. *sent.* "Things will be so bad that one will have to bribe the devil to straighten them out." (Use caution with *hell.*) □ *If I don't get this done on time, there will be hell to pay.* □ *There'll be hell to pay if we miss the plane.*

There you are. *sent.* "This is the result."; "This is the way things turned out." □ *There you are. Didn't I warn you?* □ *Well, there you are. Another first-class mess.*

There you go. **1.** *sent.* "Hooray! You did it right!" (Usually **There you go!**) □ *There you go! That's the way!* □ *Good shot, Chuck! There ya go!* **2.** *sent.* "That is the way things are, just like I told you."; "Isn't this just what you would expect?" □ *There you go. Isn't that just like a man!* □ *There you go, acting rude and ugly!* **3.** *sent.* "You are doing it again." □ *There you go! You said it again.* □ *I just told you not to put that junk on the table, and there you go.*

There's nobody home. *sent.* "There are no brains in someone's head." □ *There's lots of goodwill in that head, but there's nobody home.* □ *You twit! There's nobody home—that's for sure.*

thick **1.** *mod.* stupid; *thickheaded.* □ *She's sort of thick, but she means well.* □ *Why are you so thick about money?* **2.** *mod.* involved (with someone). □ *Sam and Mary are really thick.* □ *They're thick as can be.* **3.** *mod.* unbelievable. □ *This stuff is getting thick.* □ *This story is too thick for me. I'm cruising outa here.*

thick-skinned *mod.* able to withstand much criticism. (Compare to *thin-skinned.*) □ *You gotta be more thick-skinned if you want to be a cop.* □ *He's a real thick-skinned guy.* □ *I'm thick-skinned enough; I just don't like violence.*

thickheaded *mod.* stupid; with more bone than brain in the head. □ *He's so thickheaded he can play football without a helmet.* □ *What thickheaded dolt put scallops in the scalloped potatoes?*

thin dime *n.* a dime, thought of as a very small amount of money. (A concept eroded by inflation.) □ *For only one thin dime you will receive our exciting catalog of novelties and tricks.* □ *This whole mess isn't worth one thin dime.*

thin-skinned *mod.* sensitive to criticism. (Compare to *thick-skinned.*) □ *Don't be so thin-skinned. You can't expect everyone to like you.* □ *He's a thin-skinned guy.* □ *I'm too thin-skinned to be a bill collector.*

thing *n.* one's interest; one's *bag.* □ *This isn't exactly my thing, but I'll give it a try.* □ *This is just your thing! Enjoy it!*

thingamajig AND **thingy** ['θɪŋəmədʒɪg AND 'θɪŋi] *n.* a gadget for which the proper name has been forgotten or is unknown. □ *Hand me that thingamajig with the copper base, will you?* □ *What're ya supposed to do with this thingy?*

thingy See the previous entry.

think-box *n.* the skull; the head. ☐ *A little weak in the think-box, but other than that, okay.* ☐ *Use your think-box for something other than to hold your ears apart.*

think-piece *n.* a thoughtful piece of writing in a newspaper or magazine. ☐ *Mr. Wilson's think-piece about the need for more concern for the middle class was not well received.* ☐ *This is plain propaganda disguised as a think-piece.*

think-tank *n.* a place where great minds are assembled to try to think up solutions to problems or to envision the future. ☐ *She spent a few months in a California think-tank, then came back to teach.* ☐ *What sort of solutions are coming out of the think-tanks of the nation?*

third degree *n.* a session of questioning, usually by the police. ☐ *Max got the third degree, but—being the thoroughbred he is—he was a clam.* ☐ *They gave Bruno the third degree, but he refused to say anything.*

third wheel *n.* an extra person; a person who gets in the way. (Such a person is as useful as a third wheel on a bicycle. See also *spare tire.*) ☐ *I feel like such a third wheel around here.* ☐ *Well, let's face it. We don't need you. You are a third wheel.*

thirst-aid station *n.* a place to purchase liquor. (From *first-aid station.*) ☐ *Let's stop at the next thirst-aid station and get a snort.* ☐ *Wally stopped by the thirst-aid station for a quick snort.*

thirsty soul *n.* a drunkard; a person in need of a drink. ☐ *Yes, I'd call Bill a thirsty soul—he always seems thirsty for booze.* ☐ *There was a long line of thirsty souls waiting for the liquor joint to open.*

This is it! **1.** *exclam.* "This is exactly what I have been looking for!"; "I have found it!" ☐ *This is it! I got it right this time.* ☐ *This is it! The world's best pizza!* **2.** *exclam.* "This is the crucial moment!" ☐ *Okay, this is it, the last chance!* ☐ *Get ready, this is it! Jump now!*

This is where I came in. *sent.* "This all seems very familiar." ☐ *Okay, that's enough. This is where I came in.* ☐ *This is where I came in. It's the same thing all over again.*

thoroughbred *n.* an underworld person who is trustworthy and loyal to the underworld. (Underworld.) ☐ *Max is an A-1 thoroughbred.* ☐ *The thoroughbred clammed up during the third degree.*

thou [θaʊ] *n.* one thousand. ☐ *I managed to get a couple of thou from the bank, but I need a little more than that.* ☐ *It only costs four thou. I could borrow it from my uncle.*

threads *n.* clothing. ☐ *When'd you get new threads, man?* ☐ *Good-looking threads on Wally, huh?*

three bricks shy of a load *mod.* stupid; dense; shortchanged on intelligence. ☐ *I would never say she was dense. Just three bricks shy of a load.* ☐ *Why do you act like you're three bricks shy of a load?*

three fingers *n.* a measurement of liquor in a glass. (Compare to *two fingers.*) ☐ *I'll take three fingers. It's been a hard day.* ☐ *Your wife told me not to give you three fingers anymore.*

three point two See *three-two.*

three sheets in the wind AND **three sheets (to the wind); two sheets to the wind** *mod.* alcohol intoxicated and unsteady. (Sheets are the ropes used to manage a ship's sails. It is assumed that if these ropes were blowing in the wind, the ship would be unmanageable.) ☐ *He was three sheets to the wind and didn't pay attention to my warning.* ☐ *By midnight, he was three sheets.*

three sheets (to the wind) See the previous entry.

three squares *n.* three square meals a day. ☐ *I was glad to get back home to three squares.* ☐ *If I could limit myself to three squares, I could lose some weight.*

three-two AND **three point two** *n.* a weak beer containing 3.2 percent alcohol. ☐ *Three-two is just no good for serious sousing.* ☐ *James likes three point two because he can drink more of it without getting stoned.*

thriller-diller ['θrɪlə-'dɪlə-] *n.* something like a movie, book, or television program that is thrilling. (Compare to *whodunit.*) ☐ *The film was a real thriller-diller. I remember having to force myself to exhale.* ☐ *I can read one of these thriller-dillers in a couple of hours.*

throat *n.* an earnest student; a "cutthroat" student. (Collegiate.) ☐ *Martin is not a throat! He's not that smart.* ☐ *All the throats got A's, of course.*

throat gag *n.* liquor; strong liquor. ☐ *Pour me another of that throat gag, barkeep.* ☐ *That throat gag nearly choked me.*

throne *n.* a toilet; a toilet seat. ☐ *And there was the cat—right on the throne, just staring at me.* ☐ *Somebody'd better clean the throne pretty soon.*

throne room *n.* a restroom; a bathroom. (See also *throne.*) ☐ *Hank is in the throne room, reading, I think.* ☐ *Where's your throne room?*

through and through *mod.* thoroughly; throughout. ☐ *She's a born fighter, through and through.* ☐ *He is totally dishonest. A crook through and through.*

through the mill *mod.* abused; well-worn. ☐ *That was some convention. I've really been through the mill.* ☐ *I feel like I've gone through the mill. I'm pooped.*

throw 1. *n.* a try; a time. ☐ *Have another throw at it, why don't you?* ☐ *Just one more throw, then I'll quit.* **2.** *tr.* to confuse someone. ☐ *The question really threw me.* ☐ *When the light fixture fell, it threw us a little.*

throw a fight *tr.* to lose a boxing match on purpose. (Boxing. Other words can replace *a.*) ☐ *I just know that Wilbur didn't throw that fight.* ☐ *The guy would never throw a fight.*

throw a fit *tr.* to have a display of bad temper. ☐ *I knew you'd throw a fit when I told you.* ☐ *Oh, boy, did she ever throw a fit.*

throw a game *tr.* to lose a game on purpose. (See also *throw a fight.*) ☐ *I know Wilbur. He could never throw a game.* ☐ *There's a couple of those guys who would throw a game if they got enough money to do it.*

throw a map *tr.* to empty one's stomach; to vomit. ☐ *Somebody threw a map on the sidewalk.* ☐ *I felt like I was going to throw a map.*

throw a punch *tr.* to jab; to punch. ☐ *She tried to throw a punch at me, but I blocked it.* ☐ *Wilbur threw a punch at the thug.*

throw a technicolor yawn *tr.* to vomit. (See also *technicolor yawn.*) ☐ *One look at the food, and I almost threw a technicolor yawn.* ☐ *John stumbled into the living and threw a technicolor yawn on the new carpet.*

throw-away 1. *n.* a flyer or handbill. ☐ *The throw-away announced a big, city-wide T.G.I.F.* ☐ *I passed out the throw-aways, but not many people would take them.* **2.** *n.* a comedian's quickly uttered one-line joke. ☐ *He tossed off his best throw-away of the evening just as the curtain fell.* ☐ *She was an expert at the one-line throw-away.*

throw down *in.* to eat; to gobble one's food. (The opposite of *throw up* = to vomit.) ☐ *Man, I'm starved. Let's find a hamburger joint and throw down.* ☐ *What time are your going to throw down tonight?*

throw in the sponge See the following entry.

throw in the towel AND **throw in the sponge; toss in the sponge** *tr.* to quit; to give up. (From boxing where a towel or sponge thrown into the ring indicates that a boxer has given up.) ☐ *I can tell when it's time to throw in the towel, and this is that time.* ☐ *The candidate who was exposed by the press as a former pickpocket tossed in the sponge in a tearful press conference.*

throw money at something *tr.* to try to solve a problem by spending money on it. (Often said of the U.S. federal government.) ☐ *This agency has thrown billions at the housing problem, but it has* *been nothing but a long-term disaster.* ☐ *Don't just throw money at it.*

throw one out on one's ear *tr.* to remove someone from a place forcibly. ☐ *Straighten up, or I'll throw you out on your ear.* ☐ *The caretaker caught us and threw us out on our ear.*

throw one's cookies See *toss one's cookies.*

throw one's hat in the ring *tr.* to indicate that one is to be a contestant or a candidate. ☐ *The con claimed he needed parole so he could throw his hat in the ring for the mayoral election.* ☐ *I won't throw my hat into the ring until the last minute.*

throw one's voice *tr.* to empty one's stomach; to vomit. ☐ *Wally's in the john throwing his voice.* ☐ *Another drink of that stuff and Don'll be throwing his voice all night.*

throw one's weight around *tr.* to show off one's importance or power; to use one's rank or station to advantage. ☐ *The vice president was throwing his weight around, but that had little effect on anything.* ☐ *Don't pay any attention to her. She's just throwing her weight around.*

throw someone for a loop *tr.* to confuse or surprise someone. ☐ *The whole business threw me for a loop.* ☐ *Don't let this question throw you for a loop.*

throw something back *tr.* to eat or drink something. ☐ *Did you throw that whole beer back?* 🅃 *Jed threw back a quick snort and went on with his complaining.*

throw something together See *knock something together.*

throw the book at someone *tr.* [for the police] to charge someone with everything possible; [for a judge] to find someone guilty of everything possible. (As if one were being charged with violating all the laws in a law book.) ☐ *The judge wanted to throw the book at Bruno, but the prosecutor convinced him to go easy in hope that Bruno would lead them to Mr. Big.* ☐ *They threw the book at Rocko—he got 180 years.*

throw the bull AND **throw the crap** *tr.* to chat; to boast. (Use caution with *crap.*) ☐ *Tom could really throw the bull and sound right as rain.* ☐ *You're just throwing the crap. Can it!*

throw the crap See the previous entry.

throw up one's toenails *tr.* to wretch; to vomit a lot. ☐ *It sounded like he was throwing up his toenails.* ☐ *Who's in the john throwing up her toenails?*

thumb a ride *tr.* to beg a ride; to stand at the side of the street and signal to cars with one's thumb for a ride. ☐ *I'll thumb a ride to get there if I have to.* ☐ *I thumbed a ride to speed things up.*

thumber *n.* a beggar; a *moocher.* (As one who thumbs or begs a ride.) ☐ *Don't be a thumber, Frank. Go buy your own cancer sticks.* ☐ *There was a thumber on every corner trying to get a ride from someone.*

thumbnail sketch *n.* a quick and concise description. (One that could be written on someone's thumbnail.) ☐ *Let me give you a thumbnail sketch of what happened.* ☐ *The story—in a thumbnail sketch—deals with a family of storks and what happens to them during each of the four seasons.*

thumbs down 1. *n.* a sign of disapproval. (See also *turn thumbs down (on someone or something).*) ☐ *The board gave our proposal a thumbs down.* ☐ *Not another thumbs down!* **2.** *mod.* disapproving; negative. ☐ *It was thumbs down, and I was disappointed.* ☐ *The thumbs down decision was a victory for good sense.*

thumbs up 1. *n.* a sign of approval. ☐ *It was a thumbs up on the new filtration plant at Thursday's village board meeting.* ☐ *There was no thumbs up for the mayor as she faced certain defeat in today's balloting.* **2.** *mod.* approving; positive. ☐ *The new filtration plant got a thumbs up decision at the board meeting.* ☐ *A thumbs up vote assured another three years of financial assistance.*

thunder-boomer *n.* a thunderstorm. ☐ *There will be thunder-boomers in the* *boonies tonight.* □ *A few thunder-boomers may wake you up tonight.*

thunder-thighs *n.* big or fat thighs. (Cruel. Also a rude term of address.) □ *Here comes old thunder-thighs.* □ *Here, thunder-thighs, let me get you a chair or two.*

thunderbox *n.* a portable stereo radio, often played very loudly in public. (See also *boom box.*) □ *Someday I'm going to smash one of these thunderboxes!* □ *Why not get a thunderbox of your own?*

tick *n.* a minute; a second. (See also *sec.*) □ *I'll be with you in a tick.* □ *This won't take a tick. Sit tight.*

tick someone off *tr.* to make someone angry. □ *That really ticks me off!* 🅃 *Doesn't that tick off everyone?* (More at *ticked (off).*)

tick-tock ['tɪktɑk] **1.** *n.* a heart. (See also *ticker.*) □ *My tick-tock is as strong as an ox's.* □ *How long does an ox's tick-tock last anyway?* **2.** *n.* a watch or clock. (Juvenile.) □ *Wind your tick-tock before you forget.* □ *The tick-tock in the kitchen has broken.*

ticked (off) *mod.* angry. □ *Wow, was she ticked off!* □ *Kelly was totally ticked.*

ticker **1.** *n.* a heart. □ *I've got a good strong ticker.* □ *His ticker finally gave out.* **2.** *n.* a watch. □ *My ticker stopped. The battery must be dead.* □ *If your watch runs on a battery, can you really call it a ticker?*

ticket **1.** *n.* the exact thing; the needed thing. □ *Her smile was her ticket to a new career.* □ *This degree will be your ticket to a bright and shining future.* **2.** *n.* a license. □ *I finally got a ticket to drive a big truck.* □ *I showed her my ticket, and she let me off with a warning.*

tickle the ivories *tr.* to play the piano. □ *I used to be able to tickle the ivories real nice.* □ *She sat down to tickle the ivories for a while.*

tickled (pink) *mod.* amused; utterly delighted; pleased. □ *I am tickled pink you could come this evening.* □ *We were tickled that you thought of us.*

ticky-tacky ['tɪkitæki] *n.* cheap and shabby material. □ *Those houses are just made of ticky-tacky, and they won't even be here in twenty years.* □ *That stuff is just ticky-tacky. No one will buy it.*

tiddled *mod.* alcohol intoxicated. □ *He had a tendency to get a little tiddled.* □ *Jack's too tiddled to drive.*

tie-in *n.* a connection; a liaison. □ *And who is your tie-in with the Acme Systems Company?* □ *I got a call from Mary—my tie-in with the mayor's office—who says it's all set.*

tie it on See *tie one on.*

tie on the nosebag See *put on the feed-bag.*

tie one on AND **lay one on; tie it on** *tr.* to get drunk. □ *The boys went out to tie one on.* □ *They laid one on, but good.*

tie the knot **1.** *tr.* to marry a mate. □ *We tied the knot in a little chapel on the Arkansas border.* □ *They finally tied the knot.* **2.** *tr.* [for a cleric] to unite a couple in marriage. □ *It was hard to find somebody to tie the knot at that hour.* □ *It only took a few minutes for the ship's captain to tie the knot.*

tied up *mod.* busy. □ *I was tied up and couldn't get to the phone.* □ *The phone was tied up for more than an hour.*

tiffled ['tɪfl̩d] *mod.* alcohol intoxicated. □ *Harry was too tiffled to drive.* □ *Mary got a little tiffled, but nothing really gross.*

tiger *n.* a strong and virile man. □ *The guy's a tiger. Watch out for him.* □ *Isn't Bruno a tiger!*

tiger juice See the following entry.

tiger sweat AND **tiger juice; tiger('s) milk** *n.* bad liquor; strong liquor; any beer or liquor. □ *What is this tiger sweat anyway?* □ *How about some more of that tiger juice?* □ *This tiger milk would kill a tiger of any age or disposition.*

tiger('s) milk See the previous entry.

tight **1.** *mod.* stingy. □ *She's really tight with her cash.* □ *You're just too tight. Gimme a fiver, Dad, come on.* **2.** *mod.* alcohol intoxicated. □ *Frank was tight* *and didn't want to drive.* □ *The host got tight and had to go to bed.* **3.** *mod.* stressful; with little margin for error. □ *In a tight situation Martin can be sort of a wet rag.* □ *When the schedule is tight and we are busy as all get out, the telephone won't stop ringing.*

tight as a tick **1.** *mod.* very tight. □ *This lid is screwed on tight as a tick.* □ *The windows were closed—tight as a tick—to keep the cold out.* **2.** *mod.* alcohol intoxicated. □ *The old man was tight as a tick, but still lucid.* □ *The host got tight as a tick and fell in the pool.*

tight money *n.* money that is hard to get. □ *This is tight money. Go easy on it. It's hard to get.* □ *In these days of tight money, no new expenditures will be approved.*

tight spot *n.* a difficulty. □ *I'm in sort of a tight spot and wonder if you can help me out.* □ *Sure, I like helping people out of tight spots as long as it doesn't cost me any money.*

tight wad *n.* a stingy person; a miser. (See also *wad*.) □ *There's no need to be such a tight wad.* □ *My dad's a tight wad.*

tighten one's belt *tr.* to prepare for economies. (As if one would not be able to afford enough food to make one's stomach press against one's belt. Compare to *take one's belt in (a notch)*.) □ *Get ready to tighten your belt. I lost my job.* □ *The entire country will have to tighten its belt.*

Tijuana taxi ['tiəwɑnɑ 'tæksi] *n.* a police car. (Citizens band radio.) □ *There's a Tijuana taxi back a few cars watching you awful close.* □ *It's not a Tijuana taxi; it's a park ranger!*

till hell freezes over *mod.* forever. (Use caution with *hell*.) □ *That's all right, boss; I can wait till hell freezes over for your answer.* □ *I'll be here till hell freezes over.*

till kingdom come *mod.* until the end of the world; forever. □ *Do I have to keep assembling these units till kingdom come?* □ *I'll hate her guts till kingdom come.*

till the fat lady sings AND **when the fat lady sings** *mod.* at the end; a long time from now. (Supposedly from a tale about a child—sitting through an opera—who asks a parent when it will be over. "Not until the fat lady sings" is the answer.) □ *Relax. It won't be over till the fat lady sings.* □ *We can leave with everybody else when the fat lady sings.*

Time (out)! *exclam.* "Stop talking for a minute!" (A way of interrupting someone.) □ *Time! I have something to say.* □ *Just a minute! Time out! I want to speak!*

time to cruise *n.* "Time to leave." □ *See ya. It's time to cruise.* □ *Time to cruise. We're gone.*

tin cow *n.* canned milk. □ *This tin cow is okay in coffee or something, but you can't drink it.* □ *Tin cow was all we could get.*

tin hat *n.* a soldier's helmet. □ *Where's my tin hat?* □ *You use your tin hat for everything—washing, hauling water—you name it.*

tinkle **1.** *in.* to urinate. (Mostly juvenile use. Use caution with the topic.) □ *I gotta tinkle!* □ *Jimmy, be sure and tinkle before we leave.* **2.** *n.* urine. (Essentially juvenile. Use caution with the topic.) □ *There's tinkle on the bathroom floor.* □ *Mommy, why is tinkle warm?*

tinklebox *n.* a piano. (See also *joybox*.) □ *She's okay on the tinklebox.* □ *The tinklebox in the bar seemed to be a bit loud.*

tinsel-teeth *n.* a nickname for someone who wears dental braces. (Also a rude nickname.) □ *Tinsel-teeth is having a hard time talking.* □ *Well, tinsel-teeth, today's the day your braces come off.*

tinseled *mod.* forged or "decorated," as with a bad check. (Underworld.) □ *Gert got caught passing tinseled checks.* □ *He almost got caught kiting tinseled checks.*

tinseltown *n.* Hollywood, California. □ *Tinseltown is a very glitzy place.* □ *She's talented and has her eye on tinseltown.*

tints *n.* sunglasses. □ *Somebody sat on my tints.* □ *I have to get some prescription tints.*

tip-off *n.* a clue; an indication. □ *The tip-off was when the dog started wagging his tail. We knew you were hiding somewhere close.* □ *The broken twig was just the tip-off Barlowe needed.*

tip one's hand *tr.* to reveal what one is going to do; to reveal one's secrets. (From card playing.) □ *I didn't tip my hand at all. I left them guessing.* □ *They tried to get me to tip my hand.*

tipple 1. *n.* liquor; strong liquor. □ *This is mighty fine tipple.* □ *A little more tipple, Tom?* **2.** *tr. & in.* to drink liquor; to sip at a vessel of liquor. □ *He's been tippling beer since early morning.* □ *Actually, he's been tippling since 1943.* **3.** *n.* a drink of liquor. □ *How about a little tipple?* □ *I'll take just a little tipple—for my arthritis, you know.* **4.** *n.* a drinking bout. □ *Well, Uncle Harry's off on a tipple again.* □ *No, that's the same tipple.*

tippler 1. *n.* a tavern keeper. □ *Another beer, faithful tippler.* □ *John is the best tippler this place has ever seen. Tip me another, John.* **2.** *n.* a drunkard. □ *Uncle Ben was a tippler—a harmless one.* □ *He started drinking at fifteen and has been a tippler ever since.*

tipply *mod.* alcohol intoxicated. □ *Ben is too tipply to drive home.* □ *I feel a little tipply.*

tipster *n.* someone who gives special information; an informer. □ *We got this from a tipster who has usually proven reliable in the past.* □ *The cops got this info from their favorite tipster.*

tits *n.* the breasts. (Crude. Potentially offensive. Use only with discretion.) □ *Wow, nice tits, huh, Fred?* □ *All you think about is tits!*

tits and ass See *T. and A.*

tits up *mod.* upside down; on its or someone's back. (Potentially offensive. Use only with discretion.) □ *He landed tits up in a cornfield.* □ *Her lousy pie fell tits up onto the kitchen floor.*

tizzy ['tuzi] *n.* a state of confusion. (See also *twit.*) □ *The kind of tizzy that this place gets into drives me up the wall.* □ *The office was a tizzy when I left.*

TLC *n.* "tender loving care." (Initialism.) □ *All he needs is a little TLC.* □ *This old car will keep running as long as I give it lots of T.L.C.*

to beat the band *mod.* very hard and very fast. □ *He's selling computers to beat the band since he started advertising.* □ *She worked to beat the band to get ready for this.*

to boot *mod.* in addition. □ *For graduation, I got a new suit and a coat to boot.* □ *She got an F on her term paper and flunked the final to boot.*

to die for *mod.* important or desirable enough to die for; worth dying for. □ *This chocolate cake is to die for!* □ *We had a beautiful room at the hotel and the service was to die for.*

to-do *n.* a commotion. □ *Don't make such a to-do when you come in late.* □ *They made quite a to-do about the broken window.*

to go *mod.* packaged to be taken out; packaged to be carried home to eat. □ *Do you want it to go, or will you eat it here?* □ *This stuff is to go.*

to hell and gone *mod.* gone; ruined. (Use caution with *hell.*) □ *Fred was to hell and gone before anybody figured out what he had done.* □ *The whole plan is to hell and gone. Nothing can be salvaged.*

To hell with that! *exclam.* "That's the end of that!"; "No more of that!" (Use caution with *hell.*) □ *To hell with that! That's no excuse!* □ *I've heard stories like that before, and I don't believe any of them. To hell with that.*

to the max *mod.* maximally. (California. See also *max.*) □ *She is happy to the max.* □ *They worked to the max their whole shift.*

to the tune of something *phr.* for the sum of a specific amount of money. □ *The whole thing set me back to the tune of*

$400. ☐ *You will end up paying to the tune of twenty dollars a month.*

toast 1. *n.* a drunkard. ☐ *The old toast stumbled in front of a car.* ☐ *A couple of toasts tried to get us to buy them drinks.* **2.** *mod.* excellent. ☐ *This stuff is toast!* ☐ *Your silks are real toast.* **3.** *mod.* burned; done for. ☐ *If you don't get here in twenty minutes, you're toast.* ☐ *I told him he was toast for not being there.*

toasted *mod.* alcohol intoxicated. ☐ *The chick got toasted on two glasses of cheap white wine.* ☐ *I'm not toasted, just a little breathless.*

today *mod.* now; immediately. (Sarcastic.) ☐ *I want it done, now—today.* ☐ *Come on. Sam. Move it. Today!*

toddle off *in.* to depart; to walk away. ☐ *She said good-bye and toddled off.* ☐ *The old man toddled off somewhere and got lost.*

toddy blossom *n.* a large pimple from too much drinking. (See also *strawberry.*) ☐ *He was sporting a toddy blossom that would be the envy of any bum on skid row.* ☐ *There was nothing she could do to hide her toddy blossom.*

together *mod.* organized. ☐ *I'm not together yet. Lemme call you back.* ☐ *That chick's really got it together.*

toilet mouth See *potty mouth.*

toilet water *n.* beer; draft beer. (Alludes to the term for cologne.) ☐ *This toilet water has me running back and forth to the john.* ☐ *You want another pitcher of toilet water?*

toke [tok] **1.** *n.* a puff of marijuana smoke. (Drugs.) ☐ *After a big toke, he settled back to drift.* ☐ *Harry took a big toke and sighed.* **2.** *tr.* & *in.* to puff a marijuana cigarette. (Drugs.) ☐ *He sat on a stone to toke one before bean time.* ☐ *He tokes for a good bit of every day.* **3.** *n.* a cigarette. ☐ *You got a toke I can bum?* ☐ *I left my tokes in my jacket.* **4.** *in.* to free base. (Drugs.) ☐ *She almost blew herself up toking.* ☐ *They were toking when her mother called on the phone.* **5.** *n.* a token. ☐ *Yeah. Just a little toke of my approval.* ☐ *Nothing much. Just a toke.*

tokus AND **tukkis; tuchus** ['tokəs AND 'tʊkəs] *n.* the buttocks; the *rump.* (Yiddish.) ☐ *She fell right on her tokus!* ☐ *Look at the tukkis on that fat guy.*

tomato *n.* an attractive *girl* or woman. ☐ *There's a nice-looking tomato.* ☐ *A good-looking tomato brought me my change.*

tomcat 1. *n.* a sexually active male; a *stud.* ☐ *Old Fred's getting to be quite a tomcat.* ☐ *His goal in life is to die a tomcat at age ninety.* **2.** *in.* [for a man] to prowl around searching for sex. ☐ *Harry was out tomcatting again last night.* ☐ *He's gonna tomcat around till he catches something.*

tomfoolery ['tɑm'fuləi] *n.* foolishness. ☐ *That's enough of this tomfoolery!* ☐ *The entire evening was devoted to tomfoolery.*

tongue loosener See the following entry.

tongue oil AND **tongue loosener** *n.* liquor. ☐ *She had a little too much tongue oil and was telling all about everybody.* ☐ *Barlowe poured the pigeon another shot of tongue loosener.*

tongue-tied 1. *mod.* unable to speak from fear or confusion. (Standard English.) ☐ *I was tongue-tied and useless.* ☐ *Why do you get tongue-tied in front of a crowd?* **2.** *mod.* alcohol intoxicated. ☐ *He was tongue-tied and couldn't stand up.* ☐ *She's not just tipsy; she's tongue-tied.*

tonic *n.* liquor. ☐ *How about some more tonic?* ☐ *Just a bit of tonic. I'm cutting down.*

tons of something *n.* lots of something. ☐ *We got tons of fried chicken, so help yourself.* ☐ *You are in tons of trouble.*

tonsil bath *n.* liquor; a drink of liquor. ☐ *I could use a little tonsil bath about now.* ☐ *You want some more of that tonsil bath?*

tonsil paint AND **tonsil varnish** *n.* liquor; whiskey. ☐ *This tonsil varnish would take the paint off a barn.* ☐ *Give the man a cup of tonsil paint.*

tonsil varnish See the previous entry.

too much *mod.* overwhelming; excellent. □ *It's wonderful. It's just too much!* □ *You are so kind. This is too much.*

too rich for someone's blood **1.** *mod.* too expensive for one's budget. □ *This hotel is too rich for my blood.* □ *Europe is getting too rich for our blood.* **2.** *mod.* too high in fat content for one's diet. □ *This dessert is too rich for my blood.* □ *Most ice cream is too rich for my blood.*

Toodle(-oo). ['tudl̩('u)] *interj.* "Goodbye." □ *Take it easy. Toodle-oo.* □ *See ya! Toodle!*

tooey See the following entry.

tooie AND **tooey; tuie** ['tui] *n.* a capsule of Tuinal™, a barbiturate. □ *You got any tooies?* □ *The cops saw a few tuies on the sidewalk and made the arrest.*

took See *taken.*

tool **1.** *n.* an earnest student. (Compare to *power tool.*) □ *Of course he's a tool. See the plastic liner in his pocket?* □ *Martin is a tool, and he's proud of it.* **2.** *n.* a dupe; someone who can be victimized easily. □ *They were looking for some tool to drive the getaway car.* □ *Who's the tool with the briefcase?* **3.** *in.* to speed along (in a car). (Compare to *tool around.*) □ *We were tooling along at about seventy-five when the cop spotted us.* □ *I was tooling, and nobody could catch me.*

tool around *in.* to drive or cruise around. (Compare to *tool.*) □ *We tooled around for a while and then rented a horror movie.* □ *Let's tool around on the way home.*

toot **1.** *n.* a *binge;* a drinking spree. □ *Harry's on a toot again.* □ *He's not on one again. It's the same old toot.* **2.** *tr.* & *in.* to drink copiously. □ *She could toot booze from dusk to dawn.* □ *They tooted and tooted till they could toot no more.* **3.** *n.* an emotional *jag* of some kind. □ *She's on a toot about how nobody loves her anymore.* □ *Those toots wore everybody out.* **4.** *n.* a line or dose of cocaine; cocaine. □ *These tootheads get sort of frantic when they can't get a toot.* □ *What do you spend on a toot, anyway?* **5.** *tr.* & *in.* to *snort* a portion of cocaine. □ *She had to leave the office to toot.* □ *She tooted a couple of lines and came back.*

toot one's own horn See *blow one's own horn.*

tooter **1.** *n.* a person on a drinking spree. □ *A couple of tooters were making a lot of noise.* □ *The streets belong to the tooters on New Year's Eve.* **2.** *n.* a drunkard. □ *Hank offered the tooter a drink, which was gratefully accepted, of course.* □ *I think you are turning into a tooter.*

tootle along *in.* to depart. □ *I think I'd better tootle along now.* □ *Nice talking to you. Must tootle along.*

tootonium ['tu'toniəm] *n.* an imaginary, potent type of cocaine. (Drugs. A play on *titanium.*) □ *He called it tootonium. She called it trouble.* □ *You want some real tootonium, babe?*

tootuncommon [tutn̩'kamən] *n.* an imaginary, potent type of cocaine; any potent cocaine. (Drugs. A play on *King Tutankhamen.*) □ *Max laughed when the student asked for tootuncommon.* □ *Which is better, tootonium or tootuncommon?*

top **1.** *tr.* to surpass someone or something. □ *Can you top this one?* □ *I'll try to top your joke.* **2.** *tr.* to kill someone. □ *Max was out to top Bruno.* □ *Bruno was gonna top Max first.* **3.** *n.* the first half of a baseball inning. □ *Wilbur hit a nice double-bagger in the top half of the fourth.* □ *It's the third inning at the top; Wilbur's up.*

top banana **1.** *n.* the lead comedian in a burlesque or vaudeville act. □ *The top banana didn't show up for the gig.* □ *Let me be top banana tonight.* **2.** *n.* the boss; the leader or head of something. (See also *big cheese, big enchilada.*) □ *You'll have to ask the top banana. He's out right now.* □ *Who's top banana around here?*

top brass *n.* the highest leader(s); the boss(es). (Originally military.) □ *The top brass turned thumbs down on the proposal.* □ *You'll have to check it out* *with the top brass. She'll be home around five.*

top dog *n.* the person in charge or in power; a company officer. ☐ *The reporter tried to get hold of one of the top dogs, but couldn't get past the secretary.* ☐ *A top dog from the executive suite read a prepared statement.*

top-drawer *mod.* top-quality. ☐ *Podunk U. is a really top-drawer school.* ☐ *I want to hire a young M.B.A. who's top-drawer.*

top-flight *mod.* of the highest caliber. ☐ *This candy is top-flight in every sense.* ☐ *We are looking for a top-flight manager for our new division.*

top heavy *mod.* heavy-breasted; buxom. ☐ *Tracy gets a little top heavy when she is gaining weight.* ☐ *Who's the top heavy number in the red tent?*

top of the heap *n.* a position superior to everyone else. ☐ *For some reason, Jerry has to be at the top of the heap.* ☐ *She fought her way to the top of the heap and means to stay there.*

top story AND **upper story** *n.* the brain. ☐ *A little weak in the upper story, but other than that, a great guy.* ☐ *He has nothing for a top story.*

topless *mod.* having to do with someone wearing no clothing above the waist, usually a woman. ☐ *The topless places are beginning to dress up a little.* ☐ *The cops closed down the topless joint on Maple Street.*

topsy-boosy See the following entry.

topsy-boozy AND **topsy-boosy** ['tɑpsi'buzi] *mod.* alcohol intoxicated. ☐ *Gary drank until he was topsy-boozy.* ☐ *She was so topsy-boosy she couldn't stand up.*

topsy-turvy ['tɑpsi'tɚvi] **1.** *mod.* upside down; in disarray. ☐ *The whole office is topsy-turvy.* ☐ *He came in and turned everything topsy-turvy.* **2.** *mod.* alcohol intoxicated. ☐ *Four glasses of gin and the jerk was totally topsy-turvy.* ☐ *She was too topsy-turvy to stand up.*

tore (up) AND **torn (up)** **1.** *mod.* distraught; emotionally upset. ☐ *I knew you'd be tore up.* ☐ *Fred's really torn up about the accident.* **2.** *mod.* alcohol or drug intoxicated. ☐ *He wasn't just drunk—he was massively tore up.* ☐ *Boy, was she torn.*

torn (up) See the previous entry.

tornado juice *n.* whiskey; strong whiskey. ☐ *You want another round of tornado juice?* ☐ *This "tornado juice" smells like antifreeze.*

torpedo *n.* a drink containing chloral hydrate; a knockout drink. ☐ *Barlowe signaled the bartender to give the stoolie a torpedo.* ☐ *The stoolie never knew it was a torpedo that wrecked him.*

torqued [torkt] **1.** *mod.* angry; *bent.* ☐ *Sure I was torqued. Who wouldn't be?* ☐ *Now, now! Don't get torqued!* **2.** *mod.* drunk. (A play on *twisted.*) ☐ *Fred was really torqued and trying to pick fights with everyone.* ☐ *Mary gets torqued on just a few drinks.*

toss **1.** *in.* to empty one's stomach; to vomit. ☐ *I was afraid I was going to toss.* ☐ *She tossed right there on the steps and ran away.* **2.** *tr.* to throw something away. ☐ *Toss it. It's no good.* ☐ *I'll toss this one. It's all scratched.* **3.** *tr.* to search someone. (Underworld.) ☐ *The cops tossed him and found nothing.* ☐ *The feds have a special way of tossing somebody for drugs.* **4.** *tr.* to drink some liquor; to take a drink of liquor. ☐ *He tossed some whiskey and left.* ☐ *Toss that drink, and let's get out of here!*

toss in the sponge See *throw in the towel.*

toss one's cookies AND **throw one's cookies; toss one's lunch; toss one's tacos** *tr.* to empty one's stomach; to vomit. ☐ *Right then and there, with no warning, he tossed his cookies.* ☐ *If you feel like tossing your cookies, please leave quietly.* ☐ *Fred stepped over to the bushes and raucously tossed his tacos.*

toss one's lunch See the previous entry.

toss one's tacos See *toss one's cookies.*

toss something off **1.** *tr.* to do something quickly without much time or effort. ☐ *It was no big deal. I tossed it off in thirty minutes.* 🅃 *We can toss off the entire* *order in—let's say—three hours.* **2.** *tr.* to drink something quickly. ☐ *He tossed it off and ordered another.* 🅃 *She tossed off a scotch in one big swig.* **3.** *tr.* to ignore criticism; to ignore defeat or a setback. ☐ *She just tossed it off like nothing had happened.* 🅃 *How could she just toss off such a horrible thing?* **4.** *tr.* to resist or fight off a disease. ☐ *I caught a little cold, but tossed it off right away.* 🅃*I can't toss off these viruses like I used to.*

toss-up *n.* a matter of chance. (As predictable as the outcome of the toss of a coin.) ☐ *Nobody knew what to do. It was a toss-up.* ☐ *Who knows what will happen? It's a toss-up.*

totalled **1.** *mod.* wrecked; damaged beyond repair. (From *totally wrecked.*) ☐ *The car was totalled. There was nothing that could be saved.* ☐ *There's a place in the city that will buy totalled cars.* **2.** *mod.* alcohol intoxicated. ☐ *Tom was too totalled to talk.* ☐ *Jed was totalled and couldn't see to pay the bill.*

totally *mod.* absolutely; completely. (Standard. Achieves slang status through overuse.) ☐ *How totally gross!* ☐ *This place is totally beige.*

totally clueless *mod.* ignorant (of something). (See also *cluelessness.*) ☐ *Everybody was totally clueless as to what to do.* ☐ *Sorry, I'm totally clueless as to what to do.*

tote **1.** *n.* someone who abstains from alcohol. (From *teetotal.*) ☐ *I'm not a tote, but I do have a limit—rather low by your standards.* ☐ *Have a drink, or are you still a tote?* **2.** *n.* a small portion of cannabis. (Drugs.) ☐ *The cops found a tote when they tossed Max, but that was all.* ☐ *How much do you want for just a tote?* **3.** *n.* a small pipe for smoking cannabis. (Drugs.) ☐ *Her father found a tote in her room and really hit the ceiling.* ☐ *The cops found a tote in her purse and called in her father.*

touch **1.** *n.* a likely target for begging; someone who is asked for a loan. (See also *soft touch.*) ☐ *He was just the kind of touch we were looking for, not too bright and not too poor.* ☐ *The touch looked around him and gave the stiff two-bits.* **2.** *n.* a request for money (from a beggar); a request for a loan. ☐ *I ignored the touch and walked on by.* ☐ *Here comes Fred, and he looks like he wants to make a touch.* **3.** *tr.* to ask someone for a loan. ☐ *He touched me for a hundred bucks.* ☐ *The wino touched Martin for a fiver.* **4.** *n.* a small portion of something to eat or drink. (Folksy.) ☐ *I'll have just a touch. I'm on a diet, you know.* ☐ *Can I have another touch of that pie, please?* **5.** *tr.* to deal with or handle someone or something. (Usually in the negative.) ☐ *I wouldn't touch that problem.* ☐ *Mr. Wilson is a real pain, and I wouldn't touch his account. Find somebody else to handle it.*

touch a sore point *tr.* to mention something that upsets someone. ☐ *I touched a sore point with Larry when I mentioned taxes.* ☐ *That touched a real sore point with me.*

touch and go *mod.* chancy. ☐ *It was touch and go for a while, but we are out of the woods now.* ☐ *The place was in a real tizzy. Everything was touch and go.*

touch base (with someone) *tr.* to make contact with someone. ☐ *I wanted to touch base with you just in case something had gone wrong.* ☐ *Let's touch base on Wednesday and check on things.*

touched **1.** *mod.* flattered; honored. (Standard English.) ☐ *I was touched by your comments.* ☐ *We were both touched by your thoughtfulness.* **2.** *mod.* alcohol intoxicated. ☐ *She was acting a little touched, but we didn't smell anything on her breath.* ☐ *Jed is a mite touched, wouldn't you say? Can't talk, walk, or see.*

tough break *n.* a bit of bad luck. ☐ *Tough break. Sorry about that.* ☐ *You've had a lot of tough breaks lately.*

tough cookie *n.* a tough person. ☐ *He's a tough cookie, but I can handle him.* ☐ *There was a tough cookie in here this morning who demanded to see the manager.*

tough cookies See *tough luck.*

tough customer *n.* someone who is difficult to deal with. □ *Some of those bikers are really tough customers.* □ *Bruno is a tough customer. Just keep away from him.*

tough egg to crack AND **tough nut to crack** *n.* a person or thing that is hard to figure out or hard to deal with. □ *This problem is a tough nut to crack.* □ *I wish Jill wasn't such a tough nut to crack.*

tough guy *n.* a tough man; a man who might be part of the underworld. □ *He was your typical tough guy—jutting chin, gruff voice—but he was just our decorator checking up on the drapes.* □ *So, you want to be a tough guy, huh?*

tough luck AND **tough cookies** *interj.* "That is too bad." □ *Tough luck, but that's the way the cookie crumbles.* □ *That's too bad, tough cookies.*

tough nut to crack See *tough egg to crack.*

tough row to hoe *n.* a difficult task to carry out; a heavy set of burdens. □ *It's a tough row to hoe, but hoe it you will.* □ *This is not an easy task. This is a tough row to hoe.*

tough something out *tr.* to carry on with something despite difficulties or setbacks. □ *Sorry, you'll just have to tough it out.* □ *I think I can tough it out for another month.*

Tough titties! See the following entry.

Tough titty! AND **Tough titties!** *exclam.* "That's too bad!" (Crude. Potentially offensive. Use only with discretion.) □ *Tough titty! I told you it wouldn't be easy.* □ *So you missed the bus. Tough titty!*

tourist trap *n.* a place set up to lure tourists in to spend money. (Can be a shop, a town, or a whole country.) □ *It looked like a tourist trap, so we didn't even stop the car.* □ *What keeps these tourists traps going?*

townie ['tauni] *n.* a permanent (non-student) resident of a college town. □ *The townies get upset when we make a lot of noise on Sundays.* □ *A couple of townies won the bicycle race.*

toxic waste dump *n.* a horrible person or place. □ *Frank, stop acting like a toxic waste dump and do as you're asked.* □ *Let's get out of this toxic waste dump.*

toxicated AND **toxy** ['tɑksəkedəd AND 'tɑksi] *mod.* alcohol intoxicated. □ *He was just a tad toxy, but no one in the audience could tell.* □ *The boss showed up toxicated after lunch and shocked the secretaries.*

toxy See the previous entry.

TP AND **teepee** **1.** *n.* "toilet paper." (The abbreviation is an initialism.) □ *There's no T.P. in the john.* □ *Don't forget to get teepee at the store.* **2.** *tr.* to festoon the trees and shrubbery of a residential yard with toilet paper. (A teenage prank.) □ *All the swimmers' houses get teepeed the night before a meet.* □ *Who teepeed my spruce tree?*

track **1.** *in.* [for a laser beam, a phonograph stylus, a tape head, etc.] to successfully transfer information to or from a recording medium. □ *Something here won't track. Must be the stylus.* □ *This thing won't track. What's wrong?* **2.** *in.* [for a person] to make sense. (Usually in the negative.) □ *She wasn't tracking. There was no sense in trying to talk to her before she came out of it.* □ *I gave up on the lecturer. He wasn't tracking.* **3.** *in.* to coincide; to agree; to jibe. □ *These two things don't track. I don't know what's wrong.* □ *Your figures don't track with mine. What's wrong?*

trad [træd] *mod.* "traditional." □ *The approach is sort of trad, but so what?* □ *A more trad style might make the grown-ups more comfortable.*

traf [træf] *n.* a release of intestinal gas. (This is *fart* spelled backwards. Use caution with the topic.) □ *Who let the traf?* □ *This place smells like a traf.*

tragic-magic *n.* heroin. □ *This tragic-magic, which has swept over the land, has taken too many of our youth.* □ *This tragic-magic stuff has hurt lots of my friends.*

trammeled ['træmḷd] *mod.* alcohol intoxicated. (Collegiate.) □ *Jim came* *home trammeled and was sick on the carpet.* ☐ *Wow, is she trammeled!*

tranny ['træni] *n.* an automobile transmission. ☐ *It looks like you get a new tranny, and I get 900 bucks.* ☐ *What kind of tranny does that baby have?*

trans [trænts] *n.* an automobile. (From *transportation.*) ☐ *I don't have any trans —I can't get myself anywhere.* ☐ *What are you using for trans these days?*

trap 1. *n.* the mouth. (Crude.) ☐ *Shut your trap!* ☐ *Put this in your trap and chew it up.* **2.** *n.* a low place; a *dive.* ☐ *I want out of this trap!* ☐ *This trap is a mess. Clean it up!*

trash 1. *tr.* to throw something away. ☐ *Trash this stuff. Nobody will ever use it.* ☐ *I'll take it. Don't trash it.* **2.** *n.* a low, worthless person; worthless people. ☐ *The guy is trash! Stay away from him.* ☐ *Running around with that trash—no wonder he's in trouble.* **3.** *tr.* to vandalize something. ☐ *Somebody trashed the statue with spray paint.* ☐ *Who trashed my room?* **4.** *n.* an act of vandalism. ☐ *Who quarterbacked the bus trash?* ☐ *The trash the other night was a real travesty.* **5.** *tr.* to beat, as in a ball game. ☐ *You trashed us this game, but watch out next season!* ☐ *The Jets trashed the Wallbangers, 48-13.* **6.** *tr.* to libel someone. ☐ *He seemed content to trash the mayor.* ☐ *Who is the chick who was trashing Max in the newspapers?*

trash mouth *n.* someone who uses obscene language. ☐ *Shut up, trash mouth.* ☐ *Some trash mouth is making everybody mad over in the park.*

trashed *mod.* alcohol or drug intoxicated. (Collegiate.) ☐ *They were trashed beyond help.* ☐ *Let's all get trashed and raid the girl's dorm.*

trashy *mod.* crude; obscene. ☐ *What a trashy movie!* ☐ *Cut out the trashy talk, you guys.*

trekkie ['trɛki] *n.* a fan of *Star Trek,* the television series and the movies. ☐ *There is a convention of trekkies in Milwaukee this weekend.* ☐ *The trekkies seem to have their own language.*

trial balloon *n.* a test of someone's reaction. ☐ *It was just a trial balloon, and it didn't work.* ☐ *The trial balloon was a great success.*

trick on someone *in.* to deceive someone. ☐ *What are you doing? Are you tricking on me?* ☐ *Mary is always tricking on people and now nobody trusts her.*

tricks of the trade *n.* special skills and knowledge associated with any trade or profession. ☐ *I know a few tricks of the trade that make things easier.* ☐ *I learned the tricks of the trade from my uncle.*

trigger 1. *n.* a hired gunman. (Underworld.) ☐ *Rocko was a mob trigger for a while.* ☐ *Get your triggers outa here—then we can talk.* **2.** *tr.* to start something; to set something off. ☐ *The noise triggered an avalanche.* ☐ *One little thing triggered that blowup, and I want to find out what it is.*

trigger-happy *mod.* eager to fire a gun; eager to shoot someone or something. ☐ *Rocko is sort of trigger-happy. Watch out.* ☐ *Ask your trigger-happy hunters to be careful this year.*

trip 1. *n.* a prison sentence; a trip *up the river.* (Underworld.) ☐ *Yeah, me and Lefty both was on a little trip for a few years.* ☐ *I had a short trip, so what?* **2.** *n.* a *high* from a drug. (Drugs.) ☐ *Me and Sid went on a little trip.* ☐ *The trip was great, but once was enough.* **3.** *in.* to experience a *high* from a drug, especially *L.S.D.* ☐ *Don't bother Max. He's tripping.* ☐ *He trips about every other day.* **4.** *n.* a bad drug experience. (Drugs.) ☐ *Boy, did I ever have a trip with that stuff!* ☐ *What a trip! I thought I would die.* **5.** *n.* an annoying person or thing. ☐ *Class was a trip today.* ☐ *She is such a trip.* **6.** *in.* to leave. ☐ *I gotta trip, man.* ☐ *Time to trip. See ya.*

tripe 1. *n.* nonsense. ☐ *I don't want to hear any more of that tripe.* ☐ *That's just tripe. Pay no attention.* **2.** *n.* a bad performance; something worthless. ☐ *I know tripe when I see tripe, and that was tripe.* ☐ *The reviewer thought your play was tripe.*

triple 1. *n.* a large alcoholic drink containing three measures of hard liquor. □ *It was a hard day. Make it a triple, John.* □ *One triple, but no more. You're cutting down, remember?* 2. See *triple-bagger.*

triple-bagger 1. AND **triple** *n.* a hit in baseball that gets the batter to third base. □ *Wilbur connected for another triple-bagger in the fifth.* □ *It's a triple for Wilbur!* 2. *n.* a person whose ugly face is so frightful that three bags are required to conceal it. (Crude. See also *double-bagger, coyote-ugly.*) □ *That guy is just a triple-bagger.* □ *He's worse than a triple-bagger—if that's possible.*

triple whammy ['trɪpl̩ 'ʍæmi] *n.* a powerful treatment; a powerful shock. □ *The market crash, the trade figures, and the death of the secretary of defense was a powerful triple whammy in Washington politics this week.* □ *The tax bill served as a triple whammy to the family purse.*

tripped out *mod.* great; excellent. □ *This party is really tripped out, right?* □ *We had a tripped out time in class today. The teacher brought his pet rabbit.*

trots *n.* diarrhea; a case of diarrhea. (Always with *the.*) □ *I got the trots and can't go out tonight.* □ *There's a lot of the trots going around.*

trotters 1. *n.* pig's feet. □ *Trotters are okay if you can't tell what they are.* □ *Pickled trotters are good in the summer.* 2. *n.* the feet. □ *My trotters are sort of aching.* □ *Sit down and give your trotters a rest.*

trounce [traunts] *tr.* to beat someone; to outscore someone. (Sports.) □ *They really trounced us.* □ *Western trounced Eastern for the tenth year in a row.*

trump something up *tr.* to promote or boost something. □ *They think they have to trump something up to get people to see it.* Ⓣ *They trumped up the movie so much that many people were disappointed when it finally came out.* (More at *trumped up.*)

trumped up 1. *mod.* heavily promoted; overly praised. □ *I don't care for trumped up stuff like that movie.* □ *That movie was so trumped up. I expected to see something much better than it turned out to be.* 2. *mod.* made up; contrived. □ *They put Larry in the slammer on some trumped up charge.* □ *It was a silly, trumped up idea. Just forget it.*

trumpet spider See *barking spider.*

Trust me! *exclam.* "Believe me!"; "Honestly!" □ *It's true! Trust me!* □ *He actually said it just like Tom told you. Trust me!*

try someone back (again) *tr.* to call someone back on the telephone (again) later. □ *I'll try her back later.* □ *When should I try back?*

(T)sup? ['(t)səp] *interrog.* "What's up?"; "What is happening?"; "What have you been doing?" □ *Hi! Tsup?* □ TONY: *Sup?* TIFFANY: *Like, nothing.*

tub of guts See the following entry.

tub of lard AND **tub of guts** *n.* a fat person. (Cruel. Also a rude term of address.) □ *Who's that tub of guts who just came in?* □ *That tub of lard can hardly get through the door.*

tube 1. *n.* a can of beer. (See also *crack a tube.*) □ *Toss me a tube, will ya?* □ *How many tubes do you think we ought to get for tonight?* 2. *n.* the inner curve of a tall wave. (Surfing. See also *tubular.*) □ *I'm waiting for the best tube.* □ *A good tube will do, won't it?* 3. *in.* to fail; to *go down the tube(s).* □ *The whole plan tubed at the last minute.* □ *I tubed, and I'm sorry.* (More at *tube it.*) 4. *n.* a television set. □ *What's on the tube tonight?* □ *The tube is in the shop, so I read a book.* 5. *n.* a cigarette. □ *You got a tube I can bum?* □ *There's a pack of tubes in my jacket.*

tube it *tr.* to fail a test. (See also *tube.*) □ *I tubed it, and I'll probably get a D in the course.* □ *I was afraid I'd tube it, so I studied my head off.*

tube steak *n.* a frankfurter or a wiener. □ *Are we having tube steak again for dinner?* □ *I could live on tube steak. Nothing is better!*

tubed *mod.* alcohol intoxicated. (See also *tube*.) ☐ *They were both tubed and giggling.* ☐ *You really look tubed, man!*

tubular *mod.* excellent. (Surfing and later general youth slang. Having to do with a *tube* [wave] that is good to surf in.) ☐ *That pizza was totally tubular!* ☐ *This whole week is, like, tubular.*

tuchus See *tokus*.

tude [tud] *n.* a bad "attitude." ☐ *Hey, you really got a tude, dude.* ☐ *Are you pulling a tude with me?*

tuie See *tooie*.

tukkis See *tokus*.

tunage ['tunɪdʒ] *n.* music; *tunes*. ☐ *Why don't you come over and we'll do some tunage?* ☐ *My stereo is down and I'm running a tunage deficit.*

tune in (to something) *in.* to become alert to something. ☐ *She tuned in to the comments about acid rain.* ☐ *When I heard my name, I tuned in.*

tune out *in.* to begin to ignore everything. ☐ *I got bored and tuned out.* ☐ *The entire class had tuned out, so no one heard the teacher ask the question.*

tune someone or something out *tr.* to ignore or disregard someone or something. ☐ *I heard enough and tuned her out.* 🅃 *I managed to tune out the constant clamor in the streets.*

tuned *mod.* tipsy; drunk. ☐ *Wally was a little tuned so Sally swiped his car keys.* ☐ *Tom was too tuned to stand up, let alone drive.*

tuned in *mod.* aware; up-to-date. ☐ *Jan is tuned in and alert to what is going on around her.* ☐ *Hey, Jill! Get tuned in, why don't you?*

tunes *n.* a record; a record album; music in general. (See also *tunage*.) ☐ *I got some new tunes. Wanna come over and listen?* ☐ *The old tunes are good enough for me.*

turd [tɚd] (Potentially offensive. Use only with discretion. Colloquial.) **1.** *n.* a lump of fecal material. ☐ *There is a dog turd on the lawn.* ☐ *There are some little mouse turds in the kitchen.* **2.** *n.* a wretched person. (Also a provocative term of address.) ☐ *You stupid turd!* ☐ *The guy acts like a real turd most of the time.*

turf *n.* (one's) ground or territory. ☐ *When you're on my turf, you do what I say—savvy?* ☐ *This is my turf, and what I say goes.*

turistas [tu'ristɑs] *n.* diarrhea; a case of diarrhea. (From Spanish.) ☐ *Nobody ever died of the turistas—right away, anyway.* ☐ *Turistas can be very unpleasant.*

turkey **1.** *n.* a failure; a sham. ☐ *This whole business is a turkey.* ☐ *The turkey at the town theater closed on its first night.* **2.** *n.* a stupid person. ☐ *Who's the turkey who put the scallops in the scalloped potatoes?* ☐ *You are such a turkey!*

turn **1.** *in.* to go over to the other side, as with a spy or a criminal turning into an informer. (Underworld.) ☐ *Is there a chance that Max would turn?* ☐ *Max turn? Ha!* **2.** *tr.* to corrupt someone. ☐ *It was the booze that turned him.* ☐ *Max was trying to turn a young kid.*

turn a trick *tr.* to perform an act of prostitution. (Use caution with the topic.) ☐ *She can turn a trick and be on the streets again in six minutes flat.* ☐ *She's upstairs, turning a trick.*

turn around AND **turn over** *in.* [for something] to undergo a major, dynamic change. ☐ *Things turned around for Willard and went okay for a while.* ☐ *When life turned over and things went more smoothly, Frank was happier.*

turn belly up AND **go belly up** **1.** *in.* to fail. ☐ *I sort of felt that the whole thing would go belly up, and I was right.* ☐ *The computer—on its last legs anyway—turned belly up right in the middle of an important job.* **2.** *in.* to die. (As a fish does when it dies.) ☐ *The cat was friendly for a moment before she turned belly up.* ☐ *Every fish in Greg's tank went belly up last night.*

turn in AND **roll in** *in.* to go to bed. ☐ *Well, it's about time to turn in.* ☐ *I can't wait to roll in tonight.*

turn-off *n.* something that repels someone. ☐ *The movie was a turn-off. I couldn't stand it.* ☐ *What a turn-off!*

turn on 1. *in.* to become interested or excited. ☐ *She turned on when she heard her name called.* ☐ *He really turned on when he saw the cake.* **2.** *in.* to take a drug. (Drugs.) ☐ *Pete just can't wait to light up and turn on.* ☐ *He will turn on with anybody at the drop of a hat.* **3.** *n.* someone or something that excites someone. (Usually **turn-on.**) ☐ *The concert was a real turn-on.* ☐ *David can be a real turn on when he's in a good mood.*

turn on a dime *in.* to turn sharply; to turn in a small radius. ☐ *This baby will turn on a dime.* ☐ *A car that will turn on a dime at high speed without turning turtle is what I want.*

turn on the waterworks *in.* to begin to cry. ☐ *His lower lip was quivering, and I knew he was going to turn on the waterworks.* ☐ *Now, now! Don't turn on the waterworks. Cheer up!*

turn on, tune in, drop out *phr.* a slogan promoting the use of *L.S.D.* among young people. (Drugs.) ☐ *The key phrase in the heyday of acid was "turn on, tune in, drop out."* ☐ *Millions heard "turn on, tune in, drop out" and did just that.*

turn one's toes up *tr.* to die. ☐ *I'm too young to turn my toes up.* 🅃 *The cat turned up its toes right after church. Ah, the power of prayer.*

turn onto someone or something *in.* to become interested in someone or something. ☐ *Jeff turned onto electronics at the age of fourteen.* ☐ *I tried to get her to turn onto me, but she could only think of John.*

turn over 1. *in.* to get off of drugs. (Like *turn over a new leaf.*) ☐ *He wanted to turn over, but just couldn't.* ☐ *There is a clinic on Maple Street that'll help heads turn over.* **2.** See *turn around.*

turn someone off *tr.* to dull someone's interest in someone or something. ☐ *The prof turned me off to the subject.* 🅃 *The preacher set out to turn off the congregation to sin.*

turn someone on *tr.* to excite or interest someone. (See also *turn on.*) ☐ *Fast music with a good beat turns me on.* 🅃 *That stuff doesn't turn on anyone.*

turn someone or something upside down *tr.* to upset someone or something; to confuse someone or something. ☐ *We turned his place upside down, but never found the gun.* ☐ *The whole business turned me upside down. It'll take days to recover.*

turn someone out *tr.* to introduce someone to drugs, prostitution, homosexuality, etc. (Underworld.) ☐ *Mac tried to turn the kid out.* 🅃 *There are laws against turning out people the way Max was doing.*

turn someone's stomach *tr.* to nauseate someone. ☐ *That stuff turns my stomach. Do I have to eat it?* ☐ *Whatever that smell is, it's turning my stomach.*

turn someone's water off *tr.* to deflate someone; to silence someone. ☐ *He said you were stupid, huh? Well, I guess that turns your water off!* 🅃 *That really turned off her water.*

turn tail (and run) *tr.* to flee; to run away in fright. ☐ *I couldn't just turn tail and run, but I wasn't going to fight that monster either.* ☐ *Sometimes turning tail is the only sensible thing to do.*

turn thumbs down (on someone or something) *tr.* to reject someone or something. ☐ *The board turned thumbs down on Rocko's application for parole.* ☐ *The committee examined the proposal and turned thumbs down.*

turn turtle *in.* to turn over, as with a ship. ☐ *The old dog finally turned turtle, and that was the end.* ☐ *The car struck a pole and turned turtle.*

turn up one's nose at someone or something *tr.* to show disdain or disgust at someone or something. ☐ *This is good, wholesome food. Don't turn your nose up at it.* 🅃 *She turned up her nose at Max, which was probably a good idea.*

turned off *mod.* uninterested. □ *I'm sort of turned off to stuff like that these days. Part of getting older, I guess.* □ *I can't pay attention if I'm turned off, now can I?*

turned on 1. *mod.* made alert to what is new and exciting. □ *I want to hire someone who's really turned on—a real comer.* □ *A young, turned on M.B.A. would be just right.* 2. *mod.* drug intoxicated. (Drugs.) □ *Jerry's turned on by noon—every day.* □ *The kid over there looks sort of turned on. Let's go talk to him a bit.*

turnout *n.* an audience that has assembled for some purpose. □ *How was the turnout at the benefit?* □ *The turnout was great. We had a full house.*

turps AND **terps** [tɚps] *n.* liquor. (From *turpentine*.) □ *Don't forget to stop at the comfort station and get the turps.* □ *You got enough terps for the party?*

tux [təks] *n.* a tuxedo. □ *Do I have to wear a tux?* □ *Rent your tux well in advance.*

tweak [twik] *tr.* to adjust something slightly. □ *I just need to tweak this program a little bit; then I'll be with you.* □ *Tweak the tuner a little and see if you can get that station just a little bit clearer.*

tweased [twizd] *mod.* alcohol intoxicated. □ *Jim came in a little tweased last night.* □ *How tweased can anybody get on two beers?*

tweeked [twikt] *mod.* alcohol intoxicated. (Collegiate.) □ *They're not really bombed—just tweeked a little.* □ *Fred was too tweeked to stand up.*

twenty-twenty hindsight AND **20/20 hindsight** *n.* an ability to figure out what one should have done after it is too late to do it. □ *Everybody has twenty-twenty hindsight!* □ *Your 20/20 hindsight is just great.*

twerp See *twirp.*

twiddle one's thumbs *tr.* to do nothing; to wait nervously, playing with one's fingers. □ *I sat twiddling my thumbs while you were out doing I don't know what all!* □ *Don't just sit home twiddling your thumbs.*

twinkie [ˈtwɪŋki] *n.* a cute, teenage *girl.* (California.) □ *The mall up from the beach is usually wall-to-wall twinkies.* □ *These twinkies ought to be a little more grown up than they seem to be.*

twirp AND **twerp** [twɚp] *n.* an annoying runt of a person. (Also a term of address.) □ *Look, you twirp, get out!* □ *Some little twerp threatened to kick me in the shin.*

twist *n.* a *girl;* a woman. (Underworld. Possibly rhyming slang "twist and twirl = girl.") □ *This good-looking twist comes over to the table and asks Lefty if he'd like to dance.* □ *He says "yes," and the twist says, "Go ahead, I bet it's a scream!"*

twist (slowly) in the wind *in.* to suffer the agony of some punishment, such as hanging. (Figurative only.) □ *I'll see you twist in the wind for trying to frustrate this investigation.* □ *The prosecutor was determined that Max would twist slowly in the wind for the crime.*

twist someone's arm *tr.* to pressure someone. □ *I had to twist her arm a little, but she agreed.* □ *Do I have to twist your arm, or will you cooperate?*

twisted 1. *mod.* alcohol intoxicated. □ *She was so twisted she couldn't see.* □ *That chick is really twisted bad.* 2. *mod.* suffering from drug withdrawal. (Drugs.) □ *Frank was twisted and hurting bad.* □ *When you're twisted, your head spins, and you feel like screaming.*

twister 1. *n.* a key. (Underworld.) □ *You got the twister for this joint?* □ *Bruno snatched the jailer's twisters and waited until midnight to try something.* 2. *n.* a tornado. □ *A twister touched down yesterday at an isolated farm seventy miles north of Adamsville.* □ *The twister didn't damage any homes.* 3. *n.* a drunken spree. (See also *bender.*) □ *Harry's off on a twister again.* □ *Not again. It's the same old twister.*

twit 1. *n.* a nervous or frantic state. □ *The twit I was in made me seem sort of* *silly, I'm afraid.* □ *My confused state became a serious twit, and I didn't know what to do.* **2.** *n.* a stupid person. (Also a term of address.) □ *What a yuppie twit!* □ *Hey, you twit, get off my lawn!*

two-bit *mod.* cheap; small-time. □ *Max is just a two-bit pusher. I want Mr. Big.* □ *I'm tired of your two-bit efforts to run this office.*

two-bits *n.* twenty-five cents; a quarter coin. □ *Can I bum two-bits for the phone?* □ *Here's two-bits for your piggy bank.*

two-by-four *mod.* small. □ *A two-by-four office with a chair and a desk was where Barlowe hung out.* □ *I can't stand living in this two-by-four room!*

two fingers *n.* a measurement of liquor in a glass. (Compare to *three fingers.*) □ *I'll take two fingers of that tiger milk, John.* □ *Just two fingers tonight, John?*

two-fisted drinker *n.* a heavy drinker; someone who drinks with both hands. □ *Harry was a two-fisted drinker, a cave man, and a lady-killer.* □ *The world is filled with guys who aspire to be two-fisted drinkers.*

two shakes of a lamb's tail *mod.* quickly; rapidly. □ *I'll be there in two shakes of a lamb's tail.* □ *In two shakes of a lamb's tail, the entire pile of bricks had collapsed.*

two sheets to the wind See *three sheets in the wind.*

two-time *tr.* to deceive one's lover. □ *Sam wouldn't two-time Martha. He just wouldn't!* □ *Sam would and did two-time Martha!*

two-time loser *n.* a confirmed *loser.* □ *Poor Max is a two-time loser.* □ *Martin is a two-time loser, or at least he looks like one.*

two-timer *n.* one who deceives one's lover. □ *Sam just isn't my idea of the typical two-timer.* □ *Of course not. Two-timers rarely look like two-timers.*

two umlauts ['tu 'umlɑuts] *n.* a Löwenbräu (brand) beer. □ *I'll take a two umlauts.* □ *Calling a beer "two umlauts" is the most contrived bit of slang I have ever heard of.*

two-way street *n.* a reciprocal situation. □ *This is a two-way street, you know. You will have to help me someday in return.* □ *Friendship is a two-way street.*

twofer ['tufɚ] *n.* an item that is selling two for the price of one. □ *Here's a good deal—a twofer—only $7.98.* □ *Everything is this store is a twofer. I only want one of these. Do I have to bring a friend who wants one, too?*

type *n.* a combining form indicating a specified type of person. □ *He's a cave man type. You know, sort of hairy and smelly.* □ *Ted's the brainy type, but has no guts.*

U

ugly as sin *mod.* very ugly. ☐ *This car's as ugly as sin, but it's cheap and dependable.* ☐ *My old hound dog is ugly as sin but faithful as the dickens.*

uke AND **yuke** [juk] **1.** *in.* to empty one's stomach; to vomit. (Collegiate. Compare to *puke.*) ☐ *I think somebody yuked in the back seat, Tom.* ☐ *My friends wouldn't uke in my car!* **2.** *n.* vomit. (Collegiate.) ☐ *That is uke on the floor, isn't it?* ☐ *Tell me that the stuff in the back seat isn't uke!*

ump [əmp] *n.* an "umpire." ☐ *The ump was gonna get killed if he didn't open his eyes.* ☐ *The ump has a pretty rough job.*

umpteen ['əmptin] *mod.* many; innumerable. ☐ *I've told you umpteen times not to feed the cat right out of the can.* ☐ *There are umpteen ways to do this right. Can you manage to do one of them?*

umpteenth See the following entry.

umpty-umpth AND **umpteenth** ['əmpti-'əmpθ AND 'əmp'tintθ] *mod.* thousandth, billionth, zillionth, etc. (Represents some very large, but indefinite number.) ☐ *This is the umpty-umpth time I've told you to keep your dog out of my yard.* ☐ *This is the umpteenth meeting of the joint conference committee, but still there is no budget.*

Uncle nab *n.* a policeman. ☐ *Uncle nab is coming. Look sharp!* ☐ *Watch out for Uncle nab. He's been asking about you.*

Uncle (Sam) AND **Uncle Sugar** **1.** *n.* the personification of the U.S. ☐ *Uncle Sugar wants a little more of your money this year.* ☐ *Tell Uncle to spend a little less.* **2.** *n.* a federal agent; federal agents. ☐ *The cops called in Uncle Sam to help in the investigation.* ☐ *Uncle has some pretty strong ideas about who's in charge of this investigation.*

Uncle Sugar See the previous entry.

Uncle Whiskers See *Mr. Whiskers.*

uncool *mod. square;* dull and orthodox. ☐ *Oh, what an uncool weirdo!* ☐ *This place is uncool. Let's cruise.*

under someone's thumb *mod.* under someone's control. ☐ *You can't keep your kids under your thumb all their lives.* ☐ *I don't want all this under my thumb. I have to delegate a lot of it.*

under the affluence of incohol *mod.* alcohol intoxicated. (A deliberate spoonerism on *under the influence of alcohol.*) ☐ *Perhaps I am under the affluence of incohol just a little bit.* ☐ *You are very, very much under the affluence of incohol, as you have so aptly put it.*

under the gun *mod.* under pressure; under scrutiny. ☐ *I've been under the gun on this one long enough.* ☐ *They've got the boss under the gun to get this thing wound up by Saturday.*

under the table **1.** *mod.* alcohol intoxicated. ☐ *Jed was under the table by midnight.* ☐ *By 3:00 in the morning, everyone was under the table.* **2.** *mod.* secret; clandestine. (This is hyphenated before a nominal.) ☐ *It was strictly an under-the-table deal.* ☐ *The mayor made a few bucks under the table, too.*

under the weather **1.** *mod.* ill. ☐ *I feel sort of under the weather today.* ☐ *Whatever I ate for lunch is making me feel a bit under the weather.* **2.** *mod.* alcohol intoxicated. ☐ *Daddy's under the weather* *again.* □ *Wally's just a tad under the weather.*

under the wire *mod.* at the very last minute. □ *I got it in just under the wire.* □ *It was in under the wire. Another ten minutes and it would not have counted.*

under wraps *mod.* (held) in secret. □ *We kept it under wraps until after the election.* □ *The plan we had under wraps had to be scrapped anyway.*

underpinnings *n.* the legs. □ *He has good underpinnings—ought to be able to run faster.* □ *With underpinnings like that, he ought to be able to win the marathon.*

understanding *n.* the feet. (A pun. Always singular.) □ *The boy has a good understanding. Really big gunboats, in fact.* □ *I always had a good understanding—even when I was a kid.*

underwater basket weaving *n.* an imaginary, very easy high school or college course. □ *If I can just find a course in underwater basket weaving, I'll have an easy semester.* □ *Mary majored in underwater basket weaving.*

underwhelm *tr. & in.* to fail to impress (someone). □ *Your talents simply underwhelm me.* □ *As we were being underwhelmed by a buxom soprano, my thoughts drifted to more pleasant matters.* □ *We know you tried, but you just underwhelm.*

undies *n.* underclothing; underpants, especially women's. □ *I like red undies.* □ *Where are my clean undies?*

unearthly *mod.* weird; terrible. □ *What was that unearthly noise?* □ *There was an unearthly smell coming out of the kitchen.* □ *That's not unearthly!*

unflappable *mod.* not subject to distraction; imperturbable. □ *Isn't he great? Truly unflappable.* □ *She is totally unflappable.* □ *I wish I was that unflappable.*

ungodly *mod.* horrendous; inconceivable. □ *What is that ungodly noise?* □ *What do you want at this ungodly hour?*

unit [ˈjunət] *n.* a gadget. □ *Now, take one of the red units—put the copper strip in the slot—place the whole thing in this larger unit—and you're done.* □ *Hand me that unit on the thingy there.*

units See *(parental) units.*

unk-jay *n.* dope; *junk.* (Underworld. Pig Latin for *junk.*) □ *The creep deals in unk-jay, you know—narcotics.* □ *Stay away from the unk-jay.*

unlax [ənˈlæks] *in.* to unwind and relax. □ *I just can't wait to get home and unlax.* □ *Unlax, man. Take it easy.*

unload *tr.* to get rid of someone or something. □ *We're gonna unload all the cats and dogs during the Christmas rush.* □ *Lemme unload this dame, and then we can go out and have a little fun.*

unreal *mod.* unbelievable. □ *Your hairdo is so yummy—almost unreal.* □ *Who started this unreal argument?*

up 1. *mod.* happy; cheery; not depressed; upbeat. □ *I'm up today. Let's celebrate.* □ *This is not an up party. Let's cruise.* **2.** *tr.* to increase something. □ *She tried to up the price on me, thinking I wouldn't notice.* □ *The bank upped its rates again.* **3.** *in.* to take a stimulant drug. □ *She has to up every morning.* □ *Ted upped before going in to take the test.*

up a creek See *up the creek (without a paddle).*

up a storm *mod.* with an enthusiastic spirit. (Note syntax in examples. Usually with *sing, dance, talk, blow, play.*) □ *We talked up a storm until past midnight.* □ *Can't she dance up a storm?*

up a tree 1. *mod.* confused; without an answer to a problem; in difficulty. □ *This whole business has me up a tree.* □ *I'm up a tree, and I need some help.* **2.** *mod.* alcohol intoxicated. □ *Only two glasses of booze and he was up a tree for sure.* □ *My buddy here is up a tree and needs a crash for the night.*

up against it *mod.* having a personal crisis; having a financial crisis. □ *This is my bad season. I'm really up against* *it.* □ *Can I bum a few bucks? I'm up against it this week.*

up an' Adam See *up and at them.*

up an' at 'em See the following entry.

up and at them AND **up an' at 'em; up an' Adam** *phr.* to get up and go at people or things; to get active and get busy. ("Adam" is a misunderstanding of "at 'em.") □ *Come on, you guys! Up and at 'em! Can't sleep all day.* □ *Up and Adam! The sun is shining.*

up for grabs 1. *mod.* available for anyone; not yet claimed. □ *It's up for grabs. Everything is still very chancy.* □ *I don't know who will get it. It's up for grabs.* **2.** *mod.* in total chaos. □ *This is a madhouse. The whole place is up for grabs.* □ *When the market crashed, the whole office was up for grabs.*

up for something *mod.* agreeable to something. □ *I'm up for a pizza. Anybody want to chip in?* □ *Who's up for a swim?*

up front 1. *mod.* at the beginning; in advance. □ *She wanted $200 up front.* □ *The more you pay up front, the less you'll have to finance.* **2.** *mod.* open; honest; forthcoming. □ *She is a very up front gal—trust her.* □ *I wish the salesman had been more up front about it.* **3.** *mod.* in the forefront; under fire (at the front). □ *You guys who are up front are gonna get the most fire.* □ *You two go up front and see if you can help.*

up high *n.* a stimulating rather than a depressing drug *high.* (Drugs. See also *up pot.*) □ *She was always looking for a good up high. When she couldn't find quality, she went after quantity.* □ *Many of them have to have an up high. They are too close to clinical depression to chance anything else.*

up in arms *mod.* angry; excited. □ *The whole town was up in arms about the planned highway.* □ *Now, don't get up in arms about it.*

up in the air *mod.* (of an issue) undecided. □ *The whole matter is still up in the air.* □ *The question of who will attend is still up in the air.*

up in the air (about someone or something) *mod.* undecided about someone or something. □ *I'm sort of up in the air about whether to marry Mary or not.* □ *Mary's up in the air, too.*

up one's alley See *(right) up one's alley.*

up pot *n.* stimulating marijuana, as opposed to relaxing marijuana. (Drugs. See also *up high.*) □ *I can only handle up pot. Everything else makes me cry.* □ *Tell him you really don't want up pot unless it's cheap.*

up stakes *tr.* to prepare for leaving and then leave. (*Up* has the force of a verb here. The phrase suggests pulling up tent stakes in preparation for departure.) □ *They just upped stakes and left without saying good-bye.* □ *It's that time of the year when I feel like upping stakes and moving to the country.*

up the creek (without a paddle) AND **up a creek** *mod.* in an awkward position with no easy way out. (This creek is called "shit creek.") □ *I'm sort of up the creek and don't know what to do.* □ *You are up a creek! You got yourself into it, so get yourself out.*

up the pole *mod.* alcohol intoxicated. □ *You sound a little up the pole. Why don't you call back when you're sober?* □ *She's up the pole and shouldn't drive.*

up the river *mod.* in prison. (Underworld.) □ *Gary was up the river for a couple of years, but that doesn't make him a criminal, does it?* □ *The judge who sent him up the river was indicted for accepting bribery. If Gary had only known sooner!*

up the wall *mod.* in a very bad situation. □ *He's really up the wall about Mary's illness.* □ *We were all up the wall until the matter was resolved.*

up time *n.* the time when a computer is running. (Compare to *down time.*) □ *You'll get the maximum up time with this machine.* □ *On some systems the down time is longer than the up time.*

up to here *mod.* having as much as one can bear. □ *I'm up to here with your* *excuses!* ☐ *We are all up to here with this mystery.*

up to one's ears See the following entry.

up to one's eyeballs AND **up to one's ears** *mod.* filled up with something. ☐ *She's up to her ears in marriage proposals.* ☐ *We're up to our eyeballs in spare parts.*

up to one's knees *mod.* deep in something, such as paperwork or water. (See also *knee-deep in something.*) ☐ *We're up to our knees with orders and getting more all the time.* ☐ *The orders are up to our knees.*

up to one's neck *mod.* filled up with something. ☐ *I am up to my neck in other people's grief and anguish.* ☐ *We are all up to our necks in your problems.*

up to scratch AND **up to snuff** *mod.* satisfactory; up to what is expected. ☐ *This just isn't up to scratch. You'll have to do it again.* ☐ *The food was up to snuff, but the hotel staff was not at its usually efficient best.*

up to snuff See the previous entry.

upbeat *mod.* bright and cheery; not negative. (Compare to *downbeat.*) ☐ *I'd prefer to open the conference with an upbeat topic.* ☐ *That topic is not upbeat.* ☐ *This piece of music has an upbeat flavor to it.*

upchuck ['əptʃək] **1.** *tr. & in.* to vomit (something). ☐ *Wally upchucked his whole dinner.* ☐ *Who upchucked over there?* **2.** *n.* vomit. ☐ *Is that upchuck on your shoe?* ☐ *There is still some upchuck on the bathroom floor.*

upholstered [ə'polstəd] **1.** *mod.* alcohol intoxicated. ☐ *She was a little upholstered, but not seriously impaired.* ☐ *He drank till he was comfortably upholstered.* **2.** See *(well-)upholstered.*

upper story See *top story.*

uppity ['əpədi] *mod.* haughty. (Folksy.) ☐ *Why is she so uppity?* ☐ *Don't be uppity. Remember who you are!*

upshot (of something) *n.* the result of something; the outcome of something. (Always with *the.*) ☐ *The upshot of it all was that we don't get the new coffeepot.* ☐ *And the upshot was a new manager and raises for everyone.*

upside *n.* the good side. ☐ *On the upside, things might get better.* ☐ *There's not much to look forward to on the upside.*

uptight *mod.* anxious. ☐ *Dave always seems uptight about something.* ☐ *He is one uptight guy.* ☐ *Don't get uptight before the test.*

urge to purge *n.* the need to throw up. ☐ *Max felt the urge to purge and ran for the john.* ☐ *All this grease on the pizza gives me the urge to purge.*

urp See *earp.*

use [juz] *tr. & in.* to use (drugs); to take drugs habitually. (Drugs and now widely known.) ☐ *I tried to stop using, but I couldn't.* ☐ *I couldn't face myself if I started using the stuff again.*

Use your head! AND **Use your noggin!; Use your noodle!** *exclam.* "Think!"; "Think it through!" ☐ *You know the answer. Use your head!* ☐ *Use your noggin! It's there for more than hanging your hat on.*

Use your noggin! See the previous entry.

Use your noodle! See *Use your head!*

user *n.* a drug user; a drug addict. (Drugs.) ☐ *I want to stop being a user, but I can't do it by myself.* ☐ *I'm no user! Maybe a joint now and then, and an upper on a dreary morning—but I'm no user!*

U.V.s ['ju'viz] *n.* "ultraviolet" rays from the sun; sunshine. (Initialism.) ☐ *I wanna get some U.V.s before we go home.* ☐ *Watch out for those U.V.s.*

V

V-ball *n.* volleyball. (Compare to *B-ball.*) □ *You wanna play some V-ball?* □ *Playing V-ball is one of the best forms of exercise.*

vac 1. *n.* a vacuum cleaner. □ *Where's the vac?* □ *Bring the vac and clean this place up.* 2. *tr. & in.* to clean with a vacuum cleaner. □ *Vac while you have time!* □ *You are supposed to vac the whole house, not just your room!*

vacation *n.* a prison sentence. (Underworld.) □ *I had a little vacation upstate for a while.* □ *It was a three-year vacation, with time off for good behavior.*

vag [veg] 1. *n.* a vagrant person; a person who does not work and who wanders from place to place. □ *A couple of vags on the curb were trying to hitch a ride.* □ *You vags, move on. Go on, move it!* 2. *mod.* having to do with a charge of vagrancy. □ *They booked him on a vag charge and gave him a nice warm place to sleep that night.* □ *The vag scam didn't work like it was planned.*

vals [vælz] *n.* Valium™ tranquilizers. □ *I'm taking vals for this, but the doctor says to get off of them as soon as possible.* □ *Vals really calm you down.*

Vamoose! [væ'mus] *exclam.* "Beat it!"; "Go away!" (From Spanish.) □ *Go on, beat it! Vamoose!* □ *Vamoose! Go home!*

vanilla 1. *mod.* plain; dull. (See also *beige.*) □ *The entire production was sort of vanilla, but it was okay.* □ *No more vanilla music, please.* □ *The vacation was vanilla, but restful.* 2. *n.* a Caucasian. □ *Some vanilla's on the phone—selling something, I guess.* □ *That vanilla is looking at you sort of coplike.*

varnished *mod.* alcohol intoxicated. (Compare to *shellacked.*) □ *Really varnished, he was. Couldn't see a hole in a ladder.* □ *That lady is too varnished to drive. If you see her getting into a car, call the cops.*

varoom See *vroom.*

Vatican roulette *n.* the rhythm method of birth control. □ *My parents lost at Vatican roulette, and I am the booby prize.* □ *Father John tried to get us to refer to it as something other than Vatican roulette.*

veejay AND **V.J.; video jock** *n.* a "video jockey"; a host on a television program that features music videos. (The abbreviation is an initialism. Patterned on *deejay.* See also *disc jockey.*) □ *Sally tried out for the veejay job, but she looked too old and stuffy for that kind of work.* □ *Most of the V.J.s on cable television are untrained amateurs.* □ *Wally tried out to be a video jock, but he's too uptown.*

veep [vip] *n.* a vice president. □ *The veep is going to preside today.* □ *Now we have to elect a veep. Any nominations?*

veg [vɛdʒ] 1. *n.* a vegetable. (See also *veggy.*) □ *You want a veg with this?* □ *That's not my favorite veg.* 2. *n.* a stupid person. □ *Where is your brain, you veg?* □ *Some veg put scallops in the scalloped potatoes.* 3. See *veg (out).*

veg (out) *in.* to cease working and take it easy; to vegetate. □ *Someday, I just* *want to veg out and enjoy life.* □ *I think I'll just veg this weekend.* (More at *vegged out.*)

vegetable 1. *mod.* alcohol intoxicated. □ *He's a tad vegetable but not in a stupor.* □ *Helen drank till she was totally vegetable.* **2.** *n.* someone who is brain-dead; someone who acts brain-dead; a person almost totally destroyed by drugs. □ *You are such a vegetable!* □ *You want to end up a vegetable? Just keep shooting that stuff.* □ *Cable T.V. is turning me into a vegetable.*

vegged out *mod.* debilitated by drugs or alcohol. (Drugs.) □ *Ernie is vegged out and has quit his job and everything.* □ *Won't be long till Larry is vegged out altogether.*

veggie See the following entry.

veggy AND **veggie** ['vɛdʒi] **1.** *n.* a vegetarian. □ *We have a lovely salad bar for the veggies among you.* □ *She's a veggy, so make sure there's a nice selection of appropriate goodies.* **2.** *n.* a vegetable. (Usually plural.) □ *Do you want any veggies with this?* □ *No veggies for me.* **3.** *n.* a comatose patient in a hospital. (Medical.) □ *Mary's aunt has been a veggie in the hospital for more than a year.* □ *I don't want to lie there and rot as a veggie. I want someone to pull the plug.* **4.** *n.* someone who is tired or exhausted. □ *I want to be a veggy this weekend. I'll just stay at home and relax.* □ *I am just a veggie after all the activity of the last week.*

vent one's spleen *tr.* to release one's anger. □ *No need to vent your spleen at me. I wasn't in on it.* □ *I just feel like I have to vent my spleen at somebody.*

verboten [vɚ'botn̩] *mod.* forbidden. (German.) □ *That is strictly verboten.* □ *You said a verboten word around here.*

vest *n.* an important businessman or businesswoman. (See also *suit.*) □ *One of the vests complained to the management about the way I cleaned his office.* □ *Some vest jumped out the window this afternoon.*

vet 1. *n.* a veterinarian. (Standard English.) □ *I took the cat to the vet.* □ *The vet didn't charge much to look at the turtle.* **2.** *tr.* to give a medical examination to and treat a person (or an animal). □ *The doctor vetted me quickly and charged an unbelievable sum for it.* □ *When they vet you these days, most of the work is done in a lab.* **3.** *n.* a (war) veteran. □ *The vets in the hospitals across the land appreciate your kindness.* □ *The Vietnam vets had a very bad time of it.*

vette [vɛt] *n.* a Corvette automobile. □ *I'd rather have a vette than a caddy.* □ *Vettes aren't as popular as they once were.*

vibes [vɑɪbz] *n.* vibrations; atmosphere; feelings. (Usually with *good* or *bad.*) □ *I just don't get good vibes about this deal.* □ *The vibes are just plain bad.*

vic [vɪk] **1.** *n.* a victim. (Streets. See also *vivor.*) □ *We're all vics, but we all keep going.* □ *Harry is a con artist, not a vic.* **2.** *n.* a convict. □ *Max is a vic, but nobody cares much.* □ *We try to give the vics a chance at employment where they won't be treated badly.*

vicious ['vɪʃəs] *mod.* great; excellent. □ *Man, this burger is really vicious.* □ *That guy is one vicious driver, all right.* □ *That was a really vicious concert last night.*

vicious circle *n.* a set of actions that lead to ever more unsatisfactory consequences; a set of bad actions that are repeated in a cycle. (See also *catch-22.*) □ *It's a vicious circle, and I want out of it.* □ *Life has become one vicious circle after another.*

vicked [vɪkt] *mod.* cheated; victimized. (See also *vic.*) □ *I feel so vicked when I see where my taxes are spent.* □ *I got vicked at the stereo repair shop.*

video jock See *veejay.*

Vietnik [vi'ɛtnɪk] *n.* someone—looking like a *beatnik*—who opposed the Vietnam war. □ *The Vietniks' message was sort of distorted by the press.* □ *I knew a Vietnik who moved to Canada.*

vim and vigor *n.* energy; enthusiasm; *moxie.* □ *Show more vim and vigor! Let us know you're alive.* □ *She's sure got a lot of vim and vigor.*

vines *n.* clothing. (Black.) □ *I like those smokin' vines you're in.* □ *Good-looking vines on that guy, right?*

vinyl ['vaɪnl̩] *n.* phonograph records. □ *This is one of the best tunes on vinyl.* □ *I got some new vinyl. Come over and listen.*

V.I.P. **1.** *n.* a "very important person." (Initialism.) □ *Who's the V.I.P. in the Mercedes?* □ *That's no V.I.P.; that's the boss.* **2.** *mod.* something reserved for a *V.I.P.* (Initialism.) □ *My smile and casual manner didn't get me into the V.I.P. lounge.* □ *They gave us the V.I.P. treatment.*

visit from Flo [. . .'flo] *n.* a menstrual period. (See also *Aunt Flo.*) □ *I am expecting a visit from Flo, but she seems late.* □ *I just had a visit from Flo. I hate the old hag!*

visit from the stork *n.* the birth of a baby. □ *The last visit from the stork was in March.* □ *We are expecting a visit from the stork next June.*

visit the plumbing See *check out the plumbing.*

visiting fireman *n.* someone paying a visit to observe one's workplace. □ *We have a couple of visiting firemen coming today.* □ *Be sure to have these plans out when the visiting firemen come by.*

vital statistics *n.* the measurements of a person's body. □ *Her vital statistics must require higher math to work out!* □ *Here are his vital statistics for those who are interested.*

vivor ['vaɪvɚ] *n.* a survivor; a street person who manages to survive. (Streets. Compare to *vic.*) □ *Harry's a vivor, and I like him.* □ *She's no champ, but she's a vivor.*

viz [vaɪz] *n.* Levis; blue jeans. □ *How do you like my new viz?* □ *Those viz are too tight for her.*

V.J. See *veejay.*

vomatose ['vamətos] *mod.* drunk, vomiting, and nearly comatose. (From *vomit* and *comatose.*) □ *Claude is completely vomatose. What a party!* □ *Beavis got himself vomatose and messed up the driveway.*

vomity ['vamɪdi] *mod.* nasty. (Crude.) □ *What is this vomity stuff on my plate?* □ *Is that what you call vomity?* □ *That is a really vomity idea!*

vote with one's feet *in.* to show one's displeasure by walking out. □ *A lot of people are voting with their feet. Customers clearly don't like our goods.* □ *When the audience votes with its feet, you know you don't have a hit.*

vroom AND **varoom** [vrum AND va'rum] **1.** *interj.* the noise of a loud engine. (Onomatopoetic.) □ *Vroom, varoom went the engine as Vic gunned it over and over.* □ *Suddenly, vroom, a plane passed low overhead.* **2.** *in.* to move rapidly from place to place; to travel at high speed, making the noise of a loud engine. □ *Let's vroom over to Larry's and see what's happening.* □ *The little boy varoomed down the sidewalk on his tricycle.*

W

waa-zooed See *whazood.*

wack See *whack.*

wacky *mod.* loony; silly and giddy. ☐ *You are about the wackiest guy I ever met.* ☐ *I got a real kick out of that wacky movie we saw last night.*

wacky-tabbacky ['wækitə'bæki] *n.* marijuana. (Collegiate.) ☐ *You got any of that wacky-tabbacky?* ☐ *He gets that silly look in his eye from smoking wacky-tabbacky.*

wad [wɑd] *n.* a bundle of money; a bankroll. (Originally underworld. See also *tight wad.*) ☐ *I lost my wad on a rotten horse in the seventh race.* ☐ *You'd better not flash a wad like that around here. You won't have it long.*

waffle (around) *in.* to be indecisive. ☐ *Don't waffle around so long. Make up your mind.* ☐ *She spent three days waffling over the color of the car and finally decided on red.*

wag one's chin *tr.* to talk or jabber; to chatter aimlessly. ☐ *The two old buzzards sat on the park bench wagging their chins all afternoon.* ☐ *Stop wagging your chin for a minute and listen up!*

wagon *n.* the police wagon. ☐ *I called the wagon. It'll come and get these two thugs in about fifteen minutes.* ☐ *Look out, you guys, the wagon's coming. Don't let 'em see you!*

wail *in.* to be great. (See also *wailing.*) ☐ *Things really started to wail about midnight when the band really got going.* ☐ *This pizza really wails.*

wailing AND **whaling** *mod.* excellent. (Teens.) ☐ *Man, that's wailing!* ☐ *What a whaling guitar!*

walk 1. *n.* something easy. (Always with *a.* See also *cakewalk, sleepwalk.*) ☐ *That game was a walk!* ☐ *What a walk! I've never had such an easy time of it!* **2.** *in.* to walk out on someone. ☐ *They had a big fight, and he walked.* ☐ *Much more of this and I'm going to walk.* **3.** *in.* to walk away from something unharmed. ☐ *It couldn't have been much of an accident. Both drivers walked.* ☐ *It was a horrible meeting, but when it was over I just walked.* **4.** *in.* to get out of prison; to get off from a criminal charge. (Underworld.) ☐ *They thought they had Bruno on a vice rap, but he walked.* ☐ *I showed them my license; then I walked.*

walk heavy *in.* to be important. (Black.) ☐ *Harry's been walking heavy since he graduated.* ☐ *Why have you been walking heavy, man?*

walk-in 1. *mod.* having to do with a customer who just comes in off the street. ☐ *Two walk-in customers wanted morning papers but nothing more.* ☐ *We were hoping for more walk-in trade.* **2.** *n.* a customer who walks in off the street. ☐ *We had a couple of walk-ins this morning, but none of the hotel residents came.* ☐ *We have a new sign outside to attract walk-ins.*

walk on eggs AND **walk on thin ice** *in.* to walk very cautiously; to be in a very precarious position. ☐ *I have to remember that I'm walking on eggs when I give this speech.* ☐ *Careful with ideas like that. You're walking on thin ice.*

walk on thin ice See the previous entry.

walk soft *in.* to take it easy; to be gentle and humble. ☐ *I try to walk soft and not rock the boat.* ☐ *The guy's a tyrant. He walks soft just to mislead people.*

walk tall *in.* to be brave and self-assured. (See also *stand tall.*) ☐ *I know I can walk tall because I'm innocent.* ☐ *You go out on that stage and walk tall. There is no reason to be afraid.*

walking dandruff AND **galloping dandruff** *n.* lice. (See also *pants rabbits.*) ☐ *He's hopping around like he's got walking dandruff.* ☐ *I don't know anybody with galloping dandruff—I hope.*

walking on rocky socks *mod.* alcohol intoxicated. ☐ *She's sort of walking on rocky socks.* ☐ *He looks like he's walking on rocky socks.*

walking papers *n.* a notice of being fired, released, divorced, etc. ☐ *I hope I don't get my walking papers today. I need this job.* ☐ *Well, I got my walking papers today.*

walking wounded **1.** *n.* soldiers who are injured but still able to walk. (Standard English.) ☐ *There were enough walking wounded to start another division.* ☐ *Many of the walking wounded helped with the more seriously injured cases.* **2.** *n.* a person who is injured—mentally or physically—and still able to go about daily life. ☐ *As one of the walking wounded who has suffered the things you described, I have to disagree with you.* ☐ *The outpatient clinic was filled with the walking wounded.*

walkover *n.* an easy victory; an easy task. (From sports.) ☐ *The game was a walkover. No problem.* ☐ *Learning the computer's operating system was no walkover for me.*

wall-eyed *mod.* alcohol intoxicated. ☐ *Wow, is he ever wall-eyed!* ☐ *Who's the wall-eyed guy carrying the ham sandwich?*

wall job *n.* a car—in the shop for repairs —which is parked against the wall with no repairs done. (The customer is charged anyway.) ☐ *Places like those we surveyed may charge hundreds of dollars for what they call "wall jobs."* ☐ *Okay, Lefty, the caddy looks like another wall job. Throw some plastic over it, and we'll call the old girl and tell her it needs parts.*

wall-to-wall *mod.* expansive and comprehensive. (From "wall-to-wall carpeting.") ☐ *The guy doesn't exactly have wall-to-wall generosity.* ☐ *Old Tom is wall-to-wall hostility these days. What's wrong?*

wallet *n.* a college student's father and financial source. ☐ *My wallet won't send me another penny this semester.* ☐ *Why don't you tell your wallet you are starving?*

wallflower *n.* a shy person. ☐ *Clare was sort of a wallflower until she graduated.* ☐ *Don't be a wallflower. Come to the reception.*

wallop ['wɑləp] **1.** *n.* a hard blow. ☐ *She planted a hard wallop on his right shoulder.* ☐ *I got quite a wallop when I walked into the door.* **2.** *tr.* to strike someone or something hard. ☐ *I walloped him hard on the shoulder, but he kept on laughing.* ☐ *The door swung open and walloped me in the back.* **3.** *n.* influence; pull; clout. ☐ *The gal has a lot of wallop in city hall.* ☐ *I don't have enough wallop to make that kind of demand.*

wallpaper *n.* worthless checks. (Underworld.) ☐ *This flimflam artist has spread a lot of wallpaper in her day.* ☐ *The feds followed a trail of wallpaper from St. Louis to San Francisco and made the pinch.*

walls have ears *phr.* "Someone may be listening." (Sometimes with *the.*) ☐ *Talk softly. Walls have ears.* ☐ *The walls have ears, so be careful about what you say.*

waltz *n.* an easy task. ☐ *The job was a waltz. We did it in a day.* ☐ *The coach promised them that the game would be a waltz.*

waltz off (with something) *in.* to take something away easily. ☐ *The thieves waltzed off with a giant screen television in broad daylight.* ☐ *They just picked the* *thing up and waltzed off. Nobody asked them any questions.*

waltz through something *in.* to get through something easily. □ *I waltzed through my comps and started on my research in my second year.* □ *I tried to waltz through my assignment, but it was too hard.*

wampum ['wampəm] *n.* money. (From an Amerindian word.) □ *I don't have enough wampum to swing the deal.* □ *How much wampum do you want for this thing?*

wana ['wanə] *n.* marijuana. (Drugs.) □ *Got any wana on you?* □ *How much is this wana, man?*

wanabe AND **wanna be** ['wanə bi OR 'wənə bi] *n.* someone who wants to be something or someone. (Associated with Madonna, the singer.) □ *All these teenyboppers are wanabes, and that's why we can sell this stuff to them at any price.* □ *A wanna be came by selling chances on a raffle.*

wanna ['wanə OR 'wənə] *phr.* "want to." (Eye-dialect. Typical spoken English. Used in writing only for effect. Used in the examples of this dictionary.) □ *I will if I wanna.* □ *Do you wanna gimme the thingy and lemme go ahead with my work?*

wanna be See *wanabe.*

Wanna make sumpin' of it? See *Want to make something of it?*

want list *n.* a list of things that someone wants. (See also *laundry list, shopping list.*) □ *Some of the things on her want list we can take care of easily.* □ *Send me your want list, and I'll see what we can do.*

want out *in.* to want to remove oneself from some association or relationship. □ *Ted had had as much as he could stand, and he wanted out.* □ *I want out. This relationship is stifling me.*

Want to make something of it? AND **Wanna make sumpin' of it?** *interrog.* "Do you want to fight about it?" □ *So, I'm a little ugly. Wanna make sumpin' of it?* □ *I'm warped and smelly. Want to make something of it?*

war chest *n.* a political campaign fund. □ *They say the Vice President has over one million dollars in his war chest.* □ *When the war chest gave out, the candidate dropped out of the race.*

war paint *n.* a woman's makeup. □ *She'll be ready when she gets on her war paint.* □ *She doesn't look half bad without war paint.*

war zone *n.* an area where things get rough; a tough neighborhood. □ *Unfortunately our offices are in a war zone, and we have to be on the way home before dark.* □ *The drug dealers and the gangs have turned many of our neighborhoods into war zones.*

warhorse *n.* a tough old thing, person, or idea. □ *The conductor loves to have us play that old warhorse as an encore.* □ *What time does the old warhorse's train get in, and how long is she staying this time?*

warm body *n.* just anyone who can be counted on to stay alive. □ *See if you can get a couple of warm bodies to stand at the door and hand out programs.* □ *You mean among all these warm bodies nobody knows calculus?*

warm someone up *tr.* to prepare an audience for another—more famous—performer. □ *A famous singer came out to warm us up for Jack Benny.* Ⓣ *This man Bennett is a superb choice to warm up the audience.*

warmed over *mod.* not very original; rehashed. □ *I am not interested in reading warmed over news on a computer screen.* □ *The lecture sounded sort of warmed over, but it wasn't too dull.*

warped *mod.* drug intoxicated. (A variant of *bent.*) □ *Too many yellows made Jerry warped as the dickens.* □ *I think Max is permanently warped.*

wart 1. *n.* an annoying person. (Also a rude term of address.) □ *Who is that wart with the inch-thick glasses?* □ *Tell the wart to leave, or we will be forced to call Bruno, who doesn't care for such* *persons.* **2.** *n.* a problem or an obstruction in a plan. □ *Okay, now we come to the wart. We don't have the money to carry out this plan.* □ *It's okay except for a little wart.*

warts and all *mod.* even with the flaws. □ *It's a great performance—warts and all.* □ *Yes, we admire each other very much, warts and all.*

was had See *been had.*

wash **1.** *in.* to be believed. (As if untruth were a stain that will not *come out in the wash.*) □ *It sounds phony. It won't wash.* □ *That'll never wash! It's totally unbelievable.* **2.** *n.* a drink that follows a previous drink; a *chaser.* □ *He ordered a beer wash with his snort.* □ *Can I have a wash with this, bartender?* **3.** *n.* the almost simultaneous sale and purchase of the same stock, usually to make the stock appear to be trading actively. (Securities markets. The practice is illegal. Tax loss selling must be done in such a way to avoid appearing to be a *wash.*) □ *I sold the stock and couldn't buy it back for thirty days to avoid an illegal wash.* □ *The IRS ruled that the sale was a wash and that I couldn't take the tax loss.* **4.** *n.* a whitewash or covering up (of a problem). □ *What the administration presented was not an explanation but a wash.* □ *We don't want a wash. We want the truth.*

wash out **1.** *in.* to fail and be removed from something, such as school. (See also *washout.*) □ *I studied all I could, but I still washed out.* □ *I don't want to wash out. It's my whole future.* **2.** *in.* to have a serious wreck; to *wipe out.* □ *The little car washed out on the curve.* □ *The vehicles have a tendency to wash out when cornering.* **3.** *in.* to lose a large amount of money. □ *Fred washed out on that stock deal.* □ *Lefty and Bruno washed out at the track.* **4.** *in.* to slow down or collapse from exhaustion. □ *The whole play began to wash out during the second act. It was a lost cause by the third.* □ *Finally, after a long day, I just washed out. They had to call the paramedics.* (More at *washed out.*)

wash someone away *tr.* to kill someone. (Underworld.) □ *Bruno was charged with trying to wash Max away.* 🅃 *The mob triggers came by and tried to wash away a druggy type.*

washed out *mod.* exhausted; tired. □ *I feel too washed out to go to work today.* □ *Poor Ted really looks washed out.*

washout *n.* a failure; a fiasco. □ *The whole project was a washout. A lost cause from beginning to end.* □ *I am beginning to think that Sally's specialty is washouts.*

WASP **1.** *n.* a "white Anglo-Saxon protestant." (Usually derogatory. Acronym.) □ *Would you call Pete a WASP?* □ *Not really. The west side is where the WASPs live.* **2.** *mod.* having to do with white Anglo-Saxon protestants; *waspish.* □ *They preferred to live in a WASP neighborhood.* □ *What a silly old WASP idea.*

waspish *mod.* in the manner of a *WASP.* □ *She looks sort of waspish, but she's not.* □ *Sally is a waspish kind of yuppie.*

waste *tr.* to kill someone. (Underworld.) □ *Bruno had orders to waste Max.* □ *The mob's triggers sped by in a car and wasted four pushers.*

wasted **1.** *mod.* dead; killed. □ *Max didn't want to end up wasted.* □ *That's silly. We all end up wasted one way or another.* **2.** *mod.* alcohol or drug intoxicated. □ *I really feel wasted. What did I drink?* □ *I've never seen a bartender get wasted before.* **3.** *mod.* exhausted. □ *I worked two shifts and I'm totally wasted.* □ *Mary was wasted and went to bed.*

Watch it! *exclam.* "Be careful!"; "Watch your step!"; "Careful of what you say!" □ *Watch it, buster!* □ *You're walking on thin ice. Watch it!*

Watch my lips! AND **Read my lips!** *exclam.* "I am going to say something rude to you that I will not say out loud!" □ *You jerk! Watch my lips!* □ *Hey, chum! Read my lips!*

Watch your mouth! AND **Watch your tongue!** *exclam.* "Pay attention to what you are saying!"; "Do not say anything rude!" ☐ *Hey, don't talk that way! Watch your mouth!* ☐ *Watch your tongue, garbage mouth!*

Watch your tongue! See the previous entry.

watering hole *n.* a tavern. ☐ *Now this place is one of my favorite watering holes.* ☐ *I think you live down at that watering hole.*

wax 1. *tr.* to beat or defeat someone; to assault someone. ☐ *Those guys look like they're gonna wax us but good.* ☐ *The muggers waxed the vest and swiped his briefcase.* **2.** *n.* a phonograph recording; a substance onto which a recording is put. (Never singular or plural.) ☐ *This is one of the finest pieces of music ever put on wax.* ☐ *Now here's some wax I'll bet you've never heard before.*

waxed *mod.* alcohol intoxicated. (See also *polished (up)*.) ☐ *Tom is too waxed to talk.* ☐ *Sam got waxed and had to be taken home.*

Way! *exclam.* "Yes it can!"; "Yes it does!" (The opposite of *No way!*) ☐ TOM: *It can't be done. No way!* BILL: *Way! Yes, it can!* ☐ *Way! You will do it and you will like it!*

way *mod.* extremely; totally. ☐ *Oh, this is way gross!* ☐ *I feel way tired today.*

way down *mod.* very depressed. ☐ *Poor Clare is way down. I think she has something wrong with her.* ☐ *Pete sure looks way down.*

way off (base) *mod.* on the wrong track; completely wrong. ☐ *I think you're way off base. Try again.* ☐ *Sorry. You are way off. You should just give up.*

way out AND **way-out 1.** *mod.* extreme; arcane. ☐ *Some of your ideas are really way out.* ☐ *What a way-out hairdo.* **2.** *mod.* heavily alcohol or drug intoxicated. ☐ *That guy is way out—can't even walk.* ☐ *She was so way-out, she was almost unconscious.*

way rad *mod.* quite excellent. (California. See also *rad.*) ☐ *Oh, Tiff! That's way rad!* ☐ *You are? Way rad!*

Way to go! See *(That's the) way to go!*

WBMTTP *interj.* "Which brings me to the point." (Initialism. Used in electronic mail and computer bulletin board messages. Not pronounced aloud.) ☐ *Of course, you may not like that approach. WBMTTP You need someone to help you choose the proper method.* ☐ *I agree with what Tom said. WBMTTP. I think we spend too much time worrying about these matters.*

weak sister *n.* a timid person, usually a male. ☐ *It looks like Dave is the weak sister on the team.* ☐ *Another weak sister and we'll have to quit. We've got to pull together.*

wear *tr.* to tolerate something. (Usually negative.) ☐ *That's no good. I won't wear it.* ☐ *I don't mind, but my wife won't wear it.*

wear the pants (in the house) *tr.* to be the boss in the house; to run a household. ☐ *All right, if you have to wear the pants, have it your way.* ☐ *Well, somebody has to wear the pants.*

weasel 1. *n.* a sneaky person. ☐ *You slimy weasel! How could you!* ☐ *If Fred weren't such a weasel, we could get along better.* **2.** *n.* an earnest student. (Collegiate.) ☐ *Who's the weasel who always gets A's?* ☐ *Martin is your classic weasel.*

weasel out of something *in.* to get out of doing something; to wiggle out of a responsibility. ☐ *I know how to weasel out of something like that. You get a headache.* ☐ *You can't just weasel out now when we need you!*

wedgy ['wedʒi] *n.* a situation where one's underpants are drawn up tightly between the buttocks; a *melvin.* ☐ *Wally skipped up behind Greg and gave him a wedgy.* ☐ *I think he LIKES walking around with a wedgy all day!*

weed 1. *n.* tobacco; a cigarette or cigar. ☐ *I've about given up weed.* ☐ *This weed is gonna be the death of me.* **2.** *n.* marijuana; a marijuana cigarette. (Drugs.) ☐ *This is good weed, man.* ☐ *This weed is green but decent.*

weed-eater See the following entry.

weedhead AND **weed-eater** *n.* a smoker of marijuana. ☐ *Max is a confirmed weed-eater.* ☐ *The weedheads are taking over this neighborhood.*

weeds *n.* clothing. ☐ *Good-looking weeds you're wearing.* ☐ *These weeds came right out of the wish book. Would you believe?*

weekend warrior *n.* a member of the military reserves. ☐ *I wanted to be a weekend warrior and get some of the educational benefits.* ☐ *The weekend warriors were called into active duty.*

weenie 1. *n.* a wiener (sausage), as in a hot dog (sandwich). ☐ *They gave us some yucky beans with weenies in them.* ☐ *It's weenies again for dinner.* **2.** *n.* the penis. (Essentially juvenile and jocular. Use caution with the topic.) ☐ *Tell him to cover his weenie and run and grab a towel.* ☐ *He told some joke about a weenie, but nobody got it.* **3.** *n.* a stupid person. ☐ *Gee, you can be such a weenie!* ☐ *Who's the weenie driving the old car?* **4.** *n.* an earnest student. (Collegiate.) ☐ *That weenie keeps getting A's and raising the grade scale.* ☐ *Who's the weenie with the thick glasses?*

weeper *n.* a sad movie, novel, television program, etc. ☐ *I can't seem to get enough of these weepers.* ☐ *Not another weeper!*

weird out *in.* to become emotionally disturbed or unnerved; to *flip (out).* ☐ *The day was just gross. I thought I would weird out at noon.* ☐ *I weirded out at the news of Frankie's death.* (More at *weirded out.*)

weirded out *mod.* disturbed or unnerved by drugs or events. ☐ *I was totally weirded out and couldn't control myself.* ☐ *After the blowup, Fred was really weirded out.*

weirdo ['wɪrdo] *n.* a strange person. ☐ *She is sure a weirdo lately.* ☐ *Don't be such a weirdo!*

weisenheimer AND **wiseacre** ['waɪzn̩haɪmɚ AND 'waɪzekɚ] *n.* a presumptuous smart aleck. (Also a term of address.) ☐ *Who's the wiseacre who put sugar in the salt shaker?* ☐ *Look, weisenheimer, watch your tongue!*

welcher ['wɛltʃɚ] *n.* someone who does not pay gambling debts. ☐ *It was Bruno's job to let the welchers know that Mr. Big was angry.* ☐ *Bruno set out to teach the welcher a lesson. He didn't mean to hurt him very much.*

welk [wɛlk] *phr.* "you are welcome." ☐ TOM: *Thanks.* BOB: *Welk.* ☐ *"Welk," said Fred, accepting my thanks.*

well-fixed AND **well-heeled 1.** *mod.* rich. ☐ *His father died and left him pretty well-fixed.* ☐ *Her well-fixed uncle left her a lot of money.* ☐ *Pete is well-fixed for life.* **2.** *mod.* alcohol intoxicated. ☐ *By midnight, he was pretty well-fixed.* ☐ *You might say he is well-fixed. You might say he's dead drunk, too.*

well-heeled See the previous entry.

well-oiled 1. *mod.* alcohol intoxicated. ☐ *He was well-oiled and couldn't stand up.* ☐ *Get him well-oiled and break the news to him.* **2.** *mod.* talkative. ☐ *She was sure well-oiled. I thought she'd never stop talking.* ☐ *Get him well-oiled, and you'll find out about everything.*

(well-)upholstered *mod.* chubby; plump. ☐ *Fortunately, he was upholstered enough that the fall didn't really hurt.* ☐ *My well-upholstered brother has to go on a diet.*

wenchy AND **whenchy** ['wɛntʃi AND 'ʍɛntʃi] *mod.* bitchy; snotty. (Collegiate.) ☐ *I really wish you wouldn't be so wenchy with me!* ☐ *What's the matter with that wenchy chick?* ☐ *Then she began to get whenchy, so I left.*

Were you born in a barn? *interrog.* "Weren't you trained to close the door by yourself?" ☐ *Close the door! Were you born in a barn?* ☐ *You sure are careless with that door. Were you born in a barn?*

wet 1. *mod.* alcohol intoxicated. ☐ *The jerk is wet and can't drive home.* ☐ *He's been drinking since noon and is pretty wet.* **2.** *mod.* having to do with an area where is it legal to sell alcohol. (Compare to *dry.*) ☐ *Kansas became wet just* *a few years ago.* □ *Is it wet or dry in this county?* **3.** *mod.* feeble; in the manner of a *nerd.* □ *Tom is totally wet. What a jerk.* □ *Wayne is wet and so's his buddy.*

wet blanket *n.* someone who ruins a good time. (In the way that a wet blanket is used to put out a fire.) □ *Oh, Martin! Why do you have to be such a wet blanket?* □ *Don't be a wet blanket! Have some fun!*

wet noodle *n.* a *dupe;* a *wimp.* □ *Don't be such a wet noodle. Don't let them push you around.* □ *Martin is such a wet noodle.*

wet one *n.* a cold beer. □ *How about a wet one, Fred?* □ *I could sure use a wet one about now.*

wet rag See the following entry.

wet sock AND **wet rag** *n.* a *wimp;* a useless *jerk.* (See also *rubber sock.*) □ *Don't be such a wet sock! Stand up for your rights!* □ *Well, in a tight situation, Martin is sort of a wet rag.*

wetware ['wetwɛr] *n.* the human brain. (Compared to computer *hardware* and *software.*) □ *This isn't a hardware problem; it's a wetware problem.* □ *You need to update your wetware.*

whack AND **wack** **1.** *tr.* to strike someone or something. □ *Jed whacked the kid upside the head.* □ *Larry reached down and wacked the dog across the snout.* **2.** *n.* a blow or hit (at someone or something). □ *She tried to take a whack at me!* □ *She landed a nasty wack on his thigh.* **3.** *n.* a drink of liquor. □ *Take a whack of this stuff.* □ *Hey, give me another wack of that. It helps.*

whack someone or something (out) **1.** *tr.* [with *someone*] to kill somebody. (Underworld.) □ *Bruno made another try at whacking Max out last evening.* 🅃 *He really wants to whack out Mr. Big.* □ *He really wants to whack Mr. Big.* **2.** *tr.* [with *something*] to rob a place; to swindle a business establishment. (Underworld.) □ *Did your guys whack the church collection box?* 🅃 *Bruno's gang whacked out the bank on Maple street.*

whack someone or something up *in.* to damage someone or something. □ *Bob got mad at Greg and whacked him up.* □ *Clara whacked up her car yesterday.*

whacked *mod.* crazy; silly. □ *Greg acts whacked all the time.* □ *Garth seems whacked, but he's just putting on.*

whacked (out) *mod.* alcohol or drug intoxicated. □ *Gee, is he ever whacked!* □ *Dave was so whacked out he couldn't stand up.*

whale **1.** *n.* a very fat person. (Cruel.) □ *Tracy is getting to be such a whale.* □ *Well, Gert's the whale if you ask me.* **2.** *n.* a drunkard; a person with an enormous capacity for liquor. □ *Arthur is getting to be a regular whale. What does he drink?* □ *A pair of whales was in the corner booth tanking up.*

whale into someone or something *tr.* to attack someone or something. □ *Jimmy's dad really whaled into him.* □ *The guy whaled into the logs and had a nice woodpile by noon.*

whale on *mod.* excellent. (Confused with or in error for *wailing.*) □ *This is one whale on rally.* □ *We had a whale on time at Bob's house.*

whale the tar out of someone *tr.* to spank or beat someone. (Sometimes said to a child.) □ *My father threatened to whale the tar out of me.* □ *I'll whale the tar out of you when we get home if you don't settle down.*

whaling See *wailing.*

wham-bang ['ʍæm'bæŋ] *mod.* large; boisterous. □ *We had a really wham-bang time at your party.* □ *The overture was just too wham-bang for the tone of the play itself.*

whang(y)doodle ['ʍæŋ'dudl̩ AND 'ʍæŋi'dudl̩] **1.** *n.* a gadget. □ *Toss me one of the little whangdoodles, would ya?* □ *This whangydoodle is a little bent.* **2.** *n.* nonsense. □ *Now that's enough of your whangdoodle.* □ *All I ever hear out of you is whangydoodle.*

What (a) nerve! *exclam.* "What insolence!"; "How rude and presumptuous!" □ *Did you hear what she said?*

What nerve! □ *What a nerve! Have you ever seen such gall?*

What can I do you for? *interrog.* "How can I help you?"; "How can I serve you?" □ *Good morning. What can I do for you?* □ *Now it's your turn. What can I do for you?*

What do you say? **1.** *interrog.* "Hello, how are you?" (Most often [wədəjə'se].) □ *Hi, Jim. What do you say?* □ *What do you say, man?* **2.** *interrog.* "What is your answer?" □ *Well, what do you say?* □ *Come on, I need an answer now. What do you say?*

What else is new? *interrog.* "But isn't that what you expect?"; "What you said isn't new, so what is new?" □ *Yes, there is trouble around the world. What else is new?* □ *So, there's not enough money this week. What else is new?*

What gives? *interrog.* "What is going on?"; "What is happening?" □ *Hey! What gives? Who left this here?* □ *What gives? Who's made this mess?*

What (in) the devil? *interrog.* "What has happened?"; "What?" (Often with the force of an exclamation.) □ *What in the devil? Who put sugar in the salt shaker?* □ *What the devil? Who are you? What are you doing in my room?*

What (in) the hell? **1.** *interrog.* "What has happened?"; "What?" □ *What in the hell? Who did this?* □ *What the hell happened here?* **2.** *interrog.* "What does it matter?" (Usually with the force of an exclamation.) □ *Give her a new one. What the hell!* □ *Don't be such a cheapskate. Get the nice one. What the hell!*

What in (the) Sam Hill? *interrog.* "What has happened?"; "What?" (An elaboration of *what*. *Sam Hill* is *hell*. Often with the force of an exclamation. See examples for variations.) □ *What in Sam Hill is going on around here?* □ *What in the Sam Hill do you think you are doing?*

What is it? *interrog.* "Hello, what is happening?" □ *What is it? Tsup?* □ *What is it? What's happening?*

What someone said. *sent.* "I agree with what someone just said, although I might not have been able to say it as well or so elegantly." □ *What John said. And I agree 100 percent.* □ *What you said.*

What the deuce? *interrog.* "What has happened?"; "What?" (*Deuce* is an old word for devil.) □ *What the deuce! Who are you?* □ *What the deuce! Who did this?*

What the heck! *exclam.* "It doesn't matter!" (Often with the force of an exclamation.) □ *Oh, what the heck! Come on in. It doesn't matter.* □ *Oh, what the heck! I'll have another beer. Nobody's counting.*

What you see is what you get. **1.** *sent.* "The product you are looking at is exactly what you get if you buy it." □ *It comes just like this. What you see is what you get.* □ *What you see is what you get. The ones in the box are just like this one.* **2.** AND **WYSIWYG** ['wɪsiwɪg] *phr.* "What you see on the screen is what will print on the printer." (Computers. Acronym.) □ *This program gives you that "what you see is what you get" feature that everyone wants.* □ *I need something that's WYSIWYG. I have no imagination.*

whatchamacallit ['ʍətʃəmə'kɑlɪt] *n.* a name for a person or thing whose real name has been forgotten or is being avoided. □ *Did you invite whatchamacallit to the party?* □ *I lost my—you know—my whatchamacallit—my watch!*

whatever turns you on *phr.* "It's all right if it excites you or interests you." (Said originally about sexual matters.) □ *You really like pickled pigs feet? Whatever turns you on.* □ *I can't stand that kind of music, but whatever turns you on.*

What'll it be? *interrog.* "What do you want." (Typically said when offering someone drinks. See also *What's yours?*) □ *Okay, Mac, what'll it be?* □ *What'll it be, chum?*

What's buzzin' (cousin)? *interrog.* "What's happening?" □ *Hey, chum!*

What's buzzin' cousin? ☐ *What's buzzin' around here?*

What's cooking? *interrog.* "What is happening?"; "What's about to happen?" ☐ *What's cooking? Anything interesting?* ☐ *What's cooking anyway?*

What's eating someone? *interrog.* "What is bothering someone?" ☐ *Gee, Tom, what's eating you?* ☐ *What's eating Fred? He's in a rotten humor.*

What's going down? *interrog.* "What's happening?" ☐ *I can't figure out what's going down around here.* ☐ *Hey, man, what's going down?*

What's going on? *interrog.* "What is happening here?" ☐ *I hear a lot of noise. What's going on?* ☐ *What's all this broken glass? What's going on?*

What's happ(ening)? *interrog.* "Hello, what's new?" ☐ *Hey, dude! What's happening?* ☐ *What's happ? How's it goin'?*

what's his face AND **what's his name** *n.* someone whose name has been forgotten; someone whose name is being avoided. ☐ *Was what's his name there? I never can remember his name.* ☐ *I can't remember what's his face's name either.*

what's his name See the previous entry.

What's in it for me? *interrog.* "How do I benefit from it?" ☐ *I might help out. What's in it for me?* ☐ *I might be able to contribute a little. What's in it for me?*

What's it to you? *interrog.* "What does it matter to you?"; "Is it any of your business?" ☐ *What's it to you if I don't do it?* ☐ *So I broke my glasses. What's it to you?*

What's new? *interrog.* "Hello, how are you?"; "What has happened since I last saw you?" ☐ *Hi, Jim! What's new?* ☐ *What's new with you?*

What's poppin' *interrog.* "Hello, what is happening?" ☐ *What's poppin'? Anything new?* ☐ *What's poppin', G?*

What's shakin' (bacon)? *interrog.* "How are you?"; "What is new?" ☐ *What's shakin' bacon? What's going down?* ☐ *Hi, Jim. What's shakin'?*

What's the catch? *interrog.* "What is the drawback?"; "It sounds good. Are there any hidden problems?" ☐ *Sounds too good to be true. What's the catch?* ☐ *This looks like a good deal. What's the catch?*

What's the deal? See *What's the scam?*

What's the good word? *interrog.* "Hello, how are you?" ☐ *Hi, Jim! What's the good word?* ☐ *Haven't seen you in a long time. What's the good word?*

What's the scam? AND **What's the deal?** *interrog.* "What is going on around here?" ☐ *There's a big rumpus down the hall. What's the scam?* ☐ *I gave you a twenty, and you give me five back? What's the deal? Where's my other five?*

What's up? *interrog.* "What is going on?"; "What is happening?" (See also *(T)sup?*) ☐ *Hi, Jim! What's up?* ☐ *Haven't seen you in a month of Sundays. What's up?*

What's up, G? *interrog.* "Hello, what is up, guy?" ☐ *What's up G? How ya living?* ☐ *What's up G? Anything new?*

What's with someone or something? *interrog.* "What is wrong with someone or something?" ☐ *Hey, chum! What's with you?* ☐ *What's with this can opener? It won't turn.*

What's your age? *interrog.* "Hello, how are you?" ☐ *What's your age? Tsup?* ☐ *Yo, Sam! What's your age?*

What's yours? *interrog.* "What (or which) do you want?" (Typically said on offering drinks. See also *What'll it be?*) ☐ *"What's yours?" said the bartender.* ☐ *The nice young man behind the counter looked to the right and left at all 140 flavors and said, "What's yours?"*

whatsis AND **whatsit; whatzit; whazzit** ['mətsɪs AND 'mətsɪt, 'mətsɪt, 'məzɪt] *n.* a name for a person or thing whose real name has been forgotten or is being avoided. ☐ *Hand me that whatsis, will you?* ☐ *Put this little whatzit on the top and another on the bottom.*

whatsit See the previous entry.

whatzit See *whatsis.*

whazood AND **waa-zooed** ['ʍɑ'zud AND 'wɑ'zud] *mod.* alcohol intoxicated. □ *Man, is she whazood!* □ *Pete was too waa-zooed to stand up.*

whazzit See *whatsis.*

wheel *tr. & in.* to drive a car. □ *I'm gonna wheel over later this afternoon.* □ *Let's wheel my heap over to Marty's place.*

wheel and deal *in.* to negotiate, cajole, and connive—aggressively. (See also *wheeler-dealer.*) □ *If you can't wheel and deal, you can't run for elective office.* □ *Any crook can wheel and deal!*

wheel man *n.* the (male) driver of a criminal escape car. (Underworld.) □ *Lefty was the wheel man for the bank job.* □ *We need a new wheel man while Lefty's away.*

wheeler-dealer *n.* someone who bargains aggressively. (See also *wheel and deal.*) □ *She has turned into a real wheeler-dealer.* □ *Who's the wheeler-dealer who set up this deal?*

wheelie See *wheely.*

wheels *n.* a car; transportation by automobile. □ *I gotta get some wheels pretty soon.* □ *I'll need a ride. I don't have any wheels.*

wheely AND **wheelie** *n.* an act of rearing up on a bike or motorcycle, balancing on the rear wheel. □ *Can you do wheelies?* □ *The kid did a wheelie and scared his mother to death.*

when push comes to shove AND **if push comes to shove** *phr.* "when things get a little pressed"; "when the situation gets more active or intense." □ *When push comes to shove, you know I'll be on your side.* □ *If push comes to shove, the front office can help with some statistics.*

when the eagle flies AND **day the eagle flies** *phr.* payday. (The *eagle* is the one found on U.S. currency.) □ *I'll pay you back when the eagle flies.* □ *I'll find you the day the eagle flies.*

when the fat lady sings See *till the fat lady sings.*

whenchy See *wenchy.*

Where (have) you been keeping yourself? *interrog.* "I haven't seen you in a long time. Where have you been?" □ *Long time no see. Where've you been keeping yourself?* □ *I haven't seen you in a long time. Where you been keeping yourself?*

Where in (the) Sam Hill? *interrog.* "Where?" (An intensive form of *where. Sam Hill is hell.*) □ *Where in Sam Hill did I put my hat?* □ *Where in the Sam Hill were you?*

Where in the world? *interrog.* "Where?" (An intensive form of *where.* See examples for variations.) □ *Where in the world have you been?* □ *Where in the world did I put my glasses?*

where it's at *phr.* "what one is aiming for"; "what is needed." (This does not refer to a place.) □ *Keep on trying. That's where it's at!* □ *Good strong friends. That's where it's at.*

Where on (God's green) earth? *interrog.* "(Exactly) where?" (An intensive form of *where.* See examples for variations.) □ *Where on God's green earth did you get that ridiculous hat?* □ *Where on earth is my book?* □ *Where on God's green earth were you?*

where someone is at *phr.* "what mental condition someone is in." □ *I know where you're at. I know what you are talking about.* □ *You said it! I know just where you're at!*

where someone lives *phr.* "at one's core"; "in one's own personal situation." □ *That really hits you where you live, doesn't it?* □ *Yes, that gets me where I live.*

where someone's head is at *phr.* the state of one's mental well-being. □ *As soon as I figure where my head is at, I'll be okay.* □ *He doesn't know where his head is at.*

where the action is *phr.* "where important things are happening." □ *I want* *to be where the action is.* □ *Right there in city hall. That's where the action is.*

where the sun don't shine *phr.* in a dark place, namely the anus. (Often with *put it* or *shove it.* Part of the answer to the question *"Where shall I put it?"* Always with *don't;* never with *doesn't.*) □ *I don't care what you do with it. Just put it where the sun don't shine.* □ *For all I care you can shove it where the sun don't shine.*

Where's the beef? *interrog.* "Where is the substance?"; "Where is the content?" (From a television commercial where someone is looking for the meat in a fast-food hamburger.) □ *That's really clever and appealing, but where's the beef?* □ *Where's the beef? There's no substance in this proposal.*

Where's the fire? *interrog.* "Why are you going so fast?"; "What's the hurry?" □ *Going a little fast there, weren't you? Where's the fire?* □ *Where's the fire? We have an hour to get there.*

wherewithal ['ʍɛrwɪθɑl] **1.** *n.* money. □ *I don't have the wherewithal to invest in anything like that.* □ *I've got the interest but not the wherewithal.* **2.** *n.* motivation; gumption. □ *I just don't have the wherewithal to do the job.* □ *As soon as I get some wherewithal, I'll get a new computer.*

whiff-sniffer AND **wiff-sniffer** *n.* a prohibitionist; someone always alert for the smell of alcohol on someone's breath. (Prohibition.) □ *Martin is something of a whiff-sniffer.* □ *No wiff-sniffer is going to tell me what to do.*

whiffled ['ʍɪfl̩d] *mod.* alcohol intoxicated. □ *Jed found himself a mite whiffled, but nobody else knew.* □ *That guy really looks whiffled.*

whing-ding AND **wing-ding** **1.** *n.* a love affair; a sexual affair. □ *Sam and Martha brought their little whing-ding to an end.* □ *Somebody found out about their little wing-ding.* **2.** *n.* a gadget. □ *This whing-ding is broken. Where can I find another?* □ *I've never seen one of these little wing-dings so banged up.* **3.** AND **whinger** *n.* a wild drinking party; drinking spree. □ *Fred had one of the best whing-dings this town has ever seen.* □ *Yes, it was some whinger.*

whinger See the previous entry.

whip something into shape See *lick something into shape.*

whip something off *tr.* to finish something quickly, especially food or drink. □ *Did you just whip that whole pizza off?* Ⓣ *Lemme whip off this sandwich, and I'll be right with you.* Ⓣ *She whipped off the dishes in ten minutes.*

whipped **1.** *mod.* alcohol intoxicated. □ *He slid under the table—whipped, for sure.* □ *She was too whipped to find money to pay her bill.* **2.** *mod.* great. □ *The band was whipped and the food was unbelievable.* □ *You look whipped, Sam. Things going well?*

whipsaw **1.** *tr.* to assault a person; to gang up and beat a person. □ *The gang whipsawed the old man for about ten minutes.* □ *What kind of creeps would whipsaw an old buzzard like that?* **2.** *tr.* [for the stock market] to reduce the capital of investors by frightening them into selling when stock prices are low and encouraging them to buy when prices are high. (Securities markets.) □ *A lot of people were whipsawed in the recent market volatility.* □ *The market will whipsaw the investor who is not cautious.*

whirly bird *n.* a helicopter. □ *See that whirly bird up there? It's timing your speed. Slow down.* □ *The whirly bird landed on the roof of the hospital.*

whiskers (man) See *Mr. Whiskers.*

whiskey tenor *n.* a strained tenor. □ *He's a whiskey tenor, but a good one.* □ *Four whiskey tenors do not a barbershop quartet make.*

whistle-blower *n.* someone who calls a halt to something; an informer; an enforcer; a *stool (pigeon).* □ *I don't know who the whistle-blower was, but a good time was really ruined.* □ *Some whistle-blower put Max behind bars for a few days.*

whistle in the dark *in.* to guess aimlessly; to speculate as to a fact. □ *Am I close, or am I just whistling in the dark?* □ *She was whistling in the dark. She has no idea of what's going on.*

whistler *n.* someone who is a police informer; a *stoolie.* (Underworld. More specialized than *whistle-blower.*) □ *Tracy turned into a whistler after her last little vacation.* □ *Who's the whistler who squealed?*

white elephant *n.* a useless or unwanted object. □ *How can I get rid of this white elephant?* □ *Take all those white elephants to the flea market.*

white hat *n.* a good guy; a hero. (From Western movies where you could tell the good guys from the bad guys by the color of their hats: white for good, black for bad.) □ *He seems like a white hat, but he's a worm.* □ *The white hats don't always win, you know.*

white-knuckle 1. *mod.* having to do with an event that creates a lot of tension, especially an airplane flight. □ *I had a real white-knuckle session with the boss today.* □ *We came in during the storm on a white-knuckle flight from Chicago.* **2.** *mod.* a person who is made tense by something such as flying or sailing. □ *I'm afraid I'm a white-knuckle sailor, and you'd all be much happier if I stay on dry land.* □ *My cousin is a white-knuckle flyer and would rather take the train.*

white knuckler 1. *n.* a tense and nervous person. □ *You white knucklers are just going to have to relax.* □ *I'm such a white knuckler before a test.* **2.** *n.* a suspenseful event, such as an exciting movie or a rough airplane flight. □ *The movie was a real white knuckler.* □ *We sat through the white knuckler even without popcorn.*

whitebread *mod.* plain; dull. □ *Naw, the whole thing is too whitebread.* □ *If I wanted a whitebread vacation, I'd have gone to the beach.*

whitewash 1. *tr.* to make something look better than it really is; to conceal something bad. □ *Now, don't try to whitewash this incident. Open up about it.* □ *The mayor's office tried to whitewash the whole affair.* **2.** *n.* an act or campaign of covering up something bad. □ *They tried to give the scandal the old whitewash, but it didn't work.* □ *It was a good whitewash, but nobody believed it for a minute.*

whittled *mod.* alcohol intoxicated; filled with liquor. (Compare to *cut.*) □ *Fred's whittled and can't hardly see.* □ *Why does he keep getting so whittled?*

whiz 1. *n.* a talented or skilled person. □ *She's a real whiz with stats.* □ *I'm no math whiz, but I can find your errors.* **2.** *in.* to urinate. (Use caution with the topic.) □ *I gotta stop here and whiz.* □ *You can't whiz in the park!*

whiz kid *n.* a young *whiz.* □ *The boss's new whiz kid doesn't seem to be doing the job very well.* □ *We need a whiz kid to get things brought up to date around here.*

Who (in) the devil? See the following entry.

Who (in) the hell? AND **Who (in) the devil?** *interrog.* "Who?" (An elaboration of *who.* See examples for variations.) □ *Who in the hell was that masked man?* □ *Who the hell are you?*

who shot John *n. moonshine;* illicit whiskey. (Prohibition.) □ *You know where I can get a little of that who shot John?* □ *He's had too much of that who shot John.*

Who the deuce? *interrog.* "Who?" (An elaboration of *who.* The *deuce* is the devil. See examples for variations.) □ *Who the deuce do you think you are?* □ *Who the deuce is making all that noise?*

Whoa! [wo] *exclam.* "Stop!" (Said to a horse or any person or thing.) □ *You've gone about far enough. Whoa!* □ *Whoa, you've gone about far enough.*

whodunit [hu'dənɪt] *n.* a detective story. (Compare to *thriller-diller.*) □ *I love to read a good whodunit every now and then.* □ *I go through about three whodunits a week.*

whole bag of tricks *n.* everything; every possibility. □ *Well now. I've used my* *whole bag of tricks, and we still haven't solved this.* □ *It may take my whole bag of tricks to do it, but I'll try.*

whole ball of wax *n.* everything; the whole thing. (Always with *the*.) □ *Well, that just about ruins the whole ball of wax.* □ *Your comments threatened the whole ball of wax, that's what.*

whole bunch(es) *mod.* a whole lot; very much. (Always with *a* in the singular.) □ *I like to spend evenings at home a whole bunch.* □ *I like pizza whole bunches.*

whole enchilada [... ɛntʃəˈlɑdə] *n.* the whole thing; everything. (From Spanish. Always with *the*.) □ *Nobody, but nobody, ever gets the whole enchilada.* □ *Max wants the whole enchilada.*

whole fam damily [...ˈfæm ˈdæmli] *n.* the entire family. (Always with *the*. A deliberate spoonerism for "whole damn family.") □ *The whole fam damily has had this virus. Yuck!* □ *There's enough here for the whole fam damily.*

whole new ball game *n.* a completely different situation; something completely different. (Always with *a*.) □ *Now that you're here, it's a whole new ball game.* □ *With a faster computer, it's a whole new ball game.*

whole nine yards *n.* the entire amount; everything. (Always with *the*. Origin unknown.) □ *For you I'll go the whole nine yards.* □ *You're worth the whole nine yards.*

whole schmear [...ʃmɪr] *n.* the entire amount; the entire affair. (Yiddish. Always with *the*.) □ *You just wrecked the whole schmear, that's what.* □ *I'll take a hamburger with everything on it—the whole schmear.*

whole shebang AND **whole shooting match** [...ʃəˈbæŋ] *n.* the whole affair; everything and everyone. (Folksy. Always with *the*.) □ *The whole shebang is just about washed up.* □ *I'm fed up with the whole shooting match.*

whole shooting match See the previous entry.

whole wide world *n.* everywhere; everywhere and everything. (Always with *the*.) □ *It's the best in the whole wide world.* □ *I've searched the whole wide world for just the right hat.*

whomp See *whump*.

whooshed *mod.* alcohol intoxicated. □ *Jerry was totally whooshed by midnight.* □ *Hank was whooshed but thought he could drive home.*

whoozis AND **whoozit** [ˈhuzɪs AND ˈhuzɪt] *n.* a name for a person whose real name is forgotten or being avoided. □ *I met whoozis—you know, with the big whatsis—today.* □ *Is whoozit coming to my birthday party?*

whoozit See the previous entry.

whopper 1. *n.* something that is of relatively great size. □ *That thing's really a whopper!* □ *It was a whopper of an argument.* **2.** *n.* a very big lie. □ *That one's a whopper. I don't believe a word of it.* □ *She sure told a whopper, didn't she?*

whopping (great) *mod.* enormous. □ *Somebody showed up with a whopping great basin of chunks of pickled fish. Yummy!* □ *What a whopping fool he is!*

whump AND **whomp; womp** [ʍəmp AND ʍɑmp, wɑmp] **1.** *tr.* to beat or outscore someone. □ *They set out to whump us, and they sure did.* □ *The Redskins womped the Walleyes.* **2.** *n.* the sound made when two flat surfaces fall together. □ *I heard the whump when the shed collapsed.* □ *The whomp woke everyone up.*

wicked *mod.* excellent; impressive. □ *Now this is what I call a wicked guitar.* □ *Man, this wine is wicked!*

wide *mod.* drug intoxicated. □ *Who is that wide dude?* □ *How'd you get so wide, man?*

wide open 1. *mod.* as fast as possible; at full throttle. □ *I was driving along wide open when I became aware of a flashing red light.* □ *It was wide open and still wouldn't do better than eighty.* **2.** *mod.* vice-ridden. □ *This town is wide open!*

☐ *Because the prison is understaffed, it is wide open.*

wide place in the road *n.* a very small town. ☐ *The town is little more than a wide place in the road.* ☐ *We stopped at a wide place in the road called Adamsville.*

widget ['wɪdʒɪt] **1.** *n.* a gadget. ☐ *Now, try to fit this widget into this slot here.* ☐ *What is the real name of this widget?* **2.** *n.* a hypothetical product made by a hypothetical company. ☐ *Someone said that your company is manufacturing widgets.* ☐ *No, we stopped making widgets last year. Too much foreign competition.*

widow-maker *n.* a dangerous horse; anything dangerous: a gun, strong alcohol, etc. ☐ *I call this stuff widow-maker. It's really strong.* ☐ *That horse is a widow-maker. I won't ride it.*

wiener nose ['winɚ . . .] *n.* a simpleton. (Also a derogatory term of address.) ☐ *Look, wiener nose, mind your own business.* ☐ *Todd, you are such a wiener nose!*

wife *n.* a girlfriend. (Collegiate.) ☐ *Me and my wife are going to Fred's this Friday.* ☐ *Ask your wife if she wants to come along.*

wiff-sniffer See *whiff-sniffer.*

wig out **1.** *in.* to lose control of oneself; to *flip one's wig.* ☐ *I was afraid I would wig out if I stayed any longer.* ☐ *Take it easy, man. Don't wig out.* (More at *wigged (out).*) **2.** *in.* to have a good time at a party, etc. ☐ *We wigged out at John's do.* ☐ *Come on, let's wig out!*

wigged (out) AND **wiggy** **1.** *mod.* alcohol or drug intoxicated. ☐ *How did you get so wigged out?* ☐ *The kid got a little wigged and slipped under the table.* **2.** *mod.* having lost control of oneself; having flipped one's wig. ☐ *The kid is just too wigged to do anything these days.* ☐ *After the bad news, she was totally wigged out.*

wiggle out of something *in.* to successfully avoid doing something. ☐ *We wiggled out of the appointment.* ☐ *Don't try to wiggle out of it. I saw you with her.*

wiggy See *wigged (out).*

wild *mod.* exciting; eccentric; *cool.* ☐ *Things are really wild here.* ☐ *We had a wild time.*

wild and wooly *mod.* exciting; *hairy.* ☐ *Things get a little wild and wooly on a Friday evening at Wally's place.* ☐ *The ride home was a little wild and wooly.*

will do *phr.* "I will do it." ☐ *Will do. I'll get right on it.* ☐ *Fix the stuck window? Will do.*

willies *n.* a case of fear or anxiety. (Compare to *screaming-meemies.*) ☐ *That kind of movie always gives me the willies.* ☐ *I got the willies before the test.*

Wilma ['wɪlmə] *n.* a stupid woman. (From the Flintstones character. Also a term of address.) ☐ *She is such a Wilma! What a twit!* ☐ *Well, Wilma. I see you forgot your money again.*

WIMP [wɪmp] *mod.* "windows, icons, mouse pointer." (Acronym. Refers to a computer system, such as Macintosh or Microsoft Windows, with an elaborate user interface including resizable windows, clever icons, and a movable mouse. The term implies that such systems are for "computer weaklings.") ☐ *I am happier with a computer system that doesn't have all that WIMP stuff.* ☐ *I want all the WIMP gadgets I can get!*

wimp [wɪmp] *n.* a weak and retiring person; a *square.* ☐ *Don't be a wimp. Stand up for your rights.* ☐ *What a wimp. People walk all over her.*

wimp out (of something) *in.* to *chicken out (of something);* to get out of something, leaving others to carry the burden. ☐ *Come on! Don't wimp out now that there's all this work to be done.* ☐ *Ted wimped out on us.*

wimpy *mod.* weak; inept; *square.* ☐ *You are just a wimpy nerd!* ☐ *Come on, don't be so wimpy.*

Win a few, lose a few. *phr.* "Sometimes one wins; other times one loses." ☐ *Too bad. Sorry about that. Win a few, lose a few.* ☐ *"Win a few, lose a few," doesn't mean you never win at all.*

windbag AND **bag of wind** *n.* a talkative person; a braggart. □ *Quiet, you windbag!* □ *She's nothing but a big bag of wind.*

windy 1. *mod.* talkative. □ *She's so windy! Won't she ever let up?* □ *Here comes old windy Charlie. Once he gets started, he never stops.* 2. *mod.* flatulent; having intestinal gas. □ *I feel a little windy.* □ *If you're windy, why don't you take the day off?*

wing *in.* to travel by airplane. □ *We winged to Budapest and attended the conference.* □ *They winged from there to London.*

wing-ding See *whing-ding.*

wing heavy *mod.* alcohol intoxicated. □ *Ken's a little wing heavy and can't fly straight.* □ *From the way he's staggering, I'd say he's more than a little wing heavy.*

wing it *tr.* to improvise; to do something extemporaneously. □ *I lost my lecture notes, so I had to wing it.* □ *Don't worry. Just go out there and wing it.*

winks *n.* some sleep. (See also *forty winks.*) □ *I gotta have some winks. I'm pooped.* □ *A few winks would do you good.*

winky See *blinky.*

winner *n.* an excellent person or thing. □ *This one is a real winner.* □ *He's no winner, but he'll do.*

wino ['wɑɪno] 1. *n.* wine. □ *How about a little more wino?* □ *This is excellent wino.* 2. *n.* a wine drunkard. □ *By midnight the winos had gone into their stupors, and we got that part of town to ourselves.* □ *I gave the wino some money to help him stop the shakes.*

wipe *n.* a murder; a killing. (Underworld. See also *wipe out.*) □ *Who's responsible for that wipe downtown last night?* □ *The victim of the latest mob wipe was hauled out of the river this morning.*

Wipe it off! *exclam.* "Wipe that smile off your face!" □ *It's not funny. Wipe it off!* □ *Wipe it off! Nothing funny here, soldier.*

wipe out 1. *in.* to crash. □ *I wiped out on the curve.* □ *The car wiped out on the curve.* 2. *in.* to fall off or away from something, such as a bicycle, skates, a surfboard, a skateboard, etc. □ *I wiped out and skinned my knee.* □ *If I wipe out again, my mother says I'm through.* 3. ['wɑɪpɑʊt] *n.* a wreck. (Usually **wipe-out.**) □ *There was a four-car wipe-out on the expressway when I came in this morning.* □ *It was a pretty serious wipe-out, but no one was killed.* 4. *n.* an accident on a bicycle, skates, surfboard, skateboard, etc. (Usually **wipe-out.**) □ *I had a nasty wipe-out, but I only bruised my elbow.* □ *That last wipe-out wrecked my bike.* 5. *n.* a *loser;* someone who is likely to *wipe out.* (Usually **wipe-out.**) □ *The guy's a wipe-out, for sure.* □ *Please don't call my friend a wipe-out.*

wipe someone or something out 1. *tr.* [with *someone*] to eliminate someone; to kill someone. (Underworld.) □ *Max almost wiped Bruno out.* 🅃 *Who wiped out Lefty?* 2. *tr.* [with *someone*] to exhaust or tire someone. □ *The game wiped me out.* □ *Jogging always wipes me out.* 3. *tr.* [with *someone*] to ruin someone financially. □ *The loss of my job wiped us out.* 🅃 *The storm ruined the corn crop and wiped out everyone in the county.* 4. *tr.* [with *something*] to use up all of something. □ *I wiped the cookies out—not all at once, of course.* 🅃 *Who wiped out the strawberry preserves?* (More at *wiped (out).*)

wipe the floor up with someone See *mop the floor up with someone.*

wiped (out) 1. AND **wiped over** *mod.* alcohol or drug intoxicated. □ *Harry was too wiped out to drive.* □ *Oh, man! I'm really wiped.* 2. *mod.* (of a person or thing) exhausted. □ *I'm so wiped out that I just want to go home and go to bed.* □ *Wow, am I wiped out!* 3. *mod.* broke. □ *I'm totally wiped out. Not enough bread for grub.* □ *Medical bills left us totally wiped out.*

wiped over See the previous entry.

wire 1. *n.* a spy smuggled into a place. □ *Bruno thought Lefty was a wire.* □ *How do we know Lefty isn't a wire?* 2. *tr.* to install electronic eavesdropping equipment. ☐ *Somebody wired the mayor's office.* ☐ *They say the mayor wired his own office to make himself look like a victim.* **3.** See *(live) wire.*

wired 1. *mod.* nervous; extremely alert. ☐ *The guy is pretty wired because of the election.* ☐ *I get wired before a test.* **2.** AND **wired up** *mod.* alcohol or drug intoxicated. ☐ *Ken was so wired up he couldn't remember his name.* ☐ *Tiff is, like, totally wired up.*

wired into someone or something *mod.* concerned with someone or something; really involved with someone or something. ☐ *Mary is really wired into classical music.* ☐ *Sam and Martha are totally wired into one another.*

wired up See *wired.*

wise guy *n.* a foolish person; a *smart aleck.* (Compare to *smart guy.* Also a term of address.) ☐ *Look, wise guy, mind your own business!* ☐ *Some wise guy messed up my work.*

wise to someone or something *mod.* having found out about someone or something. (Underworld.) ☐ *The cops are wise to the plan.* ☐ *I'm wise to Lefty. He's a wire.*

wise up (to someone or something) *in.* to (finally) begin to understand someone or something; to realize and accept the facts about someone or something. (Also as a command.) ☐ *Sally finally wised up to Max.* ☐ *Come on, Sally! Wise up!*

wiseacre See *weisenheimer.*

wish book *n.* a large, mail order catalog. ☐ *The new wish book just came in the mail.* ☐ *Where's the wish book? I have to order something.*

wish list *n.* a list of things one wishes to have. (Compare to *want list.*) ☐ *I put a new car at the top of my wish list.* ☐ *I have a CD player on my wish list.*

wishy-washy ['wɪʃi'waʃi] *mod.* indecisive; insipid; weak. ☐ *Don't be such a wishy-washy wimp.* ☐ *She is so wishy-washy!*

with a bang *mod.* in a flamboyant or exciting manner. (Especially with *go out, quit, finish.*) ☐ *The party started off with a bang.* ☐ *The old year went out with a bang.*

with bells on *mod.* ready to go; eager. ☐ *She was here on time with bells on.* ☐ *I promise to be there at five in the morning with bells on.*

with flying colors *mod.* flamboyantly; boldly. ☐ *Heidi won first place with flying colors.* ☐ *Paul came home with flying colors after the match.*

with it *mod.* up-to-date; contemporary. ☐ *Martin is not exactly with it.* ☐ *Come on, chum. Get with it.*

with (one's) eyes (wide) open *mod.* totally aware of what is going on. ☐ *I went into this with my eyes open.* ☐ *We all started with eyes open but didn't realize what could happen to us.*

within an ace of (doing) something *mod.* very close to doing something. ☐ *I came within an ace of getting stoned.* ☐ *We were within an ace of beating the all-time record.*

without a hitch *mod.* with no problem(s). ☐ *Everything went off without a hitch.* ☐ *We hoped the job would go off without a hitch.*

woefits AND **woofits** ['wofɪts AND 'wufɪts] *n.* a hangover. ☐ *The poor guy is suffering from the woefits.* ☐ *That's a bad case of the woofits.*

wolf *n.* a bold and aggressive male. ☐ *He sees himself as a lady-killer. The chicks see him as an old-fashioned wolf.* ☐ *And this wolf comes up to me and starts holding my hand.*

wolf something down *tr.* to gobble something up; to bolt down food or drink. ☐ *Enjoy your food. Don't just wolf it down.* 🅃 *But I enjoy wolfing down food more than anything.*

wombat ['wɑmbæt] *n.* a strange person; a *geek.* (Collegiate.) ☐ *Why does everybody think Martin is such a wombat?* ☐ *Who's the wombat in the 1957 Chevy?*

womp See *whump.*

wonk [wɔŋk] **1.** *n.* an earnest student. (Collegiate.) □ *Who's the wonk who keeps getting the straight A's?* □ *Yes, you could call Martin a wonk. In fact, he's the classic wonk.* **2.** *n.* a bureaucrat; a flunky. □ *The State Department policy wonks were up all night putting together the report.* □ *Our office was knee-deep in wonks before the reorganization.*

wonky ['wɔŋki] *mod.* studious. (Collegiate.) □ *Martin is certainly the wonky type.* □ *You ought to get a little wonky yourself.*

wood butcher *n.* a carpenter. □ *See if you can get a wood butcher to fix this broken panel.* □ *The wood butcher tracked sawdust up the stairs.*

wood-pussy *n.* a skunk. □ *Do I smell the faint perfume of a wood-pussy?* □ *The dog had a nasty run-in with a wood-pussy.*

woods are full of ____ *phr.* "there are lots and lots of ____." (Always with *the.*) □ *The woods are full of cheap, compatible computer clones.* □ *The woods are full of nice-looking guys who'll mug you when it's too late.*

woody *n.* a wooden surfboard; a surfboard. □ *Who's the guy with the woody on his head?* □ *Get your woody, and let's get moving.*

woof [wʊf] **1.** *in.* to boast; to *sell a wolf ticket;* to chatter. (Black.) □ *They're just woofing. Ignore them.* □ *Stop woofing, Fred. You sound silly.* **2.** *in.* to vomit. (Onomatopoetic.) □ *Somebody woofed on our driveway.* □ *Beavis had to woof on the way home.*

woof cookies *tr.* to vomit. □ *Bill is in the bathroom woofing cookies.* □ *Waldo had to woof cookies in the bushes.*

woofits See *woefits.*

woofle-water AND **wozzle-water** *n.* whiskey; liquor. □ *Haven't you had just about enough woofle-water?* □ *No more wozzle-water for me.*

woofled ['wʊfl̩d] *mod.* alcohol intoxicated. □ *Good grief, was he woofled!* □ *Did I get woofled last night? I just don't remember.*

woolies *n.* long underwear. □ *It's the time of the year for woolies!* □ *I wish I'd worn my woolies today.*

woozy ['wuzi] **1.** *mod.* sleepy; disoriented. □ *Aren't you woozy at this time of day?* □ *Who is that woozy gal by the window?* □ *I'm still sort of woozy. Give me a minute or two to wake up.* **2.** *mod.* alcohol intoxicated. □ *I felt a little woozy, but that didn't stop me from having more.* □ *Woozy as I am, I can still drive. Now, give me back my keys.*

Word. 1. AND **Word up.** *interj.* "Correct."; "Right." □ *I hear you, man. Word.* □ *Word. I agree.* □ *Yes, it's time to go. Word up.* **2.** *interj.* "Hello." □ *Word. What's new.* □ *Word. Living large?*

Word up. See the previous entry.

work one's buns off See *work one's tail off.*

work one's butt off See the following entry.

work one's tail off AND **work one's buns off; work one's butt off** *tr.* to work very hard. (Use caution with *butt.*) □ *I worked my tail off to get done on time.* □ *You spend half your life working your butt off—and for what?*

work oneself up *tr.* to allow oneself to become emotionally upset. □ *Todd worked himself up, and I thought he would scream.* □ *Don't work yourself up over Tracy. She's not worth it.*

work oneself (up) into a lather 1. *tr.* to work very hard and sweat very much. (In the way that a horse works up a lather.) □ *Don't work yourself up into a lather. We don't need to finish this today.* □ *I worked myself into a lather getting this stuff ready.* **2.** *tr.* to get excited or angry. (An elaboration of *work oneself up to something.*) □ *Now, now, don't work yourself up into a lather.* □ *He had worked himself into such a lather, I was afraid he would have a stroke.*

work oneself up to something *tr.* to get oneself mentally ready to do something. □ *I spent all morning working* *myself up to taking the driver's test.* ☐ *I had to work myself up to it little by little.*

work someone over 1. *tr.* to threaten, intimidate, or beat someone. ☐ *Bruno threatened to work Sam over.* Ⓣ *Bruno had worked over Terry, and Sam knew that this was no idle threat.* **2.** *tr.* to give someone's body a thorough examination or treatment. ☐ *The doctors worked her over to the tune of $1,500, but couldn't find anything wrong with her.* Ⓣ *The dermatologist worked over her entire body looking for moles.*

workaholic *n.* someone who is obsessed with work. ☐ *Jerry is a workaholic. He can't enjoy a vacation.* ☐ *Are workaholics really productive?*

working stiff *n.* a working man; a man who must work to live. (See also *stiff.*) ☐ *But does the working stiff really care about all this economic stuff?* ☐ *All the working stiffs want is a raise.*

works *n.* the entire amount; everything. (Always with *the*.) ☐ *I'd like my hamburger with onions, pickles, catsup, mustard—the works.* ☐ *She's getting the works at the beauty shop—cut, wash, dye, and set.*

world-beater *n.* an aggressive and ambitious person. ☐ *She's not a world-beater, but she's efficient.* ☐ *They hired an alleged world-beater to manage the office.*

world-class *mod.* absolutely top rate. ☐ *Now this is a world-class computer. Lots and lots of memory.* ☐ *I want to see one of your world-class automobiles, whatever that might mean.* ☐ *This one isn't world-class.*

world is one's oyster *phr.* one rules the world; one is in charge of everything. (Always with *the*.) ☐ *I feel like the world is my oyster, today.* ☐ *The world is my oyster! I'm in love!*

worm *n.* a repellent person, usually a male. ☐ *Gad, you are a worm, Tom.* ☐ *I'd like Fred better if he wasn't such a worm.*

worm-food *n.* a corpse. ☐ *You wanna end up worm-food? Just keep smarting off.* ☐ *In the end, we're all worm-food.*

worms *n.* noodles; spaghetti. ☐ *Let's have worms tonight.* ☐ *Are the worms ready for the sauce yet?*

worms in blood *n.* spaghetti in tomato sauce. ☐ *We're having worms in blood for dinner tonight.* ☐ *I'm getting tired of worms in blood every Wednesday.*

worry wart *n.* someone who worries all the time. ☐ *Don't be such a worry wart.* ☐ *I'm sorry I'm such a worry wart.*

worship the porcelain god(dess) *tr.* to empty one's stomach; to vomit. (Collegiate.) ☐ *Somebody was in the john worshiping the porcelain god till all hours.* ☐ *I think I have to go worship the porcelain goddess. See ya.*

worst-case scenario *n.* the worse possible future outcome. ☐ *Now, let's look at the worst-case scenario.* ☐ *In the worst-case scenario, we're all dead.*

worth one's salt *mod.* worth (in productivity) what it costs to keep one. ☐ *We decided that you are worth your salt, and you can stay on as office clerk.* ☐ *You're not worth your salt. Pack up!*

would not be seen dead *phr.* would not do something under any circumstances. ☐ *I wouldn't be seen dead going out with Bruno!* ☐ *Martha would not be seen dead going into a place like that.*

Would you believe? *interrog.* "Isn't it amazing?" ☐ *He actually tried to get me to scratch his bare back! Would you believe?* ☐ *Would you believe? A three-cent per hour raise?*

wouldn't touch someone or something with a ten-foot pole *phr.* would not get involved with someone or something. ☐ *Forget it. I wouldn't touch it with a ten-foot pole.* ☐ *Tom said he wouldn't touch Tracy with a ten-foot pole.*

wow 1. *exclam.* an indication of amazement or surprise. (Usually **Wow!**) ☐ *Wow! Is he ever ugly!* ☐ *A whole quarter! Wow! Thanks, mister.* **2.** *tr.* to delight or impress someone. ☐ *She wowed them with her cleverness.* ☐ *That ought to wow them right out of their seats.* **3.** *n.* something exciting. ☐ *The game was a real wow.* ☐ *For a pretty good wow, try the Empire Theater's production of "Mame"* *this weekend.* **4.** *n.* an exclamation point. ☐ *Put a wow at the end of this sentence.* ☐ *Almost every sentence you write has a wow at the end of it.*

wozzle-water See *woofle-water.*

wrap one's car around something *tr.* to drive one's car into something at fairly high speed. ☐ *She wrapped her car around a light pole.* ☐ *If he hadn't wrapped his car around a tree, he'd be here to read his own poetry tonight.*

wrap something up *tr.* to finish something; to bring something to a conclusion. ☐ *Let's wrap this up and go home.* 🅃 *Well, that about wraps up our little session together.*

wrapped up (in someone or something) *mod.* concerned or obsessed with someone or something. ☐ *Sally is pretty wrapped up in herself.* ☐ *I'm too wrapped up in my charity work to get a job.*

wrapped up (with someone or something) *mod.* busy with someone or something. ☐ *He's wrapped up with a client right now.* ☐ *I'll talk to you when I'm not wrapped up.*

wrecked *mod.* alcohol or drug intoxicated. ☐ *Four beers and I was wrecked.* ☐ *Larry was far too wrecked to drive.*

wrinkle 1. *n.* a new idea; a new aspect of something. ☐ *Fred came up with a new wrinkle for the ad campaign.* ☐ *Here's a wrinkle for you. Nobody has ever tried this one.* **2.** *n.* a minor problem. ☐ *A wrinkle has developed in the Wilson proposal.* ☐ *What are we going to do about this wrinkle in the computer system?*

wrinkle-rod *n.* the crankshaft of an engine. ☐ *You need a new wrinkle-rod, lady.* ☐ *A wrinkle-rod'll set you back about $199, plus installation charges, of course.*

wrong side of the tracks *n.* the poor side of town. ☐ *Fred's ashamed that he's from the wrong side of the tracks, so to speak.* ☐ *I'm glad I'm from the wrong side of the tracks. I know what life is really like.*

wrongo ['rɔŋo] **1.** *mod.* wrong. ☐ *You are totally wrongo.* ☐ *Wrongo, wrongo! You lose!* **2.** *n.* an undesirable thing or person; a member of the underworld. ☐ *The guy's a total wrongo. He's got to be guilty.* ☐ *This whole business is a complete wrongo. Something's fishy.*

wuss(y) [wus AND 'wusi] *n.* a *wimp;* a weak person. ☐ *Don't be such a wuss. Stand up for your rights.* ☐ *Wussies like you will never get ahead.*

WYSIWYG See *What you see is what you get.*

X

X'd out **1.** *mod.* eliminated; crossed-out. □ *But the Babbits are X'd out.* □ *Put the X'd out Babbits back where they were.* **2.** *mod.* killed. (Underworld.) □ *Mr. Big wanted Max X'd out.* □ *He wanted Bruno to see that all these small-time punks were X'd out.*

X marks the spot. *sent.* "This is the exact place!" (A catch phrase.) □ *This is where it happened. X marks the spot.* □ *X marks the spot where we first met.*

XYZ *tr.* "examine your zipper"; make sure your fly is zipped up. (Initialism. Said to men when necessary.) □ *I say there, Wally, X.Y.Z.* □ *X.Y.Z., Fred.*

Y

ya *pro.* you. (Eye-dialect. Typical spoken English. Used in writing only for effect. Used in the examples of this dictionary.) ☐ *See ya!* ☐ *Is this all ya want?*

yack AND **yock; yuck; yuk** [jæk AND jɔk, jək] **1.** *n.* a foolish person. ☐ *Who's the yock wearing the red bandana?* ☐ *Get some yuk to do it. I'm busy.* **2.** *n.* idle chatter. ☐ *I've heard enough yack to last me a lifetime.* ☐ *Too much yock. Where's the beef?* **3.** See *yak.*

yackety-yak ['jækədi'jæk] *n.* chatter; gossip. ☐ *No more yackety-yak* ☐ *That's enough yackety-yak. Quiet!*

yahoo ['jɑhu] *n.* a rustic oaf; an uncouth *jerk.* ☐ *Ask that yahoo to close the door after him.* ☐ *What yahoo brought this dog in here?*

yak AND **yack** [jæk] **1.** *in.* to talk. ☐ *Stop yakking for a minute.* ☐ *I need to yack with you about something.* **2.** *n.* a chat. ☐ *We had a nice little yack and then left for work.* ☐ *Drop by for a yak sometime.* **3.** *n.* a joke. ☐ *That was a lousy yak.* ☐ *Don't tell that yack again. It's not a winner.* **4.** *n.* a laugh from a joke. ☐ *We had a good yack over it.* ☐ *The audience produced a feeble yak that was mostly from embarrassment.* **5.** *in.* to vomit. (Onomatopoetic.) ☐ *Hank was in the john yakking all night.* ☐ *Who yakked on the carpet?*

yak it up *tr.* to talk incessantly or a lot. ☐ *Why don't you all just yak it up while I get ready to give the talk?* ☐ *Stop yakking it up and listen.*

yakky ['jæki] *mod.* talkative. ☐ *He's a yakky old man, but I like him.* ☐ *Isn't she yakky today?*

yank **1.** *tr.* to harass someone. (See also *yank someone around.*) ☐ *Stop yanking me!* ☐ *Yank the welcher a little and see what that does.* **2.** *n.* a Yankee; a U.S. soldier. (Usually **Yank.**) ☐ *I don't care if you call me a yank. That's what I am.* ☐ *Hey, Yank! What's new?* **3.** *in.* to vomit. ☐ *Somebody or some animal yanked on the driveway.* ☐ *I think I gotta go yank.*

yank someone around *tr.* to harass someone; to give someone a hard time. (Compare to *jerk someone around.*) ☐ *Listen, I don't mean to yank you around all the time, but we have to have the drawings by Monday.* ☐ *Please stop yanking me around.*

yank someone's chain *tr.* to harass someone; to give someone a hard time. (As if one were a dog wearing a choker collar, on a leash.) ☐ *Stop yanking my chain!* ☐ *Do you really think you can just yank my chain whenever you want?*

yanked *mod.* arrested. (Underworld.) ☐ *Lefty got himself yanked one too many times.* ☐ *Everybody in the gang got yanked at least once last week.*

yap **1.** *n.* the mouth. ☐ *Shut your yap!* ☐ *You have a big yap, you know?* **2.** *in.* to chatter; to gossip. ☐ *Who's yapping so much in here?* ☐ *Did you just come here to yap?* **3.** *n.* nonsense; gibberish. ☐ *That's just yap. Forget it. They mean no harm.* ☐ *That windbag can produce an enormous amount of yap.* **4.** *in.* to empty one's stomach; to vomit. ☐ *Who yapped in the bushes?* ☐ *Ye gods, do I hear one of our guests yapping in the powder room?* **5.** *n.* a naive person; a dupe. ☐ *The poor yap was made a fool of.* ☐ *See* *if you can get that yap to bring over a left-handed monkey wrench.*

yard *n.* a one-hundred-dollar bill. (Underworld.) □ *The guy wanted a yard just to fix a little dent in the fender.* □ *Pay him a yard to shut up about what he saw.*

yard dog *n.* a repellent person; an uncouth person. □ *Is that lousy yard dog hanging around the neighborhood again?* □ *Yup. It's that yard dog, Max.*

yardbird **1.** *n.* a convict. □ *Who's the yardbird with the headphones on his noodle?* □ *So, Charlie was a yardbird. So what?* **2.** *n.* an inept soldier. (Military.) □ *You yardbirds are going to learn discipline one way or another.* □ *How many of you yardbirds would like to go home in one piece?*

yatata-yatata ['jætətə'jætətə] *n.* the sound of chatter or *yak.* □ *All I ever hear around here is yatata-yatata.* □ *He gets on the phone, and it's yatata-yatata for hours.*

yawner *n.* a boring show or performance. □ *It was a yawner from the opening curtain straight through to the end.* □ *Your lecture, sir, was a total yawner.*

yazzihamper ['jæzihæmpɚ] *n.* an obnoxious person. □ *You are the most annoying yazzihamper I know!* □ *Who's the yazzihamper in the double knit?*

Ye gods! *exclam.* "Good grief!" □ *Ye gods! What is this stuff here?* □ *Ye gods! My hair is falling out.*

yea big ['je 'bɪg] *mod.* about so big. (Accompanied by a hand gesture.) □ *Oh, it was about yea big.* □ *Do you have a panel that is about yea big?*

yeah ['jæə OR 'jæɔ] *interj.* "yes." □ LEFTY: *You okay?* BRUNO: *Yeah.* □ LEFTY: *Yeah?* BRUNO: *Yeah! I said yeah! Did you hear me say yeah?*

yeaster *n.* a beer-drinker. □ *A couple of yeasters in the back of the tavern were singing a dirty song.* □ *Who's the yeaster with the bloodshot eyes?*

Yec(c)h! [jɛk OR jɛtʃ] *exclam.* "Horrible!"; "It's yucky!" □ *Oh, yech! What's that stuff?* □ *Yecch! It's moving!*

yegg [jɛg] **1.** *n.* a tramp, thief, or safecracker. (Underworld.) □ *The cops hauled in the usual yeggs, but they all had alibis.* □ *See if you can find that yegg we worked with on the bank job. He'll do.* **2.** *n.* an obnoxious male. □ *Don't act like such a yegg, Bill.* □ *A couple of drunken yeggs were talking a little too loud, so Bruno showed them the door.*

yell one's guts out See the following entry.

yell one's head off AND **yell one's guts out** **1.** *tr.* to yell loud and long. □ *I was yelling my head off at the game.* □ *Stop yelling your guts out and listen to me.* **2.** *tr.* to complain bitterly and loudly. □ *Some lady is yelling her head off about shoddy workmanship out in the lobby.* □ *I yell my guts out about tripe when I see tripe!*

Yello. ['jɛ'lo] *interj.* "Hello." (Said with any intonation that would be appropriate with *hello.*) □ *Yello, Dave Jones speaking.* □ *Yello, Smith residence.*

yellow *mod.* cowardly. □ *Who says I'm yellow?* □ *Bruno says you're yellow. Wanna make something of it?*

yellow-bellied *mod.* cowardly. □ *You are a yellow-bellied coward!* □ *I'm not yellow-bellied!* □ *What yellow-bellied skunk ran off with my horse?*

yellow-belly *n.* a coward. □ *He's not a yellow-belly. He's cautious.* □ *Tell the yellow-belly to come outside and say that.*

yellow streak (down someone's back) *n.* a tendency toward cowardice. □ *Tim's got a yellow streak down his back a mile wide.* □ *Get rid of that yellow streak. Show some courage.*

yelper *n.* the whooping (electronic) siren on emergency vehicles. □ *The black and white rounded the corner, yelper blasting.* □ *Turn off the yelper, Chuck, we hear you.*

yench [jɛntʃ] *tr.* to swindle someone; to victimize someone. (Underworld.) □ *The flimflam artist yenched a couple of banks and then moved on.* □ *Somebody tried to yench the wrong guy at the circus.*

yenta ['jɛntə] *n.* a gossip, usually a woman. (Regarded as Yiddish.) ☐ *She can be such a yenta when she's got news.* ☐ *Tracy is a yenta if ever there was one.*

yep See *yup.*

Yes! *interj.* "Absolutely yes!" (Always with a special intonation that holds the "y " on a higher pitch and then drops the pitch sharply. The word itself is not slang, but the word with this intonation is part of many slang contexts.) ☐ *That's right! Yes!* ☐ *Yes! Exactly right!*

Yo! *interj.* "Hello!"; "Attention, please!"; "Wait a minute!" ☐ *Yo, Michael! What's new.* ☐ *Yo! Come over here.*

yo mama *interj.* "so you say." (Black.) ☐ *Not enough bread! Yo mama.* ☐ *Yo mama! The hell you say!*

yock AND **yok** [jɔk] **1.** *in.* to laugh loudly. (Compare to *yak.*) ☐ *Everybody yocked at the joke, and when things calmed down, I announced the mass firings.* ☐ *Stop yocking and listen to this.* **2.** *n.* a loud laugh. ☐ *Sue let out an enormous yock and quickly covered her mouth.* ☐ *Who came out with that uncivil yock?* **3.** See *yack.*

yodeling in a canyon *in.* talking aimlessly. ☐ *You are just yodeling in a canyon if you think I really care about it.* ☐ *Stop yodeling in a canyon and start making sense.*

yok See *yock.*

yoked [jokt] *mod.* having well-marked abdominal muscles. ☐ *That guy is really yoked. I wonder how much he works out.* ☐ *I'm too fat to ever get yoked.*

york [jork] **1.** *in.* to empty one's stomach; to vomit. ☐ *He ate the stuff, then went straight out and yorked.* ☐ *Who yorked in the flowerpot?* **2.** *n.* vomit. ☐ *Is that york I see on the living room window?* ☐ *Hey, Jimmy! Come out in the snow and see the frozen york!*

You and what army? See the following entry.

You and who else? AND **You and what army?** *interrog.* "Who besides you is threatening me?" ☐ *You're gonna whup me? You and who else?* ☐ *You and what army are gonna yank my chain?*

You asked for it! *exclam.* "Here it comes, and you deserve it!" ☐ *So you want the full treatment? You asked for it!* ☐ *So, you wanted to hear both sides of the record? You asked for it!*

you bet *interj.* "yes"; "you can bet on it." ☐ *Can you have two? You bet.* ☐ *You bet; it's all settled.*

You bet your boots! *exclam.* "You can be absolutely certain!" ☐ *Am I happy? You bet your boots!* ☐ *You bet your boots I'm mad.*

You bet your sweet life! *exclam.* "You are absolutely correct!" ☐ *Happy? You bet your sweet life!* ☐ *You bet your sweet life I am glad!*

You bet your sweet patoot(ie)! *exclam.* "You can be absolutely certain!" (*Patootie* is the buttocks.) ☐ *You bet your sweet patootie I'm serious!* ☐ *I'll be there! You bet your sweet patoot!*

You betcha! ['ju 'bɛtʃə] *interj.* "Yes!"; "You can be sure of it!" (Literally, You bet, you.) ☐ *Will I be there? You betcha.* ☐ *Can I? You betcha!*

You can say that again! *exclam.* "I agree!" ☐ *You can say that again! It's really hot!* ☐ *You can say that again! You hit the nail right on the head.*

You can't dance at two weddings. *sent.* "You cannot do two things at once." ☐ *Either go to the beach with Fred or stay here with me. You can't dance at two weddings.* ☐ *Decide which one you want to buy. You can only have one and you can't dance at two weddings.*

You can't fight city hall. *sent.* "You cannot fight a bureaucracy." ☐ *I finally gave up. You can't fight city hall.* ☐ *You can't fight city hall. Pay the parking ticket and forget it.*

You can't get there from here. *sent.* "Where you want to go is in a very remote location." (A catch phrase.) ☐ *Well, you can't get there from here.* ☐ *Adamsville? Sorry, you can't get there from here.*

You can't take it with you. *sent.* "You cannot take wealth with you when you die." ☐ *Enjoy it now. You can't take it with you.* ☐ *My uncle doesn't believe that saying, you know, "You can't take it with you." He's going to try.*

You can't win them all. AND **You can't win 'em all.** *sent.* "No one succeeds all the time." (Said when someone fails.) ☐ *Don't fret about it, Tom. You can't win them all.* ☐ *You can't win 'em all, but you can't lose 'em all, either.*

You could have knocked me over with a feather. *sent.* "I was completely surprised." ☐ *I was shocked. You could have knocked me over with a feather.* ☐ *You could have knocked me over with a feather, I was so zapped!*

You don't know the half of it. *sent.* "Things are far more complicated than you think." ☐ *You think that's bad? You don't know the half of it.* ☐ *You don't know the half of it, and I'm too much a lady to tell.*

You eat with that mouth? See *(Do) you eat with that mouth?*

You got it! 1. *exclam.* "I agree to what you asked!"; "You will get what you want!" ☐ *You want a green one? You got it!* ☐ *This one? You got it!* **2.** *exclam.* "You are right!" ☐ *That's it! You got it!* ☐ *That's the answer. You got it!*

You guys bitchin'? *interrog.* "Hello, how are you?" ☐ *Tsup? You guys bitchin'?* ☐ *You guys bitchin'? What's poppin'?*

You (had) better believe it! *exclam.* "It is true without question!" ☐ *It's true. You better believe it.* ☐ *Yes, this is the best, and you had better believe it!*

You heard the man. *sent.* "Do what the man tells you." (See also *man.*) ☐ *You heard the man. Get over there and stand still.* ☐ *Shut up! You heard the man.*

You kiss your momma with that mouth? See *(Do) you eat with that mouth?*

You want to step outside? *interrog.* "Do you intend to start a fight?"; "Shall we go outside and fight?" ☐ *So, you don't like the way I talk! You want to step outside?* ☐ *You want to step outside? We can settle this once and for all.*

You wish! See *(Don't) you wish!*

young blood 1. *n.* a newcomer. ☐ *The young blood gets a desk by the window.* ☐ *We keep young bloods so busy they never have a chance to look out the window.* **2.** *n.* a young, black male. (Black. See also *blood.*) ☐ *A young blood from two streets over came around asking for trouble today.* ☐ *Tell that young blood to beat it.*

young Turk *n.* a contentious young person who goes against the system. ☐ *The young Turks are acting up again.* ☐ *Not another young Turk!*

Your guess is as good as mine. *sent.* "I don't know either." ☐ *I don't know. Your guess is as good as mine.* ☐ *Your guess is as good as mine as to when the train will get in.*

Your place or mine? *interrog.* "Shall we carry on an affair at your dwelling or mine?" ☐ *Then I said to her, "Your place or mine?" Then she clobbered me.* ☐ *Your place or mine? It doesn't matter.*

You're the doctor. *sent.* "I will do anything you say!"; "You are in charge!" ☐ *I'll do it if you say. You're the doctor!* ☐ *Put it over here. Okay, you're the doctor.*

yours truly *n.* "me," the speaker. ☐ *If yours truly had a problem like that, it would be settled by nightfall.* ☐ *If it was up to yours truly, there wouldn't be any such problem.*

You've got another think coming. *sent.* "You have made an error. Think again." ☐ *If you think I'm going to let you get away with that, you've got another think coming.* ☐ *You've got another think coming if you think I'll do it.*

yoyo AND **yo-yo** ['jojo] **1.** *n.* a fool; an obnoxious person. ☐ *Who's the yo-yo in the plaid pants?* ☐ *Some yoyo wants to talk to you on the phone.* **2.** *mod.* stupid. ☐ *Ask that yo-yo jerk to move along.* ☐ *That is the world's yoyoest joke!* **3.** *in.* to vacillate; to be *wishy-washy.* ☐ *Stop yo-yoing and make up your mind.* ☐ *He's always got to yoyo a little before deciding.*

yuck AND **yuk** [jək] **1.** *n.* someone or something disgusting. (Also a term of address.) □ *I don't want any of that yuck on my plate!* □ *Who is that yuk in the red bandana?* **2.** *exclam.* "Horrible!" (Usually **Yuck!**) □ *Oh, yuck! Get that horrible thing out of here!* □ *Yuck! It looks alive!* **3.** *n.* a joke. □ *Come on! Chill out! It was just a yuck.* □ *Not a very good yuk if you ask me.* **4.** See *yack*.

yucky ['jəki] *mod.* nasty. □ *What is this yucky pink stuff on my plate?* □ *This tastes yucky.*

yuk See *yack; yuck*.

yuke See *uke*.

yummy ['jəmi] **1.** *mod.* delicious. □ *This stuff is really yummy.* □ *Who made this yummy cake?* **2.** *mod.* delightful; beautiful. □ *Who is that yummy blonde?* □ *This evening was just yummy.*

yup AND **yep** [jəp AND jɛp] *interj.* "yes." (Folksy.) □ *Yup, I'd say so.* □ *I think so. Yep, that's right.*

yuppie ['jəpi] **1.** *n.* a "young urban professional." □ *The yuppies are getting a lot of flack these days.* □ *Why pick on yuppies?* **2.** *mod.* having to do with yuppies. □ *I don't want to drive one of those yuppie cars.* □ *You got something against yuppie beemers?*

yutz [juts] *n.* a fool; a simpleton. □ *Don't act like such a yutz!* □ *Who is the yutz blocking the doorway?*

Z

za [zɑ] *n.* pizza. (Collegiate.) □ *I'm gonna spring for some za.* □ *Who wants some of this za?*

zagged *mod.* alcohol intoxicated. □ *How can anybody get so zagged on three beers?* □ *Wow, is she zagged!*

zany ['zeni] *mod.* silly. □ *What a zany chick!* □ *Clare is so zany.* □ *That is a zany idea, but I like it.*

zap 1. *tr.* to shock someone. □ *That fake snake zapped me for a minute.* □ *The incident zapped me, but good.* **2.** *tr.* to kill someone. □ *The stress from it all nearly zapped him.* □ *I was afraid that one of those thugs would zap me.* **3.** *tr.* to impress someone. □ *My big idea really zapped the boss. I may get a raise.* □ *I like to have something to zap the board with at every meeting.* **4.** *tr.* to stun someone with an imaginary ray gun. □ *Jimmy swung around the corner and zapped me.* □ *He zapped me with a water gun.* **5.** *exclam.* "Wow!" (Usually **Zap!**) □ *Zap! I did it again!* □ *He said, "Zap!" indicating that he really liked the present, I guess.* **6.** *tr.* to defeat someone or a team. □ *They zapped us 10-8.* □ *Fred zapped Tracy in the spelling bee.* **7.** *in.* to zip or move to somewhere very fast. □ *I'll zap over and see if the duplicating is ready yet.* □ *He's zapping to the drugstore for some aspirin.*

zapped 1. *mod.* tired; exhausted. □ *I'm too zapped to go on.* □ *I'm way zapped. Good night.* **2.** *mod.* alcohol or drug intoxicated. □ *We all got zapped and then went home.* □ *Marty is too zapped to stand up.*

zappy *mod.* energetic; *zippy.* □ *How can you be so zappy at this time of the morning?* □ *That music is a little too zappy for me.*

zarf [zɑrf] *n.* an ugly and repellent male. □ *Ooo, who is that zarf who just came in?* □ *That zarf is Martin, and he makes all A's, and he helps me with my homework, so just shut up!*

zebra *n.* a referee. (Because of the black and white striped shirt.) □ *The zebra blew the whistle on almost every play.* □ *There were not enough zebras to start the game.*

zeek out [zik . . .] *in.* to lose control of oneself. □ *I was in a pretty bad state. I almost zeeked out.* □ *Fred zeeked out and had to be calmed down.*

Zelda ['zɛldə] *n.* a dull and ugly female. (Compare to *Clyde.*) □ *I'm not as much of a Zelda as you think.* □ *Nobody's gonna call my sister a Zelda and get away with it.*

zerk [zɚk] *n.* a stupid person; a *jerk.* □ *Who's the zerk in the plaid pants?* □ *Don't be a zerk! Do what you're told.*

zerked (out) ['zɚkt . . .] *mod.* drug intoxicated; heavily drug intoxicated. □ *Gary looked really zerked out, and I thought he was really stoned.* □ *Max gets zerked out every weekend.*

zerking *mod.* strange; *zerk*-like. □ *Who is that zerking nerd over there?* □ *That zerking little guy is Martin, and I like him.*

zero *n.* an insignificant person; a nobody. □ *Pay her no mind. She is a zero around here.* □ *I want to be more in life than just another zero.*

zhlub See *schlub.*

zhlubby ['ʒləbi] *mod.* dull; boorish. (See also *schlub.*) ☐ *Who is the zhlubby type with the plaid pants?* ☐ *That guy is so zhlubby!* ☐ *I can't sit through this zhlubby thing one more minute.*

zilch [zɪltʃ] *n.* nothing. ☐ *And what do I get? Zilch, that's what!* ☐ *"Even zilch is too much," said the clerk.*

zing 1. *n.* energy; dynamism. ☐ *Put some zing into this dance number. You wanna put the audience to sleep?* ☐ *This whole business needs more zing.* **2.** *tr.* to make something penetrate; to shoot or fire something. ☐ *The crook zinged a couple of slugs into the floor and scared everyone to death.* ☐ *The kid zinged a paper clip into the wall.* **3.** *tr.* to assault someone verbally. ☐ *She zinged him with another clever remark.* ☐ *He zinged her back till he decided they were even.*

zinger 1. *n.* something nice or fine. ☐ *That set of wheels is a real zinger.* ☐ *What a zinger of a hat!* **2.** *n.* a stinging remark. ☐ *She got off another zinger at her brother.* ☐ *I did not appreciate that zinger.*

zings *n.* the delirium tremens. ☐ *The old guy was suffering from the zings.* ☐ *What can they do for the zings?*

zip 1. *n.* nothing. ☐ *There was no mail today. Nothing. Zip.* ☐ *I got zip from the booking agency all week.* **2.** *n.* a score or grade of zero. ☐ *Well, you got zip on the last test. Sorry about that.* ☐ *The prof said that zip is better than nothing, but I don't see how it could be.* **3.** *n.* vigor; spunk. ☐ *Put some zip into it. It's too ho-hum.* ☐ *This whole thing lacks the zip it needs to survive.* **4.** *in.* to move to a place fast. ☐ *I'll zip to the office and get a new form.* ☐ *He's just zipped out to get pizza.* **5.** *n.* a worthless person; a person who amounts to zero. ☐ *Who is that silly zip carrying all the books?* ☐ *Garth is such a zip. No brains in his head at all.*

zip along *in.* to move along rapidly. ☐ *Things are really zipping along here.* ☐ *Days are zipping along, and we're all getting lots done.*

zip gun *n.* a homemade handgun. (Underworld.) ☐ *The kid had a zip gun, so I didn't argue.* ☐ *Can he handle anything other than a zip gun?*

Zip it up! See the following entry.

Zip (up) your lip! AND **Zip it up!** *exclam.* "Be quiet!"; "Zip up your mouth!" ☐ *Shhhh! Zip up your lip!* ☐ *Zip your lip!* ☐ *Zip it up and listen!*

zipped *mod.* drug intoxicated. (Drugs.) ☐ *That tootsie left them zipped.* ☐ *The kid is too zipped to talk.*

zipper head *n.* a man with his hair parted in the middle. ☐ *Why are there so many zipper heads around here? Is this hair style on sale or something?* ☐ *Some zipper head behind the counter told me I couldn't come in without a shirt.*

zippy ['zɪpi] *mod.* lively; active. ☐ *Wow, is that kid zippy! Look at him dance!* ☐ *This is a real zippy number.*

zissified ['zɪsɪfaɪd] *mod.* alcohol intoxicated. ☐ *Two of them were zissified on rum. The rest just got a little wrecked.* ☐ *Man, is she zissified!*

zit [zɪt] *n.* a pimple. ☐ *Don't squeeze your zits on my mirror!* ☐ *That is one prize-winning zit on your nose.*

zit doctor *n.* a dermatologist. ☐ *The zit doctor I went to was a crater face!* ☐ *My zit doctor wears rubber gloves and has for years.*

zob [zab] *n.* a worthless person; a nobody. ☐ *Another zob came in to try out for the part.* ☐ *Who's the zob in the plaid pants?*

zod [zad] **1.** *n.* any repellent thing or person. (California.) ☐ *Wally is such a total zod.* ☐ *Is this grody zod yours or mine?* **2.** *n.* a studious person. ☐ *Quiet. You don't want to disturb the zods.* ☐ *Dave decided to be a zod for a semester and see if he could pass his courses.*

zombie ['zambi] **1.** *n.* a weird and frightening person. ☐ *Martin is practically a zombie. Doesn't he ever go out—in the daylight, I mean?* ☐ *Tracy's getting to look like a zombie. Is she well?* **2.** *n.* a very stupid person. ☐ *Is this some kind of gathering of zombies and mouth-breathers or something?* ☐ *Please ask* *one of those zombies to stand by the door.* **3.** *n.* a very tired person. ☐ *I feel like such a zombie. Maybe I'm not eating right.* ☐ *I'm just a zombie at this hour of the morning.*

zoned (out) **1.** *mod.* alcohol or drug intoxicated. ☐ *What's the matter with your eyes? Get a little zoned last night?* ☐ *Yeah, I'm sort of zoned out.* **2.** *mod.* exhausted. ☐ *After a day like this, I'm really zoned.* ☐ *Gotta get to bed. I'm just zoned out.*

zonk [zɔŋk] **1.** *tr.* to overpower someone or something. ☐ *We zonked the dog with a kick.* ☐ *It took two cops to zonk the creep.* **2.** *tr.* to tire someone out. ☐ *The pills zonked me, but they made my cold better.* ☐ *Jogging always zonks me.* (More at *zonked (out)*.)

zonk out *in.* to collapse from exhaustion; to go into a stupor from drugs or exhaustion. ☐ *I'm gonna go home and zonk out.* ☐ *I went home after the trip and just zonked out.*

zonked (out) AND **zounked (out)** [zɔŋkt . . . AND zaʊŋkt . . .] **1.** *mod.* alcohol or drug intoxicated. ☐ *She's too zonked to drive.* ☐ *Jed was almost zounked out to unconsciousness.* **2.** *mod.* exhausted; asleep. ☐ *She was totally zonked out by the time I got home.* ☐ *I'm zounked. Good night.*

zonker [ˈzɔŋkɚ] **1.** *n.* a drunkard. ☐ *The zonker just can't help himself.* ☐ *If I had known she was a confirmed zonker, I never would have given her a drink.* **2.** *n.* a marijuana smoker. (Drugs.) ☐ *A lot of these zonkers may take six years to get through high school.* ☐ *You are turning into a first-class zonker.*

zoo *n.* a confusing and chaotic place. ☐ *This place is a zoo on Monday mornings.* ☐ *Where is the person in charge of this zoo?*

zoobang [ˈzubæŋ] *mod.* alcohol intoxicated. ☐ *Boy howdy! Are you ever zoobang!* ☐ *So, you think I'm zoobang? You want to step outside?*

zooed [zud] *mod.* drunk. ☐ *Sam likes to go out and get zooed every weekend.* ☐ *Garth is so silly when he's zooed.*

zooey See the following entry.

zooie AND **zooey** [ˈzui] *mod.* confusing and chaotic. (See also *zoo*.) ☐ *I can't get anything done in this zooie place.* ☐ *It's never zooey in my office, except for a little rowdiness at closing time.*

zoom **1.** *tr.* to gain entry to someplace without paying. ☐ *Both of them zoomed the circus, and both of them got arrested.* ☐ *Let's go zoom Martha's party!* **2.** AND **zoom off** *in.* to have a drug *rush*. (Drugs.) ☐ *Sam zoomed off and thought he had gone to heaven.* ☐ *Max knows how to keep zooming for about twenty minutes.* **3.** AND **zoom off** *in.* to depart; to leave in a hurry. ☐ *Time's up. I've gotta zoom.* ☐ *Oh, you don't have to zoom off, do you?*

zoom in (on someone or something) *in.* to focus or concentrate narrowly on someone or something. ☐ *The conversation zoomed in on Sally and her recent narrow escape from drowning.* ☐ *Let's zoom in on the question of salary.*

zoom off See *zoom*.

zoom out *in.* to lose control. ☐ *I nearly zoomed out when I got the news.* ☐ *Fred zoomed out and started screaming at Ernie.*

zoom someone out *tr.* to impress someone. ☐ *You can't zoom me out, you twit!* 🅃 *Freddie is trying to zoom out Tiffany again.*

zoom up *in.* to drive or pull up to a place. ☐ *A car zoomed up, and seven kids got out.* ☐ *Let's zoom up to the door and see if she's home.*

zoomies [ˈzumiz] *n.* members of the U.S. Air Force. (A nickname used by the Army. Persian Gulf War.) ☐ *The zoomies attacked the airfield and damaged a lot of planes.* ☐ *The zoomies attacked the spy headquarters and caused a lot of damage.*

zooted [ˈzudəd] *mod.* alcohol intoxicated. ☐ *Both of them were zooted to the max.* ☐ *She was too zooted to even see straight.*

zootied [ˈzutid] *mod.* intoxicated with drugs or alcohol. ☐ *Hank seems to be* *zootied. What's he on?* □ *Garth acts like a yutz whether he's zootied or not.*

zorked ['zorkt] *mod.* alcohol intoxicated. □ *She was zorked beyond help.* □ *Everybody was essentially zorked by midnight.*

zotz [zats] **1.** AND **zot.** [zat] *n.* zero; nothing. □ *I went out to get the mail, but there was zot.* □ *All I got for a raise was little more than zotz.* **2.** *tr.* to kill someone or something. □ *Max threatened to zotz Bruno, but it was just a threat.* □ *The gunman stepped up to the wall and zotzed two of the guards.*

zounked (out) See *zonked (out).*

zowie ['zaui] **1.** *n.* energy; sparkle; zest. □ *This one sounds better because the drummer has more zowie.* □ *Put some zowie into it. It's not raining inside tonight.* **2.** *exclam.* "Wow!" (Usually **Zowie!**) □ *Zowie! They just pulled Mr. Big out of the river.* □ *Bruno had enough of the guy and wasted him, but good. Zowie!*

zozzled ['zazld] *mod.* drunk. □ *Dave was too zozzled to drive.* □ *John had a few, but he didn't get zozzled or anything like that.*

zuke [zuk] *in.* to vomit. □ *The cat zuked on the living room carpet.* □ *I hear someone zuking in the bathroom. What's going on?*

zunked [zəŋkt] *mod.* alcohol or drug intoxicated. □ *That poor guy is so zunked he can't see.* □ *The party went on and on. When the preacher got himself zunked on the punch, I knew it had reached the end.*

PHRASE-FINDER INDEX

Use this index to find the form of the phrase or compound that you want to look up in this dictionary. First, pick out any main word in the phrase you are seeking. Second, look that word up in this index to find the form of the phrase used in this dictionary. Third, look up the phrase in the main body of this dictionary. See *Uses* and *Hints* below.

Some of the words occurring in this dictionary do not occur as entries in this index. Single word entries are not indexed here and should be looked up in the dictionary directly. Some words are omitted because they occur so frequently that their lists would cover many pages. Most prepositions, most personal pronouns, and the following words do not occur as entries in the index: *a, an, and, get, have, one's, or, someone, something, that.* In these instances, you should look up the phrase under some other word.

Uses

A very high percentage of slang and colloquial expressions are noun compounds or other sequences of two or more words. This index provides a convenient way of finding the words that follow the first word in a phrasal entry. For instance, there are a number of entries beginning with *john,* but the index lists four additional entries that include *john* in some other form or position: **big John; Dear John letter; square john;** and **who shot John.**

If you were trying to find an expression that includes something about a blue flame, you could look up either word in the index. At both *blue* and *flame* you would find listed **burn with a low blue flame.** You would turn to the **B** section of this dictionary to find the entry for this expression. In fact, the index lists this expression at *burn, low, blue,* and *flame*. As explained above, the words *with* and *a* are not indexed.

You may be seeking an entry that explains the phrase *cut bait,* which you have heard in the sentence "It's time you decide whether you want to fish or cut bait." If you look up *cut*, *fish*, or *bait*, you will find that the full entry expression is **Fish or cut bait!**, which you would then look up.

Hints

1. This is an index of forms, not meanings. The expressions in an index entry do not necessarily have any meaning in common. Consult the dictionary definitions for information about meaning.
2. When you are trying to find a slang or colloquial expression in this index, try first to look up any nouns that may be part of the expression.
3. When you are looking for a noun, try first to find its singular or simplest form.
4. When you are looking for a verb, try first to find its present tense or simplest form.
5. In most expressions where a noun or pronoun is a variable part of the expression, it will be represented by the words *someone* or *something*. If you do not find the noun you want in the index, it may, in fact, be a variable word and you should look up another word.
6. When you locate the phrase you want, look it up in the main body of the dictionary.

AIM
aim for the sky

AIR
air-bags ☐ air ball ☐ air guitar ☐ air hose ☐ air one's belly ☐ air one's pores ☐ bear in the air ☐ come up for air ☐ full of hot air ☐ hot air ☐ up in the air ☐ up in the air (about someone or something)

AIRY
airy-fairy

AL
Herb and Al ☐ talk to Herb and Al

ALBERT
Prince Albert

ALECK
smart aleck

ALIVE
Look alive!

ALKIED
alkied (up)

ALL
all-nighter ☐ all right ☐ (all) shook up ☐ all that jazz ☐ all (that) meat and no potatoes ☐ all the way ☐ all the way live ☐ call (all) the shots ☐ can't win (th)em all ☐ daddy (of them all) ☐ Dash it all! ☐ drool (all) over someone or something ☐ dump all over someone or something ☐ for all I know ☐ for (all) one's trouble ☐ free for all ☐ get it (all) together ☐ go all the way ☐ (grand)daddy (of them all) ☐ Hang it all! ☐ have all one's marbles ☐ have it all together ☐ hold all the aces ☐ know all the angles ☐ know-it-all ☐ let it all hang out ☐ lose (all) one's marbles ☐ not all there ☐ Of all the nerve! ☐ once and for all ☐ pull out all the stops ☐ run on all cylinders ☐ That's all she wrote. ☐ That's all someone needs. ☐ warts and all ☐ You can't win them all.

ALLEY
alley apple ☐ (right) up one's alley ☐ up one's alley

ALLIGATOR
see you later, alligator

ALMIGHTY
almighty dollar

ALONG
buzz along ☐ hump (along) ☐ tootle along ☐ zip along

ALPHABET
alphabet soup

ALTAR
bow to the porcelain altar

AMBULANCE
ambulance chaser

AMOK
run amok

AMOUNT
pull down an amount of money ☐ shell out (an amount of money)

ANCHOR
anchor-clanker

ANCIENT
ancient history

ANGEL
angel dust ☐ angel hair ☐ dust of angels

ANGLE
know all the angles

ANIMAL
party animal ☐ study animal

ANKLE
sprain one's ankle

ANOTHER
another peep (out of you) ☐ Tell me another (one)! ☐ You've got another think coming.

ANT
have ants in one's pants ☐ piss-ant ☐ piss-ant around

ANTE
penny-ante

ANY
cannot see (any) further than the end of one's nose

APART
take someone or something apart ☐ tear someone or something apart

APE
ape hangers ☐ go ape (over someone or something)

APPLE
alley apple ☐ apple-polisher ☐ Big Apple ☐ one smart apple ☐ road apple ☐ rotten apple ☐ square apple

ARM
arm-twister ☐ arm-twisting ☐ bang in the arm ☐ long arm of the law ☐ put the arm on someone ☐ shot in the arm ☐ strong-arm ☐ strong-arm man ☐ strong-arm tactics ☐ twist someone's arm ☐ up in arms

ARMY
army brat ☐ You and what army?

AROUND
(a)round the bend ☐ blue around the gills ☐ bum around ☐ chippy around ☐ clown around ☐ drive someone around the bend ☐ galumph (around) ☐ goof around ☐ green around the gills ☐ hack around ☐ hang (around) ☐ horse around ☐ jack around ☐ jack someone around ☐ jerk around ☐ jerk someone around ☐ kick around ☐ kick some ass (around) ☐ knock around ☐ mess around (with someone or something) ☐ moist around the edges ☐ monkey around (with someone or something) ☐ mope around ☐ pal around (with someone) ☐ piddle (around) ☐ piss-ant around ☐ play around (with someone) ☐ pussyfoot (around) ☐ putz around ☐ rat around ☐ screw around ☐ screw around with someone or something ☐ scrounge (around (for someone or something)) ☐ spaz around ☐ stick around ☐ throw one's weight around ☐ tool around ☐ turn around ☐ waffle (around) ☐ wrap one's car around something ☐ yank someone around

ARROW
straight arrow

ARTICLE
genuine article

ARTILLERY
heavy artillery

ARTIST
booze artist ☐ bullshit artist ☐ burn artist ☐ castor oil artist ☐ con artist ☐ flimflam artist ☐ hype artist ☐ make-out artist ☐ off artist ☐ (rip)-off artist ☐ take-off artist

ARTSY
artsy-craftsy ☐ artsy (fartsy)

AS
clear as mud ☐ clear as vodka ☐ dry-as-dust ☐ dull as dishwater ☐ fresh as a daisy ☐ gay as pink ink ☐ jober as a sudge ☐ nutty as a fruitcake ☐ phony as a three-dollar bill ☐ queer as a three-dollar bill ☐ right as rain ☐ sober as a judge ☐ sure as hell ☐ tight as a tick ☐ ugly as sin ☐ Your guess is as good as mine.

ASK
Don't ask. ☐ Don't ask me. ☐ You asked for it!

ASLEEP
asleep at the switch

ASPHALT
asphalt jungle

ASS
bare-assed ☐ barrel ass ☐ bust ass out of some place ☐ bust (one's) ass (to do something) ☐ candy-ass ☐ dumb-ass ☐ flat on one's ass ☐ hairy-ass(ed) ☐ have one's ass in a crack ☐ have one's ass in a sling ☐ horse's ass ☐ It will be your ass! ☐ jive-ass ☐ kick in the ass ☐ kick some ass (around) ☐ kiss-ass ☐ kiss someone's ass ☐ lard ass ☐ pain in the ass ☐ smart ass ☐ sorry-ass ☐ stupid-ass ☐ tits and ass

ATTACK
Big Mac attack

ATTENTION
snap to (attention)

ATTITUDE
attitude-adjuster □ cop an attitude □ pull an attitude

AUNT
Aunt Flo

AVENUE
Madison Avenue

AW
(Aw) shucks!

AWAY
Are we away? □ blow someone away □ blowed (away) □ blown away □ fire away □ Get away! □ put someone or something away □ slave away (at something) □ squared away □ squirrel something away □ throw-away □ wash someone away

AX
battle-ax □ get the ax □ give someone the ax

AZTEC
Aztec two-step

B
B. and B. □ B-ball □ B.B. brain □ B.O. juice □ hang a BA (at someone)

BABY
baby bear □ Baby Bell □ (baby) boomer □ baby-kisser □ bottle baby □ jelly babies □ Keep the faith (baby)! □ The baby needs shoes.

BACH
bach (it)

BACK
back-door trot(s) □ back-ender □ back number □ back to square one □ back to the salt mines □ back up □ backed up □ drunk back □ get off someone's back □ have a monkey on one's back □ have a yellow streak down one's back □ juice something back □ kick back □ knock back a drink □ knock one back □ laid back □ on the back burner □ pin someone's ears back □ set someone back □ throw something back □ try someone back (again) □ yellow streak (down someone's back)

BACKFIRE
backfire (on someone)

BACKROOM
backroom boys □ boys in the backroom

BACKSEAT
backseat driver

BACON
bring home the bacon □ What's shakin' (bacon)?

BAD
bad egg □ bad hair day □ bad-mouth □ bad news □ bad paper □ bad rap □ bad trip □ get in bad (with someone) □ in a bad way □ in bad shape □ so bad one can taste it

BADGE
lost-and-found badge

BAG
air-bags □ Bag it! □ bag of bones □ bag of wind □ bag on someone □ bag some rays □ Bag that! □ Bag your face! □ barf bag □ brown-bag □ doggy bag □ double-bagger □ douche bag □ four-bagger □ half in the bag □ in the bag □ one's bag □ slime bag □ triple-bagger □ whole bag of tricks

BAGGER
double-bagger □ four-bagger □ triple-bagger

BAHAMA
Bahama-mama

BAIL
bail (out) □ jump bail

BAIT
Fish or cut bait. □ jail bait

BAKE
half-baked

BALL
air ball □ B-ball □ ball and chain □ ball-breaker □ ball-buster □ ball-busting □ ball is in someone's court □

ball of fire ☐ ball park estimate ☐ ball park figure ☐ balled up ☐ bean ball ☐ behind the eight ball ☐ break one's balls to do something ☐ break someone's balls ☐ drop the ball ☐ end of the ball game ☐ gopher ball ☐ have a ball ☐ on the ball ☐ play ball (with someone) ☐ play hardball (with someone) ☐ put balls on something ☐ That's the way the ball bounces. ☐ V-ball ☐ whole ball of wax ☐ whole new ball game

BALLOON

go over like a lead balloon ☐ trial balloon

BANANA

banana-head ☐ banana oil ☐ banana republic ☐ Cool bananas! ☐ go bananas ☐ top banana

BAND

to beat the band

BANDWAGON

on the bandwagon

BANG

(bang) dead to rights ☐ bang for the buck ☐ bang in the arm ☐ bang-up ☐ gang-bang ☐ get a bang out of someone or something ☐ slam-bang ☐ wham-bang ☐ with a bang

BANKER

banker's hours

BAR

behind bars ☐ no holds barred

BARBIE

Barbie doll

BARE

bare-assed ☐ stand there with one's bare face hanging out

BARF

barf bag ☐ Barf City ☐ Barf out! ☐ barf-out ☐ barf someone out

BARGAIN

(bargaining) chip ☐ more than one bargained for ☐ no bargain

BARK

barking spider

BARN

can't hit the (broad) side of a barn ☐ Were you born in a barn?

BARNYARD

barnyard language

BARREL

barrel ass ☐ barrel fever ☐ barrel of fun ☐ barreled (up) ☐ bottom of the barrel ☐ double-barreled slingshot ☐ loaded to the barrel ☐ scrape the bottom of the barrel

BASE

base binge ☐ free base ☐ free base party ☐ free-baser ☐ free-basing ☐ off base ☐ touch base (with someone) ☐ way off (base)

BASKET

basket case ☐ dinner basket ☐ underwater basket weaving

BASRA

Basra belly

BAT

batted out ☐ have bats in one's belfry ☐ like a bat out of hell

BATCH

ba(t)ch (it)

BATH

blood bath ☐ take a bath (on something) ☐ tonsil bath

BATHTUB

bathtub scum

BATTLE

battle-ax ☐ battle of the bulge

BAY

bay window

BEACH

beach bum ☐ beach bunny

BEAGLE

legal-beagle

BEAM
Beam me up, Scotty! ☐ beam up ☐ (I-)beam ☐ on the beam ☐ steam someone's beam

BEAN
bean ball ☐ bean-counter ☐ bean head ☐ bean time ☐ Bean Town ☐ beaned up ☐ Cool beans! ☐ full of beans ☐ not know beans (about something) ☐ not worth beans ☐ on the bean ☐ spill the beans

BEAR
baby bear ☐ bear cage ☐ bear in the air ☐ bear trap ☐ lady bear ☐ loaded for bear ☐ mama bear ☐ Smokey (the Bear)

BEAT
beat box ☐ Beat it! ☐ beat one's brains out (to do something) ☐ beat one's gums ☐ beat someone or something out ☐ beat someone's brains out ☐ beat the drum for someone or something ☐ beat up ☐ beats me ☐ egg-beater ☐ take a beating ☐ to beat the band ☐ world-beater

BEAUTY
beauty sleep

BEAVER
eager-beaver

BED
bed of roses ☐ fall out of bed ☐ make one's bed ☐ musical beds ☐ put someone to bed with a shovel ☐ put to bed with a shovel

BEDPOST
between you, me, and the bedpost

BEDROOM
bedroom eyes

BEDTIME
bedtime story

BEEF
beef-head ☐ beef something up ☐ Where's the beef?

BEER
beer and skittles ☐ beer belly ☐ beer blast ☐ beer bust ☐ beer goggles ☐ beer gut ☐ cry in one's beer ☐ hammer a beer ☐ hammer some beers ☐ near-beer ☐ pound a beer ☐ pound some beers ☐ queer-beer ☐ slam a beer ☐ slam some beers ☐ small beer

BEESWAX
mind your own beeswax ☐ none of someone's beeswax

BEET
blow beets

BEFORE
morning after (the night before)

BEHIND
behind bars ☐ behind the eight ball ☐ get behind someone or something

BELFRY
have bats in one's belfry

BELIEVE
Believe you me! ☐ I don't believe this! ☐ Would you believe? ☐ You (had) better believe it!

BELL
Baby Bell ☐ bells and whistles ☐ Hell's bells (and buckets of blood)! ☐ Ma Bell ☐ ring a bell ☐ ring the bell ☐ saved by the bell ☐ with bells on

BELLY
air one's belly ☐ Basra belly ☐ beer belly ☐ belly button ☐ belly flop ☐ belly laff ☐ belly laugh ☐ belly up ☐ belly up (to something) ☐ Delhi belly ☐ go belly up ☐ turn belly up ☐ yellow-bellied ☐ yellow-belly

BELOW
hit (someone) below the belt

BELT
belt the grape ☐ hit (someone) below the belt ☐ pull one's belt in (a notch) ☐ rust belt ☐ sun belt ☐ take one's belt in (a notch) ☐ tighten one's belt

BENCH
bench jockey ☐ bench warmer

BEND
(a)round the bend ☐ bend one's elbow

☐ bend the elbow ☐ bend the law ☐ drive someone around the bend ☐ elbow-bending ☐ fender-bender ☐ gender-bender ☐ mind-bender ☐ round the bend

BENT

bent out of shape

BERTH

soft berth

BEST

level best ☐ one's best shot ☐ Sunday best

BET

bet one's bottom dollar ☐ bet someone dollars to doughnuts ☐ you bet ☐ You bet your boots! ☐ You bet your sweet life! ☐ You bet your sweet patoot(ie)!

BETCHA

you betcha

BETTER

better half ☐ Better luck next time. ☐ seen better days ☐ You (had) better believe it!

BETWEEN

between a rock and a hard place ☐ between you, me, and the bedpost ☐ between you, me, and the lamppost ☐ put some distance between someone and someone or something

BHANG

bhang ganjah

BIBLE

swear on a stack of Bibles

BIG

Big Apple ☐ big blue ☐ big board ☐ big brother ☐ big bucks ☐ big-C. ☐ big cheese ☐ big-D. ☐ big deal ☐ big drink ☐ big drink of water ☐ big enchilada ☐ big fish ☐ big gun ☐ big-H. ☐ big house ☐ big iron ☐ big John ☐ big juice ☐ big league ☐ Big Mac attack ☐ big man on campus ☐ big mouth ☐ big name ☐ big noise ☐ big-O. ☐ big of someone ☐ big shot ☐ big spender ☐ big stink ☐ big talk ☐ big-ticket ☐ big time ☐ big-time operator ☐ big-time spender ☐ big top ☐ big wheel ☐ big with someone ☐ big Z's ☐ bite the big one ☐ buy the big one ☐ drive the big bus ☐ go over big ☐ have a (big) head ☐ have a big mouth ☐ in a big way ☐ make (it) big ☐ Mr. Big ☐ no big deal ☐ no biggie ☐ play in the big leagues ☐ talk big ☐ talk on the big white phone ☐ yea big

BIGGIE

no biggie

BIKE

On your bike!

BILGE

drain the bilge

BILL

bill and coo ☐ phony as a three-dollar bill ☐ queer as a three-dollar bill

BIN

loony bin ☐ sin-bin

BINGE

base binge

BIRD

bird-dog ☐ bird watcher ☐ boo-bird ☐ early bird ☐ flip someone the bird ☐ for the birds ☐ in the catbird seat ☐ odd bird ☐ on the bird ☐ rare bird ☐ strange bird ☐ whirly bird

BISCUIT

gorilla biscuits ☐ mystic biscuit

BIT

bit-bucket ☐ bit much ☐ bit of the action ☐ four-bits ☐ itsy-bitsy ☐ itty-bitty ☐ six-bits ☐ two-bit ☐ two-bits

BITCH

bitch box ☐ bitch of a someone or something ☐ bitch session ☐ bitch someone off ☐ bitch something up ☐ bush bitch ☐ pitch a bitch ☐ real bitch ☐ son of a bitch ☐ You guys bitchin'?

BITE

bite on something ☐ bite the big one ☐ bite the bullet ☐ bite the dust ☐ Bite the ice! ☐ Bite your tongue! ☐ I'll bite. ☐ monkey bite ☐ put the bite on someone ☐ snakebite medicine

BITSY
itsy-bitsy

BITTY
itty-bitty

BIZ
show biz

BLACK
black and blue ☐ black and white ☐ black eye ☐ in the black ☐ little black book

BLAH
blah-blah

BLANK
blankety-blank ☐ blankity-blank

BLANKET
blanket drill ☐ wet blanket

BLANKETY
blankety-blank

BLANKITY
blankity-blank

BLAST
beer blast ☐ full blast ☐ (ghetto) blaster

BLAZE
(blue) blazes ☐ Go to blazes!

BLEED
bleed for someone ☐ bleed someone dry ☐ bleed someone white ☐ on the bleeding edge

BLIMP
blimp out ☐ Have a blimp!

BLIND
blind drunk ☐ (blind) munchies ☐ half-blind ☐ rob someone blind ☐ stone blind

BLINK
on the blink

BLISS
bliss ninny ☐ bliss out ☐ blissed (out)

BLITHER
blithering idiot

BLITZ
blitzed (out)

BLOCK
knock someone's block off ☐ on the chopping block

BLOOD
abso-bloody-lutely ☐ blood and guts ☐ blood bath ☐ blood (brother) ☐ blue blood ☐ cold blood ☐ Hell's bells (and buckets of blood)! ☐ in cold blood ☐ in one's blood ☐ scream bloody murder ☐ smell blood ☐ sweat blood ☐ taste blood ☐ too rich for someone's blood ☐ worms in blood ☐ young blood

BLOODY
See *blood.*

BLOOEY
go blooey

BLOSSOM
toddy blossom

BLOT
blot someone out

BLOW
blow a fuse ☐ blow a gasket ☐ blow a hype ☐ blow beets ☐ blow chow ☐ blow chunks ☐ blow cold ☐ blow grits ☐ blow in ☐ Blow it out your ear! ☐ blow jive ☐ blow lunch ☐ blow off ☐ blow off (some) steam ☐ Blow on it! ☐ blow (one's) cookies ☐ blow one's cool ☐ blow one's cork ☐ blow one's doughnuts ☐ blow one's fuse ☐ blow one's groceries ☐ blow one's lid ☐ blow one's lines ☐ blow (one's) lunch ☐ blow one's own horn ☐ blow one's stack ☐ blow one's top ☐ blow-out ☐ blow smoke ☐ blow someone away ☐ blow someone or something off ☐ blow someone out of the water ☐ blow someone to something ☐ blow someone's cover ☐ blow someone's doors off ☐ blow someone's mind ☐ blow something wide open ☐ blow the joint ☐ blow the lid off something ☐ blow town ☐ blow up ☐ blow Z's ☐ blowed (away) ☐ blown away ☐ blown (out) ☐ blown (up) ☐ Joe Blow ☐ land a blow ☐ low-blow ☐ mind-blower ☐ whistle-blower

BLOWN

blown away □ blown (out) □ blown (up)

BLUBBER

blubber gut(s)

BLUE

big blue □ black and blue □ blue and white □ blue around the gills □ (blue) blazes □ blue blood □ blue boys □ blue chip □ blue coats □ blue devils □ blue-eyed □ blue flu □ blue funk □ blue in the face □ blue suit □ boys in blue □ burn with a low blue flame □ in a blue funk □ little boy blue □ men in blue □ once in a blue moon □ screwed, blued, and tattooed □ talk a blue streak □ talk until one is blue in the face

BOARD

big board □ boogie-board □ draft board

BOAT

just off the boat □ miss the boat

BOD

odd-bod

BODY

body count □ body shake □ over my dead body □ warm body

BOIL

boiling (mad) □ pot boiler

BOLT

nuts and bolts

BOMB

bomb (out) □ bombed (out) □ drop a bomb(shell) □ love bombs

BOMBSHELL

drop a bomb(shell)

BOND

junk bond

BONE

bag of bones □ bone factory □ bone idle □ bone orchard □ bone out □ crazy bone □ laid to the bone □ tail-bone

BONER

pull a boner

BONG

bonged (out) □ do some bongs

BONKERS

drive someone bonkers

BOO

boo-bird □ boo-boo □ make a boo-boo

BOOB

boob-tube

BOOBY

booby hatch □ booby trap

BOOGIE

boogie-board □ boogie down (to somewhere)

BOOK

book it □ crack a book □ fake book □ hit the books □ little black book □ make book on something □ pound the books □ take a page from someone's book □ throw the book at someone □ wish book

BOOM

(baby) boomer □ boom box □ boom sticks □ thunder-boomer

BOOSY

topsy-boosy

BOOT

boot someone out □ Jesus boots □ to boot □ You bet your boots!

BOOZE

booze artist □ booze it (up) □ booze up □ boozy-woozy □ hit the booze □ topsy-boosy □ topsy-boozy

BOOZY

See *booze*.

BOP

drop a bop

BORE

bore the pants off (of) someone

BORN

natural-born □ Were you born in a barn?

BOSOM
bosom buddy □ bosom chums □ bosom friends

BOSS
boss lady □ boss man □ straw boss

BOTH
both sheets in the wind □ swing both ways

BOTTLE
bottle baby □ brown bottle flu □ chief cook and bottle washer □ crack open a bottle □ head cook and bottle washer □ hit the bottle

BOTTOM
bet one's bottom dollar □ bottom dollar □ bottom fishing □ bottom line □ bottom of the barrel □ bottom of the heap □ bottom out □ Bottoms up. □ rock bottom □ scrape the bottom of the barrel

BOTTOMLESS
bottomless pit

BOUNCE
bounce for something □ bounce something off (of) someone □ deadcat bounce □ That's the way the ball bounces.

BOW
bow to the porcelain altar □ bow-wow

BOWEL
get one's bowels in an uproar

BOWL
party bowl

BOX
beat box □ bitch box □ boom box □ box someone in □ boxed in □ boxed on the table □ boxed (up) □ doc(s)-in-a-box □ eternity-box □ fuse box □ (ghetto) box □ go home in a box □ groan box □ idiot box □ knowledge-box □ squawk box □ (squeeze-)box □ think-box

BOY
backroom boys □ blue boys □ boys in blue □ boys in the backroom □ butboy □ fair-haired boy □ good old boy □ good ole boy □ little boy blue □ little boys' room □ Oh, boy! □ That-a-boy! □ That's my boy.

BRA
bra-burner

BRACK
brack-brain

BRAIN
B.B. brain □ beat one's brains out (to do something) □ beat someone's brains out □ brack-brain □ brain-burned □ brain-dead □ brain-drain □ brain-fried □ brain-teaser □ brain-twister □ feather brain □ have one's brain on a leash □ have something on the brain □ no-brainer

BRAND
(brand) spanking new □ no brand cigarette □ off-brand cigarette

BRASS
brass hat □ brass tacks □ brassed (off) □ top brass

BRAT
army brat

BREAD
bread and butter □ heavy bread □ long bread

BREAK
ball-breaker □ Break a leg! □ Break it up! □ break one's balls to do something □ break out □ break someone's balls □ break the ice □ cut someone a break □ Gimme a break! □ Give me a break! □ take a break □ tough break

BREAKFAST
breakfast of champions □ donkey's breakfast □ Mexican breakfast □ shoot one's breakfast

BREATHE
mouth-breather

BREEZE
bright and breezy □ fan the breeze □ shoot the breeze

BREW
brew-ha ☐ brew-out ☐ brews brothers ☐ home-brew ☐ quaff a brew ☐ suck (some) brew

BRICK
built like a brick outhouse ☐ built like a brick shithouse ☐ drop a brick ☐ hit the bricks ☐ like a ton of bricks ☐ one brick shy of a load ☐ three bricks shy of a load

BRIGHT
bright and breezy ☐ bright-eyed and bushy-tailed

BRING
bring-down ☐ bring home the bacon ☐ bring someone down ☐ bring someone on ☐ bring something up ☐ Earp slop, bring the mop.

BROAD
can't hit the (broad) side of a barn ☐ square john broad

BROKE
dead broke ☐ flat broke ☐ go for broke ☐ stone broke

BRONX
Bronx cheer

BROTHER
big brother ☐ blood (brother) ☐ brews brothers ☐ (soul) brother

BROW
no-brow

BROWN
brown-bag ☐ brown bottle flu ☐ brown-nose ☐ brown-noser ☐ brown out ☐ brown someone off ☐ browned (off)

BROWNIE
brownie points

BRUISE
cruisin' for a bruisin' ☐ cruising for a bruising

BRUSHOFF
give someone the brushoff

BUBBLE
bubble water ☐ half a bubble off plumb

BUCK
bang for the buck ☐ big bucks ☐ buck for something ☐ buck naked ☐ buck up ☐ fast buck ☐ pass the buck ☐ quick buck

BUCKET
bit-bucket ☐ gash bucket ☐ Hell's bells (and buckets of blood)! ☐ kick the bucket ☐ rust bucket ☐ sleaze-bucket ☐ slime bucket

BUD
sense (bud)

BUDDY
bosom buddy ☐ buddy-buddy ☐ buddy up to someone ☐ buddy up (with someone) ☐ good buddy

BUDGET
budget crunch ☐ budget squeeze

BUFF
in the buff

BUFFALO
double buffalo

BUG
Bug off! ☐ bug out ☐ crank bugs

BUILT
built like a brick outhouse ☐ built like a brick shithouse ☐ jerry-built

BULB
dim bulb ☐ light bulb

BULGE
battle of the bulge

BULL
bull-pucky ☐ bull session ☐ bullshit artist ☐ company bull ☐ full of bull ☐ hit the bull's eye ☐ shoot the bull ☐ throw the bull

BULLET
bite the bullet ☐ bullet-stopper ☐ magic bullet ☐ silver bullet ☐ sweat bullets

BULLSHIT
bullshit artist

BUM

beach bum ☐ bum around ☐ bum check ☐ bum out ☐ bum rap ☐ bum someone out ☐ bum something (off someone) ☐ bum steer ☐ bum trip ☐ bummed (out) ☐ bum's rush ☐ Hey, bum! ☐ skid row bum ☐ stew bum

BUMP

bump someone off ☐ Bump that! ☐ fanny-bumper ☐ Let's bump this place!

BUN

work one's buns off

BUNCH

bunch of fives ☐ thanks a bunch ☐ whole bunch(es)

BUNDLE

bundle from heaven ☐ bundle of joy ☐ bundle of nerves ☐ drop a bundle (on someone or something) ☐ lose a bundle ☐ make a bundle

BUNNY

beach bunny ☐ cuddle bunny ☐ dumb bunny ☐ snow bunny

BURB

burbed out

BURN

bra-burner ☐ brain-burned ☐ burn artist ☐ burn rubber ☐ burn someone down ☐ burn someone up ☐ burn with a low blue flame ☐ burned out ☐ burned up ☐ burnt offering ☐ burnt out ☐ crash and burn ☐ do a slow burn ☐ hay burner ☐ nose-burner ☐ on the back burner ☐ slow burn

BURY

bury the hatchet

BUS

drive the big bus ☐ drive the porcelain bus ☐ ride the porcelain bus

BUSH

bright-eyed and bushy-tailed ☐ bush bitch ☐ bush patrol ☐ bush pig

BUSHY

See *bush*.

BUSINESS

business end (of something) ☐ funny business ☐ give someone the business ☐ in business ☐ land office business ☐ like nobody's business ☐ mean business ☐ monkey business ☐ taking care of business ☐ That's show business (for you).

BUST

ball-buster ☐ ball-busting ☐ beer bust ☐ bust a gut (to do something) ☐ bust a move ☐ bust ass out of some place ☐ bust (one's) ass (to do something) ☐ bust one's butt to do something ☐ bust one's nuts to do something ☐ bust (some) suds ☐ bust someone one ☐ bust something up ☐ bust something wide open ☐ conk-buster ☐ fag-busting ☐ Hold it, Buster! ☐ kidney-buster ☐ skull-buster

BUT

but-boy ☐ Close, but no cigar. ☐ oldie but goodie

BUTCHER

wood butcher

BUTT

bust one's butt to do something ☐ butt naked ☐ Butt out! ☐ butt-ugly ☐ clip a butt ☐ duck butt ☐ dusty butt ☐ gunzel-butt ☐ kick in the butt ☐ pain in the butt ☐ work one's butt off

BUTTER

bread and butter

BUTTON

belly button ☐ cactus (buttons) ☐ hit the panic button ☐ on the button ☐ press the panic button ☐ push the panic button

BUY

buy it ☐ buy someone's wolf ticket ☐ buy the big one ☐ buy the farm ☐ buy time ☐ buy trouble

BUZZ

buzz along ☐ get a buzz out of someone or something ☐ give someone a buzz ☐ have a buzz on ☐ rolling buzz ☐ What's buzzin' (cousin)?

BUZZARD
buzzard meat

BY
done by mirrors ☐ fly-by-night ☐ give someone the go-by ☐ go-by ☐ have a tiger by the tail ☐ Run that by (me) again. ☐ Run that by (me) one more time. ☐ saved by the bell ☐ two-by-four

C
big-C. ☐ C-head ☐ C-note ☐ C-spot

CABOODLE
kit and caboodle

CACTUS
cactus (buttons) ☐ cactus juice

CADET
space cadet

CADILLAC
hog cadillac

CAGE
bear cage

CAIN
raise Cain

CAKE
icing on the cake ☐ nutty as a fruitcake ☐ piece of cake

CALL
call (all) the shots ☐ call earl ☐ call girl ☐ call house ☐ call hughie ☐ Call my service. ☐ call of nature ☐ call ralph ☐ call ruth ☐ call someone out ☐ close call ☐ cold call ☐ Don't call us, we'll call you. ☐ Good call! ☐ nature's call ☐ pay a call

CALM
cool, calm, and collected

CAM
cam (red)

CAMBODIAN
Cambodian red

CAME
This is where I came in.

CAMP
camp it up ☐ happy camper

CAMPUS
big man on campus ☐ campus queen

CAN
Can it! ☐ can of worms ☐ can-shaker ☐ get a can on ☐ half-canned ☐ no can do ☐ so bad one can taste it ☐ What can I do you for? ☐ You can say that again!

CANCEL
cancel someone's Christmas

CANCER
cancer stick

CANDY
candy-ass ☐ candy man ☐ candy store ☐ ear candy ☐ needle candy ☐ nose (candy) ☐ rock candy

CANITO
neato (canito)

CANNON
hash cannon ☐ loose cannon

CANNOT
See *can't*.

CAN'T
cannot see (any) further than the end of one's nose ☐ can't hit the (broad) side of a barn ☐ can't win (th)em all ☐ If you can't stand the heat, keep out of the kitchen. ☐ You can't dance at two weddings. ☐ You can't fight city hall. ☐ You can't get there from here. ☐ You can't take it with you. ☐ You can't win them all.

CANYON
yodeling in a canyon

CAPTAIN
captain of industry

CAR
wrap one's car around something

CARD
face card ☐ idiot card

CARE
I could(n't) care less. □ Take care. □ take care of number one □ take care of numero uno □ take care of someone □ taking care of business

CARPET
laugh at the carpet

CARROT
carrot top

CARRY
carry the stick □ carry weight □ carrying a (heavy) load

CART
honey cart

CARVE
carved in stone

CASE
basket case □ case of the shorts □ case the joint □ get off someone's case □ get on someone's case □ hard case □ make a federal case out of something □ on someone's case □ worst-case scenario

CASH
cash cow □ cash flow □ cash in one's checks □ cash in one's chips □ Cash is king. □ Cash is trash.

CASPER
be casper □ Casper Milquetoast

CAST
cast-iron stomach □ casting-couch □ street-casting

CASTOR
castor oil artist

CAT
cat-soup □ cats and dogs □ cat's meow □ cool cat □ fat-cat □ fraidy cat □ purr (like a cat) □ shoot the cat □ sling the cat

CATBIRD
in the catbird seat

CATCH
catch-22 □ catch hell (for something) □ catch some rays □ catch some Z's □ catch something □ catch up □ Catch you later. □ What's the catch?

CATTLE
cattle-rustler

CATTY
dead-catty

CAUSE
lost cause

CAVE
cave man

CEILING
hit the ceiling

CEMENT
cement city

CENTRAL
Grand Central Station

CENTURY
century note

CERTAIN
certain party

CHAIN
ball and chain □ chain(-smoke) □ chain-smoker □ yank someone's chain

CHAMPION
breakfast of champions

CHANCE
fat chance □ not a chance □ snowball's chance in hell

CHANGE
and change □ change the channel □ chump change □ go through the changes □ small change

CHANNEL
change the channel □ channel hopping □ channel surfer □ channel surfing □ channel zapping

CHAPTER
chapter and verse

CHARGE
charged (up)

CHARLEY
good-time Charley

CHARLIE
Charlie Irvine

CHASE
ambulance chaser ☐ chase the dragon ☐ chippy-chaser ☐ cut to the chase ☐ Go chase your tail! ☐ Go chase yourself!

CHASSIS
classis-chassis

CHASSY
classy-chassy

CHAUVINIST
male chauvinist pig

CHEAP
cheap shot ☐ dirt cheap ☐ el cheapo

CHECK
bum check ☐ cash in one's checks ☐ check out the plumbing ☐ check something out ☐ check that ☐ cut a check ☐ eternal checkout ☐ hot check ☐ rubber (check)

CHECKOUT
eternal checkout

CHEER
Bronx cheer ☐ holiday cheer

CHEESE
big cheese ☐ cheese-eater ☐ Cheese it (the cops)! ☐ cheesed off ☐ chew the cheese ☐ cut the cheese ☐ Say cheese!

CHERRY
desert cherry

CHEST
take the spear (in one's chest) ☐ war chest

CHEW
chew face ☐ chew someone out ☐ chew something over ☐ chew the cheese ☐ chew the fat ☐ chew the rag

CHI
chi-chi

CHIC
geek-chic

CHICK
slick-chick

CHICKEN
chicken feed ☐ chicken-hearted ☐ chicken out (of something) ☐ chicken powder ☐ for chicken feed ☐ spring chicken

CHIEF
chief cook and bottle washer

CHILL
chill (out) ☐ chill someone's action ☐ put the chill on someone ☐ take a chill pill

CHIMNEY
smoke like a chimney

CHIN
chin music ☐ take it on the chin ☐ wag one's chin

CHINA
China white

CHINESE
Chinese red ☐ Chinese white

CHIP
(bargaining) chip ☐ blue chip ☐ cash in one's chips ☐ cow chips ☐ in the chips

CHIPPY
chippy around ☐ chippy-chaser ☐ chippy (user)

CHOCK
chock-full

CHOP
chop-shop ☐ on the chopping block

CHOW
blow chow ☐ chow down ☐ chow hound ☐ chow something down

CHRISTMAS
cancel someone's Christmas ☐ Christmas tree

CHROME
chrome-dome

CHUCK
chuck a dummy ☐ chuck it in ☐ chuck up

CHUG
chug(-a-lug)

CHUM
bosom chums

CHUMP
chump change ☐ off one's chump

CHUNK
blow chunks

CHURCH
church key

CHUTE
go down the chute

CIGAR
Close, but no cigar.

CIGARETTE
cigarette with no name ☐ no brand cigarette ☐ no name cigarette ☐ off-brand cigarette

CINCH
dead cinch ☐ have something cinched

CIRCLE
vicious circle

CIRCULAR
circular file

CITIZEN
Joe Citizen

CITY
Barf City ☐ cement city ☐ fat city ☐ Headstone City ☐ Marble City ☐ You can't fight city hall.

CIVIL
civil serpent

CLAM
clam up

CLANKER
anchor-clanker

CLASS
class act ☐ world-class

CLASSIS
classis-chassis

CLASSY
classy-chassy

CLAY
clay pigeon

CLEAN
clean-cut ☐ clean someone out ☐ clean sweep ☐ clean up (on something) ☐ clean up one's act ☐ cleaned out ☐ come clean (with someone) (about something) ☐ keep one's nose clean ☐ squeaky clean ☐ take someone to the cleaners

CLEAR
clear as mud ☐ clear as vodka ☐ clear out ☐ clear sailing

CLICK
click (with someone)

CLIFF
cliff-dweller

CLIMB
climb the wall(s) ☐ Go climb a tree!

CLIP
clip a butt ☐ clip joint ☐ clip someone's wings ☐ roach clip

CLOCK
clock in ☐ clock watcher

CLOSE
Close, but no cigar. ☐ close call ☐ close shave

CLOWN
clown around

CLUCK
dumb cluck

CLUE
clue someone in ☐ totally clueless

CLUTCH
clutch (up)

COACH
roach-coach

COAT
blue coats

COBER
sold cober

COCKED
go off half-cocked □ half-cocked □ knock something into a cocked hat

COFFEE
coffee and □ cold coffee

COFFIN
coffin-dodger □ coffin nail □ coffin tack □ coffin varnish

COIN
do some fine coin □ hard coin

COKE
coke party

COLD
blow cold □ cold blood □ cold call □ cold coffee □ cold feet □ cold fish □ cold pop □ cold shoulder □ cold sober □ cold turkey □ freezing cold □ get one's nose cold □ in a cold sweat □ in cold blood □ in cold storage □ kick cold (turkey) □ leave someone cold □ out cold □ pour cold water on something □ stone (cold) sober

COLLAR
hot under the collar □ righteous collar

COLLECT
cool, calm, and collected

COLLEGE
Graystone College □ Joe College

COLOMBIAN
Colombian (gold)

COLOR
color of someone's money □ off color □ with flying colors

COME
come clean (with someone) (about something) □ come down □ come down hard □ come-hither look □ Come off it! □ come on □ come on like gangbusters □ come on strong □ come on to someone □ come out ahead □ come out in the wash □ come out on top □ come up for air □ coming out of one's ears □ if push comes to shove □ Johnnie-come-lately □ know where one is coming from □ till kingdom come □ when push comes to shove □ You've got another think coming.

COMEDY
Cut the comedy!

COMFORT
comfort station

COMMA
comma-counter

COMMODE
commode-hugging drunk

COMPANY
company bull □ company man

COMPLAINT
summer complaint

COMPOS
non compos □ non compos poopoo

CON
con artist □ con job □ con man □ put a con on someone

CONK
conk-buster □ conk out

CONNECT
connect (with someone or something)

CONNIPTION
conniption (fit)

COO
bill and coo □ coo-coo

COOK
chief cook and bottle washer □ cooked up □ cooking with gas □ head cook and bottle washer □ What's cooking?

COOKIE
blow (one's) cookies □ cookie pusher □ drop one's cookies □ shoot one's cookies □ smart cookie □ snap one's cookies □ That's the way the cookie crumbles. □ throw one's cookies □ toss one's cookies □ tough cookie □ tough cookies □ woof cookies

COOL
blow one's cool □ Cool bananas! □ Cool beans! □ cool, calm, and collected □ cool cat □ cool down □ Cool it! □ cool off □ cool out □ cool someone out □ cooled out □ keep cool □ keep one's cool □ lose one's cool □ play it cool

COOP
fly the coop

COP
Cheese it (the cops)! □ cop a drag □ cop a fix □ cop a head □ cop a plea □ cop a squat □ cop a tube □ cop an attitude □ cop out □ cop-shop □ cop some Z's

CORE
hard-core □ rotten to the core □ soft core

CORK
blow one's cork □ corked (up) □ liquid cork □ pop one's cork

CORKSCREW
corkscrewed (up)

CORNER
cut corners

CORRAL
corral dust

COTTON
cotton-pickin' □ cotton-picking □ in tall cotton

COUCH
casting-couch □ couch-doctor □ couch potato □ couch-turkey

COUGH
cough something up

COULD
You could have knocked me over with a feather.

COULDN'T
I could(n't) care less.

COUNT
bean-counter □ body count □ comma-counter □ down for the count □ over-the-counter □ take the (long) count

COUNTRY
country drunk

COUNTY
county-mounty

COURAGE
Dutch courage

COURSE
crib course □ snap course

COURT
ball is in someone's court □ kangaroo court

COUSIN
What's buzzin' (cousin)?

COVER
blow someone's cover □ cover-up

COW
cash cow □ cow chips □ cow-doots □ cow flop □ cow juice □ cow plop □ Don't have a cow! □ Holy cow! □ tin cow

COWBOY
drugstore cowboy

COYOTE
coyote-ugly

COZY
cozy up (to someone)

CRACK
crack a book □ crack a tube □ crack house □ crack open a bottle □ crack some suds □ crack someone up □ crack up □ cracked up to be □ dirty crack □ have a crack at something □ have one's ass in a crack □ take a crack at something □ tough egg to crack □ tough nut to crack

CRAFTSY
artsy-craftsy

CRANK
crank bugs □ crank something out □ crank something up

CRAP

crap out □ crapper dick □ Cut the crap! □ shoot the crap □ throw the crap

CRASH

crash and burn □ crash pad

CRATER

crater-face

CRAWL

crawling with someone or something

CRAZY

crazy bone □ like crazy □ stir crazy

CREAM

cream puff

CREEK

up a creek □ up the creek (without a paddle)

CREEP

creep dive □ creep joint □ creeping-crud □ Jeepers(-creepers)!

CRIB

crib course

CRICKET

not cricket

CRISPY

crispy-critter

CRITTER

crispy-critter

CROCK

crock of shit □ half-crocked

CROSS

cross-eyed (drunk) □ cross someone (up) □ cross tops □ cross up someone □ double cross □ double-crosser □ nail someone to a cross

CROTCH

crotch-pheasant □ crotch-rot

CROW

eat crow

CRUD

creeping-crud □ cruddy

CRUISE

cruisin' for a bruisin' □ cruising for a bruising □ time to cruise

CRUM

crum something up

CRUMBLE

That's the way the cookie crumbles.

CRUMP

crumped (out)

CRUNCH

budget crunch □ number-cruncher □ number crunching

CRY

cry hughie □ cry in one's beer □ cry ralph □ cry ruth □ crying drunk □ crying towel □ crying weed

CUDDLE

cuddle bunny

CUFF

cuff quote □ golden handcuffs

CULTURE

culture-vulture

CUP

cup of tea

CURB

step off the curb

CURE

Dutch cure □ take the cure

CURL

curl up and die

CUSTOMER

tough customer

CUT

able to cut something □ clean-cut □ cut a check □ cut a deal □ cut and run □ cut corners □ Cut it out! □ cut loose □ cut no ice (with someone) □ cut one's losses □ cut one's own throat □ cut one's wolf loose □ cut out □ cut-rate □ cut some Z's □ cut someone a break □ cut someone in (on something) □ cut the cheese □ Cut the comedy! □ Cut the crap! □ cut the dust □ cut the mustard ☐ cut to the chase ☐ cut (up) ☐ cut up (about someone or somehing) ☐ Fish or cut bait. ☐ It cuts two ways.

CUTIE
cutie pie

CYLINDER
run on all cylinders

D
big-D. ☐ Mickey D's

DAB
slap-dab ☐ smack (dab) in the middle

DADDY
daddy (of them all) ☐ freak daddy ☐ (grand)daddy (of them all) ☐ sugar daddy

DAGWOOD
dagwood (sandwich)

DAH
lah-di-dah ☐ Tah-dah!

DAILY
daily dozen ☐ daily grind

DAISY
fresh as a daisy ☐ pushing up daisies

DALLY
dilly-dally

DAMN
not worth a damn

DAMPER
put a damper on something

DANCE
grave-dancer ☐ tap dance like mad ☐ You can't dance at two weddings.

DANDRUFF
galloping dandruff ☐ walking dandruff

DANDY
fine and dandy

DARK
dark horse ☐ shot in the dark ☐ whistle in the dark

DASH
Dash it all! ☐ slap-dash

DATE
heavy date

DAVE
Sam and Dave

DAY
bad hair day ☐ day one ☐ day person ☐ day the eagle flies ☐ day-tripper ☐ Have a nice day. ☐ if one's a day ☐ Make my day! ☐ red-letter day ☐ seen better days ☐ That'll be the day!

DAZZLE
razzle-dazzle

DC
A.C.-D.C.

DEAD
(bang) dead to rights ☐ brain-dead ☐ dead and gone ☐ dead broke ☐ dead-catty ☐ dead cinch ☐ dead drunk ☐ dead duck ☐ dead easy ☐ dead-end kid ☐ dead from the neck up ☐ dead horse ☐ dead in the water ☐ dead issue ☐ dead letter ☐ dead man ☐ dead marine ☐ dead on ☐ dead one ☐ (dead) ringer (for someone) ☐ dead soldier ☐ dead to rights ☐ dead to the world ☐ Drop dead! ☐ drop-dead ☐ drop-dead list ☐ have someone dead to rights ☐ knock someone dead ☐ over my dead body ☐ stone dead ☐ would not be seen dead

DEADCAT
deadcat bounce

DEADLY
deadly (dull)

DEAL
big deal ☐ cut a deal ☐ deal stock ☐ dirty deal ☐ done deal ☐ Good deal! ☐ no big deal ☐ package deal ☐ raw deal ☐ sweetheart deal ☐ What's the deal? ☐ wheel and deal ☐ wheeler-dealer

DEAR
Dear John letter

DEATH
death on someone or something ☐ kiss

doctor ☐ just what the doctor ordered ☐ spin doctor ☐ You're the doctor. ☐ zit doctor

DODGE
get out of Dodge

DODGER
coffin-dodger

DODO
dumb-dodo

DOE
Jane Doe ☐ John Doe

DOG
bird-dog ☐ cats and dogs ☐ dirty dog ☐ dog and pony show ☐ dog-dew ☐ dog-do ☐ dog-doo ☐ dog-eat-dog ☐ dog meat ☐ doggy bag ☐ dog's mother ☐ Hong Kong dog ☐ Hot diggety (dog)! ☐ hot dog ☐ Hot dog! ☐ lucky dog ☐ put on the dog ☐ see a man about a dog ☐ shouldn't happen to a dog ☐ top dog ☐ yard dog

DOGGO
lie doggo

DOGGY
doggy bag

DOKEY
okey-dokey

DOLL
Barbie doll

DOLLAR
adobe dollar ☐ almighty dollar ☐ bet one's bottom dollar ☐ bet someone dollars to doughnuts ☐ bottom dollar ☐ like a million (dollars) ☐ phony as a three-dollar bill ☐ queer as a three-dollar bill ☐ sixty-four-dollar question

DOMAIN
ptomaine-domain

DOME
chrome-dome ☐ dome-doctor ☐ double-dome ☐ marble dome

DONE
done by mirrors ☐ done deal ☐ done for ☐ done over ☐ done to a turn ☐ done with mirrors

DONKEY
donkey's breakfast ☐ donkey's years

DON'T
Don't ask. ☐ Don't ask me. ☐ Don't call us, we'll call you. ☐ Don't have a cow! ☐ Don't I know it! ☐ Don't make me laugh! ☐ Don't sweat it! ☐ (Don't) you wish! ☐ do's and don'ts ☐ I don't believe this! ☐ I don't know. ☐ I don't mean maybe! ☐ where the sun don't shine ☐ You don't know the half of it.

DOO
dog-doo ☐ doo-doo ☐ in deep doo-doo

DOODLY
(doodly-)squat

DOOPER
super-dooper

DOOR
back-door trot(s) ☐ blow someone's doors off ☐ house of many doors

DOOTS
cow-doots

DOPE
do dope ☐ dope something out ☐ dope up ☐ inside dope ☐ straight dope

DORA
dumb Dora

DORK
dork off

DORKUS
dorkus maximus

DORY
hunky-dory

DOSE
go through someone like a dose of the salts

DOUBLE
double-bagger ☐ double-barreled slingshot ☐ double buffalo ☐ double cross ☐ double-crosser ☐ double-

decker □ double-deuces □ double-dipper □ double-dome □ double-gaited □ double nickels □ double saw(buck) □ double take □ double-trouble □ double up (with laughter) □ double whammy □ H-E-double-toothpicks □ on the double

DOUCHE

douche bag

DOUGH

dough head

DOUGHNUT

bet someone dollars to doughnuts □ blow one's doughnuts □ lose one's doughnuts

DOWN

be down (with someone) □ boogie down (to somewhere) □ bring-down □ bring someone down □ burn someone down □ chow down □ chow something down □ come down □ come down hard □ cool down □ down for the count □ down the drain □ Down the hatch! □ down time □ down to the wire □ down trip □ down under □ down with something □ falling-down drunk □ flake down □ garbage something down □ get down □ get down on someone □ get down to some serious drinking □ get down to the nitty-gritty □ go down □ go down in flames □ go down the chute □ go down the line □ go down the tube(s) □ hands down □ have a yellow streak down one's back □ hook something down □ hose someone down □ knock something down □ knuckle down (to something) □ lay down □ pipe down □ pull down an amount of money □ put-down □ ram something down someone's throat □ run down some lines □ run it down □ scarf something down □ shake someone down □ shoot someone down in flames □ shoot someone or something down □ shot down □ shuck down □ simmer (down) □ spaz down □ Take it down a thou(sand)! □ throw down □ thumbs down □ turn someone or something upside down □ turn thumbs down (on someone or something) □ way down □ What's going down? □ wolf something down □ yellow streak (down someone's back)

DOWNHILL

go downhill

DOZEN

daily dozen □ (dirty) dozens □ long dozen □ play the dozens □ shoot the dozens

DRAB

in dribs and drabs

DRAFT

draft board □ feel a draft

DRAG

be a drag (on someone) □ cop a drag □ dragged out □ draggin'-wagon □ in drag □ knockdown drag-out fight □ knuckle-dragger □ main drag

DRAGON

chase the dragon

DRAIN

brain-drain □ down the drain □ drain the bilge

DRAW

Do I have to draw (you) a picture? □ luck of the draw

DRAWER

droopy-drawers □ top-drawer

DRESS

dressed to kill □ dressed to the nines □ dressed to the teeth

DRIB

in dribs and drabs

DRIFT

(Do you) get my drift? □ Get my drift?

DRILL

blanket drill

DRINK

big drink □ big drink of water □ do the drink thing □ Drink up! □ get down to some serious drinking □ knock back a drink □ two-fisted drinker

DRIPP

silo drippings

☐ corral dust ☐ cut the dust ☐ dry-as-dust ☐ dust of angels ☐ dust someone off ☐ dust someone's pants ☐ dust-up ☐ ear-duster ☐ heaven dust ☐ joy dust ☐ kiss the dust

DUSTY
dusty butt ☐ rusty-dusty

DUTCH
Dutch act ☐ Dutch courage ☐ Dutch cure ☐ Dutch treat ☐ Dutch uncle ☐ go Dutch ☐ in Dutch

DUTY
rack duty

DWELLER
cliff-dweller

DYNAMIC
dynamic duo

EAGER
eager-beaver

EAGLE
day the eagle flies ☐ eagle-eye ☐ eagle freak ☐ legal-eagle ☐ when the eagle flies

EAR
Blow it out your ear! ☐ coming out of one's ears ☐ ear candy ☐ ear-duster ☐ mickey mouse ears ☐ pin someone's ears back ☐ pound one's ear ☐ sloshed (to the ears) ☐ stewed to the ears ☐ talk someone's ear off ☐ throw one out on one's ear ☐ up to one's ears ☐ walls have ears

EARFUL
give someone an earful

EARL
call earl ☐ talk to earl

EARLY
early bird

EARP
Earp slop, bring the mop.

EARTH
earth to _____ ☐ no earthly reason ☐ Where on (God's green) earth?

EARTHLY
See *earth.*

EASY
dead easy ☐ Easy does it. ☐ easy mark ☐ easy money ☐ easy street ☐ on easy street ☐ over easy ☐ take it easy ☐ take things easy

EAT
cheese-eater ☐ (Do) you eat with that mouth? ☐ dog-eat-dog ☐ eat crow ☐ eat face ☐ eat nails ☐ eat one's hat ☐ eat one's heart out ☐ eat something up ☐ eat up ☐ smoke eater ☐ weed-eater ☐ What's eating someone? ☐ You eat with that mouth?

ECO
eco freak ☐ eco nut

EDGAR
J. Edgar (Hoover)

EDGE
have an edge on ☐ moist around the edges ☐ on the bleeding edge

EGG
bad egg ☐ egg-beater ☐ egg-sucker ☐ Go fry an egg! ☐ goose egg ☐ have egg on one's face ☐ lay an egg ☐ nest egg ☐ rotten egg ☐ scrambled eggs ☐ tough egg to crack ☐ walk on eggs

EGO
ego trip ☐ ego tripper

EIGHT
behind the eight ball

EIGHTEEN
eighteen wheeler

EIGHTY
eighty-six

EL
el cheapo ☐ (el) primo

ELBOW
bend one's elbow ☐ bend the elbow ☐ elbow-bending ☐ elbow-grease ☐ lift one's elbow

ELEGANT
piss elegant

ELEPHANT
pink elephants ☐ seeing pink elephants ☐ white elephant

ELEVATOR
elevator music

ELSE
What else is new? ☐ You and who else?

EM
nail-em-and-jail-em ☐ nail-em-and-jail-em

'EM
shoot 'em up ☐ Stick 'em up! ☐ up an' at 'em

EMBALM
embalming fluid

EMBARRASS
financially embarrassed

EMPTY
empty-nesters

ENAMEL
pray to the enamel god

ENCHILADA
big enchilada ☐ whole enchilada

END
at loose ends ☐ business end (of something) ☐ cannot see (any) further than the end of one's nose ☐ dead-end kid ☐ end of the ball game ☐ go off the deep end ☐ know which end is up ☐ no end of something ☐ rear (end) ☐ see no further than the end of one's nose ☐ short end of the stick ☐ tail-end

ENDER
back-ender ☐ rear-ender

ESTIMATE
ball park estimate

ETERNAL
eternal checkout

ETERNITY
eternity-box

EVEN
even-Steven ☐ evened out

EVERYTHING
everything from soup to nuts ☐ Hold everything!

EXCUSE
Excuse my French.

EXPEDITION
fishing expedition

EXPRESS
Siberian express

EXPRESSION
if you'll pardon the expression

EYE
bedroom eyes ☐ black eye ☐ blue-eyed ☐ bright-eyed and bushy-tailed ☐ cross-eyed (drunk) ☐ eagle-eye ☐ eye-opener ☐ eye-popper ☐ four-eyes ☐ get some shut-eye ☐ glass(y)-eyed ☐ goggle-eyed ☐ goo-goo eyes ☐ googly-eyed ☐ Here's mud in your eye. ☐ hit the bull's eye ☐ pie-eyed ☐ pigeon-eyed ☐ pop-eyed ☐ private eye ☐ see eye to eye ☐ shut-eye ☐ snake eyes ☐ wall-eyed ☐ with (one's) eyes (wide) open

EYEBALL
eyeball to eyeball ☐ get an eyeball on someone or something ☐ up to one's eyeballs

FACE
Bag your face! ☐ be in someone's face ☐ blue in the face ☐ chew face ☐ crater-face ☐ eat face ☐ face card ☐ (face) fungus ☐ face man ☐ face-off ☐ face the music ☐ feed one's face ☐ frog face ☐ fungus-face ☐ fuzz-face ☐ get face ☐ get in someone's face ☐ Get out of my face! ☐ have egg on one's face ☐ in-your-face ☐ mace someone's face ☐ mess someone's face up ☐ pizza-face ☐ powder one's face ☐ put a smile on someone's face ☐ shit-faced ☐ Shut your face! ☐ slap in the face ☐ soak one's face ☐ stand there with one's bare face hanging out ☐ straight-faced ☐ suck face ☐ talk until one is blue in the face ☐ what's his face

FACT
facts of life

FACTOR
fudge factor

FACTORY
bone factory ☐ gargle factory ☐ glue factory ☐ nut factory ☐ piss factory ☐ spook factory

FADE
do a fade

FAG
fag-busting ☐ fagged out

FAIR
fair-haired boy ☐ fair shake ☐ fair-weather ☐ No fair!

FAIRY
airy-fairy ☐ fairy tale

FAITH
Keep the faith (baby)! ☐ one of the faithful

FAITHFUL
one of the faithful

FAKE
fake book ☐ fake it ☐ fake off ☐ fake someone out

FALL
fall guy ☐ fall off the wagon ☐ fall out ☐ fall out of bed ☐ falling-down drunk ☐ falling-out ☐ take a fall ☐ take the fall

FAMILIAR
in a familiar way

FAMILY
in a family way ☐ in the family way ☐ whole fam damily

FAN
fan the breeze ☐ hit the fan

FANCY
fancy footwork ☐ Fancy meeting you here. ☐ fancy-schmancy ☐ Fancy that!

FANNY
fanny-bumper ☐ fanny-dipper

FAR
far gone ☐ far out

FARM
buy the farm ☐ funny-farm

FART
fart sack

FARTSY
artsy (fartsy)

FAST
fast buck ☐ fast footwork ☐ fast one ☐ get nowhere fast ☐ play fast and loose (with someone or something) ☐ pull a fast one

FAT
chew the fat ☐ fat-cat ☐ fat chance ☐ fat city ☐ till the fat lady sings ☐ when the fat lady sings

FAX
junk fax

FEAR
I'm shaking (in fear).

FEATHER
feather brain ☐ in fine feather ☐ You could have knocked me over with a feather.

FEDERAL
federal diploma ☐ federal jug ☐ make a federal case out of something

FEDS
the feds

FEED
chicken feed ☐ feed one's face ☐ for chicken feed

FEEDBAG
put on the feedbag

FEEL
feel a draft ☐ feel groovy ☐ feeling no pain

FEET
cold feet ☐ get a load off one's feet ☐ patter of tiny feet ☐ six feet under ☐ take a load off one's feet ☐ vote with one's feet

FENCE
fence hanger ☐ straddle the fence

FLAME
burn with a low blue flame □ flame-war □ go down in flames □ old flame □ shoot someone down in flames

FLASH
flash on something □ flash the hash □ in a flash

FLAT
flat broke □ flat on one's ass □ flat out □ in nothing flat

FLESH
flesh-presser □ press (the) flesh

FLEX
flexed out of shape

FLICK
skin flick

FLIGHT
top-flight

FLIMFLAM
flimflam artist

FLING
fling up □ fling-wing

FLIP
flip-flop □ flip one's wig □ flip (out) □ flip side □ flip someone off □ flip someone out □ flip someone the bird

FLO
Aunt Flo □ visit from Flo

FLOOEY
go flooey

FLOOR
mop the floor up with someone □ wipe the floor up with someone

FLOP
belly flop □ cow flop □ flip-flop □ flop house □ flopper-stopper □ That's the way the mop flops.

FLOW
cash flow □ go with the flow

FLOWER
hearts and flowers

FLU
blue flu □ brown bottle flu

FLUB
flub something up □ flub the dub □ flub (up) □ flub-up

FLUFF
fluff-stuff

FLUID
embalming fluid

FLUNK
flunk out (of something)

FLUSHER
four-flusher

FLY
day the eagle flies □ fly-by-night □ fly kites □ fly light □ fly the coop □ fly trap □ Go fly a kite! □ I've got to fly. □ I('ve) gotta fly. □ on the fly □ straighten up and fly right □ take a flyer (on something) □ when the eagle flies □ with flying colors

FLYER
take a flyer (on something)

FOG
foggiest (idea)

FOGEY
old fogey

FOLD
folding money □ folding stuff □ green folding □ Hold some, fold some.

FOLKS
different strokes for different folks

FOO
foo-foo water

FOOD
junk food □ rabbit food □ squirrel-food □ worm-food

FOOL
play someone for a fool

FOOT
foot-in-mouth disease □ foot it □ have one foot in the grave □ My foot!

□ pussyfoot (around) □ shoot oneself in the foot □ wouldn't touch someone or something with a ten-foot pole

FOOTWORK
fancy footwork □ fast footwork

FORBIDDEN
forbidden fruit

FORGET
Forget it! □ Forget you!

FORK
fork something over □ rain pitchforks

FORM
in rare form

FORT
hold the fort

FORTUNE
small fortune

FORTY
forty winks

FOUL
foul mouth □ foul up □ fouled up

FOUND
lost-and-found badge

FOUNDRY
nut-foundry

FOUR
four-bagger □ four-bits □ four-eyes □ four-flusher □ four sheets in the wind □ four sheets (to the wind) □ four wheels □ sixty-four-dollar question □ ten-four □ two-by-four

FOX
fox trap □ foxy lady □ stone fox

FOXY
See *fox*.

FRAIDY
fraidy cat

FRAME
frame-up

FRAT
frat-rat

FREAK
eagle freak □ eco freak □ freak daddy □ freak mommy □ freak (out) □ freak someone out □ freaked (out) □ garbage freak □ juice freak □ kick freak □ pill freak □ speed freak

FREE
for free □ free base □ free base party □ free-baser □ free-basing □ free for all □ free lunch □ free ride □ free show □ free trip □ free-wheeling

FREEZE
freeze someone out □ freezing cold □ play freeze-out □ put the freeze on someone □ till hell freezes over

FRENCH
Excuse my French. □ French kiss □ Pardon my French.

FRESH
fresh and sweet □ fresh as a daisy □ funky-fresh □ stupid fresh

FRIEND
bosom friends

FRITZ
on the fritz

FROG
frog face □ frog slicing

FRONT
front man □ front money □ front off about something □ front runner □ up front

FROST
frosted (over) □ frosty one

FRUIT
forbidden fruit □ fruit loop □ hen fruit

FRUITCAKE
nutty as a fruitcake

FRY
brain-fried □ Go fry an egg! □ Kentucky fried □ small fry □ southern-fried

FUDDY
fuddy-duddy

FUDGE
fudge factor

FUEL
take on fuel

FULL
chock-full ☐ full blast ☐ full of beans ☐ full of bull ☐ full of hops ☐ full of hot air ☐ full of it ☐ full of Old Nick ☐ full of prunes ☐ full of the devil ☐ full sesh ☐ full steam ahead ☐ mouth full of South ☐ play with a full deck ☐ woods are full of. . . .

FUN
barrel of fun ☐ fun and games

FUND
slush fund

FUNERAL
It's your funeral!

FUNGUS
(face) fungus ☐ fungus-face

FUNK
blue funk ☐ funked out ☐ in a blue funk

FUNKY
funky-drunk ☐ funky-fresh

FUNNY
funny business ☐ funny-farm ☐ funny-money

FURTHER
cannot see (any) further than the end of one's nose ☐ see no further than the end of one's nose

FUSE
blow a fuse ☐ blow one's fuse ☐ fuse box ☐ have a short fuse ☐ short fuse

FUZZ
fuzz-face ☐ fuzz man ☐ fuzz station

FUZZY
fuzzy (tail)

G
G-man ☐ What's up, G?

GAB
gab room ☐ gibber-gabber ☐ gift of gab

GABBER
gibber-gabber

GAG
throat gag

GAITED
double-gaited

GALLOP
at a snail's gallop ☐ galloping dandruff

GALUMPH
galumph (around)

GAME
ahead of the game ☐ end of the ball game ☐ fun and games ☐ game plan ☐ game time ☐ name of the game ☐ skin game ☐ throw a game ☐ whole new ball game

GANDER
take a gander (at someone or something)

GANG
gang-bang

GANGBUSTERS
come on like gangbusters ☐ like gangbusters

GANJAH
bhang ganjah

GARBAGE
garbage freak ☐ garbage mouth ☐ garbage something down

GARGLE
gargle factory

GAS
cooking with gas ☐ gas-guzzler ☐ gas-passer ☐ gas up ☐ gassed (up) ☐ run out of gas ☐ take the gas pipe

GASH
gash bucket

GASKET
blow a gasket

GATE
give someone the gate

GAY
gay as pink ink

GAZOO
out the gazoo

GEAR
reverse gears ☐ swing into high gear

GEEK
geek-chic ☐ geek out

GENDER
gender-bender

GENERATION
now generation

GENUINE
genuine article

GERMAN
German goiter

GHETTO
(ghetto) blaster ☐ (ghetto) box

GHOST
ghost turd

GIANT
mental giant

GIBBER
gibber-gabber

GIDDY
Giddy up!

GIFT
get a gift ☐ gift of gab

GIGGLE
giggle goo

GILL
blue around the gills ☐ green around the gills ☐ loaded to the gills ☐ stewed to the gills

GIMME
Gimme a break!

GIN
gin dive ☐ gin mill ☐ gin palace

GIRL
call girl ☐ little girls' room ☐ old girl

GIRLIE
girlie magazine ☐ girlie show

GIT
from (the) git-go ☐ git-go

GIVE
Give it a rest! ☐ give it the gun ☐ Give it up! ☐ Give me a break! ☐ Give me a rest! ☐ Give me five! ☐ Give me (some) skin! ☐ give (out) with something ☐ give someone a buzz ☐ give someone a (good) talking to ☐ give someone a (good) working over ☐ give someone a melvin ☐ give someone a pain ☐ give someone an earful ☐ give someone five ☐ give someone hell ☐ give someone the ax ☐ give someone the brushoff ☐ give someone the business ☐ give someone the finger ☐ give someone the gate ☐ give someone the go-by ☐ give someone the nod ☐ give someone the raspberry ☐ give someone the shaft ☐ give someone the slip ☐ not give a hoot ☐ Something's got to give. ☐ What gives?

GLAD
glad-hand ☐ glad-hander ☐ glad rags

GLAMOUR
glamour puss

GLASS
glass gun

GLASSY
glass(y)-eyed

GLAZE
glazed (drunk) ☐ glazed (over)

GLOOMY
gloomy Gus

GLORY
send someone to glory

GLOSS
lip gloss

GLOVE
hand-in-glove

GLOW

glow worm □ have a glow on

GLUE

glue factory

GO

from (the) git-go □ get (out) while the goin's good □ get someone going □ get something going (with someone) □ git-go □ give someone the go-by □ go-ahead □ go all the way □ go ape (over someone or something) □ go bananas □ go belly up □ go blooey □ go-by □ Go chase your tail! □ Go chase yourself! □ Go climb a tree! □ go down □ go down in flames □ go down the chute □ go down the line □ go down the tube(s) □ go downhill □ go Dutch □ Go figure. □ go flooey □ Go fly a kite! □ go for broke □ Go for it! □ Go fry an egg! □ go-getter □ go-go □ go great guns □ go haywire □ go home in a box □ go home to mama □ go into orbit □ Go jump in the lake! □ go mental □ go off half-cocked □ go off the deep end □ Go on! □ go on (and on) about someone or something □ go over big □ go over like a lead balloon □ go over the hill □ go over the wall □ go overboard □ go-pills □ go places □ go public □ go Rinso □ Go soak your head! □ Go soak yourself! □ go sour □ go South □ go straight □ go the limit □ go through someone like a dose of the salts □ go through the changes □ Go to! □ Go to blazes! □ Go to the devil! □ go to town □ Go to your room! □ go underground □ go up □ go West □ go with it □ go with the flow □ go zonkers □ going high □ going over □ goings-on □ How goes it? □ no go □ only way to go □ pass go □ raring to go □ (That's the) way to go! □ There you go. □ to go □ touch and go □ Way to go! □ What's going down? □ What's going on?

GOAT

get someone's goat □ skin a goat

GOD

God's acre □ kiss the porcelain god □ pray to the enamel god □ pray to the porcelain god □ Where on (God's green) earth? □ Ye gods!

GODDESS

hug the porcelain god(dess) □ sex goddess □ worship the porcelain god(dess)

GOGGLE

beer goggles □ goggle-eyed

GOITER

German goiter □ Milwaukee goiter

GOLD

Colombian (gold) □ Columbian (gold) □ gold digger

GOLDEN

golden-ager □ golden handcuffs □ golden opportunity □ golden parachute

GOLDIE

goldie locks

GOLLY

Good golly, Miss Molly!

GONE

dead and gone □ far gone □ gone goose □ gone under □ real gone □ to hell and gone

GOO

giggle goo □ goo-goo eyes

GOOBER

goober-grabber □ goober-grease

GOOD

do-gooder □ get (out) while the gettin(g)'s good □ get (out) while the goin's good □ get the goods on someone □ give someone a (good) talking to □ give someone a (good) working over □ good and something □ good buddy □ Good call! □ Good deal! □ good-for-nothing □ Good golly, Miss Molly! □ Good heavens! □ good Joe □ (good) looker □ good old boy □ good ole boy □ good-time Charley □ good-time it □ good-time man □ good trip □ Have a good one. □ have good vibes □ if one knows what's good for one □ Johnny-be-good □ no-good □ oldie but goodie □ onto a good thing

☐ What's the good word? ☐ Your guess is as good as mine.

GOODBYE
kiss something goodbye

GOODNIK
no-goodnik

GOODY
goody two-shoes

GOOF
goof around ☐ goof off ☐ goof on someone ☐ goof-proof ☐ goof something up ☐ goof up ☐ goof up on something ☐ goofed (up)

GOOGLY
googly-eyed

GOON
goon-platoon ☐ goon squad

GOOSE
gone goose ☐ goose egg ☐ silver goose

GOPHER
gopher ball

GORILLA
gorilla biscuits ☐ gorilla juice ☐ gorilla pills

GORK
gorked (out)

GOSPEL
gospel (truth)

GOT
I've got to fly. ☐ I've got to split. ☐ Something's got to give. ☐ You got it! ☐ You've got another think coming.

GOTTA
I('ve) gotta fly.

GOUCH
gouch off

GOURD
stoned out of one's gourd

GRAB
goober-grabber ☐ How does that grab you? ☐ up for grabs

GRADE
grade-grubber ☐ grade-grubbing

GRAND
Grand Central Station

GRANDDADDY
(grand)daddy (of them all)

GRANDSTAND
grandstand play

GRAPE
belt the grape ☐ grape shot ☐ grapes of wrath ☐ in the grip of the grape

GRASS
grass party ☐ johnson grass ☐ snake in the grass

GRASSHOPPER
knee-high to a grasshopper

GRAVE
grave-dancer ☐ have one foot in the grave

GRAVEL
gravel-pounder

GRAVEYARD
graveyard shift

GRAVY
gravy train

GRAYBAR
Graybar Hotel

GRAYSTONE
Graystone College

GREASE
elbow-grease ☐ goober-grease ☐ grease monkey ☐ grease someone's palm ☐ grease the skids ☐ greased lightning ☐ greasy spoon

GREASY
See *grease*.

GREAT
go great guns ☐ great divide ☐ Great Scott! ☐ great unwashed ☐ no great shakes ☐ whopping (great)

GREEK
Greek to someone

come down hard ☐ hard case ☐ hard coin ☐ hard-core ☐ hard head ☐ hard liquor ☐ hard-nosed ☐ hard sell ☐ hard time ☐ hard to swallow ☐ hard up

HARDBALL

play hardball (with someone)

HARSH

harsh toke

HAS

has-been

HASH

flash the hash ☐ hash cannon ☐ hash-head ☐ hash-house ☐ hash pipe ☐ hash-slinger ☐ heavy hash ☐ settle someone's hash

HAT

brass hat ☐ eat one's hat ☐ knock something into a cocked hat ☐ old hat ☐ talk through one's hat ☐ throw one's hat in the ring ☐ tin hat ☐ white hat

HATCH

booby hatch ☐ Down the hatch!

HATCHET

bury the hatchet

HAUL

over the long haul

HAWKINS

Mr. Hawkins

HAY

hay burner ☐ hay head ☐ hit the hay

HAYWIRE

go haywire

HEAD

banana-head ☐ bean head ☐ beef-head ☐ C-head ☐ cop a head ☐ dough head ☐ get one's head together ☐ Go soak your head! ☐ hard head ☐ hash-head ☐ have a (big) head ☐ have rocks in one's head ☐ hay head ☐ head cook and bottle washer ☐ head drug ☐ head hunt ☐ head South ☐ head trip ☐ Heads up! ☐ heads will roll ☐ helium head ☐ hooch head ☐ hot head ☐ keep one's head right ☐ knock some heads together ☐ over one's head ☐ peanut head ☐ pointy-head ☐ pound someone's head in ☐ soft in the head ☐ stoned out of one's head ☐ talk someone's head off ☐ talking head ☐ Use your head! ☐ where someone's head is at ☐ yell one's head off ☐ zipper head

HEADACHE

headache department ☐ headache house ☐ headache man ☐ splitting headache

HEADSTONE

Headstone City

HEAP

bottom of the heap ☐ in a heap ☐ junk heap ☐ top of the heap

HEAR

I hear what you are saying. ☐ I hear you. ☐ talk to hear one's own voice

HEARD

You heard the man.

HEART

chicken-hearted ☐ eat one's heart out ☐ Have a heart! ☐ heart-to-heart (talk) ☐ hearts and flowers ☐ party-hearty ☐ soft-hearted ☐ sweetheart deal

HEARTY

See *heart*.

HEAT

If you can't stand the heat, keep out of the kitchen. ☐ put the heat on someone ☐ take some heat ☐ take the heat ☐ take the heat off someone

HEAVE

old heave-ho

HEAVEN

bundle from heaven ☐ Good heavens! ☐ heaven dust ☐ pig heaven ☐ smell to (high) heaven

HEAVY

carrying a (heavy) load ☐ heavy artillery ☐ heavy bread ☐ heavy date ☐ heavy-handed ☐ heavy hash ☐ heavy into someone or something ☐ heavy joint ☐ heavy metal ☐ heavy money ☐

heavy necking □ heavy scene □ heavy soul □ lay a (heavy) trip on someone □ top heavy □ walk heavy □ wing heavy

HECK
for the heck of it □ What the heck!

HEEBIE
heebie-jeebies

HEEBY
heeby-jeebies

HEEL
well-heeled

HEIL
sieg-heil someone

HEINZ
Heinz 57 (variety)

HELIUM
helium head

HELL
catch hell (for something) □ for the hell of it □ give someone hell □ hell of a mess □ hell of a note □ hell of a someone or something □ hell-on-wheels □ hell raiser □ Hell's bells (and buckets of blood)! □ helluva someone or something □ like a bat out of hell □ Like hell! □ play hell with someone or something □ quicker than hell □ raise hell □ raise hell (with someone or something) □ scare the hell out of someone □ shot to hell □ snowball's chance in hell □ someone or something from hell □ sure as hell □ There will be hell to pay. □ till hell freezes over □ to hell and gone □ To hell with that! □ What (in) the hell? □ Who (in) the hell?

HELLUVA
helluva someone or something

HELP
pitch in (and help)

HEN
hen fruit □ hen party

HEPPED
hepped (up)

HER
Let her rip!

HERB
Herb and Al □ talk to Herb and Al

HERE
Fancy meeting you here. □ get one right here □ Here's looking at you. □ Here's mud in your eye. □ I'm out of here. □ I'm outa here. □ same here □ up to here □ You can't get there from here.

HERO
hero (of the underworld)

HERPED
herped up

HEY
Hey, bum!

HI
hi-res

HIDE
nail someone('s hide) to the wall

HIGH
going high □ high and dry □ high five □ high mucky-muck □ high on something □ high-res □ high roller □ high sign □ high ups □ high, wide, and handsome □ higher ups □ hold one's high □ knee-high to a grasshopper □ on one's high horse □ smell to (high) heaven □ swing into high gear □ up high

HIGHWAY
highway robbery

HIKE
take a hike

HILL
go downhill □ go over the hill □ over the hill □ What in (the) Sam Hill? □ Where in (the) Sam Hill?

HIND
suck someone's hind tit

HINDSIGHT
20/20 hindsight □ twenty-twenty hindsight

HIP
hip-shooter □ joined at the hip □ shoot from the hip

HIRED
hired gun

HIS
what's his face □ what's his name

HISTORY
ancient history □ I'm history.

HIT
can't hit the (broad) side of a barn □ hit list □ hit man □ hit me □ hit me again □ hit on someone □ hit on something □ hit pay dirt □ hit (someone) below the belt □ hit someone (up) for something □ hit someone with something □ hit the books □ hit the booze □ hit the bottle □ hit the bricks □ hit the bull's eye □ hit the ceiling □ hit the deck □ hit the fan □ hit the hay □ hit the jackpot □ hit the panic button □ hit the pavement □ hit the road □ hit the roof □ hit the sack □ hit the skids □ hit the spot □ hit the trail □ hit under the wing □ nose hit □ smash hit

HITCH
without a hitch

HITHER
come-hither look

HITTER
pinch hitter □ power hitter □ switch-hitter

HO
gung-ho □ ho-hum □ ho-jo('s) □ old heave-ho

HOCK
hock a luggie

HOCKEY
horse hockey □ play tonsil hockey

HOE
tough row to hoe

HOG
hog cadillac □ hog-wild □ road hog □ sewer hog

HOIST
hoist one

HOLD
get a toehold □ hold all the aces □ Hold everything! □ Hold it! □ Hold it, Buster! □ hold one's high □ hold one's horses □ hold one's liquor □ Hold some, fold some. □ hold the fort □ hold water □ lose one's hold □ no holds barred

HOLE
ace in the hole □ hole in the wall □ hole up □ in the hole □ nineteenth hole □ puke hole □ square peg (in a round hole) □ watering hole

HOLIDAY
holiday cheer

HOLY
holier-than-thou □ Holy cow! □ holy Joe □ Holy mackerel! □ Holy moley! □ holy stink □ holy terror

HOME
bring home the bacon □ go home in a box □ go home to mama □ home-brew □ in the (home) stretch □ money from home □ nothing to write home about □ There's nobody home.

HONEST
honest injun

HONEY
honey cart □ honey of a something □ honey wagon

HONEYMOON
honeymoon (period) □ honeymoon stage

HONG KONG
Hong Kong dog

HOO
hoo-ha

HOOCH
hooch head □ hooch hound □ hooched (up)

HOOF
hoof it

HURT
hurt for someone or something

HUSH
hush-hush ☐ hush money ☐ hush someone or something up

HYPE
blow a hype ☐ hype artist ☐ hype something up ☐ hyped (up)

ICE
Bite the ice! ☐ break the ice ☐ cut no ice (with someone) ☐ ice queen ☐ icing on the cake ☐ on ice ☐ stink on ice ☐ walk on thin ice

ICEBERG
iceberg slim

ICKY
icky-poo

IDEA
foggiest (idea)

IDIOT
blithering idiot ☐ idiot box ☐ idiot card ☐ idiot juice ☐ idiot light ☐ idiot oil ☐ idiot pills

IDLE
bone idle

IF
if I've told you once, I've told you a thousand times ☐ if one knows what's good for one ☐ if one's a day ☐ if push comes to shove ☐ If you can't stand the heat, keep out of the kitchen. ☐ if you'll pardon the expression

INCY
incy-wincy

INDUSTRY
captain of industry

INJUN
honest injun

INK
gay as pink ink ☐ ink slinger ☐ red ink

INS
ins and outs

INSIDE
inside dope ☐ inside job ☐ inside out

INTO
get into something ☐ get one's hooks into someone or something ☐ get one's teeth into something ☐ go into orbit ☐ heavy into someone or something ☐ knock something into a cocked hat ☐ lick something into shape ☐ light into someone ☐ sail into someone ☐ sink one's teeth into something ☐ swing into high gear ☐ tear into someone or something ☐ whale into someone or something ☐ whip something into shape ☐ wired into someone or something ☐ work oneself (up) into a lather

IRON
big iron ☐ cast-iron stomach ☐ pump (some) iron ☐ shooting iron

IRVINE
Charlie Irvine

IS
ball is in someone's court ☐ Cash is king. ☐ Cash is trash. ☐ jig is up ☐ know where one is coming from ☐ know which end is up ☐ Put your money where your mouth is! ☐ quit while one is ahead ☐ talk until one is blue in the face ☐ Tell it like it is. ☐ This is it! ☐ This is where I came in. ☐ What else is new? ☐ What is it? ☐ What you see is what you get. ☐ where someone is at ☐ where someone's head is at ☐ where the action is ☐ world is one's oyster ☐ Your guess is as good as mine.

ISSUE
dead issue

ITCH
have an itch for something ☐ seven-year itch

ITEM
hot item

ITSY
itsy-bitsy

ITTY
itty-bitty

IVORY
ivory tower ☐ tickle the ivories

JAB
jab pop ☐ take a jab at someone

JACK
jack around ☐ jack someone around ☐ jack someone or something up ☐ jack-ups ☐ jacked (out) ☐ jacked up

JACKPOT
hit the jackpot

JAIL
jail bait ☐ nail-em-and-jail-em

JAM
in a jam ☐ jammed up

JANE
Jane Doe ☐ Jane Q. Public ☐ Mary Jane

JAWBONE
diarrhea of the jawbone

JAY
Peter Jay

JAY
unk-jay

JAZZ
all that jazz ☐ jazz someone or something up ☐ jazzed (up)

JEEBIES
heebie-jeebies ☐ heeby-jeebies

JEEPERS
Jeepers(-creepers)!

JELLY
jelly babies ☐ jelly sandals ☐ jelly shoes

JERK
jerk around ☐ jerk someone around ☐ jerk someone over ☐ knee-jerk ☐ tear-jerker

JERRY
jerry-built

JESUS
Jesus boots

JET
jet-set(ters)

JIFFY
in a jiff(y)

JIG
jig is up

JIVE
blow jive ☐ jive-ass ☐ jive talk ☐ jive turkey ☐ pull jive

JO
ho-jo('s)

JOB
con job ☐ do a job on someone or something ☐ do a snow job on someone ☐ inside job ☐ land a job ☐ nose job ☐ pull a job ☐ put-up job ☐ snow job ☐ wall job

JOCK
rock-jock ☐ video jock

JOCKEY
bench jockey ☐ desk jockey ☐ disc jockey ☐ disk jockey

JOE
good Joe ☐ holy Joe ☐ Joe Blow ☐ Joe Citizen ☐ Joe College ☐ Joe Doakes ☐ Joe Schmo ☐ Joe Six-pack ☐ quality Joe

JOHN
big John ☐ Dear John letter ☐ John Doe ☐ John Hancock ☐ John Q. Public ☐ square john ☐ square john broad ☐ who shot John

JOHNNIE
Johnnie-come-lately

JOHNNY
Johnny-be-good ☐ John(ny) Law

JOHNSON
johnson grass

JOIN
joined at the hip

JOINT
blow the joint ☐ case the joint ☐ clip joint ☐ creep joint ☐ get one's nose

out of joint ☐ heavy joint ☐ juice joint ☐ put someone's nose out of joint

JOKE
dirty joke

JOLLY
jolly-well

JONES
scag jones ☐ skag jones

JOY
bundle of joy ☐ joy dust ☐ joy flakes ☐ joy juice ☐ joy ride ☐ joy water

JUDGE
sober as a judge

JUG
federal jug ☐ jug up ☐ jug wine ☐ jugged (up)

JUICE
big juice ☐ B.O. juice ☐ cactus juice ☐ cow juice ☐ gorilla juice ☐ happy juice ☐ idiot juice ☐ joy juice ☐ juice freak ☐ juice house ☐ juice joint ☐ juice racket ☐ juice something back ☐ jungle juice ☐ juniper juice ☐ moo juice ☐ on the juice ☐ tiger juice ☐ tornado juice

JUMP
Go jump in the lake! ☐ jump bail ☐ jump smooth ☐ jump start ☐ jump (street) ☐ jump the gun ☐ one jump ahead of someone or something ☐ puddle jumper ☐ Take a running jump (in the lake)!

JUMPSTART
jumpstart someone or something

JUNGLE
asphalt jungle ☐ jungle juice ☐ jungle mouth

JUNIPER
juniper juice

JUNK
junk bond ☐ junk fax ☐ junk food ☐ junk heap ☐ junk mail ☐ junk squad ☐ junk tank ☐ on the junk

JUST
just off the boat ☐ just the ticket ☐ just what the doctor ordered ☐ not just whistling Dixie

KANGAROO
kangaroo court

KEEN
peachy (keen)

KEEP
for keeps ☐ If you can't stand the heat, keep out of the kitchen. ☐ keep cool ☐ Keep in touch. ☐ Keep on trucking. ☐ keep one's cool ☐ keep one's head right ☐ keep one's nose clean ☐ Keep out of this! ☐ Keep the faith (baby)! ☐ Keep your hands to yourself. ☐ Keep your pants on! ☐ Keep your shirt on! ☐ play for keeps ☐ Where (have) you been keeping yourself?

KEG
keg party

KENTUCKY
Kentucky fried

KEY
church key ☐ key figure ☐ key grip ☐ keyed (up) ☐ keyed up to the roof ☐ low-key

KIBOSH
put the kibosh on something

KICK
for kicks ☐ get a kick out of someone or something ☐ get one's kicks (from someone or something) ☐ kick around ☐ kick back ☐ kick cold (turkey) ☐ kick freak ☐ kick in the ass ☐ kick in the butt ☐ kick in the guts ☐ kick in the (seat of the) pants ☐ kick in the teeth ☐ kick in the wrist ☐ kick off ☐ kick party ☐ kick some ass (around) ☐ kick the bucket ☐ kick the habit ☐ kick up a storm

KID
dead-end kid ☐ I kid you not. ☐ I'm not kidding. ☐ kid stuff ☐ kid-vid ☐ No kidding! ☐ punk kid ☐ snotnose(d) (kid) ☐ whiz kid

KIDNEY
kidney-buster

KILL
dressed to kill ☐ fill or kill ☐ killed (off) ☐ killer-diller ☐ killer weed ☐ lady-killer ☐ make a killing

KILTER
out of kilter

KIMONO
open (up) one's kimono

KING
Cash is king. ☐ King Grod ☐ King Kong pills ☐ King Kong specials

KINGDOM
till kingdom come

KING KONG
King Kong pills ☐ King Kong specials

KISS
baby-kisser ☐ (Do) you kiss your momma with that mouth? ☐ fish-kiss ☐ French kiss ☐ kiss-ass ☐ kiss of death ☐ kiss off ☐ kiss someone or something off ☐ kiss someone's ass ☐ kiss something goodbye ☐ kiss the dust ☐ kiss the porcelain god ☐ kiss up to someone ☐ right in the kisser ☐ sealed with a kiss ☐ soul kiss ☐ You kiss your momma with that mouth?

KIT
kit and caboodle

KITCHEN
If you can't stand the heat, keep out of the kitchen.

KITE
fly kites ☐ Go fly a kite!

KITTEN
have kittens ☐ sex kitten

KNEE
knee-deep in something ☐ knee-high to a grasshopper ☐ knee-jerk ☐ up to one's knees

KNIFE
long knife

KNOCK
knock around ☐ knock back a drink ☐ Knock it off! ☐ knock off (work) ☐ knock one back ☐ knock one over ☐ knock some heads together ☐ knock someone dead ☐ knock someone or something off ☐ knock someone or something out ☐ knock someone some skin ☐ knock someone up ☐ knock someone's block off ☐ knock someone's socks off ☐ knock something down ☐ knock something into a cocked hat ☐ knock something together ☐ knock the habit ☐ knocked in ☐ knocked out ☐ knocked up ☐ You could have knocked me over with a feather.

KNOCKDOWN
knockdown drag-out fight

KNOT
tie the knot

KNOW
Don't I know it! ☐ for all I know ☐ I don't know. ☐ if one knows what's good for one ☐ in the know ☐ know all the angles ☐ know from something ☐ know-how ☐ know-it-all ☐ know shit from Shinola ☐ know the score ☐ know what's what ☐ know where it's at ☐ know where one is coming from ☐ know which end is up ☐ like, you know ☐ not know beans (about something) ☐ not know from nothing ☐ You don't know the half of it.

KNOWLEDGE
knowledge-box

KNUCKLE
knuckle down (to something) ☐ knuckle-dragger ☐ knuckle sandwich ☐ knuckle under (to someone or something) ☐ white-knuckle ☐ white knuckler

KONG
See *Hong Kong, King Kong*

LABEL
label mate

LADY
boss lady ☐ foxy lady ☐ ladies' room

☐ lady bear ☐ lady-killer ☐ Lady Snow ☐ old lady ☐ till the fat lady sings ☐ when the fat lady sings

LAFF

belly laff

LAH

lah-di-dah

LAID

laid back ☐ laid out ☐ laid to the bone

LAKE

Go jump in the lake! ☐ Take a running jump (in the lake)!

LAM

on the lam ☐ take it on the lam

LAMB

two shakes of a lamb's tail

LAME

lame duck

LAMP

between you, me, and the lamppost

LAND

land a blow ☐ land a job ☐ land office business

LANGUAGE

barnyard language ☐ speak someone's language

LAP

lap of luxury ☐ Make a lap!

LARD

lard ass ☐ tub of lard

LARGE

Living large.

LAST

last roundup ☐ last straw ☐ on one's or its last legs

LATCH

latch onto something

LATELY

Johnnie-come-lately

LATER

Catch you later. ☐ see you later ☐ see you later, alligator

LATHER

work oneself (up) into a lather

LATRINE

latrine lips ☐ latrine rumor ☐ latrine wireless

LAUGH

belly laugh ☐ Don't make me laugh! ☐ double up (with laughter) ☐ horse laugh ☐ laugh at the carpet ☐ laughing academy ☐ laughing soup ☐ laughing water ☐ liquid laugh

LAUGHTER

double up (with laughter)

LAUNCH

launch (one's lunch)

LAUNDRY

dirty laundry ☐ laundry list

LAVENDER

lay someone out in lavender

LAW

bend the law ☐ John(ny) Law ☐ long arm of the law

LAY

lay a guilt trip on someone ☐ lay a (heavy) trip on someone ☐ lay an egg ☐ lay down ☐ lay it on the line ☐ lay off (someone or something) ☐ lay one on ☐ lay (some) rubber ☐ lay some sweet lines on someone ☐ lay someone or something out ☐ lay someone out in lavender ☐ lay something on someone

LEAD

Get the lead out! ☐ go over like a lead balloon ☐ lead poisoning

LEAGUE

big league ☐ play in the big leagues

LEAK

take a leak

LEAN

lean and mean

LEASH

have one's brain on a leash ☐ on a tight leash

LEAVE
leave someone cold □ make like a tree and leave □ Take it or leave it.

LEEKY
leeky store

LEFT
hang a left □ left-handed monkey wrench □ out in left field □ out of left field

LEG
Break a leg! □ have a leg up on someone □ leg work □ loop-legged □ on one's or its last legs □ peg-leg □ pull someone's leg □ shake a leg □ stretch one's legs

LEGAL
legal-beagle □ legal-eagle

LEGREE
Simon Legree

LESS
I could(n't) care less.

LET
Let her rip! □ let it all hang out □ Let it roll! □ let off (some) steam □ let something ride □ Let's bump this place! □ Let's do lunch (sometime). □ Let's dump. □ Let's have it! □ let's say

LETTER
dead letter □ Dear John letter □ red-letter day

LEVEL
level best □ level with someone □ on the level

LICK
lick and a promise □ lick something into shape

LICKETY
lickety-split

LICORICE
licorice stick

LID
blow one's lid □ blow the lid off something □ lid poppers □ lid proppers □ skid-lid

LIE
lie doggo □ No lie! □ pack of lies

LIFE
facts of life □ Get a life! □ low-life □ You bet your sweet life!

LIFT
lift one's elbow □ lift-up

LIGHT
fly light □ green light □ idiot light □ light bulb □ light into someone □ light stuff □ lighten up (on someone or something) □ lights out □ once over lightly □ out like a light □ punch someone's lights out

LIGHTEN
lighten up (on someone or something)

LIGHTLY
once over lightly

LIGHTNING
greased lightning

LIKE
built like a brick outhouse □ built like a brick shithouse □ come on like gangbusters □ drop someone or something like a hot potato □ go over like a lead balloon □ go through someone like a dose of the salts □ like a bat out of hell □ like a million (dollars) □ like a ton of bricks □ like crazy □ like death warmed over □ like gangbusters □ Like hell! □ Like it or lump it! □ like mad □ like nobody's business □ like stink □ like there was no tomorrow □ like, you know □ make like a tree and leave □ make like someone or something □ out like a light □ purr (like a cat) □ smell like a rose □ smoke like a chimney □ stick out like a sore thumb □ swear like a trooper □ talk like a nut □ tap dance like mad □ Tell it like it is.

LILY
lily-livered

LIMIT
go the limit □ sky's the limit

LIMP
(limp) dishrag

LINE

blow one's lines ☐ bottom line ☐ do a line ☐ fire a line ☐ go down the line ☐ hook, line, and sinker ☐ lay it on the line ☐ lay some sweet lines on someone ☐ line one's own pocket(s) ☐ out of line ☐ put some sweet lines on someone ☐ run down some lines ☐ stag line

LINEN

dirty linen

LING

ding-a-ling

LION

lion's share

LIP

get lip ☐ latrine lips ☐ lip gloss ☐ Read my lips! ☐ Watch my lips! ☐ Zip (up) your lip!

LIQUID

liquid cork ☐ liquid laugh

LIQUOR

hard liquor ☐ hold one's liquor

LIST

drop-dead list ☐ hit list ☐ laundry list ☐ shopping list ☐ sucker list ☐ want list ☐ wish list

LISTEN

I'm listening. ☐ listen up

LIT

half-lit

LITTLE

have a little visitor ☐ little black book ☐ little boy blue ☐ little boys' room ☐ little girls' room ☐ (little) pinkie

LIVE

all the way live ☐ how the other half lives ☐ How ya living? ☐ (live) wire ☐ Living large. ☐ where someone lives

LIVER

lily-livered

LO

lo-res

LOAD

carrying a (heavy) load ☐ dump one's load ☐ get a load of something or someone ☐ get a load off one's feet ☐ get a load off one's mind ☐ have a load on ☐ loaded for bear ☐ loaded question ☐ loaded remark ☐ loaded to the barrel ☐ loaded to the gills ☐ one brick shy of a load ☐ take a load off one's feet ☐ three bricks shy of a load

LOCAL

local yokel

LOCK

goldie locks

LOCO

plumb loco

LONE

lone wolf

LONG

long arm of the law ☐ long bread ☐ long dozen ☐ long green ☐ long knife ☐ long shot ☐ long story short ☐ long-tall-Sally ☐ Long time no see. ☐ over the long haul ☐ so long ☐ take the (long) count

LOOK

come-hither look ☐ dirty look ☐ (good) looker ☐ Here's looking at you. ☐ look after number one ☐ Look alive! ☐ look-see ☐ Look who's talking!

LOONY

loony bin

LOOP

fruit loop ☐ loop-legged ☐ throw someone for a loop

LOOSE

at loose ends ☐ cut loose ☐ cut one's wolf loose ☐ hang loose ☐ have a loose screw ☐ have a screw loose ☐ loose cannon ☐ play fast and loose (with someone or something) ☐ stay loose ☐ tear loose (from someone or something) ☐ tongue loosener

LOOSENER

See *loose*.

LORD
drug lord □ Lord love a duck!

LOSE
lose a bundle □ lose (all) one's marbles □ lose it □ lose one's cool □ lose one's doughnuts □ lose one's grip □ lose one's hold □ lose one's lunch □ lose one's shirt □ losing streak □ two-time loser □ Win a few, lose a few.

LOSS
cut one's losses

LOST
Get lost! □ lost-and-found badge □ lost cause □ lost in the sauce

LOT
Lots of luck! □ take a lot of nerve

LOTION
motion-lotion

LOUD
loudmouth

LOUIE
hang a louie

LOUSE
louse something up

LOUSY
lousy with someone or something

LOVE
For the love of Mike! □ (I) love it! □ Lord love a duck! □ love bombs □ (love) handles □ love-in □ Love it! □ Love you! □ puppy love

LOW
burn with a low blue flame □ low-blow □ low five □ low-key □ low-life □ low rent □ low-res □ straight low

LUCK
Better luck next time. □ Lots of luck! □ luck of the draw □ luck out □ out of luck □ rotten luck □ tough luck

LUCKY
lucky dog

LUCRE
filthy lucre

LUG
chug(-a-lug)

LUGGIE
hock a luggie

LUMP
get one's lumps □ Like it or lump it! □ Lump it! □ take one's lumps

LUNCH
blow lunch □ blow (one's) lunch □ free lunch □ launch (one's lunch) □ Let's do lunch (sometime). □ lose one's lunch □ out to lunch □ spot of lunch □ toss one's lunch

LUNGER
nose-lunger

LUSH
lush up

LUXURY
lap of luxury

MA
Ma Bell

MAC
Big Mac attack □ mac out

MACE
mace someone's face

MACHINE
sex-machine

MACKEREL
Holy mackerel!

MAD
boiling (mad) □ get mad (at something) □ hopping mad □ like mad □ mad money □ tap dance like mad

MADE
have it made □ have it made in the shade □ tailor-made

MADISON
Madison Avenue

MAGAZINE
girlie magazine

MAGIC
magic bullet □ magic mushrooms □ tragic-magic

MAGNET
nerd magnet

MAIL
junk mail □ snail-mail

MAIN
main drag □ main squeeze □ main stash

MAKE
Don't make me laugh! □ make a boo-boo □ make a bundle □ make a federal case out of something □ make a killing □ Make a lap! □ make a pig of oneself □ make a pile □ make a score □ make a stink (about someone or something) □ make book on something □ make for somewhere □ make hamburger out of someone or something □ make it □ make (it) big □ make it hot for someone □ Make it snappy! □ make like a tree and leave □ make like someone or something □ make mincemeat out of someone or something □ Make my day! □ Make no mistake (about it)! □ make one's bed □ make oneself scarce □ make out □ make-out artist □ make someone □ make the scene □ make tracks □ make waves □ make with the something □ on the make □ run a make on someone □ Wanna make sumpin' of it? □ Want to make something of it? □ widow-maker

MALE
male chauvinist pig

MAMA
Bahama-mama □ go home to mama □ mama bear □ red-hot mama □ yo mama

MAN
big man on campus □ boss man □ candy man □ cave man □ company man □ con man □ dead man □ dirty old man □ face man □ front man □ fuzz man □ G-man □ good-time man □ headache man □ hit man □ man on the street □ man-size(d) □ my man □ old man □ one-man show □ point man □ repo man □ see a man about a dog □ So's your old man! □ stick man □ straight man □ strong-arm man □ T-man □ the man □ wheel man □ You heard the man.

MANIA
merger-mania

MANY
house of many doors □ one too many

MAP
throw a map

MARBLE
have all one's marbles □ lose (all) one's marbles □ Marble City □ marble dome □ marble orchard

MARE
shank's mare

MARINE
dead marine □ marine officer □ marine (recruit)

MARK
easy mark □ mark time □ skid marks □ X marks the spot.

MARKET
slave market □ spot market

MARY
Mary J. □ Mary Jane

MASH
mish-mash

MATCH
whole shooting match

MATE
label mate

MAX
grody to the max □ max out □ maxed out □ to the max

MAXIMUS
dorkus maximus

MAYBE
I don't mean maybe!

one's mind in the gutter ☐ meeting of the minds ☐ mind-bender ☐ mind-blower ☐ mind your own beeswax ☐ never mind ☐ one-track mind

MINE

back to the salt mines ☐ Your guess is as good as mine. ☐ Your place or mine?

MIRROR

done by mirrors ☐ done with mirrors ☐ smoke and mirrors

MISH

mish-mash ☐ mish-mosh

MISS

Good golly, Miss Molly! ☐ miss the boat

MISTAKE

Make no mistake (about it)!

MIX

mix it up (with someone) ☐ mixed (up)

MOBILE

nerd mobile

MOD

mod poser

MODE

in one's something mode

MOIST

moist around the edges

MOJO

on the mojo

MOLDY

moldy fig

MOLEY

Holy moley!

MOLLY

Good golly, Miss Molly!

MOMMA

(Do) you kiss your momma with that mouth? ☐ You kiss your momma with that mouth?

MOMMY

freak mommy

MONEY

color of someone's money ☐ easy money ☐ folding money ☐ front money ☐ funny-money ☐ heavy money ☐ hush money ☐ mad money ☐ money from home ☐ money grubber ☐ money talks ☐ on the money ☐ pull down an amount of money ☐ push money ☐ Put your money where your mouth is! ☐ shell an amount of money out ☐ shell out (an amount of money) ☐ smart money ☐ soft money ☐ spending money ☐ throw money at something ☐ tight money

MONKEY

grease monkey ☐ have a monkey on one's back ☐ left-handed monkey wrench ☐ monkey around (with someone or something) ☐ monkey bite ☐ monkey business ☐ monkey swill ☐ monkey talk ☐ monkey wagon ☐ monkey wards ☐ monkey with someone or something ☐ powder monkey

MONSTER

meth monster ☐ monster weed

MONTEZUMA'S

Montezuma's revenge

MOO

moo juice

MOON

once in a blue moon

MOONLIGHT

moonlight requisition

MOP

Earp slop, bring the mop. ☐ mop the floor up with someone ☐ mopping-up operation ☐ That's the way the mop flops.

MOPE

mope around

MORE

more than one bargained for ☐ Run that by (me) one more time.

MORNING

morning after (the night before)

MOSH
mish-mosh

MOSS
house moss

MOSTEST
firstest with the mostest

MOTHER
dog's mother ☐ mother nature('s)

MOTION
motion-lotion

MOTOR
get someone's motor running ☐ motor-mouth

MOUNTAIN
(mountain) dew

MOUNTY
county-mounty

MOUSE
mickey mouse ☐ mickey mouse ears ☐ mickey mouse habit

MOUTH
bad-mouth ☐ big mouth ☐ diarrhea of the mouth ☐ dirty mouth ☐ (Do) you eat with that mouth? ☐ (Do) you kiss your momma with that mouth? ☐ foot-in-mouth disease ☐ foul mouth ☐ garbage mouth ☐ have a big mouth ☐ jungle mouth ☐ loudmouth ☐ motor-mouth ☐ mouth-breather ☐ mouth full of South ☐ mouth off ☐ poor-mouth ☐ potty mouth ☐ Put your money where your mouth is! ☐ ratchet-mouth ☐ run off at the mouth ☐ shoot one's mouth off ☐ smart mouth ☐ straight from the horse's mouth ☐ toilet mouth ☐ trash mouth ☐ Watch your mouth! ☐ You eat with that mouth? ☐ You kiss your momma with that mouth?

MOVE
bust a move ☐ move on someone ☐ movers and shakers ☐ put the moves on someone

MR.
Mr. Big ☐ Mr. Hawkins ☐ Mr. Nice Guy ☐ Mr. Right ☐ Mr. Whiskers

MRS.
Mrs. Murphy

MUCH
bit much ☐ So much for that. ☐ thank you very much ☐ too much

MUCHACHOS
adios muchachos

MUCK
high mucky-muck ☐ muck something up

MUCKY
high mucky-muck

MUD
clear as mud ☐ Here's mud in your eye. ☐ stick in the mud

MUDDLE
muddled (up)

MUFFIN
meadow muffin ☐ stud-muffin

MUG
mug shot

MUNCH
(blind) munchies ☐ munch out

MUNCHIES
See *munch.*

MUNG
mung something up

MURDER
scream bloody murder

MURPHY
Mrs. Murphy

MUSHROOM
magic mushrooms ☐ sacred mushrooms

MUSIC
chin music ☐ elevator music ☐ face the music ☐ Stop the music!

MUSICAL
musical beds

MUST
(must) do

NEW
(brand) spanking new

NEW
spanking new ☐ That's a new one on me. ☐ What else is new? ☐ What's new? ☐ whole new ball game

NEWS
bad news

NEW YORK
New York's finest

NEXT
Better luck next time.

NICE
Have a nice day. ☐ Have a nice one. ☐ Mr. Nice Guy ☐ nice meeting you ☐ nice talking to you

NICK
full of Old Nick

NICKEL
double nickels ☐ nickel and dime someone (to death) ☐ not worth a plugged nickel

NIGHT
all-nighter ☐ fly-by-night ☐ morning after (the night before) ☐ night person ☐ one-night stand ☐ Saturday night special

NINE
dressed to the nines ☐ nine-to-five ☐ whole nine yards

NINETEENTH
nineteenth hole

NINNY
bliss ninny

NIP
nip and tuck

NIT
nit-picker ☐ nit-picking

NITTY
get down to the nitty-gritty ☐ nitty-gritty

NO
all (that) meat and no potatoes ☐ cigarette with no name ☐ Close, but no cigar. ☐ cut no ice (with someone) ☐ feeling no pain ☐ like there was no tomorrow ☐ Long time no see. ☐ Make no mistake (about it)! ☐ no-account ☐ no bargain ☐ no big deal ☐ no biggie ☐ no-brainer ☐ no brand cigarette ☐ no-brow ☐ no can do ☐ no dice ☐ no earthly reason ☐ no end of something ☐ No fair! ☐ no go ☐ no-good ☐ no-goodnik ☐ no great shakes ☐ no holds barred ☐ No kidding! ☐ No lie! ☐ no name cigarette ☐ no-no ☐ No nukes! ☐ no sale ☐ No Shinola! ☐ no show ☐ no soap ☐ no stress ☐ no sweat ☐ No way! ☐ no-win situation ☐ see no further than the end of one's nose

NOBODY
like nobody's business ☐ There's nobody home.

NOD
get the nod ☐ give someone the nod ☐ nodded out

NOGGIN
Use your noggin!

NOISE
big noise

NON
non compos ☐ non compos poopoo

NONE
none of someone's beeswax

NOODLE
Use your noodle! ☐ wet noodle

NOSE
brown-nose ☐ brown-noser ☐ cannot see (any) further than the end of one's nose ☐ get one's nose cold ☐ get one's nose out of joint ☐ hard-nosed ☐ keep one's nose clean ☐ nose-burner ☐ nose (candy) ☐ nose habit ☐ nose hit ☐ nose job ☐ nose-lunger ☐ nose-warmer ☐ on the nose ☐ powder one's nose ☐ put one's nose in (where it's not wanted) ☐ put someone's nose out of joint ☐ rub someone's nose in something ☐ see no further than the end of one's nose ☐ snotnose(d) (kid) ☐ stick

one's nose in (where it's not wanted) □ take it on the nose □ take it through the nose □ turn up one's nose at someone or something □ wiener nose

NOSEBAG
put on the nosebag □ tie on the nosebag

NOSEDIVE
take a nosedive

NOSH
nosh on something

NOSY
nosy parker

NOT
have-nots □ I kid you not. □ I'm not kidding. □ not a chance □ not all there □ not cricket □ not give a hoot □ not grow on trees □ not just whistling Dixie □ not know beans (about something) □ not know from nothing □ Not to worry. □ not too shabby □ not worth a damn □ not worth a plugged nickel □ not worth beans □ put one's nose in (where it's not wanted) □ stick one's nose in (where it's not wanted) □ would not be seen dead

NOTCH
pull one's belt in (a notch) □ take one's belt in (a notch)

NOTE
C-note □ century note □ hell of a note □ swap notes (on someone or something)

NOTHING
abbreviated piece of nothing □ good-for-nothing □ in nothing flat □ not know from nothing □ Nothing doing! □ Nothing to it! □ nothing to sneeze at □ nothing to write home about □ nothing upstairs □ sweet nothings

NOW
now generation □ Now what? □ Now you're talking!

NOWHERE
get nowhere fast □ middle of nowhere

NUKE
No nukes! □ nuke oneself

NUMB
numbed out

NUMBER
A number 1 □ back number □ do a number on someone □ have the wrong number □ hot number □ look after number one □ number-cruncher □ number crunching □ number one □ take care of number one

NUMERO
numero uno □ take care of numero uno

NUT
bust one's nuts to do something □ drive someone nuts □ eco nut □ everything from soup to nuts □ nut factory □ nut-foundry □ nut up □ nuts and bolts □ Nuts to you! □ nutty as a fruitcake □ off one's nut □ talk like a nut □ tough nut to crack

NUTTY
nutty as a fruitcake

O
big-O. □ B.O. juice □ O-sign

ODD
odd bird □ odd-bod □ odds-on

OFFERING
burnt offering

OFFICE
land office business

OFFICER
marine officer

OH
Oh, boy! □ Oh, yeah?

OIL
banana oil □ castor oil artist □ idiot oil □ oil it □ palm-oil □ tongue oil □ well-oiled

OINK
oink out

OK
A-OK

OKEY

okey-dokey

OLD

dirty old man ☐ full of Old Nick ☐ good old boy ☐ old flame ☐ old fogey ☐ old girl ☐ old hand (at something) ☐ old hat ☐ old heave-ho ☐ old lady ☐ old man ☐ old one-two ☐ old soldier ☐ old timer ☐ old woman ☐ rare old time ☐ same o(l)' same o(l)' ☐ same old story ☐ So's your old man!

OLDIE

oldie but goodie

OLE

good ole boy

ONCE

if I've told you once, I've told you a thousand times ☐ once and for all ☐ once in a blue moon ☐ once-over ☐ once over lightly

ONLY

one and only ☐ only way to go

ONTO

latch onto something ☐ onto a good thing ☐ onto someone or something ☐ turn onto someone or something

OPEN

blow something wide open ☐ bust something wide open ☐ crack open a bottle ☐ eye-opener ☐ open (up) one's kimono ☐ wide open ☐ with (one's) eyes (wide) open

OPERA

horse opera

OPERATION

mopping-up operation

OPERATOR

big-time operator ☐ smooth operator

OPPORTUNITY

golden opportunity

ORBIT

go into orbit ☐ in orbit

ORCHARD

bone orchard ☐ marble orchard

ORDER

doctor's orders ☐ just what the doctor ordered ☐ tall order

ORK

ork-orks

OTHER

how the other half lives

OUTA

I'm outa here.

OUTHOUSE

built like a brick outhouse

OUTSIDE

step outside ☐ You want to step outside?

OVER

chew something over ☐ done over ☐ drool (all) over someone or something ☐ dump all over someone or something ☐ fork something over ☐ frosted (over) ☐ give someone a (good) working over ☐ glazed (over) ☐ go ape (over someone or something) ☐ go over big ☐ go over like a lead balloon ☐ go over the hill ☐ go over the wall ☐ going over ☐ hand over fist ☐ jerk someone over ☐ knock one over ☐ like death warmed over ☐ once-over ☐ once over lightly ☐ over easy ☐ over my dead body ☐ over one's head ☐ over-the-counter ☐ over the hill ☐ over the hump ☐ over the long haul ☐ paper over something ☐ screw someone over ☐ till hell freezes over ☐ turn over ☐ warmed over ☐ wiped over ☐ work someone over ☐ You could have knocked me over with a feather.

OVERBOARD

go overboard

OWN

blow one's own horn ☐ cut one's own throat ☐ devil's own time ☐ do one's (own) thing ☐ line one's own pocket(s) ☐ mind your own beeswax ☐ on one's own hook ☐ talk to hear one's own voice ☐ toot one's own horn

OX

dumb ox

OYSTER
world is one's oyster

OZONE
in the ozone

PACE
at a snail's pace

PACK
Joe Six-pack ☐ nerd pack ☐ pack of lies ☐ six-pack

PACKAGE
package deal

PAD
crash pad ☐ pad out

PADDLE
up the creek (without a paddle)

PADDY
paddy wagon

PAGE
take a page from someone's book

PAIN
feeling no pain ☐ give someone a pain ☐ pain in the ass ☐ pain in the butt ☐ pain in the neck ☐ pain in the rear ☐ royal pain

PAINT
Do I have to paint (you) a picture? ☐ paint remover ☐ paint the town (red) ☐ tonsil paint ☐ war paint

PAL
pal around (with someone) ☐ palsy-walsy

PALACE
gin palace ☐ ptomaine-palace

PALLY
pally (with someone)

PALM
grease someone's palm ☐ palm-oil ☐ palm-presser ☐ palm someone or something off (on someone)

PALSY
palsy-walsy

PAMBY
namby-pamby

PAN
pan out

PANIC
hit the panic button ☐ press the panic button ☐ push the panic button

PANKY
hanky-panky

PANTS
bore the pants off (of) someone ☐ dust someone's pants ☐ have ants in one's pants ☐ Keep your pants on! ☐ kick in the (seat of the) pants ☐ pants rabbits ☐ scare the pants off someone ☐ smarty-pants ☐ sue the pants off (of) someone ☐ wear the pants (in the house)

PAPER
bad paper ☐ green paper ☐ hot paper ☐ paper-hanger ☐ paper over something ☐ paper-pusher ☐ walking papers

PARACHUTE
golden parachute

PARADE
rain on someone's parade

PARDON
if you'll pardon the expression ☐ Pardon my French.

PARENTAL
(parental) units

PARK
ball park estimate ☐ ball park figure ☐ park it (somewhere)

PARKER
nosy parker

PARLOR
sauce parlor

PART
parting shot

PARTY
certain party ☐ coke party ☐ free base

party □ grass party □ hen party □ keg party □ kick party □ party animal □ party bowl □ party-hearty □ Party on! □ party-pooper □ petting-party □ pot party □ stag-party □ tailgate party □ tea party

PASA

Que pasa?

PASS

gas-passer □ pass for something □ pass go □ pass the buck

PASSION

passion-pit

PASTE

paste someone one

PAT

stand pat (on something)

PATH

on the warpath

PATOOTIE

You bet your sweet patoot(ie)!

PATROL

bush patrol

PATTER

patter of tiny feet

PAVEMENT

hit the pavement

PAY

hit pay dirt □ pay a call □ pay one's dues □ pay one's dues to society □ strike pay dirt □ There will be hell to pay.

PEACHY

peachy (keen)

PEANUT

for peanuts □ peanut head

PEDAL

put the pedal to the metal □ soft pedal something

PEDDLER

pill-peddler

PEE'D

pee'd off

PEEP

another peep (out of you)

PEEVE

pet peeve

PEG

peg-leg □ peg someone □ square peg (in a round hole)

PENCIL

pencil-pusher

PENNY

penny-ante □ penny-pincher □ pretty penny

PEOPLE

people watching □ street people

PEP

pep pill □ pep talk □ pepped (up)

PEPPER

pepper-upper □ salt and pepper

PERCENTER

ten percenter

PERIOD

honeymoon (period)

PERK

perked (up)

PERSON

day person □ night person

PET

pet peeve □ petting-party

PETE

For Pete's sake!

PETER

Peter Jay □ peter out

PHEASANT

crotch-pheasant

PHONE

talk on the big white phone

PHONY

phony as a three-dollar bill

PICK

cotton-pickin' ☐ cotton-picking ☐ H-E-double-toothpicks ☐ nit-picker ☐ nit-picking ☐ pick-me-up ☐ pick up on something ☐ roach pick

PICTURE

Do I have to draw (you) a picture? ☐ Do I have to paint (you) a picture? ☐ Get the picture? ☐ out of the picture ☐ take pictures

PIDDLE

piddle (around)

PIE

cutie pie ☐ pie-eyed ☐ pie in the sky ☐ sweetie(-pie)

PIECE

abbreviated piece of nothing ☐ piece of cake ☐ piece (of the action) ☐ think-piece

PIG

bush pig ☐ make a pig of oneself ☐ male chauvinist pig ☐ pig heaven ☐ pig out

PIGEON

clay pigeon ☐ pigeon-eyed ☐ stool (pigeon)

PILE

make a pile

PILL

go-pills ☐ gorilla pills ☐ happy pills ☐ idiot pills ☐ King Kong pills ☐ on the pill ☐ pep pill ☐ pill-dropper ☐ pill freak ☐ pill-peddler ☐ pill-popper ☐ pill-pusher ☐ pill-roller ☐ poison pill ☐ take a chill pill

PILLAR

send someone from pillar to post

PILOT

sky-pilot

PIN

pin someone's ears back

PINCH

penny-pincher ☐ pinch hitter

PINK

gay as pink ink ☐ in the pink ☐ pink elephants ☐ pink slip ☐ pink-slipped ☐ pink spiders ☐ seeing pink elephants ☐ seeing pink spiders ☐ tickled (pink)

PINKIE

(little) pinkie

PINT

pint-sized

PIPE

hash pipe ☐ pipe down ☐ pipped (up) ☐ Put that in your pipe and smoke it! ☐ set of pipes ☐ take the gas pipe ☐ take the pipe

PIPELINE

in the pipeline

PISS

piss-ant ☐ piss-ant around ☐ piss elegant ☐ piss factory ☐ piss poor ☐ piss someone off ☐ pissed (off)

PIT

bottomless pit ☐ passion-pit ☐ pit stop

PITCH

pitch a bitch ☐ pitch in (and help) ☐ pitch (the) woo

PITCHFORK

rain pitchforks

PITY

For pity's sake!

PIZZA

pizza-face ☐ pizza-puss ☐ road pizza

PLACE

between a rock and a hard place ☐ bust ass out of some place ☐ go places ☐ Let's bump this place! ☐ wide place in the road ☐ Your place or mine?

PLAN

game plan

PLANT

plant something on someone

PLASTER

plastered to the wall ☐ pleasantly plastered

PLASTIC
plastic punk

PLATOON
goon-platoon

PLAY
grandstand play □ in play □ play around (with someone) □ play ball (with someone) □ play fast and loose (with someone or something) □ play for keeps □ play freeze-out □ play hardball (with someone) □ play hell with someone or something □ play hooky □ play in the big leagues □ play it cool □ play someone for a fool □ play the devil with someone or something □ play the dozens □ play tonsil hockey □ play with a full deck □ play with fire □ squeeze play □ the way it plays

PLEA
cop a plea

PLEASANTLY
pleasantly plastered

PLEDGE
take the pledge

PLONK
plonked (up)

PLOP
cow plop

PLOW
plowed (under)

PLUG
not worth a plugged nickel □ plug-ugly □ plugged in □ pull the plug (on someone or something)

PLUMB
half a bubble off plumb □ plumb loco

PLUMBING
check out the plumbing □ visit the plumbing

PLUNGE
take the plunge

POCKET
deep pockets □ line one's own pocket(s)

POINT
brownie points □ point man □ three point two □ touch a sore point

POINTY
pointy-head

POISON
lead poisoning □ Name your poison. □ poison pill

POLE
half up the pole □ up the pole □ wouldn't touch someone or something with a ten-foot pole

POLISH
apple-polisher □ polished (up) □ shoe polish □ spit and polish

POND
pond scum

PONY
dog and pony show

POO
icky-poo □ poo-poo

POOH
poo(h)-poo(h)

POOL
dirty pool □ pool-hopping

POOP
party-pooper □ poop out □ poop sheet □ pooped (out) □ pooper-scooper

POOPOO
non compos poopoo

POOR
piss poor □ poor-mouth

POP
cold pop □ eye-popper □ jab pop □ pill-popper □ pop-eyed □ pop for something □ pop off □ pop one's cork □ pop (some) tops □ pop the question

☐ pop wine ☐ skull-popper ☐ take a pop at someone ☐ What's poppin'

POPPER

eye-popper ☐ lid poppers ☐ pill-popper ☐ skull-popper

PORCELAIN

bow to the porcelain altar ☐ drive the porcelain bus ☐ hug the porcelain god(dess) ☐ kiss the porcelain god ☐ pray to the porcelain god ☐ ride the porcelain bus ☐ worship the porcelain god(dess)

PORE

air one's pores

PORK

pork out

POSER

mod poser

POST

between you, me, and the lamppost ☐ send someone from pillar to post

POT

pot boiler ☐ pot hound ☐ pot party ☐ pot sniffer ☐ sex pot ☐ up pot

POTATO

all (that) meat and no potatoes ☐ couch potato ☐ drop someone or something like a hot potato ☐ hot potato ☐ potato soup ☐ small potatoes

POTTY

potty mouth

POUND

gravel-pounder ☐ ground-pounder ☐ pound a beer ☐ pound one's ear ☐ pound some beers ☐ pound someone's head in ☐ pound something out ☐ pound the books

POUR

pour cold water on something

POW

pow-wow

POWDER

chicken powder ☐ powder monkey ☐ powder one's face ☐ powder one's nose ☐ powder room ☐ powder up ☐ powdered (up) ☐ take a powder

POWER

power hitter ☐ powerhouse ☐ power tool

PRAY

pray to the enamel god ☐ pray to the porcelain god

PRESS

flesh-presser ☐ palm-presser ☐ press (the) flesh ☐ press the panic button

PRETTY

pretty penny ☐ sitting pretty

PRIMO

(el) primo

PRINCE

Prince Albert

PRIVATE

private eye

PROGRAM

get with the program

PROMISE

lick and a promise

PROOF

goof-proof

PROPELLED

self-propelled sandbag

PROPPER

lid proppers

PROUD

do oneself proud

PROWL

on the prowl

PRUNE

full of prunes

PSYCH

psych out ☐ psych someone out ☐ psych someone up ☐ psyched (out) ☐ psyched (up)

PTOMAINE

ptomaine-domain ☐ ptomaine-palace

PUBLIC
go public □ Jane Q. Public □ John Q. Public □ take something public

PUCKY
bull-pucky

PUDDLE
puddle jumper

PUFF
cream puff

PUG
pug-ugly

PUKE
puke hole

PULL
pull a boner □ pull a fast one □ pull a job □ pull an attitude □ pull down an amount of money □ pull jive □ pull one's belt in (a notch) □ pull one's punches □ pull out all the stops □ pull someone's leg □ pull something off □ pull the plug (on someone or something)

PUMP
pump ship □ pump (some) iron □ pump (someone) up □ pump something up □ pumped (up)

PUMPKIN
some pumpkins

PUNCH
get one's ticket punched □ pull one's punches □ punch-drunk □ punch someone out □ punch someone's lights out □ rabbit punch □ roundhouse punch □ Sunday punch □ telegraph one's punches □ throw a punch

PUNK
plastic punk □ punk kid □ punk out

PUNKINS
some punkins

PUPPY
puppy love

PURE
pure and simple

PURGE
urge to purge

PURPOSE
accidentally-on-purpose

PURR
purr (like a cat)

PUSH
cookie pusher □ if push comes to shove □ paper-pusher □ pencil-pusher □ pill-pusher □ push money □ push off □ push the panic button □ pushing up daisies □ street pusher □ when push comes to shove

PUSS
glamour puss □ pizza-puss

PUSSY
wood-pussy

PUSSYFOOT
pussyfoot (around)

PUT
put a con on someone □ put a damper on something □ put a smile on someone's face □ Put a sock in it! □ put balls on something □ put-down □ put on the dog □ put on the feedbag □ put on the nosebag □ put on the ritz □ put one's nose in (where it's not wanted) □ put oneself straight □ put some distance between someone and someone or something □ put some sweet lines on someone □ put someone on □ put someone or something away □ put someone or something out of the way □ put someone to bed with a shovel □ put someone up □ put someone's nose out of joint □ put something on the street □ Put that in your pipe and smoke it! □ put the arm on someone □ put the bite on someone □ put the chill on someone □ put the finger on someone □ put the freeze on someone □ put the heat on someone □ put the kibosh on something □ put the moves on someone □ put the pedal to the metal □ put the screws on someone □ put the skids under someone or something □ put the squeeze on someone □ put to bed with a shovel □ put

to it □ put-up job □ Put up or shut up! □ Put your money where your mouth is!

PUTT

putt-putt

PUTZ

putz around

Q

Jane Q. Public □ John Q. Public □ Q-sign

QUAFF

quaff a brew

QUALITY

quality Joe

QUE

Que pasa?

QUEEN

campus queen □ ice queen

QUEER

queer as a three-dollar bill □ queer-beer □ queer fish □ queer for something

QUESTION

loaded question □ pop the question □ sixty-four-dollar question

QUICK

quick-and-dirty □ quick buck □ quick fix □ quick one □ quicker than hell

QUIT

quit while one is ahead

QUOTE

cuff quote □ quote, unquote

RABBIT

pants rabbits □ rabbit food □ rabbit punch

RACE

rat race

RACK

rack duty □ rack (out) □ rack something up □ rack time □ rack up □ racked (up)

RACKET

juice racket

RAD

way rad

RAG

chew the rag □ glad rags □ on the rag □ rag on someone □ rag out □ talk someone ragged □ wet rag

RAH

rah-rah

RAILROAD

railroad tracks

RAIN

rain on someone or something □ rain on someone's parade □ rain pitchforks □ right as rain

RAISE

hell raiser □ raise a stink (about someone or something) □ raise Cain □ raise hell □ raise hell (with someone or something) □ raise the devil (with someone or something)

RAKE

rake on someone □ rake something in

RALPH

call ralph □ cry ralph □ hang a ralph □ ralph something up

RAM

ram something down someone's throat

RANK

rank and file □ rank on someone □ rank someone (out)

RAP

bad rap □ bum rap □ rap session □ (rap) sheet □ take the rap (for something)

RARE

in rare form □ rare bird □ rare old time □ raring to go

RASPBERRY

give someone the raspberry

RAT

frat-rat □ rat around □ rat fink □ rat

(on someone) □ rat out □ rat race □ rug rat □ sack rat □ smell a rat

RATCHET
ratchet-mouth

RATE
cut-rate

RATTLE
rattle-trap □ slightly rattled

RAUNCH
raunch someone out

RAW
raw deal

RAY
bag some rays □ catch some rays

RAZZLE
razzle-dazzle

REACH
reach for the sky

REACTION
gut reaction (to something)

READ
Read my lips!

READY
rough and ready

REAL
for real □ Get real! □ real bitch □ real gone □ (real) McCoy

REAM
ream someone out

REAR
get off one's rear □ pain in the rear □ rear (end) □ rear-ender

REASON
no earthly reason

RECRUIT
marine (recruit)

RED
cam (red) □ Cambodian red □ Chinese red □ paint the town (red) □ red hot □ red-hot mama □ red ink □ red-letter day □ red tape □ see red

REINVENT
reinvent the wheel

REMARK
loaded remark □ snide remark

REMOVE
paint remover

RENT
low rent □ room for rent

REPELLENT
shark repellent

REPO
repo man

REPUBLIC
banana republic

REQUISITION
moonlight requisition

RES
hi-res □ high-res □ lo-res □ low-res

REST
Give it a rest! □ Give me a rest!

RESULT
net result

REV
rev something up □ revved up

REVENGE
Montezuma's revenge

REVERSE
reverse gears

RHYME
run one's rhymes

RIB
rib-tickler

RICH
filthy rich □ stinking rich □ strike it rich □ too rich for someone's blood

RIDE
free ride □ joy ride □ let something ride □ ride shotgun □ ride the porcelain bus □ thumb a ride

RIGHT
all right □ (bang) dead to rights □ dead to rights □ get one right here □ get right □ hang a right □ have someone dead to rights □ keep one's head right □ Mr. Right □ right as rain □ right guy □ right in the kisser □ (right) up one's alley □ sail (right) through something □ serve someone right □ step right up □ straighten up and fly right

RIGHTEOUS
righteous collar

RING
ring a bell □ ring off the hook □ ring the bell □ throw one's hat in the ring

RINGER
(dead) ringer (for someone) □ ringer (for someone)

RINGTAILED
ringtailed snorter

RINKY
rinky-dink

RINSO
go Rinso

RIP
Let her rip! □ rip-off □ (rip)-off artist □ rip on someone □ rip snorter □ rip someone or something off □ ripped (off) □ ripped (up)

RISE
Rise and shine!

RITZ
put on the ritz

RIVER
send someone up the river □ up the river

ROACH
roach clip □ roach-coach □ roach pick

ROAD
get the show on the road □ hit the road □ on the road □ one for the road □ road apple □ road hog □ road pizza □ smack the road □ wide place in the road

ROAR
dull roar

ROB
rob someone blind

ROBBERY
highway robbery

ROCK
between a rock and a hard place □ get one's rocks off (on something) □ have rocks in one's head □ on the rocks □ rock bottom □ rock candy □ rock-jock

ROCKER
off one's rocker

ROCKY
walking on rocky socks

ROD
(hot) rod □ wrinkle-rod

ROLL
heads will roll □ high roller □ Let it roll! □ on a roll □ pill-roller □ roll in □ rolling buzz

ROOF
hit the roof □ keyed up to the roof

ROOM
backroom boys □ boys in the backroom □ gab room □ Go to your room! □ ladies' room □ little boys' room □ little girls' room □ men's room □ powder room □ room for rent □ rumpus room □ smoke-filled room □ throne room

ROOTING
rooting-tooting

ROPE
rope someone in

ROSE
bed of roses □ smell like a rose

ROT
crotch-rot □ Rots of ruck! □ software rot

SALLY
long-tall-Sally

SALT
back to the salt mines □ go through someone like a dose of the salts □ salt and pepper □ salt horse □ worth one's salt

SAM
Sam and Dave □ Uncle (Sam) □ What in (the) Sam Hill? □ Where in (the) Sam Hill?

SAME
on the same wavelength □ same difference □ same here □ same o(l)' same o(l)' □ same old story

SANDAL
jelly sandals

SANDBAG
self-propelled sandbag

SANDWICH
dagwood (sandwich) □ knuckle sandwich

SATURDAY
Saturday night special

SAUCE
lost in the sauce □ on the sauce □ sauce parlor

SAVE
Save it! □ saved by the bell

SAW
sawed-off

SAWBUCK
double saw(buck)

SAY
I hear what you are saying. □ let's say □ Say cheese! □ say-so □ say uncle □ Say what? □ Says me! □ Says who? □ Says you! □ Smile when you say that. □ That's what I say. □ What do you say? □ You can say that again!

SCAG
scag jones

SCAM
What's the scam?

SCANDAL
scandal sheet

SCARCE
make oneself scarce

SCARE
scare someone or something up □ scare the hell out of someone □ scare the pants off someone

SCARED
run scared □ scared shitless □ scared stiff

SCARF
scarf out □ scarf something down

SCENARIO
worst-case scenario

SCENE
heavy scene □ make the scene

SCHIZZ
schiz(z) out

SCHMANCY
fancy-schmancy

SCHMEAR
whole schmear

SCHMO
Joe Schmo

SCHOOLBOY
schoolboy Scotch

SCOOP
pooper-scooper

SCOPE
scope (on) someone □ scope someone out

SCORE
know the score □ make a score

SCOTCH
schoolboy Scotch

SCOTT
Great Scott!

SCOTTY
Beam me up, Scotty!

SCRAMBLED
scrambled eggs

SCRAPE
scrape the bottom of the barrel

SCRATCH
scratch sheet □ up to scratch

SCREAM
scream bloody murder □ screaming-meemie □ screaming-meemies

SCREECH
screeching (drunk)

SCREW
have a loose screw □ have a screw loose □ put the screws on someone □ screw around □ screw around with someone or something □ screw someone or something up □ screw someone out of something □ screw someone over □ screw up □ screwed, blued, and tattooed □ screwed tight □ screwed up

SCROUNGE
scrounge (around (for someone or something)) □ scrounge someone or something up

SCUM
bathtub scum □ pond scum □ shower scum

SCUPPER
scupper up

SCUZZ
scuzz someone out

SEAL
sealed (up) □ sealed with a kiss

SEAM
seam-squirrels

SEARCH
Search me. □ skin-search □ strip-search

SEAT
backseat driver □ hot seat □ in the catbird seat □ in the driver's seat □ kick in the (seat of the) pants

SECOND
second fiddle □ second sacker

SEE
cannot see (any) further than the end of one's nose □ Long time no see. □ look-see □ see a man about a dog □ see eye to eye □ see no further than the end of one's nose □ see red □ see stars □ see ya □ see you □ see you later □ see you later, alligator □ seeing pink elephants □ seeing pink spiders □ seeing snakes □ seen better days □ What you see is what you get. □ would not be seen dead

SELF
self-propelled sandbag

SELL
hard sell □ sell a wolf ticket □ sell someone out □ sell wolf tickets □ soft sell

SEND
send someone from pillar to post □ send someone or something up □ send someone to glory □ send someone up the river □ send-up

SENSE
sense (bud)

SERIOUS
get down to some serious drinking □ serious about someone

SERPENT
civil serpent

SERVE
serve someone right

SERVICE
Call my service.

SESH
full sesh

SESSION
bitch session □ bull session □ rap session

SET
set of pipes □ set of wheels □ set someone back □ set someone up (for something)

SETTER
jet-set(ters)

SETTLE
settle someone's hash

SEVEN
seven-year itch

SEW
sew something up □ sewed up

SEWER
sewer hog

SEX
sex goddess □ sex kitten □ sex-machine □ sex pot

SEZ
Sez me! □ Sez who?

SHABBY
not too shabby

SHACK
shack up (with someone)

SHADE
have it made in the shade

SHAFT
give someone the shaft

SHAG
shag-nasty □ shag (off) □ shagged out

SHAKE
body shake □ can-shaker □ fair shake □ I'm shaking (in fear). □ movers and shakers □ no great shakes □ shake a leg □ Shake it (up)! □ shake someone down □ shake-up □ two shakes of a lamb's tail □ What's shakin' (bacon)?

SHANK
shank it □ shank's mare

SHAPE
bent out of shape □ flexed out of shape □ in bad shape □ lick something into shape □ shape up □ shape up or ship out □ strung-out shape □ whip something into shape

SHARE
lion's share

SHARK
shark repellent

SHAVE
close shave

SHEBANG
whole shebang

SHEET
both sheets in the wind □ four sheets in the wind □ four sheets (to the wind) □ poop sheet □ (rap) sheet □ scandal sheet □ scratch sheet □ swindle sheet □ three sheets in the wind □ three sheets (to the wind) □ two sheets to the wind

SHELF
off-the-shelf □ on the shelf

SHELL
drop a bomb(shell) □ shell an amount of money out □ shell out (an amount of money)

SHIFT
graveyard shift □ stick shift □ swing shift

SHINE
Rise and shine! □ shine someone □ where the sun don't shine

SHINOLA
know shit from Shinola □ No Shinola! □ tell shit from Shinola

SHIP
pump ship □ shape up or ship out

SHIRT
Keep your shirt on! □ lose one's shirt □ stuffed shirt

SHIT
bullshit artist □ crock of shit □ get one's shit together □ know shit from Shinola □ scared shitless □ shit-faced □ Shit happens. □ shoot the shit □ tell shit from Shinola

SHITHOUSE
built like a brick shithouse

SHITLESS
scared shitless

SHOCK
sticker shock

SHOE
goody two-shoes □ gym shoe □ jelly shoes □ on a shoestring □ shoe polish □ The baby needs shoes.

SHOESTRING
on a shoestring

SHOO
shoo-in

SHOOK
(all) shook up □ shook up

SHOOT
hip-shooter □ shoot 'em up □ shoot for the sky □ shoot from the hip □ shoot one's breakfast □ shoot one's cookies □ shoot one's mouth off □ shoot one's supper □ shoot one's wad □ shoot oneself in the foot □ shoot-out □ shoot someone down in flames □ shoot someone or something down □ shoot the breeze □ shoot the bull □ shoot the cat □ shoot the crap □ shoot the dozens □ shoot the shit □ shoot the works □ shoot up □ shoot up (on something) □ shooting iron □ skeet shooting □ square shooter □ straight shooter □ whole shooting match

SHOP
chop-shop □ cop-shop □ happy shop □ hook shop □ shopping list □ sweat-shop

SHORT
case of the shorts □ have a short fuse □ long story short □ short end of the stick □ short fuse □ short one □ short-snort

SHOT
big shot □ call (all) the shots □ cheap shot □ double-barreled slingshot □ grape shot □ long shot □ mug shot □ one's best shot □ parting shot □ shot down □ shot in the arm □ shot in the dark □ shot in the neck □ shot to hell □ shot up □ take a shot (at something) □ who shot John

SHOTGUN
ride shotgun □ shotgun wedding

SHOULD
shouldn't happen to a dog

SHOULDER
cold shoulder □ straight from the shoulder

SHOVE
if push comes to shove □ shove off □ when push comes to shove

SHOVEL
put someone to bed with a shovel □ put to bed with a shovel

SHOW
dog and pony show □ free show □ get the show on the road □ girlie show □ no show □ one-man show □ show and tell □ show biz □ show someone or something up □ That's show business (for you).

SHOWER
shower scum

SHUCK
(Aw) shucks! □ shuck down

SHUR
fer shur

SHUSH
shush (up)

SHUT
get some shut-eye □ Put up or shut up! □ shut-eye □ shut up □ Shut your face!

SHY
one brick shy of a load □ three bricks shy of a load

SIBERIAN
Siberian express

SICK
sick to death (of someone or something) □ sick (up)

SIDE
can't hit the (broad) side of a barn ☐ flip side ☐ on the safe side ☐ on the side ☐ sunny-side up ☐ wrong side of the tracks

SIDEWALK
sidewalk superintendent ☐ sidewalk surfing

SIEG
sieg-heil someone

SIGHT
out of sight

SIGN
high sign ☐ Nebraska sign ☐ O-sign ☐ Q-sign

SILLY
stoned silly

SILO
silo drippings

SILVER
silver bullet ☐ silver goose

SIMMER
simmer (down)

SIMON
Simon Legree

SIMPLE
pure and simple

SIN
sin-bin ☐ ugly as sin

SING
till the fat lady sings ☐ when the fat lady sings

SINK
hook, line, and sinker ☐ sink one's teeth into something

SINKER
hook, line, and sinker

SISTER
sob sister ☐ (soul) sister ☐ weak sister

SIT
sitting duck ☐ sitting pretty

SITUATION
no-win situation

SIX
deep six ☐ eighty-six ☐ Joe Six-pack ☐ six-bits ☐ six feet under ☐ six-pack

SIXTY
sixty-four-dollar question

SIZE
man-size(d) ☐ pint-sized ☐ That's about the size of it.

SKAG
skag jones ☐ skagged out

SKEET
skeet shooting

SKETCH
thumbnail sketch

SKID
grease the skids ☐ hit the skids ☐ on the skids ☐ put the skids under someone or something ☐ skid-lid ☐ skid marks ☐ skid row ☐ skid row bum

SKIN
Give me (some) skin! ☐ have a skinful ☐ knock someone some skin ☐ skin a goat ☐ skin flick ☐ skin game ☐ Skin me! ☐ skin-search ☐ thick-skinned ☐ thin-skinned

SKINFUL
See *skin*.

SKINNY
(hot) skinny ☐ skinny dip

SKIP
Skip it! ☐ skip (out)

SKITTLES
beer and skittles

SKULL
out of one's skull ☐ skull-buster ☐ skull-popper

SKUNK
skunk-drunk

SKY
aim for the sky ☐ pie in the sky ☐ reach

for the sky □ shoot for the sky □ sky hook □ sky-pilot □ sky rug □ sky's the limit

SLAM

slam a beer □ slam-bang □ slam dunk □ slam some beers

SLAP

slap-dab □ slap-dash □ slap happy □ slap in the face □ slap someone on the wrist □ slap someone's wrist

SLAVE

slave away (at something) □ slave market

SLEAZE

sleaze-bucket

SLEEP

beauty sleep □ sleep it off

SLEEVE

have an ace up one's sleeve

SLICE

frog slicing □ It's been a slice! □ slice of the action

SLICK

slick-chick

SLIGHTLY

slightly rattled

SLIM

iceberg slim

SLIME

slime bag □ slime bucket

SLING

hash-slinger □ have one's ass in a sling □ ink slinger □ sling the cat

SLINGSHOT

double-barreled slingshot

SLIP

give someone the slip □ pink slip □ pink-slipped □ Slip me five! □ slip one's trolley □ slip someone a Mickey □ slip someone five □ slip (up)

SLOB

slob up

SLOP

Earp slop, bring the mop.

SLOSH

sloshed (to the ears)

SLOUGH

sloughed (up)

SLOW

do a slow burn □ slow burn □ take it slow

SLOWLY

twist (slowly) in the wind

SLUFF

sluff (off)

SLUG

slug it out

SLUSH

slush fund □ slush up □ slushed (up)

SLY

on the sly

SMACK

smack (dab) in the middle □ smack the road

SMALL

small beer □ small change □ small fortune □ small fry □ small potatoes □ small-time

SMART

get smart (with someone) □ one smart apple □ smart aleck □ smart ass □ smart cookie □ smart guy □ smart money □ smart mouth □ smarty-pants □ street smart □ street smarts

SMARTY

See *smart*.

SMASH

smash hit

SMELL

I smell you. □ smell a rat □ smell blood □ smell fishy □ smell it up □ smell like a rose □ smell the stuff □ smell to (high) heaven

SMILE
put a smile on someone's face ☐ Smile when you say that.

SMOKE
blow smoke ☐ chain(-smoke) ☐ chain-smoker ☐ Put that in your pipe and smoke it! ☐ smoke and mirrors ☐ smoke eater ☐ smoke-filled room ☐ smoke-in ☐ smoke like a chimney ☐ Smokey (the Bear) ☐ smoking gun

SMOKEY
Smokey (the Bear)

SMOOTH
jump smooth ☐ smooth operator

SNAIL
at a snail's gallop ☐ at a snail's pace ☐ snail-mail

SNAKE
seeing snakes ☐ snake eyes ☐ snake in the grass

SNAKEBITE
snakebite medicine

SNAP
Make it snappy! ☐ snap course ☐ Snap it up! ☐ snap one's cookies ☐ snap out of something ☐ snap something up ☐ snap to (attention) ☐ Snap to it! ☐ snapped (up)

SNAPPY
Make it snappy!

SNAVED
snaved in

SNAZZ
snazz something up

SNEEZE
nothing to sneeze at

SNIDE
snide remark

SNIFF
pot sniffer ☐ whiff-sniffer ☐ wiff-sniffer

SNIT
in a snit

SNORT
ringtailed snorter ☐ rip snorter ☐ short-snort

SNOTNOSED
snotnose(d) (kid)

SNOW
do a snow job on someone ☐ Lady Snow ☐ snow bunny ☐ snow job ☐ snow stuff

SNOWBALL
snowball's chance in hell

SNOZZLE
snozzle-wobbles

SNUFF
snuff film ☐ snuff it ☐ up to snuff

SO
I am so sure! ☐ say-so ☐ so-and-so ☐ so bad one can taste it ☐ So gross! ☐ so long ☐ So much for that. ☐ so-so ☐ So what? ☐ So's your old man!

SOAK
Go soak your head! ☐ Go soak yourself! ☐ soak one's face

SOAP
no soap ☐ soft soap

SOB
sob sister ☐ sob story

SOBER
cold sober ☐ sober as a judge ☐ sober up ☐ stone (cold) sober

SOCIAL
social disease

SOCIETY
pay one's dues to society

SOCK
knock someone's socks off ☐ Put a sock in it! ☐ rubber sock ☐ sock hop ☐ Sock it to me! ☐ socked in ☐ Stuff a sock in it! ☐ sweat sock ☐ walking on rocky socks ☐ wet sock

SOFA
sofa spud

SOFT
soft berth □ soft core □ soft-hearted □ soft in the head □ soft money □ soft on someone or something □ soft pedal something □ soft sell □ soft soap □ soft touch □ walk soft

SOFTWARE
software rot

SOLD
sold cober □ sold on someone or something

SOLDIER
dead soldier □ old soldier

SOME
bag some rays □ blow off (some) steam □ bust ass out of some place □ bust (some) suds □ catch some rays □ catch some Z's □ cop some Z's □ crack some suds □ cut some Z's □ do some bongs □ do some fine coin □ get down to some serious drinking □ get some shut-eye □ Give me (some) skin! □ hammer some beers □ Hold some, fold some. □ kick some ass (around) □ knock some heads together □ knock someone some skin □ lay (some) rubber □ lay some sweet lines on someone □ let off (some) steam □ pop (some) tops □ pound some beers □ pump (some) iron □ put some distance between someone and someone or something □ put some sweet lines on someone □ run down some lines □ slam some beers □ some pumpkins □ some punkins □ suck (some) brew □ suck (some) suds □ take some doing □ take some heat

SOMETIME
Let's do lunch (sometime).

SON
son of a bitch □ son of a gun

SOP
sopping (wet)

SORE
stick out like a sore thumb □ touch a sore point

SORRY
sorry about that □ sorry-ass □ sorry 'bout that

SOUL
gripe one's soul □ heavy soul □ (soul) brother □ soul kiss □ (soul) sister □ thirsty soul

SOUND
sound off (about something)

SOUP
alphabet soup □ cat-soup □ everything from soup to nuts □ in the soup □ laughing soup □ potato soup □ soup something up □ soup-strainer □ souped up

SOUR
go sour

SOUTH
go South □ head South □ mouth full of South

SOUTHERN
southern-fried

SPACE
space cadet □ space out □ space someone out □ spaced (out)

SPADE
in spades

SPANK
(brand) spanking new □ spanking new

SPARE
spare tire

SPAZ
have a spaz □ spaz around □ spaz down □ spaz out

SPEAK
speak of the devil □ speak someone's language

SPEAR
take the spear (in one's chest)

SPECIAL
King Kong specials □ Saturday night special

SPEED
speed demon □ speed freak □ speed merchant

SPEND
big spender □ big-time spender □ spending money

SPEW
spew one's guts (out)

SPIDER
barking spider □ pink spiders □ seeing pink spiders □ trumpet spider

SPIFF
spiffed out □ spiffed up

SPILL
spill one's guts □ spill the beans □ spill the works

SPIN
spin doctor □ spin one's wheels

SPIT
spit and polish □ Spit it out! □ swap spits

SPLEEN
vent one's spleen

SPLIT
I've got to split. □ lickety-split □ split a gut □ split up □ splitting headache

SPOIL
spoiled rotten □ spoiling for a fight

SPONGE
throw in the sponge □ toss in the sponge

SPOOK
spook factory

SPOON
(flake) spoon □ greasy spoon

SPOT
C-spot □ hit the spot □ spot market □ spot of lunch □ spot someone (something) □ ten-spot □ tight spot □ X marks the spot.

SPRAIN
sprain one's ankle

SPRING
spring chicken □ spring for something □ spring someone

SPROUT
sprout wings

SPRUNG
half-sprung

SPUD
sofa spud

SQUAD
goon squad □ junk squad

SQUARE
back to square one □ square apple □ square john □ square john broad □ square (meal) □ square off □ square peg (in a round hole) □ square shooter □ square with someone □ squared away □ squared up □ three squares

SQUASH
stoned out of one's squash

SQUAT
cop a squat □ diddly-squat □ (doodly-) squat

SQUAWK
squawk box

SQUEAK
narrow squeak

SQUEAKY
squeaky clean

SQUEEZE
budget squeeze □ duck-squeezer □ main squeeze □ put the squeeze on someone □ (squeeze-)box □ squeeze play

SQUIFF
on the squiff □ squiff out

SQUIRREL
seam-squirrels □ squirrel-food □ squirrel out of something □ squirrel something away

STACK
blow one's stack □ stack the deck □ swear on a stack of Bibles

STAG
stag line □ stag-party

STAGE
honeymoon stage

STAKE
stake someone or something out □ stake someone to something □ up stakes

STALE
stale drunk

STAMP
stamping ground

STAND
If you can't stand the heat, keep out of the kitchen. □ one-night stand □ stand-in □ stand-out □ stand pat (on something) □ stand someone up □ stand tall □ stand there with one's bare face hanging out □ taco stand

STAR
see stars

STARCH
take the starch out of someone

START
jump start □ jumpstart someone or something

STASH
main stash

STATION
comfort station □ filling station □ fuzz station □ Grand Central Station □ thirst-aid station

STATISTICS
vital statistics

STAY
stay loose □ Stay tuned.

STEAK
tube steak

STEAM
blow off (some) steam □ full steam ahead □ let off (some) steam □ steam someone up □ steam someone's beam □ steam up □ steamed (up)

STEER
bum steer

STEP
Aztec two-step □ step off the curb □ step out on someone □ step outside □ step right up □ stepped on □ You want to step outside?

STEVEN
even-Steven

STEW
half-stewed □ stew bum □ stewed to the ears □ stewed to the gills □ stewed (up)

STICK
boom sticks □ cancer stick □ carry the stick □ get on the stick □ licorice stick □ short end of the stick □ stick around □ Stick 'em up! □ stick in the mud □ stick it to someone □ stick man □ stick one's nose in (where it's not wanted) □ stick out like a sore thumb □ stick shift □ stick someone with something □ swizzle-stick

STICKER
sticker shock

STICKY
sticky fingers

STIFF
scared stiff □ working stiff

STINK
big stink □ holy stink □ like stink □ make a stink (about someone or something) □ raise a stink (about someone or something) □ stink on ice □ stinking (drunk) □ stinking rich □ stinking with something

STIR
stir crazy

STOCK
deal stock □ stocking-stuffer □ story stock

STOKE
stoked (on someone or something) □ stoked out

STOMACH
cast-iron stomach ☐ turn someone's stomach

STOMP
stomp (on) someone

STONE
carved in stone ☐ stone blind ☐ stone broke ☐ stone (cold) sober ☐ stone dead ☐ stone fox ☐ stone groove ☐ stoned (out) ☐ stoned out of one's gourd ☐ stoned out of one's head ☐ stoned out of one's squash ☐ stoned silly

STOOL
stool (on someone) ☐ stool (pigeon)

STOP
bullet-stopper ☐ flopper-stopper ☐ nature stop ☐ pit stop ☐ pull out all the stops ☐ stop on a dime ☐ Stop the music!

STOPPER
bullet-stopper ☐ flopper-stopper

STORAGE
in cold storage

STORE
candy store ☐ dime store ☐ leeky store

STORK
visit from the stork

STORM
kick up a storm ☐ up a storm

STORY
bedtime story ☐ fish story ☐ long story short ☐ same old story ☐ sob story ☐ story stock ☐ top story ☐ upper story

STOW
Stow it!

STRADDLE
straddle the fence

STRAIGHT
get straight ☐ go straight ☐ put oneself straight ☐ straight arrow ☐ straight dope ☐ straight-faced ☐ straight from the horse's mouth ☐ straight from the shoulder ☐ straight low ☐ straight man ☐ straight shooter ☐ straight talk ☐ straight up ☐ straighten up and fly right

STRAINER
soup-strainer

STRANGE
strange bird

STRAP
strap someone with something ☐ super-strap

STRAW
last straw ☐ straw boss

STREAK
have a yellow streak down one's back ☐ losing streak ☐ talk a blue streak ☐ yellow streak (down someone's back)

STREET
easy street ☐ jump (street) ☐ man on the street ☐ on easy street ☐ on the street ☐ put something on the street ☐ street-casting ☐ street people ☐ street pusher ☐ street smart ☐ street smarts ☐ street time ☐ take it to the street ☐ two-way street

STRESS
no stress

STRETCH
in the (home) stretch ☐ stretch one's legs

STRICTLY
(strictly) from hunger

STRIKE
strike it rich ☐ strike out ☐ strike pay dirt

STRING
on a shoestring

STRIP
strip-search

STROKE
different strokes for different folks

STRONG
come on strong ☐ strong-arm ☐ strong-arm man ☐ strong-arm tactics

STRUNG

strung out □ strung-out shape □ strung (up)

STRUT

strut one's stuff

STUCK

stuck on someone or something □ stuck-up □ stuck with someone or something

STUD

stud-muffin

STUDY

study animal

STUFF

fluff-stuff □ folding stuff □ get one's stuff together □ green stuff □ hot stuff □ kid stuff □ light stuff □ rough stuff □ smell the stuff □ snow stuff □ stocking-stuffer □ strut one's stuff □ Stuff a sock in it! □ stuffed shirt □ That's the stuff!

STUPID

get stupid □ stupid-ass □ stupid fresh

SUCK

egg-sucker □ suck face □ suck (some) brew □ suck (some) suds □ suck someone's hind tit □ suck up to someone □ sucker for someone or something □ sucker list

SUDDEN

sudden death

SUDGE

jober as a sudge

SUDS

bust (some) suds □ crack some suds □ in the suds □ suck (some) suds □ suds-swiller

SUE

sue the pants off (of) someone

SUGAR

sugar daddy □ Uncle Sugar

SUIT

blue suit

SUMMER

summer complaint

SUMPIN'

Wanna make sumpin' of it?

SUN

sun belt □ where the sun don't shine

SUNDAY

Sunday best □ Sunday driver □ Sunday punch

SUNNY

sunny-side up

SUPER

super-dooper □ super-duper □ super-strap

SUPERINTENDENT

sidewalk superintendent

SUPPER

shoot one's supper

SURE

for sure □ I am so sure! □ sure as hell □ sure thing

SURF

channel surfer □ channel surfing □ sidewalk surfing

SUSS

suss someone out

SWALLOW

hard to swallow □ swallow the dictionary

SWAP

swap notes (on someone or something) □ swap spits

SWEAR

swear like a trooper □ swear on a stack of Bibles

SWEAT

Don't sweat it! □ in a cold sweat □ no sweat □ sweat blood □ sweat bullets □ sweat-shop □ sweat sock □ sweat something out □ tiger sweat

SWEEP

clean sweep

SWEET
fresh and sweet □ lay some sweet lines on someone □ put some sweet lines on someone □ sweet nothings □ You bet your sweet life! □ You bet your sweet patoot(ie)!

SWEETHEART
sweetheart deal

SWEETIE
sweetie(-pie)

SWILL
monkey swill □ suds-swiller □ swill-up

SWIM
swimming in something

SWINDLE
swindle sheet

SWING
swing both ways □ swing into high gear □ swing shift □ swing with someone or something

SWIPE
take a swipe at someone or something

SWITCH
asleep at the switch □ switch-hitter □ switch off □ switch on □ switched on

SWIZZLE
swizzle-stick

SYNC
out of sync

T
T. and A. □ T-man

TA
ta-ta

TABBACKY
wacky-tabbacky

TABLE
boxed on the table □ table-hop □ under the table

TACK
brass tacks □ coffin tack

TACKY
ticky-tacky

TACO
taco stand □ toss one's tacos

TACTIC
strong-arm tactics

TAH
Tah-dah!

TAIL
bright-eyed and bushy-tailed □ fuzzy (tail) □ Go chase your tail! □ have a tiger by the tail □ on someone's tail □ ringtailed snorter □ tailbone □ tail-end □ turn tail (and run) □ two shakes of a lamb's tail □ work one's tail off

TAILGATE
tailgate party

TAILOR
tailor-made

TAKE
double take □ have what it takes □ on the take □ take a bath (on something) □ take a beating □ take a break □ take a chill pill □ take a crack at something □ take a dig at someone □ take a dirt nap □ take a dive □ take a fall □ take a flyer (on something) □ take a gander (at someone or something) □ take a hike □ take a jab at someone □ take a leak □ take a load off one's feet □ take a lot of nerve □ take a nosedive □ take a page from someone's book □ take a pop at someone □ take a powder □ Take a running jump (in the lake)! □ take a shot (at something) □ take a swipe at someone or something □ take a walk □ take a whack at someone or something □ Take care. □ take care of number one □ take care of numero uno □ take care of someone □ take five □ take it □ Take it down a thou (sand)! □ take it easy □ take it on the chin □ take it on the lam □ take it on the nose □ Take it or leave it. □ take it out on someone or something □ take it slow □ take it through the nose □ take it to the street □ take names □ take off □ take-off □ take-off artist □ take on fuel □ take one's belt in (a notch) □ take one's lumps □ take pictures □ take some doing □ take

some heat □ take someone in □ take someone or something apart □ take someone or something off □ take someone or something on □ take someone or something out □ take someone to the cleaners □ take something public □ take the cure □ take the fall □ take the fifth □ take the gas pipe □ take the heat □ take the heat off someone □ take the (long) count □ take the pipe □ take the pledge □ take the plunge □ take the rap (for something) □ take the spear (in one's chest) □ take the starch out of someone □ take the wind out of someone's sails □ take things easy □ takes two to tango □ taking care of business □ You can't take it with you.

TALE

fairy tale □ fish tale □ tale of woe

TALK

big talk □ give someone a (good) talking to □ heart-to-heart (talk) □ jive talk □ Look who's talking! □ money talks □ monkey talk □ nice talking to you □ Now you're talking! □ pep talk □ straight talk □ talk a blue streak □ talk big □ talk like a nut □ talk on the big white phone □ talk someone ragged □ talk someone's ear off □ talk someone's head off □ talk through one's hat □ talk to earl □ talk to hear one's own voice □ talk to Herb and Al □ talk turkey □ talk until one is blue in the face □ talking head

TALL

in tall cotton □ long-tall-Sally □ stand tall □ tall in the saddle □ tall one □ tall order □ tall timbers □ walk tall

TANGLE

tangle with someone or something

TANGO

takes two to tango

TANK

drunk tank □ junk tank □ on a tank □ on the tank □ tank up □ tanked up □ think-tank

TAP

on tap □ tap dance like mad □ tap out □ tap someone (for something) □ tapped out

TAPE

red tape

TAR

whale the tar out of someone

TARGET

on-target

TASTE

so bad one can taste it □ taste blood

TATTOOED

screwed, blued, and tattooed

TAXI

Tijuana taxi

TEA

cup of tea □ tea party

TEACH

That'll teach someone.

TEAR

tear into someone or something □ tear-jerker □ tear loose (from someone or something) □ tear off □ tear someone or something apart □ tear someone or something up □ That tears it!

TEASER

brain-teaser

TECH

tech-nerd

TECHNICOLOR

technicolor yawn □ throw a technicolor yawn

TEE

tee someone off □ tee-tee

TEED

teed off □ teed (up)

TEENIE

teenie-weenie

TEENSY

teensy-weensy

TEENY

teeny-weeny

TEETH
dressed to the teeth □ drop one's teeth □ get one's teeth into something □ kick in the teeth □ sink one's teeth into something □ tinsel-teeth

TELEGRAPH
telegraph one's punches

TELL
Do tell. □ show and tell □ Tell it like it is. □ Tell me another (one)! □ tell shit from Shinola □ tell someone what to do with something □ tell someone where to get off □ tell the (whole) world

TEN
hang ten □ ten-four □ ten percenter □ ten-spot □ wouldn't touch someone or something with a ten-foot pole

TENOR
whiskey tenor

TERROR
holy terror

TEST
acid test

THAN
cannot see (any) further than the end of one's nose □ holier-than-thou □ more than one bargained for □ quicker than hell □ see no further than the end of one's nose

THANK
thank you very much □ thanks a bunch

THEN
then and there

THICK
thick-skinned

THIGH
thunder-thighs

THIN
thin dime □ thin-skinned □ walk on thin ice

THING
do one's (own) thing □ do the drink thing □ do the drug thing □ in thing to do □ onto a good thing □ sure thing □ take things easy

THINK
think-box □ think-piece □ think-tank □ You've got another think coming.

THIRD
third degree □ third wheel

THIRST
thirst-aid station

THIRSTY
thirsty soul

THIS
I don't believe this! □ Keep out of this! □ Let's bump this place! □ out of this world □ This is it! □ This is where I came in.

THOU
holier-than-thou

THOUSAND
if I've told you once, I've told you a thousand times □ Take it down a thou(sand)!

THREE
phony as a three-dollar bill □ queer as a three-dollar bill □ three bricks shy of a load □ three fingers □ three point two □ three sheets in the wind □ three sheets (to the wind) □ three squares □ three-two

THRILLER
thriller-diller

THROAT
cut one's own throat □ ram something down someone's throat □ throat gag

THRONE
hug the throne □ throne room

THROUGH
go through someone like a dose of the salts □ go through the changes □ sail (right) through something □ take it through the nose □ talk through one's hat □ through and through □ through the mill □ waltz through something

THROW

throw a fight ☐ throw a fit ☐ throw a game ☐ throw a map ☐ throw a punch ☐ throw a technicolor yawn ☐ throw-away ☐ throw down ☐ throw in the sponge ☐ throw in the towel ☐ throw money at something ☐ throw one out on one's ear ☐ throw one's cookies ☐ throw one's hat in the ring ☐ throw one's voice ☐ throw one's weight around ☐ throw someone for a loop ☐ throw something back ☐ throw something together ☐ throw the book at someone ☐ throw the bull ☐ throw the crap ☐ throw up one's toenails

THUMB

green thumb ☐ stick out like a sore thumb ☐ thumb a ride ☐ thumbnail sketch ☐ thumbs down ☐ thumbs up ☐ turn thumbs down (on someone or something) ☐ twiddle one's thumbs ☐ under someone's thumb

THUMBNAIL

thumbnail sketch

THUNDER

thunder-boomer ☐ thunder-thighs

TICK

tick someone off ☐ tick-tock ☐ ticked (off) ☐ tight as a tick

TICKET

big-ticket ☐ buy someone's wolf ticket ☐ get one's ticket punched ☐ just the ticket ☐ sell a wolf ticket ☐ sell wolf tickets ☐ That's the ticket!

TICKLE

rib-tickler ☐ tickle the ivories ☐ tickled (pink)

TICKY

ticky-tacky

TIE

tie-in ☐ tie it on ☐ tie on the nosebag ☐ tie one on ☐ tie the knot ☐ tied up ☐ tongue-tied

TIGER

have a tiger by the tail ☐ tiger juice ☐ tiger sweat ☐ tiger('s) milk

TIGHT

on a tight leash ☐ screwed tight ☐ tight as a tick ☐ tight money ☐ tight spot ☐ tight wad ☐ tighten one's belt

TIJUANA

Tijuana taxi

TILL

till hell freezes over ☐ till kingdom come ☐ till the fat lady sings

TIMBER

tall timbers

TIME

bean time ☐ Better luck next time. ☐ big time ☐ big-time operator ☐ big-time spender ☐ buy time ☐ devil of a time ☐ devil's own time ☐ do time ☐ down time ☐ game time ☐ good-time Charley ☐ good-time it ☐ good-time man ☐ hard time ☐ have a whale of a time ☐ if I've told you once, I've told you a thousand times ☐ Long time no see. ☐ mark time ☐ old timer ☐ rack time ☐ rare old time ☐ rough time ☐ Run that by (me) one more time. ☐ sack time ☐ small-time ☐ street time ☐ Time (out)! ☐ time to cruise ☐ two-time ☐ two-time loser ☐ two-timer ☐ up time

TIN

tin cow ☐ tin hat

TINSEL

tinsel-teeth

TINY

patter of tiny feet

TIP

hot tip ☐ tip-off ☐ tip one's hand

TIRE

spare tire

TIT

suck someone's hind tit ☐ tits and ass ☐ tits up ☐ Tough titties! ☐ Tough titty!

TITTY

See *tit*.

someone or something with a ten-foot pole

TOUGH

hang tough (on something) ☐ tough break ☐ tough cookie ☐ tough cookies ☐ tough customer ☐ tough egg to crack ☐ tough guy ☐ tough luck ☐ tough nut to crack ☐ tough row to hoe ☐ tough something out ☐ Tough titties! ☐ Tough titty!

TOURIST

tourist trap

TOWEL

crying towel ☐ throw in the towel

TOWER

ivory tower

TOWN

Bean Town ☐ blow town ☐ Get out of town! ☐ go to town ☐ one-horse town ☐ paint the town (red)

TOXIC

toxic waste dump

TRACK

make tracks ☐ off the track ☐ one-track mind ☐ railroad tracks ☐ wrong side of the tracks

TRADE

tricks of the trade

TRAGIC

tragic-magic

TRAIL

hit the trail

TRAIN

gravy train

TRAP

bear trap ☐ booby trap ☐ fly trap ☐ fox trap ☐ rattle-trap ☐ tourist trap

TRASH

Cash is trash. ☐ trash mouth

TREAT

Dutch treat

TREE

Christmas tree ☐ Go climb a tree! ☐ make like a tree and leave ☐ not grow on trees ☐ up a tree

TRIAL

trial balloon

TRICK

do the trick ☐ trick on someone ☐ tricks of the trade ☐ turn a trick ☐ whole bag of tricks

TRIGGER

trigger-happy

TRIP

bad trip ☐ bum trip ☐ day-tripper ☐ down trip ☐ ego trip ☐ ego tripper ☐ free trip ☐ good trip ☐ head trip ☐ lay a guilt trip on someone ☐ lay a (heavy) trip on someone ☐ round tripper ☐ tripped out

TRIPLE

triple-bagger ☐ triple whammy

TROLLEY

off one's trolley ☐ slip one's trolley

TROOPER

swear like a trooper

TROT

back-door trot(s)

TROUBLE

buy trouble ☐ double-trouble ☐ for (all) one's trouble

TRUCK

Keep on trucking.

TRULY

yours truly

TRUMP

trump something up ☐ trumped up

TRUMPET

trumpet spider

TRUST

Trust me!

TRUTH

gospel (truth) ☐ naked truth

TRY

try someone back (again)

TUB
tub of guts ☐ tub of lard

TUBE
boob-tube ☐ cop a tube ☐ crack a tube ☐ go down the tube(s) ☐ in the tube ☐ tube it ☐ tube steak

TUCK
nip and tuck

TUMBLE
rough and tumble

TUNE
Stay tuned. ☐ to the tune of something ☐ tune in (to something) ☐ tune out ☐ tune someone or something out ☐ tuned in ☐ turn on, tune in, drop out

TURD
ghost turd

TURK
young Turk

TURKEY
cold turkey ☐ couch-turkey ☐ jive turkey ☐ kick cold (turkey) ☐ talk turkey

TURN
done to a turn ☐ turn a trick ☐ turn around ☐ turn belly up ☐ turn in ☐ turn-off ☐ turn on ☐ turn on a dime ☐ turn on the waterworks ☐ turn on, tune in, drop out ☐ turn one's toes up ☐ turn onto someone or something ☐ turn over ☐ turn someone off ☐ turn someone on ☐ turn someone or something upside down ☐ turn someone out ☐ turn someone's stomach ☐ turn someone's water off ☐ turn tail (and run) ☐ turn thumbs down (on someone or something) ☐ turn turtle ☐ turn up one's nose at someone or something ☐ turned off ☐ turned on ☐ whatever turns you on

TURTLE
turn turtle

TURVY
topsy-turvy

TWENTY
twenty-twenty hindsight

TWIDDLE
twiddle one's thumbs

TWIST
arm-twister ☐ arm-twisting ☐ brain-twister ☐ twist (slowly) in the wind ☐ twist someone's arm

TWIT
in a twit

TWITTER
in a twitter

TWO
Aztec two-step ☐ goody two-shoes ☐ It cuts two ways. ☐ old one-two ☐ takes two to tango ☐ three point two ☐ three-two ☐ two-bit ☐ two-bits ☐ two-by-four ☐ two fingers ☐ two-fisted drinker ☐ two shakes of a lamb's tail ☐ two sheets to the wind ☐ two-time ☐ two-time loser ☐ two-timer ☐ two umlauts ☐ two-way street ☐ You can't dance at two weddings.

TWOSOME
gruesome-twosome

UGLY
butt-ugly ☐ coyote-ugly ☐ plug-ugly ☐ pug-ugly ☐ ugly as sin

UMLAUT
two umlauts

UMPTH
umpty-umpth

UMPTY
umpty-umpth

UNCLE
Dutch uncle ☐ say uncle ☐ Uncle nab ☐ Uncle (Sam) ☐ Uncle Sugar ☐ Uncle Whiskers

UNDER
down under ☐ gone under ☐ half under ☐ hit under the wing ☐ hot under the collar ☐ knuckle under (to someone or something) ☐ plowed (under) ☐ put the skids under someone or something ☐ six feet under ☐ under someone's thumb ☐ under the affluence of incohol ☐ under the gun ☐

under the table □ under the weather □ under the wire □ under wraps

UNDERGROUND
go underground

UNDERWATER
underwater basket weaving

UNDERWORLD
hero (of the underworld)

UNIT
(parental) units

UNO
numero uno □ take care of numero uno

UNQUOTE
quote, unquote

UNTIL
talk until one is blue in the face

UNWASHED
great unwashed

UPHOLSTER
(well-)upholstered

UPPER
pepper-upper □ upper story

UPROAR
get one's bowels in an uproar

UPSHOT
upshot (of something)

UPSIDE
turn someone or something upside down

UPSTAIRS
nothing upstairs

URGE
urge to purge

US
Don't call us, we'll call you.

USE
chippy (user) □ Use your head! □ Use your noggin! □ Use your noodle!

V
V-ball

VARIETY
Heinz 57 (variety)

VARNISH
coffin varnish □ tonsil varnish

VATICAN
Vatican roulette

VEG
veg (out) □ vegged out

VENT
vent one's spleen

VERSE
chapter and verse

VERY
thank you very much

VIBES
have good vibes

VICIOUS
vicious circle

VID
kid-vid

VIDEO
video jock

VIGOR
vim and vigor

VIM
vim and vigor

VISIT
visit from Flo □ visit from the stork □ visit the plumbing □ visiting fireman

VISITOR
have a little visitor

VITAL
vital statistics

VODKA
as clear as vodka

VOICE
talk to hear one's own voice □ throw one's voice

VOTE
vote with one's feet

VULTURE
culture-vulture

WACKY
wacky-tabbacky

WAD
shoot one's wad ☐ tight wad

WAFFLE
waffle (around)

WAG
wag one's chin

WAGON
draggin'-wagon ☐ fall off the wagon ☐ honey wagon ☐ meat wagon ☐ monkey wagon ☐ off the wagon ☐ on the bandwagon ☐ on the wagon ☐ paddy wagon

WAIT
hurry up and wait

WALK
take a walk ☐ walk heavy ☐ walk-in ☐ walk on eggs ☐ walk on thin ice ☐ walk soft ☐ walk tall ☐ walking dandruff ☐ walking on rocky socks ☐ walking papers ☐ walking wounded

WALL
climb the wall(s) ☐ drive someone up the wall ☐ go over the wall ☐ hole in the wall ☐ nail someone('s hide) to the wall ☐ off-the-wall ☐ plastered to the wall ☐ up the wall ☐ wall-eyed ☐ wall job ☐ wall-to-wall ☐ walls have ears

WALSY
palsy-walsy

WALTZ
waltz off (with something) ☐ waltz through something

WANNA
wanna be ☐ Wanna make sumpin' of it?

WANT
put one's nose in (where it's not wanted) ☐ stick one's nose in (where it's not wanted) ☐ want list ☐ want out ☐ Want to make something of it? ☐ You want to step outside?

WAR
flame-war ☐ on the warpath ☐ war chest ☐ war paint ☐ war zone

WARDS
monkey wards

WARM
bench warmer ☐ like death warmed over ☐ nose-warmer ☐ warm body ☐ warm someone up ☐ warmed over

WARPATH
on the warpath

WARRIOR
weekend warrior

WART
warts and all ☐ worry wart

WAS
like there was no tomorrow ☐ was had

WASH
chief cook and bottle washer ☐ come out in the wash ☐ head cook and bottle washer ☐ wash out ☐ wash someone away ☐ washed out ☐ wishy-washy

WASHY
See *wash.*

WASTE
toxic waste dump

WATCH
bird watcher ☐ clock watcher ☐ on someone's watch ☐ people watching ☐ Watch it! ☐ Watch my lips! ☐ Watch your mouth! ☐ Watch your tongue!

WATER
big drink of water ☐ blow someone out of the water ☐ bubble water ☐ dead in the water ☐ dull as dishwater ☐ foo-foo water ☐ hold water ☐ joy water ☐ laughing water ☐ pour cold water on something ☐ toilet water ☐ turn someone's water off ☐ underwater basket weaving ☐ watering hole ☐ woofle-water ☐ wozzle-water

WATERWORKS
turn on the waterworks

WAVE
finger wave ☐ make waves

WAVELENGTH
on the same wavelength

WAX
whole ball of wax

WAY
all the way ☐ all the way live ☐ go all the way ☐ in a bad way ☐ in a big way ☐ in a familiar way ☐ in a family way ☐ in the family way ☐ It cuts two ways. ☐ No way! ☐ only way to go ☐ out of the way ☐ put someone or something out of the way ☐ swing both ways ☐ that way ☐ That's the way the ball bounces. ☐ That's the way the cookie crumbles. ☐ That's the way the mop flops. ☐ (That's the) way to go! ☐ the way it plays ☐ two-way street ☐ way down ☐ way off (base) ☐ way out ☐ way rad ☐ Way to go!

WEAK
weak sister

WEAR
wear the pants (in the house)

WEASEL
weasel out of something

WEATHER
fair-weather ☐ under the weather

WEAVE
underwater basket weaving

WEDDING
shotgun wedding ☐ You can't dance at two weddings.

WEED
crying weed ☐ killer weed ☐ monster weed ☐ weed-eater

WEEKEND
weekend warrior

WEENIE
teenie-weenie

WEENSY
teensy-weensy

WEENY
teeny-weeny

WEIGHT
carry weight ☐ throw one's weight around

WEIRD
weird out ☐ weirded out

WE'LL
Don't call us, we'll call you.

WELL
jolly-well ☐ well-fixed ☐ well-heeled ☐ well-oiled ☐ (well-)upholstered

WERE
Were you born in a barn?

WEST
go West

WET
sopping (wet) ☐ wet blanket ☐ wet noodle ☐ wet one ☐ wet rag ☐ wet sock

WHACK
out of w(h)ack ☐ take a whack at someone or something ☐ whack someone or something (out) ☐ whack someone or something up ☐ whacked (out)

WHALE
have a whale of a time ☐ whale into someone or something ☐ whale on ☐ whale the tar out of someone

WHAM
wham-bang

WHAMMY
double whammy ☐ triple whammy

WHATEVER
whatever turns you on

WHEEL
big wheel ☐ eighteen wheeler ☐ fifth wheel ☐ four wheels ☐ free-wheeling ☐ hell-on-wheels ☐ reinvent the wheel ☐ set of wheels ☐ spin one's wheels ☐ third wheel ☐ wheel and deal ☐ wheel man ☐ wheeler-dealer

WHEN
Smile when you say that. ☐ when push comes to shove ☐ when the eagle flies ☐ when the fat lady sings

WHERE
know where it's at ☐ know where one is coming from ☐ put one's nose in (where it's not wanted) ☐ Put your money where your mouth is! ☐ stick one's nose in (where it's not wanted) ☐ tell someone where to get off ☐ This is where I came in. ☐ Where (have) you been keeping yourself? ☐ Where in (the) Sam Hill? ☐ Where in the world? ☐ where it's at ☐ Where on (God's green) earth? ☐ where someone is at ☐ where someone lives ☐ where someone's head is at ☐ where the action is ☐ where the sun don't shine ☐ Where's the beef? ☐ Where's the fire?

WHICH
know which end is up

WHIFF
whiff-sniffer

WHILE
get (out) while the gettin(g)'s good ☐ get (out) while the goin's good ☐ quit while one is ahead

WHING
whing-ding

WHIP
whip something into shape ☐ whip something off

WHIRLY
whirly bird

WHISKERS
Mr. Whiskers ☐ Uncle Whiskers

WHISKEY
whiskey tenor

WHISTLE
bells and whistles ☐ not just whistling Dixie ☐ whistle-blower ☐ whistle in the dark

WHITE
black and white ☐ bleed someone white ☐ blue and white ☐ China white ☐ Chinese white ☐ talk on the big white phone ☐ white elephant ☐ white hat ☐ white-knuckle ☐ white knuckler

WHIZ
whiz kid

WHO
Look who's talking! ☐ Says who? ☐ Sez who? ☐ Who (in) the devil? ☐ Who (in) the hell? ☐ who shot John ☐ Who the deuce? ☐ You and who else?

WHOLE
tell the (whole) world ☐ whole bag of tricks ☐ whole ball of wax ☐ whole bunch(es) ☐ whole enchilada ☐ whole fam damily ☐ whole new ball game ☐ whole nine yards ☐ whole schmear ☐ whole shebang ☐ whole shooting match ☐ whole wide world

WHOPPING
whopping (great)

WIDE
blow something wide open ☐ bust something wide open ☐ high, wide, and handsome ☐ whole wide world ☐ wide open ☐ wide place in the road ☐ with (one's) eyes (wide) open

WIDOW
widow-maker

WIENER
wiener nose

WIFF
wiff-sniffer

WIG
flip one's wig ☐ wig out ☐ wigged (out)

WIGGLE
Get a wiggle on! ☐ wiggle out of something

WILD
hog-wild ☐ wild and wooly

WILL
heads will roll ☐ It will be your ass! ☐ There will be hell to pay. ☐ will do

WIMP
wimp out (of something)

WIN
can't win (th)em all ☐ no-win situation ☐ Win a few, lose a few. ☐ You can't win them all.

WINCY
incy-wincy

WIND
bag of wind ☐ both sheets in the wind ☐ four sheets in the wind ☐ four sheets (to the wind) ☐ take the wind out of someone's sails ☐ three sheets in the wind ☐ three sheets (to the wind) ☐ twist (slowly) in the wind ☐ two sheets to the wind

WINDOW
bay window ☐ out the window

WINE
jug wine ☐ pop wine

WING
clip someone's wings ☐ fling-wing ☐ get one's wings ☐ hit under the wing ☐ sprout wings ☐ wing-ding ☐ wing heavy ☐ wing it

WINK
forty winks

WIPE
Wipe it off! ☐ wipe out ☐ wipe someone or something out ☐ wipe the floor up with someone ☐ wiped (out) ☐ wiped over

WIRE
down to the wire ☐ hot wire ☐ (live) wire ☐ under the wire ☐ wired into someone or something ☐ wired up

WIRELESS
latrine wireless

WISE
wise guy ☐ wise to someone or something ☐ wise up (to someone or something)

WISH
(Don't) you wish! ☐ wish book ☐ wish list ☐ You wish!

WISHY
wishy-washy

WITHIN
within an ace of (doing) something

WITHOUT
up the creek (without a paddle) ☐ without a hitch

WOBBLE
snozzle-wobbles

WOE
tale of woe

WOLF
buy someone's wolf ticket ☐ cut one's wolf loose ☐ lone wolf ☐ sell a wolf ticket ☐ sell wolf tickets ☐ wolf something down

WOMAN
old woman

WONDER
gutless wonder

WOO
pitch (the) woo

WOOD
out of the woods ☐ wood butcher ☐ wood-pussy ☐ woods are full of. . . .

WOOF
woof cookies

WOOFLE
woofle-water

WOOLY
wild and wooly

WOOZY
boozy-woozy

WORD
dirty word ☐ What's the good word? ☐ Word up.

WORK
dirty work ☐ fancy footwork ☐ fast footwork ☐ give someone a (good) working over ☐ grunt work ☐ knock off (work) ☐ leg work ☐ shoot the works ☐ spill the works ☐ work one's

buns off □ work one's butt off □ work one's tail off □ work oneself up □ work oneself (up) into a lather □ work oneself up to something □ work someone over □ working stiff

WORKS

turn on the waterworks

WORLD

dead to the world □ out of this world □ tell the (whole) world □ Where in the world? □ whole wide world □ world-beater □ world-class □ world is one's oyster

WORM

can of worms □ glow worm □ wormfood □ worms in blood

WORRY

Not to worry. □ worry wart

WORSHIP

worship the porcelain god(dess)

WORST

worst-case scenario

WORTH

not worth a damn □ not worth a plugged nickel □ not worth beans □ worth one's salt

WOULD

would not be seen dead.... □ Would you believe?

WOULDN'T

wouldn't touch someone or something with a ten-foot pole

WOUNDED

walking wounded

WOW

bow-wow □ pow-wow

WOZZLE

wozzle-water

WRAP

under wraps □ wrap one's car around something □ wrap something up □ wrapped up (in someone or something) □ wrapped up (with someone or something)

WRATH

grapes of wrath

WRENCH

left-handed monkey wrench

WRINKLE

wrinkle-rod

WRIST

kick in the wrist □ slap someone on the wrist □ slap someone's wrist

WRITE

nothing to write home about

WRONG

have the wrong number □ wrong side of the tracks

WROTE

That's all she wrote. □ That's what she wrote.

X

X marks the spot. □ X'd out

YA

How ya living? □ see ya

YACKETY

yackety-yak

YAK

yackety-yak □ yak it up

YANK

yank someone around □ yank someone's chain

YARD

barnyard language □ graveyard shift □ whole nine yards □ yard dog

YATATA

yatata-yatata

YAWN

technicolor yawn □ throw a technicolor yawn

YE

Ye gods!

YEA

yea big

YEAH
Oh, yeah?

YEAR
donkey's years ☐ seven-year itch

YELL
yell one's guts out ☐ yell one's head off

YELLOW
have a yellow streak down one's back ☐ yellow-bellied ☐ yellow-belly ☐ yellow streak (down someone's back)

YO
yo mama

YODEL
yodeling in a canyon

YOKEL
local yokel

YORK
See *New York.*

YOUNG
young blood ☐ young Turk

Z
big Z's ☐ blow Z's ☐ catch some Z's ☐ cop some Z's ☐ cut some Z's ☐ from A to Z

ZAP
channel zapping

ZEEK
zeek out

ZERK
zerked (out)

ZIGGETY
Hot ziggety!

ZIP
zip along ☐ zip gun ☐ Zip it up! ☐ Zip (up) your lip!

ZIPPER
zipper head

ZIT
zit doctor

ZONE
war zone ☐ zoned (out)

ZONK
go zonkers ☐ zonk out ☐ zonked (out)

ZOOM
zoom in (on someone or something) ☐ zoom off ☐ zoom out ☐ zoom someone out ☐ zoom up

ZOUNK
zounked (out)